Kelley Blue Book

USED CAR GUIDE
Consumer Edition
2000 – 2014 Models

Vol. 23	October—December 2015	No. 4

LES KELLEY - *Founder*
BRETT NANIGIAN - - *Sr. Product Director, Industry Solutions*
KELLY J. SALAZAR - - - - - - - - *Director, Industry Services*

Kelley Blue Book Used Car Guide, Consumer Edition is published four times per year in January, April, July and October for $9.95 per issue by Kelley Blue Book Co., P.O. Box 19691, Irvine, CA 92623. POSTMASTER: Send address changes to Kelley Blue Book Auto Market Report, P.O. Box 19691, Irvine, CA 92623.

This publication Forbes   4501

Official Guidebooks Since 1926

ORDER YOUR BLUE BOOK NOW!

Kelley Blue Book
P.O. Box 19691
Irvine, California 92623

Please accept our order for _____ copies of the Kelley Blue Book Used Car Guide Consumer Edition, at $9.95 per copy, including shipping.

NAME _____

ADDRESS _____

CITY _____

STATE _____ ZIP _____

PHONE (_____)_____

VISA or MASTER CARD # _____

EXP. DATE _____ SIGNATURE _____

Visa ☐   MasterCard ☐   Check Enclosed ☐

California residents please add sales tax. Shipping outside U.S. extra.

INTRODUCTION

Since 1926, Kelley Blue Book has provided the automotive industry with used vehicle values. Today we are the trusted resource relied upon by both the automotive industry and consumers. This **Consumer Edition** has been prepared to provide values and information relevant to the different types of consumer transactions.

What is a guidebook?

A guidebook such as this one is just that, a guide. To produce the most timely, accurate and trusted used vehicle values, Kelley Blue Book's valuation analysts constantly collect and review new and used vehicle transaction data, as well as information on each vehicle's current supply and demand. They then meticulously determine and report used car values based on real market information.

This guidebook represents the educated opinion of Kelley Blue Book's staff and each value is determined after carefully studying information we deem complete and reliable. We assume no responsibility for errors or omissions.

Is this book the same as the Kelley Blue Book trade publication?

This book contains the trusted values you have come to expect from Kelley Blue Book. The values in the Consumer Guide represent transactions relevant to consumers including Trade-In, Private Party and used Retail Values.

What is the difference between Trade-In, Private Party and Retail Values?

Kelley Blue Book provides several different values representing different types of transactions.

Trade-In Value is what consumers can expect to receive from a dealer for a Trade-In vehicle assuming an accurate appraisal of condition. This value will likely be less than the Private Party Value because the dealer incurs the cost of safety inspections, reconditioning and other costs of doing business.

Kelley Blue Book factors the following into our Trade-In values:

Safety Inspections — The dealer will incur the cost of inspecting and repairing the vehicle to ensure that it meets government requirements for safety and smog emissions.

Reconditioning — Before reselling a vehicle a dealer can spend hundreds or even thousands of dollars performing repairs, routine maintenance and cosmetic detailing and touch up.

The dealer also hopes to make a fair profit for its efforts.

INTRODUCTION

Private Party Value is what a buyer can expect to pay when buying a used car from a private party. The Private Party Value assumes the vehicle is sold "As Is" and carries no warranty (other than the continuing factory warranty). The final sales price will vary depending on the vehicle's actual condition and local market conditions. This value may also be used to derive Fair Market Value for insurance and vehicle donation purposes.

Suggested Retail Value is representative of dealers' asking prices and is the starting point for negotiation between a consumer and a dealer. This Suggested Retail Value assumes that the vehicle has been fully reconditioned and has a clean Title History. This value also takes into account the dealers' profit, costs for advertising, sales commissions and other costs of doing business. The final sales price will likely be less depending on the vehicle's actual condition, popularity, type of warranty offered and local market conditions.

How does Condition affect the value of the vehicle and what is the difference between "Good," "Very Good," and "Excellent"? There is never a single correct value for a used vehicle. The value of a vehicle depends on several factors, most importantly condition and overall appearance. Supply and demand for a particular vehicle, local market conditions and the economy also play a role in determining a car's value.

Kelley Blue Book provides additional values for used vehicles in each of the following conditions:

"Excellent" condition means that the vehicle looks new, is in excellent mechanical condition and needs no reconditioning. The vehicle has never had any body/paint work, is free of rust, has a clean title history and will pass a smog and safety inspection. The engine compartment is clean and free of visible defects, with no fluid leaks. The vehicle also has complete and verifiable service records. Roughly 3% of all used vehicles fall into this category.

"Very Good" condition means that the vehicle may have minor cosmetic defects, is in excellent mechanical condition, and requires minimal (if any) reconditioning. The vehicle is rust free and has had minor or no body/paint work. A clean title history, minimal signs of wear or visible defects, and will pass a smog and safety inspection. The vehicle also has most of its maintenance records.

"Good" condition means that the vehicle is free of any major defects. The vehicle has a clean title history with only minor (if any) paint, body and/or interior blemishes and no major mechanical problems. There should be little to no rust on the vehicle. The tires match and have substantial tread wear left. Only some reconditioning or routine servicing required to be sold at retail. Most used vehicles fall into this category.

HOW TO USE THE BLUE BOOK

Asterisks (****) may appear in place of values on certain vehicles where due to rarity in the marketplace or extreme special interest we can not yet provide accurate Trade-In or Private Party values. Some of these vehicles may be limited production or rarely traded-in. We have included retail values for these vehicles but asterisks appear in place of Trade-In and Private Party values.

FINDING A VEHICLE

There are two sections in this book, the Automobile or Car section up front and the Truck & Van Section in the back. The Truck & Van section is marked by black tabs on each page. Within each section, the makes are listed alphabetically and models are listed by size within each make. Model years are listed oldest to newest.

EQUIPMENT ADJUSTMENTS

To get the most accurate value, you will need to add or deduct from the base value depending on the equipment. "Adds" and "Deducts" appear underneath individual vehicles and in separate Equipment Schedules. A value in parentheses represents a "Deduct." More generic equipment adjustments appear in the Equipment Schedules. Schedules for cars are at the front of the book. Equipment schedules for trucks and vans are at the back of the book.

You should always add or subtract for each item that is listed separately, even if it is part of a package that you have already added for or if it was considered original standard equipment. If an equipment item is listed both underneath the vehicle listing and in the Equipment Schedule, use the value underneath the vehicle listing because it is specific to that vehicle.

MILEAGE

Mileage must also be taken into consideration to derive the most accurate valuation of a used vehicle. On page 9 we have listed an "acceptable" range of mileage for each model year. The range does not represent the average mileage driven for the model year but the point of resistance where value can be affected. As a vehicle gets older, condition is more important than mileage. Vehicles with more miles may sometimes be worth more than lower mileage vehicles if its condition is better. It is important to note that the values we list are intended for vehicles within the acceptable mileage range.

HOW TO USE THE BLUE BOOK

ABBREVIATIONS USED IN THIS BOOK

VIN — Vehicle Identification Number. The VIN may vary depending on model, engine, transmission and option packages.

W.B. — Wheelbase. This is the distance from the center of the front wheel to the center of the rear wheel.

CID/L — Engine size displacement in cubic inches or liters.

List — This is the original suggested retail price of the vehicle when it was sold new, including destination charges and equipment as indicated on the equipment schedule.

Trucks — Trucks listed in this guide have a smooth exterior with the rear wheel wells inside the bed. Value adjustments for models with the rear wheel wells on the outside of the bed can be found on the Truck Equipment Schedules under the Stepside listing.

Premium Sound — This refers to an upgraded sound system (Bose, JBL, Infinity, etc.) not simply a CD changer, equalizer or an aftermarket receiver.

VEHICLE IDENTIFICATION NUMBERS (VINs)

If you are not sure of the year or model of a vehicle, you can often determine them from the Vehicle Identification Number or VIN. Using VINs can get a bit technical. If you already know the year and the model of the vehicle you can skip this information.

Under 2013 Jaguar, you will see the heading "2013 JAGUAR — SAJ (WA0E7)-D-#." This indicates that all 2013 Jaguars have a VIN starting with SAJ and have a D in the 10th position. The fourth through eighth positions determine the specific Jaguar model and are marked by parentheses. The hyphens indicate positions which can be ignored and the # symbol represents the individual vehicle's serial number.

Please note that we do not have room in this guidebook to list all the VIN information. There are some VINs that you cannot decode using the information provided. Also there are some VINs that indicate two or more possible models. In these cases you must determine the particular model by inspecting the vehicle.

TIPS ON BUYING A USED CAR

DEALER vs PRIVATE PARTY

There are advantages and disadvantages to buying a car from a dealer vs a Private Party. With a dealer, you may get a warranty and some dealerships offer certification programs for late model vehicles that will extend the original factory warranty. While buying from a dealership provides security, buying from a Private Party can save you money. When buying from a private party, ask for all repair and maintenance records and contact information of the previous owner in case you have questions later.

TRADING-IN YOUR VEHICLE

If you are trading your vehicle to a dealer, be sure to check the Trade-In Value and the Private Party Value of your vehicle. You may find it to your benefit to sell the vehicle yourself.

CHECKING OUT A USED VEHICLE

If you are contacting a private party, be sure to ask why they are selling the vehicle. Ask them to describe the condition of the vehicle and how it was used (daily, as a second car, kids car). Ask if they have all of the repair and maintenance records for the vehicle. Ask if you can take the car to a mechanic for an inspection. This is extremely important as private party sales are "As Is" and once you have bought the vehicle, it's yours. If your state requires a smog certificate, insist that the vehicle pass a smog test before buying the car. Smog checks are the current owner's responsibility. Also be certain the vehicle's registration is current and paid to date. It can be costly to reinstate an expired registration. Registration fees vary from state to state, be sure to consult your state's Department of Motor Vehicles.

— Stand away from the vehicle and look at its body panels. Do they all match in color? Do they line up?

— Check the tires for wear. Uneven tire wear, balding on the sides or in the middle, could indicate the need for an alignment or a costly repair to the vehicle's suspension.

— Open the trunk, hood and doors. Look for paint specks or over spray, a sign that all or part of the vehicle has been repainted. If the vehicle has been repainted it is often a sign of some previous damage.

— Check the radiator fluid. If it is very dark or has oil droplets in it, there is a good chance the vehicle has a cracked head gasket meaning that coolant and oil are mixing together.

— Look at the condition of the rubber on each foot pedal and the leather on the steering wheel. Do they show heavy wear? Heavy wear in a low mileage vehicle may indicate that the vehicle has seen more mileage then the odometer indicates.

TIPS ON BUYING A USED CAR

— Spend as much time as you can inside the vehicle. Feel the seat, and we mean really feel it. Take a good long time to sit, because really, the seat is one of the most important parts of the vehicle.

— What about the steering wheel? Is it too high up or too close to the dash? When adjusted comfortably, does it cut off any or all the gauges? Look at the layout of the radio and heater controls. Can they be easily adjusted without taking your eyes off the road? Look over your shoulders, are there any blind spots that you cannot compensate for by using your mirrors? Climb into the seats, front and back. Is there enough legroom and headroom? Do the headrests come up far enough? Do they touch your head or are they raked back at an angle away from you? Does the seatbelt have an adjustable anchor or does it cut into your neck? Check to see how far the rear windows roll down. Some models have windows that only go down a few inches or are sealed in place and don't roll down at all. Take your time to explore all these areas.

— Then take it for a drive. How does it sound? A prolonged tapping could be the valves needing adjustment or a bad hydraulic lifter. Pump the brake pedal a few times and then press hard with your foot. If it slowly sinks all the way to the floor, there is either a leak in the line or the master cylinder/brake booster is dying. Shift into gear. If the vehicle is an automatic, the transmission should engage immediately and shifts should be crisp and quick. With your foot firmly on the brake, shift from drive to reverse; clunks or grinding noises could indicate a worn or broken engine/transmission mount, bad U-joints or differential wear.

— As you drive along, does the steering wheel shake or vibrate? It shouldn't. Vibration in the steering wheel can mean anything from an unbalanced wheel to a loose steering rack. Cars with ABS (anti-lock brakes) will have a slight pulsating action in the brake pedal when the brakes are applied with some force. Cars without ABS should not have a pulsating brake pedal.

— We also recommend that you contact your local Department of Motor Vehicles. Ask them what forms are required to transfer the vehicle title as well as any other required information. For example, some states require a smog certificate while others require the bill of sale from the current owner.

— Lastly, whatever you do, get it in WRITING. This means if you settle with a private party, write up a contract stating what you are paying for the vehicle and under what terms it is to be delivered. Likewise with a dealer, any work they promise to do or options they intend to add, get it in writing before you close the deal.

MILEAGE RANGES

ACCEPTABLE MILEAGE RANGES

The following are acceptable mileage ranges for each model year. They do **not** represent the average miles driven. Rather, they represent an accepted mileage range as demonstrated by market research. If a vehicle's mileage is outside of the accepted range, dollar adjustments may be necessary. Mileage higher than shown on the guidelines below can expect to encounter resistance from a buyer.

YEAR	ACCEPTABLE MILEAGE RANGE
2000 – 2002	148,000 – 153,000
2003	141,000 – 146,000
2004	132,000 – 137,000
2005	123,000 – 128,000
2006	114,000 – 119,000
2007	106,000 – 111,000
2008	96,000 – 101,000
2009	87,000 – 92,000
2010	73,000 – 78,000
2011	58,000 – 63,000
2012	45,000 – 50,000
2013	34,000 – 39,000
2014	25,000 – 30,000

PRIVATE PARTY & RETAIL EQUIPMENT VALUE CONVERSION

Use the chart below to convert Trade-In Equipment Values to Private Party and Retail Values. Simply find your total Trade-In Equipment Value under the Trade-In (TI) column then follow across to the Private Party and Retail (PP/R) column. This new figure will be your Private Party or Retail Equipment Value.

TI	PP/R	TI	PP/R	TI	PP/R	TI	PP/R	TI	PP/R
25	35	225	300	425	565	625	835	825	1100
50	65	250	335	450	600	650	865	850	1135
75	100	275	365	475	635	675	900	875	1165
100	135	300	400	500	665	700	935	900	1200
125	165	325	435	525	700	725	965	925	1235
150	200	350	465	550	735	750	1000	950	1265
175	235	375	500	575	765	775	1035	975	1300
200	265	400	535	600	800	800	1065	1000	1335

2000-2001 FACTORY EQUIPMENT TRADE-IN VALUES

Equipment	1	2	3	4	5	6
Premium Sound	25	25	25	25	25	25
Navigation System	50	—	—	—	—	—
Leather	*	*	100	100	100	100
Rear Spoiler	25	25	25	25	25	25
Parking Sensors	70	—	—	—	—	—
Alloy Wheels	*	*	25	25	25	25
Premium Wheels	100	100	50	50	50	25
Roof Rack (Wagon)	25	25	25	25	25	25
Third Seat (Wagon)	125	50	50	50	50	50
DEDUCT FOR:						
w/o ABS	—	—	(50)	(50)	(25)	(25)
w/o Power Windows	—	—	—	—	(25)	(25)
w/o Power Locks	—	—	—	—	(25)	(25)
w/o Tilt Wheel	—	—	—	—	(25)	(25)
w/o Leather	(100)	(100)	—	—	—	—
w/o Cassette	—	—	—	—	(50)	(50)

* — EQUIPMENT INCLUDED IN BASE PRICE

10   SEE PAGE 9 FOR PVT PARTY & RETAIL EQUIPMENT

2002 FACTORY EQUIPMENT TRADE-IN VALUES

Equipment	1	2	3	4	5	6
Premium Sound	25	25	25	25	25	25
Navigation System	50	110	110	115	115	115
Leather	*	*	100	100	100	100
Rear Spoiler	25	25	25	25	25	25
Parking Sensors	85	60	—	—	—	—
Alloy Wheels	*	*	25	25	25	25
Premium Wheels	100	100	50	50	50	25
Roof Rack (Wagon)	25	25	25	25	25	25
Third Seat (Wagon)	125	50	50	50	50	50
DEDUCT FOR:						
w/o ABS	—	—	(50)	(50)	(25)	(25)
w/o Power Windows	—	—	—	—	(25)	(25)
w/o Power Locks	—	—	—	—	(25)	(25)
w/o Tilt Wheel	—	—	—	—	(25)	(25)
w/o Leather	(100)	(100)	—	—	—	—
w/o Cassette	—	—	—	—	(25)	(25)

* — EQUIPMENT INCLUDED IN BASE PRICE

SEE PAGE 9 FOR PVT PARTY & RETAIL EQUIPMENT

2003 FACTORY EQUIPMENT TRADE-IN VALUES

Equipment	1	2	3	4	5	6
Premium Sound	25	25	25	25	25	25
Navigation System	65	120	120	125	125	125
Leather	*	*	100	100	100	100
Rear Spoiler	25	25	25	25	25	25
Parking Sensors	90	65	—	—	—	—
Alloy Wheels	*	*	25	25	25	25
Premium Wheels	115	115	65	65	50	25
Premium Whls 19"+	380	380	380	380	380	380
Roof Rack (Wagon)	25	25	25	25	25	25
Third Seat (Wagon)	140	65	65	65	50	50
DEDUCT FOR:						
w/o ABS	—	—	(50)	(50)	(25)	(25)
w/o Power Windows	—	—	—	—	(25)	(25)
w/o Power Locks	—	—	—	—	(25)	(25)
w/o Tilt Wheel	—	—	—	—	(25)	(25)
w/o Leather	(100)	(100)	—	—	—	—

* — EQUIPMENT INCLUDED IN BASE PRICE

2004 FACTORY EQUIPMENT TRADE-IN VALUES

Equipment	1	2	3	4	5	6
Premium Sound	25	25	25	25	25	25
Navigation System	90	135	135	135	135	135
Leather	*	*	100	100	100	100
Rear Spoiler	25	25	25	25	25	25
Parking Sensors	100	75	60	—	—	—
Alloy Wheels	*	*	25	25	25	25
Premium Wheels	140	140	90	90	50	25
Premium Whls 19"+	410	410	410	410	410	410
Roof Rack (Wagon)	25	25	25	25	25	25
Third Seat (Wagon)	185	90	90	90	50	50
DEDUCT FOR:						
w/o ABS	—	—	(50)	(50)	(25)	(25)
w/o Power Windows	—	—	—	—	(25)	(25)
w/o Power Locks	—	—	—	—	(25)	(25)
w/o Tilt Wheel	—	—	—	—	(25)	(25)
w/o Leather	(100)	(100)	—	—	—	—

* — EQUIPMENT INCLUDED IN BASE PRICE

SEE PAGE 9 FOR PVT PARTY & RETAIL EQUIPMENT

2005 FACTORY EQUIPMENT TRADE-IN VALUES

Equipment	1	2	3	4	5	6
Premium Sound	40	40	25	25	25	25
Video/DVD	100	100	100	100	100	100
Navigation System	135	145	145	145	145	145
Leather	*	*	115	115	115	115
Panorama Roof	790	—	—	—	—	—
Rear Spoiler	25	25	25	25	25	25
Parking Sensors	115	75	65	—	—	—
Backup Camera	—	—	—	—	—	—
Alloy Wheels	*	*	25	25	25	25
Premium Wheels	165	165	115	115	65	25
Premium Whls 19"+	440	440	440	440	440	440
Roof Rack (Wagon)	25	25	25	25	25	25
Third Seat (Wagon)	235	115	115	115	65	65
DEDUCT FOR:						
w/o ABS	—	—	(50)	(50)	(25)	(25)
w/o Power Windows	—	—	—	—	(40)	(25)
w/o Power Locks	—	—	—	—	(25)	(25)
w/o Tilt Wheel	—	—	—	—	(25)	(25)
w/o Leather	(115)	(115)	—	—	—	—

* — EQUIPMENT INCLUDED IN BASE PRICE

2006 FACTORY EQUIPMENT TRADE-IN VALUES

Equipment	1	2	3	4	5	6
Premium Sound	65	65	25	25	25	25
Video/DVD	120	120	120	120	120	120
Navigation System	185	185	185	185	185	185
Leather	*	*	140	140	140	140
Panorama Roof	835	—	—	—	—	—
Rear Spoiler	25	25	25	25	25	25
Parking Sensors	140	90	70	—	—	—
Backup Camera	175	175	175	—	—	—
Alloy Wheels	*	*	40	40	25	25
Premium Wheels	190	190	140	140	90	40
Premium Whls 19"+	450	450	450	450	450	450
Roof Rack (Wagon)	25	25	25	25	25	25
Third Seat (Wagon)	285	140	140	140	90	90
DEDUCT FOR:						
w/o ABS	—	—	(50)	(50)	(25)	(25)
w/o Power Windows	—	(90)	—	(90)	(65)	(25)
w/o Power Locks	—	(25)	—	(25)	(25)	(25)
w/o Tilt Wheel	—	(65)	—	(65)	(40)	(25)
w/o Leather	(140)	(140)	—	—	—	—

* — EQUIPMENT INCLUDED IN BASE PRICE

SEE PAGE 9 FOR PVT PARTY & RETAIL EQUIPMENT

2007 FACTORY EQUIPMENT TRADE-IN VALUES

Equipment	1	2	3	4	5	6
Premium Sound	90	90	40	40	40	40
Video/DVD	180	180	180	180	180	180
Navigation System	235	235	235	235	235	235
Leather	*	*	165	165	165	165
Panorama Roof	885	—	—	—	—	—
Rear Spoiler	25	25	25	25	25	25
Parking Sensors	165	115	75	—	—	—
Backup Camera	185	185	185	—	—	—
Alloy Wheels	*	*	65	65	40	25
Premium Wheels	235	235	165	165	115	65
Premium Whls 19"+	450	450	450	450	450	450
Roof Rack (Wagon)	25	25	25	25	25	25
Third Seat (Wagon)	335	165	165	165	115	115
DEDUCT FOR:						
w/o ABS	—	—	(65)	(65)	(25)	(25)
w/o Power Windows	—	—	—	—	(90)	—
w/o Power Locks	—	—	—	—	(25)	—
w/o Tilt Wheel	—	—	—	—	(65)	—
w/o Leather	(165)	(165)	—	—	—	—

* — EQUIPMENT INCLUDED IN BASE PRICE

2008 FACTORY EQUIPMENT TRADE-IN VALUES

Equipment	1	2	3	4	5	6
Premium Sound	115	115	65	65	65	65
Video/DVD	200	200	200	200	200	200
Navigation System	285	285	285	285	285	285
Leather	*	*	190	190	190	190
Panorama Roof	935	—	695	695	—	—
Rear Spoiler	25	25	25	25	25	25
Parking Sensors	190	140	90	—	—	—
Backup Camera	195	195	195	—	—	—
Alloy Wheels	*	*	90	90	65	40
Premium Wheels	285	285	190	190	140	90
Premium Whls 19"+	450	450	450	450	450	450
Roof Rack (Wagon)	25	25	25	25	25	25
Third Seat (Wagon)	385	190	190	190	140	140
DEDUCT FOR:						
w/o ABS	—	—	(90)	(90)	(40)	(40)
w/o Power Windows	—	—	—	—	(115)	(65)
w/o Power Locks	—	—	—	—	(40)	(25)
w/o Tilt Wheel	—	—	—	—	(90)	(40)
w/o Leather	(190)	(190)	—	—	—	—

* — EQUIPMENT INCLUDED IN BASE PRICE

SEE PAGE 9 FOR PVT PARTY & RETAIL EQUIPMENT

2009 FACTORY EQUIPMENT TRADE-IN VALUES

Equipment	1	2	3	4	5	6
Premium Sound	140	140	90	90	75	75
Video/DVD	235	235	235	235	235	235
Navigation System	315	315	315	315	315	315
Leather	*	*	235	235	235	235
Panorama Roof	950	—	735	735	—	—
Rear Spoiler	40	40	40	40	40	40
Parking Sensors	215	150	100	—	—	—
Backup Camera	200	200	200	—	—	—
Alloy Wheels	*	*	100	100	75	50
Premium Wheels	315	315	215	215	150	100
Premium Whls 19"+	485	485	485	485	485	485
Roof Rack (Wagon)	40	40	40	40	40	40
Third Seat (Wagon)	415	215	215	215	165	165
DEDUCT FOR:						
w/o ABS	—	—	(100)	(100)	(50)	(50)
w/o Power Windows	—	—	—	—	(125)	(75)
w/o Power Locks	—	—	—	—	(50)	—
w/o Tilt Wheel	—	—	—	—	(100)	(50)
w/o Leather	(235)	(235)	—	—	—	—

* — EQUIPMENT INCLUDED IN BASE PRICE

2010 FACTORY EQUIPMENT TRADE-IN VALUES

Equipment	1	2	3	4	5	6
Premium Sound	165	165	115	115	75	75
Video/DVD	285	285	285	285	285	285
Navigation System	340	340	340	340	340	340
Leather	*	*	285	285	285	285
Panorama Roof	950	775	775	775	—	—
Rear Spoiler	65	65	65	65	65	65
Parking Sensors	240	165	100	—	—	—
Backup Camera	200	200	200	—	—	—
Alloy Wheels	*	*	100	100	75	50
Premium Wheels	340	340	240	240	165	100
Premium Whls 19"+	535	535	535	535	535	535
Roof Rack (Wagon)	65	65	65	65	50	50
Third Seat (Wagon)	440	240	240	240	190	190
DEDUCT FOR:						
w/o ABS	—	—	(100)	(100)	(50)	(50)
w/o Power Windows	—	—	—	—	(140)	(75)
w/o Power Locks	—	—	—	—	(50)	(25)
w/o Tilt Wheel	—	—	—	—	(100)	(50)
w/o Leather	(285)	(285)	—	—	—	—

* — EQUIPMENT INCLUDED IN BASE PRICE

SEE PAGE 9 FOR PVT PARTY & RETAIL EQUIPMENT

2011 FACTORY EQUIPMENT TRADE-IN VALUES

Equipment	1	2	3	4	5	6
Premium Sound	190	190	140	140	90	75
Video/DVD	335	335	335	335	335	335
Navigation System	385	385	385	385	385	335
Leather	*	*	335	335	335	335
Panorama Roof	950	810	810	465	—	—
Rear Spoiler	90	90	90	90	90	90
Parking Sensors	265	190	100	—	—	—
Backup Camera	200	200	200	—	—	—
Alloy Wheels	*	*	100	100	75	50
Premium Wheels	385	385	265	265	190	100
Premium Whls 19"+	585	585	585	585	585	585
Roof Rack (Wagon)	—	90	90	90	50	50
Third Seat (Wagon)	—	265	265	265	215	215
DEDUCT FOR:						
w/o ABS	—	—	(100)	(100)	(50)	(50)
w/o Power Windows	—	—	—	—	(165)	(75)
w/o Power Locks	—	—	—	—	(50)	(25)
w/o Tilt Wheel	—	—	—	—	(100)	(50)
w/o Leather	(335)	(335)	—	—	—	—

* — EQUIPMENT INCLUDED IN BASE PRICE

2012 FACTORY EQUIPMENT TRADE-IN VALUES

Equipment	1	2	3	4	5	6
Premium Sound	215	215	165	165	115	75
Video/DVD	385	385	385	385	385	385
Navigation System	435	435	435	435	435	435
Leather	*	*	385	385	385	385
Panorama Roof	965	825	825	—	—	—
Rear Spoiler	100	100	100	100	100	100
Parking Sensors	290	215	115	115	—	—
Backup Camera	200	200	200	200	—	—
Alloy Wheels	*	*	115	115	90	65
Premium Wheels	435	435	290	290	215	115
Premium Whls 19"+	650	650	650	650	650	650
Roof Rack (Wagon)	—	100	100	100	50	50
Third Seat (Wagon)	—	290	290	290	240	240
DEDUCT FOR:						
w/o ABS	—	—	(115)	(115)	(65)	(50)
w/o Power Windows	—	—	—	—	(190)	(90)
w/o Power Locks	—	—	—	—	(65)	(25)
w/o Tilt Wheel	—	—	—	—	(100)	(65)
w/o Leather	(385)	(385)	—	—	—	—

* — EQUIPMENT INCLUDED IN BASE PRICE

SEE PAGE 9 FOR PVT PARTY & RETAIL EQUIPMENT **21**

2013 FACTORY EQUIPMENT TRADE-IN VALUES

Equipment	1	2	3	4	5	6
Premium Sound	240	240	190	190	140	90
Video/DVD	435	435	435	435	435	435
Navigation System	485	485	485	485	485	485
Leather	*	*	435	435	435	435
Panorama Roof	990	825	825	825	—	—
Rear Spoiler	100	100	100	100	100	100
Parking Sensors	315	240	140	140	—	—
Backup Camera	200	200	200	200	—	—
Alloy Wheels	*	*	140	140	115	90
Premium Wheels	485	485	335	335	240	140
Premium Whls 19"+	725	725	725	725	725	725
Roof Rack (Wagon)	—	100	100	100	50	50
Third Seat (Wagon)	—	335	335	335	265	265
DEDUCT FOR:						
w/o ABS	—	—	(140)	(140)	(90)	(50)
w/o Power Windows	—	—	—	—	(215)	(115)
w/o Power Locks	—	—	—	—	(90)	(40)
w/o Tilt Wheel	—	—	—	—	(115)	(90)
w/o Leather	(435)	(435)	—	—	—	—

∗ — EQUIPMENT INCLUDED IN BASE PRICE

2014 FACTORY EQUIPMENT TRADE-IN VALUES

Equipment	1	2	3	4	5	6
Premium Sound	265	265	215	215	165	115
Video/DVD	485	485	485	485	485	485
Navigation System	535	535	535	535	535	535
Leather	*	*	500	500	500	500
Panorama Roof	1015	825	825	825	—	—
Rear Spoiler	100	100	100	100	100	100
Parking Sensors	340	265	165	165	—	—
Backup Camera	200	200	200	200	—	—
Alloy Wheels	*	*	165	165	140	115
Premium Wheels	535	535	385	385	265	165
Premium Whls 19"+	800	800	800	800	800	800
Roof Rack (Wagon)	—	100	100	100	50	50
Third Seat (Wagon)	—	385	385	385	290	290
DEDUCT FOR:						
w/o ABS	—	—	(165)	(165)	(165)	(65)
w/o Power Windows	—	—	—	—	(240)	140
w/o Power Locks	—	—	—	—	(175)	(65)
w/o Tilt Wheel	—	—	—	—	(200)	(200)
w/o Leather	(500)	(500)	—	—	—	—

* — EQUIPMENT INCLUDED IN BASE PRICE

SEE PAGE 9 FOR PVT PARTY & RETAIL EQUIPMENT

Body Type	VIN	List	Trade-In Good	Very Good	Pvt-Party Good	Retail Excellent

Automobile Section

ACURA

2000 ACURA — (JH4or19U)(DB765)-Y-#

INTEGRA—4-Cyl.—Equipment Schedule 3
W.B. 101.2", 103.1" (4D); 1.8 Liter.

Body Type	VIN	List	Good	Very Good	Good	Excellent
LS Sedan 4D	DB765	21355	1700	1900	2450	4000
LS Sport Coupe 2D	DC445	20555	1750	1975	2525	4150
GS Sedan 4D	DB766	22755	1875	2100	2650	4325
GS Sport Coupe 2D	DC446	22205	1950	2200	2725	4425
GS-R Sedan 4D	DB859	22955	1925	2175	2750	4475
GS-R Sport Coupe 2D	DC239	22655	2000	2275	2800	4525
Type R Sport Cpe 2D	DC231	24805	****	****	****	8200
Manual, 5-Spd (Sedan)	3,5		(100)	(100)	(135)	(135)

TL—V6—Equipment Schedule 1
W.B. 108.1"; 3.2 Liter.

3.2 Sedan 4D	UA566	28855	1700	1975	2450	4225

RL—V6—Equipment Schedule 1
W.B. 114.6"; 3.5 Liter.

3.5 Sedan 4D	KA965	42455	1100	1275	2050	3675

NSX—V6—Equipment Schedule 2
W.B. 99.6"; 3.0 Liter, 3.2 Liter.

Sport Coupe 2D	NA123	84745	25200	26700	26100	32900
T-Targa 2D	NA126	88745	25600	27100	26200	32900

2001 ACURA — (JH4or19U)(DB765)-1-#

INTEGRA—4-Cyl.—Equipment Schedule 3
W.B. 101.2", 103.1" (4D); 1.8 Liter.

LS Sedan 4D	DB765	21480	2100	2375	2750	4300
LS Sport Coupe 2D	DC445	20680	2200	2475	2900	4600
GS Sedan 4D	DB766	22880	2425	2625	3100	4950
GS Sport Coupe 2D	DC446	22330	2425	2725	3175	5025
GS-R Sedan 4D	DB859	23080	2400	2700	3175	5025
GS-R Sport Coupe 2D	DC239	22780	2550	2850	3275	5125
Type R Sport Cpe 2D	DC231	24930	****	****	****	9450
Manual, 5-Spd (Sedan)	3,5		(175)	(175)	(225)	(225)

CL—V6—Equipment Schedule 1
W.B. 106.9"; 3.2 Liter.

3.2 Coupe 2D	YA424	28460	1725	2000	2475	3950
3.2 Type S Coupe 2D	YA426	30810	2000	2300	2825	4600

TL—V6—Equipment Schedule 1
W.B. 108.1"; 3.2 Liter.

3.2 Sedan 4D	UA566	29030	1900	2200	2725	4600

RL—V6—Equipment Schedule 1
W.B. 114.6"; 3.5 Liter.

3.5 Sedan 4D	KA965	42630	1575	1825	2650	4600

NSX—V6—Equipment Schedule 2
W.B. 99.6"; 3.0 Liter, 3.2 Liter.

Sport Coupe 2D	NA123	84845	28600	30300	29500	36700
Targa 2D	NA126	88845	29000	30700	29700	36700

2002 ACURA — (JH4or19U)(DC548)-2-#

RSX—4-Cyl.—Equipment Schedule 3
W.B. 101.2"; 2.0 Liter.

Sport Coupe 2D	DC548	21350	2900	3250	3625	5600
Type S Sport Cpe 2D	DC530	23650	3150	3525	4100	6400

CL—V6—Equipment Schedule 1
W.B. 106.9"; 3.2 Liter.

3.2 Coupe 2D	YA424	28510	2025	2325	2825	4475
3.2 Type S Coupe 2D	YA426	30860	2475	2825	3350	5325

TL—V6—Equipment Schedule 1
W.B. 108.1"; 3.2 Liter.

3.2 Sedan 4D	UA566	29360	2225	2550	3075	5075
3.2 Type S Sedan 4D	UA568	31710	2600	2975	3500	5750

RL—V6—Equipment Schedule 1
W.B. 114.6"; 3.5 Liter.

3.5 Sedan 4D	KA965	43630	1825	2075	2800	4650

Body Type	VIN	List	Trade-In Good	Very Good	Pvt-Party Good	Retail Excellent
NSX—V6—Equipment Schedule 2						
W.B. 99.6"; 3.0 Liter, 3.2 Liter.						
Targa 2D	NA126	89745	31500	33200	32400	40000

2003 ACURA — (JH4or19U)(DC548)-3-#

Body Type	VIN	List	Trade-In Good	Very Good	Pvt-Party Good	Retail Excellent
RSX—4-Cyl.—Equipment Schedule 3						
W.B. 101.2"; 2.0 Liter.						
Sport Coupe 2D	DC548	21375	3325	3700	4275	6575
Type S Sport Cpe 2D	DC530	23770	3850	4275	4800	7300
CL—V6—Equipment Schedule 1						
W.B. 106.9"; 3.2 Liter.						
3.2 Coupe 2D	YA424	28700	2475	2800	3325	5200
3.2 Type S Coupe 2D	YA426	31050	3000	3400	3925	6125
TL—V6—Equipment Schedule 1						
W.B. 108.1"; 3.2 Liter.						
3.2 Sedan 4D	UA566	29480	2750	3150	3525	5575
3.2 Type S Sedan 4D	UA568	31830	3175	3625	4000	6375
RL—V6—Equipment Schedule 1						
W.B. 114.6"; 3.5 Liter.						
3.5 Sedan 4D	KA965	43650	2100	2375	3125	5125
NSX—V6—Equipment Schedule 2						
W.B. 99.6"; 3.0 Liter, 3.2 Liter.						
Targa 2D	NA126	89765	33300	35100	34100	41900

2004 ACURA — (JH4or19U)(DC548)-4-#

Body Type	VIN	List	Trade-In Good	Very Good	Pvt-Party Good	Retail Excellent
RSX—4-Cyl.—Equipment Schedule 3						
W.B. 101.2"; 2.0 Liter.						
Sport Coupe 2D	DC548	21470	3550	3925	4450	6725
Type S Sport Cpe 2D	DC530	23865	4025	4450	5000	7550
TSX—4-Cyl.—Equipment Schedule 1						
W.B. 105.1"; 2.4 Liter.						
Sedan 4D	CL958	26990	4350	4900	5475	8325
TL—V6—Equipment Schedule 1						
W.B. 107.9"; 3.2 Liter.						
3.2 Sedan 4D	UA566	33195	4725	5350	5375	7950
A-Spec Pkg			525	525	710	710
RL—V6—Equipment Schedule 1						
W.B. 114.6"; 3.5 Liter.						
3.5 Sedan 4D	KA965	46100	3225	3625	4450	7100
NSX—V6—Equipment Schedule 2						
W.B. 99.6"; 3.0 Liter, 3.2 Liter.						
Targa 2D	NA126	89765	35600	37500	36400	44200

2005 ACURA — (JH4or19U)(DC548)-5-#

Body Type	VIN	List	Trade-In Good	Very Good	Pvt-Party Good	Retail Excellent
RSX—4-Cyl.—Equipment Schedule 3						
W.B. 101.2"; 2.0 Liter.						
Sport Coupe 2D	DC548	21745	4075	4500	5150	7525
Type S Sport Cpe 2D	DC530	24240	5075	5600	6250	9025
TSX—4-Cyl.—Equipment Schedule 1						
W.B. 105.1"; 2.4 Liter.						
Sedan 4D	CL968	27760	5550	6200	6425	8900
TL—V6—Equipment Schedule 1						
W.B. 107.9"; 3.2 Liter.						
3.2 Sedan 4D	UA662	33670	5625	6325	6475	9225
A-Spec Pkg			575	575	775	775
RL SH-AWD—V6—Equipment Schedule 1						
W.B. 110.2"; 3.5 Liter.						
3.5 Sedan 4D	KB165	49670	5800	6475	6950	9900
NSX—V6—Equipment Schedule 2						
W.B. 99.6"; 3.0 Liter, 3.2 Liter.						
Targa 2D	NA126	89765	38400	40300	39200	47100

2006 ACURA — (JH4or19U)(DC548)-6-#

Body Type	VIN	List	Trade-In Good	Very Good	Pvt-Party Good	Retail Excellent
RSX—4-Cyl.—Equipment Schedule 3						
W.B. 101.2"; 2.0 Liter.						
Sport Coupe 2D	DC548	21840	5475	5975	6550	9125
Type S Sport Cpe 2D	DC530	24460	7225	7875	8375	11650
TSX—4-Cyl.—Equipment Schedule 1						
W.B. 105.1"; 2.4 Liter.						
Sedan 4D	CL968	28505	6425	7125	7350	10000
TL—V6—Equipment Schedule 1						
W.B. 107.9"; 3.2 Liter.						

2006 ACURA

Body Type	VIN	List	Trade-In Good	Trade-In Very Good	Pvt-Party Good	Retail Excellent
3.2 Sedan 4D	UA662	33940	6850	7625	7600	10500
A-Spec Pkg			625	625	845	845
RL SH-AWD—V6—Equipment Schedule 1						
W.B. 110.2"; 3.5 Liter.						
3.5 Sedan 4D	KB165	49915	7250	8025	8150	11050
Adaptive Cruise Control			325	325	415	415
Technology Pkg			650	650	870	870

2007 ACURA — (JH4or19U)(CL968)-7-#

Body Type	VIN	List	Trade-In Good	Trade-In Very Good	Pvt-Party Good	Retail Excellent
TSX—4-Cyl. VTEC—Equipment Schedule 3						
W.B. 105.1"; 2.4 Liter.						
Sedan 4D	CL968	28760	7350	8050	8450	11350
TL—V6 VTEC—Equipment Schedule 1						
W.B. 107.9"; 3.2 Liter, 3.5 Liter.						
3.2 Sedan 4D	UA662	34295	8275	9100	9000	12000
Type S Sedan 4D	UA755	38795	10200	11200	10950	14600
RL SH-AWD—V6—Equipment Schedule 1						
W.B. 110.2"; 3.5 Liter.						
3.5 Sedan 4D	KB165	46450	8600	9400	9425	12350
Adaptive Cruise Control			350	350	435	435
Technology Pkg			675	675	860	860

2008 ACURA — (JH4or19U)(CL968)-8-#

Body Type	VIN	List	Trade-In Good	Trade-In Very Good	Pvt-Party Good	Retail Excellent
TSX—4-Cyl. VTEC—Equipment Schedule 3						
W.B. 105.1"; 2.4 Liter.						
Sedan 4D	CL968	28905	8700	9350	9875	12750
TL—V6 VTEC—Equipment Schedule 1						
W.B. 107.9"; 3.2 Liter, 3.5 Liter.						
3.2 Sedan 4D	UA662	34440	9325	10050	10350	13250
Type S Sedan 4D	UA765	38940	11800	12700	12750	16250
A-Spec Pkg			725	725	925	925
RL SH-AWD—V6—Equipment Schedule 1						
W.B. 110.2"; 3.5 Liter.						
3.5 Sedan 4D	KB165	46995	10150	10900	11350	14550
Adaptive Cruise Control			375	375	455	455
Technology Pkg			700	700	855	855

2009 ACURA — (JH4or19U)(CU266)-9-#

Body Type	VIN	List	Trade-In Good	Trade-In Very Good	Pvt-Party Good	Retail Excellent
TSX—4-Cyl. VTEC—Equipment Schedule 3						
W.B. 106.4"; 2.4 Liter.						
Sedan 4D	CU266	29720	10450	11050	11800	14650
Technology Pkg			700	700	880	880
TL—V6 VTEC—Equipment Schedule 1						
W.B. 109.3"; 3.5 Liter, 3.7 Liter.						
Sedan 4D	UA862	35765	13050	13850	14100	17100
Technology Pkg			700	700	845	845
SH-AWD			1725	1725	2070	2070
RL SH-AWD—V6—Equipment Schedule 1						
W.B. 110.2"; 3.7 Liter.						
3.5 Sedan 4D	KB265	47040	13250	14000	14950	18650
Technology Pkg			700	700	825	825

2010 ACURA — (JH4or19U)(CU2F6)-A-#

Body Type	VIN	List	Trade-In Good	Trade-In Very Good	Pvt-Party Good	Retail Excellent
TSX—4-Cyl. VTEC—Equipment Schedule 3						
W.B. 106.4"; 2.4 Liter.						
Sedan 4D	CU2F6	30070	11200	11700	12800	15450
Technology Pkg			725	725	890	890
V6, VTEC, 3.5 Liter	4		1850	1850	2300	2300
TL—V6 VTEC—Equipment Schedule 1						
W.B. 109.3"; 3.5 Liter, 3.7 Liter.						
Sedan 4D	UA8F2	35915	14450	15050	15850	18700
Technology Pkg			725	725	855	855
SH-AWD			1825	1825	2155	2155
RL SH-AWD—V6—Equipment Schedule 1						
W.B. 110.2"; 3.7 Liter.						
Sedan 4D	KB2F5	47640	16800	17550	18200	21400
Technology Pkg			725	725	830	830

2011 ACURA — (JH4or19U)(CU2F6)-B-#

TSX—4-Cyl. VTEC—Equipment Schedule 3
W.B. 106.4"; 2.4 Liter.

2011 ACURA

Body Type	VIN	List	Trade-In Good	Very Good	Pvt-Party Good	Retail Excellent
Sedan 4D	CU2F6	30470	13100	13550	14850	17600
Wagon 4D	CW2H5	31820	15350	15850	17300	20400
Technology Pkg			725	725	880	880
V6, VTEC, 3.5 Liter	4		1975	1975	2395	2395

TL—V6 VTEC—Equipment Schedule 1
W.B. 109.3"; 3.5 Liter, 3.7 Liter.

Sedan 4D	UA8F2	36165	15950	16500	17600	20300
Technology Pkg			725	725	860	860

RL SH-AWD—V6—Equipment Schedule 1
W.B. 110.2"; 3.7 Liter.

Sedan 4D	KB2F5	48060	19800	20400	21100	23900
Advance Pkg			900	900	980	980
Technology Pkg			725	725	810	810

2012 ACURA — (JH4or19U)(CU2F4)-C-#

TSX—4-Cyl. VTEC—Equipment Schedule 3
W.B. 106.4"; 2.4 Liter.

Sedan 4D	CU2F4	30695	14850	15250	16900	19700
Wagon 4D	CW2H5	32045	17150	17600	19000	21800
Technology Pkg			750	750	890	890
V6, VTEC, 3.5 Liter	4		2100	2100	2490	2490

TL—V6 VTEC—Equipment Schedule 1
W.B. 109.3"; 3.5 Liter.

Sedan 4D	UA8F2	36600	17500	17900	19250	21700
Advance Pkg			1275	1275	1490	1490
Technology Pkg			750	750	870	870

TL SH-AWD—V6 VTEC—Equipment Schedule 1
W.B. 109.3"; 3.7 Liter.

Sedan 4D	UA9F2	40150	20700	21200	22600	25400
Advance Pkg			1275	1275	1485	1485
Technology Pkg			750	750	870	870

RL SH-AWD—V6—Equipment Schedule 1
W.B. 110.2"; 3.7 Liter.

Sedan 4D	KB2F5	48585	23300	23900	25200	28600
Advance Pkg			1275	1275	1400	1400
Technology Pkg			750	750	815	815

2013 ACURA — (JH4or19U)(DE1F3)-D-#

ILX—4-Cyl. VTEC—Equipment Schedule 3
W.B. 105.1"; 2.0 Liter, 2.4 Liter.

2.0L Sedan 4D	DE1F3	26795	15450	15800	17350	19750
2.4L Sedan 4D	DE2E5	30095	15850	16200	17700	20200
Technology Pkg			1400	1400	1585	1585

ILX—4-Cyl. VTEC Hybrid—Equipment Schedule 3
W.B. 105.1"; 1.5 Liter.

Sedan 4D	DE3F3	29795	17650	18000	19450	22000
Technology Pkg			1400	1400	1565	1565

TSX—4-Cyl. VTEC—Equipment Schedule 3
W.B. 106.4"; 2.4 Liter.

Sedan 4D	CU2F4	31405	17500	17850	19400	22100
Wagon 4D	CW2H5	32775	20100	20500	22000	24800
Technology Pkg			775	775	880	880
V6, VTEC, 3.5 Liter	4		2225	2225	2560	2560

TL—V6 VTEC—Equipment Schedule 1
W.B. 109.3"; 3.5 Liter.

Sedan 4D	UA8F2	36800	21000	21300	22800	25300
Special Ed Sedan 4D	UA8F3	38300	21800	22200	23700	26300
Advance Pkg			950	950	1075	1075
Technology Pkg			775	775	870	870

TL SH-AWD—V6 VTEC—Equipment Schedule 1
W.B. 109.3"; 3.7 Liter.

Sedan 4D	UA9F2	40350	25200	25700	27300	30300
Advance Pkg			950	950	1070	1070
Technology Pkg			775	775	870	870

2014 ACURA — (JH4or19U)(DE1F5)-E-#

ILX—4-Cyl. VTEC—Equipment Schedule 3
W.B. 105.1"; 2.0 Liter.

2.0L Sedan 4D	DE1F5	27795	16700	17050	18550	21000
Premium Pkg			1225	1225	1365	1365
Technology Pkg			1475	1475	1650	1650

Body Type	VIN	List	Trade-In Good	Very Good	Pvt-Party Good	Retail Excellent
ILX—4-Cyl. VTEC—Equipment Schedule 3						
W.B. 105.1"; 2.4 Liter.						
2.4L Sedan 4D	DE2E5	30095	17700	18050	19500	22000
TSX—4-Cyl. VTEC—Equipment Schedule 3						
W.B. 106.5"; 2.4 Liter.						
Sedan 4D	CU2F4	31530	19600	19950	22100	25400
Wagon 4D	CW2H5	32880	22200	22600	24300	27500
Technology Pkg		------	775	775	905	905
V6, VTEC, 3.5 Liter		------	2350	2350	2710	2710
TL—V6 VTEC—Equipment Schedule 1						
W.B. 109.3"; 3.5 Liter.						
Sedan 4D	UA8F2	36925	24400	24900	26300	29000
Advance Pkg		------	975	975	1080	1080
Technology Pkg		------	775	775	870	870
TL—V6 VTEC—Equipment Schedule 1						
W.B. 109.3"; 3.5 Liter.						
Special Edition Sedan	UA8F3	38425	25300	25800	27300	30100
TL SH-AWD—V6 VTEC—Equipment Schedule 1						
W.B. 109.3"; 3.7 Liter.						
Sedan 4D	UA9F2	40475	28800	29300	30800	33900
Advance Pkg		------	975	975	1080	1080
Technology Pkg		------	775	775	870	870
RLX—V6 i-VTEC—Equipment Schedule 1						
W.B. 112.2"; 3.5 Liter.						
Sedan 4D	KC1F3	49345	27900	28400	30700	35100
Advance Pkg		------	975	975	1060	1060
Technology Pkg		------	775	775	860	860
RLX AWD—V6 i-VTEC Hybrid—Equipment Schedule 1						
W.B. 112.2"; 3.5 Liter.						
SH-AWD Sedan 4D	KC2F5	60870	29700	30300	32400	37000
Adaptive Cruise Control		------	500	500	535	535
Technology Pkg		------	775	775	855	855

ASTON MARTIN

2005 ASTON MARTIN — SCF(AD01A)-5-#

Body Type	VIN	List	Good	Very Good	Good	Excellent
DB9—V12—Equipment Schedule 2						
W.B. 107.9"; 6.0 Liter.						
Coupe 2D	AD01A	160000	****	****	****	60400
Volante Conv 2D	AD02A	173000	****	****	****	68500
VANQUISH S—V12—Equipment Schedule 2						
W.B. 105.9"; 6.0 Liter.						
Coupe 2D	AC243	255000	****	****	****	89100

2006 ASTON MARTIN — SCF(AD01A)-6-#

Body Type	VIN	List	Good	Very Good	Good	Excellent
DB9—V12—Equipment Schedule 2						
W.B. 107.9"; 6.0 Liter.						
Coupe 2D	AD01A	162350	****	****	****	63800
Volante Conv 2D	AD02A	176250	****	****	****	75400
VANQUISH S—V12—Equipment Schedule 2						
W.B. 105.9"; 6.0 Liter.						
Coupe 2D	AC243	261350	****	****	****	93600
VANTAGE—V8—Equipment Schedule 2						
W.B. 102.4"; 4.3 Liter.						
Coupe 2D	BB03B	108750	****	****	****	53600

2007 ASTON MARTIN — SCF(AD01A)-7-#

Body Type	VIN	List	Good	Very Good	Good	Excellent
DB9—V12—Equipment Schedule 2						
W.B. 108.0"; 6.0 Liter.						
Coupe 2D	AD01A	163400	****	****	****	74500
Volante Conv 2D	AD02A	176900	****	****	****	85600
VANTAGE—V8—Equipment Schedule 2						
W.B. 102.5"; 4.3 Liter.						
Coupe 2D	BB03B	111950	****	****	****	58300
Roadster 2D	BF04B	125150	****	****	****	69700

2008 ASTON MARTIN — SCF(AD01A)-8-#

Body Type	VIN	List	Good	Very Good	Good	Excellent
DB9—V12—Equipment Schedule 2						
W.B. 108.0"; 6.0 Liter.						
Coupe 2D	AD01A	168950	****	****	****	85200

Body Type	VIN	List	Trade-In Good	Very Good	Pvt-Party Good	Retail Excellent
Volante Conv 2D	AD02A	182450	****	****	****	106500
DBS—V12—Equipment Schedule 2						
W.B. 107.9"; 6.0 Liter.						
Coupe 2D	AB05D	266350	****	****	****	126300
VANTAGE—V8—Equipment Schedule 2						
W.B. 102.5"; 4.3 Liter.						
Coupe 2D	BF03B	114750	****	****	****	61700
Roadster 2D	BF04B	127750	****	****	****	73400

2009 ASTON MARTIN — SCF(AD01E)-9-#

Body Type	VIN	List	Trade-In Good	Very Good	Pvt-Party Good	Retail Excellent
DB9—V12—Equipment Schedule 2						
W.B. 108.0"; 6.0 Liter.						
Coupe 2D	AD01E	184685	****	****	-****	110900
Volante Conv 2D	AD02E	198185	****	****	****	130800
Bang & Olufsen Sound			****	****	****	2410
DBS—V12—Equipment Schedule 2						
W.B. 107.9"; 6.0 Liter.						
Coupe 2D	AB05D	270615	****	****	****	146000
Volante Conv 2D	AB02D	284115	****	****	****	150000
VANTAGE—V8—Equipment Schedule 2						
W.B. 102.5"; 4.3 Liter.						
Coupe 2D	BF03C	122365	****	****	****	69200
Roadster 2D	BF04C	135365	****	****	****	80200
Bang & Olufsen Sound			****	****	****	2420

2010 ASTON MARTIN — SCF(FDAAE)-A-#

Body Type	VIN	List	Trade-In Good	Very Good	Pvt-Party Good	Retail Excellent
DB9—V12—Equipment Schedule 2						
W.B. 107.9"; 6.0 Liter.						
Coupe 2D	FDAAE	187685	****	****	****	123500
Volante Conv 2D	FDABE	201185	****	****	****	142100
Bang & Olufsen Sound			****	****	****	2540
DBS—V12—Equipment Schedule 2						
W.B. 107.9"; 6.0 Liter.						
Coupe 2D	FDCBD	273615	****	****	****	167800
Volante Conv 2D	FDCCD	287115	****	****	****	171500
RAPIDE—V12—Equipment Schedule 2						
W.B. 117.7"; 6.0 Liter.						
Sedan 4D	HDDAJ	203665	****	****	****	153900
VANTAGE—V8—Equipment Schedule 2						
W.B. 102.5"; 4.7 Liter.						
Coupe 2D	EBBAC	122365	****	****	****	79300
Roadster 2D	EBBBC	135365	****	****	****	91200
N420 Coupe 2D	EBBAC	135315	****	****	****	86300
N420 Roadster 2D	EBBBC	148315	****	****	****	97200
Bang & Olufsen Sound			****	****	****	2545

2011 ASTON MARTIN — SCF(FDAAE)-B-#

Body Type	VIN	List	Trade-In Good	Very Good	Pvt-Party Good	Retail Excellent
DB9—V12—Equipment Schedule 2						
W.B. 107.9"; 6.0 Liter.						
Coupe 2D	FDAAE	192230	****	****	****	137900
Luxury Ed Coupe 2D	FDAAE	201175	****	****	****	143200
Sports Ed Coupe 2D	FDAAE	201566	****	****	****	143700
Volante Conv 2D	FDABE	205730	****	****	****	155300
Volante Luxury Conv	FDABE	214275	****	****	****	161100
Volante Sports Conv	FDABE	214666	****	****	****	161700
Bang & Olufsen BeoSound			****	****	****	2660
DBS—V12—Equipment Schedule 2						
W.B. 107.9"; 6.0 Liter.						
Coupe 2D	FDCBD	273275	****	****	****	192100
Volante Conv 2D	FDCCD	286910	****	****	****	195500
VANTAGE—V8—Equipment Schedule 2						
W.B. 102.5"; 4.7 Liter.						
Coupe 2D	EBBAK	121965	****	****	****	88100
Convertible 2D	EBBBK	134965	****	****	****	100000
N420 Coupe 2D	EBBAK	133215	****	****	****	94000
N420 Convertible 2D	EBBBK	146215	****	****	****	106600
S Coupe 2D	EKBDL	139615	****	****	****	103200
S Convertible 2D	EKBEL	152615	****	****	****	115100
Bang & Olufsen Sound			****	****	****	2660
VANTAGE—V12—Equipment Schedule 2						
W.B. 107.9"; 6.0 Liter.						
Coupe 2D	EBBCF	185150	****	****	****	138500

2011 ASTON MARTIN

Body Type	VIN	List	Trade-In Good	Trade-In Very Good	Pvt-Party Good	Retail Excellent
Carbon Black Coupe	EBBCF	196610	****	****	****	147000
Bang & Olufsen Sound						2635

2012 ASTON MARTIN — SCF(FDAAE)-C-#

DB9—V12—Equipment Schedule 2
W.B. 108.1"; 6.0 Liter.

Body Type	VIN	List	Good	Very Good	Good	Excellent
Coupe 2D	FDAAE	193730	****	****	****	151500
Luxury Ed Coupe 2D	FDAAE	199975	****	****	****	156500
Sports Ed Coupe 2D	FDAAE	200366	****	****	****	168100
Volante Conv 2D	FDABE	208730	****	****	****	173700
Volante Luxury Conv	FDABE	214975	****	****	****	174200
Volante Sports Conv	FDABE	215636	****	****	****	175100
Bang & Olufsen BeoSound						2790

RAPIDE—V12—Equipment Schedule 2
W.B. 117.7"; 6.0 Liter.

Body Type	VIN	List	Good	Very Good	Good	Excellent
Sedan 4D	HDDAJ	212110	****	****	****	167100
Luxe Sedan 4D	HDDAJ	231065	****	****	****	180500

VANTAGE—V8—Equipment Schedule 2
W.B. 102.5"; 4.7 Liter.

Body Type	VIN	List	Good	Very Good	Good	Excellent
Coupe 2D	EBBAK	122465	****	****	****	96300
Convertible 2D	EBBBK	135465	****	****	****	107900
N420 Coupe 2D	EBBAK	133715	****	****	****	101700
N420 Convertible 2D	EBBBK	146715	****	****	****	112800
S Coupe 2D	EKBDL	140115	****	****	****	110300
S Convertible 2D	EKBEL	153115	****	****	****	122200
Bang & Olufsen Sound						2785

VANTAGE—V12—Equipment Schedule 2
W.B. 107.9"; 6.0 Liter.

Body Type	VIN	List	Good	Very Good	Good	Excellent
Coupe 2D	EBBCF	185650	****	****	****	146600
Carbon Black Coupe	EBBCF	201010	****	****	****	153600
Bang & Olufsen Sound						2765

VIRAGE—V12—Equipment Schedule 2
W.B. 107.9"; 6.0 Liter.

Body Type	VIN	List	Good	Very Good	Good	Excellent
Coupe 2D	FDECN	211610	****	****	****	143400
Volante Conv 2D	FDEDN	226610	****	****	****	154500
Bang & Olufsen BeoSound						2795

2013 ASTON MARTIN — SCF(FDAAM)-D-#

DB9—V12—Equipment Schedule 2
W.B. 97.2"; 6.0 Liter.

Body Type	VIN	List	Good	Very Good	Good	Excellent
Coupe 2D	FDAAM	188225	****	****	****	158000
Volante Convertible	FDABM	203225	****	****	****	174200

VANTAGE—V8—Equipment Schedule 2
W.B. 102.4"; 4.7 Liter.

Body Type	VIN	List	Good	Very Good	Good	Excellent
Coupe 2D	EBBAK	121225	****	****	****	102900
Convertible 2D	EKBBK	135725	****	****	****	114200
S Coupe 2D	EKBDL	135225	****	****	****	116600
S Convertible 2D	EKBEL	149725	****	****	****	127700
Bang & Olufsen Sound						2925

2014 ASTON MARTIN — SCF(FDAAM)-E-#

DB9—V12—Equipment Schedule 2
W.B. 97.2"; 6.0 Liter.

Body Type	VIN	List	Good	Very Good	Good	Excellent
Coupe 2D	FDAAM	188225	****	****	****	162800
Volante Convertible	FDABM	203225	****	****	****	179200
Bang & Olufsen BeoSound						3050

VANQUISH—V12—Equipment Schedule 2
W.B. 107.9"; 6.0 Liter.

Body Type	VIN	List	Good	Very Good	Good	Excellent
Coupe 2D	LDCFP	282820	****	****	****	236100
Volante Convertible	PDCGP	300820	****	****	****	239300

RAPIDE S—V12—Equipment Schedule 2
W.B. 117.7"; 6.0 Liter.

Body Type	VIN	List	Good	Very Good	Good	Excellent
Sedan 4D	HDDAT	202775	****	****	****	164100

AUDI

2000 AUDI — (WAUorTRU)(AH28D)-Y-#

A4—V6—Equipment Schedule 3
W.B. 103.0"; 2.8 Liter.

Body Type	VIN	List	Good	Very Good	Good	Excellent
Sedan 4D	AH28D	30390	800	900	1600	2850

Body Type	VIN	List	Trade-In Good	Very Good	Pvt-Party Good	Retail Excellent
Quattro AWD	D		1100	1100	1480	1480
Manual, 5-Spd			(125)	(125)	(165)	(165)
4-Cyl, Turbo, 1.8 Liter	C		(450)	(450)	(600)	(600)
A4 AVANT QUATTRO AWD—V6—Equipment Schedule 3						
W.B. 102.6"; 2.8 Liter.						
Wagon 4D	KH28D	33140	1425	1650	2275	3850
Manual, 5-Spd			(125)	(125)	(165)	(165)
4-Cyl, Turbo, 1.8 Liter	C		(450)	(450)	(600)	(600)
S4 QUATTRO AWD—V6 Turbo—Equipment Schedule 3						
W.B. 102.6"; 2.7 Liter.						
2.7T Sedan 4D	DD68D	39625	1425	1600	2275	3750
A6—V6—Equipment Schedule 3						
W.B. 108.7"; 2.8 Liter.						
Sedan 4D	BH24B	34475	500	575	1075	1900
Quattro AWD	G,J		1100	1100	1480	1480
A6 AVANT QUATTRO AWD—V6—Equipment Schedule 3						
W.B. 108.6"; 2.8 Liter.						
Wagon 4D	LH24B	37425	1375	1550	1900	3050
A6 QUATTRO AWD—V6 Turbo—Equipment Schedule 3						
W.B. 108.7"; 2.7 Liter.						
2.7T Sedan 4D	ED24B	39075	1700	1925	2400	3900
A6 QUATTRO AWD—V8—Equipment Schedule 3						
W.B. 108.6"; 4.2 Liter.						
4.2 Sedan 4D	ZL54B	49425	1850	2100	2525	4025
A8 QUATTRO AWD—V8—Equipment Schedule 1						
W.B. 113.4", 118.5" (L); 4.2 Liter.						
Sedan 4D	FL54D	62525	650	725	1400	2350
L Sedan 4D	FL54D	68425	1625	1775	2550	4000
TT—4-Cyl. Turbo—Equipment Schedule 3						
W.B. 95.4", 95.6"; 1.8 Liter.						
Coupe 2D	TC28N	31025	1575	1750	2300	3700
Quattro AWD	U		1100	1100	1480	1480

Body Type	VIN	List	Trade-In Good	Very Good	Pvt-Party Good	Retail Excellent
A4—V6—Equipment Schedule 3						
W.B. 103.0"; 2.8 Liter.						
Sedan 4D	AH68D	30890	1050	1150	1875	3250
Quattro AWD	D		1200	1200	1585	1585
Manual, 5-Spd			(175)	(175)	(225)	(225)
4-Cyl, Turbo, 1.8 Liter	C		(500)	(500)	(670)	(670)
A4 AVANT QUATTRO AWD—V6—Equipment Schedule 3						
W.B. 102.6"; 2.8 Liter.						
Wagon 4D	KH68D	33640	1900	2175	2725	4425
Manual, 5-Spd			(175)	(175)	(225)	(225)
4-Cyl, Turbo, 1.8 Liter	C		(500)	(500)	(670)	(670)
S4 QUATTRO AWD—V6 Turbo—Equipment Schedule 3						
W.B. 102.6"; 2.7 Liter.						
2.7T Sedan 4D	RD58D	39450	2700	2975	3375	5050
2.7T Avant Wagon 4D	XD68D	41050	3650	4025	4475	6650
A6—V6—Equipment Schedule 3						
W.B. 108.7"; 2.8 Liter.						
Sedan 4D	BH54B	34950	500	575	1100	1975
Quattro AWD	E		1200	1200	1585	1585
A6 AVANT QUATTRO AWD—V6—Equipment Schedule 3						
W.B. 108.6"; 2.8 Liter.						
Wagon 4D	LH54B	37900	1400	1575	2025	3325
A6 QUATTRO AWD—V6 Turbo—Equipment Schedule 3						
W.B. 108.7"; 2.7 Liter.						
2.7T Sedan 4D	ED54B	40050	1950	2200	2700	4325
Sport Pkg			250	250	345	345
ALLROAD QUATTRO AWD—V6 Turbo—Equipment Sch 1						
W.B. 108.5"; 2.7 Liter.						
2.7T Wagon 4D	YP54B	43450	2450	2750	3225	5125
A6 QUATTRO AWD—V8—Equipment Schedule 3						
W.B. 108.6"; 4.2 Liter.						
4.2 Sedan 4D	ZL54B	49950	2100	2350	2825	4475
Sport Pkg			250	250	345	345
A8 QUATTRO AWD—V8—Equipment Schedule 1						
W.B. 113.4", 118.5" (L); 4.2 Liter.						
Sedan 4D	FL54D	62750	700	775	1500	2550
L Sedan 4D	ML54D	68450	1850	2000	2900	4550
S8 QUATTRO AWD—V8—Equipment Schedule 1						
W.B. 113.4"; 4.2 Liter.						

Body Type	VIN	List	Trade-In Good	Very Good	Pvt-Party Good	Retail Excellent
Sedan 4D	GU54D	73050	3950	4275	5000	7175
TT—4-Cyl. Turbo—Equipment Schedule 2						
W.B. 95.4"; 1.8 Liter.						
Coupe 2D	SC28N	31750	1175	1300	2050	3450
Roadster 2D	TC28N	33750	1625	1800	2450	3950
Power Folding Roof			250	250	335	335
TT QUATTRO AWD—4-Cyl. HO Turbo—Equipment Schedule 2						
W.B. 95.4"; 1.8 Liter.						
Coupe 2D	WT28N	36650	2725	3000	3600	5525
Roadster 2D	UT28N	39450	3275	3600	4100	6200

2002 AUDI — (WAUorTRU)(JC58E)–2–#

Body Type	VIN	List	Trade-In Good	Very Good	Pvt-Party Good	Retail Excellent
A4—V6—Equipment Schedule 3						
W.B. 104.3"; 3.0 Liter.						
Sedan 4D	JC58E	31965	1475	1625	2475	4175
Sport Pkg			150	150	200	200
Quattro AWD	L		1225	1225	1645	1645
Manual, 5-Spd			(175)	(175)	(235)	(235)
4-Cyl, Turbo, 1.8 Liter	C		(550)	(550)	(740)	(740)
A4 AVANT QUATTRO AWD—V6—Equipment Schedule 3						
W.B. 104.3"; 3.0 Liter.						
Wagon 4D	VC58E	34715	2550	2900	3375	5375
Sport Pkg			150	150	200	200
Manual, 5-Spd			(175)	(175)	(235)	(235)
4-Cyl, Turbo, 1.8 Liter	C		(550)	(550)	(740)	(740)
S4 QUATTRO AWD—V6 Turbo—Equipment Schedule 3						
W.B. 102.6"; 2.7 Liter.						
2.7T Sedan 4D	RD68D	39475	2725	2975	3475	5250
2.7T Avant Wagon 4D	XD68D	41075	3750	4125	4750	7100
A6—V6—Equipment Schedule 3						
W.B. 108.7"; 3.0 Liter.						
Sedan 4D	JT54B	35975	550	625	1200	2100
Quattro AWD	L		1225	1225	1645	1645
A6 AVANT QUATTRO AWD—V6—Equipment Schedule 3						
W.B. 108.6"; 3.0 Liter.						
Wagon 4D	VT54B	38925	1575	1775	2175	3475
A6 QUATTRO AWD—V6 Turbo—Equipment Schedule 3						
W.B. 108.7"; 2.7 Liter.						
2.7T Sedan 4D	LD54B	40325	2075	2325	2875	4550
Sport Pkg			275	275	360	360
ALLROAD QUATTRO AWD—V6 Turbo—Equipment Sch 1						
W.B. 108.5"; 2.7 Liter.						
2.7T Wagon 4D	YD54B	43325	2500	2800	3350	5325
A6 QUATTRO AWD—V8—Equipment Schedule 3						
W.B. 108.6"; 4.2 Liter.						
4.2 Sedan 4D	ML54B	50225	2500	2800	3500	5700
Sport Pkg			275	275	360	360
S6 AVANT QUATTRO AWD—V8—Equipment Schedule 1						
W.B. 108.6"; 4.2 Liter.						
Wagon 4D	XU54B	61375	9600	10650	11450	17550
A8 QUATTRO AWD—V8—Equipment Schedule 1						
W.B. 113.4", 118.5" (L); 4.2 Liter.						
Sedan 4D	FL44D	62775	850	925	1600	2600
L Sedan 4D	ML44D	67775	2125	2300	3075	4650
S8 QUATTRO AWD—V8—Equipment Schedule 1						
W.B. 113.4"; 4.2 Liter.						
Sedan 4D	GU44D	74775	4200	4525	5550	8150
TT—4-Cyl. Turbo—Equipment Schedule 2						
W.B. 95.4"; 1.8 Liter.						
Coupe 2D	SC28N	31755	1375	1525	2300	3700
Roadster 2D	TC28N	33775	2275	2500	3150	4875
Power Folding Roof			275	275	360	360
TT QUATTRO AWD—4-Cyl. Turbo—Equipment Schedule 2						
W.B. 95.4"; 1.8 Liter.						
180 Coupe 2D	WC28N	33595	2925	3225	3750	5650
TT QUATTRO AWD—4-Cyl. HO Turbo—Equipment Schedule 2						
W.B. 95.6"; 1.8 Liter.						
225 Coupe 2D	WT28N	36675	3500	3850	4475	6625
225 Roadster 2D	UT28N	39475	4100	4500	5125	7600
225 ALMS Comm Cpe	WT28N	40245	4875	5350	5825	8500

Body	Type	VIN	List	Trade-In Good	Trade-In Very Good	Pvt-Party Good	Retail Excellent

2003 AUDI — (WAU,WUA,WA1orTRU)(JC58E)-3-#

A4—4-Cyl. Turbo—Equipment Schedule 3
W.B. 104.3", 104.5" (Cab); 1.8 Liter.

	VIN	List	Good	Very Good	Good	Excellent
1.8T Sedan 4D	JC58E	26910	1875	2050	2825	4550
1.8T Cabriolet 2D	AC48H	35610	1675	1875	2625	4325
Sport Pkg		------	150	150	210	210
Manual, 5-Spd		------	(200)	(200)	(255)	(255)

A4 QUATTRO AWD—4-Cyl. Turbo—Equipment Schedule 3
W.B. 104.5"; 1.8 Liter.

	VIN	List	Good	Very Good	Good	Excellent
1.8T Sedan 4D	LC58E	28660	2125	2325	3100	5000

A4—V6—Equipment Schedule 3
W.B. 104.3", 104.5" (Cab); 3.0 Liter.

	VIN	List	Good	Very Good	Good	Excellent
Sedan 4D	JT58E	32250	2100	2300	3100	5000
Cabriolet 2D	AT28H	42160	2050	2300	3025	4900
Sport Pkg		------	150	150	210	210
Manual, 5-Spd		------	(200)	(200)	(255)	(255)

A4 QUATTRO AWD—V6—Equipment Schedule 3
W.B. 104.5"; 3.0 Liter.

	VIN	List	Good	Very Good	Good	Excellent
3.0 Sedan 4D	LT58E	34150	2575	2825	3625	5775
Sport Pkg		------	150	150	210	210
Manual, 5-Spd		------	(200)	(200)	(255)	(255)

A4 AVANT QUATTRO AWD—4-Cyl. Turbo—Equipment Schedule 3
W.B. 104.3"; 1.8 Liter.

	VIN	List	Good	Very Good	Good	Excellent
1.8T Wagon 4D	VC58E	29660	2675	3050	3575	5625
Manual, 5-Spd		------	(200)	(200)	(255)	(255)

A4 AVANT QUATTRO AWD—V6—Equipment Schedule 3
W.B. 104.3"; 3.0 Liter.

	VIN	List	Good	Very Good	Good	Excellent
Wagon 4D	VT58E	35000	3075	3475	4000	6250
Sport Pkg		------	150	150	210	210
Manual, 5-Spd		------	(200)	(200)	(255)	(255)

A6—V6—Equipment Schedule 3
W.B. 108.7"; 3.0 Liter.

	VIN	List	Good	Very Good	Good	Excellent
Sedan 4D	JT54B	36360	775	875	1450	2500

A6 QUATTRO AWD—V6—Equipment Schedule 3
W.B. 108.7"; 3.0 Liter.

	VIN	List	Good	Very Good	Good	Excellent
Sedan 4D	LT54B	38260	2100	2350	3050	4975

A6 AVANT QUATTRO AWD—V6—Equipment Schedule 3
W.B. 108.6"; 3.0 Liter.

	VIN	List	Good	Very Good	Good	Excellent
Wagon 4D	VT54B	39310	1775	1975	2400	3725

A6 QUATTRO AWD—V6 Turbo—Equipment Schedule 3
W.B. 108.5"; 2.7 Liter.

	VIN	List	Good	Very Good	Good	Excellent
2.7T Sedan 4D	LD54B	41510	2550	2825	3475	5550

ALLROAD QUATTRO AWD—V6 Turbo—Equipment Schedule 1
W.B. 108.5"; 2.7 Liter.

	VIN	List	Good	Very Good	Good	Excellent
2.7T Wagon 4D	YD54B	45110	2725	3025	3650	5775

A6 QUATTRO AWD—V8—Equipment Schedule 1
W.B. 108.6"; 4.2 Liter.

	VIN	List	Good	Very Good	Good	Excellent
4.2 Sedan 4D	ML54B	48460	3000	3325	4000	6350
Sport Pkg		------	275	275	375	375

S6 AVANT QUATTRO AWD—V8—Equipment Schedule 1
W.B. 108.6"; 4.2 Liter.

	VIN	List	Good	Very Good	Good	Excellent
Wagon 4D	XU54B	61060	9825	10900	11750	17800

RS6 QUATTRO AWD—V8 Bi Turbo—Equipment Schedule 1
W.B. 108.6"; 4.2 Liter.

	VIN	List	Good	Very Good	Good	Excellent
Sedan 4D	PV54B	84660	9000	9825	10100	13950

A8 QUATTRO AWD—V8—Equipment Schedule 1
W.B. 113.4", 118.5" (L); 4.2 Liter.

	VIN	List	Good	Very Good	Good	Excellent
Sedan 4D	FL44D	62860	1400	1525	2175	3325
L Sedan 4D	ML44D	67860	2700	2900	3600	5250

S8 QUATTRO AWD—V8—Equipment Schedule 1
W.B. 113.4"; 4.2 Liter.

	VIN	List	Good	Very Good	Good	Excellent
Sedan 4D	GU44D	74460	4575	4900	5775	8250

TT—4-Cyl. Turbo—Equipment Schedule 2
W.B. 95.4"; 1.8 Liter.

	VIN	List	Good	Very Good	Good	Excellent
Coupe 2D	SC28N	33145	1850	2025	2900	4675
Roadster 2D	TC28N	35145	3100	3400	4000	6025
Power Folding Roof		------	300	300	385	385

TT QUATTRO AWD—4-Cyl. HO Turbo—Equipment Schedule 2
W.B. 95.4"; 1.8 Liter.

	VIN	List	Good	Very Good	Good	Excellent
Coupe 2D	WT28N	36845	3775	4150	4875	7275
Roadster 2D	UT28N	39645	4400	4800	5475	8050

Body Type	VIN	List	Trade-In Good	Very Good	Pvt-Party Good	Retail Excellent

2004 AUDI — (WAU,WA1orTRU)(JC58E)–4–#

A4—4-Cyl. Turbo—Equipment Schedule 3
W.B. 104.3", 104.5" (Cab); 1.8 Liter.

1.8T Sedan 4D	JC58E	27420	2275	2475	3175	4950
1.8T Cabriolet 2D	AC48H	35970	2625	2900	3500	5450
Sport Pkg			175	175	220	220
Ultra Sport Pkg			725	725	950	950

A4 QUATTRO AWD—4-Cyl. Turbo—Equipment Schedule 3
W.B. 104.3"; 1.8 Liter.

1.8T Sedan 4D	LC58E	29520	2650	2900	3600	5550
Sport Pkg			175	175	220	220
Ultra Sport Pkg			725	725	950	950

A4 AVANT QUATTRO AWD—4-Cyl. Turbo—Equipment Schedule 3
W.B. 104.3"; 1.8 Liter.

1.8T Wagon 4D	VC58E	30520	3075	3450	3950	6075
Sport Pkg			175	175	220	220
Ultra Sport Pkg			725	725	950	950

A4—V6—Equipment Schedule 3
W.B. 104.3", 104.5" (Cab); 3.0 Liter.

Sedan 4D	JT58E	31840	2800	3050	3700	5700
Cabriolet 2D	AT48H	42490	3025	3350	3925	6075
Sport Pkg			175	175	220	220
Ultra Sport Pkg			725	725	950	950
Manual, 5-Spd			(200)	(200)	(265)	(265)

A4 QUATTRO AWD—V6—Equipment Schedule 3
W.B. 104.3", 104.5" (Cab); 3.0 Liter.

3.0 Sedan 4D	LT58E	35010	3100	3375	4150	6325
3.0 Cabriolet 2D	DT48H	44270	3400	3750	4450	6850
Sport Pkg			175	175	220	220
Ultra Sport Pkg			725	725	950	950
Manual, 5-Spd			(200)	(200)	(265)	(265)

A4 AVANT QUATTRO AWD—V6—Equipment Schedule 3
W.B. 104.3"; 3.0 Liter.

Wagon 4D	VT58E	35480	3350	3775	4425	6775
Sport Pkg			175	175	220	220
Ultra Sport Pkg			725	725	950	950

S4 QUATTRO AWD—V8—Equipment Schedule 1
W.B. 104.3", 104.5" (Cab); 4.2 Liter.

Sedan 4D	PL58E	47490	3925	4250	4775	6900
Cabriolet 2D	RL48H	55720	4250	4625	5225	7625

S4 AVANT QUATTRO AWD—V8—Equipment Schedule 1
W.B. 104.3"; 4.2 Liter.

Wagon 4D	XL68E	48490	4800	5225	5675	8100

A6—V6—Equipment Schedule 3
W.B. 108.7"; 3.0 Liter.

Sedan 4D	JT54B	36640	1100	1225	1750	2900

A6 QUATTRO AWD—V6—Equipment Schedule 3
W.B. 108.7"; 3.0 Liter.

Sedan 4D	LT54B	40170	2350	2600	3375	5425

A6 AVANT QUATTRO AWD—V6—Equipment Schedule 3
W.B. 108.6"; 3.0 Liter.

Wagon 4D	VT54B	40840	2225	2450	3175	5100

A6 QUATTRO AWD—V6 Turbo—Equipment Schedule 3
W.B. 108.7"; 2.7 Liter.

2.7T Sedan 4D	LD54B	42840	2800	3100	3725	5800
2.7T S-Line Sedan 4D	CD64B	43870	3400	3775	4600	7175

ALLROAD QUATTRO AWD—V6 Turbo—Equipment Schedule 1
W.B. 108.5"; 2.7 Liter.

2.7T Wagon 4D	YD54B	40640	3000	3325	4125	6575

ALLROAD QUATTRO AWD—V8—Equipment Schedule 1
W.B. 108.5"; 4.2 Liter.

4.2 Wagon 4D	YL64B	47640	3075	3400	4200	6700

A6 QUATTRO AWD—V8—Equipment Schedule 3
W.B. 108.6"; 4.2 Liter.

4.2 Sedan 4D	ML54B	49690	3600	4000	4800	7475
Sport Pkg			300	300	395	395

A8 QUATTRO AWD—V8—Equipment Schedule 1
W.B. 121.1"; 4.2 Liter.

L Sedan 4D	ML44E	69190	6200	6625	7350	9925

TT—4-Cyl. Turbo—Equipment Schedule 2
W.B. 95.4"; 1.8 Liter.

Coupe 2D	SC28N	33940	2900	3175	3825	5700

2004 AUDI

Body Type	VIN	List	Trade-In Good	Very Good	Pvt-Party Good	Retail Excellent
Roadster 2D	TC28N	35940	4000	4350	5000	7275
Power Folding Roof			300	300	395	395
TT QUATTRO AWD—V6—Equipment Schedule 2						
W.B. 95.6"; 3.2 Liter.						
Coupe 2D	WF28N	40590	5375	5850	6400	9150
Roadster 2D	UF28N	43590	6375	6925	7400	10500
4-Cyl, HO Turbo, 1.8L	T		(975)	(975)	(1245)	(1245)

2005 AUDI — (WAU, WA1 or TRU)(JC58E)-5-#

Body Type	VIN	List	Trade-In Good	Very Good	Pvt-Party Good	Retail Excellent
A4—4-Cyl. Turbo—Equipment Schedule 3						
W.B. 104.3", 104.5" (Cab); 1.8 Liter.						
1.8T Sedan 4D	JC58E	32670	2550	2775	3600	5450
1.8T Cabriolet 2D	AC48H	43020	3350	3700	4475	6725
Sport Pkg			175	175	230	230
Ultra Sport Pkg			775	775	1025	1025
S-Line Pkg			550	550	720	720
A4 QUATTRO AWD—4-Cyl. Turbo—Equipment Schedule 3						
W.B. 104.3"; 1.8 Liter.						
1.8T Sedan 4D	LC58E	30070	2925	3200	4075	6075
Sport Pkg			175	175	230	230
Ultra Sport Pkg			775	775	1025	1025
S-Line Pkg			550	550	720	720
A4—V6—Equipment Schedule 3						
W.B. 104.3", 104.5" (Cab); 3.0 Liter.						
Sedan 4D	JT58E	32670	2925	3200	4075	6075
Cabriolet 2D	AT48H	43020	3800	4175	4950	7375
Sport Pkg			175	175	230	230
Ultra Sport Pkg			775	775	1025	1025
S-Line Pkg			550	550	720	720
A4 QUATTRO AWD—V6—Equipment Schedule 3						
W.B. 104.3"; 3.0 Liter.						
3.0 Sedan 4D	JT58E	35510	3800	4150	4925	7200
3.0 Cabriolet 2D	DT48H	44970	4350	4775	5525	8175
Sport Pkg			175	175	230	230
Ultra Sport Pkg			775	775	1025	1025
S-Line Pkg			550	550	720	720
A4 AVANT QUATTRO AWD—4-Cyl. Turbo—Equipment Schedule 3						
W.B. 104.3"; 1.8 Liter.						
1.8T Wagon 4D	VC58E	31070	3175	3575	4400	6675
Sport Pkg			175	175	230	230
Ultra Sport Pkg			775	775	1025	1025
A4 AVANT QUATTRO AWD—V6—Equipment Schedule 3						
W.B. 104.3"; 3.0 Liter.						
Wagon 4D	VT58E	36510	3375	3775	4600	6975
Sport Pkg			175	175	230	230
Ultra Sport Pkg			775	775	1025	1025
A4 (2005.5)—4-Cyl. Turbo—Equipment Schedule 3						
W.B. 104.3"; 2.0 Liter.						
2.0T Sedan 4D	AF78E	29270	3250	3550	4350	6425
Sport Pkg			175	175	230	230
A4 QUATTRO AWD (2005.5)—4-Cyl. Turbo—Equipment Schedule 3						
W.B. 104.3"; 1.8 Liter.						
2.0T Sedan 4D	AF78E	31370	3775	4125	4925	7200
Sport Pkg			175	175	230	230
A4 AVANT QUATTRO AWD (2005.5)—4-Cyl. Turbo—Equip Sch 3						
W.B. 104.3"; 2.0 Liter.						
2.0T Wagon 4D	KF78E	32370	3950	4425	5100	7550
Sport Pkg			175	175	230	230
A4 QUATTRO AWD (2005.5)—V6—Equipment Schedule 3						
W.B. 104.3"; 3.2 Liter.						
3.2 Sedan 4D	DG78E	36120	4150	4500	5350	7900
Sport Pkg			175	175	230	230
A4 AVANT QUATTRO AWD (2005.5)—V6—Equipment Sch 3						
W.B. 104.3"; 3.2 Liter.						
3.2 Wagon 4D	KG78E	37120	4625	5175	5850	8625
Sport Pkg			175	175	230	230
S4 QUATTRO AWD—V8—Equipment Schedule 1						
W.B. 104.3", 104.5" (Cab); 4.2 Liter.						
Sedan 4D	PL58E	47770	5800	6275	6825	9325
Cabriolet 2D	RL48H	55870	6800	7350	8075	11200
S4 AVANT QUATTRO AWD—V8—Equipment Schedule 1						
W.B. 104.3"; 4.2 Liter.						
Wagon 4D	XL58E	48770	7550	8150	8600	11650

Body Type	VIN	List	Trade-In Good	Very Good	Pvt-Party Good	Retail Excellent
S4 QUATTRO AWD (2005.5)—V8—Equipment Schedule 1						
W.B. 104.3"; 4.2 Liter.						
Sedan 4D	GL68E	49320	6575	7100	7750	10650
S4 AVANT QUATTRO AWD (2005.5)—V8—Equipment Schedule 1						
W.B. 104.3"; 4.2 Liter.						
Wagon 4D	UL58E	50320	8500	9175	9650	13100
A6 QUATTRO AWD—V6—Equipment Schedule 3						
W.B. 111.9"; 3.2 Liter.						
Sedan 4D	DG54F	41620	4725	5200	5725	8075
Sport Pkg			300	300	380	380
A6 QUATTRO AWD—V8—Equipment Schedule 1						
W.B. 111.9"; 4.2 Liter.						
4.2 Sedan 4D	DL54F	51220	5725	6300	6775	9575
Sport Pkg			300	300	380	380
S-Line Pkg	E		550	550	665	665
ALLROAD QUATTRO AWD—V6 Turbo—Equipment Schedule 1						
W.B. 108.5"; 2.7 Liter.						
2.7T Wagon 4D	YD54B	40970	4725	5200	5550	7825
ALLROAD QUATTRO AWD—V8—Equipment Schedule 1						
W.B. 108.5"; 4.2 Liter.						
4.2 Wagon 4D	YL54B	47970	5825	6400	6675	9275
A8 QUATTRO AWD—V8—Equipment Schedule 1						
W.B. 115.9", 121.0" (L); 4.2 Liter.						
Sedan 4D	LL44E	67310	5600	5950	6925	9325
L Sedan 4D	ML44E	70620	6475	6900	7925	10650
A8 QUATTRO AWD—W12—Equipment Schedule 1						
W.B. 121.0"; 6.0 Liter.						
L Sedan 4D	MR44E	118120	10900	11600	12900	17300
TT—4-Cyl. Turbo—Equipment Schedule 2						
W.B. 95.4"; 1.8 Liter.						
Coupe 2D	SC28N	34220	4450	4825	5550	7850
Roadster 2D	TC28N	36220	5500	5975	6650	9325
Power Folding Roof			325	325	400	400
TT QUATTRO AWD—V6—Equipment Schedule 2						
W.B. 95.4", 95.6" (Cpe); 3.2 Liter.						
Coupe 2D	WF28N	40870	6975	7575	8175	11350
Roadster 2D	UF28N	43870	8150	8850	9400	13100
4-Cyl, HO Turbo, 1.8L	T		(1025)	(1025)	(1275)	(1275)

2006 AUDI — (WAU,WUAorTRU)(HF68P)-6-#

Body Type	VIN	List	Trade-In Good	Very Good	Pvt-Party Good	Retail Excellent
A3—4-Cyl. Turbo—Equipment Schedule 3						
W.B. 101.5"; 2.0 Liter.						
2.0T Wagon 4D	HF68P	26860	4400	4875	5500	7900
Sport Pkg	M		175	175	240	240
A3 QUATTRO AWD—V6—Equipment Schedule 3						
W.B. 101.5"; 3.2 Liter.						
3.2 S-Line Wagon 4D	KD78P	34700	8975	9900	9875	13250
A4—4-Cyl. Turbo—Equipment Schedule 3						
W.B. 104.3", 104.5" (Cab); 1.8 Liter, 2.0 Liter.						
2.0T Sedan 4D	AF78E	29560	4075	4400	5125	7325
1.8T Cabriolet 2D	AC48H	38060	4425	4825	5475	7875
S-Line Pkg	B,E		575	575	780	780
A4 QUATTRO AWD—4-Cyl. Turbo—Equipment Schedule 3						
W.B. 104.3"; 1.8 Liter.						
2.0T Sedan 4D	DF58E	32260	4775	5150	5875	8325
S-Line Pkg	B,E		575	575	780	780
A4—V6—Equipment Schedule 3						
W.B. 104.3"; 3.2 Liter.						
3.2 Sedan 4D	AH78H	34660	5100	5500	6375	9050
S-Line Pkg			575	575	780	780
A4 QUATTRO AWD—V6—Equipment Schedule 3						
W.B. 104.3"; 3.2 Liter.						
3.2 Sedan 4D	DG78E	37310	5750	6200	7050	9950
S-Line Pkg			575	575	780	780
A4 QUATTRO AWD—V6—Equipment Schedule 3						
W.B. 104.5"; 3.0 Liter.						
3.0 Cabriolet 2D	DT48H	46210	5575	6100	6875	9800
S-Line Pkg			575	575	780	780
A4 AVANT QUATTRO AWD—4-Cyl. Turbo—Equipment Sch 3						
W.B. 104.3"; 2.0 Liter.						
2.0T Wagon 4D	KF78E	32660	4925	5450	6125	8675
S-Line Pkg	S		575	575	780	780

1015

Body Type	VIN	List	Trade-In Good	Very Good	Pvt-Party Good	Retail Excellent
A4 AVANT QUATTRO AWD—V6—Equipment Schedule 3						
W.B. 104.3"; 3.2 Liter.						
3.2 Wagon 4D	KH78E	37760	5975	6625	7075	9850
S-Line Pkg	S		575	575	780	780
S4 QUATTRO AWD—V8—Equipment Schedule 1						
W.B. 104.3", 104.5" (Cab); 4.2 Liter.						
Sedan 4D	GL78E	49620	8575	9200	9625	12700
Special Ed Sedan 4D	GL78E	60970	9425	10100	10400	13650
Cabriolet 2D	RL48H	57860	8650	9275	9700	12800
S4 QUATTRO AWD—V8—Equipment Schedule 1						
W.B. 104.3"; 4.2 Liter.						
Wagon 4D	UL78E	50620	10400	11150	11350	14750
A6—V6—Equipment Schedule 3						
W.B. 111.9"; 3.2 Liter.						
3.2 Sedan 4D	AH74F	41540	4725	5200	5875	8275
Adaptive Cruise Control			325	325	390	390
S-Line Pkg	B		575	575	725	725
A6 QUATTRO AWD—V6—Equipment Schedule 3						
W.B. 111.9"; 3.2 Liter.						
3.2 Sedan 4D	DG74F	44690	6525	7125	7750	10900
Adaptive Cruise Control			325	325	395	395
S-Line Pkg	E		575	575	730	730
A6 AVANT QUATTRO AWD—V6—Equipment Schedule 3						
W.B. 111.9"; 3.2 Liter.						
3.2 Wagon 4D	KG74F	47590	8275	9025	9550	13300
A6 QUATTRO AWD—V8—Equipment Schedule 1						
W.B. 111.9"; 4.2 Liter.						
4.2 Sedan 4D	DL74F	54490	6850	7475	8250	11750
Adaptive Cruise Control			(325)	(325)	(400)	(400)
S-Line Pkg	E		575	575	735	735
A8 QUATTRO AWD—V8—Equipment Schedule 1						
W.B. 115.9", 121.0" (L); 4.2 Liter.						
Sedan 4D	LL44E	68850	7900	8375	9175	11900
L Sedan 4D	ML44E	72810	9100	9650	10550	13700
Adaptive Cruise Control			325	325	375	375
Premium Pkg			850	850	1020	1020
Sport Pkg			575	575	695	695
A8 QUATTRO AWD—W12—Equipment Schedule 1						
W.B. 121.0"; 6.0 Liter.						
L Sedan 4D	MR44E	120610	13400	14150	15300	19850
Adaptive Cruise Control			325	325	395	395
TT—4-Cyl. Turbo—Equipment Schedule 2						
W.B. 95.4"; 1.8 Liter.						
Coupe 2D	SC28N	34710	5400	5825	6625	9250
Roadster 2D	TC28N	36710	6900	7450	8100	11100
Power Folding Roof			350	350	420	420
TT QUATTRO AWD—V6—Equipment Schedule 2						
W.B. 95.6"; 3.2 Liter.						
Coupe 2D	WD28N	38110	7925	8575	9150	12550
Special Ed Coupe 2D	PD28N	44259	10100	10900	11300	15400
Roadster 2D	UD28N	44360	8650	9350	9925	13550
Special Ed Roadster	RD28N	47259	10900	11800	12100	16200
4-Cyl, HO, Turbo, 1.8 Liter			(1075)	(1075)	(1325)	(1325)

Body Type	VIN	List	Trade-In Good	Very Good	Pvt-Party Good	Retail Excellent
A3—4-Cyl. Turbo—Equipment Schedule 3						
W.B. 101.5"; 2.0 Liter.						
2.0T Wagon 4D	HF78P	27540	5525	6075	6725	9300
S-Line Pkg			625	625	835	835
A3 QUATTRO AWD—V6—Equipment Schedule 3						
W.B. 101.5"; 3.2 Liter.						
3.2 S-Line Wagon 4D	KD78P	34700	10350	11350	11300	14750
A4—4-Cyl. Turbo—Equipment Schedule 3						
W.B. 104.3"; 2.0 Liter.						
2.0T Sedan 4D	AF78E	30160	4700	5075	5925	8225
2.0T Cabriolet 2D	AF48H	39820	5700	6200	6850	9375
S-Line Pkg			625	625	845	845
A4 QUATTRO AWD—4-Cyl. Turbo—Equipment Schedule 3						
W.B. 104.3"; 2.0 Liter.						
2.0T Sedan 4D	DF783	32260	5525	5950	6750	9300
2.0T Cabriolet 2D	DF48H	41920	6700	7250	7900	10800
S-Line Pkg			625	625	845	845

Body Type	VIN	List	Trade-In Good	Very Good	Pvt-Party Good	Retail Excellent
A4—V6—Equipment Schedule 3						
W.B. 104.3"; 3.2 Liter.						
3.2 Sedan 4D	AH78E	38360	6325	6800	7725	10750
S-Line Pkg			625	625	845	845
A4 QUATTRO AWD—V6—Equipment Schedule 3						
W.B. 104.3"; 3.2 Liter.						
3.2 Sedan 4D	DH78E	38360	7050	7575	8500	11750
3.2 Cabriolet 2D	DH48H	47670	7800	8450	9025	12250
S-Line Pkg			625	625	835	835
A4 AVANT QUATTRO AWD—4-Cyl. Turbo—Equipment Sch 3						
W.B. 104.3"; 2.0 Liter.						
2.0T Wagon 4D	KF78E	33260	6200	6800	7350	10000
S-Line Pkg			625	625	845	845
A4 AVANT QUATTRO AWD—V6—Equipment Schedule 3						
W.B. 104.3"; 3.2 Liter.						
3.2 Wagon 4D	KH78E	39360	7600	8325	8650	11600
S-Line Pkg			625	625	825	825
RS 4 QUATTRO AWD—V8—Equipment Schedule 1						
W.B. 104.3"; 4.2 Liter.						
Sedan 4D	RU78E	68820	20800	22100	21300	26300
S4 QUATTRO AWD—V8—Equipment Schedule 1						
W.B. 104.3", 104.5" (Cab); 4.2 Liter.						
Sedan 4D	GL78E	50720	11100	11850	12050	15350
Cabriolet 2D	RU48H	58920	11550	12350	12300	15400
S4 AVANT QUATTRO AWD—V8—Equipment Schedule 1						
W.B. 104.3"; 4.2 Liter.						
Wagon 4D	UU78E	51720	12400	13200	13500	16400
A6—V6—Equipment Schedule 3						
W.B. 111.9"; 3.2 Liter.						
3.2 Sedan 4D	AH74F	42670	6250	6775	7275	9850
Adaptive Cruise Control			350	350	420	420
S-Line Pkg			625	625	780	780
A6 QUATTRO AWD—V6—Equipment Schedule 3						
W.B. 111.9"; 3.2 Liter.						
3.2 Sedan 4D	DH74F	45820	7925	8600	9225	12550
Adaptive Cruise Control			350	350	425	425
S-Line Pkg			625	625	790	790
A6 AVANT QUATTRO AWD—V6—Equipment Schedule 3						
W.B. 111.9"; 3.2 Liter.						
3.2 Wagon 4D	KH94F	48720	10000	10850	11150	14950
Adaptive Cruise Control			350	350	415	415
S-Line Pkg			625	625	770	770
A6 QUATTRO AWD—V8—Equipment Schedule 3						
W.B. 111.9"; 4.2 Liter.						
4.2 Sedan 4D	DV74F	56020	8350	9050	9625	13150
Adaptive Cruise Control			350	350	425	425
S-Line Pkg	B		625	625	790	790
S6 QUATTRO AWD—V10—Equipment Schedule 1						
W.B. 112.1"; 5.2 Liter.						
Sedan 4D	GN74F	72720	11000	11750	12000	15250
Adaptive Cruise Control			350	350	395	395
A8 QUATTRO AWD—V8—Equipment Schedule 1						
W.B. 115.9"; 121.0" (L); 4.2 Liter.						
Sedan 4D	LV44E	69620	10450	11000	11550	14250
L Sedan 4D	MV44E	73620	11600	12250	12900	15900
Adaptive Cruise Control			350	350	390	390
Premium Pkg			925	925	1060	1060
Sport Pkg			625	625	725	725
A8 QUATTRO AWD—W12—Equipment Schedule 1						
W.B. 121.0"; 6.0 Liter.						
L Sedan 4D	MR44E	121770	17150	18050	18900	23700
Adaptive Cruise Control			350	350	405	405
S8 QUATTRO AWD—V10—Equipment Schedule 1						
W.B. 115.9"; 5.2 Liter.						
Sedan 4D	PN44E	92720	18750	19700	20100	24700
Adaptive Cruise Control			350	350	400	400

2008 AUDI — (WAUorWUA)(HF78P)-8-#

Body Type	VIN	List	Trade-In Good	Very Good	Pvt-Party Good	Retail Excellent
A3—4-Cyl. Turbo—Equipment Schedule 3						
W.B. 101.5"; 2.0 Liter.						
2.0T Wagon 4D	HF78P	28185	6950	7475	8275	10900
S-Line Pkg			675	675	845	845

2008 AUDI

Body Type	VIN	List	Trade-In Good	Very Good	Pvt-Party Good	Retail Excellent
A3 QUATTRO AWD—V6—Equipment Schedule 3						
W.B. 101.5"; 3.2 Liter.						
3.2 Wagon 4D	KD78P	35690	**11200**	**12000**	**12300**	**15550**
S-Line Pkg			675	675	805	805
A4—4-Cyl. Turbo—Equipment Schedule 3						
W.B. 104.3"; 2.0 Liter.						
2.0T Sedan 4D	AF78E	30975	**7825**	**8325**	**8975**	**11650**
2.0T Cabriolet 2D	AF48H	40525	**7450**	**7975**	**8650**	**11200**
S-Line Pkg			675	675	870	870
A4 QUATTRO AWD—4-Cyl. Turbo—Equipment Schedule 3						
W.B. 104.3"; 2.0 Liter.						
2.0T Sedan 4D	DF58E	33075	**8775**	**9350**	**10050**	**13000**
2.0T Cabriolet 2D	DF48H	42625	**8775**	**9400**	**10000**	**12900**
S-Line Pkg			675	675	870	870
A4 AVANT QUATTRO AWD—4-Cyl. Turbo—Equipment Schedule 3						
W.B. 104.3"; 2.0 Liter.						
2.0T Wagon 4D	KF78E	34075	**8875**	**9550**	**10150**	**13150**
S-Line Pkg	S		675	675	860	860
A4—V6—Equipment Schedule 3						
W.B. 104.3"; 3.2 Liter.						
3.2 Sedan 4D	AH78E	37075	**9450**	**10050**	**10750**	**13950**
S-Line Pkg	B		675	675	865	865
A4 QUATTRO AWD—V6—Equipment Schedule 3						
W.B. 104.3"; 3.2 Liter.						
3.2 Sedan 4D	DH58E	39175	**10250**	**10950**	**11600**	**15000**
S-Line Pkg	B		675	675	865	865
A4 QUATTRO AWD—V6—Equipment Schedule 3						
W.B. 104.3"; 3.2 Liter.						
3.2 Cabriolet 2D	DH48H	48675	**9850**	**10500**	**11100**	**14250**
S-Line Pkg	E		675	675	855	855
A4 AVANT QUATTRO AWD—V6—Equipment Schedule 3						
W.B. 104.3"; 3.2 Liter.						
3.2 Wagon 4D	KH78E	40175	**9900**	**10600**	**11100**	**14200**
S-Line Pkg	S		675	675	860	860
RS 4 QUATTRO AWD—V8—Equipment Schedule 1						
W.B. 104.3"; 4.2 Liter.						
Sedan 4D	RU78E	69785	**22500**	**23600**	**23600**	**28700**
Cabriolet 2D	YU78E	84775	**24100**	**25300**	**25000**	**29900**
S4 QUATTRO AWD—V8—Equipment Schedule 1						
W.B. 104.3", 104.5" (Cab); 4.2 Liter.						
Sedan 4D	GL78E	51785	**13350**	**14050**	**14500**	**17700**
Cabriolet 2D	RL48H	60050	**13500**	**14200**	**14850**	**18350**
S4 AVANT QUATTRO AWD—V8—Equipment Schedule 1						
W.B. 104.3"; 4.2 Liter.						
Wagon 4D	UL78E	52785	**15200**	**16000**	**16400**	**20000**
A5 QUATTRO AWD—V6—Equipment Schedule 3						
W.B. 108.3"; 3.2 Liter.						
Coupe 2D	DH78T	41975	**13850**	**14850**	**14750**	**18250**
Bang & Olufsen Sound			325	325	390	390
S-Line Pkg	E		675	675	795	795
S5 QUATTRO AWD—V8—Equipment Schedule 1						
W.B. 108.3"; 4.2 Liter.						
Coupe 2D	RV78T	54325	**17300**	**18500**	**18150**	**22500**
Bang & Olufsen Sound			325	325	380	380
A6—V6—Equipment Schedule 3						
W.B. 111.9"; 3.2 Liter.						
3.2 Sedan 4D	AH74F	43725	**7825**	**8350**	**8850**	**11300**
S-Line Pkg	B		675	675	815	815
A6 QUATTRO AWD—V6—Equipment Schedule 3						
W.B. 111.9"; 3.2 Liter.						
3.2 Sedan 4D	DH74F	46875	**9875**	**10550**	**11050**	**14100**
S-Line Pkg	E,S		675	675	815	815
A6 AVANT QUATTRO AWD—V6—Equipment Schedule 3						
W.B. 111.9"; 3.2 Liter.						
3.2 Wagon 4D	KH94F	49775	**11600**	**12350**	**12700**	**16100**
Adaptive Cruise Control			375	375	430	430
S-Line Pkg	E,S		675	675	805	805
A6 QUATTRO AWD—V8—Equipment Schedule 3						
W.B. 111.9"; 4.2 Liter.						
4.2 Sedan 4D	DV74F	57075	**10700**	**11400**	**11900**	**15150**
Adaptive Cruise Control			375	375	435	435
S-Line Pkg	B		675	675	810	810

2008 AUDI

Body Type	VIN	List	Trade-In Good	Very Good	Pvt-Party Good	Retail Excellent
S6 QUATTRO AWD—V10—Equipment Schedule 1						
W.B. 112.1"; 5.2 Liter.						
Sedan 4D	DN74F	74425	14250	15000	15350	18600
Adaptive Cruise Control			375	375	415	415
A8 QUATTRO AWD—V8—Equipment Schedule 1						
W.B. 115.9"; 121.0" (L); 4.2 Liter.						
Sedan 4D	LV44E	71465	13450	14050	14700	17450
L Sedan 4D	MV44E	75465	15050	15700	16300	19350
Bang & Olufsen Sound			2200	2200	2465	2465
Adaptive Cruise Control			375	375	410	410
Premium Pkg			1025	1025	1140	1140
Sport Pkg			675	675	765	765
A8 QUATTRO AWD—W12—Equipment Schedule 1						
W.B. 121.0"; 6.0 Liter.						
L Sedan 4D	MR44E	122575	20800	21700	22600	27300
Bang & Olufsen Sound			2200	2200	2560	2560
Adaptive Cruise Control			375	375	425	425
R8 QUATTRO AWD—V8—Equipment Schedule 1						
W.B. 104.3"; 4.2 Liter.						
Coupe 2D	AV342	124200	****	****	****	75400
Bang & Olufsen Sound			****	****	****	350
S8 QUATTRO AWD—V10—Equipment Schedule 1						
W.B. 115.9"; 5.2 Liter.						
Sedan 4D	PN44E	96175	22600	23600	24000	28400
Bang & Olufsen Sound			2200	2200	2460	2460
Adaptive Cruise Control			375	375	410	410
TT—4-Cyl. Turbo—Equipment Schedule 2						
W.B. 97.2"; 2.0 Liter.						
Coupe 2D	AF38J	35575	9800	10450	10900	13850
Roadster 2D	MF38J	37575	10500	11150	11650	14700
Power Folding Roof			400	400	460	460
S-Line Pkg			675	675	795	795
TT QUATTRO AWD—V6—Equipment Schedule 2						
W.B. 97.2"; 3.2 Liter.						
3.2 Coupe 2D	DD38J	43675	12800	13600	14000	17700
3.2 Roadster 2D	RD38J	46675	14200	15100	15350	19400
S-Line Pkg			675	675	800	800

2009 AUDI — (WAUorWUA)(HF78P)-9-#

Body Type	VIN	List	Trade-In Good	Very Good	Pvt-Party Good	Retail Excellent
A3—4-Cyl. Turbo—Equipment Schedule 3						
W.B. 101.5"; 2.0 Liter.						
2.0T Wagon 4D	HF78P	29225	8525	9025	10000	12600
Third Row Seat			225	225	260	260
Sport Pkg			225	225	280	280
S-Line Pkg			725	725	880	880
A3 QUATTRO AWD—4-Cyl. Turbo—Equipment Schedule 3						
W.B. 101.5"; 2.0 Liter.						
2.0T Wagon 4D	KF78P	31325	11000	11650	12400	15350
Third Row Seat			225	225	255	255
Sport Pkg			225	225	275	275
S-Line Pkg			725	725	865	865
A3 QUATTRO AWD—V6—Equipment Schedule 3						
W.B. 101.5"; 3.2 Liter.						
3.2 Wagon 4D	KD78P	37800	12550	13300	13950	17050
Third Row Seat			225	225	250	250
Sport Pkg			225	225	270	270
S-Line Pkg			725	725	850	850
A4—4-Cyl. Turbo—Equipment Schedule 3						
W.B. 104.3", 110.6" (Sed); 2.0 Liter.						
2.0T Sedan 4D	AF78E	31525	9600	10150	10950	13750
2.0T Cabriolet 2D	AF48H	41575	10850	11450	12100	14850
2.0T Special Ed Cab 2D	AF48H	41575	11500	12200	12800	15700
Adaptive Cruise Control			375	375	470	470
Premium Plus Pkg			700	700	890	890
Prestige Pkg			1475	1475	1860	1860
A4 QUATTRO AWD—4-Cyl. Turbo—Equipment Schedule 3						
W.B. 104.3", 110.6" (Sed); 2.0 Liter.						
2.0T Sedan 4D	LF78K	33525	10850	11450	12250	15350
2.0T Cabriolet 2D	DF48H	41575	12300	13000	13650	16700
2.0T Special Ed Cab	DF48H	43675	12850	13600	14250	17450
Adaptive Cruise Control			375	375	465	465
Premium Plus Pkg			700	700	880	880
Prestige Pkg			1475	1475	1845	1845

1015

Body Type	VIN	List	Trade-In Good	Very Good	Pvt-Party Good	Retail Excellent
S-Line Pkg		-------	725	725	915	915
A4 AVANT QUATTRO AWD—4-Cyl. Turbo—Equipment Schedule 3						
W.B. 110.6"; 2.0 Liter.						
2.0T Wagon 4D	VF78K	35325	12900	13600	14300	17550
Adaptive Cruise Control		-------	375	375	445	445
Premium Plus Pkg		-------	700	700	845	845
Prestige Pkg		-------	1475	1475	1765	1765
S-Line Pkg	S	-------	725	725	875	875
A4 QUATTRO AWD—V6—Equipment Schedule 3						
W.B. 104.3", 110.6" (Sed); 3.2 Liter.						
3.2 Sedan 4D	LK98K	40825	12350	13050	13850	17350
3.2 Cabriolet 2D	DH48H	49625	14850	15700	16150	19650
3.2 Special Ed Cab 2D	DH48H	49625	15550	16400	16850	20500
Adaptive Cruise Control		-------	375	375	465	465
Prestige Pkg		-------	1475	1475	1830	1830
S-Line Pkg		-------	725	725	905	905
S4 QUATTRO AWD—V8—Equipment Schedule 1						
W.B. 104.5"; 4.2 Liter.						
Cabriolet 2D	RL48H	60450	17700	18450	19450	23400
A5 QUATTRO AWD—V6—Equipment Schedule 1						
W.B. 108.3"; 3.2 Liter.						
Coupe 2D	DK78T	42425	16150	17050	17300	20900
Bang & Olufsen Sound		-------	350	350	395	395
Adaptive Cruise Control		-------	375	375	435	435
S-Line Pkg		-------	725	725	850	850
S5 QUATTRO AWD—V8—Equipment Schedule 1						
W.B. 108.3"; 4.2 Liter.						
Coupe 2D	RV78T	54825	19750	20800	20900	25200
Bang & Olufsen Sound		-------	350	350	385	385
Adaptive Cruise Control		-------	375	375	425	425
A6—V6—Equipment Schedule 3						
W.B. 111.9"; 3.2 Liter.						
3.2 Sedan 4D	AH74F	45925	11950	12600	13000	15700
Premium Plus Pkg		-------	700	700	825	825
A6 QUATTRO AWD—V6 Supercharged—Equipment Schedule 3						
W.B. 111.9"; 3.0 Liter.						
3.0T Sedan 4D	DH74F	50925	13950	14700	15150	18300
Premium Plus Pkg		-------	700	700	825	825
Sport Pkg		-------	375	375	430	430
A6 AVANT QUATTRO AWD—V6 Supercharged—Equipment Schedule 3						
W.B. 111.9"; 3.0 Liter.						
3.0T Wagon 4D	KH94F	54135	15750	16600	16900	20400
Third Row Seat		-------	225	225	250	250
Premium Plus Pkg		-------	700	700	820	820
Sport Pkg		-------	375	375	425	425
A6 QUATTRO AWD—V8—Equipment Schedule 3						
W.B. 111.9"; 4.2 Liter.						
4.2 Sedan 4D	DV74F	61775	15500	16400	16750	20300
Premium Plus Pkg		-------	700	700	830	830
S6 QUATTRO AWD—V10—Equipment Schedule 1						
W.B. 112.1"; 5.2 Liter.						
Sedan 4D	DN74F	76675	19500	20300	20700	24200
A8 QUATTRO AWD—V8—Equipment Schedule 1						
W.B. 115.9", 121.0" (L); 4.2 Liter.						
Sedan 4D	LV44E	74875	18600	19250	20100	23300
L Sedan 4D	MV44E	78725	20200	20900	21700	25100
Bang & Olufsen Sound		-------	2325	2325	2525	2525
Adaptive Cruise Control		-------	375	375	405	405
Sport Pkg		-------	725	725	795	795
A8 QUATTRO AWD—W12—Equipment Schedule 1						
W.B. 121.0"; 6.0 Liter.						
L Sedan 4D	MR44E	122625	25200	26100	27200	31800
Bang & Olufsen Sound		-------	2325	2325	2595	2595
Adaptive Cruise Control		-------	375	375	420	420
R8 QUATTRO AWD—V8—Equipment Schedule 1						
W.B. 104.3"; 4.2 Liter.						
Coupe 2D	AU342	124800	****	****	****	81100
Bang & Olufsen Sound		-------	****	****	****	355
S8 QUATTRO AWD—V10—Equipment Schedule 1						
W.B. 115.9"; 5.2 Liter.						
Sedan 4D	PN44E	99125	27500	28400	29200	33600
Bang & Olufsen Sound		-------	2325	2325	2525	2525
Adaptive Cruise Control		-------	375	375	405	405

Body Type	VIN	List	Trade-In Good	Very Good	Pvt-Party Good	Retail Excellent
TT—4-Cyl. Turbo—Equipment Schedule 2						
W.B. 97.2"; 2.0 Liter.						
Coupe 2D	AF38J	36025	11750	12450	13000	15950
Roadster 2D	MF38J	38025	12250	13000	13500	16550
Power Folding Roof			400	400	455	455
S-Line Pkg			725	725	835	835
TT QUATTRO AWD—4-Cyl. Turbo—Equipment Schedule 2						
W.B. 97.2"; 2.0 Liter.						
Coupe 2D	DF38J	38125	14050	14850	15150	18400
Roadster 2D	RF38J	40125	15600	16500	17000	20900
Power Folding Roof			400	400	460	460
S-Line Pkg			725	725	830	830
TT QUATTRO AWD—V6—Equipment Schedule 2						
W.B. 97.2"; 3.2 Liter.						
3.2 Coupe 2D	DD38J	44295	16100	17000	17350	21200
3.2 Roadster 2D	RD38J	47365	17150	18100	18400	22600
S-Line Pkg			725	725	840	840
TTS QUATTRO AWD—4-Cyl. Turbo—Equipment Schedule 2						
W.B. 97.2"; 2.0 Liter.						
Coupe 2D	UF38J	46325	17100	18050	18350	22500
Roadster 2D	WF38J	48325	19600	20700	20900	25600
Power Folding Roof			400	400	455	455

2010 AUDI — (TRUorWAUorWUA)(BFBFM)–A–#

Body Type	VIN	List	Trade-In Good	Very Good	Pvt-Party Good	Retail Excellent
A3—4-Cyl. Turbo—Equipment Schedule 3						
W.B. 101.5"; 2.0 Liter.						
2.0T Wagon 4D	BFBFM	29575	10750	11250	12350	15050
Third Row Seat			250	250	280	280
Premium Plus Pkg			750	750	870	870
Sport Pkg			275	275	305	305
A3 QUATTRO AWD—4-Cyl. Turbo—Equipment Schedule 3						
W.B. 101.5"; 2.0 Liter.						
2.0T Wagon 4D	DFBFM	31675	14100	14700	15650	18600
Third Row Seat			250	250	280	280
Premium Plus Pkg			750	750	875	875
Sport Pkg			275	275	310	310
A3—4-Cyl. Turbo Diesel—Equipment Schedule 3						
W.B. 101.5"; 2.0 Liter.						
2.0 TDI Wagon 4D	BJBFM	30775	14000	14650	15550	18500
Third Row Seat			250	250	280	280
Premium Plus Pkg			750	750	870	870
Sport Pkg			275	275	310	310
A4—4-Cyl. Turbo—Equipment Schedule 3						
W.B. 110.6"; 2.0 Liter.						
2.0T Sedan 4D	AFBFL	32275	11000	11550	12500	15250
Bang & Olufsen Sound			350	350	430	430
Premium Plus Pkg			750	750	935	935
A4 QUATTRO AWD—4-Cyl. Turbo—Equipment Schedule 3						
W.B. 110.6"; 2.0 Liter.						
2.0T Sedan 4D	BFBFL	34375	12400	13050	13900	17000
Bang & Olufsen Sound			350	350	425	425
S-Line Pkg	B		775	775	965	965
Premium Plus Pkg			750	750	930	930
Prestige Pkg			1525	1525	1875	1875
A4 AVANT QUATTRO AWD—4-Cyl. Turbo—Equipment Schedule 3						
W.B. 110.6"; 2.0 Liter.						
2.0T Wagon 4D	SFBFL	36175	15050	15700	16650	19850
Bang & Olufsen Sound			350	350	410	410
Third Row Seat			250	250	285	285
Adaptive Cruise Control			400	400	460	460
S-Line Pkg			775	775	925	925
Premium Plus Pkg			750	750	885	885
Prestige Pkg			1525	1525	1790	1790
S4 QUATTRO AWD—V6 Supercharged—Equipment Schedule 1						
W.B. 110.7"; 3.0 Liter.						
Sedan 4D	BGBFL	48125	21400	22100	23300	27000
Bang & Olufsen Sound			350	350	385	385
Adaptive Cruise Control			400	400	435	435
Prestige Pkg			1525	1525	1690	1690
A5—4-Cyl. Turbo—Equipment Schedule 1						
W.B. 108.3"; 2.0 Liter.						
2.0T Cabriolet 2D	AFAFH	42825	18200	19000	19600	23000
Bang & Olufsen Sound			350	350	400	400

Body Type	VIN	List	Trade-In Good	Very Good	Pvt-Party Good	Retail Excellent
A5 QUATTRO AWD—4-Cyl. Turbo—Equipment Schedule 1						
W.B. 108.3"; 2.0 Liter.						
2.0T Coupe 2D	CFAFR	38025	17200	17950	18550	21800
2.0T Cabriolet 2D	CFAFH	44925	19400	20200	20800	24300
Bang & Olufsen Sound			350	350	400	400
Adaptive Cruise Control			400	400	450	450
Premium Plus Pkg			750	750	865	865
Prestige Pkg			1525	1525	1750	1750
S-Line Pkg			775	775	905	905
A5 QUATTRO AWD—V6—Equipment Schedule 1						
W.B. 108.3"; 3.2 Liter.						
Coupe 2D	LKAFR	44825	19500	20300	20900	24500
Bang & Olufsen Sound			350	350	400	400
Adaptive Cruise Control			400	400	450	450
Premium Plus Pkg			750	750	865	865
Prestige Pkg			1525	1525	1745	1745
S-Line Pkg			775	775	900	900
S5 QUATTRO AWD—V6 Turbo—Equipment Schedule 1						
W.B. 108.3"; 3.0 Liter.						
3.0T Cabriolet 2D	CGAFH	59075	23300	24400	24800	29000
Bang & Olufsen Sound			350	350	390	390
Adaptive Cruise Control			400	400	445	445
Prestige Pkg			1525	1525	1720	1720
S5 QUATTRO AWD—V8—Equipment Schedule 1						
W.B. 108.3"; 4.2 Liter.						
Coupe 2D	CVAFR	54425	23000	24000	24400	28600
Bang & Olufsen Sound			350	350	390	390
Adaptive Cruise Control			400	400	440	440
Prestige Pkg			1525	1525	1715	1715
A6—V6—Equipment Schedule 3						
W.B. 111.9"; 3.2 Liter.						
3.2 Sedan 4D	AKBFB	46025	13800	14450	15300	18250
Premium Plus Pkg			750	750	895	895
Sport Pkg			400	400	465	465
A6 QUATTRO AWD—V6 Supercharged—Equipment Schedule 3						
W.B. 111.9"; 3.0 Liter.						
3.0T Sedan 4D	AGBFB	51025	15950	16700	17500	21000
Premium Plus Pkg			750	750	900	900
Prestige Pkg			1525	1525	1810	1810
A6 AVANT QUATTRO AWD—V6 Supercharged—Equipment Schedule 3						
W.B. 111.9"; 3.0 Liter.						
3.0T Wagon 4D	SGBFB	54135	18150	19000	19800	23500
Third Row Seat			250	250	285	285
Premium Plus Pkg			750	750	890	890
Prestige Pkg			1525	1525	1790	1790
A6 QUATTRO AWD—V8—Equipment Schedule 3						
W.B. 111.9"; 4.2 Liter.						
4.2 Sedan 4D	BVBFB	61775	17500	18300	19200	22900
Sport Pkg			400	400	465	465
S6 QUATTRO AWD—V10—Equipment Schedule 1						
W.B. 112.1"; 5.2 Liter.						
Sedan 4D	BNBFB	78225	26100	27000	27300	30700
A8 QUATTRO AWD—V8—Equipment Schedule 1						
W.B. 115.9", 121.0" (L); 4.2 Liter.						
Sedan 4D	BVAFA	75375	20300	20900	22200	25500
L Sedan 4D	SVAFA	79225	22100	22800	24000	27400
Bang & Olufsen Sound			2450	2450	2740	2740
Adaptive Cruise Control			400	400	435	435
Sport Pkg			775	775	875	875
R8 QUATTRO AWD—V8—Equipment Schedule 1						
W.B. 104.3"; 4.2 Liter.						
4.2 Coupe 2D	AUAFG	126600	****	****	****	89500
Bang & Olufsen Sound			****	****	****	360
R8 QUATTRO AWD—V10—Equipment Schedule 1						
W.B. 104.3"; 5.2 Liter.						
5.2 Coupe 2D	ANAFG	158400	****	****	****	120800
TT QUATTRO AWD—4-Cyl. Turbo—Equipment Schedule 2						
W.B. 97.2"; 2.0 Liter.						
Coupe 2D	AFAFK	38625	17000	17850	18050	21300
Roadster 2D	SFAFK	41625	17950	18850	19100	22600
S-Line Pkg			775	775	875	875
Prestige Pkg			1525	1525	1695	1695

Body Type	VIN	List	Trade-In Good	Very Good	Pvt-Party Good	Retail Excellent
TTS QUATTRO AWD—4-Cyl. Turbo—Equipment Schedule 3						
W.B. 97.2"; 2.0 Liter.						
Coupe 2D	B1AFK	46725	20700	21800	21900	25900
Roadster 2D	S1AFK	49725	22700	23800	24000	28500
Prestige Pkg			1525	1525	1705	1705
2011 AUDI — (TRUorWAUorWUA)(BFBFM)–B–#						
A3—4-Cyl. Turbo—Equipment Schedule 3						
W.B. 101.5"; 2.0 Liter.						
2.0T Wagon 4D	BFBFM	29625	12600	13000	14350	17050
Premium Plus Pkg	------		800	800	940	940
Sport Pkg			300	300	345	345
A3 QUATTRO AWD—4-Cyl. Turbo—Equipment Schedule 3						
W.B. 101.5"; 2.0 Liter.						
2.0T Wagon 4D	DFBFM	31725	16500	17050	18250	21300
Premium Plus Pkg	------		800	800	940	940
Sport Pkg			300	300	345	345
A3—4-Cyl. Turbo Diesel—Equipment Schedule 3						
W.B. 101.5"; 2.0 Liter.						
2.0 TDI Wagon 4D	BJBFM	31125	15250	15750	17250	20400
Premium Plus Pkg	------		800	800	950	950
Sport Pkg			300	300	345	345
A4—4-Cyl. Turbo—Equipment Schedule 3						
W.B. 110.6"; 2.0 Liter.						
2.0T Sedan 4D	AFBFL	32825	14600	15250	16100	19100
Bang & Olufsen Sound			350	350	420	420
Premium Plus Pkg			800	800	955	955
A4 QUATTRO AWD—4-Cyl. Turbo—Equipment Schedule 3						
W.B. 110.6"; 2.0 Liter.						
2.0T Sedan 4D	BFBFL	35015	16050	16750	17600	20800
Bang & Olufsen Sound			350	350	425	425
Adaptive Cruise Control			425	425	500	500
S-Line Pkg			800	800	960	960
Premium Plus Pkg			800	800	955	955
Prestige Pkg			1550	1550	1845	1845
A4 AVANT QUATTRO AWD—4-Cyl. Turbo—Equipment Schedule 3						
W.B. 110.6"; 2.0 Liter.						
2.0T Wagon 4D	SFBFL	36815	17650	18250	19350	22500
Bang & Olufsen Sound			350	350	410	410
Adaptive Cruise Control			425	425	485	485
S-Line Pkg			800	800	930	930
Premium Plus Pkg			800	800	925	925
Prestige Pkg			1550	1550	1795	1795
S4 QUATTRO AWD—V6 Supercharged—Equipment Schedule 1						
W.B. 110.7"; 3.0 Liter.						
Sedan 4D	BGBFL	48875	25000	25700	27100	30700
Bang & Olufsen Sound			350	350	390	390
Adaptive Cruise Control			425	425	460	460
Prestige Pkg			1550	1550	1700	1700
A5—4-Cyl. Turbo—Equipment Schedule 1						
W.B. 108.3"; 2.0 Liter.						
2.0T Premium Cab 2D	AFAFH	42875	21300	22000	22800	26100
Bang & Olufsen Sound			350	350	405	405
Adaptive Cruise Control			425	425	475	475
Premium Plus Pkg			800	800	910	910
Prestige Pkg			1550	1550	1760	1760
S-Line Pkg			800	800	915	915
A5 QUATTRO AWD—4-Cyl. Turbo—Equipment Schedule 1						
W.B. 108.3"; 2.0 Liter.						
2.0T Premium Coupe	CFAFR	38665	20300	21000	21800	25000
2.0T Premium Cab 2D	CFAFH	45065	22500	23300	24100	27600
Bang & Olufsen Sound			350	350	405	405
Adaptive Cruise Control			425	425	475	475
S-Line Pkg			800	800	915	915
Premium Plus Pkg			800	800	910	910
Prestige Pkg			1550	1550	1765	1765
S5 QUATTRO AWD—V6 Supercharged—Equipment Schedule 1						
W.B. 108.3"; 3.0 Liter.						
3.0T Convertible 2D	CGAFH	59325	26900	27900	28600	32700
Bang & Olufsen Sound			350	350	395	395
Adaptive Cruise Control			425	425	465	465
Prestige Pkg			1550	1550	1730	1730

2011 AUDI

Body Type	VIN	List	Trade-In Good	Very Good	Pvt-Party Good	Retail Excellent
S5 QUATTRO AWD—V8—Equipment Schedule 1						
W.B. 108.3"; 4.2 Liter.						
Coupe 2D	CVAFR	55175	26300	27400	28000	32000
Bang & Olufsen Sound			350	350	395	395
Adaptive Cruise Control			425	425	465	465
Prestige Pkg			1550	1550	1730	1730
A6—V6—Equipment Schedule 3						
W.B. 111.9"; 3.2 Liter.						
3.2 Sedan 4D	AKBFB	46075	16950	17600	18700	21800
Sport Pkg			400	400	480	480
Premium Plus Pkg			800	800	955	955
A6 QUATTRO AWD—V6 Supercharged—Equipment Schedule 3						
W.B. 111.9"; 3.0 Liter.						
3.0T Sedan 4D	BGBFB	51075	19100	19850	21000	24400
Sport Pkg			400	400	480	480
Premium Plus Pkg			800	800	955	955
Prestige Pkg			1550	1550	1845	1845
A6 AVANT QUATTRO AWD—V6 Supercharged—Equipment Schedule 3						
W.B. 111.9"; 3.0 Liter.						
3.0T Wagon 4D	SGBFB	54185	21300	22200	23200	27000
Sport Pkg			400	400	475	475
Premium Plus Pkg			800	800	950	950
Prestige Pkg			1550	1550	1835	1835
A6 QUATTRO AWD—V8—Equipment Schedule 3						
W.B. 111.9"; 4.2 Liter.						
4.2 Sedan 4D	BVBFB	60025	20700	21500	22600	26300
Sport Pkg			400	400	480	480
A8 QUATTRO AWD—V8—Equipment Schedule 1						
W.B. 115.9", 121.0" (L); 4.2 Liter.						
4.2 Sedan 4D	AVAFD	78925	28600	29300	30800	34500
L 4.2 Sedan 4D	RVAFD	84875	31300	32000	33600	37500
Bang & Olufsen Sound			2575	2575	2845	2845
Adaptive Cruise Control			425	425	460	460
Sport Pkg			800	800	885	885
Premium Pkg			1400	1400	1545	1545
R8 QUATTRO AWD—V8—Equipment Schedule 1						
W.B. 104.3"; 4.2 Liter.						
4.2 Coupe 2D	AUAFG	126250	****	****	****	98800
4.2 Convertible 2D	VUAFG	139750	****	****	****	106700
Bang & Olufsen Sound			****	****	****	370
R8 QUATTRO AWD—V10—Equipment Schedule 1						
W.B. 104.3"; 5.2 Liter.						
5.2 Coupe 2D	ANAFG	159950	****	****	****	127200
5.2 Convertible 2D	VNAFG	173450	****	****	****	136400
TT QUATTRO AWD—4-Cyl. Turbo—Equipment Schedule 2						
W.B. 97.2"; 2.0 Liter.						
Coupe 2D	BFAFK	39175	20300	21200	21400	24700
Roadster 2D	SFAFK	42175	21300	22300	22500	26000
S-Line Pkg			800	800	885	885
Prestige Pkg			1550	1550	1705	1705
TTS QUATTRO AWD—4-Cyl. Turbo—Equipment Schedule 3						
W.B. 97.2"; 2.0 Liter.						
Coupe 2D	F1AFK	47875	24200	25300	25400	29400
Roadster 2D	W1AFK	50875	26700	27900	27800	32100
Prestige Pkg			1550	1550	1700	1700
2012 AUDI — (TRUorWAUorWUA)(BFAFM)-C-#						
A3—4-Cyl. Turbo—Equipment Schedule 3						
W.B. 101.5"; 2.0 Liter.						
2.0T Premium Wagon	BFAFM	29625	14500	14850	16550	19350
Sport Pkg			300	300	350	350
Premium Plus Pkg			850	850	975	975
A3 QUATTRO AWD—4-Cyl. Turbo—Equipment Schedule 3						
W.B. 101.5"; 2.0 Liter.						
2.0T Premium Wagon	DFAFM	31725	19250	19700	21500	24900
Sport Pkg			300	300	355	355
Premium Plus Pkg			850	850	1000	1000
A3—4-Cyl. Turbo Diesel—Equipment Schedule 3						
W.B. 101.5"; 2.0 Liter.						
2.0 TDI Premium Wag	BJAFM	31125	17200	17650	19500	22800
Sport Pkg			300	300	350	350
Premium Plus Pkg			850	850	985	985

2012 AUDI

Body Type	VIN	List	Trade-In Good	Very Good	Pvt-Party Good	Retail Excellent
A4—4-Cyl. Turbo—Equipment Schedule 3						
W.B. 110.6"; 2.0 Liter.						
2.0T Sedan 4D	AFAFL	33375	16800	17500	18350	21400
Bang & Olufsen Sound			350	350	425	425
S-Line Plus Pkg			800	800	945	945
Premium Plus Pkg			850	850	990	990
Prestige Pkg			1575	1575	1870	1870
A4 QUATTRO AWD—4-Cyl. Turbo—Equipment Schedule 3						
W.B. 110.6"; 2.0 Liter.						
2.0T Sedan 4D	BFAFL	35475	18750	19550	20400	23800
Bang & Olufsen Sound			350	350	410	410
Adaptive Cruise Control			450	450	505	505
S-Line Plus Pkg			800	800	945	945
Premium Plus Pkg			850	850	995	995
Prestige Pkg			1575	1575	1870	1870
A4 AVANT QUATTRO AWD—4-Cyl. Turbo—Equipment Schedule 3						
W.B. 110.6"; 2.0 Liter.						
2.0T Premium Wagon	SFAFL	37275	21200	21700	23000	26200
Bang & Olufsen Sound			350	350	410	410
Adaptive Cruise Control			450	450	505	505
S-Line Plus Pkg			800	800	915	915
Premium Plus Pkg			850	850	960	960
Prestige Pkg			1575	1575	1810	1810
S4 QUATTRO AWD—V6 Supercharged—Equipment Schedule 1						
W.B. 110.7"; 3.0 Liter.						
Premium Plus Sedan	BGAFL	49575	28500	29100	30800	34200
Bang & Olufsen Sound			350	350	390	390
Adaptive Cruise Control			450	450	480	480
Prestige Pkg			1575	1575	1730	1730
A5—4-Cyl. Turbo—Equipment Schedule 1						
W.B. 108.3"; 2.0 Liter.						
2.0T Premium Cab 2D	AFAFH	43475	24000	24600	25700	29100
Bang & Olufsen Sound			350	350	405	405
Adaptive Cruise Control			450	450	500	500
S-Line Pkg			800	800	905	905
Premium Plus Pkg			850	850	950	950
Prestige Pkg			1575	1575	1790	1790
A5 QUATTRO AWD—4-Cyl. Turbo—Equipment Schedule 1						
W.B. 108.3"; 2.0 Liter.						
2.0T Premium Coupe	CFAFR	39175	21900	22400	23600	26600
2.0T Premium Cab 2D	CFAFH	45575	25200	25900	27000	30500
Bang & Olufsen Sound			350	350	405	405
Adaptive Cruise Control			450	450	500	500
S-Line Pkg			800	800	905	905
Premium Plus Pkg			850	850	955	955
Prestige Pkg			1575	1575	1800	1800
S5 QUATTRO AWD—V6 Supercharged—Equipment Schedule 1						
W.B. 108.3"; 3.0 Liter.						
3.0T Convertible 2D	CGAFH	60175	31700	32700	33500	37600
Bang & Olufsen Sound			350	350	400	400
Adaptive Cruise Control			450	450	490	490
Prestige Pkg			1575	1575	1760	1760
S5 QUATTRO AWD—V8—Equipment Schedule 1						
W.B. 108.3"; 4.2 Liter.						
Coupe 2D	CVAFH	55975	30900	31900	32700	36600
Bang & Olufsen Sound			350	350	400	400
Adaptive Cruise Control			450	450	490	490
Prestige Pkg			1575	1575	1760	1760
A6—4-Cyl. Turbo—Equipment Schedule 3						
W.B. 114.7"; 2.0 Liter.						
2.0T Premium Sedan	AFAFC	42575	23900	24700	25600	28900
Premium Plus Pkg			850	850	930	930
Sport Pkg			400	400	440	440
A6 QUATTRO AWD—V6 Supercharged—Equipment Schedule 3						
W.B. 114.7"; 3.0 Liter.						
3.0T Premium Sedan	BGAFC	50775	25900	26700	27700	31200
Bang & Olufsen Sound			2700	2700	2975	2975
Adaptive Cruise Control			450	450	485	485
Innovation Pkg			1225	1225	1340	1340
Premium Plus Pkg			850	850	925	925
Prestige Pkg			1575	1575	1740	1740
Sport Pkg			400	400	440	440

Body Type	VIN	List	Trade-In Good	Trade-In Very Good	Pvt-Party Good	Retail Excellent
A7 QUATTRO AWD—6-Cyl. Supercharged—Equipment Schedule 1						
W.B. 114.7"; 3.0 Liter.						
Premium Sedan 4D	SGAFC	60125	37100	38300	38900	43400
Bang & Olufsen Sound			2700	2700	2960	2960
Adaptive Cruise Control			450	450	480	480
Innovation Pkg			1225	1225	1330	1330
Premium Plus Pkg			875	875	950	950
Prestige Pkg			1575	1575	1735	1735
A8 QUATTRO AWD—V8—Equipment Schedule 1						
W.B. 117.8"; 122.9" (L); 4.2 Liter.						
4.2 Sedan 4D	AVAFD	79625	33800	34500	36200	39800
L 4.2 Sedan 4D	RVAFD	85575	36300	37100	38800	42600
Bang & Olufsen Sound			2700	2700	2985	2985
Adaptive Cruise Control			450	450	485	485
Premium Pkg			1450	1450	1600	1600
A8 QUATTRO AWD—W12—Equipment Schedule 1						
W.B. 112.9"; 6.3 Liter.						
L Sedan 4D	R4AFD	136975	69200	70600	71600	77200
Bang & Olufsen Sound			2700	2700	2895	2895
Adaptive Cruise Control			450	450	470	470
Premium Pkg			1450	1450	1550	1550
R8 AWD—V8—Equipment Schedule 1						
W.B. 104.3"; 4.2 Liter.						
4.2 Coupe 2D	AUAFG	126250	****	****	****	105600
4.2 Spyder 2D	SUAFG	139750	****	****	****	113500
Bang & Olufsen Sound			****	****	****	375
Ceramic Brakes			****	****	****	4045
R8 AWD—V10—Equipment Schedule 1						
W.B. 104.3"; 5.2 Liter.						
5.2 Coupe 2D	ENAFG	161450	****	****	****	135300
5.2 Spyder 2D	VNAFG	175150	****	****	****	143100
GT Coupe 2D	9NAFG	200150	****	****	****	179700
GT Spyder Conv 2D	8NAFG	213650	****	****	****	193900
Ceramic Brakes			****	****	****	4005

2013 AUDI — (TRUorWAUorWUA)(BEAFM)-D-#

Body Type	VIN	List	Trade-In Good	Trade-In Very Good	Pvt-Party Good	Retail Excellent
A3—4-Cyl. Turbo—Equipment Schedule 3						
W.B. 101.5"; 2.0 Liter.						
2.0T Premium Wagon	BEAFM	29645	15100	15400	17350	20200
2.0T Premium Plus	KEAFM	31645	19950	20400	22300	25800
Sport Pkg			300	300	345	345
AWD	D		1275	1275	1480	1480
A3—4-Cyl. Turbo Diesel—Equipment Schedule 3						
W.B. 101.5"; 2.0 Liter.						
2.0 TDI Premium Wag	BJAFM	31145	20300	20700	22700	26100
2.0 TDI Premium Plus	KJAFM	33145	22100	22500	24400	28000
Sport Pkg			300	300	340	340
allroad QUATTRO AWD—4-Cyl. Turbo—Equipment Schedule 1						
W.B. 110.4"; 2.0 Liter.						
Premium Wagon 4D	9FAFL	40495	26400	27200	27800	30500
Premium Plus Wagon	UFAFL	43795	29200	30100	30800	33800
Prestige Wagon 4D	VFAFL	49695	30400	31300	32000	35200
Bang & Olufsen Sound			375	375	400	400
A4 QUATTRO AWD—4-Cyl. Turbo—Equipment Schedule 3						
W.B. 110.6"; 2.0 Liter.						
Premium Sedan 4D	BFAFL	35495	20100	20900	21700	25000
Premium Plus Sedan	FFAFL	39659	22800	23700	24400	27900
Prestige Sedan 4D	KFAFL	45245	25500	26400	27100	31100
Bang & Olufsen Sound			375	375	420	420
Adaptive Cruise Control			475	475	535	535
S-Line Pkg			800	800	920	920
FWD	A		(1325)	(1325)	(1550)	(1550)
S4 QUATTRO AWD—V6 Supercharged—Equipment Schedule 1						
W.B. 110.7"; 3.0 Liter.						
Premium Plus Sedan	BGAFL	49395	31400	32000	34000	37500
Prestige Sedan 4D	KGAFL	56145	32500	33100	34800	38100
Bang & Olufsen Sound			375	375	400	400
Adaptive Cruise Control			475	475	505	505
A5 QUATTRO AWD—4-Cyl. Turbo—Equipment Schedule 1						
W.B. 108.3"; 2.0 Liter.						
2.0T Premium Cab 2D	CFAFH	46345	28400	28900	30300	33800
2.0T Premium + Cab	LFAFH	49895	30400	31000	32400	36000
2.0T Prestige Cab 2D	VFAFH	55795	33100	33700	35000	38900

2013 AUDI

Body Type	VIN	List	Trade-In Good	Very Good	Pvt-Party Good	Retail Excellent
Bang & Olufsen Sound	------	------	375	375	410	410
Adaptive Cruise Control	------	------	475	475	520	520
S-Line Pkg	------	------	800	800	895	895
FWD	------	------	(1325)	(1325)	(1505)	(1505)

A5 QUATTRO AWD—4-Cyl. Turbo—Equipment Schedule 1
W.B. 108.3"; 2.0 Liter.

Body Type	VIN	List	Good	Very Good	Good	Excellent
2.0T Premium Cpe 2D	CFAFR	39945	24000	24500	25900	29000
2.0T Premium Plus 2D	LFAFR	43495	26800	27300	28600	32000
2.0T Prestige Cpe 2D	VFAFR	49395	29100	29700	31100	34700
Bang & Olufsen Sound	------	------	375	375	415	415
Adaptive Cruise Control	------	------	475	475	520	520
S-Line Pkg	------	------	800	800	895	895

S5 QUATTRO AWD—V6 Supercharged—Equipment Schedule 1
W.B. 108.3"; 3.0 Liter.

Body Type	VIN	List	Good	Very Good	Good	Excellent
Premium Plus Cpe 2D	CGAFR	53195	34100	35100	35900	39700
Prestige Coupe 2D	VGAFR	59845	35800	36900	37600	41500
Premium Plus Conv	CGAFH	60195	37100	38200	38900	42900
Prestige Convertible	VGAFH	66845	39700	40900	41600	45900
Bang & Olufsen Sound	------	------	375	375	400	400
Adaptive Cruise Control	------	------	475	475	515	515

RS 5 QUATTRO AWD—V8—Equipment Schedule 1
W.B. 108.3"; 4.2 Liter.

Body Type	VIN	List	Good	Very Good	Good	Excellent
Coupe 2D	C6AFR	69795	50600	52100	52400	57200
Convertible 2D	C6AFH	78795	53500	55100	55500	60800
Adaptive Cruise Control	------	------	475	475	505	505

A6 QUATTRO AWD—4-Cyl. Turbo—Equipment Schedule 3
W.B. 114.7"; 2.0 Liter.

Body Type	VIN	List	Good	Very Good	Good	Excellent
2.0T Premium Sedan	BFAFC	45295	27000	27800	29400	33400
2.0T Premium Plus	GFAFC	49595	27800	28700	30400	34500
Premium Plus Pkg	------	------	875	875	985	985
FWD	------	------	(1325)	(1325)	(1480)	(1480)

A6 QUATTRO AWD—V6 Supercharged—Equipment Schedule 3
W.B. 114.7"; 3.0 Liter.

Body Type	VIN	List	Good	Very Good	Good	Excellent
3.0T Premium Sed 4D	BGAFC	51295	28800	29600	31600	35600
3.0T Premium Plus	GGAFC	55595	30600	31500	33300	37800
3.0T Prestige Sed 4D	HGAFC	57845	34800	35900	37700	42700
Bang & Olufsen Sound	------	------	2825	2825	3130	3130
Adaptive Cruise Control	------	------	475	475	515	515
Innovation Pkg	------	------	1250	1250	1370	1370
Premium Plus Pkg	------	------	875	875	980	980

S6 QUATTRO AWD—V8 Twin Turbo—Equipment Schedule 1
W.B. 114.7"; 4.0 Liter.

Body Type	VIN	List	Good	Very Good	Good	Excellent
Prestige Sedan 4D	B2AFC	74095	45200	46000	47500	51500
Bang & Olufsen Sound	------	------	2825	2825	3045	3045
Adaptive Cruise Control	------	------	475	475	500	500
Innovation Pkg	------	------	1250	1250	1335	1335

A7 QUATTRO AWD—V6 Supercharged—Equipment Schedule 1
W.B. 114.7"; 3.0 Liter.

Body Type	VIN	List	Good	Very Good	Good	Excellent
Premium Sedan 4D	SGAFC	60995	38800	40000	41600	46800
Premium Plus Sedan	YGAFC	64695	39000	40100	41900	47300
Prestige Sedan 4D	2GAFC	67045	42300	43500	45200	50900
Bang & Olufsen Sound	------	------	2825	2825	3065	3065
Adaptive Cruise Control	------	------	475	475	505	505

S7 QUATTRO AWD—V8 Twin Turbo—Equipment Schedule 1
W.B. 114.7"; 4.0 Liter.

Body Type	VIN	List	Good	Very Good	Good	Excellent
Prestige Sedan 4D	S23FC	79695	54400	55400	56400	60100
Bang & Olufsen Sound	------	------	2825	2825	2975	2975
Adaptive Cruise Control	------	------	475	475	490	490
Innovation Pkg	------	------	1250	1250	1305	1305

A8 QUATTRO AWD—V6 Supercharged—Equipment Schedule 1
W.B. 117.8", 122.9" (L); 3.0 Liter.

Body Type	VIN	List	Good	Very Good	Good	Excellent
3.0T Sedan 4D	AGAFD	73095	37000	37600	39200	42600
3.0T L Sedan 4D	RGAFD	79395	38700	39400	41200	44800
Bang & Olufsen Sound	------	------	2825	2825	3050	3050
Adaptive Cruise Control	------	------	475	475	500	500

A8 QUATTRO AWD—V8 Turbo—Equipment Schedule 1
W.B. 117.8", 122.9" (L); 4.0 Liter.

Body Type	VIN	List	Good	Very Good	Good	Excellent
4.0T Sedan 4D	A2AFD	81795	38400	39100	40900	44400
4.0T L Sedan 4D	R2AFD	88095	41800	42600	44300	48100
Bang & Olufsen Sound	------	------	2825	2825	3095	3095
Adaptive Cruise Control	------	------	475	475	510	510

A8 QUATTRO AWD—W12—Equipment Schedule 1
W.B. 122.9"; 6.3 Liter.

Body Type	VIN	List	Trade-In Good	Very Good	Pvt-Party Good	Retail Excellent
L Sedan 4D	R4AFD	137495	77500	78900	80000	85500
Bang & Olufsen Sound			2825	2825	3010	3010
Adaptive Cruise Control			475	475	510	510
S8 QUATTRO AWD—V8 Twin Turbo—Equipment Schedule 1						
W.B. 117.8"; 4.0 Liter.						
Sedan 4D		110895	61900	63000	64500	69200
Bang & Olufsen Sound			2825	2825	3060	3060
Adaptive Cruise Control			475	475	505	505
TT QUATTRO AWD—4-Cyl. Turbo—Equipment Schedule 2						
W.B. 97.2"; 2.0 Liter.						
Premium Plus Coupe	BFAFK	39545	27000	28000	28400	32300
Prestige Coupe 2D	KFAFK	45645	28900	30000	30500	34600
PremiumPlus Rdstr	SFAFK	42545	28200	29300	29700	33600
Prestige Roadster 2D	4FAFK	48645	31000	32200	32600	37100
S-Line Pkg			800	800	880	880
TT RS QUATTRO AWD—5-Cyl. Turbo—Equipment Schedule 2						
W.B. 97.2"; 2.5 Liter.						
Coupe 2D	B3AFK	58095	40700	42200	42500	48300
TTS QUATTRO AWD—4-Cyl. Turbo—Equipment Schedule 3						
W.B. 97.2"; 2.0 Liter.						
Premium Plus Cpe 2D	B1AFK	48245	31300	32500	32900	37400
Prestige Coupe 2D	K1AFK	51545	32500	33700	34400	39400
PremiumPlus Rdstr	S1AFK	51245	32600	33800	34200	38900
Prestige Roadster 2D	41AFK	54545	35500	36800	37300	42500

Body Type	VIN	List	Trade-In Good	Very Good	Pvt-Party Good	Retail Excellent
allroad QUATTRO AWD—4-Cyl. Turbo—Equipment Schedule 1						
W.B. 110.4"; 2.0 Liter.						
Premium Wagon 4D	9FBFL	41595	26300	27100	27900	30600
Premium Plus Wag	UFBFL	44195	29900	30800	31600	34600
Prestige Wagon 4D	VFBFL	50095	33100	34100	34800	38100
Bang & Olufsen Sound			375	375	405	405
Sensing Cruise Control			500	500	535	535
A4 QUATTRO AWD—4-Cyl. Turbo—Equipment Schedule 3						
W.B. 110.6"; 2.0 Liter.						
Premium Sedan 4D	BFBFL	36795	23800	24700	25100	28400
FWD	A		(1400)	(1400)	(1575)	(1575)
A4 QUATTRO AWD—4-Cyl. Turbo—Equipment Schedule 3						
W.B. 110.6"; 2.0 Liter.						
Premium Plus Sedan	FFBFL	40295	27100	28100	28400	32000
Bang & Olufsen Sound			375	375	415	415
FWD			(1400)	(1400)	(1570)	(1570)
A4 QUATTRO AWD—4-Cyl. Turbo—Equipment Schedule 3						
W.B. 110.6"; 2.0 Liter.						
Prestige Sedan 4D	KFBFL	45595	29800	30900	31200	35200
Dynamic Cruise Control			500	500	550	550
Driver Assistance Pkg			675	675	745	745
S4 QUATTRO AWD—V6 Supercharged—Equipment Schedule 1						
W.B. 110.7"; 3.0 Liter.						
Premium Plus Sedan	BGAFL	50395	37200	37900	39700	43200
Bang & Olufsen Sound			375	375	405	405
S4 QUATTRO AWD—V6 Supercharged—Equipment Schedule 1						
W.B. 110.7"; 3.0 Liter.						
Prestige Sedan 4D	KGAFL	56295	38300	39000	40700	44300
Adaptive Cruise Control			500	500	530	530
Driver Assist Pkg			675	675	720	720
A5 QUATTRO AWD—4-Cyl. Turbo—Equipment Schedule 1						
W.B. 108.3"; 2.0 Liter.						
Premium Coupe 2D	CFAFR	41095	27500	28100	29300	32600
Premium Plus Cpe 2D	LFAFR	44195	30700	31300	32600	36100
Bang & Olufsen Sound			375	375	410	410
A5 QUATTRO AWD—4-Cyl. Turbo—Equipment Schedule 1						
W.B. 108.3"; 2.0 Liter.						
Prestige Coupe 2D	WFAFR	50295	34000	34700	35800	39600
Dynamic Cruise Control			500	500	540	540
Driver Assist Pkg			675	675	735	735
S-Line Pkg			800	800	885	885
A5 QUATTRO AWD—4-Cyl. Turbo—Equipment Schedule 1						
W.B. 108.3"; 2.0 Liter.						
Premium Cabriolet 2D	CFAFH	47495	31600	32300	33500	37200
Premium Plus Cab 2D	LFAFH	50595	34400	35100	36300	40100
Prestige Cabriolet 2D	WFAFH	56695	37000	37700	38800	42900
Bang & Olufsen Sound			375	375	410	410

2014 AUDI

Body Type	VIN	List	Trade-In Good	Trade-In Very Good	Pvt-Party Good	Retail Excellent
Dynamic Cruise Control			500	500	540	540
S-Line Pkg			800	800	880	880
FWD			(1400)	(1400)	(1560)	(1560)
S5 QUATTRO AWD—V6 Supercharged—Equipment Schedule 1						
W.B. 108.3"; 3.0 Liter.						
Premium Plus Cpe	CGAFR	54295	41900	43100	43500	47500
Premium Plus Cnv 2D	CGAFH	61295	44600	45900	46300	50500
Prestige Coupe 2D	VGAFR	60545	44300	45500	45800	50000
Prestige Convertible	VGAFH	67545	47100	48500	49100	53700
Sensing Cruise Control			500	500	530	530
RS 5 QUATTRO AWD—V8—Equipment Schedule 1						
W.B. 108.3"; 4.2 Liter.						
Coupe 2D	C6AFR	70495	56400	58000	58200	63400
Convertible 2D	C6AFH	78795	59400	61100	61400	67000
Active Cruise Control			500	500	530	530
Driver Assist Pkg			675	675	720	720
A6 QUATTRO AWD—4-Cyl. Turbo—Equipment Schedule 3						
W.B. 114.7"; 2.0 Liter.						
2.0T Premium Sedan	FFAFC	46095	30300	31200	33000	37400
2.0T Premium Plus Sedan	GFAFC	50395	31300	32300	34300	39100
FWD			(1400)	(1400)	(1550)	(1550)
A6 QUATTRO AWD—V6 Supercharged—Equipment Schedule 3						
W.B. 114.7"; 3.0 Liter.						
3.0T Premium Plus	FGAFC	55995	34400	35400	37600	42700
3.0T Prestige Sedan	HGAFC	58795	38200	39300	41000	46000
Bang & Olufsen Sound			2950	2950	3260	3260
Adaptive Cruise Control			500	500	545	545
A6 QUATTRO AWD—V6 Turbo Diesel—Equipment Schedule 3						
W.B. 114.7"; 3.0 Liter.						
TDI Premium Plus	FMAFC	58395	37400	38500	39600	44000
TDI Prestige Sedan	HMAFC	61195	39700	40900	41900	46400
Bang & Olufsen Sound			2950	2950	3180	3180
Adaptive Cruise Control			500	500	530	530
S6 QUATTRO AWD—V8 Twin Turbo—Equipment Schedule 1						
W.B. 114.7"; 4.0 Liter.						
Sedan 4D		74295	56000	57000	58500	62700
Bang & Olufsen Sound			2950	2950	3135	3135
Sensing Cruise Control			500	500	520	520
A7 QUATTRO AWD—V6 Supercharged—Equipment Schedule 1						
W.B. 114.7"; 3.0 Liter.						
Premium Plus Sedan	WGAFC	65395	44100	45400	46900	52500
Prestige Sedan 4D	2GAFC	68295	48000	49400	50800	56700
Bang & Olufsen Sound			2950	2950	3170	3170
Adaptive Cruise Control			500	500	525	525
Driver Assistance Pkg			675	675	715	715
A7 QUATTRO AWD—V6 Turbo Diesel—Equipment Schedule 1						
W.B. 114.7"; 3.0 Liter.						
TDI Premium Plus	WMAFC	67795	46600	48000	49500	55300
TDI Prestige Sedan	2MAFC	70695	50600	52100	53600	59600
Bang & Olufsen Sound			2950	2950	3160	3160
Adaptive Cruise Control			500	500	525	525
Driver Assistance Pkg			675	675	715	715
Innovation Pkg			1275	1275	1350	1350
S7 QUATTRO AWD—V8 Twin Turbo—Equipment Schedule 1						
W.B. 114.7"; 4.0 Liter.						
Sedan 4D		81095	61800	62900	63600	67500
Bang & Olufsen Sound			2950	2950	3085	3085
Adaptive Cruise Control			500	500	510	510
Driver Assistance Pkg			675	675	695	695
Innovation Pkg			1275	1275	1320	1320
RS 7—V8 Twin Turbo—Equipment Schedule 1						
W.B. 114.8"; 4.0 Liter.						
Prestige Sedan 4D	W2AFC	105795	89500	92500	89500	97400
Bang & Olufsen Sound			2950	2950	3100	3100
Adaptive Cruise Control			500	500	515	515
Driver Assist Plus Pkg			675	675	695	695
Carbon-Optic Pkg			1450	1450	1515	1515
Dynamic Pkg			1000	1000	1045	1045
Innovation Pkg			1275	1275	1325	1325
A8 QUATTRO AWD—V6 Supercharged—Equipment Schedule 1						
W.B. 117.8", 122.9" (L); 3.0 Liter.						
3.0T Sedan 4D	AGAFD	75995	44200	45000	46000	49100
3.0T L Sedan 4D	RGAFD	79695	49900	50800	51900	55100

Body	Type	VIN	List	Trade-In Good	Very Good	Pvt-Party Good	Retail Excellent
Adaptive Cruise Control				500	500	520	520
Driver Assistance Pkg				675	675	710	710

A8 QUATTRO AWD—V6 Turbo Diesel—Equipment Schedule 1
W.B. 122.9"; 3.0 Liter.

Body	Type	VIN	List	Good	Very Good	Good	Excellent
L TDI Sedan 4D		RMAFD	83395	55700	56700	57900	61700
Bang & Olufsen Sound				2950	2950	3110	3110
Adaptive Cruise Control				500	500	515	515
Driver Assistance Pkg				675	675	700	700
Rear Seat Comfort Pkg				1375	1375	1440	1440

A8 QUATTRO AWD—V8 Turbo—Equipment Schedule 1
W.B. 117.8", 122.9" (L); 4.0 Liter.

Body	Type	VIN	List	Good	Very Good	Good	Excellent
4.0T Sedan 4D		A2AFD	84795	49600	50500	52200	56000
4.0T L Sedan 4D		R2AFD	88495	53100	54000	55700	59700
Bang & Olufsen Sound				2950	2950	3170	3170
Adaptive Cruise Control				500	500	520	520
Driver Assistance Pkg				675	675	715	715

A8 QUATTRO AWD—W12—Equipment Schedule 1
W.B. 122.9"; 6.3 Liter.

Body	Type	VIN	List	Good	Very Good	Good	Excellent
L Sedan 4D		R4AFD	138895	90700	92300	92900	98700
Bang & Olufsen Sound				2950	2950	3115	3115
Adaptive Cruise Control				500	500	515	515
Driver Assistance Pkg				675	675	700	700
Executive Rear Comfort Pkg				1375	1375	1440	1440

S8 QUATTRO AWD—V8 Twin Turbo—Equipment Schedule 1
W.B. 117.8"; 4.0 Liter.

Body	Type	VIN	List	Good	Very Good	Good	Excellent
Sedan 4D		D2AFD	113395	73900	75200	76300	81200
Bang & Olufsen Sound				2950	2950	3155	3155
Active Cruise Control				500	500	525	525
Driver Assistance Pkg				675	675	710	710

R8 QUATTRO AWD—V8—Equipment Schedule 1
W.B. 104.3"; 4.2 Liter.

Body	Type	VIN	List	Good	Very Good	Good	Excellent
Coupe 2D		FUAFG	126550	****	****	****	113800
Convertible 2D		WUAFG	140050	****	****	****	121700
Bang & Olufsen Sound				****	****	****	390
Ceramic Brakes				****	****	****	4250

R8 QUATTRO AWD—V10—Equipment Schedule 1
W.B. 104.3"; 5.2 Liter.

Body	Type	VIN	List	Good	Very Good	Good	Excellent
Coupe 2D		ENAFG	163250	****	****	****	142900
Plus Coupe 2D		3NAFG	182595	****	****	****	153300
Convertible 2D		VNAFG	176750	****	****	****	151500
Ceramic Brakes				****	****	****	4215

TT QUATTRO AWD—4-Cyl. Turbo—Equipment Schedule 2
W.B. 97.2"; 2.0 Liter.

Body	Type	VIN	List	Good	Very Good	Good	Excellent
Coupe 2D		BFAFK	43795	28600	29700	30000	33800
Roadster 2D		SFAFK	43795	30000	31100	31700	36000
S-Line Pkg				800	800	870	870

TTS QUATTRO AWD—4-Cyl. Turbo—Equipment Schedule 2
W.B. 97.2"; 2.0 Liter.

Body	Type	VIN	List	Good	Very Good	Good	Excellent
Coupe 2D		B1AFK	49595	35000	36300	36400	41100
Roadster 2D		S1AFK	52595	37100	38500	38700	43800

BMW

2000 BMW — (4UorWB)(SorA)(AM334)-Y-#

3 SERIES—6-Cyl.—Equipment Schedule 1
W.B. 107.3"; 2.5 Liter, 2.8 Liter.

Body	Type	VIN	List	Good	Very Good	Good	Excellent
323i Sedan 4D		AM334	32680	1775	2100	2450	4075
323i Wagon 4D		AR334	32985	1875	2200	2650	4450
323Ci Coupe 2D		BM334	34280	2275	2650	2825	4525
323Ci Convertible 2D		BR334	38285	2000	2150	2925	4475
328i Sedan 4D		AM534	37670	2100	2450	2800	4625
328Ci Coupe 2D		BM534	38335	2600	3000	3225	5150
Hard Top (Conv)				300	300	400	400
Premium Pkg				150	150	200	200
Sport Pkg				175	175	220	220
Sport Premium Pkg				200	200	255	255
Manual, 5-Spd (ex 2D)				(300)	(300)	(400)	(400)

Z3—6-Cyl.—Equipment Schedule 1
W.B. 96.3"; 2.5 Liter, 2.8 Liter.

Body	Type	VIN	List	Good	Very Good	Good	Excellent
Coupe 2D		CK534	38395	4500	4975	5375	7825
2.3 Roadster 2D		CH933	34470	2600	2875	3425	5200

Body Type	VIN	List	Trade-In Good	Very Good	Pvt-Party Good	Retail Excellent
2.8 Roadster 2D	CH334	38445	**4275**	**4725**	**5050**	**7450**
Hard Top (Roadster)	------	------	300	300	400	400
M—6-Cyl.—Equipment Schedule 1						
W.B. 96.8"; 3.2 Liter.						
Coupe 2D	CM934	42670	**9900**	**10900**	**11050**	**15700**
Roadster 2D	CK934	43270	**5600**	**6200**	**6675**	**9725**
Hard Top (Roadster)	------	------	300	300	360	360
Z8—V8—Equipment Schedule 1						
W.B. 98.9"; 5.0 Liter.						
Roadster 2D	EJ134	130670	********	********	********	**53000**
5 SERIES—6-Cyl.—Equipment Schedule 1						
W.B. 111.4"; 2.8 Liter.						
528i Sedan 4D	DM634	44595	**1475**	**1650**	**2400**	**4100**
528iT Wagon 4D	DP634	46545	**900**	**1025**	**1600**	**2800**
Premium Pkg	------	------	150	150	200	200
Sport Pkg	------	------	275	275	365	365
Manual, 5-Spd	------	------	(350)	(350)	(465)	(465)
5 SERIES—V8—Equipment Schedule 1						
W.B. 111.4"; 4.4 Liter.						
540i Sedan 4D	DN634	52970	**2625**	**2975**	**3725**	**6200**
540iT Wagon 4D	DR634	55350	**2550**	**2875**	**3600**	**6000**
Sport Pkg	------	------	275	275	365	365
M5—V8—Equipment Schedule 1						
W.B. 111.4"; 5.0 Liter.						
Sedan 4D	DE934	72070	**6425**	**7075**	**7575**	**11100**
7 SERIES—V8—Equipment Schedule 1						
W.B. 115.4", 120.9" (iL); 4.4 Liter.						
740i Sedan 4D	GG834	64670	**1150**	**1275**	**1875**	**3125**
740iL Sedan 4D	GH834	66970	**1825**	**2025**	**2575**	**4025**
Sport Pkg	------	------	275	275	365	365
7 SERIES—V12—Equipment Schedule 1						
W.B. 120.9"; 5.4 Liter.						
750iL Sedan 4D	GJ034	95270	**2925**	**3225**	**3950**	**6300**

2001 BMW — WBAorWBS(AV334)-1-#

Body Type	VIN	List	Trade-In Good	Very Good	Pvt-Party Good	Retail Excellent
3 SERIES—6-Cyl.—Equipment Schedule 1						
W.B. 107.3"; 2.5 Liter, 3.0 Liter.						
325i Sedan 4D	AV334	30060	**2100**	**2425**	**2725**	**4425**
325xi AWD Sedan 4D	AV334	31810	**2375**	**2775**	**3025**	**4900**
325Ci Coupe 2D	BN334	32060	**2700**	**3150**	**3225**	**5050**
325Cic Convertible 2D	BS334	38010	**2400**	**2575**	**3400**	**5200**
325iT Wagon 4D	AW334	32470	**2100**	**2450**	**2900**	**4800**
325xiT AWD Wagon 4D	AW334	34220	**2375**	**2750**	**3200**	**5325**
330i Sedan 4D	AV334	39280	**2575**	**2975**	**3225**	**5200**
330xi AWD Sedan 4D	AV534	41030	**3025**	**3500**	**3700**	**5925**
330Ci Coupe 2D	BN534	39335	**3075**	**3550**	**3650**	**5700**
330Cic Convertible 2D	BS534	44245	**2750**	**2975**	**3800**	**5775**
Hard Top (Conv)	------	------	300	300	400	400
Premium Pkg	------	------	150	150	210	210
Sport Pkg	------	------	175	175	235	235
Manual, 5-Spd (ex 2D)	------	------	(300)	(300)	(400)	(400)
M3—6-Cyl.—Equipment Schedule 1						
W.B. 107.5"; 3.2 Liter.						
Coupe 2D	BL934	46045	**4550**	**5025**	**5700**	**8500**
Convertible 2D	BR934	54045	**5400**	**5925**	**6525**	**9650**
Hard Top (Conv)	------	------	300	300	400	400
Z3—6-Cyl.—Equipment Schedule 1						
W.B. 96.3"; 2.5 Liter, 3.0 Liter.						
2.5i Roadster 2D	CN334	34295	**3000**	**3325**	**3775**	**5600**
2.5i Coupe 2D	CK734	39845	**4900**	**5400**	**5775**	**8300**
3.0i Roadster 2D	CN534	39745	**4100**	**4525**	**5075**	**7450**
Hard Top (Roadster)	------	------	300	300	390	390
M—6-Cyl.—Equipment Schedule 1						
W.B. 96.8"; 3.2 Liter.						
Coupe 2D	CN934	45635	**11500**	**12600**	**12450**	**17400**
Roadster 2D	CL934	46635	**7575**	**8325**	**8650**	**12250**
Hard Top (Roadster)	------	------	300	300	345	345
Z8—V8—Equipment Schedule 1						
W.B. 98.6"; 5.0 Liter.						
Roadster 2D	EJ134	130745	********	********	********	**56800**
5 SERIES—6-Cyl.—Equipment Schedule 1						
W.B. 111.4"; 2.5 Liter, 3.0 Liter.						
525i Sedan 4D	DT334	40195	**1725**	**1950**	**2575**	**4225**

Body Type	VIN	List	Trade-In Good	Very Good	Pvt-Party Good	Retail Excellent
525iT Wagon 4D	DS334	41995	950	1075	1625	2800
530i Sedan 4D	DT534	44345	2375	2650	3275	5325
Premium Pkg		....	150	150	210	210
Sport Pkg		....	300	300	415	415
Manual, 5-Spd		....	(375)	(375)	(485)	(485)

5 SERIES—V8—Equipment Schedule 1
W.B. 111.4"; 4.4 Liter.

Body Type	VIN	List	Good	Very Good	Good	Excellent
540i Sedan 4D	DN634	51670	3025	3400	4025	6525
540iT Wagon 4D	DR634	54050	3025	3400	3950	6300
Sport Pkg		....	300	300	415	415

M5—V8—Equipment Schedule 1
W.B. 111.4"; 5.0 Liter.

Body Type	VIN	List	Good	Very Good	Good	Excellent
Sedan 4D	DE934	69970	7350	8075	8750	12900

7 SERIES—V8—Equipment Schedule 1
W.B. 115.4", 120.9" (iL); 4.4 Liter.

Body Type	VIN	List	Good	Very Good	Good	Excellent
740i Sedan 4D	GG834	63470	1425	1575	2500	4250
740iL Sedan 4D	GH834	67470	2250	2475	3200	5100
Sport Pkg		....	300	300	415	415

7 SERIES—V12—Equipment Schedule 1
W.B. 120.9"; 5.4 Liter.

Body Type	VIN	List	Good	Very Good	Good	Excellent
750iL Sedan 4D	GJ034	92670	3350	3675	4400	6800
Sport Pkg		....	150	150	205	205

2002 BMW — WBA,WBS,4USor5UM(ET374)-2-#

3 SERIES—6-Cyl.—Equipment Schedule 1
W.B. 107.3"; 2.5 Liter, 3.0 Liter.

Body Type	VIN	List	Good	Very Good	Good	Excellent
325i Sedan 4D	ET374	32465	2325	2700	2975	4775
325xi AWD Sedan 4D	EU334	34215	2700	3125	3375	5375
325Ci Coupe 2D	BN334	34465	3125	3625	3650	5625
325Cic Convertible 2D	BS334	39470	2975	3200	3975	5875
325iT Wagon 4D	EN334	34865	2725	3150	3450	5500
325xiT AWD Wagon 4D	EP334	36615	3100	3575	3825	6100
330i Sedan 4D	EV534	38410	2900	3350	3550	5625
330xi AWD Sedan 4D	EW534	40160	3250	3775	4050	6400
330Ci Coupe 2D	BN534	39410	3425	3950	4150	6425
330Cic Convertible 2D	BS534	46820	3375	3625	4525	6650
Hard Top		....	325	325	445	445
Premium Pkg		....	175	175	225	225
Sport Pkg		....	200	200	255	255
Manual, 5-Spd (ex 2D)		....	(325)	(325)	(420)	(420)

M3—6-Cyl.—Equipment Schedule 1
W.B. 107.5"; 3.2 Liter.

Body Type	VIN	List	Good	Very Good	Good	Excellent
Coupe 2D	BL934	49745	4975	5475	6100	8950
Convertible 2D	BR934	55545	5750	6300	6925	10050
Hard Top (Conv)		....	325	325	445	445

Z3—6-Cyl.—Equipment Schedule 1
W.B. 96.3"; 2.5 Liter, 3.0 Liter.

Body Type	VIN	List	Good	Very Good	Good	Excellent
2.5i Roadster 2D	CN334	34370	3400	3750	4175	6075
3.0i Coupe 2D	CK734	39920	5700	6250	6475	9100
3.0i Roadster 2D	CN534	39820	5125	5600	5975	8500
Hard Top (Roadster)		....	325	325	430	430
Sport Pkg		....	175	175	215	215

M—6-Cyl.—Equipment Schedule 1
W.B. 96.8"; 3.2 Liter.

Body Type	VIN	List	Good	Very Good	Good	Excellent
Coupe 2D	CN934	45635	12600	13750	13450	18500
Roadster 2D	CL934	46635	8950	9800	9950	13850
Hard Top		....	325	325	380	380

Z8—V8—Equipment Schedule 1
W.B. 98.6"; 5.0 Liter.

Body Type	VIN	List	Good	Very Good	Good	Excellent
Roadster 2D	EJ134	132745	****	****	****	62900

5 SERIES—6-Cyl.—Equipment Schedule 1
W.B. 111.4"; 2.5 Liter, 3.0 Liter.

Body Type	VIN	List	Good	Very Good	Good	Excellent
525i Sedan 4D	DT434	41070	2150	2400	3000	4825
525iT Wagon 4D	DS334	42870	1150	1300	1800	3000
530i Sedan 4D	DT634	44670	3025	3375	3950	6225
Premium Pkg		....	175	175	225	225
Sport Pkg		....	350	350	465	465
Manual, 5-Spd		....	(400)	(400)	(520)	(520)

5 SERIES—V8—Equipment Schedule 1
W.B. 111.4"; 4.4 Liter.

Body Type	VIN	List	Good	Very Good	Good	Excellent
540i Sedan 4D	DN634	53145	3375	3775	4450	6975
540iT Wagon 4D	DR634	55545	3500	3900	4525	7100
Sport Pkg		....	350	350	465	465

2002 BMW

Body Type	VIN	List	Trade-In Good	Very Good	Pvt-Party Good	Retail Excellent
M5—V8—Equipment Schedule 1						
W.B. 111.4"; 5.0 Liter.						
Sedan 4D	DE934	72645	8375	9175	10200	15200
7 SERIES—V8—Equipment Schedule 1						
W.B. 117.7", 123.2" (Li); 4.4 Liter.						
745i Sedan 4D	GL634	68495	2250	2450	3200	5100
745Li Sedan 4D	GN634	72495	3075	3375	4075	6300
Sport Pkg			350	350	465	465

2003 BMW — WBA,WBSor4US(EV334)-3-#

Body Type	VIN	List	Trade-In Good	Very Good	Pvt-Party Good	Retail Excellent
3 SERIES—6-Cyl.—Equipment Schedule 1						
W.B. 107.3"; 2.5 Liter, 3.0 Liter.						
325i Sedan 4D	EV334	32270	2675	3075	3350	5300
325xi AWD Sedan 4D	EU334	34020	3075	3525	3750	5925
325Ci Coupe 2D	BN334	34070	3500	4025	4100	6175
325Cic Convertible 2D	BS334	40120	3550	3825	4650	6700
325iT Wagon 4D	EN334	33820	2975	3375	3700	5825
325xiT AWD Wagon 4D	EP334	35570	3325	3825	4150	6550
330i Sedan 4D	EV534	39070	3250	3725	3925	6175
330xi AWD Sedan 4D	EW534	40820	3625	4175	4425	6925
330Ci Coupe 2D	BN534	40070	4025	4600	4700	7100
330Cic Convertible 2D	BS534	44870	4075	4375	5250	7500
Hard Top (Conv)			375	375	485	485
Premium Pkg			200	200	255	255
Sport Pkg			175	175	235	235
Performance Pkg			1000	1000	1345	1345
Manual, 5-Spd (ex 2D)			(350)	(350)	(455)	(455)
M3—6-Cyl.—Equipment Schedule 1						
W.B. 107.5"; 3.2 Liter.						
Coupe 2D	BL934	49345	6475	7075	7675	11000
Convertible 2D	BR934	55195	7175	7825	8475	12150
Hard Top (Conv)			375	375	485	485
Z4—6-Cyl.—Equipment Schedule 1						
W.B. 98.2"; 2.5 Liter, 3.0 Liter.						
2.5i Roadster 2D	BT334	37690	3350	3675	4500	6675
3.0i Roadster 2D	BT534	43215	3950	4325	5100	7550
Premium Pkg			200	200	245	245
Sport Pkg			175	175	225	225
Z8—V8—Equipment Schedule 1						
W.B. 98.6"; 4.8 Liter, 5.0 Liter.						
Roadster 2D	EJ134	134295	****	****	****	68100
Alpina Roadster 2D	EJ134	139295	****	****	****	91000
5 SERIES—6-Cyl.—Equipment Schedule 1						
W.B. 111.4"; 2.5 Liter, 3.0 Liter.						
525i Sedan 4D	DT334	41770	2600	2900	3525	5600
525iT Wagon 4D	DS334	43470	1150	1300	1900	3175
530i Sedan 4D	DT534	45370	3325	3700	4400	6900
Premium Pkg			200	200	255	255
Sport Pkg			375	375	515	515
Manual, 5-Spd			(250)	(250)	(345)	(345)
5 SERIES—V8—Equipment Schedule 1						
W.B. 111.4"; 4.4 Liter.						
540i Sedan 4D	DN634	52495	3800	4225	4925	7650
540iT Wagon 4D	DR634	56085	3850	4275	4950	7700
Sport Pkg			375	375	515	515
M5—V8—Equipment Schedule 1						
W.B. 111.4"; 5.0 Liter.						
Sedan 4D	DE934	73195	10100	11050	12100	17650
7 SERIES—V8—Equipment Schedule 1						
W.B. 117.7", 123.2" (Li); 4.4 Liter.						
745i Sedan 4D	GL634	70895	2600	2825	3600	5625
745Li Sedan 4D	GN634	73195	3300	3600	4425	6750
Adaptive Cruise Control			250	250	320	320
Sport Pkg			375	375	515	515
7 SERIES—V12—Equipment Schedule 1						
W.B. 123.2"; 6.0 Liter.						
760Li Sedan 4D	GN834	118195	8450	9200	10000	14600
Adaptive Cruise Control			250	250	320	320

2004 BMW — WBA,WBSor4US(EV334)-4-#

3 SERIES—6-Cyl.—Equipment Schedule 1
W.B. 107.3"; 2.5 Liter, 3.0 Liter.

1015

2004 BMW

Body Type	VIN	List	Trade-In Good	Very Good	Pvt-Party Good	Retail Excellent
325i Sedan 4D	EV334	33265	3275	3750	3950	6150
325xi AWD Sedan 4D	EU334	35015	3550	4050	4350	6725
325Ci Coupe 2D	BD334	34570	4200	4800	4775	7100
325Cic Convertible 2D	BW334	40720	4450	4750	5500	7700
325iT Wagon 4D	EN334	34815	3375	3825	4150	6350
325xiT AWD Wagon 4D	EP334	36565	3975	4550	4750	7225
330i Sedan 4D	EV534	39270	3875	4425	4675	7175
330xi AWD Sedan 4D	EW534	41020	4275	4875	5050	7750
330Ci Coupe 2D	BD534	40770	4900	5525	5525	8150
330Cic Convertible 2D	BW534	45570	4950	5275	6075	8450
Hard Top (Conv)			400	400	520	520
Premium Pkg			225	225	285	285
Sport Pkg			175	175	245	245
Performance Pkg			1100	1100	1465	1465
Manual, 5-Spd (ex 2D)			(375)	(375)	(485)	(485)
M3—6-Cyl.—Equipment Schedule 1						
W.B. 107.5"; 3.2 Liter.						
Coupe 2D	BL934	51340	7325	7950	8525	11950
Convertible 2D	BR934	56595	8150	8850	9425	13250
Hard Top (Conv)			400	400	510	510
Z4—6-Cyl.—Equipment Schedule 1						
W.B. 98.2"; 2.5 Liter, 3.0 Liter.						
2.5i Roadster 2D	BT334	37790	4400	4800	5625	8150
3.0i Roadster 2D	BT534	43315	5500	5975	6675	9550
Premium Pkg			225	225	270	270
Sport Pkg			175	175	230	230
5 SERIES—6-Cyl.—Equipment Schedule 1						
W.B. 113.7"; 2.5 Liter, 3.0 Liter.						
525i Sedan 4D	NA535	43670	4275	4725	5100	7475
530i Sedan 4D	NA735	48670	5150	5700	6125	8950
Adaptive Cruise Control			275	275	355	355
Premium Pkg			225	225	285	285
Sport Pkg			425	425	575	575
Manual, 6-Spd			(300)	(300)	(410)	(410)
5 SERIES—V8—Equipment Schedule 1						
W.B. 113.7"; 4.4 Liter.						
545i Sedan 4D	NB335	54995	5400	5975	6400	9300
Adaptive Cruise Control			275	275	355	355
Sport Pkg			425	425	575	575
6 SERIES—V8—Equipment Schedule 1						
W.B. 109.4"; 4.4 Liter.						
645Ci Coupe 2D	EH734	69995	6875	7350	8150	10600
645Cic Convertible 2D	EK734	76995	8575	9150	9775	12550
Adaptive Cruise Control			275	275	310	310
Sport Pkg			425	425	505	505
7 SERIES—V8—Equipment Schedule 1						
W.B. 117.7", 123.2" (Li); 4.4 Liter.						
745i Sedan 4D	GL634	69195	3000	3275	4175	6375
745Li Sedan 4D	GN634	73195	4125	4475	5300	7950
Adaptive Cruise Control			275	275	355	355
Sport Pkg			425	425	575	575
7 SERIES—V12—Equipment Schedule 1						
W.B. 117.7", 123.2" (Li); 6.0 Liter.						
760i Sedan 4D	GL834	111795	8200	8900	9950	14350
760Li Sedan 4D	GN834	117795	8550	9275	10250	14850
Adaptive Cruise Control			275	275	355	355

2005 BMW — WBA,WBSor4US(EV334)-5-#

Body Type	VIN	List	Trade-In Good	Very Good	Pvt-Party Good	Retail Excellent
3 SERIES—6-Cyl.—Equipment Schedule 1						
W.B. 107.3"; 2.5 Liter, 3.0 Liter.						
325i Sedan 4D	EV334	33715	3925	4475	4825	7250
325xi AWD Sedan 4D	EU334	35465	4350	4950	5250	7875
325Ci Coupe 2D	BD334	36115	4625	5250	5325	7725
325Ci Convertible 2D	BW334	42420	5275	5625	6625	8950
325i Wagon 4D	EN334	35615	4175	4700	5050	7425
325xi AWD Wagon 4D	EP334	37365	4850	5500	5650	8375
330i Sedan 4D	EV534	39120	4850	5500	5725	8550
330xi AWD Sedan 4D	EW534	40870	5025	5725	6100	9050
330Ci Coupe 2D	BD534	40720	5275	5950	6200	8900
330Ci Convertible 2D	BW534	46470	5850	6225	7250	9800
Hard Top (Conv)			425	425	555	555
Premium Pkg			250	250	320	320
Sport Pkg			200	200	260	260

2005 BMW

Body Type	VIN	List	Trade-In Good	Trade-In Very Good	Pvt-Party Good	Retail Excellent
Performance Pkg			1200	1200	1590	1590
Manual, 5-Spd (ex 2D)			(400)	(400)	(520)	(520)
M3—6-Cyl.—Equipment Schedule 1						
W.B. 107.5"; 3.2 Liter.						
Coupe 2D	BL934	51140	9775	10550	10900	14650
Convertible 2D	BR934	56495	10500	11350	11800	15950
Hard Top (Conv)			425	425	500	500
Club Sport Pkg			725	725	865	865
Competition			725	725	865	865
Z4—6-Cyl.—Equipment Schedule 1						
W.B. 98.2"; 2.5 Liter, 3.0 Liter.						
2.5i Roadster 2D	BT335	38415	4250	4625	5775	8350
3.0i Roadster 2D	BT535	44265	6325	6850	7750	10800
Premium Pkg			250	250	310	310
Sport Pkg			200	200	250	250
5 SERIES—6-Cyl.—Equipment Schedule 1						
W.B. 113.7"; 2.5 Liter, 3.0 Liter.						
525i Sedan 4D	NA535	44720	4575	5050	5650	8050
530i Sedan 4D	NA735	48820	5725	6300	6775	9625
Adaptive Cruise			300	300	385	385
Premium Pkg			250	250	320	320
Sport Pkg			475	475	645	645
5 SERIES—V8—Equipment Schedule 1						
W.B. 113.7"; 4.4 Liter.						
545i Sedan 4D	NB335	56495	5750	6325	6825	9725
Adaptive Cruise			300	300	385	385
Sport Pkg			475	475	645	645
6 SERIES—V8—Equipment Schedule 1						
W.B. 109.4"; 4.4 Liter.						
645Ci Coupe 2D	EH734	70595	9050	9650	10850	14150
645Cic Convertible 2D	EK734	78895	10650	11350	12550	16200
Adaptive Cruise Control			300	300	345	345
Sport Pkg			475	475	575	575
7 SERIES—V8—Equipment Schedule 1						
W.B. 117.7", 123.2" (Li); 4.4 Liter.						
745i Sedan 4D	GL635	70595	5075	5500	6400	9050
745Li Sedan 4D	GN635	74595	7075	7675	8375	11600
Sport Pkg			475	475	635	635
7 SERIES—V12—Equipment Schedule 1						
W.B. 117.7", 123.2" (Li); 6.0 Liter.						
760i Sedan 4D	GL835	111895	10250	11100	11800	16200
760Li Sedan 4D	GN835	119295	10500	11300	12250	17050
Adaptive Cruise Control			300	300	385	385

2006 BMW — WBA,WBSor4US(VB135)-6-#

Body Type	VIN	List	Trade-In Good	Trade-In Very Good	Pvt-Party Good	Retail Excellent
3 SERIES—6-Cyl.—Equipment Schedule 1						
W.B. 107.3", 108.7" (Sed & Wag); 2.5 Liter, 3.0 Liter.						
325i Sedan 4D	VB135	35315	5625	6325	6525	9350
325xi AWD Sedan 4D	VD135	37215	6075	6850	6975	9975
325Ci Coupe 2D	BD334	36715	5875	6600	6525	9150
325Ci Convertible 2D	BW334	43020	7150	7575	8500	11100
325xi AWD Wagon 4D	VT135	39015	6375	7175	7200	10200
330i Sedan 4D	VB335	40020	6825	7650	7700	11000
330xi AWD Sedan 4D	VD335	41920	7125	8000	8075	11500
330Ci Coupe 2D	BD534	41020	6850	7625	7600	10500
330Ci Convertible 2D	BW534	46870	7850	8300	9250	12100
Adaptive Cruise Control			325	325	420	420
Hard Top (Conv)			450	450	585	585
Premium Pkg			275	275	355	355
Sport Pkg			200	200	265	265
Performance Pkg			1275	1275	1700	1700
M3—6-Cyl.—Equipment Schedule 1						
W.B. 107.5"; 3.2 Liter.						
Coupe 2D	BL934	52640	11850	12750	12950	16850
Convertible 2D	BR934	58295	12850	13800	14000	18300
Hard Top (Conv)			450	450	525	525
Competition Pkg			775	775	910	910
Z4—6-Cyl.—Equipment Schedule 1						
W.B. 98.2"; 3.0 Liter.						
3.0i Roadster 2D	BU335	39135	7000	7525	8425	11500
3.0si Coupe 2D	DU534	40795	8725	9375	10050	13500
3.0si Roadster 2D	BU535	44485	7825	8425	9300	12650
Premium Pkg			275	275	325	325

Body Type	VIN	List	Trade-In Good	Trade-In Very Good	Pvt-Party Good	Retail Excellent
Sport Pkg			200	200	245	245
Z4 M SERIES—6-Cyl.—Equipment Schedule 1						
W.B. 98.3"; 3.2 Liter.						
Coupe 2D	DU934	49995	15350	16450	16500	21500
Roadster 2D	BT935	51995	12300	13200	13750	18200
Premium Pkg			275	275	300	300
5 SERIES—6-Cyl.—Equipment Schedule 1						
W.B. 113.7", 113.6" (Wag); 3.0 Liter.						
525i Sedan 4D	NE535	43195	5800	6325	6775	9375
525xi AWD Sedan 4D	NF535	45395	6850	7500	7950	11000
530i Sedan 4D	NE735	47495	6825	7475	7975	11050
530xi AWD Sedan 4D	NF735	49695	7275	7950	8450	11750
530xi AWD Wagon 4D	NN735	52095	8025	8750	9275	12900
Adaptive Cruise Control			325	325	415	415
Premium Pkg			275	275	350	350
Sport Pkg			525	525	700	700
5 SERIES—V8—Equipment Schedule 1						
W.B. 113.7"; 4.8 Liter.						
550i Sedan 4D	NB535	58095	7850	8575	9100	12700
Adaptive Cruise Control			325	325	420	420
Sport Pkg			525	525	710	710
M5—V10—Equipment Schedule 1						
W.B. 113.7"; 5.0 Liter.						
Sedan 4D	NB935	84895	13100	14100	14350	18850
6 SERIES—V8—Equipment Schedule 1						
W.B. 109.4"; 4.8 Liter.						
650i Coupe 2D	EH134	72495	10200	10800	11750	14850
650i Convertible 2D	EK134	79495	11750	12450	13550	17150
Adaptive Cruise Control			325	325	370	370
Sport Pkg			525	525	625	625
M6—V10—Equipment Schedule 1						
W.B. 109.5"; 5.0 Liter.						
Coupe 2D	EH934	99795	14250	15150	16100	20200
7 SERIES—V8—Equipment Schedule 1						
W.B. 117.7", 123.2" (Li); 4.8 Liter.						
750i Sedan 4D	HL835	72495	6500	7000	7625	10250
750Li Sedan 4D	HN835	76495	8175	8775	9375	12550
Adaptive Cruise Control			(350)	(350)	(430)	(430)
Sport Pkg			525	525	700	700
7 SERIES—V12—Equipment Schedule 1						
W.B. 117.7", 123.2" (Li); 6.0 Liter.						
760i Sedan 4D	HL035	113895	11650	12500	13050	17500
760Li Sedan 4D	HN035	121295	11850	12700	13350	17950
Adaptive Cruise Control			325	325	410	410

2007 BMW — WBA,WBSor4US(VA335)-7-#

Body Type	VIN	List	Trade-In Good	Trade-In Very Good	Pvt-Party Good	Retail Excellent
3 SERIES—6-Cyl.—Equipment Schedule 1						
W.B. 108.7"; 3.0 Liter.						
328i Sedan 4D	VA335	36815	6775	7550	7650	10700
328xi AWD Sedan 4D	VC935	38715	7175	8000	8125	11300
328i Coupe 2D	WB335	39715	8600	9550	9125	12300
328xi AWD Coupe 2D	WC335	41515	8700	9675	9275	12500
328i Convertible 2D	WL135	43975	10100	10650	11350	14200
328i Wagon 4D	VS135	38615	7275	8025	8250	11200
328xi AWD Wagon 4D	VT735	40515	8125	9025	8925	12350
Adaptive Cruise Control			350	350	455	455
Premium Pkg			300	300	385	385
Sport Pkg			200	200	265	265
3 SERIES—6-Cyl. Twin Turbo—Equipment Schedule 1						
W.B. 108.7"; 3.0 Liter.						
335i Sedan 4D	VB735	39675	8075	8975	9050	12650
335xi AWD Sedan 4D	VD535	41575	8450	9400	9425	13200
335i Coupe 2D	WB735	44020	9550	10500	10250	13600
335i Convertible 2D	WL735	49875	10850	11400	12200	15250
Adaptive Cruise Control			350	350	455	455
Premium Pkg			300	300	385	385
Sport Pkg			200	200	265	265
Z4—6-Cyl.—Equipment Schedule 1						
W.B. 98.2"; 3.0 Liter.						
3.0i Roadster 2D	BU335	37095	7950	8475	9425	12550
3.0si Coupe 2D	DU535	41095	10200	10900	11600	15050
3.0si Roadster 2D	BU535	43095	8675	9275	10200	13500
Premium Pkg			300	300	350	350

Body Type	VIN	List	Trade-In Good	Very Good	Pvt-Party Good	Retail Excellent
Sport Pkg			200	200	240	240
Z4 M SERIES—6-Cyl.—Equipment Schedule 1						
W.B. 98.3"; 3.2 Liter.						
Coupe 2D	DU934	50795	16850	17950	18100	23100
Roadster 2D	BT935	52795	14000	14950	15450	19950
Premium Pkg			300	300	325	325
5 SERIES—6-Cyl.—Equipment Schedule 1						
W.B. 113.7", 113.6" (Wag); 3.0 Liter.						
525i Sedan 4D	NE535	46920	6850	7450	8075	11000
525i AWD Sedan 4D	NF335	49120	7725	8375	8875	12000
530i Sedan 4D	NE735	50920	8050	8725	9250	12500
530xi AWD Sedan 4D	NF735	53120	8675	9400	9900	13350
530xi AWD Wagon 4D	NN735	55520	9375	10150	10700	14450
Adaptive Cruise Control			350	350	445	445
Premium Pkg			300	300	380	380
Sport Pkg			575	575	745	745
5 SERIES—V8—Equipment Schedule 1						
W.B. 113.7"; 4.8 Liter.						
550i Sedan 4D	NB535	60485	8950	9700	10300	14000
Adaptive Cruise Control			350	350	455	455
Sport Pkg			575	575	755	755
M5—V10—Equipment Schedule 1						
W.B. 113.7"; 5.0 Liter.						
Sedan 4D	NB935	86195	15050	16000	16050	20300
6-SERIES—V8—Equipment Schedule 1						
W.B. 109.4"; 4.8 Liter.						
650i Coupe 2D	EH135	74595	11850	12550	13550	16800
650i Convertible 2D	EK136	81605	14800	15650	16750	20800
Adaptive Cruise Control			350	350	400	400
Sport Pkg			575	575	660	660
M6—V10—Equipment Schedule 1						
W.B. 109.5"; 5.0 Liter.						
Coupe 2D	EH935	101995	15600	16500	17500	21700
Convertible 2D	EK935	108695	16850	17800	18650	22800
7 SERIES—V8—Equipment Schedule 1						
W.B. 117.7", 123.1" (Li); 4.8 Liter.						
750i Sedan 4D	HL835	75695	8825	9400	10050	13100
750Li Sedan 4D	HN835	78795	10150	10800	11550	15100
Adaptive Cruise Control			(350)	(350)	(430)	(430)
Sport Pkg			575	575	715	715
7 SERIES—V12—Equipment Schedule 1						
W.B. 123.1"; 6.0 Liter.						
760Li Sedan 4D	HN035	123795	13400	14300	14950	19500
ALPINA B7—V8 Supercharged—Equipment Schedule 1						
W.B. 117.7"; 4.4 Liter.						
Sedan 4D	HL835	115695	15900	16950	17300	22300
Adaptive Cruise Control			350	350	420	420

2008 BMW — WBA,WBS(UP735)-8-#

Body Type	VIN	List	Trade-In Good	Very Good	Pvt-Party Good	Retail Excellent
1 SERIES—6-Cyl.—Equipment Schedule 1						
W.B. 104.7"; 3.0 Liter.						
128i Coupe 2D	UP735	33095	7700	8125	9100	11650
128i Convertible 2D	UL735	33875	9250	9750	10600	13300
Premium Pkg			300	300	365	365
Sport Pkg			200	200	245	245
1 SERIES—6-Cyl. Twin Turbo—Equipment Schedule 1						
W.B. 104.7"; 3.0 Liter.						
135i Coupe 2D	UC735	39395	11750	12400	13000	16000
135i Convertible 2D	UN935	39875	11750	12400	12900	15800
Premium Pkg			300	300	345	345
Sport Pkg			200	200	230	230
3 SERIES—6-Cyl.—Equipment Schedule 1						
W.B. 108.7"; 3.0 Liter.						
328i Sedan 4D	VA335	36895	8200	9025	9025	12150
328xi AWD Sedan 4D	VC935	38795	8850	9725	9675	13000
328i Coupe 2D	WB335	39795	9850	10800	10450	13800
328xi AWD Coupe 2D	WL135	41595	10100	11100	10700	14100
328i Convertible 2D	WL135	46800	11450	11950	12900	15650
328i Wagon 4D	VS135	38695	8200	8850	9350	12200
328xi AWD Wagon 4D	VT735	40595	9350	10300	10200	13650
Adaptive Cruise Control			375	375	480	480
Premium Pkg			300	300	395	395
Sport Pkg			200	200	265	265

1015

2008 BMW

Body Type	VIN	List	Trade-In Good	Very Good	Pvt-Party Good	Retail Excellent
3 SERIES—6-Cyl. Twin Turbo—Equipment Schedule 1						
W.B. 108.7"; 3.0 Liter.						
335i Sedan 4D	VB735	42400	**10050**	**11050**	**10900**	**14650**
335xi AWD Sedan 4D	VD535	44300	**10550**	**11600**	**11400**	**15250**
335i Coupe 2D	WB735	44300	**11350**	**12250**	**12350**	**15750**
335xi AWD Coupe 2D	WC735	46100	**11800**	**13000**	**12400**	**16300**
335i Convertible 2D	WL735	51150	**12650**	**13200**	**14250**	**17250**
Adaptive Cruise Control			375	375	480	480
Premium Pkg			300	300	395	395
Sport Pkg			200	200	260	260
M3—V8—Equipment Schedule 1						
W.B. 108.7"; 4.0 Liter.						
Sedan 4D	VA935	56650	**20000**	**21000**	**21000**	**25400**
Coupe 2D	WD935	59350	**20500**	**21600**	**21600**	**26200**
Convertible 2D	WL935	68200	**21500**	**22600**	**22500**	**27200**
Premium Pkg			300	300	335	335
Z4—6-Cyl.—Equipment Schedule 1						
W.B. 98.2"; 3.0 Liter.						
3.0i Roadster 2D	BU335	40595	**9950**	**10500**	**11600**	**14650**
3.0si Coupe 2D	DU535	43445	**11700**	**12350**	**13300**	**16700**
3.0si Roadster 2D	BU535	45445	**10750**	**11350**	**12400**	**15650**
Premium Pkg			300	300	350	350
Sport Pkg			200	200	235	235
Z4 M SERIES—6-Cyl.—Equipment Schedule 1						
W.B. 98.3"; 3.2 Liter.						
Coupe 2D	DU935	52870	**18150**	**19150**	**19750**	**24400**
Roadster 2D	BT935	54870	**16550**	**17400**	**18200**	**22600**
Premium Pkg			300	300	335	335
5 SERIES—6-Cyl.—Equipment Schedule 1						
W.B. 113.7"; 3.0 Liter.						
528i Sedan 4D	NU535	46525	**9100**	**9725**	**10100**	**12750**
528xi AWD Sedan 4D	NV135	48725	**10200**	**10900**	**11150**	**14000**
Adaptive Cruise Control			375	375	455	455
Premium Pkg			300	300	370	370
Sport Pkg			600	600	730	730
5 SERIES—6-Cyl. Twin Turbo—Equipment Schedule 1						
W.B. 113.7", 113.6" (Wag); 3.0 Liter.						
535i Sedan 4D	NV135	51625	**10300**	**11050**	**11300**	**14200**
535xi AWD Sedan 4D	NV935	53825	**10750**	**11500**	**11800**	**14850**
535xi AWD Wagon 4D	PT735	56225	**11600**	**12350**	**12650**	**16000**
Adaptive Cruise Control			375	375	450	450
Premium Pkg			300	300	370	370
Sport Pkg			600	600	725	725
5 SERIES—V8—Equipment Schedule 1						
W.B. 113.7"; 4.8 Liter.						
550i Sedan 4D	NW535	61075	**12750**	**13600**	**14100**	**17950**
Adaptive Cruise Control			375	375	455	455
Sport Pkg			600	600	735	735
M5—V10—Equipment Schedule 1						
W.B. 113.7"; 5.0 Liter.						
Sedan 4D	NB935	86675	**19300**	**20300**	**20500**	**25000**
6 SERIES—V8—Equipment Schedule 1						
W.B. 109.4"; 4.8 Liter.						
650i Coupe 2D	EA535	76375	**15450**	**16200**	**17350**	**21000**
650i Convertible 2D	EB535	84775	**18400**	**19300**	**20500**	**24700**
Adaptive Cruise Control			375	375	425	425
Individual Comp			2175	2175	2510	2510
Sport Pkg			600	600	685	685
M6—V10—Equipment Schedule 1						
W.B. 109.5"; 5.0 Liter.						
Coupe 2D	EH935	103075	**18500**	**19450**	**20800**	**25200**
Convertible 2D	EK935	108875	**20200**	**21200**	**22400**	**27100**
7 SERIES—V8—Equipment Schedule 1						
W.B. 117.7", 123.2" (Li); 4.8 Liter.						
750i Sedan 4D	HL835	76575	**11000**	**11600**	**12550**	**15800**
750Li Sedan 4D	HN835	79675	**12250**	**12900**	**13950**	**17600**
Adaptive Cruise Control			375	375	450	450
Individual Comp			2175	2175	2655	2655
Sport Pkg			600	600	725	725
7 SERIES—V12—Equipment Schedule 1						
W.B. 123.2"; 6.0 Liter.						
760Li Sedan 4D	HN035	125075	**15650**	**16500**	**17600**	**22300**
Adaptive Cruise Control			375	375	450	450

Body Type	VIN	List	Trade-In Good	Very Good	Pvt-Party Good	Retail Excellent
Individual Comp			2175	2175	2675	2675

ALPINA B7—V8 Supercharged—Equipment Schedule 1
W.B. 117.7"; 4.4 Liter.

Sedan 4D	HL835	117075	18100	19050	19750	24600
Adaptive Cruise Control			375	375	445	445

2009 BMW — WBA,WBS(UP735)-9-#

1 SERIES—6-Cyl.—Equipment Schedule 1
W.B. 104.7"; 3.0 Liter.

128i Coupe 2D	UP735	31550	9200	9600	10750	13200
128i Convertible 2D	UL735	36150	11150	11650	12850	15600
Premium Pkg			325	325	395	395
Sport Pkg			225	225	275	275

1 SERIES—6-Cyl. Twin Turbo—Equipment Schedule 1
W.B. 104.7"; 3.0 Liter.

135i Coupe 2D	UC735	38000	13100	13650	14650	17550
135i Convertible 2D	UN935	42300	13650	14200	15000	17800
Premium Pkg			325	325	395	395
Sport Pkg			225	225	275	275

3 SERIES—6-Cyl.—Equipment Schedule 1
W.B. 108.7"; 3.0 Liter.

328i Sedan 4D	PH735	35750	9950	10700	10950	14000
328i xDrive Sedan 4D	PK735	37750	10750	11550	11700	14950
328i Coupe 2D	WB335	38650	11400	12300	12300	15600
328i xDrive Coupe 2D	WC335	40550	11800	12700	12700	16100
328i Convertible 2D	WL335	46700	13500	14000	15250	18000
328i Wagon 4D	UT935	37660	10500	11100	11750	14550
328i xDrive Wagon 4D	UU335	39550	12050	13000	13000	16500
Adaptive Cruise Control			375	375	475	475
Premium Pkg			325	325	420	420
Sport Pkg			225	225	295	295
M Sport Pkg			1075	1075	1350	1350

3 SERIES—6-Cyl. Twin Turbo—Equipment Schedule 1
W.B. 108.7"; 3.0 Liter.

335i Sedan 4D	PM735	41125	12250	13200	13250	16900
335i xDrive Sedan 4D	PL335	43125	12800	13800	13900	17700
335i Coupe 2D	WB735	43025	13150	13950	14600	18050
335i xDrive Coupe 2D	WC735	44925	13950	15050	14950	18950
335i Convertible 2D	WL735	51525	15150	15700	16950	20100
Adaptive Cruise Control			375	375	470	470
Premium Pkg			325	325	420	420
Sport Pkg			225	225	295	295
M Sport Pkg			1075	1075	1345	1345

3 SERIES—6-Cyl. Twin Turbo Diesel—Equipment Schedule 1
W.B. 108.7"; 3.0 Liter.

335d Sedan 4D	PN735	44725	12700	13450	14050	17400
Adaptive Cruise Control			375	375	470	470
Premium Pkg			325	325	415	415
Sport Pkg			225	225	290	290

M3—V8—Equipment Schedule 1
W.B. 108.7"; 4.0 Liter.

Sedan 4D	PM935	56975	22600	23500	24300	28800
Coupe 2D	WD935	60925	22900	23900	24700	29400
Convertible 2D	WL935	69025	24000	25000	25800	30700

Z4—6-Cyl.—Equipment Schedule 1
W.B. 98.3"; 3.0 Liter.

30i Roadster 2D	LM535	46575	15550	16250	17100	20300
Premium Pkg			325	325	375	375
Sport Pkg			225	225	260	260

Z4—6-Cyl. Twin Turbo—Equipment Schedule 1
W.B. 98.3"; 3.0 Liter

35i Roadster 2D	LM735	52475	17550	18300	19300	23200
Premium Pkg			325	325	375	375
Sport Pkg			225	225	265	265

5 SERIES—6-Cyl.—Equipment Schedule 1
W.B. 113.7"; 3.0 Liter.

528i Sedan 4D	NU535	46625	10950	11550	12450	15550
528i xDrive Sedan 4D	NV135	48925	12150	12850	13800	17100
Adaptive Cruise Control			375	375	450	450
Premium Pkg			325	325	400	400
Sport Pkg			675	675	805	805

5 SERIES—6-Cyl. Twin Turbo—Equipment Schedule 1
W.B. 113.7", 113.6" (Wag); 3.0 Liter.

2009 BMW

Body Type	VIN	List	Trade-In Good	Very Good	Pvt-Party Good	Retail Excellent
535i Sedan 4D	NW135	51925	12650	13400	14350	17900
535i xDrive Sedan 4D	NV935	54225	13600	14400	15400	19200
535i xDrive Wagon 4D	PT735	56625	14600	15400	16550	20800
Adaptive Cruise Control			375	375	445	445
Premium Pkg			325	325	395	395
Sport Pkg			675	675	795	795
5 SERIES—V8—Equipment Schedule 1						
W.B. 113.7"; 4.8 Liter.						
550i Sedan 4D	NW535	61225	17300	18250	19300	24100
Adaptive Cruise Control			375	375	450	450
Sport Pkg			675	675	805	805
M5—V10—Equipment Schedule 1						
W.B. 113.7"; 5.0 Liter.						
Sedan 4D	NB935	89325	22900	23900	24800	29600
6 SERIES—V8—Equipment Schedule 1						
W.B. 109.4"; 4.8 Liter.						
650i Coupe 2D	EA535	79025	18300	19050	20200	23800
650i Convertible 2D	EB535	87425	21500	22400	23700	27900
Adaptive Cruise Control			375	375	435	435
Individual Comp			2225	2225	2565	2565
Sport Pkg			675	675	770	770
M6—V10—Equipment Schedule 1						
W.B. 109.5"; 5.0 Liter.						
Coupe 2D	EH935	105925	20200	21000	22600	26900
Convertible 2D	EK935	111725	23800	24900	26300	31100
7 SERIES—V8 Twin Turbo—Equipment Schedule 1						
W.B. 120.9", 126.4"(Li); 4.4 Liter.						
750i Sedan 4D	KA835	82125	18950	19700	20200	23700
750Li Sedan 4D	KB835	86025	21100	22000	22400	26200
Adaptive Cruise Control			375	375	420	420
Sport Pkg			675	675	750	750

2010 BMW — WB(AorS)(UP7C5)-A-#

Body Type	VIN	List	Trade-In Good	Very Good	Pvt-Party Good	Retail Excellent
1 SERIES—6-Cyl.—Equipment Schedule 1						
W.B. 104.7"; 3.0 Liter.						
128i Coupe 2D	UP7C5	34645	11050	11400	12750	15150
128i Convertible 2D	UL7C5	38595	14100	14600	15950	18700
Premium Pkg			375	375	450	450
Sport Pkg			275	275	310	310
1 SERIES—6-Cyl. Twin Turbo—Equipment Schedule 1						
W.B. 104.7"; 3.0 Liter.						
135i Coupe 2D	UC7C5	40445	16350	16900	18300	21500
135i Convertible 2D	UN9C5	44745	17300	17900	19150	22300
Premium Pkg			375	375	445	445
Sport Pkg			275	275	310	310
3 SERIES—6-Cyl.—Equipment Schedule 1						
W.B. 108.7"; 3.0 Liter.						
328i Sedan 4D	PH7C5	33675	12050	12800	13250	16250
328i xDrive Sedan 4D	PK7C5	35675	12950	13700	14250	17450
328i Coupe 2D	WB3C5	36575	12800	13600	14150	17350
328i xDrive Coupe 2D	WC3C5	38475	13300	14100	14650	17950
328i Convertible 2D	WL1C5	45325	12000	16650	18100	20900
328i Wagon 4D	UT9C5	36225	12950	13550	14500	17400
328i xDrive Wagon 4D	UU3C5	38225	14550	15400	15850	19350
Active Cruise Control			400	400	480	480
Premium Pkg			375	375	470	470
Sport Pkg			275	275	325	325
M Sport Pkg			1100	1100	1340	1340
3 SERIES—6-Cyl. Twin Turbo—Equipment Schedule 1						
W.B. 108.7"; 3.0 Liter.						
335i Sedan 4D	PM7C5	42450	16050	16950	17250	21000
335i xDrive Sedan 4D	PL3C5	44450	16500	17500	17700	21600
335i Coupe 2D	WB7C5	44350	15950	16650	17700	21200
335i xDrive Coupe 2D	WC7C5	46250	16800	17750	18150	22300
335i Convertible 2D	WL7C5	52850	18400	18950	20300	23300
Active Cruise Control			400	400	470	470
Premium Pkg			375	375	460	460
Sport Pkg			275	275	320	320
M Sport Pkg			1100	1100	1315	1315
3 SERIES—6-Cyl. Twin Turbo Diesel—Equipment Schedule 1						
W.B. 108.7"; 3.0 Liter.						
335d Sedan 4D	PN7C5	44725	15700	16400	17350	20700
Active Cruise Control			400	400	475	475

2010 BMW

Body Type	VIN	List	Trade-In Good	Very Good	Pvt-Party Good	Retail Excellent
Premium Pkg		-------	375	375	465	465
Sport Pkg		-------	275	275	320	320
M3—V8—Equipment Schedule 1						
W.B. 108.7"; 4.0 Liter.						
Sedan 4D	PM9C5	56975	27400	28300	29700	34500
Coupe 2D	WD9C5	59975	26700	27600	28900	33600
Convertible 2D	WL9C5	69025	27500	28400	29700	34600
Z4—6-Cyl.—Equipment Schedule 1						
W.B. 98.3"; 3.0 Liter.						
30i Roadster 2D	LM5C5	46575	17500	18050	19200	22300
Premium Pkg		-------	375	375	425	425
Sport Pkg		-------	275	275	295	295
Z4—6-Cyl. Twin Turbo—Equipment Schedule 1						
W.B. 98.3"; 3.0 Liter.						
35i Roadster 2D	LM7C5	52475	19750	20400	21600	25100
Premium Pkg		-------	375	375	430	430
Sport Pkg		-------	275	275	300	300
5 SERIES—6-Cyl.—Equipment Schedule 1						
W.B. 113.7"; 3.0 Liter.						
528i Sedan 4D	NU5C5	46625	13250	13850	15000	18100
528i xDrive Sedan 4D	NV1C5	48925	14650	15300	16450	19850
Active Cruise Control		-------	400	400	475	475
Premium Pkg		-------	375	375	465	465
Sport Pkg		-------	775	775	935	935
M Sport Pkg		-------	1100	1100	1325	1325
5 SERIES—6-Cyl. Twin Turbo—Equipment Schedule 1						
W.B. 113.7", 113.6" (Wag), 120.7" (Gran Turismo); 3.0 Liter.						
535i Sedan 4D	NW1C5	51925	15250	15950	17050	20500
535i xDrive Sedan 4D	NV9C5	54225	16000	16750	17900	21600
535i xDrive Wagon 4D	PT7C5	56625	18150	19000	20200	24400
535i Gran Turismo Sed	SN2C5	56875	15700	16450	17500	21000
Active Cruise Control		-------	400	400	455	455
Premium Pkg		-------	375	375	445	445
Sport Pkg		-------	775	775	895	895
M Sport Pkg		-------	1100	1100	1270	1270
5 SERIES—V8—Equipment Schedule 1						
W.B. 113.7", 120.7" (Gran Turismo); 4.8 Liter.						
550i Sedan 4D	NW5C5	61475	19600	20500	21800	26400
550i Gran Turismo Sed	SN4C5	65775	20000	20900	21900	26100
550i GranTurismo xDrv	SP4C5	67075	21700	22700	23700	28300
Active Cruise Control		-------	400	400	465	465
Sport Pkg		-------	775	775	910	910
M Sport Pkg		-------	1100	1100	1295	1295
M5—V10—Equipment Schedule 1						
W.B. 113.7"; 5.0 Liter.						
Sedan 4D	NB9C5	89325	26300	27200	28600	33200
6 SERIES—V8—Equipment Schedule 1						
W.B. 109.4"; 4.8 Liter.						
650i Coupe 2D	EA5C5	80325	22500	23400	24600	28200
650i Convertible 2D	EB5C5	87425	27800	28900	30000	34300
Adaptive Cruise Control		-------	400	400	445	445
Individual Comp		-------	2275	2275	2575	2575
Sport Pkg		-------	775	775	870	870
M6—V10—Equipment Schedule 1						
W.B. 109.5"; 5.0 Liter.						
Coupe 2D	EH9C5	105925	27200	28300	29600	34100
Convertible 2D	EK9C5	111725	31000	32200	33400	38200
7 SERIES—V8 Twin Turbo—Equipment Schedule 1						
W.B. 120.0", 126.4" (Li); 4.4 Liter.						
750i Sedan 4D	KA8C5	82280	21400	22200	23100	26700
750i xDrive Sedan	KC6C5	85580	22500	23200	24100	27800
750Li Sedan 4D	KC8C5	86180	23900	24700	25600	29500
750Li xDrive Sedan	KC8C5	89480	24300	25100	26100	30100
Active Cruise Control		-------	400	400	450	450
Individual Comp		-------	2275	2275	2605	2605
Luxury Seating		-------	1300	1300	1495	1495
7 SERIES—V12—Equipment Schedule 1						
W.B. 126.4"; 6.0 Liter.						
760Li Sedan 4D	KB0C5	140425	41200	42500	43000	49100
Active Cruise Control		-------	(400)	(400)	(440)	(440)
Individual Comp		-------	2275	2275	2560	2560

2011 BMW

Body Type	VIN	List	Trade-In Good	Very Good	Pvt-Party Good	Retail Excellent

2011 BMW — WB(AorS)(UP7C5)–B–#

1 SERIES—6-Cyl.—Equipment Schedule 1
W.B. 104.7"; 3.0 Liter.

Body Type	VIN	List	Good	Very Good	Good	Excellent
128i Coupe 2D	UP7C5	33445	13000	13350	15000	17450
128i Convertible 2D	UL7C5	37445	17200	17650	19650	23000
Premium Pkg		------	425	425	510	510
Sport Pkg		------	300	300	345	345

1 SERIES—6-Cyl. Twin Turbo—Equipment Schedule 1
W.B. 104.7"; 3.0 Liter.

Body Type	VIN	List	Good	Very Good	Good	Excellent
135i Coupe 2D	UC9C5	39295	18450	18950	21000	24400
135i Convertible 2D	UN7C5	43795	20100	20700	22600	26300
M Coupe 2D	UR9C5	47010	40700	41700	43600	49500
Premium Pkg		------	425	425	520	520
Sport Pkg		------	300	300	350	350

3 SERIES—6-Cyl.—Equipment Schedule 1
W.B. 108.7"; 3.0 Liter.

Body Type	VIN	List	Good	Very Good	Good	Excellent
328i Sedan 4D	PH7C5	37945	14650	15300	16100	19150
328i xDrive Sedan 4D	PK7C5	39945	15800	16450	17300	20500
328i Coupe 2D	KE3C5	40000	16000	16700	17400	20600
328i xDrive Coupe 2D	KF3C5	41900	16650	17400	18100	21400
328i Convertible 2D	DW3C5	47455	19550	20000	21600	24400
328i Sport Wagon 4D	UT9C5	39445	18700	19300	20400	23400
328i xDrive Sport Wag	UU3C5	41445	20400	21300	21700	25400
Active Cruise Control		------	425	425	495	495
Premium Pkg		------	425	425	515	515
Sport Pkg		------	300	300	345	345
M Sport Pkg		------	1125	1125	1335	1335

3 SERIES—6-Cyl. Twin Turbo—Equipment Schedule 1
W.B. 108.7"; 3.0 Liter.

Body Type	VIN	List	Good	Very Good	Good	Excellent
335i Sedan 4D	PM5C5	44800	18700	19550	20200	23800
335i xDrive Sedan 4D	PL5C5	46800	19400	20200	20900	24600
335i Coupe 2D	KG7C5	46850	20700	21400	22700	26300
335i xDrive Coupe 2D	KF9C5	48750	21500	22400	23100	27200
335is Coupe 2D	KG1C5	54050	23300	24100	25300	29300
335i Convertible 2D	DX7C5	53950	22800	23400	24900	28000
335is Convertible 2D	DX1C5	61150	25500	26100	27700	31100
Active Cruise Control		------	425	425	490	490
Premium Pkg		------	425	425	510	510
Sport Pkg		------	300	300	345	345
M Sport Pkg		------	1125	1125	1320	1320

3 SERIES—6-Cyl. Twin Turbo Diesel—Equipment Schedule 1
W.B. 108.7"; 3.0 Liter.

Body Type	VIN	List	Good	Very Good	Good	Excellent
335d Sedan 4D	PN7C5	46475	19100	19700	21000	24300
Active Cruise Control		------	425	425	490	490
Premium Pkg		------	425	425	510	510
Sport Pkg		------	300	300	345	345
M Sport Pkg		------	1125	1125	1320	1320

M3—V8—Equipment Schedule 1
W.B. 108.7"; 4.0 Liter.

Body Type	VIN	List	Good	Very Good	Good	Excellent
Sedan 4D	PM9C5	59575	32700	33500	35100	39800
Coupe 2D	KG9C5	61525	31900	32800	34400	39000
Convertible 2D	DX9C5	69625	32500	33400	35000	39600

Z4—6-Cyl.—Equipment Schedule 1
W.B. 98.3"; 3.0 Liter.

Body Type	VIN	List	Good	Very Good	Good	Excellent
30i Roadster 2D	LM5C5	50995	20900	21400	23000	26200
Premium Pkg		------	425	425	480	480
Sport Pkg		------	300	300	325	325
M Sport Pkg		------	1125	1125	1240	1240

Z4—6-Cyl. Twin Turbo—Equipment Schedule 1
W.B. 98.3"; 3.0 Liter.

Body Type	VIN	List	Good	Very Good	Good	Excellent
35i Roadster 2D	LM7C5	55845	24400	25000	26500	30100
35is Roadster 2D	LM1C5	63420	26600	27400	28800	32500
Premium Pkg		------	425	425	480	480
Sport Pkg		------	300	300	325	325
M Sport Pkg		------	1125	1125	1240	1240

5 SERIES—6-Cyl.—Equipment Schedule 1
W.B. 116.9"; 3.0 Liter.

Body Type	VIN	List	Good	Very Good	Good	Excellent
528i Sedan 4D	FR1C5	46875	20200	21000	21900	25200
Active Cruise Control		------	425	425	480	480
Driver Assistance Pkg		------	600	600	680	680
Premium Pkg		------	425	425	495	495
Premium Pkg 2		------	550	550	620	620

Body Type	VIN	List	Trade-In Good	Trade-In Very Good	Pvt-Party Good	Retail Excellent
Sport Pkg	-------	-------	875	875	995	995
M Sport Pkg	-------	-------	1125	1125	1285	1285
5 SERIES—6-Cyl. Twin Turbo—Equipment Schedule 1						
W.B. 116.9", 120.9" (Gran Turismo); 3.0 Liter.						
535i Sedan 4D	FR7C5	52425	22200	23100	24000	27700
535i xDrive Sedan 4D	FU7C5	54225	24100	25000	25900	29800
535i Gran Turismo Sed	SN2C5	56875	22700	23600	24400	28100
535i GrnTurismo xDrv	SP2C5	59175	24200	25200	26000	30000
Active Cruise Control	-------	-------	425	425	465	465
Driver Assistance Pkg	-------	-------	600	600	660	660
Premium Pkg	-------	-------	425	425	485	485
Premium Pkg 2	-------	-------	550	550	605	605
Sport Pkg	-------	-------	875	875	970	970
M Sport Pkg	-------	-------	1125	1125	1250	1250
5 SERIES—V8 Twin Turbo—Equipment Schedule 1						
W.B. 116.9", 120.9" (Gran Turismo); 4.4 Liter.						
550i Sedan 4D	FR9C5	61075	26200	27200	28400	33100
550i xDrive Sedan 4D	FU9C5	63425	30000	31200	32200	37100
550i Gran Turismo Sed	SN4C5	64775	25600	26600	27700	32100
550i GrnTurismo xDrv	SP4C5	67075	26300	27300	28400	33000
Active Cruise Control	-------	-------	425	425	475	475
Driver Assistance Pkg	-------	-------	600	600	675	675
Premium Pkg	-------	-------	425	425	495	495
Premium Pkg 2	-------	-------	550	550	620	620
Sport Pkg	-------	-------	875	875	995	995
M Sport Pkg	-------	-------	1125	1125	1280	1280
7 SERIES—6-Cyl. Twin Turbo—Equipment Schedule 1						
W.B. 120.9", 126.4" (Li); 3.0 Liter.						
740i Sedan 4D	KA4C5	71525	25100	25700	27400	31200
740Li Sedan 4D	KB4C5	75925	25700	26400	28200	32300
Active Cruise Control	-------	-------	425	425	470	470
Driver Assistance Pkg	-------	-------	600	600	670	670
Individual Comp	-------	-------	2325	2325	2635	2635
M Sport Pkg	-------	-------	1125	1125	1265	1265
Luxury Seating	-------	-------	1325	1325	1495	1495
7 SERIES—V8 Twin Turbo—Equipment Schedule 1						
W.B. 120.9", 126.4" (Li); 4.4 Liter.						
750i Sedan 4D	KA8C5	84375	27300	28100	30000	34400
750i xDrive Sedan 4D	KC6C5	87675	28100	28900	30500	34700
750Li Sedan 4D	KB8C5	88275	28700	29500	31600	36400
750Li xDrive Sedan 4D	KC8C5	91575	29900	30700	32500	37000
Active Cruise Control	-------	-------	425	425	470	470
Driver Assistance Pkg	-------	-------	600	600	665	665
Individual Comp	-------	-------	2325	2325	2625	2625
M Sport Pkg	-------	-------	1125	1125	1260	1260
Luxury Seating	-------	-------	1325	1325	1490	1490
7 SERIES—V8 Twin Turbo ActiveHybrid—Equipment Schedule 1						
W.B. 120.9", 126.4" (Li); 4.4 Liter.						
750i Sedan 4D	KX6C5	103175	28500	29200	31000	35400
750Li Sedan 4D	KX8C5	107075	30700	31500	33400	38000
Driver Assistance Pkg	-------	-------	600	600	665	665
Luxury Seating	-------	-------	1325	1325	1515	1515
7 SERIES—V12 Twin Turbo—Equipment Schedule 1						
W.B. 126.4"; 6.0 Liter.						
760Li Sedan 4D	KB0C5	139975	50300	51600	52900	59000
Active Cruise Control	-------	-------	425	425	460	460
Individual Comp	-------	-------	2325	2325	2570	2570
M Sport Pkg	-------	-------	1125	1125	1235	1235
Luxury Seating	-------	-------	1325	1325	1460	1460
ALPINA B7—V8 Twin Turbo—Equipment Schedule 1						
W.B. 120.9"; 4.4 Liter.						
Sedan 4D	KA8C5	123875	43100	44200	45600	51300
xDrive Sedan 4D	KC6C5	127175	45100	46300	47600	53500
Active Cruise Control	-------	-------	425	425	460	460
Driver Assistance Pkg	-------	-------	600	600	650	650

2012 BMW — WB(AorS)(UP7C5)-C-#

Body Type	VIN	List	Trade-In Good	Trade-In Very Good	Pvt-Party Good	Retail Excellent
1 SERIES—6-Cyl.—Equipment Schedule 1						
W.B. 104.7"; 3.0 Liter.						
128i Coupe 2D	UP7C5	35320	16400	16800	19050	22100
128i Convertible 2D	UL7C5	39920	20200	20700	22700	25800
Premium Pkg	-------	-------	475	475	555	555
Sport Pkg	-------	-------	325	325	365	365

Body Type	VIN	List	Trade-In Good	Very Good	Pvt-Party Good	Retail Excellent
M Sport Pkg			1150	1150	1315	1315
1 SERIES—6-Cyl. Twin Turbo—Equipment Schedule 1						
W.B. 104.7"; 3.0 Liter.						
135i Coupe 2D	UC9C5	41825	22000	22500	24800	28500
135i Convertible 2D	UN7C5	46575	23700	24200	26500	30200
Premium Pkg			475	475	570	570
M Sport Pkg			1150	1150	1355	1355
3 SERIES—6-Cyl.—Equipment Schedule 1						
W.B. 108.7"; 3.0 Liter.						
328i Sedan 4D	3A5C5	39290	19750	20400	21400	24500
328i Coupe 2D	KE3C5	42870	18650	19250	20300	23400
328i xDrive Coupe 2D	KF3C5	47735	19600	20200	21300	24500
328i Convertible 2D	DW3C5	50820	24100	24600	26400	29300
328i Sport Wagon 4D	UT9C5	41620	22500	23000	24300	27300
328i xDrive Sport Wag	UU3C5	43620	24600	25300	26100	29600
Driver Assistance Pkg			625	625	710	710
Premium Pkg			475	475	570	570
Sport Pkg			325	325	360	360
M Sport Pkg			1150	1150	1340	1340
3 SERIES—6-Cyl. Twin Turbo—Equipment Schedule 1						
W.B. 108.7"; 3.0 Liter.						
335i Sedan 4D	3A9C5	44745	25500	26300	27000	30700
335i Coupe 2D	KG7C5	45775	23700	24200	25700	29100
335i xDrive Coupe 2D	KF9C5	47475	24900	25700	26800	30700
335is Coupe 2D	KG1C5	55275	27400	28000	29700	33600
335i Convertible 2D	DX7C5	54475	27400	27900	29800	33200
335is Convertible 2D	DX1C5	61475	32700	33400	35200	38800
Driver Assistance Pkg			625	625	705	705
Luxury Line			475	475	530	530
Premium Pkg			475	475	560	560
M Sport Pkg			1150	1150	1330	1330
M3—V8—Equipment Schedule 1						
W.B. 108.7"; 4.0 Liter.						
Coupe 2D	KG9C5	63595	36600	37400	39300	43700
Convertible 2D	DX9C5	73045	37200	38000	39900	44300
Competition Pkg			1125	1125	1255	1255
Individual Comp			2375	2375	2645	2645
Z4—4-Cyl. Twin Turbo—Equipment Schedule 1						
W.B. 98.3"; 2.0 Liter.						
28i Roadster 2D	LL5C5	51790	25300	25800	27500	30700
Premium Pkg			475	475	530	530
Sport Pkg			325	325	345	345
M Sport Pkg			1150	1150	1250	1250
Z4—6-Cyl. Twin Turbo—Equipment Schedule 1						
W.B. 98.3"; 3.0 Liter.						
35i Roadster 2D	LM7C5	56495	30300	30900	32700	36300
35is Roadster 2D	LM1C5	65095	33000	33700	35400	39200
Premium Pkg			475	475	530	530
Sport Pkg			325	325	345	345
M Sport Pkg			1150	1150	1255	1255
5 SERIES—6-Cyl.—Equipment Schedule 1						
W.B. 116.9"; 3.0 Liter.						
528i Sedan 4D	XG5C5	47575	23300	24100	25000	28200
528i xDrive Sedan 4D	XH5C5	49875	24800	25600	26700	30100
Active Cruise Control			450	450	500	500
Premium Pkg			475	475	545	545
Sport Pkg			950	950	1075	1075
M Sport Pkg			1150	1150	1290	1290
5 SERIES—6-Cyl. Twin Turbo—Equipment Schedule 1						
W.B. 116.9", 120.7" (Gran Turismo); 3.0 Liter.						
535i Sedan 4D	FR7C5	53125	28000	28900	29800	33500
535i xDrive Sedan 4D	FU7C5	55425	29400	30400	31300	35200
535i Gran Turismo Sed	SN2C5	58675	25700	26500	27600	31100
535i Grn Turismo xDrv	SP2C5	61275	28200	29100	30100	34000
Active Cruise Control			450	450	495	495
Premium Pkg			475	475	545	545
Sport Pkg			950	950	1070	1070
M Sport Pkg			1150	1150	1285	1285
5 SERIES—6-Cyl. Turbo ActiveHybrid—Equipment Schedule 1						
W.B. 116.9"; 3.0 Liter.						
Sedan 4D	FZ9C5	61845	27700	28600	29800	33900
Premium Pkg			475	475	550	550
Sport Pkg			950	950	1080	1080

Body	Type	VIN	List	Trade-In Good	Very Good	Pvt-Party Good	Retail Excellent
5 SERIES—V8 Twin Turbo—Equipment Schedule 1							
W.B. 116.9", 120.7" (Gran Turismo); 4.4 Liter.							
550i Sedan 4D	FR9C5	62575	31100	32100	33500	38100
550i xDrive Sedan 4D	FU9C5	64875	34100	35200	36400	41200
550i Gran Turismo Sed	SN4C5	67675	30800	31800	33000	37400
550i Grn Turismo xDrv	SP4C5	70275	31300	32300	33600	38100
Active Cruise Control			450	450	495	495
Sport Pkg			950	950	1070	1070
M Sport Pkg			1150	1150	1285	1285
6 SERIES—6-Cyl. Turbo—Equipment Schedule 1							
W.B. 112.4"; 3.0 Liter.							
640i Coupe 2D	LW3C5	74475	33800	34900	36500	40900
640i Convertible 2D	LW7C5	81975	36800	37900	39500	44200
Bang & Olufsen Sound			2700	2700	2990	2990
Active Cruise Control			450	450	485	485
Driver Assistance Pkg			625	625	680	680
Individual Comp			2375	2375	2625	2625
M Sport Pkg			950	950	1050	1050
6 SERIES—V8 Twin Turbo—Equipment Schedule 1							
W.B. 112.4"; 4.4 Liter.							
650i Coupe 2D	LX3C5	83875	37300	38400	40100	45000
650i xDrive Coupe 2D	LX5C5	86875	38900	40100	41700	46800
650i Convertible 2D	LZ3C5	92375	39400	40700	42200	47200
650i xDrive Convertible	LZ5C5	94375	41000	42200	43800	48900
Bang & Olufsen Sound			2700	2700	2990	2990
Active Cruise Control			450	450	485	485
Driver Assistance Pkg			625	625	680	680
Luxury Seating			1325	1325	1480	1480
Individual Comp			2375	2375	2630	2630
M Sport Pkg			950	950	1050	1050
M6—V8 Twin Turbo—Equipment Schedule 1							
W.B. 112.2"; 4.4 Liter.							
Convertible 2D	LZ9C5	115295	57300	59100	60200	66400
Bang & Olufsen Sound			2700	2700	2920	2920
7 SERIES—6-Cyl. Twin Turbo—Equipment Schedule 1							
W.B. 120.9", 126.4" (Li); 3.0 Liter.							
740i Sedan 4D	KA4C5	71875	28500	29100	31000	34600
740Li Sedan 4D	KB4C5	76375	30000	30700	32600	36300
Active Cruise Control			450	450	495	495
Driver Assistance Pkg			625	625	690	690
Individual Comp			2375	2375	2660	2660
M Sport Pkg			1150	1150	1275	1275
7 SERIES—V8 Twin Turbo—Equipment Schedule 1							
W.B. 120.9", 126.4" (Li); 4.4 Liter.							
750i Sedan 4D	KA8C5	86175	31800	32400	34300	38300
750i xDrive Sedan 4D	KC6C5	89475	32400	33100	35000	39100
750Li Sedan 4D	KB8C5	90075	34200	35000	37300	41900
750Li xDrive Sedan 4D	KC8C5	93375	35200	36000	38000	42300
Active Cruise Control			450	450	490	490
Driver Assistance Pkg			625	625	690	690
Luxury Seating			1325	1325	1490	1490
Individual Comp			2375	2375	2660	2660
7 SERIES—V8 Twin Turbo ActiveHybrid—Equipment Schedule 1							
W.B. 126.4"; 4.4 Liter.							
750i Sedan 4D	KX6C5	97875	32100	32800	34900	39100
750Li Sedan 4D	KX8C5	101875	35300	36000	38100	42600
Luxury Seating			1325	1325	1485	1485
Individual Comp			2375	2375	2645	2645
M Sport Pkg			1150	1150	1270	1270
7 SERIES—V12 Twin Turbo—Equipment Schedule 1							
W.B. 126.4"; 6.0 Liter.							
760Li Sedan 4D	KB0C5	142375	54600	55800	57600	63300
Active Cruise Control			450	450	485	485
Individual Comp			2375	2375	2610	2610
M Sport Pkg			1150	1150	1250	1250
ALPINA B7—V8 Twin Turbo—Equipment Schedule 1							
W.B. 120.9"; 4.4 Liter.							
Sedan 4D	KB8C5	124475	47800	48900	50600	56000
xDrive Sedan 4D	KC8C5	127775	49300	50300	52500	58000
Active Cruise Control			450	450	480	480
Luxury Seating			1325	1325	1460	1460

Body Type	VIN	List	Trade-In Good	Very Good	Pvt-Party Good	Retail Excellent
2013 BMW — WB(AorS)(UP7C5)-D-#						
1 SERIES—6-Cyl.—Equipment Schedule 1						
W.B. 104.7"; 3.0 Liter.						
128i Coupe 2D	UP7C5	35590	18150	18500	20900	23800
128i Convertible 2D	UL7C5	41290	22500	23000	25400	28900
Premium Pkg			525	525	605	605
M Sport Pkg			1175	1175	1330	1330
1 SERIES—6-Cyl. Turbo—Equipment Schedule 1						
W.B. 104.7"; 3.0 Liter.						
135i Coupe 2D	UC9C5	41645	24500	24900	27400	31000
135is Coupe 2D	UC9C5	45595	27900	28400	30900	34500
135i Convertible 2D	UN7C5	46445	26200	26700	29100	32700
135is Convertible 2D	UN7C5	50295	28900	29400	31800	35500
Premium Pkg			525	525	625	625
M Sport Pkg			1175	1175	1365	1365
3 SERIES—4-Cyl. Turbo—Equipment Schedule 1						
W.B. 110.6"; 2.0 Liter.						
320i Sedan 4D	3B1C5	35945	19400	19850	21200	23900
320i xDrive Sedan 4D	3C3C5	37945	20600	21100	22400	25300
328i Sedan 4D	3A5C5	38845	22100	22600	24000	27100
328i xDrive Sedan 4D	3B3C5	40845	23500	24000	25400	28700
Active Cruise Control			475	475	535	535
Driver Assistance Pkg			650	650	730	730
M Sport Line			1175	1175	1335	1335
Premium Pkg			525	525	610	610
3 SERIES—6-Cyl.—Equipment Schedule 1						
W.B. 108.7"; 3.0 Liter.						
328i Coupe 2D	KE3C5	42040	22200	22700	24000	27000
328i xDrive Coupe 2D	KF3C5	43740	24100	24600	26000	29200
328i Convertible 2D	DW3C5	50045	29200	29700	31600	34600
Active Cruise Control			475	475	535	535
Premium Pkg			525	525	615	615
M Sport Pkg			1175	1175	1345	1345
3 SERIES—6-Cyl. Turbo—Equipment Schedule 1						
W.B. 108.7", 110.6" (335i xDrive Sed); 3.0 Liter.						
335i Sedan 4D	3A9C5	45145	28100	28700	30100	33800
335i xDrive Sedan 4D	3B9C5	47145	29600	30200	31700	35500
335i Coupe 2D	KG7C5	47445	27400	27900	29700	33300
335i xDrive Coupe 2D	KF9C5	49145	28900	29500	31000	34800
335i Convertible 2D	DX7C5	54695	33300	33900	35900	39300
Active Cruise Control			475	475	525	525
Driver Assistance Pkg			650	650	725	725
Premium Pkg			525	525	610	610
M Sport Pkg			1175	1175	1340	1340
3 SERIES—6-Cyl. Twin Turbo—Equipment Schedule 1						
W.B. 108.7"; 3.0 Liter.						
335is Coupe 2D	KG1C5	54445	32100	32700	34500	38300
335is Convertible 2D	DX1C5	61695	38500	39200	41000	44800
Premium Pkg			525	525	605	605
3 SERIES—6-Cyl. Turbo ActiveHybrid—Equipment Schedule 1						
W.B. 110.6"; 3.0 Liter.						
3 Sedan 4D	3F9C5	51645	27000	27600	29000	32600
Active Cruise Control			475	475	525	525
Driver Assistance Pkg			650	650	725	725
Premium Pkg			525	525	605	605
M Sport Pkg			1175	1175	1320	1320
M3—V8—Equipment Schedule 1						
W.B. 108.7"; 4.0 Liter.						
Coupe 2D	KG9C5	62295	43600	44400	46300	50700
Convertible 2D	DX9C5	71345	44200	45000	46900	51300
Competition Pkg			1175	1175	1285	1285
M3—V8—Equipment Schedule 1						
W.B. 108.7"; 4.0 Liter.						
Lime Rock Park Ed 2D	KG9C5	73190	50700	51600	54100	59400
Frozen Limited Ed 2D	KG9C5	78590	47400	48300	50500	55400
Z4—4-Cyl. Turbo—Equipment Schedule 1						
W.B. 98.3"; 2.0 Liter.						
28i Roadster 2D	LL5C5	48245	26800	27300	29300	32400
Premium Pkg			525	525	590	590
Sport Pkg			350	350	375	375
M Sport Pkg			1175	1175	1290	1290

Body Type	VIN	List	Trade-In Good	Very Good	Pvt-Party Good	Retail Excellent
Z4—6-Cyl. Twin Turbo—Equipment Schedule 1						
W.B. 98.3"; 3.0 Liter.						
35i Roadster 2D	LM7C5	56045	32400	33000	35000	38600
35is Roadster 2D	LM1C5	65095	34600	35300	37300	41000
Premium Pkg		-------	525	525	585	585
M Sport Pkg		-------	1175	1175	1280	1280
5 SERIES—4-Cyl. Turbo—Equipment Schedule 1						
W.B. 116.9"; 2.0 Liter.						
528i Sedan 4D	XG5C5	49845	26500	27300	28700	32300
528i xDrive Sedan 4D	XH5C5	52145	28100	28900	30200	33900
Bang & Olufsen Sound		-------	2825	2825	3160	3160
Active Cruise Control		-------	475	475	520	520
Premium Pkg		-------	525	525	595	595
M Sport Pkg		-------	1175	1175	1300	1300
5 SERIES—6-Cyl. Turbo—Equipment Schedule 1						
W.B. 116.9", 120.9" (Gran Turismo); 3.0 Liter.						
535i Sedan 4D	FR7C5	53995	31700	32600	33900	38000
535i xDrive Sedan 4D	FU7C5	56285	33600	34600	35900	40100
535i Gran Turismo Sed	SN2C5	58895	29300	30200	31500	35300
535i Grn Turismo xDrv	SP2C5	61195	32100	33100	34400	38500
Bang & Olufsen Sound		-------	2825	2825	3150	3150
Active Cruise Control		-------	475	475	520	520
Driver Assistance Pkg		-------	650	650	715	715
Premium Pkg		-------	525	525	595	595
M Sport Pkg		-------	1175	1175	1295	1295
5 SERIES—6-Cyl. Turbo ActiveHybrid—Equipment Schedule 1						
W.B. 116.9"; 3.0 Liter.						
5 Sedan 4D	FZ9C5	61995	30900	31800	33200	37400
Bang & Olufsen Sound		-------	2825	2825	3220	3220
Premium Pkg		-------	525	525	605	605
Sport Pkg		-------	1025	1025	1165	1165
5 SERIES—V8 Twin Turbo—Equipment Schedule 1						
W.B. 116.9", 120.9" (Gran Turismo); 4.4 Liter.						
550i Sedan 4D	FR9C5	63295	35200	36200	37600	42200
550i xDrive Sedan 4D	FU9C5	65595	39200	40300	41600	46400
550i Gran Turismo Sed	SN0C5	68395	35200	36200	37500	42000
550i Grn Turismo xDrv	SP0C5	70695	39800	40900	42200	47000
Bang & Olufsen Sound		-------	2825	2825	3145	3145
Active Cruise Control		-------	475	475	515	515
Dynamic Handling Pkg		-------	1000	1000	1105	1105
Executive Pkg		-------	1975	1975	2200	2200
M Sport Pkg		-------	1175	1175	1295	1295
M5—V8 Twin Turbo—Equipment Schedule 1						
W.B. 116.9"; 4.4 Liter.						
Sedan 4D	FV9C5	92095	54400	55400	57700	62900
Bang & Olufsen Sound		-------	2825	2825	3010	3010
6 SERIES—6-Cyl. Turbo—Equipment Schedule 1						
W.B. 112.4", 116.9" (Gran); 3.0 Liter.						
640i Coupe 2D	LW3C5	75295	41400	42600	43800	48300
640i Convertible 2D	LW7C5	82795	45100	46400	47600	52600
640i Gran Coupe 4D	6A0C5	76895	43800	45100	46400	51200
Bang & Olufsen Sound		-------	2825	2825	3080	3080
Active Cruise Control		-------	475	475	505	505
Individual Comp		-------	2425	2425	2640	2640
M Sport Pkg		-------	1025	1025	1115	1115
6 SERIES—V8 Twin Turbo—Equipment Schedule 1						
W.B. 112.4", 116.9" (Gran); 4.4 Liter.						
650i Coupe 2D	YM9C5	86395	45600	46900	48200	53200
650i xDrive Coupe 2D	YM1C5	89395	47000	48400	49700	54900
650i Gran Coupe 4D	6B2C5	87395	48300	49800	51300	56500
650iGranCpe xDrv4D	6B4C5	90395	50100	51500	52900	58200
650i Convertible 2D	YP9C5	93395	48800	50200	51700	56900
650i xDrive Convertible	YP1C5	96895	48800	50300	51800	57100
Bang & Olufsen Sound		-------	2825	2825	3080	3080
Active Cruise Control		-------	475	475	505	505
Luxury Seating		-------	1350	1350	1450	1450
Individual Comp		-------	2425	2425	2645	2645
M Sport Pkg		-------	1025	1025	1115	1115
M6—V8 Twin Turbo—Equipment Schedule 1						
W.B. 112.2"; 4.4 Liter.						
Coupe 2D	LX9C5	108295	58000	59700	60800	66600
Convertible 2D	LZ9C5	115295	58700	60500	61700	67900
Bang & Olufsen Sound		-------	2825	2825	3010	3010

2013 BMW

Body Type	VIN	List	Trade-In Good	Very Good	Pvt-Party Good	Retail Excellent
7 SERIES—6-Cyl. Turbo—Equipment Schedule 1						
W.B. 126.4"; 3.0 Liter.						
740i Sedan 4D	YA6C5	74195	34900	35500	38100	42500
740Li Sedan 4D	YE4C5	78195	36200	36900	39000	43100
740Li xDrive Sedan 4D	YF4C5	81195	41200	42000	43900	48100
Bang & Olufsen Sound			2825	2825	3110	3110
Driver Assistance Pkg			650	650	705	705
Luxury Seating			1350	1350	1485	1485
Individual Comp			2425	2425	2665	2665
M Sport Pkg			1175	1175	1280	1280
Luxury Seating			1350	1350	1485	1485
7 SERIES—6-Cyl. Turbo ActiveHybrid—Equipment Schedule 1						
W.B. 126.4"; 3.0 Liter.						
7 Sedan 4D	YE0C5	84895	41900	42700	45400	50500
Bang & Olufsen Sound			2825	2825	3075	3075
Driver Assistance Pkg			650	650	695	695
Luxury Seating			1350	1350	1470	1470
Individual Comp			2425	2425	2640	2640
M Sport Pkg			1175	1175	1265	1265
Luxury Seating			1350	1350	1470	1470
7 SERIES—V8 Twin Turbo—Equipment Schedule 1						
W.B. 126.4"; 4.4 Liter.						
750i Sedan 4D	YA8C5	88195	40600	41300	43300	47400
750i xDrive Sedan 4D	YB6C5	91495	43500	44300	46800	51800
750Li Sedan 4D	YE8C5	91895	44100	44900	47100	51800
750Li xDrive Sedan 4D	YF8C5	95195	44600	45400	48100	53300
Bang & Olufsen Sound			2825	2825	3085	3085
Driver Assistance Pkg			650	650	695	695
Luxury Seating			1350	1350	1460	1460
Individual Comp			2425	2425	2645	2645
M Sport Pkg			1175	1175	1270	1270
Luxury Seating			1350	1350	1460	1460
ALPINA B7 AWD—V8 Twin Turbo—Equipment Schedule 1						
W.B. 126.4"; 4.4 Liter.						
Sedan 4D	YA8C5	127495	60100	61200	63200	68600
xDrive Sedan 4D	YB6C5	131495	61600	62800	64800	70300
Bang & Olufsen Sound			2825	2825	3040	3040
Driver Assistance Pkg			650	650	690	690
Luxury Seating			1350	1350	1450	1450

2014 BMW — WB(AorS)(1Z2C5)-E-#

Body Type	VIN	List	Trade-In Good	Very Good	Pvt-Party Good	Retail Excellent
i3—Electric—Equipment Schedule 1						
W.B. 101.2".						
Hatchback 4D	1Z2C5	42275	24600	25300	27000	30800
2 SERIES—4-Cyl. Turbo—Equipment Schedule 1						
W.B. 105.9"; 2.0 Liter.						
228i Coupe 2D	1F5C5	37075	24700	25100	27000	30400
Premium Pkg			575	575	630	630
M Sport Line			1200	1200	1325	1325
2 SERIES—6-Cyl. Turbo—Equipment Schedule 1						
W.B. 105.9"; 3.0 Liter.						
M235i Coupe 2D	1J7C5	44025	35600	36300	38400	42100
Premium Pkg			575	575	610	610
i8—3-Cyl. Turbo Hybrid—Equipment Schedule 1						
W.B. 110.2"; 1.5 Liter.						
Coupe 2D	2Z2C5	136625	****	****	****	145400
Full Leather			****	****	****	700
3 SERIES—4-Cyl. Turbo—Equipment Schedule 1						
W.B. 110.6"; 2.0 Liter.						
320i Sedan 4D	3B1C5	36875	19950	20300	22000	24600
320i xDrive Sedan 4D	3C3C5	38875	21400	21800	23500	26300
328i Sedan 4D	3A5C5	40725	25700	26100	27800	30900
328i xDrive Sedan 4D	3B3C5	42725	27600	28000	29700	33000
328i Grn Trsm xDrive	3X5C5	43825	29500	30000	31800	35200
328i Sport Wagon 4D	3G7C5	43825	33600	34200	35800	39400
Active Cruise Control			500	500	550	550
Driver Asst Plus Pkg			675	675	745	745
Premium Pkg			575	575	635	635
Sport Pkg			375	375	415	415
M Sport Line			1200	1200	1330	1330
3 SERIES—6-Cyl. Turbo—Equipment Schedule 1						
W.B. 108.7", 110.6" (335i xDrive Sed); 3.0 Liter.						
335i Sedan 4D	3A9C5	45775	31800	32400	34100	37800

Body Type	VIN	List	Trade-In Good	Very Good	Pvt-Party Good	Retail Excellent
335i xDrive Sedan 4D	3B9C5	47775	33400	34000	35700	39500
335i Gran Trsmo xDrv	3X9C5	49225	33500	34100	35900	39900
Active Cruise Control		------	500	500	550	550
Driver Asst Plus Pkg		------	675	675	745	745
Premium Pkg		------	575	575	630	630
M Sport Line		------	1200	1200	1330	1330

3 SERIES—6-Cyl. Turbo ActiveHybrid—Equipment Schedule 1
W.B. 110.6"; 3.0 Liter.

Body Type	VIN	List	Trade-In Good	Very Good	Pvt-Party Good	Retail Excellent
3 Sedan 4D	3F9C5	52275	32700	33300	35000	38700
Active Cruise Control		------	500	500	545	545
Driver Asst Plus Pkg		------	675	675	740	740
Premium Pkg		------	575	575	630	630
M Sport Line		------	1200	1200	1325	1325

3 SERIES—6-Cyl. Turbo Diesel—Equipment Schedule 1
W.B. 110.6"; 2.0 Liter.

Body Type	VIN	List	Trade-In Good	Very Good	Pvt-Party Good	Retail Excellent
328d Sedan 4D	3D3C5	42025	27600	28000	29700	33000
328d xDrive Sedan 4D	3D5C5	44025	29500	30000	31700	35100
328d xDrive Sport Wag	3K5C5	45325	36200	36800	38300	42100
Active Cruise Control		------	500	500	550	550
Driver Asst Plus Pkg		------	675	675	745	745
Premium Pkg		------	575	575	630	630
M Sport Line		------	1200	1200	1330	1330

4 SERIES—4-Cyl. Turbo—Equipment Schedule 1
W.B. 110.6"; 2.0 Liter.

Body Type	VIN	List	Trade-In Good	Very Good	Pvt-Party Good	Retail Excellent
428i Coupe 2D	3N3C5	41425	30000	30600	31900	35000
428i xDrive Coupe 2D	3N5C5	43425	32100	32700	34000	37300
428i Convertible 2D	3V5C5	49675	39100	39800	41500	45000
428i xDrive Conv 2D	3V9C5	51676	40900	41600	43300	47000
Active Speed Control		------	500	500	545	545
Driver Asst Plus Pkg		------	675	675	735	735
M Sport Line		------	1200	1200	1320	1320

4 SERIES—6-Cyl. Turbo—Equipment Schedule 1
W.B. 110.6"; 3.0 Liter.

Body Type	VIN	List	Trade-In Good	Very Good	Pvt-Party Good	Retail Excellent
435i Coupe 2D	3R1C5	46925	35000	35600	37100	40600
435i xDrive Coupe 2D	3R5C5	48925	37200	37900	39300	43100
435i Convertible 2D	3T3C5	55825	44500	45300	47200	51100
Active Cruise Control		------	500	500	545	545
Driver Asst Plus Pkg		------	675	675	740	740
M Sport Line		------	1200	1200	1320	1320

5 SERIES—4-Cyl. Turbo—Equipment Schedule 1
W.B. 116.9"; 2.0 Liter.

Body Type	VIN	List	Trade-In Good	Very Good	Pvt-Party Good	Retail Excellent
528i Sedan 4D	5A5C5	51875	30600	31500	32800	36600
528i xDrive Sedan 4D	5A7C5	54175	33300	34300	35400	39300
Bang & Olufsen Sound		------	2950	2950	3250	3250
Active Cruise Control		------	500	500	540	540
Premium Pkg		------	575	575	620	620
M Sport Line		------	1200	1200	1310	1310

5 SERIES—6-Cyl. Turbo—Equipment Schedule 1
W.B. 116.9"; 3.0 Liter.

Body Type	VIN	List	Trade-In Good	Very Good	Pvt-Party Good	Retail Excellent
535i Sedan 4D	5B1C5	56025	36500	37600	38600	42800
535i xDrive Sedan 4D	5B3C5	58325	39100	40300	41300	45600
Bang & Olufsen Sound		------	2950	2950	3245	3245
Active Cruise Control		------	500	500	540	540
Luxury Seating		------	1375	1375	1500	1500
Dynamic Handling Pkg		------	1000	1000	1095	1095
Individual Comp		------	2475	2475	2720	2720
Premium Pkg		------	575	575	620	620
M Sport Line		------	1200	1200	1305	1305

5 SERIES—6-Cyl. Turbo—Equipment Schedule 1
W.B. 120.9"; 3.0 Liter.

Body Type	VIN	List	Trade-In Good	Very Good	Pvt-Party Good	Retail Excellent
535i Gran Turismo Sed	5M2C5	61125	35900	37000	37900	41900
535i Grn Turismo xDrv	5M4C5	63425	40900	42100	43000	47400
Bang & Olufsen Sound		------	2950	2950	3275	3275
Luxury Seating		------	1375	1375	1515	1515
Dynamic Handling Pkg		------	1000	1000	1105	1105
M Sport Line		------	1200	1200	1315	1315

5 SERIES—6-Cyl. Turbo Diesel—Equipment Schedule 1
W.B. 116.9"; 3.0 Liter.

Body Type	VIN	List	Trade-In Good	Very Good	Pvt-Party Good	Retail Excellent
535d Sedan 4D	XA5C5	57525	38500	39600	40500	44600
535d xDrive Sedan 4D	FV3C5	59825	39200	40400	41200	45400
Bang & Olufsen Sound		------	2950	2950	3240	3240
Active Cruise Control		------	500	500	535	535
Luxury Seating		------	1375	1375	1500	1500

Body Type	VIN	List	Trade-In Good	Very Good	Pvt-Party Good	Retail Excellent
Dynamic Handling Pkg		------	1000	1000	1095	1095
Individual Comp		------	2475	2475	2715	2715
Premium Pkg		------	575	575	620	620
M Sport Line		------	1200	1200	1305	1305

5 SERIES—6-Cyl. Turbo ActiveHybrid—Equipment Schedule 1
W.B. 116.9"; 3.0 Liter.

Body Type	VIN	List	Trade-In Good	Very Good	Pvt-Party Good	Retail Excellent
5 Sedan 4D	5E1C5	62325	37200	38300	39400	43700
Bang & Olufsen Sound		------	2950	2950	3295	3295
Active Cruise Control		------	500	500	545	545
Premium Pkg		------	575	575	630	630
M Sport Line		------	1200	1200	1325	1325
Individual Comp		------	2475	2475	2765	2765

5 SERIES—V8 Twin Turbo—Equipment Schedule 1
W.B. 116.9", 120.9" (Gran Turismo); 4.4 Liter.

Body Type	VIN	List	Trade-In Good	Very Good	Pvt-Party Good	Retail Excellent
550i Sedan 4D	KN9C5	64825	42200	43400	44500	49300
550i xDrive Sedan 4D	KP9C5	67125	46400	47800	48600	53600
550i Gran Turismo Sed	5M6C5	69025	42300	43400	44700	49400
550i Grn Turismo xDrv	5M0C5	71325	46700	48100	48900	54000
Bang & Olufsen Sound		------	2950	2950	3225	3225
Active Cruise Control		------	500	500	535	535
Luxury Seating		------	1375	1375	1495	1495
Dynamic Handling Pkg		------	1000	1000	1090	1090
Executive Pkg		------	2075	2075	2255	2255
Individual Comp		------	2475	2475	2710	2710
M Sport Line		------	1200	1200	1300	1300

M5—V8 Twin Turbo—Equipment Schedule 1
W.B. 116.7"; 4.4 Liter.

Body Type	VIN	List	Trade-In Good	Very Good	Pvt-Party Good	Retail Excellent
Sedan 4D	FV9C5	95125	71500	72700	74300	80000
Bang & Olufsen Sound		------	2950	2950	3100	3100
Competition Pkg		------	1225	1225	1290	1290

6 SERIES—6-Cyl. Turbo—Equipment Schedule 1
W.B. 112.4", 116.9" (Gran), 3.0 Liter.

Body Type	VIN	List	Trade-In Good	Very Good	Pvt-Party Good	Retail Excellent
640i Coupe 2D	LW3C5	75795	47900	49300	50500	55200
640i xDrive Coupe 2D	LY1C5	78795	47700	49100	50800	55900
640i Gran Coupe 4D	6A0C5	77995	50100	51600	52800	57800
640i GranCpe xDrive	6B8C5	80995	53300	54900	56200	61500
640i Convertible 2D	LW7C5	83295	52600	54100	55300	60400
640i xDrive Convertible	YP5C5	86295	55300	56900	58100	63500
Bang & Olufsen Sound		------	2950	2950	3180	3180
Active Cruise Control		------	500	500	525	525
Driver Assistance Pkg		------	675	675	715	715
Driver Asst Plus Pkg		------	675	675	715	715
Executive Pkg		------	2075	2075	2220	2220
Individual Comp		------	2475	2475	2670	2670
M Sport Pkg		------	1100	1100	1180	1180

6 SERIES—V8 Twin Turbo—Equipment Schedule 1
W.B. 112.4", 116.9" (Gran) 4.4 Liter.

Body Type	VIN	List	Trade-In Good	Very Good	Pvt-Party Good	Retail Excellent
650i Coupe 2D	YM9C5	87095	52700	54200	55500	60900
650i xDrive Coupe 2D	YM1C5	90095	55000	56600	57800	63200
650i Gran Coupe 4D	6B2C5	89295	55700	57300	58400	63800
650i GranCpe xDrv 4D	6B4C5	92295	56800	58400	59500	64900
650i Convertible 2D	YP9C5	94595	57600	59300	60200	65700
650i xDrive Convertible	YP1C5	97595	61400	63200	64000	69800
650i Frozen White Cnv	YP9C5	106695	60400	62100	62900	68600
650i Frzn Wht xDrv Cnv	YP1C5	110095	64400	66200	66800	72600
Bang & Olufsen Sound		------	2950	2950	3180	3180
Active Cruise Control		------	500	500	530	530
Driver Assistance Pkg		------	675	675	715	715
Driver Asst Plus Pkg		------	675	675	715	715
Executive Pkg		------	2075	2075	2225	2225
Individual Comp		------	2475	2475	2670	2670
M Sport Pkg		------	1100	1100	1185	1185

M6—V8 Twin Turbo—Equipment Schedule 1
W.B. 112.2", 116.9" (4D); 4.4 Liter.

Body Type	VIN	List	Trade-In Good	Very Good	Pvt-Party Good	Retail Excellent
Coupe 2D	LX9C5	111395	77200	79400	79400	85800
Coupe 4D	6C9C5	115195	78600	80900	80700	87100
Convertible 2D	LZ9C5	117695	78800	81100	81200	87900
Bang & Olufsen Sound		------	2950	2950	3100	3100
Executive Pkg		------	2075	2075	2165	2165

7 SERIES—6-Cyl. Turbo—Equipment Schedule 1
W.B. 126.4"; 3.0 Liter.

Body Type	VIN	List	Trade-In Good	Very Good	Pvt-Party Good	Retail Excellent
740i Sedan 4D	YA6C5	74925	46000	46900	49100	53700
740Li Sedan 4D	YE4C5	78925	46700	47500	49300	53500

Body	Type	VIN	List	Trade-In Good	Very Good	Pvt-Party Good	Retail Excellent
740Li xDrive Sedan 4D		YE4C5	81925	52100	53100	54800	59000
Bang & Olufsen Sound				2950	2950	3175	3175
Active Cruise Control				500	500	525	525
Full Merino Leather				675	675	715	715
Driver Asst Plus Pkg				675	675	715	715
Executive Pkg				2075	2075	2220	2220
Luxury Seating				1375	1375	1455	1455
Individual Comp				2475	2475	2665	2665
M Sport Pkg				1200	1200	1280	1280

7 SERIES—6-Cyl. Turbo ActiveHybrid—Equipment Schedule 1
W.B. 126.4"; 3.0 Liter.

Body	Type	VIN	List	Good	Very Good	Good	Excellent
7 Sedan 4D		YE0C5	85225	52800	53800	56400	61800
Bang & Olufsen Sound				2950	2950	3155	3155
Active Cruise Control				500	500	525	525
Full Merino Leather				675	675	710	710
Driver Asst Plus Pkg				675	675	710	710
Executive Pkg				2075	2075	2205	2205
Luxury Seating				1375	1375	1460	1460
Individual Comp				2475	2475	2650	2650
M Sport Pkg				1200	1200	1270	1270

7 SERIES—V8 Twin Turbo—Equipment Schedule 1
W.B. 126.4"; 4.4 Liter.

Body	Type	VIN	List	Good	Very Good	Good	Excellent
750i Sedan 4D		YA8C5	88225	51500	52400	54300	58700
750i xDrive Sedan 4D		YB6C5	91225	54400	55400	57800	63000
750Li Sedan 4D		YE8C5	91925	55000	56000	58100	63000
750Li xDrive Sedan 4D		YF8C5	94925	55500	56500	59100	64600
Bang & Olufsen Sound				2950	2950	3145	3145
Active Cruise Control				500	500	520	520
Full Merino Leather				675	675	710	710
Driver Asst Plus Pkg				675	675	705	705
Executive Pkg				2075	2075	2195	2195
Luxury Seating				1375	1375	1455	1455
Individual Comp				2475	2475	2640	2640
M Sport Pkg				1200	1200	1265	1265

7 SERIES—V12 Twin Turbo—Equipment Schedule 1
W.B. 126.4"; 6.0 Liter.

Body	Type	VIN	List	Good	Very Good	Good	Excellent
760Li Sedan 4D		YG0C5	143825	76800	78200	79700	85600
Bang & Olufsen Sound				2950	2950	3165	3165
Active Cruise Control				500	500	525	525
Full Merino Leather				675	675	710	710
Individual Comp				2475	2475	2655	2655
M Sport Pkg				1200	1200	1275	1275

ALPINA B7—V8 Twin Turbo—Equipment Schedule 1
W.B. 120.9"; 4.4 Liter.

Body	Type	VIN	List	Good	Very Good	Good	Excellent
Sedan 4D		YA8C5	129225	73100	74400	75900	81600
xDrive Sedan 4D		YB6C5	132225	75100	76400	77900	83800
Bang & Olufsen Sound				2950	2950	3135	3135
Active Cruise Control				500	500	520	520
Full Merino Leather				675	675	705	705
Driver Asst Plus Pkg				675	675	705	705
Luxury Seating				1375	1375	1450	1450

BENTLEY

2005 BENTLEY — SCB(LC37F)-5-#

ARNAGE—V8 Twin Turbo—Equipment Schedule 2
W.B. 122.7", 132.5"; 6.8 Liter.

Body	Type	VIN	List	Good	Very Good	Good	Excellent
R Sedan 4D		LC37F	219985	****	****	****	68400
T Sedan 4D		LF34F	241985	****	****	****	77300
RL Sedan 4D		LC37F	250985	****	****	****	86400

CONTINENTAL—W12 Twin Turbo—Equipment Schedule 2
W.B. 108.0", 120.7"; 6.0 Liter.

Body	Type	VIN	List	Good	Very Good	Good	Excellent
Coupe 2D		CR63W	162285	****	****	****	63400
Flying Spur Sedan 4D		BR53W		****	****	****	57400

2006 BENTLEY — SCB(LC43F)-6-#

ARNAGE—V8 Twin Turbo—Equipment Schedule 2
W.B. 122.7", 132.5"; 6.8 Liter.

Body	Type	VIN	List	Good	Very Good	Good	Excellent
R Sedan 4D		LC43F	220985	****	****	****	83000
T Sedan 4D		LF34F	242985	****	****	****	91700
RL Sedan 4D		LC37F	251985	****	****	****	100400

2006 BENTLEY

Body Type	VIN	List	Trade-In Good	Very Good	Pvt-Party Good	Retail Excellent
CONTINENTAL AWD—W12 Twin Turbo—Equipment Schedule 2						
W.B. 108.1", 120.7"; 6.0 Liter.						
Coupe 2D	CR63W	171285	****	****	****	69600
Flying Spur Sedan 4D	BR53W	172125	****	****	****	63800

2007 BENTLEY — SCB(LC47J)-7-#

ARNAGE—V8 Twin Turbo—Equipment Schedule 2						
W.B. 122.7", 132.5"; 6.8 Liter.						
R Sedan 4D	LC47J	229985	****	****	****	98800
T Sedan 4D	LF44J	250985	****	****	****	110500
RL Sedan 4D	LF37J	271985	****	****	****	132000
AZURE—V8 Twin Turbo—Equipment Schedule 2						
W.B. 122.7"; 6.8 Liter.						
Convertible 2D	DC47L	337085	****	****	****	145800
CONTINENTAL AWD—W12 Twin Turbo—Equipment Schedule 2						
W.B. 108.1", 120.7"; 6.0 Liter.						
GT Coupe 2D	CR73W	176285	****	****	****	82100
Flying Spur Sedan 4D	BR93W	176285	****	****	****	77600
GTC Convertible 2D	DR33W	196285	****	****	****	96500

2008 BENTLEY — SCB(LC47J)-8-#

ARNAGE—V8 Twin Turbo—Equipment Schedule 2						
W.B. 122.7", 132.5"; 6.8 Liter.						
R Sedan 4D	LC47J	229085	****	****	****	116200
T Sedan 4D	LF44J	250085	****	****	****	133300
RL Sedan 4D	LE47K	271085	****	****	****	150500
AZURE—V8 Twin Turbo—Equipment Schedule 2						
W.B. 122.7"; 6.8 Liter.						
Convertible 2D	DC47L	338085	****	****	****	175000
CONTINENTAL AWD—W12 Twin Turbo—Equipment Schedule 2						
W.B. 108.1", 120.7"; 6.0 Liter.						
GT Coupe 2D	CR73W	178585	****	****	****	86400
GT Speed Coupe 2D	CP73W	202585	****	****	****	107700
Flying Spur Sedan 4D	BR93W	173585	****	****	****	83200
GTC Convertible 2D	DR33W	196585	****	****	****	102600
Ceramic Brakes			****	****	****	3595

2009 BENTLEY — SCB(LC47J)-9-#

ARNAGE—V8 Twin Turbo—Equipment Schedule 2						
W.B. 122.7", 132.5"; 6.8 Liter.						
R Sedan 4D	LC47J	227585	****	****	****	130700
T Sedan 4D	LF44J	249585	****	****	****	151100
RL Sedan 4D	LE47K	270585	****	****	****	166900
Final Series Sedan 4D	LF44J	273585	****	****	****	184900
AZURE—V8 Twin Turbo—Equipment Schedule 2						
W.B. 122.7"; 6.8 Liter.						
Convertible 2D	DC47L	342085	****	****	****	217900
BROOKLANDS—V8 Twin Turbo—Equipment Schedule 2						
W.B. 122.7"; 6.8 Liter.						
Coupe 2D	CC41N	348085	****	****	****	221400
CONTINENTAL AWD—W12 Twin Turbo—Equipment Schedule 2						
W.B. 108.1", 120.7"; 6.0 Liter.						
GT Coupe 2D	CR73W	181795	****	****	****	95000
GT Speed Coupe 2D	CP73W	206195	****	****	****	114900
Flying Spur Sedan 4D	BR93W	176695	****	****	****	87700
Flying Spur Speed Sdn	BP93W	201095	****	****	****	116500
GTC Convertible 2D	DR33W	200095	****	****	****	111000
GTC Speed Conv 2D	DP33W		****	****	****	155800
Adaptive Cruise Control			****	****	****	390

2010 BENTLEY — SCB(DC4BL)-A-#

AZURE T—V8 Twin Turbo—Equipment Schedule 2						
W.B. 122.7"; 6.8 Liter.						
Convertible 2D	DC4BL	370095	****	****	****	322200
BROOKLANDS—V8 Twin Turbo—Equipment Schedule 2						
W.B. 122.7"; 6.8 Liter.						
Coupe 2D	CC41N	348085	****	****	****	296400
CONTINENTAL AWD—W12 Twin Turbo—Equipment Schedule 2						
W.B. 108.1", 120.7"; 6.0 Liter.						
GT Coupe 2D	CR7ZA	189095	****	****	****	104900
GT Speed Cpe 2D	CP7ZA	213995	****	****	****	124900
Supersports Cpe 2D	CU8ZA	272195	****	****	****	170900

Body Type	VIN	List	Trade-In Good	Very Good	Pvt-Party Good	Retail Excellent
Flying Spur Sed 4D	BR9ZA	183895	****	****	****	96800
Flying Spur Speed Sed	BP9ZA	208795	****	****	****	127600
GTC Convertible 2D	DR3ZA	207795	****	****	****	120500
GTC Speed Conv 2D	DP3ZA	237695	****	****	****	165300
Supersports Conv 2D	CU8ZA	------	****	****	****	215700
Adaptive Cruise Control			****	****	****	405

2011 BENTLEY — SCB(BR9ZA)–B–#

CONTINENTAL AWD—W12 Twin Turbo—Equipment Schedule 2
W.B. 108.1", 120.7"; 6.0 Liter.

Body Type	VIN	List	Trade-In Good	Very Good	Pvt-Party Good	Retail Excellent
Flying Spur Sedan 4D	BR9ZA	186795	****	****	****	117700
Flying Spur Speed 4D	BP9ZA	212195	****	****	****	150000
Supersports Coupe 2D	CU7ZA	272195	****	****	****	199600
GTC Convertible 2D	DR3ZA	211195	****	****	****	135900
GTC Speed Conv 2D	DP3ZA	238695	****	****	****	188600
Supersports Conv 2D	DU3ZA	285595	****	****	****	238400
Adaptive Cruise Control			****	****	****	435

MULSANNE—V8 Twin Turbo—Equipment Schedule 2
W.B. 128.6"; 6.8 Liter.

Body Type	VIN	List	Trade-In Good	Very Good	Pvt-Party Good	Retail Excellent
Sedan 4D	BB7ZH	291295	****	****	****	221900
Adaptive Cruise Control			****	****	****	430

2012 BENTLEY — SCB(BR9ZA)–C–#

CONTINENTAL AWD—W12 Twin Turbo—Equipment Schedule 2
W.B. 108.1", 120.7"; 6.0 Liter.

Body Type	VIN	List	Trade-In Good	Very Good	Pvt-Party Good	Retail Excellent
Flying Spur Sedan 4D	BR9ZA	186795	****	****	****	122300
Flying Spur Speed 4D	BP9ZA	212195	****	****	****	154900
GT Coupe 2D	FR7ZA	192495	****	****	****	121100
Supersports Coupe 2D	CU7ZA	269595	****	****	****	209600
Supersports Conv 2D	DU3ZA	282995	****	****	****	242400
Adaptive Cruise Control			****	****	****	460

MULSANNE—V8 Twin Turbo—Equipment Schedule 2
W.B. 128.6"; 6.8 Liter.

Body Type	VIN	List	Trade-In Good	Very Good	Pvt-Party Good	Retail Excellent
Sedan 4D	BB7ZH	296295	****	****	****	232600
Adaptive Cruise Control			****	****	****	455

2013 BENTLEY — SCB(BR9ZA)–D–#

CONTINENTAL AWD—W12 Twin Turbo—Equipment Schedule 2
W.B. 108.1", 121.0"; 6.0 Liter.

Body Type	VIN	List	Trade-In Good	Very Good	Pvt-Party Good	Retail Excellent
Flying Spur Sedan 4D	BR9ZA	189925	****	****	****	129600
Flying Spur Speed 4D	BP9ZA	215325	****	****	****	160400
GT Coupe 2D	FR7ZA	198975	****	****	****	127700
GT Speed Coupe 2D	FC7ZA	220725	****	****	****	148500
GTC Convertible 2D	GR3ZA	218525	****	****	****	148000
Supersports Conv 2D	DC3ZA	297625	****	****	****	249000
Adaptive Cruise Control			****	****	****	490
Carbon Ceramic Brakes			****	****	****	4125

MULSANNE—V8 Twin Turbo—Equipment Schedule 2
W.B. 128.6"; 6.8 Liter.

Body Type	VIN	List	Trade-In Good	Very Good	Pvt-Party Good	Retail Excellent
Sedan 4D	BB7ZH	302425	****	****	****	240800
Adaptive Cruise Control			****	****	****	480

2014 BENTLEY — SCB(EC9ZA)–E–#

FLYING SPUR AWD—W12 Twin Turbo—Equipment Schedule 2
W.B. 120.7"; 6.0 Liter.

Body Type	VIN	List	Trade-In Good	Very Good	Pvt-Party Good	Retail Excellent
Sedan 4D	EC9ZA	205825	****	****	****	139700
Adaptive Cruise Control			****	****	****	515
Ceramic Brakes			****	****	****	4250

CONTINENTAL AWD—W12 Twin Turbo—Equipment Schedule 2
W.B. 108.1"; 6.0 Liter.

Body Type	VIN	List	Trade-In Good	Very Good	Pvt-Party Good	Retail Excellent
GT Speed Coupe 2D	FC7ZA	222725	****	****	****	154300
GT Speed Conv 2D	GC3ZA	241425	****	****	****	158600
Adaptive Cruise Control			****	****	****	520
Carbon Ceramic Brakes			****	****	****	4300

CONTINENTAL AWD—W12 Twin Turbo—Equipment Schedule 2
W.B. 108.1"; 6.0 Liter.

Body Type	VIN	List	Trade-In Good	Very Good	Pvt-Party Good	Retail Excellent
GT Coupe 2D	FU7ZA	204325	****	****	****	133600
GTC Convertible 2D	GU3ZA	224225	****	****	****	155200
Adaptive Cruise Control			****	****	****	500
Carbon Ceramic Brakes			****	****	****	4160
V8, Twin Turbo, 4.0 Liter			****	****	****	(10085)

2014 BENTLEY

Body Type	VIN	List	Trade-In Good	Very Good	Pvt-Party Good	Retail Excellent
MULSANNE—V8 Twin Turbo—Equipment Schedule 2						
W.B. 128.6"; 6.8 Liter.						
Sedan 4D	BB7ZH	305325	****	****	****	**248700**
Adaptive Speed Control			****	****	****	**510**

BUICK

2000 BUICK — (1,2or3)G4(WS52J)-Y-#

CENTURY—V6—Equipment Schedule 4
W.B. 109.0"; 3.1 Liter.

Custom Sedan 4D	WS52J	20592	**775**	**925**	**1450**	**2650**
Century 2000 Pkg			125	125	175	175
Limited	Y		250	250	340	340

REGAL—V6—Equipment Schedule 4
W.B. 109.0"; 3.8 Liter.

LS Sedan 4D	WB52K	22780	**850**	**1000**	**1575**	**2750**
Gran Touring Pkg			50	50	65	65

REGAL—V6 Supercharged—Equipment Schedule 4
W.B. 109.0"; 3.8 Liter.

GS Sedan 4D	WF521	25625	**1375**	**1600**	**2200**	**3775**

LeSABRE—V6—Equipment Schedule 4
W.B. 112.2"; 3.8 Liter.

Custom Sedan 4D	HP54K	24115	**875**	**1025**	**1600**	**2775**
Limited Sedan 4D	HR54K	27310	**1050**	**1225**	**1875**	**3325**
Gran Touring Pkg			50	50	65	65

PARK AVENUE—V6—Equipment Schedule 4
W.B. 113.8"; 3.8 Liter.

Sedan 4D	CW52K	32395	**875**	**1025**	**1575**	**2775**
Gran Touring Pkg			50	50	65	65

PARK AVENUE—V6 Supercharged—Equipment Schedule 4
W.B. 113.8"; 3.8 Liter.

Ultra Sedan 4D	CU521	37470	**1275**	**1500**	**2200**	**3775**
Gran Touring Pkg			50	50	65	65

2001 BUICK — (1or2)G4(WS52J)-2-#

CENTURY—V6—Equipment Schedule 4
W.B. 109.0"; 3.1 Liter.

Custom Sedan 4D	WS52J	20870	**900**	**1075**	**1650**	**2950**
Limited	Y		300	300	395	395

REGAL—V6—Equipment Schedule 4
W.B. 109.0"; 3.8 Liter.

LS Sedan 4D	WB52K	23445	**1025**	**1200**	**1775**	**3075**
Abboud Pkg			75	75	100	100
Gran Touring Pkg			50	50	65	65

REGAL—V6 Supercharged—Equipment Schedule 4
W.B. 109.0"; 3.8 Liter.

GS Sedan 4D	WF521	26695	**1350**	**1575**	**2325**	**4000**
Abboud Pkg			75	75	100	100

LeSABRE—V6—Equipment Schedule 4
W.B. 112.2"; 3.8 Liter.

Custom Sedan 4D	HP54K	24762	**1050**	**1225**	**1850**	**3200**
Limited Sedan 4D	HR54K	29451	**1125**	**1300**	**2050**	**3650**
Gran Touring Pkg			50	50	65	65

PARK AVENUE—V6—Equipment Schedule 4
W.B. 113.8"; 3.8 Liter.

Sedan 4D	CW52K	33700	**1125**	**1300**	**1875**	**3225**
Gran Touring Pkg			50	50	65	65

PARK AVENUE—V6 Supercharged—Equipment Schedule 4
W.B. 113.8"; 3.8 Liter.

Ultra Sedan 4D	CU521	38210	**1575**	**1800**	**2500**	**4225**
Gran Touring Pkg			50	50	65	65

2002 BUICK — (1or2)G4(WS52J)-2-#

CENTURY—V6—Equipment Schedule 4
W.B. 109.0"; 3.1 Liter.

Custom Sedan 4D	WS52J	21325	**1150**	**1350**	**1975**	**3550**
Limited	Y		325	325	445	445

REGAL—V6—Equipment Schedule 4
W.B. 109.0"; 3.8 Liter.

LS Sedan 4D	WB52K	23840	**1425**	**1625**	**2250**	**3700**
Abboud Pkg			75	75	105	105

Body Type	VIN	List	Trade-In Good	Very Good	Pvt-Party Good	Retail Excellent
Gran Touring Pkg			75	75	85	85
REGAL—V6 Supercharged—Equipment Schedule 4						
W.B. 109.0"; 3.8 Liter.						
GS Sedan 4D	WF521	27895	1550	1775	2550	4300
Abboud Pkg			75	75	105	105
LeSABRE—V6—Equipment Schedule 4						
W.B. 112.2"; 3.8 Liter.						
Custom Sedan 4D	HP54K	24975	1225	1425	2125	3625
Limited Sedan 4D	HR54K	30675	1475	1700	2450	4150
PARK AVENUE—V6—Equipment Schedule 4						
W.B. 113.8"; 3.8 Liter.						
Sedan 4D	CW52K	34165	1375	1575	2300	3875
Gran Touring Pkg			75	75	85	85
PARK AVENUE—V6 Supercharged—Equipment Schedule 4						
W.B. 113.8"; 3.8 Liter.						
Ultra Sedan 4D	CU521	38675	1950	2250	2975	4950
Gran Touring Pkg			75	75	85	85

Body Type	VIN	List	Trade-In Good	Very Good	Pvt-Party Good	Retail Excellent
CENTURY—V6—Equipment Schedule 4						
W.B. 109.0"; 3.1 Liter.						
Sedan 4D	WS52J	21685	1325	1550	2300	4025
Limited	Y		375	375	495	495
REGAL—V6—Equipment Schedule 4						
W.B. 109.0"; 3.8 Liter.						
LS Sedan 4D	WB52K	24230	1600	1825	2525	4175
Abboud Pkg			75	75	110	110
Gran Touring Pkg			100	100	120	120
REGAL—V6 Supercharged—Equipment Schedule 4						
W.B. 109.0"; 3.8 Liter.						
GS Sedan 4D	WF521	28175	1750	2000	2875	4875
Abboud Pkg			75	75	110	110
LeSABRE—V6—Equipment Schedule 4						
W.B. 112.2"; 3.8 Liter.						
Custom Sedan 4D	HP52K	25730	1625	1875	2525	4150
Limited Sedan 4D	HR54K	31360	1825	2075	2850	4725
Celebration Edition			325	325	445	445
PARK AVENUE—V6—Equipment Schedule 4						
W.B. 113.8"; 3.8 Liter.						
Sedan 4D	CW54K	34615	1675	1900	2600	4300
Gran Touring Pkg			100	100	120	120
PARK AVENUE—V6 Supercharged—Equipment Schedule 4						
W.B. 113.8"; 3.8 Liter.						
Ultra Sedan 4D	CU541	39915	2325	2625	3325	5375

Body Type	VIN	List	Trade-In Good	Very Good	Pvt-Party Good	Retail Excellent
CENTURY—V6—Equipment Schedule 4						
W.B. 109.0"; 3.1 Liter.						
Sedan 4D	WS52J	22415	1650	1900	2600	4375
Limited			250	250	325	325
Special Edition			400	400	550	550
REGAL—V6—Equipment Schedule 4						
W.B. 109.0"; 3.8 Liter.						
LS Sedan 4D	WB52K	24895	2125	2400	3050	4875
Abboud Pkg			100	100	120	120
Gran Touring Pkg			100	100	135	135
REGAL—V6 Supercharged—Equipment Schedule 4						
W.B. 109.0"; 3.8 Liter.						
GS Sedan 4D	WF521	28345	2600	2950	3675	5900
Abboud Pkg			100	100	120	120
LeSABRE—V6—Equipment Schedule 4						
W.B. 112.2"; 3.8 Liter.						
Custom Sedan 4D	HP54K	26470	2050	2325	3025	4875
Limited Sedan 4D	HR54K	32245	2700	3050	3750	5950
Celebration Edition			375	375	485	485
PARK AVENUE—V6—Equipment Schedule 4						
W.B. 113.8"; 3.8 Liter.						
Sedan 4D	CW52K	35545	2175	2450	3175	5075
Gran Touring Pkg			100	100	135	135
PARK AVENUE—V6 Supercharged—Equipment Schedule 4						
W.B. 113.8"; 3.8 Liter.						
Ultra Sedan 4D	CU521	40720	2775	3125	3850	6150

Body Type	VIN	List	Trade-In Good	Very Good	Pvt-Party Good	Retail Excellent

2005 BUICK — (1or2)G4(WS52J)–5–#

CENTURY—V6—Equipment Schedule 4
W.B. 109.0"; 3.1 Liter.

Body Type	VIN	List	Good	Very Good	Good	Excellent
Sedan 4D	WS52J	22950	1850	2125	3100	5175
Limited			275	275	350	350
Special Edition			475	475	635	635

LACROSSE—V6—Equipment Schedule 4
W.B. 110.5"; 3.6 Liter, 3.8 Liter.

CX Sedan 4D	WC532	23495	2150	2525	3225	5025
CXL Sedan 4D	WD532	25995	3050	3550	4150	6300
CXS Sedan 4D	WE537	28995	3600	4150	4675	7050

LeSABRE—V6—Equipment Schedule 4
W.B. 112.2"; 3.8 Liter.

Custom Sedan 4D	HP52K	27270	2425	2775	3550	5550
Limited Sedan 4D	HR54K	32930	2800	3175	4000	6250
Celebration Edition			400	400	530	530

PARK AVENUE—V6—Equipment Schedule 4
W.B. 113.8"; 3.8 Liter.

Sedan 4D	CW54K	36350	2525	2850	3650	5675

PARK AVENUE—V6 Supercharged—Equipment Schedule 4
W.B. 113.8"; 3.8 Liter.

Special Ed Ultra 4D	CU541	41525	3275	3700	4625	7100

2006 BUICK — (1or2)G4(WC582)–6–#

LACROSSE—V6—Equipment Schedule 4
W.B. 110.5"; 3.6 Liter, 3.8 Liter.

CX Sedan 4D	WC582	23595	2850	3275	3875	5800
CXL Sedan 4D	WD582	26095	3625	4175	4800	7025
CXS Sedan 4D	WE587	29095	4175	4775	5350	7825

LUCERNE—V6—Equipment Schedule 4
W.B. 115.6"; 3.8 Liter.

CX Sedan 4D	HP572	26990	3400	3625	4675	6500
CXL Sedan 4D	HD572	28990	3975	4225	5250	7225
V8, 4.6 Liter	Y		525	525	710	710

LUCERNE—V8—Equipment Schedule 4
W.B. 115.6"; 4.6 Liter.

CXS Sedan 4D	HE57Y	35990	4200	4475	5525	7600

2007 BUICK — (1or2)G4(WC582)–7–#

LACROSSE—V6—Equipment Schedule 4
W.B. 110.5"; 3.6 Liter, 3.8 Liter.

CX Sedan 4D	WC582	22915	3525	3975	4550	6550
CXL Sedan 4D	WD582	25330	4225	4750	5425	7750
CXS Sedan 4D	WE587	27545	5025	5650	6225	8825

LUCERNE—V6—Equipment Schedule 4
W.B. 115.6"; 3.8 Liter.

CX Sedan 4D	HP572	26265	4050	4275	5225	7000
CXL Sedan 4D	HD572	29280	4750	5025	6200	8275
V8, 4.6 Liter	Y		575	575	775	775

LUCERNE—V8—Equipment Schedule 4
W.B. 115.6"; 4.6 Liter.

CXS Sedan 4D	HE57Y	35295	4525	4775	5925	8050

2008 BUICK — (1or2)G4(WC582)–8–#

LACROSSE—V6—Equipment Schedule 4
W.B. 110.5"; 3.6 Liter, 3.8 Liter.

CX Sedan 4D	WC582	23995	4375	4825	5600	7625
CXL Sedan 4D	WD582	25995	5375	5900	6625	8975
CXS Sedan 4D	WE587	27995	6100	6675	7650	10550

LACROSSE—V8—Equipment Schedule 4
W.B. 110.5"; 5.3 Liter.

Super Sedan 4D	WN58C	31995	6725	7350	8350	11550

LUCERNE—V6—Equipment Schedule 4
W.B. 115.6"; 3.8 Liter.

CX Sedan 4D	HP572	26995	4875	5100	6300	8125
CXL Sedan 4D	HD572	29595	5825	6100	7350	9400
CXL Special Edition	HR572	32150	6200	6475	7725	9875
V8, 4.6 Liter			625	625	845	845

LUCERNE—V8—Equipment Schedule 4
W.B. 115.6"; 4.6 Liter.

CXS Sedan 4D	HE57Y	36595	6000	6275	7625	9875

Body Type	VIN	List	Trade-In Good	Very Good	Pvt-Party Good	Retail Excellent
Super Sedan 4D	HF579	39395	7675	8025	9425	12000

2009 BUICK — (1or2)G4(WC582)-9-#

LACROSSE—V6—Equipment Schedule 4
W.B. 110.5"; 3.8 Liter.

CX Sedan 4D	WC582	25590	5675	6075	7100	9325
CXL Sedan 4D	WD582	27960	6725	7200	8225	10800

LACROSSE—V8—Equipment Schedule 4
W.B. 110.5"; 5.3 Liter.

Super Sedan 4D	WN58C	33755	8275	8825	10000	13150

LUCERNE—V6—Equipment Schedule 4
W.B. 115.6"; 3.9 Liter.

CX Sedan 4D	HP57M	27520	7000	7250	8550	10500
CXL Sedan 4D	HD57M	30165	7825	8100	9425	11500
CXL Special Ed 4D	HR57M	32980	8350	8650	9975	12200

LUCERNE—V8—Equipment Schedule 4
W.B. 115.6"; 4.6 Liter.

Super Sedan 4D	HF579	39395	9675	10050	11500	14100

2010 BUICK — (1,2or3)G4(GB5EG)-A-#

LACROSSE—V6—Equipment Schedule 4
W.B. 111.7"; 3.0 Liter.

CX Sedan 4D	GB5EG	27835	9150	9575	10450	12850
CXL Sedan 4D	GC5EG	30395	10800	11350	12250	15000
CXS Sedan 4D	GE5EV	33765	12800	13450	14350	17500
AWD	D		950	950	1110	1110
4-Cyl, 2.4 Liter	C		(575)	(575)	(685)	(685)

LUCERNE—V6—Equipment Schedule 4
W.B. 115.6"; 3.9 Liter.

CX Sedan 4D	HA5EM	29995	8525	8775	10250	12250
CXL Sedan 4D	HC5EM	33495	9475	9750	11350	13600
CXL Special Ed 4D	HD5EM	33995	9825	10100	11700	14000
CXL Premium Rd	HC5EM	36390	10050	10350	12000	14450

LUCERNE—V8—Equipment Schedule 4
W.B. 115.6"; 4.6 Liter.

Super Sedan 4D	HH5E9	39995	12300	12650	14400	17150

2011 BUICK — (1or2)G4(GN5EC)-B-#

REGAL—4-Cyl.—Equipment Schedule 4
W.B. 107.8"; 2.4 Liter.

CXL Sedan 4D	GN5EC	26995	10050	10400	11350	13350

REGAL—4-Cyl. Turbo—Equipment Schedule 4
W.B. 107.8"; 2.0 Liter.

CXL Sedan 4D	GV5EV	29495	10900	11250	12300	14500

LACROSSE—V6—Equipment Schedule 4
W.B. 111.7"; 3.0 Liter.

CX Sedan 4D	GA5ED	27245	10550	10900	11950	14300
CXL Sedan 4D	GC5ED	30395	12350	12800	13950	16650
AWD	D		975	975	1110	1110
4-Cyl, 2.4 Liter	C		(575)	(575)	(660)	(660)

LACROSSE—V6—Equipment Schedule 4
W.B. 111.7"; 3.6 Liter.

CXS Sedan 4D	GE5ED	33765	14250	14750	15900	18950

LUCERNE—V6—Equipment Schedule 4
W.B. 115.6"; 3.9 Liter.

CX Sedan 4D	HA5EM	29995	10800	11000	12500	14650
CXL Sedan 4D	HC5EM	33495	11550	11800	13650	16000
CXL Premium Sed 4D	HJ5EM	36440	12150	12450	14350	16850

LUCERNE—V8—Equipment Schedule 4
W.B. 115.6"; 4.6 Liter.

Super Sedan 4D	HK5ES	45225	14250	14600	16650	19450

2012 BUICK — (1or2)G4(PP5SK)-C-#

VERANO—4-Cyl.—Equipment Schedule 4
W.B. 105.7"; 2.4 Liter.

Sedan 4D	PP5SK	23470	10700	11000	12450	14550
Convenience Sedan	PR5SK	24670	11150	11400	12800	14900
Leather Sedan 4D	PS5SK	26850	11550	11850	13250	15350

REGAL—4-Cyl.—Equipment Schedule 4
W.B. 107.8"; 2.4 Liter.

Sedan 4D	GR5EK	27530	11350	11600	13050	15200
Premium 1 Sedan 4D	GS5EK	28965	11800	12050	13500	15800

Body Type	VIN	List	Trade-In Good	Very Good	Pvt-Party Good	Retail Excellent
Premium 2 Sedan 4D	GT5EK	30375	12500	12800	14200	16500
REGAL—4-Cyl. Turbo—Equipment Schedule 4						
W.B. 107.8"; 2.0 Liter.						
Premium 1 Sedan 4D	GS5EV	30735	12600	12900	14300	16600
Premium 2 Sedan 4D	GT5EV	32145	13200	13500	14950	17300
Premium 3 Sedan 4D	GU5EV	33395	14050	14350	15750	18150
GS Sedan 4D	GV5EV	35310	15600	15900	17450	20200
LACROSSE—V6—Equipment Schedule 4						
W.B. 111.7"; 3.6 Liter.						
Sedan 4D	GA5ER	30820	12450	12750	14350	17100
Convenience Sedan	GB5ER	31290	13250	13550	15050	17750
Leather Sedan 4D	GC5ER	32755	14000	14350	15700	18400
Premium I Sedan 4D	GD5ER	33300	14500	14800	16300	19200
Premium II Sedan 4D	GF5E3	34725	15450	15800	17150	20100
Premium III Sedan 4D	GH5E3	36145	16000	16350	18000	21300
Touring Sedan 4D	GJ5E3	39130	16350	16700	18350	21700
AWD	L		1075	1075	1255	1255
4-Cyl, eAssist, 2.4 Liter	R		(625)	(625)	(730)	(730)

2013 BUICK — (1or2)G4(PP5SK)-D-#

VERANO—4-Cyl. Flex Fuel—Equipment Schedule 4
W.B. 105.7"; 2.4 Liter.

Body Type	VIN	List	Good	Very Good	Good	Excellent
Sedan 4D	PP5SK	23965	11450	11700	13300	15450
Convenience Sedan	PR5SK	25260	11950	12200	13900	16200
Leather Sedan	PS5SK	27640	12350	12600	14300	16700
VERANO—4-Cyl. Turbo—Equipment Schedule 4						
W.B. 105.7"; 2.0 Liter.						
Premium Sedan 4D	PT5SV	29990	13500	13800	15650	18200
REGAL—4-Cyl. eAssist—Equipment Schedule 4						
W.B. 107.8"; 2.4 Liter.						
Sedan 4D	GR5ER	29900	11800	12000	13950	16500
Premium 1 Sedan 4D	GS5ER	31520	12450	12650	14550	17150
Premium 2 Sedan 4D	GT5GR	32930	14050	14250	16250	19050
REGAL—4-Cyl. Turbo Flex Fuel—Equipment Schedule 4						
W.B. 107.8"; 2.0 Liter.						
Premium 1 Sedan 4D	GS5GV	31520	13100	13300	15400	18150
Premium 2 Sedan 4D	GT5GV	32930	14700	14950	17000	19800
Premium 3 Sedan 4D	GU5GV	34100	15250	15500	17550	20500
REGAL—4-Cyl. Turbo—Equipment Schedule 4						
W.B. 107.8"; 2.0 Liter.						
GS Sedan 4D	GV5GV	35865	17550	17800	19750	22700
LACROSSE—V6—Equipment Schedule 4						
W.B. 111.7"; 3.6 Liter.						
Sedan 4D	GA5ER	33555	14200	14400	16150	18950
Leather Sedan 4D	GC5ER	34745	15200	15450	17100	19900
Premium I Sedan 4D	GD5E3	36160	16700	17000	18700	21800
Premium II Sedan 4D	GF5E3	37580	17600	17850	19550	22700
Touring Sedan 4D	GJ5E3	40115	18450	18750	20600	24000
AWD			1175	1175	1365	1365
4-Cyl, eAssist, 2.4 Liter	R		(675)	(675)	(805)	(805)

2014 BUICK — (1or2)G4(PP5SK)-E-#

VERANO—4-Cyl. ECOTEC Flex Fuel—Equipment Schedule 4
W.B. 105.7"; 2.4 Liter.

Body Type	VIN	List	Good	Very Good	Good	Excellent
Sedan 4D	PP5SK	24625	12650	12900	14800	17200
Convenience Sedan	PR5SK	26145	13150	13400	15300	17850
Leather Sedan 4D	PS5SK	27825	14050	14350	16100	18550
VERANO—4-Cyl. ECOTEC Turbo—Equipment Schedule 4						
W.B. 105.7"; 2.0 Liter.						
Premium Sedan 4D	PT5SV	29990	14800	15100	16800	19200
REGAL—4-Cyl. Turbo—Equipment Schedule 4						
W.B. 107.8"; 2.0 Liter.						
Sedan 4D	GK5EX	30615	15650	15900	17850	20600
AWD	L		1225	1225	1380	1380
4-Cyl, 2.4 Liter	K		(725)	(725)	(820)	(820)
REGAL—4-Cyl. Turbo—Equipment Schedule 4						
W.B. 107.8"; 2.0 Liter.						
Premium II Sedan 4D	GR5GX	34685	19750	20000	21800	24800
GS Sedan 4D	GT5GX	37830	21400	21700	23500	26500
AWD	L		1225	1225	1380	1380
REGAL—4-Cyl. Turbo—Equipment Schedule 4						
W.B. 107.8"; 2.0 Liter.						

Body Type	VIN	List	Trade-In Good	Very Good	Pvt-Party Good	Retail Excellent
Premium I Sedan 4D GN5EX		32485	**16550**	**16800**	**18700**	**21500**
4-Cyl, eAssist, 2.4 Liter.......... R			**(725)**	**(725)**	**(815)**	**(815)**

LACROSSE—V6—Equipment Schedule 4
W.B. 111.7"; 3.6 Liter.

Body Type	VIN	List	Trade-In Good	Very Good	Pvt-Party Good	Retail Excellent
Sedan 4D.......... GA5G3		34060	**17950**	**18200**	**19800**	**22900**
Leather Sedan 4D.......... GB5G3		36135	**18850**	**19150**	**20600**	**23700**
Premium I Sedan 4D.......... GD5G3		39735	**21800**	**22100**	**23600**	**26900**
Premium II Sedan 4D.......... GD5G3		40280	**22800**	**23200**	**24600**	**28000**
AWD.......... C			**1225**	**1225**	**1405**	**1405**
4-Cyl, eAssist, 2.4 Liter.......... R			**(725)**	**(725)**	**(840)**	**(840)**

CADILLAC

2000 CADILLAC — (Wor1)(Gor0)6(VR52R)-Y-#

CATERA—V6—Equipment Schedule 2
W.B. 107.5"; 3.0 Liter.

Body Type	VIN	List	Trade-In Good	Very Good	Pvt-Party Good	Retail Excellent
Sedan 4D.......... VR52R		31500	**475**	**575**	**1075**	**1875**
Sport			**175**	**175**	**240**	**240**

ELDORADO—V8—Equipment Schedule 2
W.B. 108.0"; 4.6 Liter.

Body Type	VIN	List	Trade-In Good	Very Good	Pvt-Party Good	Retail Excellent
ESC Coupe 2D.......... EL12Y		39790	**1450**	**1625**	**2375**	**4050**
ETC Coupe 2D.......... ET129		43365	**2350**	**2675**	**3475**	**5725**

SEVILLE—V8—Equipment Schedule 2
W.B. 112.2"; 4.6 Liter.

Body Type	VIN	List	Trade-In Good	Very Good	Pvt-Party Good	Retail Excellent
SLS Sedan 4D.......... KS52Y		44550	**450**	**525**	**1050**	**1875**
STS Touring Sedan 4D.......... KY529		49150	**350**	**400**	**1150**	**2225**

DeVILLE—V8—Equipment Schedule 2
W.B. 115.3"; 4.6 Liter.

Body Type	VIN	List	Trade-In Good	Very Good	Pvt-Party Good	Retail Excellent
Sedan 4D.......... KD54Y		40955	**475**	**575**	**1250**	**2375**
DHS Sedan 4D.......... KE54Y		45370	**700**	**825**	**1625**	**3050**
DTS Sedan 4D.......... KF549		45370	**575**	**675**	**1575**	**3025**

2001 CADILLAC — (Wor1)(Gor0)6(VR52R)-1-#

CATERA—V6—Equipment Schedule 2
W.B. 107.4"; 3.0 Liter.

Body Type	VIN	List	Trade-In Good	Very Good	Pvt-Party Good	Retail Excellent
Sedan 4D.......... VR52R		31945	**550**	**625**	**1125**	**2000**
Sport Pkg.			**200**	**200**	**275**	**275**

ELDORADO—V8—Equipment Schedule 2
W.B. 108.0"; 4.6 Liter.

Body Type	VIN	List	Trade-In Good	Very Good	Pvt-Party Good	Retail Excellent
ESC Coupe 2D.......... EL12Y		40756	**1550**	**1750**	**2525**	**4275**
ETC Coupe 2D.......... ET129		44331	**2450**	**2750**	**3550**	**5800**

SEVILLE—V8—Equipment Schedule 2
W.B. 112.2"; 4.6 Liter.

Body Type	VIN	List	Trade-In Good	Very Good	Pvt-Party Good	Retail Excellent
SLS Sedan 4D.......... KS52Y		42655	**475**	**550**	**1100**	**1950**
STS Touring Sedan 4D.......... KY529		48765	**350**	**400**	**1175**	**2275**

DeVILLE—V8—Equipment Schedule 2
W.B. 115.3"; 4.6 Liter.

Body Type	VIN	List	Trade-In Good	Very Good	Pvt-Party Good	Retail Excellent
Sedan 4D.......... KD54Y		42000	**625**	**750**	**1450**	**2700**
DHS Sedan 4D.......... KE54Y		46987	**850**	**975**	**1850**	**3475**
DTS Sedan 4D.......... KF549		46987	**625**	**750**	**1700**	**3300**

2002 CADILLAC — 1G6(EL12Y)-2-#

ELDORADO—V8—Equipment Schedule 2
W.B. 108.0"; 4.6 Liter.

Body Type	VIN	List	Trade-In Good	Very Good	Pvt-Party Good	Retail Excellent
ESC Coupe 2D.......... EL12Y		42610	**1900**	**2125**	**2800**	**4625**
ETC Coupe 2D.......... ET129		45745	**2825**	**3150**	**3875**	**6175**
ECS Coupe 2D.......... ET129		48405	**3475**	**3875**	**4425**	**6825**

SEVILLE—V8—Equipment Schedule 2
W.B. 112.2"; 4.6 Liter.

Body Type	VIN	List	Trade-In Good	Very Good	Pvt-Party Good	Retail Excellent
SLS Sedan 4D.......... KS52Y		44269	**525**	**600**	**1150**	**2025**
STS Touring Sedan 4D.......... KY529		49825	**400**	**450**	**1250**	**2400**

DeVILLE—V8—Equipment Schedule 2
W.B. 115.3"; 4.6 Liter.

Body Type	VIN	List	Trade-In Good	Very Good	Pvt-Party Good	Retail Excellent
Sedan 4D.......... KD54Y		43070	**800**	**950**	**1675**	**3025**
DHS Sedan 4D.......... KE54Y		48000	**1000**	**1150**	**2000**	**3650**
DTS Sedan 4D.......... KF549		48000	**725**	**850**	**1850**	**3525**

2003 CADILLAC — 1G6(DM57N)-3-#

CTS—V6—Equipment Schedule 2
W.B. 113.4"; 3.2 Liter.

2003 CADILLAC

Body Type	VIN	List	Trade-In Good	Very Good	Pvt-Party Good	Retail Excellent
Sedan 4D	DM57N	31190	2125	2425	3075	4975
Luxury Sport Pkg			275	275	370	370
SEVILLE—V8—Equipment Schedule 2						
W.B. 112.2"; 4.6 Liter.						
SLS Sedan 4D	KS54Y	45270	500	575	1175	2075
STS Touring Sedan 4D	KY549	51175	625	700	1475	2725
DeVILLE—V8—Equipment Schedule 2						
W.B. 115.3"; 4.6 Liter.						
Sedan 4D	KD54Y	43995	850	1000	1750	3100
DHS Sedan 4D	KE54Y	48825	1025	1175	2150	3925
DTS Sedan 4D	KF549	48825	1000	1150	2275	4300

2004 CADILLAC — 1G6(DM57N)–4–#

Body Type	VIN	List	Trade-In Good	Very Good	Pvt-Party Good	Retail Excellent
CTS—V6—Equipment Schedule 2						
W.B. 113.4"; 3.2 Liter.						
Sedan 4D	DM57N	33155	2600	2925	3550	5575
Luxury Sport Pkg			300	300	400	400
V6, 3.6 Liter	7		450	450	595	595
CTS-V—V8—Equipment Schedule 2						
W.B. 113.4"; 5.7 Liter.						
Sedan 4D	DN57S	49995	7275	8025	8100	11450
SEVILLE—V8—Equipment Schedule 2						
W.B. 112.2"; 4.6 Liter.						
SLS Sedan 4D	KS52Y	47955	2250	2475	3300	5350
DEVILLE—V8—Equipment Schedule 2						
W.B. 115.3"; 4.6 Liter.						
Sedan 4D	KD54Y	45445	1550	1775	2450	3975
DHS Sedan 4D	KE54Y	50595	1825	2075	2975	4975
DTS Sedan 4D	KF549	50595	1800	2050	3050	5150
XLR—V8—Equipment Schedule 1						
W.B. 105.7"; 4.6 Liter.						
Hardtop Conv 2D	YV34A	76200	9225	9725	10750	13900

2005 CADILLAC — 1G6(DM56T)–5–#

Body Type	VIN	List	Trade-In Good	Very Good	Pvt-Party Good	Retail Excellent
CTS—V6—Equipment Schedule 2						
W.B. 113.4"; 2.8 Liter.						
Sedan 4D	DM56T	33595	3000	3400	4250	6500
Luxury Pkg			325	325	430	430
V6, 3.6 Liter	7		475	475	635	635
CTS-V—V8—Equipment Schedule 2						
W.B. 113.4"; 5.7 Liter.						
Sedan 4D	DN56S	49995	8225	9025	9250	12800
STS—V6—Equipment Schedule 2						
W.B. 116.6"; 3.6 Liter.						
Sedan 4D	DW677	40995	3200	3550	4375	6625
Adaptive Cruise Control			300	300	385	385
AWD			1375	1375	1835	1835
V8, 4.6 Liter	A		575	575	780	780
DEVILLE—V8—Equipment Schedule 2						
W.B. 115.3"; 4.6 Liter.						
Sedan 4D	KD54Y	46490	1575	1800	2775	4550
DHS Sedan 4D	KE54Y	52045	2175	2475	3650	6050
DTS Sedan 4D	KF549	52045	2350	2675	3725	6050
XLR—V8—Equipment Schedule 1						
W.B. 105.7"; 4.6 Liter.						
Hardtop Conv 2D	YV34A	76650	13100	13750	14500	18050

2006 CADILLAC — 1G6(DM57T)–6–#

Body Type	VIN	List	Trade-In Good	Very Good	Pvt-Party Good	Retail Excellent
CTS—V6—Equipment Schedule 2						
W.B. 113.4"; 2.8 Liter.						
Sedan 4D	DM57T	32435	4125	4575	5325	7775
Luxury Pkg			350	350	460	460
V6, 3.6 Liter	7		500	500	670	670
CTS-V—V8—Equipment Schedule 2						
W.B. 113.4"; 6.0 Liter.						
Sedan 4D	DN57U	51395	9500	10350	10500	14250
STS—V6—Equipment Schedule 2						
W.B. 116.4"; 3.6 Liter.						
Sedan 4D	DW677	41740	4075	4475	5200	7525
AWD			1500	1500	1990	1990
V8, 4.6 Liter	A		725	725	970	970

2006 CADILLAC

Body Type	VIN	List	Trade-In Good	Very Good	Pvt-Party Good	Retail Excellent
STS-V—V8 Supercharged—Equipment Schedule 2						
W.B. 116.4"; 4.4 Liter.						
Sedan 4D	DX67D	77090	11050	12050	12500	17300
DTS—V8—Equipment Schedule 2						
W.B. 115.6"; 4.6 Liter.						
Sedan 4D	KD57Y	41990	4100	4600	5575	8425
Luxury Pkg			1050	1050	1400	1400
Performance Pkg			1050	1050	1410	1410
XLR—V8—Equipment Schedule 1						
W.B. 105.7"; 4.6 Liter.						
Hardtop Conv 2D	YV36A	77295	14150	14850	15550	19150
Star Black Ltd Conv	YV36A	79795	17650	18500	19300	23800
XLR-V—V8 Supercharged—Equipment Schedule 1						
W.B. 105.7"; 4.4 Liter.						
Convertible 2D	YX36D	98300	19650	20600	21400	26300

2007 CADILLAC — 1G6(DM57T)-7-#

Body Type	VIN	List	Trade-In Good	Very Good	Pvt-Party Good	Retail Excellent
CTS—V6—Equipment Schedule 2						
W.B. 113.4"; 2.8 Liter.						
Sedan 4D	DM57T	31390	5025	5525	6250	8625
Luxury Pkg			375	375	490	490
V6, 3.6 Liter	7		525	525	710	710
CTS-V—V8—Equipment Schedule 2						
W.B. 113.4"; 6.0 Liter.						
Sedan 4D	DN57U	53205	10500	11400	11650	15500
DTS—V8—Equipment Schedule 2						
W.B 115.6"; 4.6 Liter.						
Sedan 4D	KD57Y	41990	5025	5600	6250	8775
Luxury Pkg			1125	1125	1515	1515
Performance Pkg			1150	1150	1520	1520
STS—V6—Equipment Schedule 2						
W.B. 116.4"; 3.6 Liter.						
Sedan 4D	DW677	42765	5150	5600	6525	9200
Platinum Edition			1100	1100	1475	1475
4-AWD			1600	1600	2145	2145
V8, 4.6 Liter	A		925	925	1220	1220
STS-V—V8 Supercharged—Equipment Schedule 2						
W.B. 116.4"; 4.4 Liter.						
Sedan 4D	DX67D	77485	12150	13150	13900	19000
XLR—V8—Equipment Schedule 1						
W.B. 105.7"; 4.6 Liter.						
Hardtop Conv 2D	YV36A	78495	16100	16800	17500	21200
Platinum Edition			1100	1100	1210	1210
XLR-V—V8 Supercharged—Equipment Schedule 1						
W.B. 105.7"; 4.4 Liter.						
Convertible 2D	YX36D	100000	22700	23700	24200	29200

2008 CADILLAC — 1G6(DF577)-8-#

Body Type	VIN	List	Trade-In Good	Very Good	Pvt-Party Good	Retail Excellent
CTS—V6—Equipment Schedule 2						
W.B. 113.4"; 3.6 Liter.						
Sedan 4D	DF577	34290	8600	9250	9925	12850
Luxury Pkg			400	400	500	500
Performance Pkg			1225	1225	1560	1560
Premium Luxury Collection			1225	1225	1560	1560
AWD	G,H,S,T		1725	1725	2200	2200
V6, DI, 3.6 Liter	V		1125	1125	1420	1420
DTS—V8—Equipment Schedule 2						
W.B. 115.6"; 4.6 Liter.						
Sedan 4D	KD57Y	42590	6725	7375	8025	10700
Luxury Pkg			1225	1225	1565	1565
Performance Pkg			1225	1225	1565	1565
Platinum Edition			1175	1175	1510	1510
STS—V6—Equipment Schedule 2						
W.B. 116.4"; 3.6 Liter.						
Sedan 4D	DW67V	43135	6600	7075	8000	10600
Platinum Edition			1175	1175	1515	1515
AWD	A,D,B,L		1725	1725	2215	2215
V8, 4.6 Liter	A		1100	1100	1420	1420
STS-V—V8 Supercharged—Equipment Schedule 2						
W.B. 116.4"; 4.4 Liter.						
Sedan 4D	DX67D	79000	13850	14800	15400	19800

2008 CADILLAC

Body Type	VIN	List	Trade-In Good	Very Good	Pvt-Party Good	Retail Excellent
XLR—V8—Equipment Schedule 1						
W.B. 105.7"; 4.6 Liter.						
Hartop Conv 2D	YV36A	79600	**18450**	**19200**	**20200**	**24100**
Platinum Edition			1175	1175	1280	1280
XLR-V—V8 Supercharged—Equipment Schedule 1						
W.B. 105.7"; 4.4 Liter.						
Convertible 2D	YX36D	100000	**25000**	**26000**	**26900**	**31800**

2009 CADILLAC — 1G6(DF577)-9-#

Body Type	VIN	List	Trade-In Good	Very Good	Pvt-Party Good	Retail Excellent
CTS—V6—Equipment Schedule 2						
W.B. 113.4"; 3.6 Liter.						
Sedan 4D	DF577	36080	**10200**	**10800**	**11700**	**14650**
Luxury Pkg			450	450	560	560
Performance Pkg			1300	1300	1630	1630
Premium Pkg			1300	1300	1630	1630
AWD	G,H,S,T		1850	1850	2300	2300
V6, DI, 3.6 Liter	V		1175	1175	1480	1480
CTS-V—V8—Equipment Schedule 2						
W.B. 113.4"; 6.2 Liter.						
Sedan 4D	DN57P	62595	**24300**	**25700**	**25100**	**29700**
DTS—V8—Equipment Schedule 2						
W.B. 115.6"; 4.6 Liter.						
Sedan 4D	KD57Y	44900	**8875**	**9625**	**10450**	**13550**
Performance Pkg			1300	1300	1645	1645
Platinum Edition			1250	1250	1580	1580
STS—V6—Equipment Schedule 2						
W.B. 116.4"; 3.6 Liter.						
Sedan 4D	DW67V	45290	**9250**	**9775**	**10950**	**14000**
Platinum Edition			1250	1250	1540	1540
AWD	A,D,B,L		1850	1850	2265	2265
V8, 4.6 Liter	Λ		1300	1300	1590	1590
STS-V—V8 Supercharged—Equipment Schedule 2						
W.B. 116.4"; 4.4 Liter.						
Sedan 4D	DX67D	81940	**20300**	**21400**	**22700**	**28600**
XLR—V8—Equipment Schedule 1						
W.B. 105.7"; 4.6 Liter.						
Platinum Conv 2D	YV36A	83530	**24400**	**25300**	**26400**	**30600**
XLR-V—V8 Supercharged—Equipment Schedule 1						
W.B. 105.7"; 4.4 Liter.						
Convertible 2D	YX36D	102530	**29000**	**30000**	**31300**	**36400**

2010 CADILLAC — 1G6(DA5EG)-A-#

Body Type	VIN	List	Trade-In Good	Very Good	Pvt-Party Good	Retail Excellent
CTS—V6—Equipment Schedule 2						
W.B. 113.4"; 3.0 Liter.						
Sedan 4D	DA5EG	37270	**12250**	**12800**	**13900**	**16800**
Wagon 4D	DA8EG	39090	**12900**	**13450**	**14650**	**17700**
Luxury Pkg			525	525	640	640
4-AWD	C,D,G,H		1950	1950	2385	2385
CTS—V6 DI—Equipment Schedule 2						
W.B. 113.4"; 3.6 Liter.						
3.6 Sedan 4D	DJ5EV	42390	**13950**	**14550**	**15750**	**19050**
3.6 Wagon 4D	DJ8EV	44190	**14650**	**15300**	**16450**	**19850**
4-AWD	L,M,R,S		1950	1950	2380	2380
CTS-V—V8 Supercharged—Equipment Schedule 2						
W.B. 113.4"; 6.2 Liter.						
Sedan 4D	DV5EP	64145	**27500**	**28700**	**28500**	**33000**
DTS—V8—Equipment Schedule 2						
W.B. 115.6"; 4.6 Liter.						
Sedan 4D	KA5EY	47200	**11150**	**12000**	**13000**	**16450**
Luxury Collection			1400	1400	1745	1745
Premium Collection			1200	1200	1505	1505
Platinum Collection			1325	1325	1660	1660
STS—V6—Equipment Schedule 2						
W.B. 116.4"; 3.6 Liter.						
Sedan 4D	DU6EV	47670	**10700**	**11200**	**12800**	**16050**
4-AWD			1950	1950	2385	2385
V8, 4.6 Liter	A		1475	1475	1810	1810

2011 CADILLAC — 1G6(DA5EY)-B-#

Body Type	VIN	List	Trade-In Good	Very Good	Pvt-Party Good	Retail Excellent
CTS—V6—Equipment Schedule 2						
W.B. 113.4"; 3.0 Liter.						
Sedan 4D	DA5EY	37580	**14100**	**14550**	**15850**	**18600**

Body Type	VIN	List	Trade-In Good	Very Good	Pvt-Party Good	Retail Excellent
Sport Wagon 4D	DA8EY	39090	15450	15950	17300	20300
Luxury Pkg			575	575	705	705
Performance Pkg			1475	1475	1780	1780
4-AWD	C,D		2000	2000	2415	2415
CTS—V6 DI—Equipment Schedule 2						
W.B. 113.4"; 3.6 Liter.						
3.6 Sedan 4D	D15ED	42605	16350	16900	18200	21300
3.6 Coupe 2D	DJ1ED	39230	17050	17600	18950	22200
3.6 Sport Wagon 4D	DJ8ED	44190	17100	17650	19050	22300
4-AWD	L,M		2000	2000	2410	2410
CTS-V—V8 Supercharged—Equipment Schedule 2						
W.B. 113.4"; 6.2 Liter.						
Sedan 4D	DV5EP	65820	30400	31600	32000	36300
Coupe 2D	DV1EP	65820	30800	32000	32400	36800
Wagon 4D	DV8EP	64290	31100	32300	32700	37100
DTS—V8—Equipment Schedule 2						
W.B. 115.6"; 4.6 Liter.						
Sedan 4D	KA5E6	47600	14850	15850	17100	21100
Luxury Collection			1475	1475	1740	1740
Premium Collection			1275	1275	1500	1500
Platinum Collection			1400	1400	1655	1655
STS—V6—Equipment Schedule 2						
W.B. 116.4"; 3.6 Liter.						
Sedan 4D	DU6ED	48105	14200	14750	16300	19400
AWD			2000	2000	2390	2390

2012 CADILLAC — 1G6(DA5E5)-C-#

Body Type	VIN	List	Trade-In Good	Very Good	Pvt-Party Good	Retail Excellent
CTS—V6—Equipment Schedule 2						
W.B. 113.4"; 3.0 Liter.						
Sedan 4D	DA5E5	36189	16650	17050	18450	21200
Sport Wagon 4D	DA8E5	39890	18400	18900	20300	23300
Luxury Pkg			625	625	750	750
Touring Pkg			825	825	990	990
AWD	C,D		2000	2000	2370	2370
CTS—V6 DI—Equipment Schedule 2						
W.B. 113.4"; 3.6 Liter.						
3.6 Coupe 2D	DJ1E3	39590	20300	20800	22300	25500
Touring Luxury			825	825	985	985
Performance Luxury			1175	1175	1385	1385
Performance Pkg			1500	1500	1770	1770
Premium Pkg			1950	1950	2300	2300
AWD	L		2000	2000	2355	2355
CTS—V6 DI—Equipment Schedule 2						
W.B. 113.4"; 3.6 Liter.						
3.6 Sedan 4D	DJ5E3	43165	20400	20900	22400	25600
3.6 Sport Wagon 4D	DA8E3	45065	21700	22200	23700	27200
Touring Pkg			825	825	985	985
Performance Luxury			1175	1175	1385	1385
Premium Pkg			1950	1950	2295	2295
AWD	L		2000	2000	2355	2355
CTS-V—V8 Supercharged—Equipment Schedule 2						
W.B. 113.4"; 6.2 Liter.						
Sedan 4D	DV5EP	65390	33000	34100	34900	39000
Coupe 2D	DV1EP	66710	33500	34600	35400	39600
Sport Wagon 4D	DV8EP	65390	34900	36000	36700	41000

2013 CADILLAC — 1G6(AA5SA)-D-#

Body Type	VIN	List	Trade-In Good	Very Good	Pvt-Party Good	Retail Excellent
ATS—4-Cyl.—Equipment Schedule 2						
W.B. 109.3"; 2.5 Liter.						
2.5L Standard Sedan	AA5SA	33990	16750	17300	18900	21700
2.5L Luxury Sedan 4D	AB5SA	38485	17600	18150	19850	22800
ATS—4-Cyl. Turbo—Equipment Schedule 2						
W.B. 109.3"; 2.0 Liter.						
2.0L Standard Sed	AA5SX	35795	17100	17600	19300	22200
2.0L Luxury Sed 4D	AB5SX	40290	18350	18900	20600	23700
2.0L Performance Sed	AC5SX	42790	20300	21000	22700	26100
2.0L Premium Sedan	AE5SX	45790	22000	22600	24500	28100
AWD	J		2000	2000	2295	2295
ATS—V6 Flex Fuel—Equipment Schedule 2						
W.B. 109.3"; 3.6 Liter.						
3.6L Luxury Sedan 4D	AB5S3	42090	19400	20000	21800	25100
3.6L Performance Sed	AC5S3	44590	21300	22000	23800	27400

Body Type	VIN	List	Trade-In Good	Very Good	Pvt-Party Good	Retail Excellent
3.6L Premium Sedan	AE5S3	47590	22800	23500	25300	29000
AWD	H		2000	2000	2300	2300
XTS—V6 Flex Fuel—Equipment Schedule 2						
W.B. 111.7"; 3.6 Liter.						
Sedan 4D	1N5S3	44995	22500	23200	25000	28600
Luxury Sedan 4D	1P5S3	49610	24600	25300	27300	31300
Premium Sedan 4D	1S5S3	54505	25900	26700	28600	32600
Platinum Sedan 4D	1U5S3	59080	29000	29900	31600	35800
AWD	R		2000	2000	2250	2250
CTS—V6—Equipment Schedule 2						
W.B. 113.4"; 3.0 Liter.						
3.0 Luxury Sedan 4D	DE5E5	39990	18300	18700	20400	23200
3.0 Luxury Sport Wag	DE8E5	43045	20800	21300	23000	26200
3.0 Sport Wagon 4D	DA8E5	40100	19400	19750	21400	24400
Touring Pkg			875	875	1045	1045
AWD	G,H		2000	2000	2360	2360
CTS—V6 DI—Equipment Schedule 2						
W.B. 113.4"; 3.6 Liter.						
3.6 Coupe 2D	DA1E3	39800	21100	21600	23300	26500
3.6 Performance Sedan	DJ5E3	44235	21900	22300	24000	27200
3.6 Performance Coupe	DJ1E3	44845	23100	23600	25300	28800
3.6 Performance Wag	DJ8E3	45085	23000	23500	25200	28700
3.6 Premium Sedan 4D	DP5E3	49185	23200	23700	25400	28900
3.6 Premium Coupe 2D	DP1E3	49045	25900	26400	28100	31900
3.6 Premium Wagon 4D	DP8E3	50645	25600	26100	27900	31600
Touring Pkg			875	875	1040	1040
AWD	L,M		2000	2000	2340	2340
CTS-V—V8 Supercharged—Equipment Schedule 2						
W.B. 113.4"; 6.2 Liter.						
Sedan 4D	DV5EP	65410	35800	36900	37800	42000
Coupe 2D	DV1EP	65410	37600	38700	39600	44000
Sport Wagon 4D	DV8EP	65410	38000	39200	40000	44400

2014 CADILLAC — 1G6(AA5RA)-E-#

Body Type	VIN	List	Trade-In Good	Very Good	Pvt-Party Good	Retail Excellent
ATS—4-Cyl.—Equipment Schedule 2						
W.B. 109.3"; 2.5 Liter.						
2.5L Standard Sedan	AA5RA	33990	19500	20100	21600	24400
2.5L Luxury Sedan 4D	AB5RA	38020	20900	21500	23000	26100
ATS—4-Cyl. Turbo—Equipment Schedule 2						
W.B. 109.3"; 2.0 Liter.						
2.0L Standard Sedan	AA5RX	36020	20100	20700	22200	25100
2.0L Luxury Sed 4D	AB5RX	40020	21700	22400	23900	27000
2.0L Performance Sed	AC5RX	43020	24100	24800	26300	29600
2.0L Premium Sedan	AE5RX	46020	25700	26500	28000	31600
AWD	G		2000	2000	2290	2290
ATS—V6 Flex Fuel—Equipment Schedule 2						
W.B. 109.3"; 3.6 Liter.						
3.6L Luxury Sedan 4D	AB5R3	42020	23700	24400	25900	29100
3.6L Performance Sed	AC5R3	45020	24900	25700	27200	30600
3.6L Premium Sedan	AE5R3	48020	26400	27200	28700	32400
AWD	H		2000	2000	2270	2270
XTS—V6 Flex Fuel—Equipment Schedule 2						
W.B. 111.7"; 3.6 Liter.						
Sedan 4D	1L5S3	45525	26800	27600	29300	33100
Luxury Sedan 4D	1M5S3	50435	28900	29700	31600	35700
Premium Sedan 4D	1P5S3	55380	30200	31100	32800	37000
Platinum Sedan 4D	1S5S3	62675	33400	34400	35900	40300
Sensing Cruise Control			500	500	545	545
Driver Assist Pkg			675	675	735	735
AWD	N		2000	2000	2210	2210
XTS AWD—V6 Twin Turbo—Equipment Schedule 2						
W.B. 111.7"; 3.6 Liter.						
Vsport Premium Sed	1V5S8	63020	36000	37100	38400	42800
Vsport Platinum Sed	1W5S8	70020	41300	42500	43500	48100
Adaptive Cruise Control			500	500	540	540
Driver Assist Pkg			675	675	735	735
CTS—4-Cyl. Turbo—Equipment Schedule 2						
W.B. 113.4"; 2.0 Liter.						
2.0 Standard Sedan 4D	AP5EX	46025	25800	26300	27800	31100
2.0 Luxury Sedan 4D	AR5EX	51925	29900	30500	32000	35600
2.0 Performance Sedan	AS5SX	58325	33000	33600	35000	38800
Adaptive Cruise Control			500	500	545	545
Full Leather			675	675	740	740

Body Type	VIN	List	Trade-In Good	Very Good	Pvt-Party Good	Retail Excellent
AWD	W		2000	2000	2295	2295

CTS—4-Cyl. Turbo—Equipment Schedule 2
W.B. 113.4"; 2.0 Liter.

Body Type	VIN	List	Good	Very Good	Good	Excellent
2.0 Premium Sedan 4D	AT5SX	62725	36700	37400	38600	42700
AWD	Z		2000	2000	2220	2220

CTS—V6—Equipment Schedule 2
W.B. 113.4"; 3.0 Liter, 3.6 Liter.

Body Type	VIN	List	Good	Very Good	Good	Excellent
3.6 Coupe 2D	DA1E3	40420	24200	24700	26400	29700
3.6 Performance Cpe	DC1E3	44720	26000	26500	28200	31700
3.6 Performance Wagon	DC8E3	45120	25500	26000	27600	30900
3.6 Luxury Sedan 4D	AR5S3	54625	31600	32200	33600	37400
3.0 Luxury Sport Wag	DB8E5	43120	24500	25000	26600	29800
3.6 Performance Sedan	AS5S3	61025	33600	34300	35600	39500
3.6 Premium Sedan 4D	AT5S3	65425	37400	38100	39300	43500
3.6 Premium Coupe 2D	DD1E3	48920	27800	28300	30000	33700
3.6 Premium Wagon	DD8E3	50720	27500	28000	29700	33400
Adaptive Cruise Control			500	500	550	550
Full Leather			675	675	745	745
Luxury Pkg			725	725	840	840
Performance Luxury Pkg			1300	1300	1505	1505
Touring Pkg			925	925	1070	1070
AWD	X		2000	2000	2240	2240

CTS—V6 Twin Turbo—Equipment Schedule 2
W.B. 113.4"; 3.6 Liter.

Body Type	VIN	List	Good	Very Good	Good	Excellent
3.6 Vsport Sedan 4D	AU5S8	59995	34400	35100	36600	40700
3.6 Vsport Premium 4D	AV5S8	69995	40600	41400	42600	47100

CTS-V—V8 Supercharged—Equipment Schedule 2
W.B. 113.4"; 6.2 Liter.

Body Type	VIN	List	Good	Very Good	Good	Excellent
Sedan 4D	DD5EP	65825	42800	44100	44700	49100
Coupe 2D	DV1EP	65825	44600	45900	46500	51100
Sport Wagon 4D	DV8EP	65825	45100	46400	46900	51500
RECARO Seats			575	575	630	630

ELR—Electric—Equipment Schedule 2
W.B. 106.1".

Body Type	VIN	List	Good	Very Good	Good	Excellent
Coupe 2D	RL1E4	75995	35400	36700	37200	41900
Adaptive Cruise Control			500	500	530	530
Luxury Pkg			725	725	795	795

CHEVROLET

2000 CHEVROLET — (1,2or3)(C,GorY)1(MR226)-Y-#

METRO—3-Cyl.—Equipment Schedule 6
W.B. 93.1"; 1.0 Liter.

Body Type	VIN	List	Good	Very Good	Good	Excellent
Coupe 2D	MR226	10680	475	575	1100	2100

METRO—4-Cyl.—Equipment Schedule 6
W.B. 93.1"; 1.3 Liter.

Body Type	VIN	List	Good	Very Good	Good	Excellent
LSi Sedan 4D	MR522	12395	650	775	1300	2400
LSi Coupe 2D	MR222	11530	625	750	1250	2325

PRIZM—4-Cyl.—Equipment Schedule 6
W.B. 97.1"; 1.8 Liter.

Body Type	VIN	List	Good	Very Good	Good	Excellent
Sedan 4D	SK528	14246	475	600	1125	2125
LSi Sedan 4D	SK528	16272	675	825	1375	2525

CAVALIER—4-Cyl.—Equipment Schedule 5
W.B. 104.1"; 2.2 Liter, 2.4 Liter.

Body Type	VIN	List	Good	Very Good	Good	Excellent
Sedan 4D	JC524	14275	400	500	1125	2200
Coupe 2D	JC124	14175	375	450	1075	2150
LS Sedan 4D	JF524	15220	575	700	1375	2675
Z24 Coupe 2D	JF12T	17560	900	1075	1625	2975
Z24 Convertible 2D	JF32T	21025	1225	1475	2150	3950

MALIBU—V6—Equipment Schedule 5
W.B. 107.0"; 3.1 Liter.

Body Type	VIN	List	Good	Very Good	Good	Excellent
Sedan 4D	ND52J	16995	500	625	1450	2875
LS Sedan 4D	NE52J	19625	950	1150	1875	3525

LUMINA—V6—Equipment Schedule 4
W.B. 107.5"; 3.1 Liter.

Body Type	VIN	List	Good	Very Good	Good	Excellent
Sedan 4D	WL52J	19350	550	650	1050	1800

IMPALA—V6—Equipment Schedule 4
W.B. 110.5"; 3.4 Liter, 3.8 Liter.

Body Type	VIN	List	Good	Very Good	Good	Excellent
Sedan 4D	WF52K	19787	600	700	1300	2325
LS Sedan 4D	WH52K	22925	950	1075	1725	3025

2000 CHEVROLET

Body Type	VIN	List	Trade-In Good	Very Good	Pvt-Party Good	Retail Excellent
MONTE CARLO—V6—Equipment Schedule 4						
W.B. 110.5"; 3.4 Liter, 3.8 Liter.						
LS Coupe 2D	WW12E	20090	600	700	1275	2325
SS Coupe 2D	WX12K	22295	1025	1150	1825	3275
CAMARO—V6—Equipment Schedule 4						
W.B. 101.1"; 3.8 Liter.						
Coupe 2D	FP22K	19360	1375	1550	2050	3425
Convertible 2D	FP32K	25490	2450	2775	3125	4900
T-Bar Roof			225	225	300	300
Manual, 5-Spd			(175)	(175)	(220)	(220)
CAMARO—V8—Equipment Schedule 4						
W.B. 101.1"; 5.7 Liter.						
Z28 Coupe 2D	FP22G	23515	2450	2775	3125	4900
Z28 Convertible 2D	FP32G	28900	4350	4875	5150	7875
T-Bar Roof			225	225	300	300
SS Pkg			625	625	820	820
CORVETTE—V8—Equipment Schedule 2						
W.B. 104.5"; 5.7 Liter.						
Hard Top 2D	YY12G	39205	6350	6750	7675	10400
CORVETTE—V8—Equipment Schedule 2						
W.B. 104.5"; 5.7 Liter.						
Coupe 2D	YY22G	40085	6150	6550	7500	10200
Convertible 2D	YY32G	46510	8150	8675	9350	12300
Glass Roof Panel			250	250	290	290
Dual Roof Panels			300	300	350	350
Suspension Pkg			200	200	230	230
Manual, 6-Spd			150	150	175	175

2001 CHEVROLET — (1or2)(C,GorY)(MR522)–1–#

Body Type	VIN	List	Trade-In Good	Very Good	Pvt-Party Good	Retail Excellent
METRO—4-Cyl.—Equipment Schedule 6						
W.B. 93.1"; 1.3 Liter.						
LSi Sedan 4D	MR522	12915	700	850	1400	2575
PRIZM—4-Cyl.—Equipment Schedule 6						
W.B. 97.0"; 1.8 Liter.						
Sedan 4D	SK528	14460	500	625	1175	2175
LSi Sedan 4D	SK528	16525	750	900	1425	2600
CAVALIER—4-Cyl.—Equipment Schedule 5						
W.B. 104.1"; 2.2 Liter, 2.4 Liter.						
Sedan 4D	JC524	14480	450	550	1175	2275
Coupe 2D	JC124	14380	425	525	1150	2250
LS Sedan 4D	JF524	15375	625	750	1400	2700
Z24 Coupe 2D	JF12T	17665	1025	1225	1850	3400
MALIBU—V6—Equipment Schedule 5						
W.B. 107.0"; 3.1 Liter.						
Sedan 4D	ND52J	17595	625	750	1600	3100
LS Sedan 4D	NE52J	19875	1050	1250	2000	3700
LUMINA—V6—Equipment Schedule 4						
W.B. 107.5"; 3.1 Liter.						
Sedan 4D	WL52J	19490	650	750	1150	1975
IMPALA—V6—Equipment Schedule 4						
W.B. 110.5"; 3.4 Liter, 3.8 Liter.						
Sedan 4D	WF52E	20271	725	825	1400	2425
LS Sedan 4D	WH52K	23825	1200	1350	1975	3375
MONTE CARLO—V6—Equipment Schedule 4						
W.B. 110.5"; 3.4 Liter, 3.8 Liter.						
LS Coupe 2D	WW12E	20410	750	850	1475	2675
SS Coupe 2D	WX15K	23000	1200	1375	2125	3775
CAMARO—V6—Equipment Schedule 4						
W.B. 101.1"; 3.8 Liter.						
Coupe 2D	FP22K	19635	1475	1650	2275	3800
Convertible 2D	FP32K	25760	2775	3100	3475	5425
T-Bar Roof			225	225	300	300
RS			75	75	105	105
Manual, 5-Spd			(150)	(150)	(200)	(200)
CAMARO—V8—Equipment Schedule 4						
W.B. 101.1"; 5.7 Liter.						
Z28 Coupe 2D	FP22G	23935	2900	3225	3600	5625
Z28 Convertible 2D	FP32G	29325	5175	5775	6100	9275
T-Bar Roof			225	225	300	300
SS Pkg			725	725	955	955
CORVETTE—V8—Equipment Schedule 2						
W.B. 104.5"; 5.7 Liter.						
Coupe 2D	YY22G	40475	6800	7200	8150	10900

2001 CHEVROLET

Body Type	VIN	List	Trade-In Good	Very Good	Pvt-Party Good	Retail Excellent
Z06 Hard Top 2D	YY12G	47500	7900	8400	9125	11850
Convertible 2D	YY32G	47000	8750	9300	10000	13000
Glass Roof Panel		------	250	250	285	285
Dual Roof Panels		------	300	300	345	345
Suspension Pkg		------	200	200	230	230
Z51 Handling		------	200	200	230	230
Manual, 6-Spd		------	150	150	170	170

2002 CHEVROLET — (1or2)(GorY)1(SK528)-2-#

PRIZM—4-Cyl.—Equipment Schedule 6
W.B. 97.0"; 1.8 Liter.

Body Type	VIN	List	Trade-In Good	Very Good	Pvt-Party Good	Retail Excellent
Sedan 4D	SK528	14815	600	725	1350	2575
LSi Sedan 4D	SK528	16880	750	875	1425	2600
CAVALIER—4-Cyl.—Equipment Schedule 5 W.B. 104.1"; 2.2 Liter, 2.4 Liter.						
Sedan 4D	JC124	15280	525	625	1275	2425
Coupe 2D	JC124	15180	475	600	1275	2450
LS Sedan 4D	JF524	16330	725	875	1525	2875
LS Coupe 2D	JS124	16230	650	800	1450	2725
LS Sport Sedan 4D	JF52F	17700	900	1075	1750	3250
LS Sport Coupe 2D	JS12F	17600	900	1075	1750	3250
Z24 Sedan 4D	JH52T	17900	1025	1200	1625	2775
Z24 Coupe 2D	JF12T	17800	1150	1350	2025	3725
MALIBU—V6—Equipment Schedule 5 W.B. 107.0"; 3.1 Liter.						
Sedan 4D	ND52J	18120	775	925	1725	3225
LS Sedan 4D	NE52J	20325	1150	1375	2175	3950
IMPALA—V6—Equipment Schedule 4 W.B. 110.5"; 3.4 Liter, 3.8 Liter.						
Sedan 4D	WF52E	20820	850	950	1525	2650
LS Sedan 4D	WH52K	24270	1400	1575	2225	3775
MONTE CARLO—V6—Equipment Schedule 4 W.B. 110.5"; 3.4 Liter, 3.8 Liter.						
LS Coupe 2D	WW12E	20920	875	1000	1600	2825
SS Coupe 2D	WX12K	23470	1400	1575	2350	4125
CAMARO—V6—Equipment Schedule 4 W.B. 101.1"; 3.8 Liter.						
Coupe 2D	FP22K	20640	1825	2050	2600	4175
Convertible 2D	FP32K	26650	3150	3525	3875	5825
T-Bar Roof		------	225	225	300	300
RS		------	75	75	115	115
Manual, 5-Spd		------	(175)	(175)	(245)	(245)
CAMARO—V8—Equipment Schedule 4 W.B. 101.1"; 5.7 Liter.						
Z28 Coupe 2D	FP22G	24770	3375	3775	4125	6175
Z28 Convertible 2D	FP32G	30165	6025	6700	6900	10150
T-Bar Roof		------	225	225	290	290
35th Anniversary		------	100	100	130	130
SS Pkg		------	825	825	1080	1080
CORVETTE—V8—Equipment Schedule 2 W.B. 104.5"; 5.7 Liter.						
Coupe 2D	YY22G	41650	7600	8050	8900	11700
Z06 Hard Top 2D	YY12G	50350	8550	9075	9725	12500
Convertible 2D	YY32G	48175	9550	10100	10750	13800
Glass Roof Panel		------	250	250	285	285
Dual Roof Panels		------	300	300	340	340
Suspension Pkg		------	200	200	225	225
Z51 Handling		------	200	200	225	225
Manual, 6-Spd		------	150	150	170	170

2003 CHEVROLET — (1or2)G1(JC52F)-3-#

CAVALIER—4-Cyl.—Equipment Schedule 5
W.B. 104.1"; 2.2 Liter.

Body Type	VIN	List	Trade-In Good	Very Good	Pvt-Party Good	Retail Excellent
Sedan 4D	JC52F	15520	625	750	1350	2525
Coupe 2D	JC12F	15370	625	750	1400	2625
LS Sedan 4D	JF52F	16920	975	1125	1750	3150
LS Coupe 2D	JF12F	16770	975	1125	1775	3225
LS Sport Sedan 4D	JH52F	18120	1125	1325	1925	3400
LS Sport Coupe 2D	JH12F	17970	1075	1275	1925	3450
MALIBU—V6—Equipment Schedule 5 W.B. 107.0"; 3.1 Liter.						
Sedan 4D	ND52J	18290	1000	1175	1925	3525

2003 CHEVROLET

Body Type	VIN	List	Trade-In Good	Very Good	Pvt-Party Good	Retail Excellent
LS Sedan 4D	NE52J	20575	**1300**	**1550**	**2275**	**4025**
IMPALA—V6—Equipment Schedule 4						
W.B. 110.5"; 3.4 Liter, 3.8 Liter.						
Sedan 4D	WF52E	21350	**1100**	**1225**	**1950**	**3350**
LS Sedan 4D	WH52K	24460	**1475**	**1650**	**2500**	**4225**
MONTE CARLO—V6—Equipment Schedule 4						
W.B. 110.5"; 3.4 Liter, 3.8 Liter.						
LS Coupe 2D	WW12E	21350	**1100**	**1225**	**1925**	**3350**
SS Coupe 2D	WX12K	23665	**1600**	**1800**	**2550**	**4350**
CORVETTE—V8—Equipment Schedule 2						
W.B. 104.5"; 5.7 Liter.						
Coupe 2D	YY22G	43895	**9125**	**9650**	**10400**	**13400**
Z06 Hard Top 2D	YY12S	51155	**10150**	**10700**	**11400**	**14550**
Convertible 2D	YY32G	50370	**10900**	**11550**	**12050**	**15200**
50th Anniversary			**1775**	**1775**	**1965**	**1965**
Glass Roof Panel			**250**	**250**	**275**	**275**
Dual Roof Panels			**300**	**300**	**335**	**335**
Suspension Pkg			**200**	**200**	**220**	**220**
Z51 Handling			**200**	**200**	**220**	**220**
Manual, 6-Spd			**150**	**150**	**165**	**165**

2004 CHEVROLET — (1,2orK)(GorL)1(TD526)-4-#

Body Type	VIN	List	Trade-In Good	Very Good	Pvt-Party Good	Retail Excellent
AVEO—4-Cyl.—Equipment Schedule 6						
W.B. 97.6"; 1.6 Liter.						
SVM Sedan 4D	TD526	9995	**600**	**700**	**1350**	**2425**
SVM Hatchback 4D	TD626	9995	**600**	**700**	**1375**	**2475**
Sedan 4D	TD526	11690	**950**	**1075**	**1875**	**3350**
Hatchback 4D	TD626	11690	**975**	**1100**	**1900**	**3375**
LS Sedan 4D	TJ526	12635	**1100**	**1225**	**2025**	**3475**
LS Hatchback 4D	TJ626	13435	**1175**	**1300**	**2075**	**3550**
CAVALIER—4-Cyl.—Equipment Schedule 5						
W.B. 104.1"; 2.2 Liter.						
Sedan 4D	JC52F	15995	**875**	**1025**	**1725**	**3150**
Coupe 2D	JC12F	15810	**800**	**950**	**1700**	**3125**
LS Sedan 4D	JF52F	17230	**1125**	**1300**	**2075**	**3775**
LS Coupe 2D	JF12F	17030	**1125**	**1300**	**2075**	**3775**
LS Sport Sedan 4D	JH52F	18635	**1300**	**1500**	**2275**	**4100**
LS Sport Coupe 2D	JH12F	18435	**1300**	**1500**	**2275**	**4075**
CLASSIC—4-Cyl.—Equipment Schedule 5						
W.B. 107.0" 2.2 Liter.						
Sedan 4D	ND52F	19380	**1075**	**1275**	**1825**	**3125**
MALIBU—4-Cyl.—Equipment Schedule 5						
W.B. 106.3"; 2.2 Liter.						
Sedan 4D	ZS52F	18995	**1350**	**1575**	**2150**	**3625**
V6, 3.5 Liter	8		**325**	**325**	**435**	**435**
MALIBU—V6—Equipment Schedule 5						
W.B. 106.3", 112.3" (MAXX); 3.5 Liter.						
MAXX Hatchback 4D	ZS638	21725	**1600**	**1875**	**2525**	**4225**
LS Sedan 4D	ZT528	20995	**2050**	**2400**	**3025**	**4950**
LS MAXX H'Back 4D	ZT638	22225	**1725**	**2025**	**2675**	**4425**
LT Sedan 4D	ZU528	23495	**2000**	**2325**	**2975**	**4900**
LT MAXX H'Back 4D	ZU668	24725	**2050**	**2400**	**3050**	**5025**
IMPALA—V6—Equipment Schedule 4						
W.B. 110.5"; 3.4 Liter, 3.8 Liter.						
Sedan 4D	WF52E	22150	**1375**	**1525**	**2200**	**3650**
LS Sedan 4D	WH52K	25000	**1725**	**1925**	**2775**	**4600**
IMPALA—V6 Supercharged—Equipment Schedule 4						
W.B. 110.5"; 3.8 Liter.						
SS Sedan 4D	WP521	27995	**2175**	**2425**	**3475**	**5825**
MONTE CARLO—V6—Equipment Schedule 4						
W.B. 110.5"; 3.4 Liter, 3.8 Liter.						
LS Coupe 2D	WW12E	22075	**1475**	**1650**	**2400**	**4075**
SS Coupe 2D	WX12K	24225	**1975**	**2225**	**2950**	**4850**
V6, Supercharged, 3.8L			**425**	**425**	**580**	**580**
CORVETTE—V8—Equipment Schedule 2						
W.B. 104.5"; 5.7 Liter.						
Coupe 2D	YY22G	44535	**10350**	**10900**	**11550**	**14600**
Z06 Hard Top 2D	YY12S	52385	**11850**	**12500**	**13350**	**17050**
Convertible 2D	YY32G	51535	**12300**	**12950**	**13300**	**16550**
Commemorative Ed			**450**	**450**	**490**	**490**
Glass Roof Panel			**250**	**250**	**275**	**275**
Dual Roof Panels			**300**	**300**	**330**	**330**
Suspension Pkg			**200**	**200**	**220**	**220**

Body Type	VIN	List	Trade-In Good	Very Good	Pvt-Party Good	Retail Excellent
Z51 Handling			200	200	220	220
Manual, 6-Spd			150	150	165	165

2005 CHEVROLET—(1,2orK)(GorL)1(TD526)-5-#

AVEO—4-Cyl.—Equipment Schedule 6
W.B. 97.6"; 1.6 Liter.

Body Type	VIN	List	Trade-In Good	Very Good	Pvt-Party Good	Retail Excellent
SVM Sedan 4D	TD526	9995	625	700	1550	2700
SVM Hatchback 4D	TD626	9995	625	700	1550	2700
LS Sedan 4D	TD526	12635	1000	1125	2075	3575
LS Hatchback 4D	TD626	12635	1000	1125	2075	3550
LT Sedan 4D	TG526	12760	1275	1425	2300	3800
LT Hatchback 4D	TG626	13905	1475	1650	2475	3925

COBALT—4-Cyl.—Equipment Schedule 5
W.B. 103.3"; 2.2 Liter.

Body Type	VIN	List	Trade-In Good	Very Good	Pvt-Party Good	Retail Excellent
Sedan 4D	AJ52F	15040	1425	1675	2475	4125
Coupe 2D	AJ12F	15040	1575	1850	2625	4325
LS Sedan 4D	AL52F	17335	1825	2100	2850	4650
LS Coupe 2D	AL12F	17335	1925	2225	2950	4800
LT Sedan 4D	AM52F	18760	2075	2400	3075	5000

COBALT—4-Cyl. Supercharged—Equipment Schedule 5
W.B. 103.3"; 2.0 Liter.

Body Type	VIN	List	Trade-In Good	Very Good	Pvt-Party Good	Retail Excellent
SS Coupe 2D	AP12P	21995	3175	3650	4400	7000

CAVALIER—4-Cyl.—Equipment Schedule 5
W.B. 104.1"; 2.2 Liter.

Body Type	VIN	List	Trade-In Good	Very Good	Pvt-Party Good	Retail Excellent
Sedan 4D	JC52F	16025	1025	1200	2075	3700
Coupe 2D	JC12F	15825	850	1000	1950	3550
LS Sedan 4D	JF52F	17705	1300	1525	2525	4500
LS Coupe 2D	JF12F	17505	1300	1525	2450	4325
LS Sport Sedan 4D	JH52F	19125	1450	1675	2700	4675
LS Sport Coupe 2D	JH12F	18925	1375	1625	2650	4600

CLASSIC—4-Cyl.—Equipment Schedule 5
W.B. 107.0"; 2.2 Liter.

Body Type	VIN	List	Trade-In Good	Very Good	Pvt-Party Good	Retail Excellent
Sedan 4D	ND52F	20130	1475	1725	2575	4275

MALIBU—4-Cyl.—Equipment Schedule 5
W.B. 106.3"; 2.2 Liter.

Body Type	VIN	List	Trade-In Good	Very Good	Pvt-Party Good	Retail Excellent
Sedan 4D	ZS528	19710	1525	1800	2650	4375
V6, 3.5 Liter	8		350	350	480	480

MALIBU—V6—Equipment Schedule 5
W.B. 106.3", 112.3" (MAXX); 3.5 Liter.

Body Type	VIN	List	Trade-In Good	Very Good	Pvt-Party Good	Retail Excellent
MAXX Hatchback 4D	ZS628	21475	1750	2050	2900	4725
LS Sedan 4D	ZT528	21775	2000	2325	3125	5050
LS MAXX H'Back 4D	ZT628	21975	2100	2450	3150	5050
LT Sedan 4D	ZU548	24570	2250	2625	3450	5575
LT MAXX H'Back 4D	ZU648	25120	2350	2750	3550	5725

IMPALA—V6—Equipment Schedule 4
W.B. 110.5"; 3.4 Liter, 3.8 Liter.

Body Type	VIN	List	Trade-In Good	Very Good	Pvt-Party Good	Retail Excellent
Sedan 4D	WF52E	23130	1425	1575	2750	4650
LS Sedan 4D	WH52K	25990	2225	2450	3525	5725

IMPALA—V6 Supercharged—Equipment Schedule 4
W.B. 110.5"; 3.8 Liter.

Body Type	VIN	List	Trade-In Good	Very Good	Pvt-Party Good	Retail Excellent
SS Sedan 4D	WP521	29085	3100	3425	4475	7075

MONTE CARLO—V6—Equipment Schedule 4
W.B. 110.5"; 3.4 Liter, 3.8 Liter.

Body Type	VIN	List	Trade-In Good	Very Good	Pvt-Party Good	Retail Excellent
LS Coupe 2D	WW12E	23060	1575	1800	2700	4425
LT Coupe 2D	WX12K	25220	2225	2500	3450	5600

MONTE CARLO—V6 Supercharged—Equipment Schedule 4
W.B. 110.5"; 3.8 Liter.

Body Type	VIN	List	Trade-In Good	Very Good	Pvt-Party Good	Retail Excellent
SS Coupe 2D	WZ121	28885	3275	3675	4250	6425

CORVETTE—V8—Equipment Schedule 2
W.B. 105.8"; 6.0 Liter.

Body Type	VIN	List	Trade-In Good	Very Good	Pvt-Party Good	Retail Excellent
Coupe 2D	YY22U	44245	12900	13550	14100	17300
Convertible 2D	YY34U	52245	14800	15600	15850	19250
Glass Roof Panel			250	250	275	275
Dual Roof Panels			300	300	330	330
Suspension Pkg			225	225	255	255
Z51 Handling			225	225	255	255
Manual, 6-Spd			150	150	165	165

2006 CHEVY—(1,2,3orK)(GorL)(1orN)(TD526)-6-#

AVEO—4-Cyl.—Equipment Schedule 6
W.B. 97.6"; 1.6 Liter.

Body Type	VIN	List	Trade-In Good	Very Good	Pvt-Party Good	Retail Excellent
SVM Sedan 4D	TD526	9995	850	975	1800	3000

Body Type	VIN	List	Trade-In Good	Trade-In Very Good	Pvt-Party Good	Retail Excellent
SVM Hatchback 4D	TD626	9995	850	975	1800	2975
AVEO—4-Cyl.—Equipment Schedule 6						
W.B. 97.6"; 1.6 Liter.						
LS Sedan 4D	TD526	12760	1325	1475	2550	4225
LS Hatchback 4D	TD626	12760	1325	1475	2500	4100
LT Sedan 4D	TG526	13165	1850	2050	2925	4550
LT Hatchback 4D	TG626	14180	1925	2125	2975	4600
Manual, 5-Spd			(275)	(275)	(355)	(355)
COBALT—4-Cyl.—Equipment Schedule 5						
W.B. 103.3"; 2.2 Liter, 2.4 Liter.						
LS Sedan 4D	AK55F	15340	1750	2025	2775	4475
LS Coupe 2D	AK15F	15340	1875	2175	2900	4650
LT Sedan 4D	AL55F	17640	2175	2500	3175	5000
LT Coupe 2D	AL15F	17640	2275	2600	3275	5150
LTZ Sedan 4D	AZ55F	18990	2600	2950	3575	5575
SS Sedan 4D	AM55B	19640	2925	3350	3900	6000
SS Coupe 2D	AM15B	19640	3025	3475	4100	6250
COBALT—4-Cyl. Supercharged—Equipment Schedule 5						
W.B. 103.3"; 2.0 Liter.						
SS Coupe 2D	AP15P	21990	3650	4175	5000	7800
HHR—4-Cyl.—Equipment Schedule 5						
W.B. 103.5"; 2.2 Liter.						
LS Sport Wagon 4D	A13D	16990	2400	2675	3425	5175
LT Sport Wagon 4D	A23D	17990	3025	3350	4000	5875
4-Cyl, 2.4 Liter	P		200	200	260	260
MALIBU—4-Cyl.—Equipment Schedule 5						
W.B. 106.3"; 2.2 Liter.						
LT Sedan 4D	ZT55F	19990	2675	3050	3800	5875
V6, 3.5 Liter	8		400	400	520	520
MALIBU—V6—Equipment Schedule 5						
W.B. 106.3"; 3.5 Liter.						
LS Sedan 4D	ZS558	17990	2575	2950	3650	5625
4-Cyl, 2.2 Liter	F		(250)	(250)	(320)	(320)
MALIBU—V6—Equipment Schedule 5						
W.B. 106.3", 112.3" (MAXX); 3.5 Liter, 3.9 Liter.						
LS MAXX H'Back 4D	ZS658	20835	2600	2975	3625	5550
LT MAXX H'Back 4D	ZT658	21650	3175	3600	4275	6525
SS Sedan 4D	ZW571	24490	3900	4450	5075	7550
SS MAXX H'Back 4D	ZW671	24690	4150	4725	5325	7900
LTZ Sedan 4D	ZU578	24830	3700	4200	4925	7425
LTZ MAXX H'Back 4D	ZU678	25380	4150	4725	5325	7925
IMPALA—V6—Equipment Schedule 4						
W.B. 110.5"; 3.5 Liter, 3.9 Liter.						
LS Sedan 4D	WB55K	21990	3275	3600	4575	6900
LT Sedan 4D	WC551	22520	3300	3625	4600	6900
LTZ Sedan 4D	WU551	27530	4150	4525	5525	8250
IMPALA—V8—Equipment Schedule 4						
W.B. 110.5"; 5.3 Liter.						
SS Sedan 4D	WD55C	27790	4950	5425	6375	9225
MONTE CARLO—V6—Equipment Schedule 4						
W.B. 110.5"; 3.5 Liter, 3.9 Liter.						
LS Coupe 2D	WJ15K	21990	2700	3000	3900	6125
LT Coupe 2D	WK15K	22520	3225	3600	4375	6725
LTZ Coupe 2D	WN151	26635	3750	4200	5100	7750
MONTE CARLO—V8—Equipment Schedule 4						
W.B. 110.5"; 5.3 Liter.						
SS Coupe 2D	WL15C	27790	4950	5500	6000	8675
CORVETTE—V8—Equipment Schedule 2						
W.B. 105.7"; 6.0 Liter, 7.0 Liter.						
Coupe 2D	YY22U	47345	14300	15000	15450	18750
Convertible 2D	YY32U	53585	16150	16950	17150	20600
Z06 Coupe 2D	YY25E	65800	20600	21600	22200	27100
Glass Roof Panel			250	250	270	270
Dual Roof Panels			300	300	325	325
Suspension Pkg			275	275	305	305
Z51 Handling			275	275	305	305
Manual, 6-Spd			150	150	165	165

2007 CHEVY—(1,2,3orK)(GorL)(1orN)(TD566)-7-#

AVEO—4-Cyl.—Equipment Schedule 6						
W.B. 97.6"; 1.6 Liter.						
LS Sedan 4D	TD566	13165	1775	1950	3050	4825
LT Sedan 4D	TG566	13470	2225	2425	3375	5125

Body Type	VIN	List	Trade-In Good	Trade-In Very Good	Pvt-Party Good	Retail Excellent
Manual, 5-Spd			(300)	(300)	(385)	(385)
AVEO5—4-Cyl.—Equipment Schedule 6						
W.B. 97.6"; 1.6 Liter.						
SVM Hatchback 4D	TD666	10045	950	1050	1900	3075
LS Hatchback 4D	TD666	12515	1550	1700	2800	4500
Automatic			300	300	385	385
COBALT—4-Cyl.—Equipment Schedule 5						
W.B. 103.3"; 2.2 Liter, 2.4 Liter.						
LS Sedan 4D	AK55F	14515	2200	2500	3175	4900
LS Coupe 2D	AK15F	14515	2325	2625	3300	5050
LT Sedan 4D	AL55F	15635	2600	2925	3550	5375
LT Coupe 2D	AL15F	15635	2900	3275	3850	5775
SS Sedan 4D	AM52B	19920	3500	3950	4500	6600
SS Coupe 2D	AM15B	19920	3875	4350	4825	7050
Manual, 5-Spd			(400)	(400)	(520)	(520)
COBALT—4-Cyl.—Equipment Schedule 5						
W.B. 103.3"; 2.2 Liter.						
LTZ Sedan 4D	AZ55F	18790	3000	3400	4050	6025
COBALT—4-Cyl. Supercharged—Equipment Schedule 5						
W.B. 103.3"; 2.0 Liter.						
SS Coupe 2D	AP18P	21465	4250	4775	5475	8225
HHR—4-Cyl.—Equipment Schedule 5						
W.B. 103.5"; 2.2 Liter.						
LS Sport Wagon 4D	A13D	17470	2850	3125	3950	5850
LS Panel Sport Wag 2D	A15D	17750	3000	3300	4100	6025
LT Sport Wagon 4D	A23D	18470	3300	3650	4500	6500
LT Panel Sport Wag 2D	A25P	19595	3325	3650	4500	6550
Manual, 5-Spd			(400)	(400)	(520)	(520)
4-Cyl, 2.4L (ex LT Panel)	P		225	225	285	285
MALIBU—4-Cyl.—Equipment Schedule 5						
W.B. 106.3"; 2.2 Liter.						
LT Sedan 4D	ZT58N	18930	3125	3525	4275	6350
V6, 3.5 Liter	N		425	425	565	565
MALIBU—V6—Equipment Schedule 5						
W.B. 106.3"; 3.5 Liter.						
LS Sedan 4D	ZS58N	17495	3125	3525	4175	6175
4-Cyl, 2.2 Liter	F		(250)	(250)	(335)	(335)
MALIBU—V6—Equipment Schedule 5						
W.B. 106.3", 112.3" (MAXX); 3.5 Liter, 3.9 Liter.						
LS MAXX H'Back 4D	ZS68N	20385	3200	3600	4375	6475
LT MAXX H'Back 4D	ZT68N	21130	3650	4100	4850	7125
SS Sedan 4D	ZW571	23965	4650	5225	5800	8375
SS MAXX H'Back 4D	ZW671	24265	4900	5475	6075	8750
LTZ Sedan 4D	ZU57N	24170	4300	4825	5525	8075
LTZ MAXX H'Back 4D	ZU67N	24470	4900	5475	6075	8750
IMPALA—V6—Equipment Schedule 4						
W.B. 110.5"; 3.5 Liter, 3.9 Liter.						
LS Sedan 4D	WB55K	21445	3600	3925	4850	7050
LT Sedan 4D	WT55K	22125	4000	4350	5275	7600
LTZ Sedan 4D	WU551	26935	4975	5400	6475	9250
IMPALA—V8—Equipment Schedule 4						
W.B. 110.5"; 5.3 Liter.						
SS Sedan 4D	WD55C	28540	5725	6225	7125	10000
MONTE CARLO—V6—Equipment Schedule 4						
W.B. 110.5"; 3.5 Liter.						
LS Coupe 2D	WJ15K	21515	3350	3700	4600	7000
LT Coupe 2D	WK15K	23125	3875	4300	5250	7850
MONTE CARLO—V8—Equipment Schedule 4						
W.B. 110.5"; 5.3 Liter.						
SS Coupe 2D	WL15C	28240	5625	6225	6850	9650
CORVETTE—V8—Equipment Schedule 2						
W.B. 105.7"; 6.0 Liter, 7.0 Liter.						
Coupe 2D	YY25U	46245	15200	15900	16400	19600
Convertible 2D	YY36U	54320	16900	17700	18050	21400
Z06 Coupe 2D	YY25E	70000	22200	23200	23500	28000
Glass Roof Panel			250	250	270	270
Dual Roof Panels			300	300	325	325
Suspension Pkg			325	325	360	360
Z51 Handling			325	325	360	360
Indy Pace Car Pkg			1075	1075	1175	1175
Manual, 6-Spd			150	150	160	160

Body Type	VIN	List	Trade-In Good	Very Good	Pvt-Party Good	Retail Excellent

2008 CHEVY — (1,2,3orK)(GorL)(1orN)(TD566)–8–#

AVEO—4-Cyl.—Equipment Schedule 6
W.B. 97.6"; 1.6 Liter.

Body Type	VIN	List	Good	Very Good	Good	Excellent
LS Sedan 4D	TD566	15255	2075	2250	3425	5175
LT Sedan 4D	TG566	15180	2650	2850	3900	5725
Manual, 5-Spd w/Overdrive			(350)	(350)	(460)	(460)

AVEO5—4-Cyl.—Equipment Schedule 6
W.B. 97.6"; 1.6 Liter.

SVM Hatchback 4D	TD666	10610	1200	1300	2250	3425

AVEO5—4-Cyl.—Equipment Schedule 6
W.B. 97.6"; 1.6 Liter.

LS Hatchback 4D	TD666	13620	2200	2375	3525	5300
Manual, 5-Spd w/Overdrive			(350)	(350)	(460)	(460)

COBALT—4-Cyl.—Equipment Schedule 5
W.B. 103.3"; 2.2 Liter, 2.4 Liter.

LS Sedan 4D	AK58F	15215	2825	3125	3850	5600
LS Coupe 2D	AK18F	15215	2925	3250	3950	5750
LT Sedan 4D	AL58F	15915	3225	3550	4350	6275
LT Coupe 2D	AL18F	15915	3325	3675	4425	6350
Sport Sedan 4D	AM58B	20540	4200	4625	5250	7375
Sport Coupe 2D	AM18B	20540	4525	4975	5550	7750
Manual, 5-Spd			(400)	(400)	(540)	(540)

COBALT—4-Cyl. Turbo—Equipment Schedule 5
W.B. 103.3"; 2.0 Liter.

SS Coupe 2D	AP18X	22995	5600	6175	7100	10100

HHR—4-Cyl.—Equipment Schedule 5
W.B. 103.5"; 2.2 Liter.

LS Sport Wagon 4D	A13D	17795	3525	3825	4775	6625
LS Panel Sport Wag 2D	A15D	18095	3525	3825	4800	6675
LT Sport Wagon 4D	A23D	18795	3925	4250	5175	7150
LT Panel Sport Wag 2D	A25D	19095	4025	4350	5325	7375
Manual, 5-Spd	3		(400)	(400)	(540)	(540)
4-Cyl, 2.4 Liter	P		225	225	315	315

HHR—4-Cyl. Turbo—Equipment Schedule 5
W.B. 103.5"; 2.0 Liter.

SS Sport Wagon 4D	A83X	22995	6700	7200	8250	11150
Manual, 5-Spd			(400)	(400)	(540)	(540)

MALIBU CLASSIC—4-Cyl.—Equipment Schedule 5
W.B. 106.3"; 2.2 Liter.

LS Sedan 4D	ZS58F	18495	2425	2650	3475	5050
V6, 3.5 Liter	N		450	450	610	610

MALIBU CLASSIC—V6—Equipment Schedule 5
W.B. 106.3"; 3.5 Liter.

LT Sedan 4D	ZT58N	20880	3075	3375	4300	6150

MALIBU—4-Cyl.—Equipment Schedule 4
W.B. 112.3"; 2.4 Liter.

LS Sedan 4D	ZG58B	19995	5200	5675	6475	8850
LT Sedan 4D	ZH58B	20955	5775	6325	7125	9700
V6, 3.5 Liter	N		375	375	485	485
V6, 3.6 Liter	7		725	725	975	975

MALIBU—4-Cyl. Hybrid—Equipment Schedule 4
W.B. 112.3"; 2.4 Liter.

Sedan 4D	ZF585	22790	6025	6600	7425	10150

MALIBU—V6—Equipment Schedule 4
W.B. 112.3"; 3.6 Liter.

LTZ Sedan 4D	ZK587	26995	6475	7075	7850	10700

IMPALA—V6—Equipment Schedule 4
W.B. 110.5"; 3.5 Liter, 3.9 Liter.

LS Sedan 4D	WB55K	21940	4600	4925	5925	8150
LT Sedan 4D	WT55K	22550	4825	5175	6300	8650
LT 50th Anniv Ed Sed	WV55K	25995	6025	6450	7500	10150
LTZ Sedan 4D	WU553	27515	6225	6675	7750	10500

IMPALA—V8—Equipment Schedule 4
W.B. 110.5"; 5.3 Liter.

SS Sedan 4D	WD55C	28920	6700	7175	8225	11050

CORVETTE—V8—Equipment Schedule 2
W.B. 105.7"; 6.2 Liter, 7.0 Liter.

Coupe 2D	YY25W	47245	17250	17950	18700	22000
Convertible 2D	YY36W	55585	19700	20500	21000	24400
Z06 Coupe 2D	YY25E	71000	24500	25500	26200	30800
Glass Roof Panel			250	250	270	270
Dual Roof Panels			300	300	325	325

1015   **EQUIPMENT & MILEAGE PAGE 9 TO 23**   93

Body	Type	VIN	List	Trade-In Good	Very Good	Pvt-Party Good	Retail Excellent
	Suspension Pkg			375	375	415	415
	Z51 Handling			375	375	415	415
	Indy Pace Car Pkg			1125	1125	1230	1230
	4LT			1725	1725	1880	1880
	Manual, 6-Spd			150	150	160	160

2009 CHEVY — (1,2,3orK)(GorL)(1orN)(TD56E)-9-#

AVEO—4-Cyl.—Equipment Schedule 6
W.B. 97.6"; 1.6 Liter.

Body	Type	VIN	List	Good	Very Good	Good	Excellent
	LS Sedan 4D	TD56E	12120	2400	2550	3850	5675

AVEO—4-Cyl.—Equipment Schedule 6
W.B. 97.6"; 1.6 Liter.

| | LT Sedan 4D | TG56E | 15180 | 3075 | 3275 | 4450 | 6250 |
| | Manual, 5-Spd w/Overdrive | | | (375) | (375) | (490) | (490) |

AVEO5—4-Cyl.—Equipment Schedule 6
W.B. 97.6"; 1.6 Liter.

| | LS Hatchback 4D | TD66E | 12120 | 2475 | 2650 | 3950 | 5750 |

AVEO5—4-Cyl.—Equipment Schedule 6
W.B. 97.6"; 1.6 Liter.

| | LT Hatchback 4D | TG66E | 14255 | 2850 | 3025 | 4250 | 6075 |
| | Automatic, 4-Spd | | | 325 | 325 | 445 | 445 |

COBALT—4-Cyl.—Equipment Schedule 6
W.B. 103.3"; 2.2 Liter.

	XFE Sedan 4D	AK58H	15710	3025	3300	4225	5950
	XFE Coupe 2D	AK18H	15710	2975	3250	4175	5875
	LS XFE Sedan 4D	AK58H	15670	2925	3200	4125	5800
	LS XFE Coupe 2D	AK18H	15670	2875	3125	4075	5750
	LT XFE Sedan 4D	AL58H	16370	3800	4125	5025	6975
	LT XFE Coupe 2D	AL18H	16370	3800	4125	5050	7025

COBALT—4-Cyl.—Equipment Schedule 5
W.B. 103.3"; 2.2 Liter.

	LS Sedan 4D	AS58H	16595	3325	3625	4525	6325
	LS Coupe 2D	AS18H	16595	3825	4125	4950	6800
	LT Sedan 4D	AT58H	17295	3925	4250	5200	7275
	LT Coupe 2D	AT18H	17295	4025	4350	5325	7425
	Manual, 5-Spd			(450)	(450)	(585)	(585)

COBALT—4-Cyl. Turbo—Equipment Schedule 5
W.B. 103.3"; 2.0 Liter.

| | SS Sedan 4D | AP58X | 23435 | 6400 | 6925 | 8075 | 11150 |
| | SS Coupe 2D | AP18X | 23435 | 6500 | 7025 | 7775 | 10350 |

HHR—4-Cyl.—Equipment Schedule 5
W.B. 103.5"; 2.2 Liter.

	LS Sport Wagon 4D	A13D	19590	4050	4300	5350	7125
	LS Panel Sport Wag 2D	A15D	19900	4275	4525	5550	7400
	LT Sport Wagon 4D	A23D	20590	4450	4650	5750	7725
	LT Panel Sport Wag 2D	A25D	20900	4650	4925	6000	8000
	Manual, 5-Spd			(450)	(450)	(585)	(585)
	4-Cyl, 2.4 Liter	P		250	250	340	340

HHR—4-Cyl. Turbo—Equipment Schedule 5
W.B. 103.5"; 2.0 Liter.

	SS Sport Wagon 4D	A83X	25490	7350	7800	9075	11800
	SS Panel Sport Wag 2D	A83X	25810	8025	8475	9700	12550
	Manual, 5-Spd			(450)	(450)	(585)	(585)

MALIBU—4-Cyl.—Equipment Schedule 4
W.B. 112.3"; 2.4 Liter.

	LS Sedan 4D	ZG57B	22090	6250	6675	7625	10050
	LT Sedan 4D	ZH57B	22990	6650	7100	8100	10650
	LTZ Sedan 4D	ZK57B	27365	7550	8075	9100	11950
	V6, 3.5 Liter	N		400	400	515	515
	V6, 3.6 Liter	7		775	775	1035	1035

MALIBU—4-Cyl. Hybrid—Equipment Schedule 4
W.B. 112.3"; 2.4 Liter.

| | Sedan 4D | ZF575 | 26040 | 7125 | 7625 | 8625 | 11300 |

IMPALA—V6—Equipment Schedule 4
W.B. 110.5"; 3.5 Liter, 3.9 Liter.

	LS Sedan 4D	WB55K	23795	5600	5925	7100	9300
	LT Sedan 4D	WT55K	24650	6000	6350	7500	9775
	LTZ Sedan 4D	WU553	29635	7100	7500	8775	11450

IMPALA—V8—Equipment Schedule 4
W.B. 110.5"; 5.3 Liter.

| | SS Sedan 4D | WD55C | 31140 | 7725 | 8175 | 9350 | 12050 |

CORVETTE—V8—Equipment Schedule 2
W.B. 105.7"; 6.2 Liter, 7.0 Liter.

Body Type	VIN	List	Trade-In Good	Very Good	Pvt-Party Good	Retail Excellent
Coupe 2D	YY25W	49145	**18900**	**19550**	**20400**	**23400**
Convertible 2D	YY36W	53800	21900	22700	23300	26600
Z06 Coupe 2D	YZ25E	74955	28400	29400	30500	35500
Glass Roof Panel			275	275	285	285
Dual Roof Panels			325	325	360	360
4LT			1775	1775	1930	1930
Hertz Special Ed			675	675	740	740
Suspension Pkg			425	425	470	470
Z51 Handling Pkg			425	425	470	470
Manual, 6-Spd			175	175	180	180

CORVETTE—V8 Supercharged—Equipment Schedule 2
W.B. 105.7"; 6.2 Liter.

Body Type	VIN	List	Trade-In Good	Very Good	Pvt-Party Good	Retail Excellent
ZR1 Coupe 2D	YR25R	105000	********	********	********	**59300**

2010 CHEVY — (1,2,3,6orK)(GorL)(1orN)(TD5DE)–A–#

AVEO—4-Cyl.—Equipment Schedule 6
W.B. 97.6"; 1.6 Liter.

Body Type	VIN	List	Trade-In Good	Very Good	Pvt-Party Good	Retail Excellent
LS Sedan 4D	TD5DE	12685	**3400**	**3575**	**4975**	**6775**

AVEO—4-Cyl.—Equipment Schedule 6
W.B. 97.6"; 1.6 Liter.

Body Type	VIN	List	Trade-In Good	Very Good	Pvt-Party Good	Retail Excellent
LT Sedan 4D	TD5DE	15895	**4250**	**4450**	**5750**	**7600**
Manual, 5-Spd w/Overdrive			(450)	(450)	(615)	(615)

AVEO5—4-Cyl.—Equipment Schedule 6
W.B. 97.6"; 1.6 Liter.

Body Type	VIN	List	Trade-In Good	Very Good	Pvt-Party Good	Retail Excellent
LS Hatchback 4D	TD6DE	12685	**3450**	**3650**	**5025**	**6825**

AVEO5—4-Cyl.—Equipment Schedule 6
W.B. 97.6"; 1.6 Liter.

Body Type	VIN	List	Trade-In Good	Very Good	Pvt-Party Good	Retail Excellent
LT Hatchback 4D	TD6DE	15745	**4050**	**4250**	**5500**	**7275**
Manual, 5-Spd w/Overdrive			(450)	(450)	(615)	(615)

COBALT—4-Cyl. Equipment Schedule 5
W.B. 103.3"; 2.2 Liter.

Body Type	VIN	List	Trade-In Good	Very Good	Pvt-Party Good	Retail Excellent
XFE Sedan 4D	AK58H	15710	**3900**	**4150**	**5050**	**6725**
XFE Coupe 2D	AK18H	15710	3725	4000	4875	6500
LS XFE Sedan 4D	AA5F5	16390	4100	4375	5250	7000
LS XFE Coupe 2D	AA1F5	16390	4050	4325	5200	6925
LT XFE Sedan 4D	AC5F5	17190	4900	5225	6075	8000
LT XFE Coupe 2D	AC1F5	17190	4900	5225	6125	8125

COBALT—4-Cyl.—Equipment Schedule 5
W.B. 103.3"; 2.2 Liter.

Body Type	VIN	List	Trade-In Good	Very Good	Pvt-Party Good	Retail Excellent
LS Sedan 4D	AB5F5	16390	**4125**	**4400**	**5375**	**7250**
LS Coupe 2D	AB1F5	16390	4500	4800	5775	7725

COBALT—4-Cyl.—Equipment Schedule 5
W.B. 103.3"; 2.2 Liter.

Body Type	VIN	List	Trade-In Good	Very Good	Pvt-Party Good	Retail Excellent
LT Sedan 4D	AD5F5	17190	**5125**	**5475**	**6525**	**8575**
LT Coupe 2D	AD1F5	17190	5275	5650	6675	8775
Manual, 5-Spd			(475)	(475)	(640)	(640)

COBALT—4-Cyl. Turbo—Equipment Schedule 5
W.B. 103.3"; 2.0 Liter.

Body Type	VIN	List	Trade-In Good	Very Good	Pvt-Party Good	Retail Excellent
SS Coupe 2D	AG1FX	25255	**8400**	**8950**	**9675**	**12200**

HHR—4-Cyl.—Equipment Schedule 5
W.B. 103.5"; 2.2 Liter.

Body Type	VIN	List	Trade-In Good	Very Good	Pvt-Party Good	Retail Excellent
LS Sport Wagon 4D	AADB	20440	**5350**	**5600**	**6700**	**8550**
LS Panel Wag 2D	AADB	20750	5375	5625	6925	8850
LT Sport Wagon 4D	ABDB	21440	5575	5825	7175	9200
LT Panel Sport Wag 2D	ABDB	21750	5675	5925	7250	9250
Manual, 5-Spd			(475)	(475)	(640)	(640)
4-Cyl, Flex Fuel, 2.4L	V		275	275	365	365

HHR—4-Cyl. Turbo—Equipment Schedule 5
W.B. 103.5"; 2.0 Liter.

Body Type	VIN	List	Trade-In Good	Very Good	Pvt-Party Good	Retail Excellent
SS Sport Wagon 4D	ADDM	26975	**8675**	**9050**	**10500**	**13200**
Manual, 5-Spd			(475)	(475)	(640)	(640)

MALIBU—4-Cyl.—Equipment Schedule 4
W.B. 112.3"; 2.4 Liter.

Body Type	VIN	List	Trade-In Good	Very Good	Pvt-Party Good	Retail Excellent
LS Sedan 4D	ZB5EB	22545	**7300**	**7675**	**8850**	**11250**
LT Sedan 4D	ZC5EB	23435	8075	8475	9625	12150
LTZ Sedan 4D	ZE5E7	27325	8925	9350	10600	13350
V6, 3.6 Liter	7		825	825	1070	1070

IMPALA—V6—Equipment Schedule 4
W.B. 110.5"; 3.5 Liter, 3.9 Liter.

Body Type	VIN	List	Trade-In Good	Very Good	Pvt-Party Good	Retail Excellent
LS Sedan 4D	WA5EK	24715	**6825**	**7175**	**8425**	**10600**
LT Sedan 4D	WB5EK	25880	7225	7575	8925	11250
LTZ Sedan 4D	WC5EM	30455	8475	8875	10200	12800

2010 CHEVROLET

Body Type	VIN	List	Trade-In Good	Very Good	Pvt-Party Good	Retail Excellent
CAMARO—V6—Equipment Schedule 4						
W.B. 112.3"; 3.6 Liter.						
LS Coupe 2D	FE1EV	23990	12250	12800	13500	15900
LT Coupe 2D	FF1EV	25625	13650	14300	15050	17750
RS Pkg			1225	1225	1455	1455
CAMARO—V8—Equipment Schedule 4						
W.B. 112.3"; 6.2 Liter.						
SS Coupe 2D	FS1EW	31990	16600	17350	18050	21300
CORVETTE—V8—Equipment Schedule 2						
W.B.105.7"; 6.2 Liter, 7.0 Liter.						
Coupe 2D	YE2DW	49880	21300	22000	23000	26100
Convertible 2D	YE3DW	54530	25700	26500	27200	30500
Grand Sport Cpe 2D	YP2DW	55720	25300	26100	27300	31100
Grand Sport Conv 2D	YP3DW	59530	28900	29800	30700	34700
Z06 Coupe 2D	YJ2DE	75235	31700	32700	33600	38000
Glass Roof Panel			300	300	315	315
Dual Roof Panels			375	375	415	415
Heritage			1400	1400	1565	1565
4LT			1825	1825	1975	1975
Suspension Pkg			475	475	520	520
Manual, 6-Spd			200	200	205	205
CORVETTE—V8 Supercharged—Equipment Schedule 2						
W.B. 105.7"; 6.2 Liter.						
ZR1 Coupe 2D	YM2DT	109130	****	****	****	64000

2011 CHEVY — (1,2,3,6orK)(G1,GAorL1)(TD5DG)–B–#

Body Type	VIN	List	Trade-In Good	Very Good	Pvt-Party Good	Retail Excellent
AVEO—4-Cyl.—Equipment Schedule 6						
W.B. 97.6"; 1.6 Liter.						
LS Sedan 4D	TD5DG	12685	4450	4625	6075	7925
AVEO—4-Cyl.—Equipment Schedule 6						
W.B. 97.6"; 1.6 Liter.						
LT Sedan 4D	TD5DG	15745	5100	5300	6775	8600
Manual, 5-Spd w/Overdrive			(500)	(500)	(655)	(655)
AVEO5—4-Cyl.—Equipment Schedule 6						
W.B. 97.6"; 1.6 Liter.						
LS Hatchback 4D	TD6DG	12835	4650	4850	6250	8100
AVEO5—4-Cyl.—Equipment Schedule 6						
W.B. 97.6"; 1.6 Liter.						
LT Hatchback 4D	TD6DG	15745	5100	5300	6750	8525
Manual, 5-Spd w/Overdrive			(500)	(500)	(655)	(655)
CRUZE—4-Cyl. ECOTEC—Equipment Schedule 5						
W.B. 105.7"; 1.8 Liter.						
LS Sedan 4D	PB5SH	17920	7750	8175	9125	11400
Manual, 6-Spd w/Overdrive	B		(475)	(475)	(610)	(610)
CRUZE—4-Cyl. Turbo—Equipment Schedule 5						
W.B. 105.7"; 1.4 Liter.						
LT Sedan 4D	PF5S9	18895	8525	9100	9800	12350
LTZ Sedan 4D	PH5S9	22695	9450	10100	10850	13650
CRUZE—4-Cyl. Turbo—Equipment Schedule 5						
W.B. 105.7"; 1.4 Liter.						
eco Sedan 4D	PK5S9	19820	8675	9150	10100	12500
Manual, 6-Spd w/Overdrive	K		(475)	(475)	(605)	(605)
VOLT—AC Electric—Equipment Schedule 3						
W.B. 105.7".						
Sedan 4D	RC6S4	41000	9925	10450	11400	14000
HHR—4-Cyl.—Equipment Schedule 5						
W.B. 103.5"; 2.2 Liter.						
LS Sport Wagon 4D	AEFW	19440	6425	6650	8125	10100
LS Panel Sport Wag 2D	AEFW	19750	6650	6875	8350	10400
LT Sport Wagon 4D	AFFW	20440	7025	7275	8700	10800
Manual, 5-Spd	E		(500)	(500)	(655)	(655)
4-Cyl, Flex Fuel, 2.4L	U		300	300	390	390
MALIBU—4-Cyl.—Equipment Schedule 4						
W.B. 112.3"; 2.4 Liter.						
LS Sedan 4D	ZB5E1	22695	8500	8775	10200	12650
LT Sedan 4D	ZC5E1	23545	9150	9475	10850	13450
LTZ Sedan 4D	ZE5E1	27735	10050	10400	11850	14550
V6, 3.6 Liter	7		875	875	1115	1115
IMPALA—V6—Equipment Schedule 4						
W.B. 110.5"; 3.5 Liter, 3.9 Liter.						
LS Sedan 4D	WA5EK	25215	7775	8100	9525	11650
LT Sedan 4D	WB5EK	26430	8450	8800	10250	12600
LTZ Sedan 4D	WC5EM	30755	9725	10100	11600	14100

Body Type	VIN	List	Trade-In Good	Very Good	Pvt-Party Good	Retail Excellent
CAMARO—V6—Equipment Schedule 4						
W.B. 112.3"; 3.6 Liter.						
LS Coupe 2D	FA1ED	24525	13400	13950	15000	17450
LT Coupe 2D	FB1ED	25725	15150	15750	16850	19600
LT Convertible 2D	FB3ED	30995	16500	17150	18250	21200
RS Pkg			1275	1275	1520	1520
CAMARO—V8—Equipment Schedule 4						
W.B. 112.3"; 6.2 Liter.						
SS Coupe 2D	FJ1EJ	32790	18700	19450	20500	23800
SS Convertible 2D	FJ3EJ	38495	20100	20900	21900	25300
CORVETTE—V8—Equipment Schedule 2						
W.B.105.7"; 6.2 Liter, 7.0 Liter.						
Coupe 2D	YA2DW	49900	23500	24200	25200	28200
Convertible 2D	YA3DW	54550	27100	27900	28800	31900
Grand Sport Cpe 2D	YP2DW	55740	29100	29900	31100	34900
Grand Sport Conv 2D	YP3DW	59550	32600	33600	34800	39000
Z06 Coupe 2D	YJ2DE	75255	38100	39200	40300	45100
Dual Roof Panels			425	425	465	465
Glass Roof Panel			325	325	340	340
Heritage			1475	1475	1640	1640
4LT			1875	1875	2025	2025
Magnetic Ride Suspension			525	525	575	575
Manual, 6-Spd	A		225	225	230	230
CORVETTE—V8 Supercharged—Equipment Schedule 2						
W.B. 105.7"; 6.2 Liter.						
ZR1 Coupe 2D	YM2DT	112050	****	****	****	68500

2012 CHEVY — (1,2or3)G1or(6orK)L1(JB5SH)−C−#

Body Type	VIN	List	Trade-In Good	Very Good	Pvt-Party Good	Retail Excellent
SONIC—4-Cyl.—Equipment Schedule 6						
W.B. 99.4"; 1.8 Liter.						
LS Sedan 4D	JB5SH	14495	5825	6050	7625	9450
LS Hatchback 4D	JB6SH	15395	5975	6200	7800	9700
LT Sedan 4D	JD5SH	15695	6600	6825	8400	10350
LT Hatchback 4D	JD6SH	16495	6950	7175	8850	10950
LTZ Sedan 4D	JF5SH	17295	7550	7825	9500	11650
LTZ Hatchback 4D	JF6SH	17995	7800	8075	9700	11800
Automatic, 6-Spd.	C		475	475	620	620
4-Cyl, Turbo, 1.4 Liter	B		325	325	445	445
CRUZE—4-Cyl.—Equipment Schedule 5						
W.B. 105.7"; 1.8 Liter.						
LS Sedan 4D	PD5SH	17470	8650	9050	10150	12500
Manual, 6-Spd w/Overdrive			(500)	(500)	(645)	(645)
CRUZE—4-Cyl. Turbo—Equipment Schedule 5						
W.B. 105.7"; 1.4 Liter.						
LT Sedan 4D	PL5SC	19225	9375	9875	10800	13300
eco Sedan 4D	PK5SC	19995	9625	10050	11150	13500
Manual, 6-Spd	L,M		(500)	(500)	(635)	(635)
CRUZE—4-Cyl. Turbo—Equipment Schedule 5						
W.B. 105.7"; 1.4 Liter.						
LTZ Sedan 4D	PH5SC	23860	10550	11100	12100	15050
VOLT—AC Electric—Equipment Schedule 3						
W.B. 105.7".						
Sedan 4D	RA6S4	39995	11300	11800	12850	15500
MALIBU—4-Cyl.—Equipment Schedule 4						
W.B. 112.3"; 2.4 Liter.						
LS Sedan 4D	ZB5E0	22755	9950	10200	11850	14400
LT Sedan 4D	ZC5E0	24115	10500	10750	12300	14850
LTZ Sedan 4D	ZE5E0	29245	11400	11650	13250	15950
V6, 3.6 Liter	7		925	925	1150	1150
IMPALA—V6—Equipment Schedule 4						
W.B. 110.5"; 3.6 Liter.						
LS Sedan 4D	WA5E3	26470	9100	9425	11050	13350
LT Sedan 4D	WB5E3	27995	9225	9550	11200	13550
LTZ Sedan 4D	WC5E3	31010	10200	10550	12200	14600
CAMARO—V6—Equipment Schedule 4						
W.B. 112.3"; 3.6 Liter.						
LS Coupe 2D	FA1E3	25095	14150	14650	16000	18400
LT Coupe 2D	FB1E3	27095	16100	16650	17950	20600
LT Convertible 2D	FB3E3	31995	17550	18100	19500	22400
RS Pkg			1325	1325	1570	1570
CAMARO—V8—Equipment Schedule 4						
W.B. 112.3"; 6.2 Liter.						
SS Coupe 2D	FJ1EW	37345	20200	20900	22200	25400

Body Type	VIN	List	Trade-In Good	Very Good	Pvt-Party Good	Retail Excellent
SS Convertible 2D	FJ3EW	39795	21700	22400	23600	26800
CAMARO—V8 Supercharged—Equipment Schedule 4						
W.B. 112.3"; 6.2 Liter.						
ZL1 Coupe 2D	FS1EP	54995	32700	33700	34100	37800
CORVETTE—V8—Equipment Schedule 2						
W.B.105.7"; 6.2 Liter, 7.0 Liter.						
Coupe 2D	YA2DW	51750	25400	26000	27400	30600
Convertible 2D	YA3DW	56750	29000	29800	31000	34300
Grand Sport Coupe	YP2DW	58150	31700	32600	33900	37600
Grand Sport Conv 2D	YP3DW	61750	37300	38200	39600	44000
Z06 Coupe 2D	YJ2DE	76500	41500	42600	44100	49000
Glass Roof Panel		-------	350	350	375	375
Dual Roof Panels		-------	475	475	530	530
Centennial Edition		-------	5325	5325	5920	5920
Heritage		-------	1575	1575	1745	1745
4LT		-------	1925	1925	2115	2115
Suspension Pkg		-------	575	575	640	640
Manual, 6-Spd	A,B,C,D	-------	250	250	265	265
CORVETTE—V8 Supercharged—Equipment Schedule 2						
W.B. 105.7"; 6.2 Liter.						
ZR1 Coupe 2D	YM2DT	113500	****	****	****	74500

2013 CHEVY — (1,2or3)G1or(6orK)L1(CA6S9)–D–#

Body Type	VIN	List	Trade-In Good	Very Good	Pvt-Party Good	Retail Excellent
SPARK—4-Cyl. ECOTEC—Equipment Schedule 6						
W.B. 93.5"; 1.2 Liter.						
LS Hatchback 4D	CA6S9	12995	6475	6700	8175	9900
LT Hatchback 4D	CC6S9	14495	7100	7325	8800	10550
SONIC—4-Cyl.—Equipment Schedule 6						
W.B. 99.4".						
LS Sedan 4D	JB5S4	14995	6850	7075	8700	10600
LS Hatchback 4D	JB6SH	15595	7200	7425	9125	11150
LT Sedan 4D	JD5SH	16430	7575	7825	9550	11600
LT Hatchback 4D	JD6SH	17030	7825	8075	9775	11800
LTZ Sedan 4D	JF5SH	18040	8475	8750	10450	12500
LTZ Hatchback 4D	JF6SH	18640	8700	8975	10650	12750
Automatic, 6-Spd	C	-------	500	500	655	655
4-Cyl. Turbo, 1.4 Liter	B	-------	350	350	470	470
SONIC—4-Cyl. Turbo—Equipment Schedule 6						
W.B. 99.4"; 1.4 Liter.						
RS Hatchback 4D	JH6SB	20995	10100	10400	12000	14200
Automatic, 6-Spd	G	-------	500	500	625	625
CRUZE—4-Cyl.—Equipment Schedule 5						
W.B. 105.7"; 1.8 Liter.						
LS Sedan 4D	PA5SH	19020	9350	9725	10950	13250
Manual, 6-Spd w/Overdrive	B	-------	(525)	(525)	(675)	(675)
CRUZE—4-Cyl. Turbo—Equipment Schedule 5						
W.B. 105.7"; 1.4 Liter.						
LT Sedan 4D	PC5SB	20450	10150	10650	11700	14250
eco Sedan 4D	PH5SB	21670	10300	10700	12000	14550
LTZ Sedan 4D	PG5SB	24345	11150	11650	12700	15450
Manual, 6-Spd w/OD	D,F	-------	(525)	(525)	(665)	(665)
VOLT—AC Electric—Equipment Schedule 3						
W.B. 105.7".						
Sedan 4D	RA6E4	39995	12650	13150	14350	17100
MALIBU—4-Cyl.—Equipment Schedule 4						
W.B. 107.8"; 2.5 Liter.						
LS Sedan 4D	1B5RA	23150	11300	11450	13200	15800
LT Sedan 4D	1C5RA	24765	12350	12550	14200	16750
eco Sedan 4D	1D5RR	25995	12850	13100	14750	17450
LTZ Sedan 4D	1H5RA	28590	13300	13500	15250	18000
IMPALA—V6—Equipment Schedule 4						
W.B. 110.5"; 3.6 Liter.						
LS Sedan 4D	WA5E3	26685	9450	9750	11550	13850
LT Sedan 4D	WB5E3	28210	9925	10250	12000	14350
LTZ Sedan 4D	WC5E3	31000	11000	11350	13050	15400
CAMARO—V6—Equipment Schedule 4						
W.B. 112.3"; 3.6 Liter.						
LS Coupe 2D	FA1E3	24245	15250	15700	17150	19550
LT Coupe 2D	FB1E3	26660	17600	18100	19650	22400
LT Convertible 2D	FB3D3	31560	19150	19700	21300	24300
RS Pkg		-------	1375	1375	1620	1620
CAMARO—V8—Equipment Schedule 4						
W.B. 112.3"; 6.2 Liter.						

Body Type	VIN	List	Trade-In Good	Very Good	Pvt-Party Good	Retail Excellent
SS Coupe 2D	FJ1EJ	33535	22200	22800	24200	27300
SS Convertible 2D	FJ3DJ	39585	25200	25900	27200	30600

CAMARO—V8 Supercharged—Equipment Schedule 4
W.B. 112.3"; 6.2 Liter.

Body Type	VIN	List	Trade-In Good	Very Good	Pvt-Party Good	Retail Excellent
ZL1 Coupe 2D	FL1EP	56550	35300	36300	36700	40100
ZL1 Convertible 2D	FL3DP	61745	39700	40900	41000	44600

CORVETTE—V8—Equipment Schedule 2
W.B.105.7"; 6.2 Liter, 7.0 Liter.

Body Type	VIN	List	Trade-In Good	Very Good	Pvt-Party Good	Retail Excellent
Coupe 2D	YA2DW	51825	27900	28600	30300	33700
Convertible 2D	YA3DW	56825	30100	30800	32400	35900
Grand Sport Coupe	YP2DW	58225	34500	35300	36600	40300
Grand Sport Conv 2D	YP3DW	61825	40000	41000	42400	46800
Z06 Coupe 2D	YJ2DE	76575	44000	45200	47000	52000
427 Convertible 2D	YY3DE	76900	47600	48800	50300	55100
Glass Roof Panel			375	375	400	400
Dual Roof Panels			525	525	580	580
Heritage Pkg			1675	1675	1845	1845
4LT			1975	1975	2160	2160
Suspension Pkg			625	625	690	690
Manual, 6-Spd	A,B,C,D		275	275	290	290

CORVETTE—V8 Supercharged—Equipment Schedule 2
W.B. 105.7"; 6.2 Liter.

Body Type	VIN	List	Trade-In Good	Very Good	Pvt-Party Good	Retail Excellent
ZR1 Coupe 2D	YM2DT	113575	69000	70700	71500	77700

SPARK—4-Cyl. ECOTEC—Equipment Schedule 6
W.B. 93.5"; 1.2 Liter.

Body Type	VIN	List	Trade-In Good	Very Good	Pvt-Party Good	Retail Excellent
LS Hatchback 4D	CA6S9	12995	7025	7250	8700	10350
1LT Hatchback 4D	CC6S9	14765	7525	7750	9225	10900
2LT Hatchback 4D	CE6S9	16115	8200	8450	9900	11650
Automatic, CVT	D		525	525	650	650

SPARK EV—Electric Motor—Equipment Schedule 6
W.B. 93.5".

Body Type	VIN	List	Trade-In Good	Very Good	Pvt-Party Good	Retail Excellent
1LT Hatchback 4D	CK6S0	28305	11450	11850	13350	15450
2LT Hatchback 4D	CL6S0	28630	11750	12100	13600	15750

SONIC—4-Cyl.—Equipment Schedule 6
W.B. 99.4"; 1.8 Liter.

Body Type	VIN	List	Trade-In Good	Very Good	Pvt-Party Good	Retail Excellent
LS Sedan 4D	JB5SH	14995	7500	7750	9425	11350
LS Hatchback 4D	JB6SH	15595	7575	7825	9450	11350
LT Sedan 4D	JD5SH	16605	8425	8700	10400	12400
LT Hatchback 4D	JD6SH	17205	8550	8800	10450	12500
LTZ Sedan 4D	JF5SH	18215	9550	9850	11550	13650
LTZ Hatchback 4D	JF6SH	18815	9850	10150	11800	13950
Automatic, 6-Spd	C		525	525	675	675
4-Cyl, Turbo, 1.4 Liter	B		375	375	490	490

SONIC—4-Cyl. Turbo—Equipment Schedule 6
W.B. 99.4"; 1.4 Liter.

Body Type	VIN	List	Trade-In Good	Very Good	Pvt-Party Good	Retail Excellent
RS Sedan 4D	JH5SB	20530	11100	11450	13100	15300
RS Hatchback 4D	JH6SB	21150	11500	11850	13450	15650
Automatic, 6-Spd	G		525	525	640	640

CRUZE—4-Cyl.—Equipment Schedule 5
W.B. 105.7"; 1.8 Liter.

Body Type	VIN	List	Trade-In Good	Very Good	Pvt-Party Good	Retail Excellent
LS Sedan 4D	PA5SG	19180	10300	10750	11950	14400
Manual, 6-Spd w/Overdrive	B		(550)	(550)	(700)	(700)

CRUZE—4-Cyl. Turbo—Equipment Schedule 5
W.B. 105.7"; 1.4 Liter.

Body Type	VIN	List	Trade-In Good	Very Good	Pvt-Party Good	Retail Excellent
LT Sedan 4D	PK5SB	19790	10750	11200	12400	14950
1LT Sedan 4D	PC5SB	20635	10800	11250	12350	14700
eco Sedan 4D	PH5SB	21855	11050	11500	12700	15250
2LT Sedan 4D	PE5SB	23305	11250	11650	12900	15500
LTZ Sedan 4D	PG5SB	24530	12200	12700	13850	16600
Manual, 6-Spd w/Overdrive	D		(550)	(550)	(690)	(690)

CRUZE—4-Cyl. Turbo Diesel—Equipment Schedule 5
W.B. 105.7"; 2.0 Liter.

Body Type	VIN	List	Trade-In Good	Very Good	Pvt-Party Good	Retail Excellent
Sedan 4D	P75SZ	25710	13700	14250	15450	18300

VOLT—Electric—Equipment Schedule 3
W.B. 105.7".

Body Type	VIN	List	Trade-In Good	Very Good	Pvt-Party Good	Retail Excellent
Sedan 4D	RA674	34995	16950	17600	18500	21600

MALIBU—4-Cyl.—Equipment Schedule 4
W.B. 107.8"; 2.5 Liter.

Body Type	VIN	List	Trade-In Good	Very Good	Pvt-Party Good	Retail Excellent
LS Sedan 4D	1B5SL	22965	12250	12450	14100	16600
LT Sedan 4D	1C5SL	24335	13450	13650	15350	18000
eco Sedan 4D	1F5SR	26670	14050	14250	16000	18750

Body Type	VIN	List	Trade-In Good	Very Good	Pvt-Party Good	Retail Excellent
LTZ Sedan 4D	1H5SL	28515	15000	15200	16900	19700
4-Cyl, Turbo, 2.0 Liter	X		1775	1775	2070	2070
IMPALA—4-Cyl.—Equipment Schedule 4						
W.B. 110.5"; 2.5 Liter.						
LS Sedan 4D	1Y5SL	27535	15600	16050	17650	20200
LS Eco Sedan 4D	1Z5SR	29945	17200	17700	19200	21800
LT Eco Sedan 4D	135SR	31920	19250	19850	21200	23900
IMPALA—V6—Equipment Schedule 4						
W.B. 110.5"; 3.6 Liter.						
LT Sedan 4D	125S3	30760	17650	18200	19650	22300
LTZ Sedan 4D	155S3	36580	21400	22100	23300	26100
4-Cyl, 2.5 Liter	L		(725)	(725)	(830)	(830)
IMPALA LIMITED—V6—Equipment Schedule 4						
W.B. 110.5"; 3.6 Liter.						
LS Sedan 4D	WA5E3	26655	11300	11650	13350	15600
LT Sedan 4D	WB5E3	27665	12050	12400	14100	16500
LTZ Sedan 4D	WC5E3	31360	12900	13300	15100	17500
CAMARO—V6—Equipment Schedule 4						
W.B. 112.3"; 3.6 Liter.						
LS Coupe 2D	FE1E3	24450	16850	17350	18950	21700
LT Coupe 2D	FB1E3	27935	18950	19500	21000	23900
LT Convertible 2D	FB3D3	33135	20600	21200	22800	25800
RS Pkg			1425	1425	1675	1675
CAMARO—V8—Equipment Schedule 4						
W.B. 112.3"; 6.2 Liter, 7.0 Liter.						
SS Coupe 2D	FJ1EJ	35135	24000	24800	26100	29300
SS Convertible 2D	FJ3DJ	41135	26800	27600	29000	32500
Z/28 Coupe 2D	FS1EE	75000	57100	58800	60500	67400
RS Pkg			1425	1425	1645	1645
CAMARO—V8 Supercharged—Equipment Schedule 4						
W.B. 112.3"; 6.2 Liter.						
ZL1 Coupe 2D	FL1EP	58855	38600	39700	39900	43400
ZL1 Convertible 2D	FL3DP	64055	43500	44800	45000	48900
SS—V8—Equipment Schedule 2						
W.B. 114.8"; 6.2 Liter.						
Sedan 4D	F15RW	45770	30400	31000	32400	35100
CORVETTE—V8—Equipment Schedule 2						
W.B. 106.7"; 6.2 Liter.						
Stingray Coupe 2D	YB2D7	53345	44300	45400	46400	50700
Stingray Conv 2D	YB3D7	58345	48900	50200	51300	55800
Stingray Z51 Cpe 2D	YH2D7	56145	48200	49400	50600	55100
Stingray Z51 Conv 2D	YH3D7	61145	51500	52800	53800	58400
Glass Roof Panel			400	400	420	420
3LT			2975	2975	3185	3185
Manual, 7-Spd	A,C,E		300	300	310	310

CHRYSLER

2000 CHRYSLER — (1,2,3or4)C3–(U42N)–Y–#

Body Type	VIN	List	Trade-In Good	Very Good	Pvt-Party Good	Retail Excellent
SEBRING—V6—Equipment Schedule 4						
W.B. 103.7", 106.0" (Conv); 2.5 Liter.						
LX Coupe 2D	U42N	19635	325	400	1125	2200
LXi Coupe 2D	U52N	22015	425	525	1275	2450
JX Convertible 2D	L45H	24790	350	425	850	1500
JXi Convertible 2D	L55H	27105	950	1125	1600	2700
Limited			175	175	250	250
CIRRUS—4-Cyl.—Equipment Schedule 4						
W.B. 108.0"; 2.0 Liter, 2.4 Liter.						
LX Sedan 4D	J46B	17675	525	600	1400	2700
Manual, 5-Spd			(175)	(175)	(235)	(235)
CIRRUS—V6—Equipment Schedule 4						
W.B. 108.0"; 2.5 Liter.						
LXi Sedan 4D	J56H	20480	550	650	1475	2825
CONCORDE—V6—Equipment Schedule 4						
W.B. 113.0"; 2.7 Liter, 3.2 Liter.						
LX Sedan 4D	D46R	22550	875	1000	1650	2950
LXi Sedan 4D	D36J	26480	1300	1500	2075	3525
LHS—V6—Equipment Schedule 2						
W.B. 113.0"; 3.5 Liter.						
Sedan 4D	C56G	28695	775	900	1325	2350

Body Type	VIN	List	Trade-In Good	Very Good	Pvt-Party Good	Retail Excellent

300M—V6—Equipment Schedule 2
W.B. 113.0"; 3.5 Liter.

| Sedan 4D | E66G | 29690 | 625 | 750 | 1350 | 2550 |

2001 CHRYSLER — 1C(4or8)-(Y4BB)-1-#

PT CRUISER—4-Cyl.—Equipment Schedule 4
W.B. 103.0"; 2.4 Liter.

| Sport Wagon 4D | Y4BB | 18415 | 500 | 600 | 1200 | 2200 |
| Limited Sport Wag 4D | Y4BB | 21385 | 700 | 825 | 1425 | 2500 |

SEBRING—4-Cyl.—Equipment Schedule 4
W.B. 103.7", 108.0" (Sed); 2.4 Liter.

LX Sedan 4D	L46G	18520	600	700	1500	2825
LX Coupe 2D	G42G	20495	325	375	1175	2325
V6, 2.7 Liter	R,H		100	100	135	135

SEBRING—V6—Equipment Schedule 4
W.B. 103.7", 106.0" (Conv), 108.0" (Sed); 2.7 Liter, 3.0 Liter.

LXi Sedan 4D	L66R	21405	700	800	1675	3175
LXi Coupe 2D	G62H	22685	425	500	1325	2575
LX Convertible 2D	L55U	24945	400	475	925	1625
LXi Convertible 2D	L65U	27405	1025	1200	1775	3075
Limited Convertible 2D	L65U	29490	1625	1900	2625	4450

CONCORDE—V6—Equipment Schedule 4
W.B. 113.0"; 2.7 Liter, 3.2 Liter.

| LX Sedan 4D | D46R | 22995 | 975 | 1125 | 1775 | 3150 |
| LXi Sedan 4D | D36J | 27240 | 1475 | 1675 | 2275 | 3850 |

LHS—V6—Equipment Schedule 2
W.B. 113.0"; 3.5 Liter.

| Sedan 4D | C56G | 29210 | 900 | 1050 | 1550 | 2725 |

300M—V6—Equipment Schedule 2
W.B. 113.0"; 3.5 Liter.

| Sedan 4D | E00G | 30170 | 975 | 1150 | 1700 | 3050 |

PROWLER—V6—Equipment Schedule 1
W.B. 113.3"; 3.5 Liter.

| Roadster 2D | W65G | 45400 | 14650 | 15500 | 15350 | 19100 |

2002 CHRYSLER-(1,2,3or4)C(3,4or8)-(Y48B)-2-#

PT CRUISER—4-Cyl.—Equipment Schedule 4
W.B. 103.0"; 2.4 Liter.

Sport Wagon 4D	Y48B	17590	600	700	1400	2575
Touring Sport Wag 4D	Y58B	19305	725	850	1500	2700
Limited Sport Wag 4D	Y68B	21655	900	1025	1700	3025
Dream Cruiser			375	375	505	505
Woodie Edition			150	150	200	200

SEBRING—4-Cyl.—Equipment Schedule 4
W.B. 103.7", 106.0" (Conv), 108.0" (Sed); 2.4 Liter.

LX Sedan 4D	L46X	18535	575	675	1475	2825
LX Coupe 2D	G42G	20615	325	400	1175	2325
LX Convertible 2D	L55G	23905	475	575	1025	1775
V6, 2.7 Liter	R,H		125	125	175	175

SEBRING—V6—Equipment Schedule 4
W.B. 103.7", 106.0" (Conv), 108.0" (Sed); 2.7 Liter, 3.0 Liter.

LXi Sedan 4D	L56R	20875	825	950	1825	3400
LXi Coupe 2D	G52H	23130	400	475	1300	2550
LXi Convertible 2D	L55R	26755	1225	1400	1950	3275
GTC Convertible 2D	L75R	25875	525	625	1075	1850
Limited Convertible 2D	L65R	29390	1875	2150	2850	4725

CONCORDE—V6—Equipment Schedule 4
W.B. 113.0"; 2.7 Liter, 3.5 Liter.

LX Sedan 4D	D46R	22995	1075	1225	1850	3200
LXi Sedan 4D	D36M	25600	1525	1725	2450	4150
Limited Sedan 4D	D56G	28495	2050	2300	3050	5100

300M—V6—Equipment Schedule 2
W.B. 113.0"; 3.5 Liter.

| Sedan 4D | E66G | 28995 | 1175 | 1350 | 1925 | 3350 |
| Special Sedan 4D | E76K | 32595 | 1350 | 1550 | 2125 | 3675 |

PROWLER—V6—Equipment Schedule 1
W.B. 113.3"; 3.5 Liter.

| Roadster 2D | W65G | 45400 | 16850 | 17800 | 17400 | 21300 |

2003 CHRYSLER-(1,2,3or4)C(3,4or8)-(Y48B)-3-#

PT CRUISER—4-Cyl.—Equipment Schedule 4
W.B. 103.0"; 2.4 Liter.

Body Type	VIN	List	Trade-In Good	Very Good	Pvt-Party Good	Retail Excellent
Sport Wagon 4D	Y48B	18010	725	825	1525	2700
Touring Sport Wag 4D	Y58B	19940	975	1125	1775	3050
Limited Sport Wag 4D	Y68B	22180	1025	1175	1875	3225
Woodie Edition			175	175	245	245
PT CRUISER—4-Cyl. HO Turbo—Equipment Schedule 4						
W.B. 103.0"; 2.4 Liter.						
GT Sport Wagon 4D	Y78G	23320	1200	1375	1975	3325
Dream Cruiser			400	400	540	540
SEBRING—4-Cyl.—Equipment Schedule 4						
W.B. 103.7", 106.0" (Conv), 108.0" (Sed); 2.4 Liter.						
LX Sedan 4D	L46X	19930	525	600	1450	2775
LX Coupe 2D	G42G	21560	250	300	1150	2350
LX Convertible 2D	L45X	24560	550	650	1100	1875
V6, Flex Fuel, 2.7 Liter	U,R		175	175	245	245
SEBRING—V6—Equipment Schedule 4						
W.B. 103.7", 106.0" (Conv), 108.0" (Sed); 2.7 Liter, 3.0 Liter.						
LXi Sedan 4D	L56R	21295	1200	1350	2275	4075
LXi Coupe 2D	G52H	23835	400	475	1375	2700
GTC Convertible 2D	L75R	26160	750	875	1375	2325
LXi Convertible 2D	L55T	27410	1450	1650	2150	3500
Limited Convertible 2D	L65R	30045	2050	2350	3200	5325
CONCORDE—V6—Equipment Schedule 4						
W.B. 113.0"; 2.7 Liter, 3.5 Liter.						
LX Sedan 4D	D46R	23510	1375	1550	2275	3925
LXi Sedan 4D	D36M	26240	1925	2150	3025	5100
Limited Sedan 4D	D56G	29135	2450	2750	3625	6050
300M—V6—Equipment Schedule 2						
W.B. 113.0"; 3.5 Liter.						
Sedan 4D	E66G	29245	1475	1675	2275	3925
Special Sedan 4D	E76K	32895	1425	1625	2450	4125

2004 CHRYSLER – (1,2,3or4)C(3,4or8)–(Y48B)–4–#

Body Type	VIN	List	Trade-In Good	Very Good	Pvt-Party Good	Retail Excellent
PT CRUISER—4-Cyl.—Equipment Schedule 4						
W.B. 103.0"; 2.4 Liter.						
Sport Wagon 4D	Y48B	19515	900	1025	1750	3050
Touring Sport Wag 4D	Y58B	20585	975	1125	1875	3250
Limited Sport Wag 4D	Y68B	22825	1200	1375	2150	3700
4-Cyl, Turbo, 2.4 Liter	8		425	425	575	575
PT CRUISER—4-Cyl. HO Turbo—Equipment Schedule 4						
W.B. 103.0"; 2.4 Liter.						
GT Sport Wagon 4D	Y78G	26245	1350	1525	2325	3900
SEBRING—4-Cyl.—Equipment Schedule 4						
W.B. 103.7", 106.0" (Conv), 108.0" (Sed); 2.4 Liter.						
Sedan 4D	L66R	19360	875	1000	1825	3325
Coupe 2D	G42G	22305	500	600	1450	2775
Convertible 2D	L45J	25570	275	350	925	1675
LX Sedan 4D	L46X	19500	700	800	1925	3700
LX Convertible 2D	L45X	25215	475	550	1075	1900
V6, Flex Fuel, 2.7 Liter	T		225	225	310	310
SEBRING—V6—Equipment Schedule 4						
W.B. 103.7", 106.0" (Conv), 108.0" (Sed); 2.7 Liter, 3.0 Liter.						
LXi Sedan 4D	L56R	21840	1725	1950	2875	4875
LXi Convertible 2D	L55T	28140	1225	1425	2100	3475
GTC Convertible 2D	L75R	27045	700	800	1475	2625
Touring Sedan 4D	L56R	21200	1475	1675	2575	4450
Touring Convertible 2D	L55T	28370	1450	1650	2350	3875
Limited Sedan 4D	L66R	23490	1850	2075	3050	5225
Limited Coupe 2D	G52H	24580	1000	1125	1950	3500
Limited Convertible 2D	L65R	31180	2100	2400	3325	5525
CONCORDE—V6—Equipment Schedule 4						
W.B. 113.0"; 2.7 Liter, 3.5 Liter.						
LX Sedan 4D	D46R	24130	1550	1750	2750	4800
LXi Sedan 4D	D36M	26860	2300	2575	3575	6050
Limited Sedan 4D	D56G	29755	2925	3275	4300	7175
300M—V6—Equipment Schedule 2						
W.B. 113.0"; 3.5 Liter.						
Sedan 4D	E66G	29865	1650	1900	2600	4375
Special Sedan 4D	E76K	33295	1775	2025	2775	4700
CROSSFIRE—V6—Equipment Schedule 1						
W.B. 94.5"; 3.2 Liter.						
Coupe 2D	N69L	35570	2250	2450	3275	5025

Body Type	VIN	List	Trade-In Good	Very Good	Pvt-Party Good	Retail Excellent

2005 CHRYSLER — (1,2,3or4)C(4or8)-(Y48B)-5-#

PT CRUISER—4-Cyl.—Equipment Schedule 4
W.B. 103.0"; 2.4 Liter.

Body Type	VIN	List	Good	Very Good	Good	Excellent
Sport Wagon 4D	Y48B	14820	1000	1150	1975	3300
Convertible 2D	Y45X	21685	1400	1600	2525	4125
Touring Sport Wag 4D	Y58B	13820	1175	1325	2300	3825
Limited Sport Wag 4D	Y68B	18730	1300	1500	2500	4125
4-Cyl, Turbo, 2.4 Liter	E		450	450	610	610

PT CRUISER—4-Cyl.Turbo—Equipment Schedule 4
W.B. 103.0"; 2.4 Liter.

Touring Convertible 2D	Y55X	25595	2075	2350	3250	5150
4-Cyl, 2.4 Liter	B,X		(425)	(425)	(560)	(560)

PT CRUISER—4-Cyl. HO Turbo—Equipment Schedule 4
W.B. 103.0"; 2.4 Liter.

GT Sport Wagon 4D	Y78S	23935	1975	2225	3100	4925
GT Convertible 2D	Y75S	28595	2350	2650	3425	5325

SEBRING—4-Cyl.—Equipment Schedule 4
W.B. 103.7", 106.0" (Conv), 108.0" (Sed); 2.4 Liter.

Sedan 4D	L46X	19975	775	900	1925	3475
Coupe 2D	G42G	22770	400	475	1500	2825
Convertible 2D	L45X	26035	450	550	1425	2525
V6, 2.7 Liter	R		275	275	375	375

SEBRING—V6—Equipment Schedule 4
W.B. 103.7", 106.0" (Conv), 108.0" (Sed); 2.7 Liter, 3.0 Liter.

GTC Convertible 2D	L75R	27510	800	950	1750	2950
Touring Sedan 4D	L56R	20695	1450	1650	2750	4675
Touring Convertible 2D	L55T	28835	1600	1850	2750	4425
Limited Sedan 4D	L66R	22985	2000	2250	3400	5675
Limited Coupe 2D	G52H	25045	900	1025	2075	3675
Limited Convertible 2D	L65R	31645	2300	2600	3625	5850
TSi Sedan 4D	L56R	24455	2450	2750	3975	6625

300—V6—Equipment Schedule 2
W.B. 120.0"; 2.7 Liter, 3.5 Liter.

Sedan 4D	A43R	24695	3300	3650	4400	6550
Touring Sedan 4D	A53G	27720	3975	4375	5075	7475
Signature Series			175	175	225	225
Limited			700	700	920	920
AWD			550	550	725	725

300C—V8 HEMI—Equipment Schedule 2
W.B. 120.0"; 5.7 Liter.

Sedan 4D	A63H	33495	4675	5150	5800	8500
AWD	K		550	550	725	725

300—V8 HEMI—Equipment Schedule 2
W.B. 120.0"; 6.1 Liter.

SRT8 Sedan 4D	A73W	39995	6825	7700	7425	10250

CROSSFIRE—V6—Equipment Schedule 1
W.B. 94.5"; 3.2 Liter.

Coupe 2D	N69L	29920	1750	1925	2950	4550
Roadster 2D	N65L	34960	3500	3800	4925	7200
Limited Coupe 2D	N69L	35695	3400	3675	4625	6825
Limited Roadster 2D	N65L	39995	4550	4925	5975	8625

CROSSFIRE—V6 Supercharged—Equipment Schedule 1
W.B. 94.5"; 3.2 Liter.

SRT-6 Coupe 2D	N79N	34695	6200	6725	7900	11400
SRT-6 Roadster 2D	N75N	49995	6725	7300	8425	12100

2006 CHRYSLER — (1,2,3or4)C(4or8)-(Y48B)-6-#

PT CRUISER—4-Cyl.—Equipment Schedule 4
W.B. 103.0"; 2.4 Liter.

Sport Wagon 4D	Y48B	15950	1250	1425	2300	3700
Convertible 2D	Y45X	21795	1950	2175	3075	4800
Touring Sport Wag 4D	Y58B	16995	1625	1825	2725	4325
Limited Sport Wag 4D	Y68B	20360	1750	1950	2975	4775
Route 66 Edition			100	100	130	130
Signature Series			125	125	180	180
4-Cyl, Turbo, 2.4 Liter	E,8		475	475	645	645

PT CRUISER—4-Cyl. Turbo—Equipment Schedule 4
W.B. 103.0"; 2.4 Liter.

Touring Convertible 2D	Y55X	26150	2600	2900	3750	5725
4-Cyl, 2.4 Liter	B,X		(450)	(450)	(600)	(600)

PT CRUISER—4-Cyl. Turbo—Equipment Schedule 4
W.B. 103.0"; 2.4 Liter.

Body Type	VIN	List	Trade-In Good	Very Good	Pvt-Party Good	Retail Excellent
GT Sport Wagon 4D	Y78G	24835	2300	2550	3425	5300
GT Convertible 2D	Y75S	30050	2750	3050	3875	5875
SEBRING—4-Cyl.—Equipment Schedule 4						
W.B. 106.0", 108.0" (Sed); 2.4 Liter.						
Sedan 4D	L46X	20380	1275	1450	2575	4350
Convertible 2D	L45X	26440	625	750	1625	2775
V6, 2.7 Liter	T		325	325	445	445
SEBRING—V6—Equipment Schedule 4						
W.B. 106.0", 108.0" (Sed); 2.7 Liter.						
TSi Sedan 4D	L36R	24665	3075	3425	4650	7400
GTC Convertible 2D	L75R	27915	975	1125	1975	3275
Touring Sedan 4D	L56R	21100	1825	2050	3100	5075
Touring Convertible 2D	L55R	29240	1975	2225	3100	4850
Limited Sedan 4D	L66R	23390	2450	2725	3825	6175
Limited Convertible 2D	L65R	32050	2700	3050	4000	6275
300—V6—Equipment Schedule 2						
W.B. 120.0"; 2.7 Liter, 3.5 Liter.						
Sedan 4D	A43R	24200	4325	4725	5450	7875
Touring Sedan 4D	A53G	28300	4775	5225	5875	8425
Signature Series			175	175	245	245
Limited			750	750	995	995
AWD	K		600	600	815	815
300C—V8 HEMI—Equipment Schedule 2						
W.B. 120.0"; 5.7 Liter.						
Sedan 4D	A63H	34100	5750	6300	7025	10000
Heritage			275	275	355	355
AWD	K		600	600	815	815
300—V8 HEMI—Equipment Schedule 2						
W.B. 120.0"; 6.1 Liter.						
SRT8 Sedan 4D	A73W	42695	10150	11300	10600	14200
CROSSFIRE—Equipment Schedule 1						
W.B. 94.5"; 3.2 Liter.						
Coupe 2D	N59L	30070	2450	2650	3825	5800
Roadster 2D	N55L	35110	4100	4425	5725	8325
Limited Coupe 2D	N69L	36195	3725	4025	5325	7825
Limited Roadster 2D	N65L	40545	5250	5650	6925	9975
CROSSFIRE—V6 Supercharged—Equipment Schedule 1						
W.B. 94.5"; 3.2 Liter.						
SRT-6 Coupe 2D	N79N	46085	6950	7475	8775	12500
SRT-6 Roadster 2D	N75N	50395	7825	8400	9775	13800

2007 CHRYSLER — (1,2,3or4)C(4or8)-(Y48B)-7-#

Body Type	VIN	List	Trade-In Good	Very Good	Pvt-Party Good	Retail Excellent
PT CRUISER—4-Cyl.—Equipment Schedule 4						
W.B. 103.0"; 2.4 Liter.						
Sport Wagon 4D	Y48B	15950	1500	1675	2575	4000
Convertible 2D	Y45X	22045	2475	2750	3625	5450
Touring Sport Wag 4D	Y58B	18295	1875	2075	3025	4650
Limited Sport Wag 4D	Y68B	21740	2475	2750	3725	5675
Signature Series			150	150	195	195
Street Cruiser	PCH		300	300	385	385
4-Cyl, Turbo, 2.4 Liter	8,E		500	500	680	680
PT CRUISER—4-Cyl. Turbo—Equipment Schedule 4						
W.B. 103.0"; 2.4 Liter.						
Touring Convertible 2D	Y55X	26350	3075	3375	4300	6300
GT Sport Wagon 4D	Y78G	24835	2875	3175	4150	6175
GT Convertible 2D	Y75S	30050	3275	3600	4550	6675
SEBRING—4-Cyl.—Equipment Schedule 4						
W.B. 108.9"; 2.4 Liter.						
Sedan 4D	C46K	18995	2775	3100	3900	5900
Touring Sedan 4D	C56K	20195	3225	3600	4425	6575
Limited Sedan 4D	C66K	23995	3850	4275	5175	7700
V6, Flex Fuel, 2.7 Liter	R		375	375	485	485
V6, HO, 3.5 Liter	M		500	500	680	680
300—V6—Equipment Schedule 2						
W.B. 120.0"; 2.7 Liter, 3.5 Liter.						
Sedan 4D	A43R	24480	5050	5475	6075	8450
Touring Sedan 4D	A53G	29290	5500	5975	6775	9425
Signature Series			200	200	260	260
Limited			800	800	1075	1075
AWD			675	675	905	905
300C—V8 HEMI—Equipment Schedule 2						
W.B. 120.0"; 5.7 Liter.						
Sedan 4D	A63H	34935	6975	7550	8400	11650

Body Type	VIN	List	Trade-In Good	Very Good	Pvt-Party Good	Retail Excellent
SRT Design		......	275	275	355	355
Heritage		......	300	300	385	385
AWD	K		675	675	905	905
300—V8 HEMI—Equipment Schedule 2						
W.B. 120.0"; 6.1 Liter.						
SRT8 Sedan 4D	A73W	40970	11350	12500	11850	15500
CROSSFIRE—V6—Equipment Schedule 1						
W.B. 94.5"; 3.2 Liter.						
Coupe 2D	N59L	30435	2775	2975	4100	5975
Roadster 2D	N55L	36595	4625	4950	6200	8750
Limited Coupe 2D	N69L	36560	4175	4475	5750	8150
Limited Roadster 2D	N65L	40955	5975	6375	7675	10650

2008 CHRYSLER — (1,2,3or4)C(4or8)(Y48B)-8-#

Body Type	VIN	List	Trade-In Good	Very Good	Pvt-Party Good	Retail Excellent
PT CRUISER—4-Cyl.—Equipment Schedule 4						
W.B. 103.0"; 2.4 Liter.						
Sport Wagon 4D	Y48B	16780	2225	2400	3425	5025
Convertible 2D	Y55X	19995	3150	3400	4525	6500
Touring Sport Wag 4D	Y58B	19570	2725	2950	3950	5725
Signature Series		......	175	175	220	220
4-Cyl, Turbo, 2.4 Liter	E		550	550	720	720
PT CRUISER—4-Cyl. Turbo—Equipment Schedule 4						
W.B. 103.0"; 2.4 Liter.						
Limited Sport Wag 4D	Y688	23300	3850	4150	5225	7350
SEBRING—4-Cyl.—Equipment Schedule 4						
W.B. 108.9"; 2.4 Liter.						
LX Sedan 4D	C46K	19365	3725	4100	4925	6975
LX Convertible 2D	C45K	26515	3300	3650	4575	6525
Touring Sedan 4D	C56K	20540	4000	4400	5200	7350
Limited Sedan 4D	C00K	24190	5025	5550	6475	9075
Signature Series		......	200	200	260	260
AWD	D		1050	1050	1390	1390
V6, HO, 3.5 Liter		......	550	550	730	730
SEBRING—V6—Equipment Schedule 4						
W.B. 108.9"; 2.7 Liter, 3.5 Liter.						
Touring Convertible 2D	C55R	29115	4425	4850	5725	8050
Limited Convertible 2D	C65M	32730	5725	6275	7200	9875
Power Hard Top		......	400	400	540	540
300—V6—Equipment Schedule 2						
W.B. 120.0"; 2.7 Liter, 3.5 Liter.						
Sedan 4D	A43R	25270	5400	5775	6725	9000
Touring Sedan 4D	A53G	29265	6575	7025	7900	10500
Limited Sedan 4D	A33G	32295	7375	7875	8725	11500
DUB Pkg		......	325	325	440	440
Signature Series		......	250	250	320	320
AWD	K		750	750	985	985
300C—V8 HEMI—Equipment Schedule 2						
W.B. 120.0"; 5.7 Liter.						
Sedan 4D	A63H	36070	8475	9050	9950	13150
Adaptive Cruise Control		......	375	375	480	480
SRT Design		......	300	300	380	380
Heritage		......	325	325	435	435
AWD	K		750	750	970	970
300C—V8 HEMI—Equipment Schedule 2						
W.B. 120.0"; 6.1 Liter.						
SRT8 Sedan 4D	A73W	44223	13200	14200	14100	17750
CROSSFIRE—V6—Equipment Schedule 1						
W.B. 94.5"; 3.2 Liter.						
Limited Coupe 2D	N69L	36685	5450	5750	7125	9500
Limited Roadster 2D	N65L	41130	7450	7850	9225	12150

2009 CHRYSLER — (1,2,3or4)C(4or8)(Y489)-9-#

Body Type	VIN	List	Trade-In Good	Very Good	Pvt-Party Good	Retail Excellent
PT CRUISER—4-Cyl.—Equipment Schedule 4						
W.B. 103.0"; 2.4 Liter.						
Sport Wagon 4D	Y489	18745	3100	3300	4425	6050
Touring Sport Wag 4D	Y589	20700	3325	3525	4650	6375
Dream Cruiser		......	550	550	740	740
4-Cyl, Turbo, 2.4 Liter	E		575	575	755	755
PT CRUISER—4-Cyl. Turbo—Equipment Schedule 4						
W.B. 103.0"; 2.4 Liter.						
Limited Sport Wag 4D	Y688	24430	4825	5100	6225	8325

Body Type	VIN	List	Trade-In Good	Very Good	Pvt-Party Good	Retail Excellent
SEBRING—4-Cyl.—Equipment Schedule 4						
W.B. 108.9"; 2.4 Liter.						
LX Sedan 4D	C46K	21255	4700	5125	5900	8000
LX Convertible 2D	C45K	28130	3875	4225	5175	7100
Touring Sedan 4D	C56B	21655	5000	5450	6400	8675
Limited Sedan 4D	C66B	26660	6050	6600	7550	10200
V6, HO, 3.5 Liter	V		450	450	600	600
SEBRING—V6—Equipment Schedule 4						
W.B. 108.9"; 2.7 Liter, 3.5 Liter.						
Touring Convertible 2D	C55D	30610	4950	5400	6475	8750
Limited Convertible 2D	C65V	35465	7300	7925	8800	11550
Power Hard Top			425	425	580	580
300—V6—Equipment Schedule 2						
W.B. 120.0"; 2.7 Liter, 3.5 Liter.						
LX Sedan 4D	A43D	27415	6650	7025	8050	10300
Touring Sedan 4D	A53V	29885	7500	7925	8975	11450
Limited Sedan 4D	A33V	35220	8450	8925	9950	12700
AWD			800	800	1045	1045
300C—V8 HEMI—Equipment Schedule 2						
W.B. 120.0"; 5.7 Liter.						
Sedan 4D	A63T	37585	10100	10700	11800	15050
Adaptive Cruise Control			375	375	470	470
Heritage			375	375	485	485
AWD	K		800	800	1020	1020
300—V8 HEMI—Equipment Schedule 2						
W.B. 120.0"; 6.1 Liter.						
SRT8 Sedan 4D	A73W	46361	15650	16550	16700	20100

2010 CHRYSLER — (1,2or3)(AorC)(3or4)(Y5F9)–A–#

Body Type	VIN	List	Trade-In Good	Very Good	Pvt-Party Good	Retail Excellent
PT CRUISER—4-Cyl.—Equipment Schedule 4						
W.B. 103.0"; 2.4 Liter.						
Classic Sport Wag 4D	Y5F9	18995	4825	5050	6075	7750
SEBRING—4-Cyl.—Equipment Schedule 4						
W.B. 108.9"; 2.4 Liter.						
LX Convertible 2D	C4EB	28590	5025	5425	6475	8425
Touring Sedan 4D	C4FB	20860	6325	6850	7900	10400
Limited Sedan 4D	C5FB	22855	7300	7900	8850	11500
V6, HO, 3.5 Liter	V		525	525	700	700
SEBRING—V6—Equipment Schedule 4						
W.B.108.9"; 2.7 Liter.						
Touring Convertible 2D	C5ED	29950	6700	7200	8175	10500
Limited Convertible 2D	C6EV	35445	9875	10600	11350	14150
Power Hard Top			450	450	565	565
300—V6—Equipment Schedule 2						
W.B. 120.0"; 2.7 Liter, 3.5 Liter.						
Touring Sedan 4D	A5CD	28010	8725	9125	10150	12350
Touring Plus Sed 4D	A5CV	29100	8975	9425	10400	12650
Touring Signature Sed	A5CV	31225	9050	9475	10600	12950
Limited Sedan 4D	A3CV	35860	10300	10800	11950	14550
AWD	K		950	950	1195	1195
300C—V8 HEMI—Equipment Schedule 2						
W.B. 120.0"; 5.7 Liter.						
Sedan 4D	A6CT	38760	11550	12100	13300	16200
Adaptive Cruise Control			400	400	480	480
AWD	K		950	950	1180	1180
300—V8 HEMI—Equipment Schedule 2						
W.B. 120.0"; 6.1 Liter.						
SRT8 Sedan 4D	A7CW	45615	17050	17800	18450	21800

2011 CHRYSLER — (1,2or3)(AorC)(3or4)(C4FB)–B–#

Body Type	VIN	List	Trade-In Good	Very Good	Pvt-Party Good	Retail Excellent
200—4-Cyl.—Equipment Schedule 4						
W.B. 108.9"; 2.4 Liter.						
LX Sedan 4D	C4FB	19995	7425	8000	8800	10950
Touring Convertible 2D	C2EB	27195	8750	9350	10250	12600
Limited Convertible 2D	C7EG	31990	12400	13250	13900	16800
Power Hard Top			500	500	580	580
V6, Flex Fuel, 3.6 Liter	G		825	825	1065	1065
200—V6—Equipment Schedule 4						
W.B. 108.9"; 3.6 Liter.						
Touring Sedan 4D	C1FB	23790	8475	9125	10000	12600
Limited Sedan 4D	C2FB	26290	9025	9725	10600	13300
4-Cyl, 2.4 Liter	B		(600)	(600)	(760)	(760)

Body Type	VIN	List	Trade-In Good	Very Good	Pvt-Party Good	Retail Excellent
200—V6—Equipment Schedule 4						
W.B. 108.9"; 3.6 Liter.						
S Sedan 4D	C8FG	26790	**9850**	**10600**	**11450**	**14250**
S Convertible 2D	C8EG	32490	**13050**	**13950**	**14600**	**17550**
300—V6—Equipment Schedule 2						
W.B. 120.0"; 3.6 Liter.						
Sedan 4D	A4CG	27995	**13100**	**13600**	**14500**	**16850**
Limited Sedan 4D	A5CG	31995	**13700**	**14250**	**15400**	**18000**
Adaptive Cruise Control			425	425	490	490
300C—V8 HEMI—Equipment Schedule 2						
W.B. 120.0"; 5.7 Liter.						
Sedan 4D	A6CT	38995	**15650**	**16250**	**17400**	**20300**
Adaptive Cruise Control			425	425	490	490

Body Type	VIN	List	Trade-In Good	Very Good	Pvt-Party Good	Retail Excellent
200—4-Cyl.—Equipment Schedule 4						
W.B. 108.9"; 2.4 Liter.						
LX Sedan 4D	CBAB	19745	**8875**	**9525**	**10350**	**12700**
Touring Convertible 2D	CBEB	27325	**10000**	**10600**	**11550**	**13900**
V6, Flex Fuel, 3.6 Liter	G		**875**	**875**	**1085**	**1085**
200—V6—Equipment Schedule 4						
W.B. 108.9"; 3.6 Liter.						
Touring Sedan 4D	CBBB	23915	**9600**	**10300**	**11200**	**13800**
Limited Sedan 4D	CBCB	26615	**10050**	**10800**	**11650**	**14300**
4-Cyl, 2.4 Liter	B		**(625)**	**(625)**	**(805)**	**(805)**
200—V6—Equipment Schedule 4						
W.B. 108.9"; 3.6 Liter.						
S Sedan 4D	CBHG	27115	**10850**	**11650**	**12600**	**15500**
S Convertible 2D	CBGG	32820	**14350**	**15200**	**15950**	**18850**
Limited Convertible 2D	CBFG	32320	**13500**	**14300**	**15200**	**18050**
Power Hard Top			525	525	630	630
300—V6—Equipment Schedule 4						
W.B. 120.0"; 3.6 Liter.						
Sedan 4D	CAAG	27995	**14550**	**15050**	**16400**	**18900**
Limited Sedan 4D	CACG	32995	**15600**	**16100**	**17350**	**19900**
AWD	H		1075	1075	1235	1235
300S—V6—Equipment Schedule 2						
W.B. 120.0"; 3.6 Liter.						
Sedan 4D	CABG	33995	**16700**	**17300**	**18750**	**21700**
Adaptive Cruise Control			450	450	515	515
Mopar 12			5175	5175	6060	6060
V8, HEMI, 5.7 Liter	T		1825	1825	2150	2150
300C—V8 HEMI—Equipment Schedule 2						
W.B. 120.0"; 5.7 Liter.						
300C Sedan 4D	CAET	38995	**17050**	**17600**	**19000**	**21800**
300C Luxury Series Sed	CAPT	42895	**19400**	**20000**	**21300**	**24400**
Adaptive Cruise Control			450	450	515	515
AWD	K		1075	1075	1240	1240
300—V8 HEMI—Equipment Schedule 2						
W.B. 120.0"; 6.4 Liter.						
SRT8 Sedan 4D	CAFJ	47995	**27100**	**27700**	**28800**	**32000**
Adaptive Cruise Control			450	450	490	490

Body Type	VIN	List	Trade-In Good	Very Good	Pvt-Party Good	Retail Excellent
200—4-Cyl.—Equipment Schedule 4						
W.B. 108.9"; 2.4 Liter.						
LX Sedan 4D	CBAB	19990	**9825**	**10500**	**11450**	**13900**
Touring Convertible 2D	CBEB	28095	**12050**	**12750**	**13600**	**16050**
V6, Flex Fuel, 3.6 Liter	G		**900**	**900**	**1060**	**1060**
200—V6—Equipment Schedule 4						
W.B. 108.9"; 3.6 Liter.						
LX Z Sedan 4D	CBAG	22385	**10050**	**10750**	**11650**	**14150**
Touring Sedan 4D	CBBB	22990	**10450**	**11200**	**12100**	**14700**
Limited Sedan 4D	CBCB	25680	**11050**	**11700**	**12550**	**15200**
Limited Convertible 2D	CBFG	33090	**15950**	**16850**	**17600**	**20600**
S Convertible 2D	CBGG	33590	**16600**	**17550**	**18200**	**21100**
Power Hard Top			575	575	670	670
4-Cyl, 2.4 Liter	B		**(675)**	**(675)**	**(845)**	**(845)**
300—V6—Equipment Schedule 2						
W.B. 120.0"; 3.6 Liter.						
Sedan 4D	CAAG	30840	**15950**	**16450**	**18050**	**20700**
Motown Sedan 4D	CAAG	34140	**17000**	**17500**	**19000**	**21700**

Body Type	VIN	List	Trade-In Good	Very Good	Pvt-Party Good	Retail Excellent
Adaptive Cruise Control			475	475	540	540
AWD	R		1175	1175	1350	1350

300S—V6—Equipment Schedule 2
W.B. 120.0"; 3.6 Liter.

Body Type	VIN	List	Good	Very Good	Good	Excellent
Sedan 4D	CABG	33990	17000	17500	19250	22200
Adaptive Cruise Control			475	475	545	545
AWD	G		1175	1175	1370	1370
V8, HEMI, 5.7 Liter	T		2175	2175	2565	2565

300S AWD—V6 Flex Fuel—Equipment Schedule 2
W.B. 120.0"; 3.6 Liter.

Body Type	VIN	List	Good	Very Good	Good	Excellent
Glacier Sedan 4D	CAGG	37840	19450	20000	21600	24700
Adaptive Cruise Control			475	475	540	540
V8, HEMI, 5.7 Liter	T		2175	2175	2540	2540

300C—V6—Equipment Schedule 2
W.B. 120.0"; 3.6 Liter.

Body Type	VIN	List	Good	Very Good	Good	Excellent
Sedan 4D	CACG	36990	17450	18000	19600	22500
Luxury Series Sedan	CAPG	40990	19650	20300	21800	24800
Varvatos Luxury Sedan	CADG	41490	21200	21900	23700	27200
Varvatos Limited Sed	CADG	44490	21800	22500	24100	27600
Adaptive Cruise Control			475	475	540	540
AWD	K		1175	1175	1355	1355
V8, HEMI, 5.7 Liter	T		2175	2175	2530	2530

300—V8 HEMI—Equipment Schedule 2
W.B. 120.0"; 6.4 Liter.

Body Type	VIN	List	Good	Very Good	Good	Excellent
SRT8 Core Sedan 4D	CAXJ	46275	26100	26600	28400	31700
SRT8 Sedan 4D	CAFJ	49845	30200	30700	32600	36200
Adaptive Cruise Control			475	475	520	520

2014 CHRYSLER — (1,2or3)C3–(CBEB)–E–#

200—4-Cyl.—Equipment Schedule 4
W.B. 108.9"; 2.4 Liter.

Body Type	VIN	List	Good	Very Good	Good	Excellent
Touring Convertible 2D	CBEB	28695	14850	15700	16350	18950
V6, Flex Fuel, 3.6 Liter	G		950	950	1075	1075

200—V6—Equipment Schedule 4
W.B. 108.9"; 3.6 Liter.

Body Type	VIN	List	Good	Very Good	Good	Excellent
LX Sedan 4D	CBAG	22190	10800	11550	12500	15200
Touring Sedan 4D	CBBG	23660	11250	12050	13100	15950
Limited Sedan 4D	CBCG	26350	12100	12950	13850	16700
Limited Convertible 2D	CBFG	33690	19000	20000	20500	23600
S Convertible 2D	CBDG	34190	20100	21200	21600	24800
Power Hard Top			675	675	750	750
4-Cyl. 2.4 Liter	B		(875)	(875)	(1075)	(1075)

300—V6—Equipment Schedule 2
W.B. 120.2"; 3.6 Liter.

Body Type	VIN	List	Good	Very Good	Good	Excellent
Sedan 4D	CAAG	34040	17100	17600	19300	22100
Uptown Ed Sedan 4D	CAAG	34990	18050	18550	20400	23500
Adaptive Cruise Control			500	500	565	565
AWD	R		1225	1225	1420	1420

300S—V6—Equipment Schedule 2
W.B. 120.2"; 3.6 Liter.

Body Type	VIN	List	Good	Very Good	Good	Excellent
Sedan 4D	CABG	34540	18050	18550	20400	23400
Adaptive Cruise Control			500	500	570	570
AWD	G		1225	1225	1435	1435
V8, HEMI, 5.7 Liter	T		2525	2525	2955	2955

300C—V6—Equipment Schedule 2
W.B. 120.2"; 3.6 Liter.

Body Type	VIN	List	Good	Very Good	Good	Excellent
Sedan 4D	CAEG	37540	18200	18750	20400	23400
John Varvatos Sedan	CADG	42040	22700	23300	25200	28800
John Varvatos Ltd 4D	CADG	45475	23200	23900	25900	29700
Adaptive Cruise Control			500	500	570	570
AWD	K		1225	1225	1430	1430
V8, HEMI, 5.7 Liter	T		2525	2525	2940	2940

300—V8 HEMI—Equipment Schedule 2
W.B. 120.2"; 6.4 Liter.

Body Type	VIN	List	Good	Very Good	Good	Excellent
SRT8 Core Sedan 4D	CAXJ	46520	29000	29500	31400	34900
SRT8 Sedan 4D	CAFJ	50520	33100	33700	35700	39600
Adaptive Cruise Control			500	500	545	545

2000 DODGE

Body Type	VIN	List	Trade-In Good	Very Good	Pvt-Party Good	Retail Excellent

DODGE

2000 DODGE — (1,2or4)B3–(S46C)–Y–#

NEON—4-Cyl.—Equipment Schedule 6
W.B. 105.0"; 2.0 Liter.

Body Type	VIN	List	Good	Very Good	Good	Excellent
Highline Sedan 4D	S46C	13890	400	500	975	1800
ES Sedan 4D	S56C	14680	550	675	1175	2175

AVENGER—V6—Equipment Schedule 4
W.B. 103.7"; 2.5 Liter.

| Coupe 2D | U42N | 18840 | 500 | 600 | 1150 | 2050 |
| ES Coupe 2D | U52N | 21130 | 625 | 725 | 1325 | 2425 |

STRATUS—4-Cyl.—Equipment Schedule 5
W.B. 108.0"; 2.0 Liter, 2.4 Liter.

| SE Sedan 4D | J46C | 17525 | 400 | 500 | 1000 | 1825 |

STRATUS—V6—Equipment Schedule 4
W.B. 108.0"; 2.5 Liter.

| ES Sedan 4D | J56H | 20655 | 800 | 925 | 1550 | 2750 |

INTREPID—V6—Equipment Schedule 4
W.B. 113.0"; 2.7 Liter, 3.2 Liter, 3.5 Liter.

Sedan 4D	D46R	20950	450	525	1125	2100
ES Sedan 4D	D56J	22530	825	950	1675	3050
R/T Sedan 4D	D76V	24995	1300	1475	2200	3875

VIPER—V10—Equipment Schedule 2
W.B. 96.2"; 8.0 Liter.

RT/10 Roadster 2D	R65E	70925	11650	12400	13650	18450
GTS Coupe 2D	R69E	73425	15750	16700	17750	23600
Competition			900	900	1010	1010

2001 DODGE — (1,2or4)B3–(S46C)–1–#

NEON—4-Cyl.—Equipment Schedule 6
W.B. 105.0"; 2.0 Liter.

Highline Sedan 4D	S46C	14275	450	575	1025	1850
ES Sedan 4D	S46C	15095	650	800	1300	2350
Competition Sedan 4D	S66C	15155	575	725	1200	2150
R/T Sedan 4D	S66F	16845	700	875	1400	2475

STRATUS—4-Cyl.—Equipment Schedule 4
W.B. 103.7", 108.0" (Sed); 2.4 Liter.

SE Sedan 4D	J46X	18425	400	500	1025	1875
SE Coupe 2D	G42X	19230	375	450	800	1350
Manual, 5-Spd			(200)	(200)	(265)	(265)
V6, 2.7 Liter	U,H		100	100	135	135

STRATUS—V6—Equipment Schedule 4
W.B. 103.7", 108.0" (Sed); 2.7 Liter, 3.0 Liter.

| ES Sedan 4D | J56U | 21010 | 850 | 1000 | 1600 | 2850 |
| R/T Coupe 2D | G52H | 22390 | 675 | 775 | 1375 | 2450 |

INTREPID—V6—Equipment Schedule 4
W.B. 113.0"; 2.7 Liter, 3.2 Liter, 3.5 Liter.

SE Sedan 4D	D46R	21395	600	700	1350	2500
ES Sedan 4D	D56J	23090	925	1075	1775	3175
R/T Sedan 4D	D66V	25460	1525	1725	2475	4325

VIPER—V10—Equipment Schedule 2
W.B. 96.2"; 8.0 Liter.

RT/10 Roadster 2D	R65E	67950	12050	12750	14050	18850
GTS Coupe 2D	R69E	70450	16000	16950	18050	23900
Competition			1025	1025	1150	1150

2002 DODGE — (1,2or4)B3–(S26C)–2–#

NEON—4-Cyl.—Equipment Schedule 6
W.B. 105.0"; 2.0 Liter.

S Sedan 4D	S26C	10570	325	400	800	1450
Sedan 4D	S26C	13805	325	400	800	1450
SXT Sedan 4D	S66C	15935	700	850	1425	2575
ACR Sedan 4D	S66F	14795	625	775	1300	2325
SE Sedan 4D	S46C	15405	550	675	1200	2150
ES Sedan 4D	S56C	15860	750	900	1450	2575
R/T Sedan 4D	S76F	16680	825	1000	1575	2825

STRATUS—4-Cyl.—Equipment Schedule 4
W.B. 103.7", 108.0" (Sed); 2.4 Liter.

| SE Sedan 4D | L46X | 18290 | 425 | 500 | 1050 | 1900 |
| SE Coupe 2D | G42X | 19340 | 400 | 500 | 875 | 1475 |

2002 DODGE

Body Type	VIN	List	Trade-In Good	Very Good	Pvt-Party Good	Retail Excellent
SXT Sedan 4D	L66X	19345	500	575	1225	2225
SXT Coupe 2D	G42G	19695	350	425	850	1475
Manual, 5-Spd			(200)	(200)	(265)	(265)
V6, 2.7 Liter	R,H		125	125	175	175
STRATUS—V6—Equipment Schedule 4						
W.B. 103.7", 108.0" (Sed); 2.7 Liter, 3.0 Liter.						
ES Sedan 4D	J56R	21255	975	1125	1750	3075
R/T Sedan 4D	L76R	22150	1100	1250	2000	3525
R/T Coupe 2D	G52H	22490	750	875	1450	2525
INTREPID—V6—Equipment Schedule 4						
W.B. 113.0"; 2.7 Liter, 3.5 Liter.						
SE Sedan 4D	D46R	21230	700	800	1475	2675
ES Sedan 4D	D56M	23155	1150	1325	2025	3550
SXT Sedan 4D	D56G	24170	1175	1350	2025	3500
R/T Sedan 4D	D76G	27240	1625	1850	2675	4575
VIPER—V10—Equipment Schedule 2						
W.B. 96.2"; 8.0 Liter.						
RT/10 Roadster 2D	R65E	75500	12800	13550	14600	19300
GTS Coupe 2D	R69E	76000	17200	18150	19150	25100
Competition			1150	1150	1290	1290

2003 DODGE — (1,2or4)B3-(S46C)-3-#

Body Type	VIN	List	Trade-In Good	Very Good	Pvt-Party Good	Retail Excellent
NEON—4-Cyl.—Equipment Schedule 6						
W.B. 105.0"; 2.0 Liter.						
SE Sedan 4D	S46C	13925	700	850	1475	2675
SXT Sedan 4D	S66C	16235	850	1000	1700	3100
R/T Sedan 4D	S76F	17250	950	1125	1850	3350
NEON—4-Cyl. Turbo—Equipment Schedule 6						
W.B. 105.0"; 2.4 Liter.						
SRT-4 Sedan 4D	S66S	19965	2800	3275	3575	5675
STRATUS—4-Cyl.—Equipment Schedule 4						
W.B. 103.7", 108.0" (Sed); 2.4 Liter.						
SXT Sedan 4D	L46X	18340	875	1000	1625	2825
SXT Coupe 2D	G42GX	20680	375	425	875	1500
SE Sedan 4D	L46X	18470	875	1000	1575	2725
SE Coupe 2D	G42G	20680	425	500	900	1500
Manual, 5-Spd			(225)	(225)	(310)	(310)
V6, Flex Fuel, 2.7 Liter	R,H		175	175	245	245
STRATUS—V6—Equipment Schedule 4						
W.B. 103.7", 108.0" (Sed); 2.7 Liter, 3.0 Liter.						
ES Sedan 4D	J56U	21980	1025	1175	1850	3200
R/T Sedan 4D	L76R	22340	1425	1600	2325	3975
R/T Coupe 2D	G52H	23175	825	950	1500	2575
INTREPID—V6—Equipment Schedule 4						
W.B. 113.0"; 2.7 Liter, 3.5 Liter.						
SE Sedan 4D	D46R	21720	875	1000	1825	3350
ES Sedan 4D	D56J	25515	1425	1625	2525	4375
SXT Sedan 4D	D66G	24335	1400	1575	2325	3975
VIPER—V10—Equipment Schedule 2						
W.B. 98.8"; 8.3 Liter.						
SRT10 Roadster 2D	R65Z	83795	13750	14500	15150	19350

2004 DODGE — (1,2or4)B3-(S46C)-4-#

Body Type	VIN	List	Trade-In Good	Very Good	Pvt-Party Good	Retail Excellent
NEON—4-Cyl.—Equipment Schedule 6						
W.B. 105.0"; 2.0 Liter.						
SE Sedan 4D	S46C	14495	825	975	1700	3050
SXT Sedan 4D	S66C	16805	1150	1350	2100	3750
R/T Sedan 4D	S76F	17895	1225	1450	2225	3950
NEON—4-Cyl. HO Turbo—Equipment Schedule 6						
W.B. 105.0"; 2.4 Liter.						
SRT-4 Sedan 4D	S66S	20995	3275	3800	4250	6600
STRATUS—4-Cyl.—Equipment Schedule 4						
W.B. 103.7", 108.0" (Sed); 2.4 Liter.						
SXT Sedan 4D	L66X	19350	1000	1150	1750	2925
SXT Coupe 2D	G42G	20535	600	700	1250	2150
SE Sedan 4D	L46X	20315	1000	1150	1750	2925
Manual, 5-Spd			(275)	(275)	(375)	(375)
V6, Flex Fuel, 2.7 Liter	T		225	225	310	310
STRATUS—V6—Equipment Schedule 4						
W.B. 103.7", 108.0" (Sed); 2.7 Liter, 3.0 Liter.						
ES Sedan 4D	J56R	22600	1150	1300	2025	3475
R/T Sedan 4D	L76R	23135	1700	1925	2700	4475

1015

Body Type	VIN	List	Trade-In Good	Trade-In Very Good	Pvt-Party Good	Retail Excellent
R/T Coupe 2D	G52H	23750	950	1075	1625	2750
INTREPID—V6—Equipment Schedule 4						
W.B. 113.0"; 2.7 Liter, 3.5 Liter.						
SE Sedan 4D	D46R	22270	1200	1350	2300	4100
ES Sedan 4D	D56J	26065	1775	1975	3075	5350
SXT Sedan 4D	D66G	24485	1500	1675	2725	4775
VIPER—V10—Equipment Schedule 2						
W.B. 98.8"; 8.3 Liter.						
SRT10 Roadster 2D	R65Z	84795	15350	16200	16750	21000

2005 DODGE — (1,2or4)B3–(S26C)–5–#

	VIN	List	Good	Very Good	Good	Excellent
NEON—4-Cyl.—Equipment Schedule 6						
W.B. 105.0"; 2.0 Liter.						
SE Sedan 4D	S26C	14985	875	1025	1900	3325
SXT Sedan 4D	S56C	17295	1350	1575	2500	4275
Special Edition			75	75	95	95
NEON—4-Cyl. HO Turbo—Equipment Schedule 6						
W.B. 105.0"; 2.4 Liter.						
SRT-4 Sedan 4D	S66S	21195	4050	4650	4975	7350
STRATUS—4-Cyl.—Equipment Schedule 4						
W.B. 103.7", 108.0" (Sed); 2.4 Liter.						
SXT Sedan 4D	L46J	19770	1425	1625	2325	3650
SXT Coupe 2D	G42G	21825	1025	1175	1850	2975
Special Edition			125	125	180	180
Manual, 5-Spd			(325)	(325)	(445)	(445)
V6, Flex Fuel, 2.7 Liter	T		275	275	375	375
STRATUS—V6—Equipment Schedule 4						
W.B. 103.7", 108.0" (Sed); 2.7 Liter, 3.0 Liter.						
R/T Sedan 4D	L76T	22250	2100	2375	3200	5025
R/T Coupe 2D	G52H	24320	1250	1400	2075	3325
MAGNUM—V6—Equipment Schedule 4						
W.B. 120.0"; 2.7 Liter, 3.5 Liter.						
SE Sport Wagon 4D	V48T	22495	2800	3125	3925	6050
SXT Sport Wagon 4D	V48T	22695	2950	3325	4200	6450
Special Edition			125	125	180	180
AWD	Z		575	575	765	765
MAGNUM—V8 HEMI—Equipment Schedule 4						
W.B. 120.0"; 5.7 Liter.						
R/T Sport Wagon 4D	V582	29995	4375	4900	5650	8425
AWD	Z		575	575	765	765
VIPER—V10—Equipment Schedule 2						
W.B. 98.8"; 8.3 Liter.						
SRT10 Roadster 2D	Z65Z	85395	17750	18650	19100	23600
Copperhead Edition			1425	1425	1555	1555
Mamba Edition			1225	1225	1335	1335

2006 DODGE — (1,2or4)B3–(L46X)–6–#

	VIN	List	Good	Very Good	Good	Excellent
STRATUS—4-Cyl.—Equipment Schedule 4						
W.B. 108.0"; 2.4 Liter.						
SXT Sedan 4D	L46X	20140	1575	1750	2525	3875
V6, 2.7 Liter	R		575	575	755	755
STRATUS—V6—Equipment Schedule 4						
W.B. 108.0"; 2.7 Liter.						
R/T Sedan 4D	L76R	24120	2325	2575	3425	5250
MAGNUM—V6—Equipment Schedule 4						
W.B. 120.0"; 2.7 Liter, 3.5 Liter.						
Sport Wagon 4D	V47V	22995	3000	3325	4150	6250
SXT Sport Wagon 4D	V47V	25935	3800	4200	5075	7550
AWD	Z		650	650	865	865
V8, HEMI, 5.7 Liter	2		1150	1150	1535	1535
MAGNUM—V8 HEMI—Equipment Schedule 4						
W.B. 120.0"; 5.7 Liter, 6.1 Liter.						
R/T Sport Wagon 4D	V572	30910	4775	5275	6225	9250
SRT8 Sport Wagon 4D	V773	37995	9000	9950	10100	13800
AWD	Z		650	650	865	865
CHARGER—V6—Equipment Schedule 4						
W.B. 120.0"; 2.7 Liter, 3.5 Liter.						
Sedan 4D	A43G	22295	4725	5175	5825	8350
SXT Sedan 4D	A43G	25995	5225	5700	6350	9075
V8, HEMI, 5.7 Liter	H		1150	1150	1535	1535
CHARGER—V8 HEMI—Equipment Schedule 4						
W.B. 120.0"; 5.7 Liter, 6.1 Liter.						

Body Type	VIN	List	Trade-In Good	Very Good	Pvt-Party Good	Retail Excellent
R/T Sedan 4D	A53H	29995	6800	7425	8100	11450
SRT8 Sedan 4D	A73W	38095	10950	12200	11350	15050
Daytona Edition			575	575	755	755
Performance Group			575	575	775	775
VIPER—V10—Equipment Schedule 2						
W.B. 98.8"; 8.3 Liter.						
SRT10 Coupe 2D	Z697	86995	23000	24100	24200	29300
SRT10 Convertible 2D	Z65Z	85745	19400	20300	20800	25300
First Edition Group			725	725	800	800

2007 DODGE — (1,2or4)B3—(B28C)—7—#

Body Type	VIN	List	Trade-In Good	Very Good	Pvt-Party Good	Retail Excellent
CALIBER—4-Cyl.—Equipment Schedule 6						
W.B. 103.7"; 1.8 Liter, 2.0 Liter.						
Sport Wagon 4D	B28C	14985	2650	2975	3850	5925
SXT Sport Wagon 4D	B48C	16985	2850	3200	4075	6250
Manual, 5-Spd			(300)	(300)	(385)	(385)
CALIBER AWD—4-Cyl.—Equipment Schedule 6						
W.B. 103.7"; 2.4 Liter.						
R/T Sport Wagon 4D	E78K	19985	4125	4650	5600	8425
FWD			(600)	(600)	(815)	(815)
Manual, 5-Spd			(300)	(300)	(385)	(385)
MAGNUM—V6—Equipment Schedule 4						
W.B. 120.0"; 2.7 Liter, 3.5 Liter.						
Sport Wagon 4D	V47T	23545	4125	4525	5400	7800
SXT Sport Wagon 4D	V47V	27405	4350	4775	5700	8275
AWD	Z		725	725	965	965
V8, HEMI, 5.7 Liter	2		1225	1225	1645	1645
MAGNUM—V8 HEMI—Equipment Schedule 4						
W.B. 120.0"; 5.7 Liter, 6.1 Liter.						
R/T Sport Wagon 4D	V572	31590	6250	6850	8025	11550
SRT8 Sport Wagon 4D	V773	38220	10650	11650	11650	15350
AWD	Z		725	725	965	965
CHARGER—V6—Equipment Schedule 4						
W.B. 120.0"; 2.7 Liter, 3.5 Liter.						
SE Sedan 4D	A43R	23475	5200	5650	6300	8800
SXT Sedan 4D	A43G	26580	5850	6350	7100	9850
AWD	K		725	725	965	965
V6, HO, 3.5 Liter (SE)	G		275	275	350	350
V8, HEMI, 5.7 Liter	H		1225	1225	1645	1645
CHARGER—V8 HEMI—Equipment Schedule 4						
W.B. 120.0"; 5.7 Liter, 6.1 Liter.						
R/T Sedan 4D	A53H	30890	7975	8650	9400	12950
SRT8 Sedan 4D	A73W	38695	13050	14350	13550	17650
Performance Group			625	625	830	830
Daytona Edition			625	625	830	830
Super Bee Special Ed			175	175	215	215
AWD	K		725	725	965	965

2008 DODGE — (1,2or3)B3—(B28C)—8—#

Body Type	VIN	List	Trade-In Good	Very Good	Pvt-Party Good	Retail Excellent
CALIBER—4-Cyl.—Equipment Schedule 6						
W.B. 103.7"; 1.8 Liter, 2.0 Liter.						
SE Sport Wagon 4D	B28C	15485	3225	3550	4600	6725
SXT Sport Wagon 4D	B48C	18180	3700	4050	5050	7225
Manual, 5-Spd w/Overdrive			(350)	(350)	(460)	(460)
CALIBER AWD—4-Cyl.—Equipment Schedule 6						
W.B. 103.7"; 2.4 Liter.						
R/T Sport Wagon 4D	E78K	21055	4650	5075	6200	8925
FWD			(650)	(650)	(870)	(870)
Manual, 5-Spd w/Overdrive			(350)	(350)	(460)	(460)
CALIBER—4-Cyl. Turbo—Equipment Schedule 6						
W.B. 103.7"; 2.4 Liter.						
SRT4 Sport Wagon 4D	B68F	23015	5550	6075	6850	9350
AVENGER—4-Cyl.—Equipment Schedule 4						
W.B. 108.9"; 2.4 Liter.						
SE Sedan 4D	C46K	19265	3675	3975	4900	6800
SXT Sedan 4D	C56K	20195	4325	4650	5550	7625
V6, 2.7 Liter	R		625	625	845	845
AVENGER—V6—Equipment Schedule 4						
W.B. 108.9"; 3.5 Liter.						
R/T Sedan 4D	C76M	23945	5500	5925	7050	9650
AWD	Z		800	800	1065	1065

Body Type	VIN	List	Trade-In Good	Very Good	Pvt-Party Good	Retail Excellent
MAGNUM—V6—Equipment Schedule 4						
W.B. 120.0"; 2.7 Liter, 3.5 Liter.						
Sport Wagon 4D	V47T	24095	4850	5225	6425	8875
SXT Sport Wagon 4D	V37V	27900	5375	5800	7025	9700
AWD	Z		800	800	1065	1065
V8, HEMI, 5.7 Liter	2		1325	1325	1760	1760
MAGNUM—V8 HEMI—Equipment Schedule 4						
W.B. 120.0"; 5.7 Liter, 6.1 Liter.						
R/T Sport Wagon 4D	V572	32455	8350	8975	10200	13850
SRT8 Sport Wagon 4D	V773	38580	12700	13650	14200	18150
AWD	Z		800	800	1065	1065
CHARGER—V6—Equipment Schedule 4						
W.B. 120.0"; 2.7 Liter, 3.5 Liter.						
Sedan 4D	A43R	22350	6125	6575	7550	10150
SXT Sedan 4D	A33G	26360	7075	7575	8600	11500
AWD	K		800	800	1065	1065
V6, HO, 3.5 Liter (Base)	G		275	275	370	370
V8, HEMI, 5.7 Liter	H		1325	1325	1760	1760
CHARGER—V8 HEMI—Equipment Schedule 4						
W.B. 120.0"; 5.7 Liter, 6.1 Liter.						
R/T Sedan 4D	A53H	31430	9350	10000	10950	14400
SRT8 Sedan 4D	A73W	38993	14850	16000	15600	19450
Performance Pkg			675	675	875	875
Daytona Edition			675	675	875	875
Super Bee Special Ed			200	200	225	225
AWD	K		800	800	1050	1050
CHALLENGER—V8 HEMI—Equipment Schedule 4						
W.B. 98.8"; 6.1 Liter.						
SRT8 Coupe 2D	J74W	40158	15800	16600	17350	20600
VIPER—V10—Equipment Schedule 2						
W.B. 98.8"; 8.4 Liter.						
SRT10 Coupe 2D	Z69Z	86496	30500	31700	32500	38400
SRT10 Convertible 2D	Z65Z	85746	27600	29600	29600	35200

Body Type	VIN	List	Trade-In Good	Very Good	Pvt-Party Good	Retail Excellent
CALIBER—4-Cyl.—Equipment Schedule 6						
W.B. 103.7"; 1.8 Liter, 2.0 Liter, 2.4 Liter.						
SE Sport Wagon 4D	B28C	17290	3850	4125	5175	7150
SXT Sport Wagon 4D	B48C	18660	4475	4800	5875	8050
R/T Sport Wagon 4D	B78B	21200	5500	5875	7125	9675
Manual, 5-Spd w/Overdrive			(375)	(375)	(490)	(490)
CALIBER—4-Cyl. Turbo—Equipment Schedule 6						
W.B. 103.7"; 2.4 Liter.						
SRT4 Sport Wagon 4D	B68F	24670	7250	7750	8650	11250
AVENGER—4-Cyl.—Equipment Schedule 4						
W.B. 108.9"; 2.4 Liter.						
SE Sedan 4D	C46B	20505	4675	4950	5925	7850
SXT Sedan 4D	C56B	21790	5500	5825	7050	9300
V6, 2.7 Liter	D		675	675	895	895
AVENGER—V6—Equipment Schedule 4						
W.B. 108.9"; 3.5 Liter.						
R/T Sedan 4D	C76V	25705	6175	6550	7875	10400
CHARGER—V6—Equipment Schedule 4						
W.B. 120.0"; 2.7 Liter, 3.5 Liter.						
Sedan 4D	A43D	24595	7350	7775	8925	11500
SXT Sedan 4D	A33V	26210	8375	8875	10000	12800
AWD			875	875	1130	1130
V6, HO, 3.5 Liter (Base)	V		300	300	380	380
CHARGER—V8 HEMI—Equipment Schedule 4						
W.B. 120.0"; 5.7 Liter, 6.1 Liter.						
R/T Sedan 4D	A53T	32560	11200	11850	12950	16300
SRT8 Sedan 4D	A73W	41121	17450	18500	18350	22000
Performance Pkg			700	700	895	895
Daytona Edition			700	700	895	895
Super Bee Special Ed			200	200	235	235
AWD	K		875	875	1110	1110
CHALLENGER—V6—Equipment Schedule 4						
W.B. 116.0"; 3.5 Liter.						
SE Coupe 2D	J44V	21995	11550	12050	12900	15350
CHALLENGER—V8 HEMI—Equipment Schedule 4						
W.B. 116.0"; 5.7 Liter, 6.1 Liter.						
R/T Coupe 2D	J54T	29995	13100	13650	14900	17650
SRT8 Coupe 2D	J74W	39995	18400	19200	20100	23400

2009 DODGE

Body Type	VIN	List	Trade-In Good	Trade-In Very Good	Pvt-Party Good	Retail Excellent
VIPER—V10—Equipment Schedule 2						
W.B. 98.8"; 8.4 Liter.						
SRT10 Coupe 2D	Z69Z	89021	34100	35300	36300	42000
SRT10 Convertible 2D	Z65Z	88271	29700	30700	32000	37300
VOI 10 Edition			6825	6825	7430	7430

2010 DODGE — (1or2)B3–(B1HA)–A–#

Body Type	VIN	List	Trade-In Good	Trade-In Very Good	Pvt-Party Good	Retail Excellent
CALIBER—4-Cyl.—Equipment Schedule 6						
W.B. 103.7"; 1.8 Liter, 2.0 Liter, 2.4 Liter.						
Express Sport Wag 4D	B1HA	17510	4675	4900	5950	7800
Mainstreet Spt Wag 4D	B3HA	18690	6025	6325	7425	9475
Uptown Sport Wagon	B9HA	20625	7075	7425	8725	11200
CALIBER—4-Cyl.—Equipment Schedule 6						
W.B. 103.7"; 1.8 Liter, 2.0 Liter, 2.4 Liter.						
SE Sport Wagon 4D	B2HA	18605	5200	5475	6700	8725
Heat Sport Wagon 4D	B5HA	20070	6200	6500	7625	9725
SXT Sport Wagon 4D	B4HA	20370	6275	6575	7700	9825
Rush Sport Wagon 4D	B8HB	21625	7175	7550	8825	11300
R/T Sport Wagon 4D	B7HB	22260	7600	7975	9300	11950
Manual, 5-Spd w/Overdrive			(450)	(450)	(615)	(615)
AVENGER—4-Cyl.—Equipment Schedule 4						
W.B. 108.9"; 2.4 Liter.						
SXT Sedan 4D	C4FB	20970	6175	6450	7850	10050
V6, 2.7 Liter	D		700	700	940	940
AVENGER—V6—Equipment Schedule 4						
W.B. 108.9"; 2.4 Liter.						
R/T Sedan 4D	C5FB	22470	7275	7625	9250	11950
CHARGER—V6—Equipment Schedule 4						
W.B. 120.0"; 2.7 Liter, 3.5 Liter.						
Sedan 4D	A4CD	25140	8725	9150	10350	12800
SXT Sedan 4D	A3CV	26900	9725	10200	11500	14200
Rallye Sedan 4D	A9CV	27395	10400	10900	12100	14850
AWD	K		925	925	1175	1175
V6, HO, 3.5 Liter (Base)	V		300	300	395	395
CHARGER—V8 HEMI—Equipment Schedule 4						
W.B. 120.0"; 5.7 Liter, 6.1 Liter.						
R/T Sedan 4D	A5CT	32120	13700	14350	15600	18950
SRT8 Sedan 4D	A7CW	38930	20800	21700	21900	25400
Road/Track Pkg			750	750	910	910
AWD	K		925	925	1140	1140
CHALLENGER—V6—Equipment Schedule 4						
W.B. 116.0"; 3.5 Liter.						
SE Coupe 2D	J4DV	23460	13300	13750	14950	17500
CHALLENGER—V8 HEMI—Equipment Schedule 4						
W.B. 116.0"; 5.7 Liter, 6.1 Liter.						
R/T Coupe 2D	J5DT	31585	15300	15900	17200	19950
SRT8 Coupe 2D	J7DW	41955	20600	21400	22600	25900
VIPER—V10—Equipment Schedule 4						
W.B. 98.8"; 8.4 Liter.						
SRT10 Coupe 2D	Z6JZ	94930	40300	41500	42300	48500
SRT10 Convertible 2D	Z6EZ	94180	35800	37000	38200	43500

2011 DODGE — (1or2)B3–(B1HA)–B–#

Body Type	VIN	List	Trade-In Good	Trade-In Very Good	Pvt-Party Good	Retail Excellent
CALIBER—4-Cyl.—Equipment Schedule 6						
W.B. 103.7"; 1.8 Liter, 2.0 Liter, 2.4 Liter.						
Express Sport Wag 4D	B1HA	17630	6175	6400	7675	9600
Mainstreet Spt Wag 4D	B3HA	18990	7750	8000	9275	11450
Uptown Sport Wagon	B9HA	20835	9050	9350	10650	13150
CALIBER—4-Cyl.—Equipment Schedule 6						
W.B. 103.7"; 1.8 Liter, 2.0 Liter, 2.4 Liter.						
Heat Sport Wagon 4D	B5HA	19835	8300	8600	9825	12050
Rush Sport Wagon 4D	B8HB	21835	9125	9450	10800	13300
Manual, 5-Spd w/Overdrive			(500)	(500)	(640)	(640)
AVENGER—4-Cyl.—Equipment Schedule 4						
W.B. 108.9"; 2.4 Liter.						
Express Sedan 4D	D1FB	19995	7750	8025	9700	12100
Mainstreet Sedan 4D	D1FB	21995	7950	8225	9875	12250
LUX Sedan 4D	D2FB	24295	8825	9125	10850	13450
CHARGER—V6—Equipment Schedule 4						
W.B. 120.2"; 3.6 Liter.						
Sedan 4D	L3CG	25995	13350	13850	15150	17900
Rallye			500	500	600	600

2011 DODGE

Body Type	VIN	List	Trade-In Good	Very Good	Pvt-Party Good	Retail Excellent
CHARGER—V8 HEMI—Equipment Schedule 4						
W.B. 120.2"; 5.7 Liter.						
R/T Sedan 4D	L5CT	30995	17750	18450	19700	23100
AWD	M		975	975	1155	1155
CHALLENGER—V6—Equipment Schedule 4						
W.B. 116.0"; 3.6 Liter.						
Coupe 2D	J4DG	25495	14800	15200	16550	18850
CHALLENGER—V8 HEMI—Equipment Schedule 4						
W.B. 116.0"; 5.7 Liter, 6.1 Liter.						
R/T Coupe 2D	J5DT	30495	17100	17700	19000	21600
SRT8 Coupe 2D	J7DJ	45714	25300	26100	27300	30600

2012 DODGE — (1,2or3)C3-(DWBA)-C-#

Body Type	VIN	List	Trade-In Good	Very Good	Pvt-Party Good	Retail Excellent
CALIBER—4-Cyl.—Equipment Schedule 6						
W.B. 103.7"; 2.0 Liter.						
SE Sport Wagon 4D	DWBA	18130	7800	8000	9450	11550
SXT Plus Sport Wag 4D	DWEA	19480	8700	8900	10400	12650
Automatic, CVT			475	475	595	595
CALIBER—4-Cyl.—Equipment Schedule 4						
W.B. 103.7"; 2.0 Liter.						
SXT Sport Wagon 4D	DWDA	19515	8700	8900	10400	12650
AVENGER—4-Cyl.—Equipment Schedule 4						
W.B. 108.9"; 2.4 Liter.						
SE Sedan 4D	DZAB	19745	8475	8700	10400	12600
SXT Sedan 4D	DZCB	22245	9100	9325	11050	13400
AVENGER—V6—Equipment Schedule 4						
W.B. 108.9"; 3.6 Liter.						
SXT Plus Sedan 4D	DZEG	24745	9700	9950	11750	14200
R/T Sedan 4D	DZBG	26745	10750	11050	13000	15750
CHARGER—V6—Equipment Schedule 4						
W.B. 120.2"; 3.6 Liter.						
SE Sedan 4D	DXBG	26320	14150	14650	16150	18750
SXT Sedan 4D	DXHG	29320	15850	16400	17750	20500
Rallye			500	500	585	585
CHARGER—V8 HEMI—Equipment Schedule 4						
W.B. 120.2"; 5.7 Liter, 6.4 Liter.						
R/T Sedan 4D	DXCT	30820	18800	19450	21000	24200
SRT8 Superbee Sedan 4D	DXGJ	43350	26800	27500	28500	31700
SRT8 Sedan 4D	DXEJ	47650	28800	29400	30400	33600
AWD	D		1175	1175	1385	1385
CHALLENGER—V6—Equipment Schedule 4						
W.B. 116.0"; 3.6 Liter.						
SXT Coupe 2D	DYAG	25820	16050	16400	17950	20200
CHALLENGER—V8 HEMI—Equipment Schedule 4						
W.B. 116.0"; 5.7 Liter, 6.4 Liter.						
R/T Coupe 2D	DYBT	30820	19450	20100	21300	23900
SRT8 392 Coupe 2D	DYCJ	46150	27800	28700	29900	33200

2013 DODGE — (1,2or3)C3-(DFAA)-D-#

Body Type	VIN	List	Trade-In Good	Very Good	Pvt-Party Good	Retail Excellent
DART—4-Cyl.—Equipment Schedule 6						
W.B. 106.4"; 1.4 Liter, 2.0 Liter, 2.4 Liter.						
SE Sedan 4D	DFAA	16790	8475	8625	10200	12300
SXT Sedan 4D	DFBA	18790	10350	10550	12050	14250
Rallye Sedan 4D	DFBA	19790	10400	10550	12100	14400
Limited Sedan 4D	DFCA	20790	11800	12000	13450	15750
GT Sedan 4D	DFEB	22890	11500	11700	13200	15500
Automatic, 6-Spd			500	500	620	620
4-Cyl, MltiAir Trbo, 1.4L			175	175	215	215
DART—4-Cyl. Turbo—Equipment Schedule 6						
W.B. 106.4"; 1.4 Liter.						
Aero Sedan 4D	DFAH	20090	10450	10600	12100	14350
AVENGER—4-Cyl.—Equipment Schedule 4						
W.B. 108.9"; 2.4 Liter.						
SE Sedan 4D	DZAB	19990	9900	10100	12000	14350
AVENGER—4-Cyl.—Equipment Schedule 4						
W.B. 108.9"; 2.4 Liter.						
SXT Sedan 4D	DZCB	22990	10500	10750	12650	15100
V6, Flex Fuel, 3.6 Liter	G		900	900	1140	1140
AVENGER—V6 Flex Fuel—Equipment Schedule 4						
W.B. 108.9"; 3.6 Liter.						
SE Sedan 4D	DZAG	22690	10300	10500	12450	14900
R/T Sedan 4D	DZBG	26490	11850	12100	14200	16950

Body Type	VIN	List	Trade-In Good	Very Good	Pvt-Party Good	Retail Excellent
CHARGER—V6—Equipment Schedule 4						
W.B. 120.2"; 3.6 Liter.						
SE Sedan 4D	DXBG	26790	14500	14950	16650	19200
SXT Sedan 4D	DXHG	29590	16300	16800	18400	21100
SXT Plus Sedan 4D	DXHG	31590	17800	18350	20100	23100
Rallye	F		500	500	595	595
AWD			1075	1075	1305	1305
CHARGER—V8 HEMI—Equipment Schedule 4						
W.B. 120.2"; 5.7 Liter, 6.4 Liter.						
R/T Sedan 4D	DXCT	30990	19250	19850	21600	24900
R/T Plus Sedan 4D	DXCT	32990	19400	20000	21800	25100
R/T Road/Track Sed	DXCT	34990	19600	20200	22000	25200
R/T Max Sedan 4D	DXGJ	37190	19750	20300	22000	25300
SRT8 Super Bee Sedan	DXGJ	43800	28500	29000	30600	33800
SRT8 Sedan 4D	DXEJ	47020	29800	30300	31900	35300
AWD	D		1075	1075	1285	1285
CHALLENGER—V6 Flex Fuel—Equipment Schedule 4						
W.B. 116.0"; 3.6 Liter.						
SXT Coupe 2D	DYAG	26990	17150	17450	19100	21200
SXT Plus Coupe 2D	DYAG	28990	18000	18350	20200	22600
Rallye Redline Cpe 2D	DYAG	30890	18750	19100	20800	23000
CHALLENGER—V8 HEMI—Equipment Schedule 4						
W.B. 116.0"; 5.7 Liter, 6.4 Liter.						
R/T Coupe 2D	DYBT	32190	21000	21600	23000	25700
R/T Plus Coupe 2D	DYBT	34190	21300	22000	23400	26200
R/T Classic Coupe 2D	DYBT	36190	21500	22100	23700	26500
SRT8 Core Coupe 2D	DYDJ	42220	28200	29100	30400	33700
SRT8 392 Coupe 2D	DYCJ	47120	31400	32300	33500	36900

2014 DODGE — (1,2or3)C3–(DFAA)–D–#

Body Type	VIN	List	Trade-In Good	Very Good	Pvt-Party Good	Retail Excellent
DART—4-Cyl.—Equipment Schedule 6						
W.B. 106.4"; 2.0 Liter, 2.4 Liter.						
SE Sedan 4D	DFAA	18385	9500	9650	11250	13400
SXT Sedan 4D	DFBB	19490	11050	11200	12800	15000
GT Sedan 4D	DFEB	21990	12550	12750	14200	16500
Automatic, 6-Spd			525	525	620	620
DART—4-Cyl.—Equipment Schedule 6						
W.B. 106.4"; 2.4 Liter.						
Limited Sedan 4D	DFCB	23990	12950	13150	14700	17050
DART—4-Cyl. Turbo—Equipment Schedule 6						
W.B. 106.4"; 1.4 Liter.						
Aero Sedan 4D	DFDH	20990	11600	11800	13300	15600
Auto 6-Spd Dual Dry Cltch			525	525	620	620
AVENGER—4-Cyl.—Equipment Schedule 4						
W.B. 108.9"; 2.4 Liter.						
SE Sedan 4D	DZAB	20890	10700	10900	12800	15250
SXT Sedan 4D	DZCB	23690	11650	11900	13950	16600
V6, Flex Fuel, 3.6 Liter	G		950	950	1195	1195
AVENGER—V6 Flex Fuel—Equipment Schedule 4						
W.B. 108.9"; 3.6 Liter.						
SE Sedan 4D	DZAG	22330	11050	11300	13400	16050
R/T Sedan 4D	DZBG	26790	13250	13500	15850	18800
CHARGER—V6—Equipment Schedule 4						
W.B. 120.2"; 3.6 Liter.						
SE Sedan 4D	DXBG	27290	14800	15250	17000	19600
AWD	F		1125	1125	1355	1355
CHARGER—V6—Equipment Schedule 4						
W.B. 120.2"; 3.6 Liter.						
SXT Sedan 4D	DXHG	30290	16450	16950	18600	21300
SXT Plus Sedan 4D	DXHG	32290	18950	19500	21400	24600
Adaptive Cruise Control			500	500	580	580
Rallye Appearance Group			500	500	595	595
AWD	F		1125	1125	1355	1355
CHARGER—V6—Equipment Schedule 4						
W.B. 120.2"; 3.6 Liter.						
SXT 100th Annv Ed	DXHG	34490	20200	20800	22500	25700
CHARGER—V8 HEMI—Equipment Schedule 4						
W.B. 120.2"; 5.7 Liter.						
R/T Sedan 4D	DXCT	31490	20000	20600	22500	25800
R/T Max Sedan 4D	DXCT	37990	21400	22000	23700	26900
AWD	D		1125	1125	1335	1335
CHARGER—V8 HEMI—Equipment Schedule 4						
W.B. 120.2"; 5.7 Liter.						

Body Type	VIN	List	Trade-In Good	Very Good	Pvt-Party Good	Retail Excellent
R/T Plus Sedan 4D	DXCT	33490	20100	20700	22600	25900
Adaptive Cruise Control			500	500	575	575
AWD	D		1125	1125	1330	1330
CHARGER—V8 HEMI—Equipment Schedule 4						
W.B. 120.2"; 5.7 Liter, 6.4 Liter.						
R/T Road/Track Sed	DXCT	34990	20500	21100	22900	26200
SRT8 Sedan 4D	DXEJ	47920	34600	35200	36700	40100
Adaptive Cruise Control			500	500	570	570
CHARGER—V8 HEMI—Equipment Schedule 4						
W.B. 120.2"; 5.7 Liter, 6.4 Liter.						
R/T 100th Annv Ed Sed	DXCT	35690	20700	21300	23000	26300
SRT8 Super Bee Sedan	DXGJ	44920	32300	32900	34500	37800
CHALLENGER—V6 Flex Fuel—Equipment Schedule 4						
W.B. 116.0"; 3.6 Liter.						
SXT Coupe 2D	DYAG	27290	17900	18250	20000	22200
SXT Plus Coupe 2D	DYAG	29290	18950	19300	21200	23700
SXT 100th Annv Ed	DYAG	31790	19400	19750	21600	24000
Rallye Redline Cpe 2D	DYAG	31290	19900	20300	22200	24600
CHALLENGER—V8 HEMI—Equipment Schedule 4						
W.B. 116.0"; 5.7 Liter, 6.4 Liter.						
R/T Coupe 2D	DYBT	31490	23100	23800	25200	28000
R/T Plus Coupe 2D	DYBT	33490	23700	24400	25900	28800
R/T Classic Coupe 2D	DYPT	35490	23900	24600	26100	29100
R/T 100th Annv Ed Cpe	DYBT	35990	24000	24700	26400	29600
R/T Shaker Coupe 2D	DYBT	38490	27300	28100	29700	33000
R/T Mopar '14 Shaker	DYBT	38490	27300	28100	29700	33000
SRT8 Core Coupe 2D	DYDJ	40490	26700	27500	29100	32400
SRT8 Coupe 2D	DYCJ	46220	33700	34600	35800	39400

FERRARI

2006 FERRARI — ZFF(EW58A)-6-#

F430—V8—Equipment Schedule 2
W.B. 102.4"; 4.3 Liter.

Challenge Coupe 2D	EW58A	228500	****	****	****	196200

2007 FERRARI — ZFF(EW58A)-7-#

F430—V8—Equipment Schedule 2
W.B. 102.4"; 4.3 Liter.

Coupe 2D	EW58A	174579	****	****	****	98600
Spider Convertible 2D	EW59A	202713	****	****	****	107500
599 GTB FIORANO—V12—Equipment Schedule 2						
W.B. 108.3"; 6.0 Liter.						
Coupe 2D	FC60A	275345	****	****	****	186600
612 SCAGLIETTI—V12—Equipment Schedule 2						
W.B. 116.1"; 5.7 Liter.						
Coupe 2D	JB54A	269381	****	****	****	126200

2008 FERRARI — ZFF(EW58A)-8-#

F430—V8—Equipment Schedule 2
W.B. 102.4"; 4.3 Liter.

Coupe 2D	EW58A	191425	****	****	****	107500
Spider Convertible 2D	EW59A	221810	****	****	****	116300
430 SCUDERIA—V8—Equipment Schedule 2						
W.B. 102.4"; 4.3 Liter.						
Coupe 2D	KW64A	261956	****	****	****	88700
599 GTB FIORANO—V12—Equipment Schedule 2						
W.B. 108.3"; 6.0 Liter.						
Coupe 2D	FC60A	317595	****	****	****	196200
612 SCAGLIETTI—V12—Equipment Schedule 2						
W.B. 116.1"; 5.7 Liter.						
Coupe 2D	JB54A	281887	****	****	****	133700

2009 FERRARI — ZFF(EW58A)-9-#

F430—V8—Equipment Schedule 2
W.B. 102.4"; 4.3 Liter.

Coupe 2D	EW58A	192925	****	****	****	120200
Spider Convertible 2D	EW59A	223310	****	****	****	127900
430 SCUDERIA—V8—Equipment Schedule 2						
W.B. 102.4"; 4.3 Liter.						

Body Type	VIN	List	Trade-In Good	Very Good	Pvt-Party Good	Retail Excellent
Coupe 2D	KW64A	287618	****	****	****	102300
Spider 16M Coupe 2D	KW66A	313000	****	****	****	132300
CALIFORNIA—V8—Equipment Schedule 2						
W.B. 105.1"; 4.3 Liter.						
Convertible 2D	LJ65A	197350	****	****	****	114500
599 GTB FIORANO—V12—Equipment Schedule 2						
W.B. 108.3"; 6.0 Liter.						
Coupe 2D	FC60A	326730	****	****	****	210600
612 SCAGLIETTI—V12—Equipment Schedule 2						
W.B. 116.4"; 5.7 Liter.						
Coupe 2D	JB54A	320038	****	****	****	145200

2010 FERRARI — ZFF(67NFA)-A-#

Body Type	VIN	List	Trade-In Good	Very Good	Pvt-Party Good	Retail Excellent
458 ITALIA—V8—Equipment Schedule 2						
W.B. 104.3"; 4.5 Liter.						
Coupe 2D	67NFA	230675	****	****	****	174200
CALIFORNIA—V8—Equipment Schedule 2						
W.B. 105.1"; 4.3 Liter.						
Convertible 2D	LJA5A	196450	****	****	****	132500
599 GTB FIORANO—V12—Equipment Schedule 2						
W.B. 108.3"; 6.0 Liter.						
Coupe 2D	60FCA	326730	****	****	****	228700
612 SCAGLIETTI—V12—Equipment Schedule 2						
W.B. 116.1"; 5.7 Liter.						
Coupe 2D	54JBA	315538	****	****	****	162200

2011 FERRARI — ZFF(67NFA)-B-#

Body Type	VIN	List	Trade-In Good	Very Good	Pvt-Party Good	Retail Excellent
458 ITALIA—V8—Equipment Schedule 2						
W.B. 104.3"; 4.5 Liter.						
Coupe 2D	67NFA	230675	****	****	****	195600
CALIFORNIA—V8—Equipment Schedule 2						
W.B. 105.1"; 4.3 Liter.						
Convertible 2D	65LJA	196450	****	****	****	152400
599 GTB FIORANO—V12—Equipment Schedule 2						
W.B. 108.3"; 6.0 Liter.						
Coupe 2D	60FCA	327130	****	****	****	246800
599 GTO—V12—Equipment Schedule 2						
W.B. 108.3"; 6.0 Liter.						
Coupe 2D	70RCA	416550	****	****	****	479100
612 SCAGLIETTI—V12—Equipment Schedule 2						
W.B. 116.1"; 5.7 Liter.						
Coupe 2D		315538	****	****	****	181100

2012 FERRARI — ZFF(67NFA)-C-#

Body Type	VIN	List	Trade-In Good	Very Good	Pvt-Party Good	Retail Excellent
458 ITALIA—V8—Equipment Schedule 2						
W.B. 104.3"; 4.5 Liter.						
Coupe 2D	67NFA	236182	****	****	****	225200
CALIFORNIA—V8—Equipment Schedule 2						
W.B. 105.1"; 4.3 Liter.						
Convertible 2D	65LJA	201290	****	****	****	169500
FF AWD—V12—Equipment Schedule 2						
W.B. 116.1"; 6.3 Liter.						
Coupe 2D	73SKA	298750	****	****	****	234200

2013 FERRARI — (ZFF)(67NFA)-D-#

Body Type	VIN	List	Trade-In Good	Very Good	Pvt-Party Good	Retail Excellent
458 ITALIA—V8—Equipment Schedule 2						
W.B. 104.3"; 4.5 Liter.						
Coupe 2D	67NFA	239859	****	****	****	237200
458 SPIDER—V8—Equipment Schedule 2						
W.B. 104.3"; 4.5 Liter.						
Convertible 2D	68NHA	263762	****	****	****	246900
CALIFORNIA—V8—Equipment Schedule 2						
W.B. 105.1"; 4.3 Liter.						
Convertible 2D	65TJA	203640	****	****	****	181200
F12BERLINETTA—V12—Equipment Schedule 2						
W.B. 107.1"; 6.3 Liter.						
Convertible 2D	68NHA	263762	****	****	****	246900
FF AWD—V12—Equipment Schedule 2						
W.B. 117.7"; 6.3 Liter.						
Coupe 2D	73SKA	302450	****	****	****	246600

Body Type	VIN	List	Trade-In Good	Very Good	Pvt-Party Good	Retail Excellent

2014 FERRARI — (ZFF)(67NFA)-E-#

458 ITALIA—V8—Equipment Schedule 2
W.B. 104.3"; 4.5 Liter.

Coupe 2D	67NFA 239859		****	****	****	249800

458 SPIDER—V8—Equipment Schedule 2
W.B. 104.3"; 4.5 Liter.

| Convertible 2D | 68NHA 263762 | | **** | **** | **** | 260500 |

458 SPECIALE—V8—Equipment Schedule 2
W.B. 104.3"; 4.5 Liter.

| Coupe 2D | 75VFA 294350 | | **** | **** | **** | 327800 |

CALIFORNIA—V8—Equipment Schedule 2
W.B. 105.1"; 4.3 Liter.

| Convertible 2D | 65TJA 203640 | | **** | **** | **** | 193400 |

F12BERLINETTA—V12—Equipment Schedule 2
W.B. 107.1"; 6.3 Liter.

| Coupe 2D | 74UFA 323338 | | **** | **** | **** | 294200 |

FF 4WD—V12—Equipment Schedule 2
W.B. 117.7"; 6.3 Liter.

| Coupe 2D | 73SKA 302450 | | **** | **** | **** | 275500 |

FIAT

2012 FIAT — (3C3)-(FFAR)-C-#

500—4-Cyl.—Equipment Schedule 4
W.B. 90.6"; 1.4 Liter.

Pop Hatchback 2D	FFAR	17000	6125	6400	7650	9675
Sport Hatchback 2D	FFBR	19000	6650	6975	8225	10350
Lounge Hatchback 2D	FFCR	20400	7225	7575	8750	10900
Abarth Hatchback 2D	FFFH	22700	9750	10200	11250	13650
Gucci Hatchback 2D	FFCR	24200	8600	9000	10200	12600

500C—4-Cyl.—Equipment Schedule 4
W.B. 90.6"; 1.4 Liter.

Pop Convertible 2D	FFDR	21000	7425	7775	8925	11100
Lounge Convertible 2D	FFER	24000	8425	8825	10000	12350
Gucci Convertible 2D	FFER	28200	8825	9225	10400	12850

2013 FIAT — (3C3)-(FFAR)-D-#

500—4-Cyl.—Equipment Schedule 4
W.B. 90.6"; 1.4 Liter.

Pop Hatchback 2D	FFAR	16000	7225	7525	8875	11000
Sport Hatchback 2D	FFBR	18200	7850	8175	9575	11850
Lounge Hatchback 2D	FFCR	19200	7900	8225	9550	11750
Sport Cattiva H'Back	FFBR	20400	8550	8900	10250	12600
Gucci Hatchback 2D	FFCR	25250	9675	10100	11350	13800

500—4-Cyl. Turbo—Equipment Schedule 4
W.B. 90.6"; 1.4 Liter.

Hatchback 2D	FFHH	20300	8500	8850	10200	12550
Cattiva Hatchback 2D	FFHH	21150	8900	9250	10550	12950
Abarth Hatchback 2D	FFFH	22700	10250	10700	11850	14250

500C—4-Cyl.—Equipment Schedule 4
W.B. 90.6"; 1.4 Liter.

Pop Convertible 2D	FFDR	20200	8350	8700	10000	12300
Lounge Convertible 2D	FFER	23200	9675	10050	11350	13800
Abarth Convertible 2D	FFJH	26700	11800	12250	13350	15850
Gucci Convertible 2D	FFER	29000	10350	10800	12050	14600

500e—Electric—Equipment Schedule 4
W.B. 90.6".

| Hatchback 2D | FFGE | 32600 | 10450 | 10850 | 12100 | 14600 |

2014 FIAT — (3C3)-(FFAR)-E-#

500—4-Cyl.—Equipment Schedule 4
W.B. 90.6"; 1.4 Liter.

Pop Hatchback 2D	FFAR	18245	8100	8425	9775	12050
Sport Hatchback 2D	FFBR	19550	8750	9100	10350	12600
Lounge Hatchback 2D	FFCR	20550	9550	9925	11200	13550
1957 Ed Hatchback 2D	FFCR	20550	9700	10050	11350	13700

500—4-Cyl. Turbo—Equipment Schedule 4
W.B. 90.6"; 1.4 Liter.

| Hatchback 2D | FFHH | 21550 | 10400 | 10800 | 12050 | 14500 |

2014 FIAT

Body Type	VIN	List	Trade-In Good	Very Good	Pvt-Party Good	Retail Excellent
500 ABARTH—4-Cyl. Turbo—Equipment Schedule 4						
W.B. 90.6"; 1.4 Liter.						
Hatchback 2D	FFFH	22895	11500	11950	13200	15750
Cabrio Cabriolet 2D	FFJH	26895	13850	14400	15450	18150
500C—4-Cyl. Turbo—Equipment Schedule 4						
W.B. 90.6"; 1.4 Liter.						
Pop Convertible 2D	FFDR	20495	10150	10550	11750	14150
Lounge Convertible 2D	FFER	23300	11550	12000	13150	15650
GQ Edition Conv 2D	FFJH	26895	12750	13250	14350	17000
500e—Electric—Equipment Schedule 4						
W.B. 90.6".						
Hatchback 2D	FFGE	32600	12250	12700	13850	16350
500L—4-Cyl. Turbo—Equipment Schedule 4						
W.B. 102.8"; 1.4 Liter.						
Pop Hatchback 4D	FAAH	19900	9800	10000	11850	14100
Lounge Hatchback 4D	FACH	24995	11300	11500	13400	15750
500L—4-Cyl. Turbo—Equipment Schedule 4						
W.B. 102.8"; 1.4 Liter.						
Easy Hatchback 4D	FABH	22345	10150	10350	12200	14500
Trekking Hatchback	FADH	23345	10950	11150	13100	15500

FISKER

2012 FISKER — YH4(K12AA)-C-#

KARMA—AC Electric—Equipment Schedule 2						
W.B. 124.4".						
EcoStandard Sed 4D	K12AA	103000	****	****	****	46600
EcoSport Sedan 4D	K14AA	111000	****	****	****	48300
EcoChic Sedan 4D	K16AA	116000	****	****	****	51000

FORD

2000 FORD — (1,2or3)FA-(P33P)-Y-#

FOCUS—4-Cyl.—Equipment Schedule 6						
W.B. 103.0"; 2.0 Liter.						
LX Sedan 4D	P33P	13335	350	400	1100	2100
SE Sedan 4D	P34P	13980	500	575	1375	2600
SE Wagon 4D	P36F	15795	725	825	1400	2400
Sony Special Edition			50	50	50	50
4-Cyl, 16V, 2.0 Liter	3		50	50	80	80
FOCUS—4-Cyl. 16V—Equipment Schedule 6						
W.B. 103.0"; 2.0 Liter.						
ZX3 Hatchback 2D	P313	13075	350	400	975	1800
ZTS Sedan 4D	P383	15580	675	750	1500	2750
Kona Limited Edition			50	50	50	50
ESCORT—4-Cyl.—Equipment Schedule 6						
W.B. 98.4"; 2.0 Liter.						
Sedan 4D	P13P	12440	375	450	975	1775
ZX2 Coupe 2D	P113	12970	525	625	1175	2150
S/R Performance Pkg			50	50	75	75
CONTOUR—V6—Equipment Schedule 5						
W.B. 106.5"; 2.5 Liter.						
SE Sedan 4D	P66L	17265	700	800	1400	2475
SE Sport Sedan 4D	P66L	18195	1225	1375	1950	3325
SVT Sedan 4D	P68G	23250	1900	2150	2875	4825
4-Cyl, 2.0 Liter	Z,3		(75)	(75)	(105)	(105)
MUSTANG—V6—Equipment Schedule 4						
W.B. 101.3"; 3.8 Liter.						
Coupe 2D	P404	18410	1000	1175	1625	2750
Convertible 2D	P444	23260	1500	1750	2250	3700
Manual, 5-Spd			(175)	(175)	(220)	(220)
MUSTANG—V8—Equipment Schedule 4						
W.B. 101.3"; 4.6 Liter.						
GT Coupe 2D	P42X	22905	1750	2000	2350	3675
GT Convertible 2D	P45X	27160	2775	3125	3475	5325
TAURUS—V6—Equipment Schedule 4						
W.B. 108.5"; 3.0 Liter.						
LX Sedan 4D	P52U	18995	575	675	1225	2250
SE Sedan 4D	P53U	19295	600	725	1250	2300
SE Wagon 4D	P58U	20450	925	1100	1650	2950

2000 FORD

Body Type	VIN	List	Trade-In Good	Very Good	Pvt-Party Good	Retail Excellent
SES Sedan 4D	P55U	20290	775	925	1475	2650
SES Wagon 4D	P55U	20870	925	1100	1650	2950
SEL Sedan 4D	P56U	21565	950	1125	1675	3000
V6, 24V, 3.0 Liter	S		100	100	135	135

CROWN VICTORIA—V8—Equipment Schedule 4
W.B. 114.7"; 4.6 Liter.

Body Type	VIN	List	Trade-In Good	Very Good	Pvt-Party Good	Retail Excellent
Sedan 4D	P73W	22610	425	525	1175	2300
LX Sedan 4D	P74W	24725	725	875	1500	2775

2001 FORD — (1,2or3)FA–(P33P)–1–#

FOCUS—4-Cyl.—Equipment Schedule 6
W.B. 103.0"; 2.0 Liter.

Body Type	VIN	List	Trade-In Good	Very Good	Pvt-Party Good	Retail Excellent
LX Sedan 4D	P33P	13645	375	425	1325	2600
SE Sedan 4D	P34P	14505	725	800	1600	2900
Street Edition			50	50	55	55
4-Cyl, 16V, 2.0 Liter	3		75	75	90	90

FOCUS—4-Cyl. 16V—Equipment Schedule 6
W.B. 103.0"; 2.0 Liter.

Body Type	VIN	List	Trade-In Good	Very Good	Pvt-Party Good	Retail Excellent
ZX3 Hatchback 2D	P313	13385	375	425	1125	2125
ZTS Sedan 4D	P383	15725	700	775	1575	2900
SE Wagon 4D	P363	16700	875	950	1625	2825
Street Edition			50	50	55	55
S2 Feature Car			50	50	55	55
Traction Control			125	125	170	170

ESCORT—4-Cyl.—Equipment Schedule 6
W.B. 98.4"; 2.0 Liter.

Body Type	VIN	List	Trade-In Good	Very Good	Pvt-Party Good	Retail Excellent
Sedan 4D	P13P	14230	375	450	1000	1800

ZX2—4-Cyl.—Equipment Schedule 6
W.B. 98.4"; 2.0 Liter.

Body Type	VIN	List	Trade-In Good	Very Good	Pvt-Party Good	Retail Excellent
Coupe 2D	P113	13310	525	600	1200	2150

MUSTANG—V6—Equipment Schedule 4
W.B. 101.3"; 3.8 Liter.

Body Type	VIN	List	Trade-In Good	Very Good	Pvt-Party Good	Retail Excellent
Coupe 2D	P404	17695	1125	1325	1875	3150
Deluxe Coupe 2D	P404	18260	1125	1325	1875	3150
Deluxe Convertible 2D	P444	23110	1700	1975	2500	4075
Premium Coupe 2D	P404	19490	1675	1925	2450	3950
Premium Conv 2D	P444	25675	1750	2000	2525	4125
Manual, 5-Spd			(150)	(150)	(200)	(200)

MUSTANG—V8—Equipment Schedule 4
W.B. 101.3"; 4.6 Liter.

Body Type	VIN	List	Trade-In Good	Very Good	Pvt-Party Good	Retail Excellent
GT Deluxe Coupe	P42X	23330	1925	2175	2550	3975
GT Deluxe Convertible	P45X	27585	2850	3225	3600	5525
GT Premium Coupe	P42X	24480	1925	2175	2550	3975
GT Premium Conv 2D	P45X	28735	3125	3525	3875	5900
Bullitt Coupe 2D	P42X	26580	3225	3625	3975	6050
Cobra Coupe 2D	P47V	29205	3775	4050	5025	7200
Cobra Convertible 2D	P46V	33205	5325	5750	6675	9150

TAURUS—V6—Equipment Schedule 4
W.B. 108.5"; 3.0 Liter.

Body Type	VIN	List	Trade-In Good	Very Good	Pvt-Party Good	Retail Excellent
LX Sedan 4D	P52U	19455	650	775	1325	2400
SE Sedan 4D	P53U	19635	675	800	1350	2450
SE Wagon 4D	P58U	20790	1100	1300	1850	3275
SES Sedan 4D	P55U	20850	1000	1175	1725	3075
SES Wagon 4D	P55U	21225	1175	1375	1925	3425
SEL Sedan 4D	P56U	22135	1300	1525	2100	3675
V6, 24V, 3.0 Liter	S		100	100	135	135

CROWN VICTORIA—V8—Equipment Schedule 4
W.B. 114.7"; 4.6 Liter.

Body Type	VIN	List	Trade-In Good	Very Good	Pvt-Party Good	Retail Excellent
Sedan 4D	P73W	22620	500	600	1250	2375
LX Sedan 4D	P74W	24735	850	1000	1650	3000

2002 FORD — (1,2or3)FA–(P33P)–2–#

FOCUS—4-Cyl.—Equipment Schedule 6
W.B. 103.0"; 2.0 Liter.

Body Type	VIN	List	Trade-In Good	Very Good	Pvt-Party Good	Retail Excellent
LX Sedan 4D	P33P	13220	375	425	1375	2675
SE Sedan 4D	P34P	15625	775	875	1675	3025
SE Wagon 4D	P36P	17015	1200	1325	2000	3400
4-Cyl, 16V, 2.0 Liter	3		75	75	100	100

FOCUS—4-Cyl. 16V—Equipment Schedule 6
W.B. 103.0"; 2.0 Liter.

Body Type	VIN	List	Trade-In Good	Very Good	Pvt-Party Good	Retail Excellent
ZX3 Hatchback 2D	P313	13700	400	475	1225	2325
ZTS Sedan 4D	P383	15730	825	900	1700	3075

Body Type	VIN	List	Trade-In Good	Very Good	Pvt-Party Good	Retail Excellent
ZX5 Hatchback 4D	P373	16105	775	850	1750	3225
SVT Hatchback 2D	P395	17995	1300	1475	2125	3650
ZTW Wagon 4D	P363	18195	1225	1350	2025	3425
ESCORT—4-Cyl.—Equipment Schedule 6						
W.B. 98.4"; 2.0 Liter.						
Sedan 4D	P13P	14450	450	525	1125	2025
ZX2—4-Cyl.—Equipment Schedule 6						
W.B. 98.4"; 2.0 Liter.						
Coupe 2D	P113	13655	575	650	1250	2200
MUSTANG—V6—Equipment Schedule 4						
W.B. 101.3"; 3.8 Liter.						
Coupe 2D	P404	18100	1375	1600	2075	3325
Deluxe Coupe 2D	P404	18705	1375	1600	2075	3325
Deluxe Convertible 2D	P444	23955	2025	2300	2750	4300
Premium Coupe 2D	P404	19820	1850	2125	2600	4125
Premium Conv 2D	P444	26210	2225	2550	2950	4625
Manual, 5-Spd			(175)	(175)	(245)	(245)
MUSTANG—V8—Equipment Schedule 4						
W.B. 101.3"; 4.6 Liter.						
GT Deluxe Coupe 2D	P42X	23845	2375	2650	3000	4625
GT Deluxe Convertible	P45X	28430	3250	3650	4025	6075
GT Premium Coupe 2D	P42X	25015	2725	3050	3475	5300
GT Premium Conv 2D	P45X	29270	3550	3975	4325	6500
TAURUS—V6—Equipment Schedule 4						
W.B. 108.5"; 3.0 Liter.						
LX Sedan 4D	P52U		800	925	1475	2650
SE Sedan 4D	P53U		825	975	1525	2700
SE Wagon 4D	P58U	22005	1275	1475	2050	3550
SES Sedan 4D	P55U	21085	1175	1375	1950	3375
SEL Sedan 4D	P56S	22995	1400	1625	2275	3925
SEL Wagon 4D	P59S	23265	1350	1550	2125	3700
V6, 24V, 3.0L (ex SEL)	S		125	125	155	155
CROWN VICTORIA—V8—Equipment Schedule 4						
W.B. 114.7"; 4.6 Liter.						
Sedan 4D	P73W	23435	525	625	1300	2425
LX Sedan 4D	P74W	27025	1000	1150	1775	3150
LX Sport Sedan 4D	P74W	28840	1125	1300	1950	3475
THUNDERBIRD—V8—Equipment Schedule 2						
W.B. 107.2"; 3.9 Liter.						
Soft Top Conv 2D	P60A	35495	5125	5900	5800	8525
Hard Top			425	425	545	545

2003 FORD — (1,2or3)FA–(P33P)-3-#

Body Type	VIN	List	Trade-In Good	Very Good	Pvt-Party Good	Retail Excellent
FOCUS—4-Cyl.—Equipment Schedule 6						
W.B. 103.0"; 2.0 Liter, 2.3 Liter.						
LX Sedan 4D	P33P	13505	475	550	1600	3100
SE Sedan 4D	P34P	15175	1025	1125	2050	3675
SE Wagon 4D	P36P	17525	1275	1400	2325	4050
4-Cyl, 16V, 2.3 Liter	Z		75	75	110	110
FOCUS—4-Cyl.—16V—Equipment Schedule 6						
W.B. 103.0"; 2.0 Liter, 2.3 Liter.						
ZX3 Hatchback 2D	P313	13990	575	625	1650	3175
ZX5 Hatchback 4D	P373	15900	900	1000	2050	3750
ZTS Sedan 4D	P383	16095	950	1025	1950	3500
ZTW Wagon 4D	P363	17870	1325	1450	2350	4050
ZX3 SVT Hatchback 2D	P395	19100	1425	1600	2325	3900
ZX5 SVT Hatchback 4D	P375	19600	1625	1825	2575	4250
ZX2—4-Cyl.—Equipment Schedule 6						
W.B. 98.4"; 2.0 Liter.						
Coupe 2D	P113	14250	575	650	1300	2300
MUSTANG—V6—Equipment Schedule 4						
W.B. 101.3"; 3.8 Liter.						
Coupe 2D	P404	18345	2000	2275	2675	4150
Deluxe Coupe 2D	P404	19075	2000	2275	2675	4150
Deluxe Convertible	P444	24080	2650	3000	3350	5125
Premium Coupe 2D	P404	20190	2500	2850	3200	4925
Premium Convertible 2D	P444	26665	3050	3450	3900	5925
Manual, 5-Spd			(225)	(225)	(310)	(310)
MUSTANG—V8—Equipment Schedule 4						
W.B. 101.3"; 4.6 Liter.						
GT Deluxe Coupe 2D	P42X	24330	3200	3575	3925	5800
GT Deluxe Convertible	P45X	28670	4250	4725	5125	7525
GT Premium Coupe 2D	P42X	25500	3800	4225	4500	6650

2003 FORD

Body Type	VIN	List	Trade-In Good	Very Good	Pvt-Party Good	Retail Excellent
GT Premium Conv 2D	P45X	29840	4700	5225	5575	8150
Mach 1 Coupe 2D	P42R	29810	6050	6700	6925	10050
MUSTANG—V8 Supercharged—Equipment Schedule 4						
W.B. 101.3"; 4.6 Liter.						
Cobra Coupe 2D	P48Y	34085	6725	7200	7850	10250
Cobra Convertible 2D	P49Y	38460	8600	9200	9650	12350
10th Anniversary			200	200	235	235
TAURUS—V6—Equipment Schedule 4						
W.B. 108.5"; 3.0 Liter.						
LX Sedan 4D	P52U	20230	1100	1275	2025	3675
SE Sedan 4D	P53U	20345	1175	1350	2100	3800
SE Wagon 4D	P582	21995	1425	1650	2550	4525
SES Sedan 4D	P55U	21670	1425	1650	2550	4525
SEL Sedan 4D	P56S	23570	1500	1725	2725	4875
SEL Wagon 4D	P59U	23820	1475	1700	2600	4625
V6, 24V, 3.0 Liter	S		150	150	185	185
CROWN VICTORIA—V8—Equipment Schedule 4						
W.B. 114.7"; 4.6 Liter.						
Sedan 4D	P73W	24510	1125	1275	1825	3175
LX Sedan 4D	P74W	27780	1575	1825	2375	3925
LX Sport Sedan 4D	P74W	29600	1775	2025	2675	4525
THUNDERBIRD—V8—Equipment Schedule 4						
W.B. 107.2"; 3.9 Liter.						
Soft Top Conv 2D	P60A	36895	5775	6600	6425	9375
007 Hard Top Conv 2D	P62A	43995	****	****	****	14800
Hard Top			450	450	555	555

2004 FORD — (1,2or3)FA–(P333)–4–#

Body Type	VIN	List	Trade-In Good	Very Good	Pvt-Party Good	Retail Excellent
FOCUS—4-Cyl.—Equipment Schedule 6						
W.B. 103.0"; 2.0 Liter.						
LX Sedan 4D	P333	14640	700	775	1875	3500
SE Wagon 4D	P363	18490	1750	1900	2925	4875
4-Cyl, 16V, 2.0L,2.3L	PZ		100	100	120	120
FOCUS—4-Cyl. 16V—Equipment Schedule 6						
W.B. 103.0"; 2.0 Liter, 2.3 Liter.						
ZX3 Hatchback 2D	P313	14180	825	900	1925	3525
ZX5 Hatchback 4D	P373	15580	1050	1150	2200	3950
SE Sedan 4D	P34Z	16311	1350	1475	2475	4300
ZTS Sedan 4D	P38Z	16080	1275	1375	2325	4050
ZTW Wagon 4D	P35Z	18290	1600	1750	2750	4600
SVT Hatchback 2D	P395	19375	2225	2475	2950	4525
SVT Hatchback 4D	P375	19630	2775	3075	3500	5300
MUSTANG—V6—Equipment Schedule 4						
W.B. 101.3"; 3.8 Liter, 3.9 Liter.						
Coupe 2D	P404	18775	2275	2575	3075	4750
Deluxe Coupe 2D	P404	19505	2325	2600	3100	4800
Deluxe Convertible 2D	P444	24510	2800	3150	3725	5700
Premium Coupe 2D	P404	20160	2800	3125	3600	5525
Premium Convertible 2D	P444	26635	3425	3850	4400	6675
Manual, 5-Spd			(275)	(275)	(375)	(375)
MUSTANG—V8—Equipment Schedule 4						
W.B. 101.3"; 4.6 Liter.						
GT Deluxe Coupe 2D	P42X	24300	3800	4225	4675	6950
GT Deluxe Convertible	P45X	28640	4900	5425	5975	8800
GT Premium Coupe 2D	P42X	25470	4200	4675	5250	7775
GT Premium Conv 2D	P45X	29810	5350	5925	6425	9450
Mach 1 Coupe 2D	P42R	29875	6850	7575	7900	11350
MUSTANG—V8 Supercharged—Equipment Schedule 4						
W.B. 101.3"; 4.6 Liter.						
Cobra Coupe 2D	P48Y	35485	8975	9575	10100	12800
Cobra Convertible 2D	P49Y	39575	11000	11750	12000	14950
TAURUS—V6—Equipment Schedule 4						
W.B. 108.5"; 3.0 Liter.						
LX Sedan 4D	P52U	20720	1200	1375	2175	3850
SE Sedan 4D	P53U	20855	1325	1500	2375	4200
SE Wagon 4D	P58U	22290	1650	1875	2800	4900
SES Sedan 4D	P55U	22040	1550	1775	2675	4650
SEL Sedan 4D	P56S	23965	1675	1925	2900	5100
SEL Wagon 4D	P59U	24115	1750	2000	2925	5050
V6, 24V, 3.0 Liter	S		175	175	220	220
CROWN VICTORIA—V8—Equipment Schedule 4						
W.B. 114.7"; 4.6 Liter.						
Sedan 4D	P73W	24345	1550	1775	2275	3675

Body Type	VIN	List	Trade-In Good	Very Good	Pvt-Party Good	Retail Excellent
LX Sedan 4D	P74W	27370	2000	2275	2725	4350
LX Sport Sedan 4D	P74W	30890	2350	2650	3175	5100

THUNDERBIRD—V8—Equipment Schedule 2
W.B. 107.2"; 3.9 Liter.

Body Type	VIN	List	Trade-In Good	Very Good	Pvt-Party Good	Retail Excellent
Soft Top Conv 2D	P60A	37530	6600	7475	7175	10150
Pacific Coast Conv 2D	P63A	43995	****	****	****	12550
Hard Top			450	450	565	565

2005 FORD — (1,2or3)(FAorZV)-(P31N)-5-#

FOCUS—4-Cyl.—Equipment Schedule 6
W.B. 102.9"; 2.0 Liter, 2.3 Liter.

Body Type	VIN	List	Trade-In Good	Very Good	Pvt-Party Good	Retail Excellent
ZX3 S Hatchback 2D	P31N	14545	1225	1350	2425	4075
ZX3 SE Hatchback 2D	P31N	15865	1825	2000	2950	4650
ZX3 SES Hatchback 2D	P31N	16965	1950	2125	3250	5250
ZX4 S Sedan 4D	P34N	14965	1650	1825	2900	4750
ZX4 SE Sedan 4D	P34N	16465	1850	2025	3150	5125
ZX4 SES Sedan 4D	P34N	17565	2200	2400	3525	5675
ZX4 ST Sedan 4D	P38Z	18335	2450	2675	3725	5875
ZX5 S Hatchback 4D	P35N	15665	1775	1950	3050	4950
ZX5 SE Hatchback 4D	P37N	17165	2125	2325	3425	5500
ZX5 SES H'Back 4D	P37N	18265	2425	2650	3575	5525
ZXW SE Wagon 4D	P36N	18165	2300	2525	3550	5625
ZXW SES Wagon 4D	P33N	19265	2525	2750	3875	6150

MUSTANG—V6—Equipment Schedule 4
W.B. 107.1"; 4.0 Liter.

Body Type	VIN	List	Trade-In Good	Very Good	Pvt-Party Good	Retail Excellent
Deluxe Coupe 2D	T80N	19890	4150	4650	5350	7800
Deluxe Convertible 2D	T84N	24615	4775	5350	5975	8675
Premium Coupe 2D	T80N	20765	4675	5200	5875	8525
Premium Convertible 2D	T84N	25490	5350	6000	6575	9475
Manual, 5-Spd			(325)	(325)	(435)	(435)

MUSTANG—V8—Equipment Schedule 4
W.B. 107.1"; 4.6 Liter.

Body Type	VIN	List	Trade-In Good	Very Good	Pvt-Party Good	Retail Excellent
GT Deluxe Coupe 2D	T82H	25815	6200	6825	7175	10000
GT Deluxe Convertible	T85H	30240	7850	8625	8825	12250
GT Premium Coupe 2D	T82H	26995	6850	7550	7825	10850
GT Premium Conv 2D	T85H	31420	8225	9025	9100	12500

TAURUS—V6—Equipment Schedule 4
W.B. 108.5"; 3.0 Liter.

Body Type	VIN	List	Trade-In Good	Very Good	Pvt-Party Good	Retail Excellent
SE Sedan 4D	P53U	21145	1275	1450	2525	4350
SE Wagon 4D	P58U	23015	1625	1850	2975	5100
SEL Sedan 4D	P56U	23055	1550	1775	2975	5150
SEL Wagon 4D	P59U	24005	1650	1900	3000	5150
V6, 24V, 3.0 Liter	S		200	200	255	255

FIVE HUNDRED—V6—Equipment Schedule 4
W.B. 112.9"; 3.0 Liter.

Body Type	VIN	List	Trade-In Good	Very Good	Pvt-Party Good	Retail Excellent
SE Sedan 4D	P231	22795	1775	2025	2825	4600
SEL Sedan 4D	P241	24795	2075	2375	3150	5075
Limited Sedan 4D	P251	26795	2325	2625	3425	5475
AWD	6,7,8		475	475	645	645

CROWN VICTORIA—V8—Equipment Schedule 4
W.B. 114.7"; 4.6 Liter.

Body Type	VIN	List	Trade-In Good	Very Good	Pvt-Party Good	Retail Excellent
Sedan 4D	P73W	24810	1575	1800	2475	3900
LX Sedan 4D	P74W	27945	2125	2400	2975	4625
LX Sport Sedan 4D	P74W	31270	2575	2900	3525	5475

THUNDERBIRD—V8—Equipment Schedule 2
W.B. 107.2"; 3.9 Liter.

Body Type	VIN	List	Trade-In Good	Very Good	Pvt-Party Good	Retail Excellent
Soft Top Conv 2D	P60A	38065	7075	7950	7850	11000
50th Anniv Conv 2D	P69A	44430	8775	9875	9550	13300
Hard Top			475	475	590	590

GT—V8 Supercharged—Equipment Schedule 2
W.B. 106.7"; 5.4 Liter.

Body Type	VIN	List	Trade-In Good	Very Good	Pvt-Party Good	Retail Excellent
Coupe 2D	P90S	143345	****	****	****	136000

2006 FORD-(1,2or3)(F7,FAorZV)-(P31N)-6-#

FOCUS—4-Cyl.—Equipment Schedule 6
W.B. 102.9"; 2.0 Liter, 2.3 Liter.

Body Type	VIN	List	Trade-In Good	Very Good	Pvt-Party Good	Retail Excellent
ZX3 S Hatchback 2D	P31N	14905	1475	1625	2875	4775
ZX4 ST Sedan 4D	P38Z	17585	2550	2775	3850	6000

FOCUS—4-Cyl.—Equipment Schedule 6
W.B. 102.9"; 2.0 Liter, 2.3 Liter.

Body Type	VIN	List	Trade-In Good	Very Good	Pvt-Party Good	Retail Excellent
ZX3 SE Hatchback 2D	P31N	16075	2000	2175	3250	5125
ZX3 SES Hatchback 2D	P31N	16835	2275	2475	3475	5400

2006 FORD

Body Type	VIN	List	Trade-In Good	Very Good	Pvt-Party Good	Retail Excellent
ZX4 S Sedan 4D	P34N	15265	2050	2225	3325	5275
ZX4 SE Sedan 4D	P34N	16375	2225	2400	3500	5525
ZX4 SES Sedan 4D	P34N	17135	2375	2600	3675	5750
ZX5 S Hatchback 4D	P37N	15975	2150	2350	3375	5275
ZX5 SE Hatchback 4D	P37N	17080	2475	2700	3650	5600
ZX5 SES Hatchback 4D	P37N	17815	2550	2775	3700	5650
ZXW SE Wagon 4D	P36N	18095	2750	3000	3950	6025
ZXW SES Wagon 4D	P36N	18855	2975	3225	4300	6600
Manual, 5-Spd			(275)	(275)	(355)	(355)
FUSION—4-Cyl.—Equipment Schedule 4						
W.B. 107.4"; 2.3 Liter.						
S Sedan 4D	P06Z	18620	2600	2850	3725	5700
SE Sedan 4D	P07Z	19375	2900	3175	4050	6175
Manual, 5-Spd			(375)	(375)	(510)	(510)
V6, 3.0 Liter	1		575	575	755	755
FUSION—V6—Equipment Schedule 4						
W.B. 107.4"; 3.0 Liter.						
SEL Sedan 4D	P081	22360	3650	4000	5050	7625
Manual, 5-Spd			(375)	(375)	(510)	(510)
4-Cyl, 2.3 Liter	Z		(525)	(525)	(705)	(705)
MUSTANG—V6—Equipment Schedule 4						
W.B. 107.1"; 4.0 Liter.						
Coupe 2D	T80N	19835	4950	5475	6100	8600
Convertible 2D	T84N	24660	5675	6300	6925	9725
Deluxe Coupe 2D	T80N	19935	4950	5475	6100	8600
Deluxe Convertible 2D	T84N	24760	5675	6300	6925	9725
Premium Coupe 2D	T80N	20810	5600	6200	6775	9500
Premium Convertible 2D	T84N	25635	6075	6725	7300	10250
Manual, 5-Spd			(375)	(375)	(505)	(505)
MUSTANG—V8—Equipment Schedule 4						
W.B. 107.1"; 4.6 Liter.						
GT Deluxe Coupe	T82H	25860	6950	7600	8025	11050
GT Deluxe Convertible	T85H	30685	8600	9400	9575	12950
GT Premium Coupe	T82H	27040	7675	8375	8700	11850
GT Premium Conv 2D	T85H	31865	9075	9900	10050	13600
TAURUS—6-Cyl.—Equipment Schedule 4						
W.B. 108.5"; 3.0 Liter.						
SE Sedan 4D	P53U	21515	1600	1825	2825	4650
SEL Sedan 4D	P56U	23665	2075	2325	3350	5475
FIVE HUNDRED—V6—Equipment Schedule 4						
W.B. 112.9"; 3.0 Liter.						
SE Sedan 4D	P231	22930	1975	2225	3050	4800
SEL Sedan 4D	P241	24930	2450	2750	3525	5525
Limited Sedan 4D	P251	27080	2875	3225	4000	6200
AWD	6,7,8		525	525	700	700
CROWN VICTORIA—V8—Equipment Schedule 4						
W.B. 114.7"; 4.6 Liter.						
Sedan 4D	P73W	25285	2025	2275	2850	4350
LX Sedan 4D	P74W	28830	2675	3000	3500	5175
LX Sport Sedan 4D	P74W	31605	3275	3675	4300	6400
GT—V8 Supercharged—Equipment Schedule 2						
W.B. 106.7"; 5.4 Liter.						
Coupe 2D	P90S	153345	****	****	****	154100
Heritage Coupe 2D	P90S	166345	****	****	****	179500

2007 FORD — (1,2or3)(F7,FAorZV)–(P31N)–7–#

Body Type	VIN	List	Trade-In Good	Very Good	Pvt-Party Good	Retail Excellent
FOCUS—4-Cyl.—Equipment Schedule 6						
W.B. 102.9"; 2.0 Liter, 2.3 Liter.						
S Sedan 2D	P31N	14985	1875	2050	3200	5025
ST Sedan 4D	P38Z	17690	3150	3400	4500	6650
FOCUS—4-Cyl.—Equipment Schedule 6						
W.B. 102.9"; 2.0 Liter.						
SES Wagon 4D	P36N	18145	3475	3750	4800	7050
Automatic			300	300	385	385
FOCUS—4-Cyl.—Equipment Schedule 6						
W.B. 102.9"; 2.0 Liter.						
S Sedan 4D	P34N	15110	2400	2600	3675	5650
S Hatchback 4D	P37N	15810	2525	2750	3750	5675
SE Sedan 4D	P34N	16075	2750	2975	4025	6075
SE Hatchback 2D	P31N	16075	2400	2600	3675	5600
SE Hatchback 4D	P37N	17080	3050	3300	4200	6175
SE Wagon 4D	P36N	18095	3450	3700	4750	6950
SES Sedan 4D	P34N	17135	2925	3175	4225	6250

Body Type	VIN	List	Trade-In Good	Very Good	Pvt-Party Good	Retail Excellent
SES Hatchback 2D	P31N	16835	2900	3125	4050	6025
SES Hatchback 4D	P37N	17845	3225	3475	4450	6475
Manual, 5-Spd			(300)	(300)	(385)	(385)
FUSION—4-Cyl.—Equipment Schedule 4						
W.B. 107.4"; 2.3 Liter.						
S Sedan 4D	P06Z	18845	3075	3350	4350	6400
SE Sedan 4D	P07Z	19705	3500	3825	4800	7000
AWD	1,2		750	750	1000	1000
Manual, 5-Spd			(425)	(425)	(555)	(555)
V6, 3.0 Liter	1		600	600	800	800
FUSION—V6—Equipment Schedule 4						
W.B. 107.4"; 3.0 Liter.						
SEL Sedan 4D	P081	22675	4525	4900	5875	8525
AWD	1,2		750	750	1000	1000
Manual, 5-Spd			(425)	(425)	(555)	(555)
4-Cyl, 2.3 Liter	Z		(575)	(575)	(755)	(755)
MUSTANG—V6—Equipment Schedule 4						
W.B. 107.1"; 4.0 Liter.						
Deluxe Coupe 2D	T80N	19995	5550	6100	6725	9250
Deluxe Convertible	T84N	24820	6475	7100	7700	10550
Premium Coupe 2D	T80N	20990	6325	6925	7575	10350
Premium Convertible 2D	T84N	25815	6875	7550	8150	11150
Pony Pkg			150	150	195	195
Manual, 5-Spd			(425)	(425)	(535)	(535)
MUSTANG—V8—Equipment Schedule 4						
W.B. 107.1"; 4.6 Liter.						
GT Deluxe Coupe	T82H	26440	8400	9100	9400	12500
GT Deluxe Convertible	T85H	31265	10050	10900	11100	14650
GT Premium Coupe 2D	T82H	27620	9150	9925	10200	13500
GT Premium Conv 2D	T85H	32445	10200	11050	11350	15150
Shelby Pkg			775	775	955	955
MUSTANG SHELBY GT500—V8 Supercharged—Equipment Schedule 4						
W.B. 107.1"; 5.4 Liter.						
Cobra Coupe 2D	T88S	42975	16100	17000	17050	20100
Cobra Convertible 2D	T89S	47800	17850	18900	18900	22400
TAURUS—6-Cyl.—Equipment Schedule 4						
W.B. 108.5"; 3.0 Liter.						
SE Sedan 4D	P53U	21745	2050	2300	3300	5250
SEL Sedan 4D	P56U	23895	2550	2825	3850	6050
FIVE HUNDRED—V6—Equipment Schedule 4						
W.B. 112.9"; 3.0 Liter.						
SEL Sedan 4D	P241	23420	2950	3275	4200	6325
Limited Sedan 4D	P251	26995	3775	4175	5050	7475
AWD	7,8		575	575	755	755
CROWN VICTORIA—V8—Equipment Schedule 4						
W.B. 114.6"; 4.6 Liter.						
Sedan 4D	P73W	25390	2450	2700	3250	4725
LX Sedan 4D	P74W	28385	3250	3600	4250	6125

2008 FORD — (1,2or3)(F7,FAorZV)-(P32N)-8-#

Body Type	VIN	List	Trade-In Good	Very Good	Pvt-Party Good	Retail Excellent
FOCUS—4-Cyl.—Equipment Schedule 6						
W.B. 102.9"; 2.0 Liter.						
S Coupe 2D	P32N	14695	2875	3075	4075	5850
FOCUS—4-Cyl.—Equipment Schedule 4						
W.B. 102.9"; 2.0 Liter.						
S Sedan 4D	P34N	15810	3450	3675	4850	6950
SE Coupe 2D	P35N	16510	3925	4200	5175	7200
SE Sedan 4D	P35N	16810	4125	4425	5475	7650
SES Sedan 4D	P35N	17810	4525	4825	5800	8025
SES Coupe 2D	P33N	17510	4400	4700	5775	8050
Manual, 5-Spd w/Overdrive			(350)	(350)	(460)	(460)
FUSION—4-Cyl.—Equipment Schedule 4						
W.B. 107.4"; 2.3 Liter.						
S Sedan 4D	P06Z	19370	3500	3750	4850	6850
SE Sedan 4D	P07Z	20295	4350	4650	5675	7900
AWD	1,2		800	800	1075	1075
Manual, 5-Spd			(450)	(450)	(585)	(585)
V6, 3.0 Liter	1		625	625	845	845
FUSION—4-Cyl.—Equipment Schedule 4						
W.B. 107.4"; 3.0 Liter.						
SEL Sedan 4D	P081	22875	5300	5675	6875	9450
AWD	1,2		800	800	1075	1075
Manual, 5-Spd			(450)	(450)	(585)	(585)

1015

Body Type	VIN	List	Trade-In Good	Very Good	Pvt-Party Good	Retail Excellent
4-Cyl, 2.3 Liter	Z		**(600)**	**(600)**	**(815)**	**(815)**
MUSTANG—V6—Equipment Schedule 4						
W.B. 107.1"; 4.0 Liter.						
Deluxe Coupe 2D	T80N	20990	6275	6750	7500	9800
Deluxe Convertible	T84N	25815	7425	8000	8575	11100
Premium Coupe 2D	T80N	24075	7275	7825	8525	11100
Premium Convertible	T84N	26500	7925	8525	9250	12000
Pony Pkg			150	150	200	200
Manual, 5-Spd w/Overdrive			(450)	(450)	(550)	(550)
MUSTANG—V8—Equipment Schedule 4						
W.B. 107.1"; 4.6 Liter.						
GT Deluxe Coupe	T82H	27230	9225	9850	10600	13750
GT Deluxe Convertible	T85H	32055	10850	11550	12200	15750
GT Premium Coupe	T82H	28215	10200	10950	11650	15000
GT Premium Conv 2D	T85H	33040	11300	12050	12800	16450
Bullitt Pkg			800	800	985	985
Shelby GT Pkg			825	825	1025	1025
MUSTANG SHELBY GT500—V8 Supercharged—Equipment Schedule 4						
W.B. 107.1"; 5.4 Liter.						
Coupe 2D	T88S	43975	18150	19050	19250	22300
Convertible 2D	T89S	48800	20200	21100	21100	24300
TAURUS—V6—Equipment Schedule 4						
W.B. 112.9"; 3.5 Liter.						
SEL Sedan 4D	P24W	23995	4825	5200	6025	8275
Limited Sedan 4D	P25W	27980	5175	5600	6625	9150
AWD	7,8		1225	1225	1635	1635
CROWN VICTORIA—V8—Equipment Schedule 4						
W.B. 114.7"; 4.6 Liter.						
Sedan 4D	P73V	26150	2850	3100	3850	5325
LX Sedan 4D	P74V	29145	3850	4150	4850	6625

2009 FORD — (1,2or3)(F7,FAorZV)-(P34N)-9-#

	VIN	List	Good	Very Good	Good	Excellent
FOCUS—4-Cyl.—Equipment Schedule 6						
W.B. 102.9"; 2.0 Liter.						
S Sedan 4D	P34N	16505	3950	4175	5475	7650
SE Coupe 2D	P33N	17690	4800	5100	6025	7950
SE Sedan 4D	P35N	17690	4925	5200	6275	8425
SES Coupe 2D	P33N	19080	5250	5550	6750	8950
SES Sedan 4D	P35N	19080	5175	5500	6775	9100
SEL Sedan 4D	P35N	19480	5275	5600	6825	9125
Manual, 5-Spd w/Overdrive			(375)	(375)	(490)	(490)
FUSION—4-Cyl.—Equipment Schedule 4						
W.B. 107.4"; 2.3 Liter.						
S Sedan 4D	P06Z	18860	4650	4925	6025	8025
SE Sedan 4D	P07Z	20000	5200	5525	6775	9000
AWD	1,2		875	875	1150	1150
Manual, 5-Spd w/Overdrive	1		(475)	(475)	(645)	(645)
V6, 3.0 Liter	1		675	675	895	895
FUSION—V6—Equipment Schedule 4						
W.B. 107.4"; 3.0 Liter.						
SEL Sedan 4D	P081	24065	6600	7000	8325	10900
AWD	1,2		875	875	1150	1150
4-Cyl, 2.3 Liter	Z		(650)	(650)	(875)	(875)
MUSTANG—V6—Equipment Schedule 4						
W.B. 107.1"; 4.0 Liter.						
Deluxe Coupe 2D	T80N	21525	7400	7825	8850	11250
Deluxe Convertible	T84N	26350	8425	8900	9975	12650
Premium Coupe 2D	T80N	23315	8425	8900	9975	12650
Premium Convertible 2D	T84N	28140	9025	9550	10600	13450
Pony Pkg			175	175	210	210
Manual, 5-Spd Overdrive			(475)	(475)	(600)	(600)
MUSTANG—V8—Equipment Schedule 4						
W.B. 107.1"; 4.6 Liter.						
GT Deluxe Coupe	T82H	27220	10700	11300	12450	15750
GT Deluxe Convertible	T85H	32045	12250	12900	14000	17500
GT Premium Coupe	T82H	29170	11650	12350	13550	17100
GT Premium Conv 2D	T85H	34780	12900	13600	14650	18300
Bullitt Pkg			850	850	1045	1045
MUSTANG SHELBY GT500—V8 Supercharged—Equipment Schedule 4						
W.B. 107.1"; 5.4 Liter.						
Coupe 2D	T88S	43480	21400	22400	22700	25900
Convertible 2D	T89S	48305	23500	24500	24500	28100

Body Type	VIN	List	Trade-In Good	Very Good	Pvt-Party Good	Retail Excellent
TAURUS—V6—Equipment Schedule 4						
W.B. 112.9"; 3.5 Liter.						
SE Sedan 4D	P23W	24950	5425	5750	6850	9000
SEL Sedan 4D	P24W	26250	5775	6125	7225	9475
Limited Sedan 4D	P25W	30250	6875	7300	8500	11100
AWD	6,7,8		1325	1325	1755	1755
CROWN VICTORIA—V8—Equipment Schedule 4						
W.B. 114.7"; 4.6 Liter.						
LX Sedan 4D	P74V	30080	5925	6275	7400	9725

2010 FORD — (1,2or3)(FAorZV)(P3EN)-A-#

Body Type	VIN	List	Trade-In Good	Very Good	Pvt-Party Good	Retail Excellent
FOCUS—4-Cyl.—Equipment Schedule 6						
W.B. 102.9"; 2.0 Liter.						
S Sedan 4D	P3EN	17505	5000	5275	6325	8225
SE Sedan 4D	P3CN	18385	5350	5625	6750	8650
SE Coupe 2D	P3FN	18385	5700	6000	7100	9050
SES Coupe 2D	P3DN	19995	6325	6650	7800	9950
SES Sedan 4D	P3GN	19995	6325	6675	7925	10200
SEL Sedan 4D	P3HN	19995	6475	6825	8100	10450
Manual, 5-Spd w/Overdrive			(450)	(450)	(615)	(615)
FUSION—4-Cyl.—Equipment Schedule 4						
W.B. 107.4"; 2.5 Liter.						
S Sedan 4D	P0GA	19995	5900	6200	7575	9700
SE Sedan 4D	P0HA	21270	6750	7075	8500	10850
V6, Flex Fuel, 3.0 Liter	G		700	700	935	935
FUSION—4-Cyl. Hybrid—Equipment Schedule 4						
W.B. 107.4"; 2.5 Liter.						
Sedan 4D	P0L3	27995	9400	9850	10850	13200
FUSION—V6 Flex Fuel—Equipment Schedule 4						
W.B. 107.4"; 3.0 Liter.						
SEL Sedan 4D	P0JG	26310	7900	8275	9725	12300
AWD	C,D		950	950	1265	1265
4-Cyl, 2.5 Liter	A		(625)	(625)	(820)	(820)
FUSION—V6—Equipment Schedule 4						
W.B. 107.4"; 3.5 Liter.						
Sport Sedan 4D	P0KC	26550	8625	9050	10650	13550
AWD	C,D		950	950	1250	1250
MUSTANG—V6—Equipment Schedule 4						
W.B. 107.1"; 4.0 Liter.						
Coupe 2D	P8AN	22840	9675	10100	11400	14100
Convertible 2D	P8EN	27840	10450	10950	12300	15200
Premium Coupe 2D	P8AN	25245	10700	11150	12500	15450
Premium Conv 2D	P8EN	30245	11200	11700	13100	16150
Pony Pkg			175	175	225	225
Manual, 5-Spd w/Overdrive			(500)	(500)	(620)	(620)
MUSTANG—V8—Equipment Schedule 4						
W.B. 107.1"; 4.6 Liter.						
GT Coupe 2D	P8CH	28845	13850	14500	15650	18800
GT Convertible 2D	P8FH	34840	16100	16850	17800	21300
GT Premium Coupe 2D	P8CH	31845	15050	15750	16850	20300
GT Premium Conv	P8FH	37245	16400	17200	18150	21700
MUSTANG SHELBY GT500—V8 Supercharged—Equipment Schedule 4						
W.B. 107.1"; 4.6 Liter.						
Coupe 2D	P8JS	47575	25300	26200	27000	30500
Convertible 2D	P8KS	52575	26600	27700	28400	32000
TAURUS—V6—Equipment Schedule 4						
W.B. 112.9"; 3.5 Liter.						
SE Sedan 4D	P2DW	25995	9625	10050	11100	13500
SEL Sedan 4D	P2EW	27995	10000	10450	11550	14050
Limited Sedan 4D	P2FW	31995	10750	11200	12400	15100
AWD	H,J		1400	1400	1735	1735
TAURUS AWD—V6 EcoBoost Twin Turbo—Equipment Schedule 4						
W.B. 112.9"; 3.5 Liter.						
SHO Sedan 4D	P2KT	37995	14250	14850	15750	18700
CROWN VICTORIA—V8 Flex Fuel—Equipment Schedule 4						
W.B. 114.7"; 4.6 Liter.						
LX Sedan 4D	P7EV	30780	8325	8700	9725	11900

2011 FORD — (1,2or3)(FAorZV)(P4AJ)-B-#

Body Type	VIN	List	Trade-In Good	Very Good	Pvt-Party Good	Retail Excellent
FIESTA—4-Cyl.—Equipment Schedule 6						
W.B. 98.0"; 1.6 Liter.						
S Sedan 4D	P4AJ	13995	4950	5225	6425	8500

128   DEDUCT FOR RECONDITIONING

Body Type	VIN	List	Trade-In Good	Very Good	Pvt-Party Good	Retail Excellent
SE Sedan 4D	P4EJ	14995	5800	6125	7475	9775
SE Hatchback 4D	P4EJ	15795	5875	6200	7550	9850
SEL Sedan 4D	P4CJ	16995	6350	6700	8025	10450
SES Hatchback 4D	P4FJ	17795	6525	6900	8150	10500
Automatic, 6-Spd w/OD			425	425	575	575
FOCUS—4-Cyl.—Equipment Schedule 6						
W.B. 102.9"; 2.0 Liter.						
S Sedan 4D	P3EN	18180	5975	6275	7525	9525
SE Sedan 4D	P3FN	18810	6650	6950	8200	10300
SES Sedan 4D	P3GN	20410	7800	8150	9425	11750
Manual, 5-Spd w/Overdrive			(500)	(500)	(650)	(650)
FOCUS—4-Cyl.—Equipment Schedule 6						
W.B. 102.9"; 2.0 Liter.						
SEL Sedan 4D	P3HN	20395	7650	8000	9225	11450
FUSION—4-Cyl.—Equipment Schedule 4						
W.B. 107.4"; 2.5 Liter.						
S Sedan 4D	P0GA	21295	7700	8000	9600	11950
SE Sedan 4D	P0HA	22975	8600	8950	10400	12700
AWD	C		650	650	835	835
V6, Flex Fuel, 3.0 Liter	G		750	750	935	935
FUSION—4-Cyl. Hybrid—Equipment Schedule 4						
W.B. 107.4"; 2.5 Liter.						
Sedan 4D	P0L3	28825	10750	11150	12300	14600
FUSION—V6—Equipment Schedule 4						
W.B. 107.4"; 3.5 Liter.						
SEL Sedan 4D	P0JG	27140	9675	10050	11750	14500
AWD	C		650	650	835	835
4-Cyl., 2.5 Liter	A		(650)	(650)	(845)	(845)
FUSION—V6—Equipment Schedule 4						
W.B. 107.4"; 3.5 Liter.						
Sport Sedan 4D	P0KC	27380	10550	11000	12650	15500
AWD	D		650	650	830	830
MUSTANG—V6—Equipment Schedule 4						
W.B. 107.1"; 3.7 Liter.						
Coupe 2D	P8AM	23990	11500	11900	13450	16200
Convertible 2D	P8EM	28990	12400	12800	14350	17250
Premium Coupe 2D	P8AM	26695	12350	12750	14300	17250
Premium Conv 2D	P8EM	31695	13050	13450	15200	18250
Pony Pkg			200	200	230	230
Manual, 6-Spd w/Overdrive			(550)	(550)	(665)	(665)
MUSTANG—V8—Equipment Schedule 4						
W.B. 107.1"; 5.0 Liter.						
GT Coupe 2D	P8CF	30495	16850	17500	18650	21800
GT Convertible 2D	P8FF	35495	19300	20100	21200	24600
GT Premium Coupe 2D	P8CF	36150	18150	18900	20000	23300
GT Premium Conv 2D	P8FF	38695	19700	20500	21600	25100
Brembo Brake Pkg			400	400	450	450
MUSTANG SHELBY GT500—V8 Supercharged—Equipment Schedule 4						
W.B. 107.1"; 5.4 Liter.						
Coupe 2D	P8JS	48495	30100	31100	31900	35500
Convertible 2D	P8KS	54495	32700	33800	34600	38400
TAURUS—V6—Equipment Schedule 4						
W.B. 112.9"; 3.5 Liter.						
SE Sedan 4D	P2DW	25995	11650	12000	13300	15600
SEL Sedan 4D	P2EW	28195	11950	12350	13700	16200
Limited Sedan 4D	P2FW	32595	12400	12800	14200	16800
AWD	H		1500	1500	1835	1835
TAURUS AWD—V6 EcoBoost Twin Turbo—Equipment Schedule 4						
W.B. 112.9"; 3.5 Liter.						
SHO Sedan 4D	P2KT	38595	16250	16750	17900	20600
CROWN VICTORIA—V8 Flex Fuel—Equipment Schedule 4						
W.B. 114.7"; 4.6 Liter.						
LX Sedan 4D	P7EV	30780	10250	10600	11850	14050

2012 FORD — (1,2or3)FAor1ZV-(P4AJ)-C-#

FIESTA—4-Cyl.—Equipment Schedule 4						
W.B. 98.0"; 1.6 Liter.						
S Sedan 4D	P4AJ	13995	5900	6175	7550	9650
S Hatchback 4D	P4TJ	14895	6000	6275	7700	9875
SE Sedan 4D	P4BJ	15195	6625	6950	8350	10700
SE Hatchback 4D	P4EJ	16195	6850	7175	8575	10900
SEL Sedan 4D	P4CJ	17295	7375	7700	9175	11650
SES Hatchback 4D	P4FJ	18195	7525	7875	9250	11650

Body Type	VIN	List	Trade-In Good	Very Good	Pvt-Party Good	Retail Excellent
Automatic, 6-Spd			475	475	620	620
FOCUS—4-Cyl.—Equipment Schedule 6						
W.B. 104.3"; 2.0 Liter.						
S Sedan 4D	P3E2	18090	7325	7650	8900	10950
SE Sedan 4D	P3F2	19090	8050	8400	9700	11900
SE Hatchback 4D	P3K2	19885	8400	8750	10050	12250
Titanium Sedan 4D	P3J2	22995	10350	10750	12150	14800
Titanium Hatchback 4D	P3N2	23490	10500	10950	12350	15000
Manual, 5-Spd			(475)	(475)	(610)	(610)
FOCUS—4-Cyl.—Equipment Schedule 6						
W.B. 104.3"; 2.0 Liter.						
SEL Sedan 4D	P3H2	20995	8925	9300	10550	12850
SEL Hatchback 4D	P3M2	21790	9225	9625	11000	13450
FOCUS—AC Electric—Equipment Schedule 6						
W.B. 104.3".						
Hatchback 4D	P3R4	39995	9100	9400	10750	12700
FUSION—4-Cyl.—Equipment Schedule 6						
W.B. 107.4"; 2.5 Liter.						
S Sedan 4D	P0GA	20645	9000	9300	10950	13250
SE Sedan 4D	P0HA	23625	9650	9975	11550	13800
AWD	C		675	675	850	850
V6, Flex Fuel, 3.0 Liter	G		750	750	935	935
FUSION—4-Cyl. Hybrid—Equipment Schedule 4						
W.B. 107.4"; 2.5 Liter.						
Sedan 4D	P0L3	29395	11600	12000	13350	15500
FUSION—V6—Equipment Schedule 4						
W.B. 107.4"; 3.5 Liter.						
SEL Sedan 4D	P0JG	27480	11050	11400	13200	15900
AWD	C		675	675	850	850
4-Cyl, 2.5 Liter	A		(700)	(700)	(870)	(870)
FUSION—V6—Equipment Schedule 4						
W.B. 107.4"; 3.5 Liter.						
Sport Sedan 4D	P0KC	27945	12200	12650	14450	17250
AWD	D		675	675	845	845
MUSTANG—V6—Equipment Schedule 4						
W.B. 107.1"; 3.7 Liter.						
Premium Coupe 2D	P8AM	27890	13700	14050	16050	19100
Premium Convertible	P8EM	32890	14400	14750	16800	19950
MUSTANG—V8—Equipment Schedule 4						
W.B. 107.1"; 5.0 Liter.						
GT Premium Coupe 2D	P8CF	34505	20200	20900	22200	25400
GT Premium Conv 2D	P8FF	39505	21800	22500	23800	27100
Boss 302 Coupe 2D	P8CU	40995	28000	28800	29800	33000
Brembo Brake Pkg			425	425	500	500
MUSTANG SHELBY GT500—V8 Supercharged—Equipment Schedule 4						
W.B. 107.1"; 5.4 Liter.						
Coupe 2D	P8JS	49495	33500	34500	35500	39200
Convertible 2D	P8KS	54495	36400	37500	38400	42400
TAURUS—V6—Equipment Schedule 4						
W.B. 112.9"; 3.5 Liter.						
SE Sedan 4D	P2DW	26350	12600	12900	14400	16700
SEL Sedan 4D	P2EW	28550	12800	13100	14750	17150
Limited Sedan 4D	P2FW	32950	13300	13600	15350	17750
AWD	H		1575	1575	1905	1905
TAURUS AWD—V6 EcoBoost Twin Turbo—Equipment Schedule 4						
W.B. 112.9"; 3.5 Liter.						
SHO Sedan 4D	P2KT	38950	18150	18550	20200	23000
2013 FORD — (1,2or3)FAor1ZV–(P4AJ)–D–#						
FIESTA—4-Cyl.—Equipment Schedule 6						
W.B. 98.0"; 1.6 Liter.						
S Sedan 4D	P4AJ	13995	6550	6800	8250	10400
S Hatchback 4D	P4TJ	14995	6600	6850	8400	10700
SE Sedan 4D	P4BJ	15995	7225	7525	8975	11300
SE Hatchback 4D	P4EJ	16995	7350	7650	9150	11500
Titanium Sedan 4D	P4CJ	17995	8000	8325	9775	12150
Titanium Hatchback 4D	P4FJ	18995	8500	8825	10250	12700
Automatic, 6-Spd			500	500	655	655
FOCUS—4-Cyl.—Equipment Schedule 6						
W.B. 104.3"; 2.0 Liter.						
S Sedan 4D	P3E2	16995	8150	8500	9925	12150
SE Sedan 4D	P3F2	18995	9100	9475	10900	13250
SE Hatchback 4D	P3K2	19995	9425	9825	11200	13550

Body Type	VIN	List	Trade-In Good	Very Good	Pvt-Party Good	Retail Excellent
Titanium Sedan 4D	P3J2	23995	11250	11700	13150	15800
Titanium Hatchback 4D	P3N2	24995	11550	12000	13450	16100
Manual, 5-Spd			(500)	(500)	(635)	(635)

FOCUS ST—4-Cyl. Turbo EcoBoost—Equipment Schedule 6
W.B. 104.3"; 2.0 Liter.

| Hatchback 4D | P3L9 | 24495 | 15400 | 15850 | 17300 | 19700 |

FOCUS—AC Electric—Equipment Schedule 6
W.B. 104.3"

| Hatchback 4D | P3R4 | 39995 | 10050 | 10350 | 11650 | 13800 |

C-MAX—4-Cyl. Hybrid—Equipment Schedule 4
W.B. 104.3"; 2.0 Liter.

| SE Wagon 4D | P5AU | 25995 | 11050 | 11400 | 12750 | 14800 |
| SEL Wagon 4D | P5BU | 28995 | 12250 | 12650 | 14100 | 16300 |

C-MAX ENERGI—4-Cyl. Hybrid—Equipment Schedule 3
W.B. 104.3"; 2.0 Liter.

| SEL Wagon 4D | P5CU | 33745 | 12850 | 13250 | 14800 | 17050 |

FUSION—4-Cyl.—Equipment Schedule 4
W.B. 112.2"; 2.5 Liter.

S Sedan 4D	P0G7	22495	11000	11350	13050	15400
SE Sedan 4D	P0H7	24495	12200	12600	14200	16550
4-Cyl EcoBoost Turbo 1.6L	R		150	150	170	170
4-Cyl EcoBoost Turbo 2.0L	9		175	175	210	210

FUSION—4-Cyl. Hybrid—Equipment Schedule 4
W.B. 112.2"; 2.0 Liter.

| SE Sedan 4D | P0LU | 27995 | 14100 | 14500 | 16050 | 18450 |

FUSION—4-Cyl. Turbo EcoBoost—Equipment Schedule 4
W.B. 112.2"; 2.0 Liter.

| Titanium Sedan 4D | P0K9 | 30995 | 14850 | 15300 | 17150 | 20000 |
| AWD | D | | 700 | 700 | 850 | 850 |

FUSION ENERGI—4-Cyl. Plug-In Hybrid—Equipment Schedule 4
W.B. 112.2"; 2.0 Liter.

| SE Sedan 4D | P0PU | 39495 | 16850 | 17350 | 18850 | 21500 |
| Titanium Sedan 4D | P0SU | 40995 | 19000 | 19550 | 21000 | 23900 |

MUSTANG—V6—Equipment Schedule 4
W.B. 107.1"; 3.7 Liter.

Coupe 2D	P8AM	22995	14350	14600	16450	19050
Convertible 2D	P8EM	27995	15100	15450	17300	20100
Premium Coupe 2D	P8AM	26995	15350	15650	17500	20300
Premium Conv 2D	P8EM	31995	16000	16350	18250	21200

MUSTANG—V8—Equipment Schedule 4
W.B. 107.1"; 5.0 Liter.

GT Coupe 2D	P8CF	32290	20900	21600	22600	25100
GT Convertible 2D	P8FF	37290	23700	24400	25400	28300
GT Premium Coupe 2D	P8CF	35095	22400	23100	24100	26800
GT Premium Conv 2D	P8FF	40095	24300	25000	26000	28900
Boss 302 Coupe 2D	P8CU	42995	32000	32900	33600	36500
Brembo Brake Pkg			475	475	530	530

MUSTANG SHELBY GT500—V8 Supercharged—Equipment Schedule 4
W.B. 107.1"; 5.4 Liter.

| Coupe 2D | P8JZ | 54995 | 44300 | 45600 | 46200 | 50200 |
| Convertible 2D | P8KZ | 59995 | 47200 | 48500 | 49100 | 53400 |

TAURUS—V6—Equipment Schedule 4
W.B. 112.9"; 3.5 Liter.

SE Sedan 4D	P2D8	27395	13750	14000	15800	18050
SEL Sedan 4D	P2E8	29595	14200	14450	16350	18750
Limited Sedan 4D	P2F8	33795	14850	15150	17100	19650
AWD	H		1625	1625	1950	1950
4-Cyl EcoBoost Turbo 2.0L	9		175	175	210	210

TAURUS AWD—V6 Twin Turbo EcoBoost—Equipment Schedule 4
W.B. 112.9"; 3.5 Liter.

| SHO Sedan 4D | P2KT | 39995 | 22500 | 22900 | 24700 | 27700 |

2014 FORD — (1,2or3)FAor1ZV–(P4AJ)–E–#

FIESTA—4-Cyl.—Equipment Schedule 6
W.B. 98.0"; 1.6 Liter.

S Sedan 4D	P4AJ	14795	7400	7700	9225	11550
S Hatchback 4D	P4TJ	15395	7700	8025	9550	11950
SE Sedan 4D	P4BJ	16245	8100	8425	9925	12350
SE Hatchback 4D	P4EJ	16845	8425	8775	10250	12650
Titanium Sedan 4D	P4CJ	18995	9150	9525	11000	13500
Titanium Hatchback 4D	P4FJ	19595	9450	9825	11250	13750
Auto, 6-Spd SelectShift			525	525	685	685

Body Type	VIN	List	Trade-In Good	Very Good	Pvt-Party Good	Retail Excellent
FIESTA—4-Cyl. Turbo EcoBoost—Equipment Schedule 6						
W.B. 98.0"; 1.6 Liter.						
ST Hatchback 4D	P4GX	22195	**14900**	**15450**	**16500**	**19400**
FOCUS—4-Cyl.—Equipment Schedule 6						
W.B. 104.3"; 2.0 Liter.						
S Sedan 4D	P3E2	17105	**8975**	**9325**	**10750**	**13100**
SE Sedan 4D	P3F2	19310	**9900**	**10300**	**11700**	**14100**
SE Hatchback 4D	P3K2	19910	**10100**	**10500**	**11900**	**14300**
Titanium Sedan 4D	P3J2	24310	**12100**	**12600**	**14000**	**16700**
Titanium Hatchback 4D	P3N2	24910	**12400**	**12900**	**14300**	**17000**
Manual, 5-Spd			**(525)**	**(525)**	**(655)**	**(655)**
FOCUS ST—4-Cyl. EcoBoost Turbo—Equipment Schedule 6						
W.B. 104.3"; 2.0 Liter.						
Hatchback 4D	P3L9	24910	**15950**	**16400**	**17900**	**20400**
FOCUS—AC Electric—Equipment Schedule 6						
W.B. 104.3".						
Hatchback 4D	P3R4	39995	**12300**	**12650**	**14200**	**16300**
C-MAX—4-Cyl. Hybrid—Equipment Schedule 4						
W.B. 104.3"; 2.0 Liter.						
SE Wagon 4D	P5AU	25995	**12900**	**13300**	**14750**	**16850**
SEL Wagon 4D	P5BU	29280	**14500**	**14950**	**16400**	**18700**
C-MAX ENERGI—4-Cyl. Hybrid—Equipment Schedule 3						
W.B. 104.3"; 2.0 Liter.						
SEL Wagon 4D	P5CU	33745	**15200**	**15650**	**17100**	**19400**
FUSION—4-Cyl.—Equipment Schedule 4						
W.B. 112.2"; 2.5 Liter.						
S Sedan 4D	P0G7	22695	**11550**	**11900**	**13600**	**15900**
FUSION—4-Cyl.—Equipment Schedule 4						
W.B. 112.2"; 2.5 Liter.						
SE Sedan 4D	P0H7	24650	**12700**	**13100**	**15000**	**17650**
Adaptive Cruise Control			**500**	**500**	**620**	**620**
4-Cyl EcoBoost Turbo 1.5L	D		**125**	**125**	**155**	**155**
4-Cyl EcoBoost Turbo 1.6L	R		**150**	**150**	**185**	**185**
4-Cyl EcoBoost Turbo 2.0L	9		**175**	**175**	**235**	**235**
FUSION—4-Cyl. Hybrid—Equipment Schedule 4						
W.B. 112.2"; 2.0 Liter.						
S Sedan 4D	P0UU	26995	**13650**	**14050**	**15800**	**18250**
SE Sedan 4D	P0LU	27995	**15100**	**15550**	**17150**	**19700**
Titanium Sedan 4D	P0RU	33295	**16550**	**17050**	**18700**	**21400**
FUSION—4-Cyl. Turbo EcoBoost—Equipment Schedule 4						
W.B. 112.2"; 2.0 Liter.						
Titanium Sedan 4D	P0K9	31295	**15300**	**15800**	**18100**	**21400**
AWD			**750**	**750**	**935**	**935**
FUSION ENERGI—4-Cyl. Plug-In Hybrid—Equipment Schedule 4						
W.B. 112.2"; 2.0 Liter.						
SE Luxury Sedan 4D	P0PU	39495	**19300**	**19900**	**21300**	**23900**
Titanium Sedan 4D	P0SU	41295	**20900**	**21500**	**22900**	**25700**
Adaptive Cruise Control			**500**	**500**	**550**	**550**
MUSTANG—V6—Equipment Schedule 4						
W.B. 107.1"; 3.7 Liter.						
Coupe 2D	P8AM	24190	**16050**	**16400**	**18350**	**21300**
Convertible 2D	P8EM	29190	**16850**	**17200**	**19200**	**22200**
Premium Coupe 2D	P8AM	28190	**17050**	**17400**	**19400**	**22400**
Premium Convertible	P8EM	33190	**17950**	**18350**	**20300**	**23300**
Pony Pkg			**200**	**200**	**235**	**235**
Manual, 6-Spd			**(625)**	**(625)**	**(735)**	**(735)**
MUSTANG—V8—Equipment Schedule 4						
W.B. 107.1"; 5.0 Liter.						
GT Coupe 2D	P8CF	31545	**23400**	**24100**	**25200**	**28100**
GT Convertible 2D	P8FF	37740	**25800**	**26600**	**27800**	**30900**
GT Premium Coupe 2D	P8CF	35545	**25500**	**25800**	**27000**	**30000**
GT Premium Conv 2D	P8FF	41740	**26900**	**27700**	**28900**	**32200**
Brembo Brake Pkg			**525**	**525**	**590**	**590**
MUSTANG SHELBY GT500—V8 Supercharged—Equipment Schedule 4						
W.B. 107.1"; 5.8 Liter.						
Coupe 2D	P8JZ	55445	**47400**	**48700**	**49400**	**53800**
Convertible 2D	P8KZ	60445	**50000**	**51400**	**52400**	**57000**
TAURUS—V6—Equipment Schedule 4						
W.B. 112.9"; 3.5 Liter.						
SE Sedan 4D	P2D8	27495	**14050**	**14300**	**16100**	**18350**
SEL Sedan 4D	P2E8	29695	**16350**	**16650**	**18600**	**21200**
Limited Sedan 4D	P2F8	34995	**16850**	**17100**	**19100**	**21600**
AWD	H		**1675**	**1675**	**1965**	**1965**

Body Type	VIN	List	Trade-In Good	Very Good	Pvt-Party Good	Retail Excellent
4-Cyl EcoBoost Turbo 2.0L	9		175	175	220	220

TAURUS AWD—V6 Twin Turbo EcoBoost—Equipment Schedule 4
W.B. 112.9"; 3.5 Liter.

SHO Sedan 4D	P2KT	40595	23900	24400	26500	29800
Adaptive Cruise Control			500	500	555	555

HONDA

2000 HONDA — (1HG,2HGorJHM)(ZE137)-Y-#

INSIGHT—3-Cyl. Hybrid—Equipment Schedule 3
W.B. 94.5"; 1.0 Liter.

Hatchback 2D	ZE137	20495	1250	1475	1875	3200

CIVIC—4-Cyl.—Equipment Schedule 6
W.B. 103.2"; 1.6 Liter.

CX Hatchback 2D	EJ632	11165	475	525	1175	2175
DX Sedan 4D	EJ652	13300	900	1000	1650	2900
DX Coupe 2D	EJ612	13095	775	875	1500	2600
DX Hatchback 2D	EJ634	12615	675	775	1450	2575
VP Sedan 4D	EJ661	15145	1200	1350	2075	3550
HX Coupe 2D	EJ712	13915	950	1050	1700	2950
LX Sedan 4D	EJ657	15345	1025	1150	2050	3700
EX Sedan 4D	EJ854	17245	1325	1450	2250	3950
EX Coupe 2D	EJ814	15965	1275	1400	2225	3950
Si Coupe 2D	EM115	17960	1950	2300	2775	4650

ACCORD—4-Cyl.—Equipment Schedule 3
W.B. 105.1", 106.9" (Sed); 2.3 Liter.

DX Sedan 4D	CF864	16565	625	700	1400	2525
LX Sedan 4D	CG564	19755	900	1000	1825	3300
LX Coupe 2D	CG324	19755	900	1050	1725	3100
SE Sedan 4D	CG567	20905	1075	1200	2050	3675
EX Sedan 4D	CG565	22265	1375	1500	2425	4275
EX Coupe 2D	CG325	22265	1325	1525	2325	4125
Manual, 5-Spd			(175)	(175)	(220)	(220)
V6, VTEC, 3.0 Liter			100	100	135	135

PRELUDE—4-Cyl.—Equipment Schedule 3
W.B. 101.8"; 2.2 Liter.

Coupe 2D	BB614	23915	1700	1925	2525	4150
Type SH Coupe 2D	BB615	26415	2025	2275	2900	4800
Automatic			125	125	165	165

S2000—4-Cyl.—Equipment Schedule 2
W.B. 94.5"; 2.0 Liter.

Convertible 2D	AP114	32415	4950	5600	5850	8725
Hard Top			425	425	500	500

2001 HONDA — (1HGorJHM)(ZE135)-1-#

INSIGHT—3-Cyl. Hybrid—Equipment Schedule 3
W.B. 94.5"; 1.0 Liter.

Hatchback 2D	ZE135	20620	1325	1550	2050	3575

CIVIC—4-Cyl.—Equipment Schedule 6
W.B. 103.1"; 1.7 Liter.

DX Sedan 4D	ES152	13400	1100	1200	1925	3350
DX Coupe 2D	EM212	13015	975	1100	1675	2825
HX Coupe 2D	EM217	14000	1150	1250	1875	3150
LX Sedan 4D	ES165	15015	1475	1625	2450	4225
LX Coupe 2D	EM225	15250	1425	1575	2425	4200
EX Sedan 4D	ES267	17350	1725	1900	2775	4675
EX Coupe 2D	EM229	16850	1675	1850	2650	4450
GX Sedan 4D	EN264	20670	1650	1925	2350	3925

ACCORD—4-Cyl.—Equipment Schedule 3
W.B. 105.1", 106.9" (Sed); 2.3 Liter.

DX Sedan 4D	CF864	16640	650	725	1450	2625
VP Sedan 4D	CF866	17640	700	775	1600	2900
LX Sedan 4D	CG564	20030	1050	1175	2050	3625
LX Coupe 2D	CG324	20030	1025	1200	1850	3250
EX Sedan 4D	CG565	22640	1625	1775	2750	4775
EX Coupe 2D	CG325	22640	1575	1800	2575	4475
Manual, 5-Spd	1,5		(200)	(200)	(265)	(265)
V6, VTEC, 3.0 Liter			100	100	135	135

PRELUDE—4-Cyl.—Equipment Schedule 3
W.B. 101.8"; 2.2 Liter.

Coupe 2D	BB614	24040	2125	2375	2950	4750

2001 HONDA

Body Type	VIN	List	Trade-In Good	Very Good	Pvt-Party Good	Retail Excellent
Type SH Coupe 2D	BB615	26540	2475	2775	3400	5500
Automatic			125	125	165	165
S2000—4-Cyl.—Equipment Schedule 2						
W.B. 94.5"; 2.0 Liter.						
Convertible 2D	AP114	32740	5475	6200	6425	9550
Hard Top			450	450	535	535

2002 HONDA — (1HG,SHHorJHM)(ZE135)-2-#

INSIGHT—3-Cyl. Hybrid—Equipment Schedule 3
W.B. 94.5"; 1.0 Liter.

Body Type	VIN	List	Good	Very Good	Good	Excellent
Hatchback 2D	ZE135	21720	1375	1600	2150	3725
CIVIC—4-Cyl.—Equipment Schedule 6						
W.B. 101.2", 103.1" (Sed & Cpe); 1.7 Liter, 2.0 Liter.						
DX Sedan 4D	ES151	13450	1250	1400	2175	3725
DX Coupe 2D	EM212	13250	1150	1275	2250	4025
HX Coupe 2D	EM217	14050	1350	1475	2175	3650
LX Sedan 4D	ES166	15550	1625	1800	2675	4500
LX Coupe 2D	EM225	15350	1575	1750	2650	4500
EX Sedan 4D	ES267	17450	2025	2250	3100	5150
EX Coupe 2D	EM229	16950	1975	2175	3025	5025
Si Hatchback 2D	EP335	19440	2500	2900	3300	5325
ACCORD—4-Cyl.—Equipment Schedule 3						
W.B. 105.1", 106.9" (Sed). 2.3 Liter.						
DX Sedan 4D	CF864	16740	750	825	1525	2700
VP Sedan 4D	CF866	17740	925	1025	1800	3175
LX Sedan 4D	CG564	20130	1375	1525	2350	4050
LX Coupe 2D	CG324	20130	1325	1525	2175	3700
SE Sedan 4D	CG567	21290	1625	1800	2750	4700
SE Coupe 2D	CG320	21290	1650	1875	2550	4300
EX Sedan 4D	CG566	22740	1975	2175	3175	5325
EX Coupe 2D	CG325	22740	1875	2150	2925	4925
Manual, 5-Spd	1,5		(200)	(200)	(265)	(265)
V6, VTEC, 3.0 Liter			150	150	200	200
S2000—4-Cyl.—Equipment Schedule 2						
W.B. 94.5"; 2.0 Liter.						
Convertible 2D	AP114	32840	6450	7250	7300	10600
Hard Top			475	475	565	565

2003 HONDA — (1HG,SHHorJHM)(ZE135)-3-#

INSIGHT—3-Cyl. Hybrid—Equipment Schedule 3
W.B. 94.5"; 1.0 Liter.

Body Type	VIN	List	Good	Very Good	Good	Excellent
Hatchback 2D	ZE135	21740	1525	1775	2575	4475
CIVIC—4-Cyl.—Equipment Schedule 6						
W.B. 101.2", 103.1" (Sed & Cpe); 1.7 Liter, 2.0 Liter.						
DX Sedan 4D	ES151	13470	1500	1650	2425	4050
DX Coupe 2D	EM212	13270	1400	1525	2500	4375
HX Coupe 2D	EM217	14170	1550	1700	2500	4100
LX Sedan 4D	ES166	15670	2050	2250	3125	5125
LX Coupe 2D	EM225	15470	1950	2125	3075	5075
EX Sedan 4D	ES267	17520	2375	2600	3425	5575
EX Coupe 2D	EM229	17270	2425	2650	3475	5650
Si Hatchback 2D	EP335	19460	3250	3750	3975	6175
CIVIC—4-Cyl. Hybrid—Equipment Schedule 6						
W.B. 103.2"; 1.3 Liter.						
Sedan 4D	ES966	19990	1475	1700	2475	4350
ACCORD—4-Cyl.—Equipment Schedule 3						
W.B. 105.1", 107.9" (Sed); 2.4 Liter.						
DX Sedan 4D	CM551	17060	2350	2550	3325	5325
LX Sedan 4D	CM564	20460	2675	2925	3650	5750
LX Coupe 2D	CM712	20560	2200	2500	3200	5225
EX Sedan 4D	CM556	22860	3425	3750	4700	7400
EX Coupe 2D	CM716	22960	2775	3150	3825	6100
Manual, 5-Spd	1,5		(225)	(225)	(310)	(310)
V6, VTEC, 3.0 Liter			225	225	300	300
S2000—4-Cyl.—Equipment Schedule 2						
W.B. 94.5"; 2.0 Liter.						
Convertible 2D	AP114	33060	6975	7850	7950	11500
Hard Top			525	525	600	600

2004 HONDA — (1HG,SHHorJHM)(ZE135)-4-#

INSIGHT—3-Cyl. Hybrid—Equipment Schedule 3
W.B. 94.5"; 1.0 Liter.

Body Type	VIN	List	Trade-In Good	Very Good	Pvt-Party Good	Retail Excellent
Hatchback 2D	ZE135	21870	1850	2100	2900	4900
CIVIC—4-Cyl.—Equipment Schedule 6						
W.B. 101.2", 103.1" (Sed & Cpe); 1.7 Liter, 2.0 Liter.						
DX Sedan 4D	ES151	13500	1575	1725	2600	4300
Value Sedan 4D	ES163	14900	2150	2350	3225	5200
Value Coupe 2D	EM221	13900	1925	2100	3025	4950
HX Coupe 2D	EM217	14200	1875	2050	2900	4700
LX Sedan 4D	ES166	15850	2425	2625	3475	5550
LX Coupe 2D	EM225	15650	2300	2525	3400	5500
EX Sedan 4D	ES267	17750	2825	3100	3800	5975
EX Coupe 2D	EM229	17350	2725	2975	3700	5800
Si Hatchback 2D	EP335	19560	4100	4700	4850	7250
GX Sedan 4D	EN264	21250	2875	3250	3775	6050
CIVIC—4-Cyl. Hybrid—Equipment Schedule 6						
W.B. 103.1"; 1.3 Liter.						
Sedan 4D	ES966	20140	1850	2100	2900	4900
ACCORD—4-Cyl.—Equipment Schedule 3						
W.B. 105.1", 107.9" (Sed); 2.4 Liter.						
DX Sedan 4D	CM551	17190	2575	2800	3475	5375
LX Sedan 4D	CM553	20590	3025	3275	3975	6100
LX Coupe 2D	CM712	20690	2850	3225	3775	5900
EX Sedan 4D	CM556	22990	3850	4200	5000	7625
EX Coupe 2D	CM716	23090	3475	3925	4425	6825
Manual, 5-Spd	1,5		(275)	(275)	(375)	(375)
Manual, 5-Spd	1,5		(275)	(275)	(375)	(375)
V6, VTEC, 3.0 Liter			275	275	375	375
S2000—4-Cyl.—Equipment Schedule 2						
W.B. 94.5"; 2.2 Liter.						
Convertible 2D	AP214	33290	7725	8625	8650	12350
Hard Top			550	550	640	640

Body Type	VIN	List	Trade-In Good	Very Good	Pvt-Party Good	Retail Excellent
INSIGHT—3-Cyl. Hybrid—Equipment Schedule 3						
W.B. 94.5"; 1.0 Liter.						
Hatchback 2D	ZE137	22045	1800	2050	3050	5125
CIVIC—4-Cyl.—Equipment Schedule 6						
W.B. 101.2", 103.1" (Sed & Cpe); 1.7 Liter, 2.0 Liter.						
DX Sedan 4D	ES151	13675	2175	2375	3300	5150
Value Sedan 4D	ES163	15075	2900	3150	4000	6050
Value Coupe 2D	EM221	14075	2525	2775	3675	5675
HX Coupe 2D	EM217	14375	2475	2700	3500	5325
LX Sedan 4D	ES166	16025	3075	3375	4275	6425
LX Coupe 2D	EM225	15825	3100	3375	4175	6300
LX Special Ed Sed 4D	ES155	16775	3100	3375	4175	6300
LX Special Ed Cpe 2D	EM215	16575	3000	3275	4100	6200
EX Sedan 4D	ES267	17925	3550	3850	4675	6950
EX Coupe 2D	EM220	17525	3650	3975	4725	6950
EX Special Ed Sed 4D	ES257	18375	3800	4125	4875	7125
EX Special Ed Cpe 2D	EM219	17975	3700	4025	4800	7000
Si Hatchback 2D	EP335	19735	4725	5350	5575	8125
GX Sedan 4D	EN264	20910	2975	3350	4050	6350
CIVIC—4-Cyl. Hybrid—Equipment Schedule 6						
W.B. 103.1"; 1.3 Liter.						
Sedan 4D	ES966	20315	1950	2200	3150	5200
ACCORD—4-Cyl.—Equipment Schedule 3						
W.B. 105.1", 107.9" (Sed); 2.4 Liter.						
DX Sedan 4D	CM561	17510	3100	3375	4300	6550
LX Sedan 4D	CM564	20990	3750	4100	4850	7100
LX Coupe 2D	CM723	21090	3325	3725	4375	6575
LX Special Ed Cpe 2D	CM723	25065	3725	4175	4850	7225
EX Sedan 4D	CM567	23415	4475	4875	5825	8625
EX Coupe 2D	CM726	23650	3825	4275	4975	7425
Manual, 5-Spd			(325)	(325)	(445)	(445)
V6, VTEC, 3.0 Liter			325	325	445	445
ACCORD—V6 Hybrid—Equipment Schedule 3						
W.B. 107.9"; 3.0 Liter.						
Sedan 4D	CN364	30655	5300	5725	6650	9800
S2000—4-Cyl.—Equipment Schedule 2						
W.B. 94.5"; 2.2 Liter.						
Convertible 2D	AP214	33465	10450	11600	11200	15350
Hard Top			600	600	670	670

2006 HONDA

Body Type	VIN	List	Trade-In Good	Very Good	Pvt-Party Good	Retail Excellent

2006 HONDA — (1HG,SHHorJHM)(ZE137)-6-#

INSIGHT—3-Cyl. Hybrid—Equipment Schedule 3
W.B. 94.5"; 1.0 Liter.

Body Type	VIN	List	Good	Very Good	Good	Excellent
Hatchback 2D	ZE137	22080	3225	3625	4375	6650

CIVIC—4-Cyl.—Equipment Schedule 6
W.B. 104.3", 106.3" (Sed); 1.8 Liter, 2.0 Liter.

Body Type	VIN	List	Good	Very Good	Good	Excellent
DX Sedan 4D	FA162	15110	3325	3600	4325	6300
LX Sedan 4D	FA165	17060	4300	4675	5400	7700
LX Coupe 2D	FG126	16860	4050	4400	5225	7550
EX Sedan 4D	FA168	18810	4825	5225	5875	8400
EX Coupe 2D	FG128	18810	4725	5125	5725	8200
Manual, 5-Spd			(275)	(275)	(355)	(355)

CIVIC—4-Cyl.—Equipment Schedule 6
W.B. 104.3", 106.3" (Sed); 1.8 Liter, 2.0 Liter.

Body Type	VIN	List	Good	Very Good	Good	Excellent
DX Coupe 2D	FG112	14910	2925	3150	4025	6025
Si Coupe 2D	FG215	20540	6325	7100	7125	9900
GX Sedan 4D	FA465	24990	4525	5025	5500	8025

CIVIC—4-Cyl. Hybrid—Equipment Schedule 6
W.B. 106.3"; 1.3 Liter.

Body Type	VIN	List	Good	Very Good	Good	Excellent
Sedan 4D	FA362	22400	3400	3825	4475	6700

ACCORD—4-Cyl.—Equipment Schedule 3
W.B. 105.1", 107.9" (Sed); 2.4 Liter.

Body Type	VIN	List	Good	Very Good	Good	Excellent
VP Sedan 4D	CM561	19575	3600	3900	4700	6800
LX Sedan 4D	CM564	21375	4650	5025	5675	8000
LX Coupe 2D	CM723	21725	3725	4125	4825	7025
SE Sedan 4D	CM563	22075	4725	5100	5850	8325
EX Sedan 4D	CM567	23800	5475	5925	6825	9725
EX Coupe 2D	CM726	23945	4425	4925	5575	8025
Manual, 5-Spd			(375)	(375)	(510)	(510)
Manual, 6-Spd			0	0	0	0
V6, VTEC, 3.0 Liter			375	375	510	510

ACCORD—V6 Hybrid—Equipment Schedule 3
W.B. 107.9"; 3.0 Liter.

Body Type	VIN	List	Good	Very Good	Good	Excellent
Sedan 4D	CN364	31540	6475	7000	7875	11150

S2000—4-Cyl.—Equipment Schedule 2
W.B. 94.5"; 2.2 Liter.

Body Type	VIN	List	Good	Very Good	Good	Excellent
Convertible 2D	AP214	34600	11450	12700	12300	16550
Hard Top			625	625	705	705

2007 HONDA — (1HG,SHHorJHM)(GD384)-7-#

FIT—4-Cyl. VTEC—Equipment Schedule 6
W.B. 96.5"; 1.5 Liter.

Body Type	VIN	List	Good	Very Good	Good	Excellent
Hatchback 4D	GD384	14445	3500	4025	4575	6875
Sport Hatchback 4D	GD386	15765	4125	4750	5225	7800
Manual, 5-Spd			(300)	(300)	(385)	(385)

CIVIC—4-Cyl. VTEC—Equipment Schedule 6
W.B. 104.3", 106.3" (Sed); 1.8 Liter, 2.0 Liter.

Body Type	VIN	List	Good	Very Good	Good	Excellent
DX Sedan 4D	FA162	15605	3800	4100	4925	7000
LX Sedan 4D	FA165	17555	4950	5325	6050	8425
LX Coupe 2D	FG126	17355	4900	5275	6000	8375
EX Sedan 4D	FA168	19305	5375	5825	6575	9225
EX Coupe 2D	FG128	19305	5300	5725	6450	9000
Manual, 5-Spd			(300)	(300)	(385)	(385)

CIVIC—4-Cyl. VTEC—Equipment Schedule 6
W.B. 104.3"; 1.8 Liter.

Body Type	VIN	List	Good	Very Good	Good	Excellent
DX Coupe 2D	FG112	15405	3225	3475	4425	6425
Automatic	2,6		300	300	385	385

CIVIC—4-Cyl. VTEC—Equipment Schedule 6
W.B. 104.3", 106.3" (Sed); 1.8 Liter, 2.0 Liter.

Body Type	VIN	List	Good	Very Good	Good	Excellent
Si Sedan 4D	FA555	21885	6975	7725	7900	10700
Si Coupe 2D	FG215	21685	6875	7625	7775	10500

CIVIC—4-Cyl. Hybrid—Equipment Schedule 6
W.B. 106.3"; 1.3 Liter.

Body Type	VIN	List	Good	Very Good	Good	Excellent
Sedan 4D	FA362	23195	3825	4225	4925	7150

CIVIC—4-Cyl. NGV—Equipment Schedule 6
W.B. 106.3"; 1.8 Liter.

Body Type	VIN	List	Good	Very Good	Good	Excellent
GX Sedan 4D	FA465	25185	5025	5575	6225	8800

ACCORD—4-Cyl. VTEC—Equipment Schedule 3
W.B. 105.1", 107.9" (Sed); 2.4 Liter.

Body Type	VIN	List	Good	Very Good	Good	Excellent
VP Sedan 4D	CM561	20020	4475	4825	5525	7700
LX Sedan 4D	CM564	21520	5175	5575	6200	8525

2007 HONDA

Body Type	VIN	List	Trade-In Good	Very Good	Pvt-Party Good	Retail Excellent
LX Coupe 2D	CM723	21870	4625	5075	5675	7925
SE Sedan 4D	CM563	22220	5375	5775	6675	9250
EX Sedan 4D	CM567	23945	6225	6700	7550	10450
EX Coupe 2D	CM826	24085	5600	6150	6800	9375
EX-L Sedan 4D	CM665	25685	6900	7425	8150	11150
EX-L Coupe 2D	CM726	25785	6125	6725	7400	10200
Manual, 5-Spd			(425)	(425)	(555)	(555)
V6, VTEC, 3.0 Liter			425	425	575	575

ACCORD—V6 Hybrid—Equipment Schedule 3
W.B. 107.9"; 3.0 Liter.

| Sedan 4D | CN364 | 33585 | 7400 | 7950 | 8825 | 12150 |

S2000—4-Cyl. VTEC—Equipment Schedule 2
W.B. 94.5"; 2.2 Liter.

| Convertible 2D | AP214 | 34845 | 12650 | 13950 | 13500 | 17850 |
| Hard Top | | | 650 | 650 | 735 | 735 |

2008 HONDA — (1HG,SHHorJHM)(GD384)-8-#

FIT—4-Cyl. VTEC—Equipment Schedule 6
W.B. 96.5"; 1.5 Liter.

Hatchback 4D	GD384	15385	4350	4850	5425	7675
Sport Hatchback 4D	GD386	16705	5000	5575	6125	8600
Manual, 5-Spd w/Overdrive			(350)	(350)	(460)	(460)

CIVIC—4-Cyl. VTEC—Equipment Schedule 6
W.B. 104.3", 106.3" (Sed); 1.8 Liter, 2.0 Liter.

DX Sedan 4D	FA162	15645	4225	4500	5400	7425
LX Sedan 4D	FA165	17595	5450	5825	6775	9075
LX Coupe 2D	FG126	17395	5225	5575	6600	8950
EX Sedan 4D	FA168	19345	6350	6825	7400	9950
EX Coupe 2D	FG128	19345	6475	6975	7500	10050
EX-L Sedan 4D	FA169	20545	6550	7000	7825	10350
EX-L Coupe 2D	FG129	20545	6550	7000	7800	10300
Manual, 5-Spd w/Overdrive			(350)	(350)	(460)	(460)

CIVIC—4-Cyl. VTEC—Equipment Schedule 6
W.B. 104.3"; 1.8 Liter.

| DX Coupe 2D | FG112 | 15445 | 3650 | 3925 | 4950 | 6950 |
| Automatic, 5-Spd | 2,6 | | 300 | 300 | 400 | 400 |

CIVIC—4-Cyl. VTEC—Equipment Schedule 6
W.B. 104.3", 106.3" (Sed); 2.0 Liter.

Si Sedan 4D	FA555	21925	8425	9125	9400	12150
Si Coupe 2D	FG215	21725	8225	8900	9200	11900
Si Mugen Sedan 4D	FA555	30135	11600	12500	12550	16050

CIVIC—4-Cyl. Hybrid—Equipment Schedule 6
W.B. 106.3"; 1.3 Liter.

| Sedan 4D | FA362 | 23235 | 4625 | 5000 | 5850 | 8075 |

CIVIC—4-Cyl. NGV—Equipment Schedule 6
W.B. 106.3" (Sed); 1.8 Liter.

| GX Sedan 4D | FA465 | 25225 | 6300 | 6825 | 7575 | 10150 |

ACCORD—4-Cyl. VTEC—Equipment Schedule 3
W.B. 107.9", 110.2" (Sed); 2.4 Liter.

LX Sedan 4D	CP253	21795	6675	7100	7800	10150
LX-P Sedan 4D	CP254	22795	7025	7500	8175	10700
LX-S Coupe 2D	CS113	23295	6525	7025	7700	10100
EX Sedan 4D	CP257	24495	7525	8025	8825	11600
EX Coupe 2D	CS117	24594	7325	7900	8575	11150
EX-L Sedan 4D	CP258	26495	8025	8550	9375	12300
EX-L Coupe 2D	CS118	26595	8150	8750	9425	12300
Manual, 5-Spd w/Overdrive			(450)	(450)	(570)	(570)
V6, i-VTEC, 3.5 Liter			475	475	635	635

S2000—4-Cyl. VTEC—Equipment Schedule 3
W.B. 94.5"; 2.2 Liter.

Convertible 2D	AP214	34935	14350	15700	15250	19500
CR Convertible 2D	AP212	37935	16400	17900	17050	21500
Hard Top			650	650	740	740

2009 HONDA — (1HG,SHHorJHM)(GE882)-9-#

FIT—4-Cyl. VTEC—Equipment Schedule 6
W.B. 98.4"; 1.5 Liter.

Hatchback 4D	GE882	16020	5475	5975	6750	9025
Sport Hatchback 4D	GE884	17580	6175	6725	7500	10000
Sport VSA H'Back 4D	GE876	18580	6800	7575	7725	10350
Manual, 5-Spd w/Overdrive			(375)	(375)	(490)	(490)

2009 HONDA

Body Type	VIN	List	Trade-In Good	Very Good	Pvt-Party Good	Retail Excellent
CIVIC—4-Cyl. VTEC—Equipment Schedule 6						
W.B. 104.3", 106.3" (Sed); 1.8 Liter, 2.0 Liter.						
DX Sedan 4D	FA162	16175	5000	5300	6350	8350
VP Sedan 4D	FA163	16925	5800	6150	7325	9700
LX Sedan 4D	FA165	18125	6550	6925	7925	10250
LX Coupe 2D	FG126	17925	6400	6775	7775	10100
LX-S Sedan 4D	FA166	18765	6675	7050	8100	10550
EX Sedan 4D	FA168	19975	7225	7700	8525	11200
EX Coupe 2D	FG128	19975	7250	7725	8550	11200
EX-L Sedan 4D	FA169	21525	7575	8000	8975	11500
EX-L Coupe 2D	FA129	21525	7575	8000	8925	11400
Manual, 5-Spd w/Overdrive			(375)	(375)	(490)	(490)
CIVIC—4-Cyl. VTEC—Equipment Schedule 6						
W.B. 104.3"; 1.8 Liter.						
DX Coupe 2D	FG112	15875	4675	4950	5950	7975
Automatic	2,6		325	325	445	445
CIVIC—4-Cyl. VTEC—Equipment Schedule 6						
W.B. 104.3", 106.3" (Sed); 2.0 Liter.						
Si Sedan 4D	FA555	22775	9575	10150	10750	13350
Si Coupe 2D	FG215	22575	9375	9950	10550	13150
CIVIC—4-Cyl. Hybrid—Equipment Schedule 6						
W.B. 106.3"; 1.3 Liter.						
Sedan 4D	FA362	24320	5725	6100	7150	9350
CIVIC—4-Cyl. NGV—Equipment Schedule 6						
W.B. 106.3"; 1.8 Liter.						
GX Sedan 4D	FA465	25860	6925	7350	8375	10750
ACCORD—4-Cyl. VTEC—Equipment Schedule 3						
W.B. 107.9", 110.2" (Sed); 2.4 Liter.						
LX Sedan 4D	CP253	22225	7500	7950	8800	11200
LX-P Sedan 4D	CP254	23415	7850	8300	9125	11600
LX-S Coupe 2D	CS113	23725	7350	7800	8750	11100
EX Sedan 4D	CP257	24925	8525	9025	9900	12600
EX Coupe 2D	CS117	24925	8300	8775	9650	12150
EX-L Sedan 4D	CP258	27115	8975	9475	10450	13300
EX-L Coupe 2D	CS118	27215	9125	9650	10550	13300
Manual, 5-Spd w/Overdrive			(475)	(475)	(620)	(620)
V6, i-VTEC, 3.5 Liter.			550	550	705	705
S2000—4-Cyl. VTEC—Equipment Schedule 2						
W.B. 94.5"; 2.2 Liter.						
Convertible 2D	AP214	35665	16450	17850	17350	21500
CR Convertible 2D	AP212	38665	18700	20300	19500	23900
Hard Top			675	675	760	760

2010 HONDA — (1HG,SHHorJHM)(GE8H2)-A-#

Body Type	VIN	List	Trade-In Good	Very Good	Pvt-Party Good	Retail Excellent
FIT—4-Cyl. VTEC—Equipment Schedule 6						
W.B. 98.4"; 1.5 Liter.						
Hatchback 4D	GE8H2	16410	7125	7600	8475	10750
Sport Hatchback 4D	GE8H4	17970	7775	8275	9100	11500
Sport VSA Hatchback	GE8H6	19820	8400	8950	9600	11950
Manual, 5-Spd w/Overdrive			(450)	(450)	(595)	(595)
INSIGHT—4-Cyl. VTEC Hybrid—Equipment Schedule 3						
W.B. 100.4"; 1.3 Liter.						
LX Hatchback 4D	ZE2H5	20510	6225	6500	7750	9800
EX Hatchback 4D	ZE2H7	22010	6850	7175	8550	10850
CIVIC—4-Cyl. VTEC—Equipment Schedule 6						
W.B. 104.3", 106.3" (Sed); 1.8 Liter, 2.0 Liter.						
DX Sedan 4D	FA1F2	16365	5825	6125	7275	9300
VP Sedan 4D	FA1F3	17115	6625	6975	8225	10550
LX Sedan 4D	FA1F5	18315	7450	7825	9025	11450
LX Coupe 2D	FG1B6	18115	7250	7625	8725	10950
LX-S Sedan 4D	FA1F6	18915	7550	7925	9175	11650
EX Sedan 4D	FA1F8	20165	8375	9000	9825	12400
EX Coupe 2D	FG1B8	20165	8375	8850	9675	12300
EX-L Sedan 4D	FA1F9	21715	8725	9175	10250	12900
EX-L Coupe 2D	FG1B9	21715	8625	9050	10150	12750
Manual, 5-Spd w/Overdrive			(450)	(450)	(615)	(615)
CIVIC—4-Cyl. VTEC—Equipment Schedule 6						
W.B. 104.3"; 1.8 Liter.						
DX Coupe 2D	FG1A2	16165	5250	5525	6775	8800
Automatic, 5-Spd	2,6		375	375	510	510
CIVIC—4-Cyl. VTEC—Equipment Schedule 6						
W.B. 104.3"; 1.8 Liter.						
Si Sedan 4D	FA5E5	22965	10800	11300	12100	14600

Body Type	VIN	List	Trade-In Good	Trade-In Very Good	Pvt-Party Good	Retail Excellent
Si Coupe 2D	FG2A5	22765	10600	11100	11950	14450
CIVIC—4-Cyl. Hybrid—Equipment Schedule 6						
W.B. 106.3"; 1.3 Liter.						
Sedan 4D	FA3F2	24510	6675	6975	8225	10350
CIVIC—4-Cyl. NGV—Equipment Schedule 6						
W.B. 106.3"; 1.8 Liter.						
GX Sedan 4D	FA4F5	26050	7925	8300	9525	11850
ACCORD—4-Cyl. VTEC—Equipment Schedule 3						
W.B. 107.9", 110.2" (Sed); 2.4 Liter.						
LX Sedan 4D	CP2E3	22565	8575	9025	9925	12250
LX-P Sedan 4D	CP2E4	23605	8975	9425	10300	12700
LX-S Coupe 2D	CS1A3	24065	8675	9075	10150	12450
EX Sedan 4D	CP2E7	25340	9750	10250	11200	13850
EX Coupe 2D	CS1A7	25390	9500	9925	11000	13400
EX-L Sedan 4D	CP2E8	27580	10350	10850	11850	14700
EX-L Coupe 2D	CS1A8	27630	10550	11050	12150	14800
Manual, 5-Spd w/Overdrive			(500)	(500)	(625)	(625)
V6, i-VTEC, 3.5 Liter			625	625	785	785

Body Type	VIN	List	Trade-In Good	Trade-In Very Good	Pvt-Party Good	Retail Excellent
CR-Z—4-Cyl. VTEC Hybrid—Equipment Schedule 6						
W.B. 95.9"; 1.5 Liter.						
Coupe 2D	ZF1C4	20115	7775	8075	9325	11250
EX Coupe 2D	ZF1C6	21675	8175	8500	9725	11700
FIT—4-Cyl. VTEC—Equipment Schedule 6						
W.B. 98.4"; 1.5 Liter.						
Hatchback 4D	GE8H3	16650	8425	8825	9825	12050
Sport Hatchback 4D	GE8H5	18460	8950	9375	10400	12750
Manual, 5-Spd w/Overdrive			(500)	(500)	(615)	(615)
INSIGHT—4-Cyl. VTEC Hybrid—Equipment Schedule 3						
W.B. 100.4"; 1.3 Liter.						
Hatchback 4D	ZE2H3	18950	7075	7325	8675	10600
LX Hatchback 4D	ZE2H5	20650	7625	7900	9350	11450
EX Hatchback 4D	ZE2H7	22240	8300	8575	9975	12050
CIVIC—4-Cyl. VTEC—Equipment Schedule 6						
W.B. 104.3", 106.3" (Sed); 1.8 Liter.						
DX Sedan 4D	FA1F2	16555	6575	6875	8050	10050
VP Sedan 4D	FA1F3	17305	7550	7900	9100	11250
LX Sedan 4D	FA1F5	18505	8325	8725	9900	12200
LX Coupe 2D	FG1B6	18305	8025	8425	9500	11650
LX-S Sedan 4D	FA1F6	19105	8525	8925	10100	12400
EX Sedan 4D	FA1F8	20355	9500	9975	11100	13850
EX Coupe 2D	FG1B8	20355	9375	9850	10800	13300
Manual, 5-Spd w/Overdrive			(500)	(500)	(650)	(650)
CIVIC—4-Cyl. VTEC—Equipment Schedule 6						
W.B. 104.3"; 1.8 Liter.						
DX Coupe 2D	FG1A2	16355	5900	6175	7475	9475
Automatic, 5-Spd	B		425	425	565	565
CIVIC—4-Cyl. VTEC—Equipment Schedule 6						
W.B. 104.3", 106.3" (Sed); 1.8 Liter, 2.0 Liter.						
EX-L Sedan 4D	FA1F9	22705	9725	10200	11300	13750
EX-L Coupe 2D	FG1B9	22705	9625	10050	11150	13550
Si Sedan 4D	FA5E5	23155	12300	12700	13800	16250
Si Coupe 2D	FG2A5	22955	12100	12500	13650	16100
CIVIC—4-Cyl. Hybrid—Equipment Schedule 6						
W.B. 106.3"; 1.3 Liter.						
Sedan 4D	FA3F2	24700	8575	8850	10300	12400
CIVIC—4-Cyl. NGV—Equipment Schedule 6						
W.B. 106.3"; 1.8 Liter.						
GX Sedan 4D	FA4F5	26240	9925	10250	11600	13800
ACCORD—4-Cyl. VTEC—Equipment Schedule 3						
W.B. 107.9", 110.2" (Sed); 2.4 Liter.						
LX Sedan 4D	CP2F3	22730	9925	10400	11300	13650
LX-P Sedan 4D	CP2F4	23730	10350	10850	11800	14150
LX-S Coupe 2D	CS1B3	24330	9950	10300	11550	13800
SE Sedan 4D	CP2F6	24480	10750	11250	12150	14500
EX Sedan 4D	CP2F7	25655	11250	11750	12750	15350
EX Coupe 2D	CS1B7	26005	10650	11050	12250	14550
EX-L Sedan 4D	CP2F8	28105	11650	12150	13250	16050
EX-L Coupe 2D	CS1B8	27855	11500	11850	13300	15950
Manual, 5-Spd w/Overdrive			(550)	(550)	(660)	(660)
V6, VTEC, 3.5 Liter			700	700	850	850

2012 HONDA

Body Type	VIN	List	Trade-In Good	Very Good	Pvt-Party Good	Retail Excellent

2012 HONDA — (1,2,5orJ)(9,HorK)(B,G,MorX)ZF1C4–C–#

CR-Z—4-Cyl. i-VTEC Hybrid—Equipment Schedule 6
W.B. 95.9"; 1.5 Liter.

Coupe 2D	ZF1C4	20315	9400	9725	11050	12950
EX Coupe 2D	ZF1C6	21875	10050	10400	11750	13800

FIT—4-Cyl. VTEC—Equipment Schedule 6
W.B. 98.4"; 1.5 Liter.

Hatchback 4D	GE8H3	16745	9350	9675	10850	13000
Sport Hatchback 4D	GE8H5	18530	10150	10500	11700	14050
Manual, 5-Spd	G		(475)	(475)	(575)	(575)

INSIGHT—4-Cyl. VTEC Hybrid—Equipment Schedule 3
W.B. 100.4"; 1.3 Liter.

Hatchback 4D	ZE2H3	19120	8600	8800	10300	12150
LX Hatchback 4D	ZE2H5	20895	9175	9400	10950	12950
EX Hatchback 4D	ZE2H7	22585	9975	10200	11700	13700

CIVIC—4-Cyl. VTEC—Equipment Schedule 6
W.B. 105.1"; 1.8 Liter.

LX Sedan 4D	FB2F5	18605	9375	9775	11050	13400
Manual, 5-Spd w/Overdrive	E		(550)	(550)	(690)	(690)

CIVIC—4-Cyl. VTEC—Equipment Schedule 6
W.B. 103.2", 105.1" (Sed); 1.8 Liter.

DX Sedan 4D	FB2E2	16555	7600	7925	9150	11150
DX Coupe 2D	FG3A2	18355	7400	7725	9000	11050
LX Coupe 2D	FG3A5	18405	8700	9075	10300	12450
EX Coupe 2D	FG3B8	21255	10000	10450	11550	14050
Automatic, 5-Spd			475	475	595	595

CIVIC—4-Cyl. VTEC—Equipment Schedule 6
W.B. 103.2", 105.1" (Sed); 1.8 Liter, 2.4 Liter.

HF Sedan 4D	FB2F6	20205	9725	10150	11350	13700
EX Sedan 4D	FB2F8	21255	10350	10850	11850	14350
EX-L Sedan 4D	FB2F9	22705	11100	11550	12800	15300
EX-L Coupe 2D	FG3B9	22705	10950	11400	12600	15050
Si Coupe 2D	FG4A5	22955	13250	13550	15000	17350
Si Sedan 4D	FB6E5	23155	13650	13950	15350	17750

CIVIC—4-Cyl. Hybrid—Equipment Schedule 6
W.B. 105.1"; 1.3 Liter.

Sedan 4D	FB4F2	24800	10300	10550	12100	14200

CIVIC—4-Cyl. NGV—Equipment Schedule 6
W.B. 106.3"; 1.8 Liter.

Sedan 4D	FB5F5	26925	11050	11300	12900	15050

ACCORD—4-Cyl. VTEC—Equipment Schedule 3
W.B. 107.9", 110.2" (Sed); 2.4 Liter.

LX Sedan 4D	CP2F3	23050	10750	11200	12200	14500
LX-P Sedan 4D	CP2F4	24050	11050	11500	12500	14850
LX-S Coupe 2D	CS1B3	24650	11300	11600	12950	15150
SE Sedan 4D	CP2F6	24825	11350	11800	12950	15350
EX Sedan 4D	CP2F7	25975	12000	12550	13650	16200
EX Coupe 2D	CS1B7	26325	12200	12500	13900	16200
EX-L Sedan 4D	CP2F8	28425	12650	13150	14350	17050
EX-L Coupe 2D	CS1B8	28175	12850	13200	14800	17350
Manual, 5-Spd			(575)	(575)	(655)	(655)
V6, VTEC, 3.5 Liter	2		775	775	925	925

2013 HONDA — (1,2,5orJ)(9,HorK)(B,G,MorX)ZF1C4–D–#

CR-Z—4-Cyl. i-VTEC Hybrid—Equipment Schedule 6
W.B. 95.9"; 1.5 Liter.

Coupe 2D	ZF1C4	20765	10450	10800	12150	14100
EX Coupe 2D	ZF1C6	22445	11200	11550	13100	15250

FIT—4-Cyl. VTEC—Equipment Schedule 6
W.B. 98.4"; 1.5 Liter.

Hatchback 4D	GE8G3	16115	10350	10600	11850	13950
Sport Hatchback 4D	GE8G5	17850	11200	11500	12800	15000
Automatic, 5-Spd	G		500	500	585	585

FIT EV—AC Electric—Equipment Schedule 6
W.B. 98.4".

Hatchback 4D	ZA2H4	37415				

INSIGHT—4-Cyl. Hybrid—Equipment Schedule 3
W.B. 100.4"; 1.3 Liter.

Hatchback 4D	ZE2H3	19290	9475	9650	11400	13300
LX Hatchback 4D	ZE2H5	21065	10350	10550	12300	14400
EX Hatchback 4D	ZE2H7	22755	11250	11450	13300	15450

2013 HONDA

Body Type	VIN	List	Trade-In Good	Trade-In Very Good	Pvt-Party Good	Retail Excellent
CIVIC—4-Cyl.—Equipment Schedule 6						
W.B. 105.1"; 1.8 Liter.						
LX Sedan 4D	FB2F5	19755	11400	11850	13100	15550
LX Coupe 2D	FG3B5	19555	11150	11600	12800	15050
EX Coupe 2D	FG3B8	21605	12600	13150	14000	16350
Manual, 5-Spd	E		(550)	(550)	(670)	(670)
CIVIC—4-Cyl.—Equipment Schedule 6						
W.B. 103.2", 105.1" (Sed); 1.8 Liter.						
HF Sedan 4D	FB2F6	20555	11700	12200	13250	15550
EX Sedan 4D	FB2F8	21605	12700	13250	14100	16500
EX-L Sedan 4D	FB2F9	23055	13350	13900	15000	17450
EX-L Coupe 2D	FG3B9	23055	13350	13900	15050	17600
Si Sedan 4D	FB6E5	23505	15500	15750	17350	19700
Si Coupe 2D	FB6E5	23505	15100	15350	16950	19300
CIVIC—4-Cyl. Hybrid—Equipment Schedule 6						
W.B. 105.1"; 1.3 Liter.						
Sedan 4D	FB4F2	25150	12950	13200	14950	17050
CIVIC—4-Cyl. NGV—Equipment Schedule 6						
W.B. 106.3"; 1.8 Liter.						
Sedan 4D	FB5F5	27255	13750	14000	15700	17800
ACCORD—4-Cyl.—Equipment Schedule 3						
W.B. 107.3", 109.3" (Sed); 2.4 Liter.						
LX Sedan 4D	CR2F3	23270	13700	14250	15300	17800
Sport Sedan 4D	CR2F5	24980	14950	15550	16750	19550
LX-S Coupe 2D	CT1B3	24990	14250	14900	16150	18500
EX Sedan 4D	CR2F7	26195	15500	16100	17250	20100
EX Coupe 2D	CT1B7	26685	15650	16200	17850	20400
EX-L Sedan 4D	CR2F8	28785	16450	17100	18150	21100
EX-L Coupe 2D	CT2B8	28860	17000	17350	18950	21600
Touring Sedan 4D	CR3F9	34220	18700	19450	20600	23900
Manual, 6-Spd			(600)	(600)	(700)	(700)
V6, i-VTEC, 3.5 Liter.			850	850	995	995

2014 HONDA — (1,2,5orJ)(9,HorK)(B,G,MorX)ZF1C4-E-#

Body Type	VIN	List	Trade-In Good	Trade-In Very Good	Pvt-Party Good	Retail Excellent
CR-Z—4-Cyl. i-VTEC Hybrid—Equipment Schedule 6						
W.B. 95.9"; 1.5 Liter.						
Coupe 2D	ZF1C4	20785	12600	12900	14350	16400
EX Coupe 2D	ZF1C6	22630	13000	13400	15000	17250
FIT EV—Electric—Equipment Schedule 6						
W.B. 98.4".						
Hatchback 4D	ZA2H4	37415				
INSIGHT—4-Cyl. Hybrid—Equipment Schedule 3						
W.B. 100.4"; 1.3 Liter.						
Hatchback 4D	ZE2H3	19515	11450	11650	13400	15450
LX Hatchback 4D	ZE2H5	21290	12450	12650	14300	16250
EX Hatchback 4D	ZE2H7	22980	13350	13600	15400	17450
CIVIC—4-Cyl.—Equipment Schedule 6						
W.B. 103.2", 105.1" (Sed); 1.8 Liter.						
LX Sedan 4D	FB2F5	19980	12600	13100	14300	16800
LX Coupe 2D	FG3B5	19780	12450	12950	14150	16650
HF Sedan 4D	FB2F6	20730	12900	13400	14650	17200
EX Sedan 4D	FB2F8	21880	13750	14300	15300	17750
EX Coupe 2D	FG3B8	21880	13750	14300	15350	17850
EX-L Sedan 4D	FB2F9	23550	14750	15350	16400	18950
EX-L Coupe 2D	FG3B9	23330	14450	15000	16100	18650
Manual, 5-Spd			(550)	(550)	(660)	(660)
CIVIC—4-Cyl. i-VTEC—Equipment Schedule 6						
W.B. 103.2", 105.1" (Sed); 2.4 Liter.						
Si Sedan 4D	FB6E5	23780	17500	17750	19300	21800
Si Coupe 2D	FG4A5	23580	17150	17400	18950	21400
CIVIC—4-Cyl. Hybrid—Equipment Schedule 6						
W.B. 105.1"; 1.5 Liter.						
Sedan 4D	FB4F2	25425	14650	14900	16700	18850
CIVIC—4-Cyl. Natural Gas—Equipment Schedule 5						
W.B. 105.1"; 1.8 Liter.						
Sedan 4D	FB5F5	27430	16150	16450	18100	20300
ACCORD—4-Cyl.—Equipment Schedule 3						
W.B. 107.3", 109.3" (Sed); 2.4 Liter.						
LX Sedan 4D	CR2F3	23545	15100	15700	16700	19200
LX-S Coupe 2D	CT1B3	25265	15350	15650	17300	19750
Sport Sedan 4D	CR2F5	25305	16700	17350	18400	21300
EX Sedan 4D	CR2F7	26470	17150	17850	18850	21800
EX Coupe 2D	CT1B7	26940	17050	17700	19050	21700

Body Type	VIN	List	Trade-In Good	Very Good	Pvt-Party Good	Retail Excellent
EX-L Sedan 4D	CR2F8	29060	18100	18800	19750	22700
EX-L Coupe 2D	CT1B8	29135	18200	18550	20200	22800
Manual, 6-Spd			(625)	(625)	(710)	(710)
V6, PZEV, 3.5 Liter			925	925	1070	1070

ACCORD—4-Cyl. VTEC Hybrid—Equipment Schedule 3
W.B. 109.3"; 2.0 Liter.

Sedan 4D	CR6F3	29945	20100	20900	21500	24400
EX-L Sedan 4D	CR6F5	32695	21200	22000	22500	25500
Touring Sedan 4D	CR6F7	35695	22400	23200	23600	26600

ACCORD—4-Cyl. i-VTEC Plug-In Hybrid—Equipment Schedule 3
W.B. 109.3"; 2.0 Liter.

Sedan 4D	CR5F7	40570	22400	23300	23600	26700

ACCORD—V6—Equipment Schedule 3
W.B. 109.3"; 3.5 Liter.

Touring Sedan 4D	CR3F9	34270	21500	22400	23300	26800

HYUNDAI

2000 HYUNDAI — KMH(CF35G)-Y-#

ACCENT—4-Cyl.—Equipment Schedule 6
W.B. 96.1"; 1.5 Liter.

L Hatchback 2D	CF35G	9434	350	450	1000	1925
GS Hatchback 2D	CG35G	10784	425	525	1075	2075
GL Sedan 4D	CG45G	10884	425	525	1125	2200

ELANTRA—4-Cyl.—Equipment Schedule 5
W.B. 100.4"; 2.0 Liter.

GLS Sedan 4D	JF34F	12984	375	425	1275	2475
GLS Wagon 4D	JW34F	13684	575	650	1300	2325

TIBURON—4-Cyl.—Equipment Schedule 5
W.B. 97.4"; 2.0 Liter.

Coupe 2D	JG24F	15184	450	575	1125	2075

SONATA—4-Cyl.—Equipment Schedule 5
W.B. 106.3"; 2.4 Liter.

Sedan 4D	WF14S	15934	400	525	1100	2175

SONATA—V6—Equipment Schedule 5
W.B. 106.3"; 2.5 Liter.

GLS Sedan 4D	WF34V	17934	675	850	1425	2725

2001 HYUNDAI — KMH(CF35G)-1-#

ACCENT—4-Cyl.—Equipment Schedule 6
W.B. 96.1"; 1.5 Liter, 1.6 Liter.

L Hatchback 2D	CF35G	10184	350	450	1075	2075
GS Hatchback 2D	CH35C	10584	450	575	1175	2250
GL Sedan 4D	CG45C	11084	425	550	1200	2325

ELANTRA—4-Cyl.—Equipment Schedule 5
W.B. 102.7"; 2.0 Liter.

GLS Sedan 4D	JF35D	13734	375	425	1300	2575
GT Hatchback 4D	JF35D	15234	675	750	1450	2625

TIBURON—4-Cyl.—Equipment Schedule 5
W.B. 97.4"; 2.0 Liter.

Coupe 2D	JG25D	15734	550	675	1400	2675

SONATA—4-Cyl.—Equipment Schedule 5
W.B. 106.3"; 2.4 Liter.

Sedan 4D	WF15S	15934	400	525	1150	2275

SONATA—V6—Equipment Schedule 5
W.B. 106.3"; 2.5 Liter.

GLS Sedan 4D	WF35V	17934	675	850	1425	2725

XG300—V6—Equipment Schedule 3
W.B. 108.3"; 3.0 Liter.

Sedan 4D	FU45D	23934	375	450	1000	1800
L Sedan 4D	FU45D	25434	650	725	1300	2300

2002 HYUNDAI — KMH(CF35G)-2-#

ACCENT—4-Cyl.—Equipment Schedule 6
W.B. 96.1"; 1.5 Liter, 1.6 Liter.

L Hatchback 2D	CF35G	10244	400	475	1175	2300
GS Hatchback 2D	CH35C	10744	475	575	1275	2475
GL Sedan 4D	CG45C	11144	475	575	1275	2475

ELANTRA—4-Cyl.—Equipment Schedule 5
W.B. 102.7"; 2.0 Liter.

GLS Sedan 4D	DN45D	13794	425	500	1425	2750

Body Type	VIN	List	Trade-In Good	Trade-In Very Good	Pvt-Party Good	Retail Excellent
GT Hatchback 4D	DN55D	15294	725	800	1600	2900
SONATA—4-Cyl.—Equipment Schedule 5						
W.B. 106.3"; 2.4 Liter.						
Sedan 4D	WF15S	16494	550	700	1325	2575
V6, 2.7 Liter	H		125	125	175	175
SONATA—V6—Equipment Schedule 5						
W.B. 106.3"; 2.7 Liter.						
GLS Sedan 4D	WF35H	17994	850	1050	1675	3150
LX Sedan 4D	WF35H	19319	1175	1425	2100	3925
XG350—V6—Equipment Schedule 3						
W.B. 108.3"; 3.5 Liter.						
Sedan 4D	FU45E	24494	575	650	1350	2500
L Sedan 4D	FU45E	26094	825	950	1675	3000

2003 HYUNDAI — KMH(CF35C)-3-#

Body Type	VIN	List	Trade-In Good	Trade-In Very Good	Pvt-Party Good	Retail Excellent
ACCENT—4-Cyl.—Equipment Schedule 6						
W.B. 96.1"; 1.6 Liter.						
Hatchback 2D	CF35C	10745	475	575	1275	2450
GL Hatchback 2D	CG35C	11144	650	775	1475	2775
GL Sedan 4D	CG45C	11544	650	775	1475	2775
GT Hatchback 2D	CG45C	11144	750	900	1575	2925
ELANTRA—4-Cyl.—Equipment Schedule 5						
W.B. 102.7"; 2.0 Liter.						
GLS Sedan 4D	DN45D	13794	725	800	1700	3100
GT Sedan 4D	DN55D	15444	950	1050	1900	3350
GT Hatchback 4D	DN55D	15444	950	1050	1825	3225
TIBURON—4-Cyl.—Equipment Schedule 3						
W.B. 99.6"; 2.0 Liter.						
Coupe 2D	HM65D	16494	1000	1200	1700	3450
Manual, 5-Spd			(200)	(200)	(275)	(275)
TIBURON—V6—Equipment Schedule 3						
W.B. 99.6"; 2.7 Liter.						
GT Coupe 2D	HN65F	19244	1125	1325	1900	3275
Manual, 5-Spd			(200)	(200)	(275)	(275)
SONATA—4-Cyl.—Equipment Schedule 5						
W.B. 106.3"; 2.4 Liter.						
Sedan 4D	WF15S	16494	800	1000	1700	3200
V6, 2.7 Liter	H		175	175	245	245
SONATA—V6—Equipment Schedule 5						
W.B. 106.3"; 2.7 Liter.						
GLS Sedan 4D	WF35H	18094	1150	1400	2250	4250
LX Sedan 4D	WF35H	19319	1525	1850	2625	4825
XG350—V6—Equipment Schedule 3						
W.B. 108.3"; 3.5 Liter.						
Sedan 4D	FU45E	24494	925	1025	1650	2850
L Sedan 4D	FU45E	26094	1175	1325	2000	3400

2004 HYUNDAI — KMH(CF35C)-4-#

Body Type	VIN	List	Trade-In Good	Trade-In Very Good	Pvt-Party Good	Retail Excellent
ACCENT—4-Cyl.—Equipment Schedule 6						
W.B. 96.1"; 1.6 Liter.						
Hatchback 2D	CF35C	11289	550	650	1325	2500
GL Hatchback 2D	CG35C	11439	650	775	1550	2900
GL Sedan 4D	CG45C	11839	800	925	1650	3050
GT Hatchback 2D	CG45C	11939	875	1025	1800	3350
ELANTRA—4-Cyl.—Equipment Schedule 5						
W.B. 102.7"; 2.0 Liter.						
GLS Sedan 4D	DN45D	14639	1075	1200	2125	3750
GT Sedan 4D	DN55D	16189	1375	1500	2400	4025
GT Hatchback 4D	DN55D	16189	1375	1500	2400	4075
TIBURON—4-Cyl.—Equipment Schedule 3						
W.B. 99.6"; 2.0 Liter.						
Coupe 2D	HM65D	18439	1325	1550	2225	3825
Manual, 5-Spd			(250)	(250)	(345)	(345)
TIBURON—V6—Equipment Schedule 3						
W.B. 99.6"; 2.7 Liter.						
GT Coupe 2D	HN65F	19639	1675	1975	2725	4600
GT Special Ed Cpe 2D	HN65F	20987	1950	2275	3150	5375
Manual, 5-Spd			(250)	(250)	(345)	(345)
SONATA—4-Cyl.—Equipment Schedule 5						
W.B. 106.3"; 2.4 Liter.						
Sedan 4D	WF15S	17339	925	1125	1850	3450
V6, 2.7 Liter	H		225	225	310	310

2004 HYUNDAI

Body Type	VIN	List	Trade-In Good	Very Good	Pvt-Party Good	Retail Excellent
SONATA—V6—Equipment Schedule 5						
W.B. 106.3"; 2.7 Liter.						
GLS Sedan 4D	WF35H	19339	1475	1775	2525	4600
LX Sedan 4D	WF35H	20339	1825	2175	2950	5200
XG350—V6—Equipment Schedule 3						
W.B. 108.3"; 3.5 Liter.						
Sedan 4D	FU45E	24589	1275	1425	2100	3475
L Sedan 4D	FU45E	26189	1450	1625	2400	4000

2005 HYUNDAI — KMH(CG35C)-5-#

Body Type	VIN	List	Trade-In Good	Very Good	Pvt-Party Good	Retail Excellent
ACCENT—4-Cyl.—Equipment Schedule 6						
W.B. 96.1"; 1.6 Liter.						
GLS Hatchback 2D	CG35C	11344	875	1025	1975	3575
GLS Sedan 4D	CG45C	11844	1200	1400	2275	3975
GT Hatchback 2D	CG35C	11939	1300	1525	2300	3925
ELANTRA—4-Cyl.—Equipment Schedule 5						
W.B. 102.7"; 2.0 Liter.						
GLS Sedan 4D	DN46D	14644	1450	1575	2675	4425
GLS Hatchback 4D	DN56D	14944	1550	1700	2825	4625
GT Sedan 4D	DN46D	16194	1800	1975	2900	4575
GT Hatchback 4D	DN56D	16194	1800	1975	2900	4625
TIBURON—4-Cyl.—Equipment Schedule 3						
W.B. 99.6"; 2.0 Liter.						
GS Coupe 2D	HM65D	17494	2025	2375	3000	4725
Manual, 5-Spd			(300)	(300)	(410)	(410)
TIBURON—V6—Equipment Schedule 3						
W.B. 99.6"; 2.7 Liter.						
GT Coupe 2D	HN65F	19494	2250	2625	3300	5200
SE Coupe 2D	HN65F	20594	2650	3050	3800	6075
Manual, 5-Spd			(300)	(300)	(410)	(410)
SONATA—4-Cyl.—Equipment Schedule 5						
W.B. 106.3"; 2.4 Liter.						
GL Sedan 4D	WF25S	17394	1075	1300	2125	3775
V6, 2.7 Liter	H		275	275	375	375
SONATA—V6—Equipment Schedule 5						
W.B. 106.3"; 2.7 Liter.						
GLS Sedan 4D	WF35H	19394	1550	1850	2725	4725
LX Sedan 4D	WF35H	20394	2100	2500	3325	5625
XG350—V6—Equipment Schedule 3						
W.B. 108.3"; 3.5 Liter.						
Sedan 4D	FU45E	24994	1275	1425	2325	3800
L Sedan 4D	FU45E	26594	1725	1925	2825	4500

2006 HYUNDAI — KMH(CN46C)-6-#

Body Type	VIN	List	Trade-In Good	Very Good	Pvt-Party Good	Retail Excellent
ACCENT—4-Cyl.—Equipment Schedule 6						
W.B. 98.4"; 1.6 Liter.						
GLS Sedan 4D	CN46C	13845	1900	2175	2900	4650
Manual, 5-Spd			(275)	(275)	(355)	(355)
ELANTRA—4-Cyl.—Equipment Schedule 5						
W.B. 102.7"; 2.0 Liter.						
GLS Sedan 4D	DN46D	15095	1950	2125	3150	4975
GLS Hatchback 4D	DN56D	15495	2000	2175	3275	5200
Limited Sedan 4D	DN46D	16045	2100	2275	3325	5225
GT Hatchback 4D	DN56D	16415	2275	2500	3400	5275
TIBURON—4-Cyl.—Equipment Schedule 3						
W.B. 99.6"; 2.0 Liter.						
GS Coupe 2D	HM65D	17595	2225	2550	3200	4950
Manual, 5-Spd			(350)	(350)	(475)	(475)
TIBURON—V6—Equipment Schedule 3						
W.B. 99.6"; 2.7 Liter.						
GT Coupe 2D	HN65F	19995	2625	3000	3675	5625
GT Limited Coupe 2D	HN65F	21995	3125	3550	4250	6500
SE Coupe 2D	HN65F	21595	3000	3425	4125	6300
Manual, 5-Spd			(350)	(350)	(475)	(475)
SONATA—4-Cyl.—Equipment Schedule 5						
W.B. 107.4"; 2.4 Liter.						
GL Sedan 4D	ET46C	19395	2600	3050	3500	5425
GLS Sedan 4D	EU46C	19995	3000	3500	3950	6150
V6, 3.3 Liter	F		325	325	445	445
SONATA—V6—Equipment Schedule 5						
W.B. 107.4"; 3.3 Liter.						
LX Sedan 4D	EU46F	23495	3275	3825	4425	6925

2006 HYUNDAI

Body Type	VIN	List	Trade-In Good	Very Good	Pvt-Party Good	Retail Excellent
AZERA—V6—Equipment Schedule 3						
W.B. 109.4"; 3.8 Liter.						
SE Sedan 4D	FC46F	24995	**3000**	**3400**	**3875**	**5775**
Limited Sedan 4D	FC46F	27495	**3775**	**4250**	**4775**	**7000**
Premium Pkg		------	275	275	355	355
Ultimate Pkg		------	275	275	360	360

2007 HYUNDAI — KMH(CM36C)-7-#

Body Type	VIN	List	Trade-In Good	Very Good	Pvt-Party Good	Retail Excellent
ACCENT—4-Cyl.—Equipment Schedule 6						
W.B. 98.4"; 1.6 Liter.						
GS Hatchback 2D	CM36C	11995	**1925**	**2200**	**3150**	**5125**
GLS Sedan 4D	CN46C	14145	**2275**	**2575**	**3350**	**5250**
SE Hatchback 2D	CN36C	15495	**2600**	**2950**	**3700**	**5775**
Manual, 5-Spd			**(300)**	**(300)**	**(385)**	**(385)**
ELANTRA—4-Cyl.—Equipment Schedule 6						
W.B. 104.3"; 2.0 Liter.						
GLS Sedan 4D	DU46D	16495	**3125**	**3375**	**4400**	**6450**
SE Sedan 4D	DU46D	17295	**3250**	**3500**	**4475**	**6550**
Limited Sedan 4D	DU46D	18295	**3575**	**3850**	**4900**	**7175**
Manual, 5-Spd			**(400)**	**(400)**	**(520)**	**(520)**
TIBURON—4-Cyl.—Equipment Schedule 3						
W.B. 99.6"; 2.0 Liter.						
GS Coupe 2D	HM65D	18295	**3075**	**3475**	**4150**	**6075**
Manual, 5-Spd			**(400)**	**(400)**	**(520)**	**(520)**
TIBURON—V6—Equipment Schedule 3						
W.B. 99.6"; 2.7 Liter.						
GT Coupe 2D	HN66F	20995	**3525**	**3975**	**4650**	**6775**
GT Limited Coupe 2D	HN66F	23295	**4025**	**4525**	**5175**	**7550**
SE Coupe 2D	HN66F	22595	**3350**	**3775**	**4550**	**6775**
Manual, 5-Spd			**(400)**	**(400)**	**(520)**	**(520)**
SONATA—4-Cyl.—Equipment Schedule 5						
W.B. 107.4"; 2.4 Liter.						
GLS Sedan 4D	ET46C	18895	**3300**	**3800**	**4350**	**6550**
Manual, 5-Spd			**(400)**	**(400)**	**(520)**	**(520)**
SONATA—V6—Equipment Schedule 5						
W.B. 107.4"; 3.3 Liter.						
SE Sedan 4D	EU46F	21595	**3650**	**4200**	**4750**	**7150**
Limited Sedan 4D	EU46F	23595	**4050**	**4675**	**5250**	**7925**
AZERA—V6—Equipment Schedule 3						
W.B. 109.4"; 3.3 Liter, 3.8 Liter.						
GLS Sedan 4D	FC46D	24895	**4000**	**4450**	**4900**	**6900**
SE Sedan 4D	FC46F	25195	**4275**	**4750**	**5150**	**7200**
Limited Sedan 4D	FC46F	27795	**4525**	**5000**	**5450**	**7700**
Premium Pkg			300	300	385	385
Ultimate Pkg			275	275	370	370

2008 HYUNDAI — (KMHor5NP)(CM36C)-8-#

Body Type	VIN	List	Trade-In Good	Very Good	Pvt-Party Good	Retail Excellent
ACCENT—4-Cyl.—Equipment Schedule 6						
W.B. 98.4"; 1.6 Liter.						
GS Hatchback 2D	CM36C	12395	**2475**	**2750**	**3725**	**5700**
GLS Sedan 4D	CN46C	14545	**2750**	**3050**	**3875**	**5775**
SE Hatchback 2D	CN36C	15995	**3150**	**3475**	**4275**	**6325**
Manual, 5-Spd w/Overdrive			**(350)**	**(350)**	**(460)**	**(460)**
ELANTRA—4-Cyl.—Equipment Schedule 5						
W.B. 104.3"; 2.0 Liter.						
GLS Sedan 4D	DU46D	15145	**3800**	**4050**	**5150**	**7250**
SE Sedan 4D	DU46D	17845	**4200**	**4475**	**5450**	**7500**
Manual, 5-Spd w/Overdrive			**(400)**	**(400)**	**(540)**	**(540)**
TIBURON—4-Cyl.—Equipment Schedule 3						
W.B. 99.6"; 2.0 Liter.						
GS Coupe 2D	HM65D	18595	**3625**	**3975**	**4750**	**6650**
Manual, 5-Spd			**(400)**	**(400)**	**(540)**	**(540)**
TIBURON—V6—Equipment Schedule 3						
W.B. 99.6"; 2.7 Liter.						
GT Coupe 2D	HN66F	21495	**4025**	**4425**	**5275**	**7400**
GT Limited Coupe 2D	HN66F	22995	**4800**	**5250**	**6025**	**8400**
SE Coupe 2D	HN66F	22845	**4425**	**4850**	**5700**	**8000**
Manual, 5-Spd			**(400)**	**(400)**	**(540)**	**(540)**
Manual, 6-Spd			**0**	**0**	**0**	**0**
SONATA—4-Cyl.—Equipment Schedule 5						
W.B. 107.4"; 2.4 Liter.						
GLS Sedan 4D	ET46C	19545	**3925**	**4400**	**5000**	**7075**

Body Type	VIN	List	Trade-In Good	Very Good	Pvt-Party Good	Retail Excellent
Manual, 5-Spd			(400)	(400)	(540)	(540)
V6, 3.3 Liter	F		475	475	630	630
SONATA—V6—Equipment Schedule 5						
W.B. 107.4"; 3.3 Liter.						
SE Sedan 4D	EU46F	22745	4850	5425	6100	8575
Manual, 5-Spd			(400)	(400)	(540)	(540)
4-Cyl, 2.4 Liter	C		(400)	(400)	(525)	(525)
SONATA—V6—Equipment Schedule 5						
W.B. 107.4"; 3.3 Liter.						
Limited Sedan 4D	EU46F	24695	5325	5950	6650	9375
4-Cyl, 2.4 Liter	C		(400)	(400)	(525)	(525)
AZERA—V6—Equipment Schedule 3						
W.B. 109.4"; 3.3 Liter, 3.8 Liter.						
GLS Sedan 4D	FC46D	25295	4500	4875	5475	7400
Limited Sedan 4D	FC46F	29245	5550	6025	6575	8675
Ultimate Pkg			275	275	375	375

Body Type	VIN	List	Trade-In Good	Very Good	Pvt-Party Good	Retail Excellent
ACCENT—4-Cyl.—Equipment Schedule 6						
W.B. 98.4"; 1.6 Liter.						
GS Hatchback 2D	CM36C	12745	3075	3325	4400	6425
GLS Sedan 4D	CN46C	14595	3425	3700	4750	6775
SE Hatchback 2D	CN36C	16545	3875	4200	5275	7450
Manual, 5-Spd w/Overdrive			(375)	(375)	(490)	(490)
ELANTRA—4-Cyl.—Equipment Schedule 5						
W.B. 104.3", 106.3"(Wag); 2.0 Liter.						
GLS Sedan 4D	DU46D	15795	4550	4825	5950	8050
SE Sedan 4D	DU46D	18495	5000	5300	6600	8875
Touring Wagon 4D	DC86E	19295	6075	6425	7550	9900
Manual, 5-Spd w/Overdrive			(450)	(450)	(585)	(585)
SONATA—4-Cyl.—Equipment Schedule 5						
W.B. 107.4"; 2.4 Liter.						
GLS Sedan 4D	ET46C	20195	5150	5600	6375	8525
Manual, 5-Spd w/Overdrive			(450)	(450)	(585)	(585)
V6, 3.3 Liter	F		500	500	675	675
SONATA—V6—Equipment Schedule 5						
W.B. 107.4"; 3.3 Liter.						
SE Sedan 4D	EU46F	22745	6150	6700	7425	9875
Manual, 5-Spd w/Overdrive			(450)	(450)	(585)	(585)
4-Cyl, 2.4 Liter	C		(450)	(450)	(600)	(600)
SONATA—V6—Equipment Schedule 5						
W.B. 107.4"; 3.3 Liter.						
Limited Sedan 4D	EU46F	27245	6650	7250	8075	10750
4-Cyl, 2.4 Liter	C		(450)	(450)	(595)	(595)
AZERA—V6—Equipment Schedule 3						
W.B. 109.4"; 3.3 Liter, 3.8 Liter.						
GLS Sedan 4D	FC46D	25295	5500	5850	6750	8750
Limited Sedan 4D	FC46F	29245	6500	6900	7750	9950
Ultimate Pkg			300	300	385	385
Premium Pkg			325	325	445	445
GENESIS—V6—Equipment Schedule 3						
W.B. 115.6"; 3.8 Liter.						
3.8 Sedan 4D	GB46E	33000	9625	10200	11050	13800
Technology Pkg			1125	1125	1395	1395
GENESIS—V8—Equipment Schedule 3						
W.B. 115.6"; 4.6 Liter.						
4.6 Sedan 4D	GC46F	38000	10700	11350	12350	15500
Technology Pkg			1125	1125	1400	1400

Body Type	VIN	List	Trade-In Good	Very Good	Pvt-Party Good	Retail Excellent
ACCENT—4-Cyl.—Equipment Schedule 6						
W.B. 98.4"; 1.6 Liter.						
Blue Hatchback 2D	CM3AC	10690	3000	3200	4300	6075
ACCENT—4-Cyl.—Equipment Schedule 6						
W.B. 98.4"; 1.6 Liter.						
GS Hatchback 2D	CM3AC	13715	4150	4425	5425	7350
GLS Sedan 4D	CN46C	15365	4375	4675	5775	7850
SE Hatchback 2D	CN3AC	17715	5025	5375	6500	8650
Manual, 5-Spd w/Overdrive			(450)	(450)	(615)	(615)
ELANTRA—4-Cyl.—Equipment Schedule 5						
W.B. 104.3"; 2.0 Liter.						
Blue Sedan 4D	DU4AD	14865	5050	5325	6650	8725

Body Type	VIN	List	Trade-In Good	Very Good	Pvt-Party Good	Retail Excellent
GLS Sedan 4D	DU4AD	17615	5825	6125	7475	9750
SE Sedan 4D	DU4AD	18565	6125	6450	7825	10200
ELANTRA—4-Cyl.—Equipment Schedule 5						
W.B. 106.3"; 2.0 Liter.						
GLS Touring Wagon	DB8AE	17915	5800	6100	7450	9750
SE Touring Wagon 4D	DC8AE	20515	6525	6875	8125	10450
Manual, 5-Spd w/Overdrive			(475)	(475)	(640)	(640)
SONATA—4-Cyl.—Equipment Schedule 5						
W.B. 107.4"; 3.3 Liter.						
GLS Sedan 4D	ET4AC	20620	6125	6525	7350	9375
Manual, 5-Spd w/Overdrive			(475)	(475)	(630)	(630)
SONATA—V6—Equipment Schedule 5						
W.B. 107.4"; 3.3 Liter.						
SE Sedan 4D	EU4AF	24770	7100	7575	8525	10900
Limited Sedan 4D	EU4AF	27270	7850	8350	9350	12000
4-Cyl, 2.4 Liter			(575)	(575)	(760)	(760)
AZERA—V6—Equipment Schedule 3						
W.B. 109.4"; 3.3 Liter, 3.8 Liter.						
GLS Sedan 4D	FC4DD	25745	7925	8275	9200	11250
Limited Sedan 4D	FC4DF	30345	9750	10200	11050	13450
Premium Pkg			375	375	475	475
GENESIS—4-Cyl. Turbo—Equipment Schedule 3						
W.B. 111.0"; 2.0 Liter.						
2.0T Coupe 2D	HT6KD	22750	8800	9250	10050	12650
2.0T R-Spec Coupe 2D	HT6KD	24500	9300	9750	10550	12950
2.0T Premium Coupe	HT6KD	25000	8975	9400	10250	12600
2.0T Track Coupe 2D	HT6KD	27500	9750	10250	11050	13550
GENESIS—V6—Equipment Schedule 3						
W.B. 111.0", 115.6" (Sed); 3.8 Liter.						
3.8 Sedan 4D	GC4DE	33800	11500	12000	13000	15700
3.8 Coupe 2D	HU6KH	25750	9900	10550	11150	14050
3.8 Grand Touring	HU6KH	29250	10000	10500	11450	14200
3.8 Track Coupe 2D	HU6KH	31250	10100	10600	11550	14300
Premium Pkg			975	975	1215	1215
Technology Pkg			1200	1200	1480	1480
GENESIS—V8—Equipment Schedule 3						
W.B. 115.6"; 4.6 Liter.						
4.6 Sedan 4D	GC4DF	40300	12500	13050	14300	17450
Technology Pkg			1460	1460	1460	1460

2011 HYUNDAI — 5N(MorP)orKM(8orH)(CM3AC)-B-#

Body Type	VIN	List	Trade-In Good	Very Good	Pvt-Party Good	Retail Excellent
ACCENT—4-Cyl.—Equipment Schedule 6						
W.B. 98.4"; 1.6 Liter.						
GL Hatchback 2D	CM3AC	10705	3850	4050	4975	6450
ACCENT—4-Cyl.—Equipment Schedule 6						
W.B. 98.4"; 1.6 Liter.						
GS Hatchback 2D	CM3AC	14415	5300	5575	6575	8475
GLS Sedan 4D	CN4AC	15415	5400	5675	6850	9000
SE Hatchback 2D	CN3AC	16865	6325	6675	7925	10200
Manual, 5-Spd w/Overdrive			(500)	(500)	(655)	(655)
ELANTRA—4-Cyl.—Equipment Schedule 5						
W.B. 106.3"; 1.8 Liter.						
GLS Sedan 4D	DH4AE	17800	7750	8100	9400	11750
Limited Sedan 4D	DH4AE	20700	8600	9000	10200	12600
ELANTRA—4-Cyl.—Equipment Schedule 5						
W.B. 106.3"; 2.0 Liter.						
GLS Touring Wag 4D	DB8AE	17915	7775	8125	9350	11600
Touring SE Wagon 4D	DC8AE	21015	8700	9100	10300	12700
Manual, 5-Spd w/Overdrive			(500)	(500)	(640)	(640)
SONATA—4-Cyl.—Equipment Schedule 5						
W.B. 110.0"; 2.4 Liter.						
GLS Sedan 4D	EB4AC	20915	9275	9725	10800	13250
Manual, 6-Spd w/Overdrive			(500)	(500)	(610)	(610)
SONATA—4-Cyl.—Equipment Schedule 5						
W.B. 110.0"; 2.4 Liter.						
SE Sedan 4D	EC4AC	23315	10050	10500	11600	14250
Limited Sedan 4D	EC4AC	26015	10750	11250	12250	14950
4-Cyl, Turbo, 2.0 Liter	B		1225	1225	1510	1510
SONATA—4-Cyl. Hybrid—Equipment Schedule 5						
W.B. 110.0"; 2.4 Liter.						
Sedan 4D	EC4A4	26545	10700	11200	12200	14900
AZERA—V6—Equipment Schedule 3						
W.B. 109.4"; 3.3 Liter, 3.8 Liter.						

Body Type	VIN	List	Trade-In Good	Very Good	Pvt-Party Good	Retail Excellent
GLS Sedan 4D	FC4DD	26270	10200	10550	11550	13600
Limited Sedan 4D	FC4DF	30870	11450	11800	12900	15200
Premium Pkg			425	425	520	520
GENESIS—4-Cyl. Turbo—Equipment Schedule 3						
W.B. 111.0"; 2.0 Liter.						
2.0T Coupe 2D	HT6KD	23050	10400	10750	11800	14100
2.0T R-Spec Coupe 2D	HT6KD	25300	10800	11150	12200	14600
2.0T Premium Cpe 2D	HT6KD	27550	10900	11250	12350	14900
GENESIS—V6—Equipment Schedule 3						
W.B. 111.0", 115.6" (Sed); 3.8 Liter.						
3.8 Sedan 4D	GC4DE	33800	12750	13200	14750	17750
3.8 R-Spec Coupe 2D	HU6KH	27550	11600	12150	12900	15650
3.8 Grand Touring	HU6KH	30550	12250	12700	13850	16650
3.8 Track Coupe 2D	HU6KH	31550	12400	12800	14000	16850
Premium Pkg			1050	1050	1265	1265
Technology Pkg			1275	1275	1540	1540
GENESIS—V8—Equipment Schedule 3						
W.B. 115.6"; 4.6 Liter.						
4.6 Sedan 4D	GC4DF	43800	13650	14100	15850	18750
Technology Pkg			1275	1275	1565	1565
EQUUS—V8—Equipment Schedule 3						
W.B. 119.9"; 4.6 Liter.						
Signature Sedan 4D	GH4JF	58900	19300	20000	20900	24100
Ultimate Sedan 4D	GH4JF	65400	21400	22200	23100	26500

2012 HYUNDAI — 5NPorKMH(CT4AE)-C-#

ACCENT—4-Cyl.—Equipment Schedule 6						
W.B. 98.4"; 1.6 Liter.						
GLS Sedan 4D	CT4AE	15955	7150	7475	8750	11000
GS Hatchback 4D	CT5AE	16555	7275	7625	8900	11100
Manual, 5-Spd w/Overdrive			(550)	(550)	(720)	(720)
ACCENT—4-Cyl.—Equipment Schedule 6						
W.B. 98.4"; 1.6 Liter.						
SE Hatchback 4D	CU5AE	16555	7475	7825	9125	11400
Auto, 6-Spd w/Overdrive			475	475	620	620
VELOSTER—4-Cyl.—Equipment Schedule 4						
W.B. 104.3"; 1.6 Liter.						
Coupe 3D	TC6AD	19310	10350	10800	11950	14250
Style Pkg			250	250	310	310
Tech Pkg			425	425	535	535
ELANTRA—4-Cyl.—Equipment Schedule 5						
W.B. 106.3"; 1.8 Liter, 2.0 Liter.						
GLS Sedan 4D	DH4AE	18195	8700	9075	10350	12650
Touring GLS Wagon	DB8AE	17945	8250	8625	9900	12100
Touring SE Wagon 4D	DC8AE	21045	9325	9725	11050	13450
Manual, 5-Spd w/Overdrive			(525)	(525)	(670)	(670)
Manual, 6-Spd w/Overdrive			(525)	(525)	(670)	(670)
ELANTRA—4-Cyl.—Equipment Schedule 5						
W.B. 106.3"; 1.8 Liter.						
Limited Sedan 4D	DH4AE	21195	10250	10700	11900	14350
SONATA—4-Cyl.—Equipment Schedule 5						
W.B. 110.0"; 2.4 Liter.						
GLS Sedan 4D	EB4AC	21455	10050	10400	11650	14000
Manual, 6-Spd w/Overdrive			(525)	(525)	(635)	(635)
SONATA—4-Cyl.—Equipment Schedule 5						
W.B. 110.0"; 2.4 Liter.						
SE Sedan 4D	EC4AC	23855	10700	11050	12350	14900
Limited Sedan 4D	EC4AC	27105	12150	12600	13800	16450
4-Cyl, Turbo, 2.0 Liter	B		1300	1300	1570	1570
SONATA—4-Cyl. Hybrid—Equipment Schedule 5						
W.B. 110.0"; 2.4 Liter.						
Sedan 4D	EC4A4	26625	11300	11700	13000	15550
AZERA—V6—Equipment Schedule 3						
W.B. 112.0"; 3.3 Liter.						
Sedan 4D	FH4DG	32875	14750	15050	16550	19150
GENESIS—4-Cyl. Turbo—Equipment Schedule 3						
W.B. 111.0"; 2.0 Liter.						
2.0T Coupe 2D	HT6KD	23100	12150	12400	13600	15900
2.0T R-Spec Coupe 2D	HT6KD	25350	12600	12900	14050	16450
2.0T Premium Cpe 2D	HT6KD	27600	12500	12800	14000	16400
GENESIS—V6—Equipment Schedule 3						
W.B. 111.0", 115.6" (Sed); 3.8 Liter.						
3.8 Sedan 4D	GC4DD	35050	14700	15050	16850	19750

2012 HYUNDAI

Body Type	VIN	List	Good	Trade-In Very Good	Pvt-Party Good	Retail Excellent
3.8 R-Spec Coupe 2D	HU6KH	27600	**13500**	**13950**	**14950**	**17700**
3.8 Grand Touring	HU6KII	30600	**14150**	**14500**	**15900**	**18650**
3.8 Track Coupe 2D	HU6KH	31600	**13550**	**13850**	**15350**	**18150**
Premium Pkg			**1100**	**1100**	**1310**	**1310**
Technology Pkg			**1325**	**1325**	**1590**	**1590**
GENESIS—V8—Equipment Schedule 3						
W.B. 115.6"; 4.6 Liter, 5.0 Liter.						
4.6 Sedan 4D	GC4DF	45350	**16100**	**16500**	**18400**	**21600**
5.0 Sedan 4D	GC4DH	46350	**19000**	**19500**	**21700**	**25600**
5.0 R-Spec Sedan 4D	GC4DH	47350	**20600**	**21100**	**23200**	**27200**
EQUUS—V8—Equipment Schedule 3						
W.B. 119.9".						
Signature Sedan 4D	GH4JH	59650	**22300**	**23000**	**24200**	**27500**
Ultimate Sedan 4D	GH4JH	66650	**24100**	**24900**	**26100**	**29700**

2013 HYUNDAI — 5NPorKMH(CT4AE)–D–#

Body Type	VIN	List	Good	Very Good	Good	Excellent
ACCENT—4-Cyl.—Equipment Schedule 6						
W.B. 98.4"; 1.6 Liter.						
GLS Sedan 4D	CT4AE	15320	**7725**	**8025**	**9475**	**11800**
GS Hatchback 4D	CT5AE	15570	**7900**	**8200**	**9475**	**11600**
SE Hatchback 4D	CU5AE	16870	**8725**	**9075**	**10300**	**12550**
Auto, 6-Spd w/Overdrive			**500**	**500**	**650**	**650**
VELOSTER—4-Cyl.—Equipment Schedule 4						
W.B. 104.3"; 1.6 Liter.						
Coupe 3D	TC6AD	19475	**11300**	**11750**	**13000**	**15400**
RE:MIX Coupe 3D	TC6AD	21925	**11250**	**11700**	**12950**	**15300**
Style Pkg			**275**	**275**	**325**	**325**
Tech Pkg			**450**	**450**	**555**	**555**
VELOSTER—4-Cyl. Turbo—Equipment Schedule 4						
W.B. 104.3"; 1.6 Liter.						
Coupe 3D	TC6AE	23725	**12450**	**12950**	**14050**	**16500**
ELANTRA—4-Cyl.—Equipment Schedule 5						
W.B. 106.3"; 1.8 Liter.						
GLS Sedan 4D	DH4AE	18470	**9800**	**10200**	**11550**	**13950**
GS Coupe 2D	DH6AE	19220	**10150**	**10550**	**11850**	**14150**
SE Coupe 2D	DH6AE	21520	**11150**	**11600**	**13000**	**15500**
GT Hatchback 4D	D35LE	20170	**10950**	**11400**	**12550**	**15050**
Manual, 6-Spd			**(550)**	**(550)**	**(685)**	**(685)**
ELANTRA—4-Cyl.—Equipment Schedule 5						
W.B. 106.3"; 1.8 Liter.						
Limited Sedan 4D	DH4AE	21720	**11250**	**11700**	**12950**	**15400**
SONATA—4-Cyl.—Equipment Schedule 5						
W.B. 110.0"; 2.4 Liter.						
GLS Sedan 4D	EB4AC	21670	**10900**	**11200**	**12550**	**14850**
SONATA—4-Cyl.—Equipment Schedule 5						
W.B. 110.0"; 2.4 Liter.						
SE Sedan 4D	EC4AC	24120	**11650**	**11950**	**13400**	**15900**
Limited Sedan 4D	EC4AC	26620	**13400**	**13750**	**15250**	**18000**
4-Cyl, Turbo, 2.0 Liter	B		**1350**	**1350**	**1625**	**1625**
SONATA—4-Cyl. Hybrid—Equipment Schedule 5						
W.B. 110.0"; 2.4 Liter.						
Sedan 4D	EC4A4	26445	**12100**	**12400**	**13950**	**16550**
Limited Sedan 4D	EC4A4	31345	**14050**	**14450**	**15900**	**18650**
AZERA—V6—Equipment Schedule 3						
W.B. 112.0"; 3.3 Liter.						
Sedan 4D	FG4JG	33125	**16000**	**16250**	**17900**	**20400**
Technology Pkg			**1400**	**1400**	**1630**	**1630**
GENESIS—4-Cyl. Turbo—Equipment Schedule 3						
W.B. 111.0"; 2.0 Liter.						
2.0T Coupe 2D	HT6KD	25125	**14700**	**14950**	**16250**	**18700**
2.0T R-Spec Coupe 2D	HT6KD	27375	**15250**	**15500**	**16850**	**19400**
2.0T Premium Cpe 2D	HT6KD	29625	**14850**	**15100**	**16400**	**18850**
GENESIS—V6—Equipment Schedule 3						
W.B. 111.0", 115.6" (Sed); 3.8 Liter.						
3.8 Sedan 4D	GC4DD	35075	**15250**	**15600**	**17500**	**20400**
3.8 R-Spec Coupe 2D	HU6KJ	29625	**16400**	**16800**	**17900**	**20700**
3.8 Grand Touring 2D	HU6KJ	32875	**16750**	**17050**	**18400**	**21100**
3.8 Track Coupe 2D	HU6KJ	33875	**17300**	**17600**	**19000**	**21800**
Premium Pkg			**1150**	**1150**	**1375**	**1375**
Technology Pkg			**1400**	**1400**	**1665**	**1665**
GENESIS—V8—Equipment Schedule 3						
W.B. 115.6"; 5.0 Liter.						
5.0 R-Spec Sedan 4D	GC4DH	47675	**21400**	**21800**	**24200**	**28200**

Body Type	VIN	List	Trade-In Good	Very Good	Pvt-Party Good	Retail Excellent

EQUUS—V8—Equipment Schedule 3
W.B. 119.9"; 5.0 Liter.

Signature Sedan 4D	GH4JH	60150	25700	26400	28000	31700
Ultimate Sedan 4D	GH4JH	67150	27500	28400	29900	33900

2014 HYUNDAI — 5NPorKMH(CT4AE)-E-#

ACCENT—4-Cyl.—Equipment Schedule 6
W.B. 101.2"; 1.6 Liter.

GLS Sedan 4D	CT4AE	15455	8625	8975	10250	12450
GS Hatchback 4D	CT5AE	15705	8750	9100	10300	12450
SE Hatchback 4D	CU5AE	17205	9775	10150	11300	13550
Auto, 6-Spd w/Overdrive			525	525	655	655

VELOSTER—4-Cyl.—Equipment Schedule 6
W.B. 104.3"; 1.6 Liter.

Coupe 3D	TC6AD	19860	11900	12400	13600	16000
RE:FLEX Coupe 3D	TC6AD	22460	13150	13650	14800	17200

VELOSTER—4-Cyl. Turbo—Equipment Schedule 4
W.B. 104.3"; 1.6 Liter.

R-spec Coupe 3D	TC6AE	22110	13000	13500	14650	17050
Coupe 3D	TC6AE	24110	13700	14250	15450	18050

ELANTRA—4-Cyl.—Equipment Schedule 5
W.B. 104.3" (GT), 106.3"; 1.8 Liter, 2.0 Liter.

SE Sedan 4D	DH4AE	19010	10700	11100	12450	14850
Sport Sedan 4D	DH4AH	23510	13150	13700	15000	17650
GT Hatchback 4D	D35LH	20560	11500	11950	13200	15650
Manual, 6-Spd			(575)	(575)	(705)	(705)

ELANTRA—4-Cyl.—Equipment Schedule 5
W.B. 106.3"; 1.8 Liter, 2.0 Liter.

Coupe 2D	DH6AH	20410	11450	11900	13200	15650
Limited Sedan 4D	DH4AE	22460	12200	12700	13950	16450

SONATA—4-Cyl.—Equipment Schedule 5
W.B. 110.0"; 2.4 Liter.

GLS Sedan 4D	EB4AC	22145	11950	12250	13700	16150

SONATA—4-Cyl.—Equipment Schedule 5
W.B. 110.0"; 2.4 Liter.

SE Sedan 4D	EC4A	24995	13450	13800	15250	17850
Limited Sedan 4D	EC4AC	27695	15700	16100	17450	20300
4-Cyl, Turbo, 2.0 Liter	B		1425	1425	1655	1655

SONATA—4-Cyl. Hybrid—Equipment Schedule 5
W.B. 110.0"; 2.4 Liter.

Sedan 4D	EC4A4	26810	14250	14600	16100	18850
Limited Sedan 4D	EC4A4	31345	18400	18900	20100	23100

AZERA—V6—Equipment Schedule 3
W.B. 112.0"; 3.3 Liter.

Sedan 4D	FG4JG	31895	16250	16500	18150	20700
Limited Sedan 4D	FH4JG	35645	21300	21600	23100	25900

GENESIS—4-Cyl. Turbo—Equipment Schedule 3
W.B. 111.0"; 2.0 Liter.

2.0T Coupe 2D	HT6KD	27245	17100	17350	18650	21200
2.0T R-Spec Coupe 2D	HT6KD	28095	17300	17600	18950	21600
2.0T Premium Cpe 2D	HT6KD	30195	18600	18850	20100	22700

GENESIS—V6—Equipment Schedule 3
W.B. 111.0"; 3.8 Liter.

3.8 R-Spec Coupe 2D	HU6KJ	30245	19750	20100	21300	24200
3.8 Grand Touring 2D	HU6KJ	33045	20700	21000	22200	25100
3.8 Ultimate Cpe 2D	HU6KJ	34295	21000	21300	22500	25600

GENESIS—V6—Equipment Schedule 3
W.B. 115.6"; 3.8 Liter.

3.8 Sedan 4D	GC4DD	36120	18200	18550	20400	23300
Adaptive Cruise Control			500	500	565	565
Premium Pkg			1225	1225	1405	1405
Technology Pkg			1475	1475	1705	1705

GENESIS—V8—Equipment Schedule 3
W.B. 115.6"; 5.0 Liter.

5.0 R-Spec Sedan 4D	GC4DH	48320	24100	24600	26900	31000
Adaptive Cruise Control			(500)	(500)	(570)	(570)

EQUUS—V8—Equipment Schedule 3
W.B. 119.9"; 5.0 Liter.

Signature Sedan 4D	GH4JH	61920	32000	32900	34200	38100
Ultimate Sedan 4D	GH4JH	68920	34600	35600	36800	41000

Body Type	VIN	List	Trade-In Good	Very Good	Pvt-Party Good	Retail Excellent

INFINITI

2000 INFINITI — JNK(CP11A)-Y-#

G20—4-Cyl.—Equipment Schedule 1
W.B. 102.4"; 2.0 Liter.
Sedan 4D	CP11A	24220	1050	1250	1850	3300
Touring			100	100	135	135
Manual, 5-Spd			(175)	(175)	(240)	(240)

I30—V6—Equipment Schedule 1
W.B. 108.3"; 3.0 Liter.
Sedan 4D	CA21A	29990	1425	1675	2050	3475
Touring			100	100	135	135

Q45—V8—Equipment Schedule 1
W.B. 111.4"; 4.1 Liter.
Sedan 4D	BY31A	49420	2125	2450	2950	4800
Touring			100	100	135	135
Anniversary Ed			175	175	240	240

2001 INFINITI — JNK(CP11A)-1-#

G20—4-Cyl.—Equipment Schedule 1
W.B. 102.4"; 2.0 Liter.
Sedan 4D	CP11A	24220	1375	1600	2100	3650
Touring			100	100	135	135
Manual, 5-Spd			(225)	(225)	(300)	(300)

I30—V6—Equipment Schedule 1
W.B. 108.3"; 3.0 Liter.
Sedan 4D	CA31A	29990	1675	1950	2400	3950
Touring			100	100	135	135

Q45—V8—Equipment Schedule 1
W.B. 111.4"; 4.1 Liter.
Sedan 4D	BY31A	49420	2725	3125	3475	5425
Touring			100	100	130	130

2002 INFINITI — JNK(CP11A)-2-#

G20—4-Cyl.—Equipment Schedule 1
W.B. 102.4"; 2.0 Liter.
Sedan 4D	CP11A	24340	1600	1875	2450	4150
Sport Pkg			125	125	155	155
Manual, 5-Spd			(275)	(275)	(355)	(355)

I35—V6—Equipment Schedule 1
W.B. 108.3"; 3.5 Liter.
Sedan 4D	DA31A	29295	2075	2400	2775	4500
Sport Pkg			125	125	175	175

Q45—V8—Equipment Schedule 1
W.B. 113.0"; 4.5 Liter.
Sedan 4D	BF01A	51045	3375	3850	4175	6275
Sport Pkg			125	125	175	175
Premium Pkg			600	600	785	785

2003 INFINITI — JNK(CV51E)-3-#

G35—V6—Equipment Schedule 1
W.B. 112.2"; 3.5 Liter.
Sedan 4D	CV51E	29495	2700	2950	3650	5625
Sport Coupe 2D	CV54E	32945	4650	5250	5450	8050

I35—V6—Equipment Schedule 1
W.B. 108.3"; 3.5 Liter.
Sedan 4D	DA31A	30995	2525	2875	3200	5050
Sport Pkg			175	175	245	245

M45—V8—Equipment Schedule 1
W.B. 110.2"; 4.5 Liter.
Sedan 4D	AY41E	43845	3025	3300	4575	6775
Intelligent Cruise Ctrl			250	250	320	320

Q45—V8—Equipment Schedule 1
W.B. 113.0"; 4.5 Liter.
Sedan 4D	BF01A	52545	4175	4725	4825	7000
Premium Sedan 4D	BF01A	62145	5900	6675	6725	9700
Intelligent Cruise Ctrl			250	250	300	300

Body Type	VIN	List	Trade-In Good	Trade-In Very Good	Pvt-Party Good	Retail Excellent

2004 INFINITI — JNK(CV51E)-4-#

G35—V6—Equipment Schedule 1
W.B. 112.2"; 3.5 Liter.

Body Type	VIN	List	Good	Very Good	Good	Excellent
Sedan 4D	CV51E	30690	3700	4025	4650	6800
Coupe 2D	CV54E	32140	5400	6050	6250	8950
AWD	F	-------	575	575	770	770

I35—V6—Equipment Schedule 1
W.B. 108.3"; 3.5 Liter.

Sedan 4D	DA31A	31190	3075	3475	3850	6000

M45—V8—Equipment Schedule 1
W.B. 110.2"; 4.5 Liter.

Sedan 4D	AY41E	44840	3750	4050	5375	7575

Q45—V8—Equipment Schedule 1
W.B. 113.0"; 4.5 Liter.

Sedan 4D	BF01A	52990	4575	5125	5300	7675
Premium Sedan 4D	BF01A	62190	6425	7225	7350	10550
Intelligent Cruise Ctrl		-------	275	275	345	345
Journey Pkg		-------	725	725	940	940

2005 INFINITI — JNK(CV51E)-5-#

G35—V6—Equipment Schedule 1
W.B. 112.2"; 3.5 Liter.

Sedan 4D	CV51E	31310	5100	5525	6175	8700
x AWD Sedan 4D	CV51F	34260	5150	5575	6250	8800
Coupe 2D	CV54E	31310	6475	7225	7375	10200

Q45—V8—Equipment Schedule 1
W.B. 113.0"; 4.5 Liter.

Sedan 4D	BF01A	56810	4525	5075	5575	8075
Intelligent Cruise Ctrl		-------	300	300	380	380
Premium Pkg		-------	800	800	1040	1040

2006 INFINITI — JNK(CV51E)-6-#

G35—V6—Equipment Schedule 1
W.B. 112.2"; 3.5 Liter.

Sedan 4D	CV51E	32150	6325	6800	7475	10150
x AWD Sedan 4D	CV51F	34710	6400	6875	7575	10300
Coupe 2D	CV54E	33900	8000	8850	8875	11950

M35—V6—Equipment Schedule 1
W.B. 114.2"; 3.5 Liter.

Sedan 4D	AY01E	41250	7450	7900	9450	12150
x AWD Sedan 4D	AY01F	44040	8175	8650	10100	12750
Sport Sedan 4D	AY01E	44050	7825	8300	9875	12650
Adaptive Cruise Control		-------	325	325	420	420
Journey Pkg		-------	375	375	510	510
Premium Pkg		-------	475	475	620	620

M45—V8—Equipment Schedule 1
W.B. 114.2"; 4.5 Liter.

Sedan 4D	BY01E	47560	8650	9150	10600	13400
Sport Sedan 4D	BY01E	50360	9875	10400	12300	15650
Adaptive Cruise Control		-------	325	325	420	420
Journey Pkg		-------	375	375	510	510
Premium Pkg		-------	575	575	775	775

Q45—V8—Equipment Schedule 1
W.B. 113.0"; 4.5 Liter.

Sport Sedan 4D	BF01A	58750	6050	6700	7400	10500
Adaptive Cruise Ctrl		-------	325	325	400	400
Premium Pkg		-------	850	850	1095	1095

2007 INFINITI — JNK(BV61E)-7-#

G35—V6—Equipment Schedule 1
W.B. 112.2"; 3.5 Liter.

Sedan 4D	BV61E	34500	8300	8850	9350	12150
Journey Sedan 4D	BV61E	34950	8400	8950	9475	12300
Sport Sedan 4D	BV61E	36500	8700	9275	9775	12700
x AWD Sedan 4D	BV61F	36800	8450	9025	9500	12310
Coupe 2D	CV54E	34150	9275	10150	10150	13250

M35—V6—Equipment Schedule 1
W.B. 114.2"; 3.5 Liter.

Sedan 4D	AY01E	42150	8675	9150	10850	13850
x AWD Sedan 4D	AY01F	45265	9175	9675	11500	14600
Sport Sedan 4D	AY01E	44950	9200	9700	11500	14600

2007 INFINITI

Body Type	VIN	List	Trade-In Good	Very Good	Pvt-Party Good	Retail Excellent
Intelligent Cruise Ctrl			350	350	455	455
Journey Pkg			400	400	525	525
Premium Pkg			500	500	655	655

M45—V8—Equipment Schedule 1
W.B. 114.2"; 4.5 Liter.

Body Type	VIN	List	Trade-In Good	Very Good	Pvt-Party Good	Retail Excellent
Sedan 4D	BY01E	49800	10000	10550	12400	15650
Sport Sedan 4D	BY01E	51200	11250	11800	13800	17400
Intelligent Cruise Ctrl			350	350	455	455
Premium Pkg			625	625	830	830

2008 INFINITI — JNK(BV61E)-8-#

G35—V6—Equipment Schedule 1
W.B. 112.2"; 3.5 Liter.

Body Type	VIN	List	Trade-In Good	Very Good	Pvt-Party Good	Retail Excellent
Sedan 4D	BV61E	32315	9650	10150	10950	13700
Journey Sedan 4D	BV61E	32765	9800	10350	11100	13950
Sport Sedan 4D	BV61E	33115	10100	10650	11400	14300
x AWD Sedan 4D	BV61F	34815	9800	10350	11100	13950

G37—V6—Equipment Schedule 1
W.B. 112.2"; 3.7 Liter.

Body Type	VIN	List	Trade-In Good	Very Good	Pvt-Party Good	Retail Excellent
Coupe 2D	CV64E	34965	11000	11800	12000	15050
Journey Coupe 2D	CV64E	35715	11300	12150	12350	15500
Sport Coupe 2D	CV64E	36265	11450	12300	12450	15650

M35—V6—Equipment Schedule 1
W.B. 114.2"; 3.5 Liter.

Body Type	VIN	List	Trade-In Good	Very Good	Pvt-Party Good	Retail Excellent
Sedan 4D	AY01E	43765	10650	11200	12550	15350
x AWD Sedan 4D	AY01F	45515	10850	11400	12900	15800
Adaptive Cruise Control			375	375	470	470
Premium Pkg			525	525	660	660

M45—V8—Equipment Schedule 1
W.B. 114.2"; 4.5 Liter.

Body Type	VIN	List	Trade-In Good	Very Good	Pvt-Party Good	Retail Excellent
Sedan 4D	BY01E	50065	11950	12550	14000	17050
x AWD Sedan 4D	BY01F	52565	13100	13750	15400	18750
Adaptive Cruise Control			375	375	465	465
Premium Pkg			525	525	660	660

2009 INFINITI — JNK(CV61E)-9-#

G37—V6—Equipment Schedule 1
W.B. 112.2"; 3.7 Liter.

Body Type	VIN	List	Trade-In Good	Very Good	Pvt-Party Good	Retail Excellent
Sedan 4D	CV61E	34115	11200	11700	12750	15500
Coupe 2D	CV64E	36765	12600	13300	13700	16600
Convertible 2D	CV66E	44715	14950	15800	16200	19600
Journey Sedan 4D	CV61E	34565	11400	11900	12950	15750
Journey Coupe 2D	CV64E	37515	12850	13600	14100	17100
Sport Sedan 4D	CV61E	35115	11900	12450	13450	16350
Sport Coupe 2D	CV64E	37865	13600	14440	14800	17850
Sport Convertible 2D	CV66E	44765	15650	16550	16900	20400
x AWD Sedan 4D	CV61F	36615	11400	11900	12950	15750
x AWD Coupe 2D	CV64F	39565	12750	13500	14000	16950

M35—V6—Equipment Schedule 1
W.B. 114.2"; 3.5 Liter.

Body Type	VIN	List	Trade-In Good	Very Good	Pvt-Party Good	Retail Excellent
Sedan 4D	CY01E	46615	12350	12950	14350	17400
x AWD Sedan 4D	CY01F	48765	12700	13350	14750	17800
Premium Pkg			550	550	685	685

M45—V8—Equipment Schedule 1
W.B. 114.2"; 4.5 Liter.

Body Type	VIN	List	Trade-In Good	Very Good	Pvt-Party Good	Retail Excellent
Sedan 4D	BY01E	52965	14150	14850	16650	20200
x AWD Sedan 4D	BY01F	56765	15450	16150	17900	21700
Premium Pkg			550	550	685	685

2010 INFINITI — JNK(CV6AE)-A-#

G37—V6—Equipment Schedule 1
W.B. 112.2"; 3.7 Liter.

Body Type	VIN	List	Trade-In Good	Very Good	Pvt-Party Good	Retail Excellent
Sedan 4D	CV6AE	34115	12900	13350	14750	17400
Coupe 2D	CV6EE	36915	14400	15000	15850	18800
Sport Sedan 4D	CV6AE	37865	14000	14450	15850	18650
Sport Coupe 2D	CV6EE	41265	15500	16200	17000	20100
Sport Convertible 2D	CV6FE	47815	18750	19550	20200	23900
Anniversary Ed Sed	CV6AE	44215	14800	15300	16700	19700
Anniversary Ed Cpe	CV6EE	51415	19800	20700	21200	24900
Anniversary Ed Conv	CV6FE	55765	21600	22600	23100	27100
AWD	F		0	0	0	0

2010 INFINITI

Body Type	VIN	List	Trade-In Good	Very Good	Pvt-Party Good	Retail Excellent
G37—V6—Equipment Schedule 1						
W.B. 112.2"; 3.7 Liter.						
Convertible 2D	CV6FE	45215	17750	18550	19250	22800
Journey Sedan 4D	CV6AE	36315	13000	13450	14850	17600
Journey Coupe 2D	CV6EE	39365	14900	15550	16350	19400
x AWD Sedan 4D	CV6AF	37915	13050	13500	14900	17650
x AWD Coupe 2D	CV6EF	41015	15000	15650	16500	19600
Intelligent Cruise Ctrl			400	400	470	470
Premium Pkg			575	575	690	690
Sport Pkg			550	550	680	680
M35—V6—Equipment Schedule 1						
W.B. 114.2"; 3.5 Liter.						
Sedan 4D	CY0AP	46665	15000	15650	16950	20100
x AWD Sedan 4D	CY0AR	48815	15350	16050	17400	20600
M45—V8—Equipment Schedule 1						
W.B. 114.2"; 4.5 Liter.						
Sedan 4D	BY0AP	53015	16900	17650	19050	22500
x AWD Sedan 4D	BY0AR	56815	18150	18950	20400	24100
Premium Pkg			575	575	695	695

2011 INFINITI — JN1(DV6AE)–B–#

Body Type	VIN	List	Trade-In Good	Very Good	Pvt-Party Good	Retail Excellent
G25—V6—Equipment Schedule 1						
W.B. 112.2"; 2.5 Liter.						
Sedan 4D	DV6AE	31825	12400	12750	14100	16300
Journey Sedan 4D	DV6AE	34225	12850	13200	14650	16950
x AWD Sedan 4D	DV6AF	35825	13250	13600	15150	17500
G37—V6—Equipment Schedule 1						
W.B. 112.2"; 3.7 Liter.						
Coupe 2D	CV6EE	36925	16450	16950	18100	21000
Sport Appearance Ed	CV6AE	40075	15700	16150	17850	20600
Sport Sedan 4D	CV6AE	40325	16350	16800	18450	21300
Sport Coupe 2D	CV6EE	41275	17650	18250	19350	22500
Sport Convertible 2D	CV6FE	49825	21300	21900	23100	26800
Limited Ed Sedan 4D	CV6AE	44275	17500	18000	19600	22500
x AWD Sport Appear	CV6AF	41675	16300	16700	18350	21200
G37—V6—Equipment Schedule 1						
W.B. 112.2" 3.7 Liter.						
Convertible 2D	CV6FE	45375	20200	20800	22000	25500
Journey Sedan 4D	CV6AE	36925	14750	15150	16750	19400
Journey Coupe 2D	CV6EE	39525	16550	17050	18250	21200
x AWD Sedan 4D	CV6AF	38525	15150	15550	17200	19900
x AWD Coupe 2D	CV6EF	41025	17000	17550	18700	21700
Intelligent Cruise Ctrl			425	425	505	505
Premium Pkg			600	600	715	715
Sport Pkg			600	600	735	735
G IPL—V6—Equipment Schedule 1						
W.B. 112.2"; 3.7 Liter.						
Coupe 2D	CV6EE	50725	21500	22200	23300	27100
M37—V6—Equipment Schedule 1						
W.B. 114.2"; 3.7 Liter.						
Sedan 4D	BY1AP	47115	19250	20100	21300	24900
x AWD Sedan 4D	BY1AR	49265	19500	20300	21500	25000
Premium Pkg			600	600	705	705
Technology Pkg			1275	1275	1510	1510
Sport Pkg			600	600	725	725
Sport Touring Pkg			900	900	1065	1065
Deluxe Touring Pkg			900	900	1065	1065
M56—V8—Equipment Schedule 1						
W.B. 114.2"; 5.6 Liter.						
Sedan 4D	AY1AP	58415	21000	21900	23200	27100
x AWD Sedan 4D	AY1AR	62215	22300	23200	24500	28600
Premium Pkg			600	600	700	700
Technology Pkg			1275	1275	1500	1500
Sport Pkg			600	600	720	720
Sport Touring Pkg			900	900	1060	1060
Deluxe Touring Pkg			900	900	1060	1060

2012 INFINITI — (3orJ)N1(DV6AE)–C–#

Body Type	VIN	List	Trade-In Good	Very Good	Pvt-Party Good	Retail Excellent
G25—V6—Equipment Schedule 1						
W.B. 112.2"; 2.5 Liter.						
Sedan 4D	DV6AE	33295	13600	13950	15550	17600
Journey Sedan 4D	DV6AE	35695	14700	15000	16650	18900

2012 INFINITI

Body Type	VIN	List	Trade-In Good	Very Good	Pvt-Party Good	Retail Excellent
x AWD Sedan 4D	DV6AF	37295	**14900**	**15200**	**16900**	**19150**
G37—V6—Equipment Schedule 1						
W.B. 112.2"; 3.7 Liter.						
Coupe 2D	CV6EE	38495	**19300**	**19800**	**21000**	**23900**
Sport Appearance 4D	CV6AE	40245	**17550**	**17900**	**19700**	**22300**
Sport Sedan 4D	CV6AE	41495	**18200**	**18600**	**20400**	**23000**
Sport Coupe 2D	CV6EE	44695	**21000**	**21500**	**22800**	**25900**
Sport Convertible 2D	CV6FE	51745	**24600**	**25300**	**26600**	**30200**
Limited Ed Sedan 4D	CV6AE	45445	**19850**	**20300**	**22100**	**24900**
G37—V6—Equipment Schedule 1						
W.B. 112.2"; 3.7 Liter.						
Convertible 2D	CV6FE	47295	**23800**	**24400**	**25700**	**29200**
Journey Sedan 4D	CV6AE	37095	**17050**	**17450**	**19150**	**21700**
Journey Coupe 2D	CV6EE	39945	**20000**	**20500**	**21700**	**24700**
x AWD Sedan 4D	CV6AF	38695	**17250**	**17650**	**19400**	**22000**
x AWD Coupe 2D	CV6EF	41595	**20600**	**21100**	**22400**	**25400**
Intelligent Speed Ctrl		------	450	450	520	520
Premium Pkg		------	625	625	745	745
Sport Pkg		------	675	675	795	795
G IPL—V6—Equipment Schedule 1						
W.B. 112.2"; 3.7 Liter.						
Coupe 2D	CV6EE	52145	**24800**	**25400**	**26800**	**30400**
M35—V6 Hybrid—Equipment Schedule 1						
W.B. 114.2"; 3.5 Liter.						
Sedan 4D	EY1AP	54575	**22900**	**23800**	**24800**	**28600**
Premium Pkg		------	625	625	720	720
Deluxe Touring Pkg		------	925	925	1045	1045
Technology Pkg		------	1325	1325	1520	1520
M37—V6—Equipment Schedule 1						
W.B. 114.2"; 3.7 Liter.						
Sedan 4D	BY1AP	48575	**22200**	**23100**	**24100**	**27800**
x AWD Sedan 4D	BY1AF	50725	**22800**	**23800**	**25000**	**29100**
Premium Pkg		------	625	625	725	725
Technology Pkg		------	1325	1325	1530	1530
Sport Pkg		------	675	675	775	775
Sport Touring Pkg		------	925	925	1050	1050
Deluxe Touring Pkg		------	925	925	1050	1050
M56—V8—Equipment Schedule 1						
W.B. 114.2"; 5.6 Liter.						
Sedan 4D	AY1AP	59975	**26100**	**27100**	**28100**	**32400**
x AWD Sedan 4D	AY1AF	63775	**27300**	**28400**	**29300**	**33700**
Technology Pkg		------	1325	1325	1515	1515
Sport Pkg		------	675	675	765	765
Sport Touring Pkg		------	925	925	1040	1040
Deluxe Touring Pkg		------	925	925	1040	1040

2013 INFINITI — (3orJ)N1(CV6FE)-D-#

Body Type	VIN	List	Trade-In Good	Very Good	Pvt-Party Good	Retail Excellent
G37—V6—Equipment Schedule 1						
W.B. 112.2"; 3.7 Liter.						
Sport Sedan 4D	CV6AP	42395	**20900**	**21300**	**23100**	**25700**
Sport Coupe 2D	CV6EK	46405	**22300**	**22800**	**24200**	**27200**
Sport Convertible 2D	CV6FE	52895	**27800**	**28300**	**29800**	**33400**
G37—V6—Equipment Schedule 1						
W.B. 112.2"; 3.7 Liter.						
Convertible 2D	CV6FE	48095	**26300**	**26800**	**28300**	**31700**
Journey Sedan 4D	CV6AP	37795	**18950**	**19300**	**21100**	**23500**
Journey Coupe 2D	CV6EK	41305	**21100**	**21500**	**22900**	**25700**
x AWD Sedan 4D	CV6AR	39395	**19500**	**19900**	**21700**	**24100**
x AWD Coupe 2D	CV6EL	42955	**21400**	**21900**	**23300**	**26200**
Intelligent Cruise Control		------	475	475	535	535
Premium Pkg		------	675	675	785	785
Sport Pkg		------	775	775	880	880
G IPL—V6—Equipment Schedule 1						
W.B. 112.2"; 3.7 Liter.						
Coupe 2D	CV6EK	53295	**26700**	**27300**	**28800**	**32300**
Convertible 2D	CV6FE	61495	**30300**	**30900**	**32400**	**36200**
M35—V6 Hybrid—Equipment Schedule 1						
W.B. 114.2"; 3.5 Liter.						
Sedan 4D	EY1AP	55655	**26400**	**27500**	**28400**	**32600**
Premium Pkg		------	675	675	765	765
Technology Pkg		------	1400	1400	1575	1575
Touring Pkg		------	950	950	1055	1055

Body Type	VIN	List	Trade-In Good	Very Good	Pvt-Party Good	Retail Excellent
M37—V6—Equipment Schedule 1						
W.B. 114.2"; 3.7 Liter.						
Sedan 4D	BY1AP	49605	25800	26800	27800	31900
x AWD Sedan 4D	BY1AR	51755	26400	27400	28300	32400
Premium Pkg			675	675	770	770
Sport Pkg			775	775	860	860
Technology Pkg			1400	1400	1580	1580
Touring Pkg			950	950	1060	1060
M56—V8—Equipment Schedule 1						
W.B. 114.2"; 5.6 Liter.						
Sedan 4D	AY1AP	62105	29700	30800	31700	36200
x AWD Sedan 4D	AY1AR	64605	30900	32100	33000	37600
Sport Pkg			775	775	855	855
Technology Pkg			1400	1400	1570	1570
Touring Pkg			950	950	1050	1050

2014 INFINITI — (3orJ)N1(AV7AP)-E-#

Body Type	VIN	List	Trade-In Good	Very Good	Pvt-Party Good	Retail Excellent
Q50—V6—Equipment Schedule 1						
W.B. 112.2"; 3.7 Liter.						
3.7 Sedan 4D		37605	25700	26100	27600	30500
3.7 Premium Sed		40455	26100	26600	28100	31200
3.7 S Sedan 4D		44105	28300	28900	30400	33600
Technology Pkg			750	750	840	840
Deluxe Touring Pkg			550	550	630	630
AWD			1475	1475	1645	1645
Q50—V6 Hybrid—Equipment Schedule 1						
W.B. 112.2"; 3.5 Liter.						
Premium Sedan 4D	AV7AP	44605	27100	27600	29200	32200
S Sedan 4D		47255	29000	29500	31200	34300
AWD			1475	1475	1645	1645
Q60—V6—Equipment Schedule 1						
W.B. 112.2"; 3.7 Liter.						
Journey Coupe 2D	CV6EK	41305	24500	25000	26400	29400
Convertible 2D	CV6FE	48805	31100	31700	33000	36600
S Coupe 2D	CV6EK	46405	28000	28600	29900	33200
S Convertible 2D	CV6FE	53655	32600	33200	34500	38300
IPL Convertible 2D	CV6FE	62355	34400	35100	36300	40200
Intelligent Cruise Control			500	500	550	550
Q60 AWD—V6—Equipment Schedule 1						
W.B. 112.2"; 3.7 Liter.						
Coupe 2D	CV6EK	42955	25700	26200	27600	30800
Intelligent Cruise Control			500	500	550	550
Q70—V6—Equipment Schedule 1						
W.B. 114.2"; 3.7 Liter.						
3.7 Sedan 4D	BY1AP	50405	30700	31900	32900	37600
Intelligent Cruise Control			500	500	540	540
Deluxe Touring Pkg			975	975	1065	1065
Premium Pkg			725	725	810	810
Sport Pkg			875	875	955	955
Technology Pkg			1475	1475	1630	1630
AWD	R		1475	1475	1630	1630
Q70—V6 Hybrid—Equipment Schedule 1						
W.B. 114.2"; 3.5 Liter.						
Sedan 4D	EY1AP	56455	31900	33100	34000	38700
Intelligent Cruise Control			500	500	540	540
Deluxe Touring Pkg			975	975	1060	1060
Premium Pkg			725	725	805	805
Technology Pkg			1475	1475	1625	1625
Q70—V8—Equipment Schedule 1						
W.B. 114.2"; 5.6 Liter.						
5.6 Sedan 4D	AY1AP	64205	35200	36500	37100	42000
AWD	R		1475	1475	1625	1625

JAGUAR

2000 JAGUAR — SAJ(DorJ)(A01C)-Y-#

Body Type	VIN	List	Trade-In Good	Very Good	Pvt-Party Good	Retail Excellent
S-TYPE—V6—Equipment Schedule 1						
W.B. 114.5"; 3.0 Liter.						
Sedan 4D	A01C	44980	950	1125	1525	2500
Sport Pkg			125	125	165	165

2000 JAGUAR

Body Type	VIN	List	Trade-In Good	Very Good	Pvt-Party Good	Retail Excellent
S-TYPE—V8—Equipment Schedule 1						
W.B. 114.5"; 4.0 Liter.						
Sedan 4D	A01D	48580	1575	1825	2275	3625
Sport Pkg			125	125	165	165
XJ8—V8—Equipment Schedule 1						
W.B. 113.0", 117.9" (L & Vanden Plas); 4.0 Liter.						
Sedan 4D	A14C	56245	700	850	1375	2425
L Sedan 4D	A23C	61295	1150	1325	1800	3050
Vanden Plas Sedan 4D	A24C	65345	2175	2500	2975	4825
XJR—V8 Supercharged—Equipment Schedule 1						
W.B. 113.0"; 4.0 Liter.						
Sedan 4D	A15B	69145	1200	1425	2400	4375
XJ8—V8 Supercharged—Equipment Schedule 1						
W.B. 117.9"; 4.0 Liter.						
Vanden Plas Sedan 4D	A14B	81245	1550	1775	3150	5875
XK8—V8—Equipment Schedule 2						
W.B. 101.9"; 4.0 Liter.						
Coupe 2D	A41C	66795	1875	2025	2775	4275
Convertible 2D	A42C	71795	3125	3400	4125	6050
XKR—V8 Supercharged—Equipment Schedule 2						
W.B. 101.9"; 4.0 Liter.						
Coupe 2D	A41B	77395	4500	4900	5100	6675
Convertible 2D	A42B	82395	6475	7000	7050	9150

2001 JAGUAR — SAJD(A01C)-1-#

Body Type	VIN	List	Trade-In Good	Very Good	Pvt-Party Good	Retail Excellent
S-TYPE—V6—Equipment Schedule 1						
W.B. 114.5"; 3.0 Liter.						
Sedan 4D	A01C	46250	1275	1475	1925	3100
Sport Pkg			125	125	170	170
S-TYPE—V8—Equipment Schedule 1						
W.B. 114.5"; 4.0 Liter.						
Sedan 4D	A01D	49950	1925	2200	2625	4150
Sport Pkg			125	125	170	170
XJ8—V8—Equipment Schedule 1						
W.B. 113.0", 117.9" (L & Vanden Plas); 4.0 Liter.						
Sedan 4D	A14C	56950	750	875	1475	2600
L Sedan 4D	A23C	62950	1175	1375	1975	3325
Vanden Plas Sedan 4D	A24C	68250	2350	2700	3225	5200
XJR—V8 Supercharged—Equipment Schedule 1						
W.B. 113.0"; 4.0 Liter.						
Sedan 4D	A15B	69930	1250	1450	2475	4500
XJ8—V8 Supercharged—Equipment Schedule 1						
W.B. 117.9"; 4.0 Liter.						
Vanden Plas Sedan 4D	A25B	83950	2025	2275	3375	5900
XK8—V8—Equipment Schedule 2						
W.B. 101.9"; 4.0 Liter.						
Coupe 2D	A41C	69750	2025	2200	2925	4425
Convertible 2D	A42C	74750	3225	3500	4250	6150
XKR—V8 Supercharged—Equipment Schedule 2						
W.B. 101.9"; 4.0 Liter.						
Coupe 2D	A41B	80750	5800	6275	6375	8250
Convertible 2D	A42B	85750	7600	8175	8150	10500

2002 JAGUAR — SAJ-(A51D)-2-#

Body Type	VIN	List	Trade-In Good	Very Good	Pvt-Party Good	Retail Excellent
X-TYPE AWD—V6—Equipment Schedule 2						
W.B. 106.7"; 2.5 Liter, 3.0 Liter.						
2.5L Sedan 4D	A51D	34370	1225	1450	2275	4175
2.5L Sport Sedan 4D	A53D	36370	1250	1475	2300	4200
3.0L Sedan 4D	A51C	39095	1400	1650	2425	4375
3.0L Sport Sedan 4D	A53C	41095	1525	1800	2550	4475
Manual, 5-Spd			(275)	(275)	(380)	(380)
S-TYPE—V6—Equipment Schedule 1						
W.B. 114.5"; 3.0 Liter.						
Sedan 4D	A01C	46320	1500	1750	2125	3325
Sport			575	575	760	760
Manual, 5-Spd			(275)	(275)	(380)	(380)
S-TYPE—V8—Equipment Schedule 1						
W.B. 114.5"; 4.0 Liter.						
Sedan 4D	A01D	49975	2175	2500	2900	4500
Sport			575	575	760	760
XJ8—V8—Equipment Schedule 1						
W.B. 113.0"; 4.0 Liter.						

Body Type	VIN	List	Trade-In Good	Very Good	Pvt-Party Good	Retail Excellent
Sedan 4D	A14C	56975	875	1025	1575	2725
XJ SPORT—V8—Equipment Schedule 1						
W.B. 113.0"; 4.0 Liter.						
Sedan 4D	A14C	59975	1425	1625	2200	3625
XJ VANDEN PLAS—V8—Equipment Schedule 1						
W.B. 117.9"; 4.0 Liter.						
Sedan 4D	A24C	68975	2525	2875	3325	5250
XJR—V8 Supercharged—Equipment Schedule 1						
W.B. 113.0"; 4.0 Liter.						
Sedan 4D	A15B	72475	1600	1850	2875	5100
100 Sedan 4D	A15B	....	3650	4175	5075	8250
XJ SUPER—V8 Supercharged—Equipment Schedule 1						
W.B. 117.9"; 4.0 Liter.						
Sedan 4D	A25B	79975	3250	3650	4600	7325
XK8—V8—Equipment Schedule 2						
W.B. 101.9"; 4.0 Liter.						
Coupe 2D	A41C	69975	2225	2400	3375	5175
Convertible 2D	A42C	74975	4525	4875	5700	8050
XKR—V8 Supercharged—Equipment Schedule 2						
W.B. 101.9"; 4.0 Liter.						
Coupe 2D	A41B	82975	6450	6950	7100	9175
Convertible 2D	A42B	87975	8375	9000	9000	11550
100 Coupe 2D	A41B	84000	****	****	****	17400
100 Convertible 2D	A42B	86975	****	****	****	16450

2003 JAGUAR — SAJ-(A51D)-3-#

Body Type	VIN	List	Trade-In Good	Very Good	Pvt-Party Good	Retail Excellent
X-TYPE AWD—V6—Equipment Schedule 2						
W.B. 106.7"; 2.5 Liter, 3.0 Liter.						
2.5L Sedan 4D	A51D	29950	1725	2000	2775	4800
3.0L Sedan 4D	A51C	36950	1925	2250	3000	5100
Sport Pkg		....	500	500	665	665
Manual, 5-Spd		....	(325)	(325)	(425)	(425)
S-TYPE—V6—Equipment Schedule 1						
W.B. 114.5"; 3.0 Liter.						
Sedan 4D	A01T	44975	1600	1850	2250	3475
Sport Pkg		....	650	650	855	855
Manual, 5-Spd		....	(325)	(325)	(425)	(425)
V8, 4.2 Liter	U	....	450	450	585	585
S-TYPE R—V8 Supercharged—Equipment Schedule 1						
W.B. 114.5"; 4.2 Liter.						
Sedan 4D	A03V	62400	4400	5025	5250	7775
XJ8—V8—Equipment Schedule 1						
W.B. 113.0"; 4.0 Liter.						
Sedan 4D	A14C	56975	1825	2075	2600	4150
XJ SPORT—V8—Equipment Schedule 1						
W.B. 113.0"; 4.0 Liter.						
Sedan 4D	A12C	59975	2350	2675	3275	5100
XJ VANDEN PLAS—V8—Equipment Schedule 1						
W.B. 117.9"; 4.0 Liter.						
Sedan 4D	A24C	68975	2750	3125	3825	6050
XJR—V8 Supercharged—Equipment Schedule 1						
W.B. 113.0"; 4.0 Liter.						
Sedan 4D	A15B	72475	2525	2875	3975	6650
XJ SUPER—V8 Supercharged—Equipment Schedule 1						
W.B. 117.9"; 4.0 Liter.						
Sedan 4D	A25B	79975	5575	6200	6875	10350
XK8—V8—Equipment Schedule 2						
W.B. 101.9"; 4.2 Liter.						
Coupe 2D	A41C	69975	3175	3400	4200	6050
Convertible 2D	A42C	74975	5450	5850	6475	8725
XKR—V8 Supercharged—Equipment Schedule 2						
W.B. 101.9"; 4.2 Liter.						
Coupe 2D	A41B	81975	7225	7750	8325	11050
Convertible 2D	A42B	86975	9250	9900	10100	13000
Handling Pkg		....	1225	1225	1345	1345

2004 JAGUAR — SAJ-(WA51D)-4-#

Body Type	VIN	List	Trade-In Good	Very Good	Pvt-Party Good	Retail Excellent
X-TYPE AWD—V6—Equipment Schedule 2						
W.B. 106.7"; 2.5 Liter, 3.0 Liter.						
2.5L Sedan 4D	WA51D	30520	1875	2175	2975	5050
3.0L Sedan 4D	WA51C	33995	2075	2400	3150	5300
Sport Pkg		....	550	550	735	735

Body Type	VIN	List	Trade-In Good	Very Good	Pvt-Party Good	Retail Excellent
Manual, 5-Spd		......	(350)	(350)	(475)	(475)
S-TYPE—V6—Equipment Schedule 1						
W.B. 114.5"; 3.0 Liter.						
Sedan 4D	WA01T	44995	2075	2375	2700	4050
Sport Pkg		......	725	725	950	950
Manual, 5-Spd		......	(350)	(350)	(475)	(475)
V8, 4.2 Liter		......	475	475	620	620
S-TYPE R—V8 Supercharged—Equipment Schedule 1						
W.B. 114.5"; 4.2 Liter.						
Sedan 4D	WA03V	63120	5025	5675	6175	9150
XJ8—V8—Equipment Schedule 1						
W.B. 119.4"; 4.2 Liter.						
Sedan 4D	WA71C	59995	2000	2250	2750	4275
XJ VANDEN PLAS—V8—Equipment Schedule 1						
W.B. 119.4"; 4.2 Liter.						
Sedan 4D	WA74C	68995	3825	4325	4725	7050
XJR—V8 Supercharged—Equipment Schedule 1						
W.B. 119.4"; 4.2 Liter.						
Sedan 4D	WA73B	74995	3400	3850	4575	7075
XK8—V8—Equipment Schedule 2						
W.B. 101.9"; 4.2 Liter.						
Coupe 2D	WA41C	69995	3800	4075	4950	6875
Convertible 2D	WA42C	74995	6250	6675	7325	9800
XKR—V8 Supercharged—Equipment Schedule 2						
W.B. 101.9"; 4.2 Liter.						
Coupe 2D	WA41B	82995	8150	8700	9525	12750
Convertible 2D	WA42B	87995	12050	12850	12650	15850
Handling Pkg		......	1300	1300	1475	1475

2005 JAGUAR — SAJD(WA51D)-5-#

Body Type	VIN	List	Trade-In Good	Very Good	Pvt-Party Good	Retail Excellent
X-TYPE AWD—V6—Equipment Schedule 2						
W.B. 106.7"; 2.5 Liter, 3.0 Liter.						
2.5L Sedan 4D	WA51D	32245	2175	2500	3400	5575
3.0L Sedan 4D	WA51C	34995	2275	2600	3525	5750
3.0L Wagon 4D	WA54C	36995	4050	4625	5275	8075
Sport Pkg		......	600	600	800	800
VDP Edition		......	1000	1000	1335	1335
Manual, 5-Spd		......	(400)	(400)	(520)	(520)
S-TYPE—V6—Equipment Schedule 1						
W.B. 114.5"; 3.0 Liter.						
Sedan 4D	WA01T	45995	2525	2850	3575	5525
Sport Pkg		......	775	775	1045	1045
VDP Edition		......	875	875	1165	1165
V8, 4.2 Liter		......	500	500	655	655
S-TYPE R—V8 Supercharged—Equipment Schedule 1						
W.B. 114.5"; 4.2 Liter.						
Sedan 4D	WA03V	58995	6975	7850	8750	12950
XJ8—V8—Equipment Schedule 1						
W.B. 119.4", 124.4" (L); 4.2 Liter.						
Sedan 4D	WA71C	61495	4150	4675	5300	7650
L Sedan 4D	WA79C	63495	5375	6000	6550	9325
XJ VANDEN PLAS—V8—Equipment Schedule 1						
W.B. 124.4"; 4.2 Liter.						
Sedan 4D	WA82C	70995	6900	7725	8175	11650
XJR—V8 Supercharged—Equipment Schedule 1						
W.B. 119.4"; 4.2 Liter.						
Sedan 4D	WA73B	75995	5750	6425	7600	11500
XJ SUPER—V8 Supercharged—Equipment Schedule 1						
W.B. 124.4"; 4.2 Liter.						
Sedan 4D	WA82B	89995	6500	7150	8000	11600
XK8—V8—Equipment Schedule 2						
W.B. 101.9"; 4.2 Liter.						
Coupe 2D	DA41C	70495	4950	5275	6300	8500
Convertible 2D	DA42C	75495	7175	7650	8525	11250
XKR—V8 Supercharged—Equipment Schedule 2						
W.B. 101.9"; 4.2 Liter.						
Coupe 2D	DA41B	82995	11000	11700	12400	15900
Convertible 2D	DA42B	87995	14750	15650	15850	20000
Handling Pkg		......	1400	1400	1650	1650

Body Type	VIN	List	Trade-In Good	Very Good	Pvt-Party Good	Retail Excellent

2006 JAGUAR — SAJ–(WA51A)–6–#

X-TYPE AWD—V6—Equipment Schedule 2
W.B. 106.7"; 3.0 Liter.

Body Type	VIN	List	Good	Very Good	Good	Excellent
3.0L Sedan 4D	WA51A	32995	3050	3425	4225	6575
3.0L Wagon 4D	WA54A	36995	4825	5425	5975	8825
Sport Pkg			650	650	870	870
VDP Edition			1100	1100	1460	1460

S-TYPE—V6—Equipment Schedule 1
W.B. 114.5"; 3.0 Liter.

Sedan 4D	WA01A	45995	3150	3550	4250	6300
VDP Edition			950	950	1270	1270
V8, 4.2 Liter	B		575	575	755	755

S-TYPE R—V8 Supercharged—Equipment Schedule 1
W.B. 114.5"; 4.2 Liter.

Sedan 4D	WA03C	63995	7525	8425	9225	13300
Adaptive Cruise Control			325	325	420	420

XJ8—V8—Equipment Schedule 1
W.B. 119.4", 124.4" (L); 4.2 Liter.

Sedan 4D	WA71B	62495	5125	5700	6300	8825
L Sedan 4D	WA79B	64995	7325	8125	8625	12000

XJ VANDEN PLAS—V8—Equipment Schedule 1
W.B. 124.4"; 4.2 Liter.

Sedan 4D	WA82B	74995	8425	9325	9700	13450

XJR—V8 Supercharged—Equipment Schedule 1
W.B. 119.4"; 4.2 Liter.

Sedan 4D	WA73C	79995	6750	7500	8475	12250

XJ SUPER—V8 Supercharged—Equipment Schedule 1
W.B. 124.4"; 4.2 Liter.

Sedan 4D	WA82C	91995	8800	9625	10100	13900
Portfolio Sedan 4D	WA86C	115995	23600	25600	23300	29800

XK8—V8—Equipment Schedule 2
W.B. 101.9"; 4.2 Liter.

Coupe 2D	DA41C	70495	6575	6975	8025	10550
Convertible 2D	DA42C	75495	8825	9350	10300	13350
Adaptive Cruise Control			325	325	395	395

XKR—V8 Supercharged—Equipment Schedule 2
W.B. 101.9"; 4.2 Liter.

Coupe 2D	DA41B	82995	13050	13800	14350	18000
Convertible 2D	DA42B	87995	16700	17650	17600	21600
Adaptive Cruise Control			325	325	365	365
Handling Pkg			1500	1500	1725	1725

2007 JAGUAR — SAJ–(WA51A)–7–#

X-TYPE AWD—V6—Equipment Schedule 2
W.B. 106.7"; 3.0 Liter.

3.0L Sedan 4D	WA51A	34995	4075	4525	5300	7775
3.0L Wagon 4D	WA54A	39995	5800	6450	7050	9975
Luxury Pkg			375	375	510	510

S-TYPE—V6—Equipment Schedule 1
W.B. 114.5"; 3.0 Liter.

Sedan 4D	WA01A	49000	4525	5050	5550	7775
V8, 4.2 Liter	B		675	675	885	885

S-TYPE R—V8 Supercharged—Equipment Schedule 1
W.B. 114.5"; 4.2 Liter.

Sedan 4D	WA03C	64000	9800	10900	11300	15600
Adaptive Cruise Control			350	350	450	450

XJ8—V8—Equipment Schedule 1
W.B. 119.4", 124.4" (L); 4.2 Liter.

Sedan 4D	WA71B	64250	7400	8125	8500	11350
L Sedan 4D	WA79B	67750	9725	10650	10900	14450

XJ VANDEN PLAS—V8—Equipment Schedule 1
W.B. 124.4"; 4.2 Liter.

Sedan 4D	WA82B	75500	10700	11750	11950	15850

XJR—V8 Supercharged—Equipment Schedule 1
W.B. 119.4"; 4.2 Liter.

Sedan 4D	WA73C	81500	7850	8625	9500	13150

XJ SUPER—V8 Supercharged—Equipment Schedule 1
W.B. 124.4"; 4.2 Liter.

Sedan 4D	WA82C	92000	9300	10050	10850	14850

XK—V8—Equipment Schedule 2
W.B. 108.3"; 4.2 Liter.

Body Type	VIN	List	Trade-In Good	Very Good	Pvt-Party Good	Retail Excellent
Coupe 2D	WA43B	75500	13350	14050	14800	18350
Convertible 2D	WA44B	81500	15350	16150	16900	21000
Adaptive Cruise Control			350	350	385	385
Luxury Pkg			975	975	1095	1095

XKR—V8 Supercharged—Equipment Schedule 2
W.B. 108.3"; 4.2 Liter.

Body Type	VIN	List	Trade-In Good	Very Good	Pvt-Party Good	Retail Excellent
Coupe 2D	WA43C	86500	15450	16250	16400	19800
Convertible 2D	WA44C	92500	17000	17900	18100	21900
Adaptive Cruise Control			350	350	370	370
Luxury Pkg			975	975	1045	1045

2008 JAGUAR — SAJ-(WA51A)-8-#

X-TYPE AWD—V6—Equipment Schedule 2
W.B. 106.7"; 3.0 Liter.

Body Type	VIN	List	Trade-In Good	Very Good	Pvt-Party Good	Retail Excellent
3.0L Sedan 4D	WA51A	35725	4925	5375	6400	8900
3.0L Wagon 4D	WA54A	39995	6825	7400	8125	10850
Luxury Pkg			400	400	535	535

S-TYPE—V6—Equipment Schedule 1
W.B. 114.5"; 3.0 Liter.

Body Type	VIN	List	Trade-In Good	Very Good	Pvt-Party Good	Retail Excellent
Sedan 4D	WA01A	50000	6275	6925	7725	10450
Satin Edition			1125	1125	1360	1360
V8, 4.2 Liter	B		775	775	935	935

S-TYPE R—V8 Supercharged—Equipment Schedule 1
W.B. 114.5"; 4.2 Liter.

Body Type	VIN	List	Trade-In Good	Very Good	Pvt-Party Good	Retail Excellent
Sedan 4D	WA03C	66000	11700	12800	13250	17500
Adaptive Cruise Control			375	375	435	435
Luxury Pkg			375	375	455	455

XJ8—V8—Equipment Schedule 1
W.B. 119.4", 124.4" (L); 4.2 Liter.

Body Type	VIN	List	Trade-In Good	Very Good	Pvt-Party Good	Retail Excellent
Sedan 4D	WA71B	65500	10000	10750	11300	14400
L Sedan 4D	WA79B	69000	12400	13300	13750	17500

XJ VANDEN PLAS—V8—Equipment Schedule 1
W.B. 124.4"; 4.2 Liter.

Body Type	VIN	List	Trade-In Good	Very Good	Pvt-Party Good	Retail Excellent
Sedan 4D	WA82B	77750	13500	14450	14850	18850

XJR—V8 Supercharged—Equipment Schedule 1
W.B. 119.4"; 4.2 Liter.

Body Type	VIN	List	Trade-In Good	Very Good	Pvt-Party Good	Retail Excellent
Sedan 4D	WA73C	85250	13050	14000	14800	19250

XJ SUPER—V8 Supercharged—Equipment Schedule 1
W.B. 124.4"; 4.2 Liter.

Body Type	VIN	List	Trade-In Good	Very Good	Pvt-Party Good	Retail Excellent
Sedan 4D	WA82C	95750	12900	13800	14550	18800

XK—V8—Equipment Schedule 2
W.B. 108.3"; 4.2 Liter.

Body Type	VIN	List	Trade-In Good	Very Good	Pvt-Party Good	Retail Excellent
Coupe 2D	WA43B	76500	15350	16000	16950	20500
Convertible 2D	WA44B	82500	19100	19950	21000	25400
Adaptive Cruise Control			375	375	415	415
Luxury Pkg			1000	1000	1125	1125

XKR—V8 Supercharged—Equipment Schedule 2
W.B. 108.3"; 4.2 Liter.

Body Type	VIN	List	Trade-In Good	Very Good	Pvt-Party Good	Retail Excellent
Coupe 2D	WA43C	87700	18900	19750	20100	23600
Portfolio Coupe 2D	WA45C	99700	21300	22200	22800	27000
Convertible 2D	WA44C	93700	20500	21400	21800	25600
Portfolio Conv 2D	WA46C	104800	22300	23300	23800	28200
Adaptive Cruise Control			375	375	400	400
Luxury Pkg			1000	1000	1085	1085

2009 JAGUAR — SAJ-(WA05B)-9-#

XF—V8—Equipment Schedule 1
W.B. 114.5"; 4.2 Liter.

Body Type	VIN	List	Trade-In Good	Very Good	Pvt-Party Good	Retail Excellent
Luxury Sedan 4D	WA05B	49975	11700	12400	13450	16950
Prem Luxury Sed 4D	WA06B	55975	13050	13800	14700	18350

XF—V8 Supercharged—Equipment Schedule 1
W.B. 114.5"; 4.2 Liter.

Body Type	VIN	List	Trade-In Good	Very Good	Pvt-Party Good	Retail Excellent
Sedan 4D	WA07C	62975	14400	15250	16300	20600

XJ8—V8—Equipment Schedule 1
W.B. 119.4", 124.4" (L); 4.2 Liter.

Body Type	VIN	List	Trade-In Good	Very Good	Pvt-Party Good	Retail Excellent
Sedan 4D	WA71B	66475	12350	13100	14250	17950
L Sedan 4D	WA79B	69975	14750	15600	16800	21200

VANDEN PLAS—V8—Equipment Schedule 1
W.B. 124.4"; 4.2 Liter.

Body Type	VIN	List	Trade-In Good	Very Good	Pvt-Party Good	Retail Excellent
Sedan 4D	WA82B	76850	16450	17350	18400	23000

XJR—V8 Supercharged—Equipment Schedule 1
W.B. 119.4"; 4.2 Liter.

Body Type	VIN	List	Trade-In Good	Very Good	Pvt-Party Good	Retail Excellent
Sedan 4D	WA73C	84350	14250	15050	16550	21200
XJ SUPER—V8 Supercharged—Equipment Schedule 1						
W.B. 124.4"; 4.2 Liter.						
Sedan 4D	WA82C	94850	14700	15550	16450	20400
Portfolio Sedan 4D	WA86C	105000	31100	32700	31700	37400
XK—V8—Equipment Schedule 2						
W.B. 108.3"; 4.2 Liter.						
Coupe 2D	WA43B	77775	18200	18850	20000	23400
Convertible 2D	WA44B	83775	22300	23100	24500	28700
Luxury Pkg			1025	1025	1155	1155
XKR—V8 Supercharged—Equipment Schedule 2						
W.B. 108.3"; 4.2 Liter.						
Coupe 2D	WA43C	88175	21200	22000	22800	26300
Convertible 2D	WA44C	94175	23600	24500	25300	29100
Portfolio Coupe 2D	WA45C	95975	23400	24300	25300	29500
Portfolio Conv 2D	WA46C	101975	24500	25300	26300	30600
Luxury Pkg			1025	1025	1110	1110

2010 JAGUAR — SAJ-(WA0FA)-A-#

Body Type	VIN	List	Trade-In Good	Very Good	Pvt-Party Good	Retail Excellent
XF—V8—Equipment Schedule 1						
W.B. 114.5"; 4.2 Liter, 5.0 Liter (Premium).						
Sports Sedan 4D	WA0FA	52000	15100	15750	17050	20700
Premium Sedan 4D	WA0GB	57000	16000	16700	17900	21600
XF—V8 Supercharged—Equipment Schedule 1						
W.B. 114.5"; 5.0 Liter.						
Sports Sedan 4D	WA0HE	68000	19350	20200	21500	26000
XFR—V8 Supercharged—Equipment Schedule 1						
W.B. 114.5"; 5.0 Liter.						
Sports Sedan 4D	WA0JC	80000	25400	26500	28000	33800
XK—V8—Equipment Schedule 2						
W.B. 108.3"; 5.0 Liter.						
Coupe 2D	WA4DB	83000	23800	24500	25800	29200
Convertible 2D	WA4EB	89000	28100	28900	30300	34500
XKR—V8 Supercharged—Equipment Schedule 2						
W.B. 108.3"; 5.0 Liter.						
Coupe 2D	WA4DC	96000	25500	26300	27900	32000
Convertible 2D	WA4EC	102000	28000	28800	30300	34600

2011 JAGUAR — SAJ-(WA0FB)-B-#

Body Type	VIN	List	Trade-In Good	Very Good	Pvt-Party Good	Retail Excellent
XF—V8—Equipment Schedule 1						
W.B. 114.5"; 5.0 Liter.						
Sports Sedan 4D	WA0FB	53000	18900	19500	21100	24800
Premium Sedan 4D	WA0GB	57000	19850	20500	22100	26000
XF—V8 Supercharged—Equipment Schedule 1						
W.B. 114.5"; 5.0 Liter.						
Sports Sedan 4D	WA0HE	68000	23400	24100	25900	30500
XFR—V8 Supercharged—Equipment Schedule 1						
W.B. 114.5"; 5.0 Liter.						
Sports Sedan 4D	WA0JC	80000	29700	30600	32600	38200
XJ—V8—Equipment Schedule 2						
W.B. 119.4", 124.3" (XJL); 5.0 Liter.						
XJ Sedan 4D	WA1CB	72500	26000	26900	27900	32200
XJL Sedan 4D	WA2CB	79500	27500	28400	29600	34300
Luxury Pkg			1075	1075	1190	1190
XJ—V8 Supercharged—Equipment Schedule 2						
W.B. 119.4", 124.3" (XJL); 5.0 Liter.						
XJ Sedan 4D	WA1GE	87500	31900	32900	34000	39000
XJL Sedan 4D	WA2GE	90500	32100	33100	34100	39300
XJ SUPERSPORT—V8 Supercharged—Equipment Schedule 2						
W.B. 119.4", 124.3" (XJL); 5.0 Liter.						
XJ Sedan 4D	WA1JC	110000	41800	43100	43700	50000
XJL Sedan 4D	WA2JC	113000	46000	47400	47700	54100
XK—V8—Equipment Schedule 2						
W.B. 108.3"; 5.0 Liter.						
Coupe 2D	WA4FB	83000	28200	28900	30200	33500
Convertible 2D	WA4GB	89000	32900	33600	34900	38700
XKR—V8 Supercharged—Equipment Schedule 2						
W.B. 108.3"; 5.0 Liter.						
Coupe 2D	WA4DC	96000	33300	34100	35700	39800
Convertible 2D	WA4EC	102000	35800	36600	38100	42400
XKR175—V8 Supercharged—Equipment Schedule 2						
W.B. 108.3"; 5.0 Liter.						

Body Type	VIN	List	Trade-In Good	Very Good	Pvt-Party Good	Retail Excellent
75th Anniv Coupe	WA4DC	105500	37800	38700	40300	44800

2012 JAGUAR — SAJ-(WA0FB)-C-#

XF—V8—Equipment Schedule 1
W.B. 114.5"; 5.0 Liter.

Sedan 4D	WA0FB	53875	23500	24000	25700	29300
Portfolio Sedan 4D	WA0GB	59875	26000	26600	28700	32900

XF—V8 Supercharged—Equipment Schedule 1
W.B. 114.5"; 5.0 Liter.

Sedan 4D	WA0HE	68975	31000	31700	33700	38400

XFR—V8 Supercharged—Equipment Schedule 1
W.B. 114.5" ; 5.0 Liter.

Sedan 4D	WA0JC	82875	37800	38700	40300	46300

XJ—Equipment Schedule 2
W.B. 119.4", 124.3" (XJL); 5.0 Liter.

XJ Sedan 4D	WA1CB	74575	29300	30000	31400	35600
XJL Portfolio Sedan	WA2GB	81575	34400	35300	36500	41200

XJ—V8 Supercharged—Equipment Schedule 2
W.B. 119.4", 124.3" (XJL); 5.0 Liter.

XJ Sedan 4D	WA1GE	89475	38100	39100	40200	45300
XJL Sedan 4D	WA2GE	92475	40000	40900	42000	47200

XJ SUPERSPORT—V8 Supercharged—Equipment Schedule 2
W.B. 119.4", 124.3" (XJL); 5.0 Liter.

XJ Sedan 4D	WA1JC	112075	49500	50700	51800	58000
XJL Sedan 4D	WA2JC	118575	52100	53400	54300	60600

XK—V8—Equipment Schedule 2
W.B. 108.3"; 5.0 Liter.

Coupe 2D	WA4FB	85375	36500	37300	38800	42500
Convertible 2D	WA4GB	91375	42100	42900	44400	48500

XKR—V8 Supercharged—Equipment Schedule 2
W.B. 108.3"; 5.0 Liter.

Coupe 2D	WA4DC	98375	41100	41900	43700	47900
Convertible 2D	WA4EC	104375	43800	44700	46700	51100

XKR-S—V8 Supercharged—Equipment Schedule 2
W.B. 108.3"; 5.0 Liter.

Coupe 2D	WA4HA	132875	54500	55600	57700	63300
Convertible 2D	WA4JA	138875	57800	59000	60900	66500

2013 JAGUAR — SAJ-(WA0E7)-D-#

XF—V6 Supercharged—Equipment Schedule 1
W.B. 114.5"; 3.0 Liter.

Sedan 4D	WA0E7	50875	28000	28500	30300	33900
AWD	J		1275	1275	1455	1455
4-Cyl, Turbo, 2.0 Liter	S		(1300)	(1300)	(1470)	(1470)

XF—V8 Supercharged—Equipment Schedule 1
W.B. 114.5"; 5.0 Liter.

Sedan 4D	WA0HE	68975	39300	40000	42000	46600

XFR—V8 Supercharged—Equipment Schedule 1
W.B. 114.5" ; 5.0 Liter.

Sedan 4D	WA0JC	84075	44700	45500	47800	53300

XFR-S—V8 Supercharged—Equipment Schedule 1
W.B. 114.5"; 5.0 Liter.

Sedan 4D	WA0KZ	99895				

XJ—V6 Supercharged—Equipment Schedule 2
W.B. 119.4"; 3.0 Liter.

XJ Sedan 4D	WA1C7	74075	36100	36900	38500	43300
AWD	J		1275	1275	1395	1395

XJ—V8—Equipment Schedule 2
W.B. 124.3"; 5.0 Liter.

XJL Portfolio Sedan	WA2GB	82075	41200	42000	43400	48400
AWD	J		1275	1275	1410	1410
V6, Supercharged, 3.0L	D		975	975	1065	1065

XJ—V8 Supercharged—Equipment Schedule 2
W.B. 119.4", 124.3" (XJL); 5.0 Liter.

XJ Sedan 4D	WA1GE	90475	45000	45900	47400	52900
XJL Sedan 4D	WA2GE	93475	46800	47700	49100	54800

XJ SUPERSPORT—V8 Supercharged—Equipment Schedule 2
W.B. 119.4", 124.3" (XJL); 5.0 Liter.

XJ Sedan 4D	WA1JC	113075	56300	57400	58600	64800
XJL Sedan 4D	WA2JC	119875	58900	60100	61200	67400
XJL Ultimate Sedan	WA2KC	155875	99000	100900	99900	108000

Body Type	VIN	List	Trade-In Good	Very Good	Pvt-Party Good	Retail Excellent
XK—V8—Equipment Schedule 2						
W.B. 108.3"; 5.0 Liter.						
Coupe 2D	WA4FB	85375	41100	41900	44700	49500
Convertible 2D	WA4GB	91375	45800	46600	49600	54700
Touring Coupe 2D	WA4DB	79875	41700	42400	45300	50200
Touring Conv 2D	WA4EB	85875	45200	46000	49000	54100
XKR—V8 Supercharged—Equipment Schedule 2						
W.B. 108.3"; 5.0 Liter.						
Coupe 2D	WA4DC	98375	47700	48600	50600	54800
Convertible 2D	WA4EC	104375	50700	51600	53600	58000
XKR-S—V8 Supercharged—Equipment Schedule 2						
W.B. 108.3"; 5.0 Liter.						
Coupe 2D	WA4HA	132875	61900	63000	65200	70600
Convertible 2D	WA4JA	138875	64700	65900	67900	73500

2014 JAGUAR — SAJ-(WA6E7)-E-#

Body Type	VIN	List	Trade-In Good	Very Good	Pvt-Party Good	Retail Excellent
F-TYPE—V6 Supercharged—Equipment Schedule 2						
W.B. 103.2"; 3.0 Liter.						
Convertible 2D	WA6E7	69895	47700	48600	50400	54200
S Convertible 2D	WA6FC	81895	53000	53900	55500	59500
F-TYPE AWD—V8 Supercharged—Equipment Schedule 2						
W.B. 103.2"; 5.0 Liter.						
S Convertible 2D	WA6GL	92895	62900	64100	65200	69500
XF—V6 Supercharged—Equipment Schedule 1						
W.B. 114.5"; 3.0 Liter.						
Sedan 4D	WA0EX	51395	32700	33300	35100	38800
Adaptive Cruise Control			500	500	550	550
AWD	J		1375	1375	1545	1545
4-Cyl, Turbo, 2.0 Liter	S		(1375)	(1375)	(1525)	(1525)
XF—V8 Supercharged—Equipment Schedule 1						
W.B. 114.5"; 5.0 Liter.						
Sedan 4D	WA0HP	68995	44100	44900	46800	51500
Adaptive Cruise Control			500	500	535	535
XFR—V8 Supercharged—Equipment Schedule 1						
W.B. 114.5"; 5.0 Liter.						
Sedan 4D	WA0JH	84095	50000	50800	53300	58900
Adaptive Cruise Control			500	500	545	545
XFR-S—V8 Supercharged—Equipment Schedule 1						
W.B. 114.5"; 5.0 Liter.						
Sedan 4D	WA0KH	99895	64600	65700	67300	73300
XJ—V6 Supercharged—Equipment Schedule 2						
W.B. 119.4"; 3.0 Liter.						
XJ Sedan 4D	WA1CZ	75095	49000	49900	51300	56500
Adaptive Cruise Control			500	500	525	525
Portfolio Pkg			1275	1275	1350	1350
AWD	J		1375	1375	1475	1475
XJ—V6 Supercharged—Equipment Schedule 2						
W.B. 124.3"; 3.0 Liter.						
XJL Portfolio Sedan	WA2GZ	82095	53000	54000	55600	61500
Adaptive Cruise Control			500	500	530	530
AWD	J		1375	1375	1495	1495
XJ—V8 Supercharged—Equipment Schedule 2						
W.B. 119.4", 124.3" (XJL, XJR LWB); 5.0 Liter.						
XJ Sedan 4D	WA1GT	91495	56200	57200	58500	64500
XJL Sedan 4D	WA2GT	94495	59700	60800	61900	68000
XJR Sedan 4D	WA1EK	116895	69000	70400	71200	78000
XJR LWB Sedan 4D	WA2EK	119895	71100	72400	73100	80000
Adaptive Cruise Control			500	500	525	525
XK—V8—Equipment Schedule 2						
W.B. 108.3"; 5.0 Liter.						
Coupe 2D	WA4FB	85395	55900	56900	59400	64600
Convertible 2D	WA4GB	91395	59200	60300	62800	68200
Touring Coupe 2D	WA4DB	79895	56400	57400	60000	65400
Touring Conv 2D	WA4EB	85895	60300	61400	63800	69200
Adaptive Cruise Control			500	500	525	525
Portfolio Pkg			1275	1275	1355	1355
XKR—V8 Supercharged—Equipment Schedule 2						
W.B. 108.3"; 5.0 Liter.						
Coupe 2D	WA4DC	98395	65200	66400	68200	73400
Convertible 2D	WA4EC	104395	68200	69400	70700	75500
Adaptive Cruise Control			500	500	520	520
Black Pkg			775	775	810	810
Dynamic Pkg			1000	1000	1060	1060

Body Type	VIN	List	Trade-In Good	Very Good	Pvt-Party Good	Retail Excellent
Dynamic & Black Pack			1925	1925	2050	2050
Portfolio Pkg			1275	1275	1345	1345
XKR-S—V8 Supercharged—Equipment Schedule 2						
W.B. 108.3"; 5.0 Liter.						
Coupe 2D	WA4HC	132895	77300	78700	80200	86000
Convertible 2D	WA4JC	138895	80100	81600	83000	88900
Bright Pack			850	850	905	905
XKR-S—V8 Supercharged—Equipment Schedule 2						
W.B. 108.3"; 5.0 Liter.						
GT Coupe 2D	WA4HA	174895	****	****	****	128000

KIA

2000 KIA — KNA(FA121)–Y–#

SEPHIA—4-Cyl.—Equipment Schedule 6
W.B. 100.8"; 1.8 Liter.

Body Type	VIN	List	Good	Very Good	Good	Excellent
Sedan 4D	FA121	11605	400	500	1025	1925
LS Sedan 4D	FA121	12345	550	675	1250	2325
SPECTRA—4-Cyl.—Equipment Schedule 6						
W.B. 100.8"; 1.8 Liter.						
GS Sedan 4D	FB161	11245	350	450	925	1725
GSX Sedan 4D	FB161	13445	475	600	1150	2150

2001 KIA — KNA(DC123)–1–#

RIO—4-Cyl.—Equipment Schedule 6
W.B. 94.9"; 1.5 Liter.

Body Type	VIN	List	Good	Very Good	Good	Excellent
Sedan 4D	DC123	11755	275	350	925	1775
SEPHIA—4-Cyl.—Equipment Schedule 6						
W.B. 100.8"; 1.8 Liter.						
Sedan 4D	FB121	11945	475	550	1200	2275
LS Sedan 4D	FB121	12645	675	800	1475	2775
SPECTRA—4-Cyl.—Equipment Schedule 6						
W.B. 100.8"; 1.8 Liter.						
GS Hatchback 4D	FB161	12345	375	475	1025	1775
GSX Hatchback 4D	FB161	13645	625	750	1275	2300
OPTIMA—4-Cyl.—Equipment Schedule 5						
W.B. 106.3"; 2.4 Liter.						
LX Sedan 4D	GD126	16599	350	425	1100	2100
SE Sedan 4D	GD126	18899	925	1075	1825	3275
V6, 2.5 Liter		4	100	100	135	135

2002 KIA — KNA(DC123)–2–#

RIO—4-Cyl.—Equipment Schedule 6
W.B. 94.9"; 1.5 Liter.

Body Type	VIN	List	Good	Very Good	Good	Excellent
Sedan 4D	DC123	12120	450	550	1250	2475
Cinco Wagon 4D	DC163	10465	300	375	1175	2450
SPECTRA—4-Cyl.—Equipment Schedule 6						
W.B. 100.8"; 1.8 Liter.						
Sedan 4D	FB121	12450	325	400	900	1650
GS Hatchback 4D	FB161	12850	525	650	1175	2150
LS Sedan 4D	FB121	13090	600	725	1250	2250
GSX Hatchback 4D	FB161	14090	750	900	1450	2575
OPTIMA—4-Cyl.—Equipment Schedule 5						
W.B. 106.3"; 2.4 Liter.						
LX Sedan 4D	GD126	16244	550	675	1400	2625
SE Sedan 4D	GD126	17894	1275	1450	2250	3975
V6, 2.7 Liter		8	150	150	200	200

2003 KIA — KNA(DC125)–3–#

RIO—4-Cyl.—Equipment Schedule 6
W.B. 94.9"; 1.6 Liter.

Body Type	VIN	List	Good	Very Good	Good	Excellent
Sedan 4D	DC125	12780	650	775	1650	3225
Cinco Wagon 4D	DC165	10620	475	575	1525	3100
SPECTRA—4-Cyl.—Equipment Schedule 6						
W.B. 100.8"; 1.8 Liter.						
Sedan 4D	FB121	12715	375	450	1100	2075
GS Hatchback 4D	FB161	13140	575	675	1300	2400
LS Sedan 4D	FB121	13320	675	775	1400	2550
GSX Hatchback 4D	FB161	14360	875	1000	1725	3125

Body Type	VIN	List	Trade-In Good	Very Good	Pvt-Party Good	Retail Excellent
OPTIMA—4-Cyl.—Equipment Schedule 5						
W.B. 106.3"; 2.4 Liter.						
LX Sedan 4D	GD126	16915	725	850	1650	3050
SE Sedan 4D	GD126	18590	1425	1600	2450	4300
V6, 2.7 Liter	8		225	225	300	300

2004 KIA — KNA(DC125)–4–#

RIO—4-Cyl.—Equipment Schedule 6						
W.B. 94.9"; 1.6 Liter.						
Sedan 4D	DC125	12930	825	975	1800	3400
Cinco Wagon 4D	DC165	11155	650	775	1750	3450
SPECTRA—4-Cyl.—Equipment Schedule 6						
W.B. 100.8", 102.8" (LX & EX); 1.8 Liter, 2.0 Liter.						
Sedan 4D	FB121	13320	600	700	1275	2275
GS Hatchback 4D	FB161	13580	825	950	1525	2675
LS Sedan 4D	FB121	13590	650	750	1400	2525
LX Sedan 4D	FB121	14120	825	950	1525	2675
EX Sedan 4D	FB121	14290	975	1125	1725	2975
GSX Hatchback 4D	FB161	14630	1150	1325	1900	3250
OPTIMA—4-Cyl.—Equipment Schedule 5						
W.B. 106.3"; 2.4 Liter.						
LX Sedan 4D	GD126	16960	900	1025	1850	3300
EX Sedan 4D	GD126	18635	1550	1750	2775	4800
V6, 2.7 Liter	8		275	275	375	375
AMANTI—V6—Equipment Schedule 3						
W.B. 110.2"; 3.5 Liter.						
Sedan 4D	LD124	25535	1475	1650	2350	3925

2005 KIA — KNA(DC125)–5–#

RIO—4-Cyl.—Equipment Schedule 6						
W.B. 94.9"; 1.6 Liter.						
Sedan 4D	DC125	13835	1050	1225	2150	3825
Cinco Wagon 4D	DC165	11155	950	1125	2125	3850
SPECTRA—4-Cyl.—Equipment Schedule 6						
W.B. 102.8"; 2.0 Liter.						
LX Sedan 4D	FE121	14135	1100	1250	1875	3050
EX Sedan 4D	FE121	15265	1375	1575	2275	3650
SX Sedan 4D	FE121	16510	1475	1700	2400	3825
SPECTRA5—4-Cyl.—Equipment Schedule 6						
W.B. 102.8"; 2.0 Liter.						
Hatchback 4D	FE161	16510	1600	1825	2525	4025
OPTIMA—4-Cyl.—Equipment Schedule 5						
W.B. 106.3"; 2.4 Liter.						
LX Sedan 4D	GD126	17740	1125	1275	2275	3875
EX Sedan 4D	GD126	19190	1925	2175	3425	5725
V6, 2.7 Liter	8		325	325	445	445
AMANTI—V6—Equipment Schedule 3						
W.B. 110.2"; 3.5 Liter.						
Sedan 4D	LD124	25840	1650	1875	2850	4675

2006 KIA — KNA(DE123)–6–#

RIO—4-Cyl.—Equipment Schedule 6						
W.B. 98.4"; 1.6 Liter.						
Sedan 4D	DE123	11110	1075	1250	2200	3850
RIO—4-Cyl.—Equipment Schedule 6						
W.B. 98.4"; 1.6 Liter.						
LX Sedan 4D	DE123	14125	1825	2125	2825	4625
Manual, 5-Spd			(275)	(275)	(355)	(355)
RIO5—4-Cyl.—Equipment Schedule 6						
W.B. 98.4"; 1.6 Liter.						
SX Hatchback 4D	DE163	14040	1650	1900	2850	4750
SPECTRA—4-Cyl.—Equipment Schedule 6						
W.B. 102.8"; 2.0 Liter.						
LX Sedan 4D	FE121	13475	1125	1300	2100	3375
SPECTRA—4-Cyl.—Equipment Schedule 6						
W.B. 102.8"; 2.0 Liter.						
EX Sedan 4D	FE121	15840	1650	1875	2675	4275
SX Sedan 4D	FE121	17140	1975	2225	3050	4825
Manual, 5-Spd			(275)	(275)	(355)	(355)
SPECTRA5—4-Cyl.—Equipment Schedule 6						
W.B. 102.8"; 2.0 Liter.						
Hatchback 4D	FE161	17140	2100	2350	3175	5025

Body Type	VIN	List	Trade-In Good	Very Good	Pvt-Party Good	Retail Excellent
Manual, 5-Spd.			(275)	(275)	(355)	(355)
OPTIMA—4-Cyl.—Equipment Schedule 5						
W.B. 106.3"; 2.4 Liter.						
LX Sedan 4D	GD126	18040	1500	1700	2800	4600
EX Sedan 4D	GD126	19490	2400	2675	3775	6025
V6, 2.7 Liter	8		375	375	510	510
OPTIMA (2006.5)—4-Cyl.—Equipment Schedule 5						
W.B. 107.1"; 2.4 Liter.						
LX Sedan 4D	GE123	18250	1900	2050	2975	4500
V6, 2.7 Liter	4		375	375	510	510
OPTIMA (2006.5)—V6—Equipment Schedule 5						
W.B. 107.1"; 2.7 Liter.						
EX Sedan 4D	GE124	21000	2600	2800	3775	5625
4-Cyl, 2.4 Liter	3		(450)	(450)	(600)	(600)
AMANTI—V6—Equipment Schedule 3						
W.B. 110.2"; 3.5 Liter.						
Sedan 4D	LD124	28435	2800	3100	3775	5600

2007 KIA — KNA(DE123)-7-#

Body Type	VIN	List	Trade-In Good	Very Good	Pvt-Party Good	Retail Excellent
RIO—4-Cyl.—Equipment Schedule 6						
W.B. 98.4"; 1.6 Liter.						
Sedan 4D	DE123	11350	1500	1725	2625	4300
RIO—4-Cyl.—Equipment Schedule 6						
W.B. 98.4"; 1.6 Liter.						
LX Sedan 4D	DE123	14925	2225	2550	3275	5200
SX Sedan 4D	DE123	14290	2150	2450	3250	5125
Manual, 5-Spd			(300)	(300)	(385)	(385)
RIO5—4-Cyl.—Equipment Schedule 6						
W.B. 98.4"; 1.6 Liter.						
SX Hatchback 4D	DE163	14330	2125	2400	3350	5375
Automatic			300	300	385	385
SPECTRA—4-Cyl.—Equipment Schedule 6						
W.B. 102.8"; 2.0 Liter.						
LX Sedan 4D	FE121	13495	1550	1725	2525	3900
SPECTRA—4-Cyl.—Equipment Schedule 6						
W.B. 102.8"; 2.0 Liter.						
EX Sedan 4D	FE121	16495	2375	2650	3450	5225
SX Sedan 4D	FE121	17595	2875	3175	3975	6000
Manual, 5-Spd			(300)	(300)	(385)	(385)
SPECTRA5—4-Cyl.—Equipment Schedule 6						
W.B. 102.8"; 2.0 Liter.						
SX Hatchback 4D	FE161	17595	2950	3275	4225	6350
Manual, 5-Spd			(300)	(300)	(385)	(385)
RONDO—V6—Equipment Schedule 4						
W.B. 106.3"; 2.7 Liter.						
LX Wagon 4D	FG526	19495	2875	3150	3950	5800
EX Wagon 4D	FG526	20795	3200	3525	4450	6500
4-Cyl, 2.4 Liter	5		(225)	(225)	(315)	(315)
OPTIMA—4-Cyl.—Equipment Schedule 5						
W.B. 107.1"; 2.4 Liter.						
LX Sedan 4D	GE123	18250	2825	3050	4025	5900
Manual, 5-Spd			(400)	(400)	(520)	(520)
V6, 2.7 Liter	4		425	425	575	575
OPTIMA—4-Cyl.—Equipment Schedule 5						
W.B. 107.1"; 2.4 Liter.						
EX Sedan 4D	GE123	19995	3350	3600	4775	6925
V6, 2.7 Liter	4		425	425	575	575
AMANTI—V6—Equipment Schedule 3						
W.B. 110.2"; 3.8 Liter.						
Sedan 4D	LD125	26175	3800	4175	4925	7025

2008 KIA — KNA(DE123)-8-#

Body Type	VIN	List	Trade-In Good	Very Good	Pvt-Party Good	Retail Excellent
RIO—4-Cyl.—Equipment Schedule 6						
W.B. 98.4"; 1.6 Liter.						
Sedan 4D	DE123	11515	1875	2075	3000	4600
RIO—4-Cyl.—Equipment Schedule 6						
W.B. 98.4"; 1.6 Liter.						
LX Sedan 4D	DE123	14390	2775	3125	3775	5750
SX Sedan 4D	DE123	14725	3000	3325	4100	6050
Manual, 5-Spd w/Overdrive			(350)	(350)	(460)	(460)
RIO5—4-Cyl.—Equipment Schedule 6						
W.B. 98.4"; 1.6 Liter.						

Body Type	VIN	List	Trade-In Good	Very Good	Pvt-Party Good	Retail Excellent
LX Hatchback 4D	DE163	15090	**3075**	**3375**	**4100**	**5950**
Manual, 5-Spd w/Overdrive			**(350)**	**(350)**	**(460)**	**(460)**
RIO5—4-Cyl.—Equipment Schedule 6						
W.B. 98.4"; 1.6 Liter.						
SX Hatchback 4D	DE163	14495	**2925**	**3250**	**4100**	**6100**
Automatic, 4-Spd w/OD			**300**	**300**	**400**	**400**
SPECTRA—4-Cyl.—Equipment Schedule 6						
W.B. 102.8"; 2.0 Liter.						
LX Sedan 4D	FE121	14520	**2450**	**2675**	**3475**	**4975**
EX Sedan 4D	FE121	16520	**2925**	**3175**	**4100**	**5850**
SX Sedan 4D	FE121	17620	**3400**	**3675**	**4625**	**6550**
Manual, 5-Spd w/Overdrive			**(350)**	**(350)**	**(460)**	**(460)**
SPECTRA5—4-Cyl.—Equipment Schedule 6						
W.B. 102.8"; 2.0 Liter.						
SX Hatchback 4D	FE161	17620	**3600**	**3900**	**4850**	**6850**
Manual, 5-Spd w/Overdrive			**(350)**	**(350)**	**(460)**	**(460)**
RONDO—V6—Equipment Schedule 4						
W.B. 106.3"; 2.7 Liter.						
LX Wagon 4D	FG526	19495	**3300**	**3575**	**4775**	**6850**
EX Wagon 4D	FG526	20795	**3875**	**4175**	**5350**	**7600**
4-Cyl, 2.4 Liter	5		**(250)**	**(250)**	**(340)**	**(340)**
OPTIMA—4-Cyl.—Equipment Schedule 5						
W.B. 107.1"; 2.4 Liter.						
LX Sedan 4D	GE123	18390	**3450**	**3650**	**4850**	**6750**
EX Sedan 4D	GE123	20135	**4050**	**4275**	**5525**	**7650**
Manual, 5-Spd w/Overdrive			**(400)**	**(400)**	**(540)**	**(540)**
V6, 2.7 Liter	4		**475**	**475**	**645**	**645**
AMANTI—V6—Equipment Schedule 3						
W.B. 110.2"; 3.8 Liter.						
Sedan 4D	LD125	26195	**4950**	**5325**	**6250**	**8350**

2009 KIA — KNA(DE123)-9-#

Body Type	VIN	List	Trade-In Good	Very Good	Pvt-Party Good	Retail Excellent
RIO—4-Cyl.—Equipment Schedule 6						
W.B. 98.4"; 1.6 Liter.						
Sedan 4D	DE123	12145	**2450**	**2675**	**3550**	**5125**
RIO—4-Cyl.—Equipment Schedule 6						
W.B. 98.4"; 1.6 Liter.						
LX Sedan 4D	DE223	14825	**3400**	**3750**	**4525**	**6525**
SX Sedan 4D	DE223	15390	**3600**	**3925**	**4850**	**6800**
Manual, 5-Spd w/Overdrive			**(375)**	**(375)**	**(490)**	**(490)**
RIO5—4-Cyl.—Equipment Schedule 6						
W.B. 98.4"; 1.6 Liter.						
SX Hatchback 4D	DE163	14930	**3350**	**3625**	**4675**	**6650**
Automatic, 4-Spd w/OD			**325**	**325**	**445**	**445**
RIO5—4-Cyl.—Equipment Schedule 6						
W.B. 98.4"; 1.6 Liter.						
LX Hatchback 4D	DE243	15525	**3450**	**3750**	**4650**	**6475**
Manual, 5-Spd w/Overdrive			**(375)**	**(375)**	**(490)**	**(490)**
SPECTRA—4-Cyl.—Equipment Schedule 6						
W.B. 102.8"; 2.0 Liter.						
LX Sedan 4D	FE221	14850	**3225**	**3425**	**4325**	**5775**
EX Sedan 4D	FE221	16750	**3700**	**3925**	**4900**	**6575**
SX Sedan 4D	FE221	17750	**4200**	**4475**	**5450**	**7275**
Manual, 5-Spd w/Overdrive			**(375)**	**(375)**	**(490)**	**(490)**
SPECTRA5—4-Cyl.—Equipment Schedule 6						
W.B. 102.8"; 2.0 Liter.						
SX Hatchback 4D	FE241	17995	**4425**	**4700**	**5675**	**7575**
Manual, 5-Spd w/Overdrive			**(375)**	**(375)**	**(490)**	**(490)**
RONDO—V6—Equipment Schedule 4						
W.B. 106.3"; 2.7 Liter.						
LX Wagon 4D	FG526	20145	**4700**	**4975**	**6100**	**8175**
EX Wagon 4D	FG526	22945	**5175**	**5500**	**6800**	**9050**
4-Cyl, 2.4 Liter	5		**(275)**	**(275)**	**(370)**	**(370)**
OPTIMA—4-Cyl.—Equipment Schedule 5						
W.B. 107.1"; 2.4 Liter.						
LX Sedan 4D	GE123	19625	**4825**	**5050**	**6400**	**8300**
EX Sedan 4D	GE123	21350	**5350**	**5575**	**7000**	**9100**
SX Sedan 4D	GE123	21815	**6025**	**6300**	**7750**	**10000**
Manual, 5-Spd w/Overdrive			**(450)**	**(450)**	**(585)**	**(585)**
V6, 2.7 Liter	4		**550**	**550**	**735**	**735**
AMANTI—V6—Equipment Schedule 3						
W.B. 110.2"; 3.8 Liter.						
Sedan 4D	LD225	26795	**6525**	**6925**	**7800**	**9875**

Body Type	VIN	List	Trade-In Good	Very Good	Pvt-Party Good	Retail Excellent
2010 KIA — KN(AorD)(DF4A3)–A–#						
RIO—4-Cyl.—Equipment Schedule 6 W.B. 98.4"; 1.6 Liter.						
Sedan 4D	DF4A3	12390	3150	3375	4250	5825
RIO—4-Cyl.—Equipment Schedule 6 W.B. 98.4"; 1.6 Liter.						
LX Sedan 4D	DH4A3	16790	4650	5025	5775	7825
SX Sedan 4D	DH4A3	16490	4850	5175	6150	8250
Manual, 5-Spd w/Overdrive			(450)	(450)	(615)	(615)
RIO5—4-Cyl.—Equipment Schedule 6 W.B. 98.4"; 1.6 Liter.						
LX Hatchback 4D	DG5A3	14590	4225	4525	5500	7350
Automatic, 4-Spd w/OD			375	375	510	510
RIO5—4-Cyl.—Equipment Schedule 6 W.B. 98.4"; 1.6 Liter.						
SX Hatchback 4D	DH5A3	16790	5075	5400	6350	8425
Manual, 5-Spd w/Overdrive			(450)	(450)	(615)	(615)
SOUL—4-Cyl.—Equipment Schedule 6 W.B. 100.4"; 2.0 Liter.						
Wagon 4D	JT2A1	13995	5375	5700	6700	8675
+ Wagon 4D	JT2A2	15645	6775	7200	8175	10450
Sport Wagon 4D	JT2A2	17645	7225	7550	8825	11000
! Wagon 4D	JT2A2	17645	7225	7650	8600	11000
Automatic, 4-Spd w/OD			375	375	505	505
FORTE—4-Cyl.—Equipment Schedule 6 W.B. 104.3"; 2.0 Liter, 2.4 Liter (SX).						
LX Sedan 4D	FT4A2	15390	4825	5150	6350	8425
EX Sedan 4D	FT4A2	17490	5700	6075	7100	9200
Koup EX Coupe 2D	FU6A2	18290	6600	7025	8100	10550
SX Sedan 4D	FW4A3	18890	6925	7375	8400	10800
Koup SX Coupe 2D	FW6A3	19390	7300	7775	8750	11200
OPTIMA—4-Cyl.—Equipment Schedule 5 W.B. 107.1"; 2.4 Liter.						
LX Sedan 4D	GG4A3	19890	6125	6325	7725	9575
EX Sedan 4D	GH4A3	21690	6775	7000	8475	10550
SX Sedan 4D	GH4A3	22490	7300	7575	9150	11350
Manual, 5-Spd w/Overdrive			(475)	(475)	(620)	(620)
V6, 2.7 Liter	4		625	625	810	810
RONDO—4-Cyl.—Equipment Schedule 4 W.B. 106.3"; 2.4 Liter.						
LX Wagon 4D	HG8C8	19890	6450	6750	8075	10250
2011 KIA — KN(AorD)(DF4A3)–B–#						
RIO—4-Cyl.—Equipment Schedule 6 W.B. 98.4"; 1.6 Liter.						
Sedan 4D	DF4A3	12990	4200	4425	5450	7125
LX Sedan 4D	DG4A3	15690	5450	5825	6800	8900
SX Sedan 4D	DH4A3	16790	6775	7150	8250	10450
RIO5—4-Cyl.—Equipment Schedule 6 W.B. 98.4"; 1.6 Liter.						
LX Hatchback 4D	DG5A3	15790	5550	5850	6975	8950
SX Hatchback 4D	DH5A3	17090	7225	7625	8650	10850
SOUL—4-Cyl.—Equipment Schedule 6 W.B. 100.4"; 1.6 Liter, 2.0 Liter.						
Wagon 4D	JT2A1	13995	6350	6625	7800	9775
Sport Wagon 4D	JT2A2	19190	8450	8725	10050	12100
! Wagon 4D	JT2A2	19190	8450	8825	9900	12100
SOUL—4-Cyl.—Equipment Schedule 6 W.B. 100.4"; 2.0 Liter.						
+ Wagon 4D	JT2A2	16190	7800	8150	9275	11400
Automatic, 4-Spd w/OD			425	425	565	565
FORTE—4-Cyl.—Equipment Schedule 6 W.B. 104.3"; 2.0 Liter, 2.4 Liter (SX).						
LX Sedan 4D	FT4A2	16690	6150	6450	7775	9975
Koup EX Coupe 2D	FU6A2	18690	7875	8250	9525	12000
Koup SX Coupe 2D	FW6A3	20090	8600	9000	10150	12600
SX Hatchback 4D	FW5A3	20090	8600	9000	10200	12700
Manual, 6-Spd w/Overdrive			(500)	(500)	(655)	(655)
FORTE—4-Cyl.—Equipment Schedule 6 W.B. 104.3"; 2.0 Liter, 2.4 Liter (SX).						
EX Hatchback 4D	FU5A2	17590	6500	6800	8175	10500

2011 KIA

Body Type	VIN	List	Trade-In Good	Very Good	Pvt-Party Good	Retail Excellent
EX Sedan 4D	FU4A2	18090	6925	7275	8625	10950
SX Sedan 4D	FW4A3	19590	8250	8650	9850	12300
OPTIMA—4-Cyl.—Equipment Schedule 5						
W.B. 110.0"; 2.4 Liter.						
LX Sedan 4D	GM4A7	21190	9250	9500	10950	12850
EX Sedan 4D	GN4A7	23190	10800	11100	12650	14800
Premium Pkg			325	325	380	380
Technology Pkg			400	400	470	470
Manual, 6-Spd w/Overdrive			(500)	(500)	(585)	(585)
4-Cyl, Turbo, 2.0 Liter	6		1400	1400	1675	1675
OPTIMA—4-Cyl. Turbo—Equipment Schedule 5						
W.B. 110.0"; 2.0 Liter.						
SX Sedan 4D	GR4A6	26690	12400	12700	14250	16550
Premium Pkg			325	325	370	370
Technology Pkg			400	400	465	465

2012 KIA — 5XXorKN(AorD)(JT2A5)–C–#

Body Type	VIN	List	Trade-In Good	Very Good	Pvt-Party Good	Retail Excellent
SOUL—4-Cyl.—Equipment Schedule 6						
W.B. 100.4"; 1.6 Liter, 2.0 Liter.						
Wagon 4D	JT2A5	14650	7475	7725	9125	11100
+ Wagon 4D	JT2A6	17050	8575	8850	10250	12350
Automatic, 6-Spd			475	475	605	605
SOUL—4-Cyl.—Equipment Schedule 6						
W.B. 100.4"; 2.0 Liter.						
! Wagon 4D	JT2A6	20350	9275	9600	11000	13200
RIO—4-Cyl.—Equipment Schedule 6						
W.B. 101.2"; 1.6 Liter.						
LX Sedan 4D	DM4A3	15450	7075	7475	8400	10500
Manual, 6-Spd			(525)	(525)	(705)	(705)
RIO—4-Cyl.—Equipment Schedule 6						
W.B. 101.2"; 1.6 Liter.						
LX Hatchback 4D	DM5A3	14350	6550	6850	8000	10000
Automatic, 6-Spd w/OD			475	475	620	620
RIO—4-Cyl.—Equipment Schedule 6						
W.B. 101.2"; 1.6 Liter, 2.0 Liter.						
EX Sedan 4D	DN4A3	17050	7925	8275	9400	11550
EX Hatchback 4D	DN5A3	17250	8025	8400	9500	11650
SX Sedan 4D	DN4A3	18250	8900	9300	10350	12650
SX Hatchback 4D	DN5A3	18450	8950	9350	10400	12700
FORTE—4-Cyl.—Equipment Schedule 6						
W.B. 104.3"; 2.0 Liter, 2.4 Liter (SX).						
LX Sedan 4D	FT2A4	16950	7075	7325	8800	11000
Koup EX Coupe 2D	FU6A2	18950	8525	8825	10300	12750
Koup SX Coupe 2D	FW6A3	20350	9200	9525	11000	13500
Manual, 6-Spd w/Overdrive			(550)	(550)	(720)	(720)
FORTE—4-Cyl.—Equipment Schedule 6						
W.B. 104.3"; 2.0 Liter, 2.4 Liter (SX).						
EX Hatchback 4D	FU5A2	18850	8425	8725	10200	12650
EX Sedan 4D	FU4A2	18350	8000	8275	9750	12050
SX Hatchback 4D	FW5A3	20350	9300	9625	11050	13450
SX Sedan 4D	FW4A3	19850	9025	9325	10750	13250
OPTIMA—4-Cyl.—Equipment Schedule 5						
W.B. 110.0"; 2.4 Liter.						
LX Sedan 4D	GM4A7	21750	10300	10500	12150	14100
EX Sedan 4D	GN4A7	23950	11650	11950	13650	15750
4-Cyl, Turbo, 2.0 Liter	6		1575	1575	1855	1855
OPTIMA—4-Cyl. Turbo—Equipment Schedule 5						
W.B. 110.0"; 2.0 Liter.						
SX Sedan 4D	GR4A6	27250	14600	14950	16750	19100
OPTIMA—4-Cyl. Hybrid—Equipment Schedule 5						
W.B. 110.0"; 2.4 Liter.						
Sedan 4D	GM4AD	26450	11950	12250	13900	15950

2013 KIA — 5XXorKN(AorD)(JT2A5)–D–#

Body Type	VIN	List	Trade-In Good	Very Good	Pvt-Party Good	Retail Excellent
SOUL—4-Cyl.—Equipment Schedule 6						
W.B. 100.4"; 1.6 Liter, 2.0 Liter.						
Wagon 4D	JT2A5	15175	8700	8925	10450	12400
+ Wagon 4D	JT2A6	17475	9875	10100	11750	13900
Automatic, 6-Spd			500	500	610	610
SOUL—4-Cyl.—Equipment Schedule 6						
W.B. 100.4"; 2.0 Liter.						
! Wagon 4D	JT2A6	20675	10650	10900	12450	14550

2013 KIA

Body Type	VIN	List	Trade-In Good	Very Good	Pvt-Party Good	Retail Excellent

RIO—4-Cyl.—Equipment Schedule 6
W.B. 101.2"; 1.6 Liter.

Body Type	VIN	List	Good	Very Good	Good	Excellent
LX Sedan 4D	DM4A3	14350	7425	7775	8900	10950
LX Hatchback 4D	DM5A3	14550	7525	7825	9075	11150
Automatic, 6-Spd			500	500	640	640

RIO—4-Cyl.—Equipment Schedule 6
W.B. 101.2"; 1.6 Liter.

EX Sedan 4D	DN4A3	17250	8900	9275	10450	12750
EX Hatchback 4D	DN5A3	17450	9100	9475	10650	12900
SX Sedan 4D	DN4A3	18450	9825	10250	11350	13650
SX Hatchback 4D	DN5A3	18650	10050	10450	11550	13850

FORTE—4-Cyl.—Equipment Schedule 6
W.B. 104.3"; 2.0 Liter, 2.4 Liter (SX).

LX Sedan 4D	FT4A2	17175	8100	8300	9900	12150
EX Sedan 4D	FU4A2	18575	8900	9125	10600	12850
EX Hatchback 4D	FU5A2	19075	9550	9800	11500	13950
SX Sedan 4D	FW4A3	20075	10800	11100	12550	15050
SX Hatchback 4D	FW5A3	20575	10850	11150	12700	15200
Koup SX Coupe 2D	FW6A3	19575	10450	10700	12300	14850

FORTE—4-Cyl.—Equipment Schedule 6
W.B. 104.3"; 2.0 Liter.

Koup EX Coupe 2D	FU6A2	18175	9100	9350	11050	13500
Manual, 6-Spd w/OD			(550)	(550)	(705)	(705)

OPTIMA—4-Cyl.—Equipment Schedule 5
W.B. 110.0"; 2.4 Liter.

LX Sedan 4D	GM4A7	21975	11300	11500	13350	15350
EX Sedan 4D	GM4A7	24275	12950	13200	15050	17100

OPTIMA—4-Cyl. Hybrid—Equipment Schedule 5
W.B. 110.0"; 2.4 Liter.

LX Sedan 4D	GM4AD	26675	12600	12850	14750	16900
EX Sedan 4D	GN4AD	32725	15250	15550	17450	19650

OPTIMA—4-Cyl. Turbo—Equipment Schedule 5
W.B. 110.0"; 2.0 Liter.

SX Sedan 4D	GR4A6	27575	17450	17800	19650	22000
Limited Sedan 4D		35275	18600	18950	20700	23000

2014 KIA — 5XXorKN(AorD)(DM4A3)-E-#

RIO—4-Cyl.—Equipment Schedule 6
W.B. 101.2"; 1.6 Liter.

LX Sedan 4D	DM4A3	14600	8525	8875	10000	12100
LX Hatchback 4D	DM5A3	14700	8625	8975	10150	12300
Automatic, 6-Spd			525	525	655	655

RIO—4-Cyl.—Equipment Schedule 6
W.B. 101.2"; 1.6 Liter.

EX Sedan 4D	DN4A3	17500	10650	11050	12150	14450
EX Hatchback 4D	DN5A3	17700	10850	11250	12300	14600
SX Sedan 4D	DN4A3	18600	11150	11600	12700	15050
SX Hatchback 4D	DN5A3	18790	11350	11800	12850	15200

SOUL—4-Cyl.—Equipment Schedule 6
W.B. 101.2"; 1.6 Liter.

Wagon 4D	JN3A2	15495	9900	10100	11850	13900
Automatic, 6-Spd			525	525	645	645

SOUL—4-Cyl.—Equipment Schedule 6
W.B. 104.2"; 2.0 Liter.

+ Wagon 4D	JP3A5	18995	11500	11750	13500	15600
Primo Pkg			375	375	455	455

SOUL—4-Cyl.—Equipment Schedule 6
W.B. 101.2"; 2.0 Liter.

! Wagon 4D	JX3A5	21095	13050	13300	15000	17050
The Whole Shabang			475	475	565	565

FORTE—4-Cyl.—Equipment Schedule 6
W.B. 106.3"; 1.8 Liter.

LX Sedan 4D	FK4A6	18200	9600	9850	11450	13750
Koup EX Coupe 2D	FX6A8	20400	11000	11300	12850	15350
Manual, 6-Spd			(550)	(550)	(680)	(680)

FORTE—4-Cyl.—Equipment Schedule 6
W.B. 106.3"; 2.0 Liter.

EX Sedan 4D	FX4A8	20200	10600	10900	12300	14650
EX Hatchback 4D	FX5A8	20500	11100	11400	12950	15400

FORTE—4-Cyl. Turbo—Equipment Schedule 6
W.B. 106.3"; 1.6 Liter.

Koup SX Coupe 2D	FZ6A3	22400	12200	12550	14000	16500
SX Hatchback 4D	FZ5A3	22700	12650	13000	14500	17050

Body Type	VIN	List	Trade-In Good	Trade-In Very Good	Pvt-Party Good	Retail Excellent
Manual, 6-Spd			(550)	(550)	(675)	(675)
OPTIMA—4-Cyl.—Equipment Schedule 5						
W.B. 110.0"; 2.4 Liter.						
LX Sedan 4D	GM4A7	22300	12400	12650	14500	16500
EX Sedan 4D	GN4A7	24700	14500	14800	16650	18700
SX Sedan 4D	GR4A7	26050	15650	15950	17750	19750
OPTIMA—4-Cyl. Hybrid—Equipment Schedule 5						
W.B. 110.0"; 2.4 Liter.						
LX Sedan 4D	GM4AD	26795	13800	14050	16000	18150
EX Sedan 4D	GN4AD	32795	17400	17750	19600	21800
OPTIMA—4-Cyl. Turbo—Equipment Schedule 5						
W.B. 110.0"; 2.0 Liter.						
SX Sedan 4D	GR4A6	28000	19000	19400	21200	23600
Limited Sedan 4D		37100	19900	20300	22000	24400
CADENZA—V6 GDI—Equipment Schedule 3						
W.B. 112.0"; 3.3 Liter.						
Premium Sedan 4D	LN4D7	35900	17000	17350	19550	22800
Adv. Smart Cruise Ctrl			500	500	600	600
CADENZA—V6 GDI—Equipment Schedule 3						
W.B. 112.0"; 3.3 Liter.						
Limited Sedan 4D		43200	19850	20200	22100	25300

LAMBORGHINI

2006 LAMBORGHINI — ZHW(GU12T)-6-#

Body Type	VIN	List	Good	Very Good	Good	Excellent
GALLARDO—V10—Equipment Schedule 2						
W.B. 100.8"; 5.0 Liter.						
Coupe 2D	GU12T	171300	****	****	****	72300
SE Coupe 2D	GU12T	194670	****	****	****	104800
Spyder Roadster 2D	GU22T	196300	****	****	****	101700
MURCIELAGO—V12—Equipment Schedule 2						
W.B. 104.9"; 6.2 Liter.						
Coupe 2D	BU16S	289300	****	****	****	130800
Roadster 2D	BU26S	320500	****	****	****	144300

2007 LAMBORGHINI — ZHW(GU12T)-7-#

Body Type	VIN	List	Good	Very Good	Good	Excellent
GALLARDO—V10—Equipment Schedule 2						
W.B. 100.8"; 5.0 Liter.						
Coupe 2D	GU12T	180550	****	****	****	78700
Spyder Roadster 2D	GU22T	199000	****	****	****	107000
MURCIELAGO—V12—Equipment Schedule 2						
W.B. 104.9"; 6.2 Liter.						
Coupe 2D	BU37S	313100	****	****	****	158000
Roadster 2D	BU47S	347000	****	****	****	170900

2008 LAMBORGHINI — ZHW(GU12T)-8-#

Body Type	VIN	List	Good	Very Good	Good	Excellent
GALLARDO—V10—Equipment Schedule 2						
W.B. 100.8"; 5.0 Liter.						
Coupe 2D	GU12T	196300	****	****	****	86200
Superleggera 2D	GU43T	234440	****	****	****	121000
Spyder Roadster 2D	GU22T	227760	****	****	****	113200
Ceramic Brakes			****	****	****	3610
MURCIELAGO—V12—Equipment Schedule 2						
W.B. 104.9"; 6.2 Liter.						
Coupe 2D	BU37S	347800	****	****	****	181400
Roadster 2D	BU47S	380600	****	****	****	193600
MURCIELAGO LP640—V12—Equipment Schedule 2						
W.B. 104.9"; 6.5 Liter.						
Coupe 2D	BU37S	347800	****	****	****	181400
Roadster 2D	BU47S	380600	****	****	****	193600

2009 LAMBORGHINI — ZHW(GU54T)-9-#

Body Type	VIN	List	Good	Very Good	Good	Excellent
GALLARDO AWD—V10—Equipment Schedule 2						
W.B. 100.7"; 5.2 Liter.						
LP 560-4 Coupe 2D	GU54T	205100	****	****	****	121200
LP 560-4 Roadster 2D	GU22T	223000	****	****	****	134400
MURCIELAGO AWD—V12—Equipment Schedule 2						
W.B. 104.9"; 6.5 Liter.						
Coupe 2D	BU37S	389800	****	****	****	216100
LP 640 Coupe 2D	BU37S	361400	****	****	****	204800

2010 LAMBORGHINI

Body Type	VIN	List	Trade-In Good	Very Good	Pvt-Party Good	Retail Excellent

2010 LAMBORGHINI — ZHW(GU5BZ)–A–#

GALLARDO LP 550-2—V10—Equipment Schedule 2
W.B. 100.8"; 5.2 Liter.

| Valentino Balboni Cpe | GU5BZ | 222795 | **** | **** | **** | 128400 |

GALLARDO LP 560-4 AWD—V10—Equipment Schedule 2
W.B. 100.7"; 5.2 Liter.

| Coupe 2D | GU54T | 206095 | **** | **** | **** | 133300 |
| Roadster 2D | GU6AU | 223995 | **** | **** | **** | 146200 |

MURCIELAGO AWD—V12—Equipment Schedule 2
W.B. 104.9"; 6.5 Liter.

LP 640-4 Coupe 2D	BU37S	361395	****	****	****	231500
LP 640-4 Conv 2D	BU4AN	389795	****	****	****	242000
LP 650-4 Conv 2D	BU4AN	423695	****	****	****	263000
SuperVeloce Coupe	BU8AH	456395	****	****	****	328200

2011 LAMBORGHINI — ZHW(GU5BZ)–B–#

GALLARDO—V10—Equipment Schedule 2
W.B. 100.8"; 5.2 Liter.

| LP 550-2 Bicolore Cpe | GU5BZ | 199095 | **** | **** | **** | 133500 |

GALLARDO AWD—V10—Equipment Schedule 2
W.B. 100.7" (560-4 Cpe), 100.8"; 5.2 Liter.

LP 560-4 Coupe 2D	GU54T	210095	****	****	****	144000
LP 560-4 Spyder 2D	GU6AU	235795	****	****	****	157500
LP 570-4 Superleggera	GU7AJ	245695	****	****	****	178400
LP 570-4 Performante	GU8AZ	256795	****	****	****	187700

2012 LAMBORGHINI — ZHW(GU5BZ)–C–#

GALLARDO—V10—Equipment Schedule 2
W.B. 100.8"; 5.2 Liter.

| LP 550-2 Coupe 2D | GU5BZ | 193895 | **** | **** | **** | 148000 |
| LP 550-2 Bicolore 2D | GU5BZ | 196995 | **** | **** | **** | 143500 |

GALLARDO AWD—V10—Equipment Schedule 2
W.B. 100.7" (560-4 Cpe), 100.8"; 5.2 Liter.

LP 560-4 Coupe 2D	GU5AU	207995	****	****	****	153600
LP 560-4 Spyder 2D	GU6AU	231395	****	****	****	167000
LP 570-4 Squadra	GU7AJ	243595	****	****	****	188300
LP 570-4 Performante	GU8AJ	253095	****	****	****	196300

AVENTADOR AWD—V12—Equipment Schedule 2
W.B.106.3"; 6.5 Liter.

| LP 700-4 Coupe 2D | UC1ZD | 389995 | **** | **** | **** | 373500 |

2013 LAMBORGHINI — ZHW(GU5BZ)–D–#

GALLARDO—V10—Equipment Schedule 2
W.B. 100.8"; 5.2 Liter.

| LP 550-2 Coupe 2D | GU5BZ | 196995 | **** | **** | **** | 156400 |
| LP 550-2 Spyder 2D | GU6BZ | 214595 | **** | **** | **** | 200100 |

GALLARDO AWD—V10—Equipment Schedule 2
W.B. 100.8"; 5.2 Liter.

LP 560-4 Coupe 2D	GU5AU	207095	****	****	****	161500
LP 560-4 Spyder 2D	GU6AU	230495	****	****	****	177500
LP 570-4 Superleggera	GU7AJ	246295	****	****	****	198300
LP 570-4 Performante	GU8AJ	256695	****	****	****	204100

AVENTADOR AWD—V12—Equipment Schedule 2
W.B. 106.3"; 6.5 Liter.

| LP 700-4 Coupe 2D | UC1ZD | 404195 | **** | **** | **** | 397900 |
| LP 700-4 Roadster 2D | UR1ZD | 448295 | **** | **** | **** | 403300 |

2014 LAMBORGHINI — ZHW(GU5BZ)–E–#

GALLARDO—V10—Equipment Schedule 2
W.B. 100.8"; 5.2 Liter.

LP 550-2 Coupe 2D	GU5BZ	196995	****	****	****	161700
LP 550-2 Spyder Cnv	GU6BZ	214595	****	****	****	204300
LP 560-2 50th Anv Cpe	GU5BR	204895	****	****	****	165400

GALLARDO AWD—V10—Equipment Schedule 2
W.B. 100.8"; 5.2 Liter.

LP 560-4 Coupe 2D	GU5AU	207095	****	****	****	166700
LP 560-4 Spyder Cnv	GU6BZ	214595	****	****	****	204300
LP 700-4 Roadster 2D		458295				
LP570-4Squadra Corse	GU7AJ	264195				
LP 570-4 Superleggera		246295				

2014 LAMBORGHINI

Body Type	VIN	List	Trade-In Good	Very Good	Pvt-Party Good	Retail Excellent
LP 570-4 SpydrPrfrmnt	GU8AJ	256695	****	****	****	210200
AVENTADOR—V12—Equipment Schedule 2						
W.B. 106.3"; 6.5 Liter.						
LP 700-4 Coupe 2D	UC1ZD	404695	****	****	****	408600
LP 700-4 Roadster 2D	UR1ZD	449595	****	****	****	414000
LP 720-4 50th Coupe	UD2ZD	504845	****	****	****	415800
LP 720-4 50th Rdstr	US2ZD	556795	****	****	****	418800

LEXUS

2000 LEXUS — JT8(BF28G)–Y-#

Body Type	VIN	List	Trade-In Good	Very Good	Pvt-Party Good	Retail Excellent
ES 300—V6—Equipment Schedule 1						
W.B. 105.1"; 3.0 Liter.						
Sedan 4D	BF28G	34785	2025	2275	2675	4200
Platinum Series			125	125	175	175
GS 300—6-Cyl.—Equipment Schedule 1						
W.B. 110.2"; 3.0 Liter.						
Sedan 4D	BD68S	40880	1850	2150	2650	4300
Platinum Series			125	125	175	175
GS 400—V8—Equipment Schedule 1						
W.B. 110.2"; 4.0 Liter.						
Sedan 4D	BH68X	47520	3425	3925	4350	6925
Platinum Series			125	125	175	175
SC 300—6-Cyl.—Equipment Schedule 1						
W.B. 105.9"; 3.0 Liter.						
Sport Coupe 2D	CD32Z	47140	2700	2900	3750	5450
Traction Control			100	100	135	135
SC 400—V8—Equipment Schedule 1						
W.B. 105.9"; 4.0 Liter.						
Sport Coupe 2D	CH32Y	57530	3825	4075	4950	7125
Traction Control			100	100	130	130
LS 400—V8—Equipment Schedule 1						
W.B. 112.2"; 4.0 Liter.						
Sedan 4D	BH28F	55420	3400	3675	4200	6075
Platinum Series			125	125	165	165

2001 LEXUS — JT(8orH)(BF28G)–1-#

Body Type	VIN	List	Trade-In Good	Very Good	Pvt-Party Good	Retail Excellent
ES 300—V6—Equipment Schedule 1						
W.B. 105.1"; 3.0 Liter.						
Sedan 4D	BF28G	34935	2575	2875	3225	5025
Coach Edition			150	150	190	190
IS 300—6-Cyl.—Equipment Schedule 1						
W.B. 105.1"; 3.0 Liter.						
Sedan 4D	BD182	34055	2975	3400	3725	5825
GS 300—6-Cyl.—Equipment Schedule 1						
W.B. 110.2"; 3.0 Liter.						
Sedan 4D	BD68S	41780	2450	2825	3200	5025
GS 430—V8—Equipment Schedule 1						
W.B. 110.2"; 4.3 Liter.						
Sedan 4D	BN68X	50580	3925	4475	4950	7725
LS 430—V8—Equipment Schedule 1						
W.B. 115.2"; 4.3 Liter.						
Sedan 4D	BN30F	54550	4925	5300	5925	8375
Dynamic Cruise Control			200	200	255	255
Ultra Luxury Pkg			1650	1650	2215	2215

2002 LEXUS — JT(8orH)(BF30G)–2-#

Body Type	VIN	List	Trade-In Good	Very Good	Pvt-Party Good	Retail Excellent
ES 300—V6—Equipment Schedule 1						
W.B. 107.1"; 3.0 Liter.						
Sedan 4D	BF30G	33640	3150	3525	3850	5850
IS 300—6-Cyl.—Equipment Schedule 1						
W.B. 105.1"; 3.0 Liter.						
Sedan 4D	BD192	33655	3700	4200	4500	6775
Sport Cross H'Back 4D	ED192	35195	3800	4325	4600	6950
Manual, 5-Spd			(275)	(275)	(380)	(380)
GS 300—6-Cyl.—Equipment Schedule 1						
W.B. 110.2"; 3.0 Liter.						
Sedan 4D	BD69S	41840	3000	3425	3800	5900
SportDesign			300	300	410	410
GS 430—V8—Equipment Schedule 1						
W.B. 110.2"; 4.3 Liter.						

Body Type	VIN	List	Trade-In Good	Very Good	Pvt-Party Good	Retail Excellent
Sedan 4D — BL69S		48980	4425	5025	5500	8475
LS 430—V8—Equipment Schedule 1						
W.B. 115.2"; 4.3 Liter.						
Sedan 4D — BN30F		56080	5200	5575	6475	9100
Dynamic Cruise Control			225	225	285	285
Ultra Luxury Pkg			1725	1725	2295	2295
SC 430—V8—Equipment Schedule 1						
W.B. 103.1"; 4.3 Liter.						
Convertible 2D — FN48Y		59030	6225	6625	7800	10900

2003 LEXUS — JT(8orH)(BF30G)-3-#

Body Type	VIN	List	Trade-In Good	Very Good	Pvt-Party Good	Retail Excellent
ES 300—V6—Equipment Schedule 1						
W.B. 107.1"; 3.0 Liter.						
Sedan 4D — BF30G		33780	3725	4150	4500	6650
IS 300—6-Cyl.—Equipment Schedule 1						
W.B. 105.1"; 3.0 Liter.						
Sedan 4D — BD192		32485	4625	5225	5375	7875
Sport Cross H'Back 4D — ED192		32525	4725	5350	5475	8025
SportDesign			550	550	740	740
Manual, 5-Spd			(325)	(325)	(425)	(425)
GS 300—6-Cyl.—Equipment Schedule 1						
W.B. 110.2"; 3.0 Liter.						
Sedan 4D — BD69S		40960	3800	4300	4650	7025
SportDesign			350	350	450	450
GS 430—V8—Equipment Schedule 1						
W.B. 110.2"; 4.3 Liter.						
Sedan 4D — BL69S		48400	5325	6000	6375	9625
LS 430—V8—Equipment Schedule 1						
W.B. 115.2"; 4.3 Liter.						
Sedan 4D — BN30F		56600	6400	6850	7500	10200
Dynamic Cruise Control			250	250	315	315
Ultra Luxury Pkg			1775	1775	2350	2350
SC 430—V8—Equipment Schedule 1						
W.B. 103.1"; 4.3 Liter.						
Convertible 2D — FN48Y		62600	6625	7075	8225	11400

2004 LEXUS — JT(8orH)(BA30G)-4-#

Body Type	VIN	List	Trade-In Good	Very Good	Pvt-Party Good	Retail Excellent
ES 330—V6—Equipment Schedule 1						
W.B. 107.1"; 3.3 Liter.						
Sedan 4D — BA30G		32350	4700	5175	5400	7825
IS 300—6-Cyl.—Equipment Schedule 1						
W.B. 105.1"; 3.0 Liter.						
Sedan 4D — BD192		32815	5475	6150	6375	9150
Sport Cross H'Back 4D — ED192		32855	5575	6250	6475	9300
SportDesign			600	600	800	800
Manual, 5-Spd			(350)	(350)	(475)	(475)
GS 300—6-Cyl.—Equipment Schedule 1						
W.B. 110.2"; 3.0 Liter.						
Sedan 4D — BD68S		41010	5075	5700	6000	8875
GS 430—V8—Equipment Schedule 1						
W.B. 110.2"; 4.3 Liter.						
Sedan 4D — BL69S		48450	6400	7200	7475	10850
LS 430—V8—Equipment Schedule 1						
W.B. 115.2"; 4.3 Liter.						
Sedan 4D — BN30F		55750	8775	9375	10450	14450
Dynamic Cruise Control			275	275	355	355
Ultra Luxury Pkg			1850	1850	2460	2460
SC 430—V8—Equipment Schedule 1						
W.B. 103.1"; 4.3 Liter.						
Convertible 2D — FN48Y		63200	8425	8975	10000	13550

2005 LEXUS — JT(8orH)(BA30G)-5-#

Body Type	VIN	List	Trade-In Good	Very Good	Pvt-Party Good	Retail Excellent
ES 330—V6—Equipment Schedule 1						
W.B. 107.1"; 3.3 Liter.						
Sedan 4D — BA30G		32600	5625	6200	6575	9175
IS 300—6-Cyl.—Equipment Schedule 1						
W.B. 105.1"; 3.0 Liter.						
Sedan 4D — BD192		34315	6150	6875	7225	10200
Sport Cross H'Back 4D — ED192		34355	6275	7000	7325	10350
Manual, 5-Spd			(400)	(400)	(520)	(520)
GS 300—6-Cyl.—Equipment Schedule 1						
W.B. 110.2"; 3.0 Liter.						

Body Type	VIN	List	Good	Trade-In Very Good	Pvt-Party Good	Retail Excellent
Sedan 4D	BD69S	41160	6000	6725	7050	9950
GS 430—V8—Equipment Schedule 1						
W.B. 110.2"; 4.3 Liter.						
Sedan 4D	BL69S	48600	7425	8275	8900	12850
LS 430—V8—Equipment Schedule 1						
W.B. 115.2"; 4.3 Liter.						
Sedan 4D	BN36F	56300	9350	9950	11150	15050
Dynamic Cruise Control		-------	300	300	385	385
Ultra Luxury Pkg		-------	1900	1900	2545	2545
SC 430—V8—Equipment Schedule 1						
W.B. 103.1"; 4.3 Liter.						
Convertible 2D	FN48Y	63800	10800	11500	12550	16350

2006 LEXUS — JT(8orH)(BA30G)-6-#

Body Type	VIN	List	Good	Trade-In Very Good	Pvt-Party Good	Retail Excellent
ES 330—V6—Equipment Schedule 1						
W.B. 107.1"; 3.3 Liter.						
Sedan 4D	BA30G	32950	7225	7900	8100	10950
IS 250—V6—Equipment Schedule 1						
W.B. 107.5"; 2.5 Liter.						
Sedan 4D	BK262	31750	8050	8900	8975	12150
Adaptive Cruise Control		-------	325	325	410	410
Luxury Pkg		-------	675	675	890	890
Sport Pkg		-------	675	675	865	865
AWD		-------	1000	1000	1300	1300
IS 350—V6—Equipment Schedule 1						
W.B. 107.5"; 3.5 Liter.						
Sedan 4D	BE262	36030	9650	10650	10650	14400
Adaptive Cruise Control		-------	325	325	410	410
Luxury Pkg		-------	675	675	885	885
Sport Pkg		-------	675	675	860	860
GS 300 AWD—V6—Equipment Schedule 1						
W.B. 112.2"; 3.0 Liter.						
Sedan 4D	CH96S	45545	8975	9925	10000	13650
Adaptive Cruise Control		-------	325	325	410	410
RWD	B		(575)	(575)	(730)	(730)
GS 430—V8—Equipment Schedule 1						
W.B. 112.2"; 4.3 Liter.						
Sedan 4D	BN96S	53025	10400	11500	11450	15550
Adaptive Cruise Control		-------	325	325	405	405
LS 430—V8—Equipment Schedule 1						
W.B. 115.2"; 4.3 Liter.						
Sedan 4D	BN36F	57175	10750	11350	12450	16200
Dynamic Cruise Control		-------	325	325	395	395
Ultra Luxury Pkg		-------	1975	1975	2470	2470
SC 430—V8—Equipment Schedule 1						
W.B. 103.1"; 4.3 Liter.						
Convertible 2D	FN48Y	66005	12550	13350	14150	18050
Pebble Beach Special Ed		-------	300	300	365	365

2007 LEXUS — JT(8orH)(BK262)-7-#

Body Type	VIN	List	Good	Trade-In Very Good	Pvt-Party Good	Retail Excellent
IS 250—V6—Equipment Schedule 1						
W.B. 107.5"; 2.5 Liter.						
Sedan 4D	BK262	32015	9425	10300	10350	13600
Adaptive Cruise Control		-------	350	350	430	430
Luxury Pkg		-------	725	725	930	930
AWD		-------	1075	1075	1365	1365
IS 350—V6—Equipment Schedule 1						
W.B. 107.5"; 3.5 Liter.						
Sedan 4D	BE262	36295	11050	12100	12050	15800
Adaptive Cruise Control		-------	350	350	430	430
Luxury Pkg		-------	725	725	925	925
Sport Pkg		-------	725	725	905	905
ES 350—V6—Equipment Schedule 1						
W.B. 109.3"; 3.5 Liter.						
Sedan 4D	BJ46G	35145	8750	9475	9675	12750
Premium Pkg		-------	250	250	305	305
Premium Plus Pkg		-------	475	475	615	615
Ultra Luxury Pkg		-------	350	350	430	430
GS 350 AWD—V6—Equipment Schedule 1						
W.B. 112.2"; 3.5 Liter.						
Sedan 4D	CE96S	46865	10950	11950	11950	15750
Adaptive Cruise Control		-------	350	350	420	420

Body Type	VIN	List	Trade-In Good	Trade-In Very Good	Pvt-Party Good	Retail Excellent
RWD ———————————B			**(600)**	**(600)**	**(760)**	**(760)**
GS 430—V8—Equipment Schedule 1						
W.B. 112.2"; 4.3 Liter.						
Sedan 4D	BN96S	53070	12350	13500	13200	17150
Adaptive Cruise Control			350	350	420	420
GS 450h—V6 Hybrid—Equipment Schedule 1						
W.B. 112.2"; 3.5 Liter.						
Sedan 4D	BC96S	55595	12450	13600	13250	17250
Adaptive Cruise Control			350	350	420	420
LS 460—V8—Equipment Schedule 1						
W.B. 116.9", 121.7" (L); 4.6 Liter.						
Sedan 4D	BL46F	61715	15800	16650	16850	20500
L Sedan 4D	GL46F	71715	17950	18900	18850	22800
Executive Pkg			2375	2375	2775	2775
Luxury Pkg			375	375	440	440
Touring			450	450	520	520
SC 430—V8—Equipment Schedule 1						
W.B. 103.1"; 4.3 Liter.						
Convertible 2D	FN45Y	66150	14000	14850	15600	19550
Pebble Beach Special Ed			325	325	385	385

2008 LEXUS — JT(8orH)(BK262)-8-#

Body Type	VIN	List	Trade-In Good	Trade-In Very Good	Pvt-Party Good	Retail Excellent
IS 250—V6—Equipment Schedule 1						
W.B. 107.5"; 2.5 Liter.						
Sedan 4D	BK262	32390	11000	11800	12050	15250
Adaptive Cruise Control			375	375	450	450
Luxury Plus Pkg			775	775	965	965
AWD			1150	1150	1415	1415
IS 350—V6—Equipment Schedule 1						
W.B. 107.5"; 3.5 Liter.						
Sedan 4D	BE262	36670	12650	13600	13900	17650
Adaptive Cruise Control			375	375	455	455
Luxury Plus Pkg			775	775	970	970
Sport Pkg			775	775	955	955
IS F—V8—Equipment Schedule 1						
W.B. 107.5"; 5.0 Liter.						
Sedan 4D	BP262	56765	22000	23600	22200	26800
ES 350—V6—Equipment Schedule 1						
W.B. 109.3"; 3.5 Liter.						
Sedan 4D	BJ46G	34485	10100	10800	11150	14100
Dynamic Radar Cruise Ctrl			375	375	455	455
Pebble Beach Edition			325	325	415	415
Premium Pkg			250	250	325	325
Premium Plus Pkg			525	525	650	650
Ultra Luxury Pkg			375	375	455	455
GS 350 AWD—V6—Equipment Schedule 1						
W.B. 112.2"; 3.5 Liter.						
Sedan 4D	CE96S	47375	13150	14100	14200	17750
Adaptive Cruise Control			375	375	430	430
RWD ———————————B			(650)	(650)	(775)	(775)
GS 450h—V6 Hybrid—Equipment Schedule 1						
W.B. 112.2"; 3.5 Liter.						
Sedan 4D	BC96S	55665	15400	16550	16600	20900
Adaptive Cruise Control			375	375	435	435
GS 460—V8—Equipment Schedule 1						
W.B. 112.2"; 4.6 Liter.						
Sedan 4D	BN96S	53385	15300	16450	16500	20700
Adaptive Cruise Control			375	375	430	430
LS 460—V8—Equipment Schedule 1						
W.B. 116.9", 121.7" (L); 4.6 Liter.						
Sedan 4D	BL46F	62265	17250	18000	18550	22000
L Sedan 4D	GL46F	72265	19650	20500	20800	24500
Executive Pkg			2500	2500	2880	2880
Luxury Pkg			400	400	460	460
Touring			475	475	545	545
Rear Seat Upgrade Pkg			825	825	945	945
LS 600h AWD—V8 Hybrid—Equipment Schedule 1						
W.B. 121.7"; 5.0 Liter.						
L Sedan 4D	DU46F	104765	24500	25600	26000	30800
Executive Pkg			2500	2500	2965	2965
SC 430—V8—Equipment Schedule 1						
W.B. 103.1"; 4.3 Liter.						
Convertible 2D	FN45Y	66220	16900	17850	18550	22600

Body Type	VIN	List	Trade-In Good	Very Good	Pvt-Party Good	Retail Excellent
Pebble Beach Special Ed............	....	....	325	325	395	395

2009 LEXUS — JT(8orH)(BK262)-9-#

IS 250—V6—Equipment Schedule 1
W.B. 107.5"; 2.5 Liter.

Sedan 4D....................	BK262	33200	12850	13550	14150	17250
Adaptive Cruise Control............	....	....	375	375	450	450
Luxury Plus Pkg............	....	....	825	825	1005	1005
AWD............	C	....	1225	1225	1480	1480

IS 350—V6—Equipment Schedule 1
W.B. 107.5"; 3.5 Liter.

Sedan 4D....................	BE262	37430	15700	16600	17100	20900
Luxury Plus Pkg............	....	....	825	825	1010	1010
Sport Pkg............	....	....	825	825	995	995

IS F—V8—Equipment Schedule 1
W.B. 107.5"; 5.0 Liter.

Sedan 4D....................	BP262	57435	25000	26400	25600	30000

ES 350—V6—Equipment Schedule 1
W.B. 109.3"; 3.5 Liter.

Sedan 4D....................	BJ46G	35145	11800	12450	13100	16050
Premium Pkg............	....	....	275	275	340	340
Premium Pkg............	....	....	550	550	680	680
Ultra Luxury Pkg............	....	....	400	400	475	475

GS 350 AWD—V6—Equipment Schedule 1
W.B. 112.2"; 3.5 Liter.

Sedan 4D....................	CE96S	47675	15650	16500	16950	20600
Adaptive Cruise Control............	....	....	375	375	430	430
RWD............	B	....	(700)	(700)	(810)	(810)

GS 450h—V6 Hybrid—Equipment Schedule 1
W.B. 112.2"; 3.5 Liter.

Sedan 4D....................	BC96S	57225	17850	18850	19000	22900
Adaptive Cruise Control............	....	....	375	375	430	430

GS 460—V8—Equipment Schedule 1
W.B. 112.2"; 4.6 Liter.

Sedan 4D....................	BN96S	54145	17900	18900	18950	22700
Adaptive Cruise Control............	....	....	375	375	425	425

LS 460—V8—Equipment Schedule 1
W.B. 116.9", 121.7" (L); 4.6 Liter.

Sedan 4D....................	BL46F	64500	18750	19400	20400	23900
L Sedan 4D....................	GL46F	74410	21600	22300	23600	27800
Luxury Pkg............	....	....	425	425	485	485
Touring............	....	....	500	500	580	580
Rear Seat Upgrade Pkg............	....	....	850	850	970	970
Executive Seating............	....	....	2600	2600	3005	3005
AWD............	C	....	1500	1500	1735	1735

LS 600h—V8 Hybrid—Equipment Schedule 1
W.B. 121.7"; 5.0 Liter.

L Sedan 4D....................	DU46F	106710	27100	28000	29500	34900
Dynamic Cruise Control............	....	....	375	375	445	445
Executive Seating............	....	....	2600	2600	3110	3110

SC 430—V8—Equipment Schedule 1
W.B. 103.1"; 4.3 Liter.

Convertible 2D....................	FN45Y	67630	23500	24800	25000	29400
Pebble Beach Special Ed............	....	....	350	350	405	405

2010 LEXUS — JTH(BB1BA)-A-#

HS 250h—4-Cyl. Hybrid—Equipment Schedule 1
W.B. 106.3"; 2.4 Liter.

Sedan 4D....................	BB1BA	35075	12750	13350	14450	17350
Premium Sedan 4D....................	BB1BA	37845	13500	14100	15100	18100
Dynamic Radar Cruise Ctrl............	....	....	400	400	480	480
Touring Pkg............	....	....	475	475	585	585
Technology Pkg............	....	....	600	600	735	735

IS 250—V6—Equipment Schedule 1
W.B. 107.5"; 2.5 Liter.

Sedan 4D....................	BF5C2	33890	14650	15300	16050	19000
Convertible 2D....................	FF2C2	40535	17950	18700	19400	22900
Dynamic Radar Cruise Ctrl............	....	....	400	400	465	465
Luxury Plus Pkg............	....	....	875	875	1055	1055
AWD............	C	....	1300	1300	1550	1550

IS 350—V6—Equipment Schedule 1
W.B. 107.5"; 3.5 Liter.

2010 LEXUS

Body Type	VIN	List	Trade-In Good	Very Good	Pvt-Party Good	Retail Excellent
Sedan 4D	BE5C2	38170	17600	18350	19100	22600
Convertible 2D	FE2C2	44815	19900	20800	21400	25200
Dynamic Radar Cruise Ctrl			400	400	465	465
Sport Pkg			875	875	1045	1045
Luxury Plus Value Edition			875	875	1050	1050
IS F—V8—Equipment Schedule 1						
W.B. 107.5"; 5.0 Liter.						
Sedan 4D	BP5C2	58635	28900	30100	29900	34400
ES 350—V6—Equipment Schedule 1						
W.B. 109.3"; 3.5 Liter.						
Sedan 4D	BK1EG	35675	14050	14700	15650	18700
Dynamic Radar Cruise Ctrl			400	400	470	470
Ultra Luxury Pkg			425	425	500	500
GS 350 AWD—V6—Equipment Schedule 1						
W.B. 112.2"; 3.5 Liter.						
Sedan 4D	CE1KB	47825	18050	18850	19600	23200
Adaptive Cruise Control			400	400	445	445
RWD	B		(750)	(750)	(855)	(855)
GS 450h—V6 Hybrid—Equipment Schedule 1						
W.B. 112.2"; 3.5 Liter.						
Sedan 4D	BC1KS	57425	20900	21800	22300	26300
Adaptive Cruise Control			400	400	445	445
GS 460—V8—Equipment Schedule 1						
W.B. 112.2"; 4.6 Liter.						
Sedan 4D	BL1KS	54345	21000	21900	22300	26100
Adaptive Cruise Control			400	400	445	445
LS 460—V8—Equipment Schedule 1						
W.B. 116.9", 121.7" (L); 4.6 Liter.						
Sedan 4D	BL5EF	65555	24700	25400	26800	30700
L Sedan 4D	GL5EF	71100	27500	28300	30000	34500
Dynamic Cruise Control			400	400	435	435
Sport Pkg			2225	2225	2485	2485
Rear Seat Upgrade Pkg			875	875	970	970
Executive Seating			2725	2725	3060	3060
AWD	C		1600	1600	1790	1790
LS 600h—V8 Hybrid—Equipment Schedule 1						
W.B. 121.7"; 5.0 Liter.						
L Sedan 4D	DU1EF	109675	39700	40800	42100	47700
Dynamic Cruise Control			400	400	445	445
Premium Luxury Pkg			450	450	505	505
SC 430—V8—Equipment Schedule 1						
W.B. 103.1"; 4.3 Liter.						
Convertible 2D	FN2EY	68380	26500	27900	28200	32800

2011 LEXUS — JTH(KD5BH)-B-#

Body Type	VIN	List	Trade-In Good	Very Good	Pvt-Party Good	Retail Excellent
CT 200h—4-Cyl. Hybrid—Equipment Schedule 1						
W.B. 102.4"; 1.8 Liter.						
Hatchback 4D	KD5BH	29995	13950	14400	15700	18450
Premium H'Back 4D	KD5BH	31775	14600	15050	16350	19200
Dynamic Cruise Control			425	425	495	495
HS 250h—4-Cyl. Hybrid—Equipment Schedule 1						
W.B. 106.3"; 2.4 Liter.						
Sedan 4D	BB1BA	35975	15450	15950	17200	20100
Premium Sedan 4D	BB1BA	38745	16550	17100	18200	21200
Dynamic Radar Cruise Ctrl			425	425	495	495
Touring Pkg			500	500	605	605
Technology Pkg			625	625	760	760
IS 250—V6—Equipment Schedule 1						
W.B. 107.5"; 2.5 Liter.						
Sedan 4D	BF5C2	34190	16500	17050	18000	20800
Dynamic Cruise Ctrl			425	425	490	490
Luxury Plus Value Edition			925	925	1095	1095
F-Sport Pkg			925	925	1090	1090
AWD			1375	1375	1615	1615
IS 250C—V6—Equipment Schedule 1						
W.B. 107.5"; 2.5 Liter.						
Convertible 2D	FF2C2	41935	21100	21700	22700	26200
Dynamic Cruise Ctrl			425	425	485	485
Luxury Pkg			925	925	1090	1090
IS 350—V6—Equipment Schedule 1						
W.B. 107.5"; 3.5 Liter.						
Sedan 4D	BE5C2	39445	19750	20400	21400	24700
Dynamic Cruise Ctrl			425	425	485	485

Body Type	VIN	List	Trade-In Good	Very Good	Pvt-Party Good	Retail Excellent
Luxury Plus Value Edition		-----	925	925	1090	1090
F-Sport Pkg		-----	925	925	1085	1085
AWD		-----	1375	1375	1610	1610
IS 350C—V6—Equipment Schedule 1						
W.B. 107.5"; 3.5 Liter.						
Convertible 2D	FE2C2	46215	23600	24400	25300	29100
Dynamic Cruise Ctrl		-----	425	425	485	485
Luxury Pkg		-----	925	925	1085	1085
F-Sport Pkg		-----	925	925	1080	1080
IS F—V8—Equipment Schedule 1						
W.B. 107.5"; 5.0 Liter.						
Sedan 4D	BP5C2	59335	31200	32200	32600	36900
Dynamic Radar Cruise Ctrl		-----	425	425	460	460
ES 350—V6—Equipment Schedule 1						
W.B. 109.3"; 3.5 Liter.						
Sedan 4D	BK1EG	36400	16350	17000	18100	21100
Dynamic Cruise Ctrl		-----	425	425	490	490
Ultra Luxury Pkg		-----	450	450	520	520
GS 350 AWD—V6—Equipment Schedule 1						
W.B. 112.2"; 3.5 Liter.						
Sedan 4D	CE1KS	48825	20700	21300	22300	25800
Dynamic Cruise Control		-----	425	425	470	470
RWD	B		(775)	(775)	(890)	(890)
GS 450h—V6 Hybrid—Equipment Schedule 1						
W.B. 112.2"; 3.5 Liter.						
Sedan 4D	BC1KS	58825	23400	24100	25200	29300
Dynamic Cruise Control		-----	425	425	470	470
GS 460—V8—Equipment Schedule 1						
W.B. 112.2"; 4.6 Liter.						
Sedan 4D	BL1KS	55345	23700	24400	25300	29200
Dynamic Cruise Control		-----	425	425	470	470
LS 460—V8—Equipment Schedule 1						
W.B. 116.9", 121.7" (L); 4.6 Liter.						
Sedan 4D	BL5EF	66255	27000	27600	29600	33500
L Sedan 4D	GL5EF	71800	29900	30600	32400	36500
Dynamic Radar Cruise Ctrl		-----	425	425	460	460
Sport Pkg		-----	2375	2375	2630	2630
Rear Seat Upgrade Pkg		-----	900	900	995	995
AWD	C		1700	1700	1875	1875
LS 600h—V8 Hybrid—Equipment Schedule 1						
W.B. 121.7"; 5.0 Liter.						
L Sedan 4D	DU5EF	110875	43800	44800	46400	51700
Premium Luxury Pkg		-----	475	475	525	525

Body Type	VIN	List	Trade-In Good	Very Good	Pvt-Party Good	Retail Excellent
CT 200h—4-Cyl. Hybrid—Equipment Schedule 1						
W.B. 102.4"; 1.8 Liter.						
Hatchback 4D	KD5BH	29995	15450	15850	18150	19950
Premium H'Back 4D	KD5BH	32125	16400	16800	18250	21000
Dynamic Cruise Control		-----	450	450	515	515
F Sport Pkg		-----	1475	1475	1715	1715
F Sport Special Edition		-----	425	425	500	500
HS 250h—4-Cyl. Hybrid—Equipment Schedule 1						
W.B. 106.3"; 2.4 Liter.						
Sedan 4D	BB1BA	37905	17300	17750	19050	21700
Premium Sedan 4D	BB1BA	40675	18450	18900	20200	23100
Dynamic Radar Cruise Ctrl		-----	450	450	515	515
Touring Pkg		-----	525	525	625	625
Technology Pkg		-----	675	675	790	790
IS 250—V6—Equipment Schedule 1						
W.B. 107.5"; 2.5 Liter.						
Sedan 4D	BF5C2	35640	18900	19400	20600	23300
Dynamic Cruise Ctrl		-----	450	450	510	510
Luxury Plus Value Edition		-----	975	975	1140	1140
F-Sport Pkg		-----	975	975	1135	1135
AWD		-----	1475	1475	1700	1700
IS 250C—V6—Equipment Schedule 1						
W.B. 107.5"; 2.5 Liter.						
Convertible 2D	FF2C2	43235	25000	25600	26800	30400
Dynamic Cruise Ctrl		-----	450	450	505	505
Luxury Pkg		-----	975	975	1130	1130
IS 350—V6—Equipment Schedule 1						
W.B. 107.5"; 3.5 Liter.						

2012 LEXUS

Body Type	VIN	List	Trade-In Good	Very Good	Pvt-Party Good	Retail Excellent
Sedan 4D	BE5C2	40895	22100	22700	23900	27100
Dynamic Cruise Ctrl			450	450	510	510
Luxury Plus Value Edition			975	975	1135	1135
F-Sport Pkg			975	975	1130	1130
AWD			1475	1475	1690	1690

IS 350C—V6—Equipment Schedule 1
W.B. 107.5"; 3.5 Liter.

Body Type	VIN	List	Good	Very Good	Good	Excellent
Convertible 2D	FE2C2	47515	27800	28400	29600	33500
Dynamic Cruise Ctrl			450	450	505	505
Luxury Pkg			975	975	1125	1125

IS F—V8—Equipment Schedule 1
W.B. 107.5"; 5.0 Liter.

Body Type	VIN	List	Good	Very Good	Good	Excellent
Sedan 4D	BP5C2	62175	37100	38000	38800	43300
Dynamic Cruise Ctrl			450	450	485	485

ES 350—V6—Equipment Schedule 1
W.B. 109.3"; 3.5 Liter.

Body Type	VIN	List	Good	Very Good	Good	Excellent
Sedan 4D	BK1EG	37600	19700	20300	21500	24400
Dynamic Radar Cruise Ctrl			450	450	510	510
Touring Edition			100	100	115	115
Ultra Luxury Pkg			475	475	535	535

LS 460—V8—Equipment Schedule 1
W.B. 116.9", 121.7" (L); 4.6 Liter.

Body Type	VIN	List	Good	Very Good	Good	Excellent
Sedan 4D	BL5EF	68005	30600	31200	33400	37300
L Sedan 4D	GL5EF	73650	33600	34200	36300	40300
Dynamic Cruise Ctrl			450	450	485	485
Comfort Pkg			475	475	510	510
Sport Pkg			2525	2525	2760	2760
Luxury Pkg			500	500	540	540
Rear Seat Upgrade Pkg			925	925	1010	1010
Executive Seating			2950	2950	3250	3250
AWD	C		1775	1775	1955	1955

LS 460—V8—Equipment Schedule 1
W.B. 116.9"; 4.6 Liter.

Body Type	VIN	List	Good	Very Good	Good	Excellent
Sport Special Ed 4D	BL5EF	77875	34200	34900	37200	41600

LS 600h—V8 Hybrid—Equipment Schedule 1
W.B. 121.7"; 5.0 Liter.

Body Type	VIN	List	Good	Very Good	Good	Excellent
L Sedan 4D	DU5EF	113125	47200	48100	49800	54500
Dynamic Radar Cruise Ctrl			450	450	485	485
Premium Luxury Pkg			500	500	545	545
Executive Seating			2950	2950	3255	3255

LFA—V10—Equipment Schedule 1
W.B. 102.6"; 4.8 Liter.

Body Type	VIN	List	Good	Very Good	Good	Excellent
Coupe 2D	HX8BH	377400	****	****	****	360600

2013 LEXUS — JTH(KD5BH)-D-#

CT 200h—4-Cyl. Hybrid—Equipment Schedule 1
W.B. 102.4"; 1.8 Liter.

Body Type	VIN	List	Good	Very Good	Good	Excellent
Hatchback 4D	KD5BH	32745	17550	17900	19500	22200
Dynamic Cruise			475	475	535	535
F SPORT Pkg			1575	1575	1805	1805

IS 250—V6—Equipment Schedule 1
W.B. 107.5"; 2.5 Liter.

Body Type	VIN	List	Good	Very Good	Good	Excellent
Sedan 4D	BF5C2	35960	21200	21600	23000	25800
Dynamic Cruise Control			475	475	535	535
Luxury Plus Value Edition			1025	1025	1185	1185
F Sport Pkg			1000	1000	1145	1145
AWD	C		1575	1575	1795	1795

IS 250C—V6—Equipment Schedule 1
W.B. 107.5"; 2.5 Liter.

Body Type	VIN	List	Good	Very Good	Good	Excellent
Convertible 2D	FF2C2	43405	28700	29300	30800	34500
Dynamic Cruise Control			475	475	530	530
F Sport Pkg			1000	1000	1140	1140
Luxury Pkg			1025	1025	1175	1175

IS 350—V6—Equipment Schedule 1
W.B. 107.5"; 3.5 Liter.

Body Type	VIN	List	Good	Very Good	Good	Excellent
Sedan 4D	BE5C2	41215	25500	26000	27500	30800
Dynamic Cruise Control			475	475	530	530
Luxury Plus Value Edition			1025	1025	1175	1175
F Sport Pkg			1000	1000	1140	1140
AWD	C		1575	1575	1785	1785

IS 350C—V6—Equipment Schedule 1
W.B. 107.5"; 3.5 Liter.

Body Type	VIN	List	Good	Very Good	Good	Excellent
Convertible 2D	FE2C2	47685	30700	31300	32700	36600

Body Type	VIN	List	Trade-In Good	Very Good	Pvt-Party Good	Retail Excellent
Dynamic Cruise Control	....		475	475	525	525
F Sport Pkg	....		1000	1000	1130	1130
Luxury Pkg	....		1025	1025	1170	1170
IS F—V8—Equipment Schedule 1						
W.B. 107.5"; 5.0 Liter.						
Sedan 4D	BP5C2	62495	40900	41700	42700	47200
Dynamic Cruise Control	....		475	475	510	510
ES 300h—4-Cyl. Hybrid—Equipment Schedule 1						
W.B. 111.0"; 2.5 Liter.						
Sedan 4D	BW7GG	39745	27300	28200	29200	32500
Sensing Cruise Control	....		475	475	520	520
Luxury Pkg	....		250	250	280	280
Premium Pkg	....		100	100	110	110
Ultra Luxury Pkg	....		500	500	550	550
ES 350—V6—Equipment Schedule 1						
W.B. 111.0"; 3.5 Liter.						
Sedan 4D	BK7GG	36995	25100	25900	26900	29900
Dynamic Radar Cruise Ctrl	....		475	475	520	520
Luxury Pkg	....		250	250	280	280
Premium Pkg	....		100	100	110	110
Ultra Luxury Pkg	....		500	500	550	550
GS 350—V6—Equipment Schedule 1						
W.B. 112.2"; 3.5 Liter.						
Sedan 4D	BE1BL	47775	28200	28800	30800	35000
Dynamic Cruise Control	....		475	475	555	555
Luxury Pkg	....		1125	1125	1325	1325
Premium Pkg	....		600	600	700	700
F Sport Pkg	....		1575	1575	1860	1860
AWD	C		875	875	1030	1030
GS 450h—V6 Hybrid—Equipment Schedule 1						
W.B. 112.2"; 3.5 Liter.						
Sedan 4D	BS1BL	59825	32200	32900	34900	39600
Dynamic Cruise Control	....		475	475	550	550
Luxury Pkg	....		1125	1125	1315	1315
LS 460—V8—Equipment Schedule 1						
W.B. 116.9", 121.7" (L); 4.6 Liter.						
Sedan 4D	BL1EF	72885	43700	44500	46400	50500
L Sedan 4D	GL1EF	79185	49200	50100	52100	56400
Sensing Cruise Control	....		475	475	495	495
F Sport Pkg	....		1575	1575	1675	1675
Ultra Luxury Pkg	....		2400	2400	2565	2565
AWD	C		1875	1875	2005	2005
LS 600h—V8 Hybrid—Equipment Schedule 1						
W.B. 121.7"; 5.0 Liter.						
L Sedan 4D	DU1EF	120805	64800	66000	67200	71900
Sensing Cruise Control	....		475	475	490	490
Executive Seating	....		2975	2975	3140	3140

2014 LEXUS — JTH(KD5BH)-E-#

Body Type	VIN	List	Trade-In Good	Very Good	Pvt-Party Good	Retail Excellent
CT 200h—4-Cyl. Hybrid—Equipment Schedule 1						
W.B. 102.4"; 1.8 Liter.						
Hatchback 4D	KD5BH	32960	19950	20300	21900	24700
Dynamic Cruise Control	....		500	500	555	555
F Sport Pkg	....		1675	1675	1885	1885
IS 250—V6—Equipment Schedule 1						
W.B. 110.2"; 2.5 Liter.						
Sedan 4D	BF1D2	36845	26800	27300	28400	31400
Dynamic Cruise Control	....		500	500	545	545
Luxury Pkg	....		1075	1075	1200	1200
F Sport Pkg	....		1000	1000	1105	1105
AWD	C		1600	1600	1770	1770
IS 250C—V6—Equipment Schedule 1						
W.B. 107.5"; 2.5 Liter.						
Convertible 2D	FF2C2	43620	32900	33500	34800	38600
Dynamic Cruise Control	....		500	500	545	545
Luxury Pkg	....		1075	1075	1205	1205
F Sport Pkg	....		1000	1000	1115	1115
IS 350—V6—Equipment Schedule 1						
W.B. 110.2"; 3.5 Liter.						
Sedan 4D	BE1D2	40360	30700	31300	32500	36000
Dynamic Cruise Control	....		500	500	545	545
Luxury Pkg	....		1075	1075	1200	1200
F Sport Pkg	....		1000	1000	1110	1110

Body Type	VIN	List	Trade-In Good	Very Good	Pvt-Party Good	Retail Excellent
AWD	C		1600	1600	1775	1775
IS 350C—V6—Equipment Schedule 1						
W.B. 107.5"; 3.5 Liter.						
Convertible 2D	FE2C2	47900	36400	37100	38200	42200
Dynamic Cruise Control			500	500	545	545
Luxury Pkg			1075	1075	1200	1200
F Sport Pkg			1000	1000	1110	1110
IS F—V8—Equipment Schedule 1						
W.B. 107.5"; 5.0 Liter.						
Sedan 4D	BP5C2	64260	46600	47500	48200	52900
Dynamic Cruise Control			500	500	530	530
ES 300h—4-Cyl. Hybrid—Equipment Schedule 1						
W.B. 111.0"; 2.5 Liter.						
Sedan 4D	BK1GG	40260	29700	30500	31500	34800
Dynamic Radar Cruise Ctrl			500	500	545	545
Luxury Pkg			325	325	350	350
Premium Pkg			175	175	185	185
Ultra Luxury Pkg			500	500	550	550
ES 350—V6—Equipment Schedule 1						
W.B. 111.0"; 3.5 Liter.						
Sedan 4D	BW1GG	37380	27800	28600	29500	32600
Dynamic Radar Cruise Ctrl			500	500	545	545
Luxury Pkg			325	325	350	350
Premium Pkg			175	175	185	185
Ultra Luxury Pkg			500	500	555	555
GS 350—V6—Equipment Schedule 1						
W.B. 112.2"; 3.5 Liter.						
Sedan 4D	BE1BL	48610	34100	34800	36600	41000
Adaptive Cruise Control			500	500	565	565
Luxury Pkg			1175	1175	1355	1355
Premium Pkg			625	625	710	710
F Sport Pkg			1675	1675	1920	1920
AWD	C		975	975	1115	1115
GS 450h—V6 Hybrid—Equipment Schedule 1						
W.B. 112.2"; 3.5 Liter.						
Sedan 4D	BS1BL	60510	38600	39300	41100	45900
Adaptive Cruise Control			500	500	565	565
Luxury Pkg			1175	1175	1350	1350
Premium Pkg			625	625	705	705
LS 460—V8—Equipment Schedule 1						
W.B. 116.9", 121.7" (L); 4.6 Liter.						
Sedan 4D	BL5EF	73050	52100	53000	54900	59200
L Sedan 4D	GL5EF	79350	57900	59000	60600	65100
Dynamic Cruise Control			500	500	520	520
Ultra Luxury Pkg			2450	2450	2595	2595
F Sport Pkg			1675	1675	1760	1760
Executive Class Seating			3000	3000	3140	3140
AWD	C		1975	1975	2080	2080
LS 600h—V8 Hybrid—Equipment Schedule 1						
W.B. 121.7"; 5.0 Liter.						
L Sedan 4D	DU1EF	120970	73900	75200	76200	81100
Dynamic Cruise Control			500	500	515	515
Executive Class Seating			3000	3000	3130	3130

LINCOLN

2000 LINCOLN — 1LN(HM81W)-Y-#

Body Type	VIN	List	Trade-In Good	Very Good	Pvt-Party Good	Retail Excellent
TOWN CAR—V8—Equipment Schedule 2						
W.B. 117.7", 123.7" (L Pkg); 4.6 Liter.						
Executive Sedan 4D	HM81W	39300	700	850	1425	2650
Signature Sedan 4D	HM82W	41300	925	1075	1625	2900
Cartier Sedan 4D	HM83W	43800	1000	1175	1825	3350
L Pkg			800	800	1070	1070
Touring			75	75	95	95
CONTINENTAL—V8—Equipment Schedule 2						
W.B. 117.7"; 4.6 Liter.						
Sedan 4D	HM97V	39550	1125	1300	2125	3875
LS—V6—Equipment Schedule 2						
W.B. 114.5"; 3.0 Liter.						
Sedan 4D	HM86S	31450	600	725	1350	2425
Sport Pkg			75	75	95	95

Body Type	VIN	List	Trade-In Good	Very Good	Pvt-Party Good	Retail Excellent
Manual, 5-Spd		-------	(225)	(225)	(300)	(300)
LS—V8—Equipment Schedule 2						
W.B. 114.5"; 3.9 Liter.						
Sedan 4D	HM87A	35225	1475	1725	2375	4075
Sport Pkg			75	75	95	95

2001 LINCOLN — 1LN(HM81W)-1-#

TOWN CAR—V8—Equipment Schedule 2
W.B. 117.7", 123.7" (L); 4.6 Liter.

Body Type	VIN	List	Good	Very Good	Good	Excellent
Executive Sedan 4D	HM81W	39865	875	1025	1625	2950
Executive L Sed 4D	HM84W	44225	2175	2525	3150	5375
Signature Sedan 4D	HM82W	42035	1100	1275	1850	3275
Signature Touring 4D	HM82W	42745	1150	1350	1925	3425
Cartier Sedan 4D	HM83W	44420	1425	1650	2325	4150
Cartier L Sedan 4D	HM85W	49230	3075	3550	4125	6925
CONTINENTAL—V8—Equipment Schedule 2						
W.B. 109.0"; 4.6 Liter.						
Sedan 4D	HM97V	40100	1275	1475	2275	4025
LS—V6—Equipment Schedule 2						
W.B. 114.5"; 3.0 Liter.						
Sedan 4D	HM86S	32250	1100	1275	1825	3075
Sport Pkg			75	75	105	105
Manual, 5-Spd		-------	(225)	(225)	(300)	(300)
LS—V8—Equipment Schedule 2						
W.B. 114.5"; 3.9 Liter.						
Sedan 4D	HM87A	36280	1900	2200	2825	4650
Sport Pkg			75	75	105	105

2002 LINCOLN — 1LN(HM81W)-2-#

TOWN CAR—V8—Equipment Schedule 2
W.B. 117.7", 123.7" (L); 4.6 Liter.

Body Type	VIN	List	Good	Very Good	Good	Excellent
Executive Sedan 4D	HM81W	40540	850	1000	1700	3125
Executive L Sed 4D	HM84W	44600	2575	2950	3550	5925
Signature Sedan 4D	HM82W	42710	1275	1475	2100	3700
Signature Touring 4D	HM82W	43420	1325	1550	2175	3850
Cartier Sedan 4D	HM83W	45095	1725	2000	2675	4575
Cartier L Sedan 4D	HM85W	49605	3325	3825	4500	7400
CONTINENTAL—V8—Equipment Schedule 2						
W.B. 109.0"; 4.6 Liter.						
Sedan 4D	HM97V	38555	1375	1600	2475	4325
LS—V6—Equipment Schedule 2						
W.B. 114.5"; 3.0 Liter.						
Sedan 4D	HM86S	33455	1100	1275	1875	3200
LSE			875	875	1155	1155
Manual, 5-Spd		-------	(275)	(275)	(355)	(355)
LS—V8—Equipment Schedule 2						
W.B. 114.5"; 3.9 Liter.						
Sedan 4D	HM87A	37630	2050	2375	3025	4975
LSE			875	875	1155	1155

2003 LINCOLN — 1LN(HM81W)-3-#

TOWN CAR—V8—Equipment Schedule 2
W.B. 117.7", 123.7" (L); 4.6 Liter.

Body Type	VIN	List	Good	Very Good	Good	Excellent
Executive Sedan 4D	HM81W	41140	1050	1225	1925	3450
Executive L Sed 4D	HM84W	45115	3200	3650	4425	7375
Signature Sedan 4D	HM82W	43600	1350	1575	2350	4100
Cartier Sedan 4D	HM83W	46110	2000	2300	3100	5325
Cartier L Sedan 4D	HM85W	51570	4375	4975	5475	8700
Limited Edition			325	325	445	445
LS—V8—Equipment Schedule 2						
W.B. 114.5"; 3.0 Liter.						
Sedan 4D	HM86S	40695	1700	1950	2650	4350
V6, 3.0 Liter	S		(725)	(725)	(975)	(975)

2004 LINCOLN — 1LN(HM81W)-4-#

TOWN CAR—V8—Equipment Schedule 2
W.B. 117.7", 123.7" (L); 4.6 Liter.

Body Type	VIN	List	Good	Very Good	Good	Excellent
Executive Sedan 4D	HM81W	42810	1600	1825	2475	4125
Executive L Sed 4D	HM84W	45790	3825	4325	5100	8200
Signature Sedan 4D	HM81W	41815	1800	2050	2850	4875
Ultimate Sedan 4D	HM83W	44925	2700	3075	3825	6350
Ultimate L Sedan 4D	HM85W	50470	5100	5800	6650	10550

2004 LINCOLN

Body Type	VIN	List	Trade-In Good	Trade-In Very Good	Pvt-Party Good	Retail Excellent
LS—V6—Equipment Schedule 2						
W.B. 114.5"; 3.0 Liter.						
Sedan 4D	HM86S	32495	**1800**	**2050**	**2750**	**4450**
LS—V8—Equipment Schedule 2						
W.B. 114.5"; 3.9 Liter.						
Sport Sedan 4D	HM87A	40095	**2900**	**3275**	**4025**	**6400**
LSE			**1075**	**1075**	**1420**	**1420**

2005 LINCOLN — 1LN(ForH)(M86S)-5-#

Body Type	VIN	List	Trade-In Good	Trade-In Very Good	Pvt-Party Good	Retail Excellent
LS—V6—Equipment Schedule 2						
W.B. 114.5"; 3.0 Liter.						
Sedan 4D	M86S	32965	**1775**	**2025**	**2975**	**4800**
LS—V8—Equipment Schedule 2						
W.B. 114.5"; 3.9 Liter.						
Sport Sedan 4D	M87A	40515	**2875**	**3250**	**4150**	**6525**
LSE			**1175**	**1175**	**1555**	**1555**
TOWN CAR—V8—Equipment Schedule 2						
W.B. 117.7", 123.7" (L); 4.6 Liter.						
Signature Sedan 4D	M81W	42470	**2500**	**2850**	**3750**	**6075**
Signature Ltd Sedan 4D	M83W	45310	**3225**	**3650**	**4600**	**7300**
Executive L Sedan 4D	M84W	46445	**4875**	**5475**	**6150**	**9425**
Signature L Sedan 4D	M85W	50915	**5925**	**6675**	**7475**	**11350**
Limited Edition			**225**	**225**	**305**	**305**

2006 LINCOLN — (1or3)LN(ForH)(M261)-6-#

Body Type	VIN	List	Trade-In Good	Trade-In Very Good	Pvt-Party Good	Retail Excellent
ZEPHYR—V6—Equipment Schedule 2						
W.B. 107.4"; 3.0 Liter.						
Sedan 4D	M261	29660	**3550**	**3850**	**4850**	**7150**
LS—V8—Equipment Schedule 2						
W.B. 114.5"; 3.9 Liter.						
Sedan 4D	M87A	39945	**2725**	**3075**	**3825**	**5775**
TOWN CAR—V8—Equipment Schedule 2						
W.B. 117.7", 123.7" (L); 4.6 Liter.						
Signature Sedan 4D	M81W	42875	**3275**	**3675**	**4475**	**6825**
Signature Ltd Sedan	M82W	45740	**4175**	**4675**	**5400**	**8125**
Designer Sedan 4D	M83W	46735	**4925**	**5500**	**6250**	**9225**
Executive L Sedan 4D	M84W	46990	**5875**	**6525**	**7225**	**10600**
Signature L Sedan 4D	M85W	51345	**8450**	**9400**	**9825**	**14100**

2007 LINCOLN — (1or3)LN-(M26T)-7-#

Body Type	VIN	List	Trade-In Good	Trade-In Very Good	Pvt-Party Good	Retail Excellent
MKZ—V6—Equipment Schedule 2						
W.B. 107.4"; 3.5 Liter.						
Sedan 4D	M26T	29890	**4875**	**5250**	**6025**	**8475**
AWD	8		**1000**	**1000**	**1340**	**1340**
TOWN CAR—V8—Equipment Schedule 2						
W.B. 117.7", 123.7" (L); 4.6 Liter.						
Signature Sedan 4D	M81W	42985	**4700**	**5175**	**5575**	**7800**
Signature Ltd Sedan	M82W	45850	**5125**	**5650**	**6300**	**8900**
Designer Sedan 4D	M83W	48110	**6350**	**7000**	**7325**	**10050**
Executive L Sedan 4D	M84W	47160	**8425**	**9275**	**9350**	**12650**
Signature L Sedan 4D	M85W	51455	**9550**	**10500**	**10550**	**14300**

2008 LINCOLN — (1or3)LN-(M26T)-8-#

Body Type	VIN	List	Trade-In Good	Trade-In Very Good	Pvt-Party Good	Retail Excellent
MKZ—V6—Equipment Schedule 2						
W.B. 107.4"; 3.5 Liter.						
Sedan 4D	M26T	30915	**6400**	**6825**	**7600**	**10000**
AWD			**1075**	**1075**	**1430**	**1430**
TOWN CAR—V8—Equipment Schedule 2						
W.B. 117.7", 123.7" (L); 4.6 Liter.						
Signature Ltd Sed 4D	M82W	45910	**6550**	**7075**	**8025**	**10850**
Signature L Sedan 4D	M85W	51515	**10950**	**11800**	**12100**	**15650**

2009 LINCOLN — (1or3)LN-(M26T)-9-#

Body Type	VIN	List	Trade-In Good	Trade-In Very Good	Pvt-Party Good	Retail Excellent
MKZ—V6—Equipment Schedule 2						
W.B. 107.4"; 3.5 Liter.						
Sedan 4D	M26T	32535	**7675**	**8100**	**9000**	**11450**
AWD			**1150**	**1150**	**1500**	**1500**
MKS—V6—Equipment Schedule 2						
W.B. 112.9"; 3.7 Liter.						
Sedan 4D	M93R	38465	**9850**	**10400**	**11650**	**14850**
AWD			**2050**	**2050**	**2655**	**2655**

Body Type	VIN	List	Trade-In Good	Very Good	Pvt-Party Good	Retail Excellent
TOWN CAR—V8—Equipment Schedule 2						
W.B. 117.7", 123.7" (L); 4.6 Liter.						
Signature Ltd Sedan	M82W	46760	8025	8500	9750	12750
Signature L Sedan 4D	M05W	52430	12000	12700	13850	17700

2010 LINCOLN — (1or3)LN–(L2GC)–A–#

MKZ—V6—Equipment Schedule 2						
W.B. 107.4"; 3.5 Liter.						
Sedan 4D	L2GC	34965	9500	10000	10950	13500
AWD	J		1200	1200	1545	1545
MKS—V6—Equipment Schedule 2						
W.B. 112.9"; 3.7 Liter.						
Sedan 4D	L9DR	41695	11750	12250	13750	17100
AWD	E		2175	2175	2760	2760
MKS—V6 EcoBoost Twin Turbo—Equipment Schedule 2						
W.B. 112.9"; 3.5 Liter.						
Sedan 4D	L9FT	48985	15050	15700	17550	21900
TOWN CAR—V8—Equipment Schedule 2						
W.B. 117.7", 123.7" (L); 4.6 Liter.						
Signature Ltd Sedan	L8CV	47470	11000	11500	13050	16300
Signature L Sedan 4D	L8FV	53140	15800	16450	18050	22200

2011 LINCOLN — (1or3)LN–(L2GC)–B–#

MKZ—V6—Equipment Schedule 2						
W.B. 107.4"; 3.5 Liter.						
Sedan 4D	L2GC	35180	11050	11550	12550	15100
AWD	J		1275	1275	1610	1610
MKZ—4-Cyl. Hybrid—Equipment Schedule 2						
W.B. 107.4"; 2.5 Liter.						
Sedan 4D	L2L3	35180	11900	12450	13700	16650
MKS—V6—Equipment Schedule 2						
W.B. 112.9"; 3.7 Liter.						
Sedan 4D	L9DR	42095	13450	13900	15700	19000
AWD	E		2300	2300	2890	2890
MKS—V6 EcoBoost Twin Turbo—Equipment Schedule 2						
W.B. 112.9"; 3.5 Liter.						
Sedan 4D	L9FT	48985	16850	17400	19450	23600
TOWN CAR—V8—Equipment Schedule 2						
W.B. 117.7", 123.7" (L); 4.6 Liter.						
Signature LTD Sedan	L8CV	47870	15150	15600	17550	21100
Signature L Sedan	L8FV	53540	19450	20100	21800	25700

2012 LINCOLN — (1,2or3)LN–(L2GC)–C–#

MKZ—V6—Equipment Schedule 2						
W.B. 107.4"; 3.5 Liter.						
Sedan 4D	L2GC	35630	12450	12950	14050	16650
AWD	J		1350	1350	1665	1665
MKZ—4-Cyl. Hybrid—Equipment Schedule 2						
W.B. 107.4"; 2.5 Liter.						
Sedan 4D	L2L3	35630	13800	14350	15700	18750
MKS—V6—Equipment Schedule 2						
W.B. 112.9"; 3.7 Liter.						
Sedan 4D	L9DR	42375	15600	16000	18000	21200
AWD	E		2425	2425	3015	3015
MKS AWD—V6 EcoBoost Twin Turbo—Equipment Schedule 2						
W.B. 112.9"; 3.5 Liter.						
Sedan 4D	L9FT	49265	19000	19500	21600	25400

2013 LINCOLN — (1,2or3)LN–(L2G9)–D–#

MKZ—4-Cyl. EcoBoost—Equipment Schedule 2						
W.B. 112.2"; 2.0 Liter.						
Sedan 4D	L2G9	36800	18850	19550	20600	23800
AWD	J		1400	1400	1675	1675
V6, 3.7 Liter	K		525	525	615	615
MKZ—4-Cyl. Hybrid—Equipment Schedule 2						
W.B. 107.4"; 2.0 Liter.						
Sedan 4D	L2LU	36800	20800	21600	22600	26100
MKS—V6—Equipment Schedule 2						
W.B. 112.9"; 3.7 Liter.						
Sedan 4D	L9DK	43685	18350	18750	21100	24800
AWD	E		2550	2550	3130	3130

2013 LINCOLN

Body Type	VIN	List	Trade-In Good	Very Good	Pvt-Party Good	Retail Excellent

MKS AWD—V6 EcoBoost Twin Turbo—Equipment Schedule 2
W.B. 112.9"; 3.5 Liter.

| Sedan 4D | L9FT | 50675 | 21800 | 22200 | 24700 | 28900 |

2014 LINCOLN — (1,2or3)LN-(L2G9)-E-#

MKZ—4-Cyl. EcoBoost—Equipment Schedule 2
W.B. 112.2"; 2.0 Liter.

Sedan 4D	L2G9	36820	20800	21600	22400	25600
AWD	J		1475	1475	1705	1705
V6, 3.7 Liter	K		625	625	715	715

MKZ—4-Cyl. Hybrid—Equipment Schedule 2
W.B. 112.2"; 2.0 Liter.

| Sedan 4D | L2LU | 36820 | 22900 | 23800 | 24600 | 28200 |

MKS—V6—Equipment Schedule 2
W.B. 112.9"; 3.7 Liter.

| Sedan 4D | L9DK | 41320 | 21000 | 21400 | 23300 | 26700 |
| AWD | E | | 2650 | 2650 | 3045 | 3045 |

MKS AWD—V6 EcoBoost Twin Turbo—Equipment Schedule 2
W.B. 112.9"; 3.5 Liter.

| Sedan 4D | L9FT | 48310 | 24200 | 24700 | 26400 | 29900 |

LOTUS

2005 LOTUS — SCC(PC111)-5-#

ELISE—4-Cyl.—Equipment Schedule 1
W.B. 90.5"; 1.8 Liter.

Coupe 2D	PC111	43915	****	****	****	16800
Sport Pkg			****	****	****	410
Touring Pkg			****	****	****	575

2006 LOTUS — SCC(PC111)-6-#

ELISE—4-Cyl.—Equipment Schedule 1
W.B. 90.5"; 1.8 Liter.

Coupe 2D	PC111	43915	****	****	****	19450
Sport Pkg			****	****	****	430
Touring Pkg			****	****	****	615
Track Pkg			****	****	****	1475

EXIGE—4-Cyl.—Equipment Schedule 1
W.B. 90.5"; 1.8 Liter.

Coupe 2D	PC111	51915	****	****	****	25700
Touring Pkg			****	****	****	605
Track Pkg			****	****	****	1445

2007 LOTUS — SCC(PC111)-7-#

ELISE—4-Cyl.—Equipment Schedule 2
W.B. 90.5"; 1.8 Liter.

| Coupe 2D | PC111 | 44915 | **** | **** | **** | 22700 |
| Track Pkg | | | **** | **** | **** | 1510 |

EXIGE S—4-Cyl. Supercharged—Equipment Schedule 1
W.B. 90.5"; 1.8 Liter.

| Coupe 2D | VC111 | 60815 | **** | **** | **** | 32800 |
| Track Pkg | | | **** | **** | **** | 1475 |

2008 LOTUS — SCC(PC111)-8-#

ELISE—4-Cyl.—Equipment Schedule 2
W.B. 90.5"; 1.8 Liter.

Coupe 2D	PC111	47195	****	****	****	25600
Sport Pkg			****	****	****	495
Touring Pkg			****	****	****	695

ELISE—4-Cyl. Supercharged—Equipment Schedule 2
W.B. 90.5"; 1.8 Liter.

SC Coupe 2D	ZC111	55425	****	****	****	31300
Sport Pkg			****	****	****	490
Touring Pkg			****	****	****	685

EXIGE S—4-Cyl. Supercharged—Equipment Schedule 1
W.B. 90.5"; 1.8 Liter.

Coupe 2D	VC111	61925	****	****	****	35600
240 Coupe 2D	WC111	65815	****	****	****	39700
Touring Pkg			****	****	****	680
Track Pkg			****	****	****	1520

Body Type	VIN	List	Trade-In Good	Very Good	Pvt-Party Good	Retail Excellent

2009 LOTUS — SCC(PC111)–9–#

ELISE—4-Cyl.—Equipment Schedule 2
W.B. 90.5"; 1.8 Liter.

Coupe 2D	PC111	48175	****	****	****	30100
Sport Pkg				****	****	545
Touring Pkg				****	****	735

ELISE—4-Cyl. Supercharged—Equipment Schedule 2
W.B. 90.5"; 1.8 Liter.

SC Coupe 2D	ZC111	55915	****	****	****	35500
Sport Pkg				****	****	540
Touring Pkg				****	****	725

EXIGE—4-Cyl. Supercharged—Equipment Schedule 1
W.B. 90.5"; 1.8 Liter.

S240 Coupe 2D	AC111	66615	****	****	****	43200
S260 Coupe 2D	AC111	75920	****	****	****	48300
Touring Pkg				****	****	720
Track Pkg				****	****	1560

2010 LOTUS — SCC(LHCPC)–A–#

ELISE—4-Cyl.—Equipment Schedule 2
W.B. 90.5"; 1.8 Liter.

Coupe 2D	LHCPC	48375	****	****	****	35000
Sport Pkg				****	****	595
Touring Pkg				****	****	745

ELISE—4-Cyl. Supercharged—Equipment Schedule 2
W.B. 90.5"; 1.8 Liter.

SC Coupe 2D	LHCZC	56115	****	****	****	39400
Sport Pkg				****	****	590
Touring Pkg				****	****	740

EXIGE—4-Cyl. Supercharged—Equipment Schedule 1
W.B. 90.5"; 1.8 Liter.

S240 Coupe 2D	LHHWC	66815	****	****	****	45100
Touring Pkg				****	****	735
Track Pkg				****	****	1580

EVORA—V6—Equipment Schedule 2
W.B. 101.4"; 3.5 Liter.

Coupe 2D	LMDTU	74165	****	****	****	53500
Premium Pkg				****	****	770
Sport Pkg				****	****	575
Technology Pkg				****	****	1235

2011 LOTUS — SCC(LHCPC)–B–#

ELISE—4-Cyl.—Equipment Schedule 2
W.B. 90.5"; 1.6 Liter.

Coupe 2D	LHCPC	48375	****	****	****	39100
Sport Pkg				****	****	645
Touring Pkg				****	****	745

ELISE—4-Cyl. Supercharged—Equipment Schedule 2
W.B. 90.5"; 1.8 Liter.

SC Coupe 2D	LHCZC	56115	****	****	****	42400
Sport Pkg				****	****	640
Touring Pkg				****	****	740

EXIGE—4-Cyl. Supercharged—Equipment Schedule 1
W.B. 90.5"; 1.8 Liter.

S240 Coupe 2D	LHHAC	66815	****	****	****	48800
S260 Sport Coupe 2D	LHHAC	76075	****	****	****	52700
Touring Pkg				****	****	735
Track Pkg				****	****	1575

EVORA—V6—Equipment Schedule 2
W.B. 101.4"; 3.5 Liter.

Coupe 2D	LMDTC	65175	****	****	****	57000
Sport Pkg				****	****	630
Technology Pkg				****	****	1305

2012 LOTUS — SCC(LMDTC)–C–#

EVORA—V6—Equipment Schedule 2
W.B. 101.4"; 3.5 Liter.

Coupe 2D	LMDTC	67275	****	****	****	58100
Sport Pkg				****	****	695
Technology Pkg				****	****	1380

2013 LOTUS

Body Type	VIN	List	Trade-In Good	Very Good	Pvt-Party Good	Retail Excellent

2013 LOTUS — SCC(LMDTC)-D-#

EVORA—V6—Equipment Schedule 2
W.B. 101.4"; 3.5 Liter.

Coupe 2D	LMDTC	68285	****	****	****	61300
Sport Pkg					****	790
Tech Pkg					****	1450

EVORA—V6 Supercharged—Equipment Schedule 2
W.B. 101.4"; 3.5 Liter.

S Coupe 2D	LMDSC	78585	****	****	****	63300
Sport Pkg					****	790
Tech Pkg					****	1450

2014 LOTUS — SCC(LMDTC)-E-#

EVORA—V6—Equipment Schedule 2
W.B. 101.4"; 3.5 Liter.

Coupe 2D	LMDTC	70235	****	****	****	63700
Sport Pkg					****	895
Technology Pkg					****	1525

EVORA—V6 Supercharged—Equipment Schedule 2
W.B. 101.4"; 3.5 Liter.

| S Coupe 2D | LMDSC | 80235 | **** | **** | **** | 65900 |
| Technology Pkg | | | | | **** | 1520 |

MASERATI

2005 MASERATI — ZAM(BC38A)-5-#

COUPE—V8—Equipment Schedule 1
W.B. 104.7"; 4.2 Liter.

| Cambiocorsa Coupe | BC38A | 88227 | 9750 | 10350 | 11400 | 15050 |
| GT Coupe 2D | BC38A | 99522 | 8100 | 8625 | 9950 | 13450 |

2006 MASERATI — ZAM(BC38A)-6-#

GT—V8—Equipment Schedule 1
W.B. 104.7"; 4.2 Liter.

| GT Coupe 2D | BC38A | 81250 | 10100 | 10700 | 12150 | 16050 |

CAMBIOCORSA—V8—Equipment Schedule 1
W.B. 104.7"; 4.2 Liter.

| Coupe 2D | BC38A | 88927 | 12000 | 12750 | 13600 | 17350 |

GRANSPORT—V8—Equipment Schedule 1
W.B. 104.7"; 4.2 Liter.

Coupe 2D	EC38A	100222	20600	21800	21900	27200
LE Coupe 2D	EC38A	105472	21200	22400	22500	27900
Spyder Convertible 2D	EB18A	101250	23900	25300	25000	30800

QUATTROPORTE—V8—Equipment Schedule 1
W.B. 120.6"; 4.2 Liter.

| Sedan 4D | CE39A | 105050 | 12700 | 13450 | 14200 | 18050 |
| Executive GT Sed 4D | CE39A | 117250 | 14450 | 15300 | 16150 | 20600 |

2007 MASERATI — ZAM(FE39A)-7-#

QUATTROPORTE—V8—Equipment Schedule 2
W.B. 120.6"; 4.2 Liter.

DuoSelect Sedan 4D	FE39A	111950	14650	15450	16050	19800
Sedan 4D	CE39A	113600	12300	13000	14100	17850
DuoSelect Exec GT	FE39A	121950	17950	18900	19750	24700
Executive GT Sed 4D	CE39A	123750	16550	17450	18250	22800
DuoSelect Sport GT	FE39A	120650	14250	15000	15900	19900
Sport GT Sedan 4D	CE39A	122450	16600	17450	18250	22700

2008 MASERATI — ZAM(GJ45A)-8-#

GRANTURISMO—V8—Equipment Schedule 2
W.B. 115.8"; 4.2 Liter.

| Coupe 2D | GJ45A | 113450 | 27000 | 28100 | 29000 | 34900 |

QUATTROPORTE—V8—Equipment Schedule 2
W.B. 120.6"; 4.2 Liter.

| Sedan 4D | CE39A | 119000 | 20100 | 21000 | 21800 | 26100 |
| Executive GT Sed 4D | FE39A | 129150 | 25600 | 26700 | 27100 | 32000 |

Body Type	VIN	List	Trade-In Good	Very Good	Pvt-Party Good	Retail Excellent

2009 MASERATI — ZAM(GJ45A)-9-#

GRANTURISMO—V8—Equipment Schedule 2
W.B. 115.8"; 4.2 Liter, 4.7 Liter.

Body Type	VIN	List	Good	Very Good	Good	Excellent
Coupe 2D	GJ45A	121100	31000	32100	32900	38100
S Coupe 2D	HJ45A	125600	38700	40100	40600	46400

QUATTROPORTE—V8—Equipment Schedule 2
W.B. 120.6"; 4.2 Liter.

Sedan 4D	FK39A	124150	22100	22900	24400	28800
S Sedan 4D	JK39A	130150	25700	26700	28100	33200
Sport GT S Sedan 4D	FE39A	138100	28500	29500	30800	36100

2010 MASERATI — ZAM(45GLA)-A-#

GRANTURISMO—V8—Equipment Schedule 2
W.B. 115.8"; 4.2 Liter, 4.7 Liter.

Coupe 2D	45GLA	121900	34700	35700	36900	41700
S Coupe 2D	45KLA	125900	41900	43100	44300	49800
Convertible 2D	45KMA	139700	52000	53500	54200	60700

QUATTROPORTE—V8—Equipment Schedule 2
W.B. 120.6"; 4.2 Liter, 4.7 Liter.

Sedan 4D	39FKA	124650	27300	28100	29700	34100
S Sedan 4D	39JKA	130650	30600	31500	33200	38100
Sport GT S Sedan 4D	39KKA	138600	33200	34200	35800	40900

2011 MASERATI — ZAM(45GLA)-B-#

GRANTURISMO—V8—Equipment Schedule 2
W.B. 115.8"; 4.2 Liter, 4.7 Liter.

Coupe 2D	45GLA	122800	39300	40200	41700	46300
S Coupe 2D	45KLA	126400	47800	49000	50500	55800
Convertible 2D	45KMA	140200	57000	58300	59600	65700

QUATTROPORTE—V8—Equipment Schedule 2
W.B. 120.6"; 4.2 Liter, 4.7 Liter.

Sedan 4D	39FKA	125150	35100	36000	37600	42000
S Sedan 4D	39JKA	131150	38300	39200	40900	45800
Sport GT S Sedan 4D	39KKA	139100	41300	42300	43900	49000

2012 MASERATI — ZAM(45KLA)-C-#

GRANTURISMO—V8—Equipment Schedule 2
W.B. 115.8"; 4.7 Liter.

S Coupe 2D	45KLA	126500	58900	60100	61600	66800
MC Coupe 2D	45MLA	143400	68900	70200	71600	77600
Convertible 2D	45KMA	140600	66900	68300	69700	75700
Sport Convertible 2D	45MMA	146300	73300	74800	75900	82000

QUATTROPORTE—V8—Equipment Schedule 2
W.B. 120.6"; 4.7 Liter.

| S Sedan 4D | 39JKA | 131150 | 46900 | 47900 | 49900 | 54700 |
| Sport GT S Sedan 4D | 39KKA | 139100 | 49300 | 50300 | 52400 | 57300 |

2013 MASERATI — ZAM(45VLA)-D-#

GRANTURISMO—V8—Equipment Schedule 2
W.B. 115.8"; 4.7 Liter.

Sport Coupe 2D	45VLA	129800	63500	64700	66500	71800
Sport Convertible 2D	45VMA	146600	77600	79000	80500	86400
Convertible 2D	45MMA	142100	73300	74700	76300	82100
MC Coupe 2D	45VLA	146700	72300	73600	75200	81000

QUATTROPORTE—V8—Equipment Schedule 2
W.B. 120.6"; 4.7 Liter.

| S Sedan 4D | 39NKA | 132150 | 54300 | 55300 | 57400 | 62100 |
| Sport GT S Sedan 4D | 39MKA | 140100 | 56600 | 57700 | 59700 | 64700 |

2014 MASERATI — ZAM(45VLA)-E-#

GRANTURISMO—V8—Equipment Schedule 2
W.B. 115.8"; 4.7 Liter.

Sport Coupe 2D	45VLA	130300	69400	70600	72300	77600
Sport Convertible 2D	45VMA	147100	87900	89400	90500	96600
Convertible 2D	45MMA	142600	83700	85100	86400	92400
MC Coupe 2D	45VLA	147200	78900	80300	81800	87600
MC Convertible 2D	45VMA	157200	92100	93800	95200	101300

QUATTROPORTE—V6 Twin Turbo—Equipment Schedule 2
W.B. 124.8"; 3.0 Liter.

| S Q4 Sedan 4D | 56RRA | 106900 | 69300 | 70500 | 72000 | 77000 |

Body Type	VIN	List	Trade-In Good	Very Good	Pvt-Party Good	Retail Excellent
QUATTROPORTE—V8 Twin Turbo—Equipment Schedule 2						
W.B. 124.8"; 3.8 Liter.						
GTS Sedan 4D	56PPA	144900	**73600**	**74900**	**76400**	**81700**

MAYBACH

2005 MAYBACH — WDB(VF78J)-5-#

57—V12 Twin Turbo—Equipment Schedule 1
W.B. 133.5"; 5.5 Liter.

Sedan 4D	VF78J	327250	****	****	****	**73500**

62—V12 Twin Turbo—Equipment Schedule 1
W.B. 150.7"; 5.5 Liter.

Sedan 4D	VG78J	377750	****	****	****	**124800**

2006 MAYBACH — WDB(VF78J)-6-#

57—V12 Twin Turbo—Equipment Schedule 1
W.B. 133.5"; 5.5 Liter, 6.0 Liter.

Sedan 4D	VF78J	335250	****	****	****	**103600**
S Sedan 4D	VF79J	369750	****	****	****	**131700**

62—V12 Twin Turbo—Equipment Schedule 1
W.B. 150.7"; 5.5 Liter.

Sedan 4D	VG78J	385250	****	****	****	**158300**

2007 MAYBACH — WDB(VF78J)-7-#

57—V12 Twin Turbo—Equipment Schedule 1
W.B. 133.5"; 5.5 Liter, 6.0 Liter.

Sedan 4D	VF78J	338250	****	****	****	**139400**
S Sedan 4D	VF79J	377750	****	****	****	**165500**

62—V12 Twin Turbo—Equipment Schedule 1
W.B. 133.5", 150.7"; 5.5 Liter, 6.0 Liter.

Sedan 4D	VG78J	389250	****	****	****	**191100**
S Sedan 4D	VG79J	428750	****	****	****	**217600**

2008 MAYBACH — WDB(VF78J)-8-#

57—V12 Twin Turbo—Equipment Schedule 1
W.B. 133.5", 150.7"; 5.5 Liter, 6.0 Liter.

Sedan 4D	VF78J	343250	****	****	****	**164500**
S Sedan 4D	VF79J	382750	****	****	****	**189400**

62—V12 Twin Turbo—Equipment Schedule 1
W.B. 133.5", 150.7"; 5.5 Liter, 6.0 Liter.

Sedan 4D	VG78J	394250	****	****	****	**231400**
S Sedan 4D	VG79J	433750	****	****	****	**261600**

2009 MAYBACH — WDB(VF78J)-9-#

57—V12 Twin Turbo—Equipment Schedule 1
W.B. 133.5", 150.7"; 5.5 Liter, 6.0 Liter.

Sedan 4D	VF78J	360750	****	****	****	**200700**
S Sedan 4D	VF79J	400250	****	****	****	**224100**

62—V12 Twin Turbo—Equipment Schedule 1
W.B. 150.7"; 5.5 Liter, 6.0 Liter.

Sedan 4D	VG78J	411750	****	****	****	**270200**
S Sedan 4D	VG79J	451250	****	****	****	**298600**

LANDAULET—V12 Twin Turbo—Equipment Schedule 1
W.B. 150.7"; 6.0 Liter.

Sedan 4D		1382750				

2010 MAYBACH — WDB(VF7JB)-A-#

57—V12 Twin Turbo—Equipment Schedule 1
W.B. 133.5", 150.7"; 5.5 Liter, 6.0 Liter.

Sedan 4D	VF7JB	368750	****	****	****	**278500**
S Sedan 4D	VF7KB	408250	****	****	****	**300100**
Zeppelin Sedan 4D	VG7KB	458250	****	****	****	**382400**

62—V12 Twin Turbo—Equipment Schedule 1
W.B. 150.7"; 5.5 Liter, 6.0 Liter.

Sedan 4D	VG7JB	454750	****	****	****	**343200**
S Sedan 4D		494250	****	****	****	**379700**
Zeppelin Sedan 4D	VG7KB	509250	****	****	****	**450800**

LANDAULET—V12 Twin Turbo—Equipment Schedule 1
W.B. 150.7"; 6.0 Liter.

Body Type	VIN	List	Trade-In Good	Very Good	Pvt-Party Good	Retail Excellent
Sedan 4D	VG7KB	1382750				

2011 MAYBACH — WDB(VF7JB)-B-#

57—V12 Twin Turbo—Equipment Schedule 1
W.B. 133.5", 150.7"; 5.5 Liter, 6.0 Liter.

Sedan 4D	VF7JB	375250	****	****	****	316200
S Sedan 4D	VF7HB	414750	****	****	****	336500

62—V12 Twin Turbo—Equipment Schedule 1
W.B. 150.7"; 5.5 Liter, 6.0 Liter.

Sedan 4D	VG7JB	430750	****	****	****	375300
S Sedan 4D	VG7HB	470250	****	****	****	409300

LANDAULET—V12 Twin Turbo—Equipment Schedule 1
W.B. 150.7"; 6.0 Liter.

Sedan 4D	VG7HB	1382750				

2012 MAYBACH — WDB(VF7JB)-C-#

57—V12 Twin Turbo—Equipment Schedule 1
W.B. 133.5", 150.7"; 5.5 Liter, 6.0 Liter.

Sedan 4D	VF7JB	379050	****	****	****	353900
S Sedan 4D	VF7HB	418950	****	****	****	373300

62—V12 Twin Turbo—Equipment Schedule 1
W.B. 150.7"; 5.5 Liter, 6.0 Liter.

Sedan 4D	VG7HB	430450	****	****	****	410400
S Sedan 4D	VG7HB	470350	****	****	****	442300

LANDAULET—V12 Twin Turbo—Equipment Schedule 1
W.B. 150.7"; 6.0 Liter.

Sedan 4D	VG7HB	1382750				

MAZDA

2000 MAZDA — (Jor1)(M1orYV)(BJ222)-Y-#

PROTEGE'—4-Cyl.—Equipment Schedule 6
W.B. 102.8"; 1.6 Liter, 1.8 Liter.

DX Sedan 4D	BJ222	13995	375	475	1050	1925
LX Sedan 4D	BJ222	14840	600	725	1350	2500
ES Sedan 4D	BJ221	15490	700	825	1500	2750

626—4-Cyl.—Equipment Schedule 4
W.B. 105.1"; 2.0 Liter.

LX Sedan 4D	GF2C	19695	1375	1675	2175	3725
ES Sedan 4D	GF2C	21095	1775	2150	2675	4575
Manual, 5-Spd			(175)	(175)	(220)	(220)
V6, 2.5 Liter	D		100	100	135	135

MX-5 MIATA—4-Cyl.—Equipment Schedule 6
W.B. 89.2"; 1.8 Liter.

Convertible 2D	NB353	22595	2050	2250	2800	4400
LS Convertible 2D	NB353	25345	2650	2925	3500	5475
Special Ed Conv 2D	NB353	25505	2675	2975	3675	5750
Hard Top			300	300	400	400

MILLENNIA—V6—Equipment Schedule 2
W.B. 108.3"; 2.5 Liter.

Sedan 4D	TA221	25445	725	875	1400	2450

MILLENIA—V6 Supercharged—Equipment Schedule 2
W.B. 108.3"; 2.3 Liter.

S Sedan 4D	TA222	30445	1025	1200	1750	3050
Millennium Edition			100	100	125	125

2001 MAZDA — (Jor1)(M1orYV)(BJ222)-1-#

PROTEGE'—4-Cyl.—Equipment Schedule 6
W.B. 102.8"; 1.6 Liter, 2.0 Liter.

DX Sedan 4D	BJ222	14095	400	475	1050	1950
LX Sedan 4D	BJ222	14895	650	775	1400	2525
ES Sedan 4D	BJ225	16015	775	900	1600	2875
MP3 Sedan 4D	BJ227	18500	950	1125	1525	2475

626—4-Cyl.—Equipment Schedule 4
W.B. 105.1"; 2.0 Liter.

LX Sedan 4D	GF2C	20015	1550	1875	2375	3975
ES Sedan 4D	GF2C	21415	2050	2450	2875	4775
Manual, 5-Spd			(200)	(200)	(265)	(265)
V6, 2.5 Liter	D		100	100	135	135

2001 MAZDA

Body Type	VIN	List	Trade-In Good	Very Good	Pvt-Party Good	Retail Excellent
MX-5 MIATA—4-Cyl.—Equipment Schedule 6						
W.B. 89.2"; 1.8 Liter.						
Convertible 2D	NB353	21660	**2400**	**2625**	**3125**	**4775**
LS Convertible 2D	NB353	24410	**2975**	**3275**	**3825**	**5775**
SE Convertible 2D	NB353	26195	**3100**	**3425**	**4050**	**6175**
Hard Top			**300**	**300**	**400**	**400**
MILLENIA—V6—Equipment Schedule 2						
W.B. 108.3"; 2.5 Liter.						
Sedan 4D	TA221	28505	**950**	**1100**	**1650**	**2800**
MILLENIA—V6 Supercharged—Equipment Schedule 2						
W.B. 108.3"; 2.3 Liter.						
S Sedan 4D	TA222	31505	**1250**	**1450**	**2000**	**3375**

2002 MAZDA — (Jor1)(M1orYV)(BJ222)-2-#

Body Type	VIN	List	Trade-In Good	Very Good	Pvt-Party Good	Retail Excellent
PROTEGE'—4-Cyl.—Equipment Schedule 6						
W.B. 102.8"; 2.0 Liter.						
DX Sedan 4D	BJ222	14530	**525**	**600**	**1475**	**2825**
LX Sedan 4D	BJ222	15335	**725**	**850**	**1725**	**3200**
ES Sedan 4D	BJ221	16060	**850**	**975**	**1950**	**3650**
PROTEGE5—4-Cyl.—Equipment Schedule 6						
W.B. 102.8"; 2.0 Liter.						
Hatchback 4D	BJ245	16815	**1000**	**1175**	**2350**	**4450**
626—4-Cyl.—Equipment Schedule 4						
W.B. 105.1"; 2.0 Liter.						
LX Sedan 4D	GF22C	20015	**1875**	**2225**	**2775**	**4650**
ES Sedan 4D	GF22C	22915	**2775**	**3275**	**3800**	**6275**
Manual, 5-Spd			**(200)**	**(200)**	**(265)**	**(265)**
V6, 2.5 Liter	D		**125**	**125**	**175**	**175**
MX-5 MIATA—4-Cyl.—Equipment Schedule 6						
W.B. 89.2"; 1.8 Liter.						
Convertible 2D	NB353	21660	**2650**	**2925**	**3475**	**5150**
LS Convertible 2D	NB353	24410	**3325**	**3650**	**4150**	**6100**
SE Convertible 2D	NB353	26275	**3600**	**3950**	**4475**	**6625**
Hard Top			**325**	**325**	**445**	**445**
MILLENIA—V6—Equipment Schedule 2						
W.B. 108.3"; 2.5 Liter.						
Sedan 4D	TA221	28505	**1075**	**1225**	**1800**	**3050**
MILLENIA—V6 Supercharged—Equipment Schedule 2						
W.B. 108.3"; 2.3 Liter.						
S Sedan 4D	TA222	31505	**1350**	**1550**	**2125**	**3575**

2003 MAZDA — (Jor1)(M1orYV)(BJ225)-3-#

Body Type	VIN	List	Trade-In Good	Very Good	Pvt-Party Good	Retail Excellent
PROTEGE'—4-Cyl.—Equipment Schedule 6						
W.B. 102.8"; 2.0 Liter.						
DX Sedan 4D	BJ225	14690	**775**	**900**	**1675**	**3000**
LX Sedan 4D	BJ225	15575	**1050**	**1200**	**1925**	**3350**
ES Sedan 4D	BJ225	16300	**1200**	**1350**	**2175**	**3800**
PROTEGE5—4-Cyl.—Equipment Schedule 6						
W.B. 102.8"; 2.0 Liter.						
Hatchback 4D	BJ245	17055	**1400**	**1575**	**2550**	**4525**
PROTEGE'—4-Cyl. Turbo—Equipment Schedule 6						
W.B. 102.8"; 2.0 Liter.						
Mazdaspeed Sedan 4D	BJ227	20500	**1850**	**2100**	**2600**	**4125**
6—4-Cyl.—Equipment Schedule 4						
W.B. 105.3"; 2.3 Liter.						
i Sedan 4D	FP80C	19900	**1625**	**1900**	**2550**	**4375**
Sport Pkg			**225**	**225**	**290**	**290**
Manual, 5-Spd			**(225)**	**(225)**	**(310)**	**(310)**
6—V6—Equipment Schedule 4						
W.B. 105.3"; 3.0 Liter.						
s Sedan 4D	FP80D	22520	**2025**	**2350**	**3025**	**5150**
Sport Pkg			**225**	**225**	**290**	**290**
Manual, 5-Spd			**(225)**	**(225)**	**(310)**	**(310)**
MX-5 MIATA—4-Cyl.—Equipment Schedule 6						
W.B. 89.2"; 1.8 Liter.						
Club Sport Conv 2D	NB353	20000	********	********	********	**10600**
Convertible 2D	NB353	22125	**2700**	**2975**	**3525**	**5225**
Shinsen Conv 2D	NB353	23625	**3450**	**3775**	**4225**	**6100**
LS Convertible 2D	NB353	24905	**3600**	**3925**	**4400**	**6375**
SE Convertible 2D	NB353	26550	**4125**	**4500**	**4950**	**7175**
Hard Top			**375**	**375**	**485**	**485**

2004 MAZDA

Body Type	VIN	List	Trade-In Good	Very Good	Pvt-Party Good	Retail Excellent

2004 MAZDA — (Jor1)(M1orYV)(BK12F)-4-#

MAZDA3—4-Cyl.—Equipment Schedule 6
W.B. 103.9"; 2.0 Liter, 2.3 Liter.
i Sedan 4D	BK12F	15100	1975	2225	3025	4925
s Sedan 4D	BK123	17825	2800	3150	3750	5850
s Hatchback 4D	BK143	18315	3025	3400	3900	6000

MAZDA6—4-Cyl.—Equipment Schedule 4
W.B. 105.3"; 2.3 Liter.
i Sedan 4D	FP80C	20120	2125	2450	2975	4875
i Hatchback 4D	FP84C	22165	2625	3025	3575	5850
Sport Pkg			225	225	310	310
Manual, 5-Spd			(275)	(275)	(375)	(375)

MAZDA6—V6—Equipment Schedule 4
W.B. 105.3"; 3.0 Liter.
s Sedan 4D	FP80D	22765	2625	3025	3525	5750
s Hatchback 4D	FP84D	24315	3050	3525	3950	6350
s Wagon 4D	FP82D	23645	2825	3275	3725	6050
Sport Pkg			225	225	310	310
Manual, 5-Spd			(275)	(275)	(375)	(375)

MX-5 MIATA—4-Cyl.—Equipment Schedule 6
W.B. 89.2"; 1.8 Liter.
Convertible 2D	NB353	22388	3325	3625	4125	5950
LS Convertible 2D	NB353	25193	4200	4575	5075	7275
Hard Top			400	400	520	520

MX-5 MIATA—4-Cyl. Turbo—Equipment Schedule 6
W.B. 89.2"; 1.8 Liter.
| Mazdaspeed Conv | NB354 | 26020 | 4425 | 4800 | 5450 | 7775 |

RX-8—Rotary—Equipment Schedule 3
W.B. 106.4"; 1.3 Liter.
Coupe 4D	FE173	25700	2275	2525	3300	5300
Sport Pkg			325	325	420	420
Touring			475	475	625	625
Grand Touring Pkg			625	625	845	845

2005 MAZDA — (Jor1)(M1orYV)-(K12F)-5-#

MAZDA3—4-Cyl.—Equipment Schedule 6
W.B. 103.9"; 2.0 Liter, 2.3 Liter.
i Sedan 4D	K12F	15100	2425	2725	3550	5550
s Sedan 4D	K123	18035	2900	3275	4000	6125
s Hatchback 4D	K143	18525	3025	3400	4100	6250
sp Sedan 4D	K323	20130	3225	3600	4275	6475
sp Hatchback 4D	K343	20130	3225	3600	4325	6575

MAZDA6—4-Cyl.—Equipment Schedule 4
W.B. 105.3"; 2.3 Liter.
i Sedan 4D	P80C	20590	2325	2675	3350	5375
i Sport Sedan 4D	P80C	23090	2875	3300	3825	6000
i Sport Hatchback 4D	P84C	23620	3025	3500	4125	6425
i Grand Touring Sedan	P80C	24940	3475	4000	4575	7100
Manual, 5-Spd			(325)	(325)	(445)	(445)

MAZDA6—V6—Equipment Schedule 4
W.B. 105.3"; 3.0 Liter.
s Sedan 4D	P80D	24990	2825	3250	3850	6100
s Hatchback 4D	P84D	25690	3250	3750	4375	6800
s Base Sport Wagon	P82D	24590	3025	3475	4150	6525
s Sport Wagon	P82D	25720	3425	3950	4525	7050
s Grand Touring Sedan	P80D	26870	3750	4325	4900	7625
s Grand Touring Wagon	P82D	27540	4100	4700	5225	8100
Manual, 5-Spd			(325)	(325)	(445)	(445)

MX-5 MIATA—4-Cyl.—Equipment Schedule 6
W.B. 89.2"; 1.8 Liter.
Convertible 2D	B353	22643	3425	3725	4450	6325
LS Convertible 2D	B353	25448	4225	4575	5450	7700
Hard Top			425	425	555	555

MX-5 MIATA—4-Cyl. Turbo—Equipment Schedule 6
W.B. 89.2"; 1.8 Liter.
| Mazdaspeed Conv 2D | B354 | 26325 | 5000 | 5425 | 6200 | 8700 |

RX-8—Rotary—Equipment Schedule 3
W.B. 106.4"; 1.3 Liter.
Coupe 4D	E173	26120	2650	2925	3750	5775
Shinka Special Ed 4D	E173	32220	3950	4350	5250	7950
Sport Pkg			350	350	455	455

Body Type	VIN	List	Trade-In Good	Very Good	Pvt-Party Good	Retail Excellent
Touring		....	**525**	**525**	**685**	**685**
Grand Touring Pkg		....	**675**	**675**	**910**	**910**

2006 MAZDA — (Jor1)(M1orYV)–(K12F)–6–#

MAZDA3—4-Cyl.—Equipment Schedule 6
W.B. 103.9"; 2.0 Liter, 2.3 Liter.

Body Type	VIN	List	Good	Very Good	Good	Excellent
i Sedan 4D	K12F	15170	2900	3225	4025	6050
i Touring Sedan 4D	K12F	17450	3125	3475	4300	6375
s Sedan 4D	K123	18390	3375	3750	4550	6725
s Hatchback 4D	K143	18880	3475	3875	4675	6925
s Touring Sedan 4D	K123	19125	3575	3975	4775	7000
s Touring Hatchback 4D	K143	19125	3575	3975	4800	7075
s Grand Touring Sedan	K123	20675	3800	4225	4950	7250
s Grand Touring H'Bck	K143	20675	3800	4225	5000	7350
Manual, 5-Spd			(275)	(275)	(355)	(355)

MAZDA6—4-Cyl.—Equipment Schedule 4
W.B. 105.3"; 2.3 Liter.

Body Type	VIN	List	Good	Very Good	Good	Excellent
i Sedan 4D	P80C	20570	2800	3200	3775	5850
i Sport Sedan 4D	P80C	23670	3275	3750	4375	6700
i Sport Hatchback 4D	P84C	23870	3650	4175	4800	7350
i Grand Touring Sedan	P80C	25270	4325	4925	5525	8400
i Grand Sport Sedan 4D	P80C	25770	4675	5300	5875	8925
Manual, 5-Spd			(375)	(375)	(510)	(510)

MAZDA6—V6—Equipment Schedule 4
W.B. 105.3"; 3.0 Liter.

Body Type	VIN	List	Good	Very Good	Good	Excellent
s Sedan 4D	P80D	24520	3275	3750	4400	6775
s Wagon 4D	P82D	25120	3700	4225	4875	7450
s Sport Sedan 4D	P80D	25420	3775	4275	4925	7550
s Sport Hatchback 4D	P84D	26020	4000	4550	5175	7900
s Sport Wagon 4D	P82D	26120	4200	4775	5375	8200
s Grand Touring Sedan	P80D	27820	4575	5200	5800	8825
s Grand Touring Wagon	P82D	27720	4825	5450	6025	9150
s Grand Sport Sedan	P80D	28620	4900	5550	6100	9250
s Grand Sport H'Back	P84D	29220	4725	5350	5950	9050
s Grand Sport Wag 4D	P82D	29420	5025	5725	6375	9625
Manual, 5-Spd			(375)	(375)	(510)	(510)

MAZDASPEED6 AWD—4-Cyl. Turbo—Equipment Schedule 4
W.B. 105.3"; 2.3 Liter.

Body Type	VIN	List	Good	Very Good	Good	Excellent
Sport Sedan 4D	G12L	28555	4375	4775	5300	7500
Grand Touring Sed 4D	G12L	30585	4850	5300	5975	8425

MX-5 MIATA—4-Cyl.—Equipment Schedule 6
W.B. 91.7"; 2.0 Liter.

Body Type	VIN	List	Good	Very Good	Good	Excellent
Club Spec Conv 2D	C25F	20995	4750	5100	5775	7775
Convertible 2D	C25F	21995	5000	5400	6050	8175
Touring Convertible 2D	C25F	22995	5450	5875	6525	8850
Sport Convertible 2D	C25F	23495	6075	6525	7225	9700
Grand Touring Conv	C25F	24995	6150	6625	7250	9725
3rd Generation Ltd Cnv	C25F	27260	8825	9475	10100	13500
Hard Top			450	450	550	550

RX-8—Rotary—Equipment Schedule 3
W.B. 106.4"; 1.3 Liter.

Body Type	VIN	List	Good	Very Good	Good	Excellent
Coupe 4D	E173	26995	3325	3650	4625	6050
Shinka Spcl Ed 4D	E173	33880	4600	5050	6150	9100
Sport Pkg			375	375	500	500
Touring			550	550	740	740
Grand Touring Pkg			725	725	975	975

2007 MAZDA — (Jor1)(M1orYV)–(K12F)–7–#

MAZDA3—4-Cyl.—Equipment Schedule 6
W.B. 103.9"; 2.0 Liter, 2.3 Liter.

Body Type	VIN	List	Good	Very Good	Good	Excellent
i Sport Sedan 4D	K12F	15255	3375	3700	4700	6950
i Touring Sedan 4D	K12F	17615	3625	3975	4825	6975
s Sport Sedan 4D	K123	18600	4350	4775	5550	7900
s Sport Hatchback 4D	K143	19090	4825	5300	5950	8375
s Touring Sedan 4D	K123	19835	4725	5200	6025	8450
s Touring Hatchback 4D	K143	19835	4775	5250	6050	8475
s Grand Touring Sedan	K123	21305	4850	5325	6125	8600
s Grand Touring H'Bck	K143	21305	4850	5325	6100	8500
Manual, 5-Spd			(300)	(300)	(385)	(385)

MAZDASPEED3—4-Cyl. Turbo—Equipment Schedule 6
W.B. 103.9"; 2.3 Liter.

Body Type	VIN	List	Good	Very Good	Good	Excellent
Sport Hatchback 4D	K14L	22800	5725	6275	7000	9700

2007 MAZDA

Body Type	VIN	List	Trade-In Good	Very Good	Pvt-Party Good	Retail Excellent
Grand Touring H'Back	K14L	24515	7100	7775	8225	11100

MAZDA6—4-Cyl.—Equipment Schedule 4
W.B. 105.3"; 2.3 Liter.

i Sport Sedan 4D	P80C	20425	3175	3575	4250	6350
i Sport Value Ed Sedan	P80C	20925	3400	3825	4575	6950
i Spt Value Ed H'Back	P84C	21925	4300	4850	5550	8325
i Touring Sedan 4D	P80C	23015	3925	4425	5125	7675
i Touring Hatchback 4D	P84C	24015	4975	5600	6225	9200
i Grand Touring Sedan	P80C	24585	4925	5525	6100	9025
i Grand Touring H'Back	P84C	25335	5025	5650	6425	9500
Manual, 5-Spd			(425)	(425)	(555)	(555)

MAZDA6—V6—Equipment Schedule 4
W.B. 105.3"; 3.0 Liter.

s Sport Sedan 4D	P80D	23635	3925	4425	5150	7750
s Spt Value Ed H'Back	P84D	24635	4700	5275	5975	8975
s Spt Value Ed Wagon	P82D	24685	4325	4850	5575	8400
s Touring Sedan 4D	P80D	25725	4825	5425	6050	8975
s Touring H'Back 4D	P84D	26725	5275	5950	6675	9850
s Touring Wagon 4D	P82D	26775	5750	6450	7075	10300
s Grand Touring Sedan	P80D	27595	5300	5975	6700	9875
s Grand Touring H'Back	P84D	28345	5675	6400	7025	10250
s Grand Touring Wagon	P82D	28395	5900	6625	7200	10450
Manual, 5-Spd			(425)	(425)	(555)	(555)

MAZDASPEED6 AWD—4-Cyl. Turbo—Equipment Schedule 4
W.B. 105.3"; 2.3 Liter.

Sport Sedan 4D	G12L	28590	5400	5875	6500	8900
Grand Touring Sedan	G12L	30520	6175	6700	7300	9950

MX-5 MIATA—4-Cyl.—Equipment Schedule 6
W.B. 91.7"; 2.0 Liter.

SV Convertible 2D	C25F	20995	4875	5200	5975	7925
Sport Conv Hard Top	C26F	24945	6850	7325	8100	10750

MX-5 MIATA—4-Cyl.—Equipment Schedule 6
W.B. 91.7"; 2.0 Liter.

Sport Convertible 2D	C25F	21995	5800	6200	6850	9000
Touring Convertible 2D	C25F	23800	5800	6225	6975	9225
Grand Touring Conv	C25F	25060	6575	7025	7750	10200
Touring Conv Hard Top	C26F	24789	6525	6975	7725	10250
Grand Touring HT 2D	C26F	28055	8125	8675	9325	12150

RX-8—Rotary—Equipment Schedule 3
W.B. 106.4"; 1.3 Liter.

Sport Coupe 4D	E173	27030	4225	4600	5250	7300
Touring Coupe 4D	E173	30930	5525	6000	6700	9200
Grand Touring Coupe	E173	32365	7650	8275	8700	11700
Performance Pkg			400	400	515	515

2008 MAZDA — (Jor1)(M1orYV)-(K12F)-8-#

MAZDA3—4-Cyl.—Equipment Schedule 6
W.B. 103.9"; 2.0 Liter, 2.3 Liter.

i Sport Sedan 4D	K12F	15390	4425	4750	5725	7925
i Touring Sedan 4D	K12F	17750	4700	5050	5925	8050
i Touring Value Sed 4D	K12F	17230	4600	4900	5800	7875
s Sport Sedan 4D	K123	18980	5200	5600	6600	8925
s Touring Sedan 4D	K123	19470	5500	5925	6875	9250
s Sport Hatchback 4D	K143	19470	5650	6100	7025	9425
s Touring Hatchback 4D	K123	19970	5775	6225	7150	9550
s Grand Touring Sedan	K123	21440	6325	6800	7625	10100
s Grand Touring H'Bck	K143	21440	6250	6725	7550	10050
Manual, 5-Spd w/Overdrive			(350)	(350)	(460)	(460)

MAZDASPEED3—4-Cyl. Turbo—Equipment Schedule 6
W.B. 103.9"; 2.3 Liter.

Sport Hatchback 4D	K14L	22935	7125	7675	8450	11100
Grand Touring H'Back	K14L	24650	7975	8575	9225	11950

MAZDA6—4-Cyl.—Equipment Schedule 4
W.B. 105.3"; 2.3 Liter.

i Sport Sedan 4D	P80C	19585	3850	4250	4950	7025
i Sport Value Sedan 4D	P80C	21245	4400	4825	5575	7950
i Spt Value Ed H'Back	P84C	22245	5025	5525	6500	9275
i Touring Sedan 4D	P80C	22835	4550	5000	5800	8300
i Touring Hatchback 4D	P84C	23835	5450	6000	6950	9875
i Grand Touring Sedan	P80C	24685	5975	6575	7325	10250
i Grand Touring H'Back	P84C	25435	6325	6950	7700	10800

MAZDA6—V6—Equipment Schedule 4
W.B. 105.3"; 3.0 Liter.

2008 MAZDA

Body Type	VIN	List	Trade-In Good	Very Good	Pvt-Party Good	Retail Excellent
s Sport Value Sedan 4D	P80D	23755	5075	5600	6450	9075
s Spt Value Ed H'Back	P84D	24755	5975	6575	7450	10550
s Touring Sedan 4D	P80D	25445	5725	6300	7125	10550
s Touring H'Back 4D	P84D	26445	6325	6950	7750	10900
s Grand Touring Sedan	P80D	27595	7325	8050	8675	11950
s Grand Touring H'Back	P84D	28345	7225	7925	8600	11850
Manual, 5-Spd w/Overdrive			(450)	(450)	(585)	(585)

MX-5 MIATA—4-Cyl.—Equipment Schedule 6
W.B. 91.7"; 2.0 Liter.

SV Convertible 2D	C25F	21180	5675	6000	6875	8800

MX-5 MIATA—4-Cyl.—Equipment Schedule 6
W.B. 91.7"; 2.0 Liter.

Sport Convertible 2D	C25F	22180	6525	6900	7750	9825
Touring Convertible 2D	C25F	24225	6800	7175	8075	10250
Grand Touring Conv	C25F	25485	7550	7975	8825	11150
Special Ed Conv 2D	C26F	27225	8050	8500	9400	11900
Power Hard Top			1100	1100	1325	1325

RX-8—Rotary—Equipment Schedule 6
W.B. 106.4"; 1.3 Liter.

Sport Coupe 4D	E173	27030	4550	4875	5800	7775
Touring Coupe 4D	E173	30930	7100	7600	8425	11100
Grand Touring Coupe	E173	32365	8375	8975	9675	12550
40th Anniv Coupe 4D	E173	32705	8525	9125	9950	13000
Performance Pkg			450	450	570	570

2009 MAZDA — (Jor1)(M1orYV)-(K12F)-9-#

MAZDA3—4-Cyl.—Equipment Schedule 6
W.B. 103.9"; 2.0 Liter, 2.3 Liter.

i Sport Sedan 4D	K12F	16060	5225	5550	6725	8850
i Touring Value Sed 4D	K12F	18465	5625	5975	7050	9150
s Sport Sedan 4D	K123	19455	5950	6300	7500	9850
s Sport Hatchback 4D	K143	19945	6550	6950	8075	10500
s Touring Sedan 4D	K123	20445	6575	6975	8175	10600
s Touring Hatchback 4D	K143	20445	6750	7150	8325	10750
s Grand Touring Sedan	K123	22215	7050	7450	8575	11050
s Grand Touring H'Bck	K143	22215	7200	7625	8725	11200
Manual, 5-Spd w/Overdrive			(375)	(375)	(490)	(490)

MAZDASPEED3—4-Cyl. Turbo—Equipment Schedule 6
W.B. 103.9"; 2.3 Liter.

Sport Hatchback 4D	K14L	23410	8100	8575	9525	12050
Grand Touring H'Back	K14L	25125	8875	9400	10300	12900

MAZDA6—4-Cyl.—Equipment Schedule 4
W.B. 109.8"; 2.5 Liter.

i Sport Value Sedan 4D	P80A	19220	5200	5625	6575	8900
i Sport Sedan 4D	P81A	21820	5600	6075	6825	9075
i Touring Sedan 4D	P82A	23275	5975	6475	7350	9900
i Grand Touring Sedan	P82A	26480	7225	7825	8675	11550

MAZDA6—V6—Equipment Schedule 4
W.B. 109.8"; 3.7 Liter.

s Sport Sedan 4D	P81B	24065	6650	7200	8050	10700
s Touring Sedan 4D	P82B	25745	7975	8625	9350	12350
s Grand Touring Sedan	P82B	28930	8400	9075	9850	13050

MX-5 MIATA—4-Cyl.—Equipment Schedule 6
W.B. 91.7"; 2.0 Liter.

SV Convertible 2D	C25F	22420	6325	6625	7700	9550

MX-5 MIATA—4-Cyl.—Equipment Schedule 6
W.B. 91.7"; 2.0 Liter.

Sport Convertible 2D	C25F	23420	6975	7275	8350	10300
Touring Convertible 2D	C25F	25760	7550	7875	8950	11050
Grand Touring Conv	C25F	27020	7875	8200	9325	11550
Power Hard Top			1175	1175	1415	1415

RX-8—Rotary—Equipment Schedule 6
W.B. 106.4"; 1.3 Liter.

Sport Coupe 4D	E174	27085	5725	6050	7000	8925
Touring Coupe 4D	E17M	29210	8175	8650	9550	12050
Grand Touring Coupe	E17M	32350	8950	9450	10450	13200
R3 Coupe 4D	E174	32580	9125	9650	10600	13300

2010 MAZDA — (Jor1)(M1orYV)-(L1SF)-A-#

MAZDA3—4-Cyl.—Equipment Schedule 6
W.B. 103.9"; 2.0 Liter.

i SV Sedan 4D	L1SF	16045	5775	6050	7300	9250

Body Type	VIN	List	Trade-In Good	Very Good	Pvt-Party Good	Retail Excellent
MAZDA3—4-Cyl.—Equipment Schedule 6						
W.B. 103.9"; 2.0 Liter, 2.5 Liter.						
i Sport Sedan 4D	L1SF	17495	6525	6825	8125	10300
i Touring Sedan 4D	L1EF	19020	7275	7600	8750	10850
s Sport Sedan 4D	L1S5	20210	8300	8675	9925	12350
s Sport Hatchback 4D	L1H5	21990	8300	8675	9900	12300
s Grand Touring Sed 4D	L1S5	22970	8750	9125	10350	12800
s Grand Touring H'Bck	L1H5	23550	8925	9325	10550	13000
Manual, 5-Spd w/Overdrive			(450)	(450)	(610)	(610)
MAZDASPEED3—4-Cyl. Turbo—Equipment Schedule 6						
W.B. 103.9"; 2.3 Liter.						
Sport Hatchback 4D	L1H3	24090	10800	11250	12300	14900
MAZDA6—4-Cyl.—Equipment Schedule 4						
W.B. 109.8"; 2.5 Liter.						
i Sport Value Sedan 4D	Z8BH	19200	6550	6975	7925	10250
i Sport Sedan 4D	Z8BH	21070	6775	7225	8050	10350
i Touring Sedan 4D	Z8CH	22550	7225	7700	8700	11250
i Touring Plus Sedan 4D	Z8CH	24500	7700	8200	9200	11900
i Grand Touring Sed 4D	Z8CH	26685	8425	8975	9925	12750
MAZDA6—V6—Equipment Schedule 4						
W.B. 109.8"; 3.7 Liter.						
s Touring Plus Sedan	Z8CB	27200	9000	9600	10600	13600
s Grand Touring Sed 4D	Z8CB	29140	9575	10200	11150	14300
MX-5 MIATA—4-Cyl.—Equipment Schedule 6						
W.B. 91.7"; 2.0 Liter.						
Sport Convertible 2D	C2EF	23560	9300	9625	10800	12850
Touring Convertible 2D	C2EF	25900	9425	9750	10950	13000
Grand Touring Conv 2D	C2EF	27160	9925	10300	11550	13800
Power Hard Top			1250	1250	1470	1470
RX-8—Rotary—Equipment Schedule 3						
W.B. 106.3"; 1.3 Liter.						
Sport Coupe 4D	E1CP	27245	8075	8475	9350	11300
Grand Touring Coupe	E17M	33410	10950	11450	12400	14900
R3 Coupe 4D	E1CP	32740	11300	11800	12600	15000

2011 MAZDA — 1YVorJM1-(E1HY)-B-#

Body Type	VIN	List	Trade-In Good	Very Good	Pvt-Party Good	Retail Excellent
MAZDA2—4-Cyl.—Equipment Schedule 6						
W.B. 98.0"; 1.5 Liter.						
Sport Hatchback 4D	E1HY	14730	5925	6250	7425	9525
Touring Hatchback 4D	E1HY	16185	6475	6825	7925	10100
Automatic, 4-Spd			425	425	575	575
MAZDA3—4-Cyl.—Equipment Schedule 6						
W.B. 103.9"; 2.0 Liter.						
i SV Sedan 4D	L1TF	16200	6350	6575	8075	10100
MAZDA3—4-Cyl.—Equipment Schedule 6						
W.B. 103.9"; 2.0 Liter, 2.5 Liter.						
i Sport Sedan 4D	L1UF	18350	7525	7775	9250	11350
i Touring Sedan 4D	L1VF	19745	8175	8450	9950	12200
s Sport Sedan 4D	L1U5	21140	9175	9500	11000	13350
s Sport Hatchback 4D	L1K5	21640	9575	9900	11350	13750
s Grand Touring Sedan	L1W5	24105	10150	10500	11900	14300
s Grand Touring H'Back	L1M5	24605	10350	10700	12050	14450
Manual, 5-Spd w/Overdrive			(500)	(500)	(635)	(635)
MAZDASPEED3—4-Cyl. Turbo—Equipment Schedule 6						
W.B. 103.9"; 2.3 Liter.						
Sport Hatchback 4D	L1K3	24090	11900	12300	13500	15950
MAZDA6—4-Cyl.—Equipment Schedule 4						
W.B. 109.8"; 2.5 Liter.						
i Sport Sedan 4D	Z8BH	21785	8425	8900	9925	12400
i Touring Sedan 4D	Z8CH	23430	8825	9300	10400	13000
i Touring Plus Sedan 4D	Z8CH	25035	9225	9725	10900	13650
i Grand Touring Sed 4D	Z8CH	27615	10000	10550	11700	14600
MAZDA6—V6—Equipment Schedule 4						
W.B. 109.8"; 3.7 Liter.						
s Touring Plus Sedan	Z8CB	27875	10550	11100	12250	15300
s Grand Touring Sed 4D	Z8CB	30115	10900	11500	12550	15600
MX-5 MIATA—4-Cyl.—Equipment Schedule 6						
W.B. 91.7"; 2.0 Liter.						
Sport Convertible 2D	C2JF	23710	11050	11350	12700	14700
Touring Convertible 2D	C2LF	26050	12350	12700	14100	16150
Grand Touring Conv 2D	C2NF	27310	12600	12950	14450	16650
Special Ed Conv 2D	C1SF	31720	14300	14650	16150	18550
Power Hard Top			1325	1325	1520	1520

Body Type	VIN	List	Trade-In Good	Very Good	Pvt-Party Good	Retail Excellent
RX-8—Rotary—Equipment Schedule 3						
W.B. 106.3"; 1.3 Liter.						
Sport Coupe 4D	E1RP	27590	**10050**	**10450**	**11350**	**13250**
R3 Coupe 4D	E1T4	33085	**13250**	**13800**	**15150**	**17950**
Grand Touring Coupe	E1SP	33755	**12850**	**13350**	**14450**	**16800**

2012 MAZDA — 1YVorJM1–(E1HY)–C–#

Body Type	VIN	List	Trade-In Good	Very Good	Pvt-Party Good	Retail Excellent
MAZDA2—4-Cyl.—Equipment Schedule 6						
W.B. 98.0"; 1.5 Liter.						
Sport Hatchback 4D	E1HY	15165	**6800**	**7100**	**8375**	**10550**
Touring Hatchback 4D	E1HY	16650	**7250**	**7600**	**8775**	**10950**
Automatic, 4-Spd			**475**	**475**	**620**	**620**
MAZDA3—4-Cyl.—Equipment Schedule 6						
W.B. 103.9"; 2.0 Liter.						
i SV Sedan 4D	L1TF	16595	**7600**	**7800**	**9475**	**11550**
MAZDA3—4-Cyl.—Equipment Schedule 6						
W.B. 103.9"; 2.0 Liter, 2.5 Liter.						
i Sport Sedan 4D	L1UF	18350	**8775**	**9000**	**10500**	**12600**
i Touring Sedan 4D	L1VF	19745	**9075**	**9325**	**10800**	**12900**
i Touring Hatchback 4D	L1L7	20595	**10150**	**10400**	**12000**	**14250**
i Grand Touring Sedan	L1W7	23095	**11150**	**11450**	**12950**	**15150**
i Grand Touring H'Back	L1M7	23595	**11900**	**12200**	**13700**	**16050**
s Grand Touring Sed 4D	L1W5	23865	**11950**	**12250**	**13750**	**16100**
s Grand Touring H'Back	L1M5	24365	**12250**	**12550**	**14050**	**16400**
Manual, 5-Spd			**(475)**	**(475)**	**(590)**	**(590)**
Manual, 6-Spd SKYACTIV			**0**	**0**	**0**	**0**
MAZDA3—4-Cyl.—Equipment Schedule 6						
W.B. 103.9"; 2.5 Liter.						
s Touring Sedan 4D	L1V5	21495	**10400**	**10650**	**12200**	**14500**
s Touring Hatchback 4D	L1L5	21995	**10600**	**10850**	**12350**	**14600**
Auto 5-Spd w/Manual Mode			**475**	**475**	**585**	**585**
MAZDASPEED3—4-Cyl. Turbo—Equipment Schedule 6						
W.B. 103.9"; 2.3 Liter.						
Touring Hatchback 4D	L1L3	24495	**13050**	**13400**	**14900**	**17350**
MAZDA6—4-Cyl.—Equipment Schedule 4						
W.B. 109.8"; 2.5 Liter.						
i Sport Sedan 4D	Z8BH	22035	**9350**	**9775**	**10950**	**13450**
i Touring Sedan 4D	Z8DH	23680	**10100**	**10550**	**11750**	**14400**
i Touring Plus Sedan	Z8EH	25285	**11200**	**11700**	**12950**	**15900**
i Grand Touring Sedan	Z8CH	27865	**11700**	**12250**	**13500**	**16500**
MAZDA6—V6—Equipment Schedule 4						
W.B. 109.8"; 3.7 Liter.						
s Touring Plus Sedan	Z8EB	28125	**12100**	**12650**	**14000**	**17200**
s Grand Touring Sedan	Z8CB	30365	**12700**	**13250**	**14400**	**17450**
MX-5 MIATA—4-Cyl.—Equipment Schedule 6						
W.B. 91.7"; 2.0 Liter.						
Sport Convertible 2D	C2JF	23985	**12050**	**12300**	**13800**	**15650**
Touring Convertible 2D	C2LF	26345	**13600**	**13900**	**15500**	**17500**
Grand Touring Conv 2D	C2NF	27615	**14200**	**14500**	**16150**	**18250**
Special Ed Conv 2D	C2SF	32020	**17050**	**17450**	**19050**	**21400**
Power Hard Top			**1425**	**1425**	**1595**	**1595**

2013 MAZDA — 1YVorJM1–(DE1KY)–D–#

Body Type	VIN	List	Trade-In Good	Very Good	Pvt-Party Good	Retail Excellent
MAZDA2—4-Cyl.—Equipment Schedule 6						
W.B. 98.0"; 1.5 Liter.						
Sport Hatchback 4D	DE1KY	15515	**7400**	**7700**	**9150**	**11450**
Touring Hatchback 4D	DE1LY	17005	**7725**	**8025**	**9525**	**11950**
Automatic, 4-Spd			**500**	**500**	**655**	**655**
MAZDA3—4-Cyl.—Equipment Schedule 6						
W.B. 103.9"; 2.0 Liter.						
i SV Sedan 4D	BL1TF	17495	**9000**	**9175**	**10900**	**13050**
i Touring Hatchback	BL1L7	20795	**11600**	**11850**	**13500**	**15700**
Auto, 5-Spd w/Manual Mode			**500**	**500**	**630**	**630**
MAZDA3—4-Cyl.—Equipment Schedule 6						
W.B. 103.9"; 2.0 Liter, 2.5 Liter.						
i Sport Sedan 4D	BL1U7	20020	**10300**	**10550**	**12200**	**14400**
i Touring Sedan 4D	BL1V7	21145	**11700**	**11900**	**13550**	**15800**
i Grand Touring HBk	BL1M7	24095	**13400**	**13700**	**15400**	**17800**
i Grand Touring Sedan	BL1W7	23595	**12900**	**13200**	**14800**	**17000**
s Grand Touring Sed	BL1W5	25945	**13950**	**14250**	**15950**	**18350**
s Grand Touring HBk	BL1M5	26445	**14250**	**14550**	**16250**	**18650**

2013 MAZDA

Body Type	VIN	List	Trade-In Good	Very Good	Pvt-Party Good	Retail Excellent
MAZDASPEED3—4-Cyl. Turbo—Equipment Schedule 6						
W.B. 103.9"; 2.3 Liter.						
Touring Hatchback 4D	BL1L3	24995	15250	15550	17050	19350
MAZDA6—4-Cyl.—Equipment Schedule 4						
W.B. 109.8"; 2.5 Liter.						
i Sport Sedan 4D	Z8BH	22520	11000	11450	12600	15150
i Touring Sedan 4D	Z8DH	24165	11800	12250	13550	16300
i Touring Plus Sedan	Z8EH	25965	12900	13400	14700	17700
i Grand Touring Sedan	Z8CH	28545	13850	14400	15650	18700
MAZDA6—V6—Equipment Schedule 4						
W.B. 109.8"; 3.7 Liter.						
s Grand Touring Sedan	Z8CB	30785	15000	15600	16800	19900
MX-5 MIATA—4-Cyl.—Equipment Schedule 6						
W.B. 91.7"; 2.0 Liter.						
Sport Convertible 2D	NC2JF	25595	13700	14000	15600	17450
Club Convertible 2D	NG2LF	27500	16000	16300	17900	19900
Grand Touring Conv	NC2NF	28145	16800	17100	18800	20900
Power Hard Top			1500	1500	1665	1665

2014 MAZDA — 1YVorJM1-(DE1KY)-E-#

Body Type	VIN	List	Trade-In Good	Very Good	Pvt-Party Good	Retail Excellent
MAZDA2—4-Cyl.—Equipment Schedule 6						
W.B. 98.0"; 1.5 Liter.						
Sport Hatchback 4D	DE1KY	15515	8100	8400	9850	12150
Touring Hatchback 4D	DE1LY	17005	8800	9125	10450	12750
Automatic, 4-Spd			525	525	670	670
MAZDA3—4-Cyl.—Equipment Schedule 6						
W.B. 106.3"; 2.0 Liter.						
i SV Sedan 4D	BM1T7	17740	10900	11100	12800	14900
i Sport Hatchback 4D	BM1K7	19740	12200	12450	14100	16400
i Touring Hatchback	BM1L7	20890	13550	13800	15500	17850
Auto, 6-Spd SKYACTIV			525	525	630	630
MAZDA3—4-Cyl.—Equipment Schedule 6						
W.B. 106.3"; 2.0 Liter.						
i Sport Sedan 4D	BM1U7	20290	12400	12650	14300	16600
i Touring Sedan 4D	BM1V7	21440	13800	14050	15750	18100
i Grand Touring Sed	BM1W7	24590	15300	15600	17200	19600
i Grand Touring HBk	BM1M7	25090	15800	16100	17700	20100
MAZDA3—4-Cyl.—Equipment Schedule 6						
W.B. 106.3"; 2.5 Liter.						
s Touring Sedan 4D	BM1V3	25390	15850	16150	17750	20100
s Grand Touring Sed	BM1W3	26790	17600	17950	19450	21900
s Touring Hatchback	BM1L3	25890	16400	16750	18300	20700
s Grand Touring HBk	BM1M3	27290	18450	18800	20300	22800
MAZDA6—4-Cyl.—Equipment Schedule 4						
W.B. 111.4"; 2.5 Liter.						
i Sport Sedan 4D	GJ1U6	23290	14250	14800	15950	18750
i Touring Sedan 4D	GJ1V6	25290	14950	15550	16700	19650
MAZDA6—4-Cyl.—Equipment Schedule 4						
W.B. 111.4"; 2.5 Liter.						
i Grand Touring Sedan	GJ1W6	30290	17900	18600	19550	22800
MX-5 MIATA—4-Cyl.—Equipment Schedule 6						
W.B. 91.7"; 2.0 Liter.						
Sport Convertible 2D	NC2JF	25595	16200	16500	18100	19950
Club Convertible 2D	NC2MF	27700	17300	17600	19250	21300
Grand Touring Conv	NC2NF	28345	19250	19600	21300	23400
Power Hard Top			1575	1575	1740	1740

McLAREN

2012 McLAREN — SBM(11AAA)-C-#

Body Type	VIN	List	Trade-In Good	Very Good	Pvt-Party Good	Retail Excellent
MP4-12C—V8 Twin Turbo—Equipment Schedule 2						
W.B. 105.1"; 3.8 Liter.						
Coupe 2D	11AAA	231400	****	****	****	188200

2013 McLAREN — SBM(11AAA)-D-#

Body Type	VIN	List	Trade-In Good	Very Good	Pvt-Party Good	Retail Excellent
MP4-12C—V8 Twin Turbo—Equipment Schedule 2						
W.B. 105.1"; 3.8 Liter.						
Coupe 2D	11AAA	241800	****	****	****	198400

2014 McLAREN

Body	Type	VIN	List	Trade-In Good	Very Good	Pvt-Party Good	Retail Excellent

2014 McLAREN — SMB(11AAA)-E-#

MP4-12C—V8 Twin Turbo—Equipment Schedule 2
W.B. 105.1"; 3.8 Liter.

Coupe 2D		11AAA	241900	****	****	****	204500
Spider Convertible 2D		11BAA	268250	****	****	****	217200
Ceramic Brakes				****	****	****	4150

P1—V8 Twin Turbo Hybrid—Equipment Schedule 2
W.B. 105.1"; 3.8 Liter.

Coupe 2D		12ABA	1155000				

MERCEDES-BENZ

2000 MERCEDES-BENZ — WDB(KK47F)-Y-#

SLK-CLASS—4-Cyl. Supercharged—Equipment Schedule 1
W.B. 94.5"; 2.3 Liter.

SLK230 Roadster 2D		KK47F	42495	2700	2925	3600	5250
Sport Pkg				450	450	600	600
designo Edition				400	400	545	545
Manual, 5-Spd				(225)	(225)	(305)	(305)

C-CLASS—4-Cyl. Supercharged—Equipment Schedule 1
W.B. 105.9"; 2.3 Liter.

C230 Sedan 4D		HA24G	34820	1500	1650	2275	3725
Sport Pkg				200	200	265	265

C-CLASS—V6—Equipment Schedule 1
W.B. 105.9"; 2.8 Liter.

C280 Sedan 4D		HA29G	39020	1625	1800	2525	4100
Sport Pkg				200	200	265	265

C-CLASS—V8—Equipment Schedule 1
W.B. 105.9"; 4.3 Liter.

C43 Sedan 4D		HA33G	53595	3500	3875	4200	6175

CLK-CLASS—V6—Equipment Schedule 1
W.B. 105.9"; 3.2 Liter.

CLK320 Coupe 2D		LJ65G	43505	1575	1675	2425	3675
CLK320 Cabriolet 2D		LK65G	48695	1925	2100	2800	4300
designo Edition				400	400	545	545

CLK-CLASS—V8—Equipment Schedule 1
W.B. 105.9"; 4.3 Liter.

CLK430 Coupe 2D		LJ70G	51005	2125	2275	3050	4575
CLK430 Cabriolet 2D		LK70G	56195	2375	2575	3350	5125
designo Edition				400	400	545	545

E-CLASS—V6—Equipment Schedule 1
W.B. 111.5"; 3.2 Liter.

E320 Sedan 4D		JF65G	48825	1550	1750	2125	3400
E320 AWD Sedan 4D		JF82G	51625	1475	1675	2025	3275
E320 Wagon 4D		JH65F	49675	1700	1925	2375	3825
E320 AWD Wagon 4D		JH82F	52475	1850	2075	2500	3975
designo Edition				400	400	545	545

E-CLASS—V8—Equipment Schedule 1
W.B. 111.5"; 4.3 Liter, 5.5 Liter.

E430 Sedan 4D		JF70G	54175	2350	2650	3075	4900
E430 AWD Sedan 4D		JF83G	56975	2875	3225	3600	5625
E55 Sedan 4D		JF74G	71395	3075	3325	3725	5275
Sport Pkg (E430)				450	450	600	600
designo Edition				400	400	545	545

CL-CLASS—V8—Equipment Schedule 1
W.B. 113.6"; 5.0 Liter.

CL500 Coupe 2D		PJ75J	87145	1750	1900	2600	4000

S-CLASS—V8—Equipment Schedule 1
W.B. 121.5"; 4.3 Liter, 5.0 Liter.

S430 Sedan 4D		NG70J	70295	1425	1550	2375	3750
S500 Sedan 4D		NG75J	79445	1625	1775	2625	4150
Sport Pkg				675	675	890	890
designo Edition				400	400	545	545
DISTRONIC Cruise Control				175	175	220	220

SL-CLASS—V8—Equipment Schedule 1
W.B. 99.0"; 5.0 Liter.

SL500 Roadster 2D		FA68F	84195	2650	2900	3850	5875
Sport Pkg				675	675	860	860
designo Edition				400	400	530	530
Panorama Roof				550	550	710	710

Body Type	VIN	List	Trade-In Good	Very Good	Pvt-Party Good	Retail Excellent
SL-CLASS—V12—Equipment Schedule 1						
W.B. 99.0"; 6.0 Liter.						
SL600 Roadster 2D	FA76F	132145	4275	4625	5675	8350
Sport Pkg			675	675	840	840
designo Edition			400	400	515	515
Panorama Roof			550	550	695	695

2001 MERCEDES-BENZ — WDB(KK49F)-1-#

Body Type	VIN	List	Trade-In Good	Very Good	Pvt-Party Good	Retail Excellent
SLK-CLASS—4-Cyl. Supercharged—Equipment Schedule 1						
W.B. 94.5"; 2.3 Liter.						
SLK230 Roadster 2D	KK49F	40495	2450	2650	3475	5175
Sport Pkg			525	525	700	700
designo Edition			450	450	605	605
Manual, 6-Spd			(275)	(275)	(360)	(360)
SLK-CLASS—V6—Equipment Schedule 1						
W.B. 94.5"; 3.2 Liter.						
SLK320 Roadster 2D	KK65F	45495	2075	2250	3175	4875
Sport Pkg			525	525	700	700
designo Edition			450	450	605	605
Manual, 6-Spd			(275)	(275)	(360)	(360)
C-CLASS—V6—Equipment Schedule 1						
W.B. 106.9"; 2.6 Liter, 3.2 Liter.						
C240 Sedan 4D	RF61G	34610	1725	1925	2600	4175
C320 Sedan 4D	RF64G	40310	1950	2150	2825	4525
Sport Pkg			200	200	265	265
Manual, 6-Spd			(275)	(275)	(360)	(360)
CLK-CLASS—V6—Equipment Schedule 1						
W.B. 105.9"; 3.2 Liter.						
CLK320 Coupe 2D	LJ65G	42595	1800	1950	2725	4100
CLK320 Cabriolet 2D	LK65G	49545	2275	2450	3225	4875
designo Edition			450	450	605	605
CLK-CLASS—V8—Equipment Schedule 1						
W.B. 105.9"; 4.3 Liter, 5.5 Liter.						
CLK430 Coupe 2D	LJ70G	50295	2400	2550	3350	4975
CLK430 Cabriolet 2D	LK70G	57145	2650	2875	3850	5800
CLK55 Coupe 2D	LJ74G	68045	3100	3425	4175	6450
designo Edition			450	450	605	605
E-CLASS—V6—Equipment Schedule 1						
W.B. 111.5"; 3.2 Liter.						
E320 Sedan 4D	JF65F	48495	1775	2000	2425	3825
E320 AWD Sedan 4D	JF82F	51345	1625	1850	2275	3600
E320 Wagon 4D	JH65F	49295	1900	2150	2575	4050
E320 AWD Wagon 4D	JH82F	52145	2225	2500	2900	4525
designo Edition (ex AWD)			450	450	605	605
Sport Pkg (ex AWD)			525	525	700	700
E-CLASS—V8—Equipment Schedule 1						
W.B. 111.5"; 4.3 Liter, 5.5 Liter.						
E430 Sedan 4D	JF70F	53845	2450	2725	3150	4925
E430 AWD Sedan 4D	JF83G	56695	3075	3425	3800	5925
E55 Sedan 4D	JF744	70945	3300	3575	4100	5875
designo Edition			450	450	605	605
Sport Pkg (E430 RWD)			525	525	700	700
CL-CLASS—V8—Equipment Schedule 1						
W.B. 113.6"; 5.0 Liter, 5.5 Liter.						
CL500 Coupe 2D	PJ75J	89145	2175	2350	3050	4575
CL55 Coupe 2D	PJ73J	100145	6350	6850	7800	11050
DISTRONIC Cruise Control			200	200	225	225
Sport Pkg (CL500)			775	775	895	895
designo Edition			450	450	530	530
CL-CLASS—V12—Equipment Schedule 1						
W.B. 113.6"; 5.8 Liter.						
CL600 Coupe 2D	PJ78J	119145	3425	3725	5000	7550
DISTRONIC Cruise Control			200	200	235	235
Sport Pkg			775	775	945	945
designo Edition			450	450	560	560
S-CLASS—V8—Equipment Schedule 1						
W.B. 121.5"; 4.3 Liter, 5.0 Liter, 5.5 Liter.						
S430 Sedan 4D	NG70J	71445	1875	2050	2850	4425
S500 Sedan 4D	NG75J	80595	2050	2225	3100	4775
S55 Sedan 4D	NG73J	98645	3025	3350	3875	5825
DISTRONIC Cruise Control			200	200	255	255
Sport Pkg (S430,S500)			775	775	1020	1020
designo Edition			450	450	605	605

2001 MERCEDES-BENZ

Body Type	VIN	List	Trade-In Good	Trade-In Very Good	Pvt-Party Good	Retail Excellent
S-CLASS—V12—Equipment Schedule 1						
W.B. 121.5"; 6.0 Liter.						
S600 Sedan 4D	NG78J	115985	2600	2800	3700	5700
DISTRONIC Cruise Control			200	200	255	255
Sport Pkg			775	775	1015	1015
designo Edition			450	450	605	605
SL-CLASS—V8—Equipment Schedule 1						
W.B. 99.0"; 5.0 Liter.						
SL500 Roadster 2D	FA68F	84445	3200	3475	4550	6750
designo Edition			450	450	585	585
Panorama Roof			625	625	800	800
SL-CLASS—V12—Equipment Schedule 1						
W.B. 99.0"; 6.0 Liter.						
SL600 Roadster 2D	FA76F	129595	5400	5850	6850	9775
designo Edition			450	450	570	570
Panorama Roof			625	625	785	785

2002 MERCEDES-BENZ — WDB(KK49F)-2-#

Body Type	VIN	List	Trade-In Good	Trade-In Very Good	Pvt-Party Good	Retail Excellent
SLK-CLASS—4-Cyl. Supercharged—Equipment Schedule 1						
W.B. 94.5"; 2.3 Liter.						
SLK230 Roadster 2D	KK49F	41345	2125	2300	3225	4875
Sport Pkg			600	600	800	800
designo Edition			500	500	665	665
Manual, 6-Spd			(300)	(300)	(410)	(410)
SLK-CLASS—V6—Equipment Schedule 1						
W.B. 94.5"; 3.2 Liter.						
SLK320 Roadster 2D	KK65F	46745	3050	3300	4150	6100
Sport Pkg			600	600	800	800
designo Edition			500	500	665	665
Manual, 6-Spd			(300)	(300)	(410)	(410)
SLK-CLASS—V6 Supercharged—Equipment Schedule 1						
W.B. 94.5"; 3.2 Liter.						
SLK32 Roadster 2D	KK66F	55545	6025	6475	7150	9800
designo Edition			500	500	645	645
C-CLASS—4-Cyl. Supercharged—Equipment Schedule 1						
W.B. 106.9"; 2.3 Liter.						
C230 Sport Coupe 2D	RN47J	29490	1475	1600	2225	3625
Manual, 6-Spd			(300)	(300)	(410)	(410)
C-CLASS—V6—Equipment Schedule 1						
W.B. 106.9"; 2.6 Liter, 3.2 Liter.						
C240 Sedan 4D	RF61J	33680	2075	2275	2975	4675
C320 Sedan 4D	RF64J	38780	2325	2550	3225	5075
C320 Wagon 4D	RH64J	40280	2400	2625	3325	5200
Sport Pkg			225	225	310	310
Manual, 6-Spd			(300)	(300)	(410)	(410)
C-CLASS—V6 Supercharged—Equipment Schedule 1						
W.B. 106.9"; 3.2 Liter.						
C32 Sedan 4D	RF65J	50545	4400	4825	5025	7150
CLK-CLASS—V6—Equipment Schedule 1						
W.B. 105.9"; 3.2 Liter.						
CLK320 Coupe 2D	LJ65G	44565	2225	2375	3150	4650
CLK320 Cabriolet 2D	LK65G	50245	2725	2950	3825	5650
Sport Pkg			600	600	800	800
designo Edition			500	500	665	665
CLK-CLASS—V8—Equipment Schedule 1						
W.B. 105.9"; 4.3 Liter, 5.5 Liter.						
CLK430 Coupe 2D	LJ70G	52265	2700	2900	3800	5550
CLK430 Cabriolet 2D	LK70G	57945	3250	3500	4475	6600
CLK55 Coupe 2D	LJ74G	69095	4025	4425	5150	7650
CLK55 Cabriolet 2D	LK74G	79645	4150	4550	5300	7850
designo Edition			500	500	665	665
E-CLASS—V6—Equipment Schedule 1						
W.B. 111.5"; 3.2 Liter.						
E320 Sedan 4D	JF65J	50280	2075	2325	2775	4325
E320 AWD Sedan 4D	JF82J	53130	1975	2200	2650	4175
E320 Wagon 4D	JH65J	51080	2150	2400	2850	4475
E320 AWD Wagon 4D	JH82J	53130	2750	3075	3450	5350
Sport Pkg (ex AWD)			600	600	800	800
designo Edition (ex AWD)			500	500	665	665
E-CLASS—V8—Equipment Schedule 1						
W.B. 111.5"; 4.3 Liter, 5.5 Liter.						
E430 Sedan 4D	JF70J	55680	2775	3075	3500	5425
E430 AWD Sedan 4D	JF83J	58530	3300	3675	4050	6225

Body Type	VIN	List	Trade-In Good	Very Good	Pvt-Party Good	Retail Excellent
E55 Sedan 4D	JF74J	71995	3625	3900	4600	6550
Sport Pkg (E430 RWD)			600	600	800	800
designo Edition			500	500	665	665
CL-CLASS—V8—Equipment Schedule 1						
W.B. 113.6"; 5.0 Liter, 5.5 Liter.						
CL500 Coupe 2D	PJ75J	92395	2450	2650	3400	4975
CL55 Coupe 2D	PJ73J	105145	7375	7925	8775	12150
DISTRONIC Cruise Control			225	225	255	255
Sport Pkg (CL500)			875	875	1050	1050
designo Edition			500	500	595	595
CL-CLASS—V12—Equipment Schedule 1						
W.B. 113.6"; 5.8 Liter.						
CL600 Coupe 2D	PJ78J	120895	3700	4000	5250	7825
DISTRONIC Cruise Control			225	225	270	270
Sport Pkg			875	875	1105	1105
designo Edition			500	500	625	625
S-CLASS—V8—Equipment Schedule 1						
W.B. 121.5"; 4.3 Liter, 5.0 Liter, 5.5 Liter.						
S430 Sedan 4D	NG70J	72495	2350	2525	3350	5075
S500 Sedan 4D	NG75J	81845	2450	2650	3500	5300
S55 Sedan 4D	NG73J	101145	4375	4800	5175	7325
DISTRONIC Cruise Control			225	225	285	285
Sport Pkg			875	875	1175	1175
designo Edition			500	500	665	665
S-CLASS—V12—Equipment Schedule 1						
W.B. 121.5"; 5.8 Liter.						
S600 Sedan 4D	NG78J	117545	3350	3625	4600	6825
DISTRONIC Cruise Control			225	225	280	280
Sport Pkg			875	875	1145	1145
designo Edition			500	500	645	645
SL-CLASS—V8—Equipment Schedule 1						
W.B. 99.0"; 5.0 Liter.						
SL500 Roadster 2D	FA68F	85445	4500	4850	5775	8200
Sport Pkg			875	875	1085	1085
Panorama Roof			700	700	860	860
Silver Arrow Edition			525	525	655	655
SL-CLASS—V12—Equipment Schedule 1						
W.B. 99.0"; 6.0 Liter.						
SL600 Roadster 2D	FA76F	132195	7075	7625	8475	11750
Panorama Roof			700	700	850	850
Silver Arrow Edition			525	525	650	650

2003 MERCEDES-BENZ — WDB(KK49F)-3-#

Body Type	VIN	List	Trade-In Good	Very Good	Pvt-Party Good	Retail Excellent
SLK-CLASS—4-Cyl. Supercharged—Equipment Schedule 1						
W.B. 94.5"; 2.3 Liter.						
SLK230 Roadster 2D	KK49F	40265	2275	2450	3650	5650
Sport Pkg			625	625	835	835
designo Edition			550	550	725	725
Manual, 6-Spd			(350)	(350)	(465)	(465)
SLK-CLASS—V6—Equipment Schedule 1						
W.B. 94.5"; 3.2 Liter.						
SLK320 Roadster 2D	KK65F	45715	3125	3350	4525	6850
Sport Pkg			625	625	835	835
designo Edition			550	550	725	725
Manual, 6-Spd			(350)	(350)	(465)	(465)
SLK-CLASS—V6 Supercharged—Equipment Schedule 1						
W.B. 94.5"; 3.2 Liter.						
SLK32 Roadster 2D	KK66F	56115	6875	7375	8125	11050
designo Edition			550	550	695	695
C-CLASS—4-Cyl. Supercharged—Equipment Schedule 1						
W.B. 106.9"; 1.8 Liter.						
C230 Sport Sedan 4D	RF40J	30310	2275	2475	3175	4950
C230 Sport Coupe 2D	RN40J	28270	1825	2000	2625	4050
Manual, 6-Spd			(350)	(350)	(465)	(465)
C-CLASS—V6—Equipment Schedule 1						
W.B. 106.9"; 2.6 Liter, 3.2 Liter.						
C240 Sedan 4D	RF61J	32165	2275	2475	3175	4950
C240 4MATIC Sed 4D	RF81J	33965	2500	2750	3450	5350
C240 Wagon 4D	RH61J	33544	2450	2675	3375	5200
C240 4MATIC Wag 4D	RH81J	35544	2825	3075	3775	5800
C320 Sedan 4D	RF64J	38790	2800	3050	3750	5775
C320 Sport Sedan 4D	RF64J	38790	3050	3325	4050	6250
C320 4MATIC Sed 4D	RF84J	40590	3250	3525	4250	6525

2003 MERCEDES-BENZ

Body Type	VIN	List	Trade-In Good	Very Good	Pvt-Party Good	Retail Excellent
C320 4MATIC Spt Sed	RF84J	35920	3225	3500	4225	6475
C320 Coupe 2D	RN64J	30620	1975	2150	2775	4250
C320 Wagon 4D	RH64J	38840	3000	3275	3975	6075
C320 4MATIC Wag 4D	RH84J	40640	3250	3525	4250	6525
DISTRONIC Cruise Control			250	250	320	320
Manual, 6-Spd			(350)	(350)	(465)	(465)

C-CLASS—V6 Supercharged—Equipment Schedule 1
W.B. 106.9"; 3.2 Liter.

Body Type	VIN	List	Trade-In Good	Very Good	Pvt-Party Good	Retail Excellent
C32 Sedan 4D	RF65J	52065	5125	5600	6000	8425

CLK-CLASS—V6—Equipment Schedule 1
W.B. 105.9", 106.9" (Coupe); 3.2 Liter.

Body Type	VIN	List	Trade-In Good	Very Good	Pvt-Party Good	Retail Excellent
CLK320 Coupe 2D	TJ65J	44565	2950	3150	4025	5750
CLK320 Cabriolet 2D	LK65G	50615	3625	3900	4750	6825
DISTRONIC Cruise Control			250	250	320	320
Sport Pkg (Cabriolet)			625	625	835	835
designo Edition			550	550	725	725

CLK-CLASS—V8—Equipment Schedule 1
W.B. 105.9", 106.9" (Coupe); 4.3 Liter, 5.0 Liter, 5.5 Liter.

Body Type	VIN	List	Trade-In Good	Very Good	Pvt-Party Good	Retail Excellent
CLK430 Cabriolet 2D	LK70G	58315	4025	4325	5425	7825
CLK500 Coupe 2D	TJ75J	52865	3675	3925	4775	6750
CLK55 Coupe 2D	TJ76H	69470	5075	5550	6200	9000
DISTRONIC Cruise Control			250	250	320	320
designo Edition			550	550	725	725

E-CLASS—V6—Equipment Schedule 1
W.B. 111.5", 112.4" (Sed); 3.2 Liter.

Body Type	VIN	List	Trade-In Good	Very Good	Pvt-Party Good	Retail Excellent
E320 Sedan 4D	UF65J	49165	3425	3800	4300	6575
E320 Wagon 4D	JH65J	55415	3750	4175	4725	7225
E320 4MATIC Wag 4D	JH82J	55415	3900	4325	4875	7450
DISTRONIC Cruise Control			250	250	320	320
Sport Pkg (Sedan)			625	625	835	835

E-CLASS—V8—Equipment Schedule 1
W.B. 112.4"; 5.0 Liter.

Body Type	VIN	List	Trade-In Good	Very Good	Pvt-Party Good	Retail Excellent
E500 Sedan 4D	UF70J	57065	3425	3800	4300	6550
DISTRONIC Cruise Control			250	250	320	320
Sport Pkg			625	625	835	835

E-CLASS—V8 Supercharged—Equipment Schedule 1
W.B. 112.4"; 5.5 Liter.

Body Type	VIN	List	Trade-In Good	Very Good	Pvt-Party Good	Retail Excellent
E55 Sedan 4D	UF72J	76720	6025	6450	7475	10550
DISTRONIC Cruise Control			250	250	320	320

CL-CLASS—V8—Equipment Schedule 1
W.B. 113.6"; 5.0 Liter.

Body Type	VIN	List	Trade-In Good	Very Good	Pvt-Party Good	Retail Excellent
CL500 Coupe 2D	PJ75J	93315	3075	3300	4000	5625
DISTRONIC Cruise Control			250	250	275	275
Sport Pkg			1000	1000	1160	1160
designo Edition			550	550	625	625

CL-CLASS—V8 Supercharged—Equipment Schedule 1
W.B. 113.6"; 5.5 Liter.

Body Type	VIN	List	Trade-In Good	Very Good	Pvt-Party Good	Retail Excellent
CL55 Coupe 2D	PJ74J	115265	7725	8275	9125	12500
DISTRONIC Cruise Control			250	250	280	280
designo Edition			550	550	630	630

CL-CLASS—V12 Twin Turbo—Equipment Schedule 1
W.B. 113.6"; 5.5 Liter.

Body Type	VIN	List	Trade-In Good	Very Good	Pvt-Party Good	Retail Excellent
CL600 Coupe 2D	PJ76J	127265	4175	4475	5675	8275
DISTRONIC Cruise Control			250	250	295	295
Sport Pkg			1000	1000	1240	1240
designo Edition			550	550	670	670

S-CLASS—V8—Equipment Schedule 1
W.B. 121.5"; 4.3 Liter, 5.0 Liter.

Body Type	VIN	List	Trade-In Good	Very Good	Pvt-Party Good	Retail Excellent
S430 Sedan 4D	NG70J	73265	2750	2975	3725	5500
S430 4MATIC Sed 4D	NG83J	76165	3675	3950	4725	6725
S500 Sedan 4D	NG75J	82665	2950	3150	3925	5775
S500 4MATIC Sed 4D	NG84J	85565	4475	4775	5575	7875
DISTRONIC Cruise Control			250	250	320	320
Sport Pkg			1000	1000	1345	1345
designo Edition			550	550	725	725

S-CLASS—V8 Supercharged—Equipment Schedule 1
W.B. 121.5"; 5.5 Liter.

Body Type	VIN	List	Trade-In Good	Very Good	Pvt-Party Good	Retail Excellent
S55 Sedan 4D	NG74J	107165	4725	5175	5775	8325
DISTRONIC Cruise Control			250	250	295	295
designo Edition			550	550	670	670

S-CLASS—V12—Equipment Schedule 1
W.B. 121.5"; 5.8 Liter.

Body Type	VIN	List	Trade-In Good	Very Good	Pvt-Party Good	Retail Excellent
S600 Sedan 4D	NG76J	121205	4250	4550	5350	7625

Body Type	VIN	List	Trade-In Good	Very Good	Pvt-Party Good	Retail Excellent
DISTRONIC Cruise Control	....	....	250	250	300	300
Sport Pkg	....	....	1000	1000	1265	1265
designo Edition	....	....	550	550	685	685
SL-CLASS—V8—Equipment Schedule 1						
W.B. 100.8"; 5.0 Liter.						
SL500 Roadster 2D	SK75F	87655	6575	7050	8025	11100
DISTRONIC Cruise Control	....	....	250	250	290	290
Sport Pkg	....	....	1000	1000	1210	1210
designo Edition	....	....	550	550	655	655
Launch Edition	....	....	1375	1375	1665	1665
SL-CLASS—V8 Supercharged—Equipment Schedule 1						
W.B. 100.8"; 5.5 Liter.						
SL55 Roadster 2D	SK74F	114915	8450	9075	9900	13300
DISTRONIC Cruise Control	....	....	250	250	275	275
designo Edition	....	....	550	550	620	620

2004 MERCEDES-BENZ — WDB(KK49F)-4-#

Body Type	VIN	List	Trade-In Good	Very Good	Pvt-Party Good	Retail Excellent
SLK-CLASS—4-Cyl. Supercharged—Equipment Schedule 1						
W.B. 94.5"; 2.3 Liter.						
SLK230 Roadster 2D	KK49F	40320	2950	3150	4300	6475
SLK230 Special Ed	KK49F	41920	3825	4075	5400	7925
Sport Pkg	....	....	625	625	835	835
designo Edition	....	....	600	600	785	785
Manual, 6-Spd	....	....	(375)	(375)	(515)	(515)
SLK-CLASS—V6—Equipment Schedule 1						
W.B. 94.5"; 3.2 Liter.						
SLK320 Roadster 2D	KK65F	47330	3525	3775	5125	7600
SLK320 Special Ed	KK65F	47370	4250	4550	5850	8500
Sport Pkg	....	....	625	625	835	835
designo Edition	....	....	600	600	785	785
Manual, 6-Spd	....	....	(375)	(375)	(515)	(515)
SLK-CLASS—V6 Supercharged—Equipment Schedule 1						
W.B. 94.5"; 3.2 Liter.						
SLK32 Roadster 2D	KK66F	56170	8675	9275	10050	13400
designo Edition	....	....	600	600	730	730
C-CLASS—4-Cyl. Supercharged—Equipment Schedule 1						
W.B. 106.9"; 1.8 Liter.						
C230 Sport Sedan 4D	RF40J	33180	3050	3325	3975	6000
C230 Sport Coupe 2D	RN47J	30090	2450	2650	3275	4950
Manual, 6-Spd	....	....	(375)	(375)	(515)	(515)
C-CLASS—V6—Equipment Schedule 1						
W.B. 106.9"; 2.6 Liter, 3.2 Liter.						
C240 Sedan 4D	RF61J	33920	2950	3200	3850	5800
C240 4MATIC Sed 4D	RF81J	35120	3225	3500	4150	6225
C240 Wagon 4D	RH61J	35290	3150	3425	4100	6150
C240 4MATIC Wag 4D	RH81J	36490	3375	3675	4450	6650
C320 Sedan 4D	RF64J	39270	3375	3675	4450	6650
C320 Sport Sedan 4D	RF64J	38070	3625	3950	4725	7025
C320 4MATIC Sed 4D	RF84J	40470	3925	4250	5025	7475
C320 Sport Coupe 2D	RN64J	29610	2500	2725	3325	5025
C320 Wagon 4D	RH64J	40640	3925	4250	5025	7475
C320 4MATIC Wag 4D	RH84J	41840	4250	4625	5375	7975
DISTRONIC Cruise Control	....	....	275	275	355	355
Manual, 6-Spd	....	....	(375)	(375)	(515)	(515)
C-CLASS—V6 Supercharged—Equipment Schedule 1						
W.B. 106.9"; 3.2 Liter.						
C32 Sedan 4D	RF65J	53120	6700	7275	7500	10300
CLK-CLASS—V6—Equipment Schedule 1						
W.B. 106.9"; 3.2 Liter.						
CLK320 Coupe 2D	TJ65J	46480	4025	4300	5075	7050
CLK320 Cabriolet 2D	LK65G	52120	5100	5450	6325	8725
DISTRONIC Cruise Control	....	....	275	275	355	355
designo Edition	....	....	600	600	785	785
CLK-CLASS—V8—Equipment Schedule 1						
W.B. 106.9"; 5.0 Liter, 5.5 Liter.						
CLK500 Coupe 2D	TJ75J	54520	4550	4875	5825	8025
CLK500 Cabriolet 2D	TK75G	61570	5700	6075	6950	9575
CLK55 Coupe 2D	TJ76H	70620	6300	6850	7400	10400
CLK55 Cabriolet 2D	LJ74G	80220	6500	7050	7600	10700
DISTRONIC Cruise Control	....	....	275	275	355	355
designo Edition	....	....	600	600	785	785
E-CLASS—V6—Equipment Schedule 1						
W.B. 112.4"; 3.2 Liter.						

Body Type	VIN	List	Trade-In Good	Very Good	Pvt-Party Good	Retail Excellent
E320 Sedan 4D	UF65J	49410	4150	4600	4925	7200
E320 4MATIC Sed 4D	UF82J	51910	4350	4825	5150	7525
E320 Wagon 4D	UH65J	51910	4725	5200	5600	8275
E320 4MATIC Wag 4D	UH82J	54410	5925	6550	6975	10200
DISTRONIC Cruise Control			275	275	355	355
Appearance Pkg			625	625	835	835
Sport Pkg			625	625	835	835
designo Edition			600	600	785	785
E-CLASS—V8—Equipment Schedule 1						
W.B. 112.4"; 5.0 Liter.						
E500 Sedan 4D	UF70J	58510	4150	4575	4875	7125
E500 4MATIC Sed 4D	UF83J	60545	5825	6425	6800	9850
E500 4MATIC Wag 4D	UH83J	63210	7175	7900	8200	11800
DISTRONIC Cruise Control			275	275	355	355
Appearance Pkg			625	625	835	835
Sport Pkg			625	625	835	835
designo Edition			600	600	785	785
E-CLASS—V8 Supercharged—Equipment Schedule 1						
W.B. 112.4"; 5.5 Liter.						
E55 Sedan 4D	UF76J	80070	7225	7725	8725	11950
DISTRONIC Cruise Control			275	275	355	355
designo Edition			600	600	785	785
CL-CLASS—V8—Equipment Schedule 1						
W.B. 113.6"; 5.0 Liter.						
CL500 Coupe 2D	PJ75J	94520	3775	4050	4750	6450
DISTRONIC Cruise Control			275	275	310	310
Sport Pkg			1125	1125	1310	1310
designo Edition			600	600	685	685
CL-CLASS—V8 Supercharged—Equipment Schedule 1						
W.B. 113.6"; 5.5 Liter.						
CL55 Coupe 2D	PJ74J	119520	8325	8900	9725	13100
DISTRONIC Cruise Control			275	275	305	305
designo Edition			600	600	675	675
CL-CLASS—V12 Twin Turbo—Equipment Schedule 1						
W.B. 113.6"; 5.5 Liter.						
CL600 Coupe 2D	PJ76J	129320	4700	5025	6375	9200
DISTRONIC Cruise Control			275	275	340	340
Sport Pkg			1125	1125	1440	1440
designo Edition			600	600	750	750
S-CLASS—V8—Equipment Schedule 1						
W.B. 121.5"; 4.3 Liter, 5.0 Liter.						
S430 Sedan 4D	NG72J	74320	3400	3625	4400	6200
S430 4MATIC Sed 4D	NG83J	78220	5175	5525	6450	8950
S500 Sedan 4D	NG75J	83770	3725	3975	4775	6775
S500 4MATIC Sed 4D	NG84J	86970	5225	5575	6525	9075
DISTRONIC Cruise Control			275	275	355	355
Sport Pkg			1125	1125	1510	1510
designo Edition			600	600	785	785
S-CLASS—V8 Supercharged—Equipment Schedule 1						
W.B. 121.5"; 5.5 Liter.						
S55 Sedan 4D	NG74J	111870	5425	5875	6550	9375
DISTRONIC Cruise Control			275	275	320	320
designo Edition			600	600	715	715
S-CLASS—V12 Twin Turbo—Equipment Schedule 1						
W.B. 121.5"; 5.5 Liter.						
S600 Sedan 4D	NG76J	124260	5100	5450	6525	9175
DISTRONIC Cruise Control			275	275	355	355
Sport Pkg			1125	1125	1510	1510
designo Edition			600	600	785	785
SL-CLASS—V8—Equipment Schedule 1						
W.B. 100.8"; 5.0 Liter.						
SL500 Roadster 2D	SK75F	89800	8250	8800	9650	12950
DISTRONIC Cruise Control			275	275	315	315
Sport Pkg			1125	1125	1350	1350
designo Edition			600	600	705	705
SL-CLASS—V8 Supercharged—Equipment Schedule 1						
W.B. 100.8"; 5.5 Liter.						
SL55 Roadster 2D	SK74F	121450	9825	10500	11150	14650
DISTRONIC Cruise Control			275	275	300	300
designo Edition			600	600	670	670
SL-CLASS—V12 Twin Turbo—Equipment Schedule 1						
W.B. 100.8"; 5.5 Liter.						
SL600 Roadster 2D	SK76F	128550	13150	14050	14600	19200

Body Type	VIN	List	Trade-In Good	Trade-In Very Good	Pvt-Party Good	Retail Excellent
DISTRONIC Cruise Control			275	275	315	315
Sport Pkg			1125	1125	1345	1345
designo Edition			600	600	700	700

2005 MERCEDES-BENZ — WDBorWDD(WK56F)-5-#

SLK-CLASS—V6—Equipment Schedule 1
W.B. 95.7"; 3.5 Liter.
SLK350 Roadster 2D	WK56F	47610	6900	7350	8400	11250
Sport Pkg			625	625	770	770
designo Edition			625	625	780	780
Manual, 6-Spd			(425)	(425)	(510)	(510)

SLK-CLASS—V8—Equipment Schedule 1
W.B. 95.7"; 5.5 Liter.
SLK55 Roadster 2D	WK73F	61220	9625	10250	11350	14950
designo Edition			625	625	760	760

C-CLASS—4-Cyl. Supercharged—Equipment Schedule 1
W.B. 106.9"; 1.8 Liter.
C230 Sport Sedan 4D	RF40J	34650	3875	4200	5025	7225
C230 Sport Coupe 2D	RN40J	30850	3200	3500	4325	6250
Manual, 6-Spd			(425)	(425)	(555)	(555)

C-CLASS—V6—Equipment Schedule 1
W.B. 106.9"; 2.6 Liter, 3.2 Liter.
C240 Sedan 4D	RF61J	36660	3975	4300	5125	7375
C240 4MATIC Sedan	RF87J	37860	4200	4550	5375	7700
C240 Wagon 4D	RH61J	38030	4250	4600	5425	7775
C240 4MATIC Wagon	RH81J	39230	4500	4875	5700	8150
C320 Sedan 4D	RF64J	41960	4500	4875	5700	8150
C320 4MATIC Sedan	RF84J	43160	5025	5425	6225	8900
C320 Sport Sedan 4D	RF64J	39460	4725	5100	5900	8450
C320 Sport Coupe 2D	RN64J	33250	3300	3600	4425	6400

C-CLASS—V8—Equipment Schedule 1
W.B. 106.9"; 5.5 Liter.
C55 Sedan 4D	RF76J	54620	7975	8625	9025	12200

CLK-CLASS—V6—Equipment Schedule 1
W.B. 106.9"; 3.2 Liter.
CLK320 Coupe 2D	TJ65G	47410	4700	5025	6025	8150
CLK320 Cabriolet 2D	TK65G	53420	6275	6675	7775	10500
designo Edition			625	625	845	845

CLK-CLASS—V8—Equipment Schedule 1
W.B. 106.9"; 5.0 Liter, 5.5 Liter.
CLK500 Coupe 2D	TJ75G	55910	5475	5850	6875	9275
CLK500 Cabriolet 2D	TK75G	61920	7000	7450	8475	11400
CLK55 Coupe 2D	TJ76G	71620	8100	8750	9325	12700
CLK55 Cabriolet 2D	TK76G	82870	7575	8175	8775	11950
designo Edition			625	625	845	845

E-CLASS—6-Cyl. Turbo Diesel—Equipment Schedule 1
W.B. 112.4"; 3.2 Liter.
E320 CDI Sedan 4D	UF26J	52855	7675	8425	8925	12700
designo Edition			625	625	845	845

E-CLASS—V6—Equipment Schedule 1
W.B. 112.4"; 3.2 Liter.
E320 Sedan 4D	UF65J	52280	5225	5775	6275	8900
E320 4MATIC Sedan	UF82J	54770	5425	5975	6625	9525
E320 Wagon 4D	UH65J	54400	5525	6100	6700	9600
E320 4MATIC Wagon	UH82J	56900	7075	7800	8150	11400
Appearance Pkg			625	625	830	830
Sport Pkg			625	625	830	830
designo Edition			625	625	845	845

E-CLASS—V8—Equipment Schedule 1
W.B. 112.4"; 5.0 Liter.
E500 Sedan 4D	UF70J	60480	5650	6225	6725	9550
E500 4MATIC Sedan	UF83J	61420	7425	8175	8750	12500
E500 4MATIC Wagon	UH83J	63950	8225	9025	9500	13450
Appearance Pkg			625	625	820	820
Sport Pkg			625	625	820	820
designo Edition			625	625	830	830

E-CLASS—V8 Supercharged—Equipment Schedule 1
W.B. 112.4"; 5.5 Liter.
E55 Sedan 4D	UF76J	81920	9625	10250	11050	14500
E55 Wagon 4D	UF86J	83220	12500	13250	14200	18550
DISTRONIC Cruise Control			300	300	370	370
designo Edition			625	625	810	810

Body Type	VIN	List	Trade-In Good	Very Good	Pvt-Party Good	Retail Excellent

CL-CLASS—V8—Equipment Schedule 1
W.B. 113.6"; 5.0 Liter.

CL500 Coupe 2D	PJ75J	94620	6125	6525	7250	9425
DISTRONIC Cruise Control			300	300	340	340
Sport Pkg			1250	1250	1465	1465
designo Edition			625	625	740	740

CL-CLASS—V8 Supercharged—Equipment Schedule 1
W.B. 113.6"; 5.5 Liter.

CL55 Coupe 2D	PJ74J	119620	10800	11450	12250	15850
DISTRONIC Cruise Control			300	300	340	340
designo Edition			625	625	745	745

CL-CLASS—V12 Twin Turbo—Equipment Schedule 1
W.B. 113.6"; 5.5 Liter, 6.0 Liter.

CL600 Coupe 2D	PJ76J	128620	7150	7600	8700	11700
CL65 Coupe 2D	PJ79J	178220	15500	16700	16600	22000
DISTRONIC Cruise Control			300	300	345	345
Sport Pkg			1250	1250	1495	1495
designo Edition			625	625	755	755

S-CLASS—V8—Equipment Schedule 1
W.B. 121.5"; 4.3 Liter, 5.0 Liter.

S430 Sedan 4D	NG70J	76020	5600	5975	6975	9450
S430 4MATIC Sedan	NG83J	76020	7725	8200	9225	12350
S500 Sedan 4D	NG75J	84620	6450	6875	7900	10600
S500 4MATIC Sedan	NG84J	84620	8000	8500	9550	12800
DISTRONIC Cruise Control			300	300	355	355
Sport Pkg			1250	1250	1545	1545
designo Edition			625	625	780	780

S-CLASS—V8 Supercharged—Equipment Schedule 1
W.B. 121.5"; 5.5 Liter.

S55 Sedan 4D	NG74J	112620	7850	8475	9150	12650
DISTRONIC Cruise Control			300	300	350	350
designo Edition			625	625	765	765

S-CLASS—V12 Twin Turbo—Equipment Schedule 1
W.B. 121.5"; 5.5 Liter.

S600 Sedan 4D	NG76J	125470	6275	6675	7800	10550
DISTRONIC Cruise Control			300	300	375	375
Sport Pkg			1250	1250	1635	1635
designo Edition			625	625	825	825

SL-CLASS—V8—Equipment Schedule 1
W.B. 100.8"; 5.0 Liter.

SL500 Roadster 2D	SK75F	91920	10300	10950	11900	15600
DISTRONIC Cruise Control			300	300	345	345
Sport Pkg			1250	1250	1485	1485
designo Edition			625	625	750	750

SL-CLASS—V8 Supercharged—Equipment Schedule 1
W.B. 100.8"; 5.5 Liter.

SL55 Roadster 2D	SK74F	120120	13000	13800	14250	18100
DISTRONIC Cruise Control			300	300	325	325
designo Edition			625	625	705	705

SL-CLASS—V12 Twin Turbo—Equipment Schedule 1
W.B. 100.8"; 5.5 Liter, 6.0 Liter.

SL600 Roadster 2D	SK76F	125620	18400	19550	20100	25800
SL65 Roadster 2D	SK79F	182720	23700	25200	24800	31000
DISTRONIC Cruise Control			300	300	345	345
Sport Pkg (SL600)			1250	1250	1485	1485
designo Edition			625	625	750	750

SLR-CLASS—V8 Supercharged—Equipment Schedule 1
W.B. 106.3"; 5.5 Liter.

| McLaren Coupe 2D | AJ76F | 455750 | **** | **** | **** | 158000 |

SLK-CLASS—V6—Equipment Schedule 1
W.B. 95.7"; 3.0 Liter, 3.5 Liter.

SLK280 Roadster 2D	WK54F	45085	6600	7000	8225	10950
SLK350 Roadster 2D	WK56F	49135	8050	8550	9625	12600
Sport Pkg			625	625	765	765
designo Edition			675	675	835	835
Manual, 6-Spd			(450)	(450)	(540)	(540)

SLK-CLASS—V8—Equipment Schedule 1
W.B. 95.7"; 5.5 Liter.

| SLK55 Roadster 2D | WK73F | 63575 | 11050 | 11700 | 12750 | 16450 |
| designo Edition | | | 675 | 675 | 815 | 815 |

Body Type	VIN	List	Trade-In Good	Very Good	Pvt-Party Good	Retail Excellent
C-CLASS—V6—Equipment Schedule 1						
W.B. 106.9"; 2.5 Liter, 3.0 Liter, 3.5 Liter.						
C230 Sport Sedan 4D	RF52J	33155	**5000**	**5375**	**6200**	**8675**
C280 Sedan 4D	RF54J	35515	**5100**	**5500**	**6300**	**8825**
C280 4MATIC Sedan	RF92J	37315	**5100**	**5500**	**6500**	**9125**
C350 Sedan 4D	RF56J	40715	**5525**	**5950**	**6925**	**9675**
C350 4MATIC Sedan	RF87J	42515	**6100**	**6550**	**7525**	**10500**
Manual, 6-Spd.			**(450)**	**(450)**	**(585)**	**(585)**
C-CLASS—V8—Equipment Schedule 1						
W.B. 106.9"; 5.5 Liter.						
C55 Sedan 4D	RF76J	56225	**9100**	**9775**	**10300**	**13700**
CLK-CLASS—V6—Equipment Schedule 1						
W.B. 106.9"; 3.5 Liter.						
CLK350 Coupe 2D	TJ56J	49025	**5725**	**6100**	**7250**	**9700**
CLK350 Cabriolet 2D	TK56G	55975	**7625**	**8075**	**9175**	**12100**
KEYLESS-GO			**200**	**200**	**250**	**250**
designo Edition			**675**	**675**	**910**	**910**
CLK-CLASS—V8—Equipment Schedule 1						
W.B. 106.9"; 5.0 Liter, 5.5 Liter.						
CLK500 Coupe 2D	TJ57J	57325	**6650**	**7075**	**8175**	**10900**
CLK500 Cabriolet 2D	TK75G	64275	**9025**	**9550**	**10550**	**13750**
CLK55 Cabriolet 2D	TK76G	84275	**10850**	**11650**	**12000**	**15750**
KEYLESS-GO			**200**	**200**	**250**	**250**
designo Edition			**675**	**675**	**905**	**905**
E-CLASS—6-Cyl. Turbo Diesel—Equipment Schedule 1						
W.B. 112.4"; 3.2 Liter.						
E320 CDI Sedan 4D	UF26J	54845	**8250**	**9000**	**9650**	**13600**
KEYLESS-GO			**200**	**200**	**250**	**250**
designo Edition			**675**	**675**	**910**	**910**
E-CLASS—V6—Equipment Schedule 1						
W.B. 112.4"; 3.5 Liter.						
E350 Sedan 4D	UF56J	52325	**6225**	**6825**	**7200**	**9875**
E350 4MATIC Sedan	UF87J	54825	**6675**	**7300**	**7875**	**11050**
E350 Wagon 4D	UH56J	54505	**6725**	**7350**	**7800**	**10875**
E350 4MATIC Wagon	UH87J	57005	**7775**	**8475**	**8875**	**12250**
KEYLESS-GO			**200**	**200**	**240**	**240**
Appearance Pkg			**625**	**625**	**795**	**795**
Sport Pkg			**625**	**625**	**795**	**795**
designo Edition			**675**	**675**	**870**	**870**
E-CLASS—V8—Equipment Schedule 1						
W.B. 112.4"; 5.0 Liter.						
E500 Sedan 4D	UF70J	60675	**7225**	**7875**	**8375**	**11600**
E500 4MATIC Sedan	UF83J	64475	**8425**	**9200**	**9525**	**13100**
E500 4MATIC Wagon	UH83J	65505	**9175**	**10000**	**10350**	**14250**
KEYLESS-GO			**200**	**200**	**245**	**245**
Appearance Pkg			**625**	**625**	**815**	**815**
Sport Pkg			**625**	**625**	**815**	**815**
designo Edition			**675**	**675**	**890**	**890**
E-CLASS—V8 Supercharged—Equipment Schedule 1						
W.B. 112.4"; 5.5 Liter.						
E55 Sedan 4D	UF76J	84275	**11150**	**11800**	**12700**	**16400**
E55 Wagon 4D	UH76J	83355	**14050**	**14850**	**15750**	**20200**
KEYLESS-GO			**200**	**200**	**225**	**225**
Adaptive Cruise Control			**325**	**325**	**380**	**380**
designo Edition			**675**	**675**	**820**	**820**
CL-CLASS—V8—Equipment Schedule 1						
W.B. 113.6"; 5.0 Liter.						
CL500 Coupe 2D	PJ75J	97275	**8350**	**8850**	**9950**	**13050**
Adaptive Cruise Control			**325**	**325**	**365**	**365**
designo Edition			**675**	**675**	**795**	**795**
CL-CLASS—V8 Supercharged—Equipment Schedule 1						
W.B. 113.6"; 5.5 Liter.						
CL55 Coupe 2D	PJ74J	122975	**13250**	**14000**	**14700**	**18650**
Adaptive Cruise Control			**325**	**325**	**370**	**370**
designo Edition			**675**	**675**	**800**	**800**
CL-CLASS—V12 Twin Turbo—Equipment Schedule 1						
W.B. 113.6"; 5.5 Liter, 6.0 Liter.						
CL600 Coupe 2D	PJ76J	132855	**8275**	**8775**	**10300**	**13950**
CL65 Coupe 2D	PJ79J	182975	**17750**	**19050**	**18800**	**24400**
Adaptive Cruise Control			**325**	**325**	**385**	**385**
designo Edition			**675**	**675**	**835**	**835**
CLS-CLASS—V8—Equipment Schedule 1						
W.B. 112.4"; 5.0 Liter.						

Body Type	VIN	List	Trade-In Good	Very Good	Pvt-Party Good	Retail Excellent
CLS500 Coupe 4D	DJ75X	66975	**11150**	**11850**	**12700**	**16200**
Adaptive Cruise Control			325	325	375	375
Sport Pkg			1375	1375	1645	1645
designo Edition			675	675	810	810
CLS-CLASS—V8 Supercharged—Equipment Schedule 1						
W.B. 112.4"; 5.5 Liter.						
CLS55 Coupe 4D	DJ76X	89075	**13950**	**14950**	**14800**	**19050**
Adaptive Cruise Control			325	325	365	365
designo Edition			675	675	795	795
S-CLASS—V6—Equipment Schedule 1						
W.B. 121.5"; 3.7 Liter.						
S350 Sedan 4D	NF67J	65675	**6075**	**6450**	**7375**	**9700**
KEYLESS-GO			200	200	230	230
Adaptive Cruise Control			325	325	385	385
S-CLASS—V8—Equipment Schedule 1						
W.B. 121.5"; 4.3 Liter, 5.0 Liter.						
S430 Sedan 4D	NG70J	78025	**6850**	**7250**	**8275**	**10950**
S430 4MATIC Sedan	NG83J	79025	**8825**	**9350**	**10400**	**13650**
S500 Sedan 4D	NG75J	87825	**8075**	**8550**	**9525**	**12450**
S500 4MATIC Sedan	NG84J	88125	**9550**	**10100**	**11100**	**14450**
KEYLESS-GO			200	200	230	230
Adaptive Cruise Control			325	325	390	390
Sport Pkg			1375	1375	1705	1705
designo Edition			675	675	835	835
S-CLASS—V8 Supercharged—Equipment Schedule 1						
W.B. 121.5"; 5.5 Liter.						
S55 Sedan 4D	NG74J	116625	**10100**	**10850**	**11200**	**14750**
Adaptive Cruise Control			325	325	370	370
designo Edition			675	675	800	800
S-CLASS—V12 Twin Turbo—Equipment Schedule 1						
W.B. 121.5"; 5.5 Liter, 6.0 Liter.						
S600 Sedan 4D	NG76J	131725	**7750**	**8225**	**9400**	**12550**
S65 Sedan 4D	NG79J	169775	**15350**	**16250**	**17900**	**23800**
Adaptive Cruise Control			325	325	395	395
Sport Pkg (S600)			1375	1375	1730	1730
designo Edition			675	675	855	855
SL-CLASS—V8—Equipment Schedule 1						
W.B. 100.8"; 5.0 Liter.						
SL500 Roadster 2D	SK75F	94675	**12000**	**12700**	**13700**	**17650**
KEYLESS-GO			200	200	225	225
Adaptive Cruise Control			325	325	375	375
Sport Pkg			1375	1375	1640	1640
designo Edition			675	675	810	810
SL-CLASS—V8 Supercharged—Equipment Schedule 1						
W.B. 100.8"; 5.5 Liter.						
SL55 Roadster 2D	SK74F	127875	**14650**	**15450**	**15850**	**19750**
KEYLESS-GO			200	200	210	210
Adaptive Cruise Control			325	325	350	350
Performance Pkg			3200	3200	3555	3555
designo Edition			675	675	755	755
SL-CLASS—V12 Twin Turbo—Equipment Schedule 1						
W.B. 100.8"; 5.5 Liter, 6.0 Liter.						
SL600 Roadster 2D	SK76F	134275	**20600**	**21800**	**22300**	**28100**
SL65 Roadster 2D	SK79F	188355	**25400**	**26800**	**26500**	**32700**
Adaptive Cruise Control			325	325	375	375
Sport Pkg (SL600)			1375	1375	1635	1635
designo Edition			675	675	805	805
SLR-CLASS—V8 Supercharged—Equipment Schedule 1						
W.B. 106.3"; 5.5 Liter.						
McLaren Coupe 2D	AJ76F	455750	****	****	****	197000

Body Type	VIN	List	Trade-In Good	Very Good	Pvt-Party Good	Retail Excellent
SLK-CLASS—V6—Equipment Schedule 1						
W.B. 95.7"; 3.0 Liter, 3.5 Liter.						
SLK280 Roadster 2D	WK54F	45555	**7625**	**8050**	**9300**	**12100**
SLK350 Roadster 2D	WK56F	49605	**9175**	**9675**	**10900**	**14000**
AMG Sport Pkg			625	625	755	755
designo Edition			725	725	885	885
Manual, 6-Spd			(475)	(475)	(565)	(565)
SLK-CLASS—V8—Equipment Schedule 1						
W.B. 95.7"; 5.5 Liter.						
SLK55 Roadster 2D	WK73F	64575	**14600**	**15350**	**16200**	**20200**
designo Edition			725	725	845	845

1015

Body Type	VIN	List	Trade-In Good	Very Good	Pvt-Party Good	Retail Excellent
Performance Pkg		....	**3425**	**3425**	**3935**	**3935**
C-CLASS—V6—Equipment Schedule 1						
W.B. 106.9"; 2.5 Liter, 3.0 Liter, 3.5 Liter.						
C230 Sport Sedan 4D	RF52J	34205	6700	7150	7950	10600
C280 Sedan 4D	RF54J	35965	6800	7275	8050	10750
C280 4MATIC Sedan	RF92J	37765	7250	7725	8575	11450
C350 Sedan 4D	RF56J	41165	8050	8600	9400	12500
C350 4MATIC Sedan	RF87J	42965	8650	9225	10000	13300
Manual, 6-Spd			(475)	(475)	(620)	(620)
CLK-CLASS—V6—Equipment Schedule 1						
W.B. 106.9"; 3.5 Liter.						
CLK350 Coupe 2D	TJ56J	49505	7375	7825	8825	11350
CLK350 Cabriolet 2D	TK56F	54975	9325	9825	10900	13900
KEYLESS-GO			200	200	250	250
designo Edition			725	725	930	930
CLK-CLASS—V8—Equipment Schedule 1						
W.B. 106.9"; 5.5 Liter, 6.3 Liter.						
CLK550 Coupe 2D	TJ72H	58205	9375	9950	10900	13900
CLK550 Cabriolet 2D	TK72F	63675	10950	11550	12650	16000
CLK63 Cabriolet 2D	TK77G	92575	14100	15000	15100	19100
KEYLESS-GO			200	200	245	245
designo Edition			725	725	920	920
E-CLASS—V6 Turbo Diesel—Equipment Schedule 1						
W.B. 112.4"; 3.0 Liter.						
E320 BlueTEC Sed	UF22X	52325	10150	10950	11150	14750
KEYLESS-GO			200	200	245	245
P1 Pkg			300	300	360	360
P2 Pkg			275	275	350	350
designo Edition			725	725	910	910
E-CLASS—V6—Equipment Schedule 1						
W.B. 112.4"; 3.5 Liter.						
E350 Sedan 4D	UF56X	51325	8200	8875	9050	11950
E350 4MATIC Sedan	UF87X	56475	8975	9700	9850	13000
E350 4MATIC Wagon	UH87X	53825	11650	12600	12600	16500
KEYLESS-GO			200	200	240	240
P1 Pkg			300	300	355	355
P2 Pkg			275	275	345	345
Sport Pkg (Sedan)			625	625	765	765
designo Edition			725	725	900	900
E-CLASS—V8—Equipment Schedule 1						
W.B. 112.4"; 5.5 Liter, 6.3 Liter.						
E550 Sedan 4D	UF72X	59775	9525	10300	10450	13750
E550 4MATIC Sedan	UF90X	62275	11250	12150	12250	16100
E63 Sedan 4D	UF77X	85375	14650	15450	16200	20300
E63 Wagon 4D	UH77X	86175	18250	19200	19750	24500
KEYLESS-GO			200	200	240	240
P1 Pkg			300	300	355	355
P2 Pkg			275	275	345	345
AMG Sport Pkg (E550)			625	625	765	765
designo Edition			725	725	895	895
CL-CLASS—V8—Equipment Schedule 1						
W.B. 116.3"; 5.5 Liter.						
CL550 Coupe 2D	EJ71X	100675	16700	17550	17750	21500
Adaptive Cruise Control			350	350	375	375
P1 Pkg			300	300	320	320
P2 Pkg			275	275	310	310
AMG Sport Pkg			625	625	690	690
designo Edition			725	725	810	810
CL-CLASS—V12 Twin Turbo—Equipment Schedule 1						
W.B. 116.3"; 5.5 Liter.						
CL600 Coupe 2D	EJ76X	144975	16950	17850	18400	22800
Adaptive Cruise Control			350	350	380	380
designo Edition			725	725	820	820
CLS-CLASS—V8—Equipment Schedule 1						
W.B. 112.4"; 5.5 Liter, 6.3 Liter.						
CLS550 Coupe 4D	DJ72X	68975	12350	13000	14150	18000
CLS63 Coupe 4D	DJ77X	92975	16850	17950	17600	22000
Adaptive Cruise Control			350	350	405	405
AMG Sport Pkg (CLS550)			1500	1500	1795	1795
designo Edition			725	725	870	870
S-CLASS—V8—Equipment Schedule 1						
W.B. 124.6"; 5.5 Liter.						
S550 Sedan 4D	NG71X	87175	14250	15000	15950	20100

2007 MERCEDES-BENZ

Body Type	VIN	List	Trade-In Good	Very Good	Pvt-Party Good	Retail Excellent
S550 4MATIC Sedan	NG86X	89525	15950	16800	17450	21700
KEYLESS-GO			200	200	235	235
Adaptive Cruise Control			350	350	410	410
P1 Pkg			300	300	350	350
P2 Pkg			275	275	340	340
P3 Pkg			500	500	605	605
AMG Sport Pkg			1500	1500	1820	1820
designo Edition			725	725	885	885
S-CLASS—V12 Twin Turbo—Equipment Schedule 1						
W.B. 124.6"; 5.5 Liter, 6.0 Liter.						
S600 Sedan 4D	NG76X	143675	17400	18300	19200	24100
S65 Sedan 4D	NG79X	184875	25100	26300	27000	33600
Adaptive Cruise Control			350	350	380	380
designo Edition			725	725	820	820
SL-CLASS—V8—Equipment Schedule 1						
W.B. 100.8"; 5.5 Liter.						
SL550 Roadster 2D	SK71F	97275	15250	16050	17050	21400
KEYLESS-GO			200	200	235	235
Adaptive Cruise Control			350	350	405	405
Premium Pkg I			300	300	345	345
Premium Pkg II			275	275	335	335
AMG Sport Pkg			1500	1500	1790	1790
designo Edition			725	725	870	870
SL-CLASS—V8 Supercharged—Equipment Schedule 1						
W.B. 100.8"; 5.5 Liter.						
SL55 Roadster 2D	SK72F	132175	18450	19450	19550	23700
KEYLESS-GO			200	200	215	215
Adaptive Cruise Control			350	350	375	375
designo Edition			725	725	810	810
Performance Pkg			3425	3425	3775	3775
SL-CLASS—V12 Twin Turbo—Equipment Schedule 1						
W.B. 100.8"; 5.5 Liter, 6.0 Liter.						
SL600 Roadster 2D	SK77F	135375	21400	22500	23300	29100
SL65 Roadster 2D	SK79F	189375	32400	34000	33200	39800
Adaptive Cruise Control			350	350	405	405
AMG Sport Pkg (SL600)			1500	1500	1785	1785
designo Edition			725	725	865	865
SLR-CLASS—V8 Supercharged—Equipment Schedule 1						
W.B. 106.3"; 5.5 Liter.						
McLaren 722 Edition	AJ76F	485750	****	****	****	226400

2008 MERCEDES-BENZ — WDBorWDD(WK54F)-8-#

Body Type	VIN	List	Trade-In Good	Very Good	Pvt-Party Good	Retail Excellent
SLK-CLASS—V6—Equipment Schedule 1						
W.B. 95.7"; 3.0 Liter, 3.5 Liter.						
SLK280 Roadster 2D	WK54F	46115	9325	9725	11100	13900
SLK280 Edition Rdstr	WK54F	51100	9750	10200	11700	14700
SLK350 Roadster 2D	WK56F	49975	11200	11700	13200	16500
SLK350 Edition Rdstr	WK56F	56800	16450	17150	18400	22500
AMG Sport Pkg			1625	1625	1920	1920
designo Edition			775	775	930	930
Manual, 6-Spd w/Overdrive			(400)	(400)	(480)	(480)
SLK-CLASS—V8—Equipment Schedule 1						
W.B. 95.7"; 5.5 Liter.						
SLK55 Roadster 2D	WK73F	65025	16750	17500	18600	22600
Performance Pkg			3625	3625	4140	4140
C-CLASS—V6—Equipment Schedule 1						
W.B. 108.7"; 3.0 Liter, 3.5 Liter.						
C300 Sport Sed 4D	GF54X	34915	9775	10300	11100	13950
C300 Sport 4MATIC	GF81X	36715	10250	10800	11650	14600
C300 Luxury Sedan 4D	GF54X	35175	9450	9975	10800	13550
C300 Luxury 4MATIC	GF81X	35925	9925	10450	11300	14200
C350 Sport Sedan 4D	GF56X	38775	11200	11800	12650	15850
Multimedia Pkg			225	225	295	295
P1 Pkg			300	300	380	380
P2 Pkg			300	300	380	380
Manual, 6-Spd Overdrive			(400)	(400)	(510)	(510)
C-CLASS—V8—Equipment Schedule 1						
W.B. 108.7"; 6.3 Liter.						
C63 AMG Sedan 4D	GF77X	54625	20600	21700	21500	25900
P1 Pkg			300	300	340	340
P2 Pkg			300	300	345	345
CLK-CLASS—V6—Equipment Schedule 1						
W.B. 106.9"; 3.5 Liter.						

Body Type	VIN	List	Trade-In Good	Very Good	Pvt-Party Good	Retail Excellent
CLK350 Coupe 2D	TJ56H	47275	8725	9225	10150	12700
CLK350 Cabriolet 2D	TK56F	55325	11100	11600	12900	15900
KEYLESS-GO			200	200	245	245
P1 Pkg			300	300	370	370
P2 Pkg			300	300	375	375
P3 Pkg			500	500	615	615
designo Edition			775	775	965	965
CLK-CLASS—V8—Equipment Schedule 1						
W.B. 106.9"; 5.5 Liter, 6.3 Liter.						
CLK550 Coupe 2D	TJ72H	66975	11100	11700	12600	15650
CLK550 Cabriolet 2D	TK72F	64025	13500	14100	15250	18600
CLK63 Cabriolet 2D	TK77G	90325	17500	18400	18700	22800
KEYLESS-GO			200	200	245	245
P1 Pkg			300	300	365	365
P2 Pkg			300	300	370	370
P3 Pkg			500	500	610	610
designo Edition			775	775	960	960
CLK-CLASS—V8—Equipment Schedule 1						
W.B. 106.9"; 6.3 Liter.						
CLK63 Black Series	TJ77H	135825	32800	34500	33300	39600
E-CLASS—V6 Turbo Diesel—Equipment Schedule 1						
W.B. 112.4"; 3.0 Liter.						
E320 BlueTEC Sedan	UF22X	52675	11950	12800	13000	16400
KEYLESS-GO			200	200	235	235
P1 Pkg			300	300	355	355
P2 Pkg			300	300	355	355
designo Edition			775	775	925	925
E-CLASS—V6—Equipment Schedule 1						
W.B. 112.4"; 3.5 Liter.						
E350 Sedan 4D	UF56X	51675	10050	10750	10950	13750
E350 4MATIC Sedan	UF87X	53175	10600	11350	11550	14500
E350 4MATIC Wagon	UH87X	56475	13450	14400	14500	18150
KEYLESS-GO			200	200	235	235
P1 Pkg			300	300	350	350
P2 Pkg			300	300	355	355
AMG Sport Pkg (Sedan)			625	625	735	735
designo Edition			775	775	920	920
E-CLASS—V8—Equipment Schedule 1						
W.B. 112.4"; 5.5 Liter, 6.3 Liter.						
E550 Sedan 4D	UF72X	61875	11350	12150	12850	16700
E550 4MATIC Sedan	UF90X	63375	16350	17450	17450	21800
E63 Sedan 4D	UF77X	85775	17300	18100	19000	22900
E63 Wagon 4D	UH77X	86575	20300	21200	22100	26600
KEYLESS-GO			200	200	240	240
P1 Pkg			300	300	360	360
P2 Pkg			300	300	360	360
AMG Sport Pkg			625	625	750	750
designo Edition			775	775	935	935
Performance Pkg			3625	3625	4235	4235
CL-CLASS—V8—Equipment Schedule 1						
W.B. 116.3"; 5.5 Liter.						
CL550 Coupe 2D	EJ71X	104425	19950	20800	21400	25400
Adaptive Cruise Control			375	375	400	400
Premium Pkg 1			300	300	330	330
Premium Pkg 2			300	300	335	335
AMG Sport Pkg			1625	1625	1775	1775
designo Edition			775	775	860	860
Performance Pkg			3625	3625	4030	4030
CL-CLASS—V8—Equipment Schedule 1						
W.B. 116.3"; 6.2 Liter.						
CL63 Coupe 2D	EJ77X	138325	24500	25600	26400	31600
Adaptive Cruise Control			375	375	405	405
Premium Pkg 2			300	300	335	335
designo Edition			775	775	870	870
Performance Pkg			3625	3625	4030	4030
CL-CLASS—V12 Twin Turbo—Equipment Schedule 1						
W.B. 116.3"; 5.5 Liter.						
CL600 Coupe 2D	EJ76X	148225	21300	22200	23300	28300
DISTRONIC Cruise Control			375	375	415	415
designo Edition			775	775	885	885
CL-CLASS—V12 Twin Turbo—Equipment Schedule 1						
W.B. 116.3"; 6.0 Liter.						
CL65 Coupe 2D	EJ79X	197775	46600	49000	46700	55100

Body Type	VIN	List	Trade-In Good	Very Good	Pvt-Party Good	Retail Excellent
designo Edition			775	775	850	850
CLS-CLASS—V8—Equipment Schedule 1						
W.B. 112.4"; 5.5 Liter, 6.3 Liter.						
CLS550 Coupe 4D	DJ72X	70075	**15400**	**16050**	**17250**	**21000**
CLS63 Coupe 4D	DJ77X	96975	**19650**	**20700**	**20800**	**25300**
KEYLESS-GO			200	200	235	235
Adaptive Cruise Control			375	375	425	425
designo Edition			775	775	915	915
P1 Pkg			300	300	345	345
P2 Pkg			300	300	355	355
AMG Sport Pkg (CLS550)			1625	1625	1890	1890
Performance Pkg			3625	3625	4170	4170
S-CLASS—V8—Equipment Schedule 1						
W.B. 124.6"; 5.5 Liter.						
S550 Sedan 4D	NG71X	88775	**18250**	**19000**	**19950**	**24100**
S550 4MATIC Sedan	NG86X	91775	**19800**	**20700**	**21400**	**25600**
Adaptive Cruise Control			375	375	430	430
Premium Pkg 1			300	300	350	350
Premium Pkg 2			300	300	355	355
Premium Pkg 3			500	500	585	585
AMG Sport Pkg			1625	1625	1900	1900
designo Edition			775	775	920	920
Performance Pkg			3625	3625	4380	4380
S-CLASS—V8—Equipment Schedule 1						
W.B. 124.6"; 6.3 Liter.						
S63 Sedan 4D	NG77X	127775	**22900**	**24100**	**24900**	**31000**
Adaptive Cruise Control			375	375	440	440
Premium Pkg 3			500	500	605	605
Performance Pkg			3625	3625	4380	4380
S-CLASS—V12 Twin Turbo—Equipment Schedule 1						
W.B. 124.6"; 6.0 Liter.						
S600 Sedan 4D	NG76X	147975	**19450**	**20300**	**21400**	**26100**
S65 Sedan 4D	NG79X	186575	**30800**	**32100**	**32900**	**39400**
designo Edition			775	775	865	865
SL-CLASS—V8—Equipment Schedule 1						
W.B. 100.8"; 5.5 Liter.						
SL550 Roadster 2D	SK71F	97425	**18650**	**19500**	**20800**	**25400**
KEYLESS-GO			200	200	235	235
Adaptive Cruise Control			375	375	430	430
Premium Pkg 1			300	300	355	355
AMG Sport Pkg			1625	1625	1905	1905
designo Edition			775	775	920	920
SL-CLASS—V8 Supercharged—Equipment Schedule 1						
W.B. 100.8"; 5.5 Liter.						
SL55 Roadster 2D	SK72F	132725	**22100**	**23000**	**23300**	**27300**
KEYLESS-GO			200	200	220	220
Adaptive Cruise Control			375	375	405	405
Premium Pkg 1			300	300	330	330
designo Edition			775	775	870	870
Performance Pkg			3625	3625	4015	4015
SL-CLASS—V12 Twin Turbo—Equipment Schedule 1						
W.B. 100.8"; 6.0 Liter.						
SL600 Roadster 2D	SK77F	134025	**24900**	**26000**	**27200**	**32900**
SL65 Roadster 2D	SK79F	188025	**37600**	**39200**	**38700**	**45100**
Adaptive Cruise Control			375	375	425	425
AMG Sport Pkg (SL600)			1625	1625	1885	1885
designo Edition			775	775	915	915
SLR-CLASS—V8 Supercharged—Equipment Schedule 1						
W.B. 106.3"; 5.5 Liter.						
McLaren Roadster 2D	AK76F	500750	********	********	********	**238100**

Body Type	VIN	List	Trade-In Good	Very Good	Pvt-Party Good	Retail Excellent
SLK-CLASS—V6—Equipment Schedule 1						
W.B. 95.7"; 3.0 Liter, 3.5 Liter.						
SLK300 Roadster 2D	WK54F	47285	**11000**	**11450**	**13100**	**15900**
SLK350 Roadster 2D	WK56F	50825	**13950**	**14450**	**16100**	**19400**
Multimedia Pkg			250	250	290	290
Premium Pkg I			325	325	395	395
AMG Sport Pkg			675	675	795	795
Manual, 6-Spd w/Overdrive			(425)	(425)	(515)	(515)
SLK-CLASS—V8—Equipment Schedule 1						
W.B. 95.7"; 5.5 Liter.						
SLK55 Roadster 2D	WK73F	65175	**20400**	**21100**	**22400**	**26300**

Body Type	VIN	List	Trade-In Good	Trade-In Very Good	Pvt-Party Good	Retail Excellent
Multimedia Pkg		-------	250	250	280	280
Performance Pkg		-------	3825	3825	4330	4330
C-CLASS—V6—Equipment Schedule 1						
W.B. 108.7"; 3.0 Liter.						
C300 Sport Sedan 4D	GF54X	32975	11150	11650	12750	15500
C300 Sport 4MATIC	GF81X	35715	12000	12500	13600	16500
C300 Luxury Sedan 4D	GF54X	36275	10850	11350	12450	15150
C300 Luxury 4MATIC	GF81X	35975	11650	12150	13200	16050
Multimedia Pkg		-------	250	250	305	305
Premium Pkg 1		-------	325	325	410	410
Premium Pkg 2		-------	325	325	400	400
Manual, 6-Spd Overdrive		-------	(425)	(425)	(535)	(535)
C-CLASS—V6—Equipment Schedule 1						
W.B. 108.7"; 3.5 Liter.						
C350 Sport Sedan 4D	GF56X	39075	12900	13450	14650	17800
Multimedia Pkg		-------	250	250	300	300
Premium Pkg 2		-------	325	325	395	395
C-CLASS—V8—Equipment Schedule 1						
W.B. 108.7"; 6.3 Liter.						
C63 Sedan 4D	GF77X	55975	23400	24400	24600	28800
Multimedia Pkg		-------	250	250	280	280
Premium Pkg 1		-------	325	325	365	365
Performance Pkg		-------	1300	1300	1460	1460
CLK-CLASS—V6—Equipment Schedule 1						
W.B. 106.9"; 3.5 Liter.						
CLK350 Coupe 2D	TJ56H	47675	10500	11050	12050	14700
CLK350 Cabriolet 2D	TK56F	55675	14600	15150	16500	19550
KEYLESS-GO		-------	200	200	245	245
Premium Pkg 1		-------	325	325	405	405
Premium Pkg 2		-------	325	325	395	395
AMG Sport Pkg		-------	675	675	825	825
designo Edition		-------	825	825	995	995
CLK-CLASS—V8—Equipment Schedule 1						
W.B. 106.9"; 5.5 Liter.						
CLK550 Coupe 2D	TJ72H	57375	13100	13800	14850	18000
CLK550 Cabriolet 2D	TK72F	65375	16900	17500	18750	22100
KEYLESS-GO		-------	200	200	240	240
Premium Pkg 1		-------	325	325	405	405
Premium Pkg 2		-------	325	325	390	390
designo Edition		-------	825	825	990	990
E-CLASS—V6 Turbo Diesel—Equipment Schedule 1						
W.B. 112.4"; 3.0 Liter.						
E320 BlueTEC Sedan	UF22X	53775	14750	15600	16300	20100
KEYLESS-GO		-------	200	200	240	240
Premium Pkg 1		-------	325	325	400	400
Premium Pkg 2		-------	325	325	385	385
designo Edition		-------	825	825	975	975
E-CLASS—V6—Equipment Schedule 1						
W.B. 112.4"; 3.5 Liter.						
E350 Sedan 4D	UF56X	52775	12650	13400	14300	17800
E350 4MATIC Sedan	UF87X	52775	12950	13700	14400	17700
E350 4MATIC Wagon	UH87X	56825	16350	17250	17850	21800
KEYLESS-GO		-------	200	200	235	235
Premium Pkg 1		-------	325	325	395	395
Premium Pkg 2		-------	325	325	380	380
AMG Sport Pkg (Sedan)		-------	675	675	800	800
designo Edition		-------	825	825	965	965
E-CLASS—V8—Equipment Schedule 1						
W.B. 112.4"; 5.5 Liter, 6.3 Liter.						
E550 Sedan 4D	UF72X	61275	16700	17650	18250	22400
E550 4MATIC Sedan	UF90X	64475	19400	20500	21000	25800
E63 Sedan 4D	UF77X	86875	20700	21400	22500	26300
E63 Wagon 4D	UH77X	87675	23500	24400	25500	29900
KEYLESS-GO		-------	200	200	235	235
Adaptive Cruise Control		-------	375	375	430	430
Premium Pkg 1		-------	325	325	395	395
Premium Pkg 2		-------	325	325	385	385
AMG Sport Pkg		-------	675	675	800	800
designo Edition		-------	825	825	970	970
Performance Pkg		-------	3825	3825	4380	4380
CL-CLASS—V8—Equipment Schedule 1						
W.B. 116.3"; 5.5 Liter, 6.3 Liter.						
CL550 4MATIC Coupe	EJ71X	105975	24000	24900	25900	30000

1015

Body Type	VIN	List	Trade-In Good	Very Good	Pvt-Party Good	Retail Excellent
CL63 Coupe 2D	EJ77X	140575	27400	28400	29500	34500
DISTRONIC PLUS			375	375	430	430
Premium Pkg 2			325	325	365	365
designo Edition			825	825	920	920
AMG Sport Pkg			1675	1675	1900	1900
Performance Pkg			3825	3825	4395	4395
CL-CLASS—V12 Twin Turbo—Equipment Schedule 1						
W.B. 116.3"; 5.5 Liter, 6.0 Liter.						
CL600 Coupe 2D	EJ76X	149775	31100	32200	33500	39300
CL65 Coupe 2D	EJ79X	200575	53400	55600	54100	62000
Adaptive Cruise Control			375	375	425	425
designo Edition			825	825	925	925
CLS-CLASS—V8—Equipment Schedule 1						
W.B. 112.4"; 5.5 Liter, 6.3 Liter.						
CLS550 Coupe 4D	DJ72X	69775	18200	18850	20400	24400
CLS63 Coupe 4D	DJ77X	95375	21200	22100	22900	27200
KEYLESS-GO			200	200	230	230
Adaptive Cruise Control			375	375	430	430
P1 Pkg			325	325	380	380
AMG Sport Pkg (CLS550)			1675	1675	1930	1930
designo Edition			825	825	935	935
Performance Pkg			3825	3825	4380	4380
S-CLASS—V8—Equipment Schedule 1						
W.B. 124.6"; 5.5 Liter.						
S550 Sedan 4D	NG71X	89125	21700	22500	23600	27700
S550 4MATIC Sedan	NG86X	92125	23200	24000	25200	29400
Premium Pkg 2			325	325	375	375
AMG Sport Pkg			1675	1675	1965	1965
designo Edition			825	825	950	950
S-CLASS—V8—Equipment Schedule 1						
W.B. 124.6"; 6.3 Liter.						
S63 Sedan 4D	NG77X	129225	26600	27700	28900	34700
DISTRONIC PLUS			375	375	445	445
designo Edition			825	825	970	970
Performance Pkg			3825	3825	4550	4550
S-CLASS—V12 Twin Turbo—Equipment Schedule 1						
W.B. 124.6"; 5.5 Liter, 6.0 Liter.						
S600 Sedan 4D	NG76X	148325	32700	33800	35200	41400
S65 Sedan 4D	NG79X	195825	42500	43900	44400	51200
designo Edition			825	825	890	890
SL-CLASS—V8—Equipment Schedule 1						
W.B. 100.8"; 5.5 Liter, 6.3 Liter.						
SL550 Roadster 2D	SK71F	96775	25400	26300	27800	32700
SL63 Roadster 2D	SK70F	132875	30800	31900	32600	37700
KEYLESS-GO			200	200	230	230
Adaptive Cruise Control			375	375	430	430
Premium Pkg 1			325	325	380	380
designo Edition			825	825	940	940
SL-CLASS—V12 Twin Turbo—Equipment Schedule 1						
W.B. 100.8"; 5.5 Liter, 6.0 Liter.						
SL600 Roadster 2D	SK77F	136975	35100	36300	37300	43500
SL65 Roadster 2D	SK79F	191575	54300	56100	55800	63300
KEYLESS-GO			200	200	225	225
Adaptive Cruise Control			375	375	425	425
designo Edition			825	825	920	920
SLR-CLASS—V8 Supercharged—Equipment Schedule 1						
W.B. 106.3"; 5.5 Liter.						
McLaren Roadster 2D	AK76F	500750	****	****	****	278200

Body Type	VIN	List	Trade-In Good	Very Good	Pvt-Party Good	Retail Excellent
SLK-CLASS—V6—Equipment Schedule 1						
W.B. 95.7"; 3.0 Liter, 3.5 Liter.						
SLK300 Roadster 2D	WK5EA	47775	13950	14350	16150	19050
SLK350 Roadster 2D	WK5JA	52775	16200	16700	18450	21600
Multimedia Pkg			275	275	310	310
Premium Pkg 1			375	375	445	445
AMG Sport Pkg			750	750	870	870
Manual, 6-Spd w/Overdrive			(450)	(450)	(535)	(535)
SLK-CLASS—V8—Equipment Schedule 1						
W.B. 95.7"; 5.5 Liter.						
SLK55 Roadster 2D	WK7DA	68525	25400	26100	27500	31400
Performance Pkg			3900	3900	4340	4340

Body Type	VIN	List	Trade-In Good	Very Good	Pvt-Party Good	Retail Excellent
C-CLASS—V6—Equipment Schedule 1						
W.B. 108.7"; 3.0 Liter, 3.5 Liter.						
C300 Sport Sedan 4D	GF5EB	34475	13050	13500	14700	17300
C300 Sport 4MATIC	GF8BB	37075	13900	14250	15600	18300
C300 Luxury Sedan 4D	GF5EB	36175	12600	13050	14300	16900
C300 Luxury 4MATIC	GF8BB	38175	13150	13600	14900	17550
KEYLESS-GO			200	200	240	240
Multimedia Pkg			275	275	320	320
Premium Pkg 1			375	375	465	465
Premium Pkg 2			350	350	415	415
Manual, 6-Spd Overdrive			(450)	(450)	(555)	(555)
C-CLASS—V6—Equipment Schedule 1						
W.B. 108.7"; 3.5 Liter.						
C350 Sport Sedan 4D	GF5GB	40625	15150	15700	17100	20100
KEYLESS-GO			200	200	240	240
Multimedia Pkg			275	275	320	320
Premium 2 Pkg			350	350	415	415
C-CLASS—V8—Equipment Schedule 1						
W.B. 108.7"; 6.3 Liter.						
C63 Sedan 4D	GF7HB	60325	26800	27700	28400	32500
KEYLESS-GO			200	200	225	225
Multimedia Pkg			275	275	300	300
Premium Pkg 2			350	350	385	385
Performance Pkg			1375	1375	1530	1530
E-CLASS—V6—Equipment Schedule 1						
W.B. 108.7", 113.1" (Sed); 3.5 Liter.						
E350 Sedan 4D	HF5GB	49475	17400	18200	19200	23000
E350 4MATIC Sedan	HF8HB	51975	18050	18900	19850	23700
E350 Coupe 2D	KJ5GB	48925	18250	19100	19900	23600
KEYLESS-GO			200	200	230	230
DISTRONIC Cruise Control			400	400	450	450
Driver Assistance Pkg			575	575	655	655
AMG Sport Pkg (Sedan)			750	750	865	865
E-CLASS—V8—Equipment Schedule 1						
W.B. 108.7", 113.1" (Sed); 5.5 Liter.						
E550 Sedan 4D	HF7CB	57175	20800	21800	22500	26600
E550 4MATIC Sedan	HF9AB	59675	23400	24500	25100	29700
E550 Coupe 2D	KJ7CB	55525	20400	21400	22200	26300
E63 Sedan 4D	HF7HB	88325	29700	30600	31600	35600
KEYLESS-GO			200	200	230	230
DISTRONIC Cruise Control			400	400	450	450
Driver Assistance Pkg			575	575	655	655
Premium Pkg 1			375	375	440	440
Premium Pkg 2			350	350	395	395
AMG Sport Pkg (E550)			750	750	865	865
Performance Pkg			3900	3900	4300	4300
CL-CLASS—V8—Equipment Schedule 1						
W.B. 116.3"; 5.5 Liter.						
CL550 4MATIC Coupe	EJ8GB	112575	28700	29500	30900	35200
DISTRONIC Cruise Control			400	400	440	440
designo Edition			850	850	945	945
Premium Pkg 2			350	350	385	385
CL-CLASS—V8—Equipment Schedule 1						
W.B. 116.3"; 6.3 Liter.						
CL63 Coupe 2D	EJ7HB	148675	34300	35300	37200	42900
DISTRONIC Cruise Control			400	400	450	450
Premium Pkg 2			350	350	395	395
designo Edition			850	850	965	965
Performance Pkg			3900	3900	4490	4490
CL-CLASS—V12—Equipment Schedule 1						
W.B. 116.3"; 5.5 Liter, 6.0 Liter.						
CL600 Coupe 2D	EJ7GB	158275	36800	37900	39700	45600
CL65 Coupe 2D	EJ7KB	211045	66700	68800	67500	75200
designo Edition			850	850	900	900
CLS-CLASS—V8—Equipment Schedule 1						
W.B. 112.4"; 5.5 Liter, 6.3 Liter.						
CLS550 Coupe 4D	DJ7CB	74575	21600	22300	23900	27500
CLS63 Coupe 4D	DJ7HB	101425	24400	25200	26400	30500
KEYLESS-GO			200	200	225	225
Adaptive Cruise Control			400	400	440	440
Sport Pkg Plus One			1725	1725	1960	1960
AMG Sport Pkg (CLS550)			1725	1725	1960	1960
Premium Pkg 1			375	375	435	435

Body Type	VIN	List	Trade-In Good	Very Good	Pvt-Party Good	Retail Excellent
designo Edition			850	850	950	950
Performance Pkg			3900	3900	4415	4415
S-CLASS—V6 Hybrid—Equipment Schedule 1						
W.B. 124.6"; 3.5 Liter.						
S400 Sedan 4D	NG9FB	88825	25300	26100	27800	32100
KEYLESS-GO			200	200	230	230
DISTRONIC PLUS			400	400	455	455
Driver Assistance Pkg			575	575	660	660
Premium Pkg 1			375	375	445	445
Premium Pkg 2			350	350	400	400
Sport Pkg Plus One			750	750	875	875
AMG Sport Pkg			1725	1725	2015	2015
designo Edition			850	850	980	980
S-CLASS—V8—Equipment Schedule 1						
W.B. 124.6"; 5.5 Liter, 6.3 Liter.						
S550 Sedan 4D	NG7BB	93475	28100	28900	30700	35400
S550 4MATIC Sedan	NG8GB	96475	29400	30300	32100	37000
KEYLESS-GO			200	200	230	230
DISTRONIC PLUS			400	400	450	450
Driver Assistance Pkg			575	575	650	650
Premium Pkg 2			350	350	395	395
Sport Pkg Plus One			750	750	860	860
AMG Sport Pkg			1725	1725	1990	1990
designo Edition			850	850	965	965
S-CLASS—V8—Equipment Schedule 1						
W.B. 124.6"; 6.3 Liter.						
S63 Sedan 4D	NG7HB	137425	36300	37500	38700	44700
KEYLESS-GO			200	200	230	230
DISTRONIC PLUS			400	400	445	445
Driver Assistance Pkg			575	575	645	645
designo Edition			850	850	960	960
Performance Pkg			3900	3900	4465	4465
S-CLASS—V12 Twin Turbo—Equipment Schedule 1						
W.B. 124.6"; 5.5 Liter.						
S600 Sedan 4D	NG7GB	153575	36700	37800	39600	45500
KEYLESS-GO			200	200	220	220
designo Edition			850	850	935	935
S-CLASS—V12 Twin Turbo—Equipment Schedule 1						
W.B. 124.6"; 6.0 Liter.						
S65 Sedan 4D	NG7KB	205025	47300	48700	50000	56400
designo Edition			850	850	930	930

2011 MERCEDES-BENZ — WDBorWDD(WK5EA)-B-#

Body Type	VIN	List	Trade-In Good	Very Good	Pvt-Party Good	Retail Excellent
SLK-CLASS—V6—Equipment Schedule 1						
W.B. 95.7"; 3.0 Liter, 3.5 Liter.						
SLK300 Roadster 2D	WK5EA	48525	18450	18900	20700	23700
SLK350 Roadster 2D	WK5JA	54175	20800	21300	23200	26500
Multimedia Pkg			300	300	330	330
Sport Pkg			825	825	935	935
Premium Pkg 1			850	850	955	955
Manual, 6-Spd w/Overdrive	E		(500)	(500)	(565)	(565)
C-CLASS—V6—Equipment Schedule 1						
W.B. 108.7"; 3.0 Liter.						
C300 Sport Sed 4D	GF5EB	34865	14650	15050	16600	19100
C300 Luxury Sedan 4D	GF5EB	36775	14350	14750	16250	18750
C300 Sport 4MATIC	GF8BB	38365	15200	15600	17200	19800
C300 Luxury 4MATIC	GF8BB	38775	14900	15350	16900	19500
KEYLESS-GO			200	200	240	240
Multimedia Pkg			300	300	345	345
Premium Pkg 1			425	425	515	515
Manual, 6-Spd Overdrive			(500)	(500)	(595)	(595)
C-CLASS—V6—Equipment Schedule 1						
W.B. 108.7"; 3.5 Liter.						
C350 Sport Sedan 4D	GF5GB	40865	17150	17600	19250	22100
KEYLESS-GO			200	200	240	240
Multimedia Pkg			300	300	345	345
C-CLASS—V8—Equipment Schedule 1						
W.B. 108.7"; 6.3 Liter.						
C63 AMG Sedan 4D	GF7HB	61175	31600	32400	33600	37500
KEYLESS-GO			200	200	225	225
Multimedia Pkg			300	300	325	325
E-CLASS—V6—Equipment Schedule 1						
W.B. 108.7", 113.2" (Sed); 3.5 Liter.						

Body	Type	VIN	List	Trade-In Good	Very Good	Pvt-Party Good	Retail Excellent
E350 Sedan 4D	HF5GB	50275	**19600**	**20400**	**21700**	**25500**
E350 4MATIC Sedan	HF8HB	52775	20100	20900	21800	25100
E350 Coupe 2D	KJ5GB	49725	20000	20800	21800	25200
E350 Convertible 2D	KK5GF	57725	25100	26000	27000	31200
E350 4MATIC Wagon	HH8HB	57075	23300	24200	25000	28900
KEYLESS-GO			200	200	230	230
DISTRONIC Cruise Control			425	425	480	480
Driver Assistance Pkg			600	600	685	685
Premium Pkg 1			425	425	500	500
Premium Pkg 2			375	375	420	420
AMG Sport Pkg			825	825	955	955

E-CLASS—V6 Turbo Diesel—Equipment Schedule 1
W.B. 113.2"; 3.0 Liter.

Body	Type	VIN	List	Good	Very Good	Good	Excellent
E350 BlueTEC Sed 4D	HF2EB	51775	**20800**	**21600**	**22700**	**26400**
KEYLESS-GO			200	200	230	230
DISTRONIC Cruise Control			425	425	485	485
Driver Assistance Pkg			600	600	685	685
Premium Pkg 1			425	425	505	505
Premium Pkg 2			375	375	420	420
AMG Sport Pkg			825	825	960	960

E-CLASS—V8—Equipment Schedule 1
W.B. 108.7", 113.2" (Sed); 5.5 Liter, 6.3 Liter

Body	Type	VIN	List	Good	Very Good	Good	Excellent
E550 Sedan 4D	HF7CB	57975	**23300**	**24200**	**25100**	**28900**
E550 4MATIC Sedan	HF9AB	60475	26100	27100	27900	32200
E550 Coupe 2D	KJ7CB	56325	22700	23500	24400	28200
E550 Convertible 2D	KK7CF	65675	31300	32500	33400	38500
E63 AMG Sedan 4D	HF7HB	88475	34500	35300	36700	40800
KEYLESS-GO			200	200	230	230
DISTRONIC Cruise Control			425	425	480	480
Premium Pkg 1			425	425	500	500
Premium Pkg 2			375	375	420	420
AMG Sport Pkg			825	825	950	950
Performance Pkg			3900	3900	4255	4255

CL-CLASS—V8 Twin Turbo—Equipment Schedule 1
W.B. 116.3"; 4.6 Liter, 5.5 Liter.

Body	Type	VIN	List	Good	Very Good	Good	Excellent
CL550 4MATIC Cpe	EJ9EB	114025	**35800**	**36600**	**38800**	**43800**
CL63 Coupe 2D	EJ7EB	151125	45900	47000	49100	54900
DISTRONIC PLUS			425	425	465	465
Premium Pkg 2			375	375	405	405
Performance Pkg			3900	3900	4365	4365
designo Edition			875	875	975	975

CL-CLASS—V12 Twin Turbo—Equipment Schedule 1
W.B. 116.3"; 5.5 Liter, 6.0 Liter.

Body	Type	VIN	List	Good	Very Good	Good	Excellent
CL600 Coupe 2D	EJ7GB	157875	**48500**	**49600**	**51700**	**57600**
CL65 Coupe 2D	EJ7KB	210175	83700	85800	84600	92200
designo Edition			875	875	950	950

CLS-CLASS—V8 Twin Turbo—Equipment Schedule 1
W.B. 112.4"; 5.5 Liter, 6.3 Liter.

Body	Type	VIN	List	Good	Very Good	Good	Excellent
CLS550 Coupe 4D	DJ7CB	76175	**24600**	**25200**	**27400**	**31300**
CLS63 AMG Coupe 4D	DJ7HB	102525	29700	30500	32600	37400
KEYLESS-GO			200	200	230	230
Adaptive Cruise Control			425	425	475	475
Premium Pkg 1			425	425	495	495

S-CLASS—V6 Hybrid—Equipment Schedule 1
W.B. 124.6"; 3.5 Liter.

Body	Type	VIN	List	Good	Very Good	Good	Excellent
S400 Sedan 4D	NG9FB	91875	**28900**	**29600**	**31700**	**36100**
Bang & Olufsen BeoSound			2575	2575	2965	2965
KEYLESS-GO			200	200	230	230
DISTRONIC PLUS			425	425	480	480
Driver Assistance Pkg			600	600	680	680
Premium Pkg 2			375	375	415	415
Sport Pkg Plus One			825	825	950	950
Sport Pkg			1775	1775	2050	2050

S-CLASS—V8 Twin Turbo—Equipment Schedule 1
W.B. 124.6"; 5.5 Liter, 6.3 Liter.

Body	Type	VIN	List	Good	Very Good	Good	Excellent
S550 Sedan 4D	NG7BB	94525	**31600**	**32400**	**34700**	**39500**
S550 4MATIC Sedan	NG8GB	97425	33100	33900	36100	41000
S63 Sedan 4D	NG7EB	137875	45700	46900	48400	54500
Bang & Olufsen BeoSound			2575	2575	2930	2930
DISTRONIC PLUS			425	425	470	470
KEYLESS-GO			200	200	225	225
Driver Assistance Pkg			600	600	670	670
Sport Pkg Plus One			825	825	935	935

2011 MERCEDES-BENZ

Body Type	VIN	List	Trade-In Good	Very Good	Pvt-Party Good	Retail Excellent
Premium Pkg 2			375	375	410	410
AMG Sport Pkg			1775	1775	2025	2025
Performance Pkg			3900	3900	4365	4365
S-CLASS—V12 Twin Turbo—Equipment Schedule 1						
W.B. 124.6"; 5.5 Liter, 6.0 Liter.						
S600 Sedan 4D	NG7GB	158925	53200	54400	56200	62300
S65 Sedan 4D	NG7KB	211975	69200	70800	71500	78300
DISTRONIC PLUS			425	425	455	455
SL-CLASS—V8—Equipment Schedule 1						
W.B. 100.8"; 5.5 Liter, 6.3 Liter.						
SL550 Roadster	SK7BA	104775	37900	38900	40700	45600
SL63 AMG Roadster	SK7AA	142525	42200	43200	44400	49100
KEYLESS-GO			200	200	225	225
Adaptive Cruise Control			425	425	465	465
designo Edition			875	875	970	970
Premium Pkg 1			850	850	965	965
Performance Pkg			3900	3900	4265	4265
SL-CLASS—V12 Twin Turbo—Equipment Schedule 1						
W.B. 100.8"; 6.0 Liter.						
SL65 AMG Roadster	SK7KA	202225	76700	78500	78700	85800
Adaptive Cruise Control			425	425	445	445
SLS-CLASS—V8—Equipment Schedule 1						
W.B. 105.5"; 6.3 Liter.						
AMG Coupe 2D	RJ7HA	187450	****	****	****	144200
Bang & Olufsen Sound			****	****	****	2695
Ceramic Brakes			****	****	****	3935

2012 MERCEDES-BENZ — WDBorWDD(PK4HA)-C-#

Body Type	VIN	List	Trade-In Good	Very Good	Pvt-Party Good	Retail Excellent
SLK-CLASS—4-Cyl. Turbo—Equipment Schedule 1						
W.B. 95.7"; 1.8 Liter.						
SLK250 Roadster 2D	PK4HA	43375	25300	25800	27600	30600
KEYLESS-GO			200	200	220	220
DISTRONIC PLUS			450	450	485	485
Multimedia Pkg			325	325	350	350
Premium Pkg 1			875	875	975	975
Sport Pkg			900	900	990	990
Manual, 6-Spd			(500)	(500)	(550)	(550)
SLK-CLASS—V6—Equipment Schedule 1						
W.B. 95.7"; 3.5 Liter.						
SLK350 Roadster 2D	PK5HA	55675	27700	28300	30300	33600
KEYLESS-GO			200	200	220	220
DISTRONIC PLUS			450	450	485	485
Multimedia Pkg			325	325	350	350
Premium Pkg 1			875	875	975	975
Sport Pkg			900	900	990	990
SLK-CLASS—V8—Equipment Schedule 1						
W.B. 95.7"; 5.5 Liter.						
SLK55 AMG Roadster	PK7FA	68375	38900	39700	41400	45500
KEYLESS-GO			200	200	215	215
Multimedia Pkg			325	325	345	345
C-CLASS—4-Cyl. Turbo—Equipment Schedule 1						
W.B. 108.7"; 1.8 Liter.						
C250 Coupe 2D	GJ4HB	38970	17950	18350	20100	22700
C250 Luxury Sedan	GF4HB	39770	16500	16850	18600	21000
C250 Sport Sedan 4D	GF4HB	36550	16900	17250	19000	21500
KEYLESS-GO			200	200	235	235
Multimedia Pkg			325	325	370	370
Premium Pkg			475	475	565	565
C-CLASS—V6—Equipment Schedule 1						
W.B. 108.7"; 3.0 Liter, 3.5 Liter.						
C300 4MATIC Sport	GF8BB	39770	17750	18150	19950	22600
C300 4MATIC Luxury	GF8BB	40180	17450	17850	19600	22200
C350 Sport Sedan 4D	GF5HB	42325	20000	20500	22300	25200
C350 Coupe 2D	GJ5HB	44995	20300	20800	22600	25600
KEYLESS-GO			200	200	235	235
Multimedia Pkg			325	325	370	370
Premium Pkg 1			475	475	560	560
C-CLASS—V8—Equipment Schedule 1						
W.B. 108.7"; 6.3 Liter.						
C63 AMG Sedan 4D	GF7HB	62780	37700	38500	40100	44200
C63 AMG Coupe 2D	GJ7HB	65280	38400	39200	40800	45000
C63 AMG Black Series Cpe		62305				
KEYLESS-GO			200	200	220	220

Body Type	VIN	List	Trade-In Good	Very Good	Pvt-Party Good	Retail Excellent
Multimedia Pkg			325	325	350	350
E-CLASS—V6—Equipment Schedule 1						
W.B. 108.7", 113.2" (Sed); 3.5 Liter.						
E350 Sedan 4D	HF6KB	64075	23100	23900	25200	29000
E350 4MATIC Sedan	HF8JB	55485	24300	25200	26500	30300
E350 Coupe 2D	KJ5KB	50675	24300	25100	26500	30300
E350 Convertible 2D	KK5KF	58595	30200	31200	32600	37200
E350 4MATIC Wagon	HH8JB	59645	27600	28500	29700	33700
KEYLESS-GO			200	200	230	230
Adaptive Cruise Control			450	450	510	510
Driver Assistance Pkg			625	625	710	710
Premium Pkg 1			475	475	560	560
Premium Pkg 2			375	375	445	445
Sport Pkg			900	900	1040	1040
E-CLASS—V6 Turbo Diesel—Equipment Schedule 1						
W.B. 113.2"; 3.0 Liter.						
E350 BlueTEC Sed 4D	HF2EB	54185	24300	25200	26600	30500
KEYLESS-GO			200	200	230	230
Adaptive Cruise Control			450	450	515	515
Driver Assistance Pkg			625	625	715	715
Premium Pkg 1			475	475	560	560
Premium Pkg 2			375	375	445	445
Sport Pkg			900	900	1050	1050
E-CLASS—V8 Twin Turbo—Equipment Schedule 1						
W.B. 108.7", 113.2" (Sed); 4.6 Liter, 5.5 Liter.						
E550 4MATIC Sedan	HF9BB	60665	30800	31800	33200	37800
E550 Coupe 2D	KJ7DB	57465	27500	28400	29800	33900
E550 Convertible 2D	KK7DF	65675	36300	37500	38900	44400
E63 AMG Sedan 4D	HF7EB	89775	48000	49000	50400	54900
E63 AMG Wagon 4D	HH7EB	92375	51000	52000	53600	58200
KEYLESS-GO			200	200	215	215
Adaptive Cruise Control			450	450	475	475
Driver Assistance Pkg			625	625	665	665
Premium Pkg 1			475	475	555	555
Premium Pkg 2			375	375	440	440
Performance Pkg			3900	3900	4200	4200
CL-CLASS—V8 Twin Turbo—Equipment Schedule 1						
W.B. 116.3"; 4.6 Liter, 5.5 Liter.						
CL550 Coupe 2D	EJ9EB	115850	43800	44700	46900	51900
CL63 Coupe 2D	EJ7EB	153250	54000	55100	57300	63000
DISTRONIC PLUS			450	450	485	485
Driver Assistance Pkg			625	625	680	680
Premium Pkg 2			375	375	425	425
designo Edition			900	900	985	985
Performance Pkg			3900	3900	4310	4310
CL-CLASS—V12 Twin Turbo—Equipment Schedule 1						
W.B. 116.3"; 5.5 Liter, 6.0 Liter.						
CL600 Coupe 2D	EJ7EB	163050	51800	52900	55300	60900
CL65 Coupe 2D	EJ7KB	214850	98200	100300	100000	107200
designo Edition			900	900	975	975
CLS-CLASS—V8 Twin Turbo—Equipment Schedule 1						
W.B. 113.2"; 4.6 Liter.						
CLS550 Coupe 4D	LJ7DB	72175	34700	35500	37900	42500
CLS550 4MATIC Cpe	LJ9BB	74675	37200	38000	40300	45000
KEYLESS-GO			200	200	220	220
DISTRONIC PLUS			450	450	485	485
Driver Assistance Pkg			625	625	680	680
Premium Pkg 1			475	475	535	535
designo Edition			900	900	985	985
CLS-CLASS—V8—Equipment Schedule 1						
W.B. 113.2"; 5.5 Liter.						
CLS63 AMG Coupe 4D	LJ7EB	95775	50000	51000	53200	58900
DISTRONIC PLUS			450	450	480	480
Driver Assistance Pkg			625	625	670	670
Premium Pkg 1			475	475	525	525
designo Edition			900	900	970	970
Performance Pkg			3900	3900	4255	4255
S-CLASS—V6 Hybrid—Equipment Schedule 1						
W.B. 124.6"; 3.5 Liter.						
S400 Sedan 4D	NG9FB	93600	35800	36500	39000	43600
Bang & Olufsen BeoSound			2700	2700	3035	3035
KEYLESS-GO			200	200	225	225
DISTRONIC PLUS			450	450	495	495

Body	Type	VIN	List	Trade-In Good	Trade-In Very Good	Pvt-Party Good	Retail Excellent
	Driver Assistance Pkg			625	625	690	690
	designo Edition			900	900	1000	1000
	Premium Pkg 2			375	375	430	430
	Sport Pkg			1825	1825	2060	2060
S-CLASS—V6 Turbo Diesel—Equipment Schedule 1							
W.B. 124.6"; 3.0 Liter.							
S350 BlueTec 4MATIC		NG8DB	94300	37600	38400	41000	46000
	KEYLESS-GO			200	200	225	225
	DISTRONIC PLUS			450	450	490	490
	Driver Assistance Pkg			625	625	690	690
	designo Edition			900	900	995	995
	Premium Pkg 2			375	375	425	425
	Sport Pkg Plus One			900	900	1005	1005
	Sport Pkg			1825	1825	2045	2045
S-CLASS—V8 Twin Turbo—Equipment Schedule 1							
W.B. 124.6"; 5.5 Liter.							
S550 Sedan 4D		NG7DB	96250	37100	37900	40300	45100
S550 4MATIC Sedan		NG9EB	99250	38600	39400	41800	46500
	Bang & Olufsen BeoSound			2700	2700	3025	3025
	KEYLESS-GO			200	200	225	225
	DISTRONIC PLUS			450	450	495	495
	Driver Assistance Pkg			625	625	690	690
	designo Edition			900	900	995	995
	Premium Pkg 2			375	375	430	430
	Sport Pkg Plus One			900	900	1005	1005
	Sport Pkg			1825	1825	2050	2050
S-CLASS—V8 Twin Turbo—Equipment Schedule 1							
W.B. 124.6"; 6.3 Liter.							
S63 Sedan 4D		NG7EB	141050	52700	53800	55900	61800
	DISTRONIC PLUS			450	450	485	485
	Driver Assistance Pkg			625	625	680	680
	designo Edition			900	900	985	985
	Performance Pkg			3900	3900	4305	4305
S-CLASS—V12 Twin Turbo—Equipment Schedule 1							
W.B. 124.6"; 5.5 Liter.							
S600 Sedan 4D		NG7GB	166450	55800	56900	59100	64900
	designo Edition			900	900	965	965
S-CLASS—V12 Twin Turbo—Equipment Schedule 1							
W.B. 124.6"; 6.0 Liter.							
S65 Sedan 4D		NG7KB	216850	72000	73400	74800	81100
	DISTRONIC PLUS			450	450	475	475
	designo Edition			900	900	960	960
SL-CLASS—V8—Equipment Schedule 1							
W.B. 100.8"; 5.5 Liter.							
SL550 Roadster		SK7BA	105825	51400	52500	54500	59600
	Adaptive Cruise Control			450	450	485	485
	designo Edition			900	900	975	975
SL-CLASS—V8—Equipment Schedule 1							
W.B. 100.8"; 6.3 Liter.							
SL63 AMG Roadster		SK7AA	143915	58500	59700	61000	65900
	Adaptive Cruise Control			450	450	470	470
	designo Edition			900	900	955	955
	Performance Pkg			3900	3900	4175	4175
SLS-CLASS—V8—Equipment Schedule 1							
W.B. 105.5"; 6.3 Liter.							
AMG Coupe 2D		RJ7HA	192175	****	****	****	152700
AMG Convertible 2D		RK7HA	198675	****	****	****	155600
	Bang & Olufsen Sound			****	****	****	2825
	Ceramic Brakes			****	****	****	4040

2013 MERCEDES-BENZ — WDBorWDD(PK4HA)-D-#

Body	Type	VIN	List	Trade-In Good	Trade-In Very Good	Pvt-Party Good	Retail Excellent
SLK-CLASS—4-Cyl. Turbo—Equipment Schedule 1							
W.B. 95.7"; 1.8 Liter.							
SLK250 Roadster 2D		PK4HA	43805	27800	28300	30400	33700
	KEYLESS-GO			200	200	225	225
	DISTRONIC PLUS			475	475	520	520
	Driver Assistance Pkg			650	650	715	715
	Multimedia Pkg			350	350	380	380
	Premium Pkg			900	900	1005	1005
	Sport Pkg			975	975	1085	1085
	designo Edition			900	900	1005	1005
	Manual, 6-Spd			(500)	(500)	(555)	(555)

2013 MERCEDES-BENZ

Body Type	VIN	List	Trade-In Good	Very Good	Pvt-Party Good	Retail Excellent
SLK-CLASS—V6—Equipment Schedule 1						
W.B. 95.7"; 3.5 Liter.						
SLK350 Roadster 2D	PK5HA	56305	32100	32700	35000	38600
KEYLESS-GO		-------	200	200	220	220
DISTRONIC PLUS		-------	475	475	515	515
Driver Assistance Pkg		-------	650	650	705	705
Multimedia Pkg		-------	350	350	375	375
Sport Pkg		-------	975	975	1075	1075
designo Edition		-------	900	900	990	990
SLK-CLASS—V8—Equipment Schedule 1						
W.B. 95.7"; 5.5 Liter.						
SLK55 AMG Roadster	PK7FA	68895	45900	46700	48600	52900
KEYLESS-GO		-------	200	200	215	215
Multimedia Pkg		-------	350	350	365	365
designo Edition		-------	900	900	965	965
C-CLASS—4-Cyl. Turbo—Equipment Schedule 1						
W.B. 108.7"; 1.8 Liter.						
C250 Sport Sedan 4D	GF4HB	36255	18000	18350	20200	22600
C250 Luxury Sedan	GF4HB	36675	17800	18150	20000	22400
C250 Coupe 2D	GJ4HB	38705	20200	20600	22400	25000
KEYLESS-GO		-------	200	200	230	230
DISTRONIC PLUS		-------	475	475	540	540
Driver Assistance Pkg		-------	650	650	740	740
Dynamic Sport Pkg		-------	1875	1875	2175	2175
Multimedia Pkg		-------	350	350	395	395
Premium Pkg 1		-------	525	525	615	615
Sport Pkg		-------	975	975	1125	1125
C-CLASS—V6—Equipment Schedule 1						
W.B. 108.7"; 3.5 Liter.						
C300 4MATIC Sport	GF8AB	39855	19650	20000	21900	24500
C300 4MATIC Luxury	GF8AB	40265	19350	19700	21600	24200
C350 Sport Sedan 4D	GF5HB	42305	23200	23600	25600	28500
C350 Coupe 2D	GJ5HB	44105	24000	24400	26400	29500
C350 4MATIC Coupe	GJ8JB	46105	25200	25600	27800	31000
KEYLESS-GO		-------	200	200	230	230
DISTRONIC PLUS		-------	475	475	535	535
Driver Assistance Pkg		-------	650	650	735	735
Multimedia Pkg		-------	350	350	390	390
Premium Pkg 1		-------	525	525	615	615
Sport Pkg		-------	975	975	1125	1125
C-CLASS—V8—Equipment Schedule 1						
W.B. 108.9"; 6.3 Liter.						
C63 AMG Sedan 4D	GF7HB	62405	41600	42300	44200	48300
C63 AMG Coupe 2D	GJ7HB	64935	44500	45300	47100	51400
KEYLESS-GO		-------	200	200	220	220
DISTRONIC PLUS		-------	475	475	510	510
Driver Assistance Pkg		-------	650	650	700	700
Multimedia Pkg		-------	350	350	375	375
E-CLASS—V6—Equipment Schedule 1						
W.B. 108.7", 113.2" (Sed); 3.5 Liter.						
E350 Sedan 4D	HF5KB	53525	26600	27400	28300	31400
E350 4MATIC Sedan	HF8JB	54405	27900	28700	29700	32900
E350 Coupe 2D	KJ5KB	52025	27500	28400	29300	32600
E350 4MATIC Coupe	KJ8JB	54525	28900	29700	30600	34000
E350 Convertible 2D	KK5KF	59975	33700	34700	35700	39500
E350 4MATIC Wagon	HH8JB	58605	36400	37500	38400	42600
Bang & Olufsen Sound		-------	2825	2825	3150	3150
KEYLESS-GO		-------	200	200	220	220
DISTRONIC PLUS		-------	475	475	520	520
Appearance Pkg		-------	125	125	150	150
Driver Assistance Pkg		-------	650	650	715	715
Premium Pkg 1		-------	525	525	595	595
Premium Pkg 2		-------	400	400	450	450
designo Edition		-------	900	900	1000	1000
Sport Pkg		-------	975	975	1085	1085
E-CLASS—V6 Turbo Diesel—Equipment Schedule 1						
W.B. 113.2"; 3.0 Liter.						
E350 BlueTEC Sed 4D	HF2EB	54725	27800	28700	29700	33100
Bang & Olufsen Sound		-------	2825	2825	3170	3170
KEYLESS-GO		-------	200	200	225	225
DISTRONIC PLUS		-------	475	475	520	520
Driver Assistance Pkg		-------	650	650	715	715
Premium Pkg 1		-------	525	525	595	595

1015

Body Type	VIN	List	Trade-In Good	Very Good	Pvt-Party Good	Retail Excellent
Premium Pkg 2			400	400	450	450
Sport Pkg			975	975	1090	1090
designo Edition			900	900	1005	1005
E-CLASS—V6 Hybrid—Equipment Schedule 1						
W.B. 113.2"; 3.5 Liter.						
E400 Sedan 4D	HF9FB	58325	28700	29500	30500	33900
Bang & Olufsen Sound			2825	2825	3160	3160
KEYLESS-GO			200	200	225	225
DISTRONIC PLUS			475	475	520	520
Driver Assistance Pkg			650	650	715	715
Premium Pkg 1			525	525	595	595
Premium Pkg 2			400	400	450	450
designo Edition			900	900	1005	1005
E-CLASS—V8 Twin Turbo—Equipment Schedule 1						
W.B. 108.7", 113.2" (Sed); 4.6 Liter, 5.5 Liter.						
E550 4MATIC Sedan	HF9BB	61305	36800	37900	38700	42900
E550 Coupe 2D	KJ7DB	58865	31000	31900	32900	36500
E550 Convertible 2D	KK7DF	67125	40100	41300	42200	46800
E63 AMG Sedan 4D	HF7EB	90705	54800	56300	58200	63500
E63 AMG Wagon 4D	HH7EB	93305	58100	59200	61600	67100
Bang & Olufsen Sound			2825	2825	3140	3140
KEYLESS-GO			200	200	215	215
DISTRONIC PLUS			475	475	500	500
Appearance Pkg			125	125	150	150
Driver Assistance Pkg			650	650	690	690
Premium Pkg 1			525	525	590	590
Premium Pkg 2			400	400	445	445
designo Edition			900	900	1000	1000
Performance Pkg			3900	3900	4175	4175
CL-CLASS—V8 Twin Turbo—Equipment Schedule 1						
W.B. 116.3"; 4.6 Liter, 5.5 Liter.						
CL550 4MATIC 2D	EJ9EB	116205	52100	53100	55700	60900
CL63 AMG Coupe 2D	EJ7EB	153905	66500	67700	69800	75500
DISTRONIC Cruise Control			475	475	500	500
Driver Assistance Pkg			650	650	690	690
Premium Pkg 2			400	400	440	440
designo Edition			900	900	980	980
Sport Pkg			975	975	1060	1060
Performance Pkg			3900	3900	4195	4195
CL-CLASS—V12 Twin Turbo—Equipment Schedule 1						
W.B. 116.3"; 5.5 Liter, 6.0 Liter.						
CL600 Coupe 2D	EJ7GB	161205	58000	59000	61500	67100
CL65 AMG Coupe 2D	EJ7KB	214105	103400	105200	105600	112400
designo Edition			900	900	975	975
CLS-CLASS—V8 Twin Turbo—Equipment Schedule 1						
W.B. 113.1"; 4.6 Liter, 5.5 Liter.						
CLS550 Coupe 4D	LJ7DB	72905	39700	40400	43000	47500
CLS550 4MATIC Cpe	LJ9BB	75405	42200	43000	45400	50000
CLS63 AMG Coupe 4D	LJ7EB	96805	53700	54700	57200	62700
Bang & Olufsen Sound			2825	2825	3095	3095
KEYLESS-GO			200	200	220	220
DISTRONIC PLUS			475	475	510	510
Driver Assistance Pkg			650	650	700	700
Premium Pkg 1			525	525	580	580
designo Edition			900	900	985	985
Performance Pkg			3900	3900	4230	4230
S-CLASS—V6 Hybrid—Equipment Schedule 1						
W.B. 124.6"; 3.5 Liter.						
S400 Sedan 4D	NG9FB	93225	45100	45900	48400	53300
Bang & Olufsen BeoSound			2825	2825	3075	3075
DISTRONIC PLUS			475	475	505	505
Driver Assistance Pkg			650	650	695	695
Sport Pkg Plus One			975	975	1060	1060
Sport Pkg			1875	1875	2045	2045
designo Edition			900	900	980	980
S-CLASS BlueTEC—V6 Turbo Diesel—Equipment Schedule 1						
W.B. 124.6"; 3.0 Liter.						
S350 4MATIC 4D	NG8DB	93905	46100	47000	49500	54500
Bang & Olufsen BeoSound			2825	2825	3070	3070
DISTRONIC PLUS			475	475	505	505
Driver Assistance Pkg			650	650	695	695
Sport Pkg Plus One			975	975	1055	1055
Sport Pkg			1875	1875	2040	2040

Body Type	VIN	List	Trade-In Good	Very Good	Pvt-Party Good	Retail Excellent
designo Edition			900	900	975	975

S-CLASS—V8 Twin Turbo—Equipment Schedule 1
W.B. 124.6"; 4.6 Liter.

Body Type	VIN	List	Trade-In Good	Very Good	Pvt-Party Good	Retail Excellent
S550 Sedan 4D	NG7DB	95905	45700	46500	48900	53600
S550 4MATIC Sedan	NG9EB	98905	47100	48000	50300	55100
Bang & Olufsen BeoSound			2825	2825	3075	3075
DISTRONIC PLUS			475	475	505	505
Driver Assistance Pkg			650	650	695	695
Sport Pkg Plus One			975	975	1060	1060
Sport Pkg			1875	1875	2045	2045
designo Edition			900	900	975	975

S-CLASS—V8 Twin Turbo—Equipment Schedule 1
W.B. 124.6"; 5.5 Liter.

Body Type	VIN	List	Trade-In Good	Very Good	Pvt-Party Good	Retail Excellent
S63 Sedan 4D	NG7EB	140905	61100	62200	64500	70200
Bang & Olufsen BeoSound			2825	2825	3085	3085
DISTRONIC PLUS			475	475	505	505
Driver Assistance Pkg			650	650	700	700
designo Edition			900	900	980	980
Performance Pkg			3900	3900	4250	4250

S-CLASS—V12 Twin Turbo—Equipment Schedule 1
W.B. 124.6"; 5.5 Liter.

Body Type	VIN	List	Trade-In Good	Very Good	Pvt-Party Good	Retail Excellent
S600 Sedan 4D	NG7GB	163805	65200	66400	68600	74300
DISTRONIC PLUS			475	475	500	500
designo Edition			900	900	965	965

S-CLASS—V12 Twin Turbo—Equipment Schedule 1
W.B. 124.6"; 6.0 Liter.

Body Type	VIN	List	Trade-In Good	Very Good	Pvt-Party Good	Retail Excellent
S65 Sedan 4D	NG7KB	215005	83900	85400	86800	93100
designo Edition			900	900	965	965

SL-CLASS—V8 Twin Turbo—Equipment Schedule 1
W.B. 101.8"; 4.6 Liter, 5.5 Liter.

Body Type	VIN	List	Trade-In Good	Very Good	Pvt-Party Good	Retail Excellent
SL550 Roadster	JK7DA	106405	62000	63100	65200	70600
SL63 AMG Roadster	JK7EA	146705	78700	80200	81100	86500
KEYLESS-GO			200	200	215	215
Bang & Olufsen BeoSound			2825	2825	3085	3085
Adaptive Cruise Control			475	475	505	505
Driver Assistance Pkg			650	650	700	700
Premium Pkg			950	950	995	995
designo Edition			900	900	950	950

SL-CLASS—V12 Twin Turbo—Equipment Schedule 1
W.B. 101.8"; 6.0 Liter.

Body Type	VIN	List	Trade-In Good	Very Good	Pvt-Party Good	Retail Excellent
SL65 AMG Roadster	JK7KA	214445	104100	106000	106800	113600
designo Edition			900	900	945	945
Premium Pkg			950	950	995	995

SLS-CLASS—V8—Equipment Schedule 1
W.B. 105.5"; 6.3 Liter.

Body Type	VIN	List	Trade-In Good	Very Good	Pvt-Party Good	Retail Excellent
AMG GT Coupe 2D	RJ7JA	202505	****	****	****	161000
AMG GT Convertible	RK7JA	209005	****	****	****	166400
Bang & Olufsen Sound			****	****	****	2955
Ceramic Brakes			****	****	****	4140

2014 MERCEDES-BENZ — WDBorWDD(PK4HA)-E-#

SLK-CLASS—4-Cyl. Turbo—Equipment Schedule 1
W.B. 95.7"; 1.8 Liter.

Body Type	VIN	List	Trade-In Good	Very Good	Pvt-Party Good	Retail Excellent
SLK250 Roadster 2D	PK4HA	44450	30900	31400	33500	36800
KEYLESS-GO			200	200	220	220
DISTRONIC PLUS			500	500	545	545
Driver Assistance Pkg			675	675	740	740
Premium Pkg 1			900	900	1000	1000
Multimedia Pkg			375	375	405	405
Sport Pkg			1025	1025	1150	1150
designo Edition			900	900	1000	1000

SLK-CLASS—V6—Equipment Schedule 1
W.B. 95.7"; 3.5 Liter.

Body Type	VIN	List	Trade-In Good	Very Good	Pvt-Party Good	Retail Excellent
SLK350 Roadster 2D	PK5HA	57150	36500	37200	39400	43100
KEYLESS-GO			200	200	220	220
DISTRONIC PLUS			500	500	540	540
Driver Assistance Pkg			675	675	730	730
Multimedia Pkg			375	375	400	400
Sport Pkg			1025	1025	1130	1130
designo Edition			900	900	985	985

SLK-CLASS—V8—Equipment Schedule 1
W.B. 95.7"; 5.5 Liter.

Body Type	VIN	List	Trade-In Good	Very Good	Pvt-Party Good	Retail Excellent
SLK55 AMG Roadster	PK7FA	69850	49800	50700	53500	58500

2014 MERCEDES-BENZ

Body Type	VIN	List	Trade-In Good	Very Good	Pvt-Party Good	Retail Excellent
KEYLESS-GO			200	200	220	220
Multimedia Pkg			375	375	400	400
designo Edition			900	900	990	990
B-CLASS—Electric Drive—Equipment Schedule 1						
W.B. 106.3".						
Hatchback 4D	VP9AB	42375	24100	25100	26000	30400
Multimedia Pkg			375	375	425	425
Premium Pkg			575	575	655	655
CLA-CLASS—4-Cyl. Turbo—Equipment Schedule 1						
W.B. 106.3"; 2.0 Liter.						
CLA250 Coupe 4D	SJ4EB	30825	26200	26600	27900	31000
CLA250 4MATIC 4D	SJ4GB	32825	27400	27800	29100	32200
CLA45 AMG 4MATIC	SJ5CB	48375	39500	40900	40800	45400
Driver Assistance Pkg			675	675	735	735
Multimedia Pkg			375	375	405	405
Premium Pkg			575	575	625	625
Sport Pkg			1025	1025	1140	1140
C-CLASS—4-Cyl. Turbo—Equipment Schedule 1						
W.B. 108.7"; 1.8 Liter.						
C250 Sport Sedan 4D	GF4HB	36725	20800	21200	23000	25500
C250 Luxury Sedan	GF4HB	37175	20600	21000	22900	25400
C250 Coupe 2D	GJ4HB	39125	23900	24300	26200	29000
KEYLESS-GO			200	200	230	230
DISTRONIC PLUS			500	500	560	560
Multimedia Pkg			375	375	415	415
Premium Pkg 1			575	575	645	645
Sport Pkg			1025	1025	1180	1180
C-CLASS—V6—Equipment Schedule 1						
W.B. 108.7"; 3.5 Liter.						
C300 4MATIC Sport	GF8AB	40325	23400	23800	25700	28400
C300 4MATIC Luxury	GF8AB	40775	23100	23500	25400	28100
C350 Sport Sedan 4D	GF5HB	43025	26700	27200	29100	32100
C350 Coupe 2D	GJ5HB	44775	27600	28100	30100	33300
C350 4MATIC Cpe 2D	GJ8JB	46775	28800	29300	31300	34600
KEYLESS-GO			200	200	225	225
Full Leather			500	500	565	565
DISTRONIC PLUS			500	500	555	555
Driver Assistance Pkg			675	675	755	755
Multimedia Pkg			375	375	415	415
Premium Pkg 1			575	575	640	640
Sport Pkg			1025	1025	1170	1170
C-CLASS—V8—Equipment Schedule 1						
W.B. 108.9"; 6.3 Liter.						
C63 AMG Sedan 4D	GF7HB	62875	42900	43700	45500	49500
C63 AMG Coupe 2D	GJ7HB	65375	46000	46800	48600	52700
C63 AMG Ed 507 Sed	GF7HB	72625				
C63 AMG Ed 507 Cpe	GJ7HB	75125				
KEYLESS-GO			200	200	215	215
DISTRONIC PLUS			500	500	535	535
Driver Assistance Pkg			675	675	725	725
Multimedia Pkg			375	375	400	400
E-CLASS BlueTEC—4-Cyl. Turbo Diesel—Equipment Schedule 1						
W.B. 113.2"; 2.1 Liter.						
E250 Sedan 4D	HF0EB	52305	36700	37700	38300	42000
E250 4MATIC Sedan	HF9HB	54805	39600	40800	41200	45000
KEYLESS-GO			200	200	215	215
Bang & Olufsen Sound			2950	2950	3215	3215
Premium Pkg			575	575	615	615
Sport Pkg			1025	1025	1120	1120
designo Edition			900	900	975	975
E-CLASS—V6—Equipment Schedule 1						
W.B. 108.7", 113.2" (Sed); 3.5 Liter.						
E350 Sedan 4D	HF5KB	52805	35200	36200	37200	41000
E350 4MATIC Sedan	HF8JB	55405	36800	37900	38800	42900
E350 Coupe 2D	KJ5KB	53105	36400	37400	37900	41500
E350 4MATIC 2D	KJ8JB	55605	37700	38800	39300	43000
E350 Cabriolet 2D	KK5KF	61105	43500	44800	45200	49300
E350 4MATIC Wagon	HH8JB	59505	45600	46900	47300	51800
KEYLESS-GO			200	200	215	215
Bang & Olufsen Sound			2950	2950	3225	3225
DISTRONIC PLUS			500	500	535	535
Driver Assistance Pkg			675	675	725	725
Premium Pkg 1			575	575	615	615

Body Type	VIN	List	Trade-In Good	Very Good	Pvt-Party Good	Retail Excellent
Sport Pkg			1025	1025	1125	1125
designo Edition			900	900	980	980

E-CLASS—V6 Hybrid—Equipment Schedule 1
W.B. 113.2"; 3.5 Liter.

Body Type	VIN	List	Good	Very Good	Good	Excellent
E400 Sedan 4D	HF9FB	57605	37900	39000	39500	43200
KEYLESS-GO			200	200	220	220
Bang & Olufsen Sound			2950	2950	3225	3225
DISTRONIC PLUS			500	500	535	535
Premium Pkg			575	575	615	615

E-CLASS—V8 Twin Turbo—Equipment Schedule 1
W.B. 108.7", 113.2" (Sed); 4.6 Liter, 5.5 Liter.

Body Type	VIN	List	Good	Very Good	Good	Excellent
E550 4MATIC Sedan	HF9BB	62305	45400	46800	47200	51600
E550 Coupe 2D	KJ7DB	59905	39800	41000	41400	45300
E550 Cabriolet 2D	KK7DF	68205	49700	51200	51700	56500
E63 AMG 4MATIC Sed	HF9CB	93675	59800	60900	63200	68500
KEYLESS-GO			200	200	215	215
Bang & Olufsen Sound			2950	2950	3220	3220
DISTRONIC PLUS			500	500	535	535
designo Edition			900	900	965	965
Sport Pkg			1025	1025	1125	1125
Premium Pkg			575	575	615	615
Driver Assistance Pkg			675	675	725	725

E-CLASS 4MATIC AWD—V8 Twin Turbo—Equipment Schedule 1
W.B. 113.2" (Sed); 5.5 Liter.

Body Type	VIN	List	Good	Very Good	Good	Excellent
E63 AMG S Sedan	HF7GB	100695	65400	66600	68700	74200
E63 AMG S Wagon	HH7GB	103295	67500	68600	70700	76200
DISTRONIC PLUS			500	500	520	520
Driver Assistance Pkg			675	675	710	710

CL-CLASS—V8 Twin Turbo—Equipment Schedule 1
W.B. 116.3"; 4.6 Liter.

Body Type	VIN	List	Good	Very Good	Good	Excellent
CL550 4MATIC Cpe 2D	EJ9EB	117525	60800	61800	64200	69600
CL63 AMG Coupe 2D	EJ7EB	155525	69500	70700	72800	78500
DISTRONIC PLUS			500	500	525	525
Driver Assistance Pkg			675	675	715	715
AMG Performance Pkg			3900	3900	4185	4185
designo Edition			900	900	965	965

CL-CLASS—V12 Twin Turbo—Equipment Schedule 1
W.B. 116.3"; 5.5 Liter, 6.0 Liter.

Body Type	VIN	List	Good	Very Good	Good	Excellent
CL600 Coupe 2D	EJ7GB	162925	85400	86900	88300	94500
CL65 AMG Cpe 2D	EJ7KB	216425	****	****	****	119200
designo Edition			900	900	950	950

CLS-CLASS—V8 Twin Turbo—Equipment Schedule 1
W.B. 113.1"; 4.6 Liter, 5.5 Liter.

Body Type	VIN	List	Good	Very Good	Good	Excellent
CLS550 Coupe 4D	LJ7DB	73025	46100	47000	49300	53900
CLS550 4MATIC Cpe	LJ9DB	75525	48300	49200	51800	56400
CLS63 AMG 4MATIC	LJ9CB	100425	63300	64400	66600	72200
CLS63 AMG S 4MTC	LJ7GB	107425	69300	70600	72500	78300
KEYLESS-GO			200	200	215	215
Bang & Olufsen Sound			2950	2950	3195	3195
DISTRONIC PLUS			500	500	530	530
Driver Assistance Pkg			675	675	720	720
designo Edition			900	900	970	970
Premium Pkg 1			575	575	610	610
Performance Pkg			3900	3900	4180	4180

S-CLASS—V8 Twin Turbo—Equipment Schedule 1
W.B. 124.6"; 4.6 Liter, 5.5 Liter.

Body Type	VIN	List	Good	Very Good	Good	Excellent
S550 Sedan 4D	UG8CB	93825	70300	71600	73200	78600
S550 4MATIC Sedan	UG8FB	96825	73100	74400	76000	81400
S63 AMG Sedan 4D	UG7JB	140425	104400	106300	107200	114100
DISTRONIC PLUS			500	500	515	515
Driver Assistance Pkg			675	675	700	700
designo Edition			900	900	950	950
Sport Pkg Plus One			1025	1025	1090	1090
Sport Pkg			1925	1925	2040	2040
Premium 1 Pkg			575	575	595	595

SL-CLASS—V8 Twin Turbo—Equipment Schedule 1
W.B. 101.8"; 4.6 Liter.

Body Type	VIN	List	Good	Very Good	Good	Excellent
SL550 Roadster 2D	JK7DA	107605	69000	70200	72300	77900
Bang & Olufsen BeoSound			2950	2950	3195	3195
DISTRONIC PLUS			500	500	530	530
Driver Assistance Pkg			675	675	720	720
designo Edition			900	900	970	970

2014 MERCEDES-BENZ

Body Type	VIN	List	Trade-In Good	Trade-In Very Good	Pvt-Party Good	Retail Excellent
SL-CLASS—V12 Twin Turbo—Equipment Schedule 1						
W.B. 101.8"; 6.0 Liter.						
SL63 AMG Roadster	JK7EA	148205	101800	103600	104100	110000
Bang & Olufsen BeoSound			2950	2950	3080	3080
DISTRONIC PLUS			500	500	510	510
Driver Assistance Pkg			675	675	695	695
AMG Performance Pkg			3900	3900	4060	4060
Ceramic Brakes			4075	4075	4235	4235
designo Edition			900	900	935	935
SL-CLASS—V12 Twin Turbo—Equipment Schedule 1						
W.B. 101.8"; 6.0 Liter.						
SL65AMG Roadster	JK7KA	215405	166500	169400	167700	176000
Ceramic Brakes			4075	4075	4200	4200
designo Edition			900	900	930	930
SLS-CLASS—V8—Equipment Schedule 1						
W.B. 105.5"; 6.3 Liter.						
AMG GT Coupe 2D	RJ7JA	202425	****	****	****	166500
AMG GT Convertible	RK7JA	208925	****	****	****	171800
AMG Black Series Cpe	RJ7HA	275925	****	****	****	307600
Bang & Olufsen Sound			****	****	****	3025
Ceramic Brakes			****	****	****	4240

MERCURY

2000 MERCURY — (1,2or3)(MEorZW)–(M653)–Y–#

Body Type	VIN	List	Trade-In Good	Trade-In Very Good	Pvt-Party Good	Retail Excellent
MYSTIQUE—4-Cyl.—Equipment Schedule 5						
W.B. 106.5"; 2.0 Liter.						
GS Sedan 4D	M653	17495	900	1050	1575	2725
MYSTIQUE—V6—Equipment Schedule 5						
W.B. 106.5"; 2.5 Liter.						
LS Sedan 4D	M66L	18795	1275	1450	2000	3375
SABLE—V6—Equipment Schedule 4						
W.B. 108.5"; 3.0 Liter.						
GS Sedan 4D	M50U	19395	400	500	1100	2125
GS Wagon 4D	M58U	21195	700	825	1450	2700
LS Sedan 4D	M53U	20495	600	700	1325	2475
V6, 24V, 3.0 Liter	S		100	100	135	135
SABLE—V6 24V—Equipment Schedule 4						
W.B. 108.5"; 3.0 Liter.						
LS Premium Sedan 4D	M55S	21795	775	925	1550	2875
LS Premium Wagon 4D	M59S	22895	900	1075	1700	3125
COUGAR—V6—Equipment Schedule 4						
W.B. 106.4"; 2.5 Liter.						
Coupe 2D	T61L	18880	525	600	1125	1975
Manual, 5-Spd			(125)	(125)	(150)	(150)
4-Cyl, 2.0 Liter	3		(175)	(175)	(240)	(240)
GRAND MARQUIS—V8—Equipment Schedule 4						
W.B. 114.7"; 4.6 Liter.						
GS Sedan 4D	M74W	23020	550	675	1250	2350
LS Sedan 4D	M75W	24920	725	875	1500	2825

2001 MERCURY — (1or2)(MEorZW)–(M50U)–1–#

Body Type	VIN	List	Trade-In Good	Trade-In Very Good	Pvt-Party Good	Retail Excellent
SABLE—V6—Equipment Schedule 4						
W.B. 108.5"; 3.0 Liter.						
GS Sedan 4D	M50U	19785	475	575	1200	2275
GS Wagon 4D	M58U	21585	850	1000	1650	3000
LS Sedan 4D	M53U	20885	775	900	1525	2825
V6, 24V, 3.0 Liter	S		100	100	135	135
SABLE—V6 24V—Equipment Schedule 4						
W.B. 108.5"; 3.0 Liter.						
LS Premium Sedan 4D	M55S	22185	950	1100	1750	3200
LS Premium Wagon 4D	M59S	23285	975	1150	1775	3250
COUGAR—V6—Equipment Schedule 4						
W.B. 106.4"; 2.5 Liter.						
Coupe 2D	T61L	18545	650	750	1300	2250
C2 Coupe 2D	T61L	20660	1025	1175	1675	2850
Zn Coupe 2D	T61L	21645	1150	1300	1850	3150
Manual, 5-Spd			(175)	(175)	(225)	(225)
4-Cyl, 2.0 Liter	3		(200)	(200)	(275)	(275)
GRAND MARQUIS—V8—Equipment Schedule 4						
W.B. 114.7"; 4.6 Liter.						

Body Type	VIN	List	Trade-In Good	Very Good	Pvt-Party Good	Retail Excellent
GS Sedan 4D	M74W	23460	550	700	1275	2400
LS Sedan 4D	M75W	25360	850	1025	1600	2925

2002 MERCURY — (1or2)(MEorZW)–(M50U)–2–#

SABLE—V6—Equipment Schedule 4
W.B. 108.5"; 3.0 Liter.

GS Sedan 4D	M50U	20255	600	725	1325	2450
GS Wagon 4D	M58U	21665	1050	1225	1850	3325

SABLE—V6 24V—Equipment Schedule 4
W.B. 108.5"; 3.0 Liter.

LS Premium Sedan 4D	M55S	22680	1125	1300	1975	3500
LS Premium Wagon 4D	M59S	23845	1150	1350	2000	3550

COUGAR—V6—Equipment Schedule 4
W.B. 106.4"; 2.5 Liter.

Coupe 2D	T61L	18490	775	875	1400	2400
Sport Coupe 2D	T61L	18990	950	1075	1600	2700
C2 Coupe 2D	T61L	19505	1050	1200	1750	2925
Xr Coupe 2D	T61L	19940	1125	1250	1800	3000
Manual, 5-Spd			(175)	(175)	(235)	(235)
4-Cyl, 2.0 Liter		3	(225)	(225)	(315)	(315)
35th Anniversary			50	50	65	65

GRAND MARQUIS—V8—Equipment Schedule 4
W.B. 114.7"; 4.6 Liter.

GS Sedan 4D	M74W	24325	875	1025	1600	2875
LS Sedan 4D	M75W	27800	1200	1425	2025	3575
LSE Sedan 4D	M75W	29305	1500	1750	2375	4100

2003 MERCURY — (1or2)ME–(M50U)–3–#

SABLE—V6—Equipment Schedule 4
W.B. 108.5"; 3.0 Liter.

GS Sedan 4D	M50U	20770	900	1025	1875	3475
GS Wagon 4D	M58U	22180	1275	1475	2425	4375

SABLE—V6 24V—Equipment Schedule 4
W.B. 108.5"; 3.0 Liter.

LS Premium Sedan 4D	M55S	23145	1325	1525	2425	4425
LS Premium Wagon 4D	M59S	24310	1300	1500	2500	4550

GRAND MARQUIS—V8—Equipment Schedule 4
W.B. 114.7"; 4.6 Liter.

GS Sedan 4D	M74W	24875	1200	1425	2100	3675
LS Sedan 4D	M75W	28605	1600	1875	2525	4350
LSE Sedan 4D	M75W	30110	2000	2325	2950	5000
Limited Edition			350	350	460	460

MARAUDER—V8—Equipment Schedule 4
W.B. 114.7"; 4.6 Liter.

Sedan 4D	M75V	34495	3500	4075	4525	7250

2004 MERCURY — (1or2)ME–(M50U)–4–#

SABLE—V6—Equipment Schedule 4
W.B. 108.5"; 3.0 Liter.

GS Sedan 4D	M50U	21595	1025	1175	2025	3675
GS Wagon 4D	M58U	22595	1400	1625	2575	4600

SABLE—V6 24V—Equipment Schedule 4
W.B. 108.5"; 3.0 Liter.

LS Premium Sedan 4D	M55S	23895	1500	1725	2725	4825
LS Premium Wagon 4D	M59S	24795	1500	1725	2750	4900

GRAND MARQUIS—V8—Equipment Schedule 4
W.B. 114.7"; 4.6 Liter.

GS Sedan 4D	M74W	24695	1725	2000	2600	4325
LS Sedan 4D	M75W	29595	2100	2425	3075	5175
Limited Edition			375	375	500	500

MARAUDER—V8—Equipment Schedule 2
W.B. 114.7"; 4.6 Liter.

Sedan 4D	M79V	34495	5350	6175	6500	10000

2005 MERCURY — (1or2)ME–(M50U)–5–#

SABLE—V6—Equipment Schedule 4
W.B. 108.5"; 3.0 Liter.

GS Sedan 4D	M50U	21525	1275	1450	2625	4625

SABLE—V6 24V—Equipment Schedule 4
W.B. 108.5"; 3.0 Liter.

LS Sedan 4D	M55S	24490	1475	1700	2850	4975
LS Wagon 4D	M59S	25800	1575	1825	2975	5175

2005 MERCURY

Body Type	VIN	List	Trade-In Good	Very Good	Pvt-Party Good	Retail Excellent
MONTEGO—V6—Equipment Schedule 4						
W.B. 112.9"; 3.0 Liter.						
Luxury Sedan 4D	M401	24995	**1875**	**2125**	**3000**	**4950**
Premier Sedan 4D	M421	27195	**2100**	**2400**	**3200**	**5150**
AWD			**475**	**475**	**645**	**645**
GRAND MARQUIS—V8—Equipment Schedule 4						
W.B. 114.7"; 4.6 Liter.						
GS Sedan 4D	M74W	25095	**1950**	**2250**	**2925**	**4700**
LS Sedan 4D	M75W	30150	**2600**	**3000**	**3525**	**5525**
LSE Sedan 4D	M75W	30620	**2675**	**3100**	**3725**	**5825**

2006 MERCURY — (1,2or3)ME−(M07Z)−6−#

Body Type	VIN	List	Trade-In Good	Very Good	Pvt-Party Good	Retail Excellent
MILAN—4-Cyl.—Equipment Schedule 4						
W.B. 107.4"; 2.3 Liter.						
Sedan 4D	M07Z	19820	**2250**	**2500**	**3475**	**5450**
Premier Sedan 4D	M08Z	21715	**2825**	**3100**	**4050**	**6225**
Manual, 5-Spd			**(375)**	**(375)**	**(510)**	**(510)**
V6, 3.0 Liter	1		**575**	**575**	**755**	**755**
MONTEGO—V6—Equipment Schedule 4						
W.B. 112.9"; 3.0 Liter.						
Luxury Sedan 4D	M401	25130	**2425**	**2725**	**3450**	**5350**
Premier Sedan 4D	M421	27580	**2875**	**3200**	**3950**	**6100**
AWD			**525**	**525**	**700**	**700**
GRAND MARQUIS—V8—Equipment Schedule 4						
W.B. 114.7"; 4.6 Liter.						
GS Sedan 4D	M74W	25555	**2725**	**3125**	**3700**	**5600**
LS Sedan 4D	M75V	30840	**3150**	**3600**	**4125**	**6200**
Limited Edition			**425**	**425**	**575**	**575**

2007 MERCURY—(1,2or3)ME−(M07Z)−7−#

Body Type	VIN	List	Trade-In Good	Very Good	Pvt-Party Good	Retail Excellent
MILAN—4-Cyl.—Equipment Schedule 4						
W.B. 107.4"; 2.3 Liter.						
Sedan 4D	M07Z	22465	**3000**	**3250**	**4200**	**6275**
Premier Sedan 4D	M08Z	23995	**3275**	**3550**	**4625**	**6875**
AWD			**750**	**750**	**1000**	**1000**
Manual, 5-Spd			**(425)**	**(425)**	**(555)**	**(555)**
V6, 3.0 Liter	1		**600**	**600**	**800**	**800**
MONTEGO—V6—Equipment Schedule 4						
W.B. 112.9"; 3.0 Liter.						
Sedan 4D	M401	24220	**3775**	**4175**	**4900**	**7150**
Premier Sedan 4D	M421	27995	**4000**	**4425**	**5300**	**7825**
AWD			**575**	**575**	**755**	**755**
GRAND MARQUIS—V8—Equipment Schedule 4						
W.B. 114.6"; 4.6 Liter.						
GS Sedan 4D	M74V	25660	**3425**	**3850**	**4350**	**6325**
LS Sedan 4D	M75V	30320	**3850**	**4350**	**4800**	**6950**
Palm Beach Edition			**375**	**375**	**500**	**500**

2008 MERCURY — (1,2or3)ME−(M07Z)−8−#

Body Type	VIN	List	Trade-In Good	Very Good	Pvt-Party Good	Retail Excellent
MILAN—4-Cyl.—Equipment Schedule 4						
W.B. 107.4"; 2.3 Liter.						
Sedan 4D	M07Z	20325	**3550**	**3825**	**4925**	**6950**
Premier Sedan 4D	M08Z	22020	**3975**	**4250**	**5375**	**7600**
AWD			**800**	**800**	**1075**	**1075**
Manual, 5-Spd w/Overdrive			**(450)**	**(450)**	**(585)**	**(585)**
V6, 3.0 Liter	1		**625**	**625**	**845**	**845**
SABLE—V6—Equipment Schedule 4						
W.B. 112.9"; 3.5 Liter.						
Sedan 4D	M40W	24290	**5200**	**5625**	**6525**	**8875**
Premier Sedan 4D	M42W	28080	**4925**	**5325**	**6225**	**8625**
AWD			**1225**	**1225**	**1635**	**1635**
GRAND MARQUIS—V8—Equipment Schedule 4						
W.B. 114.6"; 4.6 Liter.						
GS Sedan 4D	M74V	25830	**4350**	**4800**	**5375**	**7325**
LS Sedan 4D	M75V	28720	**4675**	**5175**	**5775**	**7950**
Palm Beach Edition			**400**	**400**	**510**	**510**

2009 MERCURY — (1,2or3)ME−(M07Z)−9−#

Body Type	VIN	List	Trade-In Good	Very Good	Pvt-Party Good	Retail Excellent
MILAN—4-Cyl.—Equipment Schedule 4						
W.B. 107.4"; 2.3 Liter.						
Sedan 4D	M07Z	20910	**4600**	**4875**	**6025**	**8125**
Premier Sedan 4D	M08Z	23160	**5250**	**5575**	**6900**	**9175**

2009 MERCURY

Body Type	VIN	List	Trade-In Good	Very Good	Pvt-Party Good	Retail Excellent
AWD			875	875	1150	1150
Manual, 5-Spd w/Overdrive			(475)	(475)	(645)	(645)
V6, 3.0 Liter	1		675	675	895	895
SABLE—V6—Equipment Schedule 4						
W.B. 112.9"; 3.5 Liter.						
Sedan 4D	M40W	25250	6025	6400	7475	9800
Premier Sedan 4D	M42W	29510	6125	6500	7675	10100
AWD			1325	1325	1755	1755
GRAND MARQUIS—V8—Equipment Schedule 4						
W.B. 114.6"; 4.6 Liter.						
LS Sedan 4D	M75V	29585	6225	6750	7500	9900

2010 MERCURY — (2or3)ME–(M0HA)–A–#

Body Type	VIN	List	Trade-In Good	Very Good	Pvt-Party Good	Retail Excellent
MILAN—4-Cyl.—Equipment Schedule 4						
W.B. 107.4"; 2.5 Liter.						
Sedan 4D	M0HA	21905	6000	6300	7725	9975
MILAN—4-Cyl. Hybrid—Equipment Schedule 4						
W.B. 107.4"; 2.5 Liter.						
Sedan 4D	M0L3	28225	8400	8800	9900	12150
MILAN—V6 Flex Fuel—Equipment Schedule 4						
W.B. 107.4"; 3.0 Liter.						
Premier Sedan 4D	M0JA	26675	6675	7000	8450	10850
AWD	C		950	950	1275	1275
4-Cyl, 2.5 Liter	A		(625)	(625)	(825)	(825)
GRAND MARQUIS—V8—Equipment Schedule 4						
W.B. 114.6"; 4.6 Liter.						
LS Sedan 4D	M7FV	30285	9700	10350	10950	13700

2011 MERCURY — (2or3)ME–(M0HA)–B–#

Body Type	VIN	List	Trade-In Good	Very Good	Pvt-Party Good	Retail Excellent
MILAN—4-Cyl.—Equipment Schedule 4						
W.B. 107.4"; 2.5 Liter.						
Sedan 4D	M0HA	22750	7700	8025	9650	12050
MILAN—4-Cyl. Hybrid—Equipment Schedule 4						
W.B. 107.4"; 2.5 Liter.						
Sedan 4D	M0L3	29070	9675	10050	11300	13500
MILAN—V6 Flex Fuel—Equipment Schedule 4						
W.B. 107.4"; 3.0 Liter.						
Premier Sedan 4D	M0JA	25890	8450	8800	10450	12950
AWD	C		650	650	845	845
4-Cyl, 2.5 Liter	A		(650)	(650)	(855)	(855)
GRAND MARQUIS—V8—Equipment Schedule 4						
W.B. 114.6"; 4.6 Liter.						
LS Sedan 4D	M7FV	30810	11200	11800	12700	15600

MINI

2002 MINI — (WMW(RC334)–2–#

Body Type	VIN	List	Trade-In Good	Very Good	Pvt-Party Good	Retail Excellent
COOPER—4-Cyl.—Equipment Schedule 3						
W.B. 97.1"; 1.6 Liter.						
Hatchback 2D	RC334	16850	1675	1925	2675	4500
Sport Pkg			225	225	300	300
COOPER—4-Cyl. Supercharged—Equipment Schedule 3						
W.B. 97.1"; 1.6 Liter.						
S Hatchback 2D	RE334	19850	2125	2300	3150	4850
Sport Pkg			225	225	300	300
John Cooper Works			1275	1275	1685	1685

2003 MINI — WMW(RC334)–3–#

Body Type	VIN	List	Trade-In Good	Very Good	Pvt-Party Good	Retail Excellent
COOPER—4-Cyl.—Equipment Schedule 3						
W.B. 97.1"; 1.6 Liter.						
Hatchback 2D	RC334	18575	1850	2100	2850	4675
Sport Pkg			250	250	325	325
COOPER—4-Cyl. Supercharged—Equipment Schedule 3						
W.B. 97.1"; 1.6 Liter.						
S Hatchback 2D	RE334	20325	2600	2800	3750	5575
Sport Pkg			250	250	325	325
John Cooper Works			1375	1375	1835	1835

Body Type	VIN	List	Trade-In Good	Very Good	Pvt-Party Good	Retail Excellent

2004 MINI — WMW(RC334)-4-#

COOPER—4-Cyl.—Equipment Schedule 3
W.B. 97.1"; 1.6 Liter.

Body Type	VIN	List	Good	Very Good	Good	Excellent
Hatchback 2D	RC334	18299	2425	2750	3400	5375
Sport Pkg			250	250	350	350

COOPER—4-Cyl. Supercharged—Equipment Schedule 3
W.B. 97.1"; 1.6 Liter.

S Hatchback 2D	RE334	19999	3050	3250	4150	6000
Sport Pkg			250	250	350	350
MC40 Pkg			1175	1175	1555	1555
John Cooper Works			1500	1500	1990	1990

2005 MINI — WMW(RC334)-5-#

COOPER—4-Cyl.—Equipment Schedule 3
W.B. 97.1"; 1.6 Liter.

Hatchback 2D	RC334	18299	2525	2875	3725	5725
Sport Pkg			275	275	375	375

COOPER CONVERTIBLE—4-Cyl.—Equipment Schedule 3
W.B. 97.1"; 1.6 Liter.

Convertible 2D	RF334	22800	2925	3300	4200	6425
Sport Pkg			275	275	375	375

COOPER—4-Cyl. Supercharged—Equipment Schedule 3
W.B. 97.1"; 1.6 Liter.

S Hatchback 2D	RE334	20449	3000	3225	4300	6150
Sport Pkg			275	275	375	375
John Cooper Works			1600	1600	2145	2145

COOPER CONVERTIBLE—4-Cyl. Supercharged—Equipment Schedule 3
W.B. 97.1"; 1.6 Liter.

S Convertible 2D	RH334	24950	3850	4125	5325	7600
Sport Pkg			275	275	375	375
John Cooper Works			1600	1600	2145	2145

2006 MINI — WMW(RC335)-6-#

COOPER—4-Cyl.—Equipment Schedule 3
W.B. 97.1"; 1.6 Liter.

Hatchback 2D	RC335	18800	2975	3300	4150	6200
Sport Pkg			300	300	400	400
Checkmate Pkg			425	425	575	575

COOPER CONVERTIBLE—4-Cyl.—Equipment Schedule 3
W.B. 97.1"; 1.6 Liter.

Convertible 2D	RF335	23300	3500	3900	4725	7000
Sport Pkg			300	300	400	400

COOPER—4-Cyl. Supercharged—Equipment Schedule 3
W.B. 97.1"; 1.6 Liter.

S Hatchback 2D	RE335	22500	3575	3800	4850	6750
S GP Hatchback 2D	RE935	31150	****	****	****	15350
Sport Pkg			300	300	400	400
Checkmate Pkg			425	425	575	575
John Cooper Works (ex GP)			1725	1725	2295	2295

COOPER CONVERTIBLE—4-Cyl. Supercharged—Equipment Schedule 3
W.B. 97.1"; 1.6 Liter.

S Convertible 2D	RH335	26800	4025	4275	5500	7725
Sport Pkg			300	300	400	400
John Cooper Works			1725	1725	2295	2295

2007 MINI — WMW(MF335)-7-#

COOPER—4-Cyl.—Equipment Schedule 3
W.B. 97.1"; 1.6 Liter.

Hatchback 2D	MF335	20050	3700	4075	4875	6975
Sport Pkg			325	325	425	425

COOPER—4-Cyl. Turbo—Equipment Schedule 3
W.B. 97.1"; 1.6 Liter.

S Hatchback 2D	MF735	23200	4200	4450	5700	7675
Sport Pkg			325	325	425	425

COOPER CONVERTIBLE—4-Cyl.—Equipment Schedule 3
W.B. 97.1"; 1.6 Liter.

Convertible 2D	RF335	23900	4000	4400	5225	7500
Sport Pkg			325	325	425	425

COOPER CONVERTIBLE—4-Cyl. Turbo—Equipment Schedule 3
W.B. 97.1"; 1.6 Liter.

S Convertible 2D	RH335	27400	5225	5525	7000	9575

2007 MINI

Body Type	VIN	List	Trade-In Good	Very Good	Pvt-Party Good	Retail Excellent
Sport Pkg			325	325	425	425
John Cooper Works			1825	1825	2450	2450

2008 MINI — WMW(MF335)-8-#

COOPER—4-Cyl.—Equipment Schedule 3
W.B. 97.1"; 1.6 Liter.

Body Type	VIN	List	Trade-In Good	Very Good	Pvt-Party Good	Retail Excellent
Hatchback 2D	MF335	19950	4350	4675	5725	7800
Sport Pkg			350	350	455	455
John Cooper Works			1950	1950	2610	2610

COOPER—4-Cyl. Turbo—Equipment Schedule 3
W.B. 97.1"; 1.6 Liter.

S Hatchback 2D	MF735	23100	5250	5475	6700	8575
Sport Pkg			350	350	455	455
John Cooper Works			1950	1950	2610	2610

COOPER CONVERTIBLE—4-Cyl.—Equipment Schedule 3
W.B. 97.1"; 1.6 Liter.

Convertible 2D	RF335	23850	4575	4925	6025	8225
Sport Pkg			350	350	455	455

COOPER CONVERTIBLE—4-Cyl. Turbo—Equipment Schedule 3
W.B. 97.1"; 1.6 Liter.

S Convertible 2D	RH335	27300	6125	6400	7800	10050
Sport Pkg			350	350	450	450
John Cooper Works			1950	1950	2575	2575

COOPER CLUBMAN—4-Cyl.—Equipment Schedule 3
W.B. 100.4"; 1.6 Liter.

Hatchback 2D	ML335	21850	5325	5575	6925	9000
Sport Pkg			350	350	455	455
John Cooper Works			1950	1950	2600	2600

COOPER CLUBMAN—4-Cyl. Turbo—Equipment Schedule 3
W.B. 100.4"; 1.6 Liter.

S Hatchback 2D	MM335	25350	6250	6525	7700	9575
Sport Pkg			350	350	420	420
John Cooper Works			1950	1950	2420	2420

2009 MINI — WMW(MF335)-9-#

COOPER HARDTOP—4-Cyl.—Equipment Schedule 3
W.B. 97.1"; 1.6 Liter.

Body Type	VIN	List	Trade-In Good	Very Good	Pvt-Party Good	Retail Excellent
Hatchback 2D	MF335	20450	5350	5675	6775	8850
Sport Pkg			375	375	510	510

COOPER HARDTOP—4-Cyl. Turbo—Equipment Schedule 3
W.B. 97.1"; 1.6 Liter.

S Hatchback 2D	MF735	22600	6100	6325	7625	9475
Sport Pkg			375	375	500	500

COOPER CONVERTIBLE—4-Cyl.—Equipment Schedule 3
W.B. 97.1"; 1.6 Liter.

Convertible 2D	MR335	25800	6175	6525	7600	9825
Sport Pkg			375	375	510	510

COOPER CONVERTIBLE—4-Cyl. Turbo—Equipment Schedule 3
W.B. 97.1"; 1.6 Liter.

S Convertible 2D	MS335	27450	7525	7800	9200	11350
Sport Pkg			375	375	485	485

COOPER CLUBMAN—4-Cyl.—Equipment Schedule 3
W.B. 100.4"; 1.6 Liter.

Hatchback 2D	ML335	22100	6000	6225	7675	9675
Sport Pkg			375	375	500	500

COOPER CLUBMAN—4-Cyl. Turbo—Equipment Schedule 3
W.B. 100.4"; 1.6 Liter.

S Hatchback 2D	MM335	25600	6875	7125	8550	10550
Sport Pkg			375	375	475	475

JOHN COOPER WORKS HARDTOP—4-Cyl. Turbo—Equipment Schedule 3
W.B. 97.1"; 1.6 Liter.

Hatchback 2D	MF935	29200	9025	9350	10800	13200

JOHN COOPER WORKS CONVERTIBLE—4-Cyl. Turbo—Equip Sch 3
W.B. 97.1"; 1.6 Liter.

Convertible 2D	MS935	34950	12000	12400	14250	17400

JOHN COOPER WORKS CLUBMAN—4-Cyl. Turbo—Equipment Sch 3
W.B. 100.4"; 1.6 Liter.

Hatchback 2D	MM935	31450	9000	9325	10700	13000

2010 MINI — WMW(MF3C5)-A-#

COOPER HARDTOP—4-Cyl.—Equipment Schedule 3
W.B. 97.1"; 1.6 Liter.

234   DEDUCT FOR RECONDITIONING

2010 MINI

Body Type	VIN	List	Trade-In Good	Very Good	Pvt-Party Good	Retail Excellent
Hatchback 2D	MF3C5	19950	6375	6675	7875	9900
Sport Pkg			425	425	575	575
Camden Pkg			875	875	1150	1150
Mayfair Pkg			700	700	920	920
COOPER HARDTOP—4-Cyl. Turbo—Equipment Schedule 3						
W.B. 97.1"; 1.6 Liter.						
S Hatchback 2D	MF7C5	23000	7950	8200	9575	11450
Sport Pkg			425	425	540	540
Camden Pkg			875	875	1080	1080
Mayfair Pkg			700	700	865	865
COOPER CONVERTIBLE—4-Cyl.—Equipment Schedule 3						
W.B. 97.1"; 1.6 Liter.						
Convertible 2D	MR3C5	26200	7575	7925	9150	11350
Sport Pkg			425	425	555	555
COOPER CONVERTIBLE—4-Cyl. Turbo—Equipment Schedule 3						
W.B. 97.1"; 1.6 Liter.						
S Convertible 2D	MS3C5	27850	10050	10350	11950	14250
Sport Pkg			425	425	525	525
COOPER CLUBMAN—4-Cyl.—Equipment Schedule 3						
W.B. 100.3"; 1.6 Liter.						
Hatchback 2D	ML3C5	22400	6950	7150	8750	10700
Sport Pkg			425	425	555	555
COOPER CLUBMAN—4-Cyl. Turbo—Equipment Schedule 3						
W.B. 100.3"; 1.6 Liter.						
S Hatchback 2D	MM3C5	26000	8250	8525	9975	12000
Sport Pkg			425	425	525	525
JOHN COOPER WORKS HARDTOP—4-Cyl. Turbo—Equipment Schedule 3						
W.B. 97.1"; 1.6 Liter.						
Hatchback 2D	MF9C5	29500	11400	11750	13350	15800
JOHN COOPER WORKS CONVERTIBLE—4-Cyl. Turbo—Equip Sch 3						
W.B. 97.1"; 1.6 Liter.						
Convertible 2D	MS9C5	34700	14550	15000	16850	19900
JOHN COOPER WORKS CLUBMAN—4-Cyl. Turbo—Equipment Sch 3						
W.B. 100.3"; 1.6 Liter.						
Hatchback 2D	MM9C5	31700	10950	11300	12900	15350

2011 MINI — WMW(SU3C5)-B-#

Body Type	VIN	List	Trade-In Good	Very Good	Pvt-Party Good	Retail Excellent
COOPER HARDTOP—4-Cyl.—Equipment Schedule 3						
W.B. 97.1"; 1.6 Liter.						
Hatchback 2D	SU3C5	21350	7925	8200	9600	11700
Sport Pkg			475	475	620	620
COOPER HARDTOP—4-Cyl. Turbo—Equipment Schedule 3						
W.B. 97.1"; 1.6 Liter.						
S Hatchback 2D	SV3C5	23700	10250	10500	12000	13950
Sport Pkg			475	475	580	580
COOPER CONVERTIBLE—4-Cyl.—Equipment Schedule 3						
W.B. 97.1"; 1.6 Liter.						
Convertible 2D	ZN3C5	26800	9725	10050	11500	13900
Sport Pkg			475	475	600	600
COOPER CONVERTIBLE—4-Cyl. Turbo—Equipment Schedule 3						
W.B. 97.1"; 1.6 Liter.						
S Convertible 2D	ZP3C5	28550	11800	12100	13800	16050
Sport Pkg			475	475	600	600
COOPER CLUBMAN—4-Cyl.—Equipment Schedule 3						
W.B. 100.3"; 1.6 Liter.						
Hatchback 2D	ZF3C5	23050	9075	9300	11000	12950
Sport Pkg			475	475	595	595
COOPER CLUBMAN—4-Cyl. Turbo—Equipment Schedule 3						
W.B. 100.3"; 1.6 Liter.						
S Hatchback 2D	ZG3C5	26750	10200	10550	12100	14250
Sport Pkg			475	475	580	580
COOPER COUNTRYMAN—4-Cyl.—Equipment Schedule 3						
W.B. 102.2"; 1.6 Liter.						
Hatchback 4D	ZB3C5	22350	12150	12500	13950	16200
Sport Pkg			475	475	565	565
COOPER COUNTRYMAN—4-Cyl. Turbo—Equipment Schedule 3						
W.B. 102.2"; 1.6 Liter.						
S Hatchback 4D	ZC3C5	25950	14050	14400	15800	18000
Sport Pkg			475	475	555	555
COOPER COUNTRYMAN AWD—4-Cyl. Turbo—Equipment Sch 3						
W.B. 102.2"; 1.6 Liter.						
S ALL4 Hatchback 4D	ZC5C5	27650	14700	15100	16450	18750
Sport Pkg			475	475	555	555

Body Type	VIN	List	Trade-In Good	Very Good	Pvt-Party Good	Retail Excellent
JOHN COOPER WORKS HARDTOP—4-Cyl. Turbo—Equipment Schedule 3						
W.B. 97.1"; 1.6 Liter.						
Hatchback 2D	SV9C5	29800	14100	14450	16200	18600
JOHN COOPER WORKS CONVERTIBLE—4-Cyl. Turbo—Equip Sch 3						
W.B. 97.1"; 1.6 Liter.						
Convertible 2D	ZP9C5	35000	15700	16100	18000	20800
JOHN COOPER WORKS CLUBMAN—4-Cyl. Turbo—Equipment Sch 3						
W.B. 100.3"; 1.6 Liter.						
Hatchback 2D	ZG9C5	32000	13750	14150	16150	19050

2012 MINI — WMW(SU3C5)-C-#

Body Type	VIN	List	Trade-In Good	Very Good	Pvt-Party Good	Retail Excellent
COOPER HARDTOP—4-Cyl.—Equipment Schedule 3						
W.B. 97.1"; 1.6 Liter.						
Hatchback 2D	SU3C5	21450	10050	10300	11800	13950
Sport Pkg			525	525	655	655
COOPER HARDTOP—4-Cyl. Turbo—Equipment Schedule 3						
W.B. 97.1"; 1.6 Liter.						
S Hatchback 2D	SV3C5	23800	12300	12550	14150	16050
Sport Pkg			525	525	625	625
COOPER COUPE—4-Cyl.—Equipment Schedule 3						
W.B. 97.1"; 1.6 Liter.						
Coupe 2D	SX1C5	22000	10100	10300	11850	13650
Sport Pkg			525	525	625	625
COOPER COUPE—4-Cyl. Turbo—Equipment Schedule 3						
W.B. 97.1"; 1.6 Liter.						
S Coupe 2D	SX3C5	25300	12000	12300	13850	15800
Sport Pkg			525	525	620	620
COOPER ROADSTER—4-Cyl.—Equipment Schedule 3						
W.B. 97.1"; 1.6 Liter.						
Roadster 2D	SY1C5	25050	13050	13350	15100	17200
Sport Pkg			525	525	625	625
COOPER ROADSTER—4-Cyl. Turbo—Equipment Schedule 3						
W.B. 97.1"; 1.6 Liter.						
S Roadster 2D	SY3C5	28050	15000	15350	17150	19500
Sport Pkg			525	525	620	620
COOPER CONVERTIBLE—4-Cyl.—Equipment Schedule 3						
W.B. 97.1"; 1.6 Liter.						
Convertible 2D	ZN3C5	26900	12250	12600	14150	16600
Sport Pkg			525	525	640	640
COOPER CONVERTIBLE—4-Cyl. Turbo—Equipment Schedule 3						
W.B. 97.1"; 1.6 Liter.						
S Convertible 2D	ZP3C5	28650	14550	14850	16750	19050
Sport Pkg			525	525	615	615
COOPER CLUBMAN—4-Cyl.—Equipment Schedule 3						
W.B. 100.3"; 1.6 Liter.						
Hatchback 2D	ZF3C5	23150	10550	10800	12500	14450
Sport Pkg			525	525	640	640
COOPER CLUBMAN—4-Cyl. Turbo—Equipment Schedule 3						
W.B. 100.3"; 1.6 Liter.						
S Hatchback 2D	ZG3C5	26850	12800	13150	14950	17350
Sport Pkg			525	525	630	630
COOPER COUNTRYMAN—4-Cyl.—Equipment Schedule 3						
W.B. 102.2"; 1.6 Liter.						
Hatchback 4D	ZB3C5	22450	13200	13500	15250	17450
Sport Pkg			525	525	620	620
COOPER COUNTRYMAN—4-Cyl. Turbo—Equipment Schedule 3						
W.B. 102.2"; 1.6 Liter.						
S Hatchback 4D	ZC3C5	26050	15200	15550	17200	19400
Sport Pkg			525	525	610	610
COOPER COUNTRYMAN AWD—4-Cyl. Turbo—Equipment Sch 3						
W.B. 102.2"; 1.6 Liter.						
S ALL4 Hatchback 4D	ZC5C5	27750	16100	16450	18200	20600
Sport Pkg			525	525	610	610
JOHN COOPER WORKS HARDTOP—4-Cyl. Turbo—Equipment Schedule 3						
W.B. 97.1"; 1.6 Liter.						
Hatchback 2D	SV9C5	30600	16600	16950	18750	21100
JOHN COOPER WORKS COUPE—4-Cyl. Turbo—Equipment Schedule 3						
W.B. 97.1"; 1.6 Liter.						
Coupe 2D	SX5C5	31900	15600	15950	17750	20200
JOHN COOPER WORKS ROADSTER—4-Cyl. Turbo—Equipment Schedule 3						
W.B. 97.1"; 1.6 Liter.						
Roadster 2D	SY5C5	35200	18400	18800	20700	23500

2012 MINI

Body Type	VIN	List	Trade-In Good	Very Good	Pvt-Party Good	Retail Excellent
JOHN COOPER WORKS CONVERTIBLE—4-Cyl. Turbo—Equipment Sch 3						
W.B. 97.1"; 1.6 Liter.						
Convertible 2D	ZP9C5	35800	19450	19850	21900	24900
JOHN COOPER WORKS CLUBMAN—4-Cyl. Turbo—Equipment Sch 3						
W.B. 100.3"; 1.6 Liter.						
Hatchback 2D	ZG9C5	32100	16600	17050	19100	22100

2013 MINI — WMW(SU3C5)—D—#

Body Type	VIN	List	Trade-In Good	Very Good	Pvt-Party Good	Retail Excellent
COOPER HARDTOP—4-Cyl.—Equipment Schedule 3						
W.B. 97.1"; 1.6 Liter.						
Hatchback 2D	SU3C5	20400	10750	11000	12550	14650
Sport Pkg			575	575	710	710
COOPER HARDTOP—4-Cyl. Turbo—Equipment Schedule 3						
W.B. 97.1"; 1.6 Liter.						
S Hatchback 2D	SV3C5	24000	14500	14800	16550	18450
Sport Pkg			575	575	670	670
COOPER COUPE—4-Cyl.—Equipment Schedule 3						
W.B. 97.1"; 1.6 Liter.						
Coupe 2D	SX1C5	22150	10850	11100	12850	14750
Sport Pkg			575	575	690	690
COOPER COUPE—4-Cyl. Turbo—Equipment Schedule 3						
W.B. 97.1"; 1.6 Liter.						
S Coupe 2D	SX3C5	25450	13300	13600	15400	17400
Sport Pkg			575	575	670	670
COOPER PACEMAN—4-Cyl.—Equipment Schedule 3						
W.B. 102.2"; 1.6 Liter.						
Hatchback 2D	SS1C5	24600	12800	13050	14950	17000
COOPER PACEMAN—4-Cyl. Turbo—Equipment Schedule 3						
W.B. 102.2"; 1.6 Liter.						
S Hatchback 2D	SS5C5	28200	15700	16000	17850	20100
Sport Pkg			575	575	665	665
COOPER PACEMAN AWD—4-Cyl. Turbo—Equipment Schedule 3						
W.B. 102.2"; 1.6 Liter.						
S ALL4 Hatchback 2D	SS7C5	29900	16350	16650	18450	20700
Sport Pkg			575	575	665	665
COOPER PACEMAN JOHN COOPER WORKS AWD—4-Cyl. Turbo—Sch 3						
W.B. 102.2"; 1.6 Liter.						
ALL4 Hatchback 2D	SS9C5	36900	21500	21900	23800	26600
COOPER CONVERTIBLE—4-Cyl.—Equipment Schedule 3						
W.B. 97.1"; 1.6 Liter.						
Convertible 2D	ZN3C5	25850	12650	12900	14600	16950
Sport Pkg			575	575	700	700
COOPER CONVERTIBLE—4-Cyl. Turbo—Equipment Schedule 3						
W.B. 97.1"; 1.6 Liter.						
S Convertible 2D	ZP3C5	28850	16750	17100	19050	21300
Sport Pkg			575	575	665	665
COOPER ROADSTER—4-Cyl.—Equipment Schedule 3						
W.B. 97.1"; 1.6 Liter.						
Roadster 2D	SY1C5	26250	14800	15100	16850	18900
Sport Pkg			575	575	675	675
COOPER ROADSTER—4-Cyl. Turbo—Equipment Schedule 3						
W.B. 97.1"; 1.6 Liter.						
S Roadster 2D	SY3C5	29250	17300	17650	19500	21900
Sport Pkg			575	575	665	665
COOPER CLUBMAN—4-Cyl.—Equipment Schedule 3						
W.B. 100.3"; 1.6 Liter.						
Hatchback 2D	ZF3C5	22100	12450	12650	14500	16500
Sport Pkg			575	575	685	685
COOPER CLUBMAN—4-Cyl. Turbo—Equipment Schedule 3						
W.B. 100.3"; 1.6 Liter.						
S Hatchback 2D	ZG3C5	25800	14250	14600	16450	18850
Sport Pkg			575	575	680	680
COOPER CLUBVAN—4-Cyl.—Equipment Schedule 3						
W.B. 100.3"; 1.6 Liter.						
Hatchback 2D	ZF3C5	25995				
Sport Pkg						
COOPER COUNTRYMAN—4-Cyl.—Equipment Schedule 3						
W.B. 102.2"; 1.6 Liter.						
Hatchback 4D	ZB3C5	22700	15000	15250	17000	19100
Sport Pkg			575	575	670	670
COOPER COUNTRYMAN—4-Cyl. Turbo—Equipment Schedule 3						
W.B. 102.2"; 1.6 Liter.						
Hatchback 4D	ZC3C5	26300	16950	17300	19050	21300
Sport Pkg			575	575	660	660

EQUIPMENT & MILEAGE PAGE 9 TO 23

2013 MINI

Body Type	VIN	List	Trade-In Good	Very Good	Pvt-Party Good	Retail Excellent
COOPER COUNTRYMAN AWD—4-Cyl. Turbo—Equipment Sch 3						
W.B. 102.2"; 1.6 Liter.						
ALL4 Hatchback 4D	ZC5C5	28000	18450	18800	20700	23100
Sport Pkg			575	575	655	655
JOHN COOPER WORKS HARDTOP—4-Cyl. Turbo—Equipment Schedule 3						
W.B. 97.1"; 1.6 Liter.						
Hatchback 2D	SU9C5	30800	19550	19900	21700	24100
JOHN COOPER WORKS COUPE—4-Cyl. Turbo—Equipment Schedule 3						
W.B. 97.1"; 1.6 Liter.						
John Cooper Works	SX9C5	32050	17400	17750	19750	22300
JOHN COOPER WORKS CONVERTIBLE—4-Cyl. Turbo—Equipment Sch 3						
W.B. 97.1"; 1.6 Liter.						
Convertible 2D	MR9C5	36000	23100	23600	25600	28600
JOHN COOPER WORKS ROADSTER—4-Cyl. Turbo—Equipment Schedule 3						
W.B. 97.1"; 1.6 Liter.						
Roadster 2D	SY9C5	36400	20900	21300	23300	26100
JOHN COOPER WORKS CLUBMAN—4-Cyl. Turbo—Equipment Sch 3						
W.B. 100.3"; 1.6 Liter.						
Hatchback 2D	MH9C5	33000	18900	19400	21400	24500
JOHN COOPER WORKS COUNTRYMAN AWD—4-Cyl. Turbo—Equip Sch 3						
W.B. 100.3"; 1.6 Liter.						
ALL4 Hatchback 4D	XD135	35550	23700	24100	26100	29000

2014 MINI — WMW(XM5C5)-E-#

Body Type	VIN	List	Trade-In Good	Very Good	Pvt-Party Good	Retail Excellent
COOPER HARDTOP—3-Cyl. Turbo—Equipment Schedule 3						
W.B. 97.1"; 1.5 Liter.						
Hatchback 2D	XM5C5	20745	13450	13700	15300	17500
Sport Pkg			625	625	745	745
COOPER HARDTOP—4-Cyl. Turbo—Equipment Schedule 3						
W.B. 97.1"; 2.0 Liter.						
S Hatchback 2D	XM7C5	24395	18850	19200	20800	22900
Sport Pkg			625	625	710	710
COOPER COUPE—4-Cyl.—Equipment Schedule 3						
W.B. 97.1"; 1.6 Liter.						
Coupe 2D	SX1C5	22245	14150	14400	16250	18250
Sport Pkg			625	625	725	725
Recaro Seats			450	450	525	525
COOPER COUPE—4-Cyl. Turbo—Equipment Schedule 3						
W.B. 97.1"; 1.6 Liter.						
S Coupe 2D	SX3C5	25545	15250	15550	17400	19450
Sport Pkg			625	625	720	720
Recaro Seats			450	450	520	520
COOPER PACEMAN—4-Cyl.—Equipment Schedule 3						
W.B. 102.2"; 1.6 Liter.						
Hatchback 2D	SS1C5	24095	14350	14650	16500	18600
Sport Pkg			625	625	735	735
COOPER PACEMAN—4-Cyl. Turbo—Equipment Schedule 3						
W.B. 102.2"; 1.6 Liter.						
S Hatchback 2D	SS5C5	27695	16150	16450	18400	20700
Sport Pkg			625	625	725	725
COOPER PACEMAN AWD—4-Cyl. Turbo—Equipment Schedule 3						
W.B. 102.2"; 1.6 Liter.						
ALL4 Hatchback 4D	SS7C5	29395	16950	17250	19150	21400
Sport Pkg			625	625	720	720
COOPER CONVERTIBLE—4-Cyl.—Equipment Schedule 3						
W.B. 97.1"; 1.6 Liter.						
Convertible 2D	ZN3C5	25945	17050	17400	19000	21500
Sport Pkg			625	625	725	725
COOPER CONVERTIBLE—4-Cyl. Turbo—Equipment Schedule 3						
W.B. 97.1"; 1.6 Liter.						
S Convertible 2D	ZP3C5	28945	20800	21200	23000	25400
Sport Pkg			625	625	705	705
COOPER ROADSTER—4-Cyl.—Equipment Schedule 3						
W.B. 97.1"; 1.6 Liter.						
Roadster 2D	SY1C5	27595	17750	18100	19900	22100
Sport Pkg			625	625	720	720
COOPER ROADSTER—4-Cyl. Turbo—Equipment Schedule 3						
W.B. 97.1"; 1.6 Liter.						
Cooper S Roadster 2D		29345	20300	20600	22500	25100
COOPER CLUBMAN—4-Cyl.—Equipment Schedule 3						
W.B. 100.3"; 1.6 Liter.						
Hatchback 2D	ZF3C5	23445	14200	14500	16400	18400
Sport Pkg			625	625	730	730

Body Type	VIN	List	Trade-In Good	Trade-In Very Good	Pvt-Party Good	Retail Excellent
Recaro Seats			450	450	530	530
COOPER CLUBMAN—4-Cyl. Turbo—Equipment Schedule 3						
W.B. 100.3"; 1.6 Liter.						
S Hatchback 2D	ZG3C5	27145	**16650**	**17050**	**18900**	**21500**
Sport Pkg			625	625	725	725
Recaro Seats			450	450	525	525
COOPER COUNTRYMAN—4-Cyl.—Equipment Schedule 3						
W.B. 102.2"; 1.6 Liter.						
Hatchback 4D	ZB3C5	24145	**15850**	**16150**	**17900**	**19950**
Sport Pkg			625	625	725	725
COOPER COUNTRYMAN—4-Cyl. Turbo—Equipment Schedule 3						
W.B. 102.2"; 1.6 Liter.						
S Hatchback 4D	ZC3C5	27745	**18500**	**18850**	**20600**	**22900**
Sport Pkg			625	625	715	715
COOPER COUNTRYMAN AWD—4-Cyl. Turbo—Equipment Sch 3						
W.B. 102.2"; 1.6 Liter.						
ALL4 Hatchback 4D	ZC5C5	29445	**21200**	**21600**	**23400**	**25900**
Sport Pkg			625	625	705	705
JOHN COOPER WORKS COUPE—4-Cyl. Turbo—Equipment Schedule 3						
W.B. 97.1"; 1.6 Liter.						
Coupe 2D	SX9C5	32145	**21100**	**21500**	**23500**	**26100**
Recaro Seats			450	450	515	515
JOHN COOPER WORKS PACEMAN AWD—4-Cyl. Turbo—Equip Sch 3						
W.B. 102.2"; 1.6 Liter.						
ALL4 Hatchback 4D	SS9C5	36395	**23500**	**23900**	**25900**	**28700**
JOHN COOPER WORKS CONVERTIBLE—4-Cyl. Turbo—Equipment Sch 3						
W.B. 97.1"; 1.6 Liter.						
Convertible 2D	MR9C5	36095	**24900**	**25400**	**27500**	**30500**
JOHN COOPER WORKS ROADSTER—4-Cyl. Turbo—Equipment Sch 3						
W.B. 97.1"; 1.6 Liter.						
Roadster 2D	SY9C5	37745	**28600**	**29200**	**31100**	**34200**
JOHN COOPER WORKS CLUBMAN—4-Cyl. Turbo—Equipment Sch 3						
W.B. 100.3"; 1.6 Liter.						
Hatchback 2D	MH9C5	34345	**22400**	**23000**	**24900**	**28200**
Recaro Seats			450	450	520	520
JOHN COOPER WORKS COUNTRYMAN AWD—4-Cyl. Turbo—Equip Sch 3						
W.B. 100.3"; 1.6 Liter.						
ALL4 Hatchback 4D	XD1C5	36995	**25600**	**26100**	**28000**	**31000**

MITSUBISHI

2000 MITSUBISHI — (J,4or6)(A3orMM)A(Y26A)-Y-#

Body Type	VIN	List	Trade-In Good	Trade-In Very Good	Pvt-Party Good	Retail Excellent
MIRAGE—4-Cyl.—Equipment Schedule 6						
W.B. 95.1", 98.4" (Sed); 1.5 Liter, 1.8 Liter.						
DE Sedan 4D	Y26A	14412	600	675	1225	2125
DE Coupe 2D	Y11A	13062	450	525	1025	1775
LS Sedan 4D	Y36C	17372	750	825	1400	2425
LS Coupe 2D	Y31C	15032	700	800	1350	2300
ECLIPSE—4-Cyl.—Equipment Schedule 4						
W.B. 100.8"; 2.4 Liter.						
RS Coupe 2D	C34G	18932	575	650	1125	1950
GS Coupe 2D	C44G	20482	700	825	1325	2275
Automatic			125	125	165	165
ECLIPSE—V6—Equipment Schedule 4						
W.B. 100.8"; 3.0 Liter.						
GT Coupe 2D	C84L	21622	875	975	1550	2625
Traction Control			100	100	135	135
Automatic			125	125	165	165
GALANT—4-Cyl.—Equipment Schedule 4						
W.B. 103.7"; 2.4 Liter.						
DE Sedan 4D	A36G	17792	475	575	1150	2050
ES Sedan 4D	A46G	18692	525	625	1175	2150
V6, 3.0 Liter	L		100	100	135	135
GALANT—V6—Equipment Schedule 4						
W.B. 103.7"; 3.0 Liter.						
LS Sedan 4D	A56L	24092	1200	1400	2200	3900
GTZ Sedan 4D	A46L	24192	1450	1675	2475	4350
DIAMANTE—V6—Equipment Schedule 4						
W.B. 107.1"; 3.5 Liter.						
ES Sedan 4D	P57P	25467	750	900	1525	2725
LS Sedan 4D	P67P	28367	1025	1200	1875	3350

2001 MITSUBISHI

Body Type	VIN	List	Trade-In Good	Very Good	Pvt-Party Good	Retail Excellent

2001 MITSUBISHI—(J,4or6)(A3orMM)A(Y11A)–1–#

MIRAGE—4-Cyl.—Equipment Schedule 6
W.B. 05.1", 98.4" (Sed); 1.5 Liter, 1.8 Liter

Body Type	VIN	List	Good	Very Good	Good	Excellent
DE Coupe 2D	Y11A	13277	475	550	1050	1800
ES Coupe 2D	Y26C	14147	725	800	1375	2375
LS Sedan 4D	Y36C	14997	800	900	1475	2500
LS Coupe 2D	Y31C	15237	850	950	1475	2500

ECLIPSE—4-Cyl.—Equipment Schedule 4
W.B. 100.8"; 2.4 Liter.

RS Coupe 2D	C31G	18507	700	825	1275	2150
GS Coupe 2D	C41G	19317	850	975	1450	2450
GS Spyder Conv 2D	E35G	23927	1350	1550	2025	3350
Automatic			125	125	165	165

ECLIPSE—V6—Equipment Schedule 4
W.B. 100.8"; 3.0 Liter.

GT Coupe 2D	C81H	21467	1050	1175	1725	2850
GT Spyder Conv 2D	E55H	26927	1550	1725	2450	4025
Traction Control			100	100	145	145
Automatic			125	125	165	165

GALANT—4-Cyl.—Equipment Schedule 4
W.B. 103.7"; 2.4 Liter.

DE Sedan 4D	A36G	18077	500	600	1150	2075
ES Sedan 4D	A46G	18927	525	625	1200	2150
V6, 3.0 Liter	H		100	100	135	135

GALANT—V6—Equipment Schedule 4
W.B. 103.7"; 3.0 Liter.

| LS Sedan 4D | A56H | 24427 | 1275 | 1450 | 2250 | 3975 |
| GTZ Sedan 4D | A46H | 24527 | 1600 | 1825 | 2675 | 4675 |

DIAMANTE—V6—Equipment Schedule 4
W.B. 107.1"; 3.5 Liter.

| ES Sedan 4D | P57P | 25907 | 800 | 950 | 1575 | 2775 |
| LS Sedan 4D | P67P | 28927 | 1125 | 1300 | 1975 | 3500 |

2002 MITSUBISHI—(J,4or6)(A3orMM)A(Y11A)–2–#

MIRAGE—4-Cyl.—Equipment Schedule 6
W.B. 95.1"; 1.5 Liter, 1.8 Liter.

| DE Coupe 2D | Y11A | 13362 | 500 | 550 | 1075 | 1825 |
| LS Coupe 2D | Y31C | 15332 | 1050 | 1175 | 1775 | 3000 |

LANCER—4-Cyl.—Equipment Schedule 4
W.B. 102.4"; 2.0 Liter.

ES Sedan 4D	J26E	15242	1100	1225	1950	3375
LS Sedan 4D	J36E	16442	1125	1250	2000	3425
OZ Rally Sedan 4D	J86E	16832	1225	1350	2125	3650

ECLIPSE—4-Cyl.—Equipment Schedule 4
W.B. 100.8"; 2.4 Liter.

RS Coupe 2D	C31G	18642	725	825	1300	2200
GS Coupe 2D	C41G	19512	975	1125	1600	2675
GS Spyder Conv 2D	E35G	24172	1425	1600	2100	3450
Automatic			125	125	165	165

ECLIPSE—V6—Equipment Schedule 4
W.B. 100.8"; 3.0 Liter.

GT Coupe 2D	C81H	21702	1125	1250	1900	3200
GT Spyder Conv 2D	E55H	27152	1775	1950	2850	4800
Automatic			125	125	165	165
Traction Control			125	125	160	160

GALANT—4-Cyl.—Equipment Schedule 4
W.B. 103.7"; 2.4 Liter.

DE Sedan 4D	A36G	18262	550	650	1200	2125
ES Sedan 4D	A46G	19072	575	675	1250	2200
LS Sedan 4D	A46G	21672	1400	1625	2375	4100
V6, 3.0 Liter	L		150	150	200	200

GALANT—V6—Equipment Schedule 4
W.B. 103.7"; 3.0 Liter.

| GTZ Sedan 4D | A46H | 24712 | 1700 | 1950 | 2825 | 4850 |

DIAMANTE—V6—Equipment Schedule 4
W.B. 107.1"; 3.5 Liter.

ES Sedan 4D	P57P	26247	900	1050	1700	2950
VR-X Sedan 4D	P67P	27557	1200	1375	2050	3575
LS Sedan 4D	P67P	29007	1275	1450	2150	3725

2003 MITSUBISHI

Body Type	VIN	List	Trade-In Good	Very Good	Pvt-Party Good	Retail Excellent

2003 MITSUBISHI — (J,4or6)(A3orMM)A(J26E)–3–#

LANCER—4-Cyl.—Equipment Schedule 6
W.B. 102.4"; 2.0 Liter.

ES Sedan 4D	J26E	15387	1325	1475	2325	4000
LS Sedan 4D	J36E	16617	1350	1475	2350	4050
OZ Rally Sedan 4D	J86E	17117	1575	1750	2775	4750

LANCER AWD—4-Cyl. Turbo—Equipment Schedule 4
W.B. 103.3"; 2.0 Liter.

Evolution Sedan 4D	H86F	29582	7400	8200	8400	12200

ECLIPSE—4-Cyl.—Equipment Schedule 4
W.B. 100.8"; 2.4 Liter.

RS Coupe 2D	C34G	18717	800	900	1400	2375
GS Coupe 2D	C44G	19617	1025	1175	1700	2850
GS Spyder Conv 2D	E45G	24397	1500	1700	2300	3775
Automatic			150	150	185	185

ECLIPSE—V6—Equipment Schedule 4
W.B. 100.8"; 3.0 Liter.

GT Coupe 2D	C84H	21807	1350	1475	2100	3425
GT Spyder Conv 2D	E85H	27592	2225	2425	3200	5100
GTS Coupe 2D	C74H	24777	2250	2475	3200	5075
GTS Spyder Conv 2D	E75H	30242	2775	3025	3800	6000
Automatic			150	150	185	185
Traction Control			125	125	175	175

GALANT—4-Cyl.—Equipment Schedule 4
W.B. 103.7"; 2.4 Liter.

DE Sedan 4D	A36G	18347	700	825	1425	2500
ES Sedan 4D	A46G	19157	750	850	1450	2500
LS Sedan 4D	A46G	21757	1525	1750	2550	4300
V6, 3.0 Liter	H		225	225	300	300

GALANT—V6—Equipment Schedule 4
W.B. 103.7"; 3.0 Liter.

GTZ Sedan 4D	A46H	25047	1950	2225	3075	5150

DIAMANTE—V6—Equipment Schedule 4
W.B. 107.1"; 3.5 Liter.

ES Sedan 4D	P57P	26557	1225	1400	2025	3375
VR-X Sedan 4D	P87P	27677	1550	1750	2400	4000
LS Sedan 4D	P67P	29027	1625	1825	2475	4150

2004 MITSUBISHI — (J,4or6)(A3)A(J26E)–4–#

LANCER—4-Cyl.—Equipment Schedule 6
W.B. 102.4"; 2.0 Liter, 2.4 Liter.

ES Sedan 4D	J26E	14972	1625	1775	2550	4100
LS Sedan 4D	J36E	16572	1850	2025	2950	4850
LS Wagon 4D	D29F	17172	1850	2025	2950	4850
OZ Rally Sedan 4D	J86E	17172	2050	2225	3200	5250
Ralliart Sedan 4D	J66F	18572	1800	1975	2675	4225
Ralliart Wagon 4D	D69F	19772	2300	2500	3175	4975

LANCER AWD—4-Cyl. Turbo—Equipment Schedule 4
W.B. 103.3"; 2.0 Liter.

Evolution RS Sedan 4D	H36D	27374	6950	7675	7950	11450
Evolution Sedan 4D	H86D	30574	8025	8850	9000	12800

ECLIPSE—4-Cyl.—Equipment Schedule 4
W.B. 100.8"; 2.4 Liter.

RS Coupe 2D	C34G	18892	775	900	1450	2475
GS Coupe 2D	C44G	19892	1350	1525	2100	3475
GS Spyder Conv 2D	E45G	24892	1725	1950	2575	4150
Automatic			175	175	220	220

ECLIPSE—V6—Equipment Schedule 4
W.B. 100.8"; 3.0 Liter.

GT Coupe 2D	C84H	22092	1600	1750	2450	3900
GT Spyder Conv 2D	E85H	28144	2675	2900	3650	5725
GTS Coupe 2D	C74H	25092	2950	3200	3950	6125
GTS Spyder Conv 2D	E75H	30794	3475	3775	4675	7225
Automatic			175	175	220	220

GALANT—4-Cyl.—Equipment Schedule 4
W.B. 108.3"; 2.4 Liter.

DE Sedan 4D	A36G	18592	1325	1525	2050	3350
ES Sedan 4D	A46G	19592	1500	1725	2325	3775
V6, 3.8 Liter	S		275	275	375	375

GALANT—V6—Equipment Schedule 4
W.B. 108.3"; 3.8 Liter.

Body Type	VIN	List	Trade-In Good	Very Good	Pvt-Party Good	Retail Excellent
LS Sedan 4D	A46H	21592	2550	2900	3575	5675
GTS Sedan 4D	A46H	26292	2875	3275	4000	6375

DIAMANTE—V6—Equipment Schedule 4
W.B. 107.2"; 3.5 Liter.

ES Sedan 4D	P57P	25594	1700	1900	2525	4100
VR-X Sedan 4D	P87P	27414	1975	2250	2950	4800
LS Sedan 4D	P67P	28214	2050	2325	3050	4950

2005 MITSUBISHI — (J,4or6)(A3)A(J26E)-5-#

LANCER—4-Cyl.—Equipment Schedule 6
W.B. 102.4"; 2.0 Liter, 2.4 Liter.

ES Sedan 4D	J26E	15474	1750	1925	2925	4700
OZ Rally Sedan 4D	J86E	17874	2325	2525	3575	5675
Ralliart Sedan 4D	J66F	18774	2125	2325	3225	4975

LANCER AWD—4-Cyl. Turbo—Equipment Schedule 4
W.B. 103.3"; 2.0 Liter.

Evolution RS Sedan 4D	H36D	28774	9275	10150	10250	14100
Evolution VIII Sedan	H76D	31074	10600	11600	11400	15600
Evolution MR Ed Sedan	H86D	35574	11800	12900	12650	17250

ECLIPSE—4-Cyl.—Equipment Schedule 4
W.B. 100.8"; 2.4 Liter.

GS Coupe 2D	C44G	20044	1725	1950	2850	4625
GS Spyder Conv 2D	E45G	25494	2275	2550	3425	5475
Automatic			200	200	255	255

ECLIPSE—V6—Equipment Schedule 4
W.B. 100.8"; 3.0 Liter.

GT Coupe 2D	C84H	23494	2000	2200	3125	4875
GT Spyder Conv 2D	E55H	28494	3100	3400	4325	6500
GTS Coupe 2D	C74H	25244	3175	3450	4300	6500
GTS Spyder Conv 2D	E75H	31094	3600	3925	4875	7275
Automatic			200	200	255	255

GALANT—4-Cyl.—Equipment Schedule 4
W.B. 108.3"; 2.4 Liter.

DE Sedan 4D	B26F	19594	1675	1900	2550	3900
ES Sedan 4D	B46F	20494	2000	2275	2900	4400
SE Sedan 4D	B46F	21594	2550	2900	3475	5225

GALANT—V6—Equipment Schedule 4
W.B. 108.3"; 3.8 Liter.

LS Sedan 4D	B46S	23094	3025	3425	4125	6300
GTS Sedan 4D	B76S	27094	3325	3775	4625	7075

2006 MITSUBISHI — (J,4or6)(A3)A(J26E)-6-#

LANCER—4-Cyl.—Equipment Schedule 6
W.B. 102.4"; 2.0 Liter, 2.4 Liter.

ES Sedan 4D	J26E	16104	2125	2325	3350	5225
SE Sedan 4D	J26E	16704	2200	2400	3400	5275
OZ Rally Sedan 4D	J86E	18404	3025	3275	4175	6300
Ralliart Sedan 4D	J66F	19574	2750	2975	3900	5875

LANCER AWD—4-Cyl. Turbo—Equipment Schedule 4
W.B. 103.3"; 2.0 Liter.

Evolution RS Sedan 4D	H36C	29274	11200	12200	12100	16250
Evolution IX Sedan 4D	H86C	31994	12800	13950	13700	18200
Evolution MR Sedan 4D	H86C	35784	14150	15450	15000	19950

ECLIPSE—4-Cyl.—Equipment Schedule 4
W.B. 101.4"; 2.4 Liter.

GS Coupe 2D	K24F	20924	3450	3850	4450	6550

ECLIPSE—V6—Equipment Schedule 4
W.B. 101.4"; 3.8 Liter.

GT Coupe 2D	K34T	25224	3625	3925	4700	6775
Special Edition	4		850	850	1135	1135

GALANT—4-Cyl.—Equipment Schedule 4
W.B. 108.3"; 2.4 Liter.

DE Sedan 4D	B26F	19994	1950	2225	2825	4200
ES Sedan 4D	B46F	20894	2600	2925	3500	5150
SE Sedan 4D	B36F	22594	3175	3575	4100	5975

GALANT—V6—Equipment Schedule 4
W.B. 108.3"; 3.8 Liter.

LS Sedan 4D	B46S	23594	3725	4200	4850	7100
GTS Sedan 4D	B76S	27594	4200	4725	5425	7950

2007 MITSUBISHI

Body Type	VIN	List	Trade-In Good	Very Good	Pvt-Party Good	Retail Excellent

2007 MITSUBISHI — (Jor4)(A3)A(J26E)-7-#

LANCER—4-Cyl.—Equipment Schedule 6
W.B. 102.4"; 2.0 Liter.

Body Type	VIN	List	Good	Very Good	Good	Excellent
ES Sedan 4D	J26E	16104	**2625**	**2825**	**3925**	**6000**
Manual, 5-Spd w/Overdrive			**(325)**	**(325)**	**(430)**	**(430)**

ECLIPSE—4-Cyl.—Equipment Schedule 4
W.B. 101.4"; 2.4 Liter.

GS Coupe 2D	K24F	21224	**3650**	**4050**	**4725**	**6825**
GS Spyder Conv 2D	L25F	26914	**4225**	**4675**	**5350**	**7775**
SE Coupe 2D	K64F	23024	**4150**	**4575**	**5250**	**7625**

ECLIPSE—V6—Equipment Schedule 4
W.B. 101.4"; 3.8 Liter.

GT Coupe 2D	K34T	24924	**4400**	**4750**	**5525**	**7775**
GT Spyder Conv 2D	L35T	29794	**4925**	**5325**	**6125**	**8425**

GALANT—4-Cyl.—Equipment Schedule 4
W.B. 108.3"; 2.4 Liter.

DE Sedan 4D	B26F	20524	**2500**	**2800**	**3475**	**5125**
ES Sedan 4D	B36F	21624	**3050**	**3425**	**4175**	**6025**
SE Sedan 4D	B36F	23324	**3825**	**4275**	**4975**	**7125**

GALANT—V6—Equipment Schedule 4
W.B. 108.3"; 3.8 Liter.

GTS Sedan 4D	B56S	25624	**4850**	**5425**	**6250**	**8925**
Ralliart Sedan 4D	B76T	27624	**5200**	**5800**	**6675**	**9550**

2008 MITSUBISHI — (1,4orJ)A3-(U16U)-8-#

LANCER—4-Cyl.—Equipment Schedule 6
W.B. 103.7"; 2.0 Liter.

DE Sedan 4D	U16U	15515	**3175**	**3400**	**4425**	**6275**
ES Sedan 4D	U26U	17515	**4025**	**4300**	**5275**	**7325**
GTS Sedan 4D	U86U	19115	**5450**	**5825**	**6975**	**9575**
Manual, 5-Spd w/Overdrive			**(350)**	**(350)**	**(460)**	**(460)**

LANCER—4-Cyl. Turbo—Equipment Schedule 4
W.B. 104.3"; 2.0 Liter.

Evolution GSR Sedan	W86V	33615	**14950**	**15950**	**15900**	**19750**
Evolution MR Sedan	W56V	38940	**18900**	**20200**	**19900**	**24800**

ECLIPSE—4-Cyl.—Equipment Schedule 4
W.B. 101.4"; 2.4 Liter.

GS Coupe 2D	K24F	21624	**4800**	**5275**	**5800**	**7925**
GS Spyder Conv 2D	L25F	27324	**4925**	**5425**	**6300**	**8750**
SE Coupe 2D	K64F	25424	**5125**	**5625**	**6475**	**8950**
V6, 3.8 Liter (SE)	T		**1775**	**1775**	**2355**	**2355**

ECLIPSE—V6—Equipment Schedule 4
W.B. 101.4"; 3.8 Liter.

GT Coupe 2D	K34T	25124	**5125**	**5475**	**6375**	**8500**
GT Spyder Conv 2D	L35T	30224	**6350**	**6775**	**7250**	**9275**

GALANT—4-Cyl.—Equipment Schedule 4
W.B. 108.3"; 2.4 Liter.

DE Sedan 4D	B26F	20624	**3100**	**3425**	**4200**	**5900**
ES Sedan 4D	B36F	21724	**3825**	**4225**	**5025**	**7000**

GALANT—V6—Equipment Schedule 4
W.B. 108.3"; 3.8 Liter.

Ralliart Sedan 4D	B76T	27774	**6375**	**7000**	**8025**	**11150**

2009 MITSUBISHI — (1,4orJ)A3-(K24F)-9-#

ECLIPSE—4-Cyl.—Equipment Schedule 4
W.B. 101.4"; 2.4 Liter.

GS Coupe 2D	K24F	20749	**5575**	**6075**	**6750**	**8825**
GS Spyder Conv 2D	L25F	26449	**6525**	**7100**	**7875**	**10450**

ECLIPSE—V6—Equipment Schedule 4
W.B. 101.4"; 3.8 Liter.

GT Coupe 2D	K34T	25799	**6975**	**7375**	**8475**	**11000**
GT Spyder Conv 2D	L35T	29649	**8350**	**8825**	**9875**	**12750**

LANCER—4-Cyl.—Equipment Schedule 4
W.B. 103.7"; 2.0 Liter, 2.4 Liter.

DE Sedan 4D	U16U	15540	**4200**	**4450**	**5450**	**7300**
ES Sedan 4D	U26U	17740	**5050**	**5350**	**6300**	**8350**
GTS Sedan 4D	U86U	19640	**6900**	**7300**	**8250**	**10650**
Manual, 5-Spd w/Overdrive			**(375)**	**(375)**	**(490)**	**(490)**

LANCER AWD—4-Cyl. Turbo—Equipment Schedule 4
W.B. 103.7"; 2.0 Liter.

Ralliart Sedan 4D	V66V	27165	**9000**	**9525**	**10250**	**12800**

2009 MITSUBISHI

Body Type	VIN	List	Trade-In Good	Very Good	Pvt-Party Good	Retail Excellent
GALANT—4-Cyl.—Equipment Schedule 4						
W.B. 108.3"; 2.4 Liter.						
ES Sedan 4D	B36F	21724	4800	5225	6100	8175
Sport Ed Sedan 4D	B36F	23124	5500	6000	7050	9475
GALANT—V6—Equipment Schedule 4						
W.B. 108.3"; 3.8 Liter.						
Sport Sedan 4D	B46T	25124	6775	7375	8775	11950
Ralliart Sedan 4D	B76T	27924	7675	8350	9500	12650

2010 MITSUBISHI — (4orJ)A3–(K2DF)–A–#

Body Type	VIN	List	Trade-In Good	Very Good	Pvt-Party Good	Retail Excellent
ECLIPSE—4-Cyl.—Equipment Schedule 4						
W.B. 101.4"; 2.4 Liter.						
GS Coupe 2D	K2DF	22419	6600	7150	7775	9850
GS Sport Coupe 2D	K5DF	25763	7300	7925	8625	10950
GS Spyder Conv 2D	L2EF	28519	8025	8675	9400	11950
ECLIPSE—V6—Equipment Schedule 4						
W.B. 101.4"; 3.8 Liter.						
GT Coupe 2D	K3DT	30128	9025	9475	10550	13150
GT Spyder Conv 2D	L3ET	33548	10050	10550	11550	14300
LANCER—4-Cyl.—Equipment Schedule 4						
W.B. 103.7"; 2.0 Liter, 2.4 Liter.						
DE Sedan 4D	U1FU	16410	5400	5700	6825	8725
ES Sedan 4D	U2FU	18610	6050	6375	7475	9525
GTS Sedan 4D	U8FW	20710	8250	8675	9700	12100
GTS Sportback 4D	X8HW	20910	8350	8775	9750	12150
Manual, 5-Spd w/Overdrive			(450)	(450)	(615)	(615)
LANCER AWD—4-Cyl. Turbo—Equipment Schedule 4						
W.B. 103.7"; 2.0 Liter.						
Ralliart Sedan 4D	V6FV	27910	12100	12750	13300	15950
Ralliart Sportback 4D	Y6HV	28310	12300	12900	13450	16050
Evolution GSR Sedan	W8FV	34310	18450	19300	19950	23600
Evolution SE Sedan	W6FV	36535	19500	20400	21200	25100
Evolution MR Sedan	W5FV	39710	21200	22200	22800	26800
Evolution MR Touring	W5FV	41710	22500	23500	24100	28400
GALANT—4-Cyl.—Equipment Schedule 4						
W.B. 108.3"; 2.4 Liter.						
FE Sedan 4D	B2FF	22260	5875	6350	7425	9650
ES Sedan 4D	B3FF	22319	6375	6875	7925	10250
SE Sedan 4D	B3FF	24719	7100	7650	8875	11550

2011 MITSUBISHI — (4orJ)A3–(K5DF)–B–#

Body Type	VIN	List	Trade-In Good	Very Good	Pvt-Party Good	Retail Excellent
ECLIPSE—4-Cyl.—Equipment Schedule 4						
W.B. 101.4"; 2.4 Liter.						
GS Coupe 2D	K5DF	20744	8375	9025	9600	11750
ECLIPSE—4-Cyl.—Equipment Schedule 4						
W.B. 101.4"; 2.4 Liter.						
GS Sport Coupe	K5DF	25673	8400	9050	9775	12150
GS Spyder Conv 2D	L5EF	28744	9175	9875	10550	13050
ECLIPSE—V6—Equipment Schedule 4						
W.B. 101.4"; 3.8 Liter.						
GT Coupe 2D	K3DT	30153	10100	10550	11600	14100
GT Spyder Conv 2D	L3ET	33573	11500	12050	13150	15850
LANCER—4-Cyl.—Equipment Schedule 6						
W.B. 103.7"; 2.0 Liter.						
DE Sedan 4D	U1FU	15740	6025	6325	7500	9400
ES Sportback 4D	X2HU	18455	7200	7525	8775	10950
LANCER—4-Cyl.—Equipment Schedule 6						
W.B. 103.7"; 2.0 Liter, 2.4 Liter.						
ES Sedan 4D	U2FU	17155	6925	7250	8450	10600
GTS Sedan 4D	U8FW	21055	9025	9425	10600	13000
GTS Sportback 4D	X8HW	21455	9150	9575	10650	12950
Manual, 5-Spd w/Overdrive			(500)	(500)	(655)	(655)
LANCER AWD—4-Cyl. Turbo—Equipment Schedule 4						
W.B. 103.7"; 2.0 Liter.						
Ralliart Sedan 4D	V6FV	28240	12850	13450	14150	16700
Ralliart Sportback 4D	Y6HV	28240	13000	13600	14400	17050
Evolution GSR Sedan	W8FV	34335	21000	21800	22500	25900
Evolution MR Sedan	W5FV	39735	23800	24800	25400	29200
GALANT—4-Cyl.—Equipment Schedule 4						
W.B. 108.3"; 2.4 Liter.						
FE Sedan 4D	B2FF	22903	7075	7550	8625	10850
ES Sedan 4D	B3FF	22344	7225	7725	8875	11150

2011 MITSUBISHI

Body Type	VIN	List	Trade-In Good	Very Good	Pvt-Party Good	Retail Excellent
SE Sedan 4D	B3FF	24744	8225	8775	10000	12650

2012 MITSUBISHI — (4orJ)A3–(K2DF)–C–#

ECLIPSE—4-Cyl.—Equipment Schedule 4
W.B. 101.4"; 2.4 Liter.

GS Coupe 2D	K2DF	21259	10250	11000	11650	14150

ECLIPSE—4-Cyl.—Equipment Schedule 4
W.B. 101.4"; 2.4 Liter.

GS Sport Coupe 2D	K5DF	25688	11200	12000	12800	15600
GS Spyder Conv 2D	L5EF	26574	11150	11950	12800	15700
GS Sport Spyder Conv	L5EF	28759	12000	12850	13700	16750
SE Coupe 2D	K5DF	25703	11550	12400	13200	16100
SE Spyder Conv 2D	L5EF	29074	12400	13250	14000	17000

ECLIPSE—V6—Equipment Schedule 4
W.B. 101.4"; 3.8 Liter.

GT Coupe 2D	K3DT	30168	11800	12300	13500	16100
GT Spyder Conv 2D	L3ET	33588	13350	13900	15250	18150

LANCER—4-Cyl.—Equipment Schedule 4
W.B. 103.7"; 2.0 Liter, 2.4 Liter.

DE Sedan 4D	U1FU	16490	7200	7525	8750	10700
ES Sportback 4D	X2HU	19190	8600	8975	10050	12100
GT Sportback 4D	X8HW	22140	10450	10850	12150	14700

LANCER—4-Cyl.—Equipment Schedule 6
W.B. 103.7"; 2.0 Liter.

ES Sedan 4D	U2FU	18690	7975	8325	9575	11700
GT Sedan 4D	U8FW	20640	9225	9625	10850	13100
Manual, 5-Spd			(500)	(500)	(635)	(635)

LANCER AWD—4-Cyl.—Equipment Schedule 6
W.B. 103.7"; 2.4 Liter.

SE Sedan 4D	V2FW	20990	9450	9875	11050	13250

LANCER AWD—4-Cyl. Turbo—Equipment Schedule 4
W.B. 103.7", 104.3"; 2.0 Liter.

Ralliart Sedan 4D	V6FV	28790	14600	15250	16050	18550
Evolution GSR Sedan	W8FV	35290	22600	23400	24400	27600
Evolution MR Sedan	W5FV	38490	25500	26300	27300	30900

GALANT—4-Cyl.—Equipment Schedule 6
W.B. 108.3"; 2.4 Liter.

FE Sedan 4D	B2FF	22903	7650	8125	9300	11500
ES Sedan 4D	B3FF	22694	8175	8700	9825	12100
SE Sedan 4D	B3FF	25094	9350	9950	11200	13850

2013 MITSUBISHI — (4orJ)A3–(U1FU)–D–#

LANCER—4-Cyl.—Equipment Schedule 6
W.B. 103.7"; 2.0 Liter.

DE Sedan 4D	U1FU	16790	7825	8150	9550	11650

LANCER—4-Cyl.—Equipment Schedule 6
W.B. 103.7"; 2.0 Liter, 2.4 Liter.

ES Sedan 4D	U2FU	17890	8675	9025	10300	12450
GT Sedan 4D	U8FW	20790	10600	11050	12250	14550
Manual, 5-Spd			(500)	(500)	(650)	(650)

LANCER—4-Cyl.—Equipment Schedule 6
W.B. 103.7"; 2.0 Liter, 2.4 Liter.

ES Hatchback 4D	X2HU	19290	9450	9825	11350	13800
GT Hatchback 4D	X8HW	22290	11450	11900	13200	15650

LANCER AWD—4-Cyl.—Equipment Schedule 6
W.B. 103.7"; 2.4 Liter.

SE Sedan 4D	V2FW	21090	10950	11400	12650	15050

LANCER AWD—4-Cyl. Turbo—Equipment Schedule 4
W.B. 103.7", 104.3"; 2.0 Liter.

Ralliart Sedan 4D	V6FV	28890	17050	17700	18500	21200
Evolution GSR Sedan	W8FV	35490	25400	26200	27400	30700
Evolution MR Sedan	W5FV	38690	28400	29200	30300	33800

2014 MITSUBISHI — (4orJ)A3–(A3HJ)–E–#

MIRAGE—3-Cyl.—Equipment Schedule 6
W.B. 96.5"; 1.2 Liter.

DE Hatchback 4D	A3HJ	13790	6950	7250	8500	10400
ES Hatchback 4D	A4HJ	14990	7425	7725	8925	10850

i-MiEV—AC Electric—Equipment Schedule 4
W.B. 100.4".

ES Hatchback 4D	215H4	23845	8775	9050	10500	12200

Body Type	VIN	List	Trade-In Good	Very Good	Pvt-Party Good	Retail Excellent

LANCER—4-Cyl.—Equipment Schedule 6
W.B. 103.7"; 2.0 Liter, 2.4 Liter.

Body Type	VIN	List	Good	Very Good	Good	Excellent
ES Sedan 4D	U2FU	18890	**9800**	**10200**	**11500**	**13750**
GT Sedan 4D	U8FW	22240	**12050**	**12550**	**13700**	**16000**
Manual, 5-Spd			**(525)**	**(525)**	**(655)**	**(655)**

LANCER AWD—4-Cyl.—Equipment Schedule 6
W.B. 103.7"; 2.4 Liter.

SE Sedan 4D	V2FW	21490	**11850**	**12300**	**13550**	**16000**

LANCER—4-Cyl.—Equipment Schedule 6
W.B. 103.7"; 2.0 Liter, 2.4 Liter.

ES Hatchback 4D	X2HU	19390	**10650**	**11100**	**12450**	**14900**
GT Hatchback 4D	X8HW	22740	**12550**	**13050**	**14150**	**16500**

LANCER AWD—4-Cyl. Turbo—Equipment Schedule 4
W.B. 103.7", 104.3" (Evolution); 2.0 Liter.

Ralliart Sedan 4D	V6FV	29190	**18900**	**19600**	**20300**	**23000**
Evolution GSR Sedan	W8FV	35790	**26700**	**27500**	**28600**	**31900**
Evolution MR Sedan	W5FV	38990	**30300**	**31200**	**32300**	**35800**

NISSAN

2000 NISSAN — (1N4,JN1or3N1)(CB51D)–Y–#

SENTRA—4-Cyl.—Equipment Schedule 6
W.B. 99.8"; 1.8 Liter, 2.0 Liter.

XE Sedan 4D	CB51D	12169	**450**	**525**	**1325**	**2500**
GXE Sedan 4D	CB51D	14019	**600**	**675**	**1525**	**2875**
CA Sedan 4D	DB51D	15319	**675**	**750**	**1475**	**2650**
SE Sedan 4D	BB51D	15419	**825**	**925**	**1675**	**3000**

ALTIMA—4-Cyl.—Equipment Schedule 4
W.B. 103.1"; 2.4 Liter.

XE Sedan 4D	DL01D	18459	**475**	**550**	**1250**	**2350**
GXE Sedan 4D	DL01D	18659	**625**	**750**	**1400**	**2550**
SE Sedan 4D	DL01D	19960	**950**	**1100**	**1800**	**3225**
GLE Sedan 4D	DL01D	20910	**1175**	**1375**	**2100**	**3700**
Manual, 5-Spd			**(175)**	**(175)**	**(220)**	**(220)**

MAXIMA—V6—Equipment Schedule 4
W.B. 108.3"; 3.0 Liter.

GXE Sedan 4D	CA31A	23269	**1075**	**1250**	**1900**	**3375**
SE Sedan 4D	CA31A	24669	**1200**	**1400**	**2075**	**3650**
GLE Sedan 4D	CA31A	26769	**1400**	**1625**	**2325**	**4075**
Manual, 5-Spd			**(175)**	**(175)**	**(220)**	**(220)**

2001 NISSAN — (1N4,JN1or3N1)(CB51D)–1–#

SENTRA—4-Cyl.—Equipment Schedule 6
W.B. 99.8"; 1.8 Liter, 2.0 Liter.

XE Sedan 4D	CB51D	13368	**525**	**575**	**1375**	**2600**
GXE Sedan 4D	CB51D	14019	**675**	**750**	**1625**	**3025**
CA Sedan 4D	DB51D	15319	**975**	**1075**	**1875**	**3325**
SE Sedan 4D	BB51D	15419	**1075**	**1175**	**2000**	**3550**

ALTIMA—4-Cyl.—Equipment Schedule 4
W.B. 103.1"; 2.4 Liter.

XE Sedan 4D	DL01D	18459	**625**	**750**	**1450**	**2675**
GXE Sedan 4D	DL01D	18659	**850**	**975**	**1650**	**2950**
SE Sedan 4D	DL01D	19960	**1325**	**1525**	**2200**	**3850**
GLE Sedan 4D	DL01D	20190	**1550**	**1775**	**2500**	**4300**
LE Pkg			**75**	**75**	**85**	**85**
Manual, 5-Spd			**(200)**	**(200)**	**(265)**	**(265)**

MAXIMA—V6—Equipment Schedule 4
W.B. 108.3"; 3.0 Liter.

GXE Sedan 4D	CA31D	23469	**1100**	**1275**	**2025**	**3625**
SE Sedan 4D	CA31D	24869	**1300**	**1500**	**2275**	**4025**
SE 20th Anniv Sed 4D	CA31A	28169	**1650**	**1900**	**2725**	**4750**
GLE Sedan 4D	CA31D	26969	**1500**	**1725**	**2525**	**4425**
Manual, 5-Spd			**(200)**	**(200)**	**(265)**	**(265)**

2002 NISSAN — (1N4,JN1or3N1)(CB51D)–2–#

SENTRA—4-Cyl.—Equipment Schedule 6
W.B. 99.8"; 1.8 Liter, 2.5 Liter.

XE Sedan 4D	CB51D	13588	**575**	**650**	**1475**	**2725**
GXE Sedan 4D	CB51D	14289	**875**	**975**	**1775**	**3175**
CA Sedan 4D	DB51D	15439	**1275**	**1400**	**2125**	**3600**
SE-R Sedan 4D	AB51A	16539	**1300**	**1425**	**2075**	**3500**

Body Type	VIN	List	Trade-In Good	Very Good	Pvt-Party Good	Retail Excellent
SE-R Spec V Sedan 4D	AB51A	17539	**1600**	**1775**	**2325**	**3750**
ALTIMA—4-Cyl.—Equipment Schedule 4						
W.B. 110.2"; 2.5 Liter.						
2.5 Sedan 4D	AL11D	17869	**1025**	**1175**	**1925**	**3400**
2.5 S Sedan 4D	AL11D	19389	**1250**	**1425**	**2175**	**3800**
2.5 SL Sedan 4D	AL11D	23239	**1800**	**2050**	**2925**	**4975**
Manual, 5-Spd			**(200)**	**(200)**	**(265)**	**(265)**
ALTIMA—V6—Equipment Schedule 4						
W.B. 110.2"; 3.5 Liter.						
3.5 SE Sedan 4D	BL11D	23689	**2075**	**2350**	**3225**	**5475**
Manual, 5-Spd			**(200)**	**(200)**	**(265)**	**(265)**
MAXIMA—V6—Equipment Schedule 4						
W.B. 108.3"; 3.5 Liter.						
GXE Sedan 4D	CA31D	25239	**1375**	**1575**	**2275**	**3925**
SE Sedan 4D	CA31D	25989	**1675**	**1900**	**2700**	**4575**
GLE Sedan 4D	CA31D	27639	**1925**	**2200**	**3000**	**5050**

2003 NISSAN — (1N4,JN1or3N1)(CB51D)-3-#

Body Type	VIN	List	Trade-In Good	Very Good	Pvt-Party Good	Retail Excellent
SENTRA—4-Cyl.—Equipment Schedule 6						
W.B. 99.8"; 1.8 Liter, 2.5 Liter.						
XE Sedan 4D	CB51D	13888	**875**	**950**	**1925**	**3525**
GXE Sedan 4D	CB51D	14639	**1175**	**1300**	**2150**	**3750**
Limited Sedan 4D	AB51D	17139	**1675**	**1850**	**2675**	**4425**
SE-R Sedan 4D	AB51D	16739	**1525**	**1675**	**2450**	**4075**
SE-R Spec V Sed 4D	AB51D	17739	**1650**	**1800**	**2575**	**4200**
ALTIMA—4-Cyl.—Equipment Schedule 4						
W.B. 110.2"; 2.5 Liter.						
2.5 Sedan 4D	AL11D	17689	**1325**	**1525**	**2225**	**3775**
2.5 S Sedan 4D	AL11D	19539	**1575**	**1775**	**2575**	**4350**
2.5 SL Sedan 4D	AL11D	23539	**2175**	**2475**	**3275**	**5425**
Manual, 5-Spd			**(225)**	**(225)**	**(310)**	**(310)**
ALTIMA—V6—Equipment Schedule 4						
W.B. 110.2"; 3.5 Liter.						
3.5 SE Sedan 4D	BL11D	23689	**2500**	**2850**	**3650**	**6025**
Manual, 5-Spd			**(225)**	**(225)**	**(310)**	**(310)**
MAXIMA—V6—Equipment Schedule 4						
W.B. 108.3"; 3.5 Liter.						
GXE Sedan 4D	DA31D	25439	**2025**	**2300**	**2925**	**4725**
SE Sedan 4D	DA31D	26189	**2250**	**2575**	**3200**	**5175**
GLE Sedan 4D	DA31D	28089	**2350**	**2675**	**3375**	**5500**
350Z—V6—Equipment Schedule 3						
W.B. 104.3"; 3.5 Liter.						
Coupe 2D	AZ34D	26809	**4025**	**4425**	**5150**	**7525**
Enthusiast Coupe 2D	AZ34D	29759	**4825**	**5275**	**5850**	**8450**
Performance Cpe 2D	AZ34D	30969	**5075**	**5550**	**6125**	**8800**
Touring Coupe 2D	AZ34D	32129	**5075**	**5550**	**6100**	**8750**
Track Coupe 2D	AZ34D	34619	**5600**	**6125**	**6600**	**9425**

2004 NISSAN—(1N4,JN1or3N1)(CB51D)-4-#

Body Type	VIN	List	Trade-In Good	Very Good	Pvt-Party Good	Retail Excellent
SENTRA—4-Cyl.—Equipment Schedule 6						
W.B. 99.8"; 1.8 Liter.						
Sedan 4D	CB51D	13760	**1325**	**1450**	**2350**	**4050**
S Sedan 4D	CB51D	14740	**1500**	**1625**	**2550**	**4350**
SE-R Sedan 4D	AB51D	17640	**1625**	**1800**	**2725**	**4525**
SE-R Spec V Sed 4D	AB51D	17840	**1800**	**1975**	**2825**	**4575**
4-Cyl, 2.5 Liter	A		**125**	**125**	**175**	**175**
ALTIMA—4-Cyl.—Equipment Schedule 4						
W.B. 110.2"; 2.5 Liter.						
2.5 Sedan 4D	AL11D	17890	**1575**	**1775**	**2575**	**4275**
2.5 S Sedan 4D	AL11D	19740	**1875**	**2125**	**2925**	**4800**
2.5 SL Sedan 4D	AL11D	23740	**2875**	**3225**	**4075**	**6550**
Manual, 5-Spd			**(275)**	**(275)**	**(375)**	**(375)**
ALTIMA—V6—Equipment Schedule 4						
W.B. 110.2"; 3.5 Liter.						
3.5 SE Sedan 4D	BL11D	23790	**3050**	**3425**	**4225**	**6800**
Manual, 5-Spd			**(275)**	**(275)**	**(375)**	**(375)**
MAXIMA—V6—Equipment Schedule 4						
W.B. 111.2"; 3.5 Liter.						
SE Sedan 4D	BA41E	27510	**2750**	**3100**	**3825**	**6075**
SL Sedan 4D	BA41E	29440	**2850**	**3200**	**3950**	**6325**
350Z—V6—Equipment Schedule 3						
W.B. 104.3"; 3.5 Liter.						

Body Type	VIN	List	Trade-In Good	Very Good	Pvt-Party Good	Retail Excellent
Coupe 2D	AZ34D	26910	4975	5425	6000	8525
Enthusiast Coupe 2D	AZ34D	29860	5800	6300	6800	9475
Enthusiast Roadster	AZ36A	35580	6650	7225	7600	10550
Performance Cpe 2D	AZ34D	31070	6050	6575	7050	9850
Track Coupe 2D	AZ34D	34720	7175	7775	8125	11250
Touring Coupe 2D	AZ34D	33820	6050	6575	7050	9850
Touring Roadster 2D	AZ36A	37950	6900	7500	7750	10600

2005 NISSAN — (1N4,JN1or3N1)(CB51D)-5-#

SENTRA—4-Cyl.—Equipment Schedule 6
W.B. 99.8"; 1.8 Liter, 2.5 Liter.

Body Type	VIN	List	Trade-In Good	Very Good	Pvt-Party Good	Retail Excellent
Sedan 4D	CB51D	14280	1600	1750	2875	4725
S Sedan 4D	CB51D	16280	1925	2100	3150	5025
SE-R Sedan 4D	AB51D	18180	2125	2325	3325	5300
SE-R Spec V Sed 4D	AB51D	18380	2325	2525	3450	5350
Special Edition			25	25	35	35

ALTIMA—4-Cyl.—Equipment Schedule 4
W.B. 110.2"; 2.5 Liter.

2.5 Sedan 4D	AL11D	17760	2350	2650	3450	5350
2.5 S Sedan 4D	AL11D	20110	2875	3225	4000	6125
SL			450	450	600	600
Manual, 5-Spd			(325)	(325)	(445)	(445)

ALTIMA—V6—Equipment Schedule 4
W.B. 110.2"; 3.5 Liter.

3.5 SE Sedan 4D	BL11D	24310	3375	3800	4725	7225
3.5 SL Sedan 4D	BL11D	27460	3900	4375	5325	8125
3.5 SE-R Sedan 4D	BL11D	29760	4800	5375	6300	9575
Manual, 5-Spd			(325)	(325)	(445)	(445)

MAXIMA—V6—Equipment Schedule 4
W.B. 111.2"; 3.5 Liter.

SE Sedan 4D	BA41E	28080	3300	3700	4475	6825
SL Sedan 4D	BA41E	29910	3475	3875	4650	7125

350Z—V6—Equipment Schedule 3
W.B. 104.3"; 3.5 Liter.

Coupe 2D	AZ35D	27060	5950	6450	7125	9800
Enthusiast Coupe 2D	AZ34D	30010	6925	7500	7950	10750
Enthusiast Roadster	AZ36A	36030	7725	8375	8750	11750
Performance Cpe 2D	AZ34D	31210	7175	7750	8200	11100
Touring Coupe 2D	AZ34D	32360	7475	8100	8525	11500
Touring Roadster 2D	AZ36A	38430	8350	9025	9250	12250
Track Coupe 2D	AZ34D	34860	8975	9700	9825	12950
35th Anniv Coupe 2D	AZ34D	37660	10500	11350	11450	15200
Grand Touring Rdstr	AZ36D	39300	8975	9700	9775	12850

2006 NISSAN — (1N4,JN1or3N1)(CB51D)-6-#

SENTRA—4-Cyl.—Equipment Schedule 6
W.B. 99.8"; 1.8 Liter, 2.5 Liter.

Body Type	VIN	List	Trade-In Good	Very Good	Pvt-Party Good	Retail Excellent
Sedan 4D	CB51D	14615	2225	2425	3500	5500
S Sedan 4D	CB51D	16615	2475	2700	3750	5800
Manual, 5-Spd			(275)	(275)	(355)	(355)

SENTRA—4-Cyl.—Equipment Schedule 6
W.B. 99.8"; 1.8 Liter, 2.5 Liter.

SE-R Sedan 4D	AB51D	18580	3075	3350	4200	6250
SE-R Spec V Sed 4D	AB51D	18780	3275	3550	4425	6475
Special Edition			25	25	45	45

ALTIMA—4-Cyl.—Equipment Schedule 4
W.B. 110.2"; 2.5 Liter.

2.5 Sedan 4D	AL11D	18230	2950	3275	3925	5800
SL			500	500	650	650

ALTIMA—4-Cyl.—Equipment Schedule 4
W.B. 110.2"; 2.5 Liter.

2.5 S Sedan 4D	AL11D	20580	3275	3650	4475	6625
SL			500	500	650	650
Manual, 5-Spd			(375)	(375)	(510)	(510)

ALTIMA—V6—Equipment Schedule 4
W.B. 110.2"; 3.5 Liter.

3.5 SE Sedan 4D	BL11D	24730	4250	4700	5525	8150
3.5 SL Sedan 4D	BL11D	27880	4800	5300	6175	9100
3.5 SE-R Sedan 4D	BL11D	30130	5500	6100	7100	10400
Manual, 5-Spd			(375)	(375)	(510)	(510)
Manual, 6-Spd			0	0	0	0

2006 NISSAN

Body Type	VIN	List	Trade-In Good	Very Good	Pvt-Party Good	Retail Excellent
MAXIMA—V6—Equipment Schedule 4						
W.B. 111.2"; 3.5 Liter.						
SE Sedan 4D	BA41E	28515	3775	4175	5000	7375
SL Sedan 4D	BA41E	30580	4150	4600	5400	7925
350Z—V6—Equipment Schedule 3						
W.B. 104.3"; 3.5 Liter.						
Coupe 2D	AZ34D	28030	6550	7050	7725	10400
Enthusiast Coupe 2D	AZ34D	30730	7450	8025	8550	11350
Enthusiast Roadster	AZ36A	35665	8350	8975	9425	12450
Touring Coupe 2D	AZ34D	33330	8175	8800	9275	12300
Touring Roadster 2D	AZ36A	39265	8900	9550	9825	12800
Track Coupe 2D	AZ34D	34930	9675	10400	10650	13850
Grand Touring Coupe	AZ34D	37465	9425	10150	10500	13800
Grand Touring Rdstr	AZ36D	41615	9425	10150	10350	13400

2007 NISSAN—(1N4,JN1or3N1)(BC11E)-7-#

Body Type	VIN	List	Trade-In Good	Very Good	Pvt-Party Good	Retail Excellent
VERSA—4-Cyl.—Equipment Schedule 6						
W.B. 102.4"; 1.8 Liter.						
S Sedan 4D	BC11E	13975	3200	3625	4400	6675
S Hatchback 4D	BC13E	13975	3225	3650	4475	6800
SL Sedan 4D	BC11E	16175	3650	4100	4800	7200
SL Hatchback 4D	BC13E	16175	3575	4025	4675	6975
Manual, 6-Spd			(350)	(350)	(455)	(455)
SENTRA—4-Cyl.—Equipment Schedule 6						
W.B. 105.7"; 2.0 Liter.						
Sedan 4D	AB61E	16175	3500	3775	4900	7225
S Sedan 4D	AB61E	17075	3600	3900	5000	7350
Manual, 6-Spd			(350)	(350)	(455)	(455)
SENTRA—4-Cyl.—Equipment Schedule 6						
W.B. 105.7"; 2.0 Liter, 2.5 Liter.						
SL Sedan 4D	AB61E	19015	3925	4225	5325	7800
SE-R Sedan 4D	BB61E	20015	4300	4625	5525	7850
SE-R Spec V Sedan	CB61E	20515	4775	5125	6000	8500
ALTIMA—4-Cyl.—Equipment Schedule 4						
W.B. 109.3"; 2.5 Liter.						
2.5 Sedan 4D	AL21E	18565	4075	4475	5150	7275
2.5 S Sedan 4D	AL21E	20925	4575	5025	5650	7900
SL			575	575	755	755
ALTIMA—4-Cyl. Hybrid—Equipment Schedule 4						
W.B. 109.3"; 2.5 Liter.						
Sedan 4D	CL21E	25015	5150	5650	6425	8975
ALTIMA—V6—Equipment Schedule 4						
W.B. 109.3"; 3.5 Liter.						
3.5 SE Sedan 4D	BL21E	25125	6150	6750	7725	10950
3.5 SL Sedan 4D	BL21E	29015	6825	7500	8575	12200
MAXIMA—V6—Equipment Schedule 4						
W.B. 111.2"; 3.5 Liter.						
SE Sedan 4D	BA41E	28665	5025	5500	6150	8625
SL Sedan 4D	BA41E	30915	5450	5975	6575	9200
Driver's Preferred Pkg			325	325	425	425
350Z—V6—Equipment Schedule 3						
W.B. 104.3"; 3.5 Liter.						
Coupe 2D	BZ34D	28515	7475	7975	8675	11400
Enthusiast Coupe 2D	BZ34D	30010	8475	9050	9650	12600
Enthusiast Roadster	BZ36A	37175	9475	10100	10600	13650
Touring Coupe 2D	BZ34D	33200	9600	10250	10700	13750
Touring Roadster 2D	BZ36A	39525	9950	10600	10950	13900
Grand Touring Coupe	BZ34A	37725	10650	11350	11750	15150
Grand Touring Rdstr	BZ36A	41875	10650	11350	11550	14650
NISMO Coupe 2D	BZ34D	38695	****	****	****	17150

2008 NISSAN — (1N4,JN1or3N1)(BC11E)-8-#

Body Type	VIN	List	Trade-In Good	Very Good	Pvt-Party Good	Retail Excellent
VERSA—4-Cyl.—Equipment Schedule 6						
W.B. 102.4"; 1.8 Liter.						
S Sedan 4D	BC11E	14170	3625	4025	4850	7000
S Hatchback 4D	BC13E	14270	3750	4150	5025	7325
SL Sedan 4D	BC11E	16120	4250	4700	5400	7675
SL Hatchback 4D	BC13E	16470	4350	4800	5500	7800
Manual, 6-Spd w/Overdrive			(375)	(375)	(485)	(485)
SENTRA—4-Cyl.—Equipment Schedule 6						
W.B. 105.7"; 2.0 Liter.						
S Sedan 4D	AB61E	17730	4225	4525	5600	7875

Body Type	VIN	List	Trade-In Good	Very Good	Pvt-Party Good	Retail Excellent
Manual, 6-Spd			(375)	(375)	(515)	(515)
SENTRA—4-Cyl.—Equipment Schedule 6						
W.B. 105.7"; 2.0 Liter, 2.5 Liter.						
Sedan 4D	AB61E	16375	4025	4300	5425	7675
SL Sedan 4D	AB61E	19305	4675	5000	6050	8425
SE-R Sedan 4D	BB61E	20305	4850	5175	6150	8450
SE-R Spec V Sedan 4D	CB61E	20805	5475	5850	6800	9150
ALTIMA—4-Cyl.—Equipment Schedule 4						
W.B. 105.3", 109.3" (Sed); 2.5 Liter.						
2.5 Sedan 4D	AL21E	18855	5100	5500	6325	8550
2.5 S Sedan 4D	AL21E	21630	5550	5975	6925	9325
2.5 S Coupe 2D	AL24E	21650	6375	6875	7900	10650
SL			675	675	890	890
ALTIMA—4-Cyl. Hybrid—Equipment Schedule 4						
W.B. 109.3"; 2.5 Liter.						
Sedan 4D	CL21E	25695	6625	7125	8175	11050
ALTIMA—V6—Equipment Schedule 4						
W.B. 105.3", 109.3" (Sed); 3.5 Liter.						
3.5 SE Sedan 4D	BL21E	25630	7325	7875	8925	11950
3.5 SE Coupe 2D	BL24E	26050	8175	8775	9900	13300
3.5 SL Sedan 4D	BL21E	28905	7875	8475	9550	12800
MAXIMA—V6—Equipment Schedule 4						
W.B. 111.2"; 3.5 Liter.						
SE Sedan 4D	BA41E	28755	5950	6400	7200	9500
SL Sedan 4D	BA41E	31005	6700	7200	8025	10600
350Z—V6—Equipment Schedule 3						
W.B. 104.3"; 3.5 Liter.						
Coupe 2D	BZ34D	28605	8900	9400	10200	12800
Enthusiast Coupe 2D	BZ34D	31305	9750	10300	11050	13750
Enthusiast Roadster	BZ36A	37940	10800	11400	12050	14950
Touring Coupe 2D	BZ34D	33935	10900	11500	12100	14900
Touring Roadster 2D	BZ36A	42490	11100	11700	12350	15200
Grand Touring Cpe 2D	BZ34D	38400	11700	12300	13100	16300
Grand Touring Rdstr	BZ36A	42640	11800	12450	13000	15900
NISMO Coupe 2D	BZ34D	38775	****	****	****	18350

Body Type	VIN	List	Trade-In Good	Very Good	Pvt-Party Good	Retail Excellent
CUBE—4-Cyl.—Equipment Schedule 6						
W.B. 99.6"; 1.8 Liter.						
Wagon 4D	AZ28R	14770	4875	5150	6075	8000
SL Sport Wagon 4D	AZ28R	17570	6000	6350	7375	9575
Krom Sport Wagon	AZ28R	20150	6900	7325	8300	10650
CUBE—4-Cyl.—Equipment Schedule 6						
W.B. 99.6"; 1.8 Liter.						
S Sport Wagon 4D	AZ28T	16410	5575	5925	6950	9050
Manual, 6-Spd			(425)	(425)	(550)	(550)
VERSA—4-Cyl.—Equipment Schedule 6						
W.B. 102.4"; 1.6 Liter.						
Sedan 4D	CC11E	11685	3275	3550	4425	6250
Automatic, 4-Spd w/OD			325	325	445	445
VERSA—4-Cyl.—Equipment Schedule 6						
W.B. 102.4"; 1.8 Liter.						
S Sedan 4D	BC11E	14685	4200	4550	5500	7675
S Hatchback 4D	BC13E	14685	4200	4550	5625	7925
Manual, 6-Spd w/Overdrive			(400)	(400)	(520)	(520)
VERSA—4-Cyl.—Equipment Schedule 6						
W.B. 102.4"; 1.8 Liter.						
SL Sedan 4D	BC11E	16650	4875	5275	6125	8375
SL Hatchback 4D	BC13E	16870	4975	5375	6275	8625
SL FE Plus Hatchback	BC13E	17050	5125	5550	6450	8850
SENTRA—4-Cyl.—Equipment Schedule 6						
W.B. 105.7"; 2.0 Liter.						
Sedan 4D	AB61E	17425	4950	5250	6450	8600
S Sedan 4D	AB61E	18455	5100	5425	6650	8900
Manual, 6-Spd			(425)	(425)	(550)	(550)
SENTRA—4-Cyl.—Equipment Schedule 6						
W.B. 105.7"; 2.0 Liter, 2.5 Liter.						
FE Plus Sedan 4D	AB61E	18000	5050	5375	6550	8700
S FE Plus Sedan 4D	AB61E	19030	5300	5625	6825	9050
SR FE Plus Sedan 4D	AB61E	19480	5275	5600	6750	8925
SL Sedan 4D	AB61E	20355	5650	6000	7150	9425
SL FE Plus Sedan 4D	AB61E	20930	5875	6225	7425	9825
SE-R Sedan 4D	BB61E	21355	6250	6625	7725	10150

Body Type	VIN	List	Trade-In Good	Very Good	Pvt-Party Good	Retail Excellent
SE-R Spec V Sedan	CB61E	21855	6650	7025	8100	10600
ALTIMA—4-Cyl.—Equipment Schedule 4						
W.B. 105.3", 109.3" (Sed); 2.5 Liter.						
2.5 Sedan 4D	AL21E	20595	6275	6650	7725	10000
2.5 S Sedan 4D	AL21E	22235	6750	7150	8225	10650
2.5 S Coupe 2D	AL24E	22945	7725	8175	9375	12100
SL			775	775	1020	1020
ALTIMA—4-Cyl. Hybrid—Equipment Schedule 4						
W.B. 109.3"; 2.5 Liter.						
Sedan 4D	CL21E	27345	8075	8550	9800	12700
ALTIMA—V6—Equipment Schedule 4						
W.B. 105.3", 109.3" (Sed); 3.5 Liter.						
3.5 SE Sedan 4D	BL21E	26375	8700	9225	10450	13550
3.5 SE Coupe 2D	BL24E	27585	9525	10050	11400	14700
3.5 SL Sedan 4D	BL21E	30075	9225	9775	11050	14250
MAXIMA—V6—Equipment Schedule 4						
W.B. 109.3"; 3.5 Liter.						
S Sedan 4D	BA41E	29985	10100	10650	11400	14200
SV Sedan 4D	BA41E	32685	10400	11000	11800	14650
350Z—V6—Equipment Schedule 3						
W.B. 104.3"; 3.5 Liter.						
Enthusiast Roadster	BZ36A	38565	13000	13600	14450	17200
Touring Roadster 2D	BZ36A	40915	13250	13800	14600	17350
Grand Touring Rdstr	BZ36A	43265	14200	14850	15550	18350
370Z—V6—Equipment Schedule 4						
W.B. 100.4"; 3.7 Liter.						
Coupe 2D	AZ44E	30650	12300	12850	13750	16350
Touring Coupe 2D	AZ44E	35180	14600	15200	15850	18700
NISMO Coupe 2D	AZ44E	39850	****	****	****	22200
Sport Pkg			1075	1075	1190	1190
LEAF—AC Electric—Equipment Schedule 3						
W.B. 106.3".						
S Hatchback 4D	AZ0CP	29650	6600	6875	8150	9975
SV Hatchback 4D	AZ0CP	32670	7425	7750	9000	10900
SL Hatchback 4D	AZ0CP	35690	8250	8575	9775	11750
GT-R AWD—V6 Turbo—Equipment Schedule 2						
W.B. 109.5"; 3.8 Liter.						
Coupe 2D	AR54M	77840	36900	38200	39000	44600
Premium Coupe 2D	AR54F	80090	36300	37600	38400	44000

2010 NISSAN — (1,3orJ)N(1,4or6)(AZ2KT)-A-#

Body Type	VIN	List	Good	Very Good	Good	Excellent
CUBE—4-Cyl.—Equipment Schedule 6						
W.B. 99.6"; 1.8 Liter.						
S Sport Wagon 4D	AZ2KT	16750	6275	6600	7700	9800
Manual, 6-Spd w/Overdrive			(450)	(450)	(615)	(615)
CUBE—4-Cyl.—Equipment Schedule 6						
W.B. 99.6"; 1.8 Liter.						
Wagon 4D	AZ2KR	14710	5500	5775	6900	8800
SL Sport Wagon 4D	AZ2KR	17850	6875	7225	8275	10450
Krom Sport Wagon	AZ2KR	20840	8000	8400	9400	11750
VERSA—4-Cyl.—Equipment Schedule 6						
W.B. 102.4"; 1.6 Liter.						
Sedan 4D	CC1AE	11710	4225	4525	5575	7525
Automatic, 4-Spd w/OD			375	375	510	510
VERSA—4-Cyl.—Equipment Schedule 6						
W.B. 102.4"; 1.8 Liter.						
S Sedan 4D	BC1AE	14820	5225	5575	6550	8700
S Hatchback 4D	BC1CE	14870	5275	5625	6750	9100
Manual, 6-Spd w/Overdrive			(450)	(450)	(615)	(615)
VERSA—4-Cyl.—Equipment Schedule 6						
W.B. 102.4"; 1.8 Liter.						
SL Sedan 4D	BC1AE	16820	5950	6350	7350	9625
SL Hatchback 4D	BC1CE	17250	6425	6850	7825	10200
SENTRA—4-Cyl.—Equipment Schedule 6						
W.B. 105.7"; 2.0 Liter.						
Sedan 4D	AB6AP	17320	5850	6175	7350	9450
Manual, 6-Spd w/Overdrive			(450)	(450)	(615)	(615)
SENTRA—4-Cyl.—Equipment Schedule 6						
W.B. 105.7"; 2.0 Liter, 2.5 Liter.						
S Sedan 4D	AB6AP	17880	6100	6425	7800	10150
SR Sedan 4D	AB6AP	17880	6100	6425	7650	9850
SL Sedan 4D	AB6AP	19280	7150	7525	8800	11250
SE-R Sedan 4D	BB6AP	20300	7725	8125	9300	11750

Body Type	VIN	List	Trade-In Good	Very Good	Pvt-Party Good	Retail Excellent
SE-R Spec V Sedan	CB6AP	20800	8025	8425	9650	12250
ALTIMA—4-Cyl.—Equipment Schedule 4						
W.B. 105.3", 109.3" (Sed); 2.5 Liter.						
2.5 Sedan 4D	AL2AP	20620	7350	7675	8975	11250
2.5 S Sedan 4D	AL2AP	22560	7750	8100	9350	11700
2.5 S Coupe 2D	AL2EP	23660	8800	9200	10600	13250
SL			875	875	1125	1125
ALTIMA—4-Cyl. Hybrid—Equipment Schedule 4						
W.B. 109.3"; 2.5 Liter.						
Sedan 4D	CL2AP	27500	9250	9650	11050	13800
Premium Pkg			975	975	1280	1280
ALTIMA—V6—Equipment Schedule 4						
W.B. 105.3", 109.3" (Sed); 3.5 Liter.						
3.5 SR Sedan 4D	BL2AP	25240	9825	10250	11750	14700
3.5 SR Coupe 2D	BL2EP	27990	10550	11000	12550	15750
Premium Pkg			975	975	1265	1265
MAXIMA—V6—Equipment Schedule 4						
W.B. 109.3"; 3.5 Liter.						
S Sedan 4D	AA5AE	31180	11900	12400	13400	16150
SV Sedan 4D	AA5AE	33900	12200	12750	13750	16600
370Z—V6—Equipment Schedule 4						
W.B. 100.4"; 3.7 Liter.						
Coupe 2D	AZ4EE	30710	14750	15250	16350	18900
Roadster 2D	AZ4FH	37690	17650	18250	19100	21900
Touring Coupe 2D	AZ4EE	35380	16900	17500	18400	21100
Touring Roadster 2D	AZ4FH	42540	18450	19100	19800	22600
NISMO Coupe 2D	AZ4EE	39910	****	****	****	24600
Sport Pkg			1175	1175	1285	1285
GT-R AWD—V6 Twin Turbo—Equipment Schedule 4						
W.B. 109.4"; 3.8 Liter.						
Coupe 2D	AR5EF	81790	42400	43800	44600	50200
Premium Coupe 2D	AR5EF	84040	42300	43600	44500	50000

2011 NISSAN — (1,3orJ)N(1or4)(AZ2KT)-B-#

Body Type	VIN	List	Trade-In Good	Very Good	Pvt-Party Good	Retail Excellent
CUBE—4-Cyl.—Equipment Schedule 6						
W.B. 99.6"; 1.8 Liter.						
S Sport Wagon 4D	AZ2KT	17430	7250	7575	8725	10800
Manual, 6-Spd w/Overdrive			(500)	(500)	(645)	(645)
CUBE—4-Cyl.—Equipment Schedule 6						
W.B. 99.6"; 1.8 Liter.						
Wagon 4D	AZ2KR	15040	6300	6600	7700	9575
SL Sport Wagon 4D	AZ2KR	18500	8275	8675	9775	11950
S Krom Sport Wagon	AZ2KR	21940	9050	9475	10600	12950
VERSA—4-Cyl.—Equipment Schedule 6						
W.B. 102.4"; 1.6 Liter.						
Sedan 4D	CC1AP	11990	5100	5375	6550	8625
Automatic, 4-Spd w/OD			425	425	575	575
VERSA—4-Cyl.—Equipment Schedule 6						
W.B. 102.4"; 1.8 Liter.						
S Sedan 4D	BC1AP	15350	5875	6225	7375	9450
S Hatchback 4D	BC1CP	15300	6075	6425	7700	9975
Manual, 6-Spd w/Overdrive			(500)	(500)	(655)	(655)
VERSA—4-Cyl.—Equipment Schedule 6						
W.B. 102.4"; 1.8 Liter.						
SL Sedan 4D	BC1AP	17220	6875	7250	8325	10550
SL Hatchback 4D	BC1CP	17650	7225	7625	8850	11300
SENTRA—4-Cyl.—Equipment Schedule 6						
W.B. 105.7"; 2.0 Liter.						
Sedan 4D	AB6AP	17104	7050	7375	8600	10800
Manual, 6-Spd w/Overdrive			(500)	(500)	(655)	(655)
SENTRA—4-Cyl.—Equipment Schedule 6						
W.B. 105.7"; 2.0 Liter, 2.5 Liter.						
S Sedan 4D	AB6AP	18200	7225	7575	8850	11150
SR Sedan 4D	AB6AP	18200	7250	7600	8950	11250
SL Sedan 4D	AB6AP	19600	8175	8550	9800	12150
SE-R Sedan 4D	BB6AP	20330	8650	9050	10250	12700
SE-R Spec V Sedan	CB6AP	20830	8950	9350	10500	12900
ALTIMA—4-Cyl.—Equipment Schedule 4						
W.B. 105.3", 109.3" (Sed); 2.5 Liter.						
2.5 Sedan 4D	AL2AP	20650	8575	8850	10300	12550
2.5 S Sedan 4D	AL2AP	22810	8950	9250	10750	13150
2.5 S Coupe 2D	AL2EP	24190	9950	10300	11950	14600
SL			900	900	1140	1140

Body Type	VIN	List	Trade-In Good	Very Good	Pvt-Party Good	Retail Excellent
ALTIMA—4-Cyl. Hybrid—Equipment Schedule 4						
W.B. 109.3"; 2.5 Liter.						
Sedan 4D	CL2AP	27530	10550	10900	12550	15300
Premium Pkg			1050	1050	1340	1340
ALTIMA—V6—Equipment Schedule 4						
W.B. 105.3", 109.3" (Sed); 3.5 Liter.						
3.5 SR Sedan 4D	BL2AP	25490	11100	11450	13100	16000
3.5 SR Coupe 2D	BL2EP	28520	11750	12150	14050	17250
Premium Pkg			1050	1050	1315	1315
MAXIMA—V6—Equipment Schedule 4						
W.B. 109.3"; 3.5 Liter.						
S Sedan 4D	AA5AP	31560	13300	13750	15050	17850
SV Sedan 4D	AA5AP	34280	13450	13900	15200	18000
370Z—V6—Equipment Schedule 4						
W.B. 100.4"; 3.7 Liter.						
Coupe 2D	AZ4EH	31360	16000	16450	17900	20400
Roadster 2D	AZ4FH	38270	18850	19350	20600	23400
Touring Coupe 2D	AZ4EH	36030	17950	18450	19750	22400
Touring Roadster 2D	AZ4FH	43150	19800	20300	21500	24300
NISMO Coupe 2D	AZ4EH	40740	****	****	****	26000
Sport Pkg			1250	1250	1390	1390
LEAF—AC Electric—Equipment Schedule 3						
W.B. 106.3".						
SV Hatchback 4D	AZ0CP	33600	4825	5075	6250	7900
SL Hatchback 4D	AZ0CP	34540	4725	4950	6150	7775
Quick Charge Port			525	525	695	695
GT-R AWD—V6 Twin Turbo—Equipment Schedule 2						
W.B. 109.4"; 3.8 Liter.						
Premium Coupe 2D	AR5EF	85060	47500	48800	49800	55200

2012 NISSAN — (1,3orJ)N(1,3or4)(AZ2KT)-C-#

Body Type	VIN	List	Trade-In Good	Very Good	Pvt-Party Good	Retail Excellent
CUBE—4-Cyl.—Equipment Schedule 6						
W.B. 99.6"; 1.8 Liter.						
S Sport Wagon 4D	AZ2KT	18200	8425	8800	10000	12200
Manual, 6-Spd			(525)	(525)	(690)	(690)
CUBE—4-Cyl.—Equipment Schedule 6						
W.B. 99.6"; 1.8 Liter.						
Wagon 4D	AZ2KT	15760	7000	7300	8525	10500
SL Sport Wagon 4D	AZ2KT	19300	9200	9600	10800	13000
VERSA—4-Cyl.—Equipment Schedule 6						
W.B. 102.4"; 1.6 Liter.						
S Sedan 4D	CN7AP	11750	6525	6825	8050	10150
Automatic, CVT			475	475	620	620
VERSA—4-Cyl.—Equipment Schedule 6						
W.B. 102.4"; 1.8 Liter.						
S Hatchback 4D	BC1CP	16260	7225	7550	8825	11050
Manual, 6-Spd			(525)	(525)	(710)	(710)
VERSA—4-Cyl.—Equipment Schedule 6						
W.B. 102.4"; 1.6 Liter, 1.8 Liter.						
SV Sedan 4D	CN7AP	15320	7025	7350	8500	10600
SL Sedan 4D	CN7AP	16320	7925	8275	9450	11650
SL Hatchback 4D	BC1CP	19150	8375	8775	9925	12250
SENTRA—4-Cyl.—Equipment Schedule 6						
W.B. 105.7"; 2.0 Liter.						
Sedan 4D	AB6AP	18210	7975	8325	9675	11900
Manual, 6-Spd			(525)	(525)	(705)	(705)
SENTRA—4-Cyl.—Equipment Schedule 6						
W.B. 105.7"; 2.0 Liter, 2.5 Liter.						
S Sedan 4D	AB6AP	18740	8125	8475	9775	12000
SR Sedan 4D	AB6AP	18740	8125	8475	9900	12250
SL Sedan 4D	AB6AP	20140	9025	9400	10550	12750
SE-R Sedan 4D	BB6AP	20870	10000	10450	11800	14350
SE-R Spec V Sedan 4D	CB6AP	21370	10400	10850	12150	14650
ALTIMA—4-Cyl.—Equipment Schedule 4						
W.B. 105.3", 109.3" (Sed); 2.5 Liter.						
2.5 Sedan 4D	AL2AP	21170	9625	9850	11450	13650
2.5 S Sedan 4D	AL2AP	23330	10000	10250	11900	14250
2.5 S Coupe 2D	AL2EP	24860	11150	11450	13350	16050
SL			900	900	1115	1115
ALTIMA—V6—Equipment Schedule 4						
W.B. 105.3", 109.3" (Sed); 3.5 Liter.						
3.5 SR Sedan 4D	BL2AP	26190	12350	12700	14550	17350
3.5 SR Coupe 2D	BL2EP	29190	13200	13550	15700	18850

Body Type	VIN	List	Trade-In Good	Very Good	Pvt-Party Good	Retail Excellent
Premium Pkg	....	....	1100	1100	1380	1380
MAXIMA—V6—Equipment Schedule 4						
W.B. 109.3"; 3.5 Liter.						
S Sedan 4D	AA5AP	32510	13750	14100	15850	18550
SV Sedan 4D	AA5AP	35210	14850	15200	16950	19850
Premium Pkg	....	....	575	575	690	690
Sport Pkg	....	....	325	325	385	385
370Z—V6—Equipment Schedule 4						
W.B. 100.4"; 3.7 Liter.						
Coupe 2D	AZ4EH	32210	18350	18750	20400	22900
Roadster 2D	AZ4FH	40260	21500	22000	23400	26000
Touring Coupe 2D	AZ4EH	36910	20100	20600	22100	24700
Touring Roadster 2D	AZ4FH	44280	22300	22800	24300	26900
NISMO Coupe 2D	AZ4EH	41590	23400	24000	25500	28300
Sport Pkg	....	....	1325	1325	1465	1465
LEAF—AC Electric—Equipment Schedule 3						
W.B. 106.3".						
SV Hatchback 4D	AZ0CP	36050	5750	6000	7200	8925
SL Hatchback 4D	AZ0CP	38100	5825	6075	7275	9000
GT-R AWD—V6 Twin Turbo—Equipment Schedule 2						
W.B. 109.4"; 3.8 Liter.						
Premium Coupe 2D	AR5EF	90950	54400	55800	56700	62100
Black Edition Coupe	AR5EF	96100	55200	56700	57500	62900

2013 NISSAN — (1,3orJ)N(1,3or4)(AZ2KT)–D–#

Body Type	VIN	List	Trade-In Good	Very Good	Pvt-Party Good	Retail Excellent
CUBE—4-Cyl.—Equipment Schedule 6						
W.B. 99.6"; 1.8 Liter.						
S Wagon 4D	AZ2KT	18450	9400	9775	11100	13300
Manual, 6-Spd	....	....	(550)	(550)	(695)	(695)
CUBE—4-Cyl.—Equipment Schedule 6						
W.B. 99.6"; 1.8 Liter.						
SL Wagon 4D	AZ2KT	19650	10250	10650	11850	14150
VERSA—4-Cyl.—Equipment Schedule 6						
W.B. 102.4"; 1.6 Liter, 1.8 Liter.						
S Sedan 4D	CN7AP	12770	7600	7900	9175	11250
S Plus Sedan 4D	CN7AP	14470	7825	8125	9325	11400
SV Sedan 4D	CN7AP	15770	8075	8400	9675	11850
SL Sedan 4D	CN7AP	17700	9050	9425	10550	12800
SENTRA—4-Cyl.—Equipment Schedule 6						
W.B. 106.3"; 1.8 Liter.						
FE+ Sedan 4D	AB7AP	18440	9500	9875	11100	13300
FE+ SV Sedan 4D	AB7AP	18600	9575	9975	11200	13350
SV Sedan 4D	AB7AP	18750	9700	10100	11350	13500
SR Sedan 4D	AB7AP	19650	10350	10750	12000	14250
SL Sedan 4D	AB7AP	20540	11000	11450	12700	15000
SENTRA—4-Cyl.—Equipment Schedule 6						
W.B. 106.3"; 1.8 Liter.						
S Sedan 4D	AB7AP	18040	9400	9775	11100	13300
Manual, 6-Spd	....	....	(550)	(550)	(695)	(695)
ALTIMA—4-Cyl.—Equipment Schedule 4						
W.B. 105.3", 109.3" (Sed); 2.5 Liter.						
2.5 Sedan 4D	AL3AP	22280	11200	11450	13100	15300
2.5 S Sedan 4D	AL3AP	23280	11550	11800	13550	15900
2.5 S Coupe 2D	AL2EP	25760	12350	12600	14450	16950
2.5 SV Sedan 4D	AL3AP	24880	12250	12500	14350	16850
2.5 SL Sedan 4D	AL3AP	28830	14050	14350	16350	19150
Premium Pkg	....	....	1150	1150	1435	1435
ALTIMA—V6—Equipment Schedule 4						
W.B. 105.3", 109.3" (Sed); 3.5 Liter.						
3.5 S Sedan 4D	BL3AP	26140	13450	13750	15800	18550
3.5 SV Sedan 4D	BL3AP	28560	13850	14150	16250	19050
3.5 SL Sedan 4D	BL3AP	30860	14750	15050	17050	19950
MAXIMA—V6—Equipment Schedule 4						
W.B. 109.3"; 3.5 Liter.						
S Sedan 4D	AA5AP	33560	14350	14650	16700	19600
SV Sedan 4D	AA5AP	35860	15550	15900	18150	21400
Premium Pkg	....	....	600	600	720	720
Sport Pkg	....	....	350	350	415	415
370Z—V6—Equipment Schedule 4						
W.B. 100.4"; 3.7 Liter.						
Coupe 2D	AZ4EH	33900	20500	20900	22800	25300
Roadster 2D	AZ4FH	42250	23500	24000	25800	28500
Touring Coupe 2D	AZ4EH	38600	22300	22700	24400	27100

2013 NISSAN

Body Type	VIN	List	Trade-In Good	Very Good	Pvt-Party Good	Retail Excellent
Touring Roadster 2D	AZ4FH	44950	**24400**	**24800**	**26600**	**29400**
NISMO Coupe 2D	AZ4EH	43800	**25500**	**26000**	**27800**	**30600**
Sport Pkg			1400	1400	1555	1555

LEAF—AC Electric—Equipment Schedule 3
W.B. 106.3".

S Hatchback 4D	AZ0CP	29650	**6600**	**6875**	**8150**	**9975**
SV Hatchback 4D	AZ0CP	32670	**7425**	**7750**	**9000**	**10900**
SL Hatchback 4D	AZ0CP	35690	**8250**	**8575**	**9775**	**11750**
Quick Charge Port			575	575	745	745

GT-R AWD—V6 Twin Turbo—Equipment Schedule 2
W.B. 109.4"; 3.8 Liter.

Premium Coupe 2D	AR5EF	97820	**59600**	**61100**	**61900**	**67300**
Black Edition Coupe	AR5EF	107320	**60400**	**61900**	**62700**	**68100**

2014 NISSAN — (1,3orJ)N(1,3or4)(AZ2KR)-E-#

CUBE—4-Cyl.—Equipment Schedule 6
W.B. 99.6"; 1.8 Liter.

S Wagon 4D	AZ2KR	18570	**10700**	**11150**	**12350**	**14600**
Manual, 6-Spd			(550)	(550)	(675)	(675)

CUBE—4-Cyl.—Equipment Schedule 6
W.B. 99.6"; 1.8 Liter.

SL Wagon 4D	AZ2KR	19670	**11450**	**11900**	**13100**	**15450**

VERSA—4-Cyl.—Equipment Schedule 6
W.B. 102.4"; 1.6 Liter.

S Sedan 4D	CN7AP	12780	**7950**	**8275**	**9525**	**11600**
Automatic, 4-Spd			525	525	675	675

VERSA—4-Cyl.—Equipment Schedule 6
W.B. 102.4"; 1.6 Liter.

S Plus Sedan 4D	CN7AP	14580	**8025**	**8350**	**9600**	**11700**
SV Sedan 4D	CN7AP	16030	**8675**	**9025**	**10250**	**12450**
SL Sedan 4D	CN7AP	17680	**9725**	**10100**	**11300**	**13550**
Note S Hatchback 4D	CE2CP	14800	**8400**	**8725**	**9925**	**12050**
Note S Plus H'Back 4D	CE2CP	16050	**8775**	**9125**	**10350**	**12550**
Note SV Hatchback 4D	CE2CP	16800	**9075**	**9450**	**10600**	**12800**

SENTRA—4-Cyl.—Equipment Schedule 6
W.B. 106.3"; 1.8 Liter.

S Sedan 4D	AB7AP	17600	**10000**	**10400**	**11700**	**14000**
Manual, 6-Spd			(550)	(550)	(680)	(680)

SENTRA—4-Cyl.—Equipment Schedule 6
W.B. 106.3"; 1.8 Liter.

FE+ S Sedan 4D	AB7AP	18000	**10250**	**10700**	**11900**	**14050**
FE+ SV Sedan 4D	AB7AP	18700	**10800**	**11250**	**12450**	**14700**
SR Sedan 4D	AB7AP	19500	**11350**	**11800**	**13100**	**15550**
SV Sedan 4D	AB7AP	18300	**10550**	**11000**	**12150**	**14350**
SL Sedan 4D	AB7AP	20400	**11800**	**12250**	**13500**	**15950**

ALTIMA—4-Cyl.—Equipment Schedule 4
W.B. 109.3"; 2.5 Liter.

2.5 Sedan 4D	AL3AP	22670	**12050**	**12350**	**13950**	**16150**
2.5 S Sedan 4D	AL3AP	23190	**12650**	**12900**	**14600**	**16950**
2.5 SV Sedan 4D	AL3AP	24990	**13300**	**13600**	**15500**	**18050**
2.5 SL Sedan 4D	AL3AP	28570	**15650**	**15950**	**17950**	**20800**

ALTIMA—V6—Equipment Schedule 4
W.B. 109.3"; 3.5 Liter.

3.5 S Sedan 4D	BL3AP	26970	**15150**	**15450**	**17450**	**20300**
3.5 SV Sedan 4D	BL3AP	29170	**15750**	**16050**	**18050**	**21000**
3.5 SL Sedan 4D	BL3AP	31470	**16650**	**17000**	**18950**	**21900**

MAXIMA—V6—Equipment Schedule 4
W.B. 109.3"; 3.5 Liter.

S Sedan 4D	AA5AP	31810	**15850**	**16150**	**18200**	**21100**
SV Sedan 4D	AA5AP	34900	**18950**	**19350**	**21600**	**25200**
Premium Pkg			625	625	745	745
Sport Pkg			375	375	440	440

370Z—V6—Equipment Schedule 4
W.B. 100.4"; 3.7 Liter.

Coupe 2D	AZ4EH	30800	**22300**	**22700**	**24600**	**27300**
Roadster 2D	AZ4FH	42280	**25300**	**25700**	**27600**	**30500**
Touring Coupe 2D	AZ4EH	36080	**23900**	**24400**	**26200**	**28900**
Touring Roadster 2D	AZ4FH	46280	**26100**	**26600**	**28400**	**31200**
NISMO Coupe 2D	AZ4EH	43830	**27300**	**27800**	**29600**	**32500**
Sport Pkg			1475	1475	1645	1645

LEAF—AC Electric—Equipment Schedule 3
W.B. 106.3".

S Hatchback 4D	AZ0CP	29830	**9250**	**9625**	**10800**	**12850**

Body Type	VIN	List	Trade-In Good	Trade-In Very Good	Pvt-Party Good	Retail Excellent
SV Hatchback 4D	AZ0CP	32850	11600	12100	13100	15300
SL Hatchback 4D	AZ0CP	35870	12350	12850	13900	16100
Quick Charge Port			625	625	750	750
GT-R AWD—V6 Twin Turbo—Equipment Schedule 2						
W.B. 109.4"; 3.8 Liter.						
Premium Coupe 2D	AR5EF	100590	64900	66500	67100	72600
Black Edition Coupe	AR5EF	110330	65700	67300	67900	73400
Track Edition Coupe	AR5EF	116710	65900	67500	68100	73600
Special Edition Pkg			2475	2475	2610	2610

OLDSMOBILE

2000 OLDSMOBILE — (1or2)G3(NK52T)-Y-#

ALERO—4-Cyl.—Equipment Schedule 5
W.B. 107.0"; 2.4 Liter.

Body Type	VIN	List	Good	Very Good	Good	Excellent
GX Sedan 4D	NK52T	16995	425	525	1050	1900
GX Coupe 2D	NK12T	16995	425	525	1050	1900
GL Sedan 4D	NL52T	18185	650	750	1350	2425
GL Coupe 2D	NL12T	18185	575	700	1275	2275
V6, 3.4 Liter	E		100	100	145	145

ALERO—V6—Equipment Schedule 4
W.B. 107.0"; 3.4 Liter.

Body Type	VIN	List	Good	Very Good	Good	Excellent
GLS Sedan 4D	NF52E	21900	900	1075	1775	3200
GLS Coupe 2D	NF12E	21900	850	1000	1700	3100

INTRIGUE—V6—Equipment Schedule 4
W.B. 109.0"; 3.5 Liter.

Body Type	VIN	List	Good	Very Good	Good	Excellent
GX Sedan 4D	WH52H	22650	800	925	1475	2650
GL Sedan 4D	WS52H	24280	925	1100	1625	2900
GLS Sedan 4D	WX52H	26280	1325	1550	2100	3700
Sterling Edition			25	25	45	45

2001 OLDSMOBILE — 1G3(NK52T)-1-#

ALERO—4-Cyl.—Equipment Schedule 5
W.B. 107.0"; 2.4 Liter.

Body Type	VIN	List	Good	Very Good	Good	Excellent
GX Sedan 4D	NK52T	17785	525	625	1200	2175
GX Coupe 2D	NK12T	17785	550	650	1250	2250
GL Sedan 4D	NL52T	19195	650	750	1375	2475
GL Coupe 2D	NL12T	19195	600	700	1300	2325
V6, 3.4 Liter	E		125	125	165	165

ALERO—V6—Equipment Schedule 4
W.B. 107.0"; 3.4 Liter.

Body Type	VIN	List	Good	Very Good	Good	Excellent
GLS Sedan 4D	NF52E	22540	1025	1175	1875	3350
GLS Coupe 2D	NF12E	22765	950	1100	1775	3175

INTRIGUE—V6—Equipment Schedule 4
W.B. 109.0"; 3.5 Liter.

Body Type	VIN	List	Good	Very Good	Good	Excellent
GX Sedan 4D	WH52H	22995	1050	1250	1775	3125
GL Sedan 4D	WS52H	24750	1400	1650	2175	3775
GLS Sedan 4D	WX52H	27115	1700	2000	2625	4500

AURORA—V6—Equipment Schedule 2
W.B. 112.2"; 3.5 Liter.

Body Type	VIN	List	Good	Very Good	Good	Excellent
Sedan 4D	GR64H	31579	1000	1175	1825	3100

AURORA—V8—Equipment Schedule 2
W.B. 112.2"; 4.0 Liter.

Body Type	VIN	List	Good	Very Good	Good	Excellent
Sedan 4D	GS64C	35314	1850	2125	2775	4600

2002 OLDSMOBILE — 1G3(NK52T)-2-#

ALERO—4-Cyl.—Equipment Schedule 5
W.B. 107.0"; 2.2 Liter.

Body Type	VIN	List	Good	Very Good	Good	Excellent
GX Sedan 4D	NK52T	18055	625	750	1375	2500
GX Coupe 2D	NK12T	18055	625	750	1375	2500
GL Sedan 4D	NL52T	20040	750	875	1525	2725
GL Coupe 2D	NL12T	20265	675	775	1425	2550
V6, 3.4 Liter	E		150	150	185	185

ALERO—V6—Equipment Schedule 4
W.B. 107.0"; 3.4 Liter.

Body Type	VIN	List	Good	Very Good	Good	Excellent
GLS Sedan 4D	NF52E	22675	1100	1250	2025	3625
GLS Coupe 2D	NF12E	22900	1000	1150	1900	3400

INTRIGUE—V6—Equipment Schedule 4
W.B. 109.0"; 3.5 Liter.

Body Type	VIN	List	Good	Very Good	Good	Excellent
GX Sedan 4D	WH52H	23427	1400	1625	2300	3975
GL Sedan 4D	WS52H	25012	1725	2000	2675	4575

Body Type	VIN	List	Trade-In Good	Very Good	Pvt-Party Good	Retail Excellent
GLS Sedan 4D	WX52H	28502	2100	2425	3125	5300

AURORA—V6—Equipment Schedule 2
W.B. 112.2"; 3.5 Liter.

| Sedan 4D | GR64H | 31665 | 1400 | 1600 | 2300 | 3875 |

AURORA—V8—Equipment Schedule 2
W.B. 112.2"; 4.0 Liter.

| Sedan 4D | GS64C | 35660 | 2125 | 2450 | 3125 | 5175 |

2003 OLDSMOBILE — 1G3(NK52F)-3-#

ALERO—4-Cyl.—Equipment Schedule 5
W.B. 107.0"; 2.2 Liter.

GX Sedan 4D	NK52F	18335	750	850	1525	2675
GX Coupe 2D	NK12F	18335	725	825	1475	2600
GL Sedan 4D	NL52F	20175	825	950	1600	2825
GL Coupe 2D	NL12F	20175	825	950	1600	2825
V6, 3.4 Liter	E		150	150	205	205

ALERO—V6—Equipment Schedule 4
W.B. 107.0"; 3.4 Liter.

| GLS Sedan 4D | NF52E | 22755 | 1400 | 1600 | 2400 | 4175 |
| GLS Coupe 2D | NF12E | 23005 | 1250 | 1425 | 2200 | 3850 |

AURORA—V8—Equipment Schedule 2
W.B. 112.2"; 4.0 Liter.

| Sedan 4D | GS64C | 34775 | 2500 | 2850 | 3500 | 5625 |

2004 OLDSMOBILE — 1G3(NK52F)-4-#

ALERO—4-Cyl.—Equipment Schedule 5
W.B. 107.0"; 2.2 Liter.

GX Sedan 4D	NK52F	18825	900	1050	1725	2975
GX Coupe 2D	NK12F	18825	800	925	1600	2750
GL Sedan 4D	NL52F	20775	1025	1150	1900	3300
GL Coupe 2D	NL12F	20775	1025	1150	1900	3300
V6, 3.4 Liter	E		175	175	225	225

ALERO—V6—Equipment Schedule 4
W.B. 107.0"; 3.4 Liter.

| GLS Sedan 4D | NF52E | 23425 | 1625 | 1825 | 2775 | 4700 |
| GLS Coupe 2D | NF12E | 23675 | 1525 | 1725 | 2550 | 4350 |

PLYMOUTH

2000 PLYMOUTH — (1or3)P3(EorH)(S46C)-Y-#

NEON—4-Cyl.—Equipment Schedule 6
W.B. 105.0"; 2.0 Liter.

| Highline Sedan 4D | S46C | 13890 | 450 | 575 | 1025 | 1825 |
| LX Sedan 4D | S46C | 14680 | 575 | 725 | 1300 | 2425 |

BREEZE—4-Cyl.—Equipment Schedule 5
W.B. 108.0"; 2.0 Liter, 2.4 Liter.

| Sedan 4D | J46C | 17525 | 250 | 250 | 1000 | 2000 |

PROWLER—V6—Equipment Schedule 1
W.B. 113.3"; 3.5 Liter.

| Roadster 2D | W65G | 43500 | 13500 | 14350 | 14250 | 17900 |

2001 PLYMOUTH — 1P3(EorH)(S46C)-1-#

NEON—4-Cyl.—Equipment Schedule 6
W.B. 105.0"; 2.0 Liter.

| Highline Sedan 4D | S46C | 14275 | 500 | 625 | 1100 | 1950 |
| LX Sedan 4D | S46C | 15095 | 625 | 775 | 1375 | 2525 |

PONTIAC

2000 PONTIAC — (1,2,3or4)G2(JB524)-Y-#

SUNFIRE—4-Cyl.—Equipment Schedule 5
W.B. 104.1"; 2.2 Liter, 2.4 Liter.

SE Sedan 4D	JB524	15120	450	575	1025	1900
SE Coupe 2D	JB124	15020	400	500	950	1775
GT Coupe 2D	JD12T	17530	725	875	1425	2625
GT Convertible 2D	JD32T	22120	1100	1300	1925	3525

GRAND AM—4-Cyl.—Equipment Schedule 5
W.B. 107.0"; 2.4 Liter.

2000 PONTIAC

Body Type	VIN	List	Trade-In Good	Very Good	Pvt-Party Good	Retail Excellent
SE Coupe 2D	NE12T	17240	625	750	1300	2325
V6, 3.4 Liter	E		125	125	165	165
GRAND AM—V6—Equipment Schedule 5						
W.B. 107.0'; 3.4 Liter.						
SE Sedan 4D	NE52T	17540	750	875	1475	2650
4-Cyl, 2.4 Liter	T		(125)	(125)	(155)	(155)
GRAND AM—V6—Equipment Schedule 5						
W.B. 107.0'; 3.4 Liter.						
GT Sedan 4D	NW52E	20385	1050	1225	1850	3275
GT Coupe 2D	NW12E	20085	1000	1175	1800	3175
FIREBIRD—V6—Equipment Schedule 4						
W.B. 101.1'; 3.8 Liter.						
Coupe 2D	FS22K	20535	1400	1550	1950	2950
Convertible 2D	FS32K	26460	2975	3300	3675	5425
T-Bar Roof			225	225	300	300
Manual, 5-Spd			(175)	(175)	(220)	(220)
FIREBIRD—V8—Equipment Schedule 4						
W.B. 101.1'; 5.7 Liter.						
Formula Coupe 2D	FV22G	24055	3200	3550	3925	5750
Trans Am Coupe 2D	FV22G	27165	4075	4500	4775	7000
Trans Am Conv 2D	FV32G	31235	5625	6200	6550	9500
T-Bar Roof			225	225	280	280
Ram Air Handling Pkg			425	425	535	535
GRAND PRIX—V6—Equipment Schedule 4						
W.B. 110.5'; 3.8 Liter.						
SE Sedan 4D	WJ52K	20610	475	575	1225	2300
GT Sedan 4D	WP52K	22105	775	925	1625	2975
GT Coupe 2D	WP12K	21955	700	825	1525	2800
V6, 3.1 Liter	J		(175)	(175)	(245)	(245)
GRAND PRIX—V6 Supercharged—Equipment Schedule 4						
W.B. 110.5'; 3.8 Liter.						
GTP Sedan 4D	WR521	24870	1250	1450	2225	4000
GTP Coupe 2D	WR121	24720	1200	1375	2175	3900
BONNEVILLE—V6—Equipment Schedule 4						
W.B. 112.2'; 3.8 Liter.						
SE Sedan 4D	HX52K	24295	750	875	1450	2550
SLE Sedan 4D	HY52K	27995	1150	1325	1950	3400
SSEi Sedan 4D	HZ52K	32250	1475	1700	2375	4125
V6, Supercharged, 3.8L	1		150	150	185	185

2001 PONTIAC — (1,2or3)G(2or7)(JB524)-1-#

Body Type	VIN	List	Trade-In Good	Very Good	Pvt-Party Good	Retail Excellent
SUNFIRE—4-Cyl.—Equipment Schedule 5						
W.B. 104.1'; 2.2 Liter, 2.4 Liter.						
SE Sedan 4D	JB524	15650	475	575	1150	2175
SE Coupe 2D	JB124	15395	425	525	1075	2050
GT Coupe 2D	JD12T	17625	725	875	1475	2725
GRAND AM—4-Cyl.—Equipment Schedule 5						
W.B. 107.0'; 2.4 Liter.						
SE Sedan 4D	NE12T	17500	725	850	1475	2650
V6, 3.4 Liter	E		125	125	165	165
GRAND AM—V6—Equipment Schedule 5						
W.B. 107.0'; 3.4 Liter.						
SE Sedan 4D	NE52E	17800	925	1100	1750	3075
4-Cyl, 2.4 Liter	T		(125)	(125)	(175)	(175)
GRAND AM—V6—Equipment Schedule 5						
W.B. 107.0'; 3.4 Liter.						
GT Sedan 4D	NW52E	21110	1375	1575	2275	3950
GT Coupe 2D	NW12E	20810	1350	1550	2250	3900
FIREBIRD—V6—Equipment Schedule 4						
W.B. 101.1'; 3.8 Liter.						
Coupe 2D	FS22K	20810	1725	1900	2275	3375
Convertible 2D	FS32K	26735	3500	3875	4200	6075
T-Bar Roof			225	225	290	290
Manual, 5-Spd			(150)	(150)	(190)	(190)
75th Anniversary			275	275	355	355
FIREBIRD—V8—Equipment Schedule 4						
W.B. 101.1'; 5.7 Liter.						
Formula Coupe 2D	FV22G	24480	3925	4325	4625	6675
Trans Am Coupe 2D	FV22G	27590	4925	5425	5775	8325
Trans Am Conv 2D	FV32G	31660	6675	7350	7625	10900
T-Bar Roof			225	225	275	275
Ram Air Handling Pkg			475	475	595	595
75th Anniversary			275	275	340	340

Body Type	VIN	List	Trade-In Good	Very Good	Pvt-Party Good	Retail Excellent
NHRA Pkg			150	150	170	170
GRAND PRIX—V6—Equipment Schedule 4						
W.B. 110.5"; 3.1 Liter, 3.8 Liter.						
SE Sedan 4D	WJ52J	21135	600	700	1375	2550
GT Sedan 4D	WP52K	22615	1000	1175	1925	3425
GT Coupe 2D	WP12K	22465	925	1075	1825	3275
Special Edition			75	75	100	100
GRAND PRIX—V6 Supercharged—Equipment Schedule 4						
W.B. 110.5"; 3.8 Liter.						
GTP Sedan 4D	WR521	26135	1425	1625	2475	4425
GTP Coupe 2D	WR121	25935	1475	1700	2525	4450
Special Edition			75	75	100	100
BONNEVILLE—V6—Equipment Schedule 4						
W.B. 112.2"; 3.8 Liter.						
SE Sedan 4D	HX52K	25730	850	1000	1625	2850
SLE Sedan 4D	HY52K	28700	1300	1500	2175	3800
BONNEVILLE—V6 Supercharged—Equipment Schedule 4						
W.B. 112.2"; 3.8 Liter.						
SSEi Sedan 4D	HZ521	33070	1700	1950	2650	4500

2002 PONTIAC — (1or2)G2(JB524)-2-#

Body Type	VIN	List	Trade-In Good	Very Good	Pvt-Party Good	Retail Excellent
SUNFIRE—4-Cyl.—Equipment Schedule 5						
W.B. 104.1"; 2.2 Liter, 2.4 Liter.						
SE Sedan 4D	JB524	16545	500	625	1225	2300
SE Coupe 2D	JB124	16045	450	550	1150	2200
GT Coupe 2D	JD12T	18205	750	900	1550	2875
GRAND AM—4-Cyl.—Equipment Schedule 5						
W.B. 107.0"; 2.2 Liter.						
SE Coupe 2D	NE12T	18210	950	1100	1800	3175
V6, 3.4 Liter	E		150	150	185	185
GRAND AM—V6—Equipment Schedule 5						
W.B. 107.0"; 3.4 Liter.						
SE Sedan 4D	NE52E	20385	1200	1375	2075	3650
4-Cyl, 2.2 Liter	F		(175)	(175)	(220)	(220)
GRAND AM—V6—Equipment Schedule 5						
W.B. 107.0"; 3.4 Liter.						
GT Sedan 4D	NW52K	21425	1600	1825	2575	4425
GT Coupe 2D	NW12E	21275	1550	1775	2525	4325
FIREBIRD—V6—Equipment Schedule 4						
W.B. 101.1"; 3.8 Liter.						
Coupe 2D	FS22K	21105	2150	2375	2700	3925
Convertible 2D	FS32K	27205	4025	4425	4850	6900
T-Bar Roof			225	225	275	275
GT Pkg			150	150	185	185
Manual, 5-Spd.			(175)	(175)	(225)	(225)
FIREBIRD—V8—Equipment Schedule 4						
W.B. 101.1"; 5.7 Liter.						
Formula Coupe 2D	FV22G	26235	4600	5050	5400	7675
Trans Am Coupe 2D	FV22G	28265	6000	6575	6875	9675
Trans Am Conv 2D	FV32G	32335	7825	8550	8700	12200
T-Bar Roof			225	225	270	270
Collector Edition			300	300	360	360
NHRA Pkg			150	150	180	180
Ram Air Handling Pkg			550	550	665	665
GRAND PRIX—V6—Equipment Schedule 4						
W.B. 110.5"; 3.1 Liter, 3.8 Liter.						
SE Sedan 4D	WJ52J	21575	750	875	1600	2875
GT Sedan 4D	WP52K	23695	1125	1300	2150	3875
GT Coupe 2D	WP12K	23545	1050	1200	2050	3700
GRAND PRIX—V6 Supercharged—Equipment Schedule 4						
W.B. 110.5"; 3.8 Liter.						
GTP Sedan 4D	WR521	26415	1450	1675	2575	4550
GTP Coupe 2D	WR121	26235	1525	1750	2675	4725
BONNEVILLE—V6—Equipment Schedule 4						
W.B. 112.2"; 3.8 Liter.						
SE Sedan 4D	HX52K	26555	1100	1275	1850	3150
SLE Sedan 4D	HY52K	29545	1625	1850	2450	4125
BONNEVILLE—V6 Supercharged—Equipment Schedule 4						
W.B. 112.2"; 3.8 Liter.						
SSEi Sedan 4D	HZ521	33605	2025	2325	3125	5250

2003 PONTIAC

Body Type	VIN	List	Trade-In Good	Very Good	Pvt-Party Good	Retail Excellent

2003 PONTIAC — (1or5)G2orY2(JB12F)-3-#

SUNFIRE—4-Cyl.—Equipment Schedule 5
W.B. 104.1"; 2.2 Liter.

Coupe 2D	JB12F	15435	900	1050	1625	2900

VIBE—4-Cyl.—Equipment Schedule 6
W.B. 102.4"; 1.8 Liter.

Sport Wagon 4D	SL628	17700	2100	2425	3000	4975
GT Sport Wagon	SN62L	19900	2275	2600	3150	5175
AWD	M		575	575	775	775

GRAND AM—V6—Equipment Schedule 5
W.B. 107.0"; 3.4 Liter.

| SE Sedan 4D | NE52E | 20620 | 1425 | 1625 | 2450 | 4250 |
| 4-Cyl, 2.2 Liter | F | | (175) | (175) | (245) | (245) |

GRAND AM—V6—Equipment Schedule 5
W.B. 107.0"; 3.4 Liter.

| GT Sedan 4D | NW52E | 21640 | 1875 | 2125 | 3125 | 5375 |
| GT Coupe 2D | NW12E | 21640 | 1825 | 2075 | 3075 | 5275 |

GRAND PRIX—V6—Equipment Schedule 4
W.B. 110.5"; 3.1 Liter, 3.8 Liter.

| SE Sedan 4D | WK52J | 22140 | 850 | 975 | 1725 | 3075 |
| GT Sedan 4D | WP52K | 23990 | 1500 | 1700 | 2500 | 4325 |

GRAND PRIX—V6 Supercharged—Equipment Schedule 4
W.B. 110.5"; 3.8 Liter.

| GTP Sedan 4D | WR521 | 26800 | 1800 | 2050 | 2975 | 5075 |

BONNEVILLE—V6—Equipment Schedule 4
W.B. 112.2"; 3.8 Liter.

| SE Sedan 4D | HX52K | 26665 | 1500 | 1700 | 2250 | 3700 |
| SLE Sedan 4D | HY52K | 29855 | 1875 | 2150 | 2825 | 4625 |

BONNEVILLE—V6 Supercharged—Equipment Schedule 4
W.B. 112.2"; 3.8 Liter.

| SSEi Sedan 4D | HZ541 | 34085 | 2475 | 2800 | 3575 | 5875 |

2004 PONTIAC — (1,2,5or6)G2orY2(JB12F)-4-#

SUNFIRE—4-Cyl.—Equipment Schedule 5
W.B. 104.1"; 2.2 Liter.

Coupe 2D	JB12F	16695	1125	1300	1925	3425

VIBE—4-Cyl.—Equipment Schedule 5
W.B. 102.4" 1.8 Liter.

Sport Wagon 4D	SL628	17895	2375	2675	3225	5225
GT Sport Wagon	SN62L	19995	2725	3075	3550	5600
AWD	M		625	625	845	845

GRAND AM—V6—Equipment Schedule 5
W.B. 107.0"; 3.4 Liter.

| SE Sedan 4D | NE52E | 21210 | 1700 | 1925 | 2850 | 4850 |
| 4-Cyl, 2.2 Liter | F | | (200) | (200) | (265) | (265) |

GRAND AM—V6—Equipment Schedule 5
W.B. 107.0"; 3.4 Liter.

| GT Sedan 4D | NW52E | 22450 | 2350 | 2650 | 3625 | 6025 |
| GT Coupe 2D | NW12E | 22450 | 2250 | 2550 | 3500 | 5850 |

GRAND PRIX—V6—Equipment Schedule 4
W.B. 110.5"; 3.8 Liter.

| GT Sedan 4D | WP52K | 22395 | 2175 | 2450 | 3325 | 5500 |

GRAND PRIX—V6 Supercharged—Equipment Schedule 4
W.B. 110.5"; 3.8 Liter.

| GTP Sedan 4D | WR524 | 26495 | 2425 | 2725 | 3675 | 6075 |

BONNEVILLE—V6—Equipment Schedule 4
W.B. 112.2"; 3.8 Liter.

| SE Sedan 4D | HX52K | 27570 | 1900 | 2125 | 2800 | 4500 |
| SLE Sedan 4D | HY52K | 30420 | 2500 | 2825 | 3525 | 5625 |

BONNEVILLE—V8—Equipment Schedule 4
W.B. 112.2"; 4.6 Liter.

| GXP Sedan 4D | HZ54Y | 35995 | 3000 | 3375 | 4350 | 7100 |

GTO—V8—Equipment Schedule 2
W.B. 109.8"; 5.7 Liter.

| Coupe 2D | VX13G | 33495 | 5750 | 6250 | 6925 | 9825 |

2005 PONTIAC — (1,2,3,5or6)G2orY2(JB12F)-5-#

SUNFIRE—4-Cyl.—Equipment Schedule 5
W.B. 104.1"; 2.2 Liter.

Coupe 2D	JB12F	15650	1300	1500	2200	3675

Body Type	VIN	List	Trade-In Good	Very Good	Pvt-Party Good	Retail Excellent
VIBE—4-Cyl.—Equipment Schedule 6						
W.B. 102.4"; 1.8 Liter.						
Sport Wagon 4D	SL628	18325	**2700**	**3075**	**3700**	**5775**
GT Sport Wagon	SN62L	20535	**3350**	**3775**	**4225**	**6400**
AWD	M		**675**	**675**	**910**	**910**
GRAND AM—V6—Equipment Schedule 5						
W.B. 107.0"; 3.4 Liter.						
SE Sedan 4D	NE52K	21210	**1900**	**2150**	**3300**	**5450**
4-Cyl, 2.2 Liter	F		**(225)**	**(225)**	**(290)**	**(290)**
GRAND AM—V6—Equipment Schedule 5						
W.B. 107.0"; 3.4 Liter.						
GT Coupe 2D	NW12E	22990	**2575**	**2900**	**4075**	**6650**
GRAND PRIX—V6—Equipment Schedule 4						
W.B. 110.5"; 3.8 Liter.						
Sedan 4D	WP522	23560	**2300**	**2575**	**3625**	**5850**
GT Sedan 4D	WS522	25045	**2700**	**3025**	**4200**	**6850**
GRAND PRIX—V6 Supercharged—Equipment Schedule 4						
W.B. 110.5"; 3.8 Liter.						
GTP Sedan 4D	WR524	27220	**3400**	**3800**	**4900**	**7775**
GRAND PRIX—V8—Equipment Schedule 4						
W.B. 110.5"; 5.3 Liter.						
GXP Sedan 4D	WC52C	29995	**3375**	**3800**	**5150**	**8275**
G6—V6—Equipment Schedule 4						
W.B. 112.3"; 3.5 Liter.						
Sedan 4D	ZG528	21700	**2400**	**2700**	**3400**	**5225**
GT Sedan 4D	ZH528	23925	**2975**	**3350**	**4075**	**6250**
BONNEVILLE—V6—Equipment Schedule 4						
W.B. 112.2"; 3.8 Liter.						
SE Sedan 4D	HX52K	28650	**2350**	**2650**	**3425**	**5275**
SLE Sedan 4D	HY52K	31035	**3075**	**3425**	**4175**	**6400**
BONNEVILLE—V8—Equipment Schedule 4						
W.B. 112.2"; 4.6 Liter.						
GXP Sedan 4D	HZ54Y	36120	**3525**	**3950**	**5025**	**7825**
GTO—V8—Equipment Schedule 2						
W.B. 109.8"; 6.0 Liter.						
Coupe 2D	VX12U	34295	**7625**	**8225**	**9000**	**12450**

2006 PONTIAC — (1,2,3,5or6)G2orY2(SL658)-6-#

Body Type	VIN	List	Trade-In Good	Very Good	Pvt-Party Good	Retail Excellent
VIBE—4-Cyl.—Equipment Schedule 6						
W.B. 102.4"; 1.8 Liter.						
Sport Wagon 4D	SL658	17840	**3450**	**3850**	**4375**	**6550**
Manual, 5-Spd			**(275)**	**(275)**	**(355)**	**(355)**
AWD	M		**725**	**725**	**975**	**975**
VIBE—4-Cyl.—Equipment Schedule 6						
W.B. 102.4"; 1.8 Liter.						
GT Sport Wagon 4D	SN65L	21015	**4575**	**5100**	**5500**	**7975**
AWD	M		**725**	**725**	**975**	**975**
SOLSTICE—4-Cyl.—Equipment Schedule 6						
W.B. 95.1"; 2.4 Liter.						
Convertible 2D	MB35B	19995	**3425**	**3775**	**4650**	**6775**
GRAND PRIX—V6—Equipment Schedule 4						
W.B. 110.5"; 3.8 Liter.						
Sedan 4D	WP552	22990	**2800**	**3125**	**4050**	**6250**
GRAND PRIX—V6 Supercharged—Equipment Schedule 4						
W.B. 110.5"; 3.8 Liter.						
GT Sedan 4D	WR554	26745	**3400**	**3775**	**4800**	**7275**
GRAND PRIX—V8—Equipment Schedule 4						
W.B. 110.5"; 5.3 Liter.						
GXP Sedan 4D	WC55C	29395	**4350**	**4825**	**5950**	**9050**
G6—4-Cyl.—Equipment Schedule 4						
W.B. 112.3"; 2.4 Liter.						
Sedan 4D	ZG558	20655	**2750**	**3050**	**3775**	**5650**
V6, 3.5 Liter	8		**375**	**375**	**490**	**490**
G6—V6—Equipment Schedule 4						
W.B. 112.3"; 3.9 Liter.						
GT Sedan 4D	ZH558	23180	**3200**	**3575**	**4425**	**6575**
GT Coupe 2D	ZH158	22955	**3625**	**4025**	**4825**	**7100**
GT Hard Top Conv 2D	ZH358	28490	**4925**	**5450**	**6625**	**10050**
GTP Sedan 4D	ZM551	24815	**3975**	**4400**	**5275**	**7850**
GTP Coupe 2D	ZM151	24610	**4075**	**4525**	**5375**	**7950**
GTP Hard Top Conv	ZM351	29990	**5900**	**6525**	**7925**	**11950**
GTO—V8—Equipment Schedule 2						
W.B. 109.8"; 6.0 Liter.						

Body Type	VIN	List	Trade-In Good	Very Good	Pvt-Party Good	Retail Excellent
Coupe 2D	VX12U	32995	8725	9375	10100	13550

2007 PONTIAC — (1,2,3,5or6)G2orY2(SL658)-7-#

VIBE—4-Cyl.—Equipment Schedule 6
W.B. 102.4"; 1.8 Liter.

Sport Wagon 4D	SL658	17995	3925	4350	5000	7175
Manual, 5-Spd			(300)	(300)	(385)	(385)

SOLSTICE—4-Cyl.—Equipment Schedule 6
W.B. 95.1"; 2.4 Liter.

Convertible 2D	MB35B	22955	4225	4600	5450	7650
Automatic			300	300	375	375

SOLSTICE—4-Cyl. Turbo—Equipment Schedule 6
W.B. 95.1"; 2.0 Liter.

GXP Convertible 2D	MG35X	27955	5475	5975	6775	9375
Automatic			300	300	375	375

GRAND PRIX—V6—Equipment Schedule 4
W.B. 110.5"; 3.8 Liter.

Sedan 4D	WP552	22315	3675	4025	4875	7025

GRAND PRIX—V6 Supercharged—Equipment Schedule 4
W.B. 110.5"; 3.8 Liter.

GT Sedan 4D	WR554	25235	4400	4825	5650	8075

GRAND PRIX—V8—Equipment Schedule 4
W.B. 110.5"; 5.3 Liter.

GXP Sedan 4D	WC55C	29315	5425	5950	6975	10000

G5—4-Cyl.—Equipment Schedule 4
W.B. 103.5"; 2.2 Liter, 2.4 Liter.

Coupe 2D	AL15F	15845	2825	3175	3850	5850
GT Coupe 2D	AN15B	18645	3400	3850	4625	7000

G6—4-Cyl.—Equipment Schedule 4
W.B. 112.3"; 2.4 Liter.

Sedan 4D	ZG55B	19265	3250	3575	4325	6175
Sport Pkg			250	250	315	315

G6—V6—Equipment Schedule 4
W.B. 112.3"; 3.5 Liter, 3.6 Liter, 3.9 Liter.

GT Sedan 4D	ZH55N	22615	3900	4300	5075	7250
GT Coupe 2D	ZH15N	22415	4250	4675	5425	7725
GT Hard Top Conv 2D	ZH35N	29215	5725	6300	7575	11050
GTP Sedan 4D	ZM557	25115	4875	5325	6125	8750
GTP Coupe 2D	ZM157	24915	4875	5325	6125	8750
Sport Pkg			200	200	270	270

2008 PONTIAC–(1,2,3or6G2,5Y2orKL2)(SL658)-8-#

VIBE—4-Cyl.—Equipment Schedule 6
W.B. 102.4"; 1.8 Liter.

Sport Wagon 4D	SL658	18195	4700	5075	5800	7925
Manual, 5-Spd w/Overdrive	P		(350)	(350)	(460)	(460)

SOLSTICE—4-Cyl.—Equipment Schedule 6
W.B. 95.1"; 2.4 Liter.

Convertible 2D	MB35B	22295	5350	5750	6700	8925
Automatic, 5-Spd			300	300	375	375

SOLSTICE—4-Cyl. Turbo—Equipment Schedule 6
W.B. 95.1"; 2.0 Liter.

GXP Convertible 2D	MG35X	27895	6550	7025	8025	10750
Automatic, 5-Spd			300	300	385	385

GRAND PRIX—V6—Equipment Schedule 4
W.B. 110.5"; 3.8 Liter.

Sedan 4D	WP552	22500	4750	5100	6025	8275

GRAND PRIX—V8—Equipment Schedule 4
W.B. 110.5"; 5.3 Liter.

GXP Sedan 4D	WC55C	29500	6250	6725	7900	10800

G5—4-Cyl.—Equipment Schedule 4
W.B. 103.5"; 2.2 Liter, 2.4 Liter.

Coupe 2D	AL15F	16450	3200	3525	4425	6450
GT Coupe 2D	AS15B	20560	4025	4450	5325	7725

G6—4-Cyl.—Equipment Schedule 4
W.B. 112.3"; 2.4 Liter.

Sedan 4D	ZG55B	19995	4275	4600	5550	7675
Sport Pkg			250	250	340	340

G6—V6—Equipment Schedule 4
W.B. 112.3"; 3.5 Liter, 3.6 Liter, 3.9 Liter.

GT Sedan 4D	ZH55N	22995	4900	5275	6200	8475
GT Coupe 2D	ZH15N	22995	5075	5475	6600	9025

2008 PONTIAC

Body Type	VIN	List	Trade-In Good	Very Good	Pvt-Party Good	Retail Excellent
GT Hard Top Conv 2D	ZH35N	29995	6675	7175	8650	12100
GXP Sedan 4D	ZM557	27310	5925	6375	7650	10550
GXP Coupe 2D	ZM157	27105	6275	6775	7975	10950
Sport Pkg			225	225	290	290
G8—V6—Equipment Schedule 4						
W.B. 114.8"; 3.6 Liter.						
Sedan 4D	EC557	27595	9125	9625	10600	13400
G8—V8—Equipment Schedule 4						
W.B. 114.8"; 6.0 Liter.						
GT Sedan 4D	ER55Y	29995	11450	12100	13050	16400

2009 PONTIAC—(1,2,3or6G2,5Y2orKL2)(SP678)-9-#

	VIN	List	Good	Very Good	Good	Excellent
VIBE—4-Cyl.—Equipment Schedule 6						
W.B. 102.4"; 1.8 Liter, 2.4 Liter.						
Sport Wagon 4D	SP678	16745	5700	6050	7050	9125
GT Sport Wagon 4D	SR670	20945	7200	7625	8500	10800
Manual, 5-Spd w/Overdrive	L		(375)	(375)	(490)	(490)
AWD	M		1350	1350	1815	1815
SOLSTICE—4-Cyl.—Equipment Schedule 6						
W.B. 95.1"; 2.4 Liter.						
Coupe 2D	MB25B	26845	8075	8550	9450	11850
Convertible 2D	MB35B	23870	7150	7575	8550	10800
Street Ed Conv 2D	MK35B	30030	8875	9400	10400	13100
Automatic, 5-Spd			325	325	400	400
SOLSTICE—4-Cyl. Turbo—Equipment Schedule 6						
W.B. 95.1"; 2.0 Liter.						
GXP Coupe 2D	MG25X	30995	9625	10150	11100	13950
GXP Convertible 2D	MG35X	29080	8725	9250	10200	12800
Automatic, 5-Spd			325	325	400	400
G3—4-Cyl.—Equipment Schedule 6						
W.B. 97.6"; 1.6 Liter.						
Hatchback 4D	TD62E	14995	3350	3625	4425	6075
Automatic, 4-Spd w/OD			325	325	445	445
G5—4-Cyl.—Equipment Schedule 4						
W.B. 103.5"; 2.2 Liter.						
Coupe 2D	AS15H	17860	3800	4125	5025	6975
GT Coupe 2D	AT15H	21160	4800	5200	6250	8575
G6—4-Cyl.—Equipment Schedule 4						
W.B. 112.3"; 2.4 Liter.						
Sedan 4D	ZG55B	20295	5375	5700	6650	8525
Sport Pkg			275	275	350	350
G6—V6—Equipment Schedule 4						
W.B. 112.3"; 3.5 Liter, 3.6 Liter, 3.9 Liter.						
GT Sedan 4D	ZH55N	24095	6025	6375	7400	9525
GT Coupe 2D	ZH15N	23995	6225	6600	7600	9800
GT Hard Top Conv 2D	ZH35N	31785	7800	8250	9675	12750
GXP Sedan 4D	ZM557	28495	6950	7375	8600	11200
GXP Coupe 2D	ZM157	28395	7425	7875	9050	11700
Sport Pkg			225	225	305	305
G6 (2009.5)—4-Cyl.—Equipment Schedule 4						
W.B. 112.3"; 2.4 Liter.						
Sedan 4D	ZG55B	21835	5650	6000	6950	8925
Coupe 2D	ZJ15B	22890	6075	6425	7400	9475
G6 (2009.5)—V6—Equipment Schedule 4						
W.B. 112.3"; 3.5 Liter, 3.6 Liter, 3.9 Liter.						
GT Sedan 4D	ZK55K	25380	5875	6225	7275	9425
GT Coupe 2D	ZK15K	25280	6675	7050	8100	10450
GT Hard Top Conv 2D	ZH35N	32970	8550	9050	10550	13900
GXP Sedan 4D	ZM557	29730	7375	7800	9100	11850
GXP Coupe 2D	ZM157	29630	7900	8350	9625	12500
G8—V6—Equipment Schedule 4						
W.B. 114.8"; 3.6 Liter.						
Sedan 4D	ER577	27995	10900	11350	12500	15100
G8—V8—Equipment Schedule 4						
W.B. 114.8"; 6.0 Liter, 6.2 Liter.						
GT Sedan 4D	EC57Y	31360	13700	14250	15300	18450
GXP Sedan 4D	EP57W	39995	20700	21600	22000	25900

2010 PONTIAC — (1,5orK)(G,LorY)2(SP6E8)-A-#

	VIN	List	Good	Very Good	Good	Excellent
VIBE—4-Cyl.—Equipment Schedule 6						
W.B. 102.4"; 1.8 Liter, 2.4 Liter.						
Sport Wagon 4D	SP6E8	17585	6775	7075	8300	10450

Body Type	VIN	List	Trade-In Good	Very Good	Pvt-Party Good	Retail Excellent
Manual, 5-Spd w/Overdrive .... N			(450)	(450)	(610)	(610)
AWD .... M			1450	1450	1910	1910
VIBE—4-Cyl.—Equipment Schedule 6						
W.B. 102.4"; 2.4 Liter.						
GT Sport Wagon 4D	SR6E0	22560	8575	8950	10100	12400
Manual, 5-Spd w/Overdrive ...... N			(450)	(450)	(605)	(605)
G3—4-Cyl.—Equipment Schedule 6						
W.B. 97.6"; 1.6 Liter.						
Hatchback 4D	TD62E	14995	4550	4850	5675	7450
Automatic, 4-Spd w/OD			375	375	510	510
G6—4-Cyl.—Equipment Schedule 4						
W.B. 112.3"; 2.4 Liter.						
Sedan 4D	ZA5EB	21995	6850	7150	8400	10550

PORSCHE

Body Type	VIN	List	Good	Very Good	Good	Excellent
BOXSTER—6-Cyl.—Equipment Schedule 1						
W.B. 95.2"; 2.7 Liter, 3.2 Liter.						
Cabriolet 2D	CA298	44745	3475	3775	4725	6900
S Cabriolet 2D	CB298	53245	5250	5675	6500	9225
Full Leather			100	100	125	125
Hard Top			300	300	360	360
Aero Kit			1075	1075	1345	1345
Sport Design			300	300	380	380
Sport Touring Pkg			725	725	910	910
Automatic w/Tiptronic ..			300	300	370	370
911 CARRERA—6-Cyl.—Equipment Schedule 1						
W.B. 92.6"; 3.4 Liter.						
Coupe 2D	AA299	71375	9675	10400	11100	14650
Cabriolet 2D	CA299	80755	11200	12050	12500	16200
Full Leather			100	100	110	110
Hard Top (Cabriolet) ...			300	300	320	320
Aero Kit			1075	1075	1220	1220
Automatic w/Tiptronic ..			300	300	335	335
911 CARRERA 4 AWD—6-Cyl.—Equipment Schedule 1						
W.B. 92.6"; 3.4 Liter.						
Coupe 2D	AA299	76805	12250	13150	13400	17250
Cabriolet 2D	CA299	86185	11800	12700	13000	16800
Full Leather			100	100	110	110
Hard Top			300	300	320	320
Aero Kit			1075	1075	1200	1200
Millennium Pkg			2550	2550	2815	2815
Automatic w/Tiptronic ..			300	300	330	330

Body Type	VIN	List	Good	Very Good	Good	Excellent
BOXSTER—6-Cyl.—Equipment Schedule 1						
W.B. 95.2"; 2.7 Liter, 3.2 Liter.						
Cabriolet 2D	CA298	42865	3475	3775	4875	7175
S Cabriolet 2D	CB298	50965	5375	5800	6725	9525
Full Leather			100	100	125	125
Hard Top			300	300	370	370
Aero Kit			1175	1175	1440	1440
Sport Design			350	350	435	435
Sport Touring Pkg			850	850	1060	1060
Automatic w/Tiptronic ..			300	300	370	370
911 CARRERA—6-Cyl.—Equipment Schedule 1						
W.B. 92.6"; 3.4 Liter.						
Coupe 2D	AA299	70275	10300	11050	11700	15250
Cabriolet 2D	CA299	79775	11800	12700	13050	16800
Full Leather			100	100	110	110
Hard Top (Cabriolet) ...			300	300	330	330
Aero Kit			1175	1175	1300	1300
Automatic w/Tiptronic ..			300	300	335	335
911 CARRERA 4 AWD—6-Cyl.—Equipment Schedule 1						
W.B. 92.6"; 3.4 Liter.						
Coupe 2D	AA299	75320	12850	13800	14000	17850
Cabriolet 2D	CA299	84820	12400	13300	13600	17400
Full Leather			100	100	110	110
Hard Top (Cabriolet) ...			300	300	330	330
Aero Kit			1175	1175	1280	1280

2001 PORSCHE

Body Type	VIN	List	Trade-In Good	Very Good	Pvt-Party Good	Retail Excellent
Automatic w/Tiptronic			300	300	330	330
911 TURBO AWD—6-Cyl. Turbo—Equipment Schedule 1						
W.B. 92.5"; 3.6 Liter.						
Coupe 2D	AB299	111765	17250	18500	18050	22400
Full Leather			100	100	110	110
Aero Kit			1175	1175	1275	1275
Automatic w/Tiptronic			300	300	325	325

2002 PORSCHE — WP0(CA298)-2-#

Body Type	VIN	List	Trade-In Good	Very Good	Pvt-Party Good	Retail Excellent
BOXSTER—6-Cyl.—Equipment Schedule 1						
W.B. 95.2"; 2.7 Liter, 3.2 Liter.						
Cabriolet 2D	CA298	43365	4000	4325	5350	7700
S Cabriolet 2D	CB298	52365	5800	6250	7450	10650
Full Leather			100	100	125	125
Hard Top			325	325	410	410
Aero Kit			1275	1275	1605	1605
Sport Design			400	400	490	490
Sport Touring Pkg			1025	1025	1255	1255
Automatic w/Tiptronic			325	325	410	410
911 CARRERA—6-Cyl.—Equipment Schedule 1						
W.B. 92.6"; 3.6 Liter.						
Coupe 2D	AA299	73450	11400	12250	12750	16400
Targa 2D	AA299	75965	14800	15850	15850	19900
Cabriolet 2D	CA299	83150	12800	13750	14000	17800
Full Leather			100	100	110	110
Hard Top (Cabriolet)			325	325	365	365
Aero Kit			1275	1275	1405	1405
Automatic w/Tiptronic			325	325	370	370
911 CARRERA 4 AWD—6-Cyl.—Equipment Schedule 1						
W.B. 92.5" (4S), 92.6"; 3.6 Liter.						
4S Coupe 2D	AA299	80965	14000	15000	15050	19000
Cabriolet 2D	CA299	88750	14350	15400	15450	19450
Full Leather			100	100	110	110
Hard Top			325	325	365	365
Aero Kit			1275	1275	1385	1385
Automatic w/Tiptronic			325	325	365	365
911 TURBO AWD—6-Cyl. Turbo—Equipment Schedule 1						
W.B. 92.6"; 3.6 Liter.						
Coupe 2D	AB299	115765	18050	19350	18800	23200
Full Leather			100	100	110	110
Aero Kit			1275	1275	1380	1380
Automatic w/Tiptronic			325	325	360	360
911 TURBO—6-Cyl. Turbo—Equipment Schedule 1						
W.B. 92.6"; 3.6 Liter.						
GT2 Coupe 2D	AB299	180665	****	****	****	55100

2003 PORSCHE — WP0(CA298)-3-#

Body Type	VIN	List	Trade-In Good	Very Good	Pvt-Party Good	Retail Excellent
BOXSTER—6-Cyl.—Equipment Schedule 1						
W.B. 95.1"; 2.7 Liter, 3.2 Liter.						
Cabriolet 2D	CA298	45485	5025	5400	6400	8950
S Cabriolet 2D	CB298	54485	8250	8825	9850	13550
Full Leather			100	100	120	120
Hard Top			375	375	445	445
Aero Kit			1375	1375	1680	1680
Sport Design			450	450	535	535
Automatic w/Tiptronic			375	375	465	465
911 CARRERA—6-Cyl.—Equipment Schedule 1						
W.B. 92.6"; 3.6 Liter.						
Coupe 2D	AA299	72435	13750	14700	15000	18850
Targa 2D	BA299	79835	17100	18300	17950	22200
Cabriolet 2D	CA299	82235	15200	16250	16250	20300
Full Leather			100	100	110	110
Hard Top (Cabriolet)			375	375	395	395
Aero Kit			1375	1375	1490	1490
Automatic w/Tiptronic			375	375	420	420
911 CARRERA 4 AWD—6-Cyl.—Equipment Schedule 1						
W.B. 92.6"; 3.6 Liter.						
4S Coupe 2D	AA299	82565	17800	19000	18650	23000
Cabriolet 2D	CA299	87835	16700	17850	17600	21800
Full Leather			100	100	110	110
Hard Top			375	375	400	400
Aero Kit			1375	1375	1490	1490

Body Type	VIN	List	Trade-In Good	Very Good	Pvt-Party Good	Retail Excellent
Automatic w/Tiptronic			375	375	415	415

911 TURBO AWD—6-Cyl. Turbo—Equipment Schedule 1
W.B. 92.6"; 3.6 Liter.

Body Type	VIN	List	Good	Very Good	Good	Excellent
Coupe 2D	AB299	118265	19450	20800	20100	24600
Full Leather			100	100	110	110
Aero Kit			1375	1375	1485	1485
Automatic w/Tiptronic			375	375	415	415

911 TURBO—6-Cyl. Turbo—Equipment Schedule 1
W.B. 92.6"; 3.6 Liter.

Body Type	VIN	List	Good	Very Good	Good	Excellent
GT2 Coupe 2D	AB299	183765	****	****	****	60300

2004 PORSCHE — WPO(CA298)-4-#

BOXSTER—6-Cyl.—Equipment Schedule 1
W.B. 95.1"; 2.7 Liter, 3.2 Liter.

Body Type	VIN	List	Good	Very Good	Good	Excellent
Cabriolet 2D	CA298	45485	6050	6450	7425	10150
S Cabriolet 2D	CB298	54485	9900	10550	11500	15400
Full Leather			100	100	120	120
Hard Top			400	400	475	475
Aero Kit			1475	1475	1775	1775
Sport Design			475	475	585	585
Special Edition			775	775	940	940
Automatic w/Tiptronic			425	425	525	525

911 CARRERA—6-Cyl.—Equipment Schedule 1
W.B. 92.6"; 3.6 Liter.

Body Type	VIN	List	Good	Very Good	Good	Excellent
Coupe 2D	AA299	72435	15450	16500	16550	20500
Targa 2D	BA299	79835	18600	19800	19450	23800
Cabriolet 2D	CA299	82235	18750	19950	19600	23900
40th Anniversary			3100	3100	3380	3380
Full Leather			100	100	110	110
Hard Top (Cabriolet)			400	400	425	425
Aero Kit			1475	1475	1600	1600
Automatic w/Tiptronic			425	425	470	470

911 CARRERA 4 AWD—6-Cyl.—Equipment Schedule 1
W.B. 92.5"; 3.6 Liter.

Body Type	VIN	List	Good	Very Good	Good	Excellent
Cabriolet 2D	CA299	86285	17900	19050	18850	23000
4S Coupe 2D	AA299	84165	20100	21400	20800	25200
4S Cabriolet 2D	CA299	93965	24900	26500	25100	30000
Full Leather			100	100	110	110
Hard Top (Cabriolet)			400	400	425	425
Aero Kit			1475	1475	1595	1595
Automatic w/Tiptronic			425	425	470	470

911 TURBO AWD—6-Cyl. Turbo—Equipment Schedule 1
W.B. 92.5"; 3.6 Liter.

Body Type	VIN	List	Good	Very Good	Good	Excellent
Coupe 2D	AB299	120465	21100	22500	21700	26300
Cabriolet 2D	CB299	130265	25300	27000	26400	32500
Full Leather			100	100	110	110
Aero Kit			1475	1475	1585	1585
Power Kit X-50			1475	1475	1590	1590
Automatic w/Tiptronic			425	425	470	470

911 GT2 TURBO—6-Cyl. Turbo—Equipment Schedule 1
W.B. 92.7"; 3.6 Liter.

Body Type	VIN	List	Good	Very Good	Good	Excellent
Coupe 2D	AB299	193765	****	****	****	69400

911 GT3—6-Cyl.—Equipment Schedule 1
W.B. 92.7"; 3.6 Liter.

Body Type	VIN	List	Good	Very Good	Good	Excellent
Coupe 2D	AC299	101965	27800	29600	29000	35800

CARRERA GT—V10—Equipment Schedule 1
W.B. 107.5"; 5.7 Liter.

Body Type	VIN	List	Good	Very Good	Good	Excellent
Roadster 2D	CA298	446165	****	****	****	295400

2005 PORSCHE — WPO(CA298)-5-#

BOXSTER—6-Cyl.—Equipment Schedule 1
W.B. 95.1"; 2.7 Liter, 3.2 Liter.

Body Type	VIN	List	Good	Very Good	Good	Excellent
Cabriolet 2D	CA298	44595	8200	8750	9900	13100
S Cabriolet 2D	CB298	53895	11550	12250	13250	17350
Full Leather			125	125	140	140
Hard Top			425	#425	495	495
Aero Kit			1550	1550	1845	1845
Sport Pkg			500	500	595	595
Automatic w/Tiptronic			475	475	575	575

911 CARRERA—6-Cyl.—Equipment Schedule 1
W.B. 92.5" (S), 92.6"; 3.6 Liter, 3.8 Liter.

Body Type	VIN	List	Good	Very Good	Good	Excellent
Coupe 2D	AA299	73165	16700	17750	17900	21900

Body Type	VIN	List	Trade-In Good	Very Good	Pvt-Party Good	Retail Excellent
Targa 2D	BA299	79865	20700	22100	21700	26100
Cabriolet 2D	CA299	82965	18700	19900	19850	24000
S Coupe 2D	AB299	79895	20600	22000	21600	26000
S Cabriolet 2D	CB299	89695	22800	24300	23500	28200
Full Leather		------	125	125	125	125
Hard Top (Cabriolet)		------	425	425	455	455
Aero Kit		------	1550	1550	1685	1685
Automatic w/Tiptronic		------	475	475	525	525

911 CARRERA 4 AWD—6-Cyl.—Equipment Schedule 1
W.B. 92.5"; 3.6 Liter.

Body Type	VIN	List	Good	Very Good	Good	Excellent
4S Coupe 2D	AA299	84195	20700	22000	21600	26000
4S Cabriolet 2D	CA299	93995	25100	26700	25600	30400
Full Leather		------	125	125	125	125
Hard Top (Cabriolet)		------	425	425	450	450
Aero Kit		------	1550	1550	1700	1700
Automatic w/Tiptronic		------	475	475	530	530

911 TURBO AWD—6-Cyl. Turbo—Equipment Schedule 1
W.B. 92.5"; 3.6 Liter.

Body Type	VIN	List	Good	Very Good	Good	Excellent
Cabriolet 2D	CB299	130295	31400	33400	32200	38800
S Coupe 2D	AB299	133495	30400	32300	31300	37800
S Cabriolet 2D	CB299	143295	32800	34800	33500	40200
Full Leather		------	125	125	125	125
Aero Kit		------	1550	1550	1670	1670
Power Kit X-50		------	1550	1550	1670	1670
Automatic w/Tiptronic		------	475	475	520	520

911 GT2—6-Cyl. Turbo—Equipment Schedule 1
W.B. 92.5"; 3.6 Liter.

Body Type	VIN	List	Good	Very Good	Good	Excellent
Coupe 2D	AB299	193795	****	****	****	78100

911 GT3—6-Cyl.—Equipment Schedule 1
W.B. 92.5"; 3.6 Liter.

Body Type	VIN	List	Good	Very Good	Good	Excellent
Coupe 2D	AC299	101995	31100	33100	32600	39600

CARRERA GT—V10—Equipment Schedule 1
W.B. 107.5"; 5.7 Liter.

Body Type	VIN	List	Good	Very Good	Good	Excellent
Roadster 2D	CA298	448400	****	****	****	343400

2006 PORSCHE — WPO(CA298)-6-#

BOXSTER—6-Cyl.—Equipment Schedule 1
W.B. 95.1"; 2.7 Liter, 3.2 Liter.

Body Type	VIN	List	Good	Very Good	Good	Excellent
Cabriolet 2D	CA298	45795	9775	10350	11450	14750
S Cabriolet 2D	CB298	55495	14000	14800	15600	19900
Full Leather		------	150	150	165	165
Hard Top		------	450	450	520	520
Aero Kit		------	1625	1625	1915	1915
Sport Pkg		------	500	500	590	590
Automatic w/Tiptronic		------	525	525	625	625

CAYMAN—6-Cyl.—Equipment Schedule 1
W.B. 95.1"; 3.4 Liter.

Body Type	VIN	List	Good	Very Good	Good	Excellent
S Coupe 2D	AB298	59695	14100	14900	15400	19300
Full Leather		------	150	150	160	160
Automatic w/Tiptronic		------	525	525	605	605

911 CARRERA—6-Cyl.—Equipment Schedule 1
W.B. 92.5"; 3.6 Liter, 3.8 Liter.

Body Type	VIN	List	Good	Very Good	Good	Excellent
Coupe 2D	AA299	73615	18500	19600	19950	24200
Cabriolet 2D	CA299	83715	21100	22300	22500	27200
S Coupe 2D	AB299	83715	22400	23700	23700	28700
S Cabriolet 2D	CB299	93745	25300	26800	26500	31900
Full Leather		------	150	150	150	150
Hard Top (Cabriolet)		------	450	450	475	475
Aero Kit		------	1625	1625	1760	1760
Automatic w/Tiptronic		------	525	525	575	575

911 CARRERA 4 AWD—6-Cyl.—Equipment Schedule 1
W.B. 92.5"; 3.6 Liter, 3.8 Liter.

Body Type	VIN	List	Good	Very Good	Good	Excellent
Coupe 2D	AA299	79415	18900	20100	20400	24800
Cabriolet 2D	CA299	89445	20800	22000	22300	27100
4S Coupe 2D	AB299	89415	22900	24200	24200	29200
4S Cabriolet 2D	CB299	99445	27000	28600	28400	34300
Full Leather		------	150	150	150	150
Hard Top (Cabriolet)		------	450	450	480	480
Aero Kit		------	1625	1625	1760	1760
Automatic w/Tiptronic		------	525	525	575	575

Body Type	VIN	List	Trade-In Good	Very Good	Pvt-Party Good	Retail Excellent

2007 PORSCHE — WPO(CA298)-7-#

BOXSTER—6-Cyl.—Equipment Schedule 1
W.B. 95.1"; 2.7 Liter, 3.4 Liter.

Body Type	VIN	List	Good	Very Good	Good	Excellent
Cabriolet 2D	CA298	46395	11550	12200	13200	16600
S Cabriolet 2D	CB298	56295	16050	16900	17650	22000
Full Leather		-----	175	175	190	190
Hard Top		-----	475	475	540	540
Aero Kit		-----	1700	1700	1970	1970
Sport Pkg		-----	500	500	580	580
Automatic w/Tiptronic		-----	575	575	655	655

CAYMAN—6-Cyl.—Equipment Schedule 1
W.B. 95.1"; 2.7 Liter, 3.4 Liter.

Body Type	VIN	List	Good	Very Good	Good	Excellent
Coupe 2D	AA298	54955	10350	10950	12200	15600
S Coupe 2D	AB298	64455	15000	15800	16650	20800
Full Leather		-----	175	175	195	195
Automatic w/Tiptronic		-----	575	575	660	660

911 CARRERA—6-Cyl.—Equipment Schedule 1
W.B. 92.5"; 3.6 Liter.

Body Type	VIN	List	Good	Very Good	Good	Excellent
Coupe 2D	AA299	73195	20700	21800	22300	26800
Cabriolet 2D	CA299	83395	23200	24500	24800	29900
Full Leather		-----	175	175	180	180
Hard Top (Cabriolet)		-----	475	475	510	510
Aero Kit		-----	1700	1700	1855	1855
PASM Sport Suspension		-----	700	700	755	755
Automatic w/Tiptronic		-----	575	575	615	615

911 CARRERA—6-Cyl.—Equipment Schedule 1
W.B. 92.5"; 3.8 Liter.

Body Type	VIN	List	Good	Very Good	Good	Excellent
S Coupe 2D	AB299	83395	26100	27500	27500	32900
S Cabriolet 2D	CB299	93595	27900	29400	29400	35300
Full Leather		-----	175	175	180	180
Hard Top		-----	475	475	510	510
Aero Kit		-----	1700	1700	1845	1845
Automatic w/Tiptronic		-----	575	575	615	615

911 CARRERA 4 AWD—6-Cyl.—Equipment Schedule 1
W.B. 92.5"; 3.6 Liter.

Body Type	VIN	List	Good	Very Good	Good	Excellent
Coupe 2D	AA299	78995	22500	23700	24000	28900
Cabriolet 2D	CA299	89195	26300	27800	27800	33200
Full Leather		-----	175	175	180	180
Hard Top (Cabriolet)		-----	475	475	510	510
Aero Kit		-----	1700	1700	1840	1840
PASM Sport Suspension		-----	700	700	745	745
Automatic w/Tiptronic		-----	575	575	610	610

911 CARRERA 4 AWD—6-Cyl.—Equipment Schedule 1
W.B. 92.5"; 3.8 Liter.

Body Type	VIN	List	Good	Very Good	Good	Excellent
4S Coupe 2D	AB299	89195	26700	28200	28200	33700
4S Cabriolet 2D	CB299	99395	31500	33200	33000	39400
Full Leather		-----	175	175	180	180
Hard Top		-----	475	475	510	510
Aero Kit		-----	1700	1700	1840	1840
Automatic w/Tiptronic		-----	575	575	610	610

911 TARGA AWD—6-Cyl.—Equipment Schedule 1
W.B. 92.5"; 3.6 Liter.

Body Type	VIN	List	Good	Very Good	Good	Excellent
4 Coupe 2D	BA299	86495	27700	29200	29100	34700
Full Leather		-----	175	175	180	180
PASM Sport Suspension		-----	700	700	755	755
Automatic w/Tiptronic		-----	575	575	615	615

911 TARGA AWD—6-Cyl.—Equipment Schedule 1
W.B. 92.5"; 3.8 Liter.

Body Type	VIN	List	Good	Very Good	Good	Excellent
4S Coupe 2D	BB299	96695	31200	33000	31800	37000
Full Leather		-----	175	175	180	180
Automatic w/Tiptronic		-----	575	575	610	610

911 GT3—6-Cyl.—Equipment Schedule 1
W.B. 92.7"; 3.6 Liter.

Body Type	VIN	List	Good	Very Good	Good	Excellent
Coupe 2D	AC299	106795	39500	41600	40800	48200
Full Leather		-----	175	175	180	180

911 TURBO AWD—6-Cyl. Turbo—Equipment Schedule 1
W.B. 92.5"; 3.6 Liter.

Body Type	VIN	List	Good	Very Good	Good	Excellent
Coupe 2D	AD299	123695	36100	38100	37700	44800
Full Leather		-----	175	175	180	180
Automatic w/Tiptronic		-----	575	575	615	615

2008 PORSCHE

Body	Type	VIN	List	Trade-In Good	Very Good	Pvt-Party Good	Retail Excellent

2008 PORSCHE — WPO(CA298)-8-#

BOXSTER—6-Cyl.—Equipment Schedule 1
W.B. 95.1"; 2.7 Liter, 3.4 Liter.

Body	Type	VIN	List	Good	Very Good	Good	Excellent
Cabriolet 2D		CA298	46660	14200	14800	16100	19750
Limited Edition Cab		CA298	50760	18000	18750	20100	24500
S Cabriolet 2D		CB298	56560	19300	20100	21300	25800
S Limited Edition		CB298	60760	21700	22600	23800	29000
Full Leather				200	200	220	220
Hard Top				500	500	560	560
Aero Kit				1775	1775	2025	2025
Sport Pkg				500	500	570	570
Automatic w/Tiptronic				600	600	675	675

CAYMAN—6-Cyl.—Equipment Schedule 1
W.B. 95.1"; 2.7 Liter, 3.4 Liter.

Body	Type	VIN	List	Good	Very Good	Good	Excellent
Coupe 2D		AA298	53470	13050	13650	14950	18400
S Coupe 2D		AB298	63170	17750	18500	19750	24000
S Design Ed 1 Cpe 2D		AB298	70760	21600	22600	23600	28500
Full Leather				200	200	220	220
Automatic w/Tiptronic				600	600	680	680

911 CARRERA—6-Cyl.—Equipment Schedule 1
W.B. 92.5"; 3.6 Liter.

Body	Type	VIN	List	Good	Very Good	Good	Excellent
Coupe 2D		AA299	74360	22400	23500	23900	27900
Cabriolet 2D		CA299	84660	27800	29100	29500	34600
Full Leather				200	200	205	205
Hard Top (Cabriolet)				500	500	535	535
Aero Kit				1775	1775	1930	1930
PASM Sport Suspension				725	725	780	780
Automatic w/Tiptronic				600	600	645	645

911 CARRERA—6-Cyl.—Equipment Schedule 1
W.B. 92.5"; 3.8 Liter.

Body	Type	VIN	List	Good	Very Good	Good	Excellent
S Coupe 2D		AB299	84660	30800	32300	32200	37400
S Cabriolet 2D		CB299	94960	32600	34100	34000	39400
Full Leather				200	200	205	205
Hard Top (Cabriolet)				500	500	525	525
Power Kit X51				1775	1775	1915	1915
Automatic w/Tiptronic				600	600	635	635

911 CARRERA 4 AWD—6-Cyl.—Equipment Schedule 1
W.B. 92.5"; 3.6 Liter.

Body	Type	VIN	List	Good	Very Good	Good	Excellent
Coupe 2D		AA299	80260	23400	24500	25000	29200
Full Leather				200	200	205	205
Aero Kit				1775	1775	1920	1920
PASM Sport Suspension				725	725	775	775
Automatic w/Tiptronic				600	600	640	640

911 CARRERA 4 AWD—6-Cyl.—Equipment Schedule 1
W.B. 92.5"; 3.6 Liter, 3.8 Liter.

Body	Type	VIN	List	Good	Very Good	Good	Excellent
Cabriolet 2D		CA299	90560	29600	31000	31100	36200
4S Coupe 2D		AB299	90560	32600	34200	33900	39300
4S Cabriolet 2D		CB299	100860	38000	39800	39600	45700
Full Leather				200	200	205	205
Hard Top (Cabriolet)				500	500	530	530
Aero Kit				1775	1775	1905	1905
Power Kit X51				1775	1775	1905	1905
Automatic w/Tiptronic				600	600	640	640

911 TARGA AWD—6-Cyl.—Equipment Schedule 1
W.B. 92.5"; 3.6 Liter.

Body	Type	VIN	List	Good	Very Good	Good	Excellent
4 Coupe 2D		BA299	87860	29400	30900	30900	36000
Full Leather				200	200	205	205
PASM Sport Suspension				725	725	780	780
Automatic w/Tiptronic				600	600	640	640

911 TARGA AWD—6-Cyl.—Equipment Schedule 1
W.B. 92.5"; 3.8 Liter.

Body	Type	VIN	List	Good	Very Good	Good	Excellent
4S Coupe 2D		BB299	98160	31800	33400	33200	38600
Full Leather				200	200	205	205
Power Kit X51				1775	1775	1910	1910
Automatic w/Tiptronic				600	600	635	635

911 TURBO AWD—6-Cyl. Turbo—Equipment Schedule 1
W.B. 92.5"; 3.6 Liter.

Body	Type	VIN	List	Good	Very Good	Good	Excellent
Coupe 2D		AD299	127060	39700	41600	41600	48500
Cabriolet 2D		CD299	137360	43100	45100	44800	52100
Full Leather				200	200	205	205
Automatic w/Tiptronic				600	600	640	640

2008 PORSCHE

Body Type	VIN	List	Trade-In Good	Very Good	Pvt-Party Good	Retail Excellent

911 GT2—6-Cyl. Twin Turbo—Equipment Schedule 1
W.B. 92.5"; 3.6 Liter.

| Coupe 2D | AD299 | 192560 | **** | **** | **** | 94900 |

911 GT3—6-Cyl.—Equipment Schedule 1
W.B. 92.5"; 3.6 Liter.

| Coupe 2D | AC299 | 108360 | 47700 | 50000 | 49000 | 56400 |

2009 PORSCHE — WPO(CA298)-9-#

BOXSTER—6-Cyl.—Equipment Schedule 1
W.B. 95.1"; 2.9 Liter, 3.4 Liter.

	VIN	List	Good	Very Good	Good	Excellent
Cabriolet 2D	CA298	50880	17050	17650	19200	22900
S Cabriolet 2D	CB298	60980	22900	23700	25200	29700
Full Leather			225	225	265	265
Hard Top			525	525	600	600
Aero Kit			1875	1875	2130	2130
Sport Pkg			550	550	620	620
Automatic, PDK			675	675	755	755

CAYMAN—6-Cyl.—Equipment Schedule 1
W.B. 95.1"; 2.9 Liter, 3.4 Liter.

Coupe 2D	AA298	51160	17200	17800	19250	22800
S Coupe 2D	AB298	64570	24700	25600	26900	31600
Full Leather			225	225	260	260
Automatic, PDK			675	675	750	750

911 CARRERA—6-Cyl.—Equipment Schedule 1
W.B. 92.5"; 3.6 Liter.

Coupe 2D	AA299	80540	27800	29000	29800	34400
Full Leather			225	225	250	250
Aero Kit			1875	1875	2035	2035
PASM Sport Suspension			750	750	800	800
Automatic, PDK			675	675	720	720

911 CARRERA—6-Cyl.—Equipment Schedule 1
W.B. 92.5"; 3.8 Liter.

S Coupe 2D	AB299	91140	36200	37700	38200	43900
Full Leather			225	225	250	250
Aero Kit			1875	1875	2040	2040
PASM Sport Suspension			750	750	800	800
Automatic, PDK			675	675	720	720

911 CARRERA—6-Cyl.—Equipment Schedule 1
W.B. 92.5"; 3.6 Liter.

Cabriolet 2D	CA299	91140	33000	34400	35000	40200
Full Leather			225	225	250	250
Hard Top			525	525	580	580
Aero Kit			1875	1875	2040	2040
Automatic, PDK			675	675	725	725

911 CARRERA—6-Cyl.—Equipment Schedule 1
W.B. 92.5"; 3.8 Liter.

S Cabriolet 2D	CB299	101740	38900	40500	41100	47200
Full Leather			225	225	250	250
Aero Kit			1875	1875	2035	2035
Automatic, PDK			675	675	720	720

911 CARRERA 4 AWD—6-Cyl.—Equipment Schedule 1
W.B. 92.5"; 3.6 Liter, 3.8 Liter.

Coupe 2D	AA299	91140	30400	31700	32400	37400
4S Coupe 2D	AB299	97240	37500	39100	39800	45700
Full Leather			225	225	250	250
Aero Kit			1875	1875	2040	2040
PASM Sport Suspension			750	750	800	800
Automatic, PDK			675	675	720	720

911 CARRERA 4 AWD—6-Cyl.—Equipment Schedule 1
W.B. 92.5"; 3.6 Liter, 3.8 Liter.

Cabriolet 2D	CA299	97240	36300	37800	38200	43800
4S Cabriolet 2D	CB299	107840	42400	44200	44400	50700
Full Leather			225	225	250	250
Hard Top			525	525	575	575
Aero Kit			1875	1875	2035	2035
Automatic, PDK			675	675	720	720

911 TARGA AWD—6-Cyl.—Equipment Schedule 1
W.B. 92.5"; 3.6 Liter.

4 Coupe 2D	BA299	94440	34700	36200	36700	42400
Full Leather			225	225	250	250
PASM Sport Suspension			750	750	805	805
Automatic, PDK			675	675	725	725

1015

Body Type	VIN	List	Trade-In Good	Trade-In Very Good	Pvt-Party Good	Retail Excellent
911 TARGA AWD—6-Cyl.—Equipment Schedule 1						
W.B. 92.5"; 3.8 Liter.						
4S Coupe 2D	BB299	105040	**37400**	**38900**	**39600**	**45600**
Full Leather			225	225	250	250
Automatic, PDK			675	675	725	725
911 TURBO AWD—6-Cyl. Turbo—Equipment Schedule 1						
W.B. 92.5"; 3.6 Liter.						
Coupe 2D	AD299	130980	**42800**	**44700**	**45000**	**51600**
Full Leather			225	225	250	250
Automatic w/Tiptronic			675	675	720	720
911 TURBO AWD—6-Cyl. Turbo—Equipment Schedule 1						
W.B. 92.5"; 3.6 Liter.						
Cabriolet 2D	CD299	143580	**48300**	**50300**	**50300**	**57300**
Full Leather			225	225	250	250
Automatic w/Tiptronic			675	675	720	720
911 GT2—6-Cyl. Twin Turbo—Equipment Schedule 1						
W.B. 92.5"; 3.6 Liter.						
Coupe 2D	AD299	194950	********	********	********	**104600**

Body Type	VIN	List	Trade-In Good	Trade-In Very Good	Pvt-Party Good	Retail Excellent
BOXSTER—6-Cyl.—Equipment Schedule 1						
W.B. 95.1"; 2.9 Liter, 3.4 Liter						
Cabriolet 2D	CA2A8	48550	**19950**	**20500**	**22200**	**25600**
S Cabriolet 2D	CB2A8	58950	**25300**	**26000**	**27800**	**32100**
Full Leather			275	275	320	320
Hard Top			575	575	630	630
SportDesign			625	625	700	700
Automatic, PDK			775	775	860	860
CAYMAN—6-Cyl.—Equipment Schedule 1						
W.B. 95.1"; 2.9 Liter, 3.4 Liter.						
Coupe 2D	AA2A8	52350	**20600**	**21200**	**22800**	**26300**
S Coupe 2D	AB2A8	65870	**28500**	**29300**	**31000**	**35500**
Full Leather			275	275	315	315
Automatic, PDK			775	775	860	860
911 CARRERA—6-Cyl.—Equipment Schedule 1						
W.B. 92.5"; 3.6 Liter.						
Coupe 2D	AA2A9	78750	**32700**	**33900**	**34900**	**39600**
Cabriolet 2D	CA2A9	89750	**38600**	**40000**	**40800**	**46300**
Full Leather			275	275	305	305
Hard Top			575	575	615	615
Aero Kit			2000	2000	2155	2155
Active Sport Suspension			775	775	820	820
PASM Sport Suspension			775	775	820	820
Automatic, PDK			775	775	820	820
911 CARRERA—6-Cyl.—Equipment Schedule 1						
W.B. 92.5"; 3.8 Liter.						
S Coupe 2D	AB2A9	89750	**41400**	**42900**	**43900**	**49700**
Full Leather			275	275	305	305
Aero Kit			2000	2000	2165	2165
PASM Sport Suspension			775	775	825	825
Power Kit X51			2000	2000	2165	2165
Automatic, PDK			775	775	825	825
911 CARRERA—6-Cyl.—Equipment Schedule 1						
W.B. 92.5"; 3.8 Liter.						
S Cabriolet 2D	CB2A9	100750	**46500**	**48200**	**48800**	**54900**
Full Leather			275	275	305	305
Hard Top			575	575	610	610
Powerkit X51			2000	2000	2165	2165
Automatic, PDK			775	775	825	825
911 CARRERA 4 AWD—6-Cyl.—Equipment Schedule 1						
W.B. 92.5"; 3.6 Liter, 3.8 Liter.						
Coupe 2D	AA2A9	85050	**35400**	**36700**	**37400**	**42300**
4S Coupe 2D	AB2A9	96050	**43000**	**44700**	**45400**	**51300**
Full Leather			275	275	305	305
Aero Kit			2000	2000	2170	2170
Powerkit X51			2000	2000	2175	2175
PASM Sport Suspension			775	775	830	830
Automatic, PDK			775	775	830	830
911 CARRERA 4 AWD—6-Cyl.—Equipment Schedule 1						
W.B. 92.5"; 3.6 Liter, 3.8 Liter.						
Cabriolet 2D	CA2A9	96050	**41500**	**43000**	**44000**	**49800**
4S Cabriolet 2D	CB2A9	107050	**48000**	**49800**	**50300**	**56600**
Full Leather			275	275	305	305

Body Type	VIN	List	Trade-In Good	Very Good	Pvt-Party Good	Retail Excellent
Hard Top		-----	575	575	615	615
Powerkit X51		-----	2000	2000	2160	2160
Automatic, PDK		-----	775	775	830	830
911 TARGA AWD—6-Cyl.—Equipment Schedule 1						
W.B. 92.5"; 3.6 Liter.						
4 Coupe 2D	BA2A9	93050	39900	41400	42400	48100
Full Leather		-----	275	275	310	310
PASM Sport Suspension		-----	775	775	835	835
Automatic, PDK		-----	775	775	835	835
911 TARGA AWD—6-Cyl.—Equipment Schedule 1						
W.B. 92.5"; 3.8 Liter.						
4S Coupe 2D	BB2A9	104050	42900	44500	45300	51100
Full Leather		-----	275	275	310	310
Powerkit X51		-----	2000	2000	2190	2190
Automatic, PDK		-----	775	775	835	835
911 TURBO AWD—6-Cyl. Turbo—Equipment Schedule 1						
W.B. 92.5"; 3.6 Liter.						
Coupe 2D	AD2A9	133750	53900	55900	56000	62600
Cabriolet 2D	CD2A9	144750	60900	63100	62700	69900
Full Leather		-----	275	275	305	305
Automatic, PDK		-----	775	775	825	825
911 GT3—6-Cyl.—Equipment Schedule 1						
W.B. 92.7"; 3.8 Liter.						
Coupe 2D	AC2A9	113150	75800	78600	76900	85000
RS Coupe 2D	AC2A9	133750	79300	82200	80700	88900
PANAMERA—V8—Equipment Schedule 1						
W.B. 115.0"; 4.8 Liter.						
S Sedan 4D	AB2A7	90775	39300	40600	41000	46600
PANAMERA AWD—V8—Equipment Schedule 1						
W.B. 115.0"; 4.8 Liter.						
4S Sedan 4D	AB2A7	94775	39300	40600	40900	46500
PANAMERA AWD—V8 Twin Turbo—Equipment Schedule 1						
W.B. 115.0"; 4.8 Liter.						
Sedan 4D	AC2A7	133575	50100	51700	51800	58400

2011 PORSCHE — WPO(CA2A8)-B-#

Body Type	VIN	List	Trade-In Good	Very Good	Pvt-Party Good	Retail Excellent
BOXSTER—6-Cyl.—Equipment Schedule 1						
W.B. 95.1"; 2.9 Liter, 3.4 Liter.						
Convertible 2D	CA2A8	49050	23100	23700	25500	28900
S Convertible 2D	CB2A8	59550	29900	30600	32500	36600
Spyder Convertible 2D	CB2A8	64510	36900	37800	39700	44500
Full Leather		-----	325	325	370	370
Hard Top		-----	600	600	660	660
SportDesign Pkg		-----	700	700	785	785
Automatic, PDK		-----	850	850	950	950
CAYMAN—6-Cyl.—Equipment Schedule 1						
W.B. 95.1"; 2.9 Liter, 3.4 Liter.						
Coupe 2D	AA2A8	54400	24400	25000	27100	30900
S Coupe 2D	AB2A8	66470	34500	35300	37100	41500
Full Leather		-----	325	325	370	370
Automatic, PDK		-----	850	850	945	945
911 CARRERA—6-Cyl.—Equipment Schedule 1						
W.B. 92.5"; 3.6 Liter.						
Coupe 2D	AA2A9	78750	38000	39300	40100	44700
Cabriolet 2D	CA2A9	89750	44000	45500	46400	51600
Full Leather		-----	325	325	355	355
Hard Top		-----	600	600	640	640
Aero Kit		-----	2125	2125	2275	2275
PASM Sport Suspension		-----	800	800	845	845
Automatic, PDK		-----	850	850	950	950
911 CARRERA—6-Cyl.—Equipment Schedule 1						
W.B. 92.5"; 3.8 Liter.						
S Coupe 2D	AB2A9	91450	47400	49000	49900	55400
Full Leather		-----	325	325	360	360
Aero Kit		-----	2125	2125	2305	2305
Powerkit		-----	2125	2125	2305	2305
PASM Sport Suspension		-----	800	800	855	855
Automatic, PDK		-----	850	850	920	920
911 CARRERA—6-Cyl.—Equipment Schedule 1						
W.B. 92.5"; 3.8 Liter.						
S Cabriolet 2D	CB2A9	102450	50600	52300	53100	59100
Full Leather		-----	325	325	355	355
Hard Top		-----	600	600	635	635

2011 PORSCHE

Body Type	VIN	List	Trade-In Good	Trade-In Very Good	Pvt-Party Good	Retail Excellent
Powerkit			2125	2125	2290	2290
Automatic, PDK			850	850	915	915
911 CARRERA 4 AWD—6-Cyl.—Equipment Schedule 1						
W.B. 92.5"; 3.6 Liter, 3.8 Liter.						
Coupe 2D	AA2A9	85050	40600	41900	43100	48000
Cabriolet 2D	CA2A9	96050	46600	48200	49000	54500
4S Coupe 2D	AB2A9	97750	47800	49400	50300	56000
Full Leather			325	325	360	360
Hard Top			600	600	640	640
Aero Kit			2125	2125	2305	2305
Powerkit			2125	2125	2305	2305
PASM Sport Suspension			800	800	850	850
Automatic, PDK			850	850	915	915
911 CARRERA 4 AWD—6-Cyl.—Equipment Schedule 1						
W.B. 92.5"; 3.8 Liter.						
4S Cabriolet 2D	CB2A9	108750	53200	55000	55700	61900
Full Leather			325	325	355	355
Hard Top			600	600	635	635
Powerkit			2125	2125	2290	2290
Automatic, PDK			850	850	910	910
911 TARGA AWD—6-Cyl.—Equipment Schedule 1						
W.B. 92.5"; 3.6 Liter.						
4 Coupe 2D	BA2A9	93050	45100	46600	47600	53000
Full Leather			325	325	360	360
PASM Sport Suspension			800	800	860	860
Automatic, PDK			850	850	920	920
911 TARGA AWD—6-Cyl.—Equipment Schedule 1						
W.B. 92.5"; 3.8 Liter.						
4S Coupe 2D	BB2A9	105750	48100	49700	50600	56300
Full Leather			325	325	360	360
Powerkit			2125	2125	2315	2315
Automatic, PDK			850	850	920	920
911 TURBO AWD—6-Cyl. Twin Turbo—Equipment Schedule 1						
W.B. 92.5"; 3.8 Liter.						
Coupe 2D	AD2A9	136450	61400	63500	63800	70600
Sport Chrono Pkg Plus			575	575	605	605
Aero Kit			2125	2125	2285	2285
Ceramic Brakes			3775	3775	4040	4040
Automatic, PDK			850	850	910	910
911 TURBO AWD—6-Cyl. Twin Turbo—Equipment Schedule 1						
W.B. 92.5"; 3.8 Liter.						
Convertible 2D	CD2A9	147750	68900	71200	70900	78100
Full Leather			325	325	355	355
Hard Top			600	600	630	630
Automatic, PDK			850	850	905	905
911 TURBO S AWD—6-Cyl. Twin Turbo—Equipment Schedule 1						
W.B. 92.5"; 3.8 Liter.						
Coupe 2D	AD2A9	161650	71400	73800	73300	80500
Convertible 2D	CD2A9	173050	78400	81000	80000	87600
Full Leather			325	325	355	355
Aero Kit			2125	2125	2275	2275
911 GT3—6-Cyl.—Equipment Schedule 1						
W.B. 92.7"; 3.8 Liter, 4.0 Liter.						
Coupe 2D	AC2A9	116650	87700	90600	89300	97300
RS Coupe 2D	AC2A9	136450	93500	96600	94900	103200
RS 4.0 Coupe 2D	AC2A9	185950	128300	132600	128200	138000
Full Leather			325	325	350	350
911 GTS—6-Cyl.—Equipment Schedule 1						
W.B. 92.5"; 3.8 Liter.						
Coupe 2D	AB2A9	104050	54000	55800	56100	61900
Aero Kit			2125	2125	2295	2295
PASM Sport Suspension			800	800	850	850
911 GTS—6-Cyl.—Equipment Schedule 1						
W.B. 92.5"; 3.8 Liter.						
Convertible 2D	CB2A9	113850	57400	59300	59600	65700
Hard Top			600	600	635	635
Aero Kit			2125	2125	2290	2290
911 SPEEDSTER—6-Cyl.—Equipment Schedule 1						
W.B. 92.5"; 3.8 Liter.						
Convertible 2D	CB2A9	204950	147200	152000	146100	156800
911 GT2 RS—6-Cyl. Twin Turbo—Equipment Schedule 1						
W.B. 92.7"; 3.6 Liter.						
Coupe 2D	AE2A9	245950	****	****	****	169700

Body Type	VIN	List	Trade-In Good	Very Good	Pvt-Party Good	Retail Excellent
PANAMERA—V6—Equipment Schedule 1						
W.B. 115.0"; 3.6 Liter.						
Sedan 4D	AA2A7	75375	37600	38600	39800	44700
Automatic, PDK			850	850	925	925
PANAMERA AWD—V6—Equipment Schedule 1						
W.B. 115.0"; 3.6 Liter.						
4 Sedan 4D	AA2A7	79875	40600	41600	42800	47800
PANAMERA—V8—Equipment Schedule 1						
W.B. 115.0"; 4.8 Liter.						
S Sedan 4D	AB2A7	90775	44200	45300	46200	51400
Automatic, PDK			850	850	920	920
PANAMERA AWD—V8—Equipment Schedule 1						
W.B. 115.0"; 4.8 Liter.						
4S Sedan 4D	AB2A7	95675	44200	45400	46400	51700
PANAMERA AWD—V8 Twin Turbo—Equipment Schedule 1						
W.B. 115.0"; 4.8 Liter.						
Sedan 4D	AC2A7	136275	55000	56400	57200	63300
2012 PORSCHE — WPO(CA2A8)–C–#						
BOXSTER—6-Cyl.—Equipment Schedule 1						
W.B. 95.1"; 2.9 Liter, 3.4 Liter.						
Convertible 2D	CA2A8	49050	30000	30600	32500	35900
S Convertible 2D	CB2A8	59550	36300	37000	39000	43200
Spyder Convertible 2D	CB2A8	62750	42600	43400	45200	49600
S Black Ed Conv 2D	CB2A8	63450	37000	37800	39800	43900
Full Leather			375	375	420	420
Hard Top			625	625	675	675
SportDesign Pkg			775	775	850	850
Auto, 7-Spd w/PDK MM			925	925	1015	1015
CAYMAN—6-Cyl.—Equipment Schedule 1						
W.B. 95.1"; 2.9 Liter, 3.4 Liter.						
Coupe 2D	AA2A8	56270	30000	30600	32800	36700
S Coupe 2D	AB2A8	70670	40100	40900	42800	47200
R Coupe 2D	AB2A8	70910	43700	44600	46900	52200
S Black Ed Coupe 2D	AB2A8	72110	41800	42600	44800	49700
Full Leather			375	375	420	420
Auto, 7-Spd w/PDK			925	925	1015	1015
911 CARRERA—6-Cyl.—Equipment Schedule 1						
W.B. 92.5"; 3.6 Liter.						
997 Coupe 2D	AA2A9	79950	44300	45700	46900	51700
Cabriolet 2D	CA2A9	91050	53700	55400	56100	61500
Full Leather			375	375	410	410
Sport Chrono Pkg Plus			400	400	430	430
Aero Kit			2250	2250	2435	2435
PASM Sport Suspension			825	825	880	880
Ceramic Brakes			3875	3875	4165	4165
Auto, 7-Spd PDK Manual			925	925	995	995
911 CARRERA—6-Cyl.—Equipment Schedule 1						
W.B. 92.5"; 3.4 Liter.						
991 Coupe 2D	AA2A9	83050	47000	48500	49500	54500
Full Leather			375	375	405	405
Premium Pkg			800	800	845	845
Premium Plus Pkg			2575	2575	2725	2725
Sport Chrono Pkg			575	575	605	605
Porsche Torque Vectoring			650	650	695	695
Ceramic Brakes			3875	3875	4090	4090
911 CARRERA BLACK EDITION—6-Cyl.—Equipment Schedule 1						
W.B. 92.5"; 3.6 Liter.						
Coupe 2D	AA2A9	82250	49900	51400	52100	57100
Convertible 2D	CA2A9	92250	50000	51600	52400	57500
Full Leather			375	375	410	410
Hard Top			625	625	665	665
Sport Chrono Pkg Plus			400	400	430	430
PASM Sport Suspension			825	825	875	875
Ceramic Brakes			3875	3875	4160	4160
Auto, 7-Spd PDK Manual			925	925	995	995
911 CARRERA 4 AWD—6-Cyl.—Equipment Schedule 1						
W.B. 92.5"; 3.6 Liter, 3.8 Liter.						
Coupe 2D	AA2A9	86350	53500	55200	55800	61100
Cabriolet 2D	CA2A9	97450	55400	57100	57500	62700
4S Coupe 2D	AA2A9	99250	59800	61700	62100	68000
GTS Coupe 2D	AB2A9	111150	64400	66400	66700	73000
Full Leather			375	375	405	405

2012 PORSCHE

Body Type	VIN	List	Trade-In Good	Very Good	Pvt-Party Good	Retail Excellent
Aero Kit			2250	2250	2395	2395
25 Yrs Exclusive Pkg			900	900	965	965
Powerkit			2250	2250	2395	2395
Sport Chrono Pkg Plus			400	400	425	425
PASM Sport Suspension			825	825	865	865
Ceramic Brakes			3875	3875	4105	4105
Auto, 7-Spd PDK Manual			925	925	980	980

911 CARRERA 4 AWD—6-Cyl.—Equipment Schedule 1
W.B. 92.5"; 3.8 Liter.

Body Type	VIN	List	Trade-In Good	Very Good	Pvt-Party Good	Retail Excellent
4S Cabriolet 2D	CB2A9	110350	61600	63500	63900	69900
GTS Convertible 2D	CB2A9	121050	69600	71700	71900	78600
Full Leather			375	375	405	405
Hard Top			625	625	660	660
25 Yrs Exclusive Pkg			900	900	970	970
Sport Chrono Pkg Plus			400	400	425	425
Powerkit			2250	2250	2405	2405
Ceramic Brakes			3875	3875	4120	4120
Auto, 7-Spd PDK Manual			925	925	995	995

911 CARRERA S—6-Cyl.—Equipment Schedule 1
W.B. 92.5"; 3.8 Liter.

Body Type	VIN	List	Trade-In Good	Very Good	Pvt-Party Good	Retail Excellent
997 Coupe 2D	AB2A9	92850	57400	59200	59500	65000
Cabriolet 2D	CB2A9	103950	59700	61600	62300	68400
Full Leather			375	375	410	410
Powerkit			2250	2250	2420	2420
Sport Chrono Pkg Plus			400	400	430	430
Ceramic Brakes			3875	3875	4150	4150
Auto, 7-Spd PDK Manual			925	925	990	990

911 CARRERA S—6-Cyl.—Equipment Schedule 1
W.B. 92.5"; 3.8 Liter.

Body Type	VIN	List	Trade-In Good	Very Good	Pvt-Party Good	Retail Excellent
991 Coupe 2D	AB2A9	97350	58500	60300	60700	66200
Full Leather			375	375	405	405
Premium Pkg			800	800	845	845
Premium Plus Pkg			2575	2575	2730	2730
Sport Chrono Pkg			575	575	605	605
PASM Sport Suspension			825	825	865	865
Ceramic Brakes			3875	3875	4095	4095
Auto, 7-Spd PDK Manual			925	925	980	980

911 TARGA AWD—6-Cyl.—Equipment Schedule 1
W.B. 92.5"; 3.6 Liter.

Body Type	VIN	List	Trade-In Good	Very Good	Pvt-Party Good	Retail Excellent
4 Coupe 2D	BA2A9	94450	54900	56500	57100	62400
Full Leather			375	375	410	410
25 Yrs Exclusive Pkg			900	900	980	980
PASM Sport Suspension			825	825	875	875
Sport Chrono Pkg Plus			400	400	430	430
Ceramic Brakes			3875	3875	4155	4155
Auto, 7-Spd PDK Manual			925	925	995	995

911 TARGA AWD—6-Cyl.—Equipment Schedule 1
W.B. 92.5"; 3.8 Liter.

Body Type	VIN	List	Trade-In Good	Very Good	Pvt-Party Good	Retail Excellent
4S Coupe 2D	BB2A9	107350	58100	59900	60500	66400
Full Leather			375	375	410	410
25 Yrs Exclusive Pkg			900	900	975	975
Powerkit			2250	2250	2425	2425
Sport Chrono Pkg Plus			400	400	430	430
Ceramic Brakes			3875	3875	4150	4150
Auto, 7-Spd PDK Manual			925	925	990	990

911 TURBO AWD—6-Cyl. Twin Turbo—Equipment Schedule 1
W.B. 92.5"; 3.8 Liter.

Body Type	VIN	List	Trade-In Good	Very Good	Pvt-Party Good	Retail Excellent
Coupe 2D	AD2A9	138450	73200	75400	75400	82300
Cabriolet 2D	CD2A9	149950	79700	82100	81700	88800
Full Leather			375	375	405	405
25 Yrs Exclusive Pkg			900	900	970	970
Sport Chrono Pkg			575	575	610	610
Hard Top			625	625	655	655
Ceramic Brakes			3875	3875	4115	4115
Auto, 7-Spd PDK Manual			925	925	985	985

911 TURBO S AWD—6-Cyl. Twin Turbo—Equipment Schedule 1
W.B. 92.5"; 3.8 Liter.

Body Type	VIN	List	Trade-In Good	Very Good	Pvt-Party Good	Retail Excellent
Coupe 2D	AD2A9	161650	81900	84400	83700	91000
Convertible 2D	CD2A9	173050	88400	91100	90500	98100
Aero Kit			2250	2250	2395	2395
Hard Top			625	625	650	650
25 Yrs Exclusive Pkg			900	900	965	965

Body Type	VIN	List	Trade-In Good	Very Good	Pvt-Party Good	Retail Excellent
911 GT3—6-Cyl.—Equipment Schedule 1						
W.B. 92.7"; 3.8 Liter, 4.0 Liter.						
Coupe 2D	AB2A9	116650	****	****	****	107500
RS Coupe 2D	AB2A9	136450	****	****	****	117300
RS 4.0 Coupe 2D	AC2A9	185950	****	****	****	150200
Ceramic Brakes			****	****	****	4035
911 CARRERA GTS—6-Cyl.—Equipment Schedule 1						
W.B. 92.5"; 3.8 Liter.						
Coupe 2D	AB2A9	104050	64000	65900	66000	71900
Convertible 2D	CB2A9	113850	67400	69500	69500	75800
Hard Top			625	625	655	655
25 Yrs Exclusive Pkg			900	900	970	970
Sport Chrono Pkg Plus			400	400	425	425
Ceramic Brakes			3875	3875	4130	4130
911 SPEEDSTER—6-Cyl.—Equipment Schedule 1						
W.B. 92.5"; 3.8 Liter.						
Convertible 2D	CB2A9	204950	****	****	****	168400
911 GT2 RS—6-Cyl. Twin Turbo—Equipment Schedule 1						
W.B. 92.7"; 3.6 Liter.						
Coupe 2D	AA2A9	245950	****	****	****	180200
PANAMERA—V6—Equipment Schedule 1						
W.B. 114.9"; 3.6 Liter.						
Sedan 4D	AA2A7	76175	43200	44100	45700	50300
Adaptive Cruise Control			450	450	475	475
PANAMERA—V6 Hybrid—Equipment Schedule 1						
W.B. 114.9"; 3.0 Liter.						
S Sedan 4D	AD2A7	95975	45000	46000	48000	53300
Adaptive Cruise Control			450	450	480	480
PANAMERA AWD—V6—Equipment Schedule 1						
W.B. 114.9"; 3.6 Liter.						
4 Sedan 4D	AA2A7	80775	45400	46300	47800	52600
Adaptive Cruise Control			450	450	475	475
PANAMERA—V8—Equipment Schedule 1						
W.B. 114.9"; 4.8 Liter.						
S Sedan 4D	AB2A7	91275	50000	51100	52900	58100
Adaptive Cruise Control			450	450	475	475
PANAMERA AWD—V8—Equipment Schedule 1						
W.B. 114.9"; 4.8 Liter.						
4S Sedan 4D	AB2A7	96175	50500	51600	53200	58300
Adaptive Cruise Control			450	450	475	475
PANAMERA AWD—V8 Twin Turbo—Equipment Schedule 1						
W.B. 115.0"; 4.8 Liter.						
Sedan 4D	AC2A7	137675	64800	66200	67300	73200
S Sedan 4D	AC2A7	174175	77200	78800	79100	85300
Adaptive Cruise Control			450	450	465	465

2013 PORSCHE — WPO(CA2A8)-D-#

Body Type	VIN	List	Trade-In Good	Very Good	Pvt-Party Good	Retail Excellent
BOXSTER—6-Cyl.—Equipment Schedule 1						
W.B. 95.1"; 2.7 Liter, 3.4 Liter.						
Convertible 2D	CA2A8	50450	35800	36500	38500	42100
S Convertible 2D	CB2A8	61850	44900	45700	48100	52400
Full Leather			425	425	470	470
Auto, 7-Spd w/PDK Manual			1000	1000	1090	1090
911 CARRERA—6-Cyl.—Equipment Schedule 1						
W.B. 92.5", 96.5" (Cab); 3.4 Liter.						
Coupe 2D	AA2A9	83050	54800	56400	57300	62600
Cabriolet 2D	CA2A9	94650	66100	68100	68200	73900
Full Leather			425	425	460	460
Premium Pkg			800	800	845	845
Premium Plus Pkg			2675	2675	2835	2835
SportDesign Pkg			1400	1400	1485	1485
PASM Sport Suspension			850	850	890	890
Ceramic Brakes			3975	3975	4205	4205
Auto, 7-Spd PDK Manual			1000	1000	1060	1060
911 CARRERA 4 AWD—6-Cyl.—Equipment Schedule 1						
W.B. 92.5"; 3.6 Liter, 3.8 Liter.						
Coupe 2D	AA2A9	86350	60400	62300	62800	68100
Cabriolet 2D	CA2A9	97450	68400	70400	70400	76100
4S Coupe 2D	AB2A9	99250	74800	77000	76900	83100
Full Leather			425	425	460	460
25 Years Exclusive Pkg			975	975	1035	1035
PASM Sport Suspension			850	850	890	890
Ceramic Brakes			3975	3975	4200	4200

2013 PORSCHE

Body Type	VIN	List	Good	Very Good	Good	Excellent
			Trade-In		**Pvt-Party**	**Retail**

Body Type	VIN	List	Good	Very Good	Good	Excellent
Auto, 7-Spd PDK Manual			1000	1000	1060	1060
911 CARRERA 4 AWD—6-Cyl.—Equipment Schedule 1						
W.B. 92.5"; 3.8 Liter.						
4S Cabriolet 2D	CB2A9	110350	79600	81900	81500	87900
Full Leather			425	425	455	455
25 Yrs Exclusive Pkg			975	975	1030	1030
Powerkit			2375	2375	2490	2490
SportDesign Pkg			1400	1400	1475	1475
Ceramic Brakes			3975	3975	4175	4175
Auto, 7-Spd PDK Manual			1000	1000	1050	1050
911 CARRERA S—6-Cyl.—Equipment Schedule 1						
W.B. 92.5", 96.5" (Cab); 3.8 Liter.						
Coupe 2D	AB2A9	97350	67300	69200	69300	75000
Cabriolet 2D	CB2A9	108950	74500	76600	76700	83200
Full Leather			425	425	455	455
Premium Pkg			800	800	840	840
Premium Plus Pkg			2675	2675	2815	2815
SportDesign Pkg			1400	1400	1475	1475
PASM Sport Suspension			850	850	885	885
Ceramic Brakes			3975	3975	4180	4180
Auto, 7-Spd PDK Manual			1000	1000	1055	1055
911 TURBO AWD—6-Cyl. Twin Turbo—Equipment Schedule 1						
W.B. 92.5"; 3.8 Liter.						
Coupe 2D	AD2A9	138450	86900	89400	88900	96000
Cabriolet 2D	CD2A9	149950	92900	95600	95200	102600
Sport Chrono Pkg			575	575	610	610
Hard Top			650	650	675	675
Ceramic Brakes			3975	3975	4190	4190
Auto, 7-Spd PDK Manual			1000	1000	1055	1055
911 TURBO S AWD—6-Cyl. Twin Turbo—Equipment Schedule 1						
W.B. 92.5"; 3.8 Liter.						
Coupe 2D	AD2A9	161650	95100	97900	97200	104700
Cabriolet 2D	CD2A9	173050	102900	105800	104800	112500
Hard Top			650	650	675	675
PANAMERA—V6—Equipment Schedule 1						
W.B. 114.9"; 3.6 Liter.						
Sedan 4D	AA2A7	76825	50300	51200	53100	57700
Platinum Ed Sedan	AA2A7	81475	51900	52800	54900	59700
Burmester Surround Sound			2825	2825	3045	3045
Adaptive Cruise Control			475	475	500	500
Full Leather			425	425	465	465
SportDesign			1400	1400	1510	1510
Premium Pkg			800	800	860	860
Premium Plus Pkg			2675	2675	2880	2880
Ceramic Brakes			3975	3975	4265	4265
PANAMERA—V6 Hybrid—Equipment Schedule 1						
W.B. 114.9"; 3.0 Liter.						
S Sedan 4D	AD2A7	97125	53300	54300	56600	61900
Adaptive Cruise Control			475	475	500	500
Full Leather			425	425	465	465
Ceramic Brakes			3975	3975	4255	4255
PANAMERA AWD—V6—Equipment Schedule 1						
W.B. 114.9"; 3.6 Liter.						
4 Sedan 4D	AA2A7	81425	52700	53700	55600	60300
4 Platinum Ed Sed	AA2A7	85575	53700	54700	56400	61000
Burmester Surround Sound			2825	2825	3040	3040
Adaptive Speed Control			475	475	500	500
Full Leather			425	425	465	465
SportDesign			1400	1400	1500	1500
Premium Pkg			800	800	860	860
Premium Plus Pkg			2675	2675	2870	2870
Ceramic Brakes			3975	3975	4255	4255
PANAMERA—V8—Equipment Schedule 1						
W.B. 114.9"; 4.8 Liter.						
S Sedan 4D	AB2A7	92325	58700	59700	61600	66700
Burmester Surround Sound			2825	2825	3020	3020
Adaptive Speed Control			475	475	495	495
Full Leather			425	425	460	460
SportDesign Pkg			1400	1400	1495	1495
Ceramic Brakes			3975	3975	4230	4230
PANAMERA AWD—V8—Equipment Schedule 1						
W.B. 114.9"; 4.8 Liter.						
4S Sedan 4D	AB2A7	97325	59900	61000	62600	67700

Body Type	VIN	List	Trade-In Good	Very Good	Pvt-Party Good	Retail Excellent
GTS Sedan 4D	AF2A7	111975	69600	70900	71600	76400
Burmester Surround Sound		......	2825	2825	3015	3015
Adaptive Cruise Control		......	475	475	495	495
Full Leather		......	425	425	460	460
Premium Pkg		......	800	800	850	850
Premium Plus Pkg		......	2675	2675	2850	2850
SportDesign		......	1400	1400	1490	1490
Ceramic Brakes		......	3975	3975	4225	4225
PANAMERA AWD—V8 Twin Turbo—Equipment Schedule 1						
W.B. 114.9"; 4.8 Liter.						
Sedan 4D	AC2A7	139625	74600	76000	77200	82900
S Sedan 4D	AC2A7	176275	87600	89200	89700	95700
Burmester Surround Sound		......	2825	2825	2975	2975
Adaptive Cruise Control		......	475	475	490	490
SportDesign		......	1400	1400	1470	1470
Sport Power Kit		......	2375	2375	2495	2495
Ceramic Brakes		......	3975	3975	4165	4165

2014 PORSCHE — WPO(CA2A8)–E–#

Body Type	VIN	List	Trade-In Good	Very Good	Pvt-Party Good	Retail Excellent
BOXSTER—6-Cyl.—Equipment Schedule 1						
W.B. 95.1"; 2.7 Liter, 3.4 Liter.						
Convertible 2D	CA2A8	51350	41300	42000	44100	48000
S Convertible 2D	CB2A8	63050	50100	51000	53200	57700
Full Leather		......	500	500	545	545
Porsche Torque Vectoring		......	675	675	745	745
Premium Pkg		......	800	800	870	870
Sport Chrono Pkg		......	600	600	640	640
Auto, 7-Spd PDK Manual		......	1075	1075	1170	1170
CAYMAN—6-Cyl.—Equipment Schedule 1						
W.B. 97.4"; 2.7 Liter.						
Coupe 2D	AA2A8	53550	43900	44700	46600	50600
S Coupe 2D	AB2A8	65700	56600	57600	59400	64000
Adaptive Cruise Control		......	500	500	525	525
Porsche Torque Vectoring		......	675	675	730	730
Auto, 7-Spd w/PDK MM		......	1075	1075	1145	1145
911 CARRERA—6-Cyl.—Equipment Schedule 1						
W.B. 96.5"; 3.4 Liter.						
Coupe 2D	AA2A9	85250	66100	68000	68400	74000
Cabriolet 2D	CA2A9	97150	82500	84800	84100	90200
50th Annv Ed Coupe	AB2A9	125050	113100	116400	114400	121900
Adaptive Cruise Control		......	500	500	515	515
Full Leather		......	500	500	530	530
Porsche Torque Vectoring		......	675	675	720	720
Sport Chrono Pkg		......	600	600	620	620
SportDesign Pkg		......	1475	1475	1560	1560
PASM Sport Suspension		......	875	875	915	915
Ceramic Brakes		......	4075	4075	4255	4255
Auto, 7-Spd PDK Manual		......	1075	1075	1135	1135
911 CARRERA 4 AWD—6-Cyl.—Equipment Schedule 1						
W.B. 96.5"; 3.4 Liter.						
Coupe 2D	AA2A9	91980	72200	74300	74100	79800
Cabriolet 2D	CA2A9	103880	85200	87700	86700	92900
4S Coupe 2D	AB2A9	106580	88300	90800	89900	96500
Adaptive Cruise Control		......	500	500	515	515
Full Leather		......	500	500	525	525
Porsche Torque Vectoring		......	675	675	720	720
Sport Chrono Pkg		......	600	600	620	620
SportDesign Pkg		......	1475	1475	1555	1555
Ceramic Brakes		......	4075	4075	4280	4280
Aero Kit		......	2475	2475	2595	2595
PASM Sport Suspension		......	875	875	910	910
Auto, 7-Spd PDK Manual		......	1075	1075	1130	1130
911 CARRERA 4 AWD—6-Cyl.—Equipment Schedule 1						
W.B. 96.5"; 3.8 Liter.						
4S Cabriolet 2D	CB2A9	118480	89700	92200	91300	98000
Adaptive Cruise Control		......	500	500	515	515
Full Leather		......	500	500	525	525
Powerkit		......	2475	2475	2585	2585
Sport Chrono Pkg		......	600	600	615	615
SportDesign Pkg		......	1475	1475	1545	1545
Ceramic Brakes		......	4075	4075	4260	4260
Auto, 7-Spd PDK Manual		......	1075	1075	1125	1125

Body Type	VIN	List	Trade-In Good	Very Good	Pvt-Party Good	Retail Excellent
911 CARRERA S—6-Cyl.—Equipment Schedule 1						
W.B. 96.5"; 3.8 Liter.						
Coupe 2D	AB2A9	99850	82600	85000	84200	90300
Cabriolet 2D	CB2A9	111750	90600	93200	92400	99300
Adaptive Cruise Control			500	500	515	515
Full Leather			500	500	525	525
Powerkit			2475	2475	2580	2580
Sport Chrono Pkg			600	600	615	615
SportDesign Pkg			1475	1475	1540	1540
Ceramic Brakes			4075	4075	4255	4255
PASM Sport Suspension			875	875	905	905
Aero Kit			2475	2475	2580	2580
Auto, 7-Spd PDK Manual			1075	1075	1125	1125
911 TURBO AWD—6-Cyl. Twin Turbo—Equipment Schedule 1						
W.B. 96.5"; 3.8 Liter.						
Coupe 2D	AD2A9	149250	119500	122900	120800	129100
Cabriolet 2D	CD2A9	161695				
Adaptive Cruise Control			500	500	510	510
Sport Chrono Pkg			600	600	610	610
Ceramic Brakes			4075	4075	4235	4235
911 TURBO S AWD—6-Cyl. Twin Turbo—Equipment Schedule 1						
W.B. 96.5"; 3.8 Liter.						
Coupe 2D	AD2A9	182050	128100	131700	129200	137700
Cabriolet 2D	CD2A9	194895				
Adaptive Cruise Control			500	500	510	510
911 TARGA 4 AWD—6-Cyl.—Equipment Schedule 1						
W.B. 96.5"; 3.4 Liter.						
Coupe 2D	BA2A9	102595				
Sensing Cruise Control		-------				
Burmester Premium Sound		-------				
Full Leather		-------				
Porsche Torque Vectoring		-------				
Sport Chrono Pkg		-------				
Ceramic Brakes		-------				
Auto, 7-Spd PDK Manual		-------				
911 TARGA 4S AWD—6-Cyl.—Equipment Schedule 1						
W.B. 96.5"; 3.8 Liter.						
Coupe 2D	BB2A9	117195				
Sensing Cruise Control		-------				
Burmester Premium Sound		-------				
Full Leather		-------				
Sport Chrono Pkg		-------				
Ceramic Brakes		-------				
Auto, 7-Spd PDK Manual		-------				
911 GT3—6-Cyl.—Equipment Schedule 1						
W.B. 96.7"; 3.8 Liter.						
Coupe 2D	AC2A9	131350	****	****	****	128400
Full Leather			****	****	****	520
Ceramic Brakes			****	****	****	4225
PANAMERA—V6—Equipment Schedule 1						
W.B. 114.9"; 3.6 Liter.						
Sedan 4D	AA2A7	79075	61200	62300	63800	68600
Adaptive Cruise Control			500	500	525	525
Full Leather			500	500	535	535
Premium Pkg			800	800	850	850
Premium Pkg Plus			2775	2775	2950	2950
Ceramic Brakes			4075	4075	4335	4335
PANAMERA—V6 Twin Turbo—Equipment Schedule 1						
W.B. 114.9"; 3.6 Liter.						
S Sedan 4D	AB2A7	94175	76400	77700	78900	84400
Adaptive Cruise Control			500	500	515	515
Full Leather			500	500	525	525
Premium Pkg			800	800	840	840
Ceramic Brakes			4075	4075	4285	4285
PANAMERA—V6 E-Hybrid—Equipment Schedule 1						
W.B. 114.9"; 3.0 Liter.						
S Sedan 4D	AD2A7	99975	75200	76600	77600	82800
Adaptive Cruise Control			500	500	515	515
Full Leather			500	500	525	525
Premium Pkg			800	800	845	845
Premium Pkg Plus			2775	2775	2915	2915
Ceramic Brakes			4075	4075	4285	4285

2014 PORSCHE

Body Type	VIN	List	Trade-In Good	Very Good	Pvt-Party Good	Retail Excellent
PANAMERA AWD—V6—Equipment Schedule 1						
W.B. 114.9"; 3.6 Liter.						
4 Sedan 4D	AA2A7	83775	66100	67300	68700	73700
Adaptive Cruise Control		——	500	500	520	520
Full Leather		——	500	500	530	530
Premium Pkg		——	800	800	850	850
Premium Pkg Plus		——	2775	2775	2935	2935
Ceramic Brakes		——	4075	4075	4315	4315
PANAMERA AWD—V6 Twin Turbo—Equipment Schedule 1						
W.B. 114.9", 120.9" (Executive); 3.0 Liter.						
4S Sedan 4D	AB2A7	99275	76100	77500	78500	83900
4S Executive Sedan	BB2A7	126575	94000	95700	95900	101700
Adaptive Cruise Control		——	500	500	515	515
Full Leather		——	500	500	525	525
Premium Pkg		——	800	800	840	840
Premium Pkg Plus		——	2775	2775	2915	2915
Ceramic Brakes		——	4075	4075	4285	4285
PANAMERA AWD—V8—Equipment Schedule 1						
W.B. 114.9"; 4.8 Liter.						
GTS Sedan 4D	AF2A7	114375	86100	87700	87800	93000
Adaptive Cruise Control		——	500	500	515	515
Full Leather		——	500	500	525	525
Premium Pkg		——	800	800	835	835
Premium Pkg Plus		——	2775	2775	2900	2900
Ceramic Brakes		——	4075	4075	4260	4260
PANAMERA AWD—V8 Twin Turbo—Equipment Schedule 1						
W.B. 114.9", 120.9" (Executive); 4.8 Liter.						
Sedan 4D	AC2A7	142275	94000	95700	96200	102400
Executive Sedan 4D	BC2A7	162075	114500	116600	116200	122600
S Sedan 4D	AC2A7	181295				
S Executive Sedan 4D	BC2A7	201495				
Adaptive Cruise Control		——	500	500	510	510
Premium Pkg Plus		——	2775	2775	2890	2890
Sport Pkg		——	1475	1475	1540	1540
Ceramic Brakes		——	4075	4075	4245	4245

ROLLS ROYCE

2005 ROLLS ROYCE — SCA(1S684)-5-#

PHANTOM—V12—Equipment Schedule 2
W.B. 140.6"; 6.8 Liter.

Sedan 4D	1S684	328750	****	****	****	94100

2006 ROLLS ROYCE — SCA(1S684) – 6-#

PHANTOM—V12—Equipment Schedule 2
2.B. 140.6"; 6.8 Liter.

Sedan 4D	1S684	329750	****	****	****	122700

2007 ROLLS ROYCE — SCA(1S685)-7-#

PHANTOM—V12—Equipment Schedule 2
W.B. 140.6", 150.4" (Ext); 6.8 Liter.

Sedan 4D	1S685	335350	****	****	****	151300
Extended Sedan 4D	1L685	387500	****	****	****	214200

2008 ROLLS ROYCE — SCA(1S685)-8-#

PHANTOM—V12—Equipment Schedule 2
W.B. 130.7"; 140.6" (Sed), 150.4" (Ext); 6.8 Liter.

Sedan 4D	1S685	345000	****	****	****	170800
Extended Sedan 4D	1L685	408000	****	****	****	230900
Drophead Coupe 2D	2D685	412000	****	****	****	275400

2009 ROLLS ROYCE — SCA(1S685)-9-#

PHANTOM—V12—Equipment Schedule 2
W.B. 130.7", 140.6" (Sed), 150.4" (Ext); 6.8 Liter.

Sedan 4D	1S685	382000	****	****	****	194000
Coupe 2D	3C675	402000	****	****	****	235000
Extended Sedan 4D	1L685	452000	****	****	****	257900
Drophead Coupe 2D	2D685	436000	****	****	****	292300

2010 ROLLS ROYCE

Body Type	VIN	List	Trade-In Good	Very Good	Pvt-Party Good	Retail Excellent

2010 ROLLS ROYCE — SCA(664S5)-A-#

GHOST—V12 Twin Turbo—Equipment Schedule 2
W.B. 129.7"; 6.6 Liter.

Sedan 4D	664S5	247000	****	****	****	151600

PHANTOM—V12—Equipment Schedule 2
W.B. 130.7", 140.6" (Sed), 150.4" (Ext); 6.8 Liter.

Sedan 4D	681S5	382000	****	****	****	231100
Coupe 2D	683C5	410000	****	****	****	268500
Extended Sedan 4D	681L5	452000	****	****	****	291000
Drophead Coupe 2D	682D5	445000	****	****	****	318100

2011 ROLLS ROYCE — SCA(664S5)-B-#

GHOST—V12 Twin Turbo—Equipment Schedule 2
W.B. 129.7"; 6.6 Liter.

Sedan 4D	664S5	250200	****	****	****	185900

PHANTOM—V12—Equipment Schedule 2
W.B. 130.7", 140.6" (Sed), 150.4" (Ext); 6.8 Liter.

Sedan 4D	681S5	385000	****	****	****	264800
Coupe 2D	673C5	413000	****	****	****	296900
Extended Sedan 4D	681L5	455000	****	****	****	318200
Drophead Conv 2D	682D5	452000	****	****	****	342500

2012 ROLLS ROYCE — SCA(664S5)-C-#

GHOST—V12 Twin Turbo—Equipment Schedule 2
W.B. 129.7", 136.4" (Ext); 6.6 Liter.

Sedan 4D	664S5	253700	****	****	****	202700
Extended Sedan 4D	664L5	292000	****	****	****	224100

PHANTOM—V12—Equipment Schedule 2
W.B. 130.7", 140.6" (Sed), 150.4" (Ext); 6.8 Liter.

Sedan 4D	681S5	385000	****	****	****	288000
Coupe 2D	683C5	413000	****	****	****	320700
Extended Sedan 4D	681L5	455000	****	****	****	336300
Drophead Conv 2D	682D5	452000	****	****	****	359200

2013 ROLLS ROYCE—SCA(664S5)-D-#

GHOST—V12 Twin Turbo—Equipment Schedule 2
W.B. 129.7", 136.4" (Ext); 6.6 Liter.

Sedan 4D	664S5	260750	****	****	****	217500
Extended Sedan 4D	664L5	298000	****	****	****	239800

PHANTOM—V12—Equipment Schedule 2
W.B. 130.7", 140.6" (Sed), 150.4" (Ext); 6.8 Liter.

Sedan 4D	681S5	403970	****	****	****	301600
Coupe 2D	683C5	434295	****	****	****	336800
Extended Sedan 4D	681L5	475295	****	****	****	351400
Drophead Conv 2D	682D5	479400	****	****	****	373200

2014 ROLLS ROYCE—SCA(665C5)-E-#

WRAITH—V12 Twin Turbo—Equipment Schedule 1
W.B. 122.5"; 6.6 Liter.

Coupe 2D	665C5	288600	****	****	****	232800

GHOST—V12 Twin Turbo—Equipment Schedule 2
W.B. 129.7", 136.4" (Ext); 6.6 Liter.

Sedan 4D	664S5	267300	****	****	****	230000
Extended Sedan 4D	664L5	305300	****	****	****	256000

PHANTOM—V12—Equipment Schedule 2
W.B. 130.7", 140.6" (Sed), 150.4" (Ext); 6.8 Liter.

Sedan 4D	681S5	407540	****	****	****	312400
Coupe 2D	683C5	438150	****	****	****	344300
Extended Sedan 4D	681L5	479590	****	****	****	360500
Drophead Cpe Conv 2D	682D5	479200	****	****	****	383800

SRT

2013 SRT — (1,2or3)C3-(DEAZ)-D-#

VIPER—V10—Equipment Schedule 2
W.B. 98.8"; 8.4 Liter.

Coupe 2D	DEAZ	104990	55100	56500	57900	63400
GTS Coupe 2D	DEBZ	124990	68400	70100	70900	77100

Body Type	VIN	List	Trade-In Good	Trade-In Very Good	Pvt-Party Good	Retail Excellent
Grand Touring Pkg			1000	1000	1065	1065
Track Package			1500	1500	1595	1595

2014 SRT — (1,2or3)C3-(DEAZ)-E-#

VIPER—V10—Equipment Schedule 2
W.B. 98.8"; 8.4 Liter.

Body Type	VIN	List	Good	Very Good	Good	Excellent
Coupe 2D	DEAZ	99390	58900	60400	61600	67100
GTS Coupe 2D	DEBZ	123890	72300	74100	74700	81000
Grand Touring Pkg			1000	1000	1060	1060

SAAB

2000 SAAB — YS3(DD35H)-Y-#

9-3—4-Cyl. Turbo—Equipment Schedule 3
W.B. 102.6"; 2.0 Liter.

Body Type	VIN	List	Good	Very Good	Good	Excellent
Hatchback 2D	DD35H	27675	325	375	925	1675
Hatchback 4D	DD55H	28115	325	375	925	1675
Convertible 2D	DD75H	41225	700	775	1350	2325
Automatic		8	125	125	165	165

9-3—4-Cyl. HO Turbo—Equipment Schedule 3
W.B. 102.6"; 2.0 Liter, 2.3 Liter.

Body Type	VIN	List	Good	Very Good	Good	Excellent
SE Hatchback 4D	DF55K	33670	525	600	1150	2050
SE Convertible 2D	DF75K	44770	750	850	1400	2425
Viggen Hatchback 2D	DP35G	38325	1650	1825	2525	4150
Viggen Hatchback 4D	DP55G	38325	1375	1525	2125	3525
Viggen Convertible 2D	DP75G	45570	1950	2150	2850	4675
Automatic		8	125	125	165	165

9-5—4-Cyl. Turbo—Equipment Schedule 2
W.B. 106.4", 106.6" (Wagon); 2.3 Liter.

Body Type	VIN	List	Good	Very Good	Good	Excellent
Sedan 4D	ED48E	35300	550	675	1175	2050
Wagon 4D	ED58E	35300	575	675	1200	2150
Gary Fisher Edition			275	275	380	380
Manual, 5-Spd		5	(175)	(175)	(240)	(240)

9-5—4-Cyl. HO Turbo—Equipment Schedule 2
W.B. 106.4", 106.6" (Wagon); 2.3 Liter.

Body Type	VIN	List	Good	Very Good	Good	Excellent
Aero Sedan 4D	EH48G	41550	1500	1725	2400	4150
Aero Wagon 4D	EH58G	44145	1700	1975	2800	4825
Manual, 5-Spd		5	(175)	(175)	(240)	(240)

9-5—V6 Turbo—Equipment Schedule 2
W.B. 106.4", 106.6" (Wagon); 3.0 Liter.

Body Type	VIN	List	Good	Very Good	Good	Excellent
SE Sedan 4D	EF48Z	38325	675	775	1375	2475
SE Wagon 4D	EF58Z	38325	875	1025	1625	2875

2001 SAAB — YS3(DD35H)-1-#

9-3—4-Cyl. Turbo—Equipment Schedule 3
W.B. 102.6"; 2.0 Liter.

Body Type	VIN	List	Good	Very Good	Good	Excellent
Hatchback 2D	DD35H	27070	375	425	1000	1825
Hatchback 4D	DD55H	27570	375	425	1000	1825
Automatic			125	125	165	165

9-3—4-Cyl. HO Turbo—Equipment Schedule 3
W.B. 102.6"; 2.0 Liter, 2.3 Liter.

Body Type	VIN	List	Good	Very Good	Good	Excellent
SE Hatchback 4D	DF55K	33170	625	700	1300	2300
SE Convertible 2D	DF75K	40570	975	1075	1675	2850
Viggen Hatchback 2D	DP35G	38570	2100	2300	2975	4775
Viggen Hatchback 4D	DP55G	38570	1675	1850	2525	4100
Viggen Convertible 2D	DP75G	45570	2375	2625	3300	5300
Automatic			125	125	165	165

9-5—4-Cyl. Turbo—Equipment Schedule 2
W.B. 106.4"; 2.3 Liter.

Body Type	VIN	List	Good	Very Good	Good	Excellent
Sedan 4D	ED48E	34570	575	675	1225	2150
Wagon 4D	ED58E	35270	600	725	1350	2425
Manual, 5-Spd			(225)	(225)	(300)	(300)

9-5—4-Cyl. HO Turbo—Equipment Schedule 2
W.B. 106.4"; 2.3 Liter.

Body Type	VIN	List	Good	Very Good	Good	Excellent
Aero Sedan 4D	EH48G	40750	1550	1775	2550	4475
Aero Wagon 4D	EH58G	41450	1825	2125	3025	5275
Manual, 5-Spd			(225)	(225)	(300)	(300)

9-5—V6 Turbo—Equipment Schedule 2
W.B. 106.4"; 3.0 Liter.

Body Type	VIN	List	Good	Very Good	Good	Excellent
SE Sedan 4D	EF48Z	39225	675	800	1500	2750
SE Wagon 4D	EF58Z	39925	950	1100	1825	3250

2002 SAAB

Body Type	VIN	List	Trade-In Good	Very Good	Pvt-Party Good	Retail Excellent

2002 SAAB — YS3(DF55K)-2-#

9-3—4-Cyl. Turbo—Equipment Schedule 3
W.B. 102.6"; 2.0 Liter.

SE Hatchback 4D	DF55K	29820	725	800	1500	2675
SE Convertible 2D	DF75K	41820	1225	1350	2025	3425
Automatic			125	125	165	165

9-3—4-Cyl. HO Turbo—Equipment Schedule 3
W.B. 102.6"; 2.3 Liter.

Viggen Hatchback 2D	DP35G	38720	2575	2825	3500	5525
Viggen Hatchback 4D	DP55G	38720	2125	2325	3000	4775
Viggen Convertible 2D	DP75G	45620	2925	3200	3875	6100

9-5—4-Cyl. Turbo—Equipment Schedule 2
W.B. 106.4"; 2.3 Liter.

Linear Sedan 4D	EB49E	35820	600	700	1250	2225
Linear Wagon 4D	EB59E	36520	700	800	1450	2625
Manual, 5-Spd		5	(275)	(275)	(355)	(355)

9-5—4-Cyl. HO Turbo—Equipment Schedule 2
W.B. 106.4"; 2.3 Liter.

Aero Sedan 4D	EH49G	40475	1550	1775	2650	4600
Aero Wagon 4D	EH59G	41175	1950	2225	3150	5400
Manual, 5-Spd		5	(275)	(275)	(355)	(355)

9-5—V6 Turbo—Equipment Schedule 2
W.B. 106.4"; 3.0 Liter.

Arc Sedan 4D	ED49Z	39275	675	800	1550	2825
Arc Wagon 4D	ED59Z	39975	975	1125	1900	3375

2003 SAAB — YS3(FB49S)-3-#

9-3—4-Cyl. Turbo—Equipment Schedule 3
W.B. 105.3"; 2.0 Liter.

Linear Sedan 4D	FB49S	27725	1075	1175	1875	3150

9-3—4-Cyl. HO Turbo—Equipment Schedule 3
W.B. 102.6", 105.3" (Sed); 2.0 Liter.

Arc Sedan 4D	FD49Y	31820	1325	1475	2225	3750
Vector Sedan 4D	FF46Y	33120	1475	1625	2450	4050
SE Convertible 2D	DF75K	40620	1475	1625	2450	4050

9-5—4-Cyl. Turbo—Equipment Schedule 2
W.B. 106.4"; 2.3 Liter.

Linear Sedan 4D	EB49E	35920	625	725	1325	2325
Linear Wagon 4D	EB59E	36620	750	875	1525	2725
Manual, 5-Spd			(250)	(250)	(345)	(345)

9-5—4-Cyl. HO Turbo—Equipment Schedule 2
W.B. 106.4"; 2.3 Liter.

Aero Sedan 4D	EH49G	40575	1900	2175	3025	5100
Aero Wagon 4D	EH59G	41275	2400	2725	3650	6100
Manual, 5-Spd			(250)	(250)	(345)	(345)

9-5—V6 Turbo—Equipment Schedule 2
W.B. 106.4"; 3.0 Liter.

Arc Sedan 4D	ED49Z	39275	900	1025	1750	3075
Arc Wagon 4D	ED59Z	39975	1200	1375	2100	3625

2004 SAAB — YS3(FB45S)-4-#

9-3—4-Cyl. Turbo—Equipment Schedule 3
W.B. 105.3"; 2.0 Liter.

Linear Sedan 4D	FB49S	28015	1350	1475	2175	3625

9-3—4-Cyl. HO Turbo—Equipment Schedule 3
W.B. 105.3"; 2.0 Liter.

Arc Sedan 4D	FD49Y	32110	1575	1725	2525	4150
Arc Convertible 2D	FD79Y	41920	2600	2825	3775	6025
Aero Sedan 4D	FH49Y	34710	2025	2200	3050	4950
Aero Convertible 2D	FH79Y	44525	3000	3250	4125	6525

9-5—4-Cyl. Turbo—Equipment Schedule 2
W.B. 106.4"; 2.3 Liter.

Linear Wagon 4D	EB59E	34225	1225	1400	1975	3250
Arc Sedan 4D	ED49G	36455	1375	1550	2175	3575
Arc Wagon 4D	ED59G	37165	1600	1800	2450	3975
Manual, 5-Spd			(300)	(300)	(410)	(410)

9-5—4-Cyl. HO Turbo—Equipment Schedule 2
W.B. 106.4"; 2.3 Liter.

Aero Sedan 4D	EH49G	41490	2650	2975	3700	5925
Aero Wagon 4D	EH59G	42195	2875	3250	4000	6375
Manual, 5-Spd			(300)	(300)	(410)	(410)

EQUIPMENT & MILEAGE PAGE 9 TO 23

Body Type	VIN	List	Trade-In Good	Very Good	Pvt-Party Good	Retail Excellent

2005 SAAB — (YS3orJF4)(GG616)–5–#

9-2X AWD—4-Cyl.—Equipment Schedule 3
W.B. 99.4"; 2.5 Liter.

Body Type	VIN	List	Good	Very Good	Good	Excellent
Linear Wagon 4D	GG616	24935	2925	3225	4200	6600

9-2X AWD—4-Cyl. Turbo—Equipment Schedule 3
W.B. 99.4"; 2.0 Liter.

Aero Wagon 4D	GG226	28895	4350	4800	5525	8150

9-3—4-Cyl. Turbo—Equipment Schedule 3
W.B. 105.3"; 2.0 Liter.

Linear Sedan 4D	FB49S	28920	1575	1725	2625	4125
Linear Convertible 2D	FB79S	39170	2725	2950	3925	6075

9-3—4-Cyl. HO Turbo—Equipment Schedule 3
W.B. 105.3"; 2.0 Liter.

Arc Sedan 4D	FD49Y	32320	1975	2150	3075	4850
Arc Convertible 2D	FD79Y	42170	3100	3375	4350	6675
Aero Sedan 4D	FH49Y	34200	2375	2600	3575	5550
Aero Convertible 2D	FH79Y	44670	3375	3675	4750	7250

9-5—4-Cyl. Turbo—Equipment Schedule 2
W.B. 106.4"; 2.3 Liter.

Linear Wagon 4D	EB59E	34620	1525	1725	2425	3775
Arc Sedan 4D	ED49A	36970	1600	1800	2550	4000
Arc Wagon 4D	ED59A	37770	1975	2225	2950	4550
Manual, 5-Spd			(350)	(350)	(475)	(475)

9-5—4-Cyl. HO Turbo—Equipment Schedule 2
W.B. 106.4"; 2.3 Liter.

Aero Sedan 4D	EH49G	42020	3075	3425	4225	6475
Aero Wagon 4D	EH59G	42820	3125	3500	4525	7025
Manual, 5-Spd			(350)	(350)	(475)	(475)

2006 SAAB — (YS3orJF4)(GG616)–6–#

9-2X AWD—4-Cyl.—Equipment Schedule 3
W.B. 99.4"; 2.5 Liter.

2.5i Wagon 4D	GG616	24960	3350	3675	4800	7350

9-2X AWD—4-Cyl. Turbo—Equipment Schedule 3
W.B. 99.4"; 2.5 Liter.

Aero Wagon 4D	GG726	28920	4975	5450	6200	8975

9-3—4-Cyl. Turbo—Equipment Schedule 3
W.B. 105.3"; 2.0 Liter.

2.0T Sedan 4D	FD49Y	27970	2250	2450	3225	4825
2.0T Convertible 2D	FD79Y	38570	3550	3825	4750	6975
2.0T SportCombi Wag	FD59Y	28970	2625	2850	3675	5475

9-3—6-Cyl. Turbo—Equipment Schedule 3
W.B. 105.3"; 2.8 Liter.

Aero Sedan 4D	FH41U	33970	3125	3400	4350	6425
Aero Convertible 2D	FH71U	43970	4300	4650	5525	8000
Aero SportCombi Wag	FH51U	34970	3600	3900	4875	7200
20th Anniversary			800	800	1075	1075

9-5—4-Cyl. Turbo—Equipment Schedule 3
W.B. 106.4"; 2.3 Liter.

2.3T Sedan 4D	ED45G	36170	2375	2650	3275	4850
2.3T SportCombi Wag	ED56G	37170	3200	3550	4300	6275
Manual, 5-Spd			(400)	(400)	(545)	(545)

2007 SAAB — (YS3orJF4)(FD49Y)–7–#

9-3—4-Cyl. Turbo—Equipment Schedule 3
W.B. 105.3"; 2.0 Liter.

2.0T Sedan 4D	FD49Y	27995	3125	3375	4100	5875
2.0T Convertible 2D	FD79Y	38595	4400	4750	5475	7625
2.0T SportCombi Wag	FD59Y	28995	3800	4100	4825	6775

9-3—V6 Turbo—Equipment Schedule 3
W.B. 105.3"; 2.8 Liter.

Aero Sedan 4D	FH41U	34295	4300	4625	5375	7525
Aero Convertible 2D	FH716	44195	5125	5525	6400	8900
Aero SportCombi Wag	FH51U	35195	4875	5250	5950	8300
4-Cyl, Turbo, 2.0L (Wag)	Y		(1200)	(1200)	(1585)	(1585)

9-5—4-Cyl. Turbo—Equipment Schedule 2
W.B. 106.4"; 2.3 Liter.

2.3T Sedan 4D	ED45G	36465	3300	3650	4375	6200
2.3T Aero Sedan 4D	EH49G	36535	3725	4100	4850	6925
2.3T SportCombi Wag	ED55G	37465	4250	4650	5425	7700
2.3T Aero SportCombi	EH59G	37535	4600	5050	5825	8275

2007 SAAB

Body Type	VIN	List	Trade-In Good	Very Good	Pvt-Party Good	Retail Excellent
Manual, 5-Spd............................			(450)	(450)	(595)	(595)

2008 SAAB — (YS3orJF4)(FB49Y)-8-#

9-3—4-Cyl. Turbo—Equipment Schedule 3
W.B. 105.3"; 2.0 Liter.
2.0T Sedan 4D	FB49Y	29735	3925	4175	5050	6925
2.0T Convertible 2D	FB79Y	41060	6150	6575	7525	10100
2.0T SportCombi Wag	FB59Y	30980	4725	5025	5825	7875

9-3—V6 Turbo—Equipment Schedule 3
W.B. 105.3"; 2.8 Liter.
Aero Sedan 4D	FH41U	36715	5350	5700	6650	8900
Aero Convertible 2D	FH71U	47015	8275	8800	9700	12800
Aero SportCombi Wag	FH51U	37615	6400	6825	7800	10450
XWD	2,7		1475	1475	1975	1975

9-3 AWD—V6 Turbo—Equipment Schedule 3
W.B. 105.3"; 2.8 Liter.
| Turbo X Sedan 4D | FM42R | 43860 | 7525 | 8025 | 9050 | 12100 |
| Turbo X SportCombi | FM57U | 44660 | 7800 | 8300 | 9225 | 12250 |

9-5—4-Cyl. Turbo—Equipment Schedule 2
W.B. 106.4"; 2.3 Liter.
2.3T Sedan 4D	ED49G	37205	4350	4675	5400	7275
2.3T Aero Sedan 4D	EH49G	38300	5200	5600	6400	8475
2.3T SportCombi Wag	ED59G	38455	5100	5500	6400	8550
2.3T Aero SportCombi	EH59G	39550	5375	5775	6725	9025
Manual, 5-Spd w/Overdrive	5		(500)	(500)	(625)	(625)

2009 SAAB — (YS3)(FB49Y)-9-#

9-3—4-Cyl. Turbo—Equipment Schedule 3
W.B. 105.3"; 2.0 Liter.
2.0T Sedan 4D	FB49Y	31535	5000	5300	6225	8200
2.0T Convertible 2D	FB79Y	44280	8150	8625	9675	12450
2.0T SportCombi Wag	FB59Y	32390	5650	5975	7050	9200
XWD			1575	1575	2105	2105

9-3 AWD—V6 Turbo—Equipment Schedule 3
W.B. 105.3"; 2.8 Liter.
| Aero Sedan 4D | FH42R | 44010 | 7950 | 8425 | 9450 | 12200 |
| Aero SportCombi Wag | FH52R | 45290 | 8275 | 8750 | 9775 | 12600 |

9-3—V6 Turbo—Equipment Schedule 3
W.B. 105.3"; 2.8 Liter.
| Aero Convertible 2D | FH71R | 51735 | 9975 | 10550 | 11550 | 14700 |

9-5—4-Cyl. Turbo—Equipment Schedule 2
W.B. 106.4"; 2.3 Liter.
2.3T Sedan 4D	ED49G	39285	7200	7625	8775	11350
2.3T SportCombi Wag	ED59G	40555	8125	8600	9750	12500
Aero Sedan 4D	EH49G	40305	8225	8700	9750	12450
Aero SportCombi Wag	EH59G	41670	8400	8900	10050	12950
Griffin Sedan 4D	EB49G	42775	8100	8575	9800	12700
Griffin SptCombi Wag	EB59G	44045	8400	8900	10200	13250
Manual, 5-Spd w/Overdrive	5		(525)	(525)	(630)	(630)

2010 SAAB — (YS3)(FA4CY)-A-#

9-3—4-Cyl. Turbo—Equipment Schedule 3
W.B. 105.3"; 2.0 Liter.
2.0T Sport Sedan 4D	FA4CY	31075	6250	6600	7675	9725
2.0T Convertible 2D	FE7CY	42165	10150	10650	11750	14650
2.0T SportCombi Wag	FA5CY	32505	7175	7550	8650	10900
Aero Sport Sedan 4D	FC4CY	37515	9900	10400	11500	14300
Aero Convertible 2D	FG7CY	47255	12550	13150	14200	17500
Aero SportCombi Wag	FC5CY	39195	10200	10750	11850	14750
XWD			1675	1675	2225	2225

9-3X AWD—4-Cyl. Turbo—Equipment Schedule 3
W.B. 105.3"; 2.0 Liter.
| SportCombi Wagon | FD5BY | 37800 | 9500 | 10000 | 11100 | 13800 |

9-5 AWD—V6 Turbo—Equipment Schedule 3
W.B. 111.7"; 2.8 Liter.
| Aero Sedan 4D | ER4BJ | 49990 | 12050 | 12550 | 13800 | 16900 |

2011 SAAB — (YS3)(FA4CY)-B-#

9-3—4-Cyl. Turbo—Equipment Schedule 3
W.B. 105.3"; 2.0 Liter.
| 2.0T Sport Sedan 4D | FA4CY | 31075 | 8175 | 8550 | 9700 | 11950 |
| 2.0T Convertible 2D | FE7CY | 42165 | 12100 | 12650 | 13850 | 16850 |

Body Type	VIN	List	Trade-In Good	Trade-In Very Good	Pvt-Party Good	Retail Excellent
2.0T SportCombi Wag	FA5CY	32505	9775	10200	11400	13900
Aero Sport Sedan 4D	FC4CY	36165	11900	12400	13650	16650
Aero Convertible 2D	FG7CY	45905	14250	14900	16100	19450
Aero SportCombi Wag	FC5CY	37845	12200	12800	14000	17000
9-3X AWD—4-Cyl. Turbo—Equipment Schedule 3						
W.B. 105.3"; 2.0 Liter.						
SportCombi Wagon	FD5BY	37800	11450	12000	13300	16250
Turbo4 XWD Sedan	FA4BZ	33220	10150	10650	11800	14400
Aero XWD Sport Sed	FC4NY	38940	12450	13050	14200	17250
Auto, 6-Spd w/Sentronic	B		275	275	325	325
9-5—4-Cyl. Turbo—Equipment Schedule 3						
W.B. 111.7"; 2.0 Liter.						
Turbo4 Sedan 4D	GN4AR	39350	11550	11950	13400	16000
Turbo4 Premium 4D	GN4AR	44260	11700	12100	13550	16250
9-5 AWD—V6 Turbo—Equipment Schedule 3						
W.B. 111.7"; 2.8 Liter.						
Turbo6 Sedan 4D	GN4BJ	48855	12950	13400	14900	17800
Aero Sedan 4D	GR4BJ	51390	13450	13900	15450	18450

SATURN

2000 SATURN — 1G8(JorZ)(F528)-Y-#

SATURN—4-Cyl.—Equipment Schedule 6
W.B. 102.4"; 1.9 Liter.

Body Type	VIN	List	Good	Very Good	Good	Excellent
SL Sedan 4D	F528	12085	400	500	1075	2050
SL1 Sedan 4D	G528	12885	400	500	1075	2050
SL2 Sedan 4D	J527	13335	450	575	1150	2225
SC1 Coupe 3D	N128	12975	375	475	1050	2025
SC2 Coupe 3D	R127	15585	550	675	1300	2475
SW2 Wagon 4D	J827	14730	525	625	1250	2400
SATURN L-SERIES—4-Cyl.—Equipment Schedule 3						
W.B. 106.5"; 2.2 Liter.						
LS Sedan 4D	R52F	16700	250	275	700	1250
LS1 Sedan 4D	T52F	18150	275	325	825	1550
LW1 Wagon 4D	U82F	19375	300	375	900	1675
Manual, 5-Spd			(175)	(175)	(220)	(220)
SATURN L-SERIES—V6—Equipment Schedule 3						
W.B. 106.5"; 3.0 Liter.						
LS2 Sedan 4D	W52R	20575	575	650	1300	2425
LW2 Wagon 4D	W82R	21800	800	925	1600	2900

2001 SATURN — 1G8(JorZ)(F528)-1-#

SATURN—4-Cyl.—Equipment Schedule 6
W.B. 102.4"; 1.9 Liter.

Body Type	VIN	List	Good	Very Good	Good	Excellent
SL Sedan 4D	F528	11995	425	525	1075	2050
SL1 Sedan 4D	G528	12910	425	525	1100	2100
SL2 Sedan 4D	J527	13360	525	650	1225	2350
SC1 Coupe 3D	N128	13960	550	675	1275	2425
SC2 Coupe 3D	R127	16110	700	850	1500	2825
SW2 Wagon 4D	J827	14755	675	825	1475	2775
SATURN L-SERIES—4-Cyl.—Equipment Schedule 3						
W.B. 106.5"; 2.2 Liter.						
L100 Sedan 4D	R52F	16245	250	300	800	1475
L200 Sedan 4D	T52F	18210	325	375	950	1800
LW200 Wagon 4D	U82F	19335	350	425	1050	2000
Manual, 5-Spd			(200)	(200)	(265)	(265)
SATURN L-SERIES—V6—Equipment Schedule 3						
W.B. 106.5"; 3.0 Liter.						
L300 Sedan 4D	W52R	19995	800	925	1675	3075
LW300 Wagon 4D	W82R	21860	1050	1225	2000	3625

2002 SATURN — 1G8(JorZ)(F528)-2-#

SATURN—4-Cyl.—Equipment Schedule 6
W.B. 102.4"; 1.9 Liter.

Body Type	VIN	List	Good	Very Good	Good	Excellent
SL Sedan 4D	F528	11995	450	575	1125	2075
SL1 Sedan 4D	G528	13275	500	625	1150	2100
SL2 Sedan 4D	J527	13800	700	825	1400	2550
SC1 Coupe 3D	N128	14325	725	850	1425	2625
SC2 Coupe 3D	R127	16545	875	1050	1625	2975
SATURN L-SERIES—4-Cyl.—Equipment Schedule 3						
W.B. 106.5"; 2.2 Liter.						

1015

Body Type	VIN	List	Trade-In Good	Very Good	Pvt-Party Good	Retail Excellent
L100 Sedan 4D	R52F	16870	275	325	875	1650
L200 Sedan 4D	T52F	19070	425	500	1200	2250
LW200 Wagon 4D	U82F	20515	550	650	1350	2500
Manual, 5-Spd			(200)	(200)	(265)	(265)
SATURN L-SERIES—V6—Equipment Schedule 3						
W.B. 106.5"; 3.0 Liter.						
L300 Sedan 4D	W52R	20920	1025	1150	1925	3450
LW300 Wagon 4D	W82R	22850	1275	1450	2250	3950

2003 SATURN — 1G8(AG54F)-3-#

ION—4-Cyl.—Equipment Schedule 6
W.B. 103.2"; 2.2 Liter.

1 Sedan 4D	AG54F	12895	575	675	1350	2525
2 Sedan 4D	AJ54F	14895	800	950	1600	2950
3 Sedan 4D	AL52F	16395	1150	1350	2000	3575
2 Quad Coupe 4D	AN12F	15395	925	1075	1750	3175
3 Quad Coupe 4D	AW12F	16895	1275	1475	2125	3800
SATURN L-SERIES—4-Cyl.—Equipment Schedule 3						
W.B. 106.5"; 2.2 Liter.						
L200 Sedan 4D	JT54F	19040	575	650	1425	2650
LW200 Wagon 4D	JU84F	20850	675	800	1550	2850
Manual, 5-Spd			(225)	(225)	(310)	(310)
SATURN L-SERIES—V6—Equipment Schedule 3						
W.B. 106.5"; 3.0 Liter.						
L300 Sedan 4D	JW54R	21255	1250	1425	2225	3925
LW300 Wagon 4D	JW84R	23185	1475	1675	2575	4475

2004 SATURN — 1G8(AG54F)-4-#

ION—4-Cyl.—Equipment Schedule 6
W.B. 103.2"; 2.2 Liter.

1 Sedan 4D	AG54F	11975	1025	1200	1800	3200
2 Sedan 4D	AJ52F	15200	1250	1475	2175	3775
3 Sedan 4D	AL52F	16725	1525	1775	2475	4250
2 Quad Coupe 4D	AN12F	15750	1375	1600	2325	4050
3 Quad Coupe 4D	AW12F	17250	1525	1775	2525	4350
ION—4-Cyl. Supercharged—Equipment Schedule 6						
W.B. 103.5"; 2.0 Liter.						
Red Line Quad Cpe 4D	AY12P	20950	1550	1800	2375	4000
SATURN L-SERIES—4-Cyl.—Equipment Schedule 3						
W.B. 106.5"; 2.2 Liter.						
L300 Sedan 4D	JC54F	16995	675	775	1625	3000
L300 Wagon 4D	JC84F	19045	875	1000	1850	3325
SATURN L-SERIES—V6—Equipment Schedule 3						
W.B. 106.5"; 3.0 Liter.						
L300 Sedan 4D	JD54R	21410	1500	1700	2600	4450
L300 Wagon 4D	JD84R	23560	1800	2025	2925	4975

2005 SATURN — 1G8(AG52F)-5-#

ION—4-Cyl.—Equipment Schedule 6
W.B. 103.2"; 2.2 Liter.

1 Sedan 4D	AG52F	12975	975	1125	1925	3325
2 Sedan 4D	AJ52F	15845	1350	1575	2400	4025
3 Sedan 4D	AL52F	17370	1700	2000	2775	4600
2 Quad Coupe 4D	AN12F	16395	1500	1750	2575	4325
3 Quad Coupe 4D	AW12F	18145	1850	2150	2900	4775
ION—4-Cyl. Supercharged—Equipment Schedule 6						
W.B. 103.2"; 2.0 Liter.						
Red Line Quad Cpe 4D	AY12P	21450	1725	2000	2725	4425
SATURN L-SERIES—V6—Equipment Schedule 3						
W.B. 106.5"; 3.0 Liter.						
L300 Sedan 4D	JD54R	21995	1625	1825	2925	4925

2006 SATURN — 1G8(AJ55F)-6-#

ION—4-Cyl.—Equipment Schedule 6
W.B. 103.2"; 2.2 Liter, 2.4 Liter.

2 Sedan 4D	AJ55F	13390	1650	1900	2750	4550
3 Sedan 4D	AL55F	15790	2225	2550	3450	5625
2 Quad Coupe 4D	AN15F	13825	1850	2125	3000	4925
3 Quad Coupe 4D	AW15F	17090	2325	2675	3575	5825
Manual, 5-Spd	M		(275)	(275)	(355)	(355)
ION—4-Cyl. Supercharged—Equipment Schedule 6						
W.B. 103.2"; 2.0 Liter.						

2006 SATURN

Body Type	VIN	List	Trade-In Good	Very Good	Pvt-Party Good	Retail Excellent
Red Line Quad Cpe 4D	AY15P	19990	2225	2525	3100	4800

2007 SATURN — 1G8(AJ55F)-7-#

ION—4-Cyl.—Equipment Schedule 6
W.B. 103.2"; 2.2 Liter, 2.4 Liter.

Body Type	VIN	List	Trade-In Good	Very Good	Pvt-Party Good	Retail Excellent
2 Sedan 4D	AJ55F	13495	2050	2325	3125	4950
3 Sedan 4D	AL55F	15915	2800	3150	3975	6200
2 Quad Coupe 4D	AN15F	14495	2450	2750	3575	5600
3 Quad Coupe 4D	AW15F	17215	2875	3250	4200	6550
Manual, 5-Spd	M		(300)	(300)	(385)	(385)

ION—4-Cyl. Supercharged—Equipment Schedule 6
W.B. 103.2"; 2.0 Liter.

Body Type	VIN	List	Trade-In Good	Very Good	Pvt-Party Good	Retail Excellent
Red Line Quad Cpe 4D	AY15P	20420	3175	3600	4300	6450

AURA—V6—Equipment Schedule 4
W.B. 112.3"; 3.5 Liter, 3.6 Liter.

Body Type	VIN	List	Trade-In Good	Very Good	Pvt-Party Good	Retail Excellent
XE Sedan 4D	ZS57N	20595	3525	3900	4650	6950
XR Sedan 4D	ZV577	24595	3850	4275	5225	7850
Panorama Roof			300	300	405	405

SKY—4-Cyl.—Equipment Schedule 3
W.B. 95.1"; 2.4 Liter.

Body Type	VIN	List	Trade-In Good	Very Good	Pvt-Party Good	Retail Excellent
Roadster 2D	MB35B	24540	5100	5550	6275	8600

SKY—4-Cyl. Turbo—Equipment Schedule 3
W.B. 95.1"; 2.0 Liter.

Body Type	VIN	List	Trade-In Good	Very Good	Pvt-Party Good	Retail Excellent
Red Line Roadster 2D	MG35X	29745	5250	5700	6575	9125

2008 SATURN — 1G8(AR671)-8-#

ASTRA—4-Cyl.—Equipment Schedule 4
W.B. 102.9"; 1.8 Liter.

Body Type	VIN	List	Trade-In Good	Very Good	Pvt-Party Good	Retail Excellent
XE Hatchback 4D	AR671	17718	2975	3300	4000	5725
XR Hatchback 2D	AT271	18870	3650	4025	4675	6575
XR Hatchback 4D	AT671	19115	3900	4300	4900	6875

AURA—4-Cyl. Hybrid—Equipment Schedule 4
W.B. 112.3"; 2.4 Liter.

Body Type	VIN	List	Trade-In Good	Very Good	Pvt-Party Good	Retail Excellent
Green Line Sedan 4D	ZR575	22790	5075	5575	6800	9950

AURA—V6—Equipment Schedule 4
W.B. 112.3"; 3.5 Liter, 3.6 Liter.

Body Type	VIN	List	Trade-In Good	Very Good	Pvt-Party Good	Retail Excellent
XE Sedan 4D	ZS57N	21495	4175	4575	5550	8025
XR Sedan 4D	ZV577	25495	4750	5200	6300	9125
4-Cyl, 2.4 Liter	B		(250)	(250)	(330)	(330)

SKY—4-Cyl.—Equipment Schedule 3
W.B. 95.1"; 2.4 Liter.

Body Type	VIN	List	Trade-In Good	Very Good	Pvt-Party Good	Retail Excellent
Roadster 2D	MC35B	26520	6425	6900	7700	10050

SKY—4-Cyl. Turbo—Equipment Schedule 3
W.B. 95.1"; 2.0 Liter.

Body Type	VIN	List	Trade-In Good	Very Good	Pvt-Party Good	Retail Excellent
Red Line Roadster 2D	MG35X	30700	7075	7575	8450	11050

2009 SATURN — 1G8(ZR575)-9-#

AURA—4-Cyl. Hybrid—Equipment Schedule 4
W.B. 112.3"; 2.4 Liter.

Body Type	VIN	List	Trade-In Good	Very Good	Pvt-Party Good	Retail Excellent
Sedan 4D	ZR575	25580	5900	6425	7750	10750

AURA—4-Cyl.—Equipment Schedule 4
W.B. 112.3"; 2.4 Liter.

Body Type	VIN	List	Trade-In Good	Very Good	Pvt-Party Good	Retail Excellent
XE Sedan 4D	ZS57B	21995	5175	5650	6550	8975

AURA—V6—Equipment Schedule 4
W.B. 112.3"; 3.6 Liter.

Body Type	VIN	List	Trade-In Good	Very Good	Pvt-Party Good	Retail Excellent
XR Sedan 4D	ZV577	26595	5825	6350	7500	10300
4-Cyl, 2.4 Liter	B		(275)	(275)	(365)	(365)

SKY—4-Cyl.—Equipment Schedule 3
W.B. 95.1"; 2.4 Liter.

Body Type	VIN	List	Trade-In Good	Very Good	Pvt-Party Good	Retail Excellent
Roadster 2D	MN35B	27780	8350	8850	9725	12150

SKY—4-Cyl. Turbo—Equipment Schedule 3
W.B. 95.1"; 2.0 Liter.

Body Type	VIN	List	Trade-In Good	Very Good	Pvt-Party Good	Retail Excellent
Red Line Roadster 2D	MG35X	32090	10150	10700	11500	14250

SCION

2004 SCION — JT(KorL)(KT624)-4-#

xA—4-Cyl.—Equipment Schedule 6
W.B. 93.3"; 1.5 Liter.

Body Type	VIN	List	Trade-In Good	Very Good	Pvt-Party Good	Retail Excellent
Hatchback 4D	KT624	13765	2225	2450	2975	4625

2004 SCION

Body Type	VIN	List	Trade-In Good	Very Good	Pvt-Party Good	Retail Excellent
xB—4-Cyl.—Equipment Schedule 6						
W.B. 98.4"; 1.5 Liter.						
Sport Wagon 4D	KT324	13765	2900	3325	3625	5750

2005 SCION — JT(KorL)(KT624)-5-#

Body Type	VIN	List	Good	Very Good	Good	Excellent
xA—4-Cyl.—Equipment Schedule 6						
W.B. 93.3"; 1.5 Liter.						
Hatchback 4D	KT624	13795	2650	2925	3575	5400
Release Series 1.0			425	425	575	575
Release Series 2.0			275	275	365	365
xB—4-Cyl.—Equipment Schedule 6						
W.B. 98.4"; 1.5 Liter.						
Sport Wagon 4D	KT334	14995	3150	3600	4025	6225
Release Series 3.0			350	350	455	455
tC—4-Cyl.—Equipment Schedule 4						
W.B. 106.3"; 2.4 Liter.						
Hatchback Coupe 2D	DE177	17265	3125	3400	4250	6325

2006 SCION — JT(KorL)(KT624)-6-#

Body Type	VIN	List	Good	Very Good	Good	Excellent
xA—4-Cyl.—Equipment Schedule 6						
W.B. 93.3"; 1.5 Liter.						
Hatchback 4D	KT624	14110	3100	3400	4150	6075
Release Series 2.0			300	300	390	390
Release Series 3.0			625	625	845	845
Manual, 5-Spd			(275)	(275)	(355)	(355)
xB—4-Cyl.—Equipment Schedule 6						
W.B. 98.4"; 1.5 Liter.						
Sport Wagon 4D	KT324	15260	3575	4075	4550	6775
Release Series 2.0			375	375	485	485
Release Series 3.0			625	625	845	845
Manual, 5-Spd	3		(275)	(275)	(355)	(355)
tC—4-Cyl.—Equipment Schedule 4						
W.B. 106.3"; 2.4 Liter.						
Hatchback Coupe 2D	DE177	17580	3750	4050	4900	7100
Release Series 2.0			625	625	845	845
Special Edition			775	775	1040	1040

2007 SCION — JT(KorL)(DE177)-7-#

Body Type	VIN	List	Good	Very Good	Good	Excellent
tC—4-Cyl.—Equipment Schedule 4						
W.B. 106.3"; 2.4 Liter.						
Spec H'Back Coupe 2D	DE177	16340	4400	4750	5500	7725
Hatchback Coupe 2D	DE177	17820	4525	4875	5625	7900
Release Series 3.0			675	675	910	910

2008 SCION — JT(KorL)(KU104)-8-#

Body Type	VIN	List	Good	Very Good	Good	Excellent
xD—4-Cyl.—Equipment Schedule 4						
W.B. 96.9"; 1.8 Liter.						
Hatchback 4D	KU104	15970	5025	5400	6300	8425
Release Series 1.0			700	700	925	925
xB—4-Cyl.—Equipment Schedule 6						
W.B. 102.4"; 2.4 Liter.						
Sport Wagon 4D	KE50E	17270	5450	6025	6600	9025
Manual, 5-Spd w/Overdrive			(350)	(350)	(460)	(460)
tC—4-Cyl.—Equipment Schedule 4						
W.B. 106.3"; 2.4 Liter.						
Spec H'Back Coupe 2D	DE167	16720	4950	5275	6075	8200
Hatchback Coupe 2D	DE167	18470	5125	5475	6425	8600
Release Series 4.0			575	575	780	780

2009 SCION — JT(KorL)(KU104)-9-#

Body Type	VIN	List	Good	Very Good	Good	Excellent
xD—4-Cyl.—Equipment Schedule 4						
W.B. 96.9"; 1.8 Liter.						
Hatchback 4D	KU104	16145	5800	6150	7150	9175
Release Series 2.0			700	700	930	930
xB—4-Cyl.—Equipment Schedule 6						
W.B. 102.4"; 2.4 Liter.						
Sport Wagon 4D	KE50E	17320	6450	6975	7575	9925
Manual, 5-Spd w/Overdrive			(375)	(375)	(490)	(490)
tC—4-Cyl.—Equipment Schedule 4						
W.B. 106.3"; 2.4 Liter.						
Hatchback Coupe 2D	DE167	18470	5850	6200	7150	9250

Body Type	VIN	List	Trade-In Good	Very Good	Pvt-Party Good	Retail Excellent
Release Series 5.0			600	600	785	785

2010 SCION — JT(KorL)(KU4B4)–A–#

xD—4-Cyl.—Equipment Schedule 4
W.B. 96.9"; 1.8 Liter.

Hatchback 4D	KU4B4	16295	6850	7175	8250	10200

xB—4-Cyl.—Equipment Schedule 6
W.B. 102.4"; 2.4 Liter.

Sport Wagon 4D	ZE4FE	17395	7475	7975	8700	11000
Manual, 5-Spd w/Overdrive			(450)	(450)	(605)	(605)

xB—4-Cyl.—Equipment Schedule 6
W.B. 102.4"; 2.4 Liter.

Release Series 7.0 Wag	ZE4FE	18990	7875	8400	9175	11650
Automatic, 4-Spd w/OD			375	375	495	495

tC—4-Cyl.—Equipment Schedule 4
W.B. 106.3"; 2.4 Liter.

Hatchback Coupe 2D	DE3B7	18520	6725	7075	8050	10100
Release Series 6.0 2D	DE3B7	19290	7775	8175	9175	11450

2011 SCION — JT(KorL)(KU4B4)–B–#

xD—4-Cyl.—Equipment Schedule 4
W.B. 96.9"; 1.8 Liter.

Hatchback 4D	KU4B4	16420	7725	8050	9275	11200
Release Series 3.0 4D	KU4B4	18425	8650	9000	10200	12250

xB—4-Cyl.—Equipment Schedule 6
W.B. 102.4"; 2.4 Liter.

Sport Wagon 4D	ZE4FE	17680	8775	9250	10050	12300
Manual, 5-Spd w/Overdrive			(500)	(500)	(625)	(625)

xB—4-Cyl.—Equipment Schedule 6
W.B. 102.4"; 2.4 Liter.

Release Series 8.0 Wag	ZE4FE	19125	9375	9900	10700	13150
Automatic, 4-Spd w/OD			425	425	545	545

tC—4-Cyl.—Equipment Schedule 4
W.B. 102.4"; 2.4 Liter.

Hatchback Coupe 2D	JF5C7	19995	8500	8900	9925	12100

2012 SCION — JT(K,LorN)(JJ1B0)–C–#

iQ—4-Cyl.—Equipment Schedule 4
W.B. 78.7"; 1.3 Liter.

Hatchback 2D	JJ1B0	15995	6750	7075	8125	10000

xD—4-Cyl.—Equipment Schedule 4
W.B. 96.9"; 1.8 Liter.

Hatchback 4D	KU4B4	16875	8750	9075	10400	12350
Release Series 4.0 4D	KU4B4	17780	9300	9625	11000	13000

xB—4-Cyl.—Equipment Schedule 6
W.B. 102.4"; 2.4 Liter.

Sport Wagon 4D	ZE4FE	17980	9825	10300	11200	13450

tC—4-Cyl.—Equipment Schedule 4
W.B. 106.3"; 2.4 Liter.

Hatchback Coupe 2D	JF5C7	20295	10050	10500	11550	13750
Release Series 7.0 2D	JF5C7	22625	10900	11350	12400	14750

2013 SCION — JT(K,LorN)(JJXB0)–D–#

iQ—4-Cyl.—Equipment Schedule 4
W.B. 78.7"; 1.3 Liter.

Hatchback 2D	JJXB0	16140	8025	8325	9425	11350

xD—4-Cyl.—Equipment Schedule 4
W.B. 96.9"; 1.8 Liter.

Hatchback 4D	KUPB4	17275	10000	10300	11700	13650
10 Series H'Back 4D	KUPB4	19710	11150	11500	12900	14900

xB—4-Cyl.—Equipment Schedule 6
W.B. 102.4"; 2.4 Liter.

Sport Wagon 4D	ZE4FE	18675	11350	11800	12750	15000
10 Series Spt Wagon	ZE4FE	20915	12500	13000	13800	16150

tC—4-Cyl.—Equipment Schedule 4
W.B. 106.3"; 2.5 Liter.

Hatchback Coupe 2D	JF5C7	20455	11200	11650	12750	15000
Release Series 8.0 2D	JF5C7	23595	12450	12900	13950	16300

FR-S—4-Cyl.—Equipment Schedule 4
W.B. 101.2"; 2.0 Liter.

Coupe 2D	ZNAA1	24930	16300	16800	18050	20300

2014 SCION

Body Type	VIN	List	Trade-In Good	Very Good	Pvt-Party Good	Retail Excellent

2014 SCION — JT(K,LorN)(JJXB0)–E–#

iQ—4-Cyl.—Equipment Schedule 4
W.B. 78.7"; 1.3 Liter.

Hatchback 2D	JJXB0	16420	**8600**	**8950**	**10050**	**12050**
10 Series H'Back 2D	JJXB0	18605	**10050**	**10450**	**11500**	**13650**

xD—4-Cyl.—Equipment Schedule 4
W.B. 96.9"; 1.8 Liter.

Hatchback 4D	KUPB4	17475	**11000**	**11350**	**12800**	**14800**

xB—4-Cyl.—Equipment Schedule 6
W.B. 102.4"; 2.4 Liter.

Sport Wagon 4D	ZE4FE	18675	**13550**	**14100**	**15000**	**17450**
10 Series Sport Wagon	ZE4FE	20915	**14550**	**15100**	**15950**	**18450**

tC—4-Cyl.—Equipment Schedule 4
W.B. 106.3"; 2.5 Liter.

Hatchback Coupe 2D	JF5C7	20965	**13000**	**13550**	**14600**	**16950**
Monogram Series 2D	JF5C7	23155	**14250**	**14800**	**15800**	**18200**
10 Series H'Back 2D	JF5C7	23195	**14500**	**15100**	**16050**	**18450**

FR-S—4-Cyl.—Equipment Schedule 4
W.B. 101.2"; 2.0 Liter.

Coupe 2D	ZNAA1	26555	**17250**	**17750**	**19050**	**21500**
Monogram Series 2D	ZNAA1	29255	**17250**	**17750**	**19050**	**21400**

SMART

2009 SMART — WME(EJ31X)–9–#

FORTWO—3-Cyl.—Equipment Schedule 3
W.B. 73.5"; 1.0 Liter.

Pure Hatchback 2D	EJ31X	12635	**2175**	**2325**	**3425**	**4975**
Passion Hatchback 2D	EJ31X	14635	**2500**	**2650**	**3850**	**5500**
Passion Cabriolet	EK31X	17635	**3225**	**3425**	**4575**	**6325**
BRABUS H'Back 2D	EJ31X	18635	**3900**	**4125**	**5250**	**7150**
BRABUS Cabriolet	EK31X	21635	**4575**	**4850**	**6200**	**8425**

2010 SMART — WME(EJ3BA)–A–#

FORTWO—3-Cyl.—Equipment Schedule 3
W.B. 73.5"; 1.0 Liter.

Pure Coupe 2D	EJ3BA	12635	**2550**	**2675**	**3850**	**5425**
Passion Coupe 2D	EJ3BA	14635	**2925**	**3100**	**4425**	**6125**
Passion Cabriolet	EK4BA	17635	**4200**	**4425**	**5450**	**7125**

2011 SMART — WME(EJ3BA)–B–#

FORTWO—3-Cyl.—Equipment Schedule 3
W.B. 73.5"; 1.0 Liter.

Pure Coupe 2D	EJ3BA	13240	**2925**	**3075**	**4325**	**5950**
Passion Coupe 2D	EJ3BA	15440	**3550**	**3725**	**5075**	**6850**
Passion Cabriolet	EK3BA	18440	**4700**	**4950**	**6275**	**8075**

2012 SMART — WME(EJ3BA)–C–#

FORTWO—3-Cyl.—Equipment Schedule 3
W.B. 73.5"; 1.0 Liter.

Pure Coupe 2D	EJ3BA	13240	**3525**	**3700**	**5075**	**6725**
Passion Coupe 2D	EJ3BA	15440	**4450**	**4625**	**5950**	**7750**
Passion Cabriolet	EK3BA	18440	**5925**	**6175**	**7500**	**9375**

2013 SMART — WME(EJ3BA)–D–#

FORTWO—3-Cyl.—Equipment Schedule 3
W.B. 73.5"; 1.0 Liter.

Pure Coupe 2D	EJ3BA	13240	**4775**	**4975**	**6325**	**8075**
Passion Hatchback 2D	EJ3BA	15640	**5250**	**5475**	**6975**	**8825**
Passion Cabriolet	EK3BA	18640	**7125**	**7400**	**8775**	**10750**

2014 SMART — WME(EJ3BA)–E–#

FORTWO—3-Cyl.—Equipment Schedule 3
W.B. 73.5"; 1.0 Liter.

Pure Coupe 2D	EJ3BA	15200	**6100**	**6350**	**7825**	**9775**
Passion Cabriolet	EK3BA	19510	**8850**	**9225**	**10500**	**12600**

FORTWO—AC Electric—Equipment Schedule 3
W.B. 73.5".

Body Type	VIN	List	Trade-In Good	Very Good	Pvt-Party Good	Retail Excellent
Coupe 2D	EJ9AA	25750	7500	7825	9400	11650
Cabriolet 2D	EK9AA	28750	9000	9375	10900	13300

SUBARU

2000 SUBARU — JF1or4S3(GC435)-Y-#

IMPREZA AWD—4-Cyl.—Equipment Schedule 5
W.B. 99.2"; 2.2 Liter, 2.5 Liter.

L Sedan 4D	GC435	17190	625	775	1250	2225
L Coupe 2D	GM435	17190	625	775	1225	2175
L Sport Wagon 4D	GF435	17590	800	975	1625	3050
Outback Sport Wag 4D	GF485	19390	1100	1350	2050	3750
2.5RS Sedan 4D	GC675	20590	1200	1450	2175	3975
2.5RS Coupe 2D	GM675	20590	1150	1375	1950	3475

LEGACY AWD—4-Cyl.—Equipment Schedule 4
W.B. 104.3"; 2.5 Liter.

Brighton Wagon 4D	BH625	19690	1075	1275	1775	3100
L Sedan 4D	BE635	20490	875	1050	1525	2725
L Wagon 4D	BH635	21190	1175	1375	1900	3325
GT Sedan 4D	BE645	24090	1650	1925	2400	4125
GT Limited Sedan 4D	BE656	25590	1825	2150	2700	4600
GT Wagon 4D	BH645	24990	1925	2275	2800	4775
Dual Moon Roofs			(75)	(75)	(105)	(105)
Manual, 5-Spd (Sedan)			(175)	(175)	(220)	(220)

OUTBACK AWD—4-Cyl.—Equipment Schedule 4
W.B. 104.3"; 2.5 Liter.

Wagon 4D	BH666	23990	900	1050	1825	3475
Limited Sedan 4D	BE686	26390	975	1175	1975	3725
Limited Wagon 4D	BH686	27390	1075	1275	2100	3925
Dual Moon Roofs			(75)	(75)	(105)	(105)

2001 SUBARU — JF1or4S3(GC435)-1-#

IMPREZA AWD—4-Cyl.—Equipment Schedule 5
W.B. 99.2"; 2.2 Liter, 2.5 Liter.

L Sedan 4D	GC435	17290	650	800	1300	2350
L Coupe 2D	GM435	17290	650	800	1275	2250
L Sport Wagon 4D	GF435	17690	825	1000	1675	3075
Outback Sport Wag 4D	GF485	19490	1400	1675	2325	4100
2.5RS Sedan 4D	GC675	20790	1375	1675	2400	4275
2.5RS Coupe 2D	GM675	20790	1375	1675	2250	3875

LEGACY AWD—4-Cyl.—Equipment Schedule 4
W.B. 104.3"; 2.5 Liter.

L Sedan 4D	BE635	20590	1075	1275	1800	3150
L Wagon 4D	BH635	21290	1375	1600	2150	3775
GT Sedan 4D	BE645	24190	1925	2250	2825	4800
GT Limited Sedan 4D	BE656	25690	2175	2550	3125	5275
GT Wagon 4D	BH645	25090	2275	2675	3225	5450
Dual Moon Roofs			75	75	115	115
Manual, 5-Spd (Sedan)			(200)	(200)	(265)	(265)

OUTBACK AWD—4-Cyl.—Equipment Schedule 4
W.B. 104.3"; 2.5 Liter.

Wagon 4D	BH665	24190	1275	1475	2175	3925
Limited Sedan 4D	BE686	26490	1425	1650	2350	4225
Limited Wagon 4D	BH686	27590	1500	1725	2450	4375
Dual Moon Roofs			(75)	(75)	(115)	(115)

OUTBACK AWD—H6—Equipment Schedule 4
W.B. 104.3"; 3.0 Liter.

L.L. Bean Wagon 4D	BH806	29990	1750	2050	2875	5100
VDC Wagon 4D	BH896	32390	2650	3075	3950	6925
Dual Moon Roofs			(75)	(75)	(115)	(115)

2002 SUBARU — JF1or4S3(GG655)-2-#

IMPREZA AWD—4-Cyl.—Equipment Schedule 5
W.B. 99.4"; 2.5 Liter.

2.5TS Sport Wagon 4D	GG655	18820	1375	1650	2425	4275
Outback Sport Wag 4D	GF485	20020	2050	2425	3025	5100
2.5RS Sedan 4D	GC675	20320	1650	1950	2675	4625

IMPREZA AWD—4-Cyl. Turbo—Equipment Schedule 4
W.B. 99.4"; 2.0 liter.

WRX Sedan 4D	GD295	25520	3175	3500	4225	6475
WRX Sport Wagon 4D	GG295	25020	2950	3250	3975	6100

Body Type	VIN	List	Trade-In Good	Trade-In Very Good	Pvt-Party Good	Retail Excellent
LEGACY AWD—4-Cyl.—Equipment Schedule 4						
W.B. 104.3"; 2.5 Liter.						
L Sedan 4D	BE635	20620	1350	1575	2100	3600
L Wagon 4D	BH635	21320	1650	1900	2475	4225
GT Sedan 4D	BE645	24220	2350	2725	3275	5450
GT Limited Sedan 4D	BE656	26020	2625	3050	3600	5950
GT Wagon 4D	BH645	25120	2600	3025	3550	5900
Dual Moon Roofs			(200)	(200)	(265)	(265)
Manual, 5-Spd (Sedan)			100	100	120	120
OUTBACK AWD—4-Cyl.—Equipment Schedule 4						
W.B. 104.3"; 2.5 Liter.						
Wagon 4D	BH665	24220	1775	2050	2775	4800
Limited Sedan 4D	BH686	26520	2025	2325	3075	5275
Limited Wagon 4D	BH686	27620	2100	2425	3150	5425
Dual Moon Roofs			(100)	(100)	(120)	(120)
OUTBACK AWD—H6—Equipment Schedule 4						
W.B. 104.3"; 3.0 Liter.						
Sedan 4D	BE896	28520	2075	2375	3125	5375
L.L. Bean Wagon 4D	BH806	30020	2450	2800	3575	6100
VDC Sedan 4D	BH806	30700	2700	3100	3900	6675
VDC Wagon 4D	BH896	32420	3225	3725	4500	7625
Dual Moon Roofs			100	100	120	120

Body Type	VIN	List	Trade-In Good	Trade-In Very Good	Pvt-Party Good	Retail Excellent
IMPREZA AWD—4-Cyl.—Equipment Schedule 5						
W.B. 99.4"; 2.5 Liter.						
2.5TS Sport Wagon 4D	GG655	18920	1550	1850	2600	4500
Outbk "Sport" Spt Wg	GG685	20220	2225	2625	3350	5675
2.5RS Sedan 4D	GD675	20420	1850	2175	3000	5175
IMPREZA AWD—4-Cyl. Turbo—Equipment Schedule 4						
W.B. 99.4"; 2.0 Liter.						
WRX Sedan 4D	GD296	25720	4175	4550	5125	7550
WRX Sport Wagon 4D	GG296	25220	3925	4275	4875	7175
LEGACY AWD—4-Cyl.—Equipment Schedule 4						
W.B. 104.3"; 2.5 Liter.						
L Sedan 4D	BE635	20820	1750	2025	2550	4225
L Wagon 4D	BH635	21520	2050	2375	2900	4775
L Special Ed Sed 4D	BE635	21320	1900	2200	2725	4475
L Special Ed Wag 4D	BH635	22420	2350	2725	3225	5250
GT Sedan 4D	BE646	26320	2850	3275	3725	6025
GT Wagon 4D	BH646	27220	3400	3925	4350	6950
Dual Moon Roofs			(100)	(100)	(130)	(130)
Manual, 5-Spd (Sedan)			(225)	(225)	(310)	(310)
OUTBACK AWD—4-Cyl.—Equipment Schedule 4						
W.B. 104.3"; 2.5 Liter.						
Wagon 4D	BH675	24370	2325	2650	3175	5175
Limited Sedan 4D	BE686	26820	2575	2950	3500	5725
Limited Wagon 4D	BH686	27920	2700	3100	3600	5875
Dual Moon Roofs			(100)	(100)	(130)	(130)
OUTBACK AWD—H6—Equipment Schedule 4						
W.B. 104.3"; 3.0 Liter.						
Sedan 4D	BE896	29020	2625	3000	3550	5825
Wagon 4D	BH896	27520	2225	2550	3100	5100
L.L. Bean Wagon 4D	BH806	30520	3100	3525	4050	6575
VDC Sedan 4D	BE896	31420	3400	3875	4400	7150
VDC Wagon 4D	BH896	32920	3900	4450	5025	8050

Body Type	VIN	List	Trade-In Good	Trade-In Very Good	Pvt-Party Good	Retail Excellent
IMPREZA AWD—4-Cyl.—Equipment Schedule 5						
W.B. 99.4"; 2.5 Liter.						
2.5TS Sport Wagon 4D	GG655	19245	1900	2225	3000	5050
Outback Sport Wag	GG685	20445	2775	3200	3875	6325
2.5RS Sedan 4D	GD675	20745	2200	2575	3300	5500
IMPREZA AWD—4-Cyl. Turbo—Equipment Schedule 4						
W.B. 99.4"; 2.0 Liter.						
WRX Sedan 4D	GD296	26045	5225	5675	6300	8975
WRX Sport Wagon 4D	GG296	25545	4900	5325	5975	8525
IMPREZA AWD—4-Cyl. HO Turbo—Equipment Schedule 4						
W.B. 100.0"; 2.5 Liter.						
WRX STi Sedan 4D	GD706	31545	10600	11500	11700	16000
LEGACY AWD—4-Cyl.—Equipment Schedule 4						
W.B. 104.3"; 2.5 Liter.						

Body Type	VIN	List	Trade-In Good	Trade-In Very Good	Pvt-Party Good	Retail Excellent
L Sedan 4D	BE635	21245	2150	2475	2950	4725
L Wagon 4D	BH635	21945	2525	2900	3325	5250
GT Sedan 4D	BE646	26645	3475	3975	4475	7025
GT Wagon 4D	BH646	27545	3875	4425	4900	7650
Dual Moon Roofs			(100)	(100)	(135)	(135)
Manual, 5-Spd			(275)	(275)	(375)	(375)

OUTBACK AWD—4-Cyl.—Equipment Schedule 4
W.B. 104.3"; 2.5 Liter.

Body Type	VIN	List	Good	Very Good	Good	Excellent
Wagon 4D	BH675	24695	2825	3200	3625	5675
Limited Sedan 4D	BE686	27145	3150	3550	3975	6275
Limited Wagon 4D	BH686	28245	3350	3775	4150	6500
Dual Moon Roofs			(100)	(100)	(135)	(135)

OUTBACK AWD—H6—Equipment Schedule 4
W.B. 104.3"; 3.0 Liter.

Body Type	VIN	List	Good	Very Good	Good	Excellent
Sedan 4D	BE896	29345	3250	3675	4075	6425
35th Anniv Wagon 4D	BH815	27645	2725	3100	3550	5625
L.L. Bean Wagon 4D	BH806	30845	3650	4150	4650	7250
VDC Sedan 4D	BE896	31545	3875	4400	4950	7775
VDC Wagon 4D	BH896	33045	4600	5200	5650	8750

2005 SUBARU — (JFor4S)(1,3or4)(GD675)-5-#

IMPREZA AWD—4-Cyl.—Equipment Schedule 5
W.B. 99.4"; 2.5 Liter.

Body Type	VIN	List	Good	Very Good	Good	Excellent
2.5RS Sedan 4D	GD675	19470	2950	3425	4150	6450
2.5RS Sport Wagon 4D	GG675	19470	3275	3800	4500	6975
Outback Sport Wag	GG685	20370	4325	4975	5325	7925
Outback Spt Spcl Ed	GG685	20320	4200	4850	5250	7800

IMPREZA AWD—4-Cyl. Turbo—Equipment Schedule 5
W.B. 99.4"; 2.0 Liter.

Body Type	VIN	List	Good	Very Good	Good	Excellent
WRX Sedan 4D	GD296	25370	7225	7825	8250	11150
WRX Sport Wagon 4D	GG296	24870	6850	7400	7875	10700

IMPREZA AWD—4-Cyl. HO Turbo—Equipment Schedule 5
W.B. 99.4"; 2.5 Liter.

Body Type	VIN	List	Good	Very Good	Good	Excellent
WRX STi Sedan 4D	GD706	32770	12800	13850	13800	18200

LEGACY AWD—4-Cyl.—Equipment Schedule 4
W.B. 105.1"; 2.5 Liter.

Body Type	VIN	List	Good	Very Good	Good	Excellent
2.5i Sedan 4D	BL616	22870	3150	3600	4150	6400
2.5i Wagon 4D	BP616	23870	3350	3800	4325	6625
2.5i Limited Sedan 4D	BL626	26120	3850	4375	5075	7850
2.5i Limited Wagon 4D	BP626	27320	3975	4525	5250	8075
Dual Moon Roofs			(125)	(125)	(155)	(155)
Manual, 5-Spd			(325)	(325)	(445)	(445)

LEGACY AWD—4-Cyl. Turbo—Equipment Schedule 4
W.B. 105.1"; 2.5 Liter.

Body Type	VIN	List	Good	Very Good	Good	Excellent
2.5GT Sedan 4D	BL686	27870	3875	4425	5175	8025
2.5GT Wagon 4D	BP686	28870	4225	4800	5550	8575
2.5GT Limited Sed 4D	BL676	30370	5400	6125	6650	9875
2.5GT Limited Wag 4D	BP676	31570	6400	7250	7800	11650
Dual Moon Roofs			(125)	(125)	(155)	(155)
Manual, 5-Spd			(325)	(325)	(445)	(445)

OUTBACK AWD—4-Cyl.—Equipment Schedule 4
W.B. 105.1"; 2.5 Liter.

Body Type	VIN	List	Good	Very Good	Good	Excellent
2.5i Wagon 4D	BP61C	25870	3825	4300	4700	6975
2.5i Limited Wagon	BP62C	28670	4275	4800	5200	7700
Dual Moon Roofs			(125)	(125)	(155)	(155)

OUTBACK AWD—4-Cyl. Turbo—Equipment Schedule 4
W.B. 105.1"; 2.5 Liter.

Body Type	VIN	List	Good	Very Good	Good	Excellent
2.5XT Wagon 4D	BP68C	29870	4475	5050	5425	8025
2.5XT Limited Wagon	BP67C	32570	5000	5625	6000	8850
Dual Moon Roofs			(125)	(125)	(155)	(155)

OUTBACK AWD—H6—Equipment Schedule 4
W.B. 105.1"; 3.0 Liter.

Body Type	VIN	List	Good	Very Good	Good	Excellent
3.0R Sedan 4D	BL84C	31670	5650	6350	6850	10150
3.0R L.L. Bean Wagon	BP86C	32870	6075	6825	7225	10600
3.0R VDC Ltd Wagon	BP85C	34070	6900	7750	8150	12050
Dual Moon Roofs			(125)	(125)	(155)	(155)

2006 SUBARU — (JFor4S)(1,3or4)(GD676)-6-#

IMPREZA AWD—4-Cyl.—Equipment Schedule 5
W.B. 99.4"; 2.5 Liter.

Body Type	VIN	List	Good	Very Good	Good	Excellent
2.5i Sedan 4D	GD676	19720	3600	4100	4775	7200
2.5i Sport Wagon	GG676	19720	3900	4425	5025	7500

2006 SUBARU

Body Type	VIN	List	Trade-In Good	Very Good	Pvt-Party Good	Retail Excellent
Outback Sport Wagon	GG686	20620	5100	5825	6200	8875
IMPREZA AWD—4-Cyl. Turbo—Equipment Schedule 4						
W.B. 99.4"; 2.5 Liter.						
WRX TR Sedan 4D	GD796	24620	7275	7800	8375	11200
WRX Sedan 4D	GD796	25620	8550	9200	9650	12750
WRX Sport Wagon 4D	GD796	25120	8125	8725	9275	12350
WRX Limited Sedan	GD796	29120	9900	10650	11100	14750
WRX Limited Spt Wag	GD796	28620	9900	10650	11100	14750
IMPREZA AWD—4-Cyl. HO Turbo—Equipment Schedule 4						
W.B. 100.0"; 2.5 Liter.						
WRX STi Sedan 4D	GD706	33620	14150	15200	15200	19750
LEGACY AWD—4-Cyl.—Equipment Schedule 4						
W.B. 105.1"; 2.5 Liter.						
i Sedan 4D	BL616	23520	3400	3825	4500	6775
i Wagon 4D	BP616	24520	3675	4150	4775	7100
i Limited Sedan 4D	BL626	26120	4675	5250	5850	8675
i Limited Wagon 4D	BP626	27320	4925	5525	6100	9025
Manual, 5-Spd			(375)	(375)	(510)	(510)
LEGACY AWD—4-Cyl. Turbo—Equipment Schedule 4						
W.B. 105.1"; 2.5 Liter.						
GT Limited Sed 4D	BL676	30620	7025	7875	8100	11500
GT Limited Wag 4D	BP676	31820	7875	8825	9200	13200
Manual, 5-Spd			(375)	(375)	(510)	(510)
OUTBACK AWD—4-Cyl.—Equipment Schedule 4						
W.B. 105.1"; 2.5 Liter.						
2.5i Wagon 4D	BP61C	26420	4750	5300	5575	7925
2.5i Limited Sedan 4D	BL62C	28020	5125	5700	5850	8250
2.5i Limited Wagon	BP62C	29220	5575	6225	6575	9375
OUTBACK AWD—4-Cyl. Turbo—Equipment Schedule 4						
W.B. 105.1"; 2.5 Liter.						
2.5XT Wagon 4D	BP68C	30420	6050	6750	7025	9900
2.5XT Limited Wagon	BP67C	32820	6775	7525	7775	11000
OUTBACK AWD—H6—Equipment Schedule 4						
W.B. 105.1"; 3.0 Liter.						
3.0R Wagon 4D	BP84C	29620	6475	7225	7450	10550
3.0R L.L. Bean Sed 4D	BL86C	31920	7250	8075	8375	11850
3.0R L.L. Bean Wagon	BP86C	33120	7600	8475	8650	12200
3.0R VDC Ltd Wagon	BP85C	36320	8550	9500	9550	13400

2007 SUBARU — (JFor4S)(1,3or4)(GD616)-7-#

Body Type	VIN	List	Trade-In Good	Very Good	Pvt-Party Good	Retail Excellent
IMPREZA AWD—4-Cyl.—Equipment Schedule 5						
W.B. 99.4"; 2.5 Liter.						
2.5i Sedan 4D	GD616	19420	4250	4750	5400	7850
2.5i Sport Wagon	GG616	19420	4450	5000	5575	8050
Outback Sport Wagon	GG626	20620	5700	6375	6800	9450
Manual, 5-Spd			(400)	(400)	(520)	(520)
IMPREZA AWD—4-Cyl. Turbo—Equipment Schedule 4						
W.B. 99.4"; 2.5 Liter.						
WRX TR Sedan 4D	GD756	24620	8450	9025	9675	12650
WRX Sedan 4D	GD746	25620	9950	10600	11000	14150
WRX Sport Wagon 4D	GG746	25120	9525	10150	10750	14000
WRX Limited Sedan	GD746	29120	11250	12000	12550	16350
WRX Limited Spt Wag	GG746	28620	11300	12050	12600	16400
IMPREZA AWD—4-Cyl. HO Turbo—Equipment Schedule 4						
W.B. 99.4"; 2.5 Liter.						
WRX STi Sedan 4D	GD766	34120	15650	16700	16650	21100
WRX STi Limited Sed	GD776	34120	16150	17200	17200	21900
LEGACY AWD—4-Cyl.—Equipment Schedule 4						
W.B. 105.1"; 2.5 Liter.						
i Sedan 4D	BL616	22120	4550	5075	5575	7925
i Wagon 4D	BP616	23620	4850	5400	5900	8375
i Limited Sedan 4D	BL626	24720	5975	6625	7200	10150
i Limited Wagon 4D	BP626	25920	6325	7000	7575	10700
Manual, 5-Spd			(425)	(425)	(555)	(555)
LEGACY AWD—4-Cyl. Turbo—Equipment Schedule 4						
W.B. 105.1"; 2.5 Liter.						
GT Limited Sedan 4D	BL676	30120	8425	9325	9475	12950
GT Limited Wagon 4D	BP676	31520	9400	10400	10700	14850
GT spec.B Sedan 4D	BL696	34620	9850	10900	10800	14550
Manual, 5-Spd			(425)	(425)	(550)	(550)
OUTBACK AWD—4-Cyl.—Equipment Schedule 4						
W.B. 105.1"; 2.5 Liter.						
2.5i Basic Wagon 4D	BP61C	23620	5175	5700	5950	8200

Body Type	VIN	List	Trade-In Good	Very Good	Pvt-Party Good	Retail Excellent
2.5i Wagon 4D	BP61C	25220	**5525**	**6100**	**6500**	**8925**
2.5i Limited Sedan 4D	BL62C	27020	**6400**	**7050**	**7350**	**10100**
2.5i Limited Wagon 4D	BP62C	28020	**7250**	**8100**	**8350**	**11400**
OUTBACK AWD—4-Cyl. Turbo—Equipment Schedule 4						
W.B. 105.1"; 2.5 Liter.						
2.5XT Limited Wagon	BP63C	32820	**8150**	**8950**	**9150**	**12500**
OUTBACK AWD—H6 HO—Equipment Schedule 4						
W.B. 105.1"; 3.0 Liter.						
3.0R L.L. Bean Sedan	BL86C	30920	**9000**	**9900**	**10000**	**13600**
3.0R L.L. Bean Wagon	BP86C	32120	**9000**	**9900**	**10000**	**13600**

2008 SUBARU — (JFor4S)(1,3or4)(GE616)-8-#

IMPREZA AWD—4-Cyl.—Equipment Schedule 5
W.B. 103.1"; 2.5 Liter.

Body Type	VIN	List	Good	Very Good	Good	Excellent
2.5i Sedan 4D	GE616	18640	**5075**	**5575**	**6625**	**9325**
2.5i Premium Sedan	GE616	20140	**6425**	**7025**	**7600**	**10150**
2.5i Sport Wagon	GH616	19140	**6175**	**6750**	**7400**	**9950**
2.5i Premium Wagon	GH616	20640	**6550**	**7175**	**7825**	**10500**
Outback Sport Wagon	GH636	21640	**7050**	**7725**	**8325**	**11100**
Manual, 5-Spd w/Overdrive			**(400)**	**(400)**	**(540)**	**(540)**
IMPREZA AWD—4-Cyl. Turbo—Equipment Schedule 4						
W.B. 103.1", 103.3" (STI); 2.5 Liter.						
WRX Sedan 4D	GE756	25995	**10500**	**11050**	**11750**	**14550**
WRX Premium Sedan	GE756	27095	**11000**	**11600**	**12250**	**15200**
WRX Sport Wagon	GH746	26495	**10800**	**11400**	**12050**	**14900**
WRX Premium Wagon	GH756	27595	**11300**	**11900**	**12550**	**15550**
WRX STI Sport Wagon	GR796	35640	**17300**	**18200**	**18500**	**22600**
LEGACY AWD—4-Cyl.—Equipment Schedule 4						
W.B. 105.1"; 2.5 Liter.						
2.5i Sedan 4D	BL616	22140	**5625**	**6125**	**6825**	**9175**
2.5i Limited Sedan 4D	BL626	24740	**7200**	**7800**	**8550**	**11450**
Manual, 5-Spd w/Overdrive			**(450)**	**(450)**	**(575)**	**(575)**
LEGACY AWD—4-Cyl. Turbo—Equipment Schedule 4						
W.B. 105.1"; 2.5 Liter.						
2.5GT Limited Sedan	BL676	30440	**9425**	**10200**	**10700**	**14000**
2.5GT spec.B Sedan	BL696	34640	**11100**	**12000**	**12250**	**15850**
Manual, 5-Spd HD w/OD			**(450)**	**(450)**	**(570)**	**(570)**
LEGACY AWD—6-Cyl.—Equipment Schedule 4						
W.B. 105.1"; 3.0 Liter.						
3.0R Limited Sedan 4D	BL856	31940	**9725**	**10550**	**10850**	**14150**
OUTBACK AWD—4-Cyl.—Equipment Schedule 4						
W.B. 105.1"; 2.5 Liter.						
Basic Wagon 4D	BP60C	23640	**6025**	**6500**	**7150**	**9450**
2.5i Wagon 4D	BP61C	25240	**6625**	**7150**	**7700**	**10100**
2.5i Limited Wagon 4D	BP62C	28040	**8475**	**9150**	**9600**	**12500**
OUTBACK AWD—4-Cyl. Turbo—Equipment Schedule 4						
W.B. 105.1"; 2.5 Liter.						
2.5XT Limited Wag	BP63C	32840	**8925**	**9625**	**10150**	**13250**
OUTBACK AWD—H6—Equipment Schedule 4						
W.B. 105.1"; 3.0 Liter.						
3.0R L.L. Bean Wagon	BP86C	32140	**9600**	**10350**	**10900**	**14250**

2009 SUBARU — (JFor4S)(1,3or4)(GE616)-9-#

IMPREZA AWD—4-Cyl.—Equipment Schedule 5
W.B. 103.1"; 2.5 Liter.

Body Type	VIN	List	Good	Very Good	Good	Excellent
2.5i Sedan 4D	GE616	19160	**6325**	**6775**	**7875**	**10500**
2.5i Sport Wagon	GH616	19660	**7400**	**7900**	**8675**	**11150**
2.5i Premium Sedan	GE606	21160	**7500**	**8025**	**8800**	**11300**
2.5i Premium Wagon	GH606	21660	**7700**	**8225**	**9075**	**11700**
Outback Sport Wagon	GH636	21660	**8350**	**8900**	**9600**	**12200**
Manual, 5-Spd w/Overdrive			**(450)**	**(450)**	**(585)**	**(585)**
IMPREZA AWD—4-Cyl. Turbo—Equipment Schedule 4						
W.B. 103.1", 103.3" (STI); 2.5 Liter.						
WRX Sedan 4D	GE766	25660	**12250**	**12800**	**13800**	**16550**
WRX Sport Wagon	GH766	26160	**12650**	**13200**	**14200**	**17000**
WRX Premium Sedan	GE766	28160	**12800**	**13350**	**14350**	**17200**
WRX Premium Wagon	GH766	28660	**13150**	**13700**	**14650**	**17550**
2.5GT Sedan 4D	GE746	27660	**11750**	**12300**	**12700**	**15850**
2.5GT Sport Wagon	GH746	28160	**11750**	**12550**	**12850**	**15900**
WRX STI Sport Wagon	GR896	35660	**19400**	**20200**	**20900**	**24800**
LEGACY AWD—4-Cyl.—Equipment Schedule 4						
W.B. 105.1"; 2.5 Liter.						

Body Type	VIN	List	Trade-In Good	Very Good	Pvt-Party Good	Retail Excellent
2.5i Sedan 4D	BL606	22460	6975	7425	8225	10500
2.5i Limited Sedan 4D	BL626	25660	8300	8825	9750	12550
Manual, 5-Spd w/Overdrive			(475)	(475)	(605)	(605)

LEGACY AWD—4-Cyl. Turbo—Equipment Schedule 4
W.B. 105.1"; 2.5 Liter.

2.5GT Limited Sedan	BL676	31060	10900	11550	12350	15600
2.5GT spec.B Sedan 4D	BL696	35260	12350	13100	13700	17100
Manual, 5-Spd HD w/OD			(475)	(475)	(605)	(605)

LEGACY AWD—6-Cyl.—Equipment Schedule 4
W.B. 105.1"; 3.0 Liter.

3.0R Sedan 4D	BL846	27260	8850	9400	10300	13200
3.0R Limited Sedan 4D	BL856	30560	11000	11650	12250	15400

OUTBACK AWD—4-Cyl.—Equipment Schedule 4
W.B. 105.1"; 2.5 Liter.

2.5i Wagon 4D	BP60C	23960	8825	9375	9975	12400
2.5i Limited Wagon 4D	BP66C	28960	10650	11300	11900	14750

OUTBACK AWD—4-Cyl. Turbo—Equipment Schedule 4
W.B. 105.1"; 2.5 Liter.

2.5XT Limited Wagon	BP63C	33460	11400	12050	12750	15850

OUTBACK AWD—H6—Equipment Schedule 4
W.B. 105.1"; 3.0 Liter.

3.0R Limited Wagon	BP85C	32760	11700	12350	12950	15950

2010 SUBARU — (JFor4S)(1,3or4)(GE6A6)–A–#

IMPREZA AWD—4-Cyl.—Equipment Schedule 5
W.B. 103.1"; 2.5 Liter.

2.5i Sedan 4D	GE6A6	18190	7575	7950	9250	11850
2.5i Sport Wagon	GH6A6	18690	8075	8475	9650	12200
2.5i Premium Sedan	GE6A6	19190	8275	8675	9825	12400
2.5i Premium Wagon	GH6A6	19690	8925	9350	10500	13150
Outback Sport Wagon	GH6D6	20690	9325	9775	10800	13400
Manual, 5-Spd w/Overdrive			(475)	(475)	(630)	(630)

IMPREZA AWD—4-Cyl. Turbo—Equipment Schedule 4
W.B. 103.1", 103.3" (STI); 2.5 Liter.

WRX Sedan 4D	GE7G6	25690	14200	14700	15900	18550
WRX Sport Wagon	GH7G6	26190	14600	15100	16250	18950
WRX Premium Sedan	GE7G6	28190	15100	15600	16750	19550
WRX Premium Wagon	GH7G6	28690	15300	15800	17000	19850
WRX Limited Sedan	GE7G6	29190	16650	17200	18450	21600
WRX Limited Wagon	GH7G6	29690	17300	17900	19100	22200
WRX STI Spec Ed Wag	GR8H6	34590	22000	22700	23600	27100
WRX STI Sport Wagon	GR8H6	35690	21700	22400	23400	27000
2.5GT Sedan 4D	GE7E6	27690	12500	13150	14100	17200
2.5GT Sport Wagon	GH7E6	28190	12750	13350	14250	17400

LEGACY AWD—4-Cyl.—Equipment Schedule 4
W.B. 108.3"; 2.5 Liter.

2.5i Sedan 4D	BMAA6	21690	8875	9275	10200	12450
2.5i Premium Sedan	BMAB6	22690	9075	9475	10450	12800
2.5i Limited Sedan 4D	BMCJ6	25660	9975	10450	11550	14300

LEGACY AWD—4-Cyl. Turbo—Equipment Schedule 4
W.B. 108.3"; 2.5 Liter.

2.5GT Premium Sed	BMFC6	28660	13850	14450	15350	18500
2.5GT Limited Sedan	BMFJ6	30660	14650	15300	16200	19550

LEGACY AWD—6-Cyl.—Equipment Schedule 4
W.B. 108.3"; 3.6 Liter.

3.6R Sedan 4D	BMDA6	25660	10100	10550	11700	14500
3.6R Premium Sedan	BMDC6	26660	11350	11850	12900	15800
3.6R Limited Sed 4D	BMDJ6	29660	13000	13600	14450	17500

OUTBACK AWD—4-Cyl.—Equipment Schedule 4
W.B. 107.9"; 2.5 Liter.

2.5i Wagon 4D	BRCAC	24690	11000	11450	12250	14600
2.5i Premium Wagon	BRCBC	26290	12100	12600	13550	16250
2.5i Limited Wagon	BRCJC	28690	13500	14050	14950	17750

OUTBACK AWD—6-Cyl.—Equipment Schedule 4
W.B. 107.9"; 3.6 Liter.

3.6R Wagon 4D	BRDAC	28690	13200	13800	14800	17850
3.6R Premium Wagon	BRECC	29690	14400	15050	16050	19150
3.6R Limited Wagon	BRDJC	31690	14900	15550	16550	19250

2011 SUBARU — (JFor4S)(1,3or4)(GE6A6)–B–#

IMPREZA AWD—4-Cyl.—Equipment Schedule 5
W.B. 103.1"; 2.5 Liter.

Body Type	VIN	List	Trade-In Good	Very Good	Pvt-Party Good	Retail Excellent
2.5i Sedan 4D	GE6A6	18220	9675	10000	11400	14050
2.5i Sport Wagon	GH6A6	18720	10150	10500	11800	14350
2.5i Premium Sedan	GE6B6	19220	10450	10800	12050	14650
2.5i Premium Wagon	GH6B6	19720	11050	11450	12700	15350
Outback Sport Wagon	GH6D6	20720	11750	12150	13250	15900
Manual, 5-Spd w/Overdrive			(500)	(500)	(615)	(615)

IMPREZA AWD—4-Cyl. Turbo—Equipment Schedule 4
W.B. 103.3"; 2.5 Liter.

Body Type	VIN	List	Trade-In Good	Very Good	Pvt-Party Good	Retail Excellent
WRX Sedan 4D	GV7E6	26220	16850	17300	18550	21000
WRX Sport Wagon	GR7E6	26220	17350	17850	19100	21600
WRX Premium Sedan	GV7F6	28720	18050	18550	19800	22400
WRX Premium Wagon	GR7E6	28720	18200	18700	19950	22600
WRX Limited Sedan	GV7F6	29720	19250	19750	21100	23900
WRX Limited Wagon	GR7E6	29720	19900	20400	21700	24500
WRX STI Sedan 4D	GV8J6	34720	23900	24500	25700	28900
WRX STI Sport Wagon	GR8H6	36720	24400	25000	26200	29400
WRX STI Limited Sed	GV8J6	38070	24200	24900	26200	29500

LEGACY AWD—4-Cyl.—Equipment Schedule 4
W.B. 108.3"; 2.5 Liter.

Body Type	VIN	List	Trade-In Good	Very Good	Pvt-Party Good	Retail Excellent
2.5i Sedan 4D	BMAA6	21720	10850	11200	12300	14500
2.5i Premium Sedan	BMAB6	22720	11250	11600	12700	15050
2.5i Limited Sedan 4D	BMCJ6	26020	12350	12750	14050	16750

LEGACY AWD—4-Cyl. Turbo—Equipment Schedule 4
W.B. 108.3"; 2.5 Liter.

Body Type	VIN	List	Trade-In Good	Very Good	Pvt-Party Good	Retail Excellent
2.5GT Limited Sedan	BMFK6	32120	16350	16850	18100	21200

LEGACY AWD—6-Cyl.—Equipment Schedule 4
W.B. 108.3"; 3.6 Liter.

Body Type	VIN	List	Trade-In Good	Very Good	Pvt-Party Good	Retail Excellent
3.6R Sedan 4D	BMDA6	25720	12350	12750	14100	16850
3.6R Premium Sedan	BMDC6	26720	13300	13700	15000	17800
3.6R Limited Sedan	BMDJ6	29020	15050	15550	16750	19650

OUTBACK AWD—4-Cyl.—Equipment Schedule 4
W.B. 107.9"; 2.5 Liter.

Body Type	VIN	List	Trade-In Good	Very Good	Pvt-Party Good	Retail Excellent
2.5i Wagon 4D	BRAAC	24920	13100	13500	14600	16950
2.5i Premium Wagon	BRCBC	26220	14100	14550	15800	18400
2.5i Limited Wagon	BRCJC	29220	15550	16050	17150	19850

OUTBACK AWD—6-Cyl.—Equipment Schedule 4
W.B. 107.9"; 3.6 Liter.

Body Type	VIN	List	Trade-In Good	Very Good	Pvt-Party Good	Retail Excellent
3.6R Wagon 4D	BRDAC	28920	15400	15900	17250	20200
3.6R Premium Wagon	BRDCC	29920	16450	16950	18250	21200
3.6R Limited Wagon	BRDJC	32220	17450	17950	18550	21300

2012 SUBARU — JF1or4S3(GJAA6)-C-#

IMPREZA AWD—4-Cyl.—Equipment Schedule 5
W.B. 104.1"; 2.0 Liter.

Body Type	VIN	List	Trade-In Good	Very Good	Pvt-Party Good	Retail Excellent
2.0i Sedan 4D	GJAA6	18245	11050	11300	12900	15550
2.0i Wagon 4D	GPAA6	18745	11300	11550	13050	15550
2.0i Premium Wagon	GPAB6	20045	12500	12750	14150	16750
2.0i Sport Prem Wag	GPAL6	21045	12900	13200	14650	17300
Manual, 5-Spd.			(525)	(525)	(635)	(635)

IMPREZA AWD—4-Cyl.—Equipment Schedule 5
W.B. 104.1"; 2.0 Liter.

Body Type	VIN	List	Trade-In Good	Very Good	Pvt-Party Good	Retail Excellent
2.0i Premium Sedan	GJAB6	19545	11950	12250	13650	16250
2.0i Limited Sedan	GJAG6	22345	13600	13900	15300	17950
2.0i Limited Wagon	GPAG6	22845	14100	14450	15800	18500
2.0i Sport Ltd Wagon	GPAR6	23345	14250	14550	15850	18550

IMPREZA AWD—4-Cyl. Turbo—Equipment Schedule 4
W.B. 103.3"; 2.5 Liter.

Body Type	VIN	List	Trade-In Good	Very Good	Pvt-Party Good	Retail Excellent
WRX Sedan 4D	GV7E6	26345	18450	18900	20300	22500
WRX Sport Wagon	GR7E6	26345	19350	19750	21200	23600
WRX Premium Sedan	GV7F6	28845	19600	20100	21500	23900
WRX Premium Wagon	GR7E6	28845	19800	20300	21700	24200
WRX Limited Sedan	GV7F6	29845	20900	21300	22800	25400
WRX Limited Wagon	GR7E6	29845	21500	21900	23400	26000
WRX STI Sedan 4D	GV8J6	34845	25800	26300	27800	30700
WRX STI Limited Sed	GV8J6	38195	26900	27500	29000	32100
WRX STI Sport Wagon	GR8H6	36845	26200	26800	28200	31200

LEGACY AWD—4-Cyl.—Equipment Schedule 4
W.B. 108.3"; 2.5 Liter.

Body Type	VIN	List	Trade-In Good	Very Good	Pvt-Party Good	Retail Excellent
2.5i Sedan 4D	BMAA6	21745	12150	12400	13700	15850
2.5i Premium Sedan	BMAB6	23045	12900	13200	14500	16800
2.5i Limited Sedan 4D	BMAJ6	26345	14300	14800	16350	19000

LEGACY AWD—4-Cyl. Turbo—Equipment Schedule 4
W.B. 108.3"; 2.5 Liter.

Body Type	VIN	List	Trade-In Good	Very Good	Pvt-Party Good	Retail Excellent
2.5GT Sedan 4D	BMFL6	32345	19600	20000	21400	24500
LEGACY AWD—6-Cyl.—Equipment Schedule 4						
W.B. 108.3"; 3.6 Liter.						
3.6R Sedan 4D	BMEA6	25845	14150	14450	16100	18750
3.6R Premium Sedan	BMEC6	27045	15500	15850	17450	20200
3.6R Limited Sedan	BMEJ6	29345	17200	17550	18950	21800
OUTBACK AWD—4-Cyl.—Equipment Schedule 4						
W.B. 107.9"; 2.5 Liter.						
2.5i Wagon 4D	BRCAC	24070	15400	15800	17300	19700
2.5i Premium Wagon	BRCBC	25570	16800	17200	18600	21100
2.5i Limited Wagon	BRCJC	29470	18300	18700	20000	22600
OUTBACK AWD—6-Cyl.—Equipment Schedule 4						
W.B. 107.9"; 3.6 Liter.						
3.6R Wagon 4D	BREAC	29070	18300	18700	20300	23100
3.6R Premium Wagon	BRECC	30270	19500	19950	21400	24300
3.6R Limited Wagon	BREJC	32470	19850	20300	21600	24300

2013 SUBARU — JF1or4S3(ZCAB1)–D–#

Body Type	VIN	List	Trade-In Good	Very Good	Pvt-Party Good	Retail Excellent
BRZ—4-Cyl.—Equipment Schedule 4						
W.B. 101.2"; 2.0 Liter.						
Premium Coupe 2D	ZCAB1	27365	16350	16850	18150	20500
Limited Coupe 2D	ZCAC1	29365	17100	17600	18900	21400
IMPREZA AWD—4-Cyl.—Equipment Schedule 5						
W.B. 104.1"; 2.0 Liter.						
2.0i Sedan 4D	GJAA6	19665	12900	13150	14750	17350
2.0i Wagon 4D	GPAA6	20165	13250	13450	15100	17650
2.0i Premium Sedan	GJAB6	21065	13850	14100	15650	18250
2.0i Premium Wagon	GPAB6	21565	14400	14650	16200	18800
2.0i Sport Prem Wag	GPAL6	22565	14950	15200	16700	19350
Manual, 5-Spd			(550)	(550)	(645)	(645)
IMPREZA AWD—4-Cyl.—Equipment Schedule 5						
W.B. 104.1"; 2.0 Liter.						
2.0i Limited Sedan	GJAG6	22765	15150	15400	16900	19550
2.0i Limited Wagon	GPAG6	23265	15300	15550	17050	19700
2.0i Sport Ltd Wagon	GPAR6	23765	15750	16000	17400	20100
IMPREZA AWD—4-Cyl. Turbo—Equipment Schedule 5						
W.B. 103.3"; 2.5 Liter.						
WRX Sedan 4D	GV7E6	26565	20100	20500	22100	24400
WRX Sport Wagon	GR7E6	26565	21000	21400	23000	25400
WRX Premium Sedan	GV7F6	29065	21400	21800	23400	25700
WRX Premium Wagon	GR7E6	29065	21500	21900	23500	25900
WRX Limited Sedan	GJ7F6	30065	22600	23000	24700	27200
WRX Limited Wagon	GR7E6	30065	23100	23500	25200	27700
WRX STI Sedan 4D	GV8J6	35065	27400	27900	29500	32300
WRX STI Limited Sed	GJ8J6	38415	28800	29300	31100	34100
WRX STI Sport Wagon	GR8H6	37065	27900	28400	30100	32900
LEGACY AWD—4-Cyl.—Equipment Schedule 4						
W.B. 108.3"; 2.5 Liter.						
2.5i Sedan 4D	BMAA6	21070	13550	13800	15450	17750
2.5i Premium Sedan	BMCB6	23270	14500	14700	16400	18850
2.5i Sport Sedan 4D			15950	16200	17800	20300
2.5i Limited Sedan 4D	BMCJ6	26670	16850	17100	18750	21300
Sensing Cruise Control			475	475	540	540
LEGACY AWD—6-Cyl.—Equipment Schedule 4						
W.B. 108.3"; 3.6 Liter.						
3.6R Sedan 4D	BMDA6	26170	16700	16950	18650	21300
3.6R Limited Sedan	BMDJ6	29670	19250	19550	21100	23800
Sensing Cruise Control			475	475	520	520
OUTBACK AWD—4-Cyl.—Equipment Schedule 4						
W.B. 107.9"; 2.5 Liter.						
2.5i Wagon 4D	BRCAC	25290	16600	16900	18550	20900
2.5i Premium Wagon	BRCBC	26790	18350	18700	20300	22700
2.5i Limited Wagon	BRCJC	29890	20300	20700	22200	24600
Adaptive Cruise Control			475	475	535	535
OUTBACK AWD—6-Cyl.—Equipment Schedule 4						
W.B. 107.9"; 3.6 Liter.						
3.6R Wagon 4D	BRDAC	29290	20100	20500	22200	24900
3.6R Limited Wagon	BRDJC	32890	22400	22800	24200	26800
Adaptive Cruise Control			475	475	520	520

2014 SUBARU

Body Type	VIN	List	Trade-In Good	Very Good	Pvt-Party Good	Retail Excellent

2014 SUBARU — JF1or4S3(ZCAB)–E–#

BRZ—4-Cyl.—Equipment Schedule 4
W.B. 101.2"; 2.0 Liter.

Premium Coupe 2D	ZCAB	26390	**17650**	**18150**	**19450**	**21900**
Limited Coupe 2D	ZCAC	29490	**18700**	**19250**	**20500**	**23100**

IMPREZA AWD—4-Cyl.—Equipment Schedule 5
W.B. 104.1"; 2.0 Liter.

2.0i Sedan 4D	GJAA	19690	**13650**	**13850**	**15600**	**18250**
2.0i Wagon 4D	GPAA	20190	**14300**	**14500**	**16200**	**18950**
2.0i Premium Sedan	GJAB	21190	**14700**	**14950**	**16500**	**19100**
2.0i Premium Wagon	GPAB	21590	**15250**	**15450**	**17000**	**19650**
2.0i Sport Prem Wag	GPAL	22590	**16050**	**16300**	**17800**	**20500**
Manual, 5-Spd			**(575)**	**(575)**	**(665)**	**(665)**

IMPREZA AWD—4-Cyl.—Equipment Schedule 5
W.B. 104.1"; 2.0 Liter.

2.0i Limited Sedan	GJAG	22990	**16150**	**16400**	**17850**	**20500**
2.0i Limited Wagon	GPAG	23490	**16450**	**16700**	**18150**	**20900**
2.0i Sport Ltd Wagon	GPAR	23990	**16950**	**17200**	**18650**	**21400**

IMPREZA AWD—4-Cyl. Turbo—Equipment Schedule 5
W.B. 103.3"; 2.5 Liter.

WRX Sedan 4D	GV7E6	26790	**21700**	**22100**	**23800**	**26100**
WRX Wagon 4D	GR7E6	26790	**22600**	**23000**	**24600**	**27000**
WRX Premium Sedan	GV7F6	29290	**23100**	**23500**	**25300**	**27800**
WRX Premium Wagon	GR7F6	29290	**23100**	**23500**	**25300**	**27800**
WRX Limited Sedan	GV7F6	30290	**24200**	**24700**	**26500**	**29100**
WRX Limited Wagon	GR7F6	30290	**24600**	**25100**	**26700**	**29100**
WRX STI Sedan 4D	GV8J6	35290	**29500**	**30000**	**31800**	**34700**
WRX STI Limited Sed	GV8J6	38640	**30500**	**31100**	**32900**	**36000**
WRX STI Sport Wagon	GR8H6	37290	**29500**	**30000**	**31900**	**34800**

LEGACY AWD—4-Cyl.—Equipment Schedule 4
W.B. 108.3"; 2.5 Liter.

2.5i Sedan 4D	BMAA6	22090	**15050**	**15250**	**16900**	**19250**
2.5i Premium Sedan	BMBC6	24090	**16450**	**16700**	**18350**	**20800**
2.5i Sport Sedan 4D	BMBG6	25490	**17650**	**17950**	**19500**	**22000**
2.5i Limited Sedan 4D	BMBK6	26690	**18300**	**18600**	**20200**	**22800**
Adaptive Cruise Control			**500**	**500**	**550**	**550**

LEGACY AWD—6-Cyl.—Equipment Schedule 4
W.B. 108.3"; 3.6 Liter.

3.6R Limited Sedan	BMDK6	29690	**21000**	**21300**	**22900**	**25700**
Adaptive Cruise Control			**500**	**500**	**545**	**545**

OUTBACK AWD—4-Cyl.—Equipment Schedule 4
W.B. 107.9"; 2.5 Liter.

2.5i Wagon 4D	BRCA	25320	**19800**	**20100**	**21700**	**24100**
2.5i Premium Wagon	BRCC	27620	**21000**	**21300**	**22900**	**25300**
2.5i Limited Wagon	ARCK	29920	**23500**	**23900**	**25300**	**27800**

OUTBACK AWD—6-Cyl.—Equipment Schedule 4
W.B. 107.9"; 3.6 Liter.

3.6R Limited Wagon	BRDK	32920	**26600**	**27100**	**28400**	**31100**

SUZUKI

2000 SUZUKI — (JSor2S)3(AB21H)–Y–#

SWIFT—4-Cyl.—Equipment Schedule 6
W.B. 93.1"; 1.3 Liter.

GA Hatchback 2D	AB21H	9499	**550**	**675**	**1200**	**2250**
GL Hatchback 2D	AB21H	10499	**525**	**650**	**1150**	**2125**

ESTEEM—4-Cyl.—Equipment Schedule 6
W.B. 97.6"; 1.6 Liter, 1.8 Liter.

GL Sedan 4D	GB31S	13349	**575**	**675**	**1225**	**2225**
GL Wagon 4D	GB31W	13849	**675**	**800**	**1400**	**2500**
GLX Sedan 4D	GB31S	14349	**750**	**875**	**1500**	**2700**
GLX Wagon 4D	GB31W	14849	**825**	**975**	**1600**	**2875**

2001 SUZUKI — (JSor2S)2(AB21H)–1–#

SWIFT—4-Cyl.—Equipment Schedule 6
W.B. 93.1"; 1.3 Liter.

GA Hatchback 2D	AB21H	9729	**625**	**750**	**1350**	**2550**
GL Hatchback 2D	AB21H	10729	**600**	**725**	**1250**	**2325**

ESTEEM—4-Cyl.—Equipment Schedule 6
W.B. 97.6"; 1.8 Liter.

Body Type	VIN	List	Trade-In Good	Trade-In Very Good	Pvt-Party Good	Retail Excellent
GL Sedan 4D	GB41S	13679	575	700	1275	2275
GL Wagon 4D	GB41W	14179	700	825	1475	2625
GLX Sedan 4D	GB41S	14479	775	925	1575	2825
GLX Wagon 4D	GB41W	14979	850	975	1650	2975

2002 SUZUKI — JS2(RA41S)-2-#

AERIO—4-Cyl.—Equipment Schedule 6
W.B. 97.6"; 2.0 Liter.

S Sedan 4D	RA41S	14999	475	550	1350	2575
GS Sedan 4D	RA41S	14999	600	700	1425	2600
SX Wagon 4D	RC41H	15999	800	925	1775	3275

ESTEEM—4-Cyl.—Equipment Schedule 6
W.B. 97.6"; 1.8 Liter.

GL Sedan 4D	GB41S	13799	700	825	1400	2475
GL Wagon 4D	GB41W	14299	800	925	1550	2725
GLX Sedan 4D	GB41S	14799	900	1050	1675	2950
GLX Wagon 4D	GB41W	15299	1000	1175	1825	3200

2003 SUZUKI — JS2(RA41S)-3-#

AERIO—4-Cyl.—Equipment Schedule 6
W.B. 97.6"; 2.0 Liter.

S Sedan 4D	RA41S	14019	625	725	1625	3025
GS Sedan 4D	RA41S	15294	650	750	1575	2925
SX Wagon 4D	RC41H	15519	950	1100	2025	3700
AWD	B		250	250	345	345

2004 SUZUKI — JS2orKL5(RA61S)-4-#

AERIO—4-Cyl.—Equipment Schedule 6
W.B. 97.6"; 2.3 Liter.

S Sedan 4D	RA61S	14299	950	1075	1975	3575
LX Sedan 4D	RA61S	15999	1075	1225	2200	3950
SX Wagon 4D	RC61H	16299	1275	1450	2425	4275
AWD	B		275	275	355	355

FORENZA—4-Cyl.—Equipment Schedule 3
W.B. 102.4"; 2.0 Liter.

S Sedan 4D	JD52Z	13799	625	725	1350	2350
LX Sedan 4D	JJ52Z	15699	800	925	1525	2575
EX Sedan 4D	JJ52Z	16499	925	1075	1700	2900
Manual, 5-Spd			(275)	(275)	(375)	(375)

VERONA—6-Cyl.—Equipment Schedule 3
W.B. 106.3"; 2.5 Liter.

S Sedan 4D	VJ52L	16999	550	650	1300	2300
LX Sedan 4D	VJ52L	18299	925	1050	1750	3025
EX Sedan 4D	VM52L	19999	1000	1150	1850	3175

2005 SUZUKI — JS2orKL5(RA62S)-5-#

AERIO—4-Cyl.—Equipment Schedule 6
W.B. 97.6"; 2.3 Liter.

S Sedan 4D	RA62S	14894	1000	1150	2200	3875
LX Sedan 4D	RA61S	16594	1225	1375	2500	4325
SX Wagon 4D	RC61H	16894	1425	1625	2750	4725
AWD	B,D		275	275	365	365

FORENZA—4-Cyl.—Equipment Schedule 3
W.B. 102.4"; 2.0 Liter.

S Sedan 4D	JD56Z	14794	575	675	1475	2550
S Wagon 4D	JD86Z	15294	675	800	1575	2625
LX Sedan 4D	JJ56Z	16694	750	875	1675	2825
LX Wagon 4D	JJ86Z	17194	950	1100	1875	3075
EX Sedan 4D	JJ56Z	17494	1050	1200	1950	3200
EX Wagon 4D	JJ86Z	17994	1150	1300	2075	3375
Manual, 5-Spd			(325)	(325)	(445)	(445)

RENO—4-Cyl.—Equipment Schedule 4
W.B. 102.4"; 2.0 Liter.

S Hatchback 4D	JD66Z	14794	750	900	1700	3025
LX Hatchback 4D	JJ66Z	16694	1675	1950	2600	4175
EX Hatchback 4D	JJ66Z	17494	1800	2075	2725	4375
Manual, 5-Spd			(325)	(325)	(445)	(445)

VERONA—6-Cyl.—Equipment Schedule 3
W.B. 106.3"; 2.5 Liter.

S Sedan 4D	VJ56L	17994	675	775	1600	2750
LX Sedan 4D	VJ56L	19794	1225	1375	2250	3775
EX Sedan 4D	VM56L	20994	1450	1625	2525	4200

Body Type	VIN	List	Trade-In Good	Very Good	Pvt-Party Good	Retail Excellent

2006 SUZUKI — JS2orKL5(RA62S)-6-#

AERIO—4-Cyl.—Equipment Schedule 6
W.B. 97.6"; 2.3 Liter.

Body Type	VIN	List	Good	Very Good	Good	Excellent
Sedan 4D	RA62S	15479	1400	1550	2525	4175
SX Wagon 4D	RC61H	15979	1900	2125	3150	5000
Manual, 5-Spd			(275)	(275)	(355)	(355)

AERIO—4-Cyl.—Equipment Schedule 6
W.B. 97.6"; 2.3 Liter.

Premium Sedan 4D	RA61S	15679	1575	1775	2750	4425
SX Premium Wagon	RA61H	15879	1825	2050	3050	4850
Automatic			275	275	355	355
AWD	B		275	275	375	375

FORENZA—4-Cyl.—Equipment Schedule 3
W.B. 102.4"; 2.0 Liter.

Sedan 4D	JD56Z	15179	725	825	1625	2700
Premium Sedan 4D	JJ56Z	16579	1525	1725	2675	4250
Wagon 4D	JD86Z	15879	950	1075	1900	3100
Premium Wagon 4D	JD86Z	17279	1650	1850	2800	4450
Manual, 5-Spd			(375)	(375)	(510)	(510)

RENO—4-Cyl.—Equipment Schedule 4
W.B. 102.4"; 2.0 Liter.

Hatchback 4D	JD66Z	14679	1000	1150	1950	3325
Convenience H'Back	JD66Z	15729	1650	1900	2625	4225
Premium Hatchback	JD66Z	16879	2150	2475	3175	5025
Manual, 5-Spd			(375)	(375)	(510)	(510)

VERONA—6-Cyl.—Equipment Schedule 3
W.B. 106.3"; 2.5 Liter.

Sedan 4D	VJ56L	18879	925	1050	2125	3675
Luxury Sedan 4D	VM56L	20879	1425	1600	2700	4575

2007 SUZUKI — JS2orKL5(RA62S)-7-#

AERIO—4-Cyl.—Equipment Schedule 6
W.B. 97.6"; 2.3 Liter.

Sedan 4D	RA62S	16594	1500	1650	2750	4400
Manual, 5-Spd			(300)	(300)	(385)	(385)

AERIO—4-Cyl.—Equipment Schedule 6
W.B. 97.6"; 2.3 Liter.

Premium Sedan 4D	RA61S	16824	2200	2425	3575	5625
AWD	B		300	300	385	385

SX4—4-Cyl.—Equipment Schedule 4
W.B. 98.4"; 2.0 Liter.

Hatchback Sedan 4D	YB413	16594	2675	3100	3575	5400
Sport H'Back Sed 4D	YB417	17994	3100	3575	4025	6050
Manual, 5-Spd			(425)	(425)	(555)	(555)

FORENZA—4-Cyl.—Equipment Schedule 3
W.B. 102.4"; 2.0 Liter.

Sedan 4D	JD56Z	15594	875	975	1775	2825
Wagon 4D	JD86Z	16294	1150	1300	2100	3275
Manual, 5-Spd			(425)	(425)	(555)	(555)

RENO—4-Cyl.—Equipment Schedule 4
W.B. 102.4"; 2.0 Liter.

Hatchback 4D	JD66Z	15094	1300	1500	2225	3600
Manual, 5-Spd			(425)	(425)	(555)	(555)

2008 SUZUKI — JS2orKL5(YC414)-8-#

SX4—4-Cyl.—Equipment Schedule 4
W.B. 98.4"; 2.0 Liter.

Sedan 4D	YC414	15395	1900	2125	2800	4125
Sport Sedan 4D	YC415	16495	3275	3675	4375	6275
Sport Road Trip Sed	YC417	17099	4150	4625	5350	7675
Road Trip Ed H'Back	YA417	17099	4225	4725	5425	7800
Manual, 5-Spd w/Overdrive			(450)	(450)	(585)	(585)

SX4 AWD—4-Cyl.—Equipment Schedule 4
W.B. 98.4"; 2.0 Liter.

Hatchback 4D	YB413	16995	3725	4150	4850	6950
FWD			(1125)	(1125)	(1510)	(1510)
Manual, 5-Spd w/Overdrive			(450)	(450)	(585)	(585)

FORENZA—4-Cyl.—Equipment Schedule 3
W.B. 102.4"; 2.0 Liter.

Sedan 4D	JD56Z	15974	1250	1350	2325	3625
Wagon 4D	JD86Z	16874	1450	1575	2625	4000

Body Type	VIN	List	Trade-In Good	Very Good	Pvt-Party Good	Retail Excellent
Manual, 5-Spd w/Overdrive			(450)	(450)	(585)	(585)
RENO—4-Cyl.—Equipment Schedule 4						
W.B. 102.4"; 2.0 Liter.						
Hatchback 4D	JD66Z	15324	1650	1850	2700	4125
Manual, 5-Spd w/Overdrive			(450)	(450)	(585)	(585)

2009 SUZUKI — JS2orKL5(YC411)-9-#

Body Type	VIN	List	Trade-In Good	Very Good	Pvt-Party Good	Retail Excellent
SX4—4-Cyl.—Equipment Schedule 4						
W.B. 98.4"; 2.0 Liter.						
Sedan 4D	YC411	13959	2275	2500	3250	4625
LE Sedan 4D	YC412	16899	3125	3425	4275	5975
Sport Sedan 4D	YC414	17499	3425	3750	4650	6500
Manual, 5-Spd w/Overdrive			(475)	(475)	(645)	(645)
SX4 AWD—4-Cyl.—Equipment Schedule 4						
W.B. 98.4"; 2.0 Liter.						
Hatchback 4D	YB413	18234	4300	4675	5525	7625
FWD			(1025)	(1025)	(1355)	(1355)
Manual, 5-Spd w/Overdrive			(475)	(475)	(645)	(645)

2010 SUZUKI — JS2(YC5A1)-A-#

Body Type	VIN	List	Trade-In Good	Very Good	Pvt-Party Good	Retail Excellent
SX4—4-Cyl.—Equipment Schedule 4						
W.B. 98.4"; 2.0 Liter.						
Sedan 4D	YC5A1	14094	2725	2900	3850	5325
Sportback 4D	YA5A9	19834	5025	5350	6400	8575
LE Sedan 4D	YC5A2	15684	3675	3925	4900	6600
Sport S Sedan 4D	YC5A4	17984	4200	4500	5525	7400
Sport SE Sedan 4D	YC5A4	18434	4500	4800	5825	7775
Sport GTS Sedan 4D	YC5A9	19584	4975	5300	6400	8625
SX4 AWD—4-Cyl.—Equipment Schedule 4						
W.B. 98.4"; 2.0 Liter.						
Hatchback 4D	YB5A3	18684	4750	5050	6100	8150
FWD	A		(1075)	(1075)	(1440)	(1440)
KIZASHI—4-Cyl.—Equipment Schedule 4						
W.B. 106.3"; 2.4 Liter.						
S Sedan 4D	RE9A1	21234	4050	4250	5225	6650
SE Sedan 4D	RE9A3	22234	4900	5125	6200	7925
GTS Sedan 4D	RE9A5	24334	6000	6275	7600	9675
SLS Sedan 4D	RE9A7	26234	6925	7250	8775	11200
AWD	F		1450	1450	1925	1925

2011 SUZUKI — JS2(YC5A1)-B-#

Body Type	VIN	List	Trade-In Good	Very Good	Pvt-Party Good	Retail Excellent
SX4—4-Cyl.—Equipment Schedule 4						
W.B. 98.4"; 2.0 Liter.						
Sedan 4D	YC5A1	14244	3975	4175	5250	6850
LE Sedan 4D	YC5A2	15940	5200	5450	6450	8250
LE Annv Ed Sedan 4D	YC5A2	17744	6250	6550	7775	9900
Sport S Sedan 4D	YC5A4	17124	5075	5325	6600	8475
Sport SE Sedan 4D	YC5A4	18494	5725	6025	7275	9325
Sport GTS Sedan 4D	YC5A9	19644	6775	7100	8350	10600
Sportback 4D	YA5A5	19894	5975	6275	7525	9600
SX4 AWD—4-Cyl.—Equipment Schedule 4						
W.B. 98.4"; 2.0 Liter.						
Hatchback 4D	YB5A3	17744	5225	5500	6825	8800
Premium H'Back 4D	YB5A3	19344	6400	6700	7950	10100
KIZASHI—4-Cyl.—Equipment Schedule 4						
W.B. 106.3"; 2.4 Liter.						
S Sedan 4D	RE9A1	21644	5150	5325	6450	7925
SE Sedan 4D	RE9A3	22644	6200	6400	7875	9775
Sport GTS Sedan 4D	RE9A6	24744	7375	7625	9250	11400
Sport SLS Sedan 4D	RE9A7	26544	8050	8300	10050	12500
AWD	F		1525	1525	2015	2015

2012 SUZUKI — JS2(YC5A1)-C-#

Body Type	VIN	List	Trade-In Good	Very Good	Pvt-Party Good	Retail Excellent
SX4—4-Cyl.—Equipment Schedule 4						
W.B. 98.4"; 2.0 Liter.						
Sedan 4D	YC5A1	14464	4400	4575	5850	7550
LE Sedan 4D	YC5A3	18314	5775	6000	7400	9350
Sport SE Sedan 4D	YC5A5	18964	6475	6700	8150	10250
Sportback 4D	YA5A5	18764	6425	6650	8100	10200
Technology H'Back 4D	YA5A5	19264	6550	6775	8375	10700
SX4 AWD—4-Cyl.—Equipment Schedule 4						
W.B. 98.4"; 2.0 Liter.						

2012 SUZUKI

Body Type	VIN	List	Good	Trade-In Very Good	Pvt-Party Good	Retail Excellent
Hatchback 4D	YB5A3	17764	6050	6275	7675	9625
Premium H'Back 4D	YB5A3	19640	7000	7250	8775	11000
Technology Value 4D	YB5A3	20414	8025	8325	9900	12350
KIZASHI—4-Cyl.—Equipment Schedule 4						
W.B. 106.3"; 2.4 Liter.						
S Sedan 4D	RE9A1	21764	6300	6450	7925	9575
SE Sedan 4D	RE9A3	23064	7550	7725	9475	11500
Sport GTS Sedan 4D	RE9A6	25164	8475	8700	10500	12750
Sport SLS Sedan 4D	RE9A8	28363	9200	9425	11450	13900
AWD	F		1625	1625	2080	2080

2013 SUZUKI — JS2(YC5A3)-D-#

SX4—4-Cyl.—Equipment Schedule 4
W.B. 98.4"; 2.0 Liter.

Body Type	VIN	List	Good	Trade-In Very Good	Pvt-Party Good	Retail Excellent
LE Sedan 4D	YC5A3	16640	6800	7000	8450	10400
LE Popular Sedan 4D	YC5A3	18644	7975	8200	9700	11800
Sport SE Sedan 4D	YC5A5	19594	8650	8900	10400	12600
SX4 4WD—4-Cyl.—Equipment Schedule 4						
W.B. 98.4"; 2.0 Liter.						
Hatchback 4D	YB5A3	17794	7325	7525	9025	11050
FWD	A		(1275)	(1275)	(1705)	(1705)
SX4 AWD—4-Cyl.—Equipment Schedule 4						
W.B. 98.4"; 2.0 Liter.						
Premium H'Back 4D	YB5A3	19970	9200	9450	11100	13500
Technology Value 4D	YB5A4	21244	9700	9950	11550	14000
KIZASHI—4-Cyl.—Equipment Schedule 4						
W.B. 106.3"; 2.4 Liter.						
Sedan 4D	RE9A1	20794	7800	7950	9975	12150
SE Sedan 4D	RE9A3	22544	8875	9050	10750	12650
Sport GTS Sedan 4D	RE9A6	26594	9925	10100	12450	15150
AWD	F		1700	1700	2020	2020
KIZASHI AWD—4-Cyl.—Equipment Schedule 4						
W.B. 106.3"; 2.4 Liter.						
Sport SLS Sedan 4D	RF9A8	29794	10700	10900	13400	16300

TESLA

2013 TESLA — 5YJ(SA-A)-D-#

MODEL S—AC Electric—Equipment Schedule 2
W.B. 116.5".

Body Type	VIN	List	Good	Trade-In Very Good	Pvt-Party Good	Retail Excellent
Sedan 4D	SA-A	68570	52300	54100	53200	58200
Performance Sedan 4D	SA-A	93570	60700	62800	61200	66600
Signature Sedan 4D	SA-D	96570	61900	64000	62300	67800
Signature Performance	SA-D	106570	67100	69300	67200	73000
85kWh Lithium-ion Battery			4425	4425	4690	4690
Performance Plus Pkg			2925	2925	3085	3085
Tech Pkg			1375	1375	1455	1455
Rear Facing Jump Seats			1500	1500	1570	1570

2014 TESLA — 5YJ(SA1S1)-E-#

MODEL S—AC Electric—Equipment Schedule 2
W.B. 116.5".

Body Type	VIN	List	Good	Trade-In Very Good	Pvt-Party Good	Retail Excellent
Sedan 4D	SA1S1	71070	56000	58000	56800	62000
P85 Sedan 4D	SA1H1	94570	65600	67800	65800	71500
85kWh Lithium-ion Battery			4575	4575	4825	4825
Performance Plus Pkg			2975	2975	3130	3130
Tech Pkg			1425	1425	1505	1505
Rear Facing Jump Seats			1575	1575	1645	1645
MODEL S AWD—AC Electric—Equipment Schedule 2						
W.B. 116.5".						
85D Sedan 4D	SA1H2	86070	64500	65700	66200	70400
P85D Sedan 4D	SA1H2	105670	70800	72100	72400	76800
Rear Facing Jump Seats			1575	1575	1645	1645

TOYOTA

2000 TOYOTA-(J,1,2or4)(NorT)(X,1,2or5)(BT123)-Y-#

ECHO—4-Cyl.—Equipment Schedule 6
W.B. 93.3"; 1.5 Liter.

Body Type	VIN	List	Trade-In Good	Very Good	Pvt-Party Good	Retail Excellent
Sedan 4D	BT123	11945	1100	1275	1950	3450
Coupe 2D	AT123	11645	950	1100	1750	3125
COROLLA—4-Cyl.—Equipment Schedule 6						
W.B. 97.0"; 1.8 Liter.						
VE Sedan 4D	BR12E	13603	550	600	1350	2475
CE Sedan 4D	BR12E	14653	700	775	1450	2575
LE Sedan 4D	BR12E	15523	950	1050	1800	3200
CAMRY—4-Cyl.—Equipment Schedule 4						
W.B. 105.2"; 2.2 Liter.						
CE Sedan 4D	BG22K	19820	1175	1300	2025	3525
LE Sedan 4D	BG22K	20743	1300	1450	2200	3800
XLE Sedan 4D	BG22K	24423	1425	1575	2375	4075
Manual, 5-Spd			(175)	(175)	(220)	(220)
V6, 3.0 Liter	F		75	75	100	100
SOLARA—4-Cyl.—Equipment Schedule 4						
W.B. 105.1"; 2.2 Liter.						
SE Coupe 2D	CG22P	20193	1300	1525	2050	3575
SE Convertible 2D	FG22P	25523	1950	2275	2875	4925
Manual, 5-Spd			(175)	(175)	(220)	(220)
V6, 3.0 Liter	F		75	75	100	100
SOLARA—V6—Equipment Schedule 4						
W.B. 105.1"; 3.0 Liter.						
SLE Coupe 2D	CF22P	26293	2025	2350	2950	5050
SLE Convertible 2D	FF22P	30943	2550	2975	3550	6025
MR2 SPYDER—4-Cyl.—Equipment Schedule 4						
W.B. 96.5"; 1.8 Liter.						
Convertible 2D	FG320	23553	2350	2650	3075	4925
CELICA—4-Cyl.—Equipment Schedule 4						
W.B. 102.3"; 1.8 Liter.						
GT Liftback 2D	DR32T	17970	1525	1725	2325	3875
GT-S Liftback 2D	DY32T	21620	2100	2375	3000	4925
Automatic			125	125	165	165
AVALON—V6—Equipment Schedule 4						
W.B. 107.1"; 3.0 Liter.						
XL Sedan 4D	BF28B	25650	1675	1850	2575	4250
XLS Sedan 4D	BF28B	30210	2000	2200	2950	4850

2001 TOYOTA—(J,1,2or4)(NorT)(D,X,1or2)(BT123)-1-#

Body Type	VIN	List	Trade-In Good	Very Good	Pvt-Party Good	Retail Excellent
ECHO—4-Cyl.—Equipment Schedule 6						
W.B. 93.3"; 1.5 Liter.						
Sedan 4D	BT123	11930	1500	1725	2350	4000
Coupe 2D	AT123	11400	1325	1525	2125	3625
COROLLA—4-Cyl.—Equipment Schedule 6						
W.B. 97.0"; 1.8 Liter.						
CE Sedan 4D	BR12E	13753	900	1025	1650	2800
S Sedan 4D	BR12E	14343	1125	1250	1900	3200
LE Sedan 4D	BR12E	14863	1150	1275	1975	3400
PRIUS—4-Cyl. Hybrid—Equipment Schedule 3						
W.B. 100.4"; 1.5 Liter.						
Sedan 4D	BK12U	20450	925	1075	1850	3475
CAMRY—4-Cyl.—Equipment Schedule 4						
W.B. 105.1"; 2.2 Liter.						
CE Sedan 4D	BG22K	19733	1500	1650	2400	4050
LE Sedan 4D	BG22K	20895	1525	1675	2425	4100
XLE Sedan 4D	BG22K	24575	1725	1900	2775	4675
Manual, 5-Spd			(200)	(200)	(265)	(265)
V6, 3.0 Liter	F		75	75	100	100
SOLARA—4-Cyl.—Equipment Schedule 4						
W.B. 105.1"; 2.2 Liter.						
SE Coupe 2D	CG22P	20245	1325	1550	2125	3700
SE Convertible 2D	FG22P	25575	2275	2625	3225	5450
Manual, 5-Spd			(200)	(200)	(265)	(265)
V6, 3.0 Liter	F		75	75	100	100
SOLARA—V6—Equipment Schedule 4						
W.B. 105.1"; 3.0 Liter.						
SLE Coupe 2D	CF22P	25645	2275	2625	3225	5450
SLE Convertible 2D	FF22P	30995	3125	3625	4100	6775
MR2 SPYDER—4-Cyl.—Equipment Schedule 4						
W.B. 96.5"; 1.8 Liter.						
Convertible 2D	FG320	24065	2450	2750	3300	5175
CELICA—4-Cyl.—Equipment Schedule 4						
W.B. 102.3"; 1.8 Liter.						
GT Liftback 2D	DR32T	18285	1800	2050	2600	4200

Body Type	VIN	List	Trade-In Good	Very Good	Pvt-Party Good	Retail Excellent
GT-S Liftback 2D	DY32T	21935	2375	2650	3225	5175
Automatic			125	125	165	165
AVALON—V6—Equipment Schedule 4						
W.B. 107.1"; 3.0 Liter.						
XL Sedan 4D	BF28B	26325	1925	2125	2825	4575
XLS Sedan 4D	BF28B	30885	2250	2475	3225	5225

2002 TOYOTA–(J,1,2or4)(NorT)(D,X,1or2)(BT123)-2-#

Body Type	VIN	List	Trade-In Good	Very Good	Pvt-Party Good	Retail Excellent
ECHO—4-Cyl.—Equipment Schedule 6						
W.B. 93.3"; 1.5 Liter.						
Sedan 4D	BT123	12265	1625	1850	2500	4250
Coupe 2D	AT123	11675	1425	1625	2250	3825
COROLLA—4-Cyl.—Equipment Schedule 6						
W.B. 97.0"; 1.8 Liter.						
CE Sedan 4D	BR12E	13533	1125	1250	1900	3225
S Sedan 4D	BR12E	14073	1350	1500	2150	3600
LE Sedan 4D	BR12E	14443	1425	1575	2350	3975
PRIUS—4-Cyl. Hybrid—Equipment Schedule 3						
W.B. 100.4"; 1.5 Liter.						
Sedan 4D	BK12U	20480	1050	1225	2025	3750
CAMRY—4-Cyl.—Equipment Schedule 4						
W.B. 107.1"; 2.4 Liter.						
LE Sedan 4D	BE32K	20285	2000	2200	3075	5100
SE Sedan 4D	BE32K	21625	2100	2325	3275	5450
XLE Sedan 4D	BF32K	25890	2650	2900	3875	6375
Manual, 5-Spd.			(200)	(200)	(265)	(265)
V6, 3.0 Liter	F		100	100	145	145
SOLARA—4-Cyl.—Equipment Schedule 4						
W.B. 105.1"; 2.4 Liter.						
SE Coupe 2D	CE22P	20650	1600	1850	2475	4250
SE Convertible 2D	FE22P	25980	2475	2850	3575	6100
Manual, 5-Spd.			(200)	(200)	(265)	(265)
V6, 3.0 Liter	F		100	100	145	145
SOLARA—V6—Equipment Schedule 4						
W.B. 105.1"; 3.0 Liter.						
SLE Coupe 2D	CF22P	25160	2550	2950	3575	6000
SLE Convertible 2D	FF22P	31010	3250	3750	4500	7475
MR2 SPYDER—4-Cyl.—Equipment Schedule 4						
W.B. 96.5"; 1.8 Liter.						
Convertible 2D	FR320	25000	3250	3650	4100	6275
CELICA—4-Cyl.—Equipment Schedule 4						
W.B. 102.4"; 1.8 Liter.						
GT Liftback 2D	DR32T	18390	2175	2425	2950	4675
GT-S Liftback 2D	DY32T	22040	2900	3225	3700	5750
Automatic			125	125	165	165
AVALON—V6—Equipment Schedule 4						
W.B. 107.1"; 3.0 Liter.						
XL Sedan 4D	BF28B	26330	2300	2525	3150	4975
XLS Sedan 4D	BF28B	30890	2825	3100	3725	5800

2003 TOYOTA–J,1,2or4(NorT)D,X,1or2(BT123)-3-#

Body Type	VIN	List	Trade-In Good	Very Good	Pvt-Party Good	Retail Excellent
ECHO—4-Cyl.—Equipment Schedule 6						
W.B. 93.3"; 1.5 Liter.						
Sedan 4D	BT123	12375	1825	2075	2725	4475
Coupe 2D	AT123	11785	1600	1850	2475	4075
COROLLA—4-Cyl.—Equipment Schedule 6						
W.B. 102.4"; 1.8 Liter.						
CE Sedan 4D	BR32E	14055	2575	2800	3400	5250
S Sedan 4D	BR32E	15000	2700	2950	3525	5450
LE Sedan 4D	BR32E	15165	2950	3225	3800	5850
Sport Pkg			75	75	105	105
TRD Pkg			150	150	195	195
PRIUS—4-Cyl. Hybrid—Equipment Schedule 3						
W.B. 100.4"; 1.5 Liter.						
Sedan 4D	BK12U	20730	1725	2000	2775	4800
MATRIX—4-Cyl.—Equipment Schedule 6						
W.B. 102.4"; 1.8 Liter.						
Sport Wagon 4D	KR32E	15985	2525	2900	3350	5425
XR Sport Wagon 4D	KR32E	17495	2825	3225	3725	6025
XRS Sport Wagon 4D	KY32E	19235	2750	3125	3600	5825
TRD Pkg			275	275	370	370
4WD			575	575	775	775

Body Type	VIN	List	Trade-In Good	Trade-In Very Good	Pvt-Party Good	Retail Excellent
CAMRY—4-Cyl.—Equipment Schedule 4						
W.B. 107.1"; 2.4 Liter.						
LE Sedan 4D	BE30K	20285	**2825**	**3075**	**3775**	**5900**
SE Sedan 4D	BE30K	21625	**3100**	**3375**	**4125**	**6425**
Manual, 5-Spd			**(225)**	**(225)**	**(310)**	**(310)**
V6, 3.0 Liter	F		**150**	**150**	**210**	**210**
CAMRY—V6—Equipment Schedule 4						
W.B. 107.1"; 3.0 Liter.						
XLE Sedan 4D	BF30K	25920	**3550**	**3875**	**4750**	**7400**
4-Cyl, 2.4 Liter	E		**(175)**	**(175)**	**(220)**	**(220)**
SOLARA—4-Cyl.—Equipment Schedule 4						
W.B. 105.1"; 2.4 Liter.						
SE Coupe 2D	CE22P	20650	**2050**	**2350**	**2825**	**4600**
SE Convertible 2D	FE22P	25980	**2925**	**3350**	**3875**	**6325**
Manual, 5-Spd			**(225)**	**(225)**	**(310)**	**(310)**
V6, 3.0 Liter	F		**150**	**150**	**210**	**210**
SOLARA—V6—Equipment Schedule 4						
W.B. 105.1"; 3.0 Liter.						
SLE Coupe 2D	CF22P	25160	**3100**	**3550**	**4125**	**6600**
SLE Convertible 2D	FF22P	31010	**3925**	**4475**	**5000**	**7975**
MR2 SPYDER—4-Cyl.—Equipment Schedule 4						
W.B. 96.5"; 1.8 Liter.						
Convertible 2D	FR320	25055	**3900**	**4350**	**4900**	**7350**
CELICA—4-Cyl.—Equipment Schedule 4						
W.B. 102.4"; 1.8 Liter.						
GT Liftback 2D	DR32T	18610	**2500**	**2775**	**3275**	**5125**
GT-S Liftback 2D	DY32T	22455	**3150**	**3500**	**4100**	**6325**
Automatic			**150**	**150**	**185**	**185**
AVALON—V6—Equipment Schedule 4						
W.B. 107.1"; 3.0 Liter.						
XL Sedan 4D	BF28B	26330	**3100**	**3375**	**3875**	**5875**
XLS Sedan 4D	BF28B	27150	**3450**	**3750**	**4375**	**6625**

2004 TOYOTA–(J,1,2or4)(NorT)D,Xor1(BT123)–4–#

Body Type	VIN	List	Trade-In Good	Trade-In Very Good	Pvt-Party Good	Retail Excellent
ECHO—4-Cyl.—Equipment Schedule 6						
W.B. 93.3"; 1.5 Liter.						
Sedan 4D	BT123	12215	**2025**	**2300**	**2975**	**4750**
Coupe 2D	AT123	11685	**1775**	**2000**	**2675**	**4300**
COROLLA—4-Cyl.—Equipment Schedule 6						
W.B. 102.4"; 1.8 Liter.						
CE Sedan 4D	BR32E	14085	**2750**	**2975**	**3525**	**5350**
S Sedan 4D	BR32E	15030	**3150**	**3425**	**3925**	**5850**
LE Sedan 4D	BR32E	15295	**3275**	**3550**	**4125**	**6250**
PRIUS—4-Cyl. Hybrid—Equipment Schedule 3						
W.B. 106.3"; 1.5 Liter.						
Hatchback Sedan 4D	KB20U	20510	**3300**	**3750**	**4150**	**6550**
MATRIX—4-Cyl.—Equipment Schedule 6						
W.B. 102.4"; 1.8 Liter.						
Sport Wagon 4D	KR32E	15985	**2825**	**3200**	**3650**	**5800**
XR Sport Wagon 4D	KR32E	17495	**3325**	**3750**	**4200**	**6600**
XRS Sport Wagon 4D	KY32E	19265	**3425**	**3875**	**4300**	**6750**
Sport Pkg			**300**	**300**	**400**	**400**
4WD	L		**625**	**625**	**845**	**845**
CAMRY—4-Cyl.—Equipment Schedule 4						
W.B. 107.1"; 2.4 Liter.						
Sedan 4D	BE32K	19390	**3000**	**3275**	**3875**	**5900**
LE Sedan 4D	BE32K	20390	**3275**	**3575**	**4175**	**6350**
SE Sedan 4D	BE32K	21220	**3475**	**3800**	**4575**	**6925**
Manual, 5-Spd			**(275)**	**(275)**	**(375)**	**(375)**
V6, 3.0 Liter	F,A		**200**	**200**	**275**	**275**
CAMRY—V6—Equipment Schedule 4						
W.B. 107.1"; 3.0 Liter.						
XLE Sedan 4D	BF32K	25920	**4300**	**4675**	**5450**	**8250**
4-Cyl, 2.4 Liter	E		**(200)**	**(200)**	**(255)**	**(255)**
SOLARA—4-Cyl.—Equipment Schedule 4						
W.B. 107.2"; 2.4 Liter.						
SE Coupe 2D	CE38P	20465	**2800**	**3175**	**3575**	**5600**
SE Sport Coupe 2D	CE38P	21960	**2825**	**3200**	**3775**	**6050**
Manual, 5-Spd			**(275)**	**(275)**	**(375)**	**(375)**
V6, 3.3 Liter	A		**200**	**200**	**275**	**275**
SOLARA—V6—Equipment Schedule 4						
W.B. 107.2"; 3.3 Liter.						
SLE Coupe 2D	CA389	26510	**3775**	**4300**	**4925**	**7825**

2004 TOYOTA

Body Type	VIN	List	Trade-In Good	Very Good	Pvt-Party Good	Retail Excellent
4-Cyl, 2.4 Liter	E		(200)	(200)	(255)	(255)
SOLARA—V6—Equipment Schedule 4						
W.B. 107.1"; 3.3 Liter.						
SE Convertible 2D	FA22P	26465	3500	3950	4600	7325
SLE Convertible 2D	FA22P	29965	4400	5000	5600	8850
MR2 SPYDER—4-Cyl.—Equipment Schedule 4						
W.B. 96.5"; 1.8 Liter.						
Convertible 2D	FR320	25410	4775	5300	5800	8500
CELICA—4-Cyl.—Equipment Schedule 4						
W.B. 102.4"; 1.8 Liter.						
GT Liftback 2D	DR32T	17905	3225	3575	4225	6425
GT-S Liftback 2D	DY32T	22570	4200	4650	5200	7825
Automatic			175	175	220	220
AVALON—V6—Equipment Schedule 4						
W.B. 107.1"; 3.0 Liter.						
XL Sedan 4D	BF28B	26560	3525	3850	4400	6475
XLS Sedan 4D	BF28B	31020	4075	4425	5025	7425

2005 TOYOTA—(J,1,2or4)(NorT)D,Xor1(BT123)-5-#

Body Type	VIN	List	Trade-In Good	Very Good	Pvt-Party Good	Retail Excellent
ECHO—4-Cyl.—Equipment Schedule 6						
W.B. 93.3"; 1.5 Liter.						
Sedan 4D	BT123	12620	2250	2525	3325	5200
Coupe 2D	AT123	12090	1975	2225	3000	4675
COROLLA—4-Cyl.—Equipment Schedule 6						
W.B. 102.4"; 1.8 Liter.						
CE Sedan 4D	BR32E	14220	3000	3250	4025	6025
S Sedan 4D	BR32E	15265	3200	3475	4250	6350
LE Sedan 4D	BR32E	15430	3425	3725	4600	6825
XRS Sedan 4D	BY32E	17995	3750	4075	4950	7350
PRIUS—4-Cyl. Hybrid—Equipment Schedule 3						
W.B. 106.3"; 1.5 Liter.						
Hatchback Sedan 4D	KB22U	21515	3450	3900	4575	7000
MATRIX—4-Cyl.—Equipment Schedule 6						
W.B. 102.4"; 1.8 Liter.						
Sport Wagon 4D	KR32E	16105	3300	3725	4200	6375
XR Sport Wagon 4D	KR32E	17615	3550	4025	4675	7175
XRS Sport Wagon 4D	KY32E	19290	3800	4300	4850	7325
4WD	L		675	675	910	910
CAMRY—4-Cyl.—Equipment Schedule 4						
W.B. 107.1"; 2.4 Liter.						
Sedan 4D	BE32K	19415	3525	3850	4600	6700
LE Sedan 4D	BE32K	20515	3975	4325	5050	7325
SE Sedan 4D	BE32K	21345	4525	4925	5675	8250
Manual, 5-Spd			(325)	(325)	(445)	(445)
V6, 3.0 Liter	F,A		250	250	345	345
CAMRY—V6—Equipment Schedule 4						
W.B. 107.1"; 3.0 Liter.						
XLE Sedan 4D	BF32K	25945	5250	5675	6425	9350
4-Cyl, 2.4 Liter	E		(250)	(250)	(335)	(335)
SOLARA—4-Cyl.—Equipment Schedule 4						
W.B. 107.1"; 2.4 Liter.						
SE Coupe 2D	CE38P	20590	3225	3650	4075	5975
SE Sport Coupe 2D	CE38P	22085	3375	3800	4400	6700
Manual, 5-Spd			(325)	(325)	(445)	(445)
V6, 3.3 Liter	A		250	250	345	345
SOLARA—V6—Equipment Schedule 4						
W.B. 107.1"; 3.3 Liter.						
SLE Coupe 2D	CA38P	26635	4450	5000	5550	8400
4-Cyl, 2.4 Liter	E		(250)	(250)	(335)	(335)
SOLARA—V6—Equipment Schedule 4						
W.B. 107.1"; 3.3 Liter.						
SE Convertible 2D	FA38P	26920	4150	4675	5225	7900
SLE Convertible 2D	FA38P	30190	4825	5450	6200	9425
MR2 SPYDER—4-Cyl.—Equipment Schedule 4						
W.B. 96.5"; 1.8 Liter.						
Convertible 2D	FR320	26685	5350	5875	6400	9050
CELICA—4-Cyl.—Equipment Schedule 4						
W.B. 102.4"; 1.8 Liter.						
GT Liftback 2D	DR32T	19830	3700	4075	4750	6975
GT-S Liftback 2D	DY32T	23575	4725	5200	5950	8675
Automatic			200	200	255	255
AVALON—V6—Equipment Schedule 4						
W.B. 111.0"; 3.5 Liter.						

Body Type	VIN	List	Trade-In Good	Very Good	Pvt-Party Good	Retail Excellent
XL Sedan 4D	BK36B	26890	4775	5175	5625	7875
Touring Sedan 4D	BK36B	29140	5500	5975	6500	9050
XLS Sedan 4D	BK36B	31340	5600	6075	6700	9400
Limited Sedan 4D	BK36B	34080	5975	6500	7075	9950

2006 TOYOTA—(1,2,4orJ)(NorT)(1,DorX)(BR32E)—6—#

COROLLA—4-Cyl.—Equipment Schedule 6
W.B. 102.4"; 1.8 Liter.

CE Sedan 4D	BR32E	14545	3375	3650	4500	6550
S Sedan 4D	BR32E	15590	3675	3975	4825	7000
LE Sedan 4D	BR32E	15755	3925	4250	5100	7375
XRS Sedan 4D	BY32E	18320	4575	4950	5750	8275

PRIUS—4-Cyl. Hybrid—Equipment Schedule 3
W.B. 106.3"; 1.5 Liter.

Hatchback Sedan 4D	KB22U	22305	4000	4475	5100	7600
Package #5			250	250	320	320

MATRIX—4-Cyl.—Equipment Schedule 6
W.B. 102.4"; 1.8 Liter.

Sport Wagon 4D	KR32E	16450	3750	4175	4775	7050
XR Sport Wagon 4D	KR32E	17960	4225	4725	5275	7775
Manual, 5-Spd			(275)	(275)	(355)	(355)
4WD	L		725	725	975	975

MATRIX—4-Cyl.—Equipment Schedule 6
W.B. 102.4"; 1.8 Liter.

XRS Sport Wagon 4D	KY32E	19640	4375	4900	5450	8000
4WD	L		725	725	975	975

CAMRY—4-Cyl.—Equipment Schedule 4
W.B. 107.1"; 2.4 Liter.

Sedan 4D	BE32K	18985	4200	4550	5225	7425
LE Sedan 4D	BE32K	20915	4600	4975	5625	7950
SE Sedan 4D	BE32K	21745	5275	5700	6550	9250
Manual, 5-Spd			(375)	(375)	(510)	(510)
V6, 3.0 Liter	F,A		300	300	410	410

CAMRY—V6—Equipment Schedule 4
W.B. 107.1"; 3.0 Liter.

XLE Sedan 4D	BF32K	26425	6025	6500	7300	10300
4-Cyl. 2.4 Liter	E		(300)	(300)	(410)	(410)

SOLARA—4-Cyl.—Equipment Schedule 4
W.B. 107.1"; 2.4 Liter.

SE Coupe 2D	CE38P	20900	3975	4425	4675	6600
SE Sport Coupe 2D	CE38P	22395	4200	4700	5050	7225
Manual, 5-Spd			(375)	(375)	(500)	(500)
V6, 3.3 Liter	A		300	300	400	400

SOLARA—V6—Equipment Schedule 4
W.B. 107.1"; 3.3 Liter.

SLE Coupe 2D	CA38P	26875	5150	5750	6275	9050
4-Cyl. 2.4 Liter	E		(300)	(300)	(410)	(410)

SOLARA—V6—Equipment Schedule 4
W.B. 107.1"; 3.3 Liter.

SE Convertible 2D	FA38P	27480	4925	5500	5975	8550
SLE Convertible 2D	FA38P	30750	6150	6850	7475	10900

AVALON—V6—Equipment Schedule 4
W.B. 111.0"; 3.5 Liter.

XL Sedan 4D	BK36B	27165	5275	5725	6250	8550
Touring Sedan 4D	BK36B	29415	6100	6600	7075	9675
XLS Sedan 4D	BK36B	31615	6650	7175	7675	10500
Limited Sedan 4D	BK36B	34355	7225	7800	8300	11350

2007 TOYOTA—(1,2,4orJ)(NorT)(1,DorX)(JT923)—7—#

YARIS—4-Cyl.—Equipment Schedule 6
W.B. 96.9", 100.4" (Sedan); 1.5 Liter.

Hatchback 2D	JT923	12430	2675	2850	4025	5825
Sedan 4D	BT923	13130	3350	3575	4700	6650
S Sedan 4D	BT923	14630	3925	4175	5300	7300
Manual, 5-Spd			(300)	(300)	(385)	(385)

COROLLA—4-Cyl.—Equipment Schedule 6
W.B. 102.4"; 1.8 Liter.

CE Sedan 4D	BR32E	14785	4175	4500	5275	7425
S Sedan 4D	BR32E	15830	4575	4925	5700	7975
LE Sedan 4D	BR32E	15995	4625	4975	5775	8100
Manual, 5-Spd			(350)	(350)	(455)	(455)

Body Type	VIN	List	Trade-In Good	Very Good	Pvt-Party Good	Retail Excellent
PRIUS—4-Cyl. Hybrid—Equipment Schedule 3						
W.B. 106.3"; 1.5 Liter.						
Hatchback Sedan 4D	KB20U	22755	4625	5100	5725	8225
Touring H'Back 4D	KB20U	23650	5150	5675	6400	9075
Package #5			250	250	350	350
Package #6			250	250	350	350
MATRIX—4-Cyl.—Equipment Schedule 6						
W.B. 102.4"; 1.8 Liter.						
Sport Wagon 4D	KR30E	16640	4250	4675	5275	7575
XR Sport Wagon 4D	KR30E	18150	5150	5650	6225	8875
Manual, 5-Spd			(300)	(300)	(385)	(385)
CAMRY—4-Cyl.—Equipment Schedule 4						
W.B. 109.3"; 2.4 Liter.						
CE Sedan 4D	BE46K	19900	5100	5475	6225	8525
LE Sedan 4D	BE46K	21355	5700	6125	6775	9200
SE Sedan 4D	BE46K	22520	6625	7125	7825	10650
XLE Sedan 4D	BE46K	25280	7225	7775	8500	11550
Manual, 5-Spd			(425)	(425)	(555)	(555)
V6, 3.5 Liter	K		350	350	475	475
CAMRY—4-Cyl. Hybrid—Equipment Schedule 4						
W.B. 109.3"; 2.4 Liter.						
Sedan 4D	BB46K	26480	5700	6275	6975	9925
SOLARA—4-Cyl.—Equipment Schedule 4						
W.B. 107.1"; 2.4 Liter.						
SE Coupe 2D	CE30P	21340	4575	5025	5325	7325
Sport Coupe 2D	CE30P	23610	4900	5400	5825	8025
Manual, 5-Spd			(425)	(425)	(525)	(525)
V6, 3.3 Liter	A		350	350	455	455
SOLARA—V6—Equipment Schedule 4						
W.B. 107.1"; 3.3 Liter.						
SLE Coupe 2D	CA309	27565	5975	6575	7050	9825
4-Cyl, 2.4 Liter	E		(350)	(350)	(445)	(445)
SOLARA—V6—Equipment Schedule 4						
W.B. 107.1"; 3.3 Liter.						
SE Convertible 2D	FA38P	27770	5850	6450	6875	9500
Sport Convertible 2D	FA38P	30040	6950	7675	8025	11050
SLE Convertible 2D	FA38P	31040	7375	8125	8500	11750
AVALON—V6—Equipment Schedule 4						
W.B. 111.0"; 3.5 Liter.						
XL Sedan 4D	BK36B	27455	5950	6400	6900	9225
Touring Sedan 4D	BK36B	29705	6825	7350	7800	10400
XLS Sedan 4D	BK36B	31905	7500	8050	8575	11450
Limited Sedan 4D	BK36B	34645	8400	9025	9425	12550

2008 TOYOTA—(1,2,4orJ)(NorT)(1,DorX)(JT923)-8-#

Body Type	VIN	List	Trade-In Good	Very Good	Pvt-Party Good	Retail Excellent
YARIS—4-Cyl.—Equipment Schedule 6						
W.B. 96.9", 100.4" (Sedan); 1.5 Liter.						
Hatchback 2D	JT923	12860	3275	3500	4800	6700
Sedan 4D	BT923	13560	3925	4175	5400	7325
S Hatchback 2D	JT923	14535	4025	4275	5525	7525
S Sedan 4D	BT923	15060	4725	5025	6175	8225
Manual, 5-Spd w/Overdrive			(350)	(350)	(460)	(460)
COROLLA—4-Cyl.—Equipment Schedule 6						
W.B. 102.4"; 1.8 Liter.						
CE Sedan 4D	BR32E	15065	4575	4875	5725	7775
S Sedan 4D	BR32E	16110	5025	5375	6225	8425
LE Sedan 4D	BR32E	16275	5100	5450	6300	8500
Manual, 5-Spd w/Overdrive			(350)	(350)	(460)	(460)
PRIUS—4-Cyl. Hybrid—Equipment Schedule 3						
W.B. 106.3"; 1.5 Liter.						
Standard H'Back Sed	KB20U	21610	5050	5450	6275	8650
Hatchback Sedan 4D	KB20U	22985	5650	6100	6950	9400
Touring H'Back 4D	KB20U	23880	6525	7050	7825	10500
Package #4			125	125	180	180
Package #5			275	275	380	380
Package #6			275	275	380	380
MATRIX—4-Cyl.—Equipment Schedule 6						
W.B. 102.4"; 1.8 Liter.						
Sport Wagon 4D	KR30E	16970	4900	5300	6025	8225
XR Sport Wagon 4D	KR30E	18480	6025	6500	7375	10000
Manual, 5-Spd			(300)	(300)	(400)	(400)
CAMRY—4-Cyl.—Equipment Schedule 4						
W.B. 109.3"; 2.4 Liter.						

Body Type	VIN	List	Trade-In Good	Very Good	Pvt-Party Good	Retail Excellent
Sedan 4D	BE46K	20280	6175	6575	7325	9625
LE Sedan 4D	BE46K	21735	6700	7150	7825	10200
SE Sedan 4D	BE46K	22900	7600	8100	8900	11700
XLE Sedan 4D	BE46K	25660	8225	8775	9575	12550
Manual, 5-Spd w/Overdrive			(450)	(450)	(565)	(565)
V6, 3.5 Liter	K		400	400	500	500
CAMRY—4-Cyl. Hybrid—Equipment Schedule 4						
W.B. 109.3"; 2.4 Liter.						
Sedan 4D	BB46K	25860	6475	7000	7725	10350
SOLARA—4-Cyl.—Equipment Schedule 4						
W.B. 107.1"; 2.4 Liter.						
SE Coupe 2D	CE30P	21420	5500	5950	6525	8575
SE Sport Coupe 2D	CE30P	23690	6125	6625	7175	9400
Manual, 5-Spd w/Overdrive			(450)	(450)	(555)	(555)
V6, 3.3 Liter	A		400	400	490	490
SOLARA—V6—Equipment Schedule 4						
W.B. 107.1"; 3.3 Liter.						
SLE Coupe 2D	CA30P	27565	7775	8400	8950	11700
4-Cyl, 2.4 Liter	E		(525)	(525)	(655)	(655)
SOLARA—V6—Equipment Schedule 4						
W.B. 107.1"; 3.3 Liter.						
SE Convertible 2D	FA38P	27850	7350	7950	8525	11200
Sport Convertible 2D	FA38P	30120	8325	8975	9475	12350
SLE Convertible 2D	FA38P	31120	8725	9425	10000	13100
AVALON—V6—Equipment Schedule 4						
W.B. 111.0"; 3.5 Liter.						
XL Sedan 4D	BK36B	27735	7100	7575	8075	10400
Touring Sedan 4D	BK36B	29985	8550	9100	9550	12200
XLS Sedan 4D	BK36B	32035	8950	9525	10050	12900
Limited Sedan 4D	BK36B	35075	9700	10300	10850	13900

2009 TOYOTA—(1,2,4orJ)(NorT)(1,DorX)(JT903)-9-#

Body Type	VIN	List	Trade-In Good	Very Good	Pvt-Party Good	Retail Excellent
YARIS—4-Cyl.—Equipment Schedule 6						
W.B. 96.9", 100.4" (Sedan); 1.5 Liter.						
Hatchback 2D	JT903	12955	3975	4200	5525	7425
Sedan 4D	BT903	14515	4700	4975	6225	8225
S Hatchback 2D	JT903	15575	4800	5075	6325	8325
S Sedan 4D	BT903	16630	5375	5700	7000	9100
Manual, 5-Spd w/Overdrive			(375)	(375)	(490)	(490)
YARIS—4-Cyl.—Equipment Schedule 6						
W.B. 96.9", 100.4" (Sedan); 1.5 Liter.						
Hatchback 4D	KT903	14025	4625	4875	6125	8125
S Hatchback 4D	KT903	15875	4975	5250	6475	8500
COROLLA—4-Cyl.—Equipment Schedule 6						
W.B. 102.4"; 1.8 Liter, 2.4 Liter.						
Sedan 4D	BU40E	15910	6125	6475	7400	9550
S Sedan 4D	BU40E	16980	6525	6900	7825	10100
XRS Sedan 4D	BE40E	19420	8075	8550	9625	12450
Manual, 5-Spd w/Overdrive			(375)	(375)	(490)	(490)
COROLLA—4-Cyl.—Equipment Schedule 6						
W.B. 102.4"; 1.8 Liter.						
LE Sedan 4D	BU40E	17310	6525	6900	7850	10100
XLE Sedan 4D	BU40E	18210	7200	7625	8775	11400
PRIUS—4-Cyl. Hybrid—Equipment Schedule 3						
W.B. 106.3"; 1.5 Liter.						
Standard H'Back Sed	KB20U	22750	5950	6325	7425	9725
Hatchback Sedan 4D	KB20U	24035	6775	7175	8175	10550
Touring H'Back 4D	KB20U	24930	7400	7850	8925	11550
Package #2			75	75	90	90
Package #3			75	75	90	90
Package #4			175	175	220	220
Package #5			300	300	410	410
Package #6			300	300	410	410
MATRIX—4-Cyl.—Equipment Schedule 6						
W.B. 102.4"; 1.8 Liter, 2.4 Liter.						
Sport Wagon 4D	KU40E	17850	5900	6250	7200	9300
XRS Sport Wagon 4D	GE40E	21320	7400	7850	8800	11250
Manual, 5-Spd w/Overdrive			(375)	(375)	(490)	(490)
MATRIX—4-Cyl.—Equipment Schedule 6						
W.B. 102.4"; 2.4 Liter.						
S Sport Wagon 4D	KE40E	18920	6625	7050	8025	10350
4WD			1100	1100	1475	1475
Automatic, 5-Spd			325	325	445	445

Body Type	VIN	List	Trade-In Good	Very Good	Pvt-Party Good	Retail Excellent
CAMRY—4-Cyl.—Equipment Schedule 4						
W.B. 109.3"; 2.4 Liter.						
Sedan 4D	BE46K	20430	7100	7525	8425	10750
LE Sedan 4D	BE46K	21885	7550	8000	8875	11300
SE Sedan 4D	BE46K	23050	8425	8925	9825	12500
XLE Sedan 4D	BE46K	25810	9050	9575	10550	13450
Manual, 5-Spd w/Overdrive			(475)	(475)	(605)	(605)
V6, 3.5 Liter	K		450	450	565	565
CAMRY—4-Cyl. Hybrid—Equipment Schedule 4						
W.B. 109.3"; 2.4 Liter.						
Sedan 4D	BB46K	26010	7900	8375	9275	11850
AVALON—V6—Equipment Schedule 4						
W.B. 111.0"; 3.5 Liter.						
XL Sedan 4D	BK36B	28505	8425	8900	9525	11850
XLS Sedan 4D	BK36B	32805	10500	11100	11700	14550
Limited Sedan 4D	BK36B	35845	11200	11800	12500	15550

2010 TOYOTA—(2,4orK)T(1,DorN)(KT4K3)–A–#

Body Type	VIN	List	Trade-In Good	Very Good	Pvt-Party Good	Retail Excellent
YARIS—4-Cyl.—Equipment Schedule 6						
W.B. 96.9", 100.4" (Sed); 1.5 Liter.						
Hatchback 4D	KT4K3	14205	5275	5550	6975	8975
Hatchback 2D	JT4K3	13905	5050	5325	6600	8575
Sedan 4D	BT4K3	14665	5525	5850	7225	9250
Manual, 5-Spd w/Overdrive			(450)	(450)	(615)	(615)
COROLLA—4-Cyl.—Equipment Schedule 6						
W.B. 102.4"; 1.8 Liter, 2.4 Liter.						
Sedan 4D	BU4EE	16070	7150	7525	8550	10700
S Sedan 4D	BU4EE	17140	7550	7925	9000	11300
XRS Sedan 4D	BE4EE	19580	8925	9375	10550	13250
Manual, 5-Spd w/Overdrive			(450)	(450)	(610)	(610)
COROLLA—4-Cyl.—Equipment Schedule 6						
W.B. 102.4"; 1.8 Liter.						
LE Sedan 4D	BU4EE	17470	7300	7675	8750	11000
XLE Sedan 4D	BU4EE	18370	8225	8650	9800	12300
PRIUS—4-Cyl. Hybrid—Equipment Schedule 3						
W.B. 106.3"; 1.8 Liter.						
I Hatchback 4D	KN3DU	22150	8425	8800	9975	12300
II Hatchback 4D	KN3DU	23150	8725	9100	10250	12600
III Hatchback 4D	KN3DU	24550	9400	9825	10900	13300
IV Hatchback 4D	KN3DU	27350	10500	11000	11900	14350
V Hatchback 4D	KN3DU	28820	11350	11850	12750	15250
MATRIX—4-Cyl.—Equipment Schedule 6						
W.B. 102.4"; 1.8 Liter, 2.4 Liter.						
Sport Wagon 4D	KU4EE	18110	7050	7375	8675	10900
XRS Sport Wagon 4D	ME4EE	21520	8525	8900	10150	12550
Manual, 5-Spd w/Overdrive			(450)	(450)	(610)	(610)
MATRIX—4-Cyl.—Equipment Schedule 6						
W.B. 102.4"; 2.4 Liter.						
S Sport Wagon 4D	KE4EE	19210	7500	7825	9050	11250
4WD			1175	1175	1515	1515
Automatic, 5-Spd			375	375	495	495
CAMRY—4-Cyl.—Equipment Schedule 4						
W.B. 109.3"; 2.5 Liter.						
Sedan 4D	BF3EK	21195	8525	8950	9925	12350
LE Sedan 4D	BF3EK	22650	8950	9400	10300	12700
SE Sedan 4D	BF3EK	23915	9675	10150	11200	13850
XLE Sedan 4D	BF3EK	26675	10350	10850	11900	14750
V6, 3.5 Liter	K		525	525	640	640
CAMRY—4-Cyl. Hybrid—Equipment Schedule 4						
W.B. 109.3"; 2.4 Liter.						
Sedan 4D	BB3EK	26900	10150	10600	11700	14200
AVALON—V6—Equipment Schedule 4						
W.B. 111.0"; 3.5 Liter.						
XL Sedan 4D	BK36B	28695	10500	11050	11700	14200
XLS Sedan 4D	BK36B	32995	12800	13450	14150	17100
Limited Sedan 4D	BK36B	36035	13500	14200	15000	18100

2011 TOYOTA—(2,3,4,5orK)T(1,4,D,KorN)(KT4K3)–B–#

Body Type	VIN	List	Trade-In Good	Very Good	Pvt-Party Good	Retail Excellent
YARIS—4-Cyl.—Equipment Schedule 6						
W.B. 96.9", 100.4" (Sed); 1.5 Liter.						
Hatchback 4D	KT4K3	14017	5950	6250	7700	9750
Hatchback 2D	JT4KE	14415	6000	6325	7775	9825

2011 TOYOTA

Body Type	VIN	List	Trade-In Good	Very Good	Pvt-Party Good	Retail Excellent
Sedan 4D	BT4KE	15175	6500	6825	8125	10100
Manual, 5-Spd w/Overdrive			(500)	(500)	(655)	(655)
COROLLA—4-Cyl.—Equipment Schedule 6						
W.B. 102.4"; 1.8 Liter.						
Sedan 4D	BU4EE	16360	8225	8600	9650	11800
S Sedan 4D	BU4EE	18230	9325	9750	10800	13100
Manual, 5-Spd w/Overdrive			(500)	(500)	(630)	(630)
COROLLA—4-Cyl.—Equipment Schedule 6						
W.B. 102.4"; 1.8 Liter.						
LE Sedan 4D	BU4EE	18060	8450	8850	9875	12050
PRIUS—4-Cyl. Hybrid—Equipment Schedule 3						
W.B. 106.3"; 1.8 Liter.						
One Hatchback 4D	KN3DU	22410	9350	9650	11150	13450
Two Hatchback 4D	KN3DU	23810	9675	10000	11500	13900
Three Hatchback 4D	KN3DU	24810	10650	11000	12400	14800
Four Hatchback 4D	KN3DU	27610	11750	12100	13350	15600
Five Hatchback 4D	KN3DU	29080	12850	13250	14450	16900
MATRIX—4-Cyl.—Equipment Schedule 6						
W.B. 102.4"; 1.8 Liter.						
Sport Wagon 4D	KU4EE	20145	8300	8550	9875	11900
Manual, 5-Spd w/Overdrive			(500)	(500)	(605)	(605)
MATRIX—4-Cyl.—Equipment Schedule 6						
W.B. 102.4"; 2.4 Liter.						
S Sport Wagon 4D	KE4EE	20025	8375	8650	9975	12000
4WD	L		1325	1325	1645	1645
Automatic, 4-Spd			425	425	535	535
CAMRY—4-Cyl.—Equipment Schedule 4						
W.B. 109.3"; 2.5 Liter.						
Sedan 4D	BF3EK	21405	9500	9925	11000	13400
LE Sedan 4D	BF3EK	22860	9750	10200	11250	13600
SE Sedan 4D	BF3EK	24125	10700	11200	12300	14900
XLE Sedan 4D	BF3EK	26885	11300	11800	12950	15750
V6, 3.5 Liter	K		575	575	705	705
CAMRY—4-Cyl. Hybrid—Equipment Schedule 4						
W.B. 109.3"; 2.4 Liter.						
Sedan 4D	BB3EK	27160	11400	11750	13150	15550
AVALON—V6—Equipment Schedule 4						
W.B. 111.0"; 3.5 Liter.						
Sedan 4D	BK3DB	33005	15500	16200	16900	19900
Limited Sedan 4D	BK3DB	36245	16300	17050	17750	20900

2012 TOYOTA—(2,4,5orJ)T(1,4,DorF)(KT4D3)-C-#

Body Type	VIN	List	Trade-In Good	Very Good	Pvt-Party Good	Retail Excellent
YARIS—4-Cyl.—Equipment Schedule 6						
W.B. 98.8"; 1.5 Liter.						
SE Hatchback 4D	KT4D3	17960	9025	9475	10700	12850
L Hatchback 2D	JT4D3	15600	7325	7700	9150	11300
Manual, 5-Spd			(500)	(500)	(665)	(665)
YARIS—4-Cyl.—Equipment Schedule 6						
W.B. 98.8"; 1.5 Liter.						
L Hatchback 4D	KT4D3	15900	7550	7950	9325	11400
LE Hatchback 4D	KT4D3	16860	8325	8750	10100	12250
LE Hatchback 2D	JT4D3	16385	8100	8500	9825	11950
Sedan 4D	BT4K3	16120	7750	8150	9550	11700
COROLLA—4-Cyl.—Equipment Schedule 6						
W.B. 102.4"; 1.8 Liter.						
L Sedan 4D	BU4EE	16890	8925	9300	10400	12500
S Sedan 4D	BU4EE	18750	10500	10900	11950	14250
Manual, 5-Spd			(550)	(550)	(685)	(685)
COROLLA—4-Cyl.—Equipment Schedule 6						
W.B. 102.4"; 1.8 Liter.						
LE Sedan 4D	BU4EE	18670	9300	9700	10800	12950
PRIUS C—4-Cyl. Hybrid—Equipment Schedule 3						
W.B. 100.4"; 1.5 Liter.						
One Hatchback 4D	KDTB3	19710	9500	9725	11250	13200
Two Hatchback 4D	KDTB3	20660	9900	10100	11600	13600
Three Hatchback 4D	KDTB3	22395	10350	10600	12050	14050
Four Hatchback 4D	KDTB3	23990	11550	11800	13250	15300
PRIUS—4-Cyl. Hybrid—Equipment Schedule 3						
W.B. 106.3"; 1.8 Liter.						
One Hatchback 4D	KN3DU	23775	10550	10800	12500	14750
Two Hatchback 4D	KN3DU	24760	10900	11200	12850	15100
Three Hatchback 4D	KN3DU	26325	11550	11850	13500	15800
Four Hatchback 4D	KN3DU	28995	12850	13150	14600	16800

Body Type	VIN	List	Trade-In Good	Very Good	Pvt-Party Good	Retail Excellent
Five Hatchback 4D	KN3DU	30565	**14000**	**14350**	**16000**	**18400**
PRIUS PLUG-IN—4-Cyl. Hybrid—Equipment Schedule 3						
W.B. 106.3"; 1.8 Liter.						
Hatchback 4D	KN3DP	32760	**12300**	**12550**	**13900**	**15850**
Advanced H'Back 4D	KN3DP	40285	**17450**	**17900**	**19250**	**21800**
PRIUS V—4-Cyl. Hybrid—Equipment Schedule 3						
W.B. 109.4"; 1.8 Liter.						
Two Wagon 4D	ZN3EU	27160	**13500**	**13850**	**15250**	**17300**
Three Wagon 4D	ZN3EU	27925	**14750**	**15100**	**16450**	**18650**
Five Wagon 4D	ZN3EU	30750	**15450**	**15800**	**17150**	**19450**
Technology Pkg			**1325**	**1325**	**1545**	**1545**
MATRIX—4-Cyl.—Equipment Schedule 6						
W.B. 102.4"; 1.8 Liter.						
Sport Wagon 4D	KU4EE	20445	**10900**	**11150**	**12450**	**14500**
Manual, 5-Spd			**(475)**	**(475)**	**(565)**	**(565)**
MATRIX—4-Cyl.—Equipment Schedule 6						
W.B. 102.4"; 2.4 Liter.						
S Sport Wagon 4D	KE4EE	20325	**10650**	**10900**	**12300**	**14200**
AWD	L		**1500**	**1500**	**1800**	**1800**
Automatic, 4-Spd			**550**	**550**	**665**	**665**
CAMRY—4-Cyl.—Equipment Schedule 4						
W.B. 109.3"; 2.5 Liter.						
L Sedan 4D	BF1FK	22715	**10950**	**11400**	**12500**	**14900**
LE Sedan 4D	BF1FK	23260	**11200**	**11650**	**12750**	**15200**
SE Sedan 4D	BF1FK	23760	**12050**	**12550**	**13750**	**16400**
XLE Sedan 4D	BF1FK	25485	**13450**	**14000**	**15200**	**18000**
V6, 3.5 Liter	K		**625**	**625**	**765**	**765**
CAMRY—4-Cyl. Hybrid—Equipment Schedule 4						
W.B. 109.3"; 2.5 Liter.						
LE Sedan 4D	BD1FK	26660	**13200**	**13500**	**15050**	**17300**
XLE Sedan 4D	BD1FK	28160	**14850**	**15200**	**16850**	**19400**
AVALON—V6—Equipment Schedule 3						
W.B. 111.0"; 3.5 Liter.						
Sedan 4D	BK3DB	33955	**16150**	**16800**	**17650**	**20500**
Limited Sedan 4D	BK3DB	37195	**17600**	**18700**	**19450**	**22500**

2013 TOYOTA—(2,4,5orJ)T(1,4,DorF)(KTLD3)–D–#

Body Type	VIN	List	Trade-In Good	Very Good	Pvt-Party Good	Retail Excellent
YARIS—4-Cyl.—Equipment Schedule 6						
W.B. 98.8"; 1.5 Liter.						
SE Hatchback 4D	KTLD3	18075	**9600**	**10050**	**11500**	**13900**
L Hatchback 2D	JTLD3	15890	**8225**	**8625**	**10150**	**12400**
Manual, 5-Spd			**(500)**	**(500)**	**(650)**	**(650)**
YARIS—4-Cyl.—Equipment Schedule 6						
W.B. 98.8"; 1.5 Liter.						
L Hatchback 4D	KTLD3	16190	**8475**	**8900**	**10250**	**12400**
LE Hatchback 4D	KTLD3	17225	**9000**	**9450**	**10900**	**13250**
LE Hatchback 2D	JTLD3	16750	**8775**	**9200**	**10700**	**13050**
COROLLA—4-Cyl.—Equipment Schedule 6						
W.B. 102.4"; 1.8 Liter.						
L Sedan 4D	BU4EE	17855	**9950**	**10350**	**11500**	**13600**
S Sedan 4D	BU4EE	19855	**11350**	**11800**	**12900**	**15150**
Manual, 5-Spd			**(500)**	**(500)**	**(610)**	**(610)**
COROLLA—4-Cyl.—Equipment Schedule 6						
W.B. 102.4"; 1.8 Liter.						
LE Sedan 4D	BU4EE	18975	**10300**	**10700**	**11800**	**14000**
PRIUS C—4-Cyl. Hybrid—Equipment Schedule 3						
W.B. 100.4"; 1.5 Liter.						
One Hatchback 4D	KDTB3	19840	**11150**	**11350**	**13050**	**15000**
Two Hatchback 4D	KDTB3	20790	**11800**	**12050**	**13700**	**15700**
Three Hatchback 4D	KDTB3	24120	**12500**	**12750**	**14350**	**16350**
Four Hatchback 4D	KDTB3	24120	**13550**	**13800**	**15500**	**17550**
PRIUS—4-Cyl. Hybrid—Equipment Schedule 3						
W.B. 106.3"; 1.8 Liter.						
One Hatchback 4D	KN3DU	23975	**11350**	**11600**	**13450**	**15650**
Two Hatchback 4D	KN3DU	24960	**12000**	**12200**	**14050**	**16250**
Three Hatchback 4D	KN3DU	26525	**12500**	**12750**	**14550**	**16800**
Persona Spcl Ed 4D	KN3DU	27890	**14100**	**14350**	**16250**	**18600**
Four Hatchback 4D	KN3DU	29195	**14700**	**14950**	**16700**	**19000**
Five Hatchback 4D	KN3DU	30765	**15850**	**16150**	**17950**	**20400**
PRIUS PLUG-IN—4-Cyl. Hybrid—Equipment Schedule 3						
W.B. 106.3"; 1.8 Liter.						
Hatchback 4D	KN3DP	32760	**14550**	**14800**	**16400**	**18450**
Advanced Hatchback	KN3DP	40285	**20400**	**20700**	**22300**	**24800**

Body Type	VIN	List	Trade-In Good	Very Good	Pvt-Party Good	Retail Excellent
PRIUS V—4-Cyl. Hybrid—Equipment Schedule 3						
W.B. 109.4"; 1.8 Liter.						
Two Wagon 4D	ZN3EU	27410	15350	15650	17150	19200
Three Wagon 4D	ZN3EU	28175	16200	16500	18000	20100
Five Wagon 4D	ZN3EU	31055	16650	16950	18450	20600
Technology Pkg			1375	1375	1590	1590
MATRIX—4-Cyl.—Equipment Schedule 6						
W.B. 102.4"; 1.8 Liter.						
L Sport Wagon 4D	KU4EE	20910	11800	12050	13650	15600
Manual, 5-Spd			(500)	(500)	(590)	(590)
MATRIX—4-Cyl.—Equipment Schedule 6						
W.B. 102.4"; 2.4 Liter.						
S Sport Wagon 4D	KE4EE	21060	11950	12200	13800	15800
Automatic, 4-Spd			500	500	580	580
AWD	L		1625	1625	1920	1920
CAMRY—4-Cyl.—Equipment Schedule 4						
W.B. 109.3"; 2.5 Liter.						
L Sedan 4D	BF1FK	22995	11700	12200	13450	15900
LE Sedan 4D	BF1FK	23440	12050	12550	13850	16450
CAMRY—4-Cyl.—Equipment Schedule 4						
W.B. 109.3"; 2.5 Liter.						
SE Sedan 4D	BF1FK	24160	12900	13400	14650	17250
XLE Sedan 4D	BF1FK	25615	14650	15250	16450	19250
V6, 3.5 Liter	K		675	675	815	815
CAMRY—4-Cyl. Hybrid—Equipment Schedule 4						
W.B. 109.3"; 2.5 Liter.						
LE Sedan 4D	BD1FK	26900	14800	15050	16750	18950
XLE Sedan 4D	BD1FK	28430	15850	16150	18000	20500
AVALON—4-Cyl. Hybrid—Equipment Schedule 4						
W.B. 111.0"; 2.5 Liter.						
XLE Premium Sedan	BD1EB	36350	21400	22200	23100	26500
XLE Touring Sedan	BD1EB	38045	21900	22800	23600	27100
Limited Sedan 4D	BD1EB	42195	22200	23100	24000	27700
AVALON—V6—Equipment Schedule 4						
W.B. 111.0"; 3.5 Liter.						
XLE Sedan 4D	BK1EB	31785	17350	18050	19050	22100
XLE Premium Sedan	BK1EB	33990	18350	19050	19950	23000
XLE Touring Sedan	BK1EB	36295	19200	19950	20900	24000
Limited Sedan 4D	BK1EB	40445	21800	22700	23400	26900
Dynamic Cruise Control			475	475	525	525
2014 TOYOTA—(2,4,5orJ)T(1,4,DorF)(KTUD3)-E-#						
YARIS—4-Cyl.—Equipment Schedule 6						
W.B. 98.8"; 1.5 Liter.						
L Hatchback 4D	KTUD3	16265	9350	9800	11150	13350
LE Hatchback 4D	KTUD3	17300	10000	10500	11900	14300
LE Hatchback 2D	JTUD3	16825	9450	9900	11400	13750
YARIS—4-Cyl.—Equipment Schedule 6						
W.B. 98.8"; 1.5 Liter.						
L Hatchback 2D	JTUD3	15965	9100	9550	11000	13350
SE Hatchback 4D	KTUD3	18150	10750	11250	12600	15050
Manual, 5-Spd			(525)	(525)	(655)	(655)
COROLLA—4-Cyl.—Equipment Schedule 6						
W.B. 102.4"; 1.8 Liter.						
L Sedan 4D	BURHE	18195	11150	11600	12750	15000
LE Sedan 4D	BURHE	19095	11750	12250	13350	15600
LE Eco Sedan 4D	BPRHE	19495	12300	12800	13850	16200
LE Plus Sedan 4D	BURHE	19495	12300	12800	13900	16300
LE Eco Plus Sedan 4D	BPRHE	20195	12850	13350	14400	16750
LE Premium Sedan	BURHE	20195	12850	13350	14450	16850
LE Eco Premium 4D	BPRHE	20895	13350	13900	14950	17300
S Sedan 4D	BURHE	19795	12600	13100	14100	16400
S Premium Sedan 4D	BURHE	21195	13650	14200	15300	17750
COROLLA—4-Cyl.—Equipment Schedule 6						
W.B. 102.4"; 1.8 Liter.						
S Plus Sedan 4D	BURHE	20495	12950	13500	14650	17050
Manual, 6-Spd			(525)	(525)	(615)	(615)
PRIUS C—4-Cyl. Hybrid—Equipment Schedule 3						
W.B. 100.4"; 1.5 Liter.						
One Hatchback 4D	KDTB3	19890	12000	12200	13950	15950
Two Hatchback 4D	KDTB3	20840	12800	13000	14700	16750
Three Hatchback 4D	KDTB3	22575	13450	13700	15400	17550
Four Hatchback 4D	KDTB3	24170	14550	14800	16500	18600

Body Type	VIN	List	Trade-In Good	Very Good	Pvt-Party Good	Retail Excellent
PRIUS—4-Cyl. Hybrid—Equipment Schedule 3						
W.B. 106.3"; 1.8 Liter.						
One Hatchback 4D	KN3DU	24025	12950	13200	15100	17350
Two Hatchback 4D	KN3DU	25010	13700	13950	15850	18100
Three Hatchback 4D	KN3DU	26575	14100	14350	16250	18500
Four Hatchback 4D	KN3DU	29245	16350	16650	18400	20700
Five Hatchback 4D	KN3DU	30815	17750	18050	19850	22300
PRIUS V—4-Cyl. Hybrid—Equipment Schedule 3						
W.B. 109.4"; 1.8 Liter.						
Two Wagon 4D	ZN3EU	27560	17450	17800	19350	21600
Three Wagon 4D	ZN3EU	28325	18150	18500	20000	22300
Five Wagon 4D	ZN3EU	31205	18950	19300	20800	23100
Dynamic Cruise Control			500	500	555	555
PRIUS PLUG-IN—4-Cyl. Hybrid—Equipment Schedule 6						
W.B. 106.3".						
Hatchback 4D	KN3DP	30800	18750	19100	20500	22700
Advanced Hatchback	KN3DP	35715	23700	24100	25500	27900
CAMRY—4-Cyl.—Equipment Schedule 4						
W.B. 109.3"; 2.5 Liter.						
L Sedan 4D	BF1FK	23045	12600	13100	14350	16950
LE Sedan 4D	BF1FK	23490	12950	13500	14800	17450
CAMRY—4-Cyl.—Equipment Schedule 4						
W.B. 109.3"; 2.5 Liter.						
SE Sedan 4D	BF1FK	24210	13550	14050	15350	18000
SE Sport Sedan 4D	BF1FK	25900	14300	14900	16100	18800
XLE Sedan 4D	BF1FK	26620	15250	15850	17050	19850
V6, 3.5 Liter	K		725	725	865	865
CAMRY—4-Cyl. Hybrid—Equipment Schedule 4						
W.B. 109.3"; 2.5 Liter.						
LE Sedan 4D	BD1FK	26950	15950	16250	17900	20100
XLE Sedan 4D	BD1FK	29435	17700	18000	19750	22200
SE Sedan 4D	BD1FK	28755	17200	17500	19250	21600
AVALON—4-Cyl. Hybrid—Equipment Schedule 4						
W.B. 111.0"; 2.5 Liter.						
XLE Premium Sedan	BD1EB	36365	23100	24000	24700	28300
XLE Touring Sedan	BD1EB	37560	23700	24600	25400	29000
Limited Sedan 4D	BD1EB	42210	24000	24900	25800	29600
AVALON—V6—Equipment Schedule 4						
W.B. 111.0"; 3.5 Liter.						
XLE Sedan 4D	BK1EB	32150	19750	20500	21400	24500
XLE Premium Sedan	BK1EB	34005	21000	21800	22500	25600
XLE Touring Sedan	BK1EB	35810	21600	22500	23200	26500
Limited Sedan 4D	BK1EB	40460	24000	25000	25600	29200
Dynamic Cruise Control			500	500	545	545

VOLKSWAGEN

2000 VOLKSWAGEN — (3orW)VW(BC21J)–Y–#

Body Type	VIN	List	Trade-In Good	Very Good	Pvt-Party Good	Retail Excellent
GOLF—4-Cyl.—Equipment Schedule 6						
W.B. 98.9"; 2.0 Liter.						
GL Hatchback 2D	BC21J	15425	500	600	1250	2275
GLS Hatchback 4D	GC21J	16875	925	1075	1625	2825
GOLF—4-Cyl. Turbo—Equipment Schedule 6						
W.B. 98.9"; 1.8 Liter.						
GLS Hatchback 4D	GH21J	18425	1150	1350	1875	3200
GOLF—4-Cyl. Turbo Diesel—Equipment Schedule 6						
W.B. 98.9"; 1.9 Liter.						
GL TDI H'Back 2D	BF21J	16720	1475	1650	2600	4500
GLS TDI H'Back 4D	GF21J	17295	2100	2325	3300	5600
GTI—4-Cyl.—Equipment Schedule 6						
W.B. 98.9"; 2.0 Liter.						
GLS Hatchback 2D	DC21J	18200	1025	1200	1725	3025
GTI—4-Cyl. Turbo—Equipment Schedule 6						
W.B. 98.9"; 1.8 Liter.						
GLS Hatchback 2D	DH21J	19750	1300	1525	2050	3600
GTI—V6—Equipment Schedule 6						
W.B. 98.9"; 2.8 Liter.						
GLX Hatchback 2D	DE21J	23145	1750	2050	2700	4675
NEW BEETLE—4-Cyl.—Equipment Schedule 6						
W.B. 98.9"; 2.0 Liter.						
GL Hatchback 2D	BC21C	16425	1075	1200	2000	3525

Body Type	VIN	List	Trade-In Good	Very Good	Pvt-Party Good	Retail Excellent
GLS Hatchback 2D	CC21C	17375	850	950	1725	3075
NEW BEETLE—4-Cyl. Turbo—Equipment Schedule 6						
W.B. 98.9"; 1.8 Liter.						
GLS Hatchback 2D	CD21C	19525	975	1075	1875	3325
GLX Hatchback 2D	DD21C	21600	975	1100	2000	3625
NEW BEETLE—4-Cyl. Turbo Diesel—Equipment Schedule 6						
W.B. 98.9"; 1.9 Liter.						
GLS TDI H'Back 2D	CF21C	18425	1375	1525	2225	3775
JETTA—4-Cyl.—Equipment Schedule 6						
W.B. 98.9"; 2.0 Liter.						
GL Sedan 4D	RC29M	17225	525	600	1225	2200
GLS Sedan 4D	SC29M	18175	675	750	1400	2500
JETTA—4-Cyl. Turbo—Equipment Schedule 6						
W.B. 98.9"; 1.8 Liter.						
GLS Sedan 4D	SD29M	19725	400	475	1075	1950
JETTA—4-Cyl. Turbo Diesel—Equipment Schedule 6						
W.B. 98.9"; 1.9 Liter.						
GLT TDI Sedan 4D	RF29M	18520	1575	1750	2400	3900
GLS TDI Sedan 4D	SF29M	19225	1875	2075	2750	4450
JETTA—V6—Equipment Schedule 6						
W.B. 98.9"; 2.8 Liter.						
GLS Sedan 4D	SE29M	20475	775	875	1500	2650
GLX Sedan 4D	TE29M	24695	950	1050	1725	3025
CABRIO—4-Cyl.—Equipment Schedule 3						
W.B. 97.4"; 2.0 Liter.						
GL Convertible 2D	CC21V	22015	525	600	1250	2250
GLS Convertible 2D	DC21V	24700	775	850	1550	2750
Manual, 5-Spd			(100)	(100)	(125)	(125)
PASSAT—4-Cyl. Turbo—Equipment Schedule 4						
W.B. 106.4"; 1.8 Liter.						
GLS Sedan 4D	MA23B	22800	775	925	1375	2475
GLS Wagon 4D	NA23B	23600	900	1075	1475	2600
Manual, 5-Spd			(175)	(175)	(220)	(220)
V6, 2.8 Liter	D		100	100	135	135
PASSAT—V6—Equipment Schedule 4						
W.B. 106.4"; 2.8 Liter.						
GLX Sedan 4D	PD23B	29255	1825	2175	2600	4425
GLX Wagon 4D	VD23B	30055	1775	2100	2550	4325
Manual, 5-Spd			(175)	(175)	(220)	(220)
PASSAT 4MOTION AWD—V6—Equipment Schedule 4						
W.B. 106.4"; 2.8 Liter.						
GLS Sedan 4D	TH23B	27050	2000	2375	2800	4725
GLS Wagon 4D	RH23B	27850	2050	2450	2875	4850
GLX Sedan 4D	UH23B	30905	2275	2675	3100	5225
GLX Wagon 4D	WH23B	31705	2300	2725	3125	5275

2001 VOLKSWAGEN — (3orW)VW(BK21J)–1–#

Body Type	VIN	List	Trade-In Good	Very Good	Pvt-Party Good	Retail Excellent
GOLF—4-Cyl.—Equipment Schedule 6						
W.B. 98.9"; 2.0 Liter.						
GL Hatchback 2D	BK21J	15425	750	875	1500	2675
GLS Hatchback 4D	GK21J	16875	1100	1275	1925	3350
GOLF—4-Cyl. Turbo—Equipment Schedule 6						
W.B. 98.9"; 1.8 Liter.						
GLS Hatchback 4D	GC21J	18425	1275	1475	2000	3375
GOLF—4-Cyl. Turbo Diesel—Equipment Schedule 6						
W.B. 98.9"; 1.9 Liter.						
GLT TDI H'Back 2D	BP21J	16720	1775	1950	2875	4875
GLS TDI H'Back 4D	GP21J	17925	2425	2650	3600	5975
GTI—4-Cyl. Turbo—Equipment Schedule 6						
W.B. 98.9"; 1.8 Liter.						
GLS Hatchback 2D	DC21J	19800	1350	1575	2075	3625
GTI—V6—Equipment Schedule 6						
W.B. 98.9"; 2.8 Liter.						
GLX Hatchback 2D	PG21J	23425	1850	2150	2775	4750
NEW BEETLE—4-Cyl.—Equipment Schedule 6						
W.B. 98.7"; 2.0 Liter.						
GL Hatchback 2D	BK21C	17325	1175	1300	2125	3725
GLS Hatchback 2D	CK21C	17375	1050	1175	2050	3650
NEW BEETLE—4-Cyl. Turbo—Equipment Schedule 6						
W.B. 98.7"; 1.8 Liter.						
GLS Hatchback 2D	CD21C	19550	1225	1350	2250	3975
Sport Hatchback 2D	ED21C	21175	1250	1375	2300	4100
GLX Hatchback 2D	DD21C	21700	1400	1550	2450	4300

2001 VOLKSWAGEN

Body	Type	VIN	List	Trade-In Good	Very Good	Pvt-Party Good	Retail Excellent

NEW BEETLE—4-Cyl. Turbo Diesel—Equipment Schedule 6
W.B. 98.7"; 1.9 Liter.

| GLS TDI H'Back 2D | CP21C | 18425 | 1550 | 1725 | 2475 | 4100 |

JETTA—4-Cyl.—Equipment Schedule 6
W.B. 98.9", 99.0" (Wag); 2.0 Liter.

GL Sedan 4D	RK29M	18125	525	600	1275	2275
GLS Sedan 4D	SK29M	19075	750	825	1525	2725
GLS Wagon 4D	SK21J	19150	600	675	1375	2475

JETTA—4-Cyl. Turbo—Equipment Schedule 6
W.B. 98.9"; 1.8 Liter.

| GLS Sedan 4D | SD29M | 19725 | 675 | 750 | 1425 | 2575 |
| Wolfsburg Edition | | | 25 | 25 | 35 | 35 |

JETTA—4-Cyl. Turbo Diesel—Equipment Schedule 6
W.B. 98.9"; 1.9 Liter.

| GL TDI Sedan 4D | RP29M | 18520 | 1700 | 1875 | 2550 | 4125 |
| GLS TDI Sedan 4D | SP29M | 19225 | 2125 | 2325 | 3000 | 4850 |

JETTA—V6—Equipment Schedule 6
W.B. 98.9", 99.0" (Wag); 2.8 Liter.

GLS Sedan 4D	SG29M	20475	825	925	1625	2875
GLS Wagon 4D	SG21J	21450	1025	1150	1875	3275
GLX Sedan 4D	TG29M	24825	1025	1150	1875	3275
GLX Wagon 4D	TG21J	25950	1150	1250	2025	3500

CABRIO—4-Cyl.—Equipment Schedule 3
W.B. 97.4"; 2.0 Liter.

GL Convertible 2D	BC21V	21625	575	650	1275	2275
GLS Convertible 2D	CC21V	22000	850	950	1600	2775
GLX Convertible 2D	DC21V	23700	1100	1200	1900	3250
Manual, 5-Spd			(175)	(175)	(225)	(225)

PASSAT—4-Cyl. Turbo—Equipment Schedule 4
W.B. 106.4"; 1.8 Liter.

GLS Sedan 4D	AD23B	23050	850	1025	1450	2575
GLS Wagon 4D	HD23B	23850	1500	1750	2125	3625
Manual, 5-Spd			(200)	(200)	(265)	(265)
V6, 2.8 Liter	H		100	100	135	135

NEW PASSAT—4-Cyl. Turbo—Equipment Schedule 4
W.B. 106.4"; 1.8 Liter.

GLS Sedan 4D	PD23B	23375	675	825	1475	2750
GLS Wagon 4D	VD23B	24175	725	875	1550	2900
Manual, 5-Spd			(200)	(200)	(265)	(265)
V6, 2.8 Liter	H		100	100	135	135

PASSAT—V6—Equipment Schedule 4
W.B. 106.4"; 2.8 Liter.

GLX Sedan 4D	BH23B	29810	2050	2425	2825	4725
GLX Wagon 4D	JH23B	30610	2050	2425	2825	4725
Manual, 5-Spd			(200)	(200)	(265)	(265)

NEW PASSAT—V6—Equipment Schedule 4
W.B. 106.4"; 2.8 Liter.

GLX Sedan 4D	RD23B	30375	1275	1500	2175	3900
GLX Wagon 4D	WD23B	31175	1775	2100	2825	4925
Manual, 5-Spd			(200)	(200)	(265)	(265)

PASSAT 4MOTION AWD—V6—Equipment Schedule 4
W.B. 106.4"; 2.8 Liter.

GLS Sedan 4D	DH23B	27400	2150	2550	2900	4825
GLS Wagon 4D	KH23B	28200	2325	2750	3125	5225
GLX Sedan 4D	EH23B	31560	2725	3200	3525	5850
GLX Wagon 4D	LH23B	32360	2800	3275	3600	5950

NEW PASSAT 4MOTION AWD—V6—Equipment Schedule 4
W.B. 106.4"; 2.8 Liter.

GLS Sedan 4D	SH23B	27625	1375	1625	2250	4000
GLS Wagon 4D	XH23B	28425	1550	1825	2575	4525
GLX Sedan 4D	TH23B	32125	1950	2300	3025	5250
GLX Wagon 4D	YH23B	32925	2275	2675	3400	5850

2002 VOLKSWAGEN—(3,9orW)(BorV)W(BK21J)-2-#

GOLF—4-Cyl.—Equipment Schedule 6
W.B. 98.9"; 2.0 Liter.

GL Hatchback 2D	BK21J	15600	850	1000	1725	3100
GL Hatchback 4D	FK21J	15800	1100	1250	1975	3450
GLS Hatchback 4D	GK21J	17150	1325	1525	2350	4125

GOLF—4-Cyl. Turbo Diesel—Equipment Schedule 6
W.B. 98.9"; 1.9 Liter.

| GL TDI H'Back 2D | BP21J | 16895 | 1825 | 2000 | 2875 | 4800 |
| GL TDI H'Back 4D | FP21J | 17095 | 2000 | 2175 | 3050 | 5025 |

Body Type	VIN	List	Trade-In Good	Very Good	Pvt-Party Good	Retail Excellent
GLS TDI H'Back 4D	GP21J	18200	**2525**	**2775**	**3625**	**5900**
GTI—4-Cyl. Turbo—Equipment Schedule 6						
W.B. 98.9"; 1.8 Liter.						
Hatchback 2D	DE61J	19460	**1800**	**2075**	**2525**	**4125**
337 Edition H'Back 2D	DE61J	22775	**2250**	**2600**	**3075**	**5075**
GTI VR6—V6—Equipment Schedule 6						
W.B. 98.9"; 2.8 Liter.						
Hatchback 2D	DH61J	20845	**2200**	**2525**	**3025**	**4975**
NEW BEETLE—4-Cyl.—Equipment Schedule 6						
W.B. 98.7"; 2.0 Liter.						
GL Hatchback 2D	BK21C	17325	**1225**	**1350**	**2175**	**3775**
GLS Hatchback 2D	CK21C	17400	**1200**	**1325**	**2175**	**3775**
NEW BEETLE—4-Cyl. Turbo—Equipment Schedule 6						
W.B. 98.7"; 1.8 Liter.						
GLS Hatchback 2D	CD21C	19750	**1350**	**1475**	**2400**	**4150**
Sport Hatchback 2D	ED21C	20800	**1375**	**1500**	**2500**	**4325**
GLX Hatchback 2D	DD21C	22050	**1475**	**1625**	**2600**	**4425**
S Hatchback 2D	FE21C	23905	**1475**	**1625**	**2600**	**4425**
NEW BEETLE—4-Cyl. Turbo Diesel—Equipment Schedule 6						
W.B. 98.7"; 1.9 Liter.						
GLS TDI H'Back 2D	CP21C	18450	**1725**	**1900**	**2725**	**4500**
JETTA—4-Cyl.—Equipment Schedule 6						
W.B. 98.9", 99.0" (Wag); 2.0 Liter.						
GL Sedan 4D	RK69M	18275	**800**	**875**	**1600**	**2850**
GL Wagon 4D	RK61J	19075	**800**	**875**	**1600**	**2850**
GLS Sedan 4D	SK69M	19325	**900**	**1000**	**1750**	**3050**
GLS Wagon 4D	SK21J	19250	**850**	**950**	**1675**	**2950**
JETTA—4-Cyl. Turbo—Equipment Schedule 6						
W.B. 98.9", 99.0" (Wag); 1.8 Liter.						
GLS Sedan 4D	SE69M	20100	**800**	**875**	**1600**	**2850**
GLS Wagon 4D	SE61J	20900	**1000**	**1125**	**1850**	**3225**
JETTA—4-Cyl. Turbo Diesel—Equipment Schedule 6						
W.B. 98.9", 99.0" (Wag); 1.9 Liter.						
GL TDI Sedan 4D	RP69M	18695	**1675**	**1850**	**2575**	**4200**
GL TDI Wagon 4D	RP69M	19495	**1850**	**2050**	**2775**	**4525**
GLS TDI Sedan 4D	SP69M	19500	**2200**	**2425**	**3175**	**5125**
GLS TDI Wagon 4D	SP69M	20300	**2750**	**3000**	**3750**	**6000**
JETTA—V6—Equipment Schedule 6						
W.B. 98.9", 99.0" (Wag); 2.8 Liter.						
GLS Sedan 4D	SH69M	20750	**950**	**1050**	**1800**	**3150**
GLS Wagon 4D	SH61J	21550	**1175**	**1275**	**2050**	**3550**
GLI Sedan 4D	VH69M	23500	**1375**	**1525**	**2325**	**3950**
GLX Sedan 4D	TH69M	25250	**1375**	**1525**	**2325**	**3950**
GLX Wagon 4D	TH61J	26050	**1475**	**1625**	**2425**	**4125**
CABRIO—4-Cyl.—Equipment Schedule 3						
W.B. 97.4"; 2.0 Liter.						
GL Convertible 2D	BC21V	21025	**625**	**700**	**1325**	**2350**
GLS Convertible 2D	CC21V	22025	**900**	**1000**	**1675**	**2900**
GLX Convertible 2D	DC21V	23725	**1175**	**1300**	**2000**	**3400**
Manual, 5-Spd			**(175)**	**(175)**	**(235)**	**(235)**
PASSAT—4-Cyl. Turbo—Equipment Schedule 4						
W.B. 106.4"; 1.8 Liter.						
GLS Sedan 4D	PD63B	23375	**1000**	**1175**	**1875**	**3425**
GLS Wagon 4D	VD63B	24175	**1050**	**1225**	**1925**	**3450**
Manual, 5-Spd			**(200)**	**(200)**	**(265)**	**(265)**
V6, 2.8 Liter	H		**125**	**125**	**175**	**175**
PASSAT—V6—Equipment Schedule 4						
W.B. 106.4"; 2.8 Liter.						
GLX Sedan 4D	RH63B	30375	**1625**	**1900**	**2725**	**4800**
GLX Wagon 4D	WH63B	31175	**2350**	**2750**	**3550**	**6150**
Manual, 5-Spd			**(200)**	**(200)**	**(265)**	**(265)**
PASSAT 4MOTION AWD—V6—Equipment Schedule 4						
W.B. 106.4"; 2.8 Liter.						
GLS Sedan 4D	SH63B	27625	**1975**	**2300**	**3100**	**5400**
GLS Wagon 4D	XH63B	28425	**2100**	**2450**	**3250**	**5625**
GLX Sedan 4D	TH63B	32125	**2475**	**2875**	**3700**	**6400**
GLX Wagon 4D	ZH63B	32925	**2950**	**3425**	**4225**	**7225**
PASSAT 4MOTION AWD—W8—Equipment Schedule 4						
W.B. 106.4"; 4.0 Liter.						
Sedan 4D	UH63B	38450	**1725**	**2050**	**2875**	**5175**
Wagon 4D	ZH63B	39250	**1850**	**2175**	**2975**	**5275**

Body Type	VIN	List	Trade-In Good	Very Good	Pvt-Party Good	Retail Excellent

2003 VOLKSWAGEN — (3,9orW)(BorV)W(BK21J)-3-#

GOLF—4-Cyl.—Equipment Schedule 6
W.B. 98.9"; 2.0 Liter.

Body Type	VIN	List	Good	Very Good	Good	Excellent
GL Hatchback 2D	BK21J	15870	1200	1375	2150	3725
GL Hatchback 4D	FK21J	16070	1325	1525	2225	3825
GLS Hatchback 4D	GK21J	18095	1650	1875	2750	4650

GOLF—4-Cyl. Turbo Diesel—Equipment Schedule 6
W.B. 98.9"; 1.9 Liter.

GL TDI H'Back 2D	BP21J	17295	2200	2400	3325	5450
GL TDI H'Back 4D	FP21J	17495	2250	2475	3275	5275
GLS TDI H'Back 4D	GP21J	19285	3000	3275	4050	6375

GTI—4-Cyl. Turbo—Equipment Schedule 6
W.B. 98.9"; 1.8 Liter.

Hatchback 2D	DE61J	19640	2025	2325	2725	4375
20th Anniv H'Back 2D	DE61J	23800	2625	3000	3450	5525

GTI VR6—V6—Equipment Schedule 6
W.B. 98.9"; 2.8 Liter.

Hatchback 2D	DH61J	22570	2625	3000	3450	5525

NEW BEETLE—4-Cyl.—Equipment Schedule 6
W.B. 98.7", 98.8" (Conv); 2.0 Liter.

GL Hatchback 2D	BK21C	16525	1250	1375	2200	3800
GL Convertible 2D	BK21Y	22200	1875	2075	2975	4925
GLS Hatchback 2D	CK21C	18390	1500	1650	2525	4250
GLS Convertible 2D	CK21Y	22425	1675	1850	2725	4525
4-Cyl. Turbo, 1.8 Liter			150	150	190	190

NEW BEETLE—4-Cyl. Turbo—Equipment Schedule 6
W.B. 98.7", 98.8" (Conv); 1.8 Liter.

GLX Hatchback 2D	DE21C	22215	1750	1900	2850	4750
GLX Convertible 2D	DD21Y	26125	2025	2225	3125	5150
S Hatchback 2D	FE21C	24115	1900	2100	3000	4950

NEW BEETLE—4-Cyl. Turbo Diesel—Equipment Schedule 6
W.B. 98.7"; 1.9 Liter.

GL TDI H'Back 2D	BP21C	17770	1475	1600	2400	3975
GLS TDI H'Back 2D	CP21C	19570	2175	2375	3150	5050

JETTA—4-Cyl.—Equipment Schedule 6
W.B. 98.9", 99.0" (Wag); 2.0 Liter.

GL Sedan 4D	RK69M	18550	1175	1300	2025	3400
GL Wagon 4D	RK61J	19350	1150	1275	1975	3350
GLS Sedan 4D	SK69M	20240	1275	1400	2150	3600
GLS Wagon 4D	SK61J	20165	1275	1400	2150	3600
4-Cyl, Turbo, 1.8 Liter	E		300	300	415	415

JETTA—4-Cyl. Turbo—Equipment Schedule 6
W.B. 98.9", 99.0" (Wag); 1.8 Liter.

Wolfsburg Sedan 4D	PE69M	20075	1200	1325	2050	3450

JETTA—4-Cyl. Turbo Diesel—Equipment Schedule 6
W.B. 98.9", 99.0" (Wag); 1.9 Liter.

GL TDI Sedan 4D	RP69M	19065	1950	2125	2875	4625
GL TDI Wagon 4D	RP61J	19865	2050	2250	3000	4800
GLS TDI Sedan 4D	SP69M	20545	2400	2625	3375	5350
GLS TDI Wagon 4D	SP61J	21345	2875	3125	3875	6125

JETTA—V6—Equipment Schedule 6
W.B. 98.9"; 2.8 Liter.

GLI Sedan 4D	VH69M	23525	1850	2050	2900	4800
GLX Sedan 4D	TH69M	27515	2125	2325	3225	5300

PASSAT—4-Cyl. Turbo—Equipment Schedule 4
W.B. 106.4"; 1.8 Liter.

GL Sedan 4D	MD63B	23400	550	675	1375	2600
GL Wagon 4D	ND63B	24200	750	900	1550	2775
GLS Sedan 4D	PD63B	24535	1275	1475	2150	3750
GLS Wagon 4D	VD63B	27835	1425	1650	2225	3825
Manual, 5-Spd			(225)	(225)	(310)	(310)
V6, 2.8 Liter	H		175	175	245	245

PASSAT—V6—Equipment Schedule 4
W.B. 106.4"; 2.8 Liter.

GLX Sedan 4D	RH63B	30400	2000	2325	3075	5225
GLX Wagon 4D	WH63B	31200	2600	3025	3775	6375
Manual, 5-Spd			(225)	(225)	(310)	(310)

PASSAT 4MOTION AWD—V6—Equipment Schedule 4
W.B. 106.4"; 2.8 Liter.

GLX Sedan 4D	TH63B	32150	2850	3275	4025	6775
GLX Wagon 4D	YH63B	32950	3250	3725	4500	7525

2003 VOLKSWAGEN

Body Type	VIN	List	Trade-In Good	Very Good	Pvt-Party Good	Retail Excellent
PASSAT 4MOTION AWD—W8—Equipment Schedule 4						
W.B. 106.4"; 4.0 Liter.						
Sedan 4D	UK63B	38475	**2250**	**2625**	**3575**	**6325**
Wagon 4D	ZK63B	39275	**2475**	**2875**	**3825**	**6725**

2004 VOLKSWAGEN—(W,3or9)(VorB)W(BK21J)-4-#

Body Type	VIN	List	Trade-In Good	Very Good	Pvt-Party Good	Retail Excellent
GOLF—4-Cyl.—Equipment Schedule 6						
W.B. 98.9"; 2.0 Liter.						
GL Hatchback 2D	BK21J	16155	**1500**	**1700**	**2425**	**4100**
GL Hatchback 4D	FK21J	16355	**1575**	**1800**	**2575**	**4275**
GLS Hatchback 4D	GK21J	18715	**1875**	**2150**	**2950**	**4900**
GOLF—4-Cyl. Turbo Diesel—Equipment Schedule 6						
W.B. 98.9"; 1.9 Liter.						
GL TDI H'Back 4D	FP21J	17775	**2575**	**2800**	**3625**	**5750**
GLS TDI H'Back 4D	GP21J	19895	**3075**	**3350**	**4275**	**6700**
GTI—4-Cyl. Turbo—Equipment Schedule 6						
W.B. 98.9"; 1.8 Liter.						
Hatchback 2D	DE61J	19825	**2550**	**2900**	**3325**	**5250**
GTI VR6—V6—Equipment Schedule 6						
W.B. 98.9"; 2.8 Liter.						
Hatchback 2D	DH61J	22645	**3275**	**3700**	**4225**	**6600**
R32 AWD—V6—Equipment Schedule 3						
W.B. 99.1"; 3.2 Liter.						
Hatchback 2D	KG61J	29675	**7800**	**8800**	**8350**	**11900**
NEW BEETLE—4-Cyl.—Equipment Schedule 6						
W.B. 98.7", 98.8" (Conv); 2.0 Liter.						
GL Hatchback 2D	BK21C	17780	**1600**	**1750**	**2600**	**4300**
GL Convertible 2D	BK21Y	22650	**2150**	**2350**	**3300**	**5350**
GLS Hatchback 2D	CK21C	19095	**1825**	**2000**	**2900**	**4725**
GLS Convertible 2D	CK21Y	23215	**2100**	**2300**	**3175**	**5100**
4-Cyl, Turbo, 1.8 Liter	D		**150**	**150**	**205**	**205**
NEW BEETLE—4-Cyl. Turbo—Equipment Schedule 6						
W.B. 98.7"; 1.8 Liter.						
S Hatchback 2D	FE21C	24425	**3100**	**3350**	**4100**	**6325**
NEW BEETLE—4-Cyl. Turbo—Equipment Schedule 6						
W.B. 98.7"; 1.9 Liter.						
GL TDI H'Back 2D	BP21C	18205	**1700**	**1850**	**2700**	**4400**
GLS TDI H'Back 2D	CP21C	20335	**2375**	**2575**	**3400**	**5400**
JETTA—4-Cyl.—Equipment Schedule 6						
W.B. 98.9", 99.0" (Wag); 2.0 Liter.						
GL Sedan 4D	RK29M	18880	**1450**	**1600**	**2275**	**3700**
GL Wagon 4D	RK61J	19880	**1525**	**1675**	**2450**	**4025**
GLS Sedan 4D	SK29M	20910	**1675**	**1850**	**2700**	**4450**
GLS Wagon 4D	SK21J	21035	**1575**	**1725**	**2500**	**4150**
4-Cyl, Turbo, 1.8 Liter	E		**350**	**350**	**460**	**460**
JETTA—4-Cyl. Turbo—Equipment Schedule 6						
W.B. 98.9"; 1.8 Liter.						
GLI Sedan 4D	VH69M	23785	**2475**	**2700**	**3650**	**5875**
V6, 2.8 Liter	H		**100**	**100**	**135**	**135**
JETTA—4-Cyl. Turbo Diesel—Equipment Schedule 6						
W.B. 98.9", 99.0" (Wag); 1.9 Liter.						
GL TDI Sedan 4D	RP29M	19245	**2425**	**2650**	**3275**	**5075**
GL TDI Wagon 4D	RP21J	20245	**2525**	**2750**	**3400**	**5225**
GLS TDI Sedan 4D	SP69M	21055	**2600**	**2850**	**3525**	**5450**
GLS TDI Wagon 4D	SP61J	22055	**3275**	**3550**	**4200**	**6400**
PASSAT—4-Cyl. Turbo—Equipment Schedule 4						
W.B. 106.4"; 1.8 Liter.						
GL Sedan 4D	MD63B	23430	**625**	**750**	**1450**	**2675**
GL Wagon 4D	ND63B	24430	**925**	**1075**	**1750**	**3100**
GLS Sedan 4D	PD63B	25030	**1450**	**1675**	**2375**	**4000**
GLS Wagon 4D	VD63B	26030	**1625**	**1875**	**2475**	**4100**
Manual, 5-Spd			**(275)**	**(275)**	**(375)**	**(375)**
PASSAT 4MOTION AWD—4-Cyl. Turbo—Equipment Schedule 4						
W.B. 106.4"; 1.8 Liter.						
GLS Sedan 4D	PD63B	26780	**2500**	**2875**	**3575**	**5925**
GLS Wagon 4D	VD63B	27780	**2875**	**3300**	**4100**	**6825**
Manual, 5-Spd			**(275)**	**(275)**	**(375)**	**(375)**
PASSAT—4-Cyl. Turbo Diesel—Equipment Schedule 4						
W.B. 106.4"; 2.0 Liter.						
GL TDI Sedan 4D	ME63B	23635	**2050**	**2375**	**2850**	**4625**
GL TDI Wagon 4D	NE63B	24635	**2150**	**2475**	**2925**	**4775**
GLS TDI Sedan 4D	PE63B	25235	**3225**	**3725**	**4125**	**6500**
GLS TDI Wagon 4D	VE63B	26235	**3400**	**3925**	**4300**	**6750**

2004 VOLKSWAGEN

Body	Type	VIN	List	Trade-In Good	Very Good	Pvt-Party Good	Retail Excellent
	Manual, 5-Spd.		------	**(275)**	**(275)**	**(375)**	**(375)**
PASSAT—V6—Equipment Schedule 4							
W.B. 106.4"; 2.8 Liter.							
GLX Sedan 4D		RH63B	31430	**2425**	**2800**	**3500**	**5825**
GLX Wagon 4D		WH63B	32430	**3125**	**3575**	**4400**	**7275**
	Manual, 5-Spd.		------	**(275)**	**(275)**	**(375)**	**(375)**
PASSAT 4MOTION AWD—V6—Equipment Schedule 4							
W.B. 106.4"; 2.8 Liter.							
GLX Sedan 4D		TH63B	33180	**3350**	**3850**	**4600**	**7475**
GLX Wagon 4D		YH63B	34180	**3600**	**4125**	**5050**	**8325**
PASSAT 4MOTION AWD—W8—Equipment Schedule 4							
W.B. 106.4"; 4.0 Liter.							
Sedan 4D		UK63B	39235	**3000**	**3450**	**4025**	**6600**
Wagon 4D		ZK63B	40235	**3100**	**3575**	**4275**	**7000**
	Sport Pkg			**175**	**175**	**220**	**220**
PHAETON AWD—V8—Equipment Schedule 1							
W.B. 118.1"; 4.2 Liter.							
Sedan 4D		AF63D	65215	**6175**	**6600**	**7275**	**9800**
	4-Passenger Seating			**250**	**250**	**325**	**325**
	W12, 6.0 Liter		H	**3450**	**3450**	**4245**	**4245**

2005 VOLKSWAGEN—(W,3or9)(VorB)W(BL61J)-5-#

Body	Type	VIN	List	Trade-In Good	Very Good	Pvt-Party Good	Retail Excellent
GOLF—4-Cyl.—Equipment Schedule 6							
W.B. 98.9"; 2.0 Liter.							
GL Hatchback 2D		BL61J	15830	**1425**	**1650**	**2600**	**4300**
GL Hatchback 4D		FL61J	16030	**1575**	**1800**	**2750**	**4475**
GLS Hatchback 4D		GL61J	18390	**1925**	**2200**	**3150**	**5075**
GOLF—4-Cyl. Turbo Diesel—Equipment Schedule 6							
W.B. 98.9"; 1.9 Liter.							
GL TDI H'Back 4D		FR61J	17450	**2725**	**2975**	**3925**	**6075**
GLS TDI H'Back 4D		GR61J	19580	**3375**	**3675**	**4600**	**6850**
GTI—4-Cyl. Turbo—Equipment Schedule 6							
W.B. 98.9"; 1.8 Liter.							
Hatchback 2D		DE61J	19510	**2700**	**3050**	**3725**	**5850**
GTI VR6—V6—Equipment Schedule 6							
W.B. 98.9"; 2.8 Liter.							
Hatchback 2D		DH61J	22330	**3500**	**3950**	**4675**	**7200**
NEW BEETLE—4-Cyl.—Equipment Schedule 6							
W.B. 98.7", 98.8" (Conv); 2.0 Liter.							
GL Hatchback 2D		BK31C	18220	**1725**	**1900**	**2875**	**4550**
GL Convertible 2D		BM31Y	22940	**2425**	**2650**	**3675**	**5775**
GLS Hatchback 2D		CK31C	19345	**2075**	**2275**	**3225**	**5075**
GLS Convertible 2D		CM31Y	23615	**2275**	**2475**	**3450**	**5375**
Bi-Color H'Back 2D		CK31C	21360	**2325**	**2550**	**3500**	**5475**
Dark Flint Ed Conv		CM31Y	26405	**2400**	**2625**	**3575**	**5550**
	4-Cyl, Turbo, 1.8 Liter		D	**175**	**175**	**225**	**225**
NEW BEETLE—4-Cyl. Turbo Diesel—Equipment Schedule 6							
W.B. 98.7"; 1.9 Liter.							
GLS TDI H'Back 2D		CR31C	20585	**2900**	**3150**	**4000**	**6075**
JETTA—4-Cyl.—Equipment Schedule 6							
W.B. 98.9", 99.0" (Wag); 2.0 Liter.							
GL Sedan 4D		RK69M	19130	**1375**	**1525**	**2400**	**3875**
GL Wagon 4D		RL61J	20130	**1550**	**1725**	**2650**	**4250**
GLS Sedan 4D		SK69M	21170	**1825**	**2000**	**2950**	**4675**
GLS Wagon 4D		SL61J	21295	**1650**	**1825**	**2775**	**4425**
	4-Cyl, Turbo, 1.8 Liter		E	**375**	**375**	**505**	**505**
JETTA—4-Cyl. Turbo—Equipment Schedule 6							
W.B. 98.9", 99.0" (Wag); 1.8 Liter.							
GLI Sedan 4D		SE69M	24645	**2700**	**2950**	**3950**	**6175**
JETTA—4-Cyl. Turbo Diesel—Equipment Schedule 6							
W.B. 98.9", 99.0" (Wag); 1.9 Liter.							
GL TDI Wagon 4D		RR61J	20505	**2550**	**2775**	**3550**	**5375**
GLS TDI Sedan 4D		SR69M	21315	**2650**	**2900**	**3675**	**5575**
GLS TDI Wagon 4D		SR61J	22315	**3275**	**3550**	**4300**	**6425**
NEW JETTA—5-Cyl.—Equipment Schedule 6							
W.B. 101.5"; 2.5 Liter.							
Value Edition Sed 4D		PF71K	18515	**1825**	**2000**	**3075**	**4925**
2.5 Sedan 4D		SF71K	21005	**2350**	**2575**	**3650**	**5800**
	Package #1			**200**	**200**	**255**	**255**
	Package #2			**400**	**400**	**515**	**515**
NEW JETTA—4-Cyl. Turbo Diesel—Equipment Schedule 6							
W.B. 101.5"; 1.9 Liter.							
TDI Sedan 4D		RT71K	22000	**3400**	**3700**	**4575**	**6800**

1015

2005 VOLKSWAGEN

Body Type	VIN	List	Trade-In Good	Very Good	Pvt-Party Good	Retail Excellent
Package #1			200	200	255	255
Package #2			400	400	515	515
PASSAT—4-Cyl. Turbo—Equipment Schedule 4						
W.B. 106.4"; 1.8 Liter.						
GL Sedan 4D	MD63B	23760	925	1100	1850	3125
GL Wagon 4D	ND63B	24760	1175	1375	2150	3550
GLS Sedan 4D	AD63B	26030	1800	2075	2800	4500
GLS Wagon 4D	CD63B	27030	1950	2250	2900	4600
Manual, 5-Spd			(325)	(325)	(445)	(445)
PASSAT 4MOTION AWD—4-Cyl. Turbo—Equipment Schedule 4						
W.B. 106.4"; 1.8 Liter.						
GLS Sedan 4D	BD63B	27780	2825	3225	4025	6400
GLS Wagon 4D	DD63B	28780	3250	3725	4575	7200
Manual, 5-Spd			(325)	(325)	(445)	(445)
PASSAT—4-Cyl. Turbo Diesel—Equipment Schedule 4						
W.B. 106.4"; 2.0 Liter.						
GL TDI Sedan 4D	ME63B	23935	2500	2875	3325	5150
GL TDI Wagon 4D	NE63B	24935	2600	3000	3425	5300
GLS TDI Sedan 4D	AE63B	26235	3750	4325	4675	7075
GLS TDI Wagon 4D	CE63B	27235	4100	4700	5000	7550
PASSAT—V6—Equipment Schedule 4						
W.B. 106.4"; 2.8 Liter.						
GLX Sedan 4D	RU63B	31440	3025	3475	4275	6675
GLX Wagon 4D	WU63B	32440	3750	4275	5125	8000
Manual, 5-Spd			(325)	(325)	(445)	(445)
PASSAT 4MOTION AWD—V6—Equipment Schedule 4						
W.B. 106.4"; 2.8 Liter.						
GLX Sedan 4D	TU63B	33190	4000	4575	5325	8275
GLX Wagon 4D	YU63B	34190	4375	4950	5775	9000
PHAETON—V8—Equipment Schedule 1						
W.B. 118.1"; 4.2 Liter.						
Sedan 4D	AF93D	68865	5950	6325	7250	9725
4-Passenger Seating			300	300	355	355
W12, 6.0 Liter	H		3700	3700	4560	4560

2006 VOLKSWAGEN–(W,3or9)(VorB)W(BR71K)–6–#

Body Type	VIN	List	Trade-In Good	Very Good	Pvt-Party Good	Retail Excellent
RABBIT—5-Cyl.—Equipment Schedule 6						
W.B. 101.5"; 2.5 Liter.						
Hatchback 2D	BR71K	16695	2325	2600	3425	5250
Hatchback 4D	DR71K	18695	2950	3300	4050	6075
Manual, 5-Spd	A		(275)	(275)	(355)	(355)
GOLF—4-Cyl.—Equipment Schedule 6						
W.B. 98.9"; 2.0 Liter.						
GL Hatchback 4D	FL61J	16645	2100	2375	3250	5100
GLS Hatchback 4D	GL61J	19005	2775	3125	3900	5950
GOLF—4-Cyl. Turbo Diesel—Equipment Schedule 6						
W.B. 98.9"; 1.9 Liter.						
GLS TDI H'Back 4D	GR61J	20195	4750	5125	5825	8250
GTI—4-Cyl. Turbo—Equipment Schedule 6						
W.B. 98.9", 101.5"; 1.8 Liter, 2.0 Liter.						
1.8T Hatchback 2D	DE61J	20955	3350	3750	4450	6675
2.0T Hatchback 2D	EV71K	22620	4475	5000	5575	8250
Package #2			725	725	965	965
NEW BEETLE—5-Cyl.—Equipment Schedule 6						
W.B. 98.7"; 98.8" (Conv); 2.5 Liter.						
2.5 Hatchback 2D	PF31C	18870	2650	2875	3875	5925
2.5 Convertible 2D	PF31Y	23610	3400	3700	4650	6900
Package #1			200	200	265	265
Package #2			400	400	540	540
Manual, 5-Spd			(275)	(275)	(355)	(355)
NEW BEETLE—4-Cyl. Turbo Diesel—Equipment Schedule 6						
W.B. 98.7"; 1.9 Liter.						
TDI Hatchback 2D	PR31C	19005	3475	3750	4625	6775
Package #1	R		200	200	265	265
Package #2	S		400	400	540	540
JETTA—5-Cyl.—Equipment Schedule 6						
W.B. 101.5"; 2.5 Liter.						
2.5 Value Ed Sedan	PF71K	19590	2550	2775	3800	5875
2.5 Sedan 4D	RF71K	21980	2875	3125	4175	6425
Package #1	S		200	200	265	265
Package #2	D		400	400	540	540
Manual, 5-Spd			(275)	(275)	(355)	(355)

2006 VOLKSWAGEN

Body Type	VIN	List	Trade-In Good	Very Good	Pvt-Party Good	Retail Excellent
JETTA—4-Cyl. Turbo—Equipment Schedule 6						
W.B. 101.5"; 2.0 Liter.						
2.0T Sedan 4D	AJ71K	25080	3375	3675	4750	7100
Package #1	K		200	200	265	265
Package #2	M		400	400	540	540
Package #3	N		575	575	780	780
Manual, 6-Spd			(300)	(300)	(390)	(390)
Manual, 6-Spd			(300)	(300)	(390)	(390)
JETTA—4-Cyl. Turbo—Equipment Schedule 6						
W.B. 101.5"; 2.0 Liter.						
GLI Sedan 4D	TJ71K	24405	3175	3450	4575	6900
Package #1	K		200	200	265	265
Package #2	M		400	400	540	540
JETTA—4-Cyl. Turbo Diesel—Equipment Schedule 6						
W.B. 101.5"; 1.9 Liter.						
TDI Sedan 4D	RT71K	22980	4275	4625	5350	7625
TDI Special Ed Sedan	FT71K	22980	4975	5375	6125	8775
Package #1			200	200	265	265
Package #2			400	400	540	540
Manual, 5-Spd			(275)	(275)	(355)	(355)
PASSAT—4-Cyl. Turbo—Equipment Schedule 4						
W.B. 106.7"; 2.0 Liter.						
2.0T Value Ed Sedan	AK73C	24640	2475	2800	3400	5150
2.0T Sedan 4D	AK73C	25590	2800	3150	3700	5550
Luxury Pkg			725	725	955	955
PASSAT—V6—Equipment Schedule 4						
W.B. 106.4"; 3.6 Liter.						
3.6 Sedan 4D	AU73C	30565	3925	4425	5125	7725
Luxury Pkg			725	725	955	955
PASSAT 4MOTION AWD—V6—Equipment Schedule 4						
W.B. 106.4"; 3.6 Liter.						
3.6 Sedan 4D	BU73C	32515	4950	5550	6200	9225
Luxury Pkg			725	725	955	955
PHAETON—V8—Equipment Schedule 1						
W.B. 118.1"; 4.2 Liter.						
Sedan 4D	AF03D	68655	7525	7975	8775	11350
4-Passenger Seating			350	350	410	410
W12, 6.0 Liter	K		4050	4050	4815	4815
2007 VOLKSWAGEN—(W,3or9)(VorB)W(BR71K)-7-#						
RABBIT—5-Cyl.—Equipment Schedule 6						
W.B. 101.5"; 2.5 Liter.						
Hatchback 2D	BR71K	16705	3150	3475	4400	6400
Hatchback 4D	DR71K	18825	3675	4050	4875	7025
Manual, 5-Spd	A		(300)	(300)	(385)	(385)
GTI—4-Cyl. Turbo—Equipment Schedule 6						
W.B. 101.5"; 2.0 Liter.						
2.0T Hatchback 2D	EV71K	22730	4800	5325	6050	8625
Package #2			775	775	1020	1020
Automatic DSG w/Tiptronic			300	300	385	385
GTI—4-Cyl. Turbo—Equipment Schedule 6						
W.B. 101.5"; 2.0 Liter.						
2.0T Hatchback 4D	HV71K	24305	5325	5875	6450	9050
Package #2			775	775	1020	1020
Manual, 6-Spd	G		(350)	(350)	(455)	(455)
EOS—4-Cyl. Turbo—Equipment Schedule 3						
W.B. 101.5"; 2.0 Liter.						
Hardtop Conv 2D	AA71F	28620	4350	5025	5300	7600
2.0T Hardtop Conv 2D	DA71F	31825	4875	5625	5800	8225
EOS—V6—Equipment Schedule 3						
W.B. 101.5"; 3.2 Liter.						
3.2L Hardtop Conv 2D	DB71F	37480	6150	7050	7000	9775
NEW BEETLE—5-Cyl.—Equipment Schedule 6						
W.B. 98.7"; 98.8" (Conv); 2.5 Liter.						
2.5 Hatchback 2D	PW31C	18885	2975	3200	4225	6200
2.5 Convertible 2D	PF31Y	23825	3775	4075	5075	7350
Package #1			200	200	280	280
Package #2			425	425	565	565
Triple White Ed (Conv)			400	400	530	530
Manual, 5-Spd			(300)	(300)	(385)	(385)
JETTA—5-Cyl.—Equipment Schedule 6						
W.B. 101.5"; 2.5 Liter.						
Sedan 4D	GF71K	19690	3125	3375	4350	6475

2007 VOLKSWAGEN

Body Type	VIN	List	Trade-In Good	Very Good	Pvt-Party Good	Retail Excellent
2.5 Sedan 4D	PF71K	19695	3275	3550	4725	7075
Wolfsburg Ed Sedan	EF71K	21175	4125	4425	5325	7600
Package #1			200	200	280	280
Package #2			425	425	565	565
Manual, 5-Spd			(300)	(300)	(385)	(385)
JETTA—4-Cyl. Turbo—Equipment Schedule 6						
W.B. 101.5"; 2.0 Liter.						
2.0T Sedan 4D	AJ71K	23695	4225	4550	5450	7750
Package #1			200	200	280	280
Package #2			425	425	565	565
Manual, 6-Spd			(350)	(350)	(455)	(455)
JETTA—4-Cyl. Turbo—Equipment Schedule 6						
W.B. 101.5"; 2.0 Liter.						
GLI Sedan 4D	TJ71K	24620	5275	5675	6525	9025
Package #1			200	200	280	280
Package #2			425	425	565	565
Automatic w/Tiptronic			300	300	385	385
PASSAT—4-Cyl. Turbo—Equipment Schedule 4						
W.B. 106.7"; 2.0 Liter.						
Sedan 4D	JK73C	24665	2250	2525	3200	4800
Wagon 4D	XK73C	26085	3150	3525	4100	5900
2.0T Sedan 4D	AK73C	25665	3350	3750	4325	6225
2.0T Value Ed Wag 4D	LK73C	25855	3375	3775	4400	6325
2.0T Wagon 4D	LK73C	26805	3425	3825	4375	6225
2.0T Wolfsburg Ed Sed	AK73C	27630	4000	4450	5100	7350
Luxury Pkg			775	775	1025	1025
Sport Pkg			825	825	1090	1090
PASSAT—V6—Equipment Schedule 4						
W.B. 106.7"; 3.6 Liter.						
3.6 Sedan 4D	AU73C	30590	5250	5850	6500	9225
3.6 Wagon 4D	LU73C	31790	6800	7550	8200	11650
Luxury Pkg			775	775	1025	1025
Sport Pkg			825	825	1090	1090
PASSAT 4MOTION AWD—V6—Equipment Schedule 4						
W.B. 106.7"; 3.6 Liter.						
3.6 Sedan 4D	BU73C	32540	6175	6850	7475	10600
3.6 Wagon 4D	MU73C	33740	7300	8100	8600	12050
Luxury Pkg			775	775	1025	1025
Sport Pkg			825	825	1090	1090

2008 VOLKSWAGEN—(W,3or9)(VorB)W(BA71K)-8-#

Body Type	VIN	List	Trade-In Good	Very Good	Pvt-Party Good	Retail Excellent
RABBIT—5-Cyl.—Equipment Schedule 6						
W.B. 101.5"; 2.5 Liter.						
Hatchback 2D	BA71K	17205	4125	4450	5375	7425
Hatchback 4D	DA71K	19200	4625	4975	5975	8275
Manual, 5-Spd w/Overdrive	A		(350)	(350)	(460)	(460)
GTI—4-Cyl. Turbo—Equipment Schedule 6						
W.B. 101.5"; 2.0 Liter.						
2.0T Hatchback 2D	EV71K	24445	6525	7050	7700	10200
Automatic, 6-Spd	F		300	300	385	385
4-Cyl, PZEV, 2.0 Liter	D		0	0	0	0
GTI—4-Cyl. Turbo—Equipment Schedule 6						
W.B. 101.5"; 2.0 Liter.						
2.0T Hatchback 4D	HV71K	24945	7000	7575	8350	11150
Manual, 6-Spd w/OD	G		(375)	(375)	(475)	(475)
4-Cyl, PZEV, 2.0 Liter	D		0	0	0	0
EOS—4-Cyl. Turbo—Equipment Schedule 3						
W.B. 101.5"; 2.0 Liter.						
Hardtop Conv 2D	AA71F	30630	5625	6300	6500	8600
Komfort HT Conv 2D	BA71F	32280	5950	6625	6800	9000
LUX Hardtop Conv 2D	FA71F	35630	7075	7875	8225	11100
EOS—V6—Equipment Schedule 3						
W.B. 101.5"; 3.2 Liter.						
VR6 Hardtop Conv 2D	DB71F	38630	7400	8250	8500	11400
NEW BEETLE—5-Cyl.—Equipment Schedule 6						
W.B. 98.8"; 2.5 Liter.						
S Hatchback 2D	PW31C	19080	3475	3725	4775	6750
S Convertible 2D	PF31Y	24840	5025	5375	6400	8700
Package #1			225	225	290	290
Manual, 5-Spd w/Overdrive			(350)	(350)	(460)	(460)
NEW BEETLE—5-Cyl.—Equipment Schedule 6						
W.B. 98.8"; 2.5 Liter.						
SE Hatchback 2D	RW31C	21080	4875	5200	6125	8400

Body Type	VIN	List	Trade-In Good	Trade-In Very Good	Pvt-Party Good	Retail Excellent
SE Convertible 2D	RF31Y	26265	5525	5900	6850	9200
Triple White Pkg			125	125	170	170
GLI—4-Cyl. Turbo—Equipment Schedule 4						
W.B. 101.5"; 2.0 Liter.						
2.0T Sedan 4D	BJ71K	25945	7075	7550	8325	10900
JETTA—5-Cyl.—Equipment Schedule 6						
W.B. 101.5"; 2.5 Liter.						
S Sedan 4D	JM71K	18705	3750	4000	5150	7300
SE Sedan 4D	RM71K	21475	4450	4750	5850	8200
Manual, 5-Spd w/Overdrive			(350)	(350)	(460)	(460)
JETTA—5-Cyl.—Equipment Schedule 6						
W.B. 101.5"; 2.5 Liter.						
SEL Sedan 4D	RM71K	23465	5450	5800	6825	9200
JETTA—4-Cyl. Turbo—Equipment Schedule 6						
W.B. 101.5"; 2.0 Liter.						
Wolfsburg Ed Sedan	RJ71A	22600	5600	5975	7125	9750
Manual, 6-Spd w/Overdrive			(375)	(375)	(485)	(485)
R32—V6—Equipment Schedule 3						
W.B. 101.5"; 3.2 Liter.						
Hatchback 2D	KC71K	33630	11300	12150	12150	15350
PASSAT—4-Cyl. Turbo—Equipment Schedule 4						
W.B. 106.7"; 2.0 Liter.						
Sedan 4D	JK73C	25630	2925	3175	4000	5600
Wagon 4D	XK73C	26830	3550	3875	4575	6300
Komfort Sedan 4D	AK73C	28430	4625	5025	5750	7850
Komfort Wagon 4D	LK73C	29630	5375	5825	6500	8700
LUX Sedan 4D	EK73C	30630	5275	5725	6275	8300
LUX Wagon 4D	TK73C	31830	7075	7650	8225	10850
PASSAT—V6—Equipment Schedule 4						
W.B. 106.7"; 3.6 Liter.						
VR6 Sedan 4D	CU73C	36630	6500	7075	7850	10550
PASSAT 4MOTION AWD—V6—Equipment Schedule 4						
W.B. 106.7"; 3.6 Liter.						
VR6 Sedan 4D	DU73C	38580	7375	7975	8725	11700
VR6 Wagon 4D	RU73C	39780	8375	9050	9050	13100

2009 VOLKSWAGEN—(W,3or9)(VorB)W(AA71K)-9-#

Body Type	VIN	List	Trade-In Good	Trade-In Very Good	Pvt-Party Good	Retail Excellent
RABBIT—5-Cyl.—Equipment Schedule 6						
W.B. 101.5"; 2.5 Liter.						
S Hatchback 2D	AA71K	16540	4625	4900	5925	7850
Auto, 6-Spd w/Overdrive			325	325	445	445
RABBIT—5-Cyl.—Equipment Schedule 6						
W.B. 101.5"; 2.5 Liter.						
S Hatchback 4D	CA71K	19640	5575	5900	7000	9100
GTI—4-Cyl. Turbo—Equipment Schedule 6						
W.B. 101.5"; 2.0 Liter.						
2.0T Hatchback 2D	EV71K	24740	7100	7550	8475	10800
Automatic, 6-Spd	F		325	325	415	415
4-Cyl, PZEV, 2.0 Liter	D		0	0	0	0
GTI—4-Cyl. Turbo—Equipment Schedule 6						
W.B. 101.5"; 2.0 Liter.						
2.0T Hatchback 4D	HV71K	25340	8350	8850	9825	12600
Manual, 6-Spd	G		(400)	(400)	(490)	(490)
4-Cyl, PZEV, 2.0 Liter	D		0	0	0	0
EOS—4-Cyl. Turbo—Equipment Schedule 3						
W.B. 101.5"; 2.0 Liter.						
Komfort HT Conv 2D	BA71F	32580	7450	8125	8775	11500
LUX Hardtop Conv 2D	FA71F	35890	8725	9475	10350	13750
NEW BEETLE—5-Cyl.—Equipment Schedule 6						
W.B. 98.8"; 2.5 Liter.						
Hatchback 2D	PW31C	19740	4725	5000	5975	7925
Manual, 5-Spd w/Overdrive			(375)	(375)	(490)	(490)
NEW BEETLE—5-Cyl.—Equipment Schedule 6						
W.B. 98.8"; 2.5 Liter.						
Convertible 2D	PF73Y	26240	7000	7425	8425	10850
GLI—4-Cyl. Turbo—Equipment Schedule 4						
W.B. 101.5"; 2.0 Liter.						
2.0T Sedan 4D	BJ71K	26340	8200	8675	9500	12050
JETTA—5-Cyl.—Equipment Schedule 6						
W.B. 101.5"; 2.5 Liter.						
S Sedan 4D	JM71K	19090	4750	5025	6150	8325
S Sportwagen 4D	KM71K	20749	5525	5850	7150	9575
SE Sedan 4D	RM71K	21670	5575	5900	7175	9625

Body Type	VIN	List	Trade-In Good	Very Good	Pvt-Party Good	Retail Excellent
California Edition			775	775	1045	1045
Panorama Roof			500	500	680	680
Manual, 5-Spd w/Overdrive			(375)	(375)	(490)	(490)
JETTA—5-Cyl.—Equipment Schedule 6						
W.B. 101.5"; 2.5 Liter.						
SE Sportwagen 4D	PM71K	21999	6125	6475	7675	10150
Panorama Roof			500	500	680	680
Automatic, 6-Spd w/OD			325	325	445	445
JETTA—5-Cyl.—Equipment Schedule 6						
W.B. 101.5"; 2.5 Liter.						
SEL Sedan 4D	RM71K	23440	6275	6650	7700	10050
JETTA—4-Cyl. Turbo—Equipment Schedule 6						
W.B. 101.5"; 2.0 Liter.						
Wolfsburg Ed Sedan 4D	RJ71K	23095	6225	6575	7775	10250
Manual, 6-Spd w/Overdrive			(400)	(400)	(520)	(520)
JETTA—4-Cyl. Turbo—Equipment Schedule 6						
W.B. 101.5"; 2.0 Liter.						
SEL Sportwagen 4D	PJ71K	26640	7700	8150	9025	11450
Panorama Roof			500	500	675	675
Automatic, 6-Spd DSG			325	325	440	440
JETTA—4-Cyl. Turbo Diesel—Equipment Schedule 6						
W.B. 101.5"; 2.0 Liter.						
TDI Sedan 4D	AL71K	23740	7100	7525	8425	10750
Loyal Ed Sedan 4D	CL71K	23140	7050	7450	8375	10750
TDI Sportwagen 4D	PL71K	25340	9050	9575	10300	12950
Panorama Roof			500	500	650	650
Manual, 6-Spd w/Overdrive			(400)	(400)	(520)	(520)
PASSAT—4-Cyl. Turbo—Equipment Schedule 4						
W.B. 106.7"; 2.0 Liter.						
Komfort Sedan 4D	AK73C	28990	6000	6375	7275	9375
Komfort Wagon 4D	LK73C	30380	6875	7300	8300	10750
CC—4-Cyl. Turbo—Equipment Schedule 4						
W.B. 106.7"; 2.0 Liter.						
Sport Sedan 4D	ML73C	28580	7275	7700	8550	10700
Luxury Sedan 4D	HL73C	32680	8125	8600	9450	11850
CC—V6—Equipment Schedule 4						
W.B. 106.7"; 3.6 Liter.						
VR6 Sport Sedan 4D	EU73C	38990	8650	9150	10050	12650
CC 4MOTION AWD—V6—Equipment Schedule 4						
W.B. 106.7"; 3.6 Liter.						
VR6 Sedan 4D	GU73C	39990	9450	10000	10900	13650

Body Type	VIN	List	Trade-In Good	Very Good	Pvt-Party Good	Retail Excellent
GOLF—5-Cyl.—Equipment Schedule 6						
W.B. 101.5"; 2.5 Liter.						
Hatchback 2D	AA7AJ	18190	6500	6800	8000	10050
Automatic, 6-Spd w/OD			375	375	495	495
GOLF—5-Cyl.—Equipment Schedule 6						
W.B. 101.5"; 2.5 Liter.						
Hatchback 4D	DB7AJ	19890	6975	7275	8475	10550
GOLF—4-Cyl. Turbo Diesel—Equipment Schedule 6						
W.B. 101.5"; 2.0 Liter.						
TDI Hatchback 2D	MM7AJ	22889	9125	9600	10400	12750
TDI Hatchback 4D	NM7AJ	23489	9725	10250	11100	13650
Automatic, 6-Spd DSG			375	375	475	475
GTI—4-Cyl. Turbo—Equipment Schedule 6						
W.B. 101.5"; 2.0 Liter.						
2.0T Hatchback 2D	EV71K	24239	9925	10350	11400	13800
Automatic, 6-Spd	F		375	375	460	460
GTI—4-Cyl. Turbo—Equipment Schedule 6						
W.B. 101.5"; 2.0 Liter.						
2.0T Hatchback 4D	HD7AJ	25690	10950	11450	12550	15200
Manual, 6-Spd	G		(450)	(450)	(550)	(550)
EOS—4-Cyl. Turbo—Equipment Schedule 3						
W.B. 101.5"; 2.0 Liter.						
Komfort HT Conv 2D	BA7AH	33840	10050	10700	11650	14650
LUX Hardtop Conv 2D	FA7AH	36240	11200	11900	12900	16250
NEW BEETLE—5-Cyl.—Equipment Schedule 6						
W.B. 98.8"; 2.5 Liter.						
Hatchback 2D	PW31C	20340	5350	5650	6800	8725
Manual, 5-Spd			(375)	(375)	(510)	(510)
NEW BEETLE—5-Cyl.—Equipment Schedule 6						
W.B. 98.8"; 2.5 Liter.						

Body Type	VIN	List	Trade-In Good	Trade-In Very Good	Pvt-Party Good	Retail Excellent
Final Edition H'Back	PW3AG	21140	6475	6800	7950	10150
Red Rock Ed H'Back	PW3AG	21140	5850	6175	7375	9475
Convertible 2D	PF31Y	27140	8475	8925	9950	12450
Final Edition Conv	RW3AL	28140	9525	10000	11000	13650
JETTA—5-Cyl.—Equipment Schedule 6						
W.B. 101.5"; 2.5 Liter.						
S Sedan 4D	JXA8J	19405	6050	6375	7575	9725
S Sportwagen 4D	KX8AJ	21065	7075	7450	8700	11100
Limited Ed Sedan 4D	JXA8J	20145	6850	7200	8325	10600
SE Sedan 4D	RX8AJ	22195	7125	7475	8725	11100
Panorama Roof			525	525	715	715
Manual, 5-Spd w/Overdrive			(450)	(450)	(615)	(615)
JETTA—5-Cyl.—Equipment Schedule 6						
W.B. 101.5"; 2.5 Liter.						
SE Sportwagen 4D	PX8AJ	23990	7950	8350	9475	11950
SEL Sedan 4D	RX8AJ	24205	8050	8450	9575	12050
Panorama Roof			525	525	705	705
JETTA—4-Cyl. Turbo—Equipment Schedule 6						
W.B. 101.5"; 2.0 Liter.						
Wolfsburg Ed Sedan	RJ8AJ	23800	8100	8500	9625	12100
Manual, 6-Spd w/Overdrive			(450)	(450)	(610)	(610)
JETTA—4-Cyl. Turbo Diesel—Equipment Schedule 6						
W.B. 101.5"; 2.0 Liter.						
TDI Sedan 4D	AL8AJ	24460	8900	9350	10200	12600
TDI Cup Ed Sedan	AL8AJ	26840	11250	11850	12600	15250
TDI Sportwagen 4D	PL8AJ	26110	10800	11350	12100	14700
Panorama Roof			525	525	665	665
Manual, 6-Spd w/Overdrive			(450)	(450)	(590)	(590)
PASSAT—4-Cyl. Turbo—Equipment Schedule 4						
W.B. 106.7"; 2.0 Liter.						
Komfort Sedan 4D	JK7AN	27695	7800	8150	9175	11350
Komfort Wagon 4D	XK7AN	29095	8800	9200	10300	12750
CC—4-Cyl. Turbo—Equipment Schedule 4						
W.B. 106.7"; 2.0 Liter.						
Sport Sedan 4D	ML7AN	29400	8800	9200	10250	12600
Luxury Sedan 4D	HL7AN	33630	9950	10400	11600	14200
R-Line Pkg			375	375	495	495
CC—V6—Equipment Schedule 4						
W.B. 106.7"; 3.6 Liter.						
VR6 Sport Sedan 4D	EU7AN	39815	11300	11800	13100	16050
CC 4MOTION AWD—V6—Equipment Schedule 4						
W.B. 106.7"; 3.6 Liter.						
VR6 Sedan 4D	GU7AN	40865	12450	13000	14250	17450

2011 VOLKSWAGEN — (Wor3)VW(AA7AJ)–B–#

Body Type	VIN	List	Trade-In Good	Trade-In Very Good	Pvt-Party Good	Retail Excellent
GOLF—5-Cyl.—Equipment Schedule 6						
W.B. 101.5"; 2.5 Liter.						
Hatchback 2D	AA7AJ	19030	7525	7800	9275	11400
Automatic, 6-Spd w/OD			425	425	550	550
GOLF—5-Cyl.—Equipment Schedule 6						
W.B. 101.5"; 2.5 Liter.						
Hatchback 4D	DA7AJ	20750	8175	8475	9850	11950
GOLF—4-Cyl. Turbo Diesel—Equipment Schedule 6						
W.B. 101.5"; 2.0 Liter.						
TDI Hatchback 2D	MM7AJ	23580	10550	11050	11900	14150
TDI Hatchback 4D	NM7AJ	24205	11250	11750	12700	15200
Automatic, 6-Spd DSG			425	425	525	525
GTI—4-Cyl. Turbo—Equipment Schedule 6						
W.B. 101.5"; 2.0 Liter.						
2.0T Hatchback 2D	FV7AJ	24460	11600	12000	13250	15550
Automatic, 6-Spd	F		425	425	505	505
GTI—4-Cyl. Turbo—Equipment Schedule 6						
W.B. 101.5"; 2.0 Liter.						
2.0T Hatchback 4D	HV7AJ	26160	12450	12850	14200	16750
Manual, 6-Spd	G		(500)	(500)	(575)	(575)
EOS—4-Cyl. Turbo—Equipment Schedule 3						
W.B. 101.5"; 2.0 Liter.						
Komfort HT Conv 2D	AD7AH	34810	12450	13000	14100	17050
LUX Hardtop Conv 2D	FD7AH	36870	13750	14400	15400	18300
JETTA—4-Cyl.—Equipment Schedule 6						
W.B. 104.4"; 2.0 Liter.						
Sedan 4D	2K8AJ	16865	6700	7025	8350	10550
S Sedan 4D	1K8AJ	17865	7400	7750	9050	11300

2011 VOLKSWAGEN

Body Type	VIN	List	Trade-In Good	Very Good	Pvt-Party Good	Retail Excellent
Manual, 5-Spd w/Overdrive	1		(500)	(500)	(655)	(655)
JETTA—5-Cyl.—Equipment Schedule 6						
W.B. 101.5"; 2.5 Liter.						
S SportWagen 4D	KX8AJ	20595	9375	9825	10950	13400
Manual, 5-Spd w/Overdrive	K		(500)	(500)	(625)	(625)
JETTA—5-Cyl.—Equipment Schedule 6						
W.B. 101.5"; 2.5 Liter.						
SE SportWagen 4D	PX8AJ	24225	10700	11200	12250	14850
Panorama Moon Roof			550	550	700	700
JETTA—5-Cyl.—Equipment Schedule 6						
W.B. 101.5"; 2.5 Liter.						
SE Sedan 4D	DX8AJ	20065	8150	8525	9775	12150
SEL Sedan 4D	LX8AJ	23265	9950	10400	11400	13750
Manual, 5-Spd w/Overdrive	B		(500)	(500)	(645)	(645)
JETTA—4-Cyl. Turbo Diesel—Equipment Schedule 6						
W.B. 101.5"; 2.0 Liter.						
TDI Sedan 4D	LL8AJ	24865	11150	11650	12550	15050
TDI SportWagen 4D	PL8AJ	26600	12900	13500	14300	16950
Panorama Moon Roof			550	550	680	680
Manual, 6-Spd w/Overdrive	3		(500)	(500)	(605)	(605)
CC—4-Cyl. Turbo—Equipment Schedule 4						
W.B. 106.7"; 2.0 Liter.						
Sport Sedan 4D	MN7AN	30120	10350	10700	11950	14250
Luxury Sedan 4D	HN7AN	31995	11850	12250	13450	15900
R-Line Sedan 4D	MN7AN	32040	10600	10950	12200	14550
Lux Plus Sedan 4D	HN7AN	34395	12000	12400	13700	16250
Lux Limited Sedan 4D	HN7AN	35195	12100	12500	13850	16450
CC 4MOTION AWD—V6—Equipment Schedule 4						
W.B. 106.7"; 3.6 Liter.						
VR6 Sedan 4D	GU7AN	40810	14350	14850	16450	19650

2012 VOLKSWAGEN — (1,3orW)VW(AA7AJ)–C–#

Body Type	VIN	List	Trade-In Good	Very Good	Pvt-Party Good	Retail Excellent
GOLF—5-Cyl.—Equipment Schedule 6						
W.B. 101.5"; 2.5 Liter.						
2.5L Hatchback 2D	AA7AJ	18765	8525	8750	10300	12350
Automatic, 6-Spd			475	475	595	595
GOLF—5-Cyl.—Equipment Schedule 6						
W.B. 101.5"; 2.5 Liter.						
2.5L Hatchback 4D	DA7AJ	20565	9050	9275	10850	13050
GOLF AWD—4-Cyl. Turbo—Equipment Schedule 6						
W.B. 101.5"; 2.0 Liter.						
R Hatchback 2D	RF7AJ	34760	22000	22500	23800	26700
R Hatchback 4D	PF7AJ	36860	22500	23000	24200	27100
GOLF—4-Cyl. Turbo Diesel—Equipment Schedule 6						
W.B. 101.5"; 2.0 Liter.						
TDI Hatchback 2D	MM7AJ	24170	11900	12400	13500	16050
TDI Hatchback 4D	DM7AJ	25465	12850	13400	14450	17100
Automatic, 6-Spd DSG			475	475	555	555
BEETLE—5-Cyl.—Equipment Schedule 6						
W.B. 99.9"; 2.5 Liter.						
Hatchback 2D	AX7AT	19765	9550	9950	11100	13300
2.5L Hatchback 2D	HX7AT	20565	9875	10300	11450	13700
BEETLE—4-Cyl. Turbo—Equipment Schedule 6						
W.B. 99.9"; 2.0 Liter.						
2.0T Hatchback 2D	487AT	24165	11850	12350	13400	15800
2.0T Launch Ed 2D	V87AT	25720	12700	13250	14200	16700
GTI—4-Cyl. Turbo—Equipment Schedule 6						
W.B. 101.5"; 2.0 Liter.						
2.0T Hatchback 2D	EV7AJ	24465	13600	13950	15500	17750
Automatic, 6-Spd	F		475	475	530	530
GTI—4-Cyl. Turbo—Equipment Schedule 6						
W.B. 101.5"; 2.0 Liter.						
2.0T Hatchback 4D	HV7AJ	26165	14500	14850	16350	18700
Manual, 6-Spd w/OD	G		(550)	(550)	(615)	(615)
EOS—4-Cyl. Turbo—Equipment Schedule 3						
W.B. 101.5"; 2.0 Liter.						
Komfort HT Conv 2D	BW7AH	34765	15150	15700	17000	20200
LUX Hardtop Conv	FW7AH	38020	16450	17000	18300	21600
Executive HT Conv	FW7AH	41175	17550	18150	19550	23200
JETTA—4-Cyl.—Equipment Schedule 6						
W.B. 104.4"; 2.0 Liter.						
2.0L Sedan 4D	1K8AJ	16135	7550	7900	9350	11650
2.0L S Sedan 4D	1K7AJ	17265	8150	8500	9950	12350

Body Type	VIN	List	Trade-In Good	Very Good	Pvt-Party Good	Retail Excellent
Manual, 5-Spd	1		(500)	(500)	(665)	(665)

JETTA—4-Cyl. Turbo—Equipment Schedule 6
W.B. 104.4"; 2.0 Liter.

Body Type	VIN	List	Good	Very Good	Good	Excellent
2.0T GLI Sedan 4D	567AJ	24515	12350	12900	13900	16400
2.0T GLI Autobahn Sed	567AJ	26565	13800	14350	15400	18100
Manual, 6-Spd	5		(500)	(500)	(605)	(605)

JETTA—4-Cyl. Turbo Diesel—Equipment Schedule 6
W.B. 104.4"; 2.0 Liter.

Body Type	VIN	List	Good	Very Good	Good	Excellent
2.0L TDI Sedan 4D	3L7AJ	23295	12650	13150	14150	16700
Manual, 6-Spd	3		(500)	(500)	(610)	(610)

JETTA—5-Cyl.—Equipment Schedule 6
W.B. 104.4"; 2.5 Liter.

Body Type	VIN	List	Good	Very Good	Good	Excellent
2.5L SE Sedan 4D	DX7AJ	20365	9175	9575	10850	13200
Manual, 5-Spd	B		(500)	(500)	(650)	(650)

JETTA—5-Cyl.—Equipment Schedule 6
W.B. 104.4"; 2.5 Liter.

Body Type	VIN	List	Good	Very Good	Good	Excellent
2.5L SEL Sedan 4D	GX7AJ	23965	11350	11800	13000	15500
Manual, 5-Spd	G		(500)	(500)	(620)	(620)

JETTA—5-Cyl.—Equipment Schedule 6
W.B. 104.4"; 2.5 Liter.

Body Type	VIN	List	Good	Very Good	Good	Excellent
2.5L SEL Premium Sed	LX7AJ	25575	13150	13700	14750	17350

JETTA SPORTWAGEN—5-Cyl.—Equipment Schedule 6
W.B. 101.5"; 2.5 Liter.

Body Type	VIN	List	Good	Very Good	Good	Excellent
2.5L S SportWagen 4D	KX7AJ	22065	10600	11050	12150	14500
Manual, 5-Spd	K		(500)	(500)	(625)	(625)

JETTA SPORTWAGEN—5-Cyl.—Equipment Schedule 6
W.B. 101.5"; 2.5 Liter.

Body Type	VIN	List	Good	Very Good	Good	Excellent
2.5L SE SportWagen	PX7AJ	24980	12650	13200	14150	16650
Panorama Moon Roof			600	600	710	710

JETTA SPORTWAGEN—4-Cyl. Turbo Diesel—Equipment Schedule 6
W.B. 101.5"; 2.0 Liter.

Body Type	VIN	List	Good	Very Good	Good	Excellent
2.0L TDI SportWagen	ML7AJ	27410	14800	15400	16350	19100
Panorama Moon Roof			600	600	695	695
Manual, 6-Spd	M		(500)	(500)	(595)	(595)

PASSAT—5-Cyl.—Equipment Schedule 4
W.B. 110.4"; 2.5 Liter.

Body Type	VIN	List	Good	Very Good	Good	Excellent
S Sedan 4D	AH7A3	23460	8675	8850	10150	11900
SE Sedan 4D	BH7A3	25595	10500	10750	12100	14200
SEL Sedan 4D	CH7A3	29185	12250	12500	14000	16400
SEL Premium Sed 4D	CH7A3	30665	13650	13950	15600	18250

PASSAT—4-Cyl. Turbo Diesel—Equipment Schedule 4
W.B. 110.4"; 2.0 Liter.

Body Type	VIN	List	Good	Very Good	Good	Excellent
TDI SE Sedan 4D	BN7A3	28665	14350	14800	16150	19150
TDI SEL Premium Sed	CN7A3	32965	15600	16100	17500	20700

PASSAT—V6—Equipment Schedule 4
W.B. 110.4"; 3.6 Liter.

Body Type	VIN	List	Good	Very Good	Good	Excellent
SE Sedan 4D	BM7A3	29765	13100	13350	15000	17550
SEL Premium Sed 4D	CM7A3	33720	13300	13750	15200	18150

CC—4-Cyl. Turbo—Equipment Schedule 4
W.B. 106.7"; 2.0 Liter.

Body Type	VIN	List	Good	Very Good	Good	Excellent
Sport Sedan 4D	MN7AN	30435	12050	12350	13900	16350
Luxury Sedan 4D	HN7AN	32240	13050	13400	14950	17550
R-Line Sedan 4D	HN7AN	32380	12650	13000	14550	17050
Lux Plus Sedan 4D	HN7AN	34685	13750	14100	15800	18450
Lux Limited Sedan 4D	HN7AN	35485	13150	13450	15200	17850

CC 4MOTION AWD—V6—Equipment Schedule 4
W.B. 106.7"; 3.6 Liter.

Body Type	VIN	List	Good	Very Good	Good	Excellent
VR6 Sedan 4D	GU7AN	41210	16750	17150	19100	22400

2013 VOLKSWAGEN — (1,3orW)VW(AB7AJ)-D-#

GOLF—5-Cyl.—Equipment Schedule 6
W.B. 101.5"; 2.5 Liter.

Body Type	VIN	List	Good	Very Good	Good	Excellent
2.5L Hatchback 2D	AB7AJ	18790	9050	9225	10850	12850
Automatic, 6-Spd DSG			500	500	620	620

GOLF—5-Cyl.—Equipment Schedule 6
W.B. 101.5"; 2.5 Liter.

Body Type	VIN	List	Good	Very Good	Good	Excellent
2.5L Hatchback 4D	DB7AJ	20590	9825	10050	11750	13950

GOLF AWD—4-Cyl. Turbo—Equipment Schedule 6
W.B. 101.5"; 2.0 Liter.

Body Type	VIN	List	Good	Very Good	Good	Excellent
R Hatchback 2D	RF7AJ	34990	24400	24800	26300	29100
R Hatchback 4D	PF7AJ	35385	24400	24800	26400	29200

GOLF—4-Cyl. Turbo Diesel—Equipment Schedule 6
W.B. 101.5"; 2.0 Liter.

Body Type	VIN	List	Trade-In Good	Trade-In Very Good	Pvt-Party Good	Retail Excellent
TDI Hatchback 2D	MM7AJ	25030	13800	14350	15550	18200
TDI Hatchback 4D	NM7AJ	25730	14700	15250	16350	19050
Automatic, 6-Spd DSG			**500**	**500**	**570**	**570**
BEETLE—5-Cyl.—Equipment Schedule 6						
W.B. 99.9"; 2.5 Liter.						
2.5L Entry Hatchback	FX7AT	19790	10850	11300	12350	14550
2.5L Hatchback 2D	HX7AT	20590	11300	11750	12950	15250
2.5L Fender Ed H'Bck	HX7AT	25235	14300	14850	15850	18400
2.5L Convertible 2D	5X7AT	25790	14750	15350	16300	18850
2.5L 50's Ed Conv 2D	5P7AT	26890	15250	15850	16800	19450
2.5L 70's Ed Conv 2D	5P7AT	29390	16750	17400	18250	21000
BEETLE—4-Cyl. Turbo—Equipment Schedule 6						
W.B. 99.9"; 2.0 Liter.						
Hatchback 2D	467AT	24190	13300	13850	15000	17500
Convertible 2D	867AT	28590	16000	16600	17550	20300
Fender Ed H'Back 2D	467AT	28925	16200	16850	17750	20500
R-Line H'Back 2D	467AT	30940	16350	17000	17850	20500
60's Ed Convertible 2D	7A7AT	33190	18400	19100	19850	22700
BEETLE—4-Cyl. Turbo Diesel—Equipment Schedule 6						
W.B. 99.9"; 2.0 Liter.						
TDI Hatchback 2D	RL7AT	24090	14000	14550	15600	18100
TDI Convertible 2D	6L7AT	28690	16100	16750	17600	20200
GTI—4-Cyl. Turbo—Equipment Schedule 6						
W.B. 101.5"; 2.0 Liter.						
Hatchback Sedan 4D	HV7AJ	25390	15850	16100	17950	20400
Wolfsburg Ed H'Back	GV7AJ	25890	16100	16400	18250	20700
Driver's Ed H'Back 4D	GV7AJ	30490	16000	16300	18450	21300
Autobahn HBack 4D	HV7AJ	31390	16950	17300	19450	22400
GTI—4-Cyl. Turbo—Equipment Schedule 6						
W.B. 101.5"; 2.0 Liter.						
Hatchback Coupe 2D	FV7AJ	24790	15150	15400	17200	19550
Autobahn HBack 2D	FV7AJ	30790	16450	16750	18850	21700
Automatic, 6-Spd	F		**500**	**500**	**560**	**560**
EOS—4-Cyl. Turbo—Equipment Schedule 3						
W.B. 101.5"; 2.0 Liter.						
Komfort Conv 2D	BW8AH	35175	17900	18350	19750	23000
Sport Conv 2D	BW8AH	37325	19100	19600	20900	24200
Lux Conv 2D	FW8AH	40025	19300	19850	21200	24600
Executive Conv 2D	FW8AH	41770	20900	21400	23100	27100
JETTA—4-Cyl.—Equipment Schedule 6						
W.B. 104.4"; 2.0 Liter.						
2.0L Sedan 4D	2K7AJ	17440	8900	9250	10550	12750
2.0L S Sedan 4D	2K7AJ	18570	9600	9975	11400	13800
Manual, 5-Spd	1		**(500)**	**(500)**	**(645)**	**(645)**
JETTA—4-Cyl. Turbo—Equipment Schedule 6						
W.B. 104.4"; 2.0 Liter.						
2.0T GLI Sedan 4D	467AJ	25840	14250	14850	15950	18550
2.0T GLI Autobahn 4D	467AJ	28090	15600	16250	17250	19950
Manual, 6-Spd	5		**(500)**	**(500)**	**(590)**	**(590)**
JETTA—4-Cyl. Turbo Diesel—Equipment Schedule 6						
W.B. 104.4"; 2.0 Liter.						
2.0L TDI Sedan 4D	LL7AJ	24885	13800	14350	15500	18100
Manual, 6-Spd	3		**(500)**	**(500)**	**(600)**	**(600)**
JETTA—4-Cyl. Turbo Hybrid—Equipment Schedule 6						
W.B. 104.4"; 1.4 Liter.						
Sedan 4D	637AJ	25790	13000	13500	14800	17400
SE Sedan 4D	637AJ	27785	13200	13750	15000	17600
SEL Sedan 4D	637AJ	30120	13900	14450	15650	18400
SEL Premium Sedan 4D	637AJ	31975	14800	15400	16550	19300
JETTA—5-Cyl.—Equipment Schedule 6						
W.B. 104.4"; 2.5 Liter.						
2.5L SE Sedan 4D	DX7AJ	20890	10300	10700	12050	14450
2.5L SEL Sedan 4D	LX7AJ	24790	12850	13350	14400	16850
Manual, 5-Spd	B		**(500)**	**(500)**	**(630)**	**(630)**
JETTA SPORTWAGEN—5-Cyl.—Equipment Schedule 6						
W.B. 101.5"; 2.5 Liter.						
2.5L S SportWagen 4D	PX7AJ	22290	11500	11950	13200	15650
2.5L SE SportWagen	PX7AJ	25005	13550	14100	15150	17600
JETTA SPORTWAGEN—4-Cyl. Turbo Diesel—Equipment Schedule 6						
W.B. 101.5"; 2.0 Liter.						
2.0L TDI SportWagen	PL7AJ	27435	16050	16700	17650	20500
PASSAT—5-Cyl.—Equipment Schedule 4						
W.B. 110.4"; 2.5 Liter.						

Body Type	VIN	List	Trade-In Good	Very Good	Pvt-Party Good	Retail Excellent
2.5L S Sedan 4D	AH7A3	23740	9600	9750	11550	13700
Wolfsburg Ed Sedan	AH783	24290	10350	10500	12250	14500
2.5L SE Sedan 4D	BH7A3	25840	11700	11850	13550	15750
2.5L SEL Sedan 4D	CH7A3	29720	14050	14250	16150	18800
2.5L SEL Premium 4D	CH7A3	31220	15000	15250	17000	19550
PASSAT—4-Cyl. Turbo Diesel—Equipment Schedule 4						
W.B. 110.4"; 2.0 Liter.						
TDI SE Sedan 4D	BN7A3	29020	16000	16350	18050	21000
TDI SEL Premium Sed	CN7A3	33710	17400	17750	19400	22500
PASSAT—V6—Equipment Schedule 4						
W.B. 110.4"; 3.6 Liter.						
SE Sedan 4D	BM7A3	30030	14400	14650	16550	19250
SEL Premium Sed 4D	CM7A3	34320	15100	15450	17200	20200
CC—4-Cyl. Turbo—Equipment Schedule 4						
W.B. 106.7"; 2.0 Liter.						
Sport Sedan 4D	BN7AN	32890	15000	15300	17200	19950
Sport Plus Sedan 4D	BN7AN	33820	15050	15350	17300	20100
R-Line Sedan 4D	BN7AN	34120	15200	15500	17450	20300
Luxury Sedan 4D	RN7AN	36460	17300	17650	19650	22800
CC—V6—Equipment Schedule 4						
W.B. 106.7"; 3.6 Liter.						
VR6 Lux Sedan 4D	HU7AN	38550	18550	18950	21000	24400
CC 4MOTION AWD—V6—Equipment Schedule 4						
W.B. 106.7"; 3.6 Liter.						
VR6 Sedan 4D	GU7AN	42240	21100	21500	23500	27000

Body Type	VIN	List	Trade-In Good	Very Good	Pvt-Party Good	Retail Excellent
GOLF—5-Cyl.—Equipment Schedule 6						
W.B. 101.5"; 2.5 Liter.						
2.5L Hatchback 4D	DB7AJ	20815	12000	12250	13800	15900
GOLF—4-Cyl. Turbo Diesel—Equipment Schedule 6						
W.B. 101.5"; 2.0 Liter.						
TDI Hatchback 4D	NM7AJ	26020	16650	17300	18250	21000
BEETLE—4-Cyl. Turbo—Equipment Schedule 6						
W.B. 100.0"; 1.8 Liter.						
1.8T Hatchback 2D	H07AT	21115	12450	12950	14050	16400
Auto, 6-Spd Tiptronic	J		525	525	620	620
BEETLE—4-Cyl. Turbo—Equipment Schedule 6						
W.B. 100.0"; 1.8 Liter.						
1.8T Convertible 2D	507AT	25990	16250	16850	17750	20300
BEETLE—5-Cyl.—Equipment Schedule 6						
W.B. 100.0"; 2.5 Liter						
2.5L Hatchback 2D	HX7AT	20815	12150	12650	13750	16100
2.5L Convertible 2D	5X7AT	25815	16150	16800	17750	20500
Auto, 6-Spd Tiptronic	J		525	525	615	615
BEETLE—4-Cyl. Turbo—Equipment Schedule 6						
W.B. 100.0"; 2.0 Liter.						
R-Line H'Back 2D	4S7AT	25615	16900	17600	18400	21000
R-Line Conv 2D	8S7AT	29815	18300	19050	19700	22400
GSR Hatchback 2D	4S7AT	30815	19100	19800	20500	23200
Auto, 6-Spd Tiptronic	V		525	525	600	600
BEETLE—4-Cyl. Turbo Diesel—Equipment Schedule 6						
W.B. 100.0"; 2.0 Liter.						
TDI Hatchback 2D	RL7AT	25015	16200	16800	17700	20300
TDI Convertible 2D	6L7AT	29315	19600	20400	21000	23700
Auto, 6-Spd Tiptronic	J		525	525	590	590
GTI—4-Cyl. Turbo—Equipment Schedule 6						
W.B. 101.5"; 2.0 Liter.						
Wolfsburg H'Back 2D	GD7AJ	25915	18600	18950	20700	23300
Driver's Ed H'Back 2D	GD7AJ	30515	19100	19450	21600	24500
Auto, 6-Spd Tiptronic	H		525	525	585	585
EOS—4-Cyl. Turbo—Equipment Schedule 3						
W.B. 101.5"; 2.0 Liter.						
Komfort Conv 2D	BW8AH	36060	20800	21300	22600	26000
Executive Conv 2D	FW8AH	42560	24400	25000	26100	29800
Sport Conv 2D	BW8AH	38790	22000	22600	23800	27400
JETTA—4-Cyl.—Equipment Schedule 4						
W.B. 104.4"; 2.0 Liter.						
2.0L Base Sedan 4D	1K5AJ	16515	9100	9475	10800	13050
JETTA—4-Cyl.—Equipment Schedule 6						
W.B. 104.4"; 2.0 Liter.						
2.0L S Sedan 4D	2K5AJ	18815	10050	10450	11750	14050
Manual, 5-Spd	1		(525)	(525)	(645)	(645)

2014 VOLKSWAGEN

Body Type	VIN	List	Trade-In Good	Very Good	Pvt-Party Good	Retail Excellent
JETTA—4-Cyl. Turbo—Equipment Schedule 6						
W.B. 104.4"; 1.8 Liter.						
1.8T SE Sedan 4D	D05AJ	20815	**11250**	**11700**	**13000**	**15450**
Manual, 5-Spd	B		**(525)**	**(525)**	**(635)**	**(635)**
JETTA—4-Cyl. Turbo—Equipment Schedule 6						
W.B. 104.4"; 1.8 Liter.						
1.8T SEL Sedan 4D	L05AJ	26410	**15400**	**16050**	**17050**	**19650**
2.0T GLI Ed 30 Sed 4D	4S5AJ	29375	**18000**	**18700**	**19500**	**22300**
JETTA—4-Cyl. Turbo—Equipment Schedule 6						
W.B. 2.0 Liter.						
2.0T GLI Sedan 4D	4S5AJ	26175	**15400**	**16050**	**16950**	**19550**
2.0T GLI Autobahn 4D	4S5AJ	28415	**17200**	**17850**	**18700**	**21400**
Manual, 6-Spd	5		**(525)**	**(525)**	**(605)**	**(605)**
JETTA—4-Cyl. Turbo Diesel—Equipment Schedule 6						
W.B. 104.4"; 2.0 Liter.						
2.0L TDI Value Ed 4D	LL5AJ	23215	**15050**	**15650**	**16700**	**19350**
JETTA—4-Cyl. Turbo Diesel—Equipment Schedule 6						
W.B. 104.4"; 2.0 Liter.						
2.0L TDI Sedan 4D	LL5AJ	25115	**16350**	**17000**	**18000**	**20800**
Manual, 6-Spd	3		**(525)**	**(525)**	**(605)**	**(605)**
JETTA—4-Cyl. Turbo Hybrid—Equipment Schedule 6						
W.B. 104.4"; 2.0 Liter.						
Sedan 4D	635AJ	26380	**16100**	**16750**	**17800**	**20600**
SE Sedan 4D	635AJ	28080	**16300**	**16950**	**18000**	**20800**
SEL Sedan 4D	635AJ	30665	**17650**	**18350**	**19300**	**22300**
SEL Premium Sedan 4D	635AJ	32265	**19150**	**19900**	**20700**	**23800**
JETTA SPORTWAGEN—5-Cyl.—Equipment Schedule 6						
W.B. 101.5"; 2.5 Liter.						
2.5L S SportWagen 4D	PX7AJ	22715	**12800**	**13300**	**14400**	**16850**
2.5L SE SportWagen 4D	PX7AJ	25415	**14000**	**14550**	**15650**	**18200**
Manual, 5-Spd	K		**(525)**	**(525)**	**(620)**	**(620)**
JETTA SPORTWAGEN—4-Cyl. Turbo Diesel—Equipment Sch 6						
W.B. 101.5"; 2.0 Liter.						
2.0L TDI SportWagen	PL7AJ	28170	**18900**	**19650**	**20500**	**23400**
Manual, 6-Spd	M		**(525)**	**(525)**	**(595)**	**(595)**
PASSAT—4-Cyl. Turbo—Equipment Schedule 4						
W.B. 110.4"; 1.8 Liter.						
1.8T S Sedan 4D	AS7A3	22915	**12450**	**12650**	**14400**	**16800**
1.8T Wolfsburg Ed 4D	AS7A3	24815	**13300**	**13500**	**15350**	**17800**
1.8T SE Sedan 4D	BS7A3	26695	**15100**	**15300**	**17250**	**20000**
1.8T Sport Sedan 4D	BS7A3	28495	**15450**	**15700**	**17550**	**20200**
1.8T SEL Premium Sed	CS7A3	32115	**18100**	**18350**	**20200**	**23200**
PASSAT—5-Cyl.—Equipment Schedule 4						
W.B. 110.4"; 2.5 Liter.						
2.5L S Sedan 4D	AH7A3	22765	**11450**	**11650**	**13450**	**15700**
2.5L Wolfsburg Ed Sed	AH7A3	24315	**12950**	**13150**	**15000**	**17350**
2.5L SE Sedan 4D	BH7A3	25865	**13450**	**13650**	**15550**	**18050**
PASSAT—4-Cyl. Turbo Diesel—Equipment Schedule 4						
W.B. 110.4"; 2.0 Liter.						
TDI SE Sedan 4D	BN7A3	29495	**17850**	**18100**	**20000**	**23000**
TDI SEL Premium 4D	CN7A3	34215	**19350**	**19650**	**21500**	**24500**
PASSAT—V6—Equipment Schedule 4						
W.B. 110.4"; 3.6 Liter.						
SE Sedan 4D	BM7A3	30485	**15950**	**16200**	**18200**	**21000**
SEL Premium Sed 4D	CM7A3	35085	**18400**	**18700**	**20500**	**23500**
CC—4-Cyl. Turbo—Equipment Schedule 4						
W.B. 106.7"; 2.0 Liter.						
2.0T Sport Sedan 4D	BN7AN	34460	**18750**	**19100**	**21100**	**24300**
2.0T R-Line Sed 4D	BN7AN	35695	**19100**	**19450**	**21500**	**24700**
2.0T Executive Sedan	RN7AN	37860	**20400**	**20800**	**22800**	**26200**
CC 4MOTION AWD—V6—Equipment Schedule 4						
W.B. 106.7"; 3.6 Liter.						
3.6 VR6 Exec Sedan	GU7AN	43310	**24600**	**25100**	**26900**	**30400**

VOLVO

2000 VOLVO — YV1(VS252)-Y-#

40 SERIES—4-Cyl. Turbo—Equipment Schedule 3						
W.B. 100.3"; 1.9 Liter.						
S40 Sedan 4D	VS252	23475	**675**	**775**	**1475**	**2725**
V40 Wagon 4D	VW252	24475	**1225**	**1400**	**1900**	**3200**

2000 VOLVO

Body	Type	VIN	List	Trade-In Good	Very Good	Pvt-Party Good	Retail Excellent
70 SERIES—5-Cyl.—Equipment Schedule 3						
W.B. 104.9"; 2.4 Liter.						
S70 Sedan 4D		LS61J	29075	**725**	**850**	**1425**	**2575**
S70 SE Sedan 4D		LS61J	30075	**625**	**750**	**1325**	**2475**
V70 Wagon 4D		LW61J	30375	**750**	**900**	**1450**	**2650**
V70 SE Wagon 4D		LW61J	31575	**925**	**1075**	**1650**	**2975**
Manual, 5-Spd.			4	**(125)**	**(125)**	**(165)**	**(165)**
70 SERIES—5-Cyl. Turbo—Equipment Schedule 1						
W.B. 104.5", 104.9" (C70, S70 & V70 ex. AWD); 2.3 Liter, 2.4 Liter.						
C70 LT Coupe 2D		NK56D	36475	**800**	**1000**	**1600**	**3050**
C70 LT Convertible 2D		NC56D	45675	**700**	**875**	**1525**	**2950**
C70 HT Coupe 2D		NK53D	40575	**1325**	**1650**	**2025**	**3600**
C70 HT Conv 2D		NC53D	47075	**1350**	**1675**	**2050**	**3625**
S70 GLT Sedan 4D		LS56D	34675	**1375**	**1600**	**2225**	**3950**
S70 GLT SE Sedan 4D		LS56D	33075	**1625**	**1900**	**2500**	**4400**
V70 GLT Wagon 4D		LW56D	35975	**1550**	**1800**	**2425**	**4275**
S70 T-5 Sedan 4D		LS53D	37275	**1575**	**1850**	**2475**	**4375**
S70 AWD Sedan 4D		LT56D	36575	**1925**	**2225**	**2950**	**5150**
V70 XC AWD Wag 4D		LZ56D	39075	**1950**	**2275**	**3000**	**5250**
V70 XC AWD SE Wag		LZ56D	37575	**1800**	**2100**	**2825**	**4975**
V70 R AWD Wagon 4D		LV60D	42075	**2725**	**3150**	**3900**	**6775**
80 SERIES—6-Cyl.—Equipment Schedule 1						
W.B. 109.9"; 2.9 Liter.						
S80 2.9 Sedan 4D		TS94D	37775	**1050**	**1250**	**1775**	**3150**
80 SERIES—6-Cyl. Turbo—Equipment Schedule 1						
W.B. 109.9"; 2.8 Liter.						
S80 T6 Sedan 4D		TS90D	42275	**1725**	**2075**	**2700**	**4800**

2001 VOLVO — YV1(VS295)-1-#

Body	Type	VIN	List	Trade-In Good	Very Good	Pvt-Party Good	Retail Excellent
40 SERIES—4-Cyl. Turbo—Equipment Schedule 3						
W.B. 100.9"; 1.9 Liter.						
S40 Sedan 4D		VS295	24075	**775**	**900**	**1625**	**2975**
S40 SE Sedan 4D		VS295	28025	**1025**	**1175**	**1800**	**3150**
V40 Wagon 4D		VW295	25075	**1375**	**1575**	**2125**	**3525**
V40 SE Wagon 4D		VW295	29025	**1425**	**1625**	**2425**	**4225**
60 SERIES—5-Cyl.—Equipment Schedule 3						
W.B. 106.9"; 2.4 Liter.						
S60 2.4 Sedan 4D		RS61N	27075	**400**	**500**	**1100**	**2150**
60 SERIES—5-Cyl. Turbo—Equipment Schedule 3						
W.B. 106.9"; 2.3 Liter, 2.4 Liter.						
S60 2.4T Sedan 4D		RS58N	30375	**625**	**750**	**1375**	**2625**
S60 T5 Sedan 4D		RS53N	33675	**1025**	**1225**	**1925**	**3575**
70 SERIES—5-Cyl.—Equipment Schedule 3						
W.B. 108.5"; 2.4 Liter.						
V70 Wagon 4D		SW61N	31075	**775**	**925**	**1500**	**2725**
70 SERIES—5-Cyl. Turbo—Equipment Schedule 1						
W.B. 104.9", 108.5" (V70 ex XC), 108.8" (XC); 2.3 Liter, 2.4 Liter.						
C70 LT Convertible 2D		NC56D	44075	**725**	**900**	**1600**	**3125**
C70 HT Coupe 2D		NK53D	38475	**1400**	**1725**	**2125**	**3800**
C70 HT Conv 2D		NC53D	47075	**1350**	**1675**	**2175**	**3850**
V70 2.4T Wagon 4D		SW58D	35375	**1625**	**1875**	**2425**	**4150**
V70 T5 Wagon 4D		SW53D	36675	**1675**	**1950**	**2675**	**4700**
V70 XC AWD Wag 4D		SZ58D	37975	**2050**	**2375**	**3100**	**5375**
80 SERIES—6-Cyl.—Equipment Schedule 1						
W.B. 109.9"; 2.9 Liter.						
S80 2.9 Sedan 4D		TS94D	38675	**1050**	**1275**	**1875**	**3425**
80 SERIES—6-Cyl. Turbo—Equipment Schedule 1						
W.B. 109.9"; 2.8 Liter.						
S80 T6A Sedan 4D		TS90D	42675	**1925**	**2250**	**2825**	**4875**
S80 T6 Executive 4D		TS90D	48075	**2075**	**2450**	**3050**	**5250**

2002 VOLVO — YV1(VS295)-2-#

Body	Type	VIN	List	Trade-In Good	Very Good	Pvt-Party Good	Retail Excellent
40 SERIES—4-Cyl. Turbo—Equipment Schedule 3						
W.B. 100.9"; 1.9 Liter.						
S40 Sedan 4D		VS295	24525	**775**	**900**	**1725**	**3225**
V40 Wagon 4D		VW295	25525	**1525**	**1725**	**2275**	**3700**
60 SERIES—5-Cyl.—Equipment Schedule 3						
W.B. 106.9"; 2.4 Liter.						
S60 2.4 Sedan 4D		RS61N	27750	**800**	**950**	**1550**	**2825**
60 SERIES—5-Cyl. Turbo—Equipment Schedule 3						
W.B. 106.9"; 2.3 Liter, 2.4 Liter.						
S60 2.4T Sedan 4D		RS58D	32250	**1125**	**1325**	**1950**	**3550**

1015

Body Type	VIN	List	Trade-In Good	Very Good	Pvt-Party Good	Retail Excellent
S60 T5 Sedan 4D	RS53D	35850	**1575**	**1850**	**2400**	**4175**
S60 2.4T AWD Sed 4D	RH58D	34000	**1550**	**1825**	**2450**	**4350**
70 SERIES—5-Cyl.—Equipment Schedule 1						
W.B. 108.5"; 2.4 Liter.						
V70 Wagon 4D	SW61R	31650	**825**	**950**	**1550**	**2800**
70 SERIES—5-Cyl. Turbo—Equipment Schedule 1						
W.B. 104.9", 108.5" (V70 ex XC), 108.8" (XC); 2.3 Liter, 2.4 Liter.						
C70 LT Convertible 2D	NC56D	44750	**775**	**975**	**1800**	**3525**
C70 HT Coupe 2D	NK53D	38150	**1400**	**1725**	**2350**	**4225**
C70 HT Convertible	NC53D	46750	**1425**	**1750**	**2375**	**4225**
V70 2.4T Wagon 4D	SW58D	36150	**1775**	**2050**	**2700**	**4575**
V70 2.4T AWD Wag 4D	SJ58D	37900	**2125**	**2450**	**3100**	**5300**
V70 T5 Wagon 4D	SW53D	38350	**1900**	**2200**	**2850**	**4875**
V70 XC AWD Wag 4D	SZ58D	38425	**2225**	**2550**	**3225**	**5475**
80 SERIES—6-Cyl.—Equipment Schedule 1						
W.B. 109.9"; 2.9 Liter.						
S80 2.9 Sedan 4D	TS94D	38775	**1575**	**1875**	**2375**	**4000**
80 SERIES—6-Cyl. Turbo—Equipment Schedule 1						
W.B. 109.9"; 2.9 Liter.						
S80 T6 Sedan 4D	TS90D	42775	**2550**	**2975**	**3375**	**5575**
S80 T6 Executive 4D	TS90D	50575	**2825**	**3300**	**3675**	**6075**

2003 VOLVO — YV1(VS275)-3-#

Body Type	VIN	List	Trade-In Good	Very Good	Pvt-Party Good	Retail Excellent
40 SERIES—4-Cyl. Turbo—Equipment Schedule 3						
W.B. 100.9"; 1.9 Liter.						
S40 Sedan 4D	VS275	24560	**1000**	**1150**	**1875**	**3300**
V40 Wagon 4D	VW275	25560	**1725**	**1950**	**2600**	**4300**
60 SERIES—5-Cyl.—Equipment Schedule 3						
W.B. 107.0"; 2.4 Liter.						
S60 2.4 Sedan 4D	RS61T	28230	**875**	**1025**	**1625**	**2900**
60 SERIES—5-Cyl. Turbo—Equipment Schedule 3						
W.B. 107.0"; 2.3 Liter, 2.4 Liter, 2.5 Liter.						
S60 2.4T Sedan 4D	RS58D	31085	**1400**	**1625**	**2200**	**3800**
S60 2.5T AWD Sed 4D	RH59H	32835	**1725**	**2025**	**2650**	**4525**
S60 T5 Sedan 4D	RS53D	34685	**1700**	**2000**	**2600**	**4400**
70 SERIES—5-Cyl.—Equipment Schedule 3						
W.B. 108.5"; 2.4 Liter.						
V70 Wagon 4D	SW61T	29530	**1000**	**1150**	**1675**	**2900**
70 SERIES—5-Cyl. Turbo—Equipment Schedule 3						
W.B. 104.9", 108.5" (V70), 108.8" (XC70); 2.3 Liter, 2.4 Liter, 2.5 Liter.						
C70 LT Convertible 2D	NC63D	44785	**1125**	**1375**	**2200**	**4175**
C70 HT Conv 2D	NC62D	47785	**1850**	**2225**	**2700**	**4625**
V70 2.4T Wagon 4D	SW58D	31530	**2000**	**2300**	**2950**	**4925**
V70 2.5T AWD Wag 4D	SJ59H	33280	**2500**	**2850**	**3425**	**5625**
V70 T5 Wagon 4D	SW53D	35730	**2025**	**2325**	**2975**	**4975**
XC70 AWD Wagon 4D	SZ59H	34530	**2725**	**3100**	**3625**	**5900**
80 SERIES—6-Cyl.—Equipment Schedule 1						
W.B. 109.9"; 2.9 Liter.						
S80 2.9 Sedan 4D	TS92D	39110	**1850**	**2150**	**2650**	**4450**
80 SERIES—6-Cyl. Turbo—Equipment Schedule 1						
W.B. 109.9"; 2.9 Liter.						
S80 T6 Sedan 4D	TS91D	44595	**2875**	**3350**	**3725**	**6075**
S80 T6 Elite Sedan 4D	TS91Z	48880	**3175**	**3675**	**4025**	**6500**

2004 VOLVO — YV1(VS275)-4-#

Body Type	VIN	List	Trade-In Good	Very Good	Pvt-Party Good	Retail Excellent
40 SERIES—4-Cyl. Turbo—Equipment Schedule 3						
W.B. 101.0"; 1.9 Liter.						
S40 Sedan 4D	VS275	25385	**1225**	**1400**	**2225**	**3825**
S40 LSE Sedan 4D	VS275	29530	**1450**	**1625**	**2450**	**4175**
V40 Wagon 4D	VW275	26385	**2350**	**2625**	**3450**	**5700**
V40 LSE Wagon 4D	VW275	30530	**2125**	**2400**	**3250**	**5450**
40 SERIES—5-Cyl.—Equipment Schedule 3						
W.B. 103.9"; 2.4 Liter.						
S40 2.4i Sedan 4D	MS382	27170	**1950**	**2200**	**3125**	**5275**
40 SERIES—5-Cyl. Turbo—Equipment Schedule 3						
W.B. 103.0"; 2.5 Liter.						
S40 T5 Sedan 4D	MS682	29970	**2325**	**2600**	**3400**	**5575**
60 SERIES—5-Cyl.—Equipment Schedule 3						
W.B. 106.9" 2.4 Liter.						
S60 2.4 Sedan 4D	RS61T	28645	**1125**	**1325**	**1775**	**3000**

Body Type	VIN	List	Trade-In Good	Very Good	Pvt-Party Good	Retail Excellent
60 SERIES—5-Cyl. Turbo—Equipment Schedule 3						
W.B. 106.9", 107.0" (R); 2.3 Liter, 2.5 Liter.						
S60 2.5T Sedan 4D	RS55V	30295	1650	1900	2375	3925
S60 T5 Sedan 4D	RS53D	34845	1800	2100	2675	4475
S60 R AWD Sedan 4D	RH52Y	38810	3225	3725	4150	6675
AWD (2.5T)			675	675	910	910
70 SERIES—5-Cyl.—Equipment Schedule 3						
W.B. 108.5"; 2.4 Liter.						
V70 Wagon 4D	SW61T	30145	1425	1625	2125	3525
70 SERIES—5-Cyl. Turbo—Equipment Schedule 1						
W.B. 104.9", 108.5" (V70), 108.8" (XC70); 2.3L, 2.4L, 2.5L.						
C70 LT Convertible 2D	NC63D	40585	1525	1825	2725	4925
C70 HT Conv 2D	NC62D	43565	2250	2700	3175	5375
V70 2.5T Wagon 4D	SW59V	35070	2600	2925	3575	5850
V70 T5 Wagon 4D	SW53D	38145	2500	2825	3475	5675
V70 R AWD Wagon 4D	SJ52Y	40060	3900	4425	5150	8225
XC70 AWD Wagon 4D	SZ59H	38145	3250	3675	4200	6725
AWD (2.5T)			675	675	910	910
80 SERIES—6-Cyl.—Equipment Schedule 1						
W.B. 109.9"; 2.9 Liter.						
S80 2.9 Sedan 4D	TS92D	39725	2825	3250	3500	5450
80 SERIES—5-Cyl. Turbo—Equipment Schedule 1						
W.B. 109.9"; 2.5 Liter.						
S80 2.5T Sedan 4D	TR59V	38630	2600	3000	3300	5225
80 SERIES—6-Cyl. Twin Turbo—Equipment Schedule 1						
W.B. 109.9"; 2.9 Liter.						
S80 T6 Sedan 4D	TS91Z	45210	3700	4275	4375	6625
S80 T6 Premier Sed 4D	TS91Z	49200	3875	4450	4650	7125

2005 VOLVO — YV1(MS392)-5-#

Body Type	VIN	List	Good	Very Good	Good	Excellent
40 SERIES—5-Cyl.—Equipment Schedule 3						
W.B. 103.9"; 2.4 Liter.						
S40 2.4i Sedan 4D	MS392	25145	2325	2600	3550	5725
40 SERIES—5-Cyl. Turbo—Equipment Schedule 3						
W.B. 103.9"; 2.5 Liter.						
S40 T5 Sedan 4D	MS682	27945	2750	3100	4000	6225
AWD	H		550	550	720	720
50 SERIES—5-Cyl.—Equipment Schedule 3						
W.B. 103.9"; 2.4 Liter.						
V50 2.4i Sport Wagon	MW382	28640	2700	3125	3850	6100
50 SERIES—5-Cyl. Turbo—Equipment Schedule 3						
W.B. 103.9"; 2.5 Liter.						
V50 T5 Sport Wagon	MW682	29145	3825	4400	4875	7475
AWD			550	550	720	720
60 SERIES—5-Cyl.—Equipment Schedule 3						
W.B. 106.9"; 2.4 Liter.						
S60 2.4 Sedan 4D	RS612	28920	2000	2300	2950	4750
60 SERIES—5-Cyl. Turbo—Equipment Schedule 3						
W.B. 106.9"; 2.4 Liter, 2.5 Liter.						
S60 2.5T Sedan 4D	RS592	30420	2350	2725	3375	5425
S60 T5 Sedan 4D	RS547	35170	2725	3125	3875	6275
S60 R AWD Sedan 4D	RH527	39185	4050	4650	5375	8500
AWD (2.5T)			725	725	955	955
70 SERIES—5-Cyl.—Equipment Schedule 3						
W.B. 108.5"; 2.4 Liter.						
V70 Wagon 4D	SW612	30445	2900	3275	3850	5950
70 SERIES—5-Cyl. Turbo—Equipment Schedule 1						
W.B. 108.5", 108.8" (XC70); 2.4 Liter, 2.5 Liter.						
V70 2.5T Wagon 4D	SW592	36895	4500	5075	5675	8600
V70 T5 Wagon 4D	SW547	39345	4450	5025	5650	8600
V70 R AWD Wagon 4D	SJ527	40685	5925	6675	7400	11200
XC70 AWD Wagon 4D	SZ592	38145	4800	5400	5975	9075
80 SERIES—5-Cyl. Turbo—Equipment Schedule 1						
W.B. 109.9"; 2.5 Liter.						
S80 2.5T Sedan 4D	TS592	39185	3400	3900	4425	6925
AWD			600	600	810	810
80 SERIES—6-Cyl. Twin Turbo—Equipment Schedule 1						
W.B. 109.9"; 2.9 Liter.						
S80 T6 Sedan 4D	TS911	45210	4900	5600	5900	8900
S80 T6 Premier Sed 4D	TR911	49200	4925	5625	6100	9375

2006 VOLVO

Body	Type	VIN	List	Trade-In Good	Very Good	Pvt-Party Good	Retail Excellent

2006 VOLVO — YV1(MS382)-6-#

40 SERIES—5-Cyl.—Equipment Schedule 3
W.B. 103.9"; 2.4 Liter.

| S40 2.4i Sedan 4D | MS382 | 25650 | 3150 | 3525 | 4525 | 7025 |

40 SERIES—5-Cyl. Turbo—Equipment Schedule 3
W.B. 103.9"; 2.5 Liter.

| S40 T5 Sedan 4D | MS682 | 28510 | 3800 | 4225 | 5125 | 7825 |
| AWD | | H | 575 | 575 | 755 | 755 |

50 SERIES—5-Cyl.—Equipment Schedule 3
W.B. 103.9"; 2.4 Liter.

| V50 2.4i Sport Wagon | MW382 | 26900 | 3525 | 4000 | 4575 | 6925 |

50 SERIES—5-Cyl. Turbo—Equipment Schedule 3
W.B. 103.9"; 2.5 Liter.

| V50 T5 Sport Wag | MW682 | 29735 | 4475 | 5100 | 5625 | 8350 |
| AWD | | J | 575 | 575 | 755 | 755 |

60 SERIES—5-Cyl. Turbo—Equipment Schedule 3
W.B. 106.9"; 2.4 Liter, 2.5 Liter.

S60 2.5T Sedan 4D	RS592	30965	2675	3050	3700	5775
S60 T5 Sedan 4D	RS547	33940	3300	3750	4425	6950
S60 R AWD Sedan 4D	RH527	39865	4750	5375	5975	9075
AWD (2.5T)			750	750	985	985

70 SERIES—5-Cyl.—Equipment Schedule 3
W.B. 108.5"; 2.4 Liter.

| V70 2.4 Wagon 4D | SW612 | 31140 | 3600 | 4025 | 4625 | 6850 |

70 SERIES—5-Cyl. Turbo—Equipment Schedule 1
W.B. 103.9" (C70), 108.5" (V70), 108.8" (XC70); 2.5 Liter.

C70 T5 Convertible 2D	MC682	40655	5075	5925	6375	9700
V70 2.5T Wagon 4D	SW592	36445	5150	5750	6250	9175
V70 R AWD Wagon 4D	SJ527	41490	7125	7950	8525	12450
XC70 AWD Wagon 4D	SZ592	39390	5525	6175	6950	10250
XC70 Ocean Race Wag	SZ592	41430	5925	6625	7800	11900

80 SERIES—5-Cyl. Turbo—Equipment Schedule 3
W.B. 109.9"; 2.5 Liter.

| S80 2.5T Sedan 4D | TS592 | 38280 | 4300 | 4875 | 5425 | 8200 |
| AWD | | | 650 | 650 | 865 | 865 |

2007 VOLVO — YV1(MS382)-7-#

40 SERIES—5-Cyl.—Equipment Schedule 3
W.B. 103.9"; 2.4 Liter.

| S40 2.4i Sedan 4D | MS382 | 26185 | 3750 | 4150 | 5250 | 7975 |

40 SERIES—5-Cyl. Turbo—Equipment Schedule 3
W.B. 103.9"; 2.5 Liter.

| S40 T5 Sedan 4D | MS682 | 30335 | 4400 | 4875 | 5875 | 8800 |
| AWD | | H | 600 | 600 | 785 | 785 |

50 SERIES—5-Cyl.—Equipment Schedule 3
W.B. 103.9"; 2.4 Liter.

| V50 2.4i Sport Wagon | MW382 | 27385 | 4200 | 4725 | 5200 | 7600 |

50 SERIES—5-Cyl. Turbo—Equipment Schedule 3
W.B. 103.9"; 2.5 Liter.

| V50 T5 Sport Wag 4D | MW682 | 30285 | 5300 | 5975 | 6600 | 9625 |
| AWD | | J | 600 | 600 | 785 | 785 |

60 SERIES—5-Cyl. Turbo—Equipment Schedule 3
W.B. 106.9"; 2.4 Liter, 2.5 Liter.

S60 2.5T Sedan 4D	RS592	31580	3550	4000	4600	6775
S60 T5 Sedan 4D	RS547	34680	4225	4750	5400	8025
S60 R AWD Sedan 4D	RH527	40930	5525	6225	6850	10050
AWD (2.5T)			750	750	995	995

70 SERIES—5-Cyl.—Equipment Schedule 3
W.B. 108.5"; 2.4 Liter.

| V70 2.4 Wagon 4D | SW612 | 31740 | 4475 | 4950 | 5475 | 7775 |

70 SERIES—5-Cyl. Turbo—Equipment Schedule 1
W.B. 103.9" (C70), 108.5" (V70), 108.8" (XC70); 2.5 Liter.

C70 T5 Convertible 2D	MC682	41035	6075	7000	7425	10850
V70 2.5T Wagon 4D	SW592	37120	6625	7300	7875	11100
V70 R AWD Wagon 4D	SJ527	42885	8575	9450	10000	14050
XC70 AWD Wagon 4D	SZ592	40110	6425	7075	7825	11200

80 SERIES—6-Cyl.—Equipment Schedule 1
W.B. 111.6"; 3.2 Liter.

S80 Sedan 4D	AS982	39400	5325	5950	6400	9350
Sport Pkg			275	275	355	355
AWD			700	700	920	920

Body Type	VIN	List	Trade-In Good	Very Good	Pvt-Party Good	Retail Excellent
2008 VOLVO — YV1(MK672)-8-#						
30 SERIES—5-Cyl. Turbo—Equipment Schedule 3						
W.B. 103.9"; 2.5 Liter.						
C30 T5 1.0 H'Back 2D	MK672	23695	5675	6250	6600	8850
C30 T5 2.0 H'Back 2D	MK672	26445	7750	8500	8550	11200
C30 T5 2.0 R-Design	MK672	26445	7800	8575	8550	11150
40 SERIES—5-Cyl.—Equipment Schedule 3						
W.B. 103.9"; 2.4 Liter.						
S40 2.4i Sedan 4D	MS382	26360	4550	5000	6225	8975
40 SERIES—5-Cyl. Turbo—Equipment Schedule 3						
W.B. 103.9"; 2.5 Liter.						
S40 T5 Sedan 4D	MS672	29260	5325	5875	7000	10000
AWD			625	625	845	845
50 SERIES—5-Cyl.—Equipment Schedule 3						
W.B. 103.9"; 2.4 Liter.						
V50 2.4i Sport Wagon	MW382	27560	4900	5400	6400	9175
50 SERIES—5-Cyl. Turbo—Equipment Schedule 3						
W.B. 103.9"; 2.5 Liter.						
V50 T5 Sport Wag 4D	MW672	30460	7550	8300	8975	12400
AWD			625	625	845	845
60 SERIES—5-Cyl. Turbo—Equipment Schedule 3						
W.B. 106.9"; 2.4 Liter, 2.5 Liter.						
S60 2.5T Sedan 4D	RS592	31630	4800	5300	5975	8400
S60 T5 Sedan 4D	RS547	34730	5400	5950	6700	9375
AWD			800	800	1055	1055
70 SERIES—5-Cyl. Turbo—Equipment Schedule 1						
W.B. 103.9"; 2.5 Liter.						
C70 T5 Convertible 2D	MC672	41235	7775	8650	9000	12300
70 SERIES—6-Cyl.—Equipment Schedule 3						
W.B. 110.9"; 3.2 Liter.						
V70 3.2 Wagon 4D	SW612	33210	6850	7400	8075	10650
Adaptive Cruise Control			375	375	450	450
70 SERIES AWD—6-Cyl.—Equipment Schedule 1						
W.B. 110.8"; 3.2 Liter.						
XC70 3.2 AWD Wagon	BZ982	37520	9000	9700	10300	13550
Adaptive Cruise Control			375	375	455	455
80 SERIES—6-Cyl.—Equipment Schedule 3						
W.B. 111.6"; 3.2 Liter.						
S80 Sedan 4D	AS982	39450	6025	6625	7025	9475
Adaptive Cruise Control			375	375	475	475
Sport Pkg			275	275	360	360
AWD			725	725	950	950
V8, 4.4 Liter			2925	2925	3795	3795
80 SERIES AWD—6-Cyl. Turbo—Equipment Schedule 1						
W.B. 111.6"; 3.0 Liter.						
S80 T6 Sedan 4D	AH992	42790	8000	8800	9025	12050
Adaptive Cruise Control			375	375	470	470
Sport Pkg			275	275	360	360
2009 VOLVO — YV1(MK672)-9-#						
30 SERIES—5-Cyl. Turbo—Equipment Schedule 3						
W.B. 103.9"; 2.5 Liter.						
C30 T5 H'Back 2D	MK672	24625	7100	7675	8350	10950
C30 T5 R-Design 2D	MK672	26775	8250	8900	9625	12650
40 SERIES—5-Cyl.—Equipment Schedule 3						
W.B. 103.9"; 2.4 Liter.						
S40 2.4i Sedan 4D	MS382	29375	6825	7425	8150	10700
40 SERIES—5-Cyl. Turbo—Equipment Schedule 3						
W.B. 103.9"; 2.5 Liter.						
S40 T5 R-Design Sedan	MS672	33175	7625	8300	9125	12050
AWD	H		675	675	860	860
50 SERIES—5-Cyl.—Equipment Schedule 3						
W.B. 103.9"; 2.4 Liter.						
V50 2.4i Sport Wagon	MW382	30595	6950	7525	8425	11300
50 SERIES AWD—5-Cyl. Turbo—Equipment Schedule 3						
W.B. 103.9"; 2.5 Liter.						
V50 T5 Sport Wagon	MJ672	36295	10200	11050	11700	15250
60 SERIES—5-Cyl. Turbo—Equipment Schedule 3						
W.B. 106.9"; 2.4 Liter, 2.5 Liter.						
S60 2.5T SE Sed 4D	RS592	31775	6050	6550	7350	9825
S60 2.5T Sedan 4D	RS592	33625	6650	7200	7950	10600

Body Type	VIN	List	Trade-In Good	Very Good	Pvt-Party Good	Retail Excellent
S60 T5 Sedan 4D	RS547	37225	7500	8100	8925	11900
AWD			850	850	1130	1130

70 SERIES—5-Cyl. Turbo—Equipment Schedule 1
W.B. 103.9"; 2.5 Liter.

Body Type	VIN	List	Good	Very Good	Good	Excellent
C70 T5 Convertible 2D	MC672	41845	9825	10650	11050	14250

70 SERIES—6-Cyl.—Equipment Schedule 3
W.B. 110.9"; 3.2 Liter.

| V70 3.2 Wagon 4D | SW612 | 33695 | 9350 | 9900 | 10550 | 13050 |

70 SERIES AWD—6-Cyl.—Equipment Schedule 1
W.B. 110.8"; 3.0 Liter, 3.2 Liter.

| XC70 3.2 Wagon 4D | BZ982 | 38045 | 11200 | 11900 | 12650 | 15800 |
| XC70 T6 Wagon 4D | BZ992 | 40295 | 12950 | 13700 | 14450 | 17900 |

80 SERIES—6-Cyl.—Equipment Schedule 1
W.B. 111.6"; 3.2 Liter.

| S80 3.2 Sedan 4D | AS982 | 40425 | 7475 | 8100 | 8575 | 11050 |

80 SERIES—6-Cyl. Turbo—Equipment Schedule 1
W.B. 111.6"; 3.0 Liter.

| S80 T6 Sedan 4D | AH992 | 42875 | 9475 | 10250 | 10750 | 14000 |

80 SERIES AWD—V8—Equipment Schedule 1
W.B. 111.6"; 4.4 Liter.

| S80 Sedan 4D | AH852 | 52675 | 13750 | 14850 | 15150 | 19450 |

2010 VOLVO — YV(1or4)(672MK)-A-#

30 SERIES—5-Cyl. Turbo—Equipment Schedule 3
W.B. 103.9"; 2.5 Liter.

| C30 T5 H'Back 2D | 672MK | 24950 | 8575 | 9150 | 10100 | 13000 |
| C30 T5 R-Design 2D | 672MK | 27150 | 10050 | 10700 | 11650 | 14950 |

40 SERIES—5-Cyl. Turbo—Equipment Schedule 3
W.B. 103.9"; 2.4 Liter.

| S40 2.4i Sedan 4D | 382MS | 28300 | 8875 | 9575 | 10200 | 12800 |

40 SERIES—5-Cyl. Turbo—Equipment Schedule 3
W.B. 103.9"; 2.5 Liter.

| S40 T5 R-Design 4D | 672MS | 32000 | 9525 | 10300 | 10900 | 13750 |
| AWD | H | | 700 | 700 | 830 | 830 |

50 SERIES—5-Cyl. Turbo—Equipment Schedule 3
W.B. 103.9"; 2.4 Liter.

| V50 2.4i Sport Wagon | 382MW | 29550 | 8950 | 9525 | 10650 | 13850 |

50 SERIES AWD—5-Cyl. Turbo—Equipment Schedule 3
W.B. 103.9"; 2.5 Liter.

| V50 T5 R-Design Wag | 672MJ | 33900 | 12450 | 13250 | 14650 | 19000 |

70 SERIES—5-Cyl. Turbo—Equipment Schedule 1
W.B. 103.9"; 2.5 Liter.

| C70 T5 Convertible 2D | 672MC | 42100 | 12300 | 13100 | 13400 | 16200 |

70 SERIES—6-Cyl.—Equipment Schedule 3
W.B. 110.8"; 3.0 Liter, 3.2 Liter.

| V70 3.2 Wagon 4D | 982BW | 34400 | 12750 | 13350 | 14200 | 16950 |
| V70 R-Design Wagon | 960BW | 38850 | 16400 | 17100 | 18100 | 21600 |

70 SERIES AWD—6-Cyl.—Equipment Schedule 1
W.B. 110.8"; 3.0 Liter, 3.2 Liter.

| XC70 3.2 Wagon 4D | 962BZ | 38800 | 14500 | 15150 | 16200 | 19500 |
| XC70 T6 Wagon 4D | 992BZ | 43650 | 16900 | 17650 | 18600 | 22200 |

80 SERIES—6-Cyl.—Equipment Schedule 1
W.B. 111.6"; 3.2 Liter.

| S80 Sedan 4D | 960AS | 40050 | 10000 | 10650 | 11300 | 14150 |

80 SERIES AWD—6-Cyl. Turbo—Equipment Schedule 1
W.B. 111.6"; 3.0 Liter.

| S80 T6 Sedan 4D | 992AH | 43800 | 12000 | 12750 | 13400 | 16750 |

80 SERIES AWD—V8—Equipment Schedule 1
W.B. 111.6"; 4.4 Liter.

| S80 Sedan 4D | 852AH | 51800 | 16300 | 17350 | 17700 | 21800 |

2011 VOLVO — YV(1or4)(672MK)-B-#

30 SERIES—5-Cyl. Turbo—Equipment Schedule 3
W.B. 103.9"; 2.5 Liter.

| C30 T5 H'Back 2D | 672MK | 25450 | 11250 | 11850 | 12850 | 15900 |
| C30 R-Design 2D | 672MK | 27800 | 12650 | 13300 | 14300 | 17600 |

40 SERIES—5-Cyl. Turbo—Equipment Schedule 3
W.B. 103.9"; 2.5 Liter.

| S40 T5 Sedan 4D | 672MS | 28600 | 10750 | 11550 | 12300 | 15250 |
| S40 T5 R-Design 4D | 672MS | 32000 | 11900 | 12800 | 13300 | 16200 |

50 SERIES—5-Cyl. Turbo—Equipment Schedule 3
W.B. 103.9"; 2.5 Liter.

Body Type	VIN	List	Trade-In Good	Trade-In Very Good	Pvt-Party Good	Retail Excellent
V50 T5 Sport Wagon	672MW	29850	12300	12950	14650	18750
V50 R-Design Wagon	672MW	33700	14450	15200	16900	21400
60 SERIES AWD—6-Cyl. Turbo—Equipment Schedule 3						
W.B. 109.3"; 3.0 Liter.						
S60 T6 Sedan 4D	902FH	38550	13650	14400	15350	18750
70 SERIES—5-Cyl. Turbo—Equipment Schedule 1						
W.B. 103.9"; 2.5 Liter.						
C70 T5 Convertible 2D	672MC	40800	15750	16500	16900	19850
70 SERIES—6-Cyl. Turbo—Equipment Schedule 1						
W.B. 110.8"; 3.2 Liter.						
XC70 3.2 Wagon 4D	952BL	32850	18350	18950	20300	23700
70 SERIES AWD—6-Cyl.—Equipment Schedule 1						
W.B. 110.8"; 3.0 Liter.						
XC70 T6 Wagon 4D	902BZ	38850	21500	22100	23400	27100
80 SERIES—6-Cyl.—Equipment Schedule 1						
W.B. 111.6"; 3.2 Liter.						
S80 Sedan 4D	952AS	37800	12700	13400	14050	17050
80 SERIES AWD—6-Cyl. Turbo—Equipment Schedule 1						
W.B. 111.6"; 3.0 Liter.						
S80 T6 Sedan 4D	902AH	41550	15900	16700	17300	20800

2012 VOLVO — YV(1or4)(672MK)–C–#

Body Type	VIN	List	Trade-In Good	Trade-In Very Good	Pvt-Party Good	Retail Excellent
30 SERIES—5-Cyl. Turbo—Equipment Schedule 3						
W.B. 103.9"; 2.5 Liter.						
C30 T5 H'Back 2D	672MK	25575	13100	13700	14900	18100
C30 R-Design 2D	672MK	27975	14400	15050	16300	19800
60 SERIES—5-Cyl. Turbo—Equipment Schedule 3						
W.B. 109.3"; 3.0 Liter.						
S60 T5 Sedan 4D	622FS	32300	12400	12950	14400	17700
60 SERIES AWD—6-Cyl. Turbo—Equipment Schedule 3						
W.B. 109.3"; 3.0 Liter.						
S60 T6 Sedan 4D	902FH	38550	17150	17900	19550	24000
S60 T6 R-Design 4D	902FH	43150	20500	21400	22800	27600
70 SERIES—5-Cyl. Turbo—Equipment Schedule 1						
W.B. 103.9"; 2.5 Liter.						
C70 T5 Convertible 2D	672MC	40825	19750	20400	20800	23600
Inscription Pkg			1000	1000	1095	1095
70 SERIES—6-Cyl.—Equipment Schedule 1						
W.B. 110.8"; 3.2 Liter.						
XC70 3.2 Wagon 4D	952BL	36375	21700	22200	23600	26600
70 SERIES AWD—6-Cyl. Turbo—Equipment Schedule 1						
W.B. 110.8"; 3.0 Liter.						
XC70 T6 Wagon 4D	902BZ	39475	24300	24800	26200	29500
80 SERIES—6-Cyl.—Equipment Schedule 1						
W.B. 111.6"; 3.2 Liter.						
S80 Sedan 4D	952AS	38425	15150	15850	16900	20300
80 SERIES AWD—6-Cyl. Turbo—Equipment Schedule 1						
W.B. 111.6"; 3.0 Liter.						
S80 T6 Sedan 4D	902AH	42175	18450	19250	20100	23900

2013 VOLVO — YV(1or4)(672MK)–D–#

Body Type	VIN	List	Trade-In Good	Trade-In Very Good	Pvt-Party Good	Retail Excellent
30 SERIES—5-Cyl. Turbo—Equipment Schedule 3						
W.B. 103.9"; 2.5 Liter.						
C30 T5 H'Back 2D	672MK	26395	17500	18150	19000	22100
C30 T5 Premier 2D	672MK	27995	19250	20000	20500	23500
C30 T5 Premier Plus	672MK	29095	19050	19800	20400	23600
C30 T5 Platinum 2D	672MK	31395	21200	22100	22400	25700
C30 T5 R-Design 2D	672MK	28745	19500	20300	20700	23800
C30 T5 R-Dsgn Prmr	672MK	30345	21200	22000	22400	25700
C30 T5 R-Dsgn Prmr +	672MK	31445	21600	22400	22700	25900
C30 T5 R Platinum	672MK	33745	22100	23000	23300	26600
S60—5-Cyl. Turbo—Equipment Schedule 3						
W.B. 109.3"; 2.5 Liter.						
T5 Sedan 4D	612FS	32645	14700	15250	16650	19950
T5 Premier Sedan	612FS	34845	15500	16100	17450	20900
T5 Premier Plus 4D	612FS	35995	15800	16450	17850	21400
T5 Platinum Sedan 4D	612FS	38695	16150	16800	18400	22200
Adaptive Cruise Control			475	475	535	535
AWD	H		1025	1025	1205	1205
S60 AWD—6-Cyl. Turbo—Equipment Schedule 3						
W.B. 109.3"; 3.0 Liter.						
T6 Sedan 4D	902FH	41345	20000	20800	22200	26400

2013 VOLVO

Body Type	VIN	List	Trade-In Good	Very Good	Pvt-Party Good	Retail Excellent
T6 Premier Plus 4D	902FH	42495	19450	20200	21800	26100
T6 Platinum Sedan	902FH	45195	21300	22100	23700	28400
T6 R-Design Sedan 4D	902FH	44795	21400	22300	23900	28800
T6 R-Design Platinum	902FH	47495	22500	23400	24800	29700
Adaptive Cruise Control			475	475	520	520
70 SERIES—5-Cyl. Turbo—Equipment Schedule 1						
W.B. 103.9"; 2.5 Liter.						
C70 T5 Convertible 2D	672MC	41885	23600	24200	24900	28200
C70 T5 Premier + Conv	672MC	43085	25200	25800	26800	30500
C70 T5 Platinum Conv	672MC	45685	25200	25900	26800	30600
70 SERIES AWD—6-Cyl.—Equipment Schedule 1						
W.B. 110.8"; 3.2 Liter.						
XC70 3.2 Wagon 4D	952BZ	36345	23800	24300	26100	29200
XC70 3.2 Premier Wagon	952BZ	39595	25200	25700	27500	30700
XC70 Premier Plus Wag	952BZ	41495	26600	27100	29100	32700
XC70 Platinum Wag 4D	952BZ	44195	27800	28300	30600	34600
Adaptive Cruise Control	L		475	475	515	515
FWD			(1200)	(1200)	(1330)	(1330)
70 SERIES AWD—6-Cyl. Turbo—Equipment Schedule 1						
W.B. 110.8"; 3.0 Liter.						
XC70 T6 Wagon 4D	902BZ	40995	27100	27600	29500	33100
XC70 T6 Premier Plus	902BZ	42995	27500	28000	30300	34200
XC70 T6 Platinum Wag	902BZ	45695	28900	29400	31700	35800
80 SERIES—6-Cyl.—Equipment Schedule 1						
W.B. 111.6"; 3.2 Liter.						
S80 Sedan 4D	952AS	39845	19700	20500	22000	26400
S80 Premier Plus Sed	952AS	40995	19800	20600	22100	26500
S80 Platinum Sed	952AS	43695	21300	22100	23500	27900
Adaptive Cruise Control			475	475	530	530
80 SERIES AWD—6-Cyl. Turbo—Equipment Schedule 1						
W.B. 111.6"; 3.0 Liter.						
S80 T6 Sedan 4D	902AH	43845	22900	23700	25000	29600
S80 T6 Premier Plus	902AH	44995	23100	24000	25500	30500
S80 T6 Platinum Sed	902AH	47695	25200	26200	27400	32400
Adaptive Cruise Control			475	475	520	520

2014 VOLVO — YV(1or4)(612FS)-E-#

Body Type	VIN	List	Trade-In Good	Very Good	Pvt-Party Good	Retail Excellent
S60—5-Cyl. Turbo—Equipment Schedule 3						
W.B. 109.3"; 2.5 Liter.						
T5 Sedan 4D	612FS	33315	17450	18150	19300	22800
T5 Premier Sedan 4D	612FS	34515	17950	18650	19850	23400
T5 Premier Plus Sedan	612FS	36465	18350	19050	20300	24000
T5 Platinum Sedan	612FS	39165	18700	19400	20800	24800
Adaptive Cruise Control			500	500	555	555
AWD	H		1225	1225	1400	1400
S60 AWD—6-Cyl. Turbo—Equipment Schedule 3						
W.B. 109.3"; 3.0 Liter.						
T6 Sedan	902FH	40165	22500	23400	24600	29000
T6 Premier Plus 4D	902FH	40815	22200	23000	24400	28900
T6 Platinum Sedan	902FH	43515	23900	24900	26300	31200
T6 R-Design Sedan	902FH	44105	24100	25000	26500	31300
T6 R-Design Platinum	902FH	46615	25000	26000	27300	32200
Adaptive Cruise Control			500	500	540	540
XC70 AWD—6-Cyl.—Equipment Schedule 1						
W.B. 110.8"; 3.2 Liter.						
3.2 Wagon 4D	952BZ	35415	25700	26100	28000	31100
3.2 Premier Wagon	952BZ	38815	27500	27900	29700	33000
3.2 Premier Plus Wag	952BZ	40365	28600	29100	31100	34700
3.2 Platinum Wagon	952BZ	42865	29300	29900	32300	36300
Adaptive Cruise Control			500	500	540	540
FWD	L		(1200)	(1200)	(1315)	(1315)
XC70 AWD—6-Cyl. Turbo—Equipment Schedule 1						
W.B. 110.8"; 3.0 Liter.						
T6 Wagon 4D	902BZ	41865	29100	29600	31600	35200
T6 Premier Plus Wag	902BZ	43865	30100	30700	32900	36900
T6 Platinum Wagon	902BZ	46565	30500	31100	33500	37600
Adaptive Cruise Control			500	500	540	540
S80—6-Cyl.—Equipment Schedule 1						
W.B. 111.6"; 3.2 Liter.						
3.2 Sedan 4D	952AS	40815	23600	24500	25500	29900
3.2 Premier Plus Sedan	952AS	42315	23700	24600	25800	30500
3.2 Platinum Sedan	952AS	45015	25100	26100	27300	32000

Body Type	VIN	List	Trade-In Good	Very Good	Pvt-Party Good	Retail Excellent
S80 AWD—6-Cyl. Turbo—Equipment Schedule 1						
W.B. 111.6"; 3.0 Liter.						
T6 Sedan 4D	902AH	44865	24800	25800	27000	31800
T6 Premier Plus Sed	902AH	46365	27000	28000	29200	34400
T6 Platinum Sedan 4D	902AH	49065	28700	29700	30800	36000

Body Type	VIN	List	Trade-In Good	Very Good	Pvt-Party Good	Retail Excellent

Truck & Van Section

ACURA

2001 ACURA — 2HN(YD182)-1-#

MDX 4WD—V6—Truck Equipment Schedule T3

Body Type	VIN	List	Good	Very Good	Good	Excellent
Sport Utility 4D	YD182	34850	2375	2750	3000	4825
Touring Spt Util 4D	YD186	37450	2875	3300	3575	5725

2002 ACURA — 2HN(YD182)-2-#

MDX 4WD—V6—Truck Equipment Schedule T3

Body Type	VIN	List	Good	Very Good	Good	Excellent
Sport Utility 4D	YD182	35180	3000	3450	3550	5525
Touring Spt Util 4D	YD186	37780	3500	4025	4150	6475

2003 ACURA — 2HN(YD182)-3-#

MDX 4WD—V6—Truck Equipment Schedule T3

Body Type	VIN	List	Good	Very Good	Good	Excellent
Sport Utility 4D	YD182	36200	3575	4075	4175	6475
Touring Spt Util 4D	YD186	38800	3875	4425	4725	7300

2004 ACURA — 2NH(YD182)-4-#

MDX 4WD—V6—Truck Equipment Schedule T3

Body Type	VIN	List	Good	Very Good	Good	Excellent
Sport Utility 4D	YD182	36945	3925	4500	4700	7200
Touring Spt Util 4D	YD186	39545	4550	5150	5425	8225

2005 ACURA — 2HN(YD182)-5-#

MDX 4WD—V6—Truck Equipment Schedule T3

Body Type	VIN	List	Good	Very Good	Good	Excellent
Sport Utility 4D	YD182	37270	5075	5775	6000	8875
Touring Spt Util 4D	YD186	40095	5625	6350	6975	10350

2006 ACURA — 2HN(YD182)-6-#

MDX 4WD—V6—Truck Equipment Schedule T3

Body Type	VIN	List	Good	Very Good	Good	Excellent
Sport Utility 4D	YD182	37740	6550	7375	7450	10550
Touring Spt Util 4D	YD186	40565	7525	8375	8675	12200

2007 ACURA — 2HN(TB182)-7-#

RDX SH-AWD—4-Cyl. Turbo—Truck Equipment Schedule T3

Body Type	VIN	List	Good	Very Good	Good	Excellent
Sport Utility 4D	TB182	33610	10050	10750	11000	13900
Technology Pkg			325	325	390	390

MDX AWD—V6 VTEC—Truck Equipment Schedule T3

Body Type	VIN	List	Good	Very Good	Good	Excellent
Sport Utility 4D	YD282	40665	11600	12900	12000	15850
Sport Pkg			325	325	395	395
Technology Pkg			800	800	940	940

2008 ACURA — 2HNor5J8(TB182)-8-#

RDX AWD—4-Cyl. Turbo—Truck Equipment Schedule T3

Body Type	VIN	List	Good	Very Good	Good	Excellent
Sport Utility 4D	TB182	33910	10900	11500	12100	14800
Technology Pkg			350	350	415	415

MDX AWD—V6 VTEC—Truck Equipment Schedule T3

Body Type	VIN	List	Good	Very Good	Good	Excellent
Sport Utility 4D	YD282	40910	12950	14200	13650	17850
Sport Pkg			350	350	420	420
Technology Pkg			850	850	1005	1005

2009 ACURA — 2HNor5J8(TB182)-9-#

RDX AWD—4-Cyl. Turbo—Truck Equipment Schedule T3

Body Type	VIN	List	Good	Very Good	Good	Excellent
Sport Utility 4D	TB182	34455	13300	13900	14800	17550
Technology Pkg			375	375	430	430

MDX AWD—V6 VTEC—Truck Equipment Schedule T3

Body Type	VIN	List	Good	Very Good	Good	Excellent
Sport Utility 4D	YD282	41550	15850	17050	16600	20700
Sport Pkg			375	375	430	430
Technology Pkg			900	900	1045	1045

2010 ACURA — 2HNor5J8(TB1H2)-A-#

RDX AWD—4-Cyl. Turbo—Truck Equipment Schedule T3

Body Type	VIN	List	Good	Very Good	Good	Excellent
Sport Utility 4D	TB1H2	35330	14800	15300	16500	19200
Technology Pkg			400	400	450	450

TRUCKS & VANS

Body Type	VIN	List	Trade-In Good	Very Good	Pvt-Party Good	Retail Excellent
FWD	2	....	(1075)	(1075)	(1240)	(1240)
MDX AWD—V6 VTEC—Truck Equipment Schedule T3						
Sport Utility 4D	YD282	43040	19300	20400	20300	24200
Advance Pkg		....	1150	1150	1305	1305
Technology Pkg		....	950	950	1080	1080
ZDX AWD—V6 VTEC—Truck Equipment Schedule T3						
Sport Utility 4D	YB1H2	46305	21300	22000	22700	25700
Advance Pkg		....	1150	1150	1255	1255
Technology Pkg		....	400	400	430	430

2011 ACURA — 2HNor5J8(TB1H2)–B–#

RDX AWD—4-Cyl. Turbo—Truck Equipment Schedule T3						
Sport Utility 4D	TB1H2	35480	17950	18400	19800	22400
Technology Pkg		....	425	425	465	465
FWD	2	....	(1075)	(1075)	(1200)	(1200)
MDX AWD—V6 VTEC—Truck Equipment Schedule T3						
Sport Utility 4D	YD2H2	43440	20800	21700	22100	25800
Advance Pkg		....	1225	1225	1365	1365
Technology Pkg		....	1000	1000	1135	1135
ZDX AWD—V6 VTEC—Truck Equipment Schedule T3						
Sport Utility 4D	YB1H2	46505	22700	23300	24200	26900
Advance Pkg		....	1225	1225	1320	1320
Technology Pkg		....	425	425	445	445

2012 ACURA — 2HNor5J8(TB2H2)–C–#

RDX—4-Cyl. Turbo—Truck Equipment Schedule T3						
Sport Utility 4D	TB2H2	33780	19150	19550	21200	23600
Technology Pkg		....	425	425	485	485
RDX SH-AWD—4-Cyl. Turbo—Truck Equipment Schedule T3						
Sport Utility 4D	TB1H2	35780	20200	20600	22300	24900
Technology Pkg		....	425	425	485	485
MDX AWD—V6 VTEC—Truck Equipment Schedule T3						
Sport Utility 4D	YD2H2	43815	23100	23800	24700	28000
Advance Pkg		....	1275	1275	1430	1430
Technology Pkg		....	1075	1075	1185	1185
ZDX AWD—V6 VTEC—Truck Equipment Schedule T3						
Sport Utility 4D	YB1H2	46905	25500	26000	27700	30900
Advance Pkg		....	1275	1275	1420	1420
Technology Pkg		....	425	425	480	480

2013 ACURA — 2HNor5J8(TB4H3)–D–#

RDX AWD—4-Cyl. Turbo—Truck Equipment Schedule T3						
Sport Utility 4D	TB4H3	36615	24000	24500	26500	29300
Technology Pkg		....	450	450	500	500
FWD	3	....	(800)	(800)	(885)	(885)
MDX AWD—V6 VTEC—Truck Equipment Schedule T3						
Sport Utility 4D	YD2H2	44175	28100	28700	29800	33100
Advance Pkg		....	1350	1350	1475	1475
Technology Pkg		....	1125	1125	1225	1225
ZDX AWD—V6 VTEC—Truck Equipment Schedule T3						
Sport Utility 4D	YB1H6	51815	28900	29500	31300	34200

2014 ACURA — 2HNor5J8(TB4H3)–E–#

RDX AWD—4-Cyl. Turbo—Truck Equipment Schedule T3						
Sport Utility 4D	TB4H3	36815	27400	27900	29800	32700
Technology Pkg		....	475	475	515	515
FWD	3	....	(800)	(800)	(875)	(875)
MDX—V6 i-VTEC—Truck Equipment Schedule T3						
Sport Utility 4D	YD4H2	43210	35100	35700	36900	40200
Adaptive Cruise Control		....	500	500	530	530
Advance Pkg		....	1425	1425	1520	1520
Technology Pkg		....	1175	1175	1265	1265
MDX SH-AWD—V6 i-VTEC—Truck Equipment Schedule T3						
Sport Utility 4D	YD4H2	45210	36200	36900	38000	41400
Adaptive Cruise Control		....	500	500	525	525
Advance Pkg		....	1425	1425	1515	1515
Technology Pkg		....	1175	1175	1260	1260

Body Type	VIN	List	Trade-In Good	Very Good	Pvt-Party Good	Retail Excellent

TRUCKS & VANS

AUDI

2009 AUDI — WA1(KF98R)-9-#

Q5 QUATTRO AWD—V6—Truck Equipment Schedule T3

Body Type	VIN	List	Good	Very Good	Good	Excellent
3.2 Premium Utility	KF98R	38025	16200	17150	17200	20500
S-Line Pkg	E		675	675	750	750

Q7 QUATTRO AWD—V6—Truck Equipment Schedule T3

3.6 Sport Utility 4D	AY74L	44325	15150	15800	16850	19650
3.6 Premium Utility	AY74L	47725	17150	17900	19000	22200
Premium Plus Pkg			750	750	865	865
Prestige Pkg			1475	1475	1710	1710

Q7 QUATTRO AWD—V6 Turbo Diesel—Truck Equipment Sch T3

3.0 TDI Sport Util	AM74L	51725	21500	22400	23400	27200
Premium Plus Pkg			750	750	855	855
Prestige Pkg			1475	1475	1700	1700

Q7 QUATTRO AWD—V8—Truck Equipment Schedule T3

4.2 Premium Utility	BV74L	60045	20600	21400	22500	26200
Bang & Olufsen Sound			2325	2325	2675	2675
S-Line Pkg	E		675	675	765	765
Adaptive Cruise Control			375	375	430	430

2010 AUDI — WA1(CKAFP)-A-#

Q5 QUATTRO AWD—V6—Truck Equipment Schedule T3

3.2 Premium Util	CKAFP	38175	19500	20300	20800	24300
Bang & Olufsen Sound			350	350	390	390
Premium Plus Pkg			775	775	890	890
S-Line Pkg	M,W		775	775	870	870

Q7 QUATTRO AWD—V6—Truck Equipment Schedule T3

3.6 Premium Util	CYAFE	47725	23400	24200	25300	28900
Premium Plus Pkg			775	775	900	900
Prestige Pkg			1525	1525	1735	1735
S-Line Pkg	M,W		775	775	880	880

Q7 QUATTRO AWD—V6 Turbo Diesel—Truck Equipment Schedule T3

3.0 TDI Premium	CMAFE	51725	26200	27200	28400	32400
Bang & Olufsen Sound			2450	2450	2805	2805
Premium Plus Pkg			775	775	900	900
Prestige Pkg			1525	1525	1735	1735
S-Line Pkg	M,W		775	775	875	875

Q7 QUATTRO AWD—V8—Truck Equipment Schedule T3

4.2 Premium Util	DVAFE	61825	26600	27700	28700	32800
Bang & Olufsen Sound			2450	2450	2810	2810
S-Line Pkg	D		775	775	880	880
Adaptive Cruise Control			400	400	450	450

2011 AUDI — WA1(CFBFP)-B-#

Q5 QUATTRO AWD—4-Cyl. Turbo—Truck Equipment Schedule T3

2.0T Premium Util	CFBFP	36075	20800	21400	22400	25700
Bang & Olufsen Sound			350	350	395	395
Premium Plus Pkg			825	825	930	930

Q5 QUATTRO AWD—V6—Truck Equipment Schedule T3

3.2 Premium Util	CKBFP	43375	24700	25500	26600	30800
Bang & Olufsen Sound			350	350	400	400
Prestige Pkg			1550	1550	1755	1755
S-Line Pkg			875	875	985	985

Q7 QUATTRO AWD—V6 Turbo Diesel—Truck Equipment Schedule T3

3.0 TDI Premium	CMAFE	51775	30300	31300	32800	37000
Bang & Olufsen Sound			2575	2575	2950	2950
Premium Plus Pkg			825	825	945	945

Q7 QUATTRO AWD—V6 Supercharged—Truck Equipment Schedule T3

3.0 Premium Util	CGAFE	46575	26100	27000	28400	32000
3.0 Prestige Utility	VGAFE	59775	30700	31700	33300	37700
Bang & Olufsen Sound			2575	2575	2970	2970
Premium Plus Pkg			825	825	950	950
S-Line Pkg			875	875	1000	1000

2012 AUDI — WA1(CFAFP)-C-#

Q5 QUATTRO AWD—4-Cyl. Turbo—Truck Equipment Schedule T3

| 2.0T Premium SUV | CFAFP | 36475 | 23800 | 24400 | 25600 | 28900 |
| Bang & Olufsen Sound | | | 350 | 350 | 395 | 395 |

2012 AUDI

Body Type	VIN	List	Trade-In Good	Very Good	Pvt-Party Good	Retail Excellent
Premium Plus Pkg			875	875	955	955
Q5 QUATTRO AWD—V6—Truck Equipment Schedule T3						
3.2 Premium Plus	DKAFP	43875	27200	27900	29200	33000
Bang & Olufsen Sound			350	350	395	395
Prestige Pkg			1575	1575	1750	1750
S-Line Pkg			975	975	1070	1070
Q7 QUATTRO AWD—V6 Turbo Diesel—Truck Equipment Schedule T3						
3.0 TDI Premium	CMAFE	52325	33600	34600	36000	40200
Bang & Olufsen Sound			2700	2700	3060	3060
Premium Plus Pkg			875	875	980	980
Prestige Pkg			1575	1575	1790	1790
S-Line Pkg			975	975	1095	1095
Q7 QUATTRO AWD—V6 Supercharged—Truck Equipment Schedule T3						
3.0 Premium Util	AGAFE	47125	29400	30400	31800	35500
3.0T S-Line Prstg	DGAFE	60825	34100	35200	36900	41400
Bang & Olufsen Sound			2700	2700	3090	3090
Premium Plus Pkg			875	875	980	980
S-Line Pkg			975	975	1105	1105

2013 AUDI — WA1(CFAFP)-D-#

Body Type	VIN	List	Trade-In Good	Very Good	Pvt-Party Good	Retail Excellent
Q5 QUATTRO AWD—4-Cyl. Turbo—Truck Equipment Schedule T3						
2.0T Premium SUV	CFAFP	36795	25300	25900	27200	30400
2.0T Premium Plus	LFAFP	41095	28000	28600	29900	33300
Bang & Olufsen Sound			375	375	400	400
Q5 QUATTRO AWD—4-Cyl. Turbo Hybrid—Truck Equipment Schedule T3						
Prestige SUV 4D	C8AFP	51795	22300	23000	34200	37900
Q5 QUATTRO AWD—V6 Turbo—Truck Equipment Schedule T3						
3.0T Premium Plus	DGAFP	44795	31500	32100	33400	36900
3.0T Prestige SUV	WGAFP	52295	33400	34100	35300	39100
Bang & Olufsen Sound			375	375	400	400
S-Line Pkg			1000	1000	1085	1085
Q7 QUATTRO AWD—V6 Supercharged—Truck Equipment Schedule T3						
3.0T Premium Util	CGAFE	47695	32600	33600	35500	39800
3.0T Premium +	LGAFE	54045	34500	35500	37500	42100
3.0TSLinePrestige	DGAFE	61445	39300	40400	42300	47200
Bang & Olufsen Sound			2825	2825	3235	3235
S-Line Pkg			1000	1000	1140	1140
Q7 QUATTRO AWD—V6 Turbo Diesel—Truck Equipment Schedule T3						
3.0 TDI Premium	CMAFE	52895	35800	36800	38700	43300
3.0 TDI Prem Plus	LMAFE	59245	37900	39000	41000	45800
3.0 TDI Prestige	VMAFE	65445	42800	44000	45700	50800
Bang & Olufsen Sound			2825	2825	3205	3205
S-Line Pkg			1000	1000	1130	1130

2014 AUDI — WA1(CFAFP)-E-#

Body Type	VIN	List	Trade-In Good	Very Good	Pvt-Party Good	Retail Excellent
Q5 QUATTRO AWD—4-Cyl. Turbo—Truck Equipment Schedule T3						
2.0T Premium	CFAFP	38195	28700	29300	30700	34100
2.0T Premium Plus	LFAFP	42095	33200	33800	35000	38600
Bang & Olufsen Sound			375	375	400	400
Q5 QUATTRO AWD—4-Cyl. Turbo Hybrid—Truck Equipment Schedule T3						
Premium Sport Util	CCAFP	52195	37400	38200	39100	42900
Q5 QUATTRO AWD—V6 Supercharged—Truck Equipment Schedule T3						
3.0T Premium Plus	DGAFP	45295	36500	37200	38200	41900
3.0T Prestige 4D	WGAFP	52795	38400	39100	40100	43900
Bang & Olufsen Sound			375	375	395	395
S-Line Pkg			1000	1000	1070	1070
Q5 QUATTRO AWD—V6 Turbo Diesel—Truck Equipment Schedule T3						
TDI Premium Plus	CMAFP	47395	37400	38100	39100	42800
TDI Prestige 4D	VMAFP	54895	40300	41100	42400	46800
Bang & Olufsen Sound			375	375	395	395
Q7 QUATTRO AWD—V6 Supercharged—Truck Equipment Schedule T3						
3.0T Premium 4D	CGAFE	48595	36800	37900	39600	44000
3.0T Premium +	LGAFE	54595	40500	41700	43500	48300
3.0TS-Line Prstg	DGAFE	61795	45900	47300	48800	54000
Bang & Olufsen Sound			2950	2950	3320	3320
S-Line Pkg			1000	1000	1120	1120
Q7 QUATTRO AWD—V6 Turbo Diesel—Truck Equipment Schedule T3						
TDI Premium 4D	CMAFE	53795	41000	42200	43900	48600
TDI Premium +	LMAFE	59795	44600	45800	47500	52600
TDI Prestige 4D	VMAFE	65795	49200	50600	52300	57600
Bang & Olufsen Sound			2950	2950	3300	3300
Sensing Cruise Control			500	500	545	545

Body Type	VIN	List	Trade-In Good	Trade-In Very Good	Pvt-Party Good	Retail Excellent
S-Line Pkg			1000	1000	1115	1115
SQ5 QUATTRO AWD—V6 Supercharged—Truck Equipment Schedule T3						
Premium Plus 4D	CGAFP	52795	41800	43300	42900	47600
Bang & Olufsen Sound			375	375	400	400
SQ5 QUATTRO AWD—V6 Supercharged—Truck Equipment Schedule T3						
Prestige Sport Util	VGAFP	60295	45800	47500	46800	51600

BMW

2000 BMW — WBA(FB335)-Y-#

Body Type	VIN	List	Good	Very Good	Good	Excellent
X5 AWD—V8—Truck Equipment Schedule T3						
4.4i Sport Utility 4D	FB335	49970	2600	2825	3425	5050
Sport Pkg			150	150	195	195

2001 BMW — WBA(FA535)-1-#

Body Type	VIN	List	Good	Very Good	Good	Excellent
X5 AWD—6-Cyl.—Truck Equipment Schedule T3						
3.0i Sport Utility 4D	FA535	42195	2750	2975	3575	5200
Sport Pkg			150	150	205	205
X5 AWD—V8—Truck Equipment Schedule T3						
4.4i Sport Utility 4D	FB335	49970	3000	3225	3875	5650
Sport Pkg			150	150	205	205

2002 BMW — 5UX(FA535)-2-#

Body Type	VIN	List	Good	Very Good	Good	Excellent
X5 AWD—6-Cyl.—Truck Equipment Schedule T3						
3.0i Sport Util 4D	FA535	42270	3050	3275	3950	5725
Sport Pkg			175	175	220	220
X5 AWD—V8—Truck Equipment Schedule T3						
4.4i Sport Util 4D	FB335	50045	3375	3625	4300	6250
4.6is Sport Util 4D	FB935	66845	4325	4625	5550	7925
Sport Pkg			175	175	220	220

2003 BMW — 5UX(FA535)-3-#

Body Type	VIN	List	Good	Very Good	Good	Excellent
X5 AWD—6-Cyl.—Truck Equipment Schedule T3						
3.0i Sport Util 4D	FA535	42920	3475	3725	4425	6375
Sport Pkg			175	175	235	235
X5 AWD—V8—Truck Equipment Schedule T3						
4.4i Sport Util 4D	FB335	50645	3675	3925	4800	6900
4.6is Sport Util 4D	FB935	67495	5600	5975	7150	10050
Sport Pkg			175	175	235	235

2004 BMW — WBXor5UX(PA734)-4-#

Body Type	VIN	List	Good	Very Good	Good	Excellent
X3 AWD—6-Cyl.—Truck Equipment Schedule T3						
2.5i Sport Utility 4D	PA734	33740	4525	4850	5450	7425
3.0i Sport Utility 4D	PA934	38270	4775	5100	5775	7975
Sport Pkg			175	175	245	245
Premium Pkg			675	675	915	915
X5 AWD—6-Cyl.—Truck Equipment Schedule T3						
3.0i Sport Utility 4D	FA135	40995	4550	4850	5600	7775
Cold Weather Pkg			125	125	155	155
Sport Pkg			175	175	245	245
X5 AWD—V8—Truck Equipment Schedule T3						
4.4i Sport Utility 4D	FB535	52195	4650	4950	5825	8200
4.8is Sport Util 4D	FA935	70495	6300	6725	7775	10750
Cold Weather Pkg			125	125	155	155
Sport Pkg			175	175	245	245

2005 BMW — WBXor5UX(PA734)-5-#

Body Type	VIN	List	Good	Very Good	Good	Excellent
X3 AWD—6-Cyl.—Truck Equipment Schedule T3						
2.5i Sport Utility 4D	PA734	34715	4550	4875	5675	7600
3.0i Sport Utility 4D	PA934	38445	4800	5125	5975	8050
Sport Pkg			200	200	260	260
Premium Pkg			750	750	990	990
X5 AWD—6-Cyl.—Truck Equipment Schedule T3						
3.0i Sport Utility 4D	FA135	45120	5075	5425	6550	8925
Cold Weather Pkg			125	125	160	160
Sport Pkg			200	200	260	260
X5 AWD—V8—Truck Equipment Schedule T3						
4.4i Sport Utility 4D	FB535	53495	5575	5950	7150	9775
4.8is Sport Util 4D	FA935	70795	6350	6775	8100	11050

TRUCKS & VANS

Body Type	VIN	List	Trade-In Good	Trade-In Very Good	Pvt-Party Good	Retail Excellent
Cold Weather Pkg			125	125	160	160
Sport Pkg			200	200	260	260

2006 BMW — WBXor5UX(PA934)–6-#

X3 AWD—6-Cyl.—Truck Equipment Schedule T3
3.0i Sport Utility 4D	PA934	38945	6025	6400	7675	10350
Sport Pkg			200	200	265	265
Premium Pkg			800	800	1070	1070

X3 AWD—6-Cyl.—Truck Equipment Schedule T3
3.0i Sport Util 4D	FA135	45920	6200	6575	7675	10200
Cold Weather Pkg			125	125	175	175
Sport Pkg			200	200	265	265

X5 AWD—V8—Truck Equipment Schedule T3
4.4i Sport Util 4D	FB535	54295	6825	7225	8400	11200
4.8is Sport Util 4D	FA935	71795	7500	7975	9225	12300
Cold Weather Pkg			125	125	175	175
Sport Pkg			200	200	265	265

2007 BMW — WBXor5UX(PC934)–7-#

X3 AWD—6-Cyl.—Truck Equipment Schedule T3
3.0si Sport Util 4D	PC934	41145	7200	7600	8900	11650
Sport Pkg			200	200	265	265
Premium Pkg			850	850	1150	1150

X5 AWD—6-Cyl.—Truck Equipment Schedule T3
3.0si Sport Util 4D	FE435	48045	11100	11700	12500	15550
Cold Weather Pkg			125	125	165	165
Sport Pkg			200	200	240	240
Third Row Seat			375	375	440	440

X5 AWD—V8—Truck Equipment Schedule T3
4.8i Sport Utility 4D	FE834	55195	11500	12100	13000	16300
Cold Weather Pkg			125	125	165	165
Sport Pkg			200	200	245	245
Third Row Seat			375	375	450	450

2008 BMW — WBXor5UX(PC934)–8-#

X3 AWD—6-Cyl.—Truck Equipment Schedule T3
3.0si Sport Util 4D	PC934	40225	9700	10150	11450	14250
Sport Pkg			200	200	255	255
Premium Pkg			925	925	1165	1165

X5 AWD—6-Cyl.—Truck Equipment Schedule T3
3.0si Sport Util 4D	FE435	46675	12800	13400	14300	17100
Cold Weather Pkg			150	150	170	170
Sport Pkg			200	200	235	235
Third Row Seat			400	400	465	465

X5 AWD—V8—Truck Equipment Schedule T3
4.8i Sport Utility 4D	FE835	55275	13700	14300	15300	18400
Cold Weather Pkg			150	150	175	175
Sport Pkg			200	200	240	240
Third Row Seat			400	400	465	465

X6 AWD—V8 Twin Turbo—Truck Equipment Schedule T3
35i Sport Utility 4D	FG435	53275	20400	21400	21100	25100
Cold Weather Pkg			150	150	160	160
Premium Pkg			700	700	790	790
Sport Pkg			200	200	225	225

X6 AWD—V8 Twin Turbo—Truck Equipment Schedule T3
50i Sport Utility 4D	FG835	63775	21800	22900	22500	26800
Cold Weather Pkg			150	150	160	160
Premium Pkg			700	700	790	790
Sport Pkg			200	200	225	225

2009 BMW — WBXor5UX(PC934)–9-#

X3 AWD—6-Cyl.—Truck Equipment Schedule T3
3.0i Sport Utility 4D	PC934	41975	11800	12250	13750	16550
Sport Pkg			225	225	285	285
Premium Pkg			975	975	1210	1210

X5 AWD—6-Cyl.—Truck Equipment Schedule T3
30i Sport Utility 4D	FE435	49775	14900	15450	16650	19500
Climate Pkg			150	150	175	175
Cold Weather Pkg			150	150	175	175
Premium Pkg			750	750	870	870
Sport Pkg			225	225	270	270
Third Row Seat			450	450	525	525

2009 BMW

Body Type	VIN	List	Trade-In Good	Very Good	Pvt-Party Good	Retail Excellent
X5 AWD—6-Cyl. Turbo Diesel—Truck Equipment Sch T3						
35d Sport Utility 4D	FF035	53475	16450	17050	18250	21400
Climate Pkg			150	150	175	175
Cold Weather Pkg			150	150	175	175
Premium Pkg			750	750	870	870
Sport Pkg			225	225	270	270
Third Row Seat			450	450	525	525
X5 AWD—V8—Truck Equipment Schedule T3						
48i Sport Utility 4D	FE835	57025	16850	17450	18650	21800
Climate Pkg			150	150	175	175
Cold Weather Pkg			150	150	175	175
Premium Pkg			750	750	870	870
Sport Pkg			225	225	270	270
Third Row Seat			450	450	525	525
X6 AWD—V6 Twin Turbo—Truck Equipment Schedule T3						
35i Sport Utility 4D	FG435	56725	23200	24200	24400	28600
Cold Weather Pkg			150	150	170	170
Premium Pkg			750	750	840	840
Sport Pkg			225	225	260	260
X6 AWD—V8 Twin Turbo—Truck Equipment Schedule T3						
50i Sport Utility 4D	FG835	67475	23900	24900	25200	29600
Cold Weather Pkg			150	150	170	170
Premium Pkg			750	750	845	845
Sport Pkg			225	225	265	265

2010 BMW — (Wor5)(B,UorY)(MorX)(PC9C4)-A-#

Body Type	VIN	List	Trade-In Good	Very Good	Pvt-Party Good	Retail Excellent
X3 AWD—6-Cyl.—Truck Equipment Schedule T3						
3.0i Sport Utility 4D	PC9C4	39575	15400	15850	17100	19500
Sport Pkg			275	275	300	300
Premium Pkg			1000	1000	1130	1130
X5 AWD—6-Cyl.—Truck Equipment Schedule T3						
xDrive30i Spt Util	FE4C	48475	18700	19250	20600	23500
Climate Pkg			150	150	185	185
Cold Weather Pkg			150	150	185	185
Premium Pkg			775	775	905	905
Sport Activity Pkg			275	275	305	305
M Sport Pkg			1100	1100	1260	1260
Third Row Seat			525	525	605	605
X5 AWD—6-Cyl. Turbo Diesel—Truck Equipment Schedule T3						
xDrive35d Spt Util	FF0C	52175	19400	19950	21400	24500
Climate Pkg			150	150	185	185
Cold Weather Pkg			150	150	185	185
Premium Pkg			775	775	910	910
Sport Activity Pkg			275	275	310	310
Third Row Seat			525	525	610	610
X5 AWD—V8—Truck Equipment Schedule T3						
xDrive48i Spt Util	FE8C	57175	19700	20300	21800	25000
Climate Pkg			150	150	185	185
Cold Weather Pkg			150	150	185	185
Premium Pkg			775	775	915	915
Sport Activity Pkg			275	275	310	310
M Sport Pkg			1100	1100	1270	1270
Third Row Seat			525	525	610	610
X5 M AWD—V8 Twin Turbo—Truck Equipment Schedule T3						
Sport Utility 4D	GY0C5	86375	29700	31200	31300	36100
Climate Pkg			150	150	180	180
Cold Weather Pkg			150	150	180	180
X6 AWD—V6 Twin Turbo—Truck Equipment Schedule T3						
35i Sport Utility 4D	FG4C5	57375	25000	25900	26600	30600
Climate Pkg			150	150	180	180
Cold Weather Pkg			150	150	180	180
Premium Pkg			775	775	885	885
Sport Pkg			275	275	300	300
X6 AWD—V8 Twin Turbo—Truck Equipment Schedule T3						
50i Sport Utility 4D	FG8C5	68075	27100	28100	28700	33000
Climate Pkg			150	150	180	180
Cold Weather Pkg			150	150	180	180
Premium Pkg			775	775	880	880
Sport Pkg			275	275	300	300
X6 M AWD—V8 Twin Turbo—Truck Equipment Schedule T3						
Sport Utility 4D	GZ0C5	89875	32000	32900	34300	39000
Climate Pkg			150	150	180	180
Cold Weather Pkg			150	150	180	180

Body Type	VIN	List	Trade-In Good	Very Good	Pvt-Party Good	Retail Excellent
Premium Pkg			775	775	880	880

X6 AWD—V8 Twin Turbo ActiveHybrid—Truck Equipment Sch T3

Body Type	VIN	List	Good	Very Good	Good	Excellent
Sport Utility 4D	FH0C5	89775	28100	28900	30300	34300
Adaptive Cruise Control			(400)	(400)	(440)	(440)
Cold Weather Pkg			150	150	180	180
Premium Pkg			775	775	885	885

2011 BMW — 5(UXorYM)(WX5C5)-B-#

X3 AWD—6-Cyl.—Truck Equipment Schedule T3

Body Type	VIN	List	Good	Very Good	Good	Excellent
xDrive28i Spt Util	WX5C5	39075	19000	19450	21200	24000
Sport Pkg			300	300	330	330
M Sport Pkg			1125	1125	1265	1265
Premium Pkg			1000	1000	1130	1130

X3 AWD—6-Cyl. Twin Turbo—Truck Equipment Schedule T3

Body Type	VIN	List	Good	Very Good	Good	Excellent
xDrive35i Spt Util	WX7C5	43375	21500	22000	23800	26900
Sport Pkg			300	300	330	330
M Sport Pkg			1125	1125	1260	1260
Premium Pkg			1000	1000	1130	1130

X5 AWD—6-Cyl. Turbo—Truck Equipment Schedule T3

Body Type	VIN	List	Good	Very Good	Good	Excellent
35i Sport Utility 4D	ZV4C5	48125	22600	23200	24800	27900
35i Premium SUV	ZV4C5	52475	23300	23900	25600	28800
35i Sport Activity	ZV4C5	54975	22900	23500	25200	28400
Active Cruise Control			425	425	470	470
Cold Weather Pkg			175	175	190	190
M Sport Pkg			1125	1125	1275	1275
Third Row Seat			575	575	660	660

X5 AWD—6-Cyl. Twin Turbo Diesel—Truck Equipment Schedule T3

Body Type	VIN	List	Good	Very Good	Good	Excellent
35d Sport Util 4D	ZW0C5	53625	23500	24000	25800	29100
Climate Pkg			175	175	190	190
Cold Weather Pkg			175	175	190	190
Premium Pkg			825	825	940	940
Sport Activity Pkg			300	300	330	330
Third Row Seat			575	575	665	665

X5 AWD—V8 Twin Turbo—Truck Equipment Schedule T3

Body Type	VIN	List	Good	Very Good	Good	Excellent
50i Sport Utility 4D	ZV8C5	59275	24500	25100	26800	30100
Active Cruise Control			425	425	470	470
Cold Weather Pkg			175	175	190	190
Premium Pkg			825	825	935	935
Sport Activity Pkg			300	300	330	330
M Sport Pkg			1125	1125	1265	1265
Third Row Seat			575	575	660	660

X5 M AWD—V8 Twin Turbo—Truck Equipment Schedule T3

Body Type	VIN	List	Good	Very Good	Good	Excellent
xDrive Sport Util	GY0C5	86575	33500	35200	35200	40100
Climate Pkg			175	175	185	185
Cold Weather Pkg			175	175	185	185

X6 AWD—V6 Twin Turbo—Truck Equipment Schedule T3

Body Type	VIN	List	Good	Very Good	Good	Excellent
35i Sport Utility 4D	FG2C5	57375	30300	31200	32400	36600
Active Cruise Control			425	425	470	470
Climate Pkg			175	175	185	185
Cold Weather Pkg			175	175	185	185
Premium Pkg			825	825	930	930
Sport Pkg			300	300	325	325

X6 AWD—V8 Twin Turbo—Truck Equipment Schedule T3

Body Type	VIN	List	Good	Very Good	Good	Excellent
50i Sport Utility 4D	FG8C5	68075	30000	30900	32300	36700
Active Cruise Control			425	425	470	470
Climate Pkg			175	175	190	190
Cold Weather Pkg			175	175	190	190
Premium Pkg			825	825	940	940
Sport Pkg			300	300	330	330

X6 AWD—V8 Twin Turbo ActiveHybrid—Truck Equipment Sch T3

Body Type	VIN	List	Good	Very Good	Good	Excellent
Sport Utility 4D	FH0C5	89775	30900	31600	33600	37900
Cold Weather Pkg			175	175	190	190
Premium Pkg			825	825	945	945

X6 M AWD—V8 Twin Turbo—Truck Equipment Schedule T3

Body Type	VIN	List	Good	Very Good	Good	Excellent
Sport Utility 4D	GZ0C5	98075	39500	40500	42100	46800
Climate Pkg			175	175	185	185
Cold Weather Pkg			175	175	185	185
Premium Pkg			825	825	915	915

2012 BMW — 5(UXorYM)(WX5C5)-C-#

X3 AWD—6-Cyl.—Truck Equipment Schedule T3

Body Type	VIN	List	Good	Very Good	Good	Excellent
xDrive28i Spt Util	WX5C5	37725	21400	21800	23500	25900

1015

Body Type	VIN	List	Trade-In Good	Very Good	Pvt-Party Good	Retail Excellent
M Sport Pkg	......	......	1150	1150	1255	1255
Sport Activity Pkg	......	......	325	325	345	345
Premium Pkg	......	......	1000	1000	1100	1100
X3 AWD—6-Cyl. Twin Turbo—Truck Equipment Schedule T3						
xDrive35i Spt Util	WX7C5	43275	25900	26400	28100	31000
Sport Activity Pkg	......	......	325	325	350	350
M Sport Pkg	......	......	1150	1150	1260	1260
Premium Pkg	......	......	1000	1000	1100	1100
X5 AWD—6-Cyl. Twin Turbo—Truck Equipment Schedule T3						
35i Sport Utility 4D	ZV4C5	48075	27200	27700	29500	32600
35i Premium Utility	ZV4C5	55675	28800	29400	31300	34500
35i Sport Activity	ZV4C5	58175	28000	28600	30600	33800
Active Speed Control	......	......	450	450	495	495
Cold Weather Pkg	......	......	175	175	195	195
Sport Pkg	......	......	325	325	355	355
M Sport Pkg	......	......	1150	1150	1280	1280
Third Row Seat	......	......	625	625	710	710
X5 AWD—6-Cyl. Twin Turbo Diesel—Truck Equipment Schedule T3						
35d Sport Utility	ZW0C5	57175	28100	28700	30800	34100
Cold Weather Pkg	......	......	175	175	195	195
Premium Pkg	......	......	875	875	975	975
Sport Activity Pkg	......	......	325	325	355	355
Third Row Seat	......	......	625	625	715	715
X5 AWD—V8 Twin Turbo—Truck Equipment Schedule T3						
50i Sport Utility 4D	ZV8C5	64675	30200	30800	32800	36400
Active Speed Control	......	......	450	450	495	495
Cold Weather Pkg	......	......	175	175	195	195
Sport Activity Pkg	......	......	325	325	355	355
Premium Pkg	......	......	875	875	975	975
M Sport Pkg	......	......	1150	1150	1285	1285
Third Row Seat	......	......	625	625	710	710
X5 M AWD—V8 Twin Turbo—Truck Equipment Schedule T3						
Sport Utility 4D	GY0C5	88145	41100	43000	42400	47300
Climate Pkg	......	......	175	175	190	190
Cold Weather Pkg	......	......	175	175	190	190
X6 AWD—V6 Twin Turbo—Truck Equipment Schedule T3						
35i Sport Utility 4D	FG2C5	59775	33700	34500	36200	40500
Active Cruise Control	......	......	450	450	495	495
Cold Weather Pkg	......	......	175	175	195	195
Premium Pkg	......	......	875	875	970	970
Sport Pkg	......	......	325	325	355	355
Active Cruise Control	......	......	450	450	495	495
X6 AWD—V8 Twin Turbo—Truck Equipment Schedule T3						
50i Sport Utility 4D	FG8C5	70375	35200	36000	37900	42500
Active Cruise Control	......	......	450	450	495	495
Cold Weather Pkg	......	......	175	175	195	195
Premium Pkg	......	......	875	875	975	975
Sport Pkg	......	......	325	325	355	355
Active Cruise Control	......	......	450	450	495	495
X6 M AWD—V8 Twin Turbo—Truck Equipment Schedule T3						
Sport Utility 4D	GZ0C5	91195	45700	46600	48400	53000
Climate Pkg	......	......	175	175	190	190
Cold Weather Pkg	......	......	175	175	190	190

2013 BMW — 5(UXorYM)(VM1C5)-D-#

Body Type	VIN	List	Good	Very Good	Good	Excellent
X1—4-Cyl. Twin Turbo—Truck Equipment Schedule T3						
sDrive28i Spt Util	VM1C5	32995	19100	19450	21300	23500
Premium Pkg	......	......	1000	1000	1100	1100
M Sport Pkg	......	......	1175	1175	1285	1285
Ultimate Pkg	......	......	2650	2650	2910	2910
X1 AWD—4-Cyl. Twin Turbo—Truck Equipment Schedule T3						
xDrive28i Spt Util	VL1C5	34695	20900	21300	23200	25800
Premium Pkg	......	......	1000	1000	1120	1120
M Sport Pkg	......	......	1175	1175	1305	1305
Ultimate Pkg	......	......	2650	2650	2960	2960
X1 AWD—6-Cyl. Twin Turbo—Truck Equipment Schedule T3						
xDrive35i Spt Util	VM5C5	40795	25100	25600	27600	30500
Premium Pkg	......	......	1000	1000	1110	1110
M Sport Pkg	......	......	1175	1175	1295	1295
Ultimate Pkg	......	......	2650	2650	2930	2930
X3 AWD—4-Cyl. Turbo—Truck Equipment Schedule T3						
xDrive28i Spt Util	WX9C5	39395	24500	24900	26700	29300
Sport Activity Pkg	......	......	350	350	375	375

Body Type	VIN	List	Trade-In Good	Very Good	Pvt-Party Good	Retail Excellent
Premium Pkg			1000	1000	1100	1100
M Sport Pkg			1175	1175	1280	1280
X3 AWD—6-Cyl. Turbo—Truck Equipment Schedule T3						
xDrive35i Spt Util	WX7C5	44495	28300	28800	30900	33900
Sport Activity Pkg			350	350	375	375
Premium Pkg			1000	1000	1105	1105
M Sport Pkg			1175	1175	1285	1285
X5 AWD—6-Cyl. Twin Turbo—Truck Equipment Schedule T3						
35i Sport Utility 4D	ZV4C5	48395	32400	33000	35100	38400
35i Premium Utility	ZV4C5	56095	34400	35000	37300	41000
35i Sport Utility	ZV4C5	58595	35100	35700	38000	41700
Active Cruise Control			475	475	520	520
Cold Weather Pkg			175	175	205	205
M Sport Pkg			1175	1175	1305	1305
Third Row Seat			675	675	760	760
X5 AWD—6-Cyl. Twin Turbo Diesel—Truck Equipment Schedule T3						
35d Sport Utility	ZW0C5	57595	34900	35500	37800	41500
Sport Activity Pkg			350	350	380	380
Premium Pkg			900	900	1015	1015
X5 AWD—V8 Twin Turbo—Truck Equipment Schedule T3						
50i Sport Utility 4D	ZV8C5	65095	37000	37600	39800	43700
Active Cruise Control			475	475	520	520
Cold Weather Pkg			175	175	205	205
Sport Activity Pkg			350	350	380	380
Premium Pkg			900	900	1010	1010
M Sport Pkg			1175	1175	1300	1300
X5 M AWD—V8 Twin Turbo—Truck Equipment Schedule T3						
Sport Utility 4D	GY0C5	89745	53500	56000	54800	60400
Climate Pkg			175	175	195	195
Cold Weather Pkg			175	175	195	195
X6 AWD—6-Cyl. Twin Turbo—Truck Equipment Schedule T3						
xDrive35i Spt Util	FG2C5	60695	38700	39500	41100	44900
Active Cruise Control			475	475	510	510
Cold Weather Pkg			175	175	200	200
Premium Pkg			900	900	990	990
X6 AWD—V8 Twin Turbo—Truck Equipment Schedule T3						
xDrive 50i Spt Util	FG8C5	71295	42300	43200	44900	49100
Active Cruise Control			475	475	510	510
Premium Pkg			900	900	990	990
Cold Weather Pkg			175	175	200	200
X6 M AWD—V8 Twin Turbo—Truck Equipment Schedule T3						
Sport Utility 4D	GZ0C5	93795	54900	55900	58500	63800
Climate Pkg			175	175	200	200
Cold Weather Pkg			175	175	200	200
2014 BMW — 5(UXorYM)(VM1C5)-E-#						
X1—4-Cyl. Twin Turbo—Truck Equipment Schedule T3						
sDrive28i Spt Util	VM1C5	33145	21800	22200	24000	26200
Premium Pkg			625	625	695	695
M Sport Line			1200	1200	1310	1310
Ultimate Pkg			2675	2675	2930	2930
X1 AWD—4-Cyl. Twin Turbo—Truck Equipment Schedule T3						
xDrive28i Spt Util	VL1C5	34845	23200	23700	25500	28100
Premium Pkg			1000	1000	1100	1100
M Sport Line			1200	1200	1310	1310
Ultimate Pkg			2675	2675	2935	2935
X1 AWD—6-Cyl. Twin Turbo—Truck Equipment Schedule T3						
xDrive35i Spt Util	VM5C5	40945	27700	28200	29900	32500
Premium Pkg			1000	1000	1080	1080
M Sport Line			1200	1200	1285	1285
Ultimate Pkg			2675	2675	2875	2875
X3 AWD—4-Cyl. Turbo—Truck Equipment Schedule T3						
xDrive28i Spt Util	WX9C5	41945	28600	29200	30900	33600
Premium Pkg			1000	1000	1070	1070
M Sport Pkg			1200	1200	1275	1275
X3 AWD—6-Cyl. Twin Turbo—Truck Equipment Schedule T3						
xDrive35i Spt Util	WX7C5	47045	34500	35100	36800	39800
Premium Pkg			1000	1000	1070	1070
M Sport Pkg			1200	1200	1275	1275
X5 AWD—6-Cyl. Twin Turbo—Truck Equipment Schedule T3						
sDrive 35i Spt Util	KR2C5	55175	43100	43800	45300	48700
xDrive 35i Spt Util	KR0C5	57475	44300	45100	46500	49900
Bang & Olufsen Sound			2950	2950	3195	3195

1015

Body Type	VIN	List	Trade-In Good	Very Good	Pvt-Party Good	Retail Excellent
Active Cruise Control			500	500	530	530
Cold Weather Pkg			200	200	205	205
Driver Asst Plus Pkg			675	675	720	720
Premium Pkg			950	950	1020	1020
M Sport Line			1200	1200	1285	1285
Third Row Seat			725	725	790	790
X5 AWD—6-Cyl. Twin Turbo Diesel—Truck Equipment Schedule T3						
xDrive 35d Spt Util	KS4C5	58975	48400	49300	50800	54300
Bang & Olufsen Sound			2950	2950	3170	3170
Active Cruise Control			500	500	525	525
Cold Weather Pkg			200	200	205	205
Driver Asst Plus Pkg			675	675	715	715
Premium Pkg			950	950	1015	1015
M Sport Line			1200	1200	1275	1275
Third Row Seat			725	725	785	785
X5 AWD—V8 Twin Turbo—Truck Equipment Schedule T3						
xDrive 50i Spt Util	KR6C5	69125	54500	55400	57000	61000
Bang & Olufsen Sound			2950	2950	3165	3165
Active Cruise Control			500	500	525	525
Cold Weather Pkg			200	200	205	205
Driver Asst Plus Pkg			675	675	715	715
M Sport Line			1200	1200	1275	1275
Third Row Seat			725	725	785	785
X6 AWD—6-Cyl. Twin Turbo—Truck Equipment Schedule T3						
xDrive35i Spt Util	FG2C5	60695	43400	44200	45500	48800
Active Cruise Control			500	500	520	520
Cold Weather Pkg			200	200	200	200
Individual Comp			2475	2475	2630	2630
Premium Pkg			950	950	1000	1000
X6 AWD—V8 Twin Turbo—Truck Equipment Schedule T3						
xDrive 50i Spt Util	FG8C5	71295	49000	49900	51500	55100
Active Cruise Control			500	500	520	520
Cold Weather Pkg			200	200	200	200
Premium Pkg			950	950	1000	1000
Individual Comp			2475	2475	2625	2625
X6 M AWD—V8 Twin Turbo—Truck Equipment Schedule T3						
Sport Utility 4D	GZ0C5	93795	66800	68000	70200	75800
Climate Pkg			200	200	205	205
Cold Weather Pkg			200	200	205	205
Driver Assistance Pkg			675	675	715	715

BUICK

2002 BUICK — 3G5-(A03E)-2-#

Body Type	VIN	List	Good	Very Good	Good	Excellent
RENDEZVOUS—V6—Truck Equipment Schedule T3						
CX Sport Utility 4D	A03E	26279	1000	1175	1575	2650
Third Row Seat			175	175	245	245
AWD	B		375	375	505	505
RENDEZVOUS AWD—V6—Truck Equipment Schedule T3						
CXL Sport Utility 4D	B03E	31502	1300	1500	2050	3550
Third Row Seat			175	175	245	245

2003 BUICK — 3G5-(A03E)-3-#

Body Type	VIN	List	Good	Very Good	Good	Excellent
RENDEZVOUS—V6—Truck Equipment Schedule T3						
CX Sport Utility 4D	A03E	26975	1175	1375	1925	3300
CXL Sport Utility 4D	B03E	30200	1475	1700	2375	4125
Third Row Seat			200	200	260	260
AWD	B		400	400	545	545

2004 BUICK — (3G5or5GA)-(A03E)-4-#

Body Type	VIN	List	Good	Very Good	Good	Excellent
RENDEZVOUS—V6—Truck Equipment Schedule T3						
CX Sport Utility 4D	A03E	26545	1550	1775	2350	3975
CXL Sport Utility 4D	A03E	31410	1975	2275	2900	4775
Third Row Seat			200	200	275	275
AWD	B		425	425	580	580
V6, 3.6 Liter	7		275	275	380	380
RENDEZVOUS AWD—V6—Truck Equipment Schedule T3						
Ultra Sport Utility 4D	B037	39695	2275	2625	3325	5525
Third Row Seat			200	200	275	275
RAINIER AWD—6-Cyl.—Truck Equipment Schedule T1						
CXL Sport Utility 4D	T13S	37895	3150	3600	4100	6550

Body Type	VIN	List	Trade-In Good	Very Good	Pvt-Party Good	Retail Excellent
2WD	S		(875)	(875)	(1155)	(1155)
V8, 5.3 Liter	P		200	200	255	255

2005 BUICK — (3G5or5GA)–(A04E)–5–#

RENDEZVOUS—V6—Truck Equipment Schedule T3
CX Sport Utility 4D	A04E	27270	1875	2175	3025	4875
CXL Sport Utility 4D	A03E	31600	2350	2700	3575	5700
Ultra Sport Util 4D	A03E	36840	2675	3075	3925	6250
Third Row Seat			225	225	295	295
AWD	B		475	475	615	615
V6, 3.6 Liter	7		300	300	410	410

TERRAZA—V6—Truck Equipment Schedule T3
CX Minivan 4D	V23L	28825	3250	3750	4425	6950
CXL Minivan 4D	V33L	31885	3550	4125	4900	7625
AWD	X		475	475	640	640

RAINIER AWD—6-Cyl.—Truck Equipment Schedule T1
CXL Sport Utility 4D	T13S	37590	3300	3775	4700	7350
2WD	S		(950)	(950)	(1260)	(1260)
V8, 5.3 Liter	M		225	225	285	285

2006 BUICK — (3G5or5GA)–(A03L)–6–#

RENDEZVOUS—V6—Truck Equipment Schedule T3
CX Sport Utility 4D	A03L	27305	2750	3100	3925	6050
CXL Sport Utility 4D	A03L	30955	3250	3675	4450	6825
Third Row Seat			225	225	310	310
AWD	B		500	500	655	655
V6, 3.6 Liter	7		325	325	435	435

TERRAZA—V6—Truck Equipment Schedule T3
CX Minivan 4D	V23L	28530	3975	4525	5350	8175
CXL Minivan 4D	V33L	31930	4525	5150	6000	9125
AWD	X		500	500	675	675

RAINIER AWD—6-Cyl.—Truck Equipment Schedule T1
CXL Sport Utility 4D	T13S	35785	4225	4750	5525	8300
2WD	S		(1025)	(1025)	(1375)	(1375)
V8, 5.3 Liter	M		250	250	320	320

2007 BUICK — (3G5or5GA)–(A03L)–7–#

RENDEZVOUS—V6—Truck Equipment Schedule T3
CX Sport Utility 4D	A03L	25795	3825	4275	5050	7325
CXL Sport Utility 4D	A03L	29370	4425	4925	5650	8125
Third Row Seat			250	250	325	325

TERRAZA—V6—Truck Equipment Schedule T3
CX Minivan 4D	V231	27275	4825	5425	6325	9425
CX Plus Minivan 4D	V231	28615	4950	5550	6450	9625
CXL Minivan 4D	V331	31395	5650	6350	7425	11000

RAINIER AWD—6-Cyl.—Truck Equipment Schedule T1
CXL Sport Utility 4D	T13S	34140	5525	6150	6925	9825
2WD	S		(1100)	(1100)	(1480)	(1480)
V8, 5.3 Liter	M		275	275	355	355

2008 BUICK — (3G5or5GA)–(R137)–8–#

ENCLAVE—V6—Truck Equipment Schedule T3
CX Sport Utility 4D	R137	34760	8800	9200	10450	13000
CXL Sport Utility 4D	R237	36990	10850	11300	12700	15750
AWD	V		700	700	900	900

2009 BUICK — (3G5or5GA)–(R13D)–9–#

ENCLAVE—V6—Truck Equipment Schedule T3
CX Sport Utility 4D	R13D	37805	10100	10500	11900	14350
CXL Sport Utility 4D	R23D	40115	12650	13100	14700	17700
AWD	V		750	750	925	925

2010 BUICK — (3G5or5GA)–(RAED)–A–#

ENCLAVE—V6—Truck Equipment Schedule T3
CX Sport Utility	RAED	35993	12850	13200	14800	17200
CXL Sport Utility	RBED	39105	14600	15050	16750	19600
AWD	V		775	775	925	925

2011 BUICK

Body	Type	VIN	List	Trade-In Good	Very Good	Pvt-Party Good	Retail Excellent

2011 BUICK — (5GA)-(RAED)-B-#

ENCLAVE—V6—Truck Equipment Schedule T3

Body Type	VIN	List	Good	Very Good	Good	Excellent
CX Sport Utility	RAED	36290	14400	14750	16400	18700
CXL Sport Utility	RBED	39405	17500	17950	19650	22300
AWD	V		825	825	950	950

2012 BUICK — (5GA)-(RAED)-C-#

ENCLAVE—V6—Truck Equipment Schedule T3

Body Type	VIN	List	Good	Very Good	Good	Excellent
Sport Utility 4D	RAED	37410	17600	17950	19850	22300
Convenience Util	RBED	38330	18400	18800	20700	23200
Leather Spt Util	RCED	40525	21600	22100	24000	26800
Premium Spt Util	RDED	43890	22900	23300	25200	28000
AWD	V		850	850	970	970

2013 BUICK — (5GA)-(JARB)-D-#

ENCORE—4-Cyl. Turbo—Truck Equipment Schedule T1

Body Type	VIN	List	Good	Very Good	Good	Excellent
Sport Utility 4D	JARB	24950	13500	13700	15250	17350
Convenience Util	JBRB	25760	14550	14750	16350	18550
Leather Sport Util	JCRB	27460	14800	15050	16700	19050
Premium Sport Util	JDRB	28940	16500	16750	18500	21000
AWD	E		925	925	1035	1035

ENCLAVE—V6—Truck Equipment Schedule T3

Body Type	VIN	List	Good	Very Good	Good	Excellent
Convenience 4D	RBED	39270	22100	22500	24800	27700
Leather Sport Util	RCED	43285	24300	24800	27200	30500
Premium Sport Util	RDED	46450	28000	28500	31000	34700
AWD	V		925	925	1050	1050

2014 BUICK — (5GA)-(JAEB)-E-#

ENCORE—4-Cyl. Turbo—Truck Equipment Schedule T1

Body Type	VIN	List	Good	Very Good	Good	Excellent
Sport Utility 4D	JAEB	25085	15250	15450	17400	19950
Convenience 4D	JBEB	26710	16250	16500	18200	20700
Leather Sport Util	JCEB	28410	17200	17450	19050	21500
Premium Sport Util	JDEB	29890	19550	19850	21300	23800
AWD	E		1000	1000	1150	1150

ENCLAVE—V6—Truck Equipment Schedule T1

Body Type	VIN	List	Good	Very Good	Good	Excellent
Convenience 4D	RAKD	39665	24300	24700	27300	30600
Leather Sport Util	RBKD	43680	28200	28700	31500	35200
Premium Sport Util	RCKD	47240	31600	32100	35000	39100
AWD	V		1000	1000	1145	1145

CADILLAC

2000 CADILLAC — 1GY-(K13R)-Y-#

ESCALADE AWD—V8—Truck Equipment Schedule T3

Body Type	VIN	List	Good	Very Good	Good	Excellent
Sport Utility 4D	K13R	46875	1650	1775	2475	3900

2001 CADILLAC — No Production

2002 CADILLAC — (1or3)GY-(K63N)-2-#

ESCALADE AWD—V8—Truck Equipment Schedule T3

Body Type	VIN	List	Good	Very Good	Good	Excellent
Sport Utility 4D	K63N	51980	4200	4500	5475	8025
2WD	C		(425)	(425)	(575)	(575)
V8, 5.3 Liter			(200)	(200)	(250)	(250)

ESCALADE EXT AWD—V8—Truck Equipment Schedule T3

Body Type	VIN	List	Good	Very Good	Good	Excellent
Sport Util Pickup 4D	K13N	49990	3875	4175	5150	7575

2003 CADILLAC — (1or3)GY-(K63N)-3-#

ESCALADE AWD—V8—Truck Equipment Schedule T3

Body Type	VIN	List	Good	Very Good	Good	Excellent
Sport Utility 4D	K63N	53950	5475	5875	6850	9650
2WD	C		(475)	(475)	(645)	(645)
V8, 5.3 Liter			(200)	(200)	(280)	(280)

ESCALADE EXT AWD—V8—Truck Equipment Schedule T3

Body Type	VIN	List	Good	Very Good	Good	Excellent
Sport Util Pickup 4D	K63N	51215	5275	5650	6475	9175

ESCALADE ESV AWD—V8—Truck Equipment Schedule T3

Body Type	VIN	List	Good	Very Good	Good	Excellent
Sport Utility 4D	K66N	56160	5500	5900	6975	9900

Body Type	VIN	List	Trade-In Good	Very Good	Pvt-Party Good	Retail Excellent

2004 CADILLAC — (1or3)GY–(E637)–4–#

SRX AWD—V6—Truck Equipment Schedule T3

Body Type	VIN	List	Good	Very Good	Good	Excellent
Sport Utility 4D	E637	40935	3750	4100	4575	6725
Third Row Seat			675	675	915	915
Luxury Performance			1075	1075	1425	1425
2WD			(425)	(425)	(580)	(580)
V8, 4.6 Liter	A		225	225	315	315

ESCALADE AWD—V8—Truck Equipment Schedule T3

Sport Utility 4D	K63N	55695	6700	7150	8075	11050
2WD	C		(525)	(525)	(710)	(710)
V8, 5.3 Liter	T		(225)	(225)	(305)	(305)

ESCALADE EXT AWD—V8—Truck Equipment Schedule T3

Sport Util Pickup 4D	K63N	52975	6275	6700	7625	10550

ESCALADE ESV AWD—V8—Truck Equipment Schedule T3

Sport Utility 4D	K66N	58095	6875	7350	8350	11550
Platinum Sport Util	K66N	69730	8750	9325	10150	13750

2005 CADILLAC — (1or3)GY–(E637)–5–#

SRX AWD—V6—Truck Equipment Schedule T3

Sport Utility 4D	E637	41895	4150	4525	5275	7700
Third Row Seat			700	700	940	940
Luxury Performance			1175	1175	1555	1555
2WD			(475)	(475)	(640)	(640)
V8, 4.6 Liter	A		250	250	340	340

ESCALADE AWD—V8—Truck Equipment Schedule T3

Sport Utility 4D	K63N	56615	7550	8025	9175	12300
2WD	C		(575)	(575)	(775)	(775)
V8, 5.3 Liter	T		(250)	(250)	(335)	(335)

ESCALADE EXT AWD—V8—Truck Equipment Schedule T3

Sport Util Pickup 4D	K62N	53895	7075	7550	8725	11700

ESCALADE ESV AWD—V8—Truck Equipment Schedule T3

Sport Utility 4D	K66N	59015	7850	8350	9550	12850
Platinum Sport Util	K66N	70385	9725	10350	11400	15100

2006 CADILLAC — (1or3)GY–(E637)–6–#

SRX AWD—V6—Truck Equipment Schedule T3

Sport Utility 4D	E637	39390	4975	5425	6150	8675
Third Row Seat			725	725	970	970
2WD			(525)	(525)	(700)	(700)
V8, 4.6 Liter	A		275	275	370	370

ESCALADE AWD—V8—Truck Equipment Schedule T3

Sport Utility 4D	K63N	57280	8925	9450	10650	13950
2WD	C		(625)	(625)	(835)	(835)

ESCALADE EXT AWD—V8—Truck Equipment Schedule T3

Sport Util Pickup 4D	K62N	54210	8575	9100	10250	13450

ESCALADE ESV AWD—V8—Truck Equipment Schedule T3

Sport Utility 4D	K66N	59680	9150	9700	10950	14450
Platinum Sport Util	K66N	71050	11000	11650	12750	16550

2007 CADILLAC — (1or3)GY–(E637)–7–#

SRX AWD—V6—Truck Equipment Schedule T3

Sport Utility 4D	E637	39595	6800	7350	7950	10800
Third Row Seat			750	750	990	990
2WD			(575)	(575)	(750)	(750)
V8, 4.6 Liter	A		300	300	395	395

ESCALADE AWD—V8—Truck Equipment Schedule T3

Sport Utility 4D	K638	57675	17500	18450	19100	23600
2WD	C		(675)	(675)	(835)	(835)

ESCALADE EXT AWD—V8—Truck Equipment Schedule T3

Sport Util Pickup 4D	K628	54605	16950	17850	18550	23000

ESCALADE ESV AWD—V8—Truck Equipment Schedule T3

Sport Utility 4D	K668	60075	16950	17850	18650	23300

2008 CADILLAC — (1or3)GY–(E437)–8–#

SRX AWD—V6—Truck Equipment Schedule T3

Sport Utility 4D	E437	41480	8800	9450	9725	12750
Third Row Seat			775	775	945	945
2WD	2,6		(675)	(675)	(830)	(830)
V8, 4.6 Liter	A		450	450	535	535

2008 CADILLAC

Body Type	VIN	List	Trade-In Good	Very Good	Pvt-Party Good	Retail Excellent
ESCALADE AWD—V8—Truck Equipment Schedule T3						
Sport Utility 4D	K638	58195	20400	21200	22000	26200
2WD	C		(725)	(725)	(860)	(860)
ESCALADE EXT AWD—V8—Truck Equipment Schedule T3						
Sport Util Pickup 4D	K628	55115	19750	20600	21300	25500
Luxury Collection			575	575	670	670
ESCALADE ESV AWD—V8—Truck Equipment Schedule T3						
Sport Utility 4D	K668	60610	19950	20800	21600	25900
Luxury Collection			575	575	670	670
Platinum Edition			1625	1625	1940	1940
2WD	C		(725)	(725)	(870)	(870)

2009 CADILLAC — (1or3)GY-(E437)-9-#

Body Type	VIN	List	Trade-In Good	Very Good	Pvt-Party Good	Retail Excellent
SRX AWD—V6—Truck Equipment Schedule T3						
Sport Utility 4D	E437	41480	10700	11400	11850	15000
Third Row Seat			800	800	950	950
2WD	2,6		(725)	(725)	(865)	(865)
V8, 4.6 Liter	A		450	450	540	540
ESCALADE AWD—V8—Truck Equipment Schedule T3						
Sport Utility 4D	K132	63305	22700	23500	24500	28600
2WD	C		(825)	(825)	(965)	(965)
ESCALADE AWD—V8 Hybrid—Truck Equipment Schedule T3						
Sport Utility 4D	K435	74325	24600	25500	26600	31000
2WD	C		(825)	(825)	(965)	(965)
ESCALADE EXT AWD—V8—Truck Equipment Schedule T3						
Sport Util Pickup 4D	K628	59690	21600	22300	23400	27300
Luxury Collection			600	600	690	690
ESCALADE ESV AWD—V8—Truck Equipment Schedule T3						
Sport Utility 4D	K668	65835	22800	23600	24800	29000
Luxury Collection			600	600	690	690
Platinum Edition			1675	1675	1960	1960
2WD	C		(825)	(825)	(970)	(970)

2010 CADILLAC — (1or3)GY-(NBEY)-A-#

Body Type	VIN	List	Trade-In Good	Very Good	Pvt-Party Good	Retail Excellent
SRX—V6—Truck Equipment Schedule T3						
Sport Utility 4D	NBEY	34155	15750	16600	17400	21600
Performance Collection			2500	2500	3030	3030
AWD	E		700	700	850	850
V6, Turbo, 2.8 Liter	4		1975	1975	2385	2385
ESCALADE AWD—V8 Flex Fuel—Truck Equipment Schedule T3						
Sport Utility 4D	KAEF	65995	24200	24900	26500	30500
2WD	C		(950)	(950)	(1105)	(1105)
ESCALADE AWD—V8 Hybrid—Truck Equipment Schedule T3						
Sport Utility 4D	KEEJ	76925	25800	26600	28100	32100
2WD	C		(950)	(950)	(1105)	(1105)
ESCALADE EXT AWD—V8—Truck Equipment Schedule T3						
Sport Util Pickup 4D	K628	62370	23600	24300	25900	29700
Luxury Pkg			625	625	710	710
Premium Pkg			1225	1225	1425	1425
ESCALADE ESV AWD—V8 Flex Fuel—Truck Equipment Schedule T3						
Sport Utility 4D	KKEF	68550	25800	26500	28000	32100
Luxury Pkg			625	625	710	710
Platinum Edition			1725	1725	1995	1995
2WD			(950)	(950)	(1100)	(1100)

2011 CADILLAC — (1or3)(GGorGY)-(NBEY)-B-#

Body Type	VIN	List	Trade-In Good	Very Good	Pvt-Party Good	Retail Excellent
SRX—V6—Truck Equipment Schedule T3						
Sport Utility 4D	NBEY	34705	17900	18800	19350	23100
Luxury Collection			650	650	745	745
Performance Pkg			2500	2500	2905	2905
Premium Pkg			2475	2475	2885	2885
AWD	E		775	775	900	900
V6, Turbo, 2.8 Liter	6		2075	2075	2400	2400
ESCALADE AWD—V8 Flex Fuel—Truck Equipment Schedule T3						
Sport Utility 4D	4AEF	65995	30400	31100	32600	36300
2WD	3		(1075)	(1075)	(1195)	(1195)
ESCALADE AWD—V8 Hybrid—Truck Equipment Schedule T3						
Sport Utility 4D	4EEJ	76925	32400	33200	34800	38800
2WD	3		(1075)	(1075)	(1200)	(1200)
ESCALADE EXT AWD—V8 Flex Fuel—Truck Equipment Schedule T3						
Sport Util Pickup 4D	4LEF	62835	29300	30000	31500	35000
Luxury Pkg			650	650	715	715

SEE BACK PAGES FOR TRUCK EQUIPMENT

TRUCKS & VANS

Body Type	VIN	List	Trade-In Good	Very Good	Pvt-Party Good	Retail Excellent
Premium Pkg			1275	1275	1435	1435
ESCALADE ESV AWD—V8 Flex Fuel—Truck Equipment Schedule T3						
Sport Utility 4D	4GEF	69215	31100	31800	33500	37500
Luxury Pkg			650	650	725	725
Platinum Edition			1775	1775	2010	2010
2WD	3		(1075)	(1075)	(1205)	(1205)

2012 CADILLAC — (1or3)GYor3GG–(NGE3)–C–#

Body Type	VIN	List	Trade-In Good	Very Good	Pvt-Party Good	Retail Excellent
SRX—V6—Truck Equipment Schedule T3						
Sport Utility 4D	NGE3	36860	20000	20900	21800	25800
Luxury Collection			675	675	770	770
Performance Collection			775	775	890	890
AWD	D,E,F,H		850	850	985	985
ESCALADE AWD—V8 Flex Fuel—Truck Equipment Schedule T3						
Sport Utility 4D	4AEF	66670	34300	35000	37000	40900
2WD	3		(1175)	(1175)	(1300)	(1300)
ESCALADE AWD—V8 Hybrid—Truck Equipment Schedule T3						
Sport Utility 4D	4EEJ	77350	37300	38000	40300	44600
2WD	2		(1175)	(1175)	(1305)	(1305)
ESCALADE EXT AWD—V8 Flex Fuel—Truck Equipment Schedule T3						
Sport Util Pickup 4D	4LEF	64010	33800	34500	36500	40300
Luxury Pkg			675	675	740	740
Premium Pkg			1325	1325	1485	1485
ESCALADE ESV AWD—V8 Flex Fuel—Truck Equipment Schedule T3						
Sport Utility 4D	4GEF	69270	36200	36900	39100	43300
Luxury Pkg			675	675	745	745
Platinum Edition			1825	1825	2055	2055
2WD	3		(1175)	(1175)	(1310)	(1310)

2013 CADILLAC — (1or3)GYor3GG–(NAE3)–D–#

Body Type	VIN	List	Trade-In Good	Very Good	Pvt-Party Good	Retail Excellent
SRX—V6 Flex Fuel—Truck Equipment Schedule T3						
Sport Utility 4D	NAE3	38050	20400	21300	22400	26300
Luxury Collection	NCE3	43425	21300	22200	23500	27800
Performance 4D	NDE3	45800	25500	26600	27700	32400
Premium Collection	NEE3	48640	26700	27800	28900	33800
AWD	G		925	925	1070	1070
ESCALADE AWD—V8 Flex Fuel—Truck Equipment Schedule T3						
Sport Utility 4D	4AEF	66715	34900	35600	37800	41500
Luxury Spt Util 4D	4BEF	70940	37500	38200	44300	44300
Premium Spt Util 4D	4CEF	75220	40400	41100	43400	47600
Platinum Ed 4D	4DEF	83490	46100	47000	49200	53800
2WD	3		(1275)	(1275)	(1405)	(1405)
ESCALADE AWD—V8 Hybrid—Truck Equipment Schedule T3						
Sport Utility 4D	4EEJ	77395	41400	42200	44500	48800
Platinum Spt Util 4D	4FEJ	86840	47700	48600	51100	55800
2WD	3		(1275)	(1275)	(1400)	(1400)
ESCALADE EXT AWD—V8 Flex Fuel—Truck Equipment Schedule T3						
Sport Util Pickup 4D	4LEF	64055	34200	34800	37000	40600
Luxury Sport Util	4MEF	68245	35900	36500	38700	42500
Premium Sport Util	4NEF	70635	37300	38000	40200	44200
ESCALADE ESV AWD—V8 Flex Fuel—Truck Equipment Schedule T3						
Sport Utility 4D	4GEF	69315	38700	39400	41800	45900
Luxury Spt Util 4D	4HEF	73540	39100	39800	42200	46300
Premium Spt Util 4D	4JEF	78420	42500	43300	45600	50100
Platinum Sport Util	4KEF	86090	46900	47800	50000	54600
2WD	3		(1275)	(1275)	(1405)	(1405)

2014 CADILLAC — (1or3)GYor3GG–(NAE3)–E–#

Body Type	VIN	List	Trade-In Good	Very Good	Pvt-Party Good	Retail Excellent
SRX—V6 Flex Fuel—Truck Equipment Schedule T3						
Sport Utility 4D	NAE3	38430	24000	24900	26100	30200
Luxury Sport Utility	NBE3	43805	29300	30400	31400	36200
Performance 4D	NCE3	46180	29700	30900	32000	36900
Premium Sport Util	NDE3	49070	33000	34200	35000	40100
AWD	E		1000	1000	1115	1115
ESCALADE AWD—V8 Flex Fuel—Truck Equipment Schedule T3						
Sport Utility 4D	4AEF	67290	41400	42200	44200	47900
Luxury Spt Util 4D	4BEF	71515	44100	44800	46800	50700
Premium Spt Util 4D	4CEF	75795	47100	48000	49900	54000
Platinum Ed Spt Utl	4DEF	84065	53000	53900	56000	60400
2WD	3		(1375)	(1375)	(1495)	(1495)
ESCALADE ESV AWD—V8 Flex Fuel—Truck Equipment Schedule T3						
Sport Utility 4D	4GEF	69890	45400	46200	48000	52000

Body Type	VIN	List	Trade-In Good	Very Good	Pvt-Party Good	Retail Excellent
Luxury Spt Util 4D	4HEF	74115	45800	46600	48500	52600
Premium Spt Util 4D	4JEF	78995	49300	50200	52400	56600
Platinum Sport Util	4KEF	86665	53500	54400	56600	61100
2WD	3	......	(1500)	(1500)	(1625)	(1625)

CHEVROLET/GMC

2000 CHEVY/GMC–(1,2or3)(CorG)(1,B,CorN)–J186–Y–#

TRACKER 4WD—4-Cyl.—Truck Equipment Schedule T2

Sport Util Conv 2D	J186	15425	925	1075	1625	2825
Sport Utility 4D	J13C	16650	1375	1600	2250	3900
2WD	E	......	(275)	(275)	(355)	(355)

BLAZER/JIMMY 4WD—V6—Truck Equipment Schedule T1

Sport Utility 2D	T18W	23495	700	825	1425	2525
Sport Utility 4D	T13W		1000	1175	1825	3200
2WD	S	......	(525)	(525)	(715)	(715)

ENVOY 4WD—V6—Truck Equipment Schedule T3

Sport Utility 4D	T13W	34695	1950	2250	2925	4925

TAHOE 4WD—V8 4.8L Engine (New)—Truck Equipment Schedule T1

Sport Utility 4D	K13V	29441	2075	2350	3225	5550
Third Row Seat			200	200	265	265
2WD	C		(325)	(325)	(445)	(445)
V8, 5.3 Liter	T		75	75	100	100

TAHOE 4WD—V8 5.7L Engine—Truck Equipment Schedule T1

Sport Utility 4D	K13R	39544	1900	2150	2950	5050
2WD	C		(325)	(325)	(445)	(445)

YUKON 4WD—V8 (New)—Truck Equipment Schedule T1

SLE Sport Utility 4D	K13V	35835	2525	2850	3750	6375
Third Row Seat			200	200	265	265
2WD	C		(325)	(325)	(445)	(445)
V8, 5.3 Liter	T		75	75	100	100

YUKON DENALI 4WD—V8—Truck Equipment Schedule T3

Sport Utility 4D	K13R	44185	2200	2550	3050	5125

SUBURBAN 4WD—V8—Truck Equipment Schedule T1

K1500 Sport Utility	K16T	29362	1750	1975	3025	5375
K2500 Sport Utility	K26U	31330	1875	2100	3200	5675
Third Row Seat			200	200	265	265
2WD	C		(525)	(525)	(715)	(715)

YUKON XL 4WD—V8—Truck Equipment Schedule T1

1500 Sport Utility	K13T	38081	2150	2450	3625	6475
2500 Sport Utility	K23U	39683	2250	2550	3775	6725
Third Row Seat			200	200	265	265
2WD	C		(525)	(525)	(715)	(715)

VENTURE—V6—Truck Equipment Schedule T2

Cargo Minivan 4D	U05E	22330	925	1100	1475	2525

VENTURE—V6—Truck Equipment Schedule T1

Minivan 4D	U05E	21230	625	775	1175	2025
Extended Minivan	X09E	24930	750	900	1300	2250

ASTRO/SAFARI—V6—Truck Equipment Schedule T2

Cargo/SL Cargo	M19W	20635	1200	1425	1900	3325
Dutch Doors			50	50	65	65
AWD	L		250	250	335	335

ASTRO/SAFARI—V6—Truck Equipment Schedule T1

Minivan/SL Minivan	M19W	21982	950	1175	1625	2825
Dutch Doors			50	50	65	65
AWD	L		250	250	335	335

EXPRESS/SAVANA—V8—Truck Equipment Schedule T1

1500 Passenger Van	G15M	24240	1925	2325	2725	4525
2500 Passenger Van	G25R	26245	2025	2425	2825	4675
3500 Passenger Van	G35R	26534	2125	2550	2950	4925
5-Passenger Seating	9		(200)	(200)	(265)	(265)
155" WB			50	50	65	65
V6, 4.3 Liter	W		(200)	(200)	(265)	(265)
V8, 5.7 Liter (1500)	R		150	150	200	200
V8, 454/7.4 Liter	J		100	100	135	135
V8, Turbo Dsl, 6.5L	F		100	100	115	115

EXPRESS/SAVANA—V6—Truck Equipment Schedule T1

1500 Cargo Van	G15W	21910	1200	1425	1825	3175
2500 Cargo Van	G25W	22360	1250	1500	1900	3275
155" WB			50	50	65	65
V8, 5.0 Liter	M		100	100	135	135

2000 CHEVROLET/GMC

Body Type	VIN	List	Trade-In Good	Very Good	Pvt-Party Good	Retail Excellent
V8, 5.7 Liter	R		150	150	200	200
V8, Turbo Diesel, 6.5L	F		125	125	175	175
EXPRESS/SAVANA—V8—Truck Equipment Schedule T1						
3500 Cargo Van	G35R	23894	1300	1550	1950	3375
155" WB			50	50	65	65
V8, 454/7.4 Liter	J		200	200	265	265
V8, Turbo Diesel, 6.5L	J		125	125	175	175
S10/SONOMA PICKUP—4-Cyl.—Truck Equipment Schedule T2						
Short Bed	S144	12610	1025	1150	1900	3375
Long Bed	S144	12661	825	925	1650	2925
Extended Cab	S194	15309	1700	1900	2900	5025
Third Door			100	100	135	135
4WD	T		400	400	535	535
V6, 4.3 Liter	W		200	200	265	265
SILVERADO/SIERRA REGULAR CAB—V8 (New)—Truck Schedule T1						
1500 Short Bed	C14V	18510	1875	2225	2650	4425
1500 Long Bed	C14V	18810	1725	2025	2425	4075
2500 Short Bed	C24T	21950	1950	2175	2700	4250
2500 HD Long Bed	C24T	23074	2650	2925	3375	5150
4WD	K		625	625	820	820
V6, 4.3 Liter	W		(350)	(350)	(455)	(455)
V8, 5.3 Liter (1500)	T		75	75	100	100
V8, 6.0 Liter	U		150	150	200	200
SILVERADO/SIERRA EXTENDED CAB—V8 (New)—Truck Schedule T1						
1500 Short Bed	C19V	22884	2750	3250	3650	6050
1500 Long Bed	C19V	23184	2475	2900	3300	5600
2500 Short Bed	C29T	24400	3325	3650	4300	6725
Fourth Door			125	125	160	160
4WD	K		625	625	820	820
V6, 4.3 Liter	W		(350)	(350)	(455)	(455)
V8, 5.3 Liter (1500)	T		75	75	100	100
V8, 6.0 Liter	U		150	150	200	200
SILVERADO/SIERRA EXTENDED CAB—V8 (New)—Truck Schedule T1						
2500 HD Short Bed	C29U	28324	3575	3925	4600	7175
2500 HD Long Bed	C29U	25524	3375	3725	4350	6800
Fourth Door			125	125	160	160
4WD	K		625	625	820	820
REGULAR CAB PICKUP—V8—Truck Equipment Schedule T1						
2500 HD Long Bed	C24R	21837	2075	2425	3000	5125
3500 Long Bed	C34R	22435	2100	2450	3050	5225
4WD	K		625	625	820	820
V8, 454/7.4 Liter	J		150	150	200	200
V8, Turbo Diesel, 6.5L	F		275	275	365	365
EXTENDED CAB PICKUP 4WD—V8—Truck Equipment Schedule T1						
2500 HD Short Bed	K29R	26547	3000	3475	4250	7350
V8, 454/7.4 Liter	J		150	150	200	200
V8, Turbo Diesel, 6.5L	F		275	275	365	365
EXTENDED CAB PICKUP—V8—Truck Equipment Schedule T1						
2500 HD Long Bed	C29R	23441	2700	3125	3875	6700
3500 Long Bed	C39R	25861	2875	3325	4000	6850
4WD	K		625	625	820	820
V8, 454/7.4 Liter	J		150	150	200	200
V8, Turbo Diesel, 6.5L	F		275	275	365	365
CREW CAB PICKUP—V8—Truck Equipment Schedule T1						
2500 Short Bed	C23R	24826	2850	3300	4050	7025
3500 Short Bed	C33R	27045	3700	4300	5200	8875
3500 Long Bed	C33R	25565	3525	4100	4825	8275
4WD	K		625	625	820	820
V8, 454/7.4 Liter	J		150	150	200	200
V8, Turbo Diesel, 6.5L	F		275	275	365	365

2001 CHEVY/GMC—(1,2or3)(CorG)(A,B,CorN)—J18C-1-#

Body Type	VIN	List	Trade-In Good	Very Good	Pvt-Party Good	Retail Excellent
TRACKER 4WD—4-Cyl.—Truck Equipment Schedule T2						
Sport Util Conv 2D	J18C	16760	1250	1450	2000	3350
Sport Utility 4D	J13C	17380	1675	1925	2625	4400
ZR2 Spt Util Conv 2D	J78C	18835	1725	2000	2700	4525
2WD	E		(300)	(300)	(385)	(385)
TRACKER 4WD—V6—Truck Equipment Schedule T2						
ZR2 Sport Utility 4D	J734	21200	2050	2350	2825	4550
LT Sport Utility 4D	J634	21880	2500	2875	3350	5325
2WD	E		(300)	(300)	(385)	(385)
BLAZER/JIMMY 4WD—V6—Truck Equipment Schedule T1						
Sport Utility 2D	T18W	23745	875	1025	1600	2825

TRUCKS & VANS

Body Type	VIN	List	Trade-In Good	Trade-In Very Good	Pvt-Party Good	Retail Excellent
Sport Utility 4D	T13W	27345	**1200**	**1375**	**2025**	**3525**
2WD			(625)	(625)	(820)	(820)
TAHOE 4WD—V8—Truck Equipment Schedule T1						
Sport Utility 4D	K13V	31021	**2850**	**3200**	**3775**	**6075**
Third Row Seat			200	200	265	265
2WD	C		(375)	(375)	(510)	(510)
V8, 5.3 Liter	T		75	75	100	100
YUKON 4WD—V8—Truck Equipment Schedule T1						
SLE Sport Utility 4D	K13V	36128	**3150**	**3525**	**4150**	**6700**
Third Row Seat			200	200	265	265
2WD	C		(375)	(375)	(510)	(510)
V8, 5.3 Liter	T,Z		75	75	100	100
YUKON DENALI AWD—V8—Truck Equipment Schedule T3						
Sport Utility 4D	K13U	46680	**3125**	**3600**	**3875**	**6200**
SUBURBAN 4WD—V8—Truck Equipment Schedule T1						
K1500 Sport Utility	K16T	29602	**2200**	**2475**	**3400**	**5825**
K2500 Sport Utility	K26U	31545	**2325**	**2600**	**3550**	**6075**
Third Row Seat			200	200	265	265
2WD			(625)	(625)	(820)	(820)
V8, 8.1 Liter	G		175	175	235	235
YUKON XL 4WD—V8—Truck Equipment Schedule T1						
1500 Sport Utility	K13T	36287	**2775**	**3100**	**4125**	**7025**
2500 Sport Utility	K23U	37659	**2900**	**3225**	**4275**	**7275**
2WD	C		(625)	(625)	(820)	(820)
V8, 8.1 Liter	G		175	175	235	235
YUKON XL DENALI AWD—V8—Truck Equipment Schedule T3						
1500 Sport Utility 4D	K16U	48185	**2775**	**3250**	**3475**	**5550**
VENTURE—V6—Truck Equipment Schedule T1						
Minivan 4D	U05E	21605	**800**	**975**	**1400**	**2425**
Extended Minivan	X09E	26085	**900**	**1100**	**1525**	**2625**
ASTRO/SAFARI—V6—Truck Equipment Schedule T2						
Cargo/SL Cargo	M19W	21238	**1375**	**1650**	**2125**	**3625**
Dutch Doors			50	50	65	65
AWD	L		250	250	335	335
ASTRO/SAFARI—V6—Truck Equipment Schedule T1						
Minivan 3D	M19W	23886	**1275**	**1525**	**2000**	**3425**
Dutch Doors			50	50	65	65
AWD	L		250	250	335	335
EXPRESS/SAVANA VAN—V8—Truck Equipment Schedule T1						
1500 Passenger Van	G15M	24725	**2400**	**2875**	**3125**	**5000**
2500 Passenger Van	G25R	26735	**2525**	**3000**	**3250**	**5200**
3500 Passenger Van	G35R	27024	**2675**	**3175**	**3425**	**5500**
155" WB			50	50	65	65
V6, 4.3 Liter	W		(200)	(200)	(265)	(265)
V8, 5.7 Liter (1500)	R		150	150	200	200
V8, 8.1 Liter	G		100	100	135	135
V8, Turbo Dsl, 6.5L	F		100	100	130	130
EXPRESS/SAVANA VAN—V8—Truck Equipment Schedule T1						
1500 Cargo Van	G15M	22520	**1475**	**1750**	**2225**	**3875**
2500 Cargo Van	G25M	22650	**1525**	**1800**	**2275**	**3975**
3500 Cargo Van	G35R	24929	**1575**	**1850**	**2325**	**4100**
155" WB			50	50	65	65
V6, 4.3 Liter	W		(200)	(200)	(265)	(265)
V8, 5.7 Liter (ex 3500)	R		150	150	200	200
V8, 8.1 Liter	G		200	200	265	265
V8, Turbo Diesel, 6.5L	F		150	150	195	195
S10/SONOMA PICKUP—4-Cyl. Flex Fuel—Truck Equipment Schedule T2						
Short Bed	S145	12859	**1325**	**1450**	**2125**	**3600**
Long Bed	S145	13210	**1100**	**1200**	**1850**	**3150**
Extended Cab	S195	16203	**2050**	**2250**	**3125**	**5150**
Third Door			125	125	160	160
4WD	T		400	400	535	535
V6, 4.3 Liter	W		200	200	265	265
S10/SONOMA CREW CAB 4WD—V6—Truck Equip Schedule T1						
LS/SLS Short Bed	T13W	25369	**3525**	**3875**	**5050**	**8225**
SILVERADO/SIERRA REGULAR CAB—V8—Truck Equip Schedule T1						
1500 Short Bed	C14V	19185	**2250**	**2650**	**3025**	**4950**
1500 Long Bed	C14V	19485	**1950**	**2300**	**2725**	**4500**
2500 Long Bed	C24U	23689	**2600**	**2850**	**3225**	**4800**
2500 HD Long Bed	C24U	24109	**3375**	**3700**	**3950**	**5750**
3500 Long Bed	C34U	25361	**3050**	**3350**	**3675**	**5425**
4WD	K		725	725	955	955
V6, 4.3 Liter	W		(350)	(350)	(465)	(465)

Body Type	VIN	List	Trade-In Good	Trade-In Very Good	Pvt-Party Good	Retail Excellent
V8, 5.3 Liter	T	....	75	75	100	100
V8, 8.1 Liter	G	....	175	175	235	235
V8, Turbo Diesel, 6.6L	1	....	2475	2475	3295	3295
SILVERADO/SIERRA EXTENDED CAB—V8—Truck Equip Schedule T1						
1500 Short Bed	C19V	23589	3100	3600	4025	6625
1500 Long Bed	C19V	23889	2875	3350	3775	6225
2500 HD Short Bed	C29U	26614	4100	4525	5050	7550
2500 HD Long Bed	C29U	26859	3925	4325	4850	7250
3500 Long Bed	C39U	28141	4000	4400	4950	7400
4WD	K	....	725	725	955	955
V6, 4.3 Liter	W	....	(350)	(350)	(465)	(465)
V8, 5.3 Liter	T	....	75	75	100	100
V8, 8.1 Liter	G	....	175	175	235	235
V8, Turbo Diesel, 6.6L	1	....	2475	2475	3295	3295
SILVERADO/SIERRA EXTENDED CAB 4WD—V8—Truck Equip Sch T1						
2500 Short Bed	K29U	29039	3900	4300	4825	7225
SIERRA EXTENDED CAB PICKUP AWD—Truck Equip Schedule T1						
1500 C3 Short Bed	C19U	33995	5375	6275	6825	11000
SILVERADO/SIERRA CREW CAB—V8—Truck Equipment Schedule T1						
1500 HD Short Bed	C13U	28912	3625	4225	4725	7725
2500 HD Short Bed	C23U	27084	4375	4800	5350	8025
2500 HD Long Bed	C23U	28284	4300	4725	5275	7900
3500 Long Bed	C33U	30766	4425	4875	5425	8100
4WD	K	....	725	725	955	955
V8, 8.1 Liter	G	....	175	175	235	235
V8, Turbo Diesel, 6.6L	1	....	2475	2475	3295	3295

Body Type	VIN	List	Trade-In Good	Trade-In Very Good	Pvt-Party Good	Retail Excellent
TRACKER 4WD—4-Cyl.—Truck Equipment Schedule T2						
Sport Util Conv 2D	J18C	17415	1675	1925	2550	4200
Sport Utility 4D	J13C	18105	2300	2625	3325	5425
ZR2 Spt Utl Conv 2D	J78C	19395	2350	2700	3400	5575
2WD	E	....	(350)	(350)	(465)	(465)
V6, 2.5 Liter	4	....	250	250	335	335
TRACKER 4WD—V6—Truck Equipment Schedule T2						
ZR2 Sport Utility 4D	J734	21845	2700	3075	3525	5575
LT Sport Utility 4D	J634	22270	3125	3550	4000	6275
2WD	E	....	(350)	(350)	(465)	(465)
BLAZER 4WD—V6—Truck Equipment Schedule T1						
Sport Utility 2D	T18W	....	1125	1300	1875	3150
Sport Utility 4D	T13W	26130	1525	1750	2375	3975
2WD	S	....	(700)	(700)	(935)	(935)
TRAILBLAZER 4WD—6-Cyl.—Truck Equipment Schedule T1						
Sport Utility 4D	T1S3	28130	1650	1925	2375	3975
Ext Spt Util 4D	T16S	33610	2050	2350	2900	4625
2WD	S	....	(425)	(425)	(575)	(575)
ENVOY 4WD—6-Cyl.—Truck Equipment Schedule T1						
Sport Utility 4D	T13S	31770	2150	2500	3025	5050
2WD	S	....	(425)	(425)	(575)	(575)
ENVOY XL 4WD—6-Cyl.—Truck Equipment Schedule T1						
Sport Utility 4D	T16S	33820	2300	2625	3250	5300
2WD	S	....	(425)	(425)	(575)	(575)
TAHOE 4WD—V8—Truck Equipment Schedule T1						
Sport Utility 4D	K13V	36345	3525	3925	4325	6650
Third Row Seat		....	225	225	310	310
2WD	C	....	(425)	(425)	(575)	(575)
V8, 5.3 Liter	T,Z	....	100	100	145	145
YUKON 4WD—V8—Truck Equipment Schedule T1						
Sport Utility 4D	K13V	37000	3650	4075	4675	7275
Third Row Seat		....	225	225	310	310
2WD	C	....	(425)	(425)	(575)	(575)
V8, 5.3 Liter	T,Z	....	100	100	145	145
YUKON DENALI 4WD—V8—Truck Equipment Schedule T3						
Sport Utility 4D	K63U	47355	3750	4325	4575	7125
SUBURBAN 4WD—V8—Truck Equipment Schedule T1						
K1500 Sport Utility	K16T	39219	2750	3075	4000	6650
K2500 Sport Utility	K26U	40916	2900	3225	4175	6925
2WD	C	....	(700)	(700)	(935)	(935)
V8, 8.1 Liter	G	....	200	200	255	255
YUKON XL 4WD—V8—Truck Equipment Schedule T1						
1500 Sport Utility	K13T	37047	3325	3700	4675	7725
2500 Sport Utility	K23U	38419	3450	3850	4825	7975
2WD	C	....	(700)	(700)	(935)	(935)

Body Type	VIN	List	Trade-In Good	Trade-In Very Good	Pvt-Party Good	Retail Excellent
V8, 8.1 Liter	G		200	200	255	255
YUKON XL DENALI AWD—V8—Truck Equipment Schedule T3						
1500 Sport Utility 4D	K66U	48890	3450	4000	4150	6500
VENTURE—V6—Truck Equipment Schedule T2						
Cargo Minivan 4D	U05E	24697	1250	1475	1950	3300
VENTURE—V6—Truck Equipment Schedule T1						
Minivan 4D	U03E	22035	925	1100	1550	2700
Ext Minivan 4D	X03E	26255	1150	1375	1850	3150
5-Passenger Seating			(225)	(225)	(310)	(310)
AWD			275	275	375	375
ASTRO/SAFARI—V6—Truck Equipment Schedule T2						
Cargo/SL Cargo	M19W	21768	1650	1950	2400	4025
Dutch Doors			75	75	85	85
AWD	L		275	275	375	375
ASTRO/SAFARI—V6—Truck Equipment Schedule T1						
Minivan 3D	M19X	24416	1625	1925	2375	3975
Dutch Doors			75	75	85	85
AWD	L		275	275	375	375
EXPRESS/SAVANA VAN—V8—Truck Equipment Schedule T1						
1500 Passenger Van	G15M	25287	3025	3575	3900	6275
2500 Passenger Van	G25R	27292	3100	3650	4000	6425
3500 Passenger Van	G35R	27581	3300	3875	4200	6750
155" WB			75	75	85	85
V6, 4.3 Liter	W		(225)	(225)	(310)	(310)
V8, 5.7 Liter (1500)	R		175	175	220	220
V8, 8.1 Liter	G		125	125	155	155
V8, Turbo Dsl, 6.5L	F		125	125	155	155
EXPRESS/SAVANA VAN—V8—Truck Equipment Schedule T1						
1500 Cargo Van	G15M	22948	1925	2250	2875	4950
2500 Cargo Van	G25M	23078	2000	2350	2975	5125
3500 Cargo Van	G35R	25357	2075	2425	3075	5300
155" WB			75	75	85	85
V6, 4.3 Liter	W		(225)	(225)	(310)	(310)
V8, 5.7 Liter (ex 3500)	R		175	175	220	220
V8, 8.1 Liter	G		225	225	310	310
V8, Turbo Diesel, 6.5L	F		175	175	245	245
S10/SONOMA PICKUP—4-Cyl. Flex Fuel—Truck Equipment Sch T2						
Short Bed	S145	14327	1725	1900	2700	4450
Long Bed	S145	15772	1350	1475	2150	3600
Extended Cab	S195	16309	2375	2625	3450	5625
4WD	T		500	500	665	665
V6, 4.3 Liter	W		225	225	310	310
S10/SONOMA CREW CAB PICKUP 4WD—V6—Truck Equipment Sch T1						
LS/SLS Short Bed	T13W	24584	4125	4525	5650	9050
AVALANCHE 4WD—V8—Truck Equipment Schedule T1						
1500 Spt Util Pickup	C13T	33965	4700	5350	5950	9275
2500 Spt Util Pickup	C23G	35865	5325	6050	6900	10850
2WD			(700)	(700)	(935)	(935)
North Face Edition			425	425	575	575
SILVERADO/SIERRA REGULAR CAB—V8—Truck Equipment Schedule T1						
1500 Short Bed	C14V	20028	2275	2650	3125	5150
1500 Long Bed	C14V	20328	2050	2400	2900	4800
2500 Long Bed	C24U	24182	3125	3425	3750	5475
2500 HD Long Bed	C24U	24672	4025	4400	4700	6700
3500 Long Bed	C34U	29017	3675	4025	4400	6400
4WD	K		850	850	1135	1135
V6, 4.3 Liter	W,X		(375)	(375)	(485)	(485)
V8, 5.3 Liter	T		100	100	145	145
V8, 8.1 Liter	G		200	200	255	255
V8, Turbo Diesel, 6.6L	1		2650	2650	3525	3525
SILVERADO/SIERRA EXTENDED CAB—V8—Truck Equipment Schedule T1						
1500 Short Bed	C19V	23952	3225	3775	4225	6925
1500 Long Bed	C19V	25052	3050	3550	4025	6575
2500 HD Short Bed	K29U	27177	5125	5600	6025	8800
2500 HD Long Bed	C29U	27452	4775	5225	5700	8350
3500 Long Bed	C39U	28734	4900	5375	5825	8550
Quadrasteer			325	325	445	445
4WD	K		850	850	1135	1135
V6, 4.3 Liter	W,X		(375)	(375)	(485)	(485)
V8, 5.3 Liter	T		100	100	145	145
V8, 8.1 Liter	G		200	200	255	255
V8, Turbo Diesel, 6.6L	1		2650	2650	3525	3525

TRUCKS & VANS

Body Type	VIN	List	Trade-In Good	Very Good	Pvt-Party Good	Retail Excellent
SILVERADO/SIERRA EXTENDED CAB 4WD—V8—Truck Equipment Sch T1						
2500 Short Bed	K29U	29407	4625	5075	5550	8125
SIERRA DENALI EXT CAB PICKUP AWD—V8—Truck Equipment Schedule T3						
1500 Short Bed	K69U	44105	7700	8425	8725	12400
SILVERADO/SIERRA CREW CAB PICKUP—V8—Truck Equipment Sch T1						
1500 HD Short Bed	C13U	29425	4075	4725	5225	8425
2500 HD Short Bed	C23U	28577	5250	5750	6225	9125
2500 HD Long Bed	C23U	28877	5175	5675	6150	9000
3500 Long Bed	C33U	30159	5325	5825	6300	9250
4WD	K		850	850	1135	1135
V8, 8.1 Liter	G		200	200	255	255
V8, Turbo Diesel, 6.6L	1		2650	2650	3525	3525

2003 CHEVY/GMC—(1,2or3)(CorG)(A,B,CorN)—(J18C)—3—#

Body Type	VIN	List	Trade-In Good	Very Good	Pvt-Party Good	Retail Excellent
TRACKER 4WD—4-Cyl.—Truck Equipment Schedule T2						
Sport Utl Conv 2D	J18C	17815	2175	2475	3025	4800
Sport Utility 4D	J13C	18505	2925	3325	3900	6175
ZR2 Spt Utl Conv 2D	J78C	19675	2950	3350	3950	6250
2WD	E		(425)	(425)	(565)	(565)
V6, 2.5 Liter	4		275	275	365	365
TRACKER 4WD—V6—Truck Equipment Schedule T2						
ZR2 Sport Utility 4D	J734	22125	3300	3725	4100	6250
LT Sport Utility 4D	J634	22550	3700	4175	4650	7100
2WD	E		(425)	(425)	(565)	(565)
BLAZER—V6—Truck Equipment Schedule T1						
Xtreme Sport Utl 2D	T18X	24170	1075	1250	1850	3150
BLAZER 4WD—V6—Truck Equipment Schedule T1						
LS Sport Utility 2D	T18X	24705	1425	1625	2275	3850
LS Sport Utility 4D	T13X	26585	1775	2050	2825	4725
2WD	T		(775)	(775)	(1040)	(1040)
TRAILBLAZER 4WD—6-Cyl.—Truck Equipment Schedule T1						
LS Sport Utility 4D	T13S	28800	1925	2225	2850	4725
LS Extended Spt Utl	T16S	33510	2325	2625	3375	5525
LT Sport Utility 4D	T13S	32345	2250	2625	3250	5425
LT Extended Spt Utl	T16S	34295	2575	2925	3650	5925
LTZ Sport Utility 4D	T13S	36195	2575	2950	3600	5975
2WD	T		(775)	(775)	(1040)	(1040)
V8, 5.3 Liter	P		150	150	210	210
ENVOY 4WD—6-Cyl.—Truck Equipment Schedule T1						
SLE Sport Utility 4D	T13S	31495	2575	2950	3600	5975
SLT Sport Utility 4D	T13S	36345	2500	2900	3525	5875
2WD	S		(775)	(775)	(1040)	(1040)
ENVOY XL 4WD—6-Cyl.—Truck Equipment Schedule T1						
SLE Sport Utility 4D	T16S	33795	2775	3125	3925	6425
SLT Sport Utility 4D	T16S	38145	2925	3300	4100	6700
2WD	S		(775)	(775)	(1040)	(1040)
V8, 5.3 Liter	P		150	150	210	210
TAHOE 4WD—V8—Truck Equipment Schedule T1						
LS Sport Utility 4D	K13V	37387	3875	4300	4675	6975
LT Sport Utility 4D	K13V	41380	4450	4925	5275	7875
Third Row Seat			275	275	355	355
2WD	C		(475)	(475)	(645)	(645)
V8, 5.3 Liter	T		150	150	210	210
YUKON—V8—Truck Equipment Schedule T1						
SLE Sport Utility 4D	C13V	35027	3600	4000	4400	6550
Third Row Seat			275	275	355	355
4WD	K		475	475	635	635
V8, 5.3 Liter	T		150	150	210	210
YUKON 4WD—V8—Truck Equipment Schedule T1						
SLT Sport Utility 4D	K13V	40300	4600	5100	5575	8450
Third Row Seat			275	275	355	355
2WD	C		(475)	(475)	(645)	(645)
V8, 5.3 Liter	T		150	150	210	210
YUKON DENALI 4WD—V8—Truck Equipment Schedule T3						
Sport Utility 4D	K63U	49195	5100	5825	5850	8850
SUBURBAN 4WD—V8—Truck Equipment Schedule T1						
K1500 LS Sport Util	K16T	43875	3375	3725	4250	6575
K1500 LT Sport Util	K16T	40630	4025	4475	5100	7850
K2500 LS Sport Util	K26U	45575	4125	4575	5200	8000
K2500 LT Sport Util	K26U	42230	4950	5475	6100	9375
Quadrasteer			375	375	495	495
2WD	C		(775)	(775)	(1040)	(1040)
V8, 8.1 Liter	G		200	200	270	270

364   **DEDUCT FOR RECONDITIONING**

1015

Body Type	VIN	List	Trade-In Good	Very Good	Pvt-Party Good	Retail Excellent
YUKON XL—V8—Truck Equipment Schedule T1						
1500 SLE Sport Util	C16T	37967	**3175**	**3525**	**4025**	**6225**
4WD	K		**775**	**775**	**1020**	**1020**
YUKON XL 4WD—V8—Truck Equipment Schedule T1						
1500 SLT Sport Util	K16Z	43590	**4850**	**5375**	**5975**	**9175**
2500 SLE Sport Util	K26U	42875	**4175**	**4650**	**5275**	**8100**
2500 SLT Sport Util	K26U	46165	**5100**	**5650**	**6275**	**9625**
Quadrasteer			**375**	**375**	**495**	**495**
2WD	C		**(775)**	**(775)**	**(1040)**	**(1040)**
V8, 8.1 Liter	G		**200**	**200**	**270**	**270**
YUKON XL DENALI AWD—V8—Truck Equipment Schedule T3						
1500 Sport Utility 4D	K16U	50859	**4425**	**5100**	**5225**	**7975**
YUKON XL Equipment Schedule T2						
Cargo Minivan 4D	U03E	22925	**1550**	**1800**	**2300**	**3850**
VENTURE—V6—Truck Equipment Schedule T1						
Minivan 4D	U03E	23139	**1325**	**1550**	**2025**	**3400**
Ext Minivan 4D	X03E	24509	**1400**	**1625**	**2125**	**3550**
LS Minivan 4D	U13E	25845	**1750**	**2050**	**2525**	**4200**
LS Ext Minivan	X03E	26845	**1725**	**2025**	**2600**	**4300**
LT Ext Minivan	X03E	29745	**2125**	**2500**	**3075**	**5075**
WarnerBros Ext	X13E	31995	**2225**	**2625**	**3175**	**5250**
5-Passenger Seating			**(275)**	**(275)**	**(355)**	**(355)**
AWD	V		**325**	**325**	**445**	**445**
ASTRO/SAFARI—V6—Truck Equipment Schedule T2						
Cargo/SL Cargo 3D	M19X	21952	**1925**	**2250**	**2850**	**4725**
Dutch Doors			**100**	**100**	**120**	**120**
AWD	L		**325**	**325**	**445**	**445**
ASTRO/SAFARI—V6—Truck Equipment Schedule T1						
Minivan 3D	M19X	23801	**1900**	**2225**	**2825**	**4675**
LS Minivan 3D	M19X	25390	**2000**	**2350**	**2925**	**4850**
LT Minivan 3D	M19X	29291	**2175**	**2550**	**3150**	**5200**
Dutch Doors			**100**	**100**	**120**	**120**
AWD	L		**325**	**325**	**445**	**445**
EXPRESS/SAVANA VAN—V8—Truck Equipment Schedule T1						
1500 Passenger	G15T	27005	**3625**	**4225**	**4525**	**7025**
1500 LS Passenger	G15T	28240	**3750**	**4375**	**4675**	**7250**
2500 Passenger	G25U	28000	**3675**	**4300**	**4575**	**7100**
2500 Extended	G29U	28995	**3875**	**4525**	**4825**	**7475**
2500 LS Passenger	G25U	30740	**3950**	**4625**	**4900**	**7600**
2500 LS Extended	G29U	31590	**4100**	**4800**	**5075**	**7875**
3500 Passenger	G35U	29499	**3975**	**4650**	**4925**	**7650**
3500 Extended	G39U	29499	**4075**	**4750**	**5050**	**7825**
3500 LS Passenger	G35U	31244	**4225**	**4950**	**5225**	**8100**
3500 LS Extended	G39U	32094	**4300**	**5025**	**5300**	**8225**
AWD	H		**325**	**325**	**445**	**445**
V6, 4.3 Liter	X		**(275)**	**(275)**	**(355)**	**(355)**
EXPRESS VAN—V6—Truck Equipment Schedule T1						
1500 Cargo Van	G15X	23185	**2550**	**2975**	**3400**	**5600**
AWD	H		**400**	**400**	**540**	**540**
V8, 5.3 Liter	T		**250**	**250**	**345**	**345**
EXPRESS VAN—V8—Truck Equipment Schedule T1						
1500 Cargo Van	G15X	23265	**2825**	**3275**	**3750**	**6200**
AWD	H		**400**	**400**	**540**	**540**
V6, 4.3 Liter	X		**(275)**	**(275)**	**(355)**	**(355)**
EXPRESS/SAVANA VAN—V8—Truck Equipment Schedule T1						
2500 Cargo Van	G25V	23415	**2900**	**3350**	**3850**	**6350**
2500 Ext Cargo	G29V	24695	**2975**	**3450**	**3950**	**6500**
3500 Cargo Van	G35U	25969	**3000**	**3475**	**3975**	**6550**
3500 Ext Cargo	G39U	27249	**3425**	**3975**	**4475**	**7375**
V6, 4.3 Liter	X		**(275)**	**(275)**	**(355)**	**(355)**
V8, 5.3 Liter (ex 1500)	T		**150**	**150**	**185**	**185**
V8, 6.0 Liter (ex 3500)	U		**275**	**275**	**355**	**355**
S10/SONOMA REGULAR CAB PICKUP—4-Cyl.—Truck Equip Sch T2						
2D 6'	S14H	14771	**1075**	**1200**	**1775**	**2925**
2D 7 1/3'	S14H	16216	**1175**	**1275**	**1875**	**3075**
LS/SLS 2D 6'	S14H	16495	**1425**	**1575**	**2150**	**3500**
LS/SLS 2D 7 1/3'	S14H	17945	**1500**	**1650**	**2250**	**3625**
S10/SONOMA EXTENDED CAB PICKUP—4-Cyl.—Truck Equip Sch T2						
3D 6'	S19H	16593	**1775**	**1950**	**2625**	**4200**
4WD	T		**625**	**625**	**820**	**820**
V6, 4.3 Liter	X		**275**	**275**	**355**	**355**
S10/SONOMA CREW CAB PICKUP 4WD—V6—Truck Equipment Sch T1						
LS/SLS 4D 4 1/2'	T13X	24404	**3900**	**4275**	**5150**	**7975**

TRUCKS & VANS

TRUCKS & VANS

Body Type	VIN	List	Trade-In Good	Very Good	Pvt-Party Good	Retail Excellent
SSR REGULAR CAB PICKUP—V8—Truck Equipment Schedule T3						
LS Convertible 2D	S14P	41995	15850	17250	15450	20100
AVALANCHE 4WD—V8—Truck Equipment Schedule T1						
1500 Spt Util Pickup	K13T	35139	5675	6425	6950	10450
2500 Spt Util Pickup	K23G	37039	6050	6825	7600	11650
2WD	C		(775)	(775)	(1040)	(1040)
North Face Edition			450	450	610	610
SILVERADO REGULAR CAB PICKUP—V6—Truck Equipment Sch T1						
1500 2D 6 1/2'	C14X	20031	2775	3225	3400	5275
1500 LS/SLE 2D 6 1/2'	C14X	23584	3200	3675	3800	5800
4WD	K		1025	1025	1380	1380
V8, 4.8 Liter	V		325	325	435	435
V8, 5.3 Liter	T		525	525	710	710
SIERRA REGULAR CAB PICKUP—V8—Truck Equipment Sch T1						
1500 2D 6 1/2'	C14V	20726	3350	3875	3950	6000
4WD	K		1025	1025	1380	1380
V6, 4.3 Liter	X		(400)	(400)	(520)	(520)
V8, 5.3 Liter	T		150	150	210	210
SILVERADO/SIERRA REGULAR CAB PICKUP—V8—Truck Equipment Sch T1						
1500 2D 8'	C14V	21026	2650	3075	3275	5050
1500 LS/SLE 2D 8'	C14V	24310	3125	3600	3775	5800
2500 Work Trk 8'	C24U	24810	2150	2375	2975	4575
2500 HD Wrk Trk 8'	C24U	25060	3425	3725	4125	6025
2500 2D 8'	C24U	23627	2875	3150	3725	5650
2500 HD 2D 8'	C24U	23877	4225	4600	5075	7375
2500 LS/SLE 2D 8'	C24U	27460	3350	3650	4225	6375
2500 HD LS/SLE 8'	C24U	27710	4425	4825	5275	7650
4WD	K		1025	1025	1380	1380
V6, 4.3 Liter	X		(400)	(400)	(520)	(520)
V8, 5.3 Liter	T		150	150	210	210
V8, 8.1 Liter	G		200	200	270	270
V8, Turbo Diesel, 6.6L	1		2900	2900	3880	3880
SILVERADO/SIERRA REGULAR CAB 4WD—V8 Turbo Diesel—Truck Sch T1						
3500 2D 8'	K341	29317	7350	8000	8775	12800
3500 LS/SLE 2D 8'	K341	31960	8025	8750	9500	13800
V8, 6.0 Liter	U		(3575)	(3575)	(4755)	(4755)
V8, 8.1 Liter	G		(2875)	(2875)	(3825)	(3825)
SILVERADO/SIERRA EXTENDED CAB PICKUP—V8—Truck Equip Sch T1						
1500 Work Trk 6 1/2'	C19V	24110	3500	4025	4325	6700
1500 4D 8'	C19V	24465	3825	4400	4700	7275
1500 4D 8'	C19V	26565	3625	4175	4450	6900
1500 LS/SLE 4D 6 1/2'	C19V	27265	4325	4975	5225	8075
1500 LS/SLE 4D 8'	C19V	27565	4325	5000	5200	8000
1500 LT/SLT 4D 6 1/2'	C19V	32475	4825	5550	5725	8800
1500 LT/SLT 4D 8'	C19V	32775	4375	5050	5275	8125
2500 HD 4D 6 1/2'	C29U	26257	4675	5100	5800	8625
2500 HD 4D 8'	C29U	26532	4875	5300	6000	8925
2500HD LS/SLE 8'	C29U	30560	5175	5625	6325	9375
2500HD LT/SLT 8'	C29U	34743	5400	5875	6550	9725
Quadrasteer			375	375	495	495
4WD	K		1025	1025	1380	1380
V6, 4.3 Liter	X		(400)	(400)	(520)	(520)
V8, 5.3 Liter	T		150	150	210	210
V8, 8.1 Liter	G		200	200	270	270
V8, Turbo Diesel, 6.6L	1		2900	2900	3880	3880
SILVERADO/SIERRA EXTENDED CAB PICKUP 4WD—V8—Truck Sch T1						
2500 4D 6 1/2'	K29U	29822	4425	4825	5525	8225
2500 LS/SLE 6 1/2'	K29U	32765	5200	5650	6350	9425
2500 LT/SLT 6 1/2'	K29U	37285	5200	5650	6350	9425
SILVERADO/SIERRA EXTENDED CAB PICKUP 4WD—V8—Truck Equip T1						
2500HD LS/SLE 6 1/2'	K29U	30260	6625	7225	8050	11850
2500HD LT/SLT 6 1/2'	K29U	34443	6700	7300	8125	11950
3500 LS/SLE 4D 8'	K39U	31510	6925	7550	8375	12300
2WD	C		(1150)	(1150)	(1525)	(1525)
V8, 8.1 Liter	G		200	200	270	270
V8, Turbo Diesel, 6.6L	1		2900	2900	3880	3880
SILVERADO/SIERRA EXTENDED CAB 4WD—V8 Turbo Diesel—Truck Sch T1						
3500 4D 8'	K391	28999	10100	11000	11850	17250
3500 LT/SLT 4D 8'	K391	35310	10800	11750	12700	18500
2WD	C		(1150)	(1150)	(1525)	(1525)
V8, 6.0 Liter	U		(3575)	(3575)	(4755)	(4755)
V8, 8.1 Liter	G		(2875)	(2875)	(3825)	(3825)

TRUCKS & VANS

Body Type	VIN	List	Trade-In Good	Very Good	Pvt-Party Good	Retail Excellent
SILVERADO SS EXTENDED CAB PICKUP AWD—V8—Truck Equip Sch T3						
1500 4D 6 1/2'	K19U	39995	9025	10350	10300	15600
SIERRA DENALI EXTENDED CAB PICKUP AWD—V8—Truck Equip Sch T3						
1500 4D 6 1/2'	K19U	44995	7200	7850	8425	12150
SILVERADO/SIERRA CREW CAB 4WD—V8 Turbo Diesel—Truck Equip T1						
2500HD LT/SLT 6 1/2'	K231	46435	10550	11500	12200	17600
2WD	C		(1150)	(1150)	(1525)	(1525)
V8, 6.0 Liter	U		(3575)	(3575)	(4755)	(4755)
V8, 8.1 Liter	G		(2875)	(2875)	(3825)	(3825)
SILVERADO CREW CAB PICKUP 4WD—V8—Truck Equip Schedule T1						
1500HD LS 6 1/2	K13U	32900	7200	8275	8400	12850
1500HD LT 6 1/2	K13U	38140	7425	8525	8700	13300
Quadrasteer			375	375	495	495
2WD	S		(775)	(775)	(1040)	(1040)
SIERRA CREW CAB PICKUP—V8—Truck Equip Schedule T1						
1500 HD SLE 6 1/2'	C13U	30442	5800	6700	6950	10650
4WD	K		1025	1025	1380	1380
SIERRA CREW CAB PICKUP 4WD—V8—Truck Equip Schedule T1						
1500 HD SLT 6 1/2'	K13U	33348	7850	9025	9175	14000
2WD	C		(1150)	(1150)	(1525)	(1525)
SILVERADO/SIERRA CREW CAB PICKUP 4WD—V8—Truck Equip Sch T1						
2500 4WD 8'	K23U	32640	6425	7000	7850	11550
2500HD LS/SLE 6 1/2	K23U	34629	6825	7425	8225	12050
3500 4D 8'	K33U	31620	6475	7050	7900	11650
2WD	C		(1150)	(1150)	(1525)	(1525)
V8, 8.1 Liter	G		200	200	270	270
V8, Turbo Diesel, 6.6L	1		2900	2900	3880	3880
SILVERADO/SIERRA CREW CAB PICKUP—V8—Truck Equip Schedule T1						
2500 4WD 8'	C23U	29577	5175	5625	6325	9375
2500HD LS/SLE 8'	C23U	32410	5425	5900	6775	10000
2500HD LT/SLT 8'	C23U	36831	5600	6100	6950	10250
4WD	K		1025	1025	1380	1380
V8, 8.1 Liter	G		200	200	270	270
V8, Turbo Diesel, 6.6L	1		2900	2900	3880	3880
SILVERADO/SIERRA CREW CAB 4WD—V8 Turbo Diesel—Truck Equip T1						
3500 LS/SLE 4D 8'	K331	33372	10950	11900	12800	18600
3500 LT/SLT 4D 8'	K331	37410	11100	12050	12900	18700
2WD	C		(1150)	(1150)	(1525)	(1525)
V8, 6.0 Liter	U		(3575)	(3575)	(4755)	(4755)
V8, 8.1 Liter	G		(2875)	(2875)	(3825)	(3825)

2004 CHEVY/GMC—(1,2or3)(CorG)(A,B,CorN)—(J134)—4—#

Body Type	VIN	List	Trade-In Good	Very Good	Pvt-Party Good	Retail Excellent
TRACKER 4WD—V6—Truck Equipment Schedule T2						
Sport Utility 4D	J134	21355	3525	3975	4500	6925
ZR2 Sport Utility 4D	J734	22705	3775	4250	4775	7225
LT Sport Utility 4D	J634	23105	4350	4875	5400	8150
2WD	E		(500)	(500)	(665)	(665)
BLAZER—V6—Truck Equipment Schedule T1						
Xtreme Spt Utility 2D	S18X	24940	1550	1750	2350	3875
BLAZER 4WD—V6—Truck Equipment Schedule T1						
LS Sport Utility 2D	T18X	25395	1775	2025	2725	4450
LS Sport Utility 4D	T13X	27345	2275	2600	3350	5425
2WD	S		(875)	(875)	(1155)	(1155)
TRAILBLAZER 4WD—6-Cyl.—Truck Equipment Schedule T1						
LS Sport Utility 4D	T13S	30045	2300	2625	3200	5175
LT Sport Utility 4D	T13S	32855	2800	3225	3775	6075
LS Ext Sport Util	T16S	32595	2975	3350	3925	6100
LT Ext Sport Util	T16S	34805	3200	3600	4175	6475
2WD	S		(875)	(875)	(1155)	(1155)
V8, 5.3 Liter	P		200	200	255	255
ENVOY 4WD—6-Cyl.—Truck Equipment Schedule T1						
SLE Sport Utility 4D	T13S	34655	3150	3600	4150	6650
SLT Sport Utility 4D	T13S	36905	3125	3575	4150	6650
2WD	S		(875)	(875)	(1155)	(1155)
ENVOY XL 4WD—6-Cyl.—Truck Equipment Schedule T1						
SLE Sport Utility 4D	T16S	36455	3400	3825	4475	6975
SLT Sport Utility 4D	T16S	38705	3575	4025	4775	7450
2WD	S		(875)	(875)	(1155)	(1155)
V8, 5.3 Liter	P		200	200	255	255
ENVOY XUV 4WD—6-Cyl.—Truck Equipment Schedule T1						
SLE Sport Utility 4D	T12S	34150	3275	3675	4000	5975
2WD	S		(875)	(875)	(1155)	(1155)
V8, 5.3 Liter	P		200	200	255	255

TRUCKS & VANS

Body Type	VIN	List	Trade-In Good	Very Good	Pvt-Party Good	Retail Excellent
ENVOY XUV 4WD—V8—Truck Equipment Schedule T1						
SLT Sport Utiltiy 4D	T12P	40215	3925	4425	4925	7400
2WD	S		(875)	(875)	(1155)	(1155)
6-Cyl, 4.2 Liter	S		(200)	(200)	(280)	(280)
TAHOE 4WD—V8—Truck Equipment Schedule T1						
LS Sport Utility 4D	K13V	38425	5200	5725	6050	8875
LT Sport Utility 4D	K13V	44600	5750	6350	6825	9975
Third Row Seat			300	300	385	385
2WD	C		(525)	(525)	(710)	(710)
V8, 5.3 Liter	T		200	200	255	255
YUKON—V8—Truck Equipment Schedule T1						
SLE Sport Utility 4D	C13V	35725	4875	5375	5725	8400
Third Row Seat			300	300	385	385
4WD	K		525	525	705	705
V8, 5.3 Liter	T		200	200	255	255
YUKON 4WD—V8—Truck Equipment Schedule T1						
SLT Sport Utility 4D	K13V	41315	6100	6725	7250	10700
Third Row Seat			300	300	385	385
2WD	C		(525)	(525)	(710)	(710)
V8, 5.3 Liter	T		200	200	255	255
YUKON DENALI AWD—V8—Truck Equipment Schedule T3						
Sport Utility 4D	K13U	50125	5950	6750	6925	10350
SUBURBAN 4WD—V8—Truck Equipment Schedule T1						
K1500 LS Sport Util	K16T	45870	4400	4875	5400	8075
K1500 LT Sport Util	K16T	43070	5175	5725	6225	9275
K2500 LS Sport Util	K26U	42600	5275	5825	6350	9475
K2500 LT Sport Util	K26U	47570	6275	6925	7575	11300
Quadrasteer			400	400	540	540
2WD	C		(875)	(875)	(1155)	(1155)
V8, 8.1 Liter	G		225	225	290	290
YUKON XL—V8—Truck Equipment Schedule T1						
1500 SLE Sport Util	C16T	38775	4025	4450	4975	7475
4WD	K		850	850	1135	1135
YUKON XL 4WD—V8—Truck Equipment Schedule T1						
1500 SLT Sport Util	K16Z	44765	5800	6425	7075	10550
2500 SLE Sport Util	K26U	43210	5325	5875	6375	9525
2500 SLT Sport Util	K26U	46500	6125	6750	7425	11050
Quadrasteer			400	400	540	540
2WD	C		(875)	(875)	(1155)	(1155)
V8, 8.1 Liter	G		225	225	290	290
YUKON XL DENALI AWD—V8—Truck Equipment Schedule T3						
1500 Sport Utility 4D	K16U	51775	5375	6150	6375	9500
VENTURE—V6—Truck Equipment Schedule T2						
Cargo Minivan 4D	U03E	23120	1775	2075	2675	4375
VENTURE—V6—Truck Equipment Schedule T1						
Minivan 4D	U03E	21995	1650	1925	2450	4050
LS Minivan 4D	U13E	26040	2050	2375	3025	4950
Ext Minivan 4D	X03E	23570	1725	2000	2550	4200
LS Ext Minivan 4D	X03E	27390	2150	2500	3125	5150
LT Ext Minivan 4D	X13E	31290	2425	2800	3450	5650
5-Passenger Seating	V		(300)	(300)	(385)	(385)
AWD			375	375	510	510
ASTRO/SAFARI—V6—Truck Equipment Schedule T2						
Cargo 3D	M19X	22965	2425	2825	3475	5675
Dutch Doors			100	100	135	135
AWD	L		375	375	510	510
ASTRO/SAFARI—V6—Truck Equipment Schedule T1						
Minivan 3D	M19X	24395	2350	2750	3400	5550
LS/SLE Minivan	M19X	25970	2500	2900	3550	5800
LT/SLT Minivan	M19X	29870	2725	3175	3800	6200
Dutch Doors			100	100	135	135
AWD	L		375	375	510	510
EXPRESS/SAVANA VAN—V8—Truck Equipment Schedule T1						
1500 Passenger	G15T	27280	4400	5075	5425	8325
1500 LS Passenger	G15T	28905	4550	5275	5600	8575
2500 Passenger	G25U	28685	4475	5175	5500	8450
2500 LS Passenger	G25U	31805	4850	5600	5875	9000
3500 Passenger	G35U	28089	4800	5550	5875	9000
3500 LS Passenger	G35U	32209	5075	5850	6175	9450
3500 Extended	G39U	30409	4925	5700	6000	9200
3500 LS Extended	G39U	33004	5200	6000	6300	9650
AWD	H		425	425	575	575
V6, 4.3 Liter	X		(300)	(300)	(385)	(385)

Body Type	VIN	List	Trade-In Good	Trade-In Very Good	Pvt-Party Good	Retail Excellent
EXPRESS VAN—V6—Truck Equipment Schedule T1						
1500 Cargo Van	G15X	23575	3600	4125	4325	6750
AWD	H		425	425	575	575
V8, 5.3 Liter	T		275	275	380	380
SAVANA VAN—V8—Truck Equipment Schedule T1						
1500 Cargo Van	G15T	23185	3625	4175	4575	7225
AWD	H		425	425	575	575
V6, 4.3 Liter	X		(300)	(300)	(385)	(385)
EXPRESS/SAVANA VAN—V8—Truck Equipment Schedule T1						
2500 Cargo Van	G25V	23965	3775	4350	4750	7500
2500 Extended	G29V	25040	3875	4475	4875	7700
3500 Cargo Van	G35U	27194	3900	4500	4900	7725
3500 Extended	G39U	28414	4375	5025	5400	8525
AWD	H		425	425	575	575
V6, 4.3 Liter	X		(300)	(300)	(385)	(385)
V8, 5.3 Liter (2500)	T		175	175	220	220
V8, 6.0 Liter (2500)	U		300	300	385	385
S10/SONOMA CREW CAB PICKUP 4WD—V6—Truck Equipment Sch T1						
LS/SLS 4D 4 1/2'	T13X	25095	4950	5375	5925	8700
COLORADO/CANYON REGULAR CAB PICKUP—4-Cyl.—Truck Equip Sch T2						
Base/SL 2D 6'	S148	17295	3300	3725	3925	5950
LS/SLE 2D 6'	S148	18135	3625	4100	4375	6625
4WD	T		750	750	960	960
5-Cyl, 3.5 Liter	6		150	150	195	195
COLORADO/CANYON EXT CAB PICKUP—4-Cyl.—Truck Equip Sch T2						
LS 4D 6'	S198	21235	5350	6075	6350	9525
SL 4D 6'	S198	22210	4725	5325	5500	8300
4WD	T		750	750	945	945
5-Cyl, 3.5 Liter	6		150	150	190	190
COLORADO/CANYON EXT CAB PICKUP—5-Cyl.—Truck Equip Sch T2						
Base 4D 6'	S196	20640	4150	4700	5050	7775
SLE 4D 6'	S196	24555	5550	6275	6550	9825
4WD	T		750	750	975	975
4-Cyl, 2.8 Liter	8		(150)	(150)	(190)	(190)
COLORADO/CANYON CREW CAB PICKUP—5-Cyl.—Truck Equip Sch T2						
LS/SLE 4D 5'	S136	23505	6300	7125	7375	11100
4WD	T		750	750	945	945
4-Cyl, 2.8 Liter	8		(150)	(150)	(185)	(185)
SSR REGULAR CAB PICKUP—V8—Truck Equipment Schedule T3						
Convertible 2D	S14P	41995	17100	18550	17100	22400
AVALANCHE 4WD—V8—Truck Equipment Schedule T1						
1500 Spt Util Pickup	K12T	36100	6925	7750	8025	11700
2500 Spt Util Pickup	K22G	37935	8525	9575	9750	14150
2WD	C		(875)	(875)	(1155)	(1155)
SILVERADO REGULAR CAB PICKUP—V6—Truck Equipment Sch T1						
1500 2D 6 1/2'	C14X	21905	2850	3275	3550	5450
4WD	K		1175	1175	1555	1555
V8, 4.8 Liter	V		375	375	485	485
V8, 5.3 Liter	T		550	550	750	750
SIERRA REGULAR CAB PICKUP—V8—Truck Equipment Sch T1						
1500 2D 6 1/2'	C14V	23400	3850	4400	4500	6675
4WD	K		1175	1175	1555	1555
V6, 4.3 Liter	X		(425)	(425)	(555)	(555)
V8, 5.3 Liter	T		200	200	255	255
SILVERADO/SIERRA REGULAR CAB PICKUP—V8—Truck Equipment Sch T1						
1500 Work Trk 6 1/2'	C14V	21185	2150	2475	2700	4100
1500 Work Truck 8'	C14V	21285	1825	2100	2400	3725
1500 2D 8'	C14V	23700	2975	3400	3600	5475
1500 LS/SLE 2D 6 1/2'	C14V	25585	3925	4500	4600	6825
1500 LS/SLE 2D 8'	C14V	25585	3550	4050	4125	6200
2500 Wrk Trk 2D 8'	C24U	25465	4475	4850	5150	7200
2500 2D 8'	C24U	26660	5400	5875	6125	8550
2500 LS/SLE 2D 8'	C24U	28215	5550	6025	6475	9025
2500 HD Work Trk 8'	C24U	25940	5425	5875	6025	8300
2500 HD 2D 8'	C24T	26910	6875	7450	7625	10450
2500 HD LS/SLE 8'	C24U	28690	7275	7900	8100	11100
4WD	K		1175	1175	1555	1555
V6, 4.3 Liter	X		(425)	(425)	(555)	(555)
V8, 5.3 Liter	T		200	200	255	255
V8, 8.1 Liter	G		225	225	260	260
V8, 6.6L Turbo Dsl	1,2		3225	3225	3820	3820
SILVERADO/SIERRA REGULAR CAB 4WD—V8—Truck Equipment Sch T1						
3500 Wrk Trk 2D 8'	K34U	29595	5200	5650	5875	8175

Body Type	VIN	List	Trade-In Good	Trade-In Very Good	Pvt-Party Good	Retail Excellent
V8, 8.1 Liter	G		225	225	265	265
V8, 6.6L Turbo Dsl	1,2		3225	3225	3900	3900
SILVERADO/SIERRA REGULAR CAB 4WD—V8 Turbo Diesel—Truck Equipment Sch T1						
3500 2D 8'	K341,2	30940	10450	11300	11600	16100
3500 LS/SLE 2D 8'	K341,2	31845	10950	11850	12150	16800
V8, 6.0 Liter	U		(3900)	(3900)	(4715)	(4715)
V8, 8.1 Liter	G		(3300)	(3300)	(3990)	(3990)
SILVERADO REGULAR CAB PICKUP 4WD—V8—Truck Equipment Sch T1						
1500 Z71 2D 6 1/2'	K14V	30235	5400	6150	6150	9150
1500 Z71 2D 8'	K14V	30535	5200	5925	5950	8850
V8, 5.3 Liter	T		200	200	255	255
SILVERADO/SIERRA EXT CAB PICKUP—V8—Truck Equipment Schedule T1						
1500 Work Trk 6 1/2'	C19V	25090	3950	4525	4725	7125
1500 Work Truck 8'	C19V	25740	3500	4000	4150	6275
1500 4D 6 1/2'	C19V	26260	4750	5425	5525	8300
1500 4D 8'	C19V	26815	4250	4875	5050	7600
1500 LS/SLE 4D 6 1/2'	C19V	28145	4900	5600	5725	8575
1500 LS/SLE 4D 8'	C19V	28995	4800	5475	5600	8425
2500 HD Wk Tk 6 1/2'	C29U	28590	6700	7275	7725	10850
2500 HD Wrk Trk 8'	C29U	28890	6675	7250	7675	10750
2500 HD 4D 6 1/2'	C29U	29160	7475	8125	8575	12000
2500 HD 4D 8'	C29U	29460	7800	8475	8925	12450
2500 HD LS/SLE 8'	C29U	31540	8125	8800	9225	12900
2500HD LT/SLT 6 1/2'	K29U	35423	10250	11100	11500	16100
2500 HD LT/SLT 8'	C29U	35723	8250	8950	9375	13100
3500 Wrk Trk 4D 8'	C39U	30150	6850	7450	7800	10900
4WD	K		1175	1175	1555	1555
V6, 4.3 Liter	X		(425)	(425)	(555)	(555)
V8, 5.3 Liter	T		200	200	255	255
V8, 6.0 Liter	N		375	375	505	505
V8, 8.1 Liter	G		225	225	265	265
V8, 6.6L Turbo Dsl	1,2		3225	3225	3925	3925
SILVERADO/SIERRA EXT CAB 4WD PICKUP—V8—Truck Equipment Sch T1						
2500 Wrk Trk 6 1/2'	K29U	30820	6350	6900	7300	10200
2500 4D 6 1/2'	K29U	31615	7275	7900	8350	11700
2500 LS/SLE 6 1/2'	K29U	33520	7725	8375	8825	12300
2500 LT/SLT 6 1/2'	K29U	38040	7825	8475	8950	12550
2500HD LS/SLE 6 1/2'	K29U	31240	9950	10750	11200	15700
3500 LS/SLE 6 1/2'	K39U	32490	10600	11500	11950	16650
2WD	C		(1475)	(1475)	(1795)	(1795)
V8, 8.1 Liter	G		225	225	265	265
V8, 6.6L Turbo Dsl	1,2		3225	3225	3925	3925
SILVERADO/SIERRA EXT CAB 4WD—V8 Turbo Diesel—Truck Equip Sch T1						
3500 4D 8'	K391,2	30400	13300	14450	14950	20900
3500 LT/SLT 4D 8'	K391,2	36290	14450	15650	16100	22500
2WD	C		(1475)	(1475)	(1795)	(1795)
V8, 6.0 Liter	U		(3900)	(3900)	(4755)	(4755)
V8, 8.1 Liter	G		(3300)	(3300)	(4025)	(4025)
SILVERADO/SIERRA EXT CAB PICKUP—V8—Truck Equipment Schedule T1						
1500 LT/SLT 4D 6 1/2'	C19T	33455	5600	6425	6625	9900
1500 LT/SLT 4D 8'	C19T	33755	5325	6075	6150	9225
4WD	K		1175	1175	1555	1555
V8, 6.0 Liter	N		375	375	505	505
SILVERADO EXTENDED CAB PICKUP 4WD—V8—Truck Equipment Sch T1						
1500 Z71 4D 6 1/2'	K19V	32202	6200	7075	7225	10800
V8, 5.3 Liter	T		200	200	255	255
SILVERADO EXTENDED CAB PICKUP 4WD—V8—Truck Equipment Sch T1						
1500 Z71 4D 8'	K19T	32502	6000	6850	7025	10500
SILVERADO SS EXT CAB PICKUP AWD—V8—Truck Equipment Schedule T3						
1500 4D 6 1/2'	K19N	40195	9825	11200	11550	16350
SIERRA DENALI EXT CAB PICKUP AWD—V8—Truck Equip Schedule T3						
1500 4D 6 1/2'	K69U	41995	8025	8700	9400	13400
SILVERADO/SIERRA CREW CAB PICKUP—V8—Truck Equipment Sch T1						
1500 Work Truck 5 3/4'	C13T	31020	6650	7575	7690	11250
1500 LT/SLT 4D 5 3/4'	C13T	35023	7200	8225	8150	12050
2500 LS/SLE 4D 6 1/2'	C23U	31540	8850	9575	10000	14000
2500 LT/SLT 4D 6 1/2'	C23U	36366	9075	9850	10250	14300
2500HD Wk Trk 6 1/2'	C23U	30590	7300	7925	8375	11700
2500 HD Wrk Trk 8'	C23U	30890	7275	7875	8275	11550
2500 HD 4D 8'	C23U	31160	8550	9275	9700	13550
2500 HD LS/SLE 8'	C23U	33390	8850	9575	10000	14000
2500 HD LT/SLT 8'	C23U	37811	9075	9850	10250	14300
3500 Work Truck 8'	C33U	32150	7425	8050	8500	11900

Body Type	VIN	List	Trade-In Good	Very Good	Pvt-Party Good	Retail Excellent
Quadrasteer			400	400	540	540
4WD	K		1175	1175	1555	1555
V8, 8.1 Liter	G		225	225	265	265
V8, 6.6L Turbo Dsl	1,2		3225	3225	3930	3930
SIERRA CREW CAB PICKUP—V8—Truck Equipment Sch T1						
3500 4D 8'	C33U	31710	8750	9475	9900	13850
4WD	K		1175	1175	1425	1425
V8, Turbo Diesel, 6.6L	1,2		3225	3225	3935	3935
V8, 8.1 Liter	G		225	225	265	265
SILVERADO CREW CAB PICKUP 4WD—V8—Truck Equipment Sch T1						
3500 4D 8'	K33U	31710	10150	10950	11450	16050
2WD			(1475)	(1475)	(1800)	(1800)
V8, 6.6L Turbo Dsl	1,2		3225	3225	3945	3945
V8, 8.1 Liter	G		225	225	265	265
SILVERADO/SIERRA CREW CAB 4WD—V8—Truck Equipment Sch T1						
2500HD LT/SLT 6 1/2'	K23U	34210	10350	11200	11600	16250
2500HD LS/SLE 6 1/2'	K23U	35735	10300	11200	11600	16150
2WD	C		(1475)	(1475)	(1795)	(1795)
V8, 8.1 Liter	G		225	225	265	265
V8, 6.6L Turbo Dsl	1,2		3225	3225	3930	3930
SILVERADO/SIERRA CREW CAB 4WD—V8 Turbo Diesel—Truck Sch T1						
2500HD LT/SLT 6'	K231,2	47618	14550	15750	15950	22000
3500 LS/SLE 4D 8'	K331,2	34352	14650	15850	16350	22800
3500 LT/SLT 4D 8'	K331,2	38390	14950	16200	16600	23100
2WD	C		(1475)	(1475)	(1800)	(1800)
V8, 6.0 Liter	G		(3900)	(3900)	(4765)	(4765)
V8, 8.1 Liter	G		(3300)	(3300)	(4030)	(4030)
SILVERADO CREW CAB PICKUP 4WD—V8—Truck Equipment Sch T1						
1500 Z71 4D 5 3/4'	K13T	35040	7050	8050	8025	11900

Body Type	VIN	List	Good	Very Good	Good	Excellent
BLAZER—V6—Truck Equipment Schedule T1						
Xtreme Spt Util 2D	S18X	24940	1825	2100	3050	4850
BLAZER 4WD—V6—Truck Equipment Schedule T1						
LS Sport Utility 2D	T18X	25850	2125	2450	3425	5425
LS Sport Utility 4D	T13X	28025	2400	2750	3850	6175
2WD	S		(950)	(950)	(1260)	(1260)
EQUINOX—V6—Truck Equipment Schedule T1						
LS Sport Utility 4D	L13F	21660	2300	2625	3425	5425
LT Sport Utility 4D	L63F	23600	2825	3200	4000	6275
AWD	2,7		550	550	715	715
TRAILBLAZER 4WD—6-Cyl.—Truck Equipment Schedule T1						
LS Sport Utility 4D	T13S	30655	2550	2925	3675	5800
LT Sport Utility 4D	T13S	33305	3125	3575	4350	6775
LS Ext Sport Util	T16S	32775	3300	3700	4500	6675
LT Ext Sport Util	T16S	34955	3550	3975	4750	7075
2WD	S		(950)	(950)	(1260)	(1260)
V8, 5.3 Liter	M		225	225	285	285
ENVOY 4WD—6-Cyl.—Truck Equipment Schedule T1						
SLE Sport Utility 4D	T13S	32685	3275	3750	4525	7100
SLT Sport Utility 4D	T13S	37025	3350	3850	4800	7550
2WD	S		(950)	(950)	(1260)	(1260)
ENVOY DENALI 4WD—V8—Truck Equipment Schedule T3						
Sport Utility 4D	T63M	39640	4725	5300	6000	8775
2WD	S		(950)	(950)	(1260)	(1260)
ENVOY XL 4WD—6-Cyl.—Truck Equipment Schedule T1						
SLE Sport Utility 4D	T16S	34355	3450	3875	4775	7225
SLT Sport Utility 4D	T16S	38675	4000	4500	5350	8000
2WD	S		(950)	(950)	(1260)	(1260)
V8, 5.3 Liter	M		225	225	285	285
ENVOY XL DENALI 4WD—V8—Truck Equipment Schedule T3						
Sport Utility 4D	T16M	40920	4825	5425	6200	9000
2WD	S		(950)	(950)	(1260)	(1260)
ENVOY XUV 4WD—6-Cyl.—Truck Equipment Schedule T1						
SLE Sport Utility 4D	T12S	34440	3100	3500	4450	6925
2WD	S		(950)	(950)	(1260)	(1260)
V8, 5.3 Liter	M		225	225	285	285
ENVOY XUV 4WD—V8—Truck Equipment Schedule T1						
SLT Sport Utility 4D	T12M	39975	4250	4775	5725	8625
2WD	S		(950)	(950)	(1260)	(1260)
6-Cyl, 4.2 Liter	S		(225)	(225)	(305)	(305)
TAHOE 4WD—V8—Truck Equipment Schedule T1						
LS Sport Utility 4D	K13V	39185	5000	5525	6350	9225

TRUCKS & VANS

Body	Type	VIN	List	Trade-In Good	Very Good	Pvt-Party Good	Retail Excellent
LT Sport Utility 4D		K13V	45155	6400	7050	7725	11050
Third Row Seat				325	325	420	420
2WD		C	......	(575)	(575)	(775)	(775)
V8, 5.3 Liter		T	......	225	225	285	285
YUKON—V8—Truck Equipment Schedule T1							
SLE Sport Utility 4D		C13V	36310	5050	5575	6350	9175
Third Row Seat				325	325	420	420
4WD		K	......	575	575	775	775
V8, 5.3 Liter		T	......	225	225	285	285
YUKON 4WD—V8—Truck Equipment Schedule T1							
SLT Sport Utility 4D		K13V	42075	6900	7575	8275	11900
Third Row Seat				325	325	420	420
2WD		C	......	(575)	(575)	(775)	(775)
V8, 5.3 Liter		T	......	225	225	285	285
YUKON DENALI AWD—V8—Truck Equipment Schedule T3							
Sport Utility 4D		K63U	50885	8200	9200	9175	13050
SUBURBAN 4WD—V8—Truck Equipment Schedule T1							
K1500 LS Sport Util		K16Z	42415	5100	5625	6275	9100
K1500 LT Sport Util		K16Z	48005	5900	6500	7275	10500
K2500 LS Sport Util		K26U	43690	6000	6600	7375	10650
K2500 LT Sport Util		K26U	48890	7125	7850	8625	12450
Quadrasteer			......	450	450	590	590
2WD		C	......	(950)	(950)	(1260)	(1260)
V8, 8.1 Liter		G	......	225	225	305	305
YUKON XL—V8—Truck Equipment Schedule T1							
1500 SLE Sport Util		C16Z	39360	4400	4875	5550	8075
Quadrasteer			......	450	450	590	590
4WD		K	......	925	925	1245	1245
YUKON XL 4WD—V8—Truck Equipment Schedule T1							
1500 SLT Sport Util		K16Z	46295	6750	7425	8150	11750
2500 SLE Sport Util		K26U	43560	6050	6650	7450	10750
2500 SLT Sport Util		K26U	47370	7250	7975	8775	12650
Quadrasteer			......	450	450	590	590
2WD		C	......	(950)	(950)	(1260)	(1260)
V8, 8.1 Liter		G	......	225	225	305	305
YUKON XL DENALI AWD—V8—Truck Equipment Schedule T3							
1500 Sport Utility 4D		K66U	52535	7025	7975	8150	11800
VENTURE—V6—Truck Equipment Schedule T2							
Cargo Minivan 4D		V13E	23880	1975	2300	3025	4850
VENTURE—V6—Truck Equipment Schedule T1							
Ext Minivan 4D		V03E	24080	1775	2075	2800	4500
LS Ext Minivan		V23E	27550	2300	2675	3425	5475
LT Ext Minivan		V33E	31475	2675	3100	3850	6100
5-Passenger Seating				(325)	(325)	(420)	(420)
ASTRO/SAFARI—V6—Truck Equipment Schedule T2							
Cargo 3D		M19X	23540	2925	3400	4150	6575
Dutch Doors				100	100	135	135
AWD		L	......	425	425	575	575
ASTRO/SAFARI—V6—Truck Equipment Schedule T1							
Minivan 3D		M19X	25040	2900	3325	4100	6500
LS Minivan 3D		M19X	28535	3150	3650	4400	6950
LT Minivan 3D		M19X	30185	3425	3950	4700	7400
Dutch Doors				100	100	135	135
AWD		L	......	425	425	575	575
UPLANDER—V6—Truck Equipment Schedule T2							
Cargo Minivan 4D		V13L	21415	1900	2225	3000	4825
UPLANDER—V6—Truck Equipment Schedule T1							
Extended Minivan		V03L	24350	1925	2250	2925	4600
LS Extended		V23L	26955	2075	2425	3100	4875
LT Extended		V33L	29385	2625	3025	3675	5775
AWD		X	......	375	375	495	495
EXPRESS/SAVANA VAN—V8—Truck Equipment Schedule T1							
1500 Passenger		G15T	26305	4950	5700	6125	9050
1500 LS Passenger		G15T	26690	5000	5775	6175	9150
2500 Passenger		G25V	29405	5175	5950	6350	9400
2500 LS Passenger		G25V	29540	5225	6025	6425	9500
3500 Passenger		G35U	30009	5250	6075	6625	9800
3500 LS Passenger		G35U	30624	5350	6175	6725	9950
3500 Extended		G39U	31594	5325	6150	6725	9950
3500 LS Extended		G39U	31594	5475	6325	6850	10150
V6, 4.3 Liter		X	......	(325)	(325)	(420)	(420)
EXPRESS VAN—V6—Truck Equipment Schedule T1							
1500 Cargo Van		G15X	23980	4100	4725	5200	7875

Body Type	VIN	List	Trade-In Good	Very Good	Pvt-Party Good	Retail Excellent
AWD	H		450	450	610	610
V8, 5.3 Liter	T		325	325	415	415
SAVANA VAN—V8—Truck Equipment Schedule T1						
1500 Cargo Van	G15X	23575	4425	5075	5550	8425
AWD	H		450	450	610	610
V6, 4.3 Liter	X		(325)	(325)	(420)	(420)
EXPRESS/SAVANA VAN—V8—Truck Equipment Schedule T1						
2500 Cargo Van	G25T	24275	4700	5400	5850	8875
3500 Cargo Van	G35V	26809	4850	5550	6000	9100
V8, 6.0 Liter	U		325	325	420	420
EXPRESS/SAVANA VAN—V8—Truck Equipment Schedule T1						
2500 Extended	G29T	25415	4800	5500	5950	9025
3500 Extended	G39V	28014	5000	5725	6150	9350
V6, 4.3 Liter	X		(325)	(325)	(420)	(420)
V8, 6.0 Liter	U		325	325	420	420
COLORADO/CANYON REGULAR CAB PICKUP—4-Cyl.—Truck Equip Sch T2						
Base/SL 2D 6'	S148	17425	3250	3675	4150	6225
LS 2D 6'	S148	18425	3600	4075	4700	7075
4WD	T		875	875	1155	1155
5-Cyl, 3.5 Liter	6		150	150	215	215
CANYON REGULAR CAB PICKUP—5-Cyl.—Truck Equip Sch T2						
SLE 2D 6'	S146	19870	3850	4350	4875	7200
4WD	T		875	875	1155	1155
4-Cyl, 2.8 Liter	8		(150)	(150)	(205)	(205)
COLORADO EXTENDED CAB PICKUP—4-Cyl.—Truck Equipment Sch T2						
LS 4D 6'	S198	21545	5450	6150	6775	10050
4WD	T		875	875	1155	1155
5-Cyl, 3.5 Liter	6		150	150	215	215
COLORADO EXTENDED CAB PICKUP—5-Cyl.—Truck Equipment Sch T2						
Base 4D 6'	S196	20770	4700	5300	5825	8675
4WD	T		875	875	1155	1155
4-Cyl, 2.8 Liter	8		(150)	(150)	(205)	(205)
CANYON EXTENDED CAB PICKUP—4-Cyl.—Truck Equipment Sch T2						
SL 4D 6'	S198	20100	4675	5275	5800	8625
4WD	T		875	875	1155	1155
5-Cyl, 3.5 Liter	6		150	150	215	215
CANYON EXTENDED CAB PICKUP—5-Cyl.—Truck Equipment Sch T2						
SLE 4D 6'	S196	22990	5625	6350	6925	10250
4WD	T		875	875	1155	1155
4-Cyl, 2.8 Liter	8		(150)	(150)	(205)	(205)
COLORADO/CANYON CREW CAB PICKUP—5-Cyl.—Truck Equip Sch T2						
LS/SLE 4D 5'	S136	23915	6625	7475	8025	11900
4WD	T		875	875	1155	1155
4-Cyl, 2.8 Liter	8		(150)	(150)	(205)	(205)
SSR REGULAR CAB PICKUP—V8—Truck Equipment Schedule T3						
Convertible 2D	S14H	43055	18400	19900	18600	24100
AVALANCHE 4WD—V8—Truck Equipment Schedule T1						
1500 LS Util Pickup	K12Z	37765	7600	8500	8925	12650
1500 LT Util Pickup	K12Z	41805	8175	9125	9475	13350
2500 LS Util Pickup	K22G	39175	8575	9550	10050	14300
2500 LT Util Pickup	K22G	43215	8725	9750	10300	14650
2WD	C		(950)	(950)	(1260)	(1260)
SILVERADO/SIERRA REGULAR CAB PICKUP—V6—Truck Equipment Sch T1						
1500 2D 6 1/2'	C14X	22555	3725	4275	4625	6725
4WD	K		1275	1275	1690	1690
V8, 4.8 Liter	V		400	400	535	535
V8, 5.3 Liter	T		625	625	825	825
V8, FFV, 5.3 Liter	Z		575	575	760	760
SILVERADO/SIERRA REGULAR CAB PICKUP—V8—Truck Equipment Sch T1						
1500 Work Trk 6 1/2'	C14V	21830	3275	3775	4050	5800
1500 Work Truck 8'	C14V	21930	3100	3550	3775	5400
1500 2D 8'	C14V	23935	4000	4575	4825	6950
1500 LS/SLE 2D 6 1/2'	C14V	26585	4925	5600	5725	8200
1500 LS/SLE 2D 8'	C14V	26585	4650	5275	5450	7800
2500 HD Wrk Trk 8'	C24U	26350	5300	5750	6500	8975
2500 HD 2D 8'	C24U	27700	6725	7275	7900	10850
2500 HD LS/SLE 8'	C24U	29100	7375	7975	8700	11950
4WD	K		1275	1275	1690	1690
V6, 4.3 Liter	X		(450)	(450)	(585)	(585)
V8, 5.3 Liter	T		225	225	285	285
V8, 8.1 Liter	G		225	225	275	275
V8, 6.6L Turbo Dsl	2		3525	3525	4180	4180

TRUCKS & VANS

TRUCKS & VANS

Body Type	VIN	List	Trade-In Good	Very Good	Pvt-Party Good	Retail Excellent
SILVERADO REGULAR CAB PICKUP 4WD—V8—Truck Equipment Sch T1						
1500 Z71 2D 6 1/2'	K14V	30570	6800	7725	7825	11150
1500 Z71 2D 8'	K14V	30870	6600	7500	7600	10850
V8, 5.3 Liter	T		225	225	285	285
SILVERADO/SIERRA REGULAR CAB PICKUP 4WD—V8—Truck Equip Sch T1						
3500 Work Truck 8'	K34U	30855	5075	5500	6100	8425
V8, 8.1 Liter	G		225	225	280	280
V8, 6.6L Turbo Dsl	2		3525	3525	4265	4265
SILVERADO/SIERRA REGULAR CAB 4WD—V8 Turbo Diesel—Sch T1						
3500 2D 8'	K342	31730	10300	11100	11800	16150
3500 LS/SLE 2D 8'	K342	32510	10900	11750	12550	17250
V8, 6.0 Liter	U		(4275)	(4275)	(5075)	(5075)
V8, 8.1 Liter	G		(3625)	(3625)	(4300)	(4300)
SILVERADO/SIERRA EXTENDED CAB—V8 Hybrid—Truck Equipment Sch T1						
1500 LS/SLE 6 1/2'	C19T	28845	10800	12200	12050	17300
4WD			1275	1275	1690	1690
SILVERADO/SIERRA EXTENDED CAB PICKUP—V8—Truck Equip Sch T1						
1500 Work Trk 6 1/2'	C19V	25790	5275	6000	6200	8975
1500 Work Truck 8'	C19V	24790	4525	5150	5400	7775
1500 4D 6 1/2'	C19V	27295	5400	6150	6525	9475
1500 4D 8'	C19V	28295	5325	6050	6400	9225
1500 LS/SLE 4D 6 1/2'	C19V	28845	6375	7225	7400	10600
1500 LS/SLE 4D 8'	C19V	30045	5975	6800	7025	10100
1500 LT/SLT 4D 6 1/2'	C19T	33985	7150	8125	8300	11950
1500 LT/SLT 4D 8'	C19T	34285	6525	7400	7600	10950
2500HD Wk Trk 6 1/2'	C29U	29050	6550	7075	7950	11100
2500 HD Wrk Trk 8'	C29U	29350	6500	7025	7875	11000
2500 HD 4D 6 1/2'	C29U	30000	7725	8350	9275	12950
2500 HD 4D 8'	C29U	30300	7775	8400	9275	12900
2500 HD LS/SLE 8'	C29U	32000	8450	9125	9975	13850
2500 HD LT/SLT 8'	C29U	37280	8675	9400	10200	14300
3500 Work Truck 8'	C39U	30610	6975	7550	8425	11750
Quadrasteer			450	450	590	590
4WD	K		1275	1275	1690	1690
V6, 4.3 Liter	X		(450)	(450)	(585)	(585)
V8, 5.3L (ex LT/SLT)	T		225	225	285	285
V8, 8.1 Liter	G		225	225	280	280
V8, 6.6L Turbo Dsl	2		3525	3525	4265	4265
SILVERADO/SIERRA EXTENDED CAB PICKUP 4WD—V8—Truck Sch T1						
2500HD LS/SLE 6 1/2	K29U	31700	10700	11550	12350	17100
2500HD LT/SLT 6 1/2	K29U	36980	10950	11850	12700	17550
3500 LS/SLE 4D 8'	K39U	32950	11650	12600	13450	18600
2WD	C		(1625)	(1625)	(1950)	(1950)
V8, 8.1 Liter	G		225	225	275	275
V8, 6.6L Turbo Dsl	2		3525	3525	4225	4225
SILVERADO/SIERRA EXTENDED CAB 4WD—V8 Turbo Diesel—Truck Sch T1						
3500 4D 8'	K392	31240	14850	16050	17000	23600
3500 LT/SLT 4D 8'	K392	37845	15900	17150	17700	24600
2WD	C		(1625)	(1625)	(1910)	(1910)
V8, 6.0 Liter	U		(4275)	(4275)	(5005)	(5005)
V8, 8.1 Liter	G		(3625)	(3625)	(4240)	(4240)
SILVERADO EXTENDED CAB PICKUP 4WD—V8—Truck Equipment Sch T1						
1500 Z71 4D 6 1/2'	K19V	32485	7450	8475	8700	12600
1500 Z71 4D 8'	K19V	33685	7550	8550	8725	12600
V8, 5.3 Liter	T		225	225	285	285
SILVERADO SS EXT CAB PICKUP—V8—Truck Equipment Schedule T3						
1500 4D 6 1/2'	C19N	36440	11300	12800	12700	18300
AWD			1275	1275	1690	1690
SILVERADO/SIERRA CREW CAB PICKUP—V8—Truck Equip Schedule T1						
1500 LS/SLE 4D 5 3/4'	C13T	30875	8100	9175	9175	13100
1500 LT/SLT 4D 5 3/4'	C13T	35555	8500	9625	9625	13750
2500HD Wk Trk 6 1/2	C23U	31150	8025	8675	9475	13150
2500 HD Wrk Trk 8'	C23U	31450	7825	8450	9300	12900
2500 HD 4D 8'	C23U	32400	9150	9900	10750	14900
2500 HD LS/SLE 8'	C23U	33950	9450	10200	11100	15450
2500 HD LT/SLT 8'	C23U	38370	9975	10750	11650	16150
3500 Work Truck 8'	C33U	32710	8025	8675	9500	13200
Quadrasteer			450	450	590	590
4WD	K		1275	1275	1690	1690
V8, 8.1 Liter	G		225	225	275	275
V8, 6.6L Turbo Dsl	2		3525	3525	4235	4235
SILVERADO/SIERRA CREW CAB PICKUP 4WD—V8—Truck Equip Sch T1						
1500HD LS/SLE 6 1/2	K13U	35795	11050	12500	12400	17800

Body Type	VIN	List	Trade-In Good	Very Good	Pvt-Party Good	Retail Excellent
1500HD LT/SLT 6 1/2'	K13U	40035	11200	12700	12700	18350
2500 HD 4D 6 1/2'	K23U	35015	11200	12100	13000	18050
2500HD LS/SLE 6 1/2'	K23U	36395	11550	12500	13100	17900
3500 4D 8'	K33U	33340	11350	12300	13200	18300
2WD	C		(1625)	(1625)	(2175)	(2175)
V8, 6.6L Turbo Dsl	2		3525	3525	4230	4230
V8, 8.1 Liter			225	225	275	275
SILVERADO/SIERRA CREW CAB 4WD—V8 Turbo Diesel—Truck Sch T1						
2500HD LT/SLT 6 1/2'	K232	48580	15900	17150	17650	24000
3500 LS/SLE 4D 8'	K332	34910	15650	16850	17600	24100
3500 LT/SLT 4D 8'	K332	38950	16750	18050	18550	25300
2WD	C		(1625)	(1625)	(1960)	(1960)
V8, 6.0 Liter	U		(4275)	(4275)	(5125)	(5125)
V8, 8.1 Liter			(3625)	(3625)	(4345)	(4345)
SILVERADO CREW CAB PICKUP 4WD—V8—Truck Equipment Sch T1						
1500 Z71 4D 5 3/4'	K13T	35385	8750	9900	9800	13950
SIERRA DENALI CREW CAB PICKUP AWD—V8—Truck Equip Schedule T3						
1500 4D 5 3/4'	K63N	42585	11050	11950	12600	17250

2006 CHEVY/GMC—(1,2or3)(CorG)(A,B,CorN)—(L13F)—6—#

Body Type	VIN	List	Trade-In Good	Very Good	Pvt-Party Good	Retail Excellent
EQUINOX—V6—Truck Equipment Schedule T1						
LS Sport Utility 4D	L13F	22345	3475	3900	4675	6975
LT Sport Utility 4D	L63F	22990	3625	4075	4950	7500
AWD	2,7		575	575	765	765
TRAILBLAZER 4WD—6-Cyl.—Truck Equipment Schedule T1						
LS Sport Utility 4D	T13S	27240	3325	3750	4450	6700
LT Sport Utility 4D	T13S	29535	3800	4275	5075	7625
LS Ext Sport Util	T16S	28840	3775	4225	5100	7500
LT Ext Sport Util	T16S	30940	4175	4650	5525	8075
2WD	S		(1025)	(1025)	(1375)	(1375)
V8, 5.3 Liter	M		250	250	320	320
TRAILBLAZER 4WD—V8—Truck Equipment Schedule T1						
SS Sport Util 4D	T13H	33505	8050	8925	9550	13400
2WD	S		(1025)	(1025)	(1375)	(1375)
ENVOY 4WD—6-Cyl.—Truck Equipment Schedule T1						
SLE Sport Utility 4D	T13S	31550	4075	4600	5400	8075
SLT Sport Utility 4D	T13S	32585	4475	5025	5825	8750
2WD	S		(1025)	(1025)	(1375)	(1375)
ENVOY DENALI 4WD—V8—Truck Equipment Schedule T3						
Sport Utility 4D	T63M	39395	6000	6675	7525	10800
2WD	S		(1025)	(1025)	(1375)	(1375)
ENVOY XL 4WD—6-Cyl.—Truck Equipment Schedule T1						
SLE Sport Utility 4D	T16S	32880	4475	4975	5925	8750
SLT Sport Utility 4D	T16S	33870	4875	5425	6325	9275
2WD	S		(1025)	(1025)	(1375)	(1375)
V8, 5.3 Liter	M		250	250	320	320
ENVOY XL DENALI 4WD—V8—Truck Equipment Schedule T3						
Sport Utility 4D	T66M	40825	6150	6825	7525	10650
2WD	S		(1025)	(1025)	(1375)	(1375)
TAHOE 4WD—V8—Truck Equipment Schedule T1						
LS Sport Utility 4D	K13V	40750	5725	6275	7050	10000
LT Sport Utility 4D	K13V	45625	7450	8125	8925	12600
Third Row Seat			350	350	455	455
2WD	C		(625)	(625)	(845)	(845)
V8, 5.3 Liter	T		250	250	320	320
YUKON—V8—Truck Equipment Schedule T1						
SLE Sport Utility 4D	C13V	37280	6025	6600	7400	10500
Third Row Seat			350	350	455	455
4WD	K		625	625	845	845
V8, 5.3 Liter	T		250	250	320	320
YUKON 4WD—V8—Truck Equipment Schedule T1						
SL Sport Utility 4D	K13V	37640	6425	7025	7800	11050
SLT Sport Utility 4D	K13V	42210	8350	9125	9850	13850
Third Row Seat			350	350	455	455
2WD	C		(625)	(625)	(845)	(845)
V8, 5.3 Liter	T		250	250	320	320
YUKON DENALI AWD—V8—Truck Equipment Schedule T3						
Sport Utility 4D	K63U	51160	10350	11500	11350	15700
SUBURBAN 4WD—V8—Truck Equipment Schedule T1						
K1500 LS Sport Util	K16Z	42440	6200	6775	7675	10950
K1500 LT Sport Util	K16Z	47935	7150	7825	8800	12600
K1500 LTZ Spt Util	K16Z	53400	7850	8825	8950	12550
K2500 LS Sport Util	K26U	48820	7300	7975	8950	12800

Body Type	VIN	List	Trade-In Good	Very Good	Pvt-Party Good	Retail Excellent
K2500 LT Sport Util	K26U	44920	8375	9150	10050	14300
2WD	C		(1025)	(1025)	(1375)	(1375)
V8, 8.1 Liter	G		250	250	325	325
YUKON XL—V8—Truck Equipment Schedule T1						
1500 SLE Sport Util	C16Z	40330	5825	6375	7325	10550
4WD	K		1025	1025	1355	1355
YUKON XL 4WD—V8—Truck Equipment Schedule T1						
1500 SL Sport Util	K16Z	40413	6250	6825	7775	11150
1500 SLT Sport Util	K16Z	46320	8150	8900	9825	14000
2500 SLE Sport Util	K26U	44105	7375	8075	9050	12950
2500 SLT Sport Util	K26U	47395	9375	9350	10300	14650
2WD	C		(1025)	(1025)	(1375)	(1375)
V8, 8.1 Liter	G		250	250	325	325
YUKON XL DENALI AWD—V8—Truck Equipment Schedule T3						
1500 Sport Utility 4D	K66U	52810	8225	9250	9450	13350
UPLANDER—V6—Truck Equipment Schedule T2						
Cargo Minivan 4D	V13L	21640	2075	2375	3275	5275
UPLANDER—V6—Truck Equipment Schedule T1						
LS Minivan 4D	U23L	21990	2050	2350	3050	4750
LS Extended 4D	V23L	24575	2450	2800	3500	5400
LT Extended 4D	V33L	28385	3275	3725	4400	6750
AWD	X		400	400	545	545
EXPRESS/SAVANA VAN—V8—Truck Equipment Schedule T1						
1500 LS Passenger	G15T	26770	5475	6250	6750	9700
1500 LT Passenger	G15T	28580	5775	6575	7050	10150
2500 LS Passenger	G25V	28625	5650	6425	6925	9950
2500 LT Passenger	G25V	30435	6050	6900	7350	10550
3500 LS Passenger	G35U	30704	6150	7000	7475	10750
3500 LS Extended	G39U	29574	6475	7350	7825	11300
3500 LT Passenger	G35U	32119	6575	7475	7900	11350
3500 LT Extended	G39U	29914	7000	7950	8375	12000
AWD	H		475	475	645	645
V6, 4.3 Liter	X		(350)	(350)	(455)	(455)
EXPRESS VAN—V6—Truck Equipment Schedule T1						
1500 Cargo Van	G15X	22660	5250	5950	6225	9100
AWD	H		475	475	645	645
V8, 5.3 Liter	T		350	350	455	455
SAVANA VAN—V8—Truck Equipment Schedule T1						
1500 Cargo Van	G15T	23980	5400	6125	6600	9650
AWD	H		475	475	645	645
V6, 4.3 Liter	X		(350)	(350)	(455)	(455)
EXPRESS/SAVANA VAN—V8—Truck Equipment Schedule T1						
2500 Cargo Van	G25V	25750	5750	6550	7000	10250
2500 Extended	G29V	24175	5925	6725	7175	10500
3500 Cargo Van	G35V	27434	5975	6800	7200	10550
3500 Extended	G39V	26729	6425	7300	7700	11300
V8, 6.0 Liter	U		350	350	455	455
V8, 6.6L Turbo Dsl	2		3850	3850	5125	5125
COLORADO/CANYON REGULAR CAB PICKUP—4-Cyl.—Truck Equip Sch T1						
Work Truck 2D 6'	S148	17085	2875	3225	3750	5500
LS/SL 2D 6'	S148	17085	3450	3875	4500	6575
LT 2D 6'	S148	18715	4000	4475	5025	7325
4WD	T		975	975	1290	1290
5-Cyl, 3.5 Liter	6		175	175	225	225
CANYON REGULAR CAB PICKUP—5-Cyl.—Truck Equipment Sch T1						
SLE 2D 6'	S146	20410	4175	4675	5200	7525
4WD	T		975	975	1280	1280
4-Cyl, 2.8 Liter	8		(175)	(175)	(220)	(220)
CANYON EXTENDED CAB PICKUP—4-Cyl.—Truck Equipment Sch T1						
Work Truck 4D 6'	S198	19460	4400	4925	5450	7925
4WD	T		975	975	1285	1285
5-Cyl, 3.5 Liter	6		175	175	225	225
COLORADO/CANYON EXTENDED CAB PICKUP—4-Cyl.—Truck Sch T1						
LS/SL 4D 6'	S198	19460	5000	5575	6125	8950
4WD	T		975	975	1280	1280
5-Cyl, 3.5 Liter	6		175	175	225	225
COLORADO/CANYON EXTENDED CAB PICKUP—5-Cyl.—Truck Sch T1						
LT/SLE 4D 6'	S196	22090	6050	6750	7325	10550
4WD	T		975	975	1275	1275
4-Cyl, 2.8 Liter	8		(175)	(175)	(220)	(220)
COLORADO/CANYON CREW CAB PICKUP—5-Cyl.—Truck Equip T1						
LT/SLE 4D 5 1/4'	S136	23900	7300	8125	8700	12500
4WD	T		975	975	1265	1265

Body Type	VIN	List	Trade-In Good	Very Good	Pvt-Party Good	Retail Excellent
4-Cyl, 2.8 Liter	8		(175)	(175)	(220)	(220)
CANYON CREW CAB PICKUP—5-Cyl.—Truck Equipment Sch T2						
SLT 4D 5'	S136	26810	7400	8250	8800	12650
4WD	T		975	975	1265	1265
SSR REGULAR CAB PICKUP—V8—Truck Equipment Schedule T3						
Convertible 2D	S314H	39990	20900	22500	20900	26500
AVALANCHE 4WD—V8—Truck Equipment Schedule T1						
1500 LS Util Pickup	K12Z	37885	8600	9525	9875	13600
1500 LT Util Pickup	K12Z	41730	8975	9925	10250	14050
2500 LS Util Pickup	K22G	39295	10750	11900	12200	16750
2500 LT Util Pickup	K22G	43140	11100	12250	12400	16900
2WD	C		(1025)	(1025)	(1375)	(1375)
SILVERADO REGULAR CAB PICKUP—V6—Truck Equipment Sch T1						
1500 LS/SL 2D 6 1/2'	C14X	23345	3550	4025	4600	6725
4WD	K		1500	1500	2000	2000
V8, 4.8 Liter	V		450	450	585	585
V8, 5.3 Liter	T		675	675	910	910
V8, FFV, 5.3 Liter	Z		625	625	830	830
SILVERADO/SIERRA REGULAR CAB PICKUP—V8—Truck Equipment Sch T1						
1500 Work Trk 6 1/2'	C14V	18755	2625	2975	3475	5075
1500 Work Truck 8'	C14V	19030	2325	2650	3175	4650
1500 LS/SL 2D 8'	C14V	24690	3775	4250	4800	7000
1500 LT/SLE 6 1/2'	C14V	23875	4500	5025	5100	7300
1500 LT/SLE 8'	C14V	24185	4100	4625	5100	7350
2500 HD Wrk Trk 8'	C24U	23795	5800	6250	6925	9300
2500 HD LS/SL 8'	C24U	27295	7375	7925	8700	11700
3500 Wrk Trk 2D 8'	C34U	24060	5400	5825	6600	8925
3500 SL 8'	C34U	30275	6225	6700	7600	10400
3500 LT/SLE 2D 8'	C34U	26355	7075	7625	8400	11300
4WD	K		1500	1500	2000	2000
V6, 4.3 Liter	X		(450)	(450)	(600)	(600)
V8, 5.3 Liter	T		250	250	320	320
V8, 8.1 Liter	G		250	250	285	285
V8, 6.6L Turbo Dsl	2,D		3850	3850	4490	4490
SILVERADO/SIERRA REGULAR CAB PICKUP 4WD—V8—Truck Equip Sch T1						
2500 HD LT/SLE 8'	K24U	25455	10000	10750	11350	15150
2WD	C		(2000)	(2000)	(2330)	(2330)
V8, 8.1 Liter	G		250	250	285	285
V8, 6.6L Turbo Dsl	2,D		3850	3850	4470	4470
SILVERADO REGULAR CAB PICKUP—V8 Turbo Diesel—Truck Equip Sch T1						
3500 LS 2D 8'	C342,D	30275	10900	11700	12550	17000
4WD	K		1500	1500	1770	1770
V8, 6.0 Liter	U		(4600)	(4600)	(5425)	(5425)
V8, 8.1 Liter	G		(3975)	(3975)	(4680)	(4680)
SILVERADO/SIERRA EXTENDED CAB PICKUP—V8—Truck Equip Sch T1						
1500 LT/SLE 4D 8'	C19V	27660	6025	6775	7350	10600
4WD	K		1500	1500	2000	2000
SILVERADO EXTENDED CAB—V8 Hybrid—Truck Equip Sch T1						
1500 LT 4D 6 1/2'	C19K	26485	10100	11300	11650	16700
4WD	K		1500	1500	2000	2000
SIERRA EXTENDED CAB 4WD—V8 Hybrid—Truck Equip Sch T1						
1500 SLE 4D 6 1/2'	K19T	26485	12150	13600	13650	19250
2WD	C		(2000)	(2000)	(2675)	(2675)
SILVERADO/SIERRA EXTENDED CAB PICKUP—V8—Truck Equip Sch T1						
1500 Work Trk 6 1/2'	C19V	22935	4225	4750	5325	7775
1500 Work Truck 8'	C19V	25040	3875	4375	4925	7175
1500 LS 4D 6 1/2'	C19V	27195	5725	6450	7100	10300
1500 LS/SL 4D 8'	C19V	28125	5500	6175	6825	9925
1500 LT/SLE 4D 6 1/2'	C19V	26485	6550	7350	7900	11400
4WD	K		1500	1500	2000	2000
V8, 5.3 Liter	T,B,Z		250	250	320	320
SILVERADO/SIERRA EXTENDED CAB PICKUP—V8—Truck Equip Sch T1						
1500 LT 4D 5 3/4'	C19T	30130	6675	7525	8050	11600
1500 SLT 4D 5 3/4'	C19T	31200	8475	9500	9850	14050
1500 SLT 4D 8'	C19T	31640	6575	7375	7900	11400
2500HD Wk Trk 6 1/2'	C29U	26485	7375	7950	8850	12050
2500HD Work Trk 8'	C29U	26780	7175	7725	8650	11800
2500 HD SL 4D 6 1/2'	C29U	29570	9100	9775	10650	14400
2500 HD SL/SLE 4D 8'	C29U	29860	9000	9675	10550	14250
2500 HD SLT 8'	C29U	33400	10350	11100	11900	16150
3500 Work Truck 8'	C39U	27350	7850	8450	9275	12600
4WD	K		1500	1500	1785	1785
V8, 6.6L Turbo Dsl	2,D		3850	3850	4580	4580

Body Type	VIN	List	Trade-In Good	Very Good	Pvt-Party Good	Retail Excellent
V8, 8.1 Liter	G	......	250	250	290	290
SIERRA EXTENDED CAB PICKUP—V8 Turbo Diesel—Truck Equip Sch T1						
3500 SL 4D 8'	C392,D	32790	14050	15050	15750	21000
4WD	K	......	1500	1500	1755	1755
V8, 6.0 Liter	U	......	(4600)	(4600)	(5385)	(5385)
V8, 8.1 Liter	G	......	(3975)	(3975)	(4640)	(4640)
SIERRA EXTENDED CAB PICKUP 4WD—V8—Truck Equip Sch T1						
1500 SL 4D 6 1/2'	K19V	27195	8075	9050	9375	13300
2WD	C	......	(2000)	(2000)	(2675)	(2675)
V6, 4.3 Liter	X	......	(450)	(450)	(600)	(600)
V8, 5.3 Liter	T	......	250	250	320	320
SIERRA EXTENDED CAB PICKUP 4WD—V8—Truck Equip Sch T1						
1500 SLT 4D 6 1/2'	K19B	31350	9450	10600	11050	15850
2WD	C	......	(2000)	(2000)	(2675)	(2675)
V8, HO, 6.0 Liter	N	......	450	450	590	590
SILVERADO/SIERRA EXTENDED CAB PICKUP 4WD—V8—Truck Sch T1						
2500 HD LS 6 1/2'	K29U	29570	11250	12050	12900	17450
2500HD LT/SLE 6 1/2	K29U	29200	11800	12650	13600	18500
2500 HD SLT 6 1/2'	K29U	33110	12650	13600	14400	19450
3500 LS 4D 8'	K39U	28000	11150	11950	12850	17400
2WD	C	......	(2000)	(2000)	(2375)	(2375)
V8, 8.1 Liter	G	......	250	250	290	290
V8, 6.6L Turbo Dsl	2,D	......	3850	3850	4560	4560
SIERRA EXTENDED CAB—V8 Turbo Diesel—Truck Equipment Sch T1						
3500 SL 4D 8'	C392,D	32790	14050	15050	15750	21000
4WD	K	......	1500	1500	1755	1755
V8, 6.0 Liter	U	......	(4600)	(4600)	(5385)	(5385)
V8, 8.1 Liter	G	......	(3975)	(3975)	(4640)	(4640)
SILVERADO/SIERRA EXTENDED CAB 4WD—V8 Turbo Diesel—Truck Sch T1						
3500 LT/SLE 4D 8'	K392,D	29900	16250	17450	18250	24700
2WD	C	......	(2000)	(2000)	(2360)	(2360)
V8, 6.0 Liter	U	......	(4600)	(4600)	(5415)	(5415)
V8, 8.1 Liter	G	......	(3975)	(3975)	(4670)	(4670)
SILVERADO SS EXTENDED CAB PICKUP—V8—Truck Equip Schedule T3						
1500 4D 6 1/2'	C19N	36625	11450	12800	12950	18400
SILVERADO/SIERRA CREW CAB PICKUP—V8—Truck Equip Schedule T1						
1500 LS/SL 4D 5 3/4'	C13V	27990	8775	9825	10100	14350
1500 LT/SLE 4D 5 3/4'	C13T	29040	8975	10050	10100	14100
1500 HD SLE 6 1/2'	C13U	32855	8900	9975	10400	15000
2500 HD Wk Tk 6 1/2	C23U	28480	9000	9675	10550	14250
2500 HD Wk Trk 8'	C23U	28770	8900	9575	10450	14150
2500 HD LS/SL 8'	C23U	31830	10550	11300	12050	16300
2500 HD LT/SLE 8'	C23U	31415	11550	12400	13100	17650
2500 HD SLT 8'	C23U	35475	11700	12550	13400	18150
4WD	K	......	1500	1500	2000	2000
V8, HO, 6.0 Liter	N	......	450	450	590	590
V8, 8.1 Liter	G	......	250	250	290	290
V8, 6.6L Turbo Dsl	2,D	......	3850	3850	4570	4570
SILVERADO/SIERRA CREW CAB PICKUP 4WD—V8—Truck Equip Sch T1						
1500 SLT 4D 5 3/4'	K13T	33215	11700	13100	13150	18600
1500 HD LT 6 1/2'	K13U	36305	10850	12150	12200	17150
1500 HD SLT 6 1/2'	K13U	34205	11900	13350	13400	19000
2500HD LS/SL 6 1/2'	K23U	34485	12750	13700	14600	19750
2WD	C	......	(2000)	(2000)	(2370)	(2370)
V8, 8.1 Liter	G	......	250	250	290	290
V8, 6.6L Turbo Dsl	2,D	......	3850	3850	4545	4545
SILVERADO CREW CAB 4WD—V8 Turbo Diesel—Truck Equip Sch T1						
3500 LS 4D 8'	K332,D	35005	17250	18500	19250	25900
2WD	C	......	(2000)	(2000)	(2360)	(2360)
V8, 6.0 Liter	U	......	(4600)	(4600)	(5420)	(5420)
V8, 8.1 Liter	G	......	(3975)	(3975)	(4670)	(4670)
SIERRA CREW CAB—V8 Turbo Diesel—Truck Equipment Sch T1						
3500 SL 4D 8'	C332,D	35005	15000	16100	16950	22800
3500 SLE 4D 8'	C332,D	32515	15400	16500	17200	23000
4WD	K	......	1500	1500	1770	1770
V8, 6.0 Liter	U	......	(4600)	(4600)	(5420)	(5420)
V8, 8.1 Liter	G	......	(3975)	(3975)	(4675)	(4675)
SILVERADO/SIERRA CREW CAB 4WD—V8 Turbo Diesel—Truck Sch T1						
2500HD LT/SLE 6'	K232,D	43415	17450	18700	19200	25650
2500 HD SLT 6 1/2'	K232,D	48050	18200	19500	20000	26600
3500 LT 4D 8'	K332,D	32015	17250	18500	19250	25900
3500 SLT 4D 8'	K332,D	35885	18300	19600	20200	27000
2WD	C	......	(2000)	(2000)	(2360)	(2360)

2006 CHEVROLET/GMC

Body Type	VIN	List	Trade-In Good	Very Good	Pvt-Party Good	Retail Excellent
V8, 6.0 Liter	U		(4600)	(4600)	(5420)	(5420)
V8, 8.1 Liter	G		(3975)	(3975)	(4670)	(4670)
SIERRA DENALI CREW CAB PICKUP AWD—V8—Truck Equip Schedule T3						
1500 4D 5 3/4'	K63N	42610	11700	12550	13350	17950

2007 CHEVY/GMC—(1,2or3)(CorG)(A,B,CorN)—(L13F)—7—#

Body Type	VIN	List	Good	Very Good	Good	Excellent
EQUINOX—V6—Truck Equipment Schedule T1						
LS Sport Utility 4D	L13F	22680	4250	4700	5450	7875
LT Sport Utility 4D	L63F	23655	4950	5475	6275	9050
AWD	2,7		600	600	810	810
TRAILBLAZER 4WD—6-Cyl.—Truck Equipment Schedule T1						
LS Sport Utility 4D	T13S	27735	4675	5200	5825	8300
LT Sport Utility 4D	T13S	30945	5275	5850	6450	9200
2WD	S		(1100)	(1100)	(1480)	(1480)
V8, 5.3 Liter	M		275	275	355	355
TRAILBLAZER AWD—V8—Truck Equipment Schedule T1						
SS Sport Utility 4D	T13H	34015	10050	11000	11300	15100
2WD	S		(1100)	(1100)	(1425)	(1425)
ENVOY 4WD—6-Cyl.—Truck Equipment Schedule T1						
SLE Sport Utility 4D	T13S	29330	5275	5875	6700	9575
SLT Sport Utility 4D	T13S	33695	5675	6300	7150	10250
2WD	S		(1100)	(1100)	(1480)	(1480)
ENVOY DENALI 4WD—V8—Truck Equipment Schedule T3						
Sport Utility 4D	T63M	37570	7475	8200	8850	12050
2WD	C		(1100)	(1100)	(1480)	(1480)
ACADIA—V6—Truck Equipment Schedule T1						
SLE Sport Utility 4D	R137	29990	7600	8325	8875	12000
AWD	V		675	675	885	885
ACADIA AWD—V6—Truck Equipment Schedule T1						
SLT Sport Utility 4D	V237	35960	9350	10250	10900	14850
2WD	R		(625)	(625)	(840)	(840)
TAHOE—V8—Truck Equipment Schedule T1						
LS Sport Utility 4D	C13C	34755	12050	13050	13000	16950
Third Row Seat			375	375	455	455
4WD	K		1100	1100	1370	1370
V8, 5.3 Liter	J		275	275	330	330
TAHOE 4WD—V8—Truck Equipment Schedule T1						
LT Sport Utility 4D	K130	40120	14800	16000	15850	20700
LTZ Sport Utility 4D	K130	48980	15300	16800	16050	21200
Third Row Seat			375	375	455	455
2WD	C		(1100)	(1100)	(1390)	(1390)
YUKON—V8—Truck Equipment Schedule T1						
SLE Sport Utility 4D	C130	34690	12900	13950	13950	18350
Third Row Seat			375	375	465	465
4WD	K		1100	1100	1405	1405
V8, 4.8 Liter	C		(275)	(275)	(360)	(360)
YUKON 4WD—V8—Truck Equipment Schedule T1						
SLT Sport Utility 4D	K130	41670	15650	16900	16650	21600
Third Row Seat			375	375	450	450
2WD	C		(1100)	(1100)	(1375)	(1375)
V8, 4.8 Liter	C		(275)	(275)	(350)	(350)
YUKON DENALI AWD—V8—Truck Equipment Schedule T3						
Sport Utility 4D	K638	48370	16900	18550	17600	23100
SUBURBAN 4WD—V8—Truck Equipment Schedule T1						
K1500 LS Sport Util	R163	39790	11200	12100	12500	16650
K1500 LT Sport Util	R163	40540	12600	13650	14000	18650
K1500 LTZ Sport Util	R163	48455	14000	15500	14950	19800
K2500 LS Sport Util	K26K	41715	12700	13750	14100	18750
K2500 LT Sport Util	K26K	39705	13900	15050	15300	20400
2WD	C		(1100)	(1100)	(1455)	(1455)
V8, 6.0 Liter	Y		475	475	620	620
YUKON XL 4WD—V8—Truck Equipment Schedule T1						
1500 SLE Sport Util	R163	37790	11650	12600	12950	17300
1500 SLT Sport Util	R163	44170	13600	14700	15000	20000
2500 SLE Sport Util	K26K	41765	12500	13550	13850	18450
2500 SLT Sport Util	K26K	45345	14600	15800	16000	21200
2WD	C		(1100)	(1100)	(1455)	(1455)
V8, 6.0 Liter	Y		475	475	620	620
YUKON XL DENALI AWD—V8—Truck Equipment Schedule T3						
1500 Sport Utility 4D	K168	50870	14850	16450	15850	21100
UPLANDER—V6—Truck Equipment Schedule T2						
Cargo Minivan 4D	V131	22670	2550	2875	3875	6100

Body Type	VIN	List	Trade-In Good	Very Good	Pvt-Party Good	Retail Excellent
UPLANDER—V6—Truck Equipment Schedule T1						
LS Minivan 4D	U231	20770	2675	3025	3775	5700
LS Extended Minivan	V231	23845	3275	3675	4450	6675
LT Extended Minivan	V331	27970	4375	4925	5775	8600
EXPRESS/SAVANA VAN—V8—Truck Equipment Schedule T1						
1500 LS Passenger	G15T	26460	6225	7000	7375	10200
1500 LT Passenger	G15Z	27955	6500	7300	7650	10600
2500 LS Passenger	G25V	27265	6425	7200	7575	10450
2500 LT Passenger	G25V	29075	6875	7725	8000	11050
3500 LS Passenger	G35U	29299	7000	7875	8250	11400
3500 LS Extended	G39U	31529	8250	9250	9525	13150
3500 LT Passenger	G35U	30714	8025	8975	9275	12800
3500 LT Extended	G39U	31869	8600	9625	9875	13650
AWD	H		500	500	655	655
EXPRESS VAN—V6—Truck Equipment Schedule T1						
1500 Cargo Van	G15X	23130	6150	6900	7275	10250
AWD	H		500	500	680	680
V8, 5.3 Liter	T		375	375	485	485
SAVANA VAN—V8—Truck Equipment Schedule T1						
1500 Cargo Van	G15T	22720	6650	7475	7800	11050
AWD	H		500	500	680	680
V6, 4.3 Liter	X		(375)	(375)	(485)	(485)
EXPRESS/SAVANA VAN—V8—Truck Equipment Schedule T1						
2500 Cargo Van	G25V	23495	7075	7950	8325	11750
2500 Extended	G29V	24595	7275	8175	8500	12000
3500 Cargo Van	G35V	26099	7425	8325	8675	12250
3500 Extended	G39V	27674	7775	8700	9025	12750
3500 Van Cab-Ch	G31Z	24773	7200	8100	8700	12250
V8, 6.0 Liter	U		375	375	485	485
V8, 6.6L Turbo Dsl	2,6		4050	4050	5400	5400
COLORADO/CANYON REGULAR CAB PICKUP—4-Cyl.—Truck Equip Sch T1						
Work Truck 2D 6'	S149	17455	3700	4075	4725	6750
LS/SL 2D 6'	S149	19455	4150	4575	5225	7400
LT/SLE 2D 6'	S149	21085	4675	5175	5775	8175
4WD	T		1075	1075	1395	1395
5-Cyl, 3.7 Liter	E		175	175	230	230
CANYON REGULAR CAB PICKUP—5-Cyl.—Truck Equipment Sch T1						
SLE 2D 6'	S14E	19135	4825	5325	5925	8375
4WD	T		1075	1075	1405	1405
4-Cyl, 2.9 Liter	9		(175)	(175)	(220)	(220)
CANYON EXTENDED CAB PICKUP—4-Cyl.—Truck Equipment Sch T1						
Work Truck 4D 6'	S199	19455	5250	5800	6550	9250
4WD	T		1075	1075	1395	1395
5-Cyl, 3.7 Liter	E		175	175	235	235
COLORADO/CANYON EXTENDED CAB PICKUP—4-Cyl.—Truck Sch T1						
LS/SL 4D 6'	S199	19455	5750	6350	7075	9975
4WD	T		1075	1075	1395	1395
5-Cyl, 3.7 Liter	E		175	175	230	230
COLORADO/CANYON EXTENDED CAB PICKUP—5-Cyl.—Truck Sch T1						
LT/SLE 4D 6'	S19E	22085	7200	7925	8650	12150
4WD	T		1075	1075	1375	1375
4-Cyl, 2.9 Liter	9		(175)	(175)	(215)	(215)
COLORADO/CANYON CREW CAB PICKUP—5-Cyl.—Truck Equip Sch T2						
LT/SLE 4D 5 1/4'	S13E	23360	8325	9175	9825	13800
4WD	T		1075	1075	1385	1385
4-Cyl, 2.9 Liter	9		(175)	(175)	(215)	(215)
CANYON CREW CAB PICKUP—5-Cyl.—Truck Equipment Sch T2						
SLT 4D 5'	S13E	25720	9975	10950	11350	15650
4WD	T		1075	1075	1330	1330
AVALANCHE 4WD—V8—Truck Equipment Schedule T1						
LS Spt Util Pickup	K123	36810	11750	12850	12800	16800
LT Spt Util Pickup	K123	36940	12600	13750	13650	17850
LTZ Spt Util Pickup	K123	43670	13850	15150	15050	19750
2WD	C		(1100)	(1100)	(1435)	(1435)
SILVERADO CLASSIC REGULAR CAB—V6—Truck Equipment Sch T1						
1500 LS 2D 6 1/2'	C14X	22070	3725	4150	4600	6350
4WD	K		1875	1875	2490	2490
V8, 4.8 Liter	V		450	450	600	600
V8, 5.3 Liter	T		750	750	1000	1000
SILVERADO/SIERRA CLASSIC REGULAR CAB—V8—Truck Equipment Sch T1						
1500 Work Trk 6 1/2'	C14V	19350	3450	3875	4300	5925
1500 Work Truck 8'	C14V	19625	3175	3525	3875	5350
1500 SL 2D 6 1/2'	C14V	23015	4925	5475	5800	7975

Body Type	VIN	List	Trade-In Good	Trade-In Very Good	Pvt-Party Good	Retail Excellent
1500 LS/SL 2D 8'	C14V	23455	3650	4075	4525	6250
1500 LT/SLE 2D 6 1/2'	C14V	24250	5075	5650	5950	8150
1500 LT/SLE 2D 8'	C14V	24540	5000	5550	5850	8025
2500 HD Wrk Trk 8'	C24U	24220	4700	5025	5900	8050
2500 HD LT/SLE 8'	C24U	25880	6500	6950	7975	10750
3500 Work Truck 8'	C34U	25355	4700	5025	5875	8000
3500 LS/SL 2D 8'	C34U	25410	6050	6475	7425	9975
3500 SLE 2D 8'	C34U	27185	6725	7175	8100	10850
4WD	K		1875	1875	2490	2490
V6, 4.3 Liter	X		(450)	(450)	(600)	(600)
V8, 5.3 Liter	T		275	275	355	355
V8, 8.1 Liter	G		275	275	335	335
V8, 6.6L Turbo Dsl	D		4050	4050	5130	5130
SIERRA CLASSIC REGULAR CAB 4WD—V8—Truck Equipment Sch T1						
2500 HD SL 2D 8'	K24U	24915	8525	9100	10050	13350
2WD	C		(2175)	(2175)	(2605)	(2605)
V8, 8.1 Liter	G		275	275	315	315
V8, 6.6L Turbo Dsl	D		4050	4050	4835	4835
SILVERADO CLASSIC REGULAR CAB—V8 Turbo Diesel—Truck Sch T1						
2500 HD LS 2D 8'	C24D	33240	10100	10800	11850	15850
4WD	K		1875	1875	2225	2225
V8, 6.0 Liter	U		(4825)	(4825)	(5765)	(5765)
V8, 8.1 Liter	G		(4175)	(4175)	(4985)	(4985)
SILVERADO CLASSIC REGULAR CAB—V8—Truck Equipment Sch T1						
3500 LT 2D 8'	C34U	26780	6300	6725	7725	10400
4WD	K		1875	1875	2270	2270
V8, 8.1 Liter	G		275	275	325	325
SILVERADO/SIERRA CLASSIC EXTENDED CAB—V8—Truck Equip Sch T1						
1500 LT/SLE 4D 5 3/4'	C19T	27830	7850	8700	9000	12350
1500 LT/SLE 4D 8'	C19T	28035	6950	7725	8025	11000
1500 SLT 4D 5 3/4'	C19T	31575	9000	9975	10150	13800
1500 SLT 4D 8'	C19T	32015	8150	9025	9250	12600
4WD	K		1875	1875	2480	2480
SILVERADO/SIERRA CLASSIC EXTENDED 4WD—V8 Hybrid—Truck Sch T1						
1500 LT/SLE 6 1/2'	K19T	33105	13900	15350	15350	20900
2WD	C		(2175)	(2175)	(2850)	(2850)
SILVERADO/SIERRA CLASSIC EXTENDED CAB—V8—Truck Equip Sch T1						
1500 Work Trk 6 1/2'	C19V	23310	5400	6000	6650	9325
1500 Work Truck 8'	C19V	25415	5150	5725	6000	8225
1500 LS 4D 6 1/2'	C19V	25785	6850	7625	7925	10900
1500 LS/SL 4D 8'	C19V	26815	6200	6900	7325	10100
1500 LT/SLE 4D 6 1/2'	C19V	26860	6975	7750	8125	11150
2500HD WkTrk 6 1/2'	C29V	26910	7425	7925	9025	12200
2500HD Wrk Trk 8'	C29U	27205	7275	7775	8800	11900
2500 HD LS 6 1/2'	C29U	28310	8800	9375	10400	13950
2500 HD LS/SL 4D 8'	C29U	28605	8700	9275	10300	13800
2500 HD SLE 6 1/2'	C29U	30125	9200	9825	10900	14550
2500 HD LT/SLE 8'	C29U	28825	8850	9425	10450	14000
2500 HD SLT 6 1/2'	C29U	33485	10100	10800	11850	15800
2500 HD SLT 4D 8'	C29U	33775	9875	10550	11600	15500
3500 Work Truck 8'	C39U	27775	6650	7100	8300	11350
3500 LS/SL 4D 8'	C39U	29520	8150	8725	9950	13550
3500 SLE 4D 8'	C39U	30825	9300	9925	11200	15200
4WD	K		1875	1875	2480	2480
V6, 4.3 Liter	X		(450)	(450)	(595)	(595)
V8, 5.3 Liter	T		275	275	355	355
V8, 8.1 Liter	G		275	275	320	320
V8, 6.6L Turbo Dsl	D		4050	4050	4875	4875
SILVERADO CLASSIC EXTENDED CAB—V8 Turbo Diesel—Truck Sch T1						
3500 LT 4D 8'	C39D	38080	12150	12950	14350	19400
4WD	K		1875	1875	2260	2260
V8, 6.0 Liter	U		(4825)	(4825)	(5850)	(5850)
V8, 8.1 Liter	G		(4175)	(4175)	(5065)	(5065)
SILVERADO CLASSIC EXTENDED CAB 4WD—V8—Truck Equip Sch T1						
2500 HD LT 6 1/2'	K29U	28530	11900	12700	13750	18300
2WD	C		(2175)	(2175)	(2600)	(2600)
V8, 8.1 Liter	G		275	275	315	315
V8, 6.6L Turbo Dsl	D		4050	4050	4825	4825
SIERRA CLASSIC EXTENDED CAB 4WD—V8—Truck Equipment Sch T1						
1500 SL 4D 6 1/2'	K19V	25785	9925	11000	11050	15000
1500 SLT 4D 6 1/2'	K19Z	31725	11600	12850	12800	17350
2500 HD SL 4D 6 1/2'	K29U	30850	11300	12100	13150	17500
2WD	C		(2175)	(2175)	(2860)	(2860)

TRUCKS & VANS

Body Type	VIN	List	Trade-In Good	Very Good	Pvt-Party Good	Retail Excellent
V6, 4.3 Liter	X	......	(450)	(450)	(590)	(590)
V8, 5.3 Liter	T,B	......	275	275	350	350
V8, 6.6L Turbo Dsl	D	......	4050	4050	4845	4845
V8, 8.1 Liter	G	......	275	275	320	320
SILVERADO SS CLASSIC EXTENDED CAB—V8—Truck Equip Sch T3						
1500 4D 6 1/2'	C19N	34180	12850	14200	14300	19500
SILVERADO/SIERRA CLASSIC CREW CAB—V8—Truck Equip Schedule T1						
1500 LS/SL 4D 5 3/4'	C13V	25595	8425	9325	9575	13100
1500 LT 4D 5 3/4'	C13Z	29415	9200	10200	10450	14300
1500 SLT 4D 5 3/4'	C13Z	33590	9325	10300	10550	14400
4WD	K	......	1875	1875	2470	2470
V8, 6.0 Liter	N	......	475	475	625	625
SIERRA CLASSIC CREW CAB—V8—Truck Equipment Schedule T1						
1500 SLE 4D 8'	C19J	28205	9125	10100	10300	14000
4WD	K	......	1875	1875	2475	2475
SILVERADO/SIERRA CLASSIC CREW CAB—V8—Truck Equip Schedule T1						
1500 HD LT 6 1/2'	C13Z	30545	9325	10300	10550	14400
1500 HD SLT 6 1/2'	C13U	34580	10450	11600	11700	16000
2500HD WrkTrk 6 1/2'	C23U	28905	8650	9225	10250	13750
2500 HD Wrk Trk 8'	C23U	29195	8550	9125	10150	13600
2500 HD LS/SL 4D 8'	C23U	30595	10100	10800	11850	15800
2500HD LT/SLE 8'	C23U	30745	10650	11350	12400	16550
2500 HD SLT 4D 8'	C23U	35850	11750	12550	13550	18050
3500 Work Truck 8'	C33U	30015	8850	9425	10450	14000
3500 SLE 4D/DR 8'	C33U	32940	10850	11550	12600	16800
3500 SLT 4D 8'	C33U	36260	11700	12500	13550	18100
4WD	K	......	1875	1875	2300	2300
V8, 8.1 Liter	K	......	275	275	325	325
V8, 6.6L Turbo Dsl	D	......	4050	4050	4980	4980
SIERRA CLASSIC CREW CAB 4WD—V8—Truck Equip Schedule T1						
1500 SLE 4D 5 3/4'	K13Z	29915	11050	12250	12400	16950
1500 HD SLT 6 1/2'	K13U	30545	11900	13150	13250	18100
2500 HD SL 4D 6 1/2'	K23U	30295	12800	13650	14800	19700
2WD	C	......	(2175)	(2175)	(2890)	(2890)
V8, 8.1 Liter	G	......	275	275	315	315
V8, 6.6L Turbo Dsl	D	......	4050	4050	4830	4830
SIERRA CLASSIC CREW CAB 4WD—V8 Turbo Diesel—Truck Sch T1						
2500 HD SLE 6 1/2'	K23D	32045	17650	18800	19900	26400
3500 SL 4D 8'	K33D	31515	19200	20400	21200	27800
2WD	C	......	(2175)	(2175)	(2585)	(2585)
V8, 6.0 Liter	U	......	(4825)	(4825)	(5730)	(5730)
V8, 8.1 Liter	G	......	(4175)	(4175)	(4955)	(4955)
SILVERADO CLASSIC CREW CAB—V8 Turbo Diesel—Truck Sch T1						
2500 HD LS 6 1/2'	C23D	37525	14550	15500	16550	21900
3500 LS 4D 8'	C33D	38745	14550	15500	16650	22100
4WD	K	......	1875	1875	2220	2220
V8, 6.0 Liter	U	......	(4825)	(4825)	(5750)	(5750)
V8, 8.1 Liter	G	......	(4175)	(4175)	(4975)	(4975)
SILVERADO/SIERRA CLASSIC CREW CAB 4WD—V8 Turbo Diesel—Sch T1						
2500 HD LT 6 1/2'	K23D	39590	17650	18800	19750	26100
2500 HD SLT 6 1/2'	K23D	35560	18650	19850	20600	27000
3500 LT 4D 8'	K33D	42975	17650	18800	19850	26300
2WD	C	......	(2175)	(2175)	(2585)	(2585)
V8, 6.0 Liter	U	......	(4825)	(4825)	(5725)	(5725)
V8, 8.1 Liter	G	......	(4175)	(4175)	(4955)	(4955)
SIERRA DENALI CLASSIC CREW CAB AWD—V8—Truck Equip Sch T3						
1500 4D 5 3/4'	K63N	40025	12700	13550	14350	19050
SILVERADO/SIERRA REGULAR CAB—V8—Truck Equipment Schedule T1						
1500 Work Trk 6 1/2'	C140	10360	5850	6525	6750	9100
4WD	K	......	1875	1875	2405	2405
V6, 4.3 Liter	X	......	(450)	(450)	(580)	(580)
V8, 5.3 Liter	J	......	275	275	340	340
SILVERADO REGULAR CAB—V6—Truck Equipment Schedule T1						
1500 Work Truck 8'	C14X	19055	5150	5700	5850	7900
4WD	K	......	1875	1875	2385	2385
V8, 4.8 Liter	C	......	450	450	575	575
V8, 5.3 Liter	J	......	750	750	955	955
SIERRA REGULAR CAB—V8—Truck Equipment Schedule T1						
1500 Work Truck 8'	C14C	20525	6050	6725	6825	9125
4WD	K	......	1875	1875	2360	2360
V6, 4.3 Liter	X	......	(450)	(450)	(570)	(570)
V8, 5.3 Liter	J	......	275	275	335	335

Body Type	VIN	List	Trade-In Good	Very Good	Pvt-Party Good	Retail Excellent
SILVERADO/SIERRA REGULAR CAB—V8—Truck Equipment Schedule T1						
2500 HD Work Trk 8'	C24K	25443	5200	5575	6475	8675
2500 HD LT/SLE 8'	C24U	24575	8500	9075	9850	12950
3500 HD Wrk Trk 8'	C34K	25665	5175	5550	6325	8525
3500 SLE 2D 8'	C34K	28060	8075	8600	9450	12500
4WD	K		1875	1875	2465	2465
V8, 6.6L Turbo Dsl	6		4050	4050	4795	4795
SILVERADO/SIERRA REGULAR CAB 4WD—V8 Turbo Diesel—Truck Equip SchT1						
3500 HD LT 8'	K346	28060	15400	16400	17100	22300
2WD	C		(2175)	(2175)	(2575)	(2575)
V8, 6.0 Liter	K		(4825)	(4825)	(5705)	(5705)
SILVERADO/SIERRA EXTENDED CAB PICKUP—V6—Truck Equipment Sch T1						
1500 Work Truck 6'	C19X	23900	6450	7175	7525	10300
4WD	K		1875	1875	2490	2490
V8, 4.8 Liter	J		(275)	(275)	(375)	(375)
V8, 5.3 Liter	J		475	475	635	635
SIERRA EXTENDED CAB PICKUP—V8—Truck Equip Sch T1						
1500 Work Truck 6'	C19C	24500	6950	7725	8000	10900
4WD	K		1875	1875	2485	2485
V6, 4.3 Liter	X		(450)	(450)	(600)	(600)
V8, 5.3 Liter	J		275	275	355	355
SILVERADO/SIERRA EXTENDED CAB PICKUP—V8—Truck Equip Sch T1						
1500 Work Truck 5 3/4'	C190	23605	7075	7850	8225	11250
1500 Work Truck 8'	C190	25245	7175	7975	8275	11300
1500 LT/SLE 4D 8'	C19J	28205	9125	10100	10300	14050
1500 LTZ/SLT 5 3/4'	C19J	32105	10100	11150	11350	15550
1500 LTZ/SLT 4D 8'	C19J	32695	9600	10650	10850	14800
4WD	K		1875	1875	2490	2490
V6, 4.3 Liter	X		(450)	(450)	(600)	(600)
V8, 6.0 Liter	Y		475	475	630	630
V6, 4.3 Liter	X		(450)	(450)	(600)	(600)
SILVERADO/SIERRA EXTENDED CAB PICKUP 4WD—V8—Truck Equip Sch T1						
1500 LTZ/SLT 6 1/2'	K19J	35500	12100	13350	13500	18500
2WD	C		(2175)	(2175)	(2840)	(2840)
V8, 6.0 Liter	Y		475	475	620	620
SILVERADO/SIERRA EXTENDED CAB PICKUP—V8—Truck Equip Sch T1						
1500 LT/SLE 4D 5 3/4'	C19C	26565	9400	10450	10600	14500
1500 LT/SLE 4D 6 1/2'	C19C	26860	8900	9850	10050	13800
4WD	K		1875	1875	2475	2475
V8, 5.3 Liter	J		275	275	350	350
V8, 6.0 Liter	Y		475	475	630	630
SILVERADO/SIERRA EXTENDED CAB PICKUP—V8—Truck Equip Sch T1						
2500 HD Work Trk 6'	C29K	27475	8650	9225	10250	13750
2500 HD Work Trk 8	C29K	27770	8550	9125	10050	13400
3500 HD Wrk Trk 8'	C39K	28785	8925	9550	10550	14150
3500 HD LTZ/SLT 8'	C39K	36045	11950	12750	13750	18200
4WD	K		1875	1875	2475	2475
V8, 6.6L Turbo Dsl	6		4050	4050	4870	4870
SILVERADO/SIERRA EXTENDED CAB PICKUP 4WD—V8—Truck Sch T1						
2500HD LT/SLE 6 1/2'	K29K	30470	13400	14400	15450	20500
2500 HD LT/SLE 8'	K29K	30765	13250	14150	15200	20200
2500 HD LTZ/SLT 6'	K29K	35395	14350	15300	16350	21700
2500 HD LTZ/SLT 8'	K29K	35690	14150	15100	16100	21300
2WD	C		(2175)	(2175)	(2595)	(2595)
V8, 6.6L Turbo Dsl	6		4050	4050	4815	4815
SILVERADO/SIERRA EXTENDED CAB PICKUP 4WD—V8 Turbo Diesel—Truck Sch T1						
3500 HD LT/SLE 8'	K396	31790	18050	19200	20000	26300
2WD	C		(2175)	(2175)	(2590)	(2590)
V8, 6.0 Liter	K		(4825)	(4825)	(5730)	(5730)
SILVERADO/SIERRA CREW CAB PICKUP—V8—Truck Equip Schedule T1						
1500 Wrk Trk 5 3/4'	C133	27045	9600	10650	10700	14500
1500 LT/SLE 5 3/4'	C13C	29415	12050	13350	13050	17550
2500 HD LT/SLE 8'	C23K	32840	12900	13750	14850	19650
2500 HD LTZ/SLT 8'	C23K	37680	13600	14500	15500	20500
4WD	K		1875	1875	2425	2425
V8, 5.3 Liter	J,M		275	275	345	345
V8, 6.0 Liter	Y		475	475	615	615
V8, 6.6L Turbo Dsl	6		4050	4050	4810	4810
SIERRA CREW CAB PICKUP—V8—Truck Equip Schedule T1						
2500 HD Work Trk 6'	C23K	28750	10800	11500	12550	16750
2500 HD Work Trk 8'	C23K	29045	10650	11350	12300	16350
3500 Work Truck 8'	C33K	29975	11100	11850	12950	17250
4WD	K		1875	1875	2235	2235

Body Type	VIN	List	Trade-In Good	Very Good	Pvt-Party Good	Retail Excellent
V8, 6.6L Turbo Dsl	6		4050	4050	4855	4855
SILVERADO/SIERRA CREW CAB 4WD—V8—Truck Equip Sch T1						
1500 LTZ/SLT 5 3/4'	K13M	33520	15050	16650	16350	22100
2WD	C		(2175)	(2175)	(2805)	(2805)
V8, 6.0 Liter	Y		475	475	610	610
SILVERADO/SIERRA CREW CAB 4WD—V8 Turbo Diesel—Truck Sch T1						
3500 HD LT/SLE 8'	K336	32380	21000	22300	22900	29900
3500 HD LTZ/SLT 8'	K336	37010	22200	23600	24000	31100
2WD	C		(2175)	(2175)	(2565)	(2565)
V8, 6.0 Liter	K		(4825)	(4825)	(5680)	(5680)
SILVERADO CREW CAB PICKUP—V8—Truck Equipment Sch T1						
2500 HD Work Trk 6'	C23K	31850	10800	11500	12550	16750
4WD	K		1875	1875	2240	2240
V8, 6.6L Turbo Dsl	6		4050	4050	4855	4855
SILVERADO CREW CAB—V8 Turbo Diesel—Truck Equip Sch T1						
2500 HD Work Trk 8'	C236	37440	14950	15900	16950	22400
3500 HD Wrk Trk 8'	C336	29975	16050	17100	18000	23700
4WD	K		1875	1875	2200	2200
V8, 6.0 Liter	K		(4825)	(4825)	(5695)	(5695)
SILVERADO/SIERRA CREW CAB 4WD—V8 Turbo Diesel—Truck Sch T1						
2500 HD LT/SLE 6'	K236	44040	19950	21200	21700	28100
2500 HD LTZ/SLT 6'	K236	48880	20900	22200	22800	29800
2WD	C		(2175)	(2175)	(2580)	(2580)
V8, 6.0 Liter	K		(4825)	(4825)	(5730)	(5730)
SIERRA DENALI CREW CAB PICKUP AWD—V8—Truck Equip Schedule T3						
1500 4D 5 3/4'	K638	42095	18050	19250	19550	25200
2WD	C		(675)	(675)	(800)	(800)

2008 CHEVY/GMC—(1,2or3)(CorG)(A,B,CorN)—(L13F)—8—#

Body Type	VIN	List	Trade-In Good	Very Good	Pvt-Party Good	Retail Excellent
EQUINOX—V6—Truck Equipment Schedule T1						
LS Sport Utility 4D	L13F	22995	5100	5525	6225	8325
LT Sport Utility 4D	L33F	23855	5525	6000	6900	9275
AWD	2,4,6,8,0		650	650	845	845
EQUINOX AWD—V6—Truck Equipment Schedule T1						
LTZ Sport Utility 4D	L83F	29295	7850	8475	9450	12750
Sport SUV 4D	L037	29595	8275	8925	9925	13350
FWD	7		(650)	(650)	(875)	(875)
TRAILBLAZER 4WD—6-Cyl.—Truck Equipment Schedule T1						
LS Sport Utility 4D	T13S	29650	5275	5725	6725	9225
LT Sport Utility 4D	T13S	28415	5850	6375	7375	10100
2WD	S		(1200)	(1200)	(1595)	(1595)
V8, 5.3 Liter	M		300	300	385	385
TRAILBLAZER AWD—V8—Truck Equipment Schedule T1						
SS Sport Utility 4D	T33H	33990	12200	13100	13600	17400
2WD	S		(1200)	(1200)	(1455)	(1455)
ENVOY 4WD—6-Cyl.—Truck Equipment Schedule T1						
SLE Sport Utility 4D	T23S	29850	6275	6800	7850	10750
SLT Sport Utility 4D	T33S	33795	6650	7225	8300	11400
2WD	S		(1200)	(1200)	(1595)	(1595)
ENVOY DENALI 4WD—V8—Truck Equipment Schedule T3						
Sport Utility 4D	T43M	36730	9050	9750	10600	13850
2WD	S		(1200)	(1200)	(1510)	(1510)
ACADIA—V6—Truck Equipment Schedule T1						
SLE Sport Utility 4D	R137	29845	8975	9650	10200	13050
AWD	V		700	700	885	885
ACADIA AWD—V6—Truck Equipment Schedule T1						
SLT Sport Utility 4D	V237	36310	11100	11900	12550	16100
2WD	R		(675)	(675)	(850)	(850)
TAHOE—V8—Truck Equipment Schedule T1						
LS Sport Utility 4D	C13C	34995	12600	13500	13700	17250
Third Row Seat			400	400	475	475
4WD			1175	1175	1445	1445
V8, FFV, 5.3L	0		300	300	355	355
TAHOE 4WD—V8—Truck Equipment Schedule T1						
LT Sport Utility 4D	K130	40650	16200	17300	17350	21700
LTZ Sport Utility 4D	K130	48230	18350	19750	18900	23400
Third Row Seat			400	400	475	475
2WD	C		(1200)	(1200)	(1450)	(1450)
V8, 6.2 Liter	8		500	500	570	570
TAHOE 4WD—V8 Hybrid—Truck Equipment Schedule T1						
Sport Utility 4D	K135	53295	15650	16700	17100	21700
Third Row Seat			400	400	490	490
2WD	C		(1200)	(1200)	(1490)	(1490)

Body Type	VIN	List	Trade-In Good	Very Good	Pvt-Party Good	Retail Excellent
YUKON—V8—Truck Equipment Schedule T1						
SLE Sport Utility 4D	C230	36490	13600	14550	14850	18650
Third Row Seat			400	400	475	475
4WD	K		1175	1175	1445	1445
V8, 4.8 Liter	C		(300)	(300)	(370)	(370)
YUKON 4WD—V8—Truck Equipment Schedule T1						
SLT Sport Utility 4D	K330	42700	17000	18150	18300	23000
Third Row Seat			400	400	480	480
2WD	C		(1200)	(1200)	(1460)	(1460)
YUKON 4WD—V8 Hybrid—Truck Equipment Schedule T1						
Sport Utility 4D	K135	53755	15850	16900	17300	21900
Third Row Seat			400	400	485	485
2WD	C		(1200)	(1200)	(1490)	(1490)
YUKON DENALI AWD—V8—Truck Equipment Schedule T3						
Sport Utility 4D	K038	49420	18700	20100	19300	23900
2WD	C		(1200)	(1200)	(1385)	(1385)
SUBURBAN 4WD—V8—Truck Equipment Schedule T1						
K1500 LS Sport Utl	K163	41080	13400	14300	14750	18650
K1500 LT Spt Utl	K263	42005	15000	16050	16350	20700
K1500 LTZ Spt Utl	K363	49320	15700	17000	16700	21100
K2500 LS Sport Utl	K46K	43375	15200	16250	16600	21000
K2500 LT Sport Utl	K26K	40575	16400	17550	17800	22500
2WD	C		(1200)	(1200)	(1480)	(1480)
V8, 6.0 Liter	Y		500	500	625	625
YUKON XL 4WD—V8—Truck Equipment Schedule T1						
1500 SLE Sport Util	K263	43590	13950	14900	15300	19350
1500 SLT Sport Util	K363	45215	16150	17200	17500	22100
2500 SLE Sport Util	K56K	43190	14800	15800	16200	20500
2500 SLT Sport Util	K66K	46585	16900	18000	18250	23100
2WD	C		(1200)	(1200)	(1475)	(1475)
V8, 6.0 Liter	Y		500	500	625	625
YUKON XL DENALI AWD—V8—Truck Equipment Schedule T3						
1500 Sport Utility 4D	K068	51980	16550	17850	17550	22200
2WD	C		(1200)	(1200)	(1435)	(1435)
UPLANDER—V6—Truck Equipment Schedule T2						
Cargo Minivan 4D	V131	23385	3350	3675	4950	7375
UPLANDER—V6—Truck Equipment Schedule T1						
LS Minivan 4D	U231	21870	3550	3900	4725	6675
LS Extended Minivan	V231	24540	4150	4550	5425	7650
LT Extended Minivan	V331	29540	5300	5800	6700	9375
EXPRESS/SAVANA VAN—V8—Truck Equipment Schedule T1						
1500 LS Passenger	G154	26710	7200	7875	8550	11400
1500 LT Passenger	G154	28560	7600	8300	8975	11950
2500 LS Passenger	G25K	28195	7450	8150	8825	11750
2500 LT Passenger	G25K	30045	8025	8775	9400	12500
3500 LS Passenger	G35K	29914	8125	8900	9525	12700
3500 LS Extended	G39K	32429	9000	9825	10400	13850
3500 LT Passenger	G35K	31369	8825	9625	10250	13650
3500 LT Extended	G39K	32799	9625	10500	11100	14750
AWD	H		550	550	675	675
EXPRESS VAN—V6—Truck Equipment Schedule T1						
1500 Cargo Van	G15X	24650	8075	8900	9275	12500
AWD	H		550	550	680	680
V8, 5.3 Liter	4		525	525	645	645
SAVANA VAN—V8—Truck Equipment Schedule T1						
1500 Cargo	G154	23130	8525	9375	9775	13150
AWD	H		550	550	680	680
V6, 4.3 Liter	X		(400)	(400)	(495)	(495)
EXPRESS/SAVANA VAN—V8—Truck Equipment Schedule T1						
2500 Cargo Van	G25C	24205	9000	9900	10250	13800
2500 Extended	G29C	25240	9525	10500	10850	14650
3500 Cargo Van	G35C	26809	9525	10500	10900	14700
3500 Extended	G39C	27784	9725	10700	11100	14950
V8, 6.0 Liter	K		400	400	495	495
V8, 6.6L Turbo Dsl	6		4200	4200	5315	5315
COLORADO/CANYON REGULAR CAB PICKUP—4-Cyl.—Truck Equip Sch T1						
Work Truck 2D 6'	S149	16290	4625	5000	5650	7575
LT 2D 6'	S349	17530	5725	6175	7025	9400
4WD	T		1225	1225	1515	1515
5-Cyl, 3.7 Liter	E		175	175	230	230
COLORADO/CANYON REGULAR CAB PICKUP—4-Cyl.—Truck Equip Sch T1						
LS/SL 2D 6'	S249	16565	5300	5725	6550	8750
4WD	T		1225	1225	1550	1550

Body Type	VIN	List	Trade-In Good	Very Good	Pvt-Party Good	Retail Excellent
5-Cyl, 3.7 Liter	E		**175**	**175**	**235**	**235**
CANYON REGULAR CAB PICKUP—5-Cyl.—Truck Equipment Sch T1						
SLE 2D 6'	S34E	18335	**6025**	**6525**	**7350**	**9825**
4WD	T		**1225**	**1225**	**1515**	**1515**
4-Cyl, 2.9 Liter	9		**(175)**	**(175)**	**(215)**	**(215)**
CANYON EXTENDED CAB PICKUP—4-Cyl.—Truck Equipment Sch T1						
Work Truck 4D 6'	S199	18365	**7000**	**7575**	**8450**	**11300**
4WD	T		**1225**	**1225**	**1515**	**1515**
5-Cyl, 3.7 Liter	E		**175**	**175**	**230**	**230**
COLORADO/CANYON EXTENDED CAB PICKUP—4-Cyl.—Truck Equip T1						
LS/SL 4D 6'	S299	18855	**7225**	**7800**	**8675**	**11600**
4WD	T		**1225**	**1225**	**1515**	**1515**
5-Cyl, 3.7 Liter	E		**175**	**175**	**230**	**230**
COLORADO EXTENDED CAB PICKUP—5-Cyl.—Truck Equipment Sch T2						
LT 4D 6'	S39E	21990	**8500**	**9150**	**10050**	**13450**
4WD	T		**1225**	**1225**	**1525**	**1525**
4-Cyl, 2.9 Liter	9		**(175)**	**(175)**	**(215)**	**(215)**
CANYON EXTENDED CAB PICKUP—5-Cyl.—Truck Equipment Sch T1						
SLE 4D 6'	S39E	20760	**8500**	**9150**	**10050**	**13450**
4WD	T		**1225**	**1225**	**1535**	**1535**
4-Cyl, 2.9 Liter	9		**(175)**	**(175)**	**(220)**	**(220)**
COLORADO/CANYON CREW CAB PICKUP—5-Cyl.—Truck Equip Sch T1						
LT/SLE 4D 5 1/4'	S33E	22600	**10350**	**11150**	**12100**	**16150**
4WD	T		**1225**	**1225**	**1515**	**1515**
4-Cyl, 2.9 Liter	9		**(175)**	**(175)**	**(215)**	**(215)**
CANYON CREW CAB PICKUP—5-Cyl.—Truck Equipment Sch T2						
SLT 4D 5'	S53E	27240	**11150**	**12000**	**12900**	**17100**
4WD	T		**1225**	**1225**	**1510**	**1510**
AVALANCHE 4WD—V8—Truck Equipment Schedule T1						
LS Spt Util Pickup	K123	37385	**14150**	**15150**	**15350**	**19200**
LT Spt Util Pickup	K223	37465	**14600**	**15650**	**15900**	**20100**
LTZ Spt Util Pickup	K333	38255	**15850**	**17000**	**17250**	**21900**
2WD	C		**(1200)**	**(1200)**	**(1415)**	**(1415)**
SILVERADO/SIERRA REGULAR CAB PICKUP—V8—Truck Equipment Sch T1						
1500 Work Trk 6 1/2'	C140	19540	**7750**	**8400**	**8800**	**11350**
4WD	K		**2125**	**2125**	**2635**	**2635**
V6, 4.3 Liter	X		**(450)**	**(450)**	**(555)**	**(555)**
V8, 5.3 Liter	J		**300**	**300**	**360**	**360**
SILVERADO REGULAR CAB PICKUP—V6—Truck Equipment Sch T1						
1500 Work Truck 8'	C14X	18380	**8150**	**8850**	**9025**	**11450**
4WD	K		**2125**	**2125**	**2535**	**2535**
V8, 4.8 Liter	C		**450**	**450**	**535**	**535**
V8, 5.3 Liter	J		**850**	**850**	**1010**	**1010**
SIERRA REGULAR CAB PICKUP—V8—Truck Equipment Sch T1						
1500 Work Truck 8'	C14C	18485	**8200**	**8900**	**9150**	**11700**
4WD	K		**2125**	**2125**	**2570**	**2570**
V6, 4.3 Liter	X		**(450)**	**(450)**	**(540)**	**(540)**
V8, 5.3 Liter	J		**300**	**300**	**350**	**350**
SILVERADO/SIERRA REGULAR CAB PICKUP—V8—Truck Equipment Sch T1						
1500 LT/SLE 2D 6 1/2'	C24C	24955	**8425**	**9125**	**9675**	**12650**
1500 LT/SLE 2D 8'	C24C	27880	**8025**	**8700**	**9300**	**12200**
2500 HD Wrk Trk 8'	C54K	24755	**6575**	**6950**	**7875**	**10000**
2500 HD LT/SLE 8'	C54K	28400	**9150**	**9650**	**10750**	**13650**
3500 HD Wrk Trk 8'	C74K	24975	**6325**	**6675**	**7650**	**9775**
3500 SLE 2D 8'	C84K	28340	**8850**	**9325**	**10400**	**13300**
4WD	K		**2125**	**2125**	**2735**	**2735**
V6, 4.3 Liter	X		**(450)**	**(450)**	**(555)**	**(555)**
V8, 5.3 Liter	J		**300**	**300**	**370**	**370**
V8, 6.6L Turbo Dsl	6		**4200**	**4200**	**4920**	**4920**
SILVERADO REGULAR CAB 4WD—V8 Turbo Diesel—Truck Equip Sch T1						
3500 HD LT 8'	K846	28340	**16500**	**17400**	**18550**	**23400**
2WD	C		**(2400)**	**(2400)**	**(2770)**	**(2770)**
V8, 6.0 Liter			**(5025)**	**(5025)**	**(5825)**	**(5825)**
SILVERADO/SIERRA EXTENDED CAB PICKUP—V8—Truck Equip Sch T1						
1500 Work Truck 4D 8'	C190	29810	**8375**	**9075**	**9625**	**12600**
1500 LT/SLE 4D 8'	C290	28125	**10250**	**11100**	**11600**	**15250**
1500 LTZ/SLT 5 3/4'	C390	32135	**11800**	**12750**	**13300**	**17500**
1500 LTZ/SLT 4D 8'	C390	32725	**11200**	**12100**	**12650**	**16550**
4WD	K		**2125**	**2125**	**2725**	**2725**
V8, 6.0 Liter			**500**	**500**	**650**	**650**
SILVERADO/SIERRA EXTENDED CAB PICKUP 4WD—V8—Truck Sch T1						
1500 LTZ/SLT 6 1/2'	K39J	35530	**13550**	**14650**	**15300**	**20200**
2WD	C		**(2400)**	**(2400)**	**(3045)**	**(3045)**

Body Type	VIN	List	Trade-In Good	Trade-In Very Good	Pvt-Party Good	Retail Excellent
V8, 6.0 Liter	Y	.....	500	500	645	645
SILVERADO EXTENDED CAB PICKUP—V6—Truck Equipment Sch T1						
1500 Work Trk 6 1/2'	C19X	23325	7900	8550	9150	12050
4WD	K	.....	2125	2125	2720	2720
V8, 4.8 Liter	C	.....	450	450	575	575
V8, 5.3 Liter	J	.....	850	850	1085	1085
SIERRA EXTENDED CAB PICKUP—V8—Truck Equipment Sch T1						
1500 Work Trk 6 1/2'	C19C	23430	8100	8775	9375	12350
4WD	K	.....	2125	2125	2755	2755
V6, 4.3 Liter	X	.....	(450)	(450)	(580)	(580)
V8, 5.3 Liter	J	.....	300	300	375	375
SILVERADO/SIERRA EXTENDED CAB PICKUP—V8—Truck Equip Sch T1						
1500 Work Trk 5 3/4'	C19C	23975	8300	9000	9600	12650
1500 LS/SL 4D 6 1/2'	C19C	24425	9625	10400	11100	14600
1500 LT/SLE 4D 5 3/4'	C29C	26935	10550	11400	11950	15700
1500 LT/SLE 4D 6 1/2'	C29C	30035	10350	11200	11700	15350
2500HD Wk Tk 6 1/2'	C49K	28050	9900	10450	11550	14650
2500 HD Wrk Trk 8'	C49K	29180	9825	10350	11450	14550
3500 HD Wrk Trk 8'	C79K	29675	10150	10700	11800	15000
3500 HD LTZ/SLT 8'	C99K	36885	13150	13850	15100	19150
4WD	K	.....	2125	2125	2740	2740
V6, 4.3 Liter	X	.....	(450)	(450)	(580)	(580)
V8, 5.3 Liter	J	.....	300	300	375	375
V8, 6.0 Liter	Y	.....	500	500	650	650
V8, 6.6L Turbo Dsl	6	.....	4200	4200	4905	4905
SILVERADO EXTENDED CAB PICKUP 4WD—V8—Truck Sch T1						
2500HD LT/SLE 6 1/2	K59K	30750	14750	15550	16750	21200
2500 HD LT/SLE 8'	K59K	31045	14350	15100	16300	20600
2500 HD LTZ/SLT 6'	K69K	35425	15800	16650	17850	22500
2500 HD LTZ/SLT 8'	K69K	35720	15650	16450	17650	22300
2WD	C	.....	(2400)	(2400)	(2800)	(2800)
V8, 6.6L Turbo Dsl	6	.....	4200	4200	4905	4905
SILVERADO/SIERRA EXTENDED CAB 4WD—V8 Turbo Diesel—Truck Sch T1						
3500 HD LT/SLE 8'	K896	40005	19700	20700	21800	27500
2WD	C	.....	(2400)	(2400)	(2795)	(2795)
V8, 6.0 Liter	K	.....	(5025)	(5025)	(5870)	(5870)
SILVERADO CREW CAB PICKUP—V8—Truck Equipment Schedule T1						
1500 Work Trk 5 3/4'	C130	31220	11500	12450	12850	16650
4WD	K	.....	2125	2125	2690	2690
V8, 4.8 Liter	C	.....	(300)	(300)	(380)	(380)
SIERRA CREW CAB PICKUP—V8—Truck Equipment Schedule T1						
1500 Work Trck 5 3/4'	C13C	28195	12450	13500	13650	17550
4WD	K	.....	2125	2125	2645	2645
V8, 5.3 Liter	J	.....	300	300	360	360
SILVERADO/SIERRA CREW CAB PICKUP—V8—Truck Equipment Sch T1						
1500 LS/SL 5 3/4'	C13C	30015	12650	13700	14050	18350
4WD	K	.....	2125	2125	2700	2700
SILVERADO/SIERRA CREW CAB PICKUP—V8—Truck Equipment Sch T1						
1500 LT/SLE 5 3/4'	C23C	29785	14100	15250	15400	19800
2500 HD Wk Tk 6 1/2	C23K	32280	12100	12750	13850	17600
2500 HD LT/SLE 8'	C23K	33120	14600	15350	16500	20900
2500HD LTZ/SLT 8'	C23K	37710	15350	16150	17350	21900
4WD	K	.....	2125	2125	2675	2675
V8, 6.0 Liter	Y	.....	500	500	635	635
V8, 6.6L Turbo Dsl	6	.....	4200	4200	4905	4905
SILVERADO/SIERRA CREW CAB PICKUP 4WD—V8—Truck Equip Sch T1						
1500 LTZ/SLT 5 3/4'	K33M	39620	18300	19750	19800	25600
2WD	C	.....	(2400)	(2400)	(2980)	(2980)
V8, 6.0 Liter	Y	.....	500	500	630	630
SILVERADO CREW CAB—V8 Turbo Diesel—Truck Equip Schedule T1						
2500 HD Work Trk 8'	C436	40970	16450	17350	18500	23400
3500 HD Work Trk 8'	C736	39830	17800	18750	19800	24900
4WD	K	.....	2125	2125	2480	2480
V8, 6.0 Liter	K	.....	(5025)	(5025)	(5885)	(5885)
SILVERADO/SIERRA CREW CAB 4WD—V8 Turbo Diesel—Truck Sch T1						
2500HD LT/SLE 6 1/2	K536	44320	22100	23200	23900	29800
2WD	C	.....	(2400)	(2400)	(2785)	(2785)
V8, 6.0 Liter	K	.....	(5025)	(5025)	(5850)	(5850)
SIERRA CREW CAB PICKUP—V8—Truck Equipment Schedule T1						
3500 Work Truck 8'	C73K	31435	12800	13450	14550	18450
4WD	K	.....	2125	2125	2500	2500
V8, 6.6L Turbo Dsl	6	.....	4200	4200	4925	4925

TRUCKS & VANS

Body Type	VIN	List	Trade-In Good	Very Good	Pvt-Party Good	Retail Excellent
SILVERADO/SIERRA CREW CAB 4WD—V8 Turbo Diesel—Truck Sch T1						
2500HD LTZ/SLT 6'	K636	48910	23600	24800	25700	32100
3500 HD LT/SLE 8'	K836	43735	23100	24300	25200	31500
3500 HD LTZ/SLT 8'	K936	47455	24100	25400	26300	32900
2WD	C		(2400)	(2400)	(2770)	(2770)
V8, 6.0 Liter	K		(5025)	(5025)	(5815)	(5815)
SIERRA DENALI CREW CAB PICKUP AWD—V8—Truck Equip Schedule T3						
1500 4D 5 3/4'	K638	42120	19550	20600	21400	26700
2WD	C		(725)	(725)	(855)	(855)

2009 CHEVY/GMC–(1,2or3)(CorG)(A,B,CorN)–(L13F)–9–#

Body Type	VIN	List	Trade-In Good	Very Good	Pvt-Party Good	Retail Excellent
EQUINOX—V6—Truck Equipment Schedule T1						
LS Sport Utility 4D	L13F	24250	6500	6900	7850	10000
LT Sport Utility 4D	L33F	25170	7200	7650	8725	11150
AWD	2,4,6,8,0		675	675	865	865
EQUINOX AWD—V6—Truck Equipment Schedule T1						
LTZ Sport Utility 4D	L83F	30700	9175	9725	10850	13800
Sport SUV 4D	L037	31005	9850	10450	11500	14650
FWD	7		(700)	(700)	(890)	(890)
TRAILBLAZER 4WD—6-Cyl.—Truck Equipment Schedule T1						
LT Sport Utility 4D	T33S	31165	7550	8025	9250	12100
2WD	C		(1275)	(1275)	(1700)	(1700)
TRAILBLAZER AWD—V8—Truck Equipment Schedule T1						
SS Sport Utility 4D	T53H	39165	15300	16150	16950	20900
2WD	C		(1275)	(1275)	(1540)	(1540)
ENVOY 4WD—6-Cyl.—Truck Equipment Schedule T1						
SLE Sport Utility 4D	T33S	32550	8225	8750	9950	13000
SLT Sport Utility 4D	T43S	36360	9050	9625	10850	14100
2WD	C		(1275)	(1275)	(1685)	(1685)
ENVOY DENALI 4WD—V8—Truck Equipment Schedule T3						
Sport Utility 4D	T53M	38460	12200	12900	14000	17500
2WD	C		(1275)	(1275)	(1580)	(1580)
ACADIA—V6—Truck Equipment Schedule T1						
SLE Sport Utility 4D	R137	31685	10400	11000	11750	14450
AWD	V		750	750	885	885
ACADIA AWD—V6—Truck Equipment Schedule T1						
SLT Sport Utility 4D	V23D	38085	12350	13050	13850	17100
2WD	R		(725)	(725)	(865)	(865)
TRAVERSE—V6—Truck Equipment Schedule T1						
LS Sport Utility 4D	R13D	28900	8675	9200	10200	12950
AWD	V		1275	1275	1635	1635
TRAVERSE AWD—V6—Truck Equipment Schedule T1						
LT Sport Utility 4D	V23D	33545	11050	11700	12750	16100
LTZ Sport Utility 4D	V33D	41810	13200	14000	15100	19000
2WD	R		(1275)	(1275)	(1630)	(1630)
TAHOE—V8—Truck Equipment Schedule T1						
LS XFE Sport Utility 4D	C133	39115	14600	15450	16100	19600
LT XFE Sport Util	C233	40465	15300	16200	16800	20500
TAHOE—V8—Truck Equipment Schedule T1						
LS Sport Utility 4D	C13C	37915	13650	14400	15150	18500
Third Row Seat			450	450	545	545
4WD	K		1275	1275	1530	1530
V8, 5.3 Liter	0		325	325	380	380
TAHOE 4WD—V8—Truck Equipment Schedule T1						
LT Sport Utility 4D	K230	43115	18050	19050	19600	23900
LTZ Sport Utility 4D	K320	52350	21800	23100	22800	27400
Third Row Seat			450	450	540	540
2WD	C		(1275)	(1275)	(1525)	(1525)
V8, 6.2 Liter	2		525	525	595	595
TAHOE 4WD—V8 Hybrid—Truck Equipment Schedule T1						
Sport Utility 4D	K135	54210	17950	18950	19650	24200
Third Row Seat			450	450	545	545
2WD	C		(1275)	(1275)	(1540)	(1540)
YUKON—V8—Truck Equipment Schedule T1						
SLE XFE Sport Util	C23C	39855	16100	17000	17550	21400
SLT XFE Sport Util	C330	44295	17250	18250	18800	22900
YUKON—V8—Truck Equipment Schedule T1						
SLE Sport Utility 4D	C260	38405	15200	16100	16700	20400
Third Row Seat			450	450	540	540
4WD	K		1275	1275	1520	1520
V8, 4.8 Liter	C		(325)	(325)	(385)	(385)
YUKON 4WD—V8—Truck Equipment Schedule T1						
SLT Sport Utility 4D	K360	45700	19250	20300	20800	25400

Body Type	VIN	List	Trade-In Good	Very Good	Pvt-Party Good	Retail Excellent
Third Row Seat		......	450	450	535	535
2WD	C	......	(1275)	(1275)	(1520)	(1520)
YUKON 4WD—V8 Hybrid—Truck Equipment Schedule T3						
Sport Utility 4D	K135	54680	18150	19150	19850	24400
Third Row Seat		......	450	450	545	545
2WD	C	......	(1275)	(1275)	(1540)	(1540)
YUKON DENALI AWD—V8—Truck Equipment Schedule T3						
Sport Utility 4D	K032	52880	21500	22700	22600	27100
2WD	C	......	(1275)	(1275)	(1470)	(1470)
YUKON DENALI 4WD—V8 Hybrid—Truck Equipment Schedule T3						
Sport Utility 4D	K035	54080	21400	22600	22500	27100
2WD	C	......	(1275)	(1275)	(1480)	(1480)
SUBURBAN 4WD—V8—Truck Equipment Schedule T1						
K1500 LS Sport Util	K163	44165	14100	14900	15950	19800
K1500 LT Sport Util	K263	45175	16150	17100	18000	22300
K1500 LTZ Sport Util	K363	54410	20700	21900	21900	26700
K2500 LS Sport Util	K46K	45975	16450	17400	18300	22700
K2500 LT Sport Util	K56K	46065	17650	18650	19500	24100
2WD	C	......	(1275)	(1275)	(1590)	(1590)
V8, 6.0 Liter	Y	......	550	550	665	665
YUKON XL 4WD—V8—Truck Equipment Schedule T1						
1500 SLE Sport Util	K263	40855	14800	15600	16600	20600
1500 SLT Sport Util	K363	47780	17100	18050	18950	23400
2500 SLE Sport Util	K56K	46435	15800	16700	17650	21900
2500 SLT Sport Util	K66K	50490	18150	19150	20000	24700
2WD	C	......	(1275)	(1275)	(1585)	(1585)
V8, 6.0 Liter	Y	......	550	550	665	665
YUKON XL DENALI AWD—V8—Truck Equipment Schedule T3						
1500 Sport Utility 4D	K168	55605	20800	22100	22100	27000
2WD	C	......	(1275)	(1275)	(1500)	(1500)
EXPRESS/SAVANA VAN—V8—Truck Equipment Schedule T1						
1500 LS Passenger	G154	28760	8150	8725	9575	12300
1500 LT Passenger	G154	31305	8925	9500	10400	13300
2500 LS Passenger	G25K	29865	8450	9025	9900	12700
2500 LT Passenger	G25K	32410	9250	9900	10800	13800
3500 LS Passenger	G35K	32160	9350	1000	10900	13950
3500 LT Passenger	G35K	34310	10200	10900	11850	15200
3500 LS Extended	G39K	34725	10300	11000	11950	15300
3500 LT Extended	G39K	35095	10850	11550	12500	16050
AWD	H	......	575	575	700	700
EXPRESS VAN—V6—Truck Equipment Schedule T1						
1500 Cargo Van	G15X	25635	9650	10400	11000	14200
AWD	H	......	575	575	695	695
V8, 5.3 Liter	4	......	550	550	675	675
SAVANA VAN—V8—Truck Equipment Schedule T1						
1500 Cargo Van	G154	26340	10150	10950	11500	14900
AWD	H	......	575	575	690	690
V6, 4.3 Liter	X	......	(450)	(450)	(550)	(550)
EXPRESS/SAVANA VAN—V8—Truck Equipment Schedule T1						
2500 Cargo Van	G25C	25520	10750	11600	12150	15700
2500 Extended	G29C	28075	11000	11900	12500	16150
3500 Cargo Van	G35C	28940	10950	11850	12450	16100
3500 Extended	G39C	30520	11350	12250	12800	16550
V8, 6.0L	K	......	425	425	530	530
V8, 6.6L Turbo Dsl	6	......	4400	4400	5390	5390
COLORADO/CANYON REGULAR CAB PICKUP—4-Cyl.—Truck Equip Sch T1						
Work Truck 2D 6'	S149	18000	6300	6700	7750	9975
LT/SLE 2D 6'	S349	19125	6425	6825	7875	10100
4WD	T	......	1425	1425	1690	1690
5-Cyl, 3.7 Liter	E	......	200	200	230	230
CANYON REGULAR CAB PICKUP—5-Cyl.—Truck Equip Sch T1						
SLE 2D 6'	S34E	20195	6750	7150	8175	10500
4WD	T	......	1425	1425	1685	1685
4-Cyl, 2.9 Liter	9	......	(175)	(175)	(220)	(220)
COLORADO/CANYON EXTENDED CAB PICKUP—4-Cyl.—Truck Sch T1						
Work Truck 4D 6'	S199	23545	8475	9000	10100	12900
4WD	T	......	1425	1425	1675	1675
5-Cyl, 3.7 Liter	E	......	200	200	230	230
COLORADO/CANYON EXTENDED CAB PICKUP—5-Cyl—Truck Equip Sch T1						
LT/SLE 4D 6'	S39E	24000	8950	9475	10650	13600
4WD	T	......	1425	1425	1705	1705
4-Cyl, 2.9 Liter	9	......	(175)	(175)	(220)	(220)
V8, 5.3 Liter	L	......	625	625	755	755

Body Type	VIN	List	Trade-In Good	Very Good	Pvt-Party Good	Retail Excellent
CANYON EXTENDED CAB PICKUP—5-Cyl.—Truck Equip Schedule T2						
SLT 4D 6'	S59E	21255	10500	11100	12250	15650
4WD	T		1425	1425	1670	1670
V8, 5.3 Liter	L		750	750	880	880
COLORADO/CANYON CREW CAB PICKUP—5-Cyl.—Truck Equip Sch T2						
LT/SLE 4D 5 1/4'	S32E	25830	11950	12650	13850	17650
4WD	T		1425	1425	1670	1670
4-Cyl, 2.9 Liter	9		(175)	(175)	(215)	(215)
V8, 5.3 Liter	L		625	625	735	735
CANYON CREW CAB PICKUP—5-Cyl.—Truck Equipment Schedule T2						
SLT 4D 5'	S53E	24200	12150	12850	14050	17900
4WD	T		1425	1425	1665	1665
V8, 5.3 Liter	L		750	750	880	880
AVALANCHE 4WD—V8—Truck Equipment Schedule T1						
LS Spt Util Pickup	K120	39125	15200	16050	16650	20300
LT Spt Util Pickup	K220	39125	16100	17000	17650	21600
LTZ Spt Util Pickup	K320	46495	18600	19650	20200	24700
2WD	C		(1275)	(1275)	(1470)	(1470)
SILVERADO/SIERRA REGULAR CAB PICKUP—V8—Truck Equipment Sch T1						
1500 Work Trk 6 1/2'	C140	19620	8900	9475	10150	12650
4WD	K		2475	2475	2975	2975
V6, 4.3 Liter	X		(500)	(500)	(600)	(600)
V8, 5.3 Liter	J		325	325	380	380
SILVERADO REGULAR CAB PICKUP—V6—Truck Equipment Sch T1						
1500 Work Truck 8'	C14X	19410	7725	8225	8900	11100
4WD	K		2475	2475	2975	2975
V8, 4.8 Liter	C		500	500	605	605
V8, 5.3 Liter	J		900	900	1100	1100
SIERRA REGULAR CAB PICKUP—V8—Truck Equipment Sch T1						
1500 Work Truck 8'	C14C	21685	8325	8850	9500	11850
4WD	K		2475	2475	2985	2985
V6, 4.3 Liter	X		(500)	(500)	(605)	(605)
V8, 5.3 Liter	J		325	325	380	380
SILVERADO/SIERRA REGULAR CAB PICKUP—V8—Truck Equipment Sch T1						
1500 LT/SLE 6 1/2'	C24C	26135	10400	11050	11750	14700
1500 LT/SLE 8'	C24C	27220	9900	10500	11250	14100
2500 HD Work Trk 8'	C44K	25890	7600	7925	9075	11200
2500 HD LT/SLE 8'	C54K	25890	10000	10450	11700	14300
3500 Work Truck 8'	C74K	26110	7350	7675	8850	10950
3500 SLE 2D 8'	C84K	26135	9675	10100	11350	13950
4WD	K		2475	2475	3015	3015
V6, 4.3 Liter	X		(500)	(500)	(600)	(600)
V8, 5.3 Liter	J		325	325	385	385
V8, 6.6L Turbo Dsl	6		4400	4400	5015	5015
SILVERADO REGULAR CAB 4WD—V8 Turbo Diesel—Truck Equip Sch T1						
3500 LT 2D 8'	K846	38220	17500	18400	19900	24300
2WD	C		(2600)	(2600)	(2905)	(2905)
V8, 6.0 Liter	K		(5225)	(5225)	(5870)	(5870)
SILVERADO EXTENDED CAB PICKUP—V6—Truck Equipment Sch T1						
1500 Work Trk 6 1/2'	C19X	40200	9575	10200	10950	13800
4WD	K		2475	2475	3025	3025
V8, 4.8 Liter	C		500	500	610	610
V8, 5.3 Liter	J		900	900	1115	1115
SIERRA EXTENDED CAB PICKUP—V6—Truck Equipment Sch T1						
1500 Work Trk 6 1/2'	C19C	26710	9725	10350	11100	13900
4WD	K		2475	2475	3030	3030
V6, 4.3 Liter	X		(500)	(500)	(615)	(615)
V8, 5.3 Liter	J		325	325	385	385
SILVERADO/SIERRA EXTENDED CAB PICKUP—V8—Truck Equip Sch T1						
1500 Work Truck 4D 8'	C19J	28835	10150	10800	11500	14400
1500 LT/SLE 4D 8'	C29J	30710	12400	13150	13900	17400
1500 LTZ/SLT 5 3/4'	C39J	34055	14050	14950	15850	19900
1500 LTZ/SLT 4D 8'	C39J	34655	12600	13400	14150	17750
4WD	K		2475	2475	3020	3020
V8, 6.0 Liter	Y		550	550	660	660
SILVERADO/SIERRA EXTENDED CAB PICKUP 4WD—V8—Truck Sch T1						
1500 LTZ/SLT 6 1/2'	K39J	37505	16200	17200	18050	22700
2WD	C		(2600)	(2600)	(3145)	(3145)
V8, 6.0 Liter	Y		550	550	655	655
SILVERADO/SIERRA EXTENDED CAB PICKUP—V8—Truck Equip Sch T1						
1500 Work Trk 5 3/4'	C19C	25080	10500	11150	11900	14950
1500 LS/SL 4D 6 1/2'	C19C	29780	11800	12500	13400	16850
1500 LT/SLE 4D 5 3/4'	C29C	28150	12650	13450	14300	18000

1015

Body Type	VIN	List	Trade-In Good	Very Good	Pvt-Party Good	Retail Excellent
1500 LT/SLE 4D 6 1/2'	C29C	28795	12450	13200	13950	17500
2500HD WrkTrk 6 1/2'	C49K	29190	11550	12050	13450	16600
2500 HD Work Trk 8'	C49K	29235	11250	11750	13150	16250
3500 Work Truck 8'	C79K	30270	11850	12350	13750	16900
3500 LTZ/SLT 4D 8'	C99K	37640	14950	15600	17050	20800
4WD	K	----	2475	2475	3015	3015
V6, 4.3 Liter	X	----	(500)	(500)	(610)	(610)
V8, 5.3 Liter	J	----	325	325	385	385
V8, 6.0 Liter	Y	----	550	550	660	660
V8, 6.6L Turbo Dsl	6	----	4400	4400	4970	4970

SILVERADO/SIERRA EXTENDED CAB PICKUP 4WD—V8—Truck Sch T1

Body Type	VIN	List	Trade-In Good	Very Good	Pvt-Party Good	Retail Excellent
2500HD LT/SLE 6 1/2'	K59K	32000	16550	17250	18900	23300
2500 HD LT/SLE 8'	K59K	32045	16550	17250	18900	23200
2500HD LTZ/SLT 6'	K69K	37235	17750	18500	20000	24500
2500HD LTZ/SLT 8'	K69K	37280	17550	18300	19850	24300
2WD	C	----	(2600)	(2600)	(2925)	(2925)
V8, 6.6L Turbo Dsl	6	----	4400	4400	4965	4965

SILVERADO/SIERRA EXTENDED CAB PICKUP 4WD—V8 Turbo Diesel—Truck Sch T1

Body Type	VIN	List	Trade-In Good	Very Good	Pvt-Party Good	Retail Excellent
3500 LT/SLE 4D 8'	K896	44165	21700	22600	24200	29600
2WD	C	----	(2600)	(2600)	(2905)	(2905)
V8, 6.0 Liter	K	----	(5225)	(5225)	(5870)	(5870)

SILVERADO/SIERRA CREW CAB PICKUP—V8—Truck Equipment Sch T1

Body Type	VIN	List	Trade-In Good	Very Good	Pvt-Party Good	Retail Excellent
1500 Wrk Trck 5 3/4'	C13C	30030	13250	14100	14800	18400
1500 XFE 5 3/4'	C233	33080	15350	16300	16950	21100
1500 LS/SL 5 3/4'	C13C	29685	14150	15050	15850	19900
1500 LT/SLE 5 3/4'	C23C	32120	15350	16300	16950	21100
2500 HD Work Trk 6	C43K	34790	13800	14400	16000	19700
2500 HD LT/SLE 8'	C53K	34155	16050	16750	18350	22600
2500 HD LTZ/SLT 8'	C63K	39300	17100	17800	19300	23600
4WD	K	----	2475	2475	3010	3010
V8, 6.0 Liter	Y	----	550	550	655	655
V8, 6.6L Turbo Dsl	6	----	4400	4400	4985	4985

SIERRA CREW CAB PICKUP—V8—Truck Equipment Schedule T1

Body Type	VIN	List	Trade-In Good	Very Good	Pvt-Party Good	Retail Excellent
2500 Work Truck 8'	C43K	32385	13500	14100	15700	19300
3500 Work Truck 8'	C73K	33640	14500	15100	16700	20600
4WD	K	----	2475	2475	2810	2810
V8, Turbo Diesel, 6.6L	6	----	4400	4400	5015	5015

SILVERADO/SIERRA CREW CAB PICKUP 4WD—V8—Truck Equip Sch T1

Body Type	VIN	List	Trade-In Good	Very Good	Pvt-Party Good	Retail Excellent
1500 LTZ/SLT 5 3/4'	K33M	41650	20700	22000	22440	27700
2WD	C	----	(2600)	(2600)	(3095)	(3095)
V8, 6.0 Liter	Y	----	550	550	645	645

SILVERADO/SIERRA CREW CAB 4WD—V8 Turbo Diesel—Truck Equip Sch T1

Body Type	VIN	List	Trade-In Good	Very Good	Pvt-Party Good	Retail Excellent
2500 HD LT/SLE 6'	K535	50800	23800	24800	26300	31800
2500 HD LTZ/SLT 6'	K636	47650	25500	26600	28100	34100
3500 HD LT/SLE 8'	K836	45230	25300	26400	27900	33900
3500 HD LTZ/SLT 8'	K936	50165	26800	27900	29300	35500
2WD	C	----	(2600)	(2600)	(2900)	(2900)
V8, 6.0 Liter	K	----	(5225)	(5225)	(5860)	(5860)

SILVERADO CREW CAB PICKUP—V8 Turbo Diesel—Truck Equip Sch T1

Body Type	VIN	List	Trade-In Good	Very Good	Pvt-Party Good	Retail Excellent
2500 HD Work Trk 8'	C436	39080	18300	19100	20500	24900
3500 HD Work Trk 8'	C736	40025	20000	20800	22500	27500
4WD	K	----	2475	2475	2770	2770
V8, 6.0 Liter	K	----	(5225)	(5225)	(5870)	(5870)

SILVERADO CREW CAB PICKUP—V8 Hybrid—Truck Equip Sch T1

Body Type	VIN	List	Trade-In Good	Very Good	Pvt-Party Good	Retail Excellent
1500 4D 5 3/4'	C135	38995	16450	17450	18150	22700
4WD	K	----	2475	2475	3010	3010

SIERRA CREW CAB PICKUP 4WD—V8 Hybrid—Truck Equip Sch T1

Body Type	VIN	List	Trade-In Good	Very Good	Pvt-Party Good	Retail Excellent
1500 4D 5 3/4'	K135	38995	19450	20600	21100	26200
2WD	C	----	(2600)	(2600)	(3125)	(3125)

SIERRA DENALI CREW CAB PICKUP AWD—V8—Truck Equip Schedule T3

Body Type	VIN	List	Trade-In Good	Very Good	Pvt-Party Good	Retail Excellent
1500 4D 5 3/4'	K032	43665	22400	23400	23900	28100
2WD	C	----	(825)	(825)	(920)	(920)

2010 CHEVY/GMC — (1,2or3)(CorG)(A,B,CorN)—(LBEW)—A

EQUINOX—4-Cyl.—Truck Equipment Schedule T1

Body Type	VIN	List	Trade-In Good	Very Good	Pvt-Party Good	Retail Excellent
LS Sport Utility 4D	LBEW	23185	9575	10000	11250	13800
AWD	C,E,N,G	----	725	725	860	860

EQUINOX—4-Cyl.—Truck Equipment Schedule T1

Body Type	VIN	List	Trade-In Good	Very Good	Pvt-Party Good	Retail Excellent
LT Sport Utility 4D	LDEW	24105	10200	10650	11900	14500
AWD	E,N	----	725	725	865	865
V6, 3.0 Liter	Y	----	825	825	1000	1000

EQUINOX AWD—V6—Truck Equipment Schedule T1

Body Type	VIN	List	Trade-In Good	Very Good	Pvt-Party Good	Retail Excellent
LTZ Sport Utility	LGEY	32040	12700	13250	14650	17800

Body Type	VIN	List	Trade-In Good	Very Good	Pvt-Party Good	Retail Excellent
FWD	F		(750)	(750)	(905)	(905)
4-Cyl, 2.4 Liter	W		(675)	(675)	(805)	(805)
TERRAIN—4-Cyl.—Truck Equipment Schedule T1						
SLE Sport Util 4D	LBEW	24995	10850	11300	12300	14800
SLT Sport Util 4D	LFEW	28195	12300	12850	13900	16650
AWD	C,E,G		725	725	830	830
V6, 3.0 Liter	Y		450	450	525	525
ACADIA—V6—Truck Equipment Schedule T1						
SL Sport Utility 4D	RKED	32515	11250	11750	12950	15700
SLE Sport Utility 4D	RLED	35090	12300	12850	13950	16750
AWD	V		775	775	915	915
ACADIA AWD—V6—Truck Equipment Schedule T1						
SLT Sport Util 4D	VMED	41360	15300	15950	17150	20600
2WD	R		(775)	(775)	(885)	(885)
TRAVERSE—V6—Truck Equipment Schedule T1						
LS Sport Utility 4D	REED	29999	10050	10500	11850	14650
AWD	V		1350	1350	1720	1720
TRAVERSE AWD—V6—Truck Equipment Schedule T1						
LT Sport Utility 4D	VFED	34520	12600	13200	14750	18050
LTZ Sport Utility	VHED	40760	14750	15400	17000	20800
2WD	R		(1350)	(1350)	(1705)	(1705)
TAHOE—V8—Truck Equipment Schedule T1						
LS Sport Utility 4D	CAE3,0	38230	16400	17150	18000	21300
Third Row Seat			525	525	615	615
4WD	K		1350	1350	1590	1590
TAHOE 4WD—V8—Truck Equipment Schedule T1						
LT Sport Utility 4D	KBE0	45930	21100	22100	22800	27000
LTZ Sport Utility 4D	KCE0	54565	26000	27100	27200	31500
Third Row Seat			525	525	615	615
2WD	C		(1350)	(1350)	(1590)	(1590)
TAHOE 4WD—V8 Hybrid—Truck Equipment Schedule T1						
Sport Utility 4D	KDDJ	54475	21500	22500	23400	27700
Third Row Seat			525	525	610	610
2WD	C		(1350)	(1350)	(1585)	(1585)
YUKON—V8—Truck Equipment Schedule T1						
SLE Sport Utility	CAE0,3	38970	17750	18600	19400	23000
Third Row Seat			525	525	615	615
4WD	K		1350	1350	1585	1585
YUKON 4WD—V8—Truck Equipment Schedule T1						
SLT Sport Utility	KCE0	47615	22200	23200	24000	28400
Third Row Seat			525	525	610	610
2WD	C		(1350)	(1350)	(1580)	(1580)
YUKON 4WD—V8 Hybrid—Truck Equipment Schedule T1						
Sport Utility 4D	KFDJ	54945	22800	23800	24600	29100
Third Row Seat			525	525	610	610
2WD	C		(1350)	(1350)	(1580)	(1580)
YUKON DENALI AWD—V8—Truck Equipment Schedule T3						
Sport Utility 4D	KEEF	56945	25500	26600	26800	31200
Third Row Seat			525	525	595	595
2WD	C		(1350)	(1350)	(1535)	(1535)
YUKON DENALI 4WD—V8 Hybrid—Truck Equipment Schedule T3						
Sport Utility 4D	KGEJ	62295	25100	26100	26500	30900
Third Row Seat			525	525	595	595
2WD	C		(1350)	(1350)	(1545)	(1545)
SUBURBAN 4WD—V8—Truck Equipment Schedule T1						
K1500 LS Sport Util	KHE0	44430	17400	18200	19300	23100
K1500 LT Sport Util	KJE0	47940	19550	20400	21500	25700
2WD	C		(1350)	(1350)	(1650)	(1650)
SUBURBAN 4WD—V8—Truck Equipment Schedule T1						
K1500 LTZ Spt Util	KKE0	56575	23600	24600	25100	29700
K1500 75th Dmnd	KKE3	58740	24500	25600	26100	30800
K2500 LS Spt Util	KLEG	46035	19800	20700	21700	25900
2WD	C		(1350)	(1350)	(1570)	(1570)
SUBURBAN 4WD—V8—Truck Equipment Schedule T1						
K2500 LT Spt Util	KMEG	49530	21400	22400	23300	27800
2WD	C		(1350)	(1350)	(1640)	(1640)
YUKON XL 4WD—V8—Truck Equipment Schedule T1						
1500 SLE Sport Util	KHE0	43030	17950	18800	19900	23900
1500 SLT Sport Util	KKE0	47615	20500	21400	22400	26800
2500 SLE Sport Util	KNEG	46900	19350	20200	21300	25400
2500 SLT Sport Util	KREG	51305	21900	22900	23800	28400
Third Row Seat			525	525	640	640

1015

Body Type	VIN	List	Trade-In Good	Trade-In Very Good	Pvt-Party Good	Retail Excellent
2WD	C		(1350)	(1350)	(1655)	(1655)
V8, Flex Fuel, 6.2 Liter	2		550	550	665	665
YUKON XL DENALI AWD—V8—Truck Equipment Schedule T3						
1500 Sport Util	KMEF	59700	24900	26000	26500	31300
Third Row Seat			525	525	610	610
2WD	C		(1350)	(1350)	(1575)	(1575)
EXPRESS/SAVANA VAN—V8—Truck Equipment Schedule T1						
1500 LS Passenger	GBD4	29495	9475	9950	11000	13650
1500 LT Passenger	GCD4	31345	10300	10800	11850	14700
2500 LS Passenger	GPDG	31000	9750	10250	11300	14000
2500 LT Passenger	GRDG	32850	10450	11000	12050	14900
3500 LS Passenger	GXDG	33295	10800	11350	12400	15350
3500 LT Passenger	GYDG	34750	11700	12250	13400	16550
3500 LS Extended	GZDG	35165	12150	12700	13900	17200
3500 LT Extended	G1DG	35535	12500	13100	14250	17600
AWD	H		625	625	760	760
EXPRESS VAN—V6—Truck Equipment Schedule T1						
1500 Cargo Van	GADX	25840	11150	11900	12700	16000
AWD	H		625	625	745	745
V8, Flex Fuel, 5.3 Liter	4		550	550	640	640
SAVANA VAN—V8—Truck Equipment Schedule T1						
1500 Cargo Van	GAD4	25635	11600	12350	13150	16550
AWD	H		625	625	745	745
V6, 4.3 Liter	X		(525)	(525)	(630)	(630)
EXPRESS/SAVANA VAN—V8—Truck Equipment Schedule T1						
2500 Cargo Van	GFBA	26755	12250	13050	13900	17500
2500 Extended	GGBA	28615	12550	13350	14200	17850
3500 Cargo Van	GTBA	30075	12600	13400	14200	17850
3500 Extended	GUBA	30960	12800	13650	14550	18350
V8, Flex Fuel, 6.0 Liter	K		475	475	560	560
V8, 6.6L Turbo Dsl	6		5175	5175	6210	6210
EXPRESS/SAVANA VAN—V8 Turbo Diesel—Truck Equipment Sch T1						
2500 Cargo Van	GFBL	38750	17450	18250	19550	24200
2500 Extended	GGBL	40610	17700	18550	19850	24500
3500 Cargo Van	GTBL	42070	17900	18750	20000	24700
3500 Extended	GUBL	42955	18300	19150	20400	25200
COLORADO/CANYON REGULAR CAB PICKUP—4-Cyl.—Truck Equip Sch T1						
Work Truck 2D 6'	SBD9	18860	7650	7975	9175	11300
LT/SLE 2D 6'	SCD9	19985	8200	8575	9750	12000
4WD	T		1625	1625	1910	1910
5-Cyl, 3.7 Liter	E		200	200	235	235
CANYON REGULAR CAB PICKUP—5-Cyl.—Truck Equipment Sch T1						
SLE 2D 6'	SCDE	21055	8800	9200	10400	12750
4WD	T		1625	1625	1910	1910
4-Cyl, 2.9 Liter	9		(200)	(200)	(230)	(230)
COLORADO/CANYON EXTENDED CAB PICKUP—4-Cyl.—Truck Sch T1						
Work Truck 4D 6'	SBD9	24405	10150	10600	11850	14550
4WD	T		1625	1625	1905	1905
5-Cyl, 3.7 Liter	E		200	200	235	235
COLORADO/CANYON EXTENDED CAB PICKUP—5-Cyl.—Truck Sch T1						
LT/SLE 4D 6'	SCDE	24860	11150	11650	12950	15850
4WD	T		1625	1625	1900	1900
4-Cyl, 2.9 Liter	9		(200)	(200)	(225)	(225)
V8, 5.3 Liter	P		675	675	795	795
CANYON EXTENDED CAB PICKUP—5-Cyl.—Truck Equipment Sch T2						
SLT 4D 6'	SFDE	26410	12150	12700	14050	17200
4WD	T		1625	1625	1895	1895
V8, 5.3 Liter	P		850	850	995	995
COLORADO/CANYON CREW CAB PICKUP—5-Cyl.—Truck Equip Sch T2						
LT/SLE 4D 5'	SCDE	25865	13450	14050	15550	19000
4WD	T		1625	1625	1895	1895
4-Cyl, 2.9 Liter	9		(200)	(200)	(225)	(225)
V8, 5.3 Liter	P		675	675	790	790
CANYON CREW CAB PICKUP—5-Cyl.—Truck Equipment Schedule T2						
SLT 4D 5'	SFDE	27960	14100	14750	16200	19800
4WD	T		1625	1625	1895	1895
V8, 5.3 Liter	P		850	850	995	995
AVALANCHE 4WD—V8—Truck Equipment Schedule T1						
LS Spt Util Pickup	KEE0	39725	17650	18450	19300	22900
LT Spt Util Pickup	KFE0	42830	19550	20400	21300	25200
LTZ Spt Util Pickup	KGE0	49815	22100	23100	23900	28400
2WD	C		(1350)	(1350)	(1540)	(1540)

TRUCKS & VANS

TRUCKS & VANS

Body Type	VIN	List	Good	Trade-In Very Good	Pvt-Party Good	Retail Excellent
SILVERADO REGULAR CAB PICKUP—V6—Truck Equipment Sch T1						
1500 Work Truck 8'	CPEX	22235	**8850**	**9250**	**10200**	**12350**
4WD	K		2725	2725	3290	3290
V8, Flex Fuel, 4.8 Liter	A		650	650	795	795
V8, Flex Fuel, 5.3 Liter	0		975	975	1170	1170
SIERRA REGULAR CAB PICKUP—V8—Truck Equipment Schedule T1						
1500 Work Truck 8'	CTEA	22235	**9675**	**10100**	**11050**	**13400**
4WD	K		2725	2725	3280	3280
V6, 4.3 Liter	X		(575)	(575)	(690)	(690)
V8, Flex Fuel, 5.3 Liter	0		350	350	410	410
SILVERADO/SIERRA REGULAR CAB PICKUP—V8—Truck Equipment Sch T1						
1500 Wrk Trk 6 1/2'	CPEA	21845	**9975**	**10400**	**11400**	**13800**
1500 LT/SLE 6 1/2'	CSEA	27805	**11250**	**11750**	**12850**	**15600**
1500 LT/SLE 8'	CSEA	27930	**10850**	**11350**	**12350**	**15000**
2500 HD Wrk Trk 8'	CVBG	28460	**8400**	**8700**	**10000**	**11950**
2500 HD LT/SLE 8'	CXBG	31255	**11100**	**11500**	**12950**	**15400**
3500 Work Truck 8'	CZBK	28680	**8200**	**8500**	**9825**	**11800**
3500 SLE 2D 8'	C3BK	31610	**10800**	**11200**	**12700**	**15150**
4WD	K		2725	2725	3285	3285
V6, 4.3 Liter	X		(575)	(575)	(690)	(690)
V8, Flex Fuel, 5.3 Liter	0		350	350	410	410
V8, 6.6L Turbo Dsl	6		5175	5175	6085	6085
SILVERADO REGULAR CAB 4WD—V8 Turbo Diesel—Truck Equip Sch T1						
3500 LT 2D 8'	K0B6	39590	**19100**	**19750**	**21500**	**25600**
2WD	C		(2775)	(2775)	(3115)	(3115)
V8, 6.0 Liter	G,K		(5425)	(5425)	(6100)	(6100)
SILVERADO/SIERRA EXTENDED CAB—V6—Truck Equipment Sch T1						
1500 Wrk Trk 6 1/2'	CPEX	26390	**10550**	**11050**	**12050**	**14650**
4WD	K		2725	2725	3300	3300
V8, Flex Fuel, 4.8 Liter	A		650	650	795	795
V8, Flex Fuel, 5.3 Liter	0,3		975	975	1170	1170
SILVERADO/SIERRA EXTENDED CAB PICKUP—V8—Truck Equip Sch T1						
1500 Work Truck 8'	CPE0	31580	**10800**	**11300**	**12350**	**15050**
1500 LT/SLE 8'	CSE0	31230	**13300**	**13900**	**15150**	**18450**
1500 LTZ/SLT 8'	CTE0	36575	**13650**	**14300**	**15550**	**18900**
4WD	K		2725	2725	3310	3310
SILVERADO/SIERRA EXTENDED CAB 4WD—V8—Truck Equip Sch T1						
1500 LTZ/SLT 6 1/2'	KTE3	39425	**18450**	**19300**	**20500**	**25000**
2WD	C		(2775)	(2775)	(3320)	(3320)
V8, Flex Fuel, 6.2 Liter	2		550	550	660	660
SILVERADO/SIERRA EXTENDED CAB PICKUP—V8—Truck Equip Sch T1						
1500 LS/SL 6 1/2'	CSEA	29135	**12650**	**13200**	**14500**	**17750**
1500 LT/SLE 6 1/2'	CSEA	30120	**13500**	**14100**	**15300**	**18600**
2500 HD WrkTrk 6'	CVBG	30890	**12550**	**12950**	**14450**	**17050**
2500 HD Wrk Trk 8'	CVBK	30935	**12450**	**12900**	**14300**	**16950**
3500 Wrk Trk 4D 8'	CZBG	31970	**12900**	**13350**	**14800**	**17400**
3500 LTZ/SLT 8'	C1BG	39590	**16450**	**17000**	**18800**	**22400**
4WD	K		2725	2725	3325	3325
V8, 5.3L Flex Fuel	0,3		350	350	410	410
V8, Flex Fuel, 6.2 Liter	2		550	550	665	665
V8, 6.6L Turbo Dsl	6		5175	5175	5855	5855
SILVERADO/SIERRA EXTENDED CAB 4WD—V8—Truck Equip Sch T1						
2500 HD LT/SLE 6'	KXBG	33900	**18000**	**18650**	**20500**	**24500**
2500 HD LT/SLE 8'	KXBG	33945	**18250**	**18850**	**20700**	**24600**
2500HD LTZ/SLT 6	KYBG	39185	**19550**	**20200**	**22000**	**26200**
2500HD LTZ/SLT 8'	KYBG	39230	**19350**	**20000**	**21900**	**26000**
2WD	C		(2775)	(2775)	(3135)	(3135)
V8, 6.6L Turbo Dsl	6		5175	5175	5855	5855
SILVERADO/SIERRA EXTENDED CAB 4WD—V8 Turbo Diesel—Truck Equip Sch T1						
3500 LT/SLE 8'	K0B6	46065	**23300**	**24100**	**26200**	**31100**
2WD	C		(2775)	(2775)	(3110)	(3110)
V8, 6.0 Liter	G,K		(5425)	(5425)	(6090)	(6090)
SILVERADO/SIERRA CREW CAB PICKUP—V8—Truck Equipment Sch T1						
1500 XFE 5 3/4'	CSE3	34220	**15900**	**16600**	**17750**	**21500**
SILVERADO/SIERRA CREW CAB PICKUP 4WD—V8—Truck Equip Sch T1						
1500 LTZ/SLT 5 3/4'	KTE3	43570	**22000**	**22900**	**24000**	**29000**
2WD	C		(2775)	(2775)	(3310)	(3310)
V8, Flex Fuel, 6.2 Liter	2		550	550	655	655
SILVERADO CREW CAB PICKUP—V8 Hybrid—Truck Equip Sch T1						
1500 4D 5 3/4'	CUEJ	39335	**18450**	**19250**	**20400**	**24700**
4WD	K		2725	2725	3285	3285
SIERRA CREW CAB PICKUP 4WD—V8 Hybrid—Truck Equip Sch T1						
1500 4D 5 3/4'	KYEJ	39705	**20700**	**21600**	**22700**	**27500**

Body Type	VIN	List	Trade-In Good	Very Good	Pvt-Party Good	Retail Excellent
2WD	C		(2775)	(2775)	(3330)	(3330)
SILVERADO/SIERRA CREW CAB PICKUP—V8—Truck Equip Sch T1						
1500 Wrk Trk 5 3/4'	CTEA	30370	13800	14450	15600	18950
1500 LS/SL 5 3/4'	CREA	31355	15350	16050	17250	21000
1500 LT/SLE 5 3/4'	CSEA	32460	16800	17550	18600	22400
2500 HD WrkTrk 6'	CVBG	35490	15150	15700	17050	20000
2500 HD LT/SLE 8'	CXBG	36055	17650	18250	20100	23900
2500 HD LTZ/SLT 8'	CYBG	41250	18800	19400	21300	25300
4WD	K		2725	2725	3300	3300
V8, Flex Fuel, 5.3 Liter	0,3		350	350	410	410
V8, Flex Fuel, 6.2 Liter	2		550	550	660	660
V8, 6.6L Turbo Dsl	6		5175	5175	5840	5840
SILVERADO/SIERRA CREW CAB 4WD—V8 Turbo Diesel—Truck Sch T1						
2500 HD LT 6'	KXB6	47550	25500	26400	28100	33100
2500 HD LTZ/SLT 6'	KYB6	52750	27700	28600	30600	36300
2WD	C		(2775)	(2775)	(3100)	(3100)
V8, 6.0 Liter	G		(5425)	(5425)	(6070)	(6070)
SIERRA CREW CAB PICKUP—V8—Truck Equipment Sch T1						
3500 Work Trk 8'	C2B6	33640	15750	16250	18050	21500
4WD			2725	2725	3105	3105
V8, 6.6L Turbo Dsl	6		5175	5175	5885	5885
SILVERADO CREW CAB—V8 Turbo Diesel—Truck Equipment Sch T1						
2500 HD Wrk Trk 8'	CVB6	40780	19900	20600	21800	25300
3500 Work Truck 8'	CZB6	41725	21800	22500	24400	29000
4WD			2725	2725	3065	3065
V8, 6.0 Liter	G,K		(5425)	(5425)	(6090)	(6090)
SILVERADO CREW CAB 4WD—V8 Turbo Diesel—Truck Equip Sch T1						
3500 LTZ 4D 8'	K1B6	51120	29300	30300	32300	38100
2WD	C		(2775)	(2775)	(3115)	(3115)
V8, 6.0 Liter	G		(5425)	(5425)	(6100)	(6100)
SILVERADO/SIERRA CREW CAB 4WD—V8 Turbo Diesel—Truck Sch T1						
3500 LT/SLE 8'	K0B6	47130	27000	27900	29900	35300
2WD	C		(2775)	(2775)	(3135)	(3135)
V8, 6.0 Liter	G,K		(5425)	(5425)	(6140)	(6140)
SIERRA CREW CAB PICKUP—V8 Turbo Diesel—Truck Equip Sch T1						
3500 SLT 4D 8'	C4B6	42265	24500	25300	27400	32600
4WD	K		2725	2725	3070	3070
V8, 6.0 Liter	G,K		(5425)	(5425)	(6105)	(6105)
SIERRA DENALI CREW CAB PICKUP AWD—V8—Truck Equip Schedule T3						
1500 4D 5 3/4'	KXE2	47430	24700	25500	26400	30300
2WD	C		(950)	(950)	(1055)	(1055)

2011 CHEVY/GMC — (1,2or3)(CorG)(A,B,CorN)-(LBEC)-B

Body Type	VIN	List	Trade-In Good	Very Good	Pvt-Party Good	Retail Excellent
EQUINOX—4-Cyl.—Truck Equipment Schedule T1						
LS Sport Utility 4D	LBEC	23490	10750	11100	12550	14850
AWD	C		775	775	905	905
EQUINOX—4-Cyl.—Truck Equipment Schedule T1						
LT Sport Utility 4D	LDEC	24655	11550	11950	13350	15700
AWD	E,N		775	775	910	910
V6, Flex Fuel, 3.0 Liter	5		925	925	1085	1085
EQUINOX AWD—V6—Truck Equipment Schedule T1						
LTZ Sport Utility 4D	LGE5	32315	13900	14350	15850	18600
FWD	F		(1000)	(1000)	(1175)	(1175)
4-Cyl, 2.4 Liter	C		(775)	(775)	(895)	(895)
TERRAIN—4-Cyl.—Truck Equipment Schedule T1						
SLE Sport Utility	LMEC	24995	12100	12500	14050	16800
SLT Sport Utility	LUEC	28595	13800	14300	16000	19050
AWD	R		775	775	920	920
V6, Flex Fuel, 3.0 Liter	5		525	525	625	625
ACADIA—V6—Truck Equipment Schedule T1						
SL Sport Util 4D	RKED	32615	13500	13950	15250	17750
SLE Sport Util 4D	RNED	35240	14300	14750	16050	18750
Denali Sport Util.	RTED	43995	21300	22000	23100	26600
AWD	V		825	825	935	935
ACADIA AWD—V6—Truck Equipment Schedule T1						
SLT Sport Util 4D	VRED	40960	18000	18550	19800	23000
2WD	R		(825)	(825)	(925)	(925)
TRAVERSE—V6—Truck Equipment Schedule T1						
LS Sport Utility 4D	REED	29999	12000	12400	13950	16550
AWD	V		1450	1450	1735	1735
TRAVERSE AWD—V6—Truck Equipment Schedule T1						
LT Sport Utility 4D	VGED	34640	15150	15650	17350	20600
LTZ Sport Utility	VLED	40750	16800	17350	19250	22900

TRUCKS & VANS

Body Type	VIN	List	Trade-In Good	Very Good	Pvt-Party Good	Retail Excellent
2WD	R		(1450)	(1450)	(1730)	(1730)
TAHOE—V8—Truck Equipment Schedule T1						
LS Sport Util 4D	CAE0	38520	19200	19950	20900	24100
Third Row Seat			575	575	665	665
4WD	K		1450	1450	1640	1640
TAHOE 4WD—V8—Truck Equipment Schedule T1						
LT Sport Util 4D	KBE0	46220	23900	24900	25900	29800
LTZ Sport Util 4D	KCE0	55110	27900	28700	29500	33400
Third Row Seat			575	575	665	665
2WD	C		(1450)	(1450)	(1640)	(1640)
TAHOE 4WD—V8 Hybrid—Truck Equipment Schedule T1						
Sport Utility 4D	KDFJ	54490	25600	26600	27700	32000
Third Row Seat			575	575	670	670
2WD	C		(1450)	(1450)	(1655)	(1655)
YUKON—V8—Truck Equipment Schedule T1						
SLE Sport Utility 4D	2AE0	39485	20500	21300	22300	25700
Third Row Seat			575	575	665	665
4WD	2		1450	1450	1640	1640
YUKON 4WD—V8—Truck Equipment Schedule T1						
SLT Sport Utility 4D	2CE0	47855	24700	25600	26600	30600
Third Row Seat			575	575	665	665
2WD	1		(1450)	(1450)	(1640)	(1640)
YUKON 4WD—V8 Hybrid—Truck Equipment Schedule T1						
Sport Utility 4D	2FFJ	54960	26400	27400	28500	32900
Third Row Seat			575	575	670	670
2WD	1		(1450)	(1450)	(1655)	(1655)
YUKON DENALI AWD—V8—Truck Equipment Schedule T3						
Sport Utility 4D	2EEF	57185	26900	27700	28600	32500
Third Row Seat			575	575	650	650
2WD	1		(1450)	(1450)	(1615)	(1615)
YUKON DENALI 4WD—V8 Hybrid—Truck Equipment Schedule T3						
Sport Utility 4D	2GEJ	62310	29000	29900	30900	35100
Third Row Seat			575	575	650	650
2WD	1		(1450)	(1450)	(1610)	(1610)
SUBURBAN 4WD—V8—Truck Equipment Schedule T1						
K1500 LS Sport Util	KHE0	44720	20800	21600	22700	26200
K1500 LT Sport Util	KJE0	48230	23100	24000	25100	29000
K1500 LTZ Spt Utl	KKE0	57120	26700	27500	28400	32600
K2500 LS Spt Utl	KLEG	46325	23400	24300	25300	29300
K2500 LT Spt Utl	KMEG	49820	25500	26500	27500	31800
Third Row Seat			575	575	675	675
2WD	C		(1450)	(1450)	(1675)	(1675)
YUKON XL 4WD—V8—Truck Equipment Schedule T1						
1500 SLE Sport Util	2HE0	46205	21500	22400	23400	27100
1500 SLT Sport Util	2KE0	50365	24000	24900	26000	30000
2500 SLE Sport Util	2NEG	47565	23000	23800	24800	28700
2500 SLT Sport Util	2REG	51695	25800	26800	27900	32300
Third Row Seat			575	575	675	675
2WD	1		(1450)	(1450)	(1675)	(1675)
YUKON XL DENALI AWD—V8—Truck Equipment Schedule T3						
1500 Sport Utility	2MEF	59940	28000	28800	29700	34200
Third Row Seat			575	575	660	660
2WD	1		(1450)	(1450)	(1635)	(1635)
EXPRESS/SAVANA VAN—V8—Truck Equipment Schedule T1						
1500 LS Passenger	GBF4	29690	10900	11300	12400	14850
1500 LT Passenger	GCF4	31540	12050	12500	13700	16400
2500 LS Passenger	GPFA	30200	11100	11500	12700	15250
2500 LT Passenger	GRFA	32050	12450	12850	14050	16800
AWD	H		700	700	840	840
V8, Flex Fuel, 6.0 Liter	G		500	500	575	575
EXPRESS/SAVANA VAN—V8 Flex Fuel—Truck Equipment Sch T1						
3500 LS Passenger	GXFG	33490	12250	12650	13900	16650
3500 LT Passenger	GYFG	34945	13350	13800	15100	18100
3500 LS Extended	GZFG	35360	13800	14300	15600	18650
3500 LT Extended	G1FG	35730	14100	14550	15900	19050
EXPRESS/SAVANA VAN—V8 Turbo Diesel—Truck Equipment Sch T1						
3500 LS Passenger	GXFL	45355	18000	18600	20000	23900
3500 LT Passenger	GYFL	46940	18800	19450	20900	25000
3500 LS Extended	GZFL	47385	18800	19500	20900	25000
3500 LT Extended	G1FL	47725	19400	20100	21500	25700
EXPRESS VAN—V6—Truck Equipment Schedule T1						
1500 Cargo Van	GAFX	26070	12550	13200	14250	17500
AWD	H		700	700	820	820

Body Type	VIN	List	Trade-In Good	Very Good	Pvt-Party Good	Retail Excellent
V8, Flex Fuel, 5.3 Liter	4	....	650	650	775	775
SAVANA VAN—V8—Truck Equipment Schedule T1						
1500 Cargo Van	7AF4	25840	12900	13600	14750	18200
AWD	8	....	700	700	820	820
V6, 4.3 Liter	X	....	(575)	(575)	(685)	(685)
EXPRESS/SAVANA VAN—V8—Truck Equipment Schedule T1						
2500 Cargo Van	GFCB	31275	13750	14450	15650	19300
3500 Cargo Van	GTCB	31445	14600	15400	16600	20400
V8, Flex Fuel, 4.8 Liter	A	....	(475)	(475)	(565)	(565)
EXPRESS/SAVANA VAN—V8—Truck Equipment Schedule T1						
2500 Extended	GGCA	32820	14250	15000	16200	19950
3500 Extended	GUCA	31165	14800	15600	16750	20600
3500 Van Cab-Ch	G4CA	27210	13850	14300	16150	19850
V8, Flex Fuel, 6.0 Liter	G	....	500	500	575	575
V8, Turbo Diesel, 6.6L	L	....	4825	4825	6050	6050
EXPRESS/SAVANA VAN—V8 Diesel—Truck Equipment Sch T1						
2500 Cargo Van	GFCL	38955	19100	19750	21500	26100
2500 Extended	GGCL	40815	19500	20100	21900	26500
3500 Cargo Van	GTCL	42275	19700	20400	22100	26800
3500 Extended	GUCL	43160	20000	20700	22500	27200
COLORADO/CANYON REGULAR CAB PICKUP—4-Cyl.—Truck Equip Sch T1						
Work Truck 2D 6'	SBF9	18920	9025	9325	10700	12750
LT 2D 6'	SCF9	20045	9725	10050	11450	13600
4WD	T	....	1825	1825	2125	2125
5-Cyl, 3.7 Liter	E	....	200	200	230	230
CANYON REGULAR CAB PICKUP—5-Cyl.—Truck Equip Sch T1						
SLE 2D 6'	5MFE	21115	9950	10300	11700	13900
4WD	6	....	1825	1825	2115	2115
4-Cyl, 2.9 Liter	9	....	(200)	(200)	(230)	(230)
COLORADO/CANYON EXTENDED CAB PICKUP—4-Cyl.—Truck Sch T1						
Work Truck 4D 6'	SBF9	24465	11350	11700	13250	15700
4WD	T	....	1825	1825	2120	2120
5-Cyl, 3.7 Liter	E	....	200	200	230	230
COLORADO/CANYON EXTENDED CAB—5-Cyl.—Truck Equip Sch T1						
LT/SLE 4D 6'	SCFE	24920	12550	12950	14500	17250
4WD	T	....	1825	1825	2115	2115
4-Cyl, 2.9 Liter	9	....	(200)	(200)	(230)	(230)
V8, 5.3 Liter	P	....	725	725	845	845
COLORADO/CANYON CREW CAB PICKUP—5-Cyl.—Truck Equip Sch T2						
LT/SLE 4D 5'	SCFE	27240	15550	16050	17750	20900
4WD	T	....	1825	1825	2100	2100
4-Cyl, 2.9 Liter	9	....	(200)	(200)	(230)	(230)
V8, 5.3 Liter	P	....	725	725	840	840
CANYON CREW CAB PICKUP—5-Cyl.—Truck Equipment Schedule T2						
SLT 4D 5'	5NFE	28020	16000	16500	18250	21600
4WD	6	....	1825	1825	2110	2110
V8, 5.3 Liter	P	....	950	950	1100	1100
AVALANCHE 4WD—V8—Truck Equipment Schedule T1						
LS Spt Util Pickup	KEE3	40110	20000	20700	21800	25300
LT Spt Util Pickup	KFE3	43215	22500	23200	24300	27900
LTZ Spt Util Pickup	KGE3	50260	24900	25700	26800	30900
2WD	C	....	(1450)	(1450)	(1605)	(1605)
SILVERADO/SIERRA REGULAR CAB PICKUP—V8—Truck Equipment Sch T1						
1500 Work Trk 6 1/2'	CPEA	23175	11750	12100	13400	15850
1500 Work Truck 8'	CPEA	23500	10700	11050	12250	14450
1500 LT/SLE 6 1/2'	CSEA	27805	12800	13200	14650	17300
1500 LT/SLE 8'	CSEA	27930	12350	12750	14050	16650
1500 HD Wrk Trk 8'	CVCG	28960	12100	12450	13600	16350
2500 LT/SLE 8'	CXCG	32155	15150	15550	16900	19150
3500 Work Truck 8'	CZCG	29800	12250	12550	13750	16550
4WD	K	....	2925	2925	3470	3470
V6, 4.3 Liter	X	....	(650)	(650)	(770)	(770)
V8, Flex Fuel, 5.3 Liter	0	....	375	375	430	430
V8, Turbo Diesel, 6.6L	8,L	....	4825	4825	5455	5455
SILVERADO/SIERRA REGULAR CAB 4WD—V8 Turbo Diesel—Truck Sch T1						
3500 LT/SLE 8'	K0C8,L	44335	23600	24200	25800	29300
2WD	C	....	(2950)	(2950)	(3265)	(3265)
V8, 6.0 Liter	G	....	(5625)	(5625)	(6220)	(6220)
SILVERADO/SIERRA EXTENDED CAB PICKUP—V8—Truck Equip Sch T1						
1500 LT/SLE 8'	CSE0	31230	14300	14750	16350	19450
1500 LTZ/SLT 8'	CTE0	36575	15950	16450	18000	21300
4WD	K	....	2925	2925	3510	3510

TRUCKS & VANS

Body Type	VIN	List	Trade-In Good	Very Good	Pvt-Party Good	Retail Excellent
SILVERADO/SIERRA EXTENDED CAB PICKUP—V6—Truck Equip Sch T1						
1500 Work Trk 6 1/2'	CPEA	26390	12300	12650	14000	16550
4WD	K		2925	2925	3480	3480
V8, Flex Fuel, 4.8 Liter	A		700	700	830	830
V8, Flex Fuel, 5.3 Liter	0,3		1025	1025	1220	1220
SILVERADO/SIERRA EXTENDED CAB PICKUP—V8—Truck Equip Sch T1						
1500 Work Truck 8'	CPE0	31580	12150	12500	13850	16400
4WD	K		2925	2925	3485	3485
SILVERADO/SIERRA EXTENDED CAB PICKUP 4WD—V8—Truck Equip T1						
1500 LTZ/SLT 6 1/2'	KTE3	39425	20500	21100	22900	27200
2WD	C		(2950)	(2950)	(3485)	(3485)
V8, Flex Fuel, 6.2 Liter	2		550	550	650	650
SILVERADO/SIERRA EXTENDED CAB PICKUP—V8—Truck Equip Sch T1						
1500 LS/SL 6 1/2'	CREA	29135	14000	14450	16050	19150
1500 LT/SLE 6 1/2'	CSEA	30120	15400	15900	17400	20700
2500 HD Wrk Trk 6'	CVCG	31140	16300	16750	18250	20800
2500 HD Wrk Trk 8'	CVCG	31335	15350	15800	17350	19850
3500 Work Truck 8'	CZCG	33025	16750	17200	18650	21200
1500 LTZ/SLT 8'	C1CG	40615	20700	21200	22700	25800
4WD	K		2925	2925	3520	3520
V8, Flex Fuel, 5.3 Liter	0,3		375	375	435	435
V8, Flex Fuel, 6.2 Liter	2		550	550	655	655
V8, Turbo Diesel, 6.6L	8		4825	4825	5355	5355
SILVERADO/SIERRA EXTENDED CAB PICKUP—V8—Truck Equip Sch T1						
2500 HD LT/SLE 6'	KXCG	34450	22500	23100	24800	28300
2500 HD LT/SLE 8'	KXCG	34645	22600	23200	24900	28400
2500 HD LTZ/SLT 6'	KYCG	39185	23800	24500	26100	29700
2500 HD LTZ/SLT 8'	KYCG	39380	23700	24300	25900	29500
2WD	C		(2950)	(2950)	(3280)	(3280)
V8, Turbo Diesel, 6.6L	8		4825	4825	5360	5360
SILVERADO/SIERRA EXTENDED CAB 4WD—V8 Turbo Diesel—Truck Sch T1						
3500 LT/SLE 8'	K0C8,L	47770	28100	28900	30600	34700
2WD	C		(2950)	(2950)	(3275)	(3275)
V8, 6.0 Liter	G		(5625)	(5625)	(6245)	(6245)
SILVERADO/SIERRA CREW CAB PICKUP—V8—Truck Equipment Sch T1						
1500 XFE 5 3/4'	CSE3	34220	17800	18350	19850	23400
SILVERADO/SIERRA CREW CAB PICKUP 4WD—V8—Truck Equip Sch T1						
1500 LTZ 4D 5 3/4'	KTE3	43550	24300	25000	26500	31100
1500 SLT 4D 5 3/4'	2WE3	40120	23200	23900	25300	29800
2WD	C		(2950)	(2950)	(3485)	(3485)
V8, Flex Fuel, 6.2 Liter	2		550	550	650	650
SILVERADO CREW CAB PICKUP—V8 Hybrid—Truck Equip Sch T1						
1500 4D 5 3/4'	CUEJ	39335	20400	21100	22600	26800
4WD	K		2925	2925	3485	3485
SIERRA CREW CAB PICKUP 4WD—V8 Hybrid—Truck Equip Sch T1						
1500 4D 5 3/4'	2YEJ	46035	23100	23800	25400	29900
2WD	1		(2950)	(2950)	(3525)	(3525)
SILVERADO/SIERRA CREW CAB PICKUP—V8—Truck Equipment Sch T1						
1500 Wrk Trk 5 3/4'	CPEA	33520	15650	16150	17650	20900
1500 LS 4D 5 3/4'	CREA	31355	17200	17700	19300	22900
1500 LT 4D 5 3/4'	CSEA	32460	18900	19500	20900	24500
2500 HD Wrk Trk 6'	CVCG	35995	18700	19200	20700	23500
2500 HD LT/SLE 8'	CXCG	36900	22100	22700	24300	27700
2500 HD LTZ/SLT 8'	CYCG	42100	23800	24400	26000	29600
3500 Work Trk 6 1/2'	CZCG	34560	21300	21800	23300	26400
3500 LT/SLE 6 1/2'	C0CG	37915	23900	24500	26200	29800
3500 LTZ/SLT 6 1/2'	C1CG	42600	25000	25700	27400	31200
4WD	K		2925	2925	3490	3490
V8, Flex Fuel, 5.3 Liter	0,3		375	375	435	435
V8, Flex Fuel, 6.2 Liter	2		550	550	655	655
V8, Turbo Diesel, 6.6L	8		4825	4825	5365	5365
SILVERADO/SIERRA CREW CAB 4WD—V8 Turbo Diesel—Truck Sch T1						
2500 HD LT/SLE 6'	KXC8	48250	30300	31100	33000	37500
2WD	C		(2950)	(2950)	(3270)	(3270)
V8, 6.0 Liter	G		(5625)	(5625)	(6235)	(6235)
SIERRA CREW CAB PICKUP—V8—Truck Equipment Sch T1						
2500 Work Truck 8'	1ZCG	33235	19000	19500	21200	24200
3500 Work Truck 8'	12CG	34960	19950	20500	22000	25000
4WD			2925	2925	3265	3265
V8, 6.6L Turbo Dsl			4825	4825	5380	5380
SILVERADO CREW CAB—V8 Turbo Diesel—Truck Equip Sch T1						
2500 HD Wrk Trk 8'	CVC8,L	41630	23100	23700	25500	29200
3500 Work Truck 8'	CZC8,6	42955	26000	26700	28300	32100

Body Type	VIN	List	Trade-In Good	Very Good	Pvt-Party Good	Retail Excellent
4WD .... K			2925	2925	3245	3245
V8, 6.0 Liter .... G			(5625)	(5625)	(6230)	(6230)
SILVERADO CREW CAB PICKUP 4WD—V8 Turbo Diesel—Truck Sch T1						
2500 HD LTZ/SLT 6' KYC8	53450		33100	34000	35700	40500
3500 LT 4D 8' K0C8,L	49460		31700	32600	34600	39600
3500 LTZ 4D 8' KNC8,L	54145		34100	35000	36700	41600
2WD			(2950)	(2950)	(3265)	(3265)
V8, 6.0 Liter .... G			(5625)	(5625)	(6230)	(6220)
SIERRA DENALI CREW CAB PICKUP AWD—V8—Truck Equip Schedule T3						
1500 4D 5 3/4' 2XE2	47430		26200	26900	28100	31500
2WD 1			(1075)	(1075)	(1170)	(1170)
SIERRA DENALI CREW CAB PICKUP—V8—Truck Equip Schedule T3						
3500 4D 6 1/2' 16CG	44410		25400	26100	27700	31400
3500 4D 8' 16CG	44595		25600	26300	27900	31500
4WD 2			2925	2925	3255	3255
V8, Turbo Diesel, 6.6L ... 8			4825	4825	5365	5365
SIERRA DENALI CREW CAB 4WD—V8 Turbo Diesel—Truck Equip Sch T3						
2500 4D 6 1/2' 25C8	55255		34200	35100	36700	41400
2WD 1			(2950)	(2950)	(3270)	(3270)
V8, 6.0 Liter .... G			(5625)	(5625)	(6230)	(6230)

2012 CHEVY/GMC — (1,2or3)(CorG)(A,B,CorN)–(L1EK)–C

Body Type	VIN	List	Trade-In Good	Very Good	Pvt-Party Good	Retail Excellent
CAPTIVA SPORT—4-Cyl.—Truck Equipment Schedule T1						
LS Sport Utility 4D L1EK	24245		10450	10700	12500	14700
CAPTIVA SPORT—V6—Truck Equipment Schedule T1						
LT Sport Utility 4D L3E5	27395		11050	11300	13350	15850
CAPTIVA SPORT AWD—V6—Truck Equipment Schedule T1						
LTZ Sport Utility 4D L4E5	32845		12550	12850	14850	17600
EQUINOX—4-Cyl.—Truck Equipment Schedule T1						
LS Sport Utility 4D .... LBEK	24260		12350	12650	14100	16100
AWD C			850	850	990	990
EQUINOX—V6—Truck Equipment Schedule T1						
LT Sport Utility 4D .... LDEK	25780		13800	14100	15750	18050
AWD .... E			850	850	990	990
4-Cyl, Flex Fuel, 2.4L ..... K			(875)	(875)	(1010)	(1010)
EQUINOX AWD—V6—Truck Equipment Schedule T1						
LTZ Sport Utility 4D LGE5	33200		16000	16400	18250	21100
FWD .... F			(1075)	(1075)	(1250)	(1250)
TERRAIN—4-Cyl.—Truck Equipment Schedule T1						
SLE Sport Utility 4D .... LMEK	26290		13850	14200	15850	18350
SLT Sport Utility 4D .... LUEK	29240		15550	15950	17750	20700
AWD .... R,T			850	850	965	965
V6, Flex Fuel, 3.0 Liter ... 5			625	625	700	700
ACADIA—V6—Truck Equipment Schedule T1						
SL Sport Utility 4D .... RNED	33415		16550	17000	18300	20800
SLE Sport Utility 4D .... RPED	35890		17300	17750	19050	21600
Denali Sport Util. .... RTED	44690		24000	24600	25900	29200
AWD V			850	850	970	970
ACADIA AWD—V6—Truck Equipment Schedule T1						
SLT Sport Utility .... VRED	41640		20700	21200	22600	25600
2WD .... R			(850)	(850)	(975)	(975)
TRAVERSE—V6—Truck Equipment Schedule T1						
LS Sport Utility 4D .... REED	30240		14250	14600	16550	19250
AWD V			1525	1525	1810	1810
TRAVERSE AWD—V6—Truck Equipment Schedule T1						
LT Sport Utility 4D .... VGED	35340		17300	17700	19650	22700
LTZ Sport Utility 4D .... VLED	41615		18450	18900	21000	24300
2WD .... R			(1525)	(1525)	(1780)	(1780)
TAHOE—V8—Truck Equipment Schedule T1						
LS Sport Util 4D CAE0	39400		21800	22500	23600	26700
Third Row Seat			625	625	710	710
4WD .... K			1525	1525	1715	1715
TAHOE 4WD—V8—Truck Equipment Schedule T1						
LT Sport Util 4D KBE0	47400		25700	26600	27800	31500
LTZ Sport Util 4D KGE0	56720		31700	32400	33600	37300
Third Row Seat			625	625	710	710
2WD C			(1525)	(1525)	(1715)	(1715)
TAHOE 4WD—V8 Hybrid—Truck Equipment Schedule T1						
Sport Utility 4D .... KDFJ	55420		28200	29100	30400	34400
Third Row Seat			625	625	715	715
2WD C			(1525)	(1525)	(1725)	(1725)
YUKON—V8—Truck Equipment Schedule T1						
SLE Sport Utility 4D 1AE0	40730		22500	23300	24400	27700

TRUCKS & VANS

Body	Type	VIN	List	Trade-In Good	Very Good	Pvt-Party Good	Retail Excellent
Third Row Seat				625	625	710	710
4WD		2		1525	1525	1715	1715

YUKON 4WD—V8—Truck Equipment Schedule T1

Body	Type	VIN	List	Good	Very Good	Good	Excellent
SLT Sport Utility 4D		2CE0	49150	26900	27800	28800	32500
Third Row Seat				625	625	710	710
2WD		1		(1525)	(1525)	(1715)	(1715)

YUKON 4WD—V8 Hybrid—Truck Equipment Schedule T1

Sport Utility 4D		2FFJ	56005	29800	30800	32000	36200
Third Row Seat				625	625	715	715
2WD		1		(1525)	(1525)	(1720)	(1720)

YUKON DENALI AWD—V8—Truck Equipment Schedule T3

Sport Utility 4D		2EEF	58730	32200	33000	34200	38000
Third Row Seat				625	625	700	700
2WD		1		(1525)	(1525)	(1680)	(1680)

YUKON DENALI 4WD—V8 Hybrid—Truck Equipment Schedule T3

Sport Utility 4D		2GFJ	63855	31500	32200	33600	37400
Third Row Seat				625	625	700	700
2WD		1		(1525)	(1525)	(1690)	(1690)

SUBURBAN 4WD—V8—Truck Equipment Schedule T1

K1500 LS Sport Util		KHE7	42865	23500	24300	25500	28800
K1500 LT Sport Util		KJE7	46625	25300	26100	27200	30800
K1500 LTZ Util		KKE7	55760	30900	31500	32600	36600
K2500 LS Spt Util		KLEG	44475	25700	26600	27700	31300
K2500 LT Spt Util		KMEG	48215	28000	28900	30000	33900
Third Row Seat				625	625	710	710
2WD		C		(1525)	(1525)	(1705)	(1705)

YUKON XL 4WD—V8—Truck Equipment Schedule T1

1500 SLE Sport Util		2HE7	47115	24900	25700	26900	30400
1500 SLT Sport Util		2KE7	51295	26200	27100	28200	31800
2500 SLE Sport Util		2NEG	48655	26000	26900	28000	31600
2500 SLT Sport Util		2REG	53035	28100	29000	30100	34000
Third Row Seat				625	625	710	710
2WD		1		(1525)	(1525)	(1710)	(1710)

YUKON XL DENALI AWD—V8—Truck Equipment Schedule T3

1500 Sport Utility		2MEF	61530	31800	32500	33600	37700
Third Row Seat				625	625	700	700
2WD		1		(1525)	(1525)	(1690)	(1690)

EXPRESS/SAVANA VAN—V8—Truck Equipment Schedule T1

1500 LS Passenger		GBF4	29920	12450	12750	14100	16600
1500 LT Passenger		GCF4	31770	13450	13750	15300	18000
2500 LS Passenger		GPFA	30710	12600	12900	14250	16800
2500 LT Passenger		GRFA	32560	13850	14150	15650	18400
AWD		H		775	775	905	905
V8, Flex Fuel, 6.0 Liter		5		525	525	605	605

EXPRESS/SAVANA VAN—V8 Flex Fuel—Truck Equipment Sch T1

3500 LS Passenger		GXFA	33005	13750	14050	15600	18350
3500 LT Passenger		GYFA	34460	14900	15250	16800	19750
3500 LS Extended		GZFA	34875	15300	15700	17250	20300
3500 LT Extended		G1FA	35245	16100	16450	18050	21200

EXPRESS/SAVANA VAN—V8 Turbo Diesel—Truck Equipment Sch T1

3500 LS Passenger		GXFL	45935	20200	20600	22300	26200
3500 LT Passenger		GYFL	47400	20900	21400	23100	27100
3500 LS Extended		GZFL	47815	21200	21600	23400	27500
3500 LT Extended		G1FL	48185	21500	22000	23700	27900

EXPRESS VAN—V6—Truck Equipment Schedule T1

1500 Cargo Van		GAFX	28195	14400	15050	16200	19450
AWD		H		775	775	905	905
V8, Flex Fuel, 5.3 Liter		4		675	675	785	785

SAVANA VAN—V8—Truck Equipment Schedule T1

1500 Cargo Van		7AF4	27080	14600	15250	16450	19750
AWD		H		775	775	915	915
V6, 4.3 Liter		X		(625)	(625)	(725)	(725)

EXPRESS/SAVANA VAN—V8—Truck Equipment Schedule T1

2500 Cargo Van		GFCA	27590	15350	16000	17250	20700
2500 Extended		GGCA	29450	16600	17350	18600	22300
3500 Cargo Van		GFCA	30790	17050	17850	19050	22900
3500 Extended		GGCA	31675	18200	19000	20100	24000
V8, Cmprssd NG, 6.0L		B		775	775	900	900
V8, Flex Fuel, 6.0 Liter		5		525	525	600	600

EXPRESS/SAVANA VAN—V8 Turbo Diesel—Truck Equipment Sch T1

2500 Cargo Van		GFCL	39535	20800	21300	23100	27300
2500 Extended		GGCL	41395	21200	21700	23500	27700
3500 Cargo Van		GFCL	42735	21400	21900	23700	28000

1015

TRUCKS & VANS

Body Type	VIN	List	Trade-In Good	Very Good	Pvt-Party Good	Retail Excellent
3500 Extended	GGCL	43620	21900	22400	24300	28600
EXPRESS/SAVANA COMMERCIAL CUTAWAY—V8—Truck Equipment Sch T1						
3500 Van Cab-Ch	G2CA	27840	16050	16400	18500	22200
V8, 6.0 Liter	G		525	525	645	645
COLORADO REGULAR CAB PICKUP—4-Cyl.—Truck Equip Sch T1						
LT 2D 6'	SCF9	21100	11200	11450	13100	15200
4WD	T		2100	2100	2380	2380
5-Cyl, 3.7 Liter	E		200	200	225	225
COLORADO/CANYON REGULAR CAB PICKUP—4-Cyl.—Truck Equip Sch T1						
Work Truck 2D 6'	SBF9	19300	10000	10250	11800	13700
4WD	T		2100	2100	2385	2385
5-Cyl, 3.7 Liter	E		200	200	225	225
CANYON REGULAR CAB PICKUP—5-Cyl.—Truck Equipment Sch T1						
SLE 2D 6'	5MEE	23280	11450	11750	13400	15600
4WD	6		2100	2100	2385	2385
4-Cyl, 2.9 Liter	9		(200)	(200)	(225)	(225)
COLORADO/CANYON EXTENDED CAB—4-Cyl.—Truck Equip Sch T1						
Work Truck 4D 6'	SBF9	24855	12650	12950	14800	17150
4WD	T		2100	2100	2380	2380
5-Cyl, 3.7 Liter	E		200	200	225	225
COLORADO/CANYON EXTENDED CAB PICKUP—5-Cyl.—Truck Sch T1						
LT/SLE 4D 6'	SCFE	25985	14800	15150	17100	19800
4WD	T		2100	2100	2380	2380
4-Cyl, 2.9 Liter	9		(200)	(200)	(225)	(225)
V8, 5.3 Liter	P		775	775	885	885
COLORADO/CANYON CREW CAB PICKUP—5-Cyl.—Truck Equip Sch T1						
LT/SLE 4D 5'	SCFE	27600	16900	17300	19200	22200
4WD	T		2100	2100	2360	2360
4-Cyl, 2.9 Liter	9		(200)	(200)	(225)	(225)
V8, 5.3 Liter	P		775	775	880	880
CANYON CREW CAB PICKUP 4WD—5-Cyl.—Truck Equipment Schedule T1						
SLT 4D 5'	6NFE	32520	18400	18800	20800	24100
V8, 5.3 Liter	P		975	975	1095	1095
AVALANCHE 4WD—V8—Truck Equipment Schedule T1						
LS Spt Util Pickup	KEE7	40720	22200	22700	24000	27200
LT Sport Util Pickup	KFE7	44115	24700	25300	26600	30100
LTZ Spt Util Pickup	KGE7	51175	28200	28900	30100	34000
2WD	C		(1525)	(1525)	(1695)	(1695)
SILVERADO REGULAR CAB PICKUP—V6—Truck Equipment Schedule T1						
1500 Work Truck 8'	CPEX	23330	12350	12600	14200	16550
4WD	K		3125	3125	3760	3760
V8, Flex Fuel, 4.8 Liter	A		750	750	890	890
V8, Flex Fuel, 5.3 Liter	0		1125	1125	1340	1340
SIERRA REGULAR CAB PICKUP—V8—Truck Equipment Schedule T1						
1500 Work Truck 8'	1TEA	23330	13050	13350	15050	17500
4WD	K		3125	3125	3735	3735
V6, 4.3 Liter	X		(725)	(725)	(865)	(865)
V8, Flex Fuel, 5.3 Liter	0		400	400	465	465
SILVERADO/SIERRA REGULAR CAB PICKUP—V8—Truck Equipment Sch T1						
1500 Work Trk 6 1/2'	CPEA	25240	13400	13650	15300	17800
1500 LT/SLE 6 1/2'	CSEA	28295	14800	15100	16750	19450
1500 LT/SLE 8'	CSEA	28420	14100	14400	16050	18650
2500 Work Truck 8'	CVCG	29410	14600	14950	16350	18200
2500 LT 8'	CXCG	32255	18300	18700	20200	22500
3500 Work Truck 8'	CZCG	31155	14400	14700	16150	17950
3500 SLE 2D 8'	13CG	33905	16750	17150	18650	20800
4WD	K		3125	3125	3710	3710
V6, 4.3 Liter	X		(725)	(725)	(860)	(860)
V8, Flex Fuel, 5.3 Liter	0		400	400	460	460
V8, Turbo Diesel, 6.6L	8,L		5025	5025	5620	5620
SIERRA REGULAR CAB PICKUP—V8—Truck Equipment Schedule T1						
2500 Work Truck 8'	1ZCG	29795	14450	14800	16250	18050
2500 HD SLE 2D 8'	10CG	32815	18200	18600	20200	22500
3500 Work Truck 8'	12CG	31155	14400	14700	16150	17950
3500 SLE 2D 8'	13CG	33905	16750	17150	18650	20800
4WD	2		3125	3125	3480	3480
V8, 6.6L Turbo Dsl	8,L		5025	5025	5595	5595
SILVERADO REGULAR CAB 4WD—V8 Turbo Diesel—Truck Sch T1						
3500 LT 8'	K0CG	45035	25400	26000	27800	31000
2WD	C		(3150)	(3150)	(3430)	(3430)
V8, Flex Fuel, 6.0 Liter	G		(5825)	(5825)	(6375)	(6375)
SILVERADO/SIERRA EXTENDED CAB PICKUP—V8—Truck Equip Sch T1						
1500 Work Truck 8'	1TE0	29375	13550	13850	15550	18150

Body Type	VIN	List	Trade-In Good	Very Good	Pvt-Party Good	Retail Excellent
1500 LT/SLE 8'	CSE0	32160	16800	17150	19000	22100
1500 LTZ/SLT 8'	CTE0	37350	18250	18650	20600	24000
4WD			3125	3125	3740	3740
SILVERADO/SIERRA EXTENDED CAB 4WD—V8—Truck Equip Sch T1						
1500 LTZ/SLT 6 1/2'	KTE7	40200	22600	23100	24700	28500
2WD	C		(3150)	(3150)	(3570)	(3570)
V8, Flex Fuel, 6.2 Liter	2		550	550	625	625
SILVERADO/SIERRA EXTENDED CAB—V6—Truck Equipment Schedule T1						
1500 Work Trk 6 1/2'	CPEX	27335	14050	14350	16100	18850
4WD			3125	3125	3555	3555
V8, Flex Fuel, 4.8 Liter	A		750	750	845	845
V8, Flex Fuel, 5.3 Liter	0,7		1125	1125	1265	1265
SILVERADO/SIERRA EXTENDED CAB PICKUP—V8—Truck Equip Sch T1						
1500 LS/SL 6 1/2'	CREA	30525	16300	16650	18550	21700
1500 LT/SLE 6 1/2'	CSEA	31050	17450	17800	19650	22900
2500 HD Wrk Trk 6'	CVCG	31825	18000	18400	19950	22300
2500 HD Wrk Trk 8'	CVCG	32020	17800	18200	19800	22100
3500 Work Truck 8'	CZCG	34230	17800	18200	19800	22100
3500 LTZ/SLT 8'	C1CG	41795	22200	22700	24400	27300
4WD	K		3125	3125	3755	3755
V8, Flex Fuel, 5.3 Liter	0,7		400	400	465	465
V8, Flex Fuel, 6.2 Liter	2		550	550	655	655
V8, Turbo Diesel, 6.6L	8		5025	5025	5530	5530
SILVERADO/SIERRA EXTENDED CAB PICKUP 4WD—V8—Truck Sch T1						
2500 HD LT/SLE 6'	KXCG	34995	24400	24900	26800	30000
2500 HD LT/SLE 8'	KXCG	35190	24200	24700	26600	29700
2500 HD LTZ/SLT 6'	KYCG	40385	25700	26300	28200	31500
2500 HD LTZ/SLT 8'	KYCG	40560	25500	26100	27900	31200
3500 LT/SLE 8'	K0CG	48770	29900	30500	32600	36400
2WD	C		(3150)	(3150)	(3440)	(3440)
V8, Turbo Diesel, 6.6L	8		5025	5025	5520	5520
SILVERADO/SIERRA CREW CAB PICKUP—V8—Truck Equipment Sch T1						
1500 Wrk Trk 5 3/4'	CPEA	34465	18100	18500	20400	23700
1500 LS 4D 5 3/4'	CREA	32840	18850	19250	20900	24100
1500 LT 4D 5 3/4'	CSEA	33390	20800	21300	22700	26000
4WD	K		3125	3125	3630	3630
V8, Flex Fuel, 5.3 Liter	0,7		400	400	450	450
V8, Flex Fuel, 6.2 Liter	2		550	550	630	630
SILVERADO CREW CAB PICKUP—V8 Hybrid—Truck Equipment Sch T1						
1500 4D 5 3/4'	CUEJ	40260	22800	23300	24900	28600
4WD			3125	3125	3600	3600
SIERRA CREW CAB PICKUP 4WD—V8 Hybrid—Truck Equipment Sch T1						
1500 4D 5 3/4'	2YEJ	46630	25400	26000	27800	32000
2WD	C		(3150)	(3150)	(3595)	(3595)
SILVERADO/SIERRA CREW CAB PICKUP—V8—Truck Equip Sch T1						
1500 XFE 5 3/4'	CSE7	35145	20700	21200	22700	25900
SILVERADO/SIERRA CREW CAB PICKUP—V8—Truck Equip Sch T1						
2500 HD LT/SLE 8'	CXCG	37345	24500	25000	26800	30000
2500 HD LTZ/SLT 8'	CYCG	43230	27100	27600	29500	32900
3500 Work Trk 8'	CZCG	35865	22800	23300	25000	27900
3500 LT/SLE 6 1/2'	C0CG	38815	25800	26400	28300	31700
3500 LTZ/SLT 6 1/2'	C1CG	43730	26900	27500	29400	32900
4WD	K		3125	3125	3435	3435
V8, 6.6L Turbo Dsl	8,L		5025	5025	5520	5520
SILVERADO/SIERRA CREW CAB PICKUP 4WD—V8—Truck Equip Sch T1						
1500 LTZ 4D 5 3/4'	KTE7	43260	26300	26900	28400	32300
1500 SLT 4D 5 3/4'	2WE7	40785	23600	24100	25900	29900
2WD	C		(3150)	(3150)	(3555)	(3555)
V8, Flex Fuel, 6.2 Liter	2		550	550	625	625
SILVERADO/SIERRA CREW CAB 4WD—V8 Turbo Diesel—V8—Truck Sch T1						
2500 HD SLE 6 1/2'	20C8	49650	31700	32400	34400	38800
2500 HD LTZ 6 1/2'	KYC8	53735	35200	35900	38100	42600
2500 HD SLT 6 1/2'	21C8	55435	34800	35600	37700	42100
2WD	C		(3150)	(3150)	(3430)	(3430)
V8, Flex Fuel, 6.0 Liter	G		(4775)	(4775)	(5205)	(5205)
SILVERADO/SIERRA CREW CAB 4WD—V8 Turbo Diesel—Truck Sch T1						
3500 LT/SLE 8'	K0CG	50555	33400	34200	36600	41100
3500 LTZ 8'	K1CG	55275	35900	36700	38800	43300
2WD	C		(3150)	(3150)	(3480)	(3480)
V8, Flex Fuel, 6.0 Liter	G		(5825)	(5825)	(6465)	(6465)
SILVERADO/SIERRA CREW CAB—V8—Truck Equipment Sch T1						
2500 HD Wrk Trk 6'	CVCG	34030	20200	20600	22300	24900
3500 Work Truck 8'	CZCG	44455	27800	28400	30200	33700

1015

Body Type	VIN	List	Trade-In Good	Very Good	Pvt-Party Good	Retail Excellent
4WD	K		3125	3125	3470	3470
V8, Turbo Diesel, 6.6L	8		5025	5025	5570	5570
SIERRA CREW CAB PICKUP—V8—Truck Equipment Sch T1						
2500 Work Truck 8'	1ZC8	34020	21200	21600	23300	26100
4WD	K		3125	3125	3455	3455
V8, 6.6L Turbo Dsl	8		5025	5025	5545	5545
SILVERADO/SIERRA CREW CAB—V8 Turbo Diesel—Truck Equip Sch T1						
2500 HD Wrk Trk 8'	CVC8,L	42620	25000	25500	27400	30500
3500 SLT Pickup 8'	14CG	52825	31300	31900	34000	38000
4WD	K		3125	3125	3430	3430
V8, Flex Fuel, 6.0 Liter	G		(5825)	(5825)	(6400)	(6400)
SILVERADO CREW CAB 4WD—V8 Turbo Diesel—Truck Equip Sch T1						
2500 HD LT 6 1/2'	KXC8	48695	32100	32800	35000	39100
2WD	C		(3150)	(3150)	(3455)	(3455)
V8, Flex Fuel, 6.0 Liter	G		(4775)	(4775)	(5220)	(5220)
SIERRA DENALI CREW CAB PICKUP AWD—V8—Truck Equip Schedule T3						
1500 4D 5 3/4'	2XE2	49605	29000	29600	31400	34900
2WD	1		(1500)	(1500)	(1670)	(1670)

2013 CHEVY/GMC — (1,2or3)(CorG)(A,B,CorN)—(L1EK)—D

Body Type	VIN	List	Trade-In Good	Very Good	Pvt-Party Good	Retail Excellent
CAPTIVA SPORT—4-Cyl. Flex Fuel—Truck Equipment Schedule T1						
LS Sport Utility 4D	L1EK	24580	11300	11550	13850	16250
LT Sport Utility 4D	L3EK	26595	11650	11900	14300	17000
LTZ Sport Utility 4D	L4EK	30440	12700	12950	15300	18100
EQUINOX—4-Cyl.—Truck Equipment Schedule T1						
LS Sport Utility 4D	LBEK	24580	13400	13650	15800	18300
AWD	C		925	925	1130	1130
EQUINOX—V6—Truck Equipment Schedule T1						
LT Sport Utility 4D	LDERK	26225	15400	15650	17950	20800
LTZ Sport Utility 4D	LFE3	31340	16750	17050	19750	23200
AWD	E,N		925	925	1110	1110
4-Cyl, 2.4 Liter	K		(975)	(975)	(1160)	(1160)
TERRAIN—4-Cyl.—Truck Equipment Schedule T1						
SLE-1 Sport Utility	LMEK	26660	14950	15300	17350	20200
SLE-2 Sport Utility	LSEK	28160	15800	16100	18200	21200
SLT-1 Sport Utility	LUEK	29710	16750	17100	19300	22500
SLT-2 Sport Utility	LEEK	32955	17050	17400	19700	23000
Denali Sport Utility	LYEK	35350	21000	21400	23800	27700
AWD	R		925	925	1100	1100
V6, 3.6 Liter	3		675	675	810	810
ACADIA—V6—Truck Equipment Schedule T1						
SLE-1 Sport Util	RNED	34875	20300	20700	22300	25300
SLE-2 Sport Util	RPED	36765	21300	21700	23500	26700
AWD	V		925	925	1040	1040
ACADIA AWD—V6—Truck Equipment Schedule T1						
SLT-1 Sport Util	VRED	42605	25500	26000	27900	31700
SLT-2 Sport Util	VSED	44025	26600	27100	29100	33000
Denali Sport Util	VTED	48770	29900	30500	31900	35500
2WD	R		(925)	(925)	(1050)	(1050)
TRAVERSE—V6—Truck Equipment Schedule T1						
LS Sport Utility 4D	RFED	31335	16200	16500	18200	20500
AWD	V		1600	1600	1790	1790
TRAVERSE AWD—V6—Truck Equipment Schedule T1						
LT Sport Utility 4D	VGED	36550	20700	21100	22900	25700
LTZ Sport Utility	VLED	43250	25200	25700	27800	31300
2WD	R		(1600)	(1600)	(1790)	(1790)
TAHOE—V8 Flex Fuel—Truck Equipment Schedule T1						
LS Sport Util 4D	KAE0	44135	23400	24000	25400	28600
4WD	K		1600	1600	1820	1820
TAHOE 4WD—V8 Flex Fuel—Truck Equipment Schedule T1						
Commercial 4D	K4E0	42840				
LT Sport Util 4D	KBE0	48075	27500	28300	29700	33300
LTZ Sport Util 4D	KCX0	57395	32100	32600	34200	37700
Third Row Seat			675	675	775	775
2WD	C		(1600)	(1600)	(1820)	(1820)
TAHOE 4WD—V8 Hybrid—Truck Equipment Schedule T1						
Sport Utility 4D	KDEJ	56095	30900	31800	33300	37400
Third Row Seat			675	675	775	775
2WD	C		(1600)	(1600)	(1820)	(1820)
YUKON 4WD—V8 Flex Fuel—Truck Equipment Schedule T1						
Commercial 4D	2BE0	42980				
SLE Sport Utility 4D	2AE0	45440	24300	25100	26500	29900
SLT Sport Utility 4D	2CE0	49770	28300	29200	30700	34500

Body Type	VIN	List	Trade-In Good	Very Good	Pvt-Party Good	Retail Excellent
Third Row Seat			675	675	775	775
2WD	1		(1600)	(1600)	(1820)	(1820)
YUKON 4WD—V8 Hybrid—Truck Equipment Schedule T1						
Sport Utility 4D	2FEJ	56625	31700	32600	34100	38300
Third Row Seat			675	675	775	775
2WD	1		(1600)	(1600)	(1820)	(1820)
YUKON DENALI AWD—V8 Flex Fuel—Truck Equipment Schedule T3						
Sport Utility 4D	2EEF	59350	35000	35600	37100	40800
Third Row Seat			675	675	745	745
2WD	1		(1600)	(1600)	(1755)	(1755)
YUKON DENALI 4WD—V8 Hybrid—Truck Equipment Schedule T3						
Sport Utility 4D	2GEJ	64475	36000	36600	38200	42100
2WD	1		(1600)	(1600)	(1765)	(1765)
SUBURBAN 4WD—V8 Flex Fuel—Truck Equipment Schedule T1						
K1500 Commercial	K5E0	45090				
K1500 LS Sport Util	KHE0	46385	26000	26700	28000	31300
K1500 LT Sport Util	KJE0	50145	28100	28900	30200	33800
K1500 LTZ Utility	KKE0	59435	30900	31400	33100	37000
Third Row Seat			675	675	765	765
2WD	C		(1600)	(1600)	(1795)	(1795)
SUBURBAN 4WD—V8—Truck Equipment Schedule T1						
K2500 Commercial	K5EG	46695				
K2500 LS Spt Util	KLEG	47990	28500	29400	30800	34500
K2500 LT Spt Util	KMEG	51735	30800	31700	33100	37000
2WD	C		(1600)	(1600)	(1800)	(1800)
YUKON XL 4WD—V8 Flex Fuel—Truck Equipment Schedule T1						
1500 Commercial	S2JE7	45145				
1500 SLE Sport Util	S2HE7	47990	25300	26100	27600	31000
1500 SLT Sport Util	S2KE7	51870	28700	29600	31000	34700
Third Row Seat			675	675	765	765
2WD	1		(1600)	(1600)	(1795)	(1795)
YUKON XL DENALI AWD—V8 Flex Fuel—Truck Equipment Schedule T3						
1500 Sport Utility	S2MEF	62105	34000	34500	36100	40200
Third Row Seat			675	675	755	755
2WD	1		(1600)	(1600)	(1780)	(1780)
YUKON XL 4WD—V8—Truck Equipment Schedule T1						
2500 Commercial	W2PEG	46765				
2500 SLE Spt Util	W2NRG	49230	27200	28000	29400	33100
2500 SLT Spt Util	W2REG	53610	·31000	32000	33400	37300
Third Row Seat			675	675	770	770
2WD	1		(1600)	(1600)	(1810)	(1810)
EXPRESS/SAVANA VAN—V8 Flex Fuel—Truck Equipment Schedule T1						
1500 LS Passenger	GBF4	29965	14250	14450	16200	18900
1500 LT Passenger	GCF4	32270	15200	15450	17200	20000
2500 LS Passenger	GPFA	30860	14350	14550	16250	18950
2500 LT Passenger	GRFA	33165	15750	16050	17800	20700
3500 LS Passenger	GXFA	33155	15700	15950	17700	20600
3500 LT Passenger	GYFA	35065	16800	17050	18850	22000
3500 LS Extended	GZFA	35025	17500	17800	19600	22800
3500 LT Extended	G1FA	35850	18100	18400	20200	23600
AWD	H		850	850	985	985
V8, Flex Fuel, 6.0 Liter	G		550	550	625	625
EXPRESS/SAVANA VAN—V8 Turbo Diesel—Truck Equipment Sch T1						
3500 LS Passenger	GXFL	46095	22000	22400	24300	28300
3500 LT Passenger	GYFL	48005	22900	23200	25300	29400
3500 LS Extended	GZFL	47965	23100	23400	25400	29600
3500 LT Extended	G1FL	48790	23500	23800	25800	30100
EXPRESS VAN—V6—Truck Equipment Schedule T1						
1500 Cargo Van	GAF4	26315	16050	16700	17750	20900
AWD	H		850	850	975	975
V8, Flex Fuel, 5.3 Liter	4		675	675	775	775
SAVANA VAN—V8—Truck Equipment Schedule T1						
1500 Cargo Van	7AF4	26315	16250	16850	18000	21200
AWD	8		850	850	980	980
V6, 4.3 Liter	X		(650)	(650)	(735)	(735)
EXPRESS/SAVANA VAN—V8 Flex Fuel—Truck Equipment Schedule T1						
2500 Cargo Van	GFCA	27820	17000	17650	18800	22100
2500 Extended	GGCA	29680	18450	19150	20300	23800
3500 Cargo Van	GTCA	31140	19200	19950	21100	24800
3500 Extended	GUCA	32025	20100	20900	22100	26000
V8, CNG, 6.0 Liter	B		825	825	935	935
V8, Flex Fuel, 6.0 Liter	G		550	550	620	620

TRUCKS & VANS

Body Type	VIN	List	Trade-In Good	Very Good	Pvt-Party Good	Retail Excellent
EXPRESS/SAVANA VAN—V8 Turbo Diesel—Truck Equipment Sch T1						
2500 Cargo Van	GFCL	39765	22800	23100	25000	28900
2500 Extended	GGCL	41625	23200	23500	25300	29300
3500 Cargo Van	GTCL	43085	23400	23800	25600	29600
3500 Extended	GUCL	43970	23800	24200	26200	30300
AVALANCHE 4WD—V8 Flex Fuel—Truck Equipment Schedule T1						
Black Diamond LS	KEE7	40025	24900	25400	27000	30400
Black Diamond LT	KFE7	42670	29500	30100	31700	35600
Black Diamond LTZ	KGE7	48880	33100	33800	35400	39600
2WD	C		(1600)	(1600)	(1755)	(1755)
SIERRA REGULAR CAB PICKUP—V8—Truck Equipment Schedule T1						
1500 Work Truck 8'	1TEA	23980	14450	14700	16500	18900
4WD	2		3275	3275	3690	3690
V6, 4.3 Liter	X		(775)	(775)	(885)	(885)
V8, Flex Fuel, 5.3 Liter	0		400	400	455	455
SILVERADO/SIERRA REGULAR CAB—V8 Flex Fuel—Truck Sch T1						
1500 Work Trk 6 1/2'	CPEX	23590	15050	15300	17150	19650
1500 LT/SLE 6 1/2'	CSEA	28945	16550	16800	18600	21300
1500 LT/SLE 8'	CSEA	29070	16050	16300	18100	20700
2500 Work Truck 8'	CVEG	30295	16400	16750	18400	20400
2500 LT/SLE 2D 8'	CXEG	33475	19900	20300	22100	24500
3500 Work Truck 8'	CZCG	31790	16250	16550	18250	20200
3500 SLE 2D 8'	13CG	34640	18600	18950	20900	23200
4WD	K		3275	3275	3705	3705
V8, Flex Fuel, 5.3 Liter	0		400	400	455	455
V8, Turbo Diesel, 6.6L	8,L		5225	5225	5855	5855
SILVERADO REGULAR CAB PICKUP 4WD—V8 Turbo Diesel—Truck Sch T1						
3500 LT 8'	K0CG	46420	26300	26800	28900	32100
2WD	C		(3275)	(3275)	(3570)	(3570)
V8, Flex Fuel, 6.0 Liter	G		(6025)	(6025)	(6600)	(6600)
SILVERADO/SIERRA EXTENDED CAB PICKUP—V8 Flex Fuel—Truck Sch T1						
1500 Work Truck 8'	CPE0	29775	16250	16500	18100	20500
1500 LS/SL 6 1/2'	CREA	31520	17150	17400	19400	22300
1500 LT/SLE 8'	CSE0	32660	18400	18700	20600	23300
1500 LTZ/SLT 6 1/2'	CTE0	41020	24600	25000	26800	30300
1500 LTZ/SLT 8'	CTE0	37425	20200	20600	22400	25600
4WD			3275	3275	3765	3765
V8, Flex Fuel, 6.2 Liter	2		550	550	620	620
SILVERADO/SIERRA EXTENDED CAB—V6—Truck Equipment Schedule T1						
1500 Work Trk 6 1/2'	CPEX	27735	15400	15600	17250	19650
4WD	K		3275	3275	3710	3710
V8, Flex Fuel, 4.8 Liter	A		400	400	455	455
V8, Flex Fuel, 5.3 Liter	0,7		400	400	455	455
SILVERADO/SIERRA EXTENDED CAB—V8 Flex Fuel—Truck Equip Sch T1						
1500 LT/SLE 6 1/2'	CSEA	31550	19050	19350	21100	23900
2500 HD Wrk Trk 6'	CVCG	32325	19100	19500	21400	23900
2500 HD Wrk Trk 8'	CVCG	32520	18900	19300	21200	23700
3500 Work Truck 8'	CZCG	34965	20500	20900	22800	25400
3500 LTZ/SLT 8'	C1CG	42630	24100	24500	26600	29600
4WD			3275	3275	3745	3745
V8, Flex Fuel, 5.3 Liter	0,7		400	400	460	460
V8, Flex Fuel, 6.2 Liter	2		550	550	630	630
V8, Turbo Diesel, 6.6L	8,L		5225	5225	5750	5750
SILVERADO EXTENDED CAB PICKUP 4WD—V8—Truck Equip Schedule T1						
2500 HD LT/SLE 6'	KXCG	39345	26000	26500	28600	31700
2500 HD LT 8'	KXCG	39540	25800	26300	28400	31500
2500 HD LTZ/SLT 6'	KYCG	44470	28100	28600	30900	34300
2500 HD LTZ 8'	KYCG	44665	27900	28400	30600	34000
3500 LT 8'	K0CG	51660	32000	32600	34900	38800
2WD	C		(3275)	(3275)	(3575)	(3575)
V8, Turbo Diesel, 6.6L	8,L		5225	5225	5730	5730
SIERRA EXTENDED CAB PICKUP—V8—Truck Equipment Schedule T1						
2500 HD SLE 4D 8'	10CG	36635	23100	23500	25500	28400
2500 SLT 4D 8'	11CG	42040	24900	25400	27500	30400
4WD	2		3275	3275	3585	3585
V8, Turbo Diesel, 6.6L	8		5225	5225	5750	5750
SIERRA EXTENDED CAB PICKUP 4WD—V8 Turbo Diesel—Truck Sch T1						
3500 SLE 4D 8'	23C8	50800	33200	33900	36300	40400
2WD			(3275)	(3275)	(3565)	(3565)
V8, Flex Fuel, 6.0 Liter	G		(6025)	(6025)	(6590)	(6590)
SILVERADO/SIERRA CREW CAB PICKUP—V8 Flex Fuel—Truck Equip Sch T1						
1500 Wrk Trk 5 3/4'	CPEA	31615	18550	18850	20800	23900
1500 LS/SL 4D 5 3/4'	CREA	33290	19800	20100	22200	25500

Body Type	VIN	List	Trade-In Good	Very Good	Pvt-Party Good	Retail Excellent
1500 LT/SLE 5 3/4'	CSEA	34015	22500	22900	24600	27800
4WD	K		3275	3275	3735	3735
V8, Flex Fuel, 5.3 Liter	0,7		400	400	450	450
V8, Flex Fuel, 6.2 Liter	2		550	550	620	620
SILVERADO CREW CAB PICKUP 4WD—V8 Flex Fuel—Truck Equip Sch T1						
1500 LTZ 4D 5 3/4'	CTE0	44380	28000	28400	30300	34100
2WD	C		(3275)	(3275)	(3690)	(3690)
V8, Flex Fuel, 6.2 Liter	2		550	550	620	620
SILVERADO CREW CAB PICKUP—V8 Hybrid—Truck Equipment Schedule T1						
1500 4D 5 3/4'	CUEJ	40885	23900	24200	26200	29800
4WD	K		3275	3275	3680	3680
SIERRA CREW CAB PICKUP 4WD—V8 Hybrid—Truck Equipment Sch T1						
1500 4D 5 3/4'	2YEJ	44705	27000	27400	29500	33500
2WD	1		(3275)	(3275)	(3680)	(3680)
SILVERADO/SIERRA CREW CAB PICKUP—V8 Flex Fuel—Truck Equip Sch T1						
1500 XFE 5 3/4'	CSE7	35770	21800	22100	23800	26900
SIERRA CREW CAB PICKUP 4WD—V8 Flex Fuel—Truck Equipment Sch T1						
1500 SLT 4D 5 3/4'	2WET	44085	27600	28000	30100	34200
2WD	1		(3275)	(3275)	(3685)	(3685)
V8, Flex Fuel, 6.2 Liter	2		550	550	620	620
SIERRA DENALI CREW CAB PICKUP AWD—V8 Flex Fuel—Truck Sch T3						
1500 Denali 4D 5 3/4'	2XE2	49630	30800	31400	33600	37200
2WD	1		(1275)	(1275)	(1425)	(1425)
SILVERADO CREW CAB PICKUP—V8 Truck Equipment Schedule T1						
2500 Work Truck 8'	1ZCG	34525	21600	22000	24000	26800
Tool Box			200	200	210	210
4WD	2		3275	3275	3610	3610
V8, Turbo Dsl, 6.6L			5225	5225	5780	5780
SILVERADO/SIERRA CREW CAB PICKUP—V8—Truck Equipment Sch T1						
2500 HD Wrk Trk 6'	CVCG	34330	21100	21500	23500	26300
2500 HD LT/SLE 8'	CXCG	38140	25400	25900	28000	31000
3500 HD LTZ/SLT 8'	CYCG	43860	28700	29200	31400	34800
3500 Work Trk 8 1/2'	CZCG	36600	23800	24200	26300	29300
3500 Work Truck 8'	ZZCG	36795	23800	24200	26400	29300
3500 LT/SLE 6 1/2'	C0CG	39650	26500	27000	29100	32400
3500 LTZ/SLT 6 1/2'	C1CG	44440	27300	27800	30100	33500
Tool Box			200	200	210	210
4WD	K		3275	3275	3585	3585
V8, Turbo Diesel, 6.6L	L,8		5225	5225	5740	5740
SILVERADO CREW CAB PICKUP—V8 Turbo Diesel—Truck Equip Sch T1						
2500 HD Wrk Trk 8'	CVC8	42920	27000	27500	29800	33100
Tool Box			200	200	210	210
4WD	K		3275	3275	3585	3585
V8, Flex Fuel, 6.0 Liter	G		(5050)	(5050)	(5540)	(5540)
SILVERADO/SIERRA CREW CAB 4WD—V8 Turbo Diesel—Truck Sch T1						
2500 HD LT/SLE 6'	KXC8	49635	33300	33900	36500	40600
2500 HD LTZ/SLT 6'	KYCG	55860	36700	37400	39800	44100
Tool Box			200	200	210	210
2WD	G		(3275)	(3275)	(3595)	(3595)
V8, Flex Fuel, 6.0 Liter	G		(5050)	(5050)	(5555)	(5555)
SILVERADO/SIERRA CREW CAB 4WD—V8 Turbo Diesel—Truck Sch T1						
3500 LT/SLE 8'	K0CG	51390	35400	36000	38700	43200
3500 LTZ/SLT 8'	K1CG	56180	38500	39200	41800	46300
Tool Box			200	200	210	210
2WD	C		(3275)	(3275)	(3620)	(3620)
V8, Flex Fuel, 6.0 Liter	G		(6025)	(6025)	(6685)	(6685)
SIERRA CREW CAB PICKUP 4WD—V8 Turbo Diesel—Truck Equip Sch T1						
2500 HD SLE 4D 6 1/2'	20C8	50750	33200	33800	36400	40500
2500 SLT 4D 6 1/2'	21CG	56360	36500	37200	39600	43900
Tool Box			200	200	210	210
2WD	1		(3275)	(3275)	(3585)	(3585)
V8, Flex Fuel, 6.0 Liter	G		(5050)	(5050)	(5540)	(5540)

2014 CHEVY/GMC — (1,2or3)(CorG)(A,B,CorN)-(L1EK)-E

	VIN	List	Good	Very Good	Good	Excellent
CAPTIVA SPORT—4-Cyl. Flex Fuel—Truck Equipment Schedule T1						
LS Sport Utility 4D	L1EK	25235	13100	13350	16150	19250
LT Sport Utility 4D	L3EK	26850	14000	14250	16950	20000
LTZ Sport Utility 4D	L4EK	30370	14600	14900	17750	21100
EQUINOX—4-Cyl.—Truck Equipment Schedule T1						
LS Sport Utility 4D	LAEK	25235	15100	15350	17250	19500
AWD	E		1000	1000	1140	1140
EQUINOX—V6—Truck Equipment Schedule T1						
LT Sport Utility 4D	LBE3	26880	17750	18100	19950	22400

Body Type	VIN	List	Trade-In Good	Very Good	Pvt-Party Good	Retail Excellent
LTZ Sport Utility 4D	LHE3	34195	23300	23700	25700	28800
AWD	F,G		1000	1000	1120	1120
4-Cyl, 2.4 Liter	K		(1075)	(1075)	(1195)	(1195)
TERRAIN—4-Cyl.—Truck Equipment Schedule T1						
SLE-1 Sport Utility	LMEK	27390	16150	16450	18850	22100
SLE-2 Sport Utility	LREK	28890	17350	17650	20100	23400
SLT-1 Sport Utility	LSEK	30440	20800	21200	23600	27200
SLT-2 Sport Utility	LTEK	33685	20500	20900	23400	27300
Denali Sport Utility	LUEK	36080	23800	24300	27100	31500
AWD	V		1000	1000	1205	1205
V6, 3.6 Liter	3		725	725	880	880
ACADIA—V6—Truck Equipment Schedule T1						
SLE-1 Sport Util	RNKD	35260	21900	22300	24100	27300
SLE-2 Sport Util	RPKD	37150	23700	24200	26000	29400
AWD	V		1000	1000	1130	1130
ACADIA AWD—V6—Truck Equipment Schedule T1						
SLT-1 Sport Util	VRKD	43315	28200	28700	30700	34600
SLT-2 Sport Util	VSKD	44410	28900	29500	31500	35500
Denali Sport Util	VTKD	49600	33200	33800	35600	39800
2WD	R		(1000)	(1000)	(1120)	(1120)
TRAVERSE—V6—Truck Equipment Schedule T1						
LS Sport Utility 4D	RFED	31670	17300	17600	19850	22600
AWD	V		1700	1700	1990	1990
TRAVERSE AWD—V6—Truck Equipment Schedule T1						
LT Sport Utility 4D	VGED	36885	23400	23800	26000	29400
LTZ Sport Utility 4D	VJED	44130	28000	28500	30700	34300
2WD	R		(1700)	(1700)	(1950)	(1950)
TAHOE—V8 Flex Fuel—Truck Equipment Schedule T1						
LS Sport Util 4D	CAE0	42595	27600	28500	29700	33000
Third Row Seat			725	725	815	815
4WD	K		1700	1700	1880	1880
TAHOE 4WD—V8 Flex Fuel—Truck Equipment Schedule T1						
Commercial 4D	K4E0	44300	26700	27500	28700	31800
LT Sport Util 4D	KBE0	49985	31800	32800	34000	37800
LTZ Sport Util 4D	KCE0	58855	37000	37700	39300	43100
Third Row Seat			725	725	815	815
2WD	C		(1700)	(1700)	(1880)	(1880)
YUKON 4WD—V8 Flex Fuel—Truck Equipment Schedule T1						
Commercial 4D	2BE0	44440	26900	27700	28900	32100
SLE Sport Utility 4D	2AE0	47960	28500	29300	30600	34100
SLT Sport Utility 4D	2CE0	51230	32800	33800	35100	39000
2WD	1		(1700)	(1700)	(1885)	(1885)
Third Row Seat			725	725	815	815
YUKON DENALI AWD—V8 Flex Fuel—Truck Equipment Schedule T3						
Sport Utility 4D	2EEF	60810	38400	39100	40800	44700
2WD	1		(1700)	(1700)	(1845)	(1845)
SUBURBAN 4WD—V8 Flex Fuel—Truck Equipment Schedule T1						
1500 Commercial	K5E7	47940	28400	29200	30400	33600
1500 LS Sport Util	KHE7	50295	30500	31400	32600	36000
1500 LT Sport Util	KJE7	53555	33400	34400	35500	39300
1500 LTZ Sport Util.	KKE7	62395	37800	38400	39800	44100
2WD	C		(1700)	(1700)	(1860)	(1860)
YUKON XL 4WD—V8 Flex Fuel—Truck Equipment Schedule T1						
1500 SLE Sport Util	2HE7	50210	32100	33000	34200	37900
1500 SLT Sport Util	2KE7	53330	32400	33300	34600	38400
2WD	1		(1700)	(1700)	(1870)	(1870)
YUKON XL DENALI AWD—V8 Flex Fuel—Truck Equipment Sch T1						
1500 Sport Utility	2MEF	63565	40600	41200	42700	47300
2WD	1		(1700)	(1700)	(1855)	(1855)
EXPRESS PASSENGER VAN—V8 Flex Fuel—Truck Equipment Sch T1						
1500 LS Passenger	GBF4	31965	16600	16850	18500	21300
1500 LT Passenger	GCF4	37340	17900	17650	19250	22100
AWD	H		925	925	1060	1060
EXPRESS PASSENGER VAN—V8 Flex Fuel—Truck Equipment Sch T1						
3500 LS Passenger	GXFA	35155	18100	18350	19900	22800
3500 LT Passenger	GYFA	36585	19250	19550	21000	24000
3500 LS Extended	GZFA	37025	19950	20300	21700	24700
3500 LT Extended	G1FA	37370	20400	20800	22200	25200
V8, Flex Fuel, 6.0L	G		575	575	640	640
EXPRESS PASSENGER VAN—V8 Turbo Diesel—Truck Equipment Sch T1						
3500 LS Passenger	GXFL	48095	24600	24900	26700	30700
3500 LT Passenger	GYFL	49525	25500	25900	27600	31600
3500 LS Extended	GZFL	49965	25700	26100	27800	31800

TRUCKS & VANS

Body Type	VIN	List	Trade-In Good	Very Good	Pvt-Party Good	Retail Excellent
3500 LT Extended	G1FL	50310	26100	26500	28200	32200
SAVANA PASSENGER VAN—V8 Flex Fuel—Truck Equipment Sch T1						
1500 LS Passenger	7BF4	31465	16550	16800	18400	21200
1500 LT Passenger	7CF4	33765	17600	17850	19450	22300
2500 LS Passenger	7PFA	32360	16700	16950	18600	21400
2500 LT Passenger	7RFA	34660	18200	18450	20000	22900
3500 LS Passenger	7XFA	34655	18100	18350	19900	22800
3500 LT Passenger	7YFA	36560	19250	19550	21000	24000
3500 LS Extended	7ZFA	36525	20000	20300	21700	24700
3500 LT Extended	71FA	37345	20400	20700	22100	25100
AWD	8		925	925	1050	1050
V8, Flex Fuel, 6.0 Liter	G		575	575	635	635
SAVANA PASSENGER VAN—V8 Turbo Diesel—Truck Equipment Sch T1						
3500 LS Passenger	7XFL	47595	24600	24900	26700	30700
3500 LT Passenger	7YFL	49500	25400	25700	27500	31500
3500 LS Extended	7ZFL	49465	25700	26100	27800	31800
3500 LT Extended	71FL	50285	26000	26400	28100	32200
EXPRESS CARGO VAN—V6—Equipment Schedule T1						
1500 Cargo Van	GAFX	27705	17400	18050	19100	22300
AWD	H		925	925	1065	1065
V8, Flex Fuel, 5.3 Liter	4		675	675	775	775
EXPRESS CARGO VAN—V8 Flex Fuel—Truck Equipment Schedule T1						
2500 Cargo Van	GFCA	29210	18750	19500	20400	23700
2500 Extended	GGCA	31070	20400	21100	22000	25600
3500 Cargo Van	GTCA	32680	21000	21900	22800	26500
3500 Extended	GUCA	33565	22000	22900	23900	27900
V8, CNG, 6.0 Liter	B		850	850	970	970
V8, Flex Fuel, 6.0 Liter	G		575	575	645	645
EXPRESS CARGO VAN—V8 Turbo Diesel—Truck Equipment Sch T1						
2500 Cargo Van	GFCL	41155	25900	26300	28000	32000
2500 Extended	GGCL	43015	26400	26800	28500	32500
3500 Cargo Van	GTCL	44625	26600	27000	28700	32700
3500 Extended	GUCL	45510	27200	27600	29300	33300
SAVANA CARGO VAN—V8 Flex Fuel—Truck Equipment Schedule T1						
1500 Cargo Van	S7AF4	29700	18400	19100	20000	23300
AWD	8		925	925	1060	1060
V6, 4.3 Liter	X		(675)	(675)	(760)	(760)
SAVANA CARGO VAN—V8 Flex Fuel—Truck Equipment Schedule T1						
2500 Cargo Van	7FFA	30210	19050	19800	20700	24000
2500 Extended	7GFA	32070	20500	21300	22200	25800
3500 Cargo Van	7TCA	33530	22000	22900	23600	27200
3500 Extended	7TUA	34415	23000	23900	24600	28500
V8, CNG, 6.0 Liter	B		850	850	970	970
V8, Flex Fuel, 6.0 Liter	G		575	575	645	645
SAVANA CARGO VAN—V8 Turbo Diesel—Truck Equipment Schedule T1						
2500 Cargo Van	7FFL	42155	26100	26500	28200	32200
2500 Extended	7GFL	44015	26700	27100	28800	32800
3500 Cargo Van	7TCL	45475	26600	27000	28700	32700
3500 Extended	7TUL	46360	27200	27600	29300	33400
SILVERADO REGULAR CAB—V6 Flex Fuel EcoTec3—Truck Sch T1						
1500 Work Trk 6 1/2'	CPEH	24585	17200	17450	19250	21900
1500 Work Truck 8'	CPEH	24975	16900	17150	18950	21500
4WD	K		3500	3500	3975	3975
V8, EcoTec3, FF, 5.3L	C		400	400	455	455
SIERRA REGULAR CAB—V6 Flex Fuel EcoTec3—Truck Equipment Sch T1						
1500 2D 6 1/2'	1TEH	25085	18600	18900	20400	23300
1500 2D 8'	1TEH	25475	18050	18350	20100	22700
4WD	K		3500	3500	3935	3935
V8, EcoTec3, FF, 5.3L	C		400	400	450	450
SIERRA REGULAR CAB—V6 Flex Fuel EcoTec3—Truck Equipment Sch T1						
1500 SLE 6 1/2'	1UEH	31410	20400	20700	22300	25100
1500 SLE 2D 8'	1UEH	31535	20100	20400	22000	24800
4WD	K		3500	3500	3885	3885
V8, EcoTec3, FF, 5.3L	C		400	400	450	450
SILVERADO REGULAR CAB PICKUP 4WD—V6—Truck Equipment Sch T1						
1500 LT 6 1/2'	KREH	33650	20100	20400	22000	24800
1500 LT 8'	KREH	33950	19750	20000	21700	24500
1500 Z71 LT 6'	KREH	35340	21700	22100	23900	27000
1500 Z71 LT 8'	KREH	35640	21400	21700	23600	26700
2WD	C		(3500)	(3500)	(3925)	(3925)
V8, EcoTec3, FF, 5.3L	C		400	400	450	450
SILVERADO/SIERRA REGULAR CAB—V8 Flex Fuel—Truck Equip Sch T1						
2500 Work Truck 8'	CVCG	30805	17600	17900	19600	21600

TRUCKS & VANS

Body Type	VIN	List	Trade-In Good	Very Good	Pvt-Party Good	Retail Excellent
2500 LT 8'	CXCG	34435	21800	22200	24100	26600
2500 HD SLE 8'	10CG	34875	21800	22200	24100	26700
3500 Work Truck 8'	CZCG	32300	19100	19450	21200	23600
3500 SLE 2D 8'	13CG	35600	21400	21800	23600	26000
Tool Box			225	225	240	240
4WD	K		3500	3500	3890	3890
V8, Turbo Diesel, 6.6L	8		5425	5425	6035	6035
SILVERADO REGULAR CAB PICKUP 4WD—V8 Turbo Diesel—Truc Sch T1						
3500 LT 8'	K0CG	46680	27800	28300	30600	33900
Tool Box			225	225	235	235
2WD	C		(3500)	(3500)	(3825)	(3825)
V8, Flex Fuel, 6.0 Liter	G		(6225)	(6225)	(6810)	(6810)
SILVERADO/SIERRA DOUBLE CAB—V6 Flex Fuel EcoTec3—Truck Sch T1						
1500 Work Truck 6'	CPEH	28610	18800	19050	20900	23600
1500 4D 6 1/2'	1TEH	29110	19050	19350	21100	23900
4WD	K		3500	3500	3955	3955
V8, EcoTec3, FF, 5.3L	C		400	400	450	450
SILVERADO DOUBLE CAB 4WD—V8 Flex Fuel EcoTec3—Truck Equip Sch T1						
1500 LT 6 1/2'	KREC	37140	26400	26700	28500	31900
1500 Z71 LT 6 1/2'	KREC	38830	26400	26800	28400	31700
2WD	C		(3500)	(3500)	(3880)	(3880)
V6, EcoTec3, FF, 4.3L	H		(625)	(625)	(700)	(700)
SILVERADO DOUBLE CAB 4WD—V8 Flex Fuel EcoTec3—Truck Equip Sch T1						
1500 LTZ 6 1/2'	KSEC	41020	29700	30200	31900	35600
1500 Z71 LTZ 6 1/2'	KSEC	41800	29400	29800	31300	34800
1500 SLT 6 1/2'	2VEC	41760	30000	30500	32200	36000
2WD	C		(3500)	(3500)	(3860)	(3860)
V8, EcoTec3, FF, 6.2L	J		825	825	920	920
SIERRA DOUBLE CAB 4WD—V8 Flex Fuel EcoTec3—Truck Equip Sch T1						
1500 SLE 6 1/2'	2UEC	39155	26800	27100	28800	32100
2WD	1		(3500)	(3500)	(3860)	(3860)
V6, EcoTec3, 4.3L FF	H		(625)	(625)	(700)	(700)
SILVERADO/SIERRA CREW CAB—V6 Flex Fuel EcoTec3—Truck Equip Sch T1						
1500 Wrk Trk 5 3/4'	CPEH	32710	20800	21100	23000	26000
1500 Wrk Trk 6 1/2'	CROH	33010	19650	19950	21900	24900
1500 4D 5 3/4 ft	1TEH	33210	20700	21000	22900	25900
1500 4D 6 1/2 ft	1TEH	33510	20400	20700	22600	25700
4WD	2		3500	3500	3980	3980
V8, EcoTec3, FF, 5.3L	C		400	400	450	450
SIERRA CREW CAB 4WD—V6 Flex Fuel EcoTec3—Truck Equipment Sch T1						
1500 SLE 4D 5 3/4'	2UEC	41545	29700	30100	31800	35400
1500 SLE 4D 6 1/2'	2UEC	41845	29900	30300	32100	35700
2WD	1		(3500)	(3500)	(3850)	(3850)
V6, EcoTec3, 4.3L FF	H		(625)	(625)	(695)	(695)
SILVERADO CREW CAB PICKUP—V8 Flex Fuel EcoTec3—Truck Sch T1						
1500 LT 4D 5 3/4'	CREC	36155	23800	24100	26000	29300
1500 LT 4D 6 1/2'	CREC	36455	22000	22400	23800	26600
4WD	K		3500	3500	3915	3915
V6, EcoTec3, FF, 4.3L	H		(625)	(625)	(710)	(710)
SILVERADO CREW CAB 4WD—V8 Flex Fuel EcoTec3—Truck Equip Sch T1						
1500 Z71 LT 5 3/4'	KREC	41420	25800	26200	27800	31100
2WD	C		(3500)	(3500)	(3875)	(3875)
V6, EcoTec3, FF, 4.3L	H		(625)	(625)	(700)	(700)
SILVERADO CREW CAB 4WD—V8 Flex Fuel EcoTec3—Truck Equip Sch T1						
1500 Z71 LT 4D 6'	KREC	41720	25500	25800	27500	30800
2WD	C		(3500)	(3500)	(3880)	(3880)
V6, EcoTec3, FF, 4.3L	H		(625)	(625)	(700)	(700)
SILVERADO CREW CAB 4WD—V8 Flex Fuel EcoTec3—Truck Equip Sch T1						
1500 LTZ 4D 5 3/4'	KSEC	43380	33200	33700	35400	39400
1500 LTZ 4D 6 1/2'	KSEC	43680	32400	32900	34600	38600
1500 SLT 4D 5 3/4'	2VEC	44120	32300	32800	34400	38300
1500 SLT 4D 6 1/2'	2VEC	44420	32000	32500	34100	38000
1500 Z71 LTZ 4D 5'	KSEC	44460	33400	33900	35600	39500
1500 Z71 LTZ 4D 6 1/2'	KSEC	44460	33600	34100	35600	39500
1500 HighCountry 5'	KTEC	48475	34300	34800	36100	39700
1500 HighCountry 6'	KTEC	48775	34100	34600	35900	39500
2WD	C		(3500)	(3500)	(3855)	(3855)
V8, EcoTec3, FF, 6.2L	J		825	825	915	915
SIERRA DENALI CREW CAB PICKUP 4WD—V8 Flex Fuel EcoTec3—Sch T1						
1500 4D 5 3/4'	2WEC	51060	37000	37700	39800	43600
1500 4D 6 1/2'	2WEC	51360	36800	37500	39900	43900
2WD	1		(1375)	(1375)	(1520)	(1520)
V8 EcoTec3 FF 6.2L	J		550	550	610	610

2014 CHEVROLET/GMC

Body Type	VIN	List	Trade-In Good	Very Good	Pvt-Party Good	Retail Excellent
SILVERADO/SIERRA CREW CAB PICKUP—V8 Flex Fuel—Truck Equip Sch T1						
2500 HD Wrk Trk 6'	CVCG	34590	23200	23600	25600	28400
2500 HD LT/SLE 8'	CXCG	39050	27000	27500	29700	32800
2500 HD LTZ/SLT 8'	CYCG	44770	31600	32200	34400	37900
Tool Box			225	225	240	240
4WD	K		3500	3500	3820	3820
V8, Natural Gas, 6.0L	B		5125	5125	5595	5595
V8, Turbo Diesel, 6.6L	8		5425	5425	5930	5930
SIERRA CREW CAB PICKUP—V8 Flex Fuel—Truck Equipment Sch T1						
2500 Work Truck 8'	1ZCG	34785	23500	23900	25900	28700
4WD	2		3500	3500	3855	3855
V8, CNG, 6.0L	G		5125	5125	5645	5645
V8, Turbo Dsl, 6.6L	8		5425	5425	5980	5980
SILVERADO/SIERRA CREW CAB PICKUP 4WD—V8 Turbo Diesel—Truck Equip Sch T1						
2500 HD SLE 4D 6 1/2'	20C8	49810	36100	36700	39300	43500
2500 SLT 4D 6 1/2'	21C8	55420	41400	42100	44500	48900
2500 HD Denali 6'	25E8	55735	42300	43000	45500	50100
Tool Box			225	225	235	235
2WD	1		(3500)	(3500)	(3825)	(3825)
V8, Flex Fuel, 6.0 Liter	G		(5325)	(5325)	(5820)	(5820)
V8, Natural Gas, 6.0L	B		5125	5125	5605	5605
SILVERADO/SIERRA CREW CAB—V8 Turbo Diesel—Truck Equipment Sch T1						
2500 HD Wrk Trk 8'	CVC8	41980	28900	29500	31800	35300
2500 HD LTZ/SLT 6'	KYC8	54920	40800	41500	43900	48300
Tool Box			225	225	235	235
4WD	K		3500	3500	3845	3845
V8, Flex Fuel, 6.0 Liter	G		(5325)	(5325)	(5850)	(5850)
V8, Natural Gas, 6.0L	B		5125	5125	5635	5635
SILVERADO/SIERRA CREW CAB 4WD—V8 Turbo Diesel—Truck Sch T1						
2500 HD LT/SLE 6'	KXC8	49345	35600	36200	38700	42800
Tool Box			225	225	235	235
2WD	C		(3500)	(3500)	(3800)	(3800)
V8, Flex Fuel, 6.0 Liter	G		(5325)	(5325)	(5785)	(5785)
V8, Natural Gas, 6.0L	B		5125	5125	5570	5570
SILVERADO/SIERRA CREW CAB—V8 Flex Fuel—Truck Equip Sch T1						
3500 Work Trk 6 1/2'	CZCG	36860	24800	25300	27400	30400
3500 Work Truck 8'	C2CG	37055	25000	25500	27600	30600
3500 LT/SLE 6 1/2'	C0CG	40540	27700	28200	30200	33200
3500 LTZ/SLT 6 1/2'	C1CG	45350	29100	29700	32100	35600
Tool Box			225	225	235	235
4WD	K		3500	3500	3820	3820
V8, Turbo Diesel, 6.6L	8		5425	5425	5930	5930
SILVERADO/SIERRA CREW CAB 4WD—V8 Turbo Diesel—Truck Sch T1						
3500 LT/SLE 8'	K0CG	52300	36400	37000	39800	44300
3500 LTZ/SLT 8'	K1CG	57090	39700	40500	43100	47700
Tool Box			225	225	240	240
2WD	C		(3500)	(3500)	(3870)	(3870)
V8, Flex Fuel, 6.0 Liter	G		(6225)	(6225)	(6890)	(6890)
SIERRA CREW CAB PICKUP—V8 Flex Fuel—Truck Equipment Schedule T1						
3500 Work Trk 6 1/2	12CG	36860	26500	27000	29000	32000
3500 Work Truck 8'	12CG	37055	26800	27300	29400	32400
3500 SLE 6 1/2'	13CG	41000	28800	29300	31700	35000
3500 SLT 6 1/2'	14CG	45855	30100	30700	33000	36400
Tool Box			225	225	240	240
4WD	2		3500	3500	3875	3875
V8, Turbo Diesel, 6.6L	8		5425	5425	6015	6015
SIERRA CREW CAB PICKUP 4WD—V8 Turbo Diesel—Truck Sch T1						
3500 SLE 4D 8'	23C8	54315	37900	38500	40500	44100
Tool Box			225	225	235	235
2WD	1		(3500)	(3500)	(3820)	(3820)
V8, Flex Fuel, 6.0 Liter	G		(6225)	(6225)	(6800)	(6800)
SIERRA CREW CAB PICKUP—V8 Turbo Diesel—Truck Equip Sch T1						
3500 SLT 4D 8'	14C8	54435	35600	36200	38200	41700
Tool Box			225	225	235	235
4WD	2		3500	3500	3810	3810
V8, Flex Fuel, 6.0 Liter	G		(6225)	(6225)	(6785)	(6785)
SIERRA DENALI CREW CAB PICKUP—V8 Flex Fuel—Truck Equip Sch T1						
3500 4D 6 1/2'	16EG	48640	31600	32200	34500	38100
3500 4D 8'	16CG	48835	31400	32000	34300	37900
Tool Box			225	225	240	240
4WD	2		3500	3500	3860	3860
V8, Turbo Diesel, 6.6L	8		5425	5425	5990	5990

410 DEDUCT FOR RECONDITIONING 1015

Body Type	VIN	List	Trade-In Good	Very Good	Pvt-Party Good	Retail Excellent

CHRYSLER

2000 CHRYSLER — 1C4–(J253)–Y–#

VOYAGER—V6—Truck Equipment Schedule T1

Body Type	VIN	List	Good	Very Good	Good	Excellent
Minivan 4D	J253	20895	375	475	800	1400
SE Minivan 4D	J453	23840	375	475	800	1400
Grand Minivan 4D	J243	22545	350	450	800	1400
SE Grand Minivan 4D	J443	24835	350	450	800	1400
5-Passenger Seating			(200)	(200)	(265)	(265)
Second Sliding Door			50	50	60	60
4-Cyl, 2.4 Liter	B		(250)	(250)	(340)	(340)

TOWN & COUNTRY—V6—Truck Equipment Schedule T3

LX Minivan	P44R	26950	425	525	900	1575
LXi Minivan	P54L	31530	550	675	1050	1825
Limited Minivan	P64L	34855	950	1150	1550	2650
Air Conditioning, Rear			100	100	135	135
AWD			250	250	335	335

2001 CHRYSLER — 1C(4or8)–(J24G)–1–#

VOYAGER—V6—Truck Equipment Schedule T1

Minivan	J24G	20770	425	525	875	1475
LX Minivan	J54G	24165	425	525	875	1475
5-Passenger Seating			(200)	(200)	(265)	(265)
4-Cyl, 2.4 Liter	B		(300)	(300)	(385)	(385)

TOWN & COUNTRY—V6—Truck Equipment Schedule T3

LX Minivan	P44G	26155	675	825	1175	2000
EX Minivan	P54L	26830	800	950	1300	2200
LXi Minivan	P64G	30705	950	1125	1475	2500
Limited Minivan	P64L	35490	1350	1600	1975	3300
Quad Seating			100	100	130	130
Air Conditioning, Rear			100	100	135	135
AWD	T		250	250	335	335

2002 CHRYSLER — 1C(4or8)–(J15B)–2–#

VOYAGER—4-Cyl.—Truck Equipment Schedule T1

eC Minivan	J15B	16995	375	475	775	1325
5-Passenger Seating			(225)	(225)	(310)	(310)

VOYAGER—V6—Truck Equipment Schedule T1

Minivan	J253	19995	475	600	925	1550
LX Minivan	J453	24060	475	600	925	1550
5-Passenger Seating			(225)	(225)	(310)	(310)
4-Cyl, 2.4 Liter	B		(350)	(350)	(465)	(465)

TOWN & COUNTRY—V6—Truck Equipment Schedule T3

eL Minivan	P343	24330	425	525	875	1500
LX Minivan	P443	27065	900	1075	1425	2375
EX Minivan	P74L	26830	1125	1325	1675	2775
LXi Minivan	P543	30970	1175	1400	1750	2875
Limited Minivan	P64L	35990	1675	1950	2325	3800
Quad Seating			125	125	155	155
Air Conditioning, Rear			125	125	155	155
AWD	T		275	275	375	375

2003 CHRYSLER — 1C(4or8)–(J453)–3–#

VOYAGER—V6—Truck Equipment Schedule T1

LX Minivan	J453	24025	525	650	1150	2025
5-Passenger Seating			(275)	(275)	(355)	(355)
4-Cyl, 2.4 Liter	B		(425)	(425)	(565)	(565)

TOWN & COUNTRY—V6—Truck Equipment Schedule T3

eL Minivan	P343	24330	575	675	1225	2225
Minivan	P24R	25975	575	675	1225	2225
LX Minivan	P443	27010	975	1150	1725	3025
EX Minivan	P74L	27235	1350	1575	2175	3775
LXi Minivan	P54L	34080	1450	1700	2300	3975
Limited Minivan	P64L	36535	2000	2325	3075	5250
Quad Seating			150	150	185	185
Air Conditioning, Rear			150	150	185	185
AWD	T		325	325	445	445

TRUCKS & VANS

Body Type	VIN	List	Trade-In Good	Very Good	Pvt-Party Good	Retail Excellent
2004 CHRYSLER — (1or2)C(4or8)–(P45R)–4–#						
TOWN & COUNTRY—V6—Truck Equipment Schedule T3						
Minivan	P45R	23520	800	925	1425	2425
LX Minivan	P44R	27490	1400	1625	2200	3700
EX Minivan	P74L	30110	1875	2150	2850	4750
Touring Minivan	P54L	33245	1975	2275	2975	4950
Limited Minivan	P64L	38380	2650	3025	3775	6275
Quad Seating			150	150	200	200
Air Conditioning, Rear			175	175	220	220
AWD	T		375	375	510	510
PACIFICA—V6—Truck Equipment Schedule T3						
Sport Wagon 4D	M684	30410	1875	2125	2650	4175
AWD	F		425	425	580	580
2005 CHRYSLER — (1or2)C(4or8)–(P45R)–4–#						
TOWN & COUNTRY—V6—Truck Equipment Schedule T3						
Minivan	P45R	21185	825	950	1625	2700
LX Minivan	P44R	25640	1375	1575	2375	3950
Touring Minivan	P54L	27940	2250	2575	3350	5375
Limited Minivan	P64L	35940	2950	3350	4125	6550
Quad Seating			150	150	200	200
Air Conditioning, Rear			200	200	255	255
Signature Series			275	275	360	360
PACIFICA—V6—Truck Equipment Schedule T3						
Sport Wagon 4D	M48L	24995	1500	1725	2450	3825
Touring Spt Wag 4D	M684	28525	2200	2500	3325	5100
Signature Series			250	250	335	335
AWD	F		475	475	615	615
PACIFICA AWD—V6—Truck Equipment Schedule T3						
Limited Sport Wag	F784	36995	3450	3875	4700	6975
2006 CHRYSLER — (1or2)C(4or8)–(P45R)–6–#						
TOWN & COUNTRY—V6—Truck Equipment Schedule T3						
Minivan	P45R	21735	1175	1350	1975	3175
LX Minivan	P44R	26100	2000	2250	2975	4650
Touring Minivan	P54L	28590	2950	3325	4025	6175
Limited Minivan	P64L	36465	3925	4425	5200	7875
Quad Seating			150	150	200	200
Signature Series			300	300	390	390
PACIFICA—V6—Truck Equipment Schedule T3						
Sport Wagon 4D	M484	25895	1850	2100	3075	4800
Touring Spt Wag 4D	M684	29095	2725	3050	3925	5900
Signature Series			275	275	360	360
AWD	F		500	500	655	655
PACIFICA AWD—V6—Truck Equipment Schedule T3						
Limited Sport Wag	M784	37415	3800	4225	5200	7700
Signature Series			275	275	360	360
FWD			(500)	(500)	(675)	(675)
2007 CHRYSLER — (1or2)C(4or8)–(W58N)–7–#						
ASPEN 4WD—V8—Truck Equipment Schedule T1						
Limited Spt Util 4D	W58N	34265	7325	8050	9050	12650
2WD	X		(1100)	(1100)	(1480)	(1480)
V8, HEMI, 5.7 Liter	2		625	625	820	820
TOWN & COUNTRY—V6—Truck Equipment Schedule T3						
Minivan	P45R	21985	1500	1675	2325	3600
LX Minivan	P44R	26350	2250	2525	3200	4825
Touring Minivan	P54L	28790	3625	4025	4775	7025
Limited Minivan	P64L	36860	5200	5775	6700	9775
Quad Seating			150	150	200	200
Signature Series			325	325	445	445
PACIFICA—V6—Truck Equipment Schedule T3						
Sport Wagon 4D	M48L	24890	2625	2900	3900	5850
Touring Spt Wag 4D	M68X	27980	3475	3850	4950	7250
Signature Series			300	300	390	390
AWD	F		525	525	685	685
PACIFICA AWD—V6—Truck Equipment Schedule T3						
Limited Spt Wag 4D	M78X	36205	5050	5550	6550	9450
FWD			(575)	(575)	(775)	(775)

Body Type	VIN	List	Trade-In Good	Very Good	Pvt-Party Good	Retail Excellent

2008 CHRYSLER — (1or2)C(4or8)–(W58N)–8–#

ASPEN 4WD—V8—Truck Equipment Schedule T1
Limited Spt Util 4D	W58N	35625	8825	9500	10300	13400
2WD	X		(1200)	(1200)	(1575)	(1575)
V8, HEMI, 5.7 Liter	2		650	650	860	860

TOWN & COUNTRY—V6—Truck Equipment Schedule T3
LX Minivan	R44H	23190	4975	5400	6025	8175
Touring Minivan	R54P	28430	6800	7375	8075	10850
Limited Minivan	R64X	36400	8650	9375	10100	13550
Quad Seating			150	150	200	200

PACIFICA—V6—Truck Equipment Schedule T3
Sport Wagon 4D	M48L	27310	3375	3650	4775	6700
Touring Spt Wag 4D	M68X	30435	4475	4825	5975	8325
Signature Series			325	325	445	445
AWD	F		550	550	720	720

PACIFICA AWD—V6—Truck Equipment Schedule T3
Limited Spt Wag 4D	M78X	36925	6200	6700	7925	10800
FWD			(650)	(650)	(880)	(880)

2009 ASPEN — (1or2)C(4or8)–(W58P)–9–#

ASPEN 4WD—V8—Truck Equipment Schedule T1
Limited Sport Util	W58P	37415	10500	11100	12250	15550
2WD	X		(1275)	(1275)	(1670)	(1670)
V8, HEMI, 5.7 Liter	T		700	700	900	900

ASPEN 4WD—V8 Hybrid—Truck Equipment Schedule T1
Limited Sport Util	W18T	45570	10600	11200	12900	16750

TOWN & COUNTRY—V6—Truck Equipment Schedule T3
LX Minivan	R44E	26500	5875	6250	7325	9650
Touring Minivan	R541	29665	7850	8350	9350	12100
Limited Minivan	R64X	37300	10600	11250	12400	16000
Quad Seating			175	175	245	245

2010 CHRYSLER — (1or2)C(4or8)–(R4DE)–A–#

TOWN & COUNTRY—V6—Truck Equipment Schedule T3
LX Minivan	R4DE	25995	7175	7500	8850	11250
Touring Minivan	R5D1	29245	8675	9075	10300	12850
Limited Minivan	R6DX	35880	12550	13100	14600	18250
Quad Seating			225	225	305	305

2011 CHRYSLER — (1or2)C(4or8)–(R5DG)–B–#

TOWN & COUNTRY—V6—Truck Equipment Schedule T3
Touring Minivan	R5DG	30995	10850	11150	12550	15100
Touring-L Minivan	R8DG	32995	12950	13350	15050	18150
Limited Minivan	R6DG	39495	14900	15400	17350	21100

2012 CHRYSLER — (1,2or3)C(4or6)–(C1BG)–C–#

TOWN & COUNTRY—V6—Truck Equipment Schedule T3
Touring Minivan	C1BG	30830	12700	12950	14500	16950
Touring-L Minivan	C1CG	33330	15200	15550	17300	20300
Limited Minivan	C1GG	39830	17350	17750	19650	23000

2013 CHRYSLER — (1,2or3)C(4or6)–(C1BG)–D–#

TOWN & COUNTRY—V6—Truck Equipment Schedule T3
Touring Minivan	C1BG	30990	14800	15050	16750	19200
Touring-L Minivan	C1CG	34290	17450	17750	19650	22600
S Minivan 4D	C1HG	32090	17300	17550	19200	21900
Limited Minivan	C1GG	40990	19950	20200	22100	25400

2014 CHRYSLER — (1,2or3)C(4or6)–(C1BG)–E–#

TOWN & COUNTRY—V6—Truck Equipment Schedule T3
Touring Minivan	C1BG	31760	17150	17400	19000	21600
Touring-L Minivan	C1CG	34990	20300	20600	22400	25400
Touring-L 30th Anv	C1CG	36690	20800	21100	22700	25500
S Minivan 4D	C1HG	33190	19700	20000	21600	24400
Limited Minivan	C1GG	42290	23500	23900	25700	29100

Body Type	VIN	List	Trade-In Good	Very Good	Pvt-Party Good	Retail Excellent

TRUCKS & VANS

DODGE/PLYMOUTH

2000 DODGE/PLYM–(1,2,3or4)B4–(S28N)–Y–#

Body Type	VIN	List	Good	Very Good	Good	Excellent
DURANGO 4WD—V8—Truck Equipment Schedule T1						
SLT Sport Utility 4D	S28N	29060	775	950	1525	2775
R/T Sport Utility 4D	S28Z	33810	1075	1300	1975	3600
Third Row Seat			200	200	265	265
2WD	R		(525)	(525)	(715)	(715)
V8, 4.7 Liter (ex R/T)	Z		100	100	145	145
CARAVAN/VOYAGER—V6—Truck Equipment Schedule T1						
Minivan 4D	P243	21905	600	700	1100	1875
SE Minivan 4D	P443	23675	900	1050	1475	2425
Grand Minivan 4D	P243	22380	800	950	1350	2250
SE Grand Minivan	P443	24670	500	600	1000	1725
LE Grand Minivan	P54R	27785	1125	1325	1800	3000
5-Passenger Seating			(200)	(200)	(265)	(265)
Second Sliding Door			50	50	60	60
AWD	T		250	250	335	335
4-Cyl, 2.4 Liter	B		(250)	(250)	(340)	(340)
V6, 3.8 Liter	L		50	50	65	65
CARAVAN—V6—Truck Equipment Schedule T1						
ES Grand Minivan	P54L	29995	1525	1775	2275	3800
Second Sliding Door			50	50	60	60
AWD	T		250	250	335	335
GRAND CARAVAN AWD—V6—Truck Equipment Schedule T1						
Sport Minivan 4D	T44L	28670	1200	1400	1900	3200
5-Passenger Seating			(200)	(200)	(265)	(265)
RAM WAGON—V8—Truck Equipment Schedule T1						
1500 Passenger Van	B15Y	22245	1200	1425	1950	3525
2500 Passenger Van	B25Y	23670	1325	1575	2125	3825
3500 Maxi Passenger	B35Y	26675	1550	1825	2425	4350
V6, 3.9 Liter	X		(200)	(200)	(265)	(265)
V8, 5.9 Liter	Z		50	50	65	65
RAM VAN—V6—Truck Equipment Schedule T1						
1500 Cargo Van	B11X	19575	950	1150	1575	2800
Maxi-Van			50	50	65	65
V8, 5.2 Liter	T,Y		100	100	135	135
V8, 5.9 Liter	Z		200	200	265	265
RAM VAN—V8—Truck Equipment Schedule T1						
2500 Cargo Van	B21Y	21075	1225	1450	1975	3500
3500 Cargo Van	B31Y	23260	1525	1800	2350	4200
Maxi-Van			50	50	65	65
V8, 5.9 Liter	Z		50	50	65	65
DAKOTA PICKUP—4-Cyl.—Truck Equipment Schedule T1						
Short Bed	L26P	15850	450	525	825	1350
R/T Short Bed	L26Z	20090	800	925	1425	2450
4WD	G		400	400	535	535
V6, 3.9 Liter	X		125	125	165	165
V8, 4.7 Liter	Y		150	150	200	200
V8, 5.9 Liter (ex R/T)	Z		250	250	325	325
DAKOTA PICKUP—V6—Truck Equipment Schedule T1						
Club Cab	L22X	19045	1275	1450	2000	3425
R/T Club Cab	L22Z	22340	1675	1900	2500	4225
Quad Cab	L2AX	20290	900	1025	1550	2725
4WD	G		400	400	535	535
4-Cyl, 2.5 Liter	P		(100)	(100)	(120)	(120)
V8, 4.7 Liter	N		100	100	135	135
V8, 5.9 Liter (ex R/T)	Z		200	200	255	255
RAM REGULAR CAB PICKUP—V8—Truck Equipment Schedule T1						
1500 Short Bed	C16Y	19695	1225	1425	1825	2975
1500 Long Bed	C16Y	19980	1075	1250	1650	2725
2500 Long Bed	C26Z	22570	1050	1200	1650	2775
3500 Long Bed	C36Z	24330	1275	1475	1925	3225
Work Special			(250)	(250)	(335)	(335)
4WD	F		625	625	820	820
V6, 3.9 Liter	X		(350)	(350)	(455)	(455)
6-Cyl, Turbo Diesel	6		1475	1475	1955	1955
V8, 5.9 Liter	Z,5		75	75	100	100
V10, 8.0 Liter	W		100	100	135	135

TRUCKS & VANS

Body Type	VIN	List	Trade-In Good	Trade-In Very Good	Pvt-Party Good	Retail Excellent
RAM CLUB CAB PICKUP—V8—Truck Equipment Schedule T1						
1500 Short Bed	C12Y	21890	1450	1675	2300	3925
4WD	F	......	625	625	820	820
V8, 5.9 Liter	Z	......	75	75	100	100
RAM QUAD CAB PICKUP—V8—Truck Equipment Schedule T1						
1500 Short Bed	C13Y	22750	1775	2050	2700	4550
1500 Long Bed	C13Y	23030	1675	1925	2500	4225
4WD	F	......	625	625	820	820
V8, 5.9 Liter	Z,5	......	75	75	100	100
RAM QUAD CAB PICKUP 4WD—6-Cyl. Turbo Diesel—Truck Equip Sch T1						
2500 Short Bed	F23X	31500	5500	6325	7475	12200
2500 Long Bed	F23X	31690	5350	6150	7275	11850
3500 Long Bed	F33X	34260	5625	6450	7575	12400
2WD	C	......	(725)	(725)	(980)	(980)
V8, 5.9 Liter	Z,5	......	(1450)	(1450)	(1945)	(1945)
V10, 8.0 Liter	W	......	100	100	135	135

2001 DODGE—(1or2)B(4,7or8)—(S28N)—1—#

Body Type	VIN	List	Trade-In Good	Trade-In Very Good	Pvt-Party Good	Retail Excellent
DURANGO 4WD—V8—Truck Equipment Schedule T1						
SLT Sport Utility 4D	S28N	30740	975	1200	1700	3000
R/T Sport Utility 4D	S28Z	30990	1425	1700	2325	4075
Third Row Seat		......	200	200	265	265
2WD	R	......	(625)	(625)	(820)	(820)
V8, 5.9 Liter (ex R/T)	Z	......	125	125	160	160
CARAVAN—V6—Truck Equipment Schedule T1						
SE Minivan 4D	P44G	20740	950	1100	1550	2600
Sport Minivan 4D	P64G	24165	1000	1175	1650	2775
SE Grand Minivan	P44G	22440	650	775	1200	2050
Sport Grand 4D	P64G	24915	1150	1350	1875	3125
5-Passenger Seating		......	(200)	(200)	(265)	(265)
AWD	T	......	250	250	335	335
4-Cyl, 2.4 Liter	B	......	(300)	(300)	(385)	(385)
V6, 3.8 Liter		......	250	250	345	345
CARAVAN—V6—Truck Equipment Schedule T1						
EX Grand Minivan	P44L	26725	1300	1500	2025	3425
ES Grand Minivan	P54L	29750	1700	1975	2650	4425
5-Passenger Seating		......	(200)	(200)	(265)	(265)
AWD		......	250	250	335	335
RAM WAGON—V8—Truck Equipment Schedule T1						
1500 Passenger Van	B15Y	22615	1500	1750	2325	4150
2500 Passenger Van	B25Y	24040	1625	1900	2500	4450
3500 Maxi Passenger	B35Y	27055	1800	2125	2825	5000
V6, 3.9 Liter	X	......	(200)	(200)	(265)	(265)
V8, 5.9 Liter	Z	......	50	50	65	65
RAM VAN—V6—Truck Equipment Schedule T1						
1500 Cargo Van	B11X	19890	1175	1400	1900	3350
2500 Cargo Van	B21X	21390	1450	1700	2250	3975
Maxi-Van		......	50	50	65	65
V8, 5.2 Liter	Y	......	100	100	135	135
V8, 5.9 Liter	Z	......	200	200	265	265
RAM VAN—V8—Truck Equipment Schedule T1						
3500 Cargo Van	B31Y	23575	1700	2000	2575	4525
Maxi-Van		......	50	50	65	65
V8, 5.9 Liter	Z	......	50	50	65	65
DAKOTA PICKUP—4-Cyl.—Truck Equipment Schedule T1						
Short Bed	L26P	16255	475	550	900	1475
R/T Short Bed	L26Z	20505	850	975	1500	2575
4WD	G	......	400	400	535	535
V6, 3.9 Liter	X	......	125	125	165	165
V8, 4.7 Liter	N	......	150	150	200	200
V8, 5.9 Liter (ex R/T)	Z	......	275	275	370	370
DAKOTA PICKUP—V6—Truck Equipment Schedule T1						
Club Cab	L22X	19580	1375	1550	2125	3575
R/T Club Cab	L22Z	22885	1675	1900	2550	4275
Quad Cab	L23X	21950	1300	1475	2050	3475
4WD	G	......	400	400	535	535
4-Cyl, 2.5 Liter	P	......	(125)	(125)	(155)	(155)
V8, 4.7 Liter	N	......	100	100	135	135
V8, 5.9 Liter	Z	......	225	225	285	285
RAM REGULAR CAB PICKUP—V8—Truck Equipment Schedule T1						
1500 Short Bed	C16Y	20145	1450	1675	2075	3375
1500 Long Bed	C16Y	20430	1275	1475	1825	2925
2500 Long Bed	C26Z	23475	1225	1425	1875	3075

TRUCKS & VANS

Body Type	VIN	List	Trade-In Good	Very Good	Pvt-Party Good	Retail Excellent
3500 Long Bed	C36Z	25360	1350	1550	2025	3350
Work Special			(250)	(250)	(335)	(335)
4WD	F		725	725	955	955
V6, 3.9 Liter	X		(350)	(350)	(465)	(465)
6-Cyl, Turbo Diesel	6		1600	1600	2120	2120
6-Cyl, HO Turbo Dsl	7		3075	3075	4110	4110
V8, 5.9 Liter (1500)			75	75	100	100
V10, 8.0 Liter	W		100	100	135	135
RAM CLUB CAB PICKUP—V8—Truck Equipment Schedule T1						
1500 Short Bed	C12Y	21465	1800	2075	2750	4575
4WD	F		725	725	955	955
V8, 5.9 Liter			75	75	100	100
RAM QUAD CAB PICKUP—V8—Truck Equipment Schedule T1						
1500 Short Bed	C13Y	23375	2225	2550	3150	5150
1500 Long Bed	C13Y	23655	2025	2325	2975	4900
4WD	F		725	725	955	955
V8, 5.9 Liter			75	75	100	100
RAM QUAD CAB PICKUP 4WD—6-Cyl. Turbo Diesel—Truck Equip Sch T1						
2500 Short Bed	F236	32390	7000	7975	8775	13800
2500 Long Bed	F236	32580	7275	8300	9225	14600
3500 Long Bed	C33Z	35080	7475	8525	9500	15050
2WD	C		(875)	(875)	(1165)	(1165)
6-Cyl, HO Turbo Dsl	7		425	425	580	580
V8, 5.9 Liter	Z		(1750)	(1750)	(2330)	(2330)
V10, 8.0 Liter	W		100	100	135	135

2002 DODGE — 1B(4,7or8)–(S38N)-2–#

Body Type	VIN	List	Trade-In Good	Very Good	Pvt-Party Good	Retail Excellent
DURANGO 4WD—V8—Truck Equipment Schedule T1						
Sport Utility 4D	S38N	27595	1300	1550	2125	3675
R/T Sport Utility 4D	S78Z	37070	1850	2175	2975	5175
Third Row Seat			225	225	310	310
2WD	R		(700)	(700)	(935)	(935)
V8, 5.9 Liter (ex R/T)	Z		125	125	175	175
CARAVAN—4-Cyl.—Truck Equipment Schedule T1						
eC Minivan 4D	P15B	16995	450	550	950	1600
5-Passenger Seating			(225)	(225)	(310)	(310)
CARAVAN—V6—Truck Equipment Schedule T1						
SE Minivan 4D	P44R	19795	1025	1200	1675	2800
Sport Minivan 4D	P64G	24060	1075	1250	1775	2975
SE Grand Minivan	P44G	22440	800	925	1450	2475
eL Grand Minivan	P34R	24175	1025	1200	1750	2950
Sport Grand 4D	P64G	24930	1325	1525	2100	3550
5-Passenger Seating			(225)	(225)	(310)	(310)
AWD	T		275	275	375	375
V6, 3.8 Liter	L		300	300	395	395
CARAVAN—V6—Truck Equipment Schedule T1						
EX Grand Minivan	P44L	26725	1450	1675	2275	3825
ES Grand Minivan	P54L	30135	2025	2325	3075	5150
5-Passenger Seating			(225)	(225)	(310)	(310)
AWD	T		275	275	375	375
RAM WAGON—V8—Truck Equipment Schedule T1						
1500 Passenger Van	B15Y	22035	1750	2075	2650	4525
2500 Passenger Van	B25Y	24050	1900	2250	2825	4850
3500 Maxi Passenger	B35Y	27055	2150	2525	3125	5375
V6, 3.9 Liter	X		(225)	(225)	(310)	(310)
V8, 5.9 Liter	Z		50	50	65	65
RAM VAN—V6—Truck Equipment Schedule T1						
1500 Cargo Van	B11X	20050	1400	1650	2200	3875
2500 Cargo Van	B21X	21595	1700	2000	2650	4675
Maxi-Van			75	75	85	85
V8, 5.2 Liter	Y		125	125	155	155
V8, 5.9 Liter	Z		225	225	310	310
RAM VAN—V8—Truck Equipment Schedule T1						
3500 Cargo Van	B31Y	23780	1850	2175	2950	5175
Maxi-Van			75	75	85	85
V8, 5.9 Liter	Z		50	50	65	65
DAKOTA PICKUP—4-Cyl.—Truck Equipment Schedule T1						
Short Bed	L26P	16370	500	600	975	1600
R/T Short Bed	L26Z	21290	1250	1425	1800	2900
4WD	G		500	500	665	665
V6, 3.9 Liter	X		150	150	185	185
V8, 4.7 Liter	N		175	175	245	245
V8, 5.9 Liter (ex R/T)	Z		300	300	410	410

TRUCKS & VANS

Body Type	VIN	List	Trade-In Good	Very Good	Pvt-Party Good	Retail Excellent
DAKOTA PICKUP—V6—Truck Equipment Schedule T1						
Club Cab	L22X	19695	**1900**	**2150**	**2600**	**4150**
R/T Club Cab	L22Z	23585	**2525**	**2850**	**3300**	**5200**
Quad Cab	L23X	21985	**1925**	**2175**	**2700**	**4350**
4WD	G		**500**	**500**	**665**	**665**
4-Cyl, 2.5 Liter	P		**(150)**	**(150)**	**(185)**	**(185)**
V8, 4.7 Liter	N		**125**	**125**	**155**	**155**
V8, 5.9 Liter (ex R/T)	Z		**250**	**250**	**320**	**320**
RAM REGULAR CAB PICKUP—V8—Truck Equipment Schedule T1						
1500 Short Bed	C16Y	19620	**2450**	**2800**	**2975**	**4450**
1500 Long Bed	C16Y	19905	**2025**	**2325**	**2525**	**3775**
2500 HD Long Bed	C26Z	23490	**1275**	**1475**	**1875**	**3050**
3500 Long Bed	C36Z	25375	**1425**	**1650**	**2150**	**3525**
4WD	F		**850**	**850**	**1135**	**1135**
V6, 3.7 Liter	K		**(375)**	**(375)**	**(485)**	**(485)**
6-Cyl, Turbo Diesel	6		**1800**	**1800**	**2400**	**2400**
6-Cyl, HO Turbo Dsl	7		**3275**	**3275**	**4365**	**4365**
V8, 5.9 Liter (1500)	Z		**100**	**100**	**145**	**145**
V10, 8.0 Liter	W		**125**	**125**	**155**	**155**
RAM QUAD CAB PICKUP—V8—Truck Equipment Schedule T1						
1500 Short Bed	C13Y	23840	**3525**	**4000**	**4275**	**6550**
1500 Long Bed	C13Y	24120	**3300**	**3750**	**4025**	**6125**
4WD	F		**850**	**850**	**1135**	**1135**
V8, 5.9 Liter	Z		**100**	**100**	**145**	**145**
RAM QUAD CAB PICKUP 4WD—6-Cyl, Turbo Diesel—Truck Equip Sch T1						
2500 Short Bed	F23G	32595	**8850**	**10050**	**10400**	**15750**
2500 Long Bed	F23G	32785	**8550**	**9700**	**10400**	**16050**
3500 Long Bed	C03Z	35470	**8950**	**10150**	**10850**	**16750**
2WD	C		**(1000)**	**(1000)**	**(1345)**	**(1345)**
6-Cyl, HO Turbo Dsl	7		**500**	**500**	**670**	**670**
V8, 5.9 Liter	Z		**(2050)**	**(2050)**	**(2720)**	**(2720)**
V10, 8.0 Liter	W		**125**	**125**	**155**	**155**

2003 DODGE — (1,2or3)D(3,4,7or8)-(S38N)-3-#

Body Type	VIN	List	Trade-In Good	Very Good	Pvt-Party Good	Retail Excellent
DURANGO 4WD—V8—Truck Equipment Schedule T1						
Sport SUV 4D	S38N	29640	**1575**	**1875**	**2525**	**4350**
SXT Sport Utility 4D	S38N	30545	**1600**	**1900**	**2550**	**4425**
SLT Sport Utility 4D	S48N	33565	**1700**	**2025**	**2775**	**4800**
R/T Sport Utility 4D	S78Z	39240	**2450**	**2875**	**3750**	**6425**
Third Row Seat			**275**	**275**	**355**	**355**
2WD	R		**(775)**	**(775)**	**(1040)**	**(1040)**
V8, 5.9 Liter (ex R/T)	Z		**150**	**150**	**195**	**195**
CARAVAN—V6—Truck Equipment Schedule T2						
Cargo Minivan	P253	21965	**700**	**825**	**1325**	**2225**
Grand Cargo Minivan	P253	22850	**800**	**925**	**1400**	**2375**
CARAVAN—V6—Truck Equipment Schedule T1						
SE Minivan 4D	P25R	21440	**1175**	**1350**	**1875**	**3125**
Sport Minivan 4D	P453	25110	**1500**	**1700**	**2300**	**3800**
SE Grand Minivan	P24R	22890	**1225**	**1400**	**1975**	**3300**
eL Grand Minivan	P343	24425	**1525**	**1750**	**2375**	**3925**
Sport Grand 4D	P44R	28040	**1850**	**2125**	**2900**	**4775**
5-Passenger Seating			**(275)**	**(275)**	**(355)**	**(355)**
AWD	T		**325**	**325**	**445**	**445**
4-Cyl, 2.4 Liter	B		**(425)**	**(425)**	**(565)**	**(565)**
V6, 3.8 Liter	L		**325**	**325**	**440**	**440**
CARAVAN—V6—Truck Equipment Schedule T1						
EX Grand Minivan	P74L	26400	**1800**	**2075**	**2825**	**4675**
ES Grand Minivan	P54L	33335	**2500**	**2850**	**3725**	**6175**
5-Passenger Seating			**(275)**	**(275)**	**(355)**	**(355)**
AWD	T		**325**	**325**	**445**	**445**
RAM VAN—V6—Truck Equipment Schedule T1						
1500 Cargo Van	B11X	20540	**1800**	**2100**	**2850**	**4975**
1500 Ext Cargo Van	B11X	21175	**1875**	**2175**	**2950**	**5150**
2500 Cargo Van	B21X	21640	**1900**	**2200**	**2975**	**5200**
Maxi-Van			**100**	**100**	**120**	**120**
V8, 5.2 Liter	Y		**150**	**150**	**185**	**185**
V8, 5.9 Liter	Z		**275**	**275**	**355**	**355**
RAM VAN—V8—Truck Equipment Schedule T1						
3500 Cargo Van	B31Y	24415	**2150**	**2500**	**3375**	**5900**
Maxi-Van			**100**	**100**	**120**	**120**
V8, 5.9 Liter	Z		**50**	**50**	**65**	**65**
DAKOTA REGULAR CAB PICKUP—V6—Truck Equipment Sch T1						
2D 6 1/2'	L16X	17680	**950**	**1100**	**1450**	**2325**

Body Type	VIN	List	Trade-In Good	Trade-In Very Good	Pvt-Party Good	Retail Excellent
SXT 2D 6 1/2'	L16X	18420	1125	1275	1625	2575
Sport 2D 6 1/2'	L36X	19000	1075	1225	1575	2500
SLT 2D 6 1/2'	L46X	19000	1175	1350	1700	2675
4WD	G		625	625	820	820
V8, 4.7 Liter	N		150	150	185	185
DAKOTA REGULAR CAB PICKUP—V8—Truck Equipment Sch T1						
R/T 2D 6 1/2'	L76Z	22800	2075	2350	2750	4275
DAKOTA CLUB CAB PICKUP—V6—Truck Equipment Schedule T1						
2D 6 1/2'	L12X	19375	2125	2375	2800	4350
SXT 2D 6 1/2'	L12X	20825	2350	2650	3025	4700
Sport 2D 6 1/2'	L32X	20840	2525	2825	3225	5000
SLT 2D 6 1/2'	L42X	20840	2625	2950	3350	5200
4WD	G		625	625	820	820
V8, 4.7 Liter	N		150	150	185	185
V8, 5.9 Liter	Z		275	275	355	355
DAKOTA CLUB CAB PICKUP—V8—Truck Equipment Schedule T1						
R/T 2D 6 1/2'	L72Z	25100	3425	3850	.4225	6500
DAKOTA QUAD CAB PICKUP—V6—Truck Equipment Schedule T1						
Sport 4D 5'	L38X	22550	2275	2550	3100	4925
SXT 4D 5'	L18X	23415	2625	2950	3425	5375
SLT 4D 5'	L48X	23025	2725	3050	3550	5550
4WD	G		625	625	820	820
V8, 4.7 Liter	N		150	150	185	185
V8, 5.9 Liter	Z		275	275	355	355
RAM REGULAR CAB PICKUP—V6—Truck Equipment Schedule T1						
1500 ST 2D 6 1/4'	A16K	19635	2475	2825	2975	4400
4WD	U		1025	1025	1380	1380
V8, 4.7 Liter	N		325	325	435	435
V8, 5.9 Liter	Z		450	450	600	600
V8, HEMI, 5.7 Liter	D		925	925	1220	1220
RAM REGULAR CAB PICKUP—V8—Truck Equipment Schedule T1						
1500 ST 2D 8'	A16N	20510	2275	2575	2775	4100
1500 SLT 2D 6 1/4'	A16N	23525	3700	4200	4325	6250
1500 SLT 2D 8'	A16N	23810	3475	3925	3950	5700
1500 Laramie 6 1/4'	U16N	30590	4500	5075	5325	7900
1500 Laramie 2D 8'	A16N	27965	2675	3025	3250	4850
4WD	U		1025	1025	1380	1380
V6, 3.7 Liter	K		(400)	(400)	(520)	(520)
V8, 5.9 Liter	Z		150	150	185	185
V8, HEMI, 5.7 Liter	D		575	575	765	765
RAM REGULAR CAB PICKUP 4WD—V8 HEMI—Truck Equipment Sch T1						
2500 ST 2D 8'	U26D	27460	5650	6400	6825	10150
2500 SLT 2D 8'	U26D	29115	6000	6775	6975	10200
2500 Laramie 2D 8'	U26D	33350	6700	7575	7825	11550
2WD	A		(1150)	(1150)	(1525)	(1525)
V10, 8.0 Liter	W		150	150	185	185
6-Cyl, Turbo Diesel	6		2125	2125	2835	2835
6-Cyl, HO Turbo Diesel	C		3475	3475	4620	4620
RAM REGULAR CAB PICKUP—V8 HEMI—Truck Equipment Schedule T1						
3500 ST 2D 8'	A36D	26140	4525	5125	5450	8200
4WD	U		1025	1025	1380	1380
6-Cyl, Turbo Diesel	6		2125	2125	2835	2835
6-Cyl, HO Turbo Dsl	C		3475	3475	4620	4620
V10, 8.0 Liter	W		150	150	185	185
RAM REGULAR CAB PICKUP—6-Cyl. Turbo Diesel—Truck Sch T1						
3500 ST 2D 8'	A466	27890	7975	9000	9125	13350
3500 Laramie 2D 8'	A466	31450	7975	9000	9250	13650
4WD	U		1025	1025	1380	1380
V8, HEMI, 5.7 Liter	D		(2325)	(2325)	(3105)	(3105)
6-Cyl, HO Turbo Dsl	C		575	575	760	760
V10, 8.0 Liter	W		(2175)	(2175)	(2900)	(2900)
RAM QUAD CAB PICKUP—V8—Truck Equipment Schedule T1						
1500 ST 4D 6 1/4'	A18N	26920	3725	4200	4550	6850
1500 ST 4D 8'	A18N	27275	3550	4000	4250	6375
1500 SLT 4D 6 1/4'	A18N	27325	4275	4825	5150	7725
1500 SLT 4D 8'	A18N	27605	3975	4500	4850	7275
1500 Laramie 4D 8'	A18N	31970	4450	5025	5400	8100
4WD	U		1025	1025	1380	1380
V6, 3.7 Liter	K		(400)	(400)	(520)	(520)
V8, HEMI, 5.7 Liter	D		575	575	765	765
V8, 5.9 Liter	Z		150	150	185	185
RAM QUAD CAB PICKUP 4WD—V8—Truck Equipment Schedule T1						
1500 Laramie 6 1/4'	U18N	34435	5175	5850	6575	10050

Body Type	VIN	List	Trade-In Good	Trade-In Very Good	Pvt-Party Good	Retail Excellent
2WD	A	......	(1150)	(1150)	(1525)	(1525)
V6, 3.7 Liter	K	......	(400)	(400)	(520)	(520)
V8, HEMI, 5.7 Liter	D	......	575	575	765	765
V8, 5.9 Liter	Z	......	150	150	185	185
RAM QUAD CAB PICKUP 4WD—V8 HEMI—Truck Equipment Sch T1						
2500 ST 4D 6 1/4'	U28D	29715	6675	7525	7925	11850
2500 Laramie 6 1/4'	U28D	36280	7575	8550	9025	13500
3500 ST 4D 8'	U48D	29315	6600	7450	7950	11950
2WD	A	......	(1150)	(1150)	(1525)	(1525)
6-Cyl, Turbo Diesel	6	......	2125	2125	2835	2835
6-Cyl, HO Turbo Dsl	C	......	3475	3475	4620	4620
RAM QUAD CAB PICKUP 4WD—6-Cyl. Turbo Diesel—Truck Equip Sch T1						
3500 SLT 4D 8'	U486	37255	10100	11400	11650	17200
3500 Laramie 4D 8'	U486	41990	9625	10850	11050	16250
2WD	A	......	(1150)	(1150)	(1525)	(1525)
6-Cyl, HO Turbo Dsl	C	......	575	575	760	760
V8, HEMI, 5.7 Liter	D	......	(2325)	(2325)	(3105)	(3105)
V10, 8.0 Liter	W	......	(2175)	(2175)	(2900)	(2900)
RAM QUAD CAB PICKUP 4WD—V8 Turbo Diesel—Truck Equipment Sch T1						
2500 SLT 4D 6 1/4'	U286	35195	10050	11250	11550	17000
2WD	A	......	(1150)	(1150)	(1525)	(1525)
V8, HEMI, 5.7 Liter	D	......	(2325)	(2325)	(3105)	(3105)
V10, 8.0 Liter	W	......	(2175)	(2175)	(2900)	(2900)
6-Cyl, HO Turbo Dsl	C	......	575	575	760	760
RAM QUAD CAB PICKUP—V8 HEMI—Truck Equipment Schedule T1						
2500 ST 4D 8'	A28D	26790	5175	5825	6225	9375
2500 SLT 4D 8'	A28D	29345	5475	6200	6750	10200
2500 Laramie 4D 8'	A28D	33405	6175	6975	7375	11000
4WD	U	......	1025	1025	1380	1380
6-Cyl, Turbo Diesel	6	......	2125	2125	2835	2835
6-Cyl, HO Turbo Dsl	C	......	3475	3475	4620	4620
V10, 8.0 Liter	W	......	150	150	185	185
RAM QUAD CAB PICKUP—6-Cyl. Turbo Diesel—Truck Schedule T1						
3500 ST 4D 6 1/2'	A386	32405	8900	10050	10250	15200
3500 SLT 4D 6 1/2'	A386	34305	9825	11050	11400	16900
3500 Laramie 4D 6 1/2'	A386	38365	10100	11400	11750	17500
4WD	U	......	1025	1025	1380	1380
6-Cyl, HO Turbo Dsl	C	......	250	250	320	320

2004 DODGE—(1,3orW)D(2,3,4,5,7or8)—(B38N)—4—#

Body Type	VIN	List	Trade-In Good	Trade-In Very Good	Pvt-Party Good	Retail Excellent
DURANGO 4WD—V8—Truck Equipment Schedule T1						
ST Sport Utility 4D	B38N	29745	2125	2475	3175	5250
SLT Sport Utility 4D	B48N	32160	2775	3225	3825	6175
Limited Sport Utility	B58N	35470	3325	3550	4175	5900
Third Row Seat		......	300	300	385	385
2WD	D	......	(875)	(875)	(1155)	(1155)
V6, 3.7 Liter	K	......	(325)	(325)	(445)	(445)
V8, 5.7 Liter	D	......	500	500	680	680
CARAVAN CARGO—V6—Truck Equipment Schedule T2						
Minivan	P21R	22585	825	950	1550	2675
Grand Minivan	P23R	23455	850	975	1600	2775
CARAVAN PASSENGER—4-Cyl.—Truck Equipment Schedule T1						
SE Minivan 4D	P25B	21795	1250	1425	2050	3450
5-Passenger Seating		......	(300)	(300)	(385)	(385)
CARAVAN PASSENGER—V6—Truck Equipment Schedule T1						
SXT Minivan 4D	P45R	24850	1425	1625	2350	3950
SE Grand Minivan	P24R	24975	1375	1550	2300	3900
5-Passenger Seating		......	(300)	(300)	(385)	(385)
CARAVAN PASSENGER—V6—Truck Equipment Schedule T1						
EX Grand Minivan	P74L	27225	2025	2300	3275	5475
SXT Grand Minivan	P44L	30335	2025	2300	3275	5475
AWD	T	......	375	375	510	510
DAKOTA REGULAR CAB PICKUP—V6—Truck Equipment Schedule T1						
Pickup 2D 6 1/2'	L16K	18940	1550	1750	2175	3475
SXT 2D 6 1/2'	L16X	19205	1650	1850	2375	3750
Sport 2D 6 1/2'	L36K	19785	1700	1900	2350	3725
SLT 2D 6 1/2'	L46K	19785	1825	2075	2600	4100
4WD	G	......	750	750	1000	1000
V8, 4.7 Liter	N	......	275	275	375	375
DAKOTA CLUB CAB PICKUP—V6—Truck Equipment Schedule T1						
2D 6 1/2'	L12K	21610	2400	2700	3075	4675
SXT 2D 6 1/2'	L22X	21615	2875	3225	3725	5825
Sport 2D 6 1/2'	L32K	21625	3075	3425	3950	6150

2004 DODGE/PLYMOUTH

Body Type	VIN	List	Trade-In Good	Trade-In Very Good	Pvt-Party Good	Retail Excellent
SLT 2D 6 1/2'	L42K	21625	3325	3700	4125	6325
4WD	G		750	750	1000	1000
V8, 4.7 Liter	N		275	275	375	375
DAKOTA QUAD CAB PICKUP—V6—Truck Equipment Schedule T1						
Sport 4D 5 1/2'	L38K	23810	2900	3250	3875	6100
SXT 4D 5 1/2'	L23X	23810	3350	3750	4400	6925
SLT 4D 5 1/2'	L48K	23810	3450	3850	4500	7100
4WD	G		750	750	1000	1000
V8, 4.7 Liter	N		275	275	375	375
RAM REGULAR CAB PICKUP—V6—Truck Equipment Schedule T1						
1500 ST 2D 6 1/4'	A16K	20860	3225	3600	3725	5350
4WD	N		1175	1175	1555	1555
V8, 4.7 Liter	N		375	375	485	485
V8, Flex Fuel, 4.7 Liter			350	350	450	450
V8, HEMI, 5.7 Liter			900	900	1200	1200
RAM REGULAR CAB PICKUP—V8—Truck Equipment Schedule T1						
1500 ST 2D 8'	A16N	22580	2950	3325	3475	5025
1500 SLT 2D 6 1/4'	A16N	25400	4375	4900	4975	7125
1500 SLT 2D 8'	A16N	25685	4025	4525	4600	6575
1500 Laramie 2D 8'	A16N	28620	3500	3950	4075	5950
4WD	U		1175	1175	1555	1555
V6, 3.7 Liter	K		(425)	(425)	(555)	(555)
V8, HEMI, 5.7 Liter	D		625	625	820	820
RAM REGULAR CAB PICKUP 4WD—V8—Truck Equipment Schedule T1						
1500 Laramie 6 1/4'	U16N	32010	5575	6250	6625	9650
2WD			(1475)	(1475)	(1960)	(1960)
V8, HEMI, 5.7 Liter	D		625	625	820	820
RAM REGULAR CAB PICKUP 4WD—V8 HEMI—Truck Equipment Schedule T1						
2500 ST 2D 8'	U26D	28825	7400	8300	8375	12000
2500 SLT 2D 8'	U26D	30530	7850	8800	8875	12150
2500 Laramie 2D 8'	U26D	34835	8625	9675	9550	13500
2WD	C		(1475)	(1475)	(1860)	(1860)
6-Cyl, Turbo Diesel	6		2475	2475	3140	3140
6-Cyl, HO Turbo Dsl	D		3650	3650	4620	4620
RAM REGULAR CAB PICKUP—V8 HEMI—Truck Equipment Schedule T1						
3500 ST 2D 8'	A36D	27975	5975	6700	6875	9850
4WD	U		1175	1175	1485	1485
6-Cyl, Turbo Diesel	6		2475	2475	3160	3160
6-Cyl, HO Turbo Dsl	D		3650	3650	4650	4650
RAM REGULAR CAB PICKUP—V8 Turbo Diesel—Truck Equipment Sch T1						
3500 SLT 2D 8'	A466	29050	9425	10550	10500	14900
3500 Laramie 2D 8'	A466	32680	9950	11150	11050	15700
4WD	U		1175	1175	1470	1470
V8, HEMI, 5.7 Liter	D		(2625)	(2625)	(3300)	(3300)
6-Cyl, HO Turbo Dsl	D		475	475	610	610
RAM REGULAR CAB PICKUP—V10—Truck Equipment Schedule T1						
1500 SRT-10 2D 6 1/4'	A16H	47635	11500	12450	12500	17000
Manual, 6-Spd			0	0	0	0
RAM QUAD CAB PICKUP—V8—Truck Equipment Schedule T1						
1500 ST 4D 6 1/4'	A18N	26455	4725	5300	5600	8275
1500 ST 4D 8'	A18N	26735	4400	4950	5275	7750
1500 SLT 4D 6 1/4'	A18N	28470	5300	5950	6200	9050
1500 SLT 4D 8'	A18N	28750	4900	5500	5800	8550
1500 Laramie 8'	A18N	31070	5350	6000	6475	9575
4WD	U		1175	1175	1555	1555
V6, 3.7 Liter	K		(425)	(425)	(555)	(555)
V8, HEMI, 5.7 Liter	D		625	625	820	820
RAM QUAD CAB PICKUP 4WD—V8—Truck Equipment Schedule T1						
1500 Laramie 6 1/4'	U18N	35965	6450	7250	7925	11950
2WD			(1475)	(1475)	(1960)	(1960)
V8, HEMI, 5.7 Liter	D		625	625	820	820
RAM QUAD CAB PICKUP—V8 HEMI—Truck Equipment Schedule T1						
2500 ST 4D 8'	A28D	28660	7025	7875	7975	11500
2500 SLT 4D 8'	A28D	30540	7375	8275	8475	12200
2500 Laramie 4D 8'	A28D	33055	8000	8975	9025	12900
4WD	U		1175	1175	1500	1500
6-Cyl, Turbo Diesel	6		2475	2475	3195	3195
6-Cyl, HO Turbo Dsl	D		3650	3650	4700	4700
RAM QUAD CAB PICKUP 4WD—V8 HEMI—Truck Equipment Schedule T1						
2500 ST 4D 6 1/4'	U28D	31115	8875	9950	9950	14250
2500 Laramie 6 1/4'	U28D	37990	9775	10950	11000	15800
3500 ST 4D 8'	U48D	33860	8775	9850	9900	14200
2WD	C		(1475)	(1475)	(1875)	(1875)

Body Type	VIN	List	Trade-In Good	Trade-In Very Good	Pvt-Party Good	Retail Excellent
6-Cyl, Turbo Diesel	6		2475	2475	3170	3170
6-Cyl, HO Turbo Dsl	C		3650	3650	4660	4660
RAM QUAD CAB PICKUP 4WD—6-Cyl. Turbo Diesel—Truck Sch T1						
2500 SLT 4D 6 1/4'	U286	38335	12500	13950	13700	19500
3500 SLT 4D 8'	U486	39660	12750	14250	14000	19950
3500 Laramie 4D 8'	U486	43850	11150	12450	12300	17600
2WD	C		(1475)	(1475)	(1865)	(1865)
6-Cyl, HO Turbo Dsl	D		475	475	610	610
V8, HEMI, 5.7 Liter	D		(2625)	(2625)	(3325)	(3325)
RAM QUAD CAB PICKUP—6-Cyl. Turbo Diesel—Truck Schedule T1						
3500 SLT 4D 6 1/4'	A386	35060	11050	12350	12200	17400
4WD	U		1175	1175	1480	1480
6-Cyl, HO Turbo Dsl	D		275	275	335	335
RAM QUAD CAB PICKUP 4WD—6-Cyl. Turbo Diesel—Truck Sch T1						
3500 SLT 4D 6 1/4'	U386	38120	13200	14800	14400	20400
3500 Laramie 6 1/4'	U386	42925	13600	15250	14950	21300
2WD	A		(1475)	(1475)	(1865)	(1865)

2005 DODGE — (1,3orW)D(2,3,4,5,7or8)-(B38N)-5-#

Body Type	VIN	List	Trade-In Good	Trade-In Very Good	Pvt-Party Good	Retail Excellent
DURANGO 4WD—V8—Truck Equipment Schedule T1						
ST Sport Utility 4D	B38N	30610	3225	3725	4325	6625
SXT Sport Utility	B38N	30900	3200	3700	4325	6625
SLT Sport Utility	B48N	33380	3450	4000	4750	7300
Limited Sport Utility	B58N	36560	3700	3950	5075	7125
Third Row Seat			325	325	420	420
2WD	D		(950)	(950)	(1260)	(1260)
V6, 3.7 Liter	K		(375)	(375)	(510)	(510)
V8, HEMI, 5.7 Liter	D		550	550	725	725
CARAVAN CARGO—V6—Truck Equipment Schedule T2						
Minivan	P21R	20185	975	1125	1825	3000
Grand Minivan	P23R	20885	975	1150	1925	3200
CARAVAN PASSENGER—V6—Truck Equipment Schedule T1						
Minivan 4D	P25R	18995	1300	1500	2275	3700
SXT Minivan 4D	P45R	22485	1600	1850	2775	4525
Grand Minivan 4D	P24R	22185	1650	1875	2850	4650
SXT Grand Minivan	P44L	27185	2150	2475	3500	5700
5-Passenger Seating			(325)	(325)	(420)	(420)
4-Cyl, 2.4 Liter	B		(575)	(575)	(765)	(765)
DAKOTA CLUB CAB PICKUP—V6—Truck Equipment Schedule T1						
ST 2D 6 1/2'	E22K	21400	2950	3300	3850	5725
SLT 2D 6 1/2'	E42K	23155	3800	4250	4875	7175
4WD	W		875	875	1155	1155
V8, 4.7 Liter	N		325	325	420	420
V8, HO, 4.7 Liter	J		325	325	420	420
DAKOTA CLUB CAB PICKUP 4WD—V8—Truck Equipment Schedule T1						
Laramie 2D 6 1/2'	W52N	28619	5850	6550	7150	10400
2WD	E		(1000)	(1000)	(1320)	(1320)
V6, 3.7 Liter	K		(325)	(325)	(435)	(435)
DAKOTA QUAD CAB PICKUP—V6—Truck Equipment Schedule T1						
ST 4D 5 1/2'	E28K	22800	3325	3725	4575	7000
4WD	W		875	875	1155	1155
V8, 4.7 Liter	N		325	325	420	420
DAKOTA QUAD CAB PICKUP 4WD—V8—Truck Equipment Schedule T1						
SLT 4D 5 1/2'	W48N	28490	5450	6125	6875	10150
Laramie 4D 5 1/2'	W58N	30695	6125	6850	7575	11150
2WD	E		(1000)	(1000)	(1320)	(1320)
V6, 3.7 Liter	K		(325)	(325)	(435)	(435)
RAM REGULAR CAB PICKUP—V6—Truck Equipment Schedule T1						
1500 ST 2D 6 1/4'	A16K	22125	3850	4325	4800	6850
4WD	U		1275	1275	1690	1690
V8, 4.7 Liter	N		400	400	535	535
V8, Flex Fuel, 4.7 Liter	P		375	375	495	495
V8, HEMI, 5.7 Liter	D		1000	1000	1320	1320
RAM REGULAR CAB PICKUP—V8—Truck Equipment Schedule T1						
1500 ST 2D 8'	A16N	23520	3750	4225	4700	6725
1500 SLT 2D 6 1/4'	A16N	25650	4600	5150	5650	8075
1500 SLT 2D 8'	A16N	25935	4350	4875	5350	7600
1500 Laramie 8'	A16N	30085	4600	5175	5625	8000
4WD	U		1275	1275	1690	1690
V6, 3.7 Liter	K		(450)	(450)	(585)	(585)
V8, HEMI, 5.7 Liter	D		650	650	880	880
RAM REGULAR CAB PICKUP 4WD—V8—Truck Equipment Schedule T1						
1500 Laramie 6 1/4'	U16N	33120	6800	7625	8275	11850

SEE BACK PAGES FOR TRUCK EQUIPMENT

TRUCKS & VANS

Body Type	VIN	List	Trade-In Good	Very Good	Pvt-Party Good	Retail Excellent
2WD	A	......	(1625)	(1625)	(2175)	(2175)
V6, 3.7 Liter	K	......	(450)	(450)	(585)	(585)
V8, HEMI, 5.7 Liter	D	......	650	650	880	880
RAM REGULAR CAB PICKUP 4WD—V8 HEMI—Truck Equipment Sch T1						
2500 ST 2D 8'	S26D	29790	7900	8825	9050	12650
2500 SLT 2D 8'	S26D	31495	8500	9500	9525	13100
2500 Laramie 8'	S26D	34040	8750	9775	9925	13750
Power Wagon		......	4175	4175	5110	5110
2WD	R	......	(1625)	(1625)	(2015)	(2015)
6-Cyl, HO Turbo Dsl	C	......	3850	3850	4755	4755
RAM REGULAR CAB PICKUP 4WD—V8 HEMI—Truck Equipment Sch T1						
3500 ST 2D 8' DR	R36D	28720	7125	7975	8275	11550
4WD	S	......	1275	1275	1565	1565
6-Cyl, HO Turbo Dsl	C	......	3850	3850	4745	4745
RAM REGULAR CAB PICKUP—V8 Turbo Diesel—Truck Equip Sch T1						
3500 SLT 2D 8' DR	R46C	29795	11750	13050	12800	17550
3500 Laramie 8' DR	R46C	33425	12400	13800	13550	18650
4WD	S	......	1275	1275	1515	1515
V8, HEMI, 5.7 Liter	D	......	(2925)	(2925)	(3490)	(3490)
RAM REGULAR CAB PICKUP—V10—Truck Equipment Schedule T1						
1500 SRT-10 2D 6 1/4'	A16H	45850	12200	13150	13900	19050
Manual, 6-Spd		......	0	0	0	0
RAM QUAD CAB PICKUP—V8—Truck Equipment Schedule T1						
1500 ST 4D 6 1/4'	A18N	27305	5850	6550	7175	10300
1500 ST 4D 8'	A18N	27660	5600	6275	6875	9825
1500 SLT 4D 6 1/4'	A18N	29395	6375	7150	7700	11000
1500 SLT 4D 8'	A18N	29675	6025	6750	7350	10550
1500 Laramie 8'	A18N	31995	6550	7325	7900	11350
4WD	U	......	1275	1275	1690	1690
V6, 3.7 Liter	K	......	(450)	(450)	(585)	(585)
V8, HEMI, 5.7 Liter	D	......	650	650	880	880
RAM QUAD CAB PICKUP 4WD—V8—Truck Equipment Schedule T1						
1500 Laramie 6 1/4'	U18N	35925	8325	9300	10050	14600
2WD	A	......	(1625)	(1625)	(2175)	(2175)
V6, 3.7 Liter	K	......	(450)	(450)	(585)	(585)
V8, HEMI, 5.7 Liter	D	......	650	650	880	880
RAM QUAD CAB PICKUP—V10—Truck Equipment Schedule T1						
1500 SRT-10 2D 6 1/4'	A18H	50850	12600	13600	13950	18800
RAM QUAD CAB PICKUP—V8 HEMI—Truck Equipment Schedule T1						
2500 ST 4D 8'	R28D	29605	7275	8125	8525	12000
2500 SLT 4D 8'	R28D	31485	7850	8775	9100	12800
2500 Laramie 8'	R28D	35615	8625	9625	9850	13750
4WD	S	......	1275	1275	1599	1599
6-Cyl, HO Turbo Dsl	C	......	3850	3850	4825	4825
RAM QUAD CAB PICKUP 4WD—V8 HEMI—Truck Equipment Schedule T1						
2500 Laramie 6 1/4'	S28D	38765	10700	1950	12100	16950
2500 SLT 4D 6 1/4'	S28D	32080	9625	10750	10850	15100
3500 SLT 4D 8'	S48D	34825	9625	10750	11050	15500
2WD	R	......	(1625)	(1625)	(1960)	(1960)
6-Cyl, HO Turbo Dsl	C	......	3850	3850	4625	4625
RAM QUAD CAB PICKUP 4WD—6-Cyl. HO Turbo Diesel—Truck Sch T1						
2500 SLT 4D 6 1/4'	S28C	39345	14200	15850	15600	21600
3500 SLT 4D 8'	S48C	41440	14950	16600	16350	22600
3500 Laramie 8'	S48C	44105	15250	16950	16600	22900
2WD	R	......	(1625)	(1625)	(1965)	(1965)
Power Wagon		......	4175	4175	5050	5050
V8, HEMI, 5.7 Liter	D	......	(2925)	(2925)	(3515)	(3515)
RAM QUAD CAB PICKUP—6-Cyl. HO Turbo Diesel—Truck Schedule T1						
3500 SLT 4D 6 1/4'	R38C	36500	11950	13300	13300	18500
4WD	S	......	1275	1275	1555	1555
RAM QUAD CAB PICKUP 4WD—6-Cyl. HO Turbo Diesel—Truck Sch T1						
3500 SLT 4D 6 1/4'	S38C	39820	15150	16850	16500	22700
3500 Laramie 6 1/4'	S38C	42465	16000	17800	17400	24000
2WD	R	......	(1625)	(1625)	(1970)	(1970)

2006 DODGE — (1,3orW)D(2,3,4,5,7or8)-(B38N)-6-#

DURANGO 4WD—V8—Truck Equipment Schedule T1						
SXT Sport Utility 4D	B38N	31825	4075	4650	5325	7900
SLT Sport Utility 4D	B48N	34275	4400	5000	5700	8500
Limited Sport Utility	B58N	38155	4775	5075	6175	8400
Third Row Seat		......	350	350	455	455
2WD	D	......	(1025)	(1025)	(1375)	(1375)
V6, 3.7 Liter	K	......	(425)	(425)	(575)	(575)

Body Type	VIN	List	Trade-In Good	Very Good	Pvt-Party Good	Retail Excellent
V8, HEMI, 5.7 Liter	2	......	575	575	775	775
CARAVAN CARGO—V6—Truck Equipment Schedule T2						
Minivan	P21R	20645	1075	1225	2000	3275
Grand Minivan	P23R	21345	1300	1500	2275	3675
CARAVAN PASSENGER—V6—Truck Equipment Schedule T1						
SE Minivan 4D	P25R	19095	1475	1675	2475	3950
SXT Minivan 4D	P45R	23035	2000	2275	3150	4975
Grand Minivan 4D	P24R	23745	2175	2450	3425	5400
SXT Grand Minivan	P44L	27830	2800	3150	4175	6550
5-Passenger Seating			(350)	(350)	(455)	(455)
4-Cyl, 2.4 Liter	B		(625)	(625)	(845)	(845)
DAKOTA CLUB CAB PICKUP—V6—Truck Equipment Schedule T1						
ST 2D 6 1/2'	E22K	21750	3025	3400	3950	5775
SLT 2D 6 1/2'	E42K	23685	4425	4925	5400	7675
4WD	W		975	975	1290	1290
V8, 4.7 Liter	N		350	350	455	455
V8, HO, 4.7 Liter	J		350	350	455	455
DAKOTA CLUB CAB PICKUP 4WD—V8—Truck Equipment Schedule T1						
Laramie 2D 6 1/2'	W52N	29450	6750	7500	7950	11250
2WD	E		(1075)	(1075)	(1445)	(1445)
V6, 3.7 Liter	K		(350)	(350)	(475)	(475)
DAKOTA QUAD CAB PICKUP—V6—Truck Equipment Schedule T1						
ST 4D 5 1/2'	E28K	23150	3950	4400	4975	7200
4WD	W		975	975	1290	1290
V8, 4.7 Liter	N		350	350	455	455
DAKOTA QUAD CAB PICKUP 4WD—V8—Truck Equipment Schedule T1						
SLT 4D 5 1/2'	W58N	28540	6425	7125	7725	11050
Laramie 4D 5 1/2'	W58N	31015	7875	8750	9325	13350
2WD	E		(1075)	(1075)	(1445)	(1445)
V6, 3.7 Liter	K		(350)	(350)	(475)	(475)
RAM REGULAR CAB PICKUP—V6—Truck Equipment Schedule T1						
1500 ST 2D 6 1/4'	A16K	22795	4625	5125	5550	7675
4WD	U		1500	1500	2000	2000
V8, 4.7 Liter	N		450	450	585	585
V8, Flex Fuel, 4.7 Liter	P		400	400	540	540
V8, HEMI, 5.7 Liter	2		1100	1100	1455	1455
RAM REGULAR CAB PICKUP—V8—Truck Equipment Schedule T1						
1500 ST 2D 8'	A16N	23865	4300	4800	5250	7300
1500 SLT 2D 6 1/4'	A16N	26220	5125	5700	6300	8775
1500 SLT 2D 8'	A16N	26505	4950	5500	5925	8225
1500 Laramie 6 1/4'	U16N	34855	7850	8675	9250	12900
1500 Laramie 8'	A16N	30505	5250	5850	6425	8925
4WD	U		1500	1500	2000	2000
V6, 3.7 Liter	K		(450)	(450)	(600)	(600)
V8, HEMI, 5.7 Liter	2		700	700	935	935
RAM REGULAR CAB PICKUP—V8 HEMI—Truck Equipment Schedule T1						
3500 ST 2D 8' DR	L36D	29065	10650	11750	11450	15200
4WD	S,X		1500	1500	1755	1755
6-Cyl, HO Turbo Dsl	C		4025	4025	4725	4725
RAM REGULAR CAB 4WD—V8 HEMI—Truck Equipment Schedule T1						
2500 ST 2D 8'	S26D	30460	11200	12400	12100	16050
2500 SLT 2D 8'	S26D	32115	11700	12950	12450	16450
2500 Laramie 2D 8'	S26D	34635	12300	13600	13150	17400
Power Wagon			4375	4375	5110	5110
2WD	R,L		(2000)	(2000)	(2330)	(2330)
6-Cyl, HO Turbo Dsl	C		4025	4025	4695	4695
RAM REGULAR CAB—6-Cyl, HO Turbo Diesel—Truck Equipment Sch T1						
3500 SLT 2D 8' DR	L46C	30621	15500	17100	16300	21500
3500 Laramie 8' DR	L46C	31615	16100	17750	17000	22500
4WD	S,X		1500	1500	1735	1735
V8, HEMI, 5.7 Liter	D		(3200)	(3200)	(3710)	(3710)
RAM REGULAR CAB PICKUP—V10—Truck Equipment Schedule T1						
1500 SRT-10 6 1/4'	A16H	48505	13050	14000	14400	18950
Manual, 6-Spd			0	0	0	0
RAM QUAD CAB PICKUP—V8—Truck Equipment Schedule T1						
1500 ST 4D 6 1/4'	A18N	27650	6850	7600	8150	11400
1500 ST 4D 8'	A18N	28005	6650	7375	7950	11100
1500 SLT 4D 6 1/4'	A18N	29710	7450	8250	8800	12300
1500 SLT 4D 8'	A18N	29990	7125	7900	8525	11950
1500 Laramie 8'	A18N	33700	7700	8525	9075	12650
4WD	U		1500	1500	2000	2000
V6, 3.7 Liter	K		(450)	(450)	(600)	(600)
V8, HEMI, 5.7 Liter	2		700	700	935	935

TRUCKS & VANS

Body Type	VIN	List	Trade-In Good	Very Good	Pvt-Party Good	Retail Excellent
RAM QUAD CAB PICKUP 4WD—V8—Truck Equipment Schedule T1						
1500 Laramie 6 1/4'	U18N	37500	9700	10700	11450	16200
2WD	A		(2000)	(2000)	(2675)	(2675)
V8, HEMI, 5.7 Liter	2		700	700	935	935
RAM QUAD CAB PICKUP—V10—Truck Equipment Schedule T1						
1500 SRT-10 6 1/4'	A18H	52710	14300	15350	15700	20700
RAM QUAD CAB PICKUP—V8 HEMI—Truck Equipment Schedule T1						
2500 ST 4D 8'	R28D	30245	11100	12250	12050	16050
2500 SLT 4D 8'	R28D	32400	11550	12750	12550	16750
2500 Laramie 8'	R28D	34825	12250	13500	13150	17500
4WD	S,X		1500	1500	1770	1770
6-Cyl, HO Turbo Dsl	C		4025	4025	4765	4765
RAM QUAD CAB PICKUP 4WD—V8 HEMI—Truck Equipment Schedule T1						
2500 ST 4D 6 1/4'	S28D	38600	13600	15000	14600	19400
2500 Laramie 6 1/4'	S28D	37355	14550	16050	15650	20900
3500 ST 4D 8'	X48D	35915	13600	15000	14750	19750
2WD	R,L		(2000)	(2000)	(2340)	(2340)
6-Cyl, HO Turbo Dsl	C		4025	4025	4715	4715
RAM QUAD CAB 4WD—6-Cyl. HO Turbo Diesel—Truck Equipment Schedule T1						
3500 SLT 4D 8'	X48C	42615	18850	20800	19900	26600
3500 Laramie 8'	X48C	44950	19400	21400	20400	27100
2WD	R,L		(2000)	(2000)	(2340)	(2340)
V8, HEMI, 5.7 Liter	D		(3200)	(3200)	(3745)	(3745)
RAM QUAD CAB 4WD—6-Cyl. HO Turbo Diesel—Truck Equipment Sch T1						
2500 SLT 4D 6 1/4'	S28C	40500	18400	20300	19400	25800
Power Wagon			4375	4375	5115	5115
2WD	R,L		(2000)	(2000)	(2340)	(2340)
V8, HEMI, 5.7 Liter	D		(3200)	(3200)	(3740)	(3740)
RAM QUAD CAB PICKUP—6-Cyl. HO Turbo Diesel—Truck Schedule T1						
3500 ST 4D 6 1/4'	L38C	37065	16050	17700	17150	22900
4WD	S,X		1500	1500	1770	1770
RAM QUAD CAB 4WD—6-Cyl. HO Turbo Diesel—Truck Equipment Schedule T1						
3500 SLT 4D 6 1/4'	X38C	41375	19300	21300	20300	27000
3500 Laramie 6 1/4'	X38C	43710	19850	21900	20900	27900
2WD	R,L		(2000)	(2000)	(2345)	(2345)
RAM MEGA CAB PICKUP 4WD—V8 HEMI—Truck Equipment Schedule T1						
1500 SLT 4D 6 1/4'	S19D	35980	12700	14050	14550	20300
1500 Laramie 6 1/4'	S19D	41075	12450	13750	14200	19800
2WD	R		(2000)	(2000)	(2675)	(2675)
RAM MEGA CAB 4WD—6-Cyl. HO Turbo Diesel—Truck Equipment Sch T1						
2500 SLT 4D 6 1/4'	S29C	40500	22100	24300	22900	30300
2500 Laramie 6 1/4'	S29C	42835	22500	24800	23300	30800
2WD	R		(2000)	(2000)	(2325)	(2325)
V8, HEMI, 5.7 Liter	D		(3200)	(3200)	(3715)	(3715)
RAM MEGA CAB 4WD—6-Cyl. HO Turbo Diesel—Truck Schedule T1						
3500 SLT 4D 6 1/4'	X39C	44595	21200	23300	22200	29500
3500 Laramie 6 1/4'	X39C	49690	22400	24700	23200	30600
2WD	R		(2000)	(2000)	(2345)	(2345)

2007 DODGE — (1,2or3)D(2,3,4,5,7or8)–(U28K)–7–#

Body Type	VIN	List	Trade-In Good	Very Good	Pvt-Party Good	Retail Excellent
NITRO 4WD—V6—Truck Equipment Schedule T1						
SXT Sport Utility 4D	U28K	22495	5850	6425	7125	9750
SLT Sport Utility 4D	U58K	24805	6575	7225	7875	10800
R/T Sport Utility 4D	U586	25795	8175	8975	9625	13150
2WD	T		(675)	(675)	(910)	(910)
DURANGO 4WD—V8—Truck Equipment Schedule T1						
SXT Sport Util 4D	B38N	29855	5050	5675	6450	9225
SLT Sport Util 4D	B48N	32675	5450	6125	6875	9800
Limited Sport Util	B58N	36670	6700	7075	8225	10700
Third Row Seat	K		375	375	485	485
2WD	D		(1100)	(1100)	(1480)	(1480)
V6, 3.7 Liter	K		(475)	(475)	(645)	(645)
V8, HEMI, 5.7 Liter	2		625	625	820	820
CARAVAN CARGO—V6—Truck Equipment Schedule T2						
Minivan	P21R	20845	2050	2300	3200	4925
Grand Minivan	P23R	21545	2200	2450	3475	5200
CARAVAN PASSENGER—V6—Truck Equipment Schedule T1						
Minivan 4D	P25R	19345	2325	2600	3500	5375
SXT Minivan 4D	P45R	23235	2900	3250	4175	6350
Grand Minivan 4D	P24R	23995	3075	3425	4400	6700
SXT Grand Minivan	P44L	28030	3875	4325	5500	8325
5-Passenger Seating			(375)	(375)	(485)	(485)
4-Cyl, 2.4 Liter	B		(675)	(675)	(910)	(910)

2007 DODGE/PLYMOUTH

Body Type	VIN	List	Trade-In Good	Very Good	Pvt-Party Good	Retail Excellent
DAKOTA CLUB CAB PICKUP—V6—Truck Equipment Schedule T1						
ST 2D 6 1/2'	E22K	20840	3325	3725	4350	6175
SLT 2D 6 1/2'	E42K	24630	5300	5875	6525	9175
4WD	W		1075	1075	1420	1420
V8, 4.7 Liter	N		375	375	485	485
V8, HO, 4.7 Liter	J		375	375	485	485
DAKOTA CLUB CAB PICKUP 4WD—V8—Truck Equipment Schedule T1						
Laramie 2D 6 1/2'	W52N	29285	7850	8675	9200	12850
2WD	E		(1625)	(1625)	(2155)	(2155)
V6, 3.7 Liter	K		(375)	(375)	(515)	(515)
DAKOTA QUAD CAB PICKUP—V6—Truck Equipment Schedule T1						
ST 4D 5 1/2'	E28K	23540	4875	5400	6025	8575
4WD	N		1075	1075	1420	1420
V8, 4.7 Liter	N		375	375	485	485
DAKOTA QUAD CAB PICKUP 4WD—V8—Truck Equipment Schedule T1						
SLT 4D 5 1/2'	W48N	29975	7725	8550	9250	13050
2WD	E		(1625)	(1625)	(2155)	(2155)
V6, 3.7 Liter	K		(375)	(375)	(515)	(515)
DAKOTA QUAD CAB PICKUP 4WD—V8—Truck Equipment Schedule T1						
Laramie 4D 5 1/2'	W58N	31070	8400	9275	9950	14050
2WD	E		(1625)	(1625)	(2155)	(2155)
V6, 3.7 Liter	K		(375)	(375)	(515)	(515)
RAM REGULAR CAB PICKUP—V6—Truck Equipment Schedule T1						
1500 ST 2D 6 1/4'	A16K	23375	5200	5725	6200	8450
4WD	U		1875	1875	2440	2440
V8, 4.7 Liter	N		450	450	590	590
V8, Flex Fuel, 4.7 Liter	P		450	450	575	575
V8, HEMI, 5.7 Liter	2		1175	1175	1545	1545
RAM REGULAR CAB PICKUP—V8—Truck Equipment Schedule T1						
1500 ST 2D 8'	A16N	24265	4675	5125	5700	7850
1500 SLT 2D 6 1/4'	A16N	26750	5675	6225	6900	9425
1500 SLT 2D 8'	A16N	27035	5525	6075	6750	9200
4WD	U		1875	1875	2485	2485
V6, 3.7 Liter	K		(450)	(450)	(600)	(600)
V8, HEMI, 5.7 Liter	2		750	750	985	985
RAM REGULAR CAB PICKUP—V8 HEMI—Truck Equipment Schedule T1						
3500 ST 2D 8' DR	L36D	29425	9675	10600	10850	14450
Power Wagon			4575	4575	5430	5430
4WD	S,X		1875	1875	2225	2225
6-Cyl, HO Trb Dsl 5.9L	C		4225	4225	5040	5040
6-Cyl, Turbo Dsl 6.7L	A		4550	4550	5405	5405
RAM REGULAR CAB 4WD—V8 HEMI—Truck Equipment Schedule T1						
2500 ST 2D 8'	S26D	30820	10350	11300	11500	15250
2500 SLT 2D 8'	S26D	32520	10950	11950	11950	15600
2WD	C		(2175)	(2175)	(2595)	(2595)
6-Cyl, HO Trb Dsl 5.9L	C		4225	4225	5035	5035
6-Cyl, Turbo Dsl 6.7L	A		4550	4550	5395	5395
RAM REGULAR CAB—6-Cyl. Turbo Diesel—Truck Equipment Sch T1						
3500 ST 2D 8' DR	L46A	30570	14300	15600	15450	20300
4WD	S,X		1875	1875	2210	2210
6-Cyl, HO Trb Dsl 5.9L	C		(250)	(250)	(300)	(300)
V8, HEMI, 5.7 Liter	D		(4125)	(4125)	(4870)	(4870)
RAM QUAD CAB PICKUP—V8—Truck Equipment Schedule T1						
1500 ST 4D 6 1/4'	A18N	28010	7400	8125	8800	12050
1500 ST 4D 8'	A18N	28365	7250	7950	8675	11900
1500 SLT 4D 6 1/4'	A18N	30320	8375	9150	9800	13400
1500 SLT 4D 8'	A18N	30600	7650	8400	9175	12600
4WD	U		1875	1875	2480	2480
V6, 3.7 Liter	K		(450)	(450)	(595)	(595)
V8, HEMI, 5.7 Liter	2		750	750	985	985
RAM QUAD CAB PICKUP 4WD—V8 HEMI—Truck Equipment Schedule T1						
1500 Laramie 6 1/4'	U182	37565	11500	12600	13250	18100
2WD	R		(2175)	(2175)	(2910)	(2910)
RAM QUAD CAB PICKUP 4WD—V8 HEMI—Truck Equipment Schedule T1						
2500 ST 4D 8'	R28D	30530	9725	10650	10950	14550
2500 SLT 4D 8'	R28D	32530	10250	11250	11550	15450
2500 Laramie 8'	R28D	35011	11000	12050	12300	16300
4WD	S,X		1875	1875	2280	2280
6-Cyl, HO Trb Dsl 5.9L	C		4225	4225	5165	5165
6-Cyl, Turbo Dsl 6.7L	A		4550	4550	5535	5535
RAM QUAD CAB PICKUP 4WD—V8 HEMI—Truck Equipment Schedule T1						
2500 ST 4D 6 1/4'	S28D	37860	12800	14000	14050	18550
2500 Laramie 6 1/4'	S28D	37860	13300	14550	14800	19750

Body Type	VIN	List	Trade-In Good	Very Good	Pvt-Party Good	Retail Excellent
3500 ST 4D 8'	X48D	36275	12700	13900	14100	18850
2WD	R		(2175)	(2175)	(2625)	(2625)
6-Cyl, HO Trb Dsl 5.9L	C		4225	4225	5055	5055
6-Cyl, Turbo Dsl 6.7L	A		4550	4550	5460	5460
RAM QUAD CAB 4WD—6-Cyl. Turbo Diesel—Truck Equipment Sch T1						
3500 Laramie 8'	X48A	45014	19100	20800	20500	27000
2WD	R		(2175)	(2175)	(2590)	(2590)
6-Cyl, HO Trb Dsl 5.9L	C		(250)	(250)	(300)	(300)
V8, HEMI, 5.7 Liter	8		(4125)	(4125)	(4885)	(4885)
RAM QUAD CAB PICKUP—6-Cyl. Turbo Diesel—Truck Schedule T1						
3500 ST 4D 6 1/4'	L38A	37425	15100	16500	16500	21900
4WD	S,X		1875	1875	2230	2230
6-Cyl, HO Trb Dsl 5.9L	C		(300)	(300)	(360)	(360)
RAM QUAD CAB 4WD—6-Cyl. Turbo Diesel—Truck Equipment Sch T1						
2500 SLT 4D 6 1/4'	X28A	40985	18050	19700	19400	25600
3500 SLT 4D 6 1/4'	X38A	41810	18700	20400	20100	26400
3500 SLT 4D 8'	X48A	43100	18650	20300	20000	26500
3500 Laramie 6 1/4'	X38A	43315	19200	20900	20600	27300
Power Wagon			4575	4575	5450	5450
2WD	R		(2175)	(2175)	(2585)	(2585)
6-Cyl, HO Trb Dsl 5.9L	C		(250)	(250)	(300)	(300)
V8, HEMI, 5.7 Liter	8		(4125)	(4125)	(4880)	(4880)
RAM MEGA CAB PICKUP 4WD—V8 HEMI—Truck Equipment Schedule T1						
1500 SLT 4D 6 1/4'	S19D	36845	14650	16000	16500	22400
1500 Laramie 6 1/4'	S19D	42050	14800	16150	16650	22500
2WD			(2175)	(2175)	(2785)	(2785)
RAM MEGA CAB PICKUP 4WD—6-Cyl. Turbo Diesel—Truck Equip Sch T1						
2500 SLT 4D 6 1/4'	S29A	44120	23000	25100	24000	31300
2WD	R		(2175)	(2175)	(2530)	(2530)
6-Cyl, HO Trb Dsl 5.9L	C		(250)	(250)	(295)	(295)
V8, HEMI, 5.7 Liter	8		(4125)	(4125)	(4775)	(4775)
RAM MEGA CAB 4WD—6-Cyl. HO Turbo Diesel—Truck Equipment Sch T1						
2500 Laramie 6 1/4'	S29C	49090	23200	25300	24300	31700
2WD	R		(2175)	(2175)	(2555)	(2555)
6-Cyl, Turbo Dsl 6.7L	A		250	250	300	300
V8, HEMI, 5.7 Liter	8		(3525)	(3525)	(4140)	(4140)
RAM MEGA CAB 4WD—6-Cyl. HO Turbo Diesel—Truck Schedule T1						
3500 SLT 4D 6 1/4'	X39C	46245	21400	23400	22800	30100
3500 Laramie 6 1/4'	X39C	50515	22800	24900	23800	31000
2WD	L		(2175)	(2175)	(2555)	(2555)
6-Cyl, Turbo Dsl 6.7L	A		200	200	235	235

2008 DODGE — (1,3orW)D(2,3,4,5,7or8)–(U28K)–8–#

Body Type	VIN	List	Trade-In Good	Very Good	Pvt-Party Good	Retail Excellent
NITRO 4WD—V6—Truck Equipment Schedule T1						
SXT Sport Utility 4D	U28K	21915	6575	7100	7950	10450
SLT Sport Utility 4D	U58K	25325	7425	8000	8925	11750
R/T Sport Utility 4D	U586	28500	9375	10100	11000	14450
2WD	T		(725)	(725)	(975)	(975)
DURANGO 4WD—V8—Truck Equipment Schedule T1						
SXT Sport Utility 4D	B38N	30480	6275	6875	7850	10800
Adventurer Spt Util	B68N	35610	7475	8150	9150	12500
Third Row Seat			400	400	520	520
2WD	D		(1200)	(1200)	(1595)	(1595)
V6, 3.7 Liter	K		(525)	(525)	(710)	(710)
V8, HEMI, 5.7 Liter	2		650	650	870	870
DURANGO 4WD—V8 HEMI—Truck Equipment Schedule T1						
SLT Sport Utility 4D	B482	34800	6900	7550	8625	11850
Limited Sport Util	B582	38870	8250	8625	9925	12450
2WD			(1200)	(1200)	(1595)	(1595)
V6, 3.7 Liter	K		(1450)	(1450)	(1925)	(1925)
V8, Flex Fuel, 4.7 Liter	N		(725)	(725)	(975)	(975)
CARAVAN CARGO—V6—Truck Equipment Schedule T2						
SE Grand Minivan	N11H	22470	4325	4775	5650	7925
GRAND CARAVAN—V6—Truck Equipment Schedule T1						
SE Minivan	N44H	22470	5225	5750	6825	9550
SXT Minivan	N54P	27535	6225	6850	7975	11150
DAKOTA EXTENDED CAB PICKUP—V6—Truck Equipment Schedule T1						
ST 4D 6 1/2'	E22K	21215	3550	3925	4725	6575
SLT 4D 6 1/2'	E42K	25730	5050	5525	6250	8600
SXT 4D 6 1/2'	E32K	26730	5075	5600	6450	8850
Sport 4D 6 1/2'	E62K	25780	5150	5650	6325	8700
TRX 4D 6 1/2'	E72K	26100	5300	5825	6675	9175
4WD	W		1225	1225	1645	1645

TRUCKS & VANS

Body Type	VIN	List	Trade-In Good	Very Good	Pvt-Party Good	Retail Excellent
V8, Flex Fuel, 4.7 Liter	N		400	400	545	545
DAKOTA EXTENDED CAB PICKUP 4WD—V8—Truck Equipment Schedule T1						
Laramie 4D 6 1/2'	W52N	33795	7950	8725	9475	12850
2WD	E		(1650)	(1650)	(2185)	(2185)
DAKOTA CREW CAB PICKUP—V6—Truck Equipment Schedule T1						
SXT 4D 5 1/4'	E38K	25420	7700	8450	9200	12500
4WD	W		1225	1225	1645	1645
V8, Flex Fuel, 4.7 Liter	N		400	400	545	545
DAKOTA CREW CAB PICKUP 4WD—V6—Truck Equipment Schedule T1						
ST 4D 5 1/4'	W28K	25730	8500	9300	10000	13550
2WD	E		(1650)	(1650)	(2185)	(2185)
V8, Flex Fuel, 4.7 Liter	N		400	400	545	545
DAKOTA CREW CAB PICKUP—V8 Flex Fuel—Truck Equipment Schedule T1						
SLT 4D 5 1/4'	E48N	27875	8600	9425	10100	13700
4WD	W		1225	1225	1645	1645
V6, 3.7 Liter	K		(425)	(425)	(555)	(555)
DAKOTA CREW CAB 4WD—V8 Flex Fuel—Truck Equipment Sch T1						
TRX 4D 5 1/4'	W78N	31450	10100	11050	11700	15800
Sport 4D 5 1/4'	W68N	31180	10750	11800	12400	16650
2WD	E		(1650)	(1650)	(2185)	(2185)
V6, 3.7 Liter	K		(425)	(425)	(555)	(555)
DAKOTA CREW CAB PICKUP 4WD—V8 HEMI—Truck Equipment Schedule T1						
Laramie 4D 5 1/4'	W58N	31745	10250	11200	11850	16000
2WD	E		(1650)	(1650)	(2185)	(2185)
RAM REGULAR CAB PICKUP—V6—Truck Equipment Schedule T1						
1500 ST 2D 6 1/4'	A16K	23150	5100	5525	6400	8475
1500 SXT 2D 6 1/4'	A16K	25095	5775	6225	7175	9525
4WD	U		2125	2125	2800	2800
V8, 4.7 Liter	N		625	625	805	805
V8, HEMI, 5.7 Liter	2		1275	1275	1675	1675
RAM REGULAR CAB PICKUP—V8—Truck Equipment Schedule T1						
1500 ST 2D 8'	A16N	24480	5025	5400	6175	8200
1500 ST 2D 8'	A16N	26425	5775	6325	7250	9625
1500 SLT 2D 6 1/4'	A16N	26570	6050	6525	7475	9925
1500 SLT 2D 8'	A16N	26855	6075	6550	7400	9750
4WD	U		2125	2125	2820	2820
V6, 3.7 Liter	K		(450)	(450)	(595)	(595)
V8, HEMI, 5.7 Liter	2		775	775	1040	1040
RAM REGULAR CAB PICKUP—V8 HEMI—Truck Equipment Schedule T1						
2500 SXT 2D 8'	R26D	29685	9275	9975	10500	13350
3500 SLT 2D 8' DR	L36D	29610	10850	11650	12100	15450
4WD	S,X		2125	2125	2505	2505
6-Cyl, Turbo Dsl 6.7L	A		4750	4750	5585	5585
RAM REGULAR CAB PICKUP—6-Cyl. Turbo Diesel—Truck Equip Sch T1						
3500 SLT 2D 8' DR	L46A	31860	16850	18100	18200	22900
4WD	S,X		2125	2125	2495	2495
V8, HEMI, 5.7 Liter	D		(4450)	(4450)	(5220)	(5220)
RAM REGULAR CAB PICKUP 4WD—V8 HEMI—Truck Equipment Schedule T1						
3500 SXT 2D 8' DR	L46D	31305	14150	15200	15650	20000
2WD	C		(2400)	(2400)	(2825)	(2825)
6-Cyl, Turbo Dsl 6.7L	C		4750	4750	5605	5605
RAM REGULAR CAB 4WD—V8 HEMI—Truck Equipment Schedule T1						
2500 ST 2D 8'	S26D	32130	11750	12600	13100	16700
2500 ST 2D 8'	S26D	34725	12150	13050	13350	16800
Power Wagon			4775	4775	5560	5560
2WD	C		(2400)	(2400)	(2795)	(2795)
6-Cyl, HO Trb Dsl 5.9L	C		4425	4425	5175	5175
6-Cyl, Turbo Dsl 6.7L	A		4750	4750	5550	5550
RAM QUAD CAB PICKUP—V8—Truck Equipment Schedule T1						
1500 ST 2D 6 1/4'	A18N	28365	8150	8775	9775	12950
1500 ST 2D 8'	A18N	29900	8000	8600	9600	12700
1500 SXT 4D 6 1/4'	A18N	30470	8950	9625	10700	14150
1500 SLT 4D 8'	A18N	32005	8500	9150	10150	13450
1500 SLT 4D 6 1/4'	A18N	30740	9100	9775	10750	14200
1500 SLT 4D 8'	A18N	31410	8700	9350	10350	13700
4WD	U		2125	2125	2790	2790
V6, 3.7 Liter	K		(450)	(450)	(585)	(585)
V8, HEMI, 5.7 Liter	2		775	775	1025	1025
RAM QUAD CAB PICKUP 4WD—V8 HEMI—Truck Equipment Schedule T1						
1500 Laramie 6 1/4'	U182	40680	12450	13400	14550	19150
2WD	R		(2400)	(2400)	(3145)	(3145)
RAM QUAD CAB PICKUP—V8 HEMI—Truck Equipment Schedule T1						
2500 ST 4D 8'	R28D	30740	11700	12600	13050	16600

Body Type	VIN	List	Trade-In Good	Very Good	Pvt-Party Good	Retail Excellent
2500 SXT 4D 8'	R28D	32860	12450	13350	13750	17500
2500 SLT 4D 8'	R28D	34105	12600	13550	13950	17800
2500 Laramie 8'	R28D	37235	13150	14100	14600	18650
3500 SXT 4D 8'	L48D	35295	12600	13500	14050	18000
4WD	S		2125	2125	2525	2525
6-Cyl, Turbo Dsl 6.7L	A		4750	4750	5625	5625
RAM QUAD CAB PICKUP 4WD—V8 HEMI—Truck Equipment Schedule T1						
2500 ST 4D 6 1/4'	S282	34840	14850	15950	16350	20800
2500 Laramie 6 1/4'	S282	41575	16200	17400	17750	22600
3500 ST 4D 8'	X48D	36160	14750	15850	16400	21000
2WD	R		(2400)	(2400)	(2810)	(2810)
6-Cyl, Turbo Dsl 6.7L	A		4750	4750	5580	5580
6-Cyl, HO Trb Dsl 5.9L	C		4425	4425	5205	5205
RAM QUAD CAB 4WD—6-Cyl. Turbo Diesel— Equipment Schedule T1						
2500 SXT 4D 6 1/4'	S28A	36970	20500	22000	22000	27700
2500 SLT 4D 6 1/4'	S28A	44765	20700	22200	22200	28100
3500 SLT 4D 8'	X48A	44560	21200	22800	22900	29200
3500 Laramie 8'	X48A	48665	21700	23200	23300	29600
Power Wagon			4775	4775	5610	5610
2WD	R		(2400)	(2400)	(2825)	(2825)
V8, HEMI, 5.7 Liter	D		(4450)	(4450)	(5255)	(5255)
RAM QUAD CAB PICKUP—6-Cyl. Turbo Diesel—Truck Equipment Sch T1						
3500 SXT 4D 6 1/4'	L38A	38105	17600	18850	19200	24500
3500 SXT 4D 6 1/4'	L38A	40565	17950	19300	19500	24800
4WD	X		2125	2125	2505	2505
6-Cyl, HO Trb Dsl 5.9L	C		(300)	(300)	(350)	(350)
RAM QUAD CAB 4WD—6-Cyl. Turbo Diesel—Truck Equipment Sch T1						
3500 SLT 4D 6 1/4'	X38A	44645	21400	23000	23000	29200
3500 Laramie 6 1/4'	X38A	48075	21800	23400	23500	30000
2WD	L,R		(2400)	(2400)	(2815)	(2815)
RAM MEGA CAB PICKUP—V8 HEMI—Truck Equipment Schedule T1						
1500 SXT 4D 6 1/4'	A19D	33695	12550	13450	14450	19000
4WD	S,U		2125	2125	2740	2740
RAM MEGA CAB PICKUP 4WD—V8 HEMI—Truck Equipment Schedule T1						
1500 SLT 4D 6 1/4'	S19D	38665	15400	16500	17550	23000
1500 Laramie 6 1/4'	S19D	42250	16100	17300	18200	23700
2WD	A,R		(2400)	(2400)	(3035)	(3035)
RAM MEGA CAB 4WD—6-Cyl. Turbo Diesel—Truck Equipment Schedule T1						
2500 SXT 4D 6 1/4'	S29A	45530	25600	27400	26900	33700
2500 SLT 4D 6 1/4'	S29A	46315	25900	27700	27300	34300
2500 Laramie 6 1/4'	S29A	49630	26300	28200	27800	35000
2WD	R		(2400)	(2400)	(2765)	(2765)
V8, HEMI, 5.7 Liter	D		(4450)	(4450)	(5155)	(5155)
RAM MEGA CAB PICKUP 4WD—6-Cyl. Turbo Diesel—Truck Equip Sch T1						
3500 SXT 4D 6 1/4'	X39A	47750	24600	26300	26100	33000
3500 SLT 4D 6 1/4'	X39A	48260	24800	26500	26400	33500
3500 Laramie 6 1/4'	X39C	51400	25600	27400	27000	33900
2WD	L		(2400)	(2400)	(2780)	(2780)

2009 DODGE — (1,3orW)D(2,3,4,5,7or8)—(U28K)—9—#

Body Type	VIN	List	Trade-In Good	Very Good	Pvt-Party Good	Retail Excellent
NITRO 4WD—V6—Truck Equipment Schedule T1						
SE Sport Utility 4D	U28K	23795	8625	9150	10200	12950
SLT Sport Utility 4D	U58K	26115	9300	9850	11000	14000
R/T Sport Utility 4D	U58X	29290	12100	12800	13850	17400
2WD	T		(825)	(825)	(1070)	(1070)
JOURNEY—4-Cyl.—Truck Equipment Schedule T1						
SE Sport Utility 4D	G47B	19985	5525	5775	7275	9400
JOURNEY—V6—Truck Equipment Schedule T1						
SXT Sport Utility 4D	G57V	22985	6500	6800	8275	10600
AWD	H		900	900	1200	1200
JOURNEY AWD—V6—Truck Equipment Schedule T1						
R/T Sport Utility 4D	H67V	26545	8525	9025	10250	13100
FWD	G		(1200)	(1200)	(1595)	(1595)
DURANGO 4WD—V8—Truck Equipment Schedule T1						
SE Sport Utility 4D	B38P	31710	7900	8450	9475	12300
Third Row Seat			450	450	580	580
2WD	D		(1275)	(1275)	(1650)	(1650)
V6, 3.7 Liter	K		(625)	(625)	(815)	(815)
DURANGO 4WD—V8 HEMI—Truck Equipment Schedule T1						
SLT Sport Utility 4D	B48T	35835	9325	9975	11050	14400
Limited Sport Utility	B58T	41075	9425	9775	11300	13850
Third Row Seat			450	450	585	585
2WD	D		(1275)	(1275)	(1665)	(1665)

2009 DODGE

Body Type	VIN	List	Trade-In Good	Very Good	Pvt-Party Good	Retail Excellent
V6, 3.7 Liter	K	......	(1550)	(1550)	(2020)	(2020)
V8, Flex Fuel, 4.7 Liter	P	......	(775)	(775)	(1020)	(1020)
DURANGO 4WD—V8 HEMI Hybrid—Truck Equipment Schedule T1						
Limited Sport Utility	B18T	45340	10300	10650	12400	15350
Third Row Seat		......	450	450	570	570
GRAND CARAVAN—V6—Truck Equipment Schedule T1						
SE Minivan	N44E	24300	6300	6850	7900	10550
SXT Minivan	N541	28595	7200	7825	9025	12100
DAKOTA EXTENDED CAB PICKUP—V6—Truck Equipment Schedule T1						
ST 4D 6 1/2'	E38K	24515	5675	6200	7050	9350
Big Horn/Lone Star	E32K	24090	6400	7400	8200	10800
4WD	W	......	1425	1425	1910	1910
V8, FFV, 4.7 Liter	P	......	450	450	610	610
DAKOTA EXTENDED CAB PICKUP 4WD—V6—Truck Equipment Schedule T1						
Laramie 4D 6 1/2'	W52K	29995	9450	10300	11100	14550
2WD	E	......	(2200)	(2200)	(2930)	(2930)
V8, FFV, 4.7 Liter	P	......	450	450	610	610
DAKOTA EXTENDED CAB PICKUP 4WD—V6—Truck Equipment Sch T1						
TRX 4D 6 1/2'	W72K	30375	7550	8225	9075	11950
V8, FFV, 4.7 Liter	P	......	450	450	610	610
DAKOTA CREW CAB PICKUP—V6—Truck Equipment Schedule T1						
Big Horn/Lone Star	E38K	26795	9350	10200	11000	14400
4WD	W	......	1425	1425	1910	1910
V8, FFV, 4.7 Liter	P	......	450	450	610	610
DAKOTA CREW CAB PICKUP 4WD—V6—Truck Equipment Schedule T1						
ST 4D 5 1/4'	W32K	27440	10600	11500	12300	16050
2WD	E	......	(2200)	(2200)	(2920)	(2920)
V8, FFV, 4.7 Liter	P	......	450	450	605	605
DAKOTA CREW CAB 4WD—V8 Flex Fuel—Truck Equipment Schedule T1						
Laramie 4D 5 1/4'	W58N	32530	12700	13800	14550	19000
2WD	E	......	(2200)	(2200)	(2875)	(2875)
V6, 3.7 Liter	K	......	(450)	(450)	(600)	(600)
DAKOTA CREW CAB PICKUP 4WD—V8 Flex Fuel—Truck Equipment Sch T1						
TRX 4D 5 1/4'	W78P	31945	11650	12650	13400	17450
V6, 3.7 Liter	K	......	(450)	(450)	(605)	(605)
RAM REGULAR CAB PICKUP—V6—Truck Equipment Schedule T1						
1500 ST 2D 6 1/4'	A16K	22170	7525	7975	8775	10850
4WD	V	......	2475	2475	2945	2945
V8, 4.7 Liter	P	......	650	650	785	785
V8, HEMI, 5.7L	T	......	1375	1375	1635	1635
RAM REGULAR CAB PICKUP—V8—Truck Equipment Schedule T1						
1500 ST 2D 8'	B16P	23705	7100	7500	8300	10300
1500 SLT 2D 6 1/4'	B16P	26615	9325	9850	10600	13150
1500 SLT 2D 8'	B16P	26915	8475	8975	9775	12150
4WD	V	......	2475	2475	2975	2975
V6, 3.7 Liter	K	......	(500)	(500)	(600)	(600)
V8, HEMI, 5.7 Liter	T	......	850	850	1025	1025
RAM REGULAR CAB PICKUP—V8 HEMI—Truck Equipment Schedule T1						
2500 SXT 2D 8'	R26T	31980	10150	10750	11550	14250
4WD	S	......	2475	2475	2865	2865
6-Cyl, Turbo Dsl 6.7L	L	......	4975	4975	5775	5775
RAM REGULAR CAB 4WD—V8 HEMI—Truck Equipment Schedule T1						
2500 ST 2D 8'	S26T	35185	12650	13350	14150	17450
2500 SLT 2D 8'	S26T	35185	13100	13900	14600	17900
2WD	R,L	......	(2600)	(2600)	(2940)	(2940)
6-Cyl, Turbo Dsl 6.7L	L	......	4975	4975	5640	5640
RAM REGULAR CAB PICKUP—6-Cyl. Turbo Diesel—Truck Equip Schedule T1						
3500 ST 2D 8' DR	L36L	39034	17050	18000	18700	23000
3500 SLT 2D 8' DR	L36L	41284	17850	18850	19500	23900
4WD	X	......	2475	2475	2790	2790
RAM REGULAR CAB 4WD—6-Cyl. Turbo Diesel—Truck Equip Sch T1						
3500 SXT 2D 8' DR	L46L	39654	20800	22000	22600	27800
2WD	L	......	(2600)	(2600)	(2920)	(2920)
RAM QUAD CAB PICKUP—V8—Truck Equipment Schedule T1						
1500 ST 4D 6 1/4'	B18P	27460	11150	11800	12700	15800
1500 SLT 4D 6 1/4'	B18P	30625	11950	12650	13500	16750
4WD	V	......	2475	2475	2975	2975
V6, 3.7 Liter	K	......	(500)	(500)	(600)	(600)
V8, HEMI, 5.7 Liter	T	......	850	850	1025	1025
RAM QUAD CAB PICKUP 4WD—V8 HEMI—Truck Equipment Schedule T1						
1500 Laramie 6 1/4'	V18T	42785	15750	16650	17650	21900
2WD	B	......	(2600)	(2600)	(3170)	(3170)

Body Type	VIN	List	Trade-In Good	Very Good	Pvt-Party Good	Retail Excellent
RAM QUAD CAB PICKUP—V8 HEMI—Truck Equipment Schedule T1						
2500 ST 4D 8'	R28T	33125	**12750**	**13500**	**14400**	**17750**
2500 SXT 8'	R28T	35155	**13300**	**14100**	**15050**	**18600**
2500 SLT 4D 8'	R28T	36400	**13750**	**14500**	**15550**	**19300**
2500 Laramie 8'	R28T	39830	**14200**	**15000**	**15900**	**19650**
Power Wagon	S,V		4975	4975	5625	5625
4WD			2475	2475	2810	2810
6-Cyl, Turbo Dsl 6.7L	L		4975	4975	5665	5665
RAM QUAD CAB PICKUP 4WD—V8 HEMI—Truck Equipment Schedule T1						
2500 Laramie 6 1/4'	S28T	35000	**15950**	**16850**	**17650**	**21800**
2500 Laramie 6 1/4'	S28T	42035	**17150**	**18150**	**19000**	**23500**
2WD	B,R		(2600)	(2600)	(2950)	(2950)
6-Cyl, Turbo Dsl 6.7L	L		4975	4975	5665	5665
RAM QUAD CAB 4WD—6-Cyl. Turbo Diesel—Truck Equipment Sch T1						
2500 SLT 4D 6 1/4'	S28L	44925	**22000**	**23200**	**23900**	**29400**
2500 SLT 4D 6 1/4'	S28L	48165	**22200**	**23400**	**23900**	**29300**
Power Wagon			4975	4975	5625	5625
2WD	B,R		(2600)	(2600)	(2935)	(2935)
V8, HEMI, 5.7 Liter	T		(4800)	(4800)	(5440)	(5440)
RAM QUAD CAB PICKUP—6-Cyl. Turbo Diesel—Truck Equipment Sch T1						
3500 SLT 4D 6 1/4'	L38L	41429	**18750**	**19850**	**20700**	**25500**
3500 SXT 6 1/4'	L38L	42334	**19250**	**20300**	**21100**	**26100**
3500 SXT 4D 8'	L38L	43444	**19050**	**20100**	**21000**	**25900**
4WD			2475	2475	2800	2800
RAM QUAD CAB 4WD—6-Cyl. Turbo Diesel—Truck Equipment Sch T1						
2500 SLT 4D 6 1/4'	S28L	44925	**22000**	**23200**	**23900**	**29400**
3500 SLT 4D 8'	X48L	42664	**21800**	**23000**	**23300**	**28200**
3500 SLT 4D 6 1/4'	X38L	45915	**22600**	**23900**	**24500**	**30100**
3500 SLT 4D 8'	X38L	46250	**22400**	**23700**	**24300**	**29800**
3500 Laramie 6 1/4'	X38L	49530	**23200**	**24500**	**25100**	**30900**
3500 Laramie 8'	X48L	50720	**22900**	**24200**	**24800**	**30400**
Power Wagon			4975	4975	5625	5625
2WD	B,R		(2600)	(2600)	(2935)	(2935)
V8, HEMI, 5.7 Liter	T		(4800)	(4800)	(5445)	(5445)
RAM CREW CAB PICKUP—V8—Truck Equipment Schedule T1						
1500 SLT 4D 5 1/2'	B13P	32780	**13750**	**14550**	**15550**	**19350**
4WD	V,S		2475	2475	2970	2970
V8, HEMI, 5.7 Liter	T		850	850	1020	1020
RAM CREW CAB PICKUP 4WD—V8—Truck Equipment Schedule T1						
1500 SLT 4D 5 1/2'	V13P	33040	**16350**	**17300**	**18250**	**22600**
2WD	B,R		(2600)	(2600)	(3120)	(3120)
V8, HEMI, 5.7 Liter	T		850	850	1025	1025
RAM CREW CAB PICKUP 4WD—V8 HEMI—Truck Equipment Schedule T1						
1500 Laramie 5 1/2'	V13T	44935	**17900**	**18950**	**20000**	**25000**
2WD	B,R		(2600)	(2600)	(3155)	(3155)
RAM MEGA CAB 4WD—6-Cyl. Turbo Diesel—Truck Equipment Sch T1						
2500 SXT 4D 6 1/4'	S29L	47165	**26600**	**28000**	**28300**	**34600**
2500 Laramie 6 1/4'	S29L	51450	**27500**	**29100**	**29300**	**35800**
2WD	B,R		(2600)	(2600)	(2915)	(2915)
V8, HEMI, 5.7 Liter	T		(4800)	(4800)	(5405)	(5405)
RAM MEGA CAB 4WD—6-Cyl. Turbo Diesel—Truck Equipment Sch T1						
3500 SXT 4D 6 1/4'	X39L	50070	**25600**	**27000**	**27600**	**33900**
3500 Laramie 6 1/4'	X39L	49530	**27000**	**28500**	**28900**	**35400**
2WD			(2600)	(2600)	(2935)	(2935)

Body Type	VIN	List	Good	Very Good	Good	Excellent
NITRO 4WD—V6—Truck Equipment Schedule T1						
SE Sport Util 4D	U2GK	23995	**9650**	**10100**	**11400**	**13950**
Heat Sport Util 4D	U4GK	23995	**10200**	**10650**	**11950**	**14650**
SXT Sport Util 4D	U5GK	25640	**10300**	**10750**	**12050**	**14800**
2WD			(950)	(950)	(1200)	(1200)
V6, 4.0 Liter	X		1325	1325	1675	1675
NITRO 4WD—V6—Truck Equipment Schedule T1						
Detonator Spt Utl	U6GX	28155	**11450**	**11950**	**13400**	**16500**
Shock Sport Util	U7GX	29155	**12100**	**12650**	**14100**	**17300**
2WD	T		(950)	(950)	(1205)	(1205)
JOURNEY—4-Cyl.—Truck Equipment Schedule T1						
SE Sport Utility 4D	G4FB	21165	**6975**	**7225**	**8850**	**10950**
JOURNEY—V6 HO—Truck Equipment Schedule T1						
SXT Sport Utility	G5FV	24465	**7775**	**8050**	**9700**	**12000**
AWD	H		975	975	1285	1285
JOURNEY AWD—V6 HO—Truck Equipment Schedule T1						
R/T Sport Utility	H6FV	28870	**10150**	**10650**	**11900**	**14600**

Body Type	VIN	List	Trade-In Good	Very Good	Pvt-Party Good	Retail Excellent
FWD	G	......	(1075)	(1075)	(1330)	(1330)
CARAVAN CARGO—V6—Truck Equipment Schedule T2						
Grand Minivan	N1AE	22620	6000	6450	7450	9625
GRAND CARAVAN—V6—Truck Equipment Schedule T1						
SE Minivan	N4DE	23995	7500	8075	9150	11750
Hero Minivan	N3D1	25675	8025	8650	9700	12400
SXT Minivan	N5D1	27300	8550	9200	10250	13150
5-Passenger Seating			(525)	(525)	(700)	(700)
V6, 4.0 Liter	X		300	300	415	415
GRAND CARAVAN—V6—Truck Equipment Schedule T1						
Crew Minivan	N6DX	28795	8600	9250	10400	13350
DAKOTA EXTENDED CAB PICKUP—V6—Truck Equipment Sch T1						
ST 4D 6 1/2'	E2BK	23495	6900	7475	8200	10400
Big Horn/Lone Star	E3BK	24370	8475	9175	9925	12550
4WD	W		1625	1625	2105	2105
V8, FFV, 4.7 Liter	P		525	525	675	675
DAKOTA CREW CAB PICKUP—V6—Truck Equipment Schedule T1						
Big Horn/Lone Star	E3GK	27065	10850	11750	12550	15850
4WD	W		1625	1625	2075	2075
V8, FFV, 4.7 Liter	P		525	525	665	665
DAKOTA CREW CAB PICKUP 4WD—V6—Truck Equipment Schedule T1						
ST 4D 5 1/4'	W5GK	29075	12150	13150	13800	17300
2WD	E		(2200)	(2200)	(2760)	(2760)
V8, FFV, 4.7 Liter	P		525	525	660	660
DAKOTA CREW CAB 4WD—V8 Flex Fuel—Truck Equipment Sch T1						
Laramie 4D 5 1/4'	W5GP	33795	14200	15350	16150	20400
2WD	E		(2200)	(2200)	(2790)	(2790)
V6, 3.7 Liter	K		(525)	(525)	(665)	(665)
DAKOTA CREW CAB PICKUP 4WD—V8 Flex Fuel—Truck Equipment Sch T1						
TRX4 4D 5 1/4'	W7GP	32105	12300	13300	14050	17750
RAM REGULAR CAB PICKUP—V6—Truck Equipment Schedule T1						
1500 ST 2D 6 1/3'	B1EK	21510	8275	8650	9675	11750
4WD	V		2725	2725	3220	3220
V8, Flex Fuel, 4.7 Liter	P		775	775	920	920
V8, HEMI, 5.7 Liter	T		1500	1500	1765	1765
RAM REGULAR CAB PICKUP—V8—Truck Equipment Schedule T1						
1500 ST 2D 8'	B1EP	21810	7775	8150	9200	11150
1500 SLT 2D 6 1/3'	B1EP	25755	9675	10100	11250	13650
1500 SLT 2D 8'	B1EP	26055	9075	9500	10650	13000
4WD	V		2725	2725	3230	3230
V6, 3.7 Liter	K		(575)	(575)	(680)	(680)
V8, HEMI, 5.7 Liter	T		925	925	1095	1095
RAM REGULAR CAB PICKUP—V8 HEMI—Truck Equipment Schedule T1						
2500 SLT 2D 8'	P2ET	31310	12450	13000	14050	16900
4WD	T		2725	2725	3170	3170
6-Cyl, Turbo Dsl 6.7L	L		5200	5200	6015	6015
RAM REGULAR CAB 4WD—V8 HEMI—Truck Equipment Schedule T1						
2500 ST 2D 8'	T2ET	30475	14600	15200	16300	19450
2WD	P		(2775)	(2775)	(3125)	(3125)
6-Cyl, Turbo Dsl 6.7L	L		5200	5200	5845	5845
RAM REGULAR CAB PICKUP—6-Cyl. Turbo Diesel—Truck Equip Sch T1						
3500 ST 2D 8' DR	M4EL	35630	19500	20300	21400	25400
3500 SLT 2D 8' DR	M4EL	39270	20100	21000	22000	26200
4WD	Y		2725	2725	3075	3075
RAM QUAD CAB PICKUP—V8—Truck Equipment Schedule T1						
1500 SLT 4D 6 1/3'	B1GP	29765	12650	13200	14350	17400
4WD	V		2725	2725	3220	3220
V8, HEMI, 5.7 Liter	T		925	925	1090	1090
RAM QUAD CAB PICKUP 4WD—V8—Truck Equipment Schedule T1						
1500 ST 4D 6 1/3'	V1GP	29975	15100	15750	17050	20600
2WD	B		(2775)	(2775)	(3265)	(3265)
V6, 3.7 Liter	K		(575)	(575)	(675)	(675)
V8, HEMI, 5.7 Liter	T		925	925	1090	1090
RAM QUAD CAB PICKUP—V8 HEMI—Truck Equipment Schedule T1						
1500 Laramie 6 1/3'	B1GT	37780	15250	15900	17200	20700
4WD	V		2725	2725	3205	3205
RAM CREW CAB PICKUP—V8 HEMI—Truck Equipment Schedule T1						
1500 SLT 4D 5 1/2'	B1CT	33230	15200	15850	17400	21300
4WD	T,V		2725	2725	3265	3265
V8, Flex Fuel, 4.7 Liter	P		(825)	(825)	(995)	(995)
RAM CREW CAB PICKUP 4WD—V8 HEMI—Truck Equipment Schedule T1						
1500 ST 4D 5 1/2'	V1CT	34880	18400	19200	20600	24900
1500 Laramie 5 1/2'	V1CT	45470	19750	20600	22200	27000

TRUCKS & VANS

Body Type	VIN	List	Trade-In Good	Very Good	Pvt-Party Good	Retail Excellent
2WD	B	......	(2775)	(2775)	(3280)	(3280)
V8, Flex Fuel, 4.7 Liter	P	......	(825)	(825)	(985)	(985)
RAM CREW CAB PICKUP 4WD—V8 HEMI—Truck Equipment Schedule T1						
2500 ST 4D 6 1/3'	T2CT	34085	18800	19650	20700	24700
2500 ST 4D 8'	T2CT	31615	15250	15900	17000	20300
2500 SLT 4D 8'	T2CT	36365	16300	17000	18200	21800
2500 Laramie 8'	T2CT	40440	17550	18300	19350	23100
2WD	B	......	(2775)	(2775)	(3120)	(3120)
6-Cyl, Turbo Dsl 6.7L	L	......	5200	5200	5835	5835
RAM CREW CAB 4WD—6-Cyl. Turbo Diesel—Truck Equipment Sch T1						
2500 SLT 4D 6 1/3'	T2CL	46245	25400	26400	27500	32700
2500 Laramie 6 1/3'	T2CL	50950	26900	28100	28900	34200
Power Wagon	P	......	5150	5150	5815	5815
2WD	P	......	(2775)	(2775)	(3125)	(3125)
V8, HEMI, 5.7 Liter	T	......	(5150)	(5150)	(5805)	(5805)
RAM CREW CAB PICKUP—6-Cyl. Turbo Diesel—Truck Equipment Sch T1						
3500 ST 4D 6 1/3'	M3CL	40775	22300	23300	24300	29000
3500 ST 4D 8' DR	M3CL	40975	21800	22800	23700	28100
4WD	Y	......	2725	2725	3080	3080
RAM CREW CAB 4WD—6-Cyl. Turbo Diesel—Truck Equipment Sch T1						
3500 SLT 4D 6 1/3'	Y3CL	48320	26100	27200	28200	33600
3500 SLT 4D 8' DR	Y3CL	48520	25900	27000	28100	33500
3500 Laramie 6 1/3'	Y3CL	52860	27300	28400	29400	35000
3500 Laramie 8' DR	Y3CL	53060	26500	27600	28600	34000
2WD			(2775)	(2775)	(3125)	(3125)
RAM MEGA CAB 4WD—6-Cyl. Turbo Diesel—Truck Equipment Sch T1						
2500 SLT 6 4D 1/3'	S2HL	46945	28600	29800	30700	36500
2WD	P	......	(2775)	(2775)	(3135)	(3135)
V8, HEMI, 5.7 Liter	T	......	(5150)	(5150)	(5815)	(5815)
RAM MEGA CAB PICKUP—V8 HEMI—Truck Equipment Schedule T1						
2500 Laramie 6 1/3'	P2HT	40940	20700	21600	22600	26900
4WD	Y	......	2725	2725	3080	3080
6-Cyl, Turbo Dsl 6.7L	L	......	5200	5200	5850	5850
RAM MEGA CAB PICKUP—6-Cyl. Turbo Diesel—Truck Equipment Sch T1						
3500 Laramie 6 DR	M4HL	48715	26200	27300	28300	33600
4WD	Y	......	2725	2725	3100	3100
RAM MEGA CAB 4WD—6-Cyl. Turbo Diesel—Truck Equipment Sch T1						
3500 SLT 6 1/3' DR	Y4HL	49020	28000	29200	30400	36300
2WD	M	......	(2775)	(2775)	(3130)	(3130)

2011 DODGE — 1D4–(U2GK)–B–#

Body Type	VIN	List	Trade-In Good	Very Good	Pvt-Party Good	Retail Excellent
NITRO 4WD—V6—Truck Equipment Schedule T1						
SE Sport Utility 4D	U2GK	24090	10800	11150	12600	15100
Heat Sport Utility	U4GK	24000	11800	12200	13750	16400
SXT Sport Util 4D	U5GK	25735	11600	11950	13550	16250
2WD	T	......	(1075)	(1075)	(1300)	(1300)
V6, 4.0 Liter	X	......	1425	1425	1735	1735
NITRO 4WD—V6—Truck Equipment Schedule T1						
Detonator Spt Util	U6GX	28745	14250	14700	16400	19500
Shock Sport Utility	U7GX	29745	14400	14900	16650	19900
2WD	T	......	(1075)	(1075)	(1295)	(1295)
JOURNEY—4-Cyl.—Truck Equipment Schedule T1						
Express Sport Util	G4FB	22995	8825	9075	10800	12850
Third Row Seat			375	375	470	470
JOURNEY—V6—Truck Equipment Schedule T1						
Mainstreet Utility	G1FG	23655	9325	9600	11350	13500
Crew Sport Utility	G3FG	29175	11950	12400	13700	16200
Third Row Seat			375	375	470	470
AWD	H	......	975	975	1200	1200
JOURNEY AWD—V6—Truck Equipment Schedule T1						
R/T Sport Utility	G6FG	28995	11600	12100	13500	16100
LUX Sport Utility	G9FG	33490	15200	15800	17150	20100
Third Row Seat			375	375	460	460
FWD	G	......	(1075)	(1075)	(1275)	(1275)
DURANGO AWD—V6—Truck Equipment Schedule T1						
Express Sport Util	E2GG	32045	15450	16000	17150	20300
Heat Sport Utility	E3GG	33145	16000	16550	17650	20900
2WD	D	......	(1450)	(1450)	(1700)	(1700)
DURANGO AWD—V6—Truck Equipment Schedule T1						
Crew Sport Utility	E4GG	36045	16900	17500	18650	22000
2WD	D	......	(1450)	(1450)	(1700)	(1700)
V8, HEMI, 5.7 Liter	T	......	1775	1775	2085	2085

2011 DODGE

Body Type	VIN	List	Trade-In Good	Very Good	Pvt-Party Good	Retail Excellent
DURANGO AWD—V8 HEMI—Truck Equipment Schedule T1						
R/T Sport Utility 4D	E6GT	38715	20600	21300	22500	26700
Citadel Sport Utl	E5GT	44645	20100	20500	22200	25100
2WD	D		(1450)	(1450)	(1645)	(1645)
V6, 3.6 Liter	G		(875)	(875)	(990)	(990)
CARAVAN CARGO—V6—Truck Equipment Schedule T2						
Grand Minivan	N1AG	23375	6875	7325	8425	10650
GRAND CARAVAN—V6—Truck Equipment Schedule T1						
Express Minivan	N4DG	25830	8700	9300	10450	13100
Mainstreet Minivan	N3DG	26830	9150	9775	11000	13750
Crew Minivan	N5DG	29530	9750	10400	11650	14650
R/T Minivan	N7DG	31430	11900	12700	13950	17350
5-Passenger Seating			(575)	(575)	(765)	(765)

2012 DODGE — (1,2or3)C4-(DCAB)-C-#

Body Type	VIN	List	Trade-In Good	Very Good	Pvt-Party Good	Retail Excellent
JOURNEY—4-Cyl.—Truck Equipment Schedule T1						
American Value	DCAB	19795	9525	9750	11550	13550
SE Sport Utility 4D	DCAB	21795	10500	10750	12600	14750
Third Row Seat			425	425	500	500
JOURNEY AWD—V6—Truck Equipment Schedule T1						
SXT Sport Utility	DCBG	25295	12400	12650	14700	17100
Crew Sport Utility	DCDG	29295	14200	14700	16300	18950
R/T Sport Utility	DCEG	30795	15100	15650	17300	20200
Third Row Seat			425	425	505	505
FWD	C		(1175)	(1175)	(1415)	(1415)
4-Cyl, 2.4 Liter	B		(875)	(875)	(1050)	(1050)
DURANGO AWD—V6—Truck Equipment Schedule T1						
SXT Sport Util 4D	DJAG	31845	18050	18500	19750	22800
2WD	H		(1525)	(1525)	(1745)	(1745)
DURANGO AWD—V6—Truck Equipment Schedule T1						
Crew Sport Utility	DJDG	36545	19350	19800	21100	24400
2WD	H		(1525)	(1525)	(1755)	(1755)
V8, HEMI, 5.7 Liter	T		1075	1075	1235	1235
DURANGO AWD—V8 HEMI—Truck Equipment Schedule T1						
R/T Sport Utility 4D	DJCT	38845	22500	23000	24400	28300
Citadel Sport Util	DJET	43845	23200	23700	25400	28200
2WD	H		(1525)	(1525)	(1710)	(1710)
V6, 3.6 Liter	G		(975)	(975)	(1085)	(1085)
GRAND CARAVAN—V6—Truck Equipment Schedule T1						
SE Minivan	DGBG	23830	10050	10700	11950	14700
SXT Minivan	DGCG	27330	11000	11700	12950	15900
Crew Minivan	DGDG	29330	11550	12300	13700	16900
R/T Minivan	DGEG	30830	13250	14050	15500	19000
5-Passenger Seating			(625)	(625)	(815)	(815)

2013 DODGE — (1,2or3)C4-(DCAB)-D-#

Body Type	VIN	List	Trade-In Good	Very Good	Pvt-Party Good	Retail Excellent
JOURNEY—4-Cyl.—Truck Equipment Schedule T1						
AVP Sport Utility	DCAB	19990	10350	10550	12450	14400
SE Sport Utility 4D	DCAB	21990	11850	12100	14150	16350
Third Row Seat			450	450	520	520
JOURNEY AWD—V6—Truck Equipment Schedule T1						
SXT Sport Utility	DDBG	27390	13600	13850	16150	18600
Third Row Seat			450	450	520	520
FWD	C		(1275)	(1275)	(1495)	(1495)
4-Cyl, 2.4 Liter	B		(975)	(975)	(1140)	(1140)
JOURNEY AWD—V6—Truck Equipment Schedule T1						
Crew Sport Utility	DDDG	30790	16150	16650	18300	20900
R/T Sport Utility	DDEG	31790	16950	17500	19150	21900
Third Row Seat			450	450	510	510
FWD	C		(1275)	(1275)	(1465)	(1465)
DURANGO AWD—V6—Truck Equipment Schedule T1						
SXT Sport Util 4D	DJAG	32190	21100	21500	22800	26000
2WD	H		(1600)	(1600)	(1815)	(1815)
DURANGO AWD—V8 HEMI—Truck Equipment Schedule T1						
Crew Sport Utility	DJDT	37790	23500	23900	25300	28800
Citadel Sport Util	DJET	43190	25800	26300	28300	31200
2WD	H		(1600)	(1600)	(1815)	(1815)
V6, 3.6 Liter	G		(1075)	(1075)	(1205)	(1205)
DURANGO AWD—V8 HEMI—Truck Equipment Schedule T1						
R/T Sport Utility 4D	DJCT	39590	26700	27200	28600	32600
2WD	H		(1600)	(1600)	(1815)	(1815)

Body Type	VIN	List	Trade-In Good	Trade-In Very Good	Pvt-Party Good	Retail Excellent
GRAND CARAVAN—V6 Flex Fuel—Truck Equipment Schedule T1						
AVP Minivan	DGBG	20990	10150	10750	11950	14450
SE Minivan	DGBG	23900	11500	12150	13450	16250
SXT Minivan	DGCG	27490	12650	13400	14650	17700
Crew Minivan	DGDG	29490	13150	13900	15400	18650
R/T Minivan	DGEG	30990	14950	15800	17250	20900

2014 DODGE — (1,2or3)C4-(DCAB)-E-#

Body Type	VIN	List	Trade-In Good	Trade-In Very Good	Pvt-Party Good	Retail Excellent
JOURNEY—4-Cyl.—Truck Equipment Schedule T1						
AVP Sport Utility	DCAB	20490	12600	12850	14950	17150
SE Sport Utility 4D	DDAG	25890	15000	15300	17450	19800
Third Row Seat			475	475	540	540
JOURNEY AWD—V6—Truck Equipment Schedule T1						
SXT Sport Utility	DDBG	27690	15750	16050	18300	20800
Third Row Seat			475	475	540	540
FWD	C		(1375)	(1375)	(1590)	(1590)
4-Cyl, 2.4 Liter	B		(1075)	(1075)	(1240)	(1240)
JOURNEY AWD—V6—Truck Equipment Schedule T1						
SXT Plus Sport Util 4D		28685	16150	16450	18700	21200
Crossroad Spt Util	DDGB	29390	18000	18300	20400	22900
Third Row Seat			475	475	540	540
FWD			(1375)	(1375)	(1585)	(1585)
4-Cyl, 2.4 Liter			(1075)	(1075)	(1240)	(1240)
JOURNEY AWD—V6—Truck Equipment Schedule T1						
Limited Sport Util	DDDG	31190	19000	19350	21700	24500
R/T Sport Utility	DDEG	31790	19800	20400	22100	25100
Third Row Seat			475	475	540	540
FWD	C		(1375)	(1375)	(1595)	(1595)
DURANGO AWD—V6 Flex Fuel—Truck Equipment Schedule T1						
SXT Sport Util 4D	DJAG	33190	23000	23300	24800	28300
SXT Plus Sport Util	DJAG	34890	22600	22900	24500	27900
Citadel Sport Util	DJET	44390	31400	32000	34000	37100
2WD	H		(1700)	(1700)	(1910)	(1910)
DURANGO AWD—V8 HEMI—Truck Equipment Schedule T1						
Special Serv Spt Util	DJFT	34290				
Limited Sport Util	DJDT	39390	26700	27200	29300	32300
2WD	G		(1700)	(1700)	(1885)	(1885)
V6, Flex Fuel, 3.6 Liter	H		(1175)	(1175)	(1305)	(1305)
DURANGO AWD—V8 HEMI—Truck Equipment Schedule T1						
R/T Sport Utility 4D	DJCT	42390	29900	30400	31900	36000
2WD	G		(1700)	(1700)	(1895)	(1895)
GRAND CARAVAN—V6 Flex Fuel—Truck Equipment Schedule T1						
AVP Minivan 4D	DGBG	20990	11650	12350	13450	16050
SE Minivan 4D	DGBG	24390	13500	14300	15500	18450
SE 30th Anniv	DGBG	25690	14500	15350	16450	19450
SXT Minivan 4D	DGCG	27690	14900	15750	17000	20300
SXT 30th Anniv	DGCG	28990	16000	16900	18150	21600
R/T Minivan 4D	DGEG	30990	17200	18150	19450	23200

FORD

2000 FORD-(1,2or3)F(B,MorT)-(U70X)-Y-#

Body Type	VIN	List	Trade-In Good	Trade-In Very Good	Pvt-Party Good	Retail Excellent
EXPLORER SPORT 4WD—V6—Truck Equipment Schedule T1						
Utility 2D	U70X	24690	475	600	1075	1950
2WD	6		(525)	(525)	(715)	(715)
V6, SOHC, 4.0 Liter	E		75	75	110	110
EXPLORER 4WD—V6—Truck Equipment Schedule T1						
XL Sport Utility 4D	U72X	26790	575	725	1250	2300
Eddie Bauer Spt Util	U74P	34470	875	1050	1675	3050
2WD	6		(525)	(525)	(715)	(715)
AWD	8		0	0	0	0
V6, SOHC, 4.0 Liter	E		75	75	110	110
V8, 5.0 Liter	P		100	100	125	125
EXPEDITION 4WD—V8—Truck Equipment Schedule T1						
XLT Sport Utility 4D	U166	33165	1075	1275	1825	3250
Eddie Bauer Spt Util	U186	40575	1575	1825	2500	4475
Third Row Seat			(125)	(125)	(155)	(155)
2WD	5,7		(325)	(325)	(445)	(445)
V8, 5.4 Liter	L		75	75	100	100
EXCURSION 4WD—V10—Truck Equipment Schedule T1						
XLT Sport Utility 4D	U41S	38090	2800	3200	3725	6025

Body Type	VIN	List	Trade-In Good	Trade-In Very Good	Pvt-Party Good	Retail Excellent
Third Row Seat			225	225	310	310
2WD			(325)	(325)	(445)	(445)
V8, 5.4 Liter	L		(250)	(250)	(335)	(335)
V8, Turbo Diesel, 7.3L	F		3325	3325	4445	4445
WINDSTAR—V6—Truck Equipment Schedule T2						
Cargo Minivan	A544	20395	900	1050	1475	2575
WINDSTAR—V6—Truck Equipment Schedule T1						
Minivan	A504	23080	550	675	1150	2075
LX Minivan	A514	25045	725	850	1350	2450
SE Minivan	A524	28195	1075	1250	1825	3250
SEL Minivan	A534	31095	1175	1375	1950	3475
Limited Minivan	A534	33990	1350	1575	2150	3850
Second Sliding Door			50	50	60	60
V6, 3.0 Liter	U		(100)	(100)	(115)	(115)
ECONOLINE WAGON—V8—Truck Equipment Schedule T1						
E150 Passenger Van	E11L	23810	1550	1825	2075	3375
E350 Super Duty Van	E31L	25900	1650	1950	2200	3600
E350 Super Duty Ext	S31L	27570	1725	2050	2400	3950
V6, 4.2 Liter	2		(200)	(200)	(265)	(265)
V8, Turbo Diesel, 7.3L	F		1100	1100	1470	1470
V10, 6.8 Liter	S		225	225	285	285
ECONOLINE VAN—V6—Truck Equipment Schedule T1						
E150 Cargo Van	E142	20950	1150	1300	1800	3025
E250 Cargo Van	E242	22055	1200	1375	1875	3175
E250 Extended	E242	22900	1625	1850	2500	4300
V8, 4.6 Liter	W		75	75	100	100
V8, 5.4 Liter	L		100	100	135	135
ECONOLINE VAN—V8—Truck Equipment Schedule T1						
E350 Super Cargo	E34L	24500	1450	1650	2225	3775
E350 Ext SD Cargo	S34L	25475	1725	1950	2650	4575
V8, Turbo Diesel, 7.3L	F		1100	1100	1470	1470
V10, 6.8 Liter	S		225	225	285	285
RANGER PICKUP—4-Cyl.—Truck Equipment Schedule T2						
Short Bed	R10C	11995	850	1025	1275	2100
Long Bed	R10C	12465	775	925	1175	1975
Super Cab 2D	R14C	15655	975	1175	1475	2475
Super Cab 4D	R14C	16230	1650	1975	2375	4025
4WD	1,5		400	400	535	535
V6, Flex Fuel, 3.0 Liter	V		125	125	165	165
V6, 4.0 Liter	X		150	150	200	200
REGULAR CAB PICKUP—V8—Truck Equipment Schedule T1						
F150 Short Bed	F17W	19510	1700	2000	2400	4075
F150 Long Bed	F17W	19810	1450	1700	2100	3550
4WD	6,8		625	625	820	820
Work Truck			(250)	(250)	(335)	(335)
V6, 4.2 Liter	2		(350)	(350)	(455)	(455)
V8, 5.4 Liter	L		75	75	100	100
REGULAR CAB—V8 Supercharged—Truck Equip Schedule T1						
F150 Lightning	F073	30895	5650	6500	6550	9775
SUPER CAB PICKUP—V8—Truck Equipment Schedule T1						
F150 Short Bed	X17W	22195	2400	2650	3725	6250
F150 Long Bed	X17W	22495	1775	1975	2900	4900
4WD	6,8		625	625	820	820
Work Truck			(250)	(250)	(335)	(335)
V6, 4.2 Liter	2		(350)	(350)	(455)	(455)
V8, 5.4 Liter	L		75	75	100	100
SUPER CAB PICKUP—V8—Truck Equipment Schedule T1						
F150 Harley	X17L	33800	5075	5825	5875	8900
SUPER DUTY REGULAR CAB PICKUP—V8—Truck Equip Schedule T1						
F250 Long Bed	F20L	22450	2525	2900	3150	4900
F350 Long Bed	F30L	23175	2650	3050	3350	5225
4WD	1		625	625	820	820
V8, Turbo Diesel, 7.3L	F		3325	3325	4445	4445
V10, 6.8 Liter	S		225	225	305	305
SUPER DUTY SUPER CAB PICKUP—V8—Truck Equip Schedule T1						
F250 Short Bed	X20L	24620	3375	3875	4300	6825
F250 Long Bed	X20L	24820	3200	3675	4000	6275
F350 Short Bed	X30L	25410	3550	4075	4475	7125
F350 Long Bed	X30L	25610	3450	3950	4350	6925
4WD	1		625	625	820	820
V8, Turbo Diesel, 7.3L	F		3325	3325	4445	4445
V10, 6.8 Liter	S		225	225	305	305

Body Type	VIN	List	Trade-In Good	Very Good	Pvt-Party Good	Retail Excellent
SUPER DUTY CREW CAB PICKUP—V8—Truck Equipment Schedule T1						
F250 Short Bed	W20L	25930	3850	4425	4925	7775
F250 Long Bed	W20L	26130	3700	4250	4775	7550
F350 Short Bed	W30L	26590	4425	5075	5525	8675
F350 Long Bed	W30L	26790	4000	4600	5100	8100
4WD	1		625	625	820	820
V8, Turbo Diesel, 7.3L	F		3325	3325	4445	4445
V10, 6.8 Liter	S		225	225	305	305

2001 FORD — (1or2)F(B,MorT)-(U011)-1-#

Body Type	VIN	List	Trade-In Good	Very Good	Pvt-Party Good	Retail Excellent
ESCAPE—V6—Truck Equipment Schedule T1						
XLS Sport Utility 4D	U011	19975	775	875	1550	2800
4WD			375	375	485	485
4-Cyl, 2.0 Liter	B		(275)	(275)	(375)	(375)
ESCAPE 4WD—V6—Truck Equipment Schedule T1						
XLT Sport Utility 4D	U041	22815	1250	1425	2150	3725
2WD			(275)	(275)	(510)	(510)
4-Cyl, 2.0 Liter	B		(275)	(275)	(375)	(375)
EXPLORER SPORT 4WD—V6—Truck Equipment Schedule T1						
Sport Utility 2D	U70E	24435	625	750	1200	2125
2WD	6		(625)	(625)	(820)	(820)
EXPLORER 4WD—V6—Truck Equipment Schedule T1						
XLS Sport Utility 4D	U71E	27570	650	775	1275	2325
Eddie Bauer Spt Util	U74E	34590	975	1175	1725	3075
2WD	6		(625)	(625)	(820)	(820)
AWD	8		0	0	0	0
V8, 5.0 Liter	P		100	100	130	130
EXPLORER SPORT TRAC 4WD—V6—Truck Equipment Sch T1						
Utility Pickup 4D	U77E	25010	3050	3275	4325	6650
2WD	6		(625)	(625)	(820)	(820)
EXPEDITION 4WD—V8—Truck Equipment Schedule T1						
XLT Sport Util 4D	U16W	33405	1275	1475	2050	3575
Eddie Bauer Util	U18W	41410	1850	2125	2875	5000
Third Row Seat			(150)	(150)	(185)	(185)
2WD	5		(375)	(375)	(510)	(510)
V8, 5.4 Liter	L		75	75	100	100
EXCURSION 4WD—V10—Truck Equipment Schedule T1						
XLT Sport Utility 4D	U41S	38925	3350	3850	4425	7075
Third Row Seat			250	250	350	350
2WD	0,2		(375)	(375)	(510)	(510)
V8, 5.4 Liter	L		(275)	(275)	(380)	(380)
V8, Turbo Diesel, 7.3L	F		3525	3525	4710	4710
WINDSTAR—V6—Truck Equipment Schedule T2						
Cargo Minivan	A544	20540	1100	1275	1750	3000
WINDSTAR—V6—Truck Equipment Schedule T1						
LX Minivan	A514	25320	775	925	1450	2600
SE Sport Minivan	A574	27755	1175	1375	1975	3475
SE Minivan	A524	28915	1350	1550	2150	3825
SEL Minivan	A534	31435	1450	1675	2300	4075
Limited Minivan	A584	34085	1575	1825	2475	4350
Second Sliding Door			50	50	65	65
ECONOLINE WAGON—V8—Truck Equipment Schedule T1						
E150 Passenger Van	E11W	24060	1825	2150	2500	4100
E350 Super Duty	E31L	26350	1950	2275	2675	4375
E350 Super Duty Ext	S31L	27970	2100	2450	2875	4700
V6, 4.2 Liter	2		(200)	(200)	(265)	(265)
V8, 5.4 Liter (E150)	L		100	100	135	135
V8, Turbo Diesel, 7.3L	F		1125	1125	1500	1500
V10, 6.8 Liter	S		250	250	320	320
ECONOLINE VAN—V6—Truck Equipment Schedule T1						
E150 Cargo Van	E142	21445	1450	1650	2150	3600
E250 Cargo Van	E242	22565	1500	1700	2225	3725
E250 Extended	S242	23410	1875	2125	2925	4975
Crew Van Pkg			150	150	200	200
V8, 4.6 Liter	W		75	75	100	100
V8, 5.4 Liter	L		100	100	135	135
ECONOLINE VAN—V8—Truck Equipment Schedule T1						
E350 Super Cargo	E34L	24995	1725	1950	2550	4325
E350 Ext SD Cargo	S34L	25970	2000	2275	3100	5300
V8, Turbo Diesel, 7.3L	F		1125	1125	1500	1500
V10, 6.8 Liter	S		250	250	320	320
RANGER PICKUP—4-Cyl.—Truck Equipment Schedule T2						
Short Bed	R10C	12400	950	1125	1400	2325

Body Type	VIN	List	Trade-In Good	Very Good	Pvt-Party Good	Retail Excellent
Long Bed	R10C	13515	875	1050	1325	2200
Super Cab 2D	R14C	16465	1250	1475	1850	3150
Super Cab 4D	R14C	20960	1950	2300	2825	4800
4WD	1,5		400	400	535	535
V6, 3.0 Liter	U		125	125	165	165
V6, 4.0 Liter	E		150	150	200	200
REGULAR CAB PICKUP—V8—Truck Equipment Schedule T1						
F150 Short Bed	F17W	20170	1750	2050	2525	4200
F150 Long Bed	F17W	20470	1575	1850	2200	3675
Work Truck			(250)	(250)	(335)	(335)
4WD	6,8		725	725	955	955
V6, 4.2 Liter	2		(350)	(350)	(465)	(465)
V8, 5.4 Liter	L,Z		75	75	100	100
REGULAR CAB PICKUP—V8 Supercharged—Truck Schedule T1						
F150 Lightning	P073	32460	7125	8150	7950	11650
SUPER CAB PICKUP—V8—Truck Equipment Schedule T1						
F150 Short Bed	X17W	22855	1925	2125	3000	4950
F150 Long Bed	X17W	23155	2250	2475	3475	5775
Work Truck			(250)	(250)	(335)	(335)
4WD	6,8		725	725	955	955
V6, 4.2 Liter	2		(350)	(350)	(465)	(465)
V8, 5.4 Liter	L,Z		75	75	100	100
SUPERCREW PICKUP—V8—Truck Equipment Schedule T1						
F150 Short Bed 4D	W07W	26940	3400	3725	4725	7650
F150 King Ranch	W07W	31455	4275	4700	6025	9750
4WD	8		725	725	955	955
V8, 5.4 Liter	L		75	75	100	100
SUPERCREW PICKUP—V8—Truck Equipment Schedule T1						
F150 Harley	W07L	34495	5800	6625	6775	10100
SUPER DUTY REGULAR CAB—V8—Truck Equipment Schedule T1						
F250 Long Bed	F20L	23155	2675	3050	3300	5050
F350 Long Bed	F30L	23580	2875	3300	3525	5400
4WD	1		725	725	955	955
V8, Turbo Diesel, 7.3L	F		3525	3525	4710	4710
V10, 6.8 Liter	S		250	250	340	340
SUPER DUTY SUPER CAB—V8—Truck Equipment Schedule T1						
F250 Short Bed	X20L	25295	3525	4000	4325	6750
F250 Long Bed	X20L	25495	3525	4025	4275	6600
F350 Short Bed	X30L	26085	3825	4375	4750	7325
F350 Long Bed	X30L	26285	3700	4225	4600	7100
4WD	1		725	725	955	955
V8, Turbo Diesel, 7.3L	F		3525	3525	4710	4710
V10, 6.8 Liter	S		250	250	340	340
SUPER DUTY CREW CAB—V8—Truck Equipment Schedule T1						
F250 Short Bed	W20L	25295	4275	4900	5275	8150
F250 Long Bed	W20L	26805	4150	4725	5100	7850
F350 Short Bed	W30L	27265	4850	5550	5775	8775
F350 Long Bed	W30L	27465	4450	5100	5425	8325
Platinum Edition			75	75	100	100
4WD	1		725	725	955	955
V8, Turbo Diesel, 7.3L	F		3525	3525	4710	4710
V10, 6.8 Liter	S		250	250	340	340

2002 FORD — (1or2)F(B,MorU)–(U011)–2–#

Body Type	VIN	List	Trade-In Good	Very Good	Pvt-Party Good	Retail Excellent
ESCAPE—V6—Truck Equipment Schedule T1						
XLS Sport Utility 4D	U011	20465	975	1100	1725	3000
4WD			425	425	560	560
4-Cyl, 2.0 Liter	B		(300)	(300)	(415)	(415)
ESCAPE 4WD—V6—Truck Equipment Schedule T1						
XLT Sport Utility 4D	U041	23935	2075	2300	2900	4650
2WD			(425)	(425)	(575)	(575)
4-Cyl, 2.0 Liter	B		(300)	(300)	(415)	(415)
EXPLORER SPORT 4WD—V6—Truck Equipment Schedule T1						
Sport Utility 2D	U70E	24785	925	1100	1675	2950
2WD	6		(700)	(700)	(935)	(935)
EXPLORER 4WD—V6—Truck Equipment Schedule T1						
XLS Sport Utility 4D	U72E	27775	1200	1425	2125	3800
Eddie Bauer Spt Util	U74E	35135	1550	1800	2575	4600
Third Row Seat			225	225	310	310
2WD	6		(700)	(700)	(935)	(935)
V8, 4.6 Liter	W		125	125	155	155
EXPLORER SPORT TRAC 4WD—V6—Truck Equipment Schedule T1						
Utility Pickup 4D	U77E	25410	3550	3825	5025	7625

TRUCKS & VANS

TRUCKS & VANS

Body Type	VIN	List	Trade-In Good	Very Good	Pvt-Party Good	Retail Excellent
2WD	6	......	(700)	(700)	(935)	(935)
EXPEDITION 4WD—V8—Truck Equipment Schedule T1						
XLT Sport Utility	U16W	33810	1575	1800	2325	3950
Eddie Bauer Spt Ut	U18W	41825	2150	2500	3175	5450
Third Row Seat		......	(175)	(175)	(220)	(220)
2WD	5,7	......	(425)	(425)	(575)	(575)
V8, 5.4 Liter	L	......	100	100	145	145
EXCURSION 4WD—V10—Truck Equipment Schedule T1						
XLT Sport Utility 4D	U41S	38985	3925	4475	5025	7800
Third Row Seat		......	300	300	385	385
2WD		......	(425)	(425)	(575)	(575)
V8, 5.4 Liter	L	......	(325)	(325)	(420)	(420)
V8, Turbo Diesel, 7.3L	F	......	3725	3725	4980	4980
WINDSTAR—V6—Truck Equipment Schedule T2						
Cargo Minivan	A544	20905	1400	1625	2075	3475
WINDSTAR—V6—Truck Equipment Schedule T1						
LX Minivan	A514	22995	925	1075	1600	2800
SE Minivan	A524	29280	1600	1850	2450	4200
SEL Minivan	A534	31950	1725	1975	2575	4450
Limited Minivan	A584	34360	1775	2050	2750	4725
Second Sliding Door		......	50	50	65	65
ECONOLINE WAGON—V6—Truck Equipment Schedule T1						
E150 Passenger Van	E112	24660	2150	2500	2875	4675
V8, 4.6 Liter	W	......	125	125	155	155
V8, 5.4 Liter	L	......	125	125	155	155
ECONOLINE WAGON—V8—Truck Equipment Schedule T1						
E350 Super Duty	E31L	26950	2325	2700	3075	4950
E350 Super Duty Ext	S31L	28370	2475	2875	3300	5350
V8, Turbo Diesel, 7.3L	F	......	1250	1250	1655	1655
V10, 6.8 Liter	S	......	275	275	355	355
ECONOLINE VAN—V6—Truck Equipment Schedule T1						
E150 Cargo Van	E142	21880	1750	1975	2600	4275
E250 Cargo Van	E242	22750	1800	2025	2650	4375
E250 Extended	E242	23960	2275	2575	3300	5475
Crew Van Pkg		......	150	150	215	215
V8, 4.6 Liter	W	......	75	75	100	100
V8, 5.4 Liter	L	......	125	125	155	155
ECONOLINE VAN—V8—Truck Equipment Schedule T1						
E350 Super Duty Cargo	E34L	25230	2050	2325	3000	4975
E350 Ext SD Cargo	E34L	26520	2425	2725	3500	5800
Crew Van Pkg		......	150	150	215	215
V8, Turbo Diesel, 7.3L	F	......	1250	1250	1655	1655
V10, 6.8 Liter	S	......	275	275	355	355
RANGER PICKUP—4-Cyl.—Truck Equipment Schedule T2						
Short Bed	R10C	12725	1125	1325	1725	2925
Long Bed	R10C	13655	1050	1225	1600	2750
Super Cab 2D	R14C	16400	1900	2225	2750	4650
Super Cab 4D	R14C	18075	2650	3100	3675	6250
4WD	1,5	......	500	500	665	665
V6, 3.0 Liter	U	......	150	150	185	185
V6, Flex Fuel, 3.0 Liter	V	......	150	150	185	185
V6, 4.0 Liter	E	......	175	175	245	245
REGULAR CAB PICKUP—V8—Truck Equipment Schedule T1						
F150 Short Bed	F17W	20640	2200	2575	2950	4750
F150 Long Bed	F17W	20940	1975	2300	2650	4250
Work Truck		......	(275)	(275)	(375)	(375)
4WD	6,8	......	850	850	1135	1135
V6, 4.2 Liter	2	......	(375)	(375)	(485)	(485)
V8, 5.4 Liter	L,Z	......	100	100	145	145
V8, Flex Fuel, 5.4 Liter	M	......	100	100	145	145
REGULAR CAB PICKUP—V8 Supercharged—Truck Equipment Schedule T1						
F150 Lightning	F073	32490	7300	8300	8200	11900
SUPER CAB PICKUP—V8—Truck Equipment Schedule T1						
F150 Short Bed	X17W	23290	2250	2475	3325	5400
F150 Long Bed	X17W	22840	2250	2475	3500	5775
F150 King Ranch	X17W	29735	3650	4000	5100	8125
Work Truck		......	(275)	(275)	(375)	(375)
4WD	6,8	......	850	850	1135	1135
V6, 4.2 Liter	2	......	(375)	(375)	(485)	(485)
V8, 5.4 Liter	L,Z	......	100	100	145	145
SUPERCREW PICKUP—V8—Truck Equipment Schedule T1						
F150 Short Bed 4D	W07W	27660	3600	3950	5050	8025
F150 King Ranch 4D	W07W	32135	4775	5225	6500	10300

1015

Body Type	VIN	List	Trade-In Good	Very Good	Pvt-Party Good	Retail Excellent
4WD	8		850	850	1135	1135
V8, 5.4 Liter	L		100	100	145	145
SUPERCREW PICKUP—V8 Supercharged—Truck Equipment Schedule T1						
F150 Harley	W073	36520	5400	6150	6500	9775
SUPER DUTY REGULAR CAB PICKUP—V8—Truck Equipment Schedule T1						
F250 Long Bed	F20L	22725	3075	3475	3675	5550
F350 Long Bed	F30L	23985	3625	4100	4150	6150
4WD	1		850	850	1135	1135
V8, Turbo Diesel, 7.3L	F		3725	3725	4980	4980
V10, 6.8 Liter	S		275	275	380	380
SUPER DUTY SUPER CAB PICKUP—V8—Truck Equipment Schedule T1						
F250 Short Bed	X20L	25715	4475	5100	5200	7675
F250 Long Bed	X20L	25915	4250	4850	4950	7325
F350 Short Bed	X30L	26505	4675	5325	5400	7975
F350 Long Bed	X30L	26705	4550	5175	5275	7775
4WD	1		850	850	1135	1135
V8, Turbo Diesel, 7.3L	F		3725	3725	4980	4980
V10, 6.8 Liter	S		275	275	380	380
SUPER DUTY CREW CAB PICKUP—V8—Truck Equipment Schedule T1						
F250 Short Bed	W20L	27025	5250	5950	6000	8875
F250 Long Bed	W20L	27225	5050	5725	5800	8550
F350 Short Bed	W30L	27685	5600	6350	6350	9325
F350 Long Bed	W30L	27885	6150	7000	6925	10000
4WD	1		850	850	1135	1135
V8, Turbo Diesel, 7.3L	F		3725	3725	4980	4980
V10, 6.8 Liter	S		275	275	380	380

2003 FORD — (1or2)F(B,D,MorT)–(U021)–3–#

Body Type	VIN	List	Trade-In Good	Very Good	Pvt-Party Good	Retail Excellent
ESCAPE—V6—Truck Equipment Schedule T1						
XLS Sport Utility 4D	U021	20925	1125	1275	1875	3175
4WD	B		475	475	635	635
4-Cyl, 2.0 Liter	B		(350)	(350)	(460)	(460)
ESCAPE 4WD—V6—Truck Equipment Schedule T1						
XLT Sport Utility 4D	U931	25475	2150	2400	3175	5200
Limited Spt Util 4D	U941	27475	2550	2850	3625	5925
2WD	0		(475)	(475)	(645)	(645)
EXPLORER SPORT 4WD—V6—Truck Equipment Schedule T1						
XLS Sport Util 2D	U70E	26055	1400	1625	2100	3525
XLT Spt Util 2D	U70E	27405	1500	1725	2275	3850
2WD	6		(775)	(775)	(1040)	(1040)
EXPLORER 4WD—V6 Flex Fuel—Truck Equipment Schedule T1						
XLS Sport Utility 4D	U72K	29155	1400	1625	2150	3650
XLT Utility 4D	U73K	31695	1625	1875	2500	4200
NBX Sport Utility	U73K	32870	1800	2100	2725	4575
Eddie Bauer 4D	U74K	35970	2325	2700	3325	5550
Limited Sport Util	U75K	36645	2375	2750	3400	5650
Third Row Seat			275	275	355	355
2WD	6		(775)	(775)	(1040)	(1040)
AWD	8		0	0	0	0
V8, 4.6 Liter	W		150	150	185	185
EXPLORER SPORT TRAC 4WD—V6—Truck Equipment Schedule T1						
XLS Util Pickup 4D	U77E	26285	3100	3575	4125	6725
XLT Sport Pickup	U77K	27880	4200	4500	5800	8700
2WD	6		(775)	(775)	(1040)	(1040)
EXPEDITION—V8—Truck Equipment Schedule T1						
XLT Sport Util 4D	U15W	31295	2275	2600	3000	4775
Third Row Seat			(200)	(200)	(255)	(255)
4WD	6,8		475	475	635	635
V8, 5.4 Liter	L		150	150	210	210
EXPEDITION 4WD—V8—Truck Equipment Schedule T1						
FX4 Off-Rd Spt Util	U16W	38470	3275	3750	4125	6575
Eddie Bauer Spt Ut	U18W	42055	3525	4025	4550	7200
Third Row Seat			(200)	(200)	(255)	(255)
2WD	5,7		(475)	(475)	(645)	(645)
V8, 5.4 Liter	L		150	150	210	210
EXCURSION 4WD—V10—Truck Equipment Schedule T1						
XLT Sport Utility 4D	U41S	40340	4400	5000	5450	8300
Eddie Bauer Spt Util	U45S	44405	6075	6925	7325	11000
Limited Spt Util 4D	U43S	45465	6100	6950	7400	11150
Third Row Seat			325	325	445	445
2WD	0,2,4		(475)	(475)	(645)	(645)
V8, 5.4 Liter	L		(350)	(350)	(465)	(465)
V8, Turbo Diesel, 6.0L	P		2625	2625	3505	3505

TRUCKS & VANS

TRUCKS & VANS

Body Type	VIN	List	Trade-In Good	Very Good	Pvt-Party Good	Retail Excellent
V8, Turbo Diesel, 7.3L	F		3925	3925	5245	5245
WINDSTAR—V6—Truck Equipment Schedule T2						
Cargo Minivan	A544	21360	1700	1925	2600	4475
WINDSTAR—V6—Truck Equipment Schedule T1						
LX Minivan	A514	23365	1150	1325	2050	3675
SE Minivan	A524	29675	1800	2075	3025	5350
SEL Minivan	A534	32405	1925	2200	3175	5600
Limited Minivan	A584	35110	2075	2375	3375	5950
Second Sliding Door	0		50	50	65	65
ECONOLINE WAGON—V6—Truck Equipment Schedule T1						
E150 XL Passenger	E112	24595	2450	2825	3000	4600
E150 XLT Passenger	E112	27435	2850	3275	3550	5575
E150 Chateau Pass	W	29600	3250	3750	3900	6000
V8, 4.6 Liter	W		100	100	120	120
V8, 5.4 Liter	M,L		150	150	185	185
ECONOLINE WAGON—V8—Truck Equipment Schedule T1						
E350 XL Super Duty	E31L	27635	2750	3175	3475	5475
E350 XLT Passenger	E31L	30440	3350	3875	4025	6175
E350 Chateau Pass	E31L	32240	3600	4150	4400	6800
E350 SD Ext	S31L	29055	3375	3875	4050	6275
E350 XLT Extended	S31L	30910	3525	4050	4325	6650
V8, Turbo Diesel, 7.3L	F		1425	1425	1890	1890
V10, 6.8 Liter	S		325	325	435	435
ECONOLINE VAN—V6—Truck Equipment Schedule T1						
E150 Super Cargo	E142	22420	2150	2425	3150	5200
E250 Super Cargo	E242	23290	2200	2475	3200	5300
E250 Extended SD	E242	24200	2850	3200	4000	6675
Crew Van Pkg	W		175	175	225	225
V8, 4.6 Liter	W		100	100	120	120
V8, 5.4 Liter	L,M		150	150	185	185
ECONOLINE VAN—V8—Truck Equipment Schedule T1						
E350 Super Cargo	E34L	25770	2675	3000	3825	6300
E350 Extended SD	E34L	26760	3275	3650	4575	7550
Crew Van Pkg			175	175	225	225
V8, Turbo Diesel, 7.3L	F		1425	1425	1890	1890
V10, 6.8 Liter	S		325	325	435	435
RANGER REGULAR CAB PICKUP—4-Cyl.—Truck Equipment Schedule T2						
XL 2D 6'	R10D	14620	1325	1550	1825	2925
XL 2D 7'	R10D	14655	975	1150	1425	2300
XLT 2D 6'	R10D	16280	2050	2400	2725	4375
XLT 2D 7'	R10D	17705	1525	1775	2025	3275
4WD	1,5		625	625	820	820
V6, 3.0 Liter	U		175	175	220	220
V6, 4.0 Liter	E		225	225	285	285
RANGER REGULAR CAB PICKUP—V6 4WD—Truck Equipment Schedule T2						
Edge Plus 2D 6'	R11U	20450	2050	2400	2725	4375
V6, 4.0 Liter	E		225	225	285	285
RANGER SUPER CAB—4-Cyl.—Truck Equipment Schedule T2						
XLT 4D 6'	R44D	21645	3300	3800	4125	6625
4WD	1,5		625	625	820	820
V6, 3.0 Liter	U		175	175	220	220
V6, Flex Fuel, 3.0 Liter	V		175	175	220	220
V6, 4.0 Liter	E		225	225	285	285
RANGER SUPER CAB—V6—Truck Equipment Schedule T2						
XLT 2D 6'	R14U	20560	2725	3150	3475	5600
4WD	1,5		625	625	820	820
4-Cyl, 2.3 Liter	D		(200)	(200)	(250)	(250)
V6, 4.0 Liter	E		50	50	65	65
RANGER SUPER CAB—V6—Truck Equipment Schedule T2						
XL 2D 6'	R14U	18320	2375	2750	3075	4975
XL 4D 6'	R44U	18905	2600	3025	3350	5375
Edge 2D 6'	R14U	19235	3025	3525	3825	6175
Edge 4D 6'	R44U	21645	3375	3900	4225	6775
Edge Plus 4D 6'	R44U	20990	2950	3425	3725	6000
Tremor 2D 6'	R14U	19775	2725	3150	3475	5600
Tremor Plus 4D 6'	R44U	22075	2425	2825	3150	5075
4WD	1,5		625	625	820	820
V6, 4.0 Liter	E		225	225	285	285
RANGER SUPER CAB—V6 4WD—Truck Equipment Schedule T2						
XLT FX4 Off-Road 6'	R45E	25425	5225	6050	5950	9075
XLT FX4 Level II 6'	R44E	25890	5125	5925	5850	8925
REGULAR CAB PICKUP—V8—Truck Equipment Schedule T1						
F150 XL 2D 6 1/2'	F17W	21450	2050	2375	2975	4925

Body Type	VIN	List	Trade-In Good	Very Good	Pvt-Party Good	Retail Excellent
F150 XL 2D 8'	F17W	21750	1850	2150	2750	4550
F150 XL STX 6 1/2'	F17W	22445	2250	2625	3200	5325
F150 XL STX 2D 8'	F17W	22745	2100	2450	3050	5050
F150 XLT 2D 6 1/2'	F17W	24120	2525	2900	3500	5800
F150 XLT 2D 8'	F17W	24415	2425	2800	3400	5625
F150 XLT STX 6 1/2'	F17W	25115	2700	3125	3700	6075
F150 XLT STX 2D 8'	F17W	25410	2550	2950	3550	5850
4WD	8		1025	1025	1380	1380
V6, 4.2 Liter	2		(400)	(400)	(520)	(520)
V8, 5.4 Liter	L		150	150	210	210
V8, Flex Fuel, 5.4 Liter	Z		150	150	210	210
REGULAR CAB PICKUP—V8 Supercharged—Truck Equipment Schedule T1						
F150 Lightning	F073	33255	9850	11100	10300	14200
SUPER CAB PICKUP—V8—Truck Equipment Schedule T1						
F150 XL 4D 6 1/2'	X17W	24100	3200	3475	4125	6300
F150 XL 4D 8'	X17W	24400	2925	3175	3825	5825
F150 XL STX 4D 6 1/2'	X17W	25095	3250	3525	4200	6375
F150 XL STX 4D 8'	X17W	25395	3050	3325	3975	6050
F150 XLT 4D 6 1/2'	X17W	26965	3575	3900	4650	7000
F150 XLT 4D 8'	X17W	27265	3425	3725	4325	6550
F150 XLT STX 6 1/2'	X17W	29250	3525	3850	4525	6900
F150 XLT STX 8'	X17W	28560	3275	3550	4225	6425
F150 Heritage 6 1/2'	X17W	28165	3500	3825	4500	6850
F150 Lariat 6 1/2'	X17W	28680	3575	3925	4725	7150
F150 King Ranch 4D	X07W	31660	4675	5100	5975	9075
4WD	8		1025	1025	1380	1380
V6, 4.2 Liter	2		(400)	(400)	(520)	(520)
V8, 5.4 Liter	L		150	150	210	210
SUPERCREW PICKUP—V8—Truck Equipment Schedule T1						
F150 XL 4D 6 1/2'	W076	28965	4950	5375	6200	9350
F150 Lariat 4D 6 1/2'	W076	31055	5675	6200	7375	11200
F150 King Ranch 4D	W076	33115	5925	6450	7700	11750
4WD	8		1025	1025	1380	1380
V8, 5.4 Liter	L		150	150	210	210
SUPERCREW PICKUP—V8 Supercharged—Truck Equipment Schedule T1						
F150 Harley 5 1/2'	W073	37295	8325	9375	9025	12750
SUPER DUTY REGULAR CAB PICKUP—V8—Truck Equipment Schedule T1						
F250 XL 8'	F20L	23335	2475	2800	3250	5050
F250 XLT 4D 8'	F20L	26590	2900	3275	3700	5725
F350 XL 4D 8'	F30L	23790	2750	3100	3500	5350
F350 XLT 4D 8'	F30L	27395	3075	3500	3900	6025
4WD	1		1025	1025	1380	1380
V8, Turbo Diesel, 6.0L	P		2625	2625	3505	3505
V8, Turbo Diesel, 7.3L	F		3925	3925	5245	5245
V10, 6.8 Liter	S		325	325	415	415
SUPER DUTY SUPER CAB PICKUP—V8—Truck Equipment Schedule T1						
F250 XL 4D 6 3/4'	X20L	25520	3725	4225	4725	7250
F250 XL 4D 8'	X20L	25720	3550	4025	4425	6800
F250 XLT 4D 6 3/4'	X20L	29510	4000	4525	5075	7775
F250 XLT 4D 8'	X20L	29710	3800	4325	4850	7450
F250 Lariat 4D 6 3/4'	X20L	31630	4175	4725	5250	8050
F250 Lariat 4D 8'	X20L	31830	3950	4475	5025	7700
F350 XL 4D 6 1/2'	X20L	26310	3925	4450	5000	7650
F350 XL 4D 8'	X20L	26510	3800	4325	4850	7450
F350 XL 4D 6 1/2'	X30L	30655	4225	4775	5300	8125
F350 XL 4D 8'	X30L	30855	3900	4425	4950	7600
F350 Lariat 4D 6 1/2'	X30L	32630	4425	5000	5500	8425
F350 Lariat 4D 8'	X30L	32830	4275	4850	5350	8200
4WD	1		1025	1025	1380	1380
V8, Turbo Diesel, 6.0L	P		2625	2625	3505	3505
V8, Turbo Diesel, 7.3L	F		3925	3925	5245	5245
V10, 6.8 Liter	S		325	325	415	415
SUPER DUTY CREW CAB PICKUP—V8—Truck Equipment Schedule T1						
F250 XL 4D 6 1/2'	W20L	26930	4600	5200	5700	8725
F250 XL 4D 8'	W20L	30005	4375	4950	5450	8350
F250 XLT 4D 6 1/2'	W20L	31430	5250	5900	6375	9725
F250 XLT 4D 8'	W20L	31630	5100	5750	6225	9475
F250 Lariat 4D 6 1/2'	W20L	33850	5475	6175	6650	10100
F250 Lariat 4D 8'	W20L	34050	5225	5875	6350	9675
F250 King Ranch 6'	W20L	36460	5575	6325	6925	10500
F250 King Ranch 8'	W20L	36660	5375	6075	6700	10150
F350 XL 4D 6 1/2'	W30L	27590	4825	5450	5950	9075
F350 XL 4D 8'	W30L	27790	4800	5425	5900	9025

SEE BACK PAGES FOR TRUCK EQUIPMENT

Body Type	VIN	List	Trade-In Good	Very Good	Pvt-Party Good	Retail Excellent
F350 XLT 4D 6 1/2'	W30L	32440	5500	6225	6650	10100
F350 XLT 4D 8'	W30L	32640	5400	6100	6550	9975
F350 Lariat 4D 6 1/2'	W30L	34715	6525	7375	7725	11500
F350 Lariat 4D 8'	W30L	34915	6500	7350	7675	11400
F350 King Ranch 6'	W30L	37325	6000	6775	7375	11150
F350 King Ranch 8'	W30L	37525	5775	6550	7125	10800
4WD	1,3		1025	1025	1380	1380
V8, Turbo Diesel, 6.0L	P		2625	2625	3505	3505
V8, Turbo Diesel, 7.3L	P		3925	3925	5245	5245
V10, 6.8 Liter	S		325	325	415	415

2004 FORD—(1or2)F(B,MorT)—(U021)—4—#

Body Type	VIN	List	Trade-In Good	Very Good	Pvt-Party Good	Retail Excellent
ESCAPE—V6—Truck Equipment Schedule T1						
XLS Sport Utility 4D	U021	20890	1500	1675	2250	3675
4WD			525	525	705	705
4-Cyl, 2.0 Liter	B		(375)	(375)	(500)	(500)
ESCAPE 4WD—V6—Truck Equipment Schedule T1						
XLT Sport Utility 4D	U931	24770	2350	2600	3375	5425
Limited Sport Util	U941	26830	2850	3150	3975	6375
2WD	0		(525)	(525)	(710)	(710)
EXPLORER 4WD—V6 Flex Fuel—Truck Equipment Schedule T1						
XLS Utility 4D	U72K	29620	1625	1875	2675	4575
XLS "Sport" SUV	U72K	30795	1875	2150	2925	4950
XLT Sport Utility 4D	U73K	32260	2075	2375	3175	5375
XLT "Sport" 4D	U73K	33535	2150	2450	3275	5550
NBX Sport Utility	U73K	33535	2225	2575	3375	5725
Eddie Bauer Spt Util	U74K	36435	2775	3175	4025	6725
Third Row Seat			300	300	385	385
2WD	6		(875)	(875)	(1155)	(1155)
AWD	8		0	0	0	0
V8, 4.6 Liter	W		175	175	220	220
EXPLORER 4WD—V8—Truck Equipment Schedule T1						
Limited Sport Util	U75W	37645	3175	3625	4500	7475
2WD	6		(875)	(875)	(1155)	(1155)
AWD	8		0	0	0	0
V6, Flex Fuel, 4.0 Liter	K		(150)	(150)	(210)	(210)
EXPLORER SPORT TRAC 4WD—V6 Flex Fuel—Truck Equipment Schedule T1						
XLS Utility Pickup	U77K	26460	3525	4025	4900	8025
XLT Spt Util Pickup	U77K	28185	5200	5550	7050	10450
Adrenalin Util Pkup	U77K	27380	4350	4650	6475	10000
2WD	6		(875)	(875)	(1155)	(1155)
EXPEDITION—V8—Truck Equipment Schedule T1						
XLS Sport Utility	U15W	32735	2175	2475	2950	4700
XLT Sport Utility	U15W	34560	2750	3125	3600	5700
Third Row Seat			(225)	(225)	(285)	(285)
4WD	4,6,8		525	525	705	705
V8, 5.4 Liter	L		200	200	255	255
EXPEDITION 4WD—V8—Truck Equipment Schedule T1						
XLT "Sport" SUV	U16W	38485	3750	4250	4825	7625
XLT NBX Spt Util	U16W	39280	3875	4400	5000	7850
Eddie Bauer Util	U18W	42790	4325	4900	5475	8600
Third Row Seat			(225)	(225)	(285)	(285)
2WD	3,5,7		(525)	(525)	(710)	(710)
V8, 5.4 Liter	L		200	200	255	255
EXCURSION 4WD—V10—Truck Equipment Schedule T1						
XLS Sport Utility 4D	U41S	40485	5025	5675	6075	9075
XLT Sport Utility 4D	U41S	41795	5425	6150	6650	9900
Eddie Bauer Spt Util	U45S	44985	7150	8075	8500	12600
Limited Sport Util	U43S	46050	7275	8225	8700	12900
Third Row Seat			375	375	510	510
2WD	0,2,4		(525)	(525)	(710)	(710)
V8, 5.4 Liter	L		(375)	(375)	(505)	(505)
V8, Turbo Dsl 6.0L	P		2875	2875	3845	3845
FREESTAR—V6—Truck Equipment Schedule T2						
Cargo Minivan	A546	22070	475	550	1150	2100
FREESTAR—V6—Truck Equipment Schedule T1						
S Minivan	A506	24460	850	1000	1675	3025
SE Minivan	A516	26930	1050	1225	1950	3425
SES Minivan	A576	28750	1300	1500	2250	3925
SEL Minivan	A522	29995	1475	1700	2475	4300
Limited Minivan	A582	33630	1875	2125	3050	5275
ECONOLINE WAGON—V8—Truck Equipment Schedule T1						
E150 XL Passenger	E11W	25255	3100	3550	3700	5575

Body	Type	VIN	List	Trade-In Good	Trade-In Very Good	Pvt-Party Good	Retail Excellent
E150 XLT Passenger	E11W	28095	3625	4125	4250	6425
E150 Chateau	E11W	30095	4000	4575	4775	7225
E350 XL Super Duty	E31L	27995	3500	4000	4125	6225
E350 XLT Passenger	E31L	30800	4175	4775	4975	7500
E350 Chateau	E31L	32605	4625	5275	5450	8225
E350 XL S.D. Ext	S31L	29415	4075	4650	4875	7375
E350 XLT Extended	S31L	31270	4450	5075	5275	7950
V8, 5.4 Liter (E150)	M		175	175	220	220
V8, Turbo Dsl 6.0L	P		1600	1600	2120	2120
V10, 6.8 Liter	S		375	375	510	510
ECONOLINE VAN—V8—Truck Equipment Schedule T1							
E150 Super Cargo	E14W	23060	2650	2975	3625	5775
E250 Super Cargo	E24W	24105	2900	3250	3925	6250
E250 Ext SD Cargo	S24W	25220	3650	4050	4775	7575
E350 Super Cargo	E34L	26110	3425	3825	4475	7100
E350 Ext SD Cargo	S34L	27705	3950	4400	5250	8300
Crew Van Pkg			175	175	235	235
V8, 5.4 Liter (ex E350)	L		175	175	220	220
V8, Turbo Dsl 6.0L	P		1600	1600	2120	2120
V10, 6.8 Liter	S		375	375	510	510
RANGER REGULAR CAB PICKUP—4-Cyl.—Truck Equipment Schedule T2							
XL 2D 6'	R10D	15385	1875	2150	2550	4075
XL 2D 7'	R10D	15135	1475	1700	2025	3275
Edge 2D 6'	R10D	17470	2275	2650	3000	4825
XLT 2D 6'	R10D	16850	2650	3050	3400	5425
XLT 2D 7'	R10D	18570	2075	2425	2775	4450
4WD	1,5		750	750	1000	1000
V6, 3.0 Liter	U		200	200	255	255
V6, 4.0 Liter	E		250	250	320	320
RANGER SUPER CAB PICKUP—V6—Truck Equipment Schedule T2							
XLT 2D 6'	R14U	19365	3525	4075	4525	7150
4WD	1,5		750	750	1000	1000
4-Cyl, 2.3 Liter	D		(200)	(200)	(275)	(275)
V6, 4.0 Liter	E		50	50	65	65
RANGER SUPER CAB PICKUP—V6—Truck Equipment Schedule T2							
XL 2D 6'	R14U	19120	3050	3500	3850	6100
XL 4D 6'	R44U	19405	3200	3700	4025	6400
Edge 2D 6'	R14U	19765	3725	4300	4750	7500
Edge 4D 6'	R44U	22905	3875	4450	4900	7750
Tremor 2D 6'	R14U	21055	3550	4075	4400	6975
Tremor 4D 6'	R44U	23030	3950	4550	4975	7875
4WD	1,5		750	750	1000	1000
V6, 4.0 Liter	E		250	250	320	320
RANGER SUPER CAB PICKUP 4WD—V6—Truck Equipment Schedule T2							
XLT FX4 Off-Road	R45E	25970	5800	6675	6625	9925
XLT FX4 Level II	R45E	26515	5600	6450	6450	9675
HERITAGE REGULAR CAB PICKUP—V8—Truck Equipment Sch T1							
F150 XL 2D 6 1/2'	F17W	21765	2675	3050	3550	5675
F150 XL 2D 8'	F17W	22065	2200	2550	3025	4850
F150 XL STX 6 1/2'	F17W	22260	2800	3200	3700	5900
F150 XL STX 8'	F17W	22560	2500	2850	3350	5350
F150 XLT 6 1/2'	F17W	23935	3325	3775	4300	6850
F150 XLT 8'	F17W	24235	2675	3050	3550	5675
F150 XLT STX 6 1/2'	F17W	24930	3425	3900	4400	7025
F150 XLT STX 8'	F17W	25230	2875	3300	3800	6050
Work Truck			(375)	(375)	(510)	(510)
4WD	8		1175	1175	1555	1555
V6, 4.2 Liter	2		(425)	(425)	(555)	(555)
V8, Flex Fuel, 5.4 Liter	Z		200	200	255	255
HERITAGE REGULAR CAB PICKUP—V8 Supercharged—Truck Equip Sch T1							
F150 Lightning 1/2'	F073	33560	10400	11650	11050	15250
HERITAGE SUPER CAB PICKUP—V8—Truck Equipment Schedule T1							
F150 XL 4D 6 1/2'	X17W	24415	3800	4150	4825	7075
F150 XL 4D 8'	X17W	24715	3725	4050	4675	6850
F150 XLT 4D 6 1/2'	X17W	26780	4550	4925	5600	8175
F150 XLT 4D 8'	X17W	27080	4350	4725	5375	7825
Work Truck			(375)	(375)	(510)	(510)
4WD	8		1175	1175	1555	1555
V6, 4.2 Liter	2		(425)	(425)	(555)	(555)
V8, Flex Fuel, 5.4 Liter	Z		200	200	255	255
REGULAR CAB PICKUP—V8—Truck Equipment Schedule T1							
F150 XL 2D 6 1/2'	F12W	22010	2975	3400	3825	6025
F150 XL 2D 8'	F12W	22310	2650	3025	3450	5450

TRUCKS & VANS

Body Type	VIN	List	Trade-In Good	Very Good	Pvt-Party Good	Retail Excellent
F150 STX 2D 6 1/2'	F12W	22810	3650	4150	4475	6925
F150 XLT 2D 6 1/2'	F12W	25120	3625	4150	4675	7350
F150 XLT 2D 8'	F12W	25420	3325	3800	4200	6625
4WD	4		1175	1175	1555	1555
V8, 5.4 Liter	5		200	200	255	255
REGULAR CAB PICKUP 4WD—V8—Truck Equipment Schedule T1						
F150 FX4 2D 6 1/2'	F14W	30635	6050	6900	7675	12050
SUPER CAB PICKUP—V8—Truck Equipment Schedule T1						
F150 XL 4D 6 1/2'	X12W	24860	4050	4400	5050	7350
F150 XL 4D 8'	X12W	24960	3725	4050	4700	6900
F150 STX 4D 5 1/2'	X12W	25010	4350	4725	5325	7750
F150 XLT 4D 5 1/2'	X12W	27665	4575	4950	5550	8075
F150 Lariat 4D 5 1/2'	X12W	30395	5050	5475	6075	8800
F150 Lariat 4D 5 1/2'	X12W	30695	5200	5625	6250	9075
4WD	4		1175	1175	1555	1555
V8, 5.4 L (ex XLT 8')	5		200	200	255	255
SUPER CAB PICKUP 4WD—V8—Truck Equipment Schedule T1						
F150 STX 4D 6 1/2'	X14W	28845	5400	5850	6775	9950
F150 XLT 4D 6 1/2'	X14W	31300	6000	6525	7375	10750
2WD	2		(1475)	(1475)	(1960)	(1960)
V8, 5.4 Liter	5		200	200	255	255
SUPER CAB PICKUP 4WD—V8—Truck Equipment Schedule T1						
F150 XLT 4D 8'	X145	31600	5750	6250	7075	10300
2WD	2		(1475)	(1475)	(1960)	(1960)
SUPER CAB PICKUP 4WD—V8—Truck Equipment Schedule T1						
F150 FX4 4D 6 1/2'	X12W	32830	7075	7675	8450	12200
F150 FX4 4D 6 1/2'	X14W	33130	6700	7250	8175	11900
SUPERCREW PICKUP—V8—Truck Equipment Schedule T1						
F150 XLT 4D 5 1/2'	W12W	29815	5950	6450	7275	10550
4WD	4		1175	1175	1555	1555
V8, 5.4 Liter	5		200	200	255	255
SUPERCREW PICKUP 4WD—V8—Truck Equipment Schedule T1						
F150 Lariat 4D 5 1/2'	W14W	36785	8100	8775	10000	14800
2WD	2		(1475)	(1475)	(1960)	(1960)
V8, 5.4 Liter	5		200	200	255	255
SUPERCREW PICKUP 4WD—V8—Truck Equipment Schedule T1						
F150 FX4 4D 5 1/2'	X130	35130	8175	8875	9950	14550
SUPER DUTY REGULAR CAB PICKUP—V8—Truck Equipment Schedule T1						
F250 XL 2D 8'	F20L	24430	2875	3225	3600	5425
F250 XLT 2D 8'	F20L	27015	2975	3325	3925	6100
F350 XL 2D 8'	F30L	24885	2500	2800	3300	5100
F350 XLT 2D 8'	F30L	27820	3175	3575	4125	6400
4WD	1		1175	1175	1555	1555
V8, Turbo Dsl 6.0L	P		2875	2875	3845	3845
V10, 6.8 Liter	S		350	350	455	455
SUPER DUTY SUPER CAB PICKUP—V8—Truck Equipment Schedule T1						
F250 XL 4D 6 3/4'	X20L	26815	3675	4125	4800	7375
F250 XL 4D 8'	X20L	26815	3525	3950	4375	6675
F250 XLT 4D 6 3/4'	X20L	29935	4325	4875	5550	8525
F250 XLT 4D 8'	X20L	30135	4150	4650	5050	7500
F250 Lariat 4D 6 3/4'	X20L	32105	4675	5250	5925	9075
F250 Lariat 4D 8'	X20L	32305	4275	4800	5275	7925
F350 XL 4D 6 3/4'	X30L	27405	3850	4325	5025	7725
F350 XL 4D 8'	X30L	27605	3700	4175	4775	7300
F350 XLT 4D 6 3/4'	X30L	30455	4250	4775	5450	8400
F350 XLT 4D 8'	X30L	30655	4075	4575	5275	8150
F350 Lariat 4D 6 3/4'	X30L	32480	4575	5150	5825	8925
F350 Lariat 4D 8'	X30L	32680	4400	4950	5625	8625
4WD	1		1175	1175	1555	1555
V8, Turbo Dsl 6.0L	P		2875	2875	3845	3845
V10, 6.8 Liter	S		350	350	455	455
SUPER DUTY SUPER CAB PICKUP 4WD—V8 Turbo Diesel—Truck Sch T1						
F250 Harley 6 3/4'	X20P	39890	9225	10000	10450	14600
F250 Harley 8'	X20P	40090	9050	9800	10250	14300
F350 Harley 6 3/4'	X31P	40895	9425	10200	10650	14850
F350 Harley 8'	X31P	41095	9050	9800	10250	14300
V10, 6.8 Liter	S		(400)	(400)	(495)	(495)
SUPER DUTY CREW CAB PICKUP—V8—Truck Equipment Schedule T1						
F250 XL 4D 6 3/4'	W20L	28025	4600	5175	5775	8800
F250 XL 4D 8'	W20L	28225	4300	4850	5525	8500
F250 XLT 4D 6 3/4'	W20L	32265	5400	6050	6650	10100
F250 XLT 4D 8'	W20L	32465	5150	5775	6425	9800
F250 Lariat 4D 6 3/4'	W20L	34735	6000	6725	7400	11100

TRUCKS & VANS

Body Type	VIN	List	Trade-In Good	Very Good	Pvt-Party Good	Retail Excellent
F250 Lariat 4D 8'	W20L	34935	5350	6000	6625	10100
F250 KingRnch 6 3/4'	W20L	37350	5950	6700	7425	11250
F250 King Ranch 8'	W20L	37550	5500	6175	6900	10400
F350 XL 4D 6 3/4'	W30L	28685	5075	5700	6350	9700
F350 XL 4D 8'	W30L	38415	4825	5400	5950	8975
F350 XLT 4D 6 3/4'	W30L	33275	5375	6050	6850	10450
F350 XLT 4D 8'	W30L	33475	5450	6100	6750	10250
F350 Lariat 4D 6 3/4'	W30L	35600	6625	7425	7975	11850
F350 Lariat 4D 8'	W30L	35800	6550	7350	7925	11800
F350 KingRnch 6 3/4'	W30L	38215	6100	6850	7600	11500
F350 King Ranch 8'	W30L	38415	5750	6475	7275	11050
4WD	1		1175	1175	1555	1555
V8, Turbo Dsl 6.0L	P		2875	2875	3845	3845
V10, 6.8 Liter	S		350	350	455	455
SUPER DUTY CREW CAB PICKUP 4WD—V8 Turbo Diesel—Truck Sch T1						
F250 Harley 6 3/4'	W21P	42385	11400	12250	12650	17550
F250 Harley 8'	W21P	42585	11300	12250	12600	17500
F350 Harley 6 3/4'	W35P	43000	11600	12550	12900	17900
F350 Harley 8'	W35P	43200	11500	12450	12800	17800
V10, 6.8 Liter	S		(400)	(400)	(495)	(495)
SUPER DUTY CAB-CHASSIS—6-Cyl. Turbo Diesel—Truck Equip Sch T1						
F450 Cab-Ch DR	F46P	30540	6700	7525	8150	12200
F450 Crew Ch DR	W46P	31240	8125	9125	9775	14600
F550 Cab-Ch	F56P	30810	5450	6125	6750	10100
F550 Crew Ch DR	W56P	33655	9050	10150	10650	15750
4WD	7		1175	1175	1555	1555
V10, 6.8 Liter	S		(2725)	(2725)	(3640)	(3640)

2005 FORD — (1or2)F(B,MorT)—(U96H)—5—#

Body Type	VIN	List	Trade-In Good	Very Good	Pvt-Party Good	Retail Excellent
ESCAPE 4WD—4-Cyl. Hybrid—Truck Equipment Schedule T1						
Sport Utility 4D	U96H	28595	2550	2875	3675	5600
2WD	0		(575)	(575)	(775)	(775)
ESCAPE—4-Cyl.—Truck Equipment Schedule T1						
XLS Sport Utility 4D	U02Z	19995	1475	1650	2625	4200
4WD	9		575	575	775	775
ESCAPE 4WD—V6—Truck Equipment Schedule T1						
XLT Utility 4D	U931	25545	2800	3100	4000	6150
XLT "Sport" SUV	U931	26505	3225	3550	4425	6750
Limited Sport Util	U941	27145	3325	3675	4550	6925
2WD	0		(575)	(575)	(775)	(775)
4-Cyl, 2.3 Liter	Z		(400)	(400)	(540)	(540)
FREESTYLE—V6—Truck Equipment Schedule T1						
SE Sport Utility 4D	K011	25595	1150	1325	2225	3600
SEL Sport Utility 4D	K021	26995	1475	1700	2625	4150
AWD	4		925	925	1245	1245
FREESTYLE AWD—V6—Truck Equipment Schedule T1						
Limited Sport Util	K061	30895	2200	2475	3475	5475
2WD	3		(950)	(950)	(1260)	(1260)
EXPLORER 4WD—V6 Flex Fuel—Truck Equipment Schedule T1						
XLS Sport Utility 4D	U72K	29880	1900	2200	3125	5075
XLS "Sport" SUV	U72K	31135	2025	2350	3350	5525
XLT Sport Utility 4D	U73K	32520	2375	2725	3725	6075
XLT "Sport" 4D	U73K	34265	2525	2900	3900	6325
Eddie Bauer Spt Util	U74K	36995	3275	3750	4825	7725
Third Row Seat	6		325	325	420	420
2WD	6		(950)	(950)	(1260)	(1260)
V8, 4.6 Liter	W		200	200	255	255
EXPLORER 4WD—V8—Truck Equipment Schedule T1						
Limited Sport Util	U75W	38175	3400	3900	5050	8075
2WD	6		(950)	(950)	(1260)	(1260)
V6, 4.0 Liter	K		(175)	(175)	(225)	(225)
EXPLORER SPORT TRAC 4WD—V6 Flex Fuel—Truck Equipment Sch T1						
XLS Utility Pickup	U77K	27125	4375	4975	5850	9075
XLT Utility Pickup	U77K	28685	5800	6175	7800	11050
Adrenalin Utility	U77K	31885	5850	6225	7950	11300
2WD	6		(950)	(950)	(1260)	(1260)
EXPEDITION—V8—Truck Equipment Schedule T1						
XLS Sport Utility 4D	U135	33365	2175	2475	3175	4975
XLT Sport Utility 4D	U155	35390	2850	3225	3950	6125
Third Row Seat			(250)	(250)	(320)	(320)
4WD	0,4,6,8		575	575	775	775
EXPEDITION 4WD—V8—Truck Equipment Schedule T1						
XLT "Sport" SUV	U165	39320	3825	4325	5150	7950

Body Type	VIN	List	Trade-In Good	Very Good	Pvt-Party Good	Retail Excellent
XLT NBX Sport Util	U165	39540	3775	4275	5125	7950
Eddie Bauer Spt Util	U185	43725	4425	5000	5850	9050
Limited Sport Util	U205	44835	4600	5175	5875	9600
King Ranch Spt Util	U185	46560	5200	5850	6725	9875
Third Row Seat			(250)	(250)	(320)	(320)
2WD	3,5,7,9		(575)	(575)	(775)	(775)
EXCURSION 4WD—V10—Truck Equipment Schedule T1						
XLS Sport Utility 4D	U41S	41395	6475	7300	7900	11450
XLT Sport Utility 4D	U41S	42385	6950	7850	8475	12250
Eddie Bauer Spt Util	U45S	45315	9225	10400	10700	15150
Limited Sport Util	U43S	46640	8925	10050	10450	14850
Third Row Seat			425	425	575	575
2WD	0,2,4		(575)	(575)	(775)	(775)
V8, 5.4 Liter	L		(425)	(425)	(550)	(550)
V8, Turbo Dsl 6.0L	P		3150	3150	4190	4190
FREESTAR—V6—Truck Equipment Schedule T2						
Cargo Minivan	A546	22295	925	1075	1800	3025
FREESTAR—V6—Truck Equipment Schedule T1						
S Minivan	A506	24595	1325	1525	2325	3875
SE Minivan	A516	27195	1525	1750	2550	4250
SES Minivan	A576	28695	1650	1875	2775	4600
SEL Minivan	A522	29695	1850	2100	3000	4975
Limited Minivan	A582	33395	2300	2625	3575	5875
ECONOLINE WAGON—V8—Truck Equipment Schedule T1						
E150 XL Super Duty	E11W	25525	3500	4025	4625	6950
E150 XLT S.D.	E11W	28515	4300	4900	5475	8200
E150 Chateau S.D.	E11W	30515	4575	5200	5775	8650
E350 XL Super Duty	E31L	28685	4000	4575	5150	7750
E350 XLT S.D.	E31L	31220	4850	5500	6050	9075
E350 Chateau S.D.	E31L	33025	5225	5950	6475	9675
E350 XL S.D. Ext	S31L	30865	4800	5450	6000	9000
E350 XLT S.D. Ext	S31L	32490	4975	5675	6225	9325
V8, 5.4 Liter (E150)	L		200	200	255	255
V8, Turbo Dsl 6.0L	P		1750	1750	2335	2335
V10, 6.8 Liter	S		425	425	575	575
ECONOLINE VAN—V8—Truck Equipment Schedule T1						
E150 Super Cargo	E14W	23330	3425	3825	4575	7000
E250 Super Cargo	E24W	24375	3625	4075	4950	7525
E250 Extended SD	E24W	25695	4500	5025	5875	8900
E350 Super Cargo	E34L	27160	4025	4500	5350	8125
E350 Extended SD	E34L	28295	4875	5450	6350	9625
Crew Van Pkg			175	175	250	250
V8, 5.4L (E150/E250)	L		200	200	255	255
V8, Turbo Dsl 6.0L	P		1750	1750	2335	2335
V10, 6.8 Liter	S		425	425	575	575
RANGER REGULAR CAB PICKUP—4-Cyl.—Truck Equipment Schedule T2						
XL 2D 6'	R10D	15985	2050	2400	3025	4750
XL 2D 7'	R10D	17865	1450	1700	2325	3675
STX 2D 6'	R10D	16640	2325	2700	3325	5175
XLT 2D 6'	R10D	17700	3050	3525	4075	6300
XLT 2D 7'	R10D	18100	2325	2700	3325	5175
Edge 2D 6'	R10U	18050	3300	3800	4450	6875
4WD	1,5		875	875	1155	1155
V6, 3.0 Liter (ex Edge)	U		225	225	285	285
V6, 4.0 Liter	E		275	275	355	355
RANGER SUPER CAB PICKUP—V6—Truck Equipment Schedule T2						
XL 2D 6'	R14U	19110	3950	4550	5025	7600
STX 2D 6'	R14U	19680	3925	4525	5100	7850
STX 4D 6'	R44U	20845	5175	5925	6425	9825
XLT 2D 6'	R14U	19735	4475	5150	5700	8725
XLT 4D 6'	R44U	20900	5475	6275	6750	10150
Edge 2D 6'	R14U	20085	5075	5850	6500	9925
Edge 4D 6'	R44U	21250	4975	5700	6225	9500
4WD	1,5		875	875	1155	1155
V6, 4.0 Liter	E		275	275	355	355
RANGER SUPER CAB PICKUP 4WD—V6—Truck Equipment Schedule T2						
XLT FX4 Off-Road	R45E	26365	6650	7600	7650	11100
XLT FX4 Level II	R45E	26685	6525	7475	7525	10950
REGULAR CAB PICKUP—V6—Truck Equipment Schedule T1						
F150 XL 2D 6 1/2'	F122	21295	3575	4075	4775	7250
F150 STX 2D 6 1/2'	F122	22135	4150	4750	5350	8025
4WD	4		1275	1275	1690	1690
V8, 4.6 Liter	W		350	350	460	460

Body Type	VIN	List	Trade-In Good	Very Good	Pvt-Party Good	Retail Excellent
V8, 5.4 Liter	5		575	575	760	760
REGULAR CAB PICKUP—V8—Truck Equipment Schedule T1						
F150 XL 2D 8'	F12W	21736	3750	4300	4800	7150
F150 XLT 2D 6 1/2'	F12W	25676	4950	5625	6225	9350
F150 XLT 2D 8'	F12W	25976	4500	5150	5800	8750
4WD	4		1275	1275	1690	1690
V6, 4.2 Liter	2		(450)	(450)	(585)	(585)
V8, 5.4 Liter	5		225	225	285	285
REGULAR CAB PICKUP 4WD—V8—Truck Equipment Schedule T1						
F150 FX4 2D 6 1/2'	F145	33086	7425	8425	9325	14150
SUPER CAB PICKUP—V8—Truck Equipment Schedule T1						
F150 XL 4D 6 1/2'	X12W	26060	4200	4550	5450	7825
F150 XL 4D 8'	X12W	26360	3900	4250	5150	7375
F150 STX 4D 5 1/2'	X12W	26410	4500	4875	5675	8050
F150 XLT 4D 5 1/2'	X12W	28285	4800	5200	6050	8600
F150 Lariat 4D 6 1/2'	X12W	31250	5125	5575	6700	9625
4WD	4		1275	1275	1690	1690
V8, 5.4 Liter	5		225	225	285	285
SUPER CAB PICKUP 4WD—V8—Truck Equipment Schedule T1						
F150 STX 4D 6 1/2'	X14W	29840	6425	6975	8050	11450
F150 XLT 4D 6 1/2'	X14W	32225	6525	7075	8175	11700
2WD	0		(1625)	(1625)	(2175)	(2175)
V8, 5.4 Liter	5		225	225	285	285
SUPER CAB PICKUP—V8—Truck Equipment Schedule T1						
F150 Lariat 4D 5 1/2'	X125	30950	5225	5675	6725	9575
4WD	4		1275	1275	1690	1690
SUPER CAB PICKUP 4WD—V8—Truck Equipment Schedule T1						
F150 XLT 4D 8'	X145	32505	6650	7200	8150	11450
2WD	0		(1625)	(1625)	(2175)	(2175)
SUPER CAB PICKUP 4WD—V8—Truck Equipment Schedule T1						
F150 FX4 4D 5 1/2'	X145	33500	8150	8800	9825	13850
F150 FX4 4D 6 1/2'	X145	33800	7975	8625	9625	13550
SUPERCREW PICKUP—V8—Truck Equipment Schedule T1						
F150 XLT 4D 5 1/2'	W12W	30185	6425	6950	7975	11300
F150 Lariat 4D 5 1/2'	W145	37760	9200	9950	11350	16300
F150 KingRnch 1/2'	W145	40910	10500	11350	12650	17950
4WD	4		1275	1275	1690	1690
V8, 5.4 Liter (XLT)	5		225	225	285	285
SUPER DUTY REGULAR CAB PICKUP—V8—Truck Equipment Schedule T1						
F250 XL 4D 8'	F205	25525	3325	3750	4275	6225
F350 XL 4D 8'	F305	26270	2725	3075	3800	5725
4WD	1		1275	1275	1690	1690
V8, Turbo Dsl 6.0L	P		3150	3150	4190	4190
V10, 6.8 Liter	Y		375	375	510	510
SUPER DUTY REGULAR CAB PICKUP 4WD—V8—Truck Equipment Sch T1						
F250 XLT 2D 8'	F215	28270	5175	5775	6375	9275
2WD	0		(1625)	(1625)	(2150)	(2150)
V8, Turbo Dsl 6.0L	P		3150	3150	4145	4145
V10, 6.8 Liter	Y		375	375	505	505
SUPER DUTY REGULAR CAB PICKUP 4WD—V8 Turbo Diesel—Truck Sch T1						
F350 XLT 2D 8'	F31P	29365	9300	10350	10850	15450
2WD	0,2		(1625)	(1625)	(2055)	(2055)
V8, 5.4 Liter	5		(3000)	(3000)	(3785)	(3785)
V10, 6.8 Liter	Y		(2625)	(2625)	(3315)	(3315)
SUPER DUTY SUPER CAB PICKUP—V8—Truck Equipment Schedule T1						
F250 XL 4D 6 3/4'	X205	27710	3950	4425	5325	8000
F250 XL 4D 8'	X205	27910	3800	4275	4950	7250
F250 XLT 4D 8'	X205	31390	4525	5075	5900	8800
F250 Lariat 4D 8'	X205	33560	4775	5350	6050	8900
F350 XL 4D 8'	X305	28990	4050	4550	5275	7800
F350 XLT 4D 8'	X305	32825	4825	5400	6050	8825
F350 Lariat 4D 8'	X305	34850	5075	5700	6500	9450
4WD	1		1275	1275	1690	1690
V8, Turbo Dsl 6.0L	P		3150	3150	4190	4190
V10, 6.8 Liter	Y		375	375	510	510
SUPER DUTY SUPER CAB 4WD—V8—Truck Equipment Schedule T1						
F250 XLT 4D 6 3/4'	X215	31190	7050	7900	8675	12600
F350 XL 4D 6 3/4'	X315	28790	5825	6525	7325	10650
F350 Lariat 4D 6 3/4'	X315	34650	7000	7850	8550	12350
2WD	0		(1625)	(1625)	(2135)	(2135)
V8, Turbo Dsl 6.0L	P		3150	3150	4120	4120
V10, 6.8 Liter	Y		375	375	500	500

TRUCKS & VANS

Body Type	VIN	List	Trade-In Good	Very Good	Pvt-Party Good	Retail Excellent
SUPER DUTY SUPER CAB PICKUP 4WD—V8 Turbo Diesel—Truck Sch T1						
F250 Lariat 4D 6 3/4'	X21P	33360	10550	11750	12450	18000
F350 XLT 4D 6 3/4'	X31P	32625	10850	12100	12600	18050
2WD	0		(1625)	(1625)	(2125)	(2125)
V8, 5.4 Liter	5		(3000)	(3000)	(3905)	(3905)
V10, 6.8 Liter	Y		(2625)	(2625)	(3420)	(3420)
SUPER DUTY CREW CAB PICKUP—V8—Truck Equipment Schedule T1						
F250 XL 4D 6 3/4'	W205	29120	5200	5825	6500	9500
F250 XL 4D 8'	W205	29320	4875	5450	6150	9025
F250 XLT 4D 8'	W205	33720	5675	6375	7125	10350
F250 King Ranch 8'	W205	37505	6550	7325	8075	11700
F350 XL 4D 8'	W305	30270	5100	5725	6500	9475
F350 Lariat 4D 8'	W305	37345	7350	8200	8750	12500
4WD	1		1275	1275	1690	1690
V8, Turbo Dsl 6.0L	P		3150	3150	4190	4190
V10, 6.8 Liter	Y		375	375	510	510
SUPER DUTY CREW CAB PICKUP 4WD—V8—Truck Equipment Sch T1						
F350 XLT 4D 8'	W315	35020	8400	9375	9950	14250
F350 King Ranch 8'	W315	38650	8800	9800	10450	15050
2WD	0		(1625)	(1625)	(2125)	(2125)
V8, Turbo Dsl 6.0L	P		3150	3150	4095	4095
V10, 6.8 Liter	Y		375	375	500	500
SUPER DUTY CREW CAB PICKUP—V8 Turbo Diesel—Truck Sch T1						
F250 XL 4D 6 3/4'	W30P	30070	9075	10100	10800	15550
4WD	1		1275	1275	1650	1650
V8, 5.4 Liter	5		(3000)	(3000)	(3905)	(3905)
V10, 6.8 Liter	Y		(2625)	(2625)	(3420)	(3420)
SUPER DUTY CREW CAB PICKUP 4WD—V8 Turbo Diesel—Truck Sch T1						
F350 XLT 4D 6 3/4'	W31P	34820	12000	13350	13850	19750
F350 Lariat 4D 6 3/4'	W31P	37145	12700	14100	14500	20700
F350 KingRnch 6 3/4'	W31P	38450	12700	14100	14350	20300
2WD	0		(1625)	(1625)	(2100)	(2100)
V8, 5.4 Liter	5		(3000)	(3000)	(3870)	(3870)
V10, 6.8 Liter	Y		(2625)	(2625)	(3390)	(3390)
SUPER DUTY CREW CAB PICKUP 4WD—V8 Turbo Diesel—Truck Sch T1						
F250 XLT 4D 6 3/4'	W21P	33520	11100	12400	12950	18600
F250 Lariat 4D 6 3/4'	W21P	35990	11500	12800	13400	19250
F250 Lariat 4D 8'	W21P	36190	11200	12450	13100	18850
F250 KingRnch 4D 8'	W21P	37105	12100	13450	13950	19950
2WD	0		(1625)	(1625)	(2110)	(2110)
V8, 5.4 Liter	5		(3000)	(3000)	(3885)	(3885)
V10, 6.8 Liter	Y		(2625)	(2625)	(3400)	(3400)
SUPER DUTY CREW CAB PICKUP 4WD—V8 Turbo Diesel—Truck Sch T1						
F250 Harley 6 3/4'	W215	41835	13100	14150	14600	19700
F250 Harley 8'	W215	42035	12950	13950	14400	19450
F350 Harley 6 3/4'	W315	42610	13400	14450	14900	20100
F350 Harley 8'	W315	42810	13200	14250	14700	19800
V10, 6.8 Liter	Y		(425)	(425)	(505)	(505)

2006 FORD — (1,2or3)F(D,MorT)–(U021)–6–#

Body Type	VIN	List	Trade-In Good	Very Good	Pvt-Party Good	Retail Excellent
ESCAPE—4-Cyl.—Truck Equipment Schedule T1						
XLS Sport Utility 4D	U021	20685	1825	2025	2925	4500
4WD	9		625	625	845	845
ESCAPE 4WD—V6—Truck Equipment Schedule T1						
XLT Utility 4D	U931	25755	3350	3675	4725	7075
XLT "Sport" SUV	U931	26550	3925	4325	5350	7925
Limited Sport Util	U941	27295	4225	4625	5700	8450
2WD	0		(625)	(625)	(845)	(845)
4-Cyl, 2.3 Liter	Z		(450)	(450)	(585)	(585)
ESCAPE 4WD—4-Cyl. Hybrid—Truck Equipment Schedule T1						
Sport Utility 4D	U96H	29140	3325	3700	4575	6850
2WD	5		(625)	(625)	(845)	(845)
FREESTYLE—V6—Truck Equipment Schedule T1						
SE Sport Utility 4D	K011	25780	1500	1700	2650	4175
SEL Sport Utility 4D	K021	27180	2125	2375	3275	5000
AWD			700	700	920	920
FREESTYLE AWD—V6—Truck Equipment Schedule T1						
Limited Sport Utility	K061	31280	2950	3300	4275	6500
2WD	1,2,3		(625)	(625)	(845)	(845)
EXPLORER—V6—Truck Equipment Schedule T1						
XLS Sport Utility 4D	U62E	27175	2850	3225	3950	6025
Third Row Seat			350	350	455	455
4WD	7		1025	1025	1355	1355

1015

TRUCKS & VANS

Body Type	VIN	List	Trade-In Good	Very Good	Pvt-Party Good	Retail Excellent
V8, 4.6 Liter	8		200	200	265	265
EXPLORER 4WD—V6—Truck Equipment Schedule T1						
XLT Sport Util 4D	U73E	31095	4175	4725	5475	8175
Eddie Bauer Spt Util	U74E	33070	5150	5800	6550	9775
Third Row Seat			350	350	455	455
2WD	6		(1025)	(1025)	(1375)	(1375)
V8, 4.6 Liter	8		200	200	265	265
EXPLORER 4WD—V8—Truck Equipment Schedule T1						
Limited Sport Util	U75W	36585	5375	6050	6925	10250
Third Row Seat			350	350	455	455
2WD	6		(1025)	(1025)	(1375)	(1375)
V6, 4.0 Liter	E		(175)	(175)	(245)	(245)
EXPEDITION—V8—Truck Equipment Schedule T1						
XLS Sport Utility 4D	U135	34275	2775	3125	3875	5875
XLT Sport Utility 4D	U155	36325	3525	3950	4775	7225
Third Row Seat			(275)	(275)	(355)	(355)
4WD	4		625	625	845	845
EXPEDITION 4WD—V8—Truck Equipment Schedule T1						
XLT "Sport" Util	U165	39000	4950	5525	6250	9300
Eddie Bauer Spt Util	U185	42710	5725	6400	7275	10800
Limited Sport Util	U205	44460	5575	6200	7025	10050
King Ranch Spt Util	U185	46060	6350	7025	7925	11400
Third Row Seat			(275)	(275)	(355)	(355)
2WD	5		(625)	(625)	(845)	(845)
FREESTAR—V6—Truck Equipment Schedule T2						
Cargo Minivan	A546	20380	1150	1300	2075	3400
FREESTAR—V6—Truck Equipment Schedule T2						
SE Minivan	A516	24385	1800	2025	2875	4625
SEL Minivan	A522	27345	2275	2550	3450	5475
Limited Minivan	A582	30305	2950	3300	4200	6600
ECONOLINE WAGON—V8—Truck Equipment Schedule T1						
E150 XL Super Duty	E11W	26170	4650	5250	5750	8325
E150 XLT S.D.	E11W	28945	5425	6125	6750	9750
E150 Chateau S.D.	E11W	31015	6000	6750	7325	10600
E350 XL Super Duty	E31L	28610	5000	5625	6100	8850
E350 XLT S.D.	E31L	31415	6125	6875	7475	10800
E350 Chateau S.D.	E31L	33220	6750	7575	8150	11800
E350 XL S.D. Ext	S31L	30600	5825	6550	7125	10300
E350 XLT S.D. Ext	S31L	32460	6625	7450	7975	11500
V8, 5.4 Liter (E150)	L		200	200	265	265
V8, Turbo Dsl 6.0L	P		1900	1900	2520	2520
V10, 6.8 Liter	S		475	475	640	640
ECONOLINE VAN—V8—Truck Equipment Schedule T1						
E150 Super Cargo	E14W	23975	4725	5275	5950	8700
E250 Super Cargo	E24W	25045	5025	5600	6250	9125
E250 Extended SD	S24W	25740	5725	6375	7225	10550
E350 Super Cargo	E34L	27380	5375	5975	6625	9675
E350 Extended SD	S34L	28310	6175	6850	7675	11200
Crew Van Pkg			200	200	260	260
V8, 5.4L (E150/E250)	L		200	200	265	265
V8, Turbo Dsl 6.0L	P		1900	1900	2535	2535
V10, 6.8 Liter	S		475	475	645	645
RANGER REGULAR CAB PICKUP—4-Cyl.—Truck Equipment Schedule T1						
XL 2D 6'	R10D	16245	2600	2975	3500	5300
XLT 2D 6'	R10D	18165	3450	3925	4500	6750
4WD	1,5		975	975	1290	1290
V6, 3.0 Liter	U		250	250	320	320
V6, 4.0 Liter	E		300	300	385	385
RANGER REGULAR CAB PICKUP—4-Cyl.—Truck Equipment Schedule T2						
XL 2D 7'	R10D	16190	1750	2025	2675	4100
4WD	1,5		975	975	1290	1290
V6, 3.0 Liter	U		250	250	320	320
V6, 4.0 Liter	E		300	300	385	385
RANGER REGULAR CAB PICKUP—V6—Truck Equipment Schedule T2						
STX 2D 6'	R10U	19905	2750	3150	3675	5525
RANGER REGULAR CAB PICKUP—V6—Truck Equipment Schedule T2						
Sport 2D 6'	R10U	18870	3975	4550	5050	7525
4WD	1,5		975	975	1290	1290
RANGER REGULAR CAB PICKUP—V6—Truck Equipment Schedule T2						
XLT 2D 7'	R11U	17935	3275	3725	4200	6300
4WD	1,5		975	975	1290	1290
V6, 4.0 Liter	E		300	300	385	385

SEE BACK PAGES FOR TRUCK EQUIPMENT

TRUCKS & VANS

Body Type	VIN	List	Trade-In Good	Very Good	Pvt-Party Good	Retail Excellent
RANGER SUPER CAB PICKUP—4-Cyl.—Truck Equipment Schedule T1						
XL 2D 6'	R14D	18745	4325	4925	5425	8050
XLT 2D 6'	R14D	20000	5150	5875	6450	9500
4WD	1,5		975	975	1290	1290
V6, 3.0 Liter	U		250	250	320	320
V6, 4.0 Liter	E		300	300	385	385
RANGER SUPER CAB PICKUP—V6—Truck Equipment Schedule T1						
STX 2D 6'	R14U	19905	4675	5325	5775	8550
STX 4D 6'	R44U	21300	6125	6975	7450	11000
Sport 2D 6'	R14U	20705	5875	6675	7175	10550
Sport 4D 6'	R44U	22100	6275	7125	7575	11150
XLT 4D 6'	R44U	21600	5950	6750	7250	10650
4WD	1,5		975	975	1290	1290
V6, 4.0 Liter	E		300	300	385	385
RANGER SUPER CAB PICKUP 4WD—V6—Truck Equipment Schedule T2						
XLT FX4 Level II 6'	R45E	27305	7225	8175	8275	11800
RANGER SUPER CAB PICKUP 4WD—V6—Truck Equipment Schedule T1						
XLT FX4 Off-Rd 2D	R15E	26225	6350	7425	7475	10550
XLT FX4 Off-Rd 4D	R45E	27620	7425	8425	8475	12050
REGULAR CAB PICKUP—V6—Truck Equipment Schedule T1						
F150 XL 2D 6 1/2'	F122	19805	3700	4175	4950	7400
F150 STX 2D 6 1/2'	F122	22105	4075	4600	5350	7975
4WD	4		1500	1500	2000	2000
V8, 4.6 Liter	W		400	400	550	550
V8, 5.4 Liter	5		625	625	830	830
REGULAR CAB PICKUP—V8—Truck Equipment Schedule T1						
F150 XL 2D 8'	F12W	21945	3600	4075	4800	7175
F150 XLT 2D 6 1/2'	F12W	25095	5250	5900	6525	9650
F150 XLT 2D 8'	F12W	25390	4700	5300	6025	8950
4WD	4		1500	1500	2000	2000
V6, 4.2 Liter	2		(450)	(450)	(600)	(600)
V8, 5.4 Liter	5		250	250	320	320
REGULAR CAB PICKUP 4WD—V8—Truck Equipment Schedule T1						
F150 FX4 2D 6 1/2'	F14W	32020	8025	9000	9900	14650
SUPER CAB PICKUP—V8—Truck Equipment Schedule T1						
F150 XL 4D 6 1/2'	X12W	24985	5175	5575	6275	8575
F150 XL 4D 8'	X12W	25280	4800	5175	5875	8075
F150 STX 4D 5 1/2'	X12W	26300	5250	5650	6475	8825
F150 XLT 4D 6 1/2'	X12W	28735	5675	6100	7000	9600
F150 Lariat 4D 6 1/2'	X12W	31630	6550	7050	7950	10900
4WD	4		1500	1500	1980	1980
V8, 5.4 Liter	5		250	250	315	315
SUPER CAB PICKUP 4WD—V8—Truck Equipment Schedule T1						
F150 STX 4D 6 1/2'	X14W	29695	7575	8150	9075	12350
F150 XLT 4D 6 1/2'	X14W	32050	7750	8325	9275	12700
2WD	2		(2000)	(2000)	(2615)	(2615)
V8, 5.4 Liter	5		250	250	320	320
SUPER CAB PICKUP 4WD—V8—Truck Equipment Schedule T1						
F150 XLT 4D 8'	X145	32350	7675	8275	9200	12600
2WD	2		(2000)	(2000)	(2635)	(2635)
SUPER CAB PICKUP—V8—Truck Equipment Schedule T1						
F150 Lariat 4D 5 1/2'	X125	31350	6350	6825	7675	10450
F150 Harley 6 1/2'	X125	35645	10250	11000	11950	16300
4WD	4		1500	1500	1965	1965
SUPER CAB PICKUP 4WD—V8—Truck Equipment Schedule T1						
F150 FX4 4D 5 1/2'	X145	34215	9275	9975	10900	14850
F150 FX4 4D 6 1/2'	X145	34520	9225	9900	10800	14700
SUPERCREW PICKUP—V8—Truck Equipment Schedule T1						
F150 XLT 4D 5 1/2'	W12W	31335	7425	8000	8925	12200
F150 XLT 4D 6 1/2'	W14W	34500	9200	9900	10950	15000
F150 KingRnch 6 3/4'	W125	37480	10650	11400	12350	16800
4WD	4		1500	1500	1965	1965
V8, 5.4 Liter (XLT)	5		250	250	320	320
SUPERCREW PICKUP 4WD—V8—Truck Equipment Schedule T1						
F150 XLT 4D 6 1/2'	W14W	34500	9200	9900	10950	15000
F150 Lariat 4D 5 1/2'	W145	37465	11200	12000	13250	18250
F150 Lariat 4D 6 1/2'	W145	37765	11500	12350	13400	18300
F150 KingRnch 5 1/2'	W145	40630	11800	12700	13800	19000
2WD	2		(2000)	(2000)	(2605)	(2605)
SUPERCREW PICKUP 4WD—V8—Truck Equipment Schedule T1						
F150 FX4 4D 5 1/2'	W145	36510	11000	11850	12900	17600
F150 FX4 4D 6 1/2'	W145	36810	10900	11700	12550	17000

Body Type	VIN	List	Trade-In Good	Trade-In Very Good	Pvt-Party Good	Retail Excellent
SUPER DUTY REGULAR CAB PICKUP—V8—Truck Equipment Schedule T1						
F250 XL 2D 6 3/4'	F205	24835	3225	3575	4250	6175
F350 XL 2D 8'	F305	25565	2425	2700	3575	5425
4WD	1		1500	1500	2000	2000
V8, Turbo Dsl 6.0L	P		3400	3400	4535	4535
V10, 6.8 Liter	Y		425	425	575	575
SUPER DUTY REGULAR CAB 4WD—V8—Truck Equipment Schedule T1						
F250 XLT 2D 8'	F215	28575	5425	6025	6800	9650
2WD	0		(2000)	(2000)	(2585)	(2585)
V8, Turbo Dsl 6.0L	P		3400	3400	4385	4385
V10, 6.8 Liter	Y		425	425	560	560
SUPER DUTY REGULAR CAB 4WD—V8 Turbo Diesel—Truck Equip Sch T1						
F350 XLT 2D 8'	F31P	29665	9275	10250	10900	15300
2WD	0		(2000)	(2000)	(2560)	(2560)
V8, 5.4 Liter	5		(3300)	(3300)	(4210)	(4210)
V10, 6.8 Liter	Y		(2900)	(2900)	(3690)	(3690)
SUPER DUTY SUPER CAB PICKUP—V8—Truck Equipment Schedule T1						
F250 XL 4D 6 3/4'	X205	26965	3925	4375	5250	7675
F250 XL 4D 8'	X205	27165	3700	4125	4925	7150
F250 XLT 4D 8'	X205	31690	4875	5425	6150	8850
F250 Lariat 4D 8'	X205	34130	4850	5400	6300	9050
F350 XL 4D 6 3/4'	X305	28025	6425	7125	7925	11250
F350 XL 4D 8'	X305	29065	4275	4750	5500	7950
F350 XLT 4D 8'	X305	33135	5000	5550	6450	9250
F350 Lariat 4D 8'	X305	35630	5300	5900	6750	9675
4WD	1		1500	1500	2000	2000
V8, Turbo Dsl 6.0L	P		3400	3400	4535	4535
V10, 6.8 Liter	Y		425	425	575	575
SUPER DUTY SUPER CAB PICKUP 4WD—V8—Truck Equipment Schedule T1						
F250 XLT 4D 6 3/4'	X215	31445	7075	7825	8675	12350
F350 Lariat 4D 6 3/4'	X315	35425	7350	8150	8950	12700
2WD	0		(2000)	(2000)	(2590)	(2590)
V8, Turbo Dsl 6.0L	P		3400	3400	4390	4390
V10, 6.8 Liter	Y		425	425	560	560
SUPER DUTY SUPER CAB 4WD—V8 Turbo Diesel—Truck Equipment Sch T1						
F350 XLT 4D 6 3/4'	X31P	32930	11350	12550	13200	18550
2WD	0		(2000)	(2000)	(2535)	(2535)
V8, 5.4 Liter	5		(3300)	(3300)	(4175)	(4175)
V10, 6.8 Liter	Y		(2900)	(2900)	(3655)	(3655)
SUPER DUTY SUPER CAB 4WD—V8 Turbo Diesel—Truck Equipment Sch T1						
F250 Lariat 4D 6 3/4'	X21P	34130	11100	12300	13000	18350
2WD	0		(2000)	(2000)	(2545)	(2545)
V8, 5.4 Liter	5		(3300)	(3300)	(4190)	(4190)
V10, 6.8 Liter	Y		(2900)	(2900)	(3670)	(3670)
SUPER DUTY CREW CAB PICKUP—V8—Truck Equipment Schedule T1						
F250 XL 4D 6 3/4'	W205	28345	5325	5925	6800	9725
F250 XL 4D 8'	W205	28540	4950	5500	6400	9200
F250 XLT 4D 8'	W205	34020	6050	6700	7525	10750
F250 King Ranch 8'	W205	40145	6750	7500	8275	11800
F350 XL 4D 8'	W305	29475	5450	6050	6900	9875
F350 Lariat 4D 8'	W305	38120	7750	8575	9200	12900
4WD	1		1500	1500	1950	1950
V8, Turbo Dsl 6.0L	P		3400	3400	4425	4425
V10, 6.8 Liter	Y		425	425	565	565
SUPER DUTY CREW CAB 4WD—V8—Truck Equipment Schedule T1						
F350 XLT 4D 8'	W315	35325	8700	9600	10250	14450
F350 King Ranch 8'	W315	41305	9350	10350	11100	15650
2WD	0,2		(2000)	(2000)	(2555)	(2555)
V8, Turbo Dsl 6.0L	P		3400	3400	4330	4330
V10, 6.8 Liter	Y		425	425	550	550
SUPER DUTY CREW CAB 4WD—V8 Turbo Diesel—Truck Equipment Sch T1						
F250 XLT 4D 6 3/4'	W21P	33825	12250	13500	14100	19700
F250 Lariat 4D 6 3/4'	W21P	36765	12750	14100	14750	20700
F250 Lariat 4D 8'	W21P	36960	12400	13700	14300	20100
F250 KingRnch 6 3/4'	W21P	39150	13450	14500	15100	21100
F350 XL 4D 6 3/4'	W30P	29275	10150	11200	11850	16700
F350 XLT 4D 6 3/4'	W31P	33130	12550	13850	14550	20400
F350 Lariat 4D 6 3/4'	W31P	37925	13350	14700	15350	21500
F350 KingRnch 6 3/4'	W31P	41110	13500	14900	15400	21400
2WD	0		(2000)	(2000)	(2520)	(2520)
V8, 5.4 Liter	5		(3300)	(3300)	(4150)	(4150)
V10, 6.8 Liter	Y		(2900)	(2900)	(3630)	(3630)

TRUCKS & VANS

Body Type	VIN	List	Trade-In Good	Very Good	Pvt-Party Good	Retail Excellent
SUPER DUTY CREW CAB PICKUP 4WD—V8 Turbo Diesel—Schedule T1						
F250 Harley 6 3/4'	W21P	50780	15300	16450	16850	22300
F250 Harley 8'	W21P	50985	15150	16250	16650	22000
F350 Harley 6 3/4'	W31P	51555	15700	16850	17250	22800
F350 Harley 8'	W31P	51760	15500	16650	17050	22600

2007 FORD—(1,2or3)F(D,MorT)—(U02Z)—7-#

Body Type	VIN	List	Trade-In Good	Very Good	Pvt-Party Good	Retail Excellent
ESCAPE—4-Cyl.—Truck Equipment Schedule T1						
XLS Sport Utility 4D	U02Z	20560	2725	3000	3725	5325
4WD	5,9		975	975	1310	1310
ESCAPE 4WD—4-Cyl. Hybrid—Truck Equipment Schedule T1						
Sport Utility 4D	U59H	27925	4375	4825	6025	8875
2WD	0		(675)	(675)	(910)	(910)
ESCAPE 4WD—V6—Truck Equipment Schedule T1						
XLT Sport Utility 4D	U931	25525	4575	4975	5825	8225
XLT "Sport" SUV 4D	U931	26310	5025	5475	6225	8700
Limited Sport Util	U941	27045	5350	5825	6725	9400
2WD	0		(675)	(675)	(910)	(910)
4-Cyl, 2.3 Liter			(475)	(475)	(620)	(620)
EDGE—V6—Truck Equipment Schedule T1						
SE Sport Utility 4D	K36C	25995	6350	6800	7875	10700
SEL Sport Utility 4D	K38C	27990	7275	7775	8900	12000
SEL Plus Spt Util 4D	K39C	29745	7825	8350	9575	13000
AWD	4		525	525	685	685
FREESTYLE—V6—Truck Equipment Schedule T1						
SEL Sport Utility 4D	K021	26245	2500	2775	3725	5575
AWD	5,6		775	775	1020	1020
FREESTYLE AWD—V6—Truck Equipment Schedule T1						
Limited Sport Utility	K061	31405	3425	3775	4850	7125
2WD	2,3		(675)	(675)	(910)	(910)
EXPLORER 4WD—V6—Truck Equipment Schedule T1						
XLT Sport Utility 4D	U73E	28290	5175	5775	6400	8975
Eddie Bauer Spt Util	U74E	31290	6450	7175	7750	10900
Third Row Seat			375	375	485	485
2WD	6		(1100)	(1100)	(1480)	(1480)
V8, 4.6 Liter	8		200	200	265	265
EXPLORER 4WD—V8—Truck Equipment Schedule T1						
Limited Sport Util	U758	35690	7950	8825	9275	12900
Third Row Seat			375	375	485	485
2WD	6		(1100)	(1100)	(1480)	(1480)
V6, 4.0 Liter	E		(200)	(200)	(260)	(260)
EXPLORER SPORT TRAC—V6—Truck Equipment Schedule T1						
XLT Utility Pickup	U31K	24940	8400	8875	9925	12700
4WD	5		1100	1100	1395	1395
V8, 4.6 Liter	8		200	200	255	255
EXPLORER SPORT TRAC 4WD—V6—Truck Equipment Schedule T1						
Limited Util Pickup	U53K	29270	10450	11050	12050	15300
2WD	3		(1100)	(1100)	(1395)	(1395)
V8, 4.6 Liter	8		200	200	250	250
EXPEDITION 4WD—V8—Truck Equipment Schedule T1						
XLT Sport Utility 4D	U165	32985	6525	7200	7850	11050
Eddie Bauer Spt Util	U185	39295	9025	9950	10450	14550
Limited Spt Util	U205	40745	9850	10800	11250	15150
Third Row Seat			(300)	(300)	(385)	(385)
2WD	3,5,7,9		(675)	(675)	(910)	(910)
EXPEDITION EL 4WD—V8—Truck Equipment Schedule T1						
XLT Sport Utility 4D	K165	37345	7650	8425	9075	12750
Eddie Bauer Spt Util	K185	41945	9850	10850	11400	15900
Limited Sport Util	K205	43395	10800	11800	12200	16450
Third Row Seat			(300)	(300)	(385)	(385)
2WD	5,7,9		(675)	(675)	(910)	(910)
FREESTAR—V6—Truck Equipment Schedule T2						
Cargo Minivan	A542	20480	1650	1850	2825	4475
FREESTAR—V6—Truck Equipment Schedule T1						
SE Minivan	A512	24485	2375	2625	3600	5650
SEL Minivan	A522	27445	2925	3225	4225	6550
Limited Minivan	A582	30355	3625	4025	5150	7875
ECONOLINE WAGON—V8—Truck Equipment Schedule T1						
E150 XL Super Duty	E11W	26460	5825	6475	7000	9725
E150 XLT S.D.	E11W	29220	6875	7625	8100	11300
E150 Chateau S.D.	E11W	31290	7475	8300	8925	12550
E350 XL Super Duty	E31L	28485	6275	6975	7500	10450
E350 XLT S.D.	E31L	32155	7725	8575	9200	12900

Body Type	VIN	List	Trade-In Good	Very Good	Pvt-Party Good	Retail Excellent
E350 XL S.D. Ext	S31L	31190	7225	8025	8550	11900
E350 XLT Extended	S31L	32635	8400	9325	9975	14100
V8, 5.4 Liter (E150)	L		200	200	250	250
V8, Turbo Dsl 6.0L	P		2050	2050	2590	2590
ECONOLINE VAN—V8—Truck Equipment Schedule T1						
E150 Super Cargo	E14W	24250	5975	6600	7200	10050
E250 Super Cargo	E24W	24865	6425	7125	7650	10650
E250 Ext SD Cargo	E24W	26550	7325	8125	8700	12150
E350 Super Cargo	E34L	27745	6725	7450	8000	11150
E350 Ext SD Cargo	E34L	29120	7875	8700	9275	13000
Crew Van Pkg			200	200	265	265
V8, 5.4L (E150/E250)	L		200	200	265	265
V8, Turbo Dsl 6.0L	P		2050	2050	2715	2715
V10, 6.8 Liter	S		525	525	705	705
RANGER REGULAR CAB PICKUP—4-Cyl.—Truck Equipment Schedule T2						
XL 2D 7'	R10D	15700	1825	2100	2800	4275
XLT 2D 7'	R10D	16365	3175	3600	4300	6350
4WD	1,5		1075	1075	1420	1420
V6, 3.0 Liter	U		250	250	335	335
V6, 4.0 Liter	E		325	325	420	420
RANGER REGULAR CAB PICKUP—4-Cyl.—Truck Equipment Schedule T1						
XL 2D 6'	R10D	15495	2675	3050	3675	5475
XLT 2D 6'	R10D	16970	3575	4025	4700	6925
4WD	1,5		1075	1075	1420	1420
V6, 3.0 Liter	U		250	250	335	335
V6, 4.0 Liter	E		325	325	420	420
RANGER REGULAR CAB PICKUP—V6—Truck Equipment Schedule T2						
STX 2D 6'	R10U	15865	2825	3200	3825	5675
4WD	1,5		1075	1075	1420	1420
4-Cyl, 2.3 Liter	D		(250)	(250)	(335)	(335)
RANGER REGULAR CAB PICKUP—V6—Truck Equipment Schedule T1						
Sport 2D 6'	R10U	17605	4000	4525	5150	7575
4WD	1,5		1075	1075	1420	1420
V6, 4.0 Liter	E		325	325	420	420
RANGER SUPER CAB PICKUP—4-Cyl.—Truck Equipment Schedule T1						
XL 2D 6'	R14D	16865	4425	4975	5575	8150
4WD	1,5		1075	1075	1420	1420
V6, 3.0 Liter	U		250	250	335	335
V6, 4.0 Liter	E		325	325	420	420
RANGER SUPER CAB PICKUP—V6—Truck Equipment Schedule T1						
STX 2D 6'	R14U	17835	4825	5425	6025	8800
4WD	1,5		1075	1075	1420	1420
4-Cyl, 2.3 Liter	D		(250)	(250)	(335)	(335)
V6, 4.0 Liter	E		75	75	85	85
RANGER SUPER CAB PICKUP—V6—Truck Equipment Schedule T1						
XLT 2D 6'	R14U	18365	5450	6150	6850	10000
XLT 4D 6'	R44U	19820	5975	6725	7375	10700
Sport 2D 6'	R14U	19000	6000	6750	7375	10650
Sport 4D 6'	R44U	20255	6475	7275	7900	11450
STX 4D 6'	R14U	19045	6275	7050	7700	11150
4WD	1,5		1075	1075	1420	1420
V6, 4.0 Liter	E		325	325	420	420
RANGER SUPER CAB PICKUP 4WD—V6—Truck Equipment Schedule T2						
FX4 Off-Road 2D 6'	R15E	22620	7475	8400	8550	11900
FX4 Off-Road Lvl II	R45E	24950	8450	9475	9525	13250
RANGER SUPER CAB PICKUP 4WD—V6—Truck Equipment Schedule T1						
FX4 Off-Road 4D 6'	R45E	24705	8725	9750	9775	13600
REGULAR CAB PICKUP—V6—Truck Equipment Schedule T1						
F150 XL 2D 6 1/2'	F122	19200	4325	4825	5575	8050
F150 XL 2D 8'	F122	19500	4025	4475	5225	7525
4WD	4		1875	1875	2490	2490
V8, 4.6 Liter	W		450	450	595	595
V8, 5.4 Liter	5		675	675	905	905
REGULAR CAB PICKUP—V8—Truck Equipment Schedule T1						
F150 STX 4D 6 1/2'	F12W	23750	5400	6000	6775	9650
F150 XLT 4D 6 1/2'	F12W	26050	5975	6650	7425	10600
F150 XLT 4D 8'	F12W	26350	5450	6075	6725	9450
4WD	4		1875	1875	2490	2490
V6, 4.2 Liter	2		(450)	(450)	(600)	(600)
V8, 5.4 Liter	5		275	275	355	355
REGULAR CAB PICKUP 4WD—V8—Truck Equipment Schedule T1						
F150 FX4 4D 6 1/2'	F145	30750	9875	10950	11950	17150

SEE BACK PAGES FOR TRUCK EQUIPMENT

TRUCKS & VANS

TRUCKS & VANS

Body Type	VIN	List	Trade-In Good	Very Good	Pvt-Party Good	Retail Excellent
SUPER CAB PICKUP—V8—Truck Equipment Schedule T1						
F150 XL 4D 6 1/2'	X12W	24295	5175	5550	6475	8700
F150 XL 4D 8'	X12W	24595	5375	5750	6650	8850
F150 STX 4D 5 1/2'	X12W	25850	6050	6475	7300	9675
F150 XLT 4D 5 1/2'	X12W	28150	6700	7175	8000	10650
4WD	4		1875	1875	2470	2470
V8, 5.4 Liter	5		275	275	350	350
SUPER CAB PICKUP 4WD—V8—Truck Equipment Schedule T1						
F150 STX 4D 5 1/2'	X14W	29150	8650	9225	10100	13450
F150 XLT 4D 6 1/2'	X14W	31450	8775	9375	10350	13800
2WD	2		(2175)	(2175)	(2825)	(2825)
V8, 5.4 Liter	5		275	275	345	345
SUPER CAB PICKUP—V8—Truck Equipment Schedule T1						
F150 Lariat 4D 5 1/2'	X125	30750	7225	7700	8600	11400
F150 Lariat 4D 6 1/2'	X125	31050	7850	8375	9225	12250
4WD	4		1875	1875	2405	2405
SUPER CAB PICKUP 4WD—V8—Truck Equipment Schedule T1						
F150 XLT 4D 8'	X145	31750	8800	9400	10400	13800
2WD	2		(2175)	(2175)	(2805)	(2805)
SUPER CAB PICKUP 4WD—V8—Truck Equipment Schedule T1						
F150 FX4 4D 5 1/2'	X145	32850	10800	11500	12300	16200
F150 FX4 4D 6 1/2'	X145	33150	10900	11650	12450	16350
SUPERCREW PICKUP—V8—Truck Equipment Schedule T1						
F150 XLT 4D 5 1/2'	W12W	30490	8900	9500	10300	13650
F150 KingRnch 6 1/2	W125	36590	11750	12500	13500	17950
F150 Harley 5 1/2'	W125	37150	12900	13800	14850	19700
4WD	4		1875	1875	2395	2395
V8, 5.4 Liter (XLT)	5		275	275	340	340
SUPERCREW PICKUP 4WD—V8—Truck Equipment Schedule T1						
F150 XLT 4D 6 1/2'	W14W	33850	11050	11800	12800	16950
2WD	2		(2175)	(2175)	(2855)	(2855)
V8, 5.4 Liter	5		275	275	340	340
SUPERCREW PICKUP 4WD—V8—Truck Equipment Schedule T1						
F150 Lariat 4D 5 1/2'	W145	36220	12300	13100	14350	19300
F150 Lariat 4D 6 1/2'	W145	36450	13100	13950	15150	20100
F150 KingRnch 5 1/2	W145	39420	13650	14550	15400	20200
2WD	2		(2175)	(2175)	(2855)	(2855)
SUPERCREW PICKUP 4WD—V8—Truck Equipment Schedule T1						
F150 FX4 4D 5 1/2'	W125	35250	12250	13050	14000	18550
F150 FX4 4D 6 1/2'	W125	35550	12150	12950	13900	18350
SUPER DUTY REGULAR CAB PICKUP—V8—Truck Equipment Schedule T1						
F250 XL 2D 8'	F205	25795	4450	4875	5425	7400
F350 XL 2D 8'	F305	26525	3375	3700	4475	6450
4WD	1		1875	1875	2375	2375
V8, Turbo Dsl 6.0L	P		3650	3650	4650	4650
V10, 6.8 Liter	Y		475	475	590	590
SUPER DUTY REGULAR CAB PICKUP—V8—Truck Equipment Schedule T1						
F250 XLT 2D 8'	F215	28685	6700	7350	8125	11250
2WD	0		(2175)	(2175)	(2685)	(2685)
V8, Turbo Dsl 6.0L	P		3650	3650	4500	4500
V10, 6.8 Liter	Y		475	475	575	575
SUPER DUTY REGULAR CAB 4WD—V8 Turbo Diesel—Truck Equip Sch T1						
F350 XLT 2D 8'	F31P	29775	10900	11950	12600	17350
2WD	0		(2175)	(2175)	(2600)	(2600)
V8, 5.4 Liter	5		(3600)	(3600)	(4290)	(4290)
V10, 6.8 Liter	Y		(3800)	(3800)	(4515)	(4515)
SUPER DUTY SUPER CAB PICKUP—V8—Truck Equipment Schedule T1						
F250 XL 4D 6 3/4'	X205	27925	5150	5650	6600	9275
F250 XL 4D 8'	X205	28125	4875	5350	6150	8675
F250 XLT 4D 8'	X205	31800	6000	6600	7500	10500
F250 Lariat 4D 8'	X205	34445	6300	6900	7800	10850
F350 XL 4D 6 3/4'	X315	28135	8075	8850	9700	13450
F350 XL 4D 8'	X315	29175	5250	5775	6700	9400
F350 XLT 4D 8'	X305	33245	6400	7025	7900	11000
F350 Lariat 4D 8'	X305	35740	6950	7600	8475	11800
4WD	1		1875	1875	2330	2330
V8, Turbo Dsl 6.0L	P		3650	3650	4565	4565
V10, 6.8 Liter	Y		475	475	580	580
SUPER DUTY SUPER CAB PICKUP 4WD—V8—Truck Equipment Schedule T1						
F250 XLT 4D 6 3/4'	X315	31605	8825	9675	10500	14550
F350 Lariat 4D 6 3/4'	X315	35740	8925	9775	10600	14650
2WD	0		(2175)	(2175)	(2640)	(2640)
V8, Turbo Dsl 6.0L	P		3650	3650	4420	4420

Body Type	VIN	List	Trade-In Good	Trade-In Very Good	Pvt-Party Good	Retail Excellent
V10, 6.8 Liter	Y		475	475	565	565
SUPER DUTY SUPER CAB 4WD—V8 Turbo Diesel—Truck Equip Sch T1						
F250 Lariat 4D 6 3/4'	X21P	34240	13050	14300	15050	20600
F350 XLT 4D 6 3/4'	X31P	33040	13300	14550	15300	20900
2WD	0		(2175)	(2175)	(2610)	(2610)
V8, 5.4 Liter	5		(3600)	(3600)	(4305)	(4305)
V10, 6.8 Liter	Y		(3800)	(3800)	(4530)	(4530)
SUPER DUTY CREW CAB PICKUP—V8—Truck Equipment Schedule T1						
F250 XL 4D 6 3/4'	W205	29305	6650	7300	8150	11350
F250 XL 4D 8'	W205	29500	6300	6900	7800	10850
F250 XLT 4D 8'	W205	33755	7300	8000	8900	12400
F250 King Ranch 8'	W205	40255	8025	8800	9675	13400
F350 XL 4D 8'	W305	30435	6700	7350	8225	11450
F350 Lariat 4D 8'	W305	38230	9400	10300	10950	14950
4WD	1		1875	1875	2335	2335
V8, Turbo Dsl 6.0L	P		3650	3650	4575	4575
V10, 6.8 Liter	Y		475	475	580	580
SUPER DUTY CREW CAB PICKUP—V8 Turbo Diesel—Truck Equip Sch T1						
F350 XL 4D 6 3/4'	W30P	30235	11100	12150	12900	17700
4WD	1		1875	1875	2290	2290
V8, 5.4 Liter	5		(3600)	(3600)	(4410)	(4410)
V10, 6.8 Liter	Y		(3800)	(3800)	(4645)	(4645)
SUPER DUTY CREW CAB PICKUP 4WD—V8—Truck Equipment Schedule T1						
F350 XLT 4D 8'	W315	35435	10200	11150	11750	16000
F350 King Ranch 8'	W315	41415	11100	12150	12950	17800
2WD	0		(2175)	(2175)	(2620)	(2620)
V8, Turbo Dsl 6.0L	P		3650	3650	4390	4390
V10, 6.8 Liter	Y		475	475	560	560
SUPER DUTY CREW CAB 4WD—V8 Turbo Diesel—Truck Equipment Sch T1						
F250 XLT 4D 6 3/4'	W21P	33570	14300	15650	16250	22100
F250 Lariat 4D 6 3/4'	W21P	36740	15950	17400	17950	24400
F250 Lariat 4D 8'	W21P	36935	14350	15700	16450	22600
F250 KingRnch 6 3/4'	W21P	40060	15650	17100	17650	23900
F350 XLT 4D 6 3/4'	W31P	35240	14850	16200	16750	22800
F350 Lariat 4D 8'	W31P	38905	15900	17350	17850	24200
F350 KingRnch 6 3/4'	W31P	41220	16200	17700	18000	24300
2WD	0		(2175)	(2175)	(2610)	(2610)
V8, 5.4 Liter	5		(3600)	(3600)	(4305)	(4305)
V10, 6.8 Liter	Y		(3800)	(3800)	(4530)	(4530)
SUPER DUTY CREW CAB PICKUP 4WD—V8 Turbo Diesel—Schedule T1						
F250 Harley 6 3/4'	W21P	50890	18300	19450	19750	25400
F250 Harley 8'	W21P	51095	18100	19300	19550	25100
F350 Harley 6 3/4'	W31P	51665	18650	19850	20100	25900
F350 Harley 8'	W31P	51870	18450	19650	20000	25700

Body Type	VIN	List	Trade-In Good	Trade-In Very Good	Pvt-Party Good	Retail Excellent
ESCAPE—4-Cyl.—Truck Equipment Schedule T1						
XLS Sport Utility 4D	U02Z	20245	4450	4775	5625	7550
4WD			1075	1075	1425	1425
ESCAPE 4WD—4-Cyl. Hybrid—Truck Equipment Schedule T1						
Sport Utility 4D	U59H	27680	6025	6500	7825	10750
2WD	0,4		(725)	(725)	(975)	(975)
ESCAPE 4WD—V6—Truck Equipment Schedule T1						
XLT Sport Utility 4D	U931	24485	6175	6625	7725	10350
Limited Sport Util	U941	26185	7550	8100	9275	12450
2WD	0,4		(725)	(725)	(975)	(975)
4-Cyl, 2.3 Liter	Z		(500)	(500)	(655)	(655)
EDGE—V6—Truck Equipment Schedule T1						
SE Sport Utility 4D	K36C	26025	6875	7250	8425	11000
SEL Sport Utility 4D	K38C	28020	7925	8375	9625	12500
Limited Spt Util 4D	K39C	29775	8725	9200	10550	13700
AWD	4		550	550	720	720
TAURUS X—V6—Truck Equipment Schedule T1						
SEL Sport Utility	K03W	27365	5100	5500	6425	8675
AWD	5,8,6		800	800	1065	1065
TAURUS X AWD—V6—Truck Equipment Schedule T1						
Eddie Bauer Spt Utl	K08W	31955	6950	7475	8725	11900
Limited Sport Util	K06W	32935	7125	7675	9050	12350
2WD	2,3,7		(725)	(725)	(975)	(975)
EXPLORER 4WD—V6—Truck Equipment Schedule T1						
XLT Sport Utility 4D	U73E	28895	5950	6475	7225	9650
Eddie Bauer Spt Util	U74E	31130	7475	8100	8875	11800
Third Row Seat			400	400	515	515

TRUCKS & VANS

Body Type	VIN	List	Trade-In Good	Very Good	Pvt-Party Good	Retail Excellent
2WD	6	......	(1200)	(1200)	(1575)	(1575)
AWD	8	......	0	0	0	0
V8, 4.6 Liter	8	......	200	200	265	265
EXPLORER 4WD—V8—Truck Equipment Schedule T1						
Limited Sport Util	U758	36195	8150	8825	9650	12900
Third Row Seat		......	400	400	520	520
2WD	6	......	(1200)	(1200)	(1585)	(1585)
AWD	8	......	0	0	0	0
V6, 4.0 Liter	E	......	(200)	(200)	(265)	(265)
EXPLORER SPORT TRAC—V6—Truck Equipment Schedule T1						
XLT Utility Pickup	U31K	25435	9675	10100	11250	13800
4WD	8	......	1175	1175	1440	1440
V8, 4.6 Liter	8	......	200	200	240	240
EXPLORER SPORT TRAC 4WD—V6—Truck Equipment Schedule T1						
Limited Util Pickup	U53K	29995	13350	13950	15100	18400
2WD	3	......	(1200)	(1200)	(1430)	(1430)
AWD		......	0	0	0	0
V8, 4.6 Liter	8	......	200	200	240	240
EXPEDITION 4WD—V8—Truck Equipment Schedule T1						
XLT Sport Utility 4D	U165	34420	8400	9075	9725	12750
Eddie Bauer Spt Util	U185	39665	11600	12500	13050	17050
Limited Sport Util	U205	41825	12000	12900	13150	16600
King Ranch Spt Util	U185	43765	12400	13300	13550	17100
Third Row Seat		......	(325)	(325)	(400)	(400)
2WD	5,7,9	......	(725)	(725)	(930)	(930)
EXPEDITION EL 4WD—V8—Truck Equipment Schedule T1						
XLT Sport Utility 4D	K165	37945	9600	10350	11000	14400
Eddie Bauer Spt Util	K185	42315	12100	13000	13550	17600
Limited Sport Util	K205	44475	12650	13600	13950	17600
King Ranch Spt Util	K185	46415	12850	13800	14200	17950
Third Row Seat		......	(325)	(325)	(400)	(400)
2WD	5,7,9	......	(725)	(725)	(930)	(930)
ECONOLINE WAGON—V8—Truck Equipment Schedule T1						
E150 XL Super Duty	E11W	26790	7250	7875	8475	11150
E150 XLT S.D.	E11W	29565	8525	9225	9675	12600
E350 XL Super Duty	E31L	30320	7775	8450	9050	11950
E350 XLT S.D.	E31L	33125	9550	10350	10800	14100
E350 XL S.D. Ext	S31L	32710	9000	9750	10300	13500
E350 XLT Extended	S31L	34470	10150	11000	11550	15200
V8, 5.4 Liter (E150)	L	......	200	200	245	245
V8, Turbo Dsl 6.0L	P	......	2200	2200	2715	2715
ECONOLINE VAN—V8—Truck Equipment Schedule T1						
E150 Cargo Van	E14W	24595	7100	7800	8425	11300
E150 Extended	S14W	25595	7800	8575	9175	12300
E250 Cargo Van	E24W	25925	7900	8675	9225	12300
E250 Extended	E24W	27075	8950	9800	10350	13850
E350 Super Cargo	E34L	28715	8325	9125	9675	12900
E350 Extended SD	E34L	29645	9525	10450	10950	14650
Crew Van Pkg		......	200	200	255	255
V8, 5.4L (E150/E250)	L	......	200	200	255	255
V8, Turbo Dsl 6.0L	P	......	2200	2200	2790	2790
V10, 6.8 Liter	S	......	575	575	740	740
RANGER REGULAR CAB PICKUP—4-Cyl.—Truck Equipment Schedule T2						
XL 2D 7'	R10D	15925	3150	3475	4400	6475
XLT 2D 7'	R10D	17505	4150	4575	5575	8100
4WD	1,5	......	1225	1225	1645	1645
V6, 3.0 Liter	U	......	250	250	335	335
V6, 4.0 Liter	E	......	350	350	455	455
RANGER REGULAR CAB PICKUP—4-Cyl.—Truck Equipment Schedule T1						
XL 2D 6'	R10D	15655	3675	4050	5075	7400
XLT 2D 6'	R10D	17380	4675	5150	6175	8950
4WD	1,5	......	1225	1225	1620	1620
V6, 3.0 Liter	U	......	250	250	330	330
V6, 4.0 Liter	E	......	350	350	445	445
RANGER REGULAR CAB PICKUP—V6—Truck Equipment Schedule T1						
Sport 2D 6'	R10U	17915	5100	5625	6575	9475
4WD	1,5	......	1225	1225	1590	1590
V6, 4.0 Liter	E	......	350	350	440	440
RANGER SUPER CAB PICKUP—4-Cyl.—Truck Equipment Schedule T1						
XL 2D 6'	R14D	17130	5575	6150	7275	10400
4WD	1,5	......	1225	1225	1580	1580
V6, 3.0 Liter	U	......	250	250	320	320
V6, 4.0 Liter	E	......	350	350	435	435

Body Type	VIN	List	Trade-In Good	Very Good	Pvt-Party Good	Retail Excellent
RANGER SUPER CAB PICKUP—V6—Truck Equipment Schedule T1						
XLT 2D 6'	R14U	18780	6500	7150	8075	11350
4WD	1,5		1225	1225	1570	1570
4-Cyl, 2.3 Liter	D		(275)	(275)	(340)	(340)
V6, 4.0 Liter	E		350	350	435	435
RANGER SUPER CAB PICKUP—V6—Truck Equipment Schedule T1						
Sport 2D 6'	R14U	19570	7575	8325	9475	13450
Sport 4D 6'	R44U	20825	8100	8900	10050	14250
XLT 4D 6'	R44U	20235	7775	8550	9700	13750
4WD	1,5		1225	1225	1560	1560
V6, 4.0 Liter	E		350	350	430	430
RANGER SUPER CAB PICKUP 4WD—V6—Truck Equipment Schedule T2						
FX4 Off-Road 2D 6'	R15E	23145	8475	9325	9850	13400
RANGER SUPER CAB PICKUP 4WD—V6—Truck Equipment Schedule T1						
FX4 Off-Road 4D 6'	R45E	25400	9375	10300	10800	14650
REGULAR CAB PICKUP—V6—Truck Equipment Schedule T1						
F150 XL 2D 6 1/2'	F122	18270	5075	5525	6625	9200
F150 XL 2D 8'	F122	18570	4825	5250	6175	8575
4WD	4		2125	2125	2845	2845
V8, 4.6 Liter	W		475	475	640	640
V8, 5.4 Liter	5		725	725	975	975
REGULAR CAB PICKUP—V8—Truck Equipment Schedule T1						
F150 STX 2D 6 1/2'	F12W	25960	6650	7200	8100	10950
F150 XLT 2D 6 1/2'	F12W	26120	7175	7800	8775	11850
F150 XLT 2D 8'	F12W	26420	6650	7200	8150	11050
4WD	4		2125	2125	2845	2845
V6, 4.2 Liter	2		(450)	(450)	(600)	(600)
V8, 5.4 Liter	5		300	300	385	385
REGULAR CAB PICKUP 4WD—V8—Truck Equipment Schedule T1						
F150 FX4 2D 6 1/2'	F145	32665	11650	12600	13900	19050
SUPER CAB PICKUP—V8—Truck Equipment Schedule T1						
F150 XL 4D 5 1/2'	X12W	24365	6250	6625	7625	9775
F150 STX 4D 5 1/2'	X12W	25920	6775	7150	8125	10400
F150 XLT 4D 5 1/2'	X12W	28220	7100	7500	8575	11050
F150 XLT 60th 6 1/2'	X12W	31500	7175	7575	8625	11000
4WD	4		2125	2125	2700	2700
V8, 5.4 Liter	5		300	300	370	370
SUPER CAB PICKUP 4WD—V8—Truck Equipment Schedule T1						
F150 STX 4D 6 1/2'	X14W	29220	9525	10050	11000	13900
F150 XLT 4D 6 1/2'	X14W	31520	10150	10700	11700	14750
2WD	2		(2400)	(2400)	(2970)	(2970)
V8, 5.4 Liter	5		300	300	360	360
SUPER CAB PICKUP—V8—Truck Equipment Schedule T1						
F150 XL 4D 8'	X125	24665	6275	6625	7600	9700
F150 Lariat 4D 5 1/2'	X125	30820	8325	8800	9825	12550
F150 Lariat 4D 6 1/2'	X125	31120	8525	9000	10000	12700
4WD	4		2125	2125	2715	2715
SUPER CAB PICKUP 4WD—V8—Truck Equipment Schedule T1						
F150 XLT 4D 8'	X145	31820	10150	10700	11850	15150
2WD	2		(2400)	(2400)	(2995)	(2995)
SUPER CAB PICKUP 4WD—V8—Truck Equipment Schedule T1						
F150 FX4 4D 5 1/2'	X145	32920	11000	11600	12750	16200
F150 FX4 4D 6 1/2'	X145	33220	11100	11700	12850	16300
SUPERCREW PICKUP—V8—Truck Equipment Schedule T1						
F150 XL 4D 5 1/2'	W12W	27820	9675	10200	11300	14350
F150 XL 4D 6 1/2'	W12W	28120	9475	10000	11050	14050
F150 XLT 4D 5 1/2'	W12W	31205	10250	10800	11850	15050
F150 XLT 60th 5 1/3'	W12W	33600	10550	11100	12200	15500
F150 XLT 60th 6 1/2'	W12W	33900	10250	10800	11850	15100
4WD	4		2125	2125	2690	2690
V8, 5.4 Liter	5		300	300	365	365
SUPERCREW PICKUP 4WD—V8—Truck Equipment Schedule T1						
F150 XLT 4D 6 1/2'	W14W	33920	12750	13400	14600	18600
2WD	2		(2400)	(2400)	(3000)	(3000)
V8, 5.4 Liter	5		300	300	365	365
SUPERCREW PICKUP—V8—Truck Equipment Schedule T1						
F150 KingRnch 6 1/2'	W125	36720	13100	13800	15150	19300
4WD	4		2125	2125	2685	2685
SUPERCREW PICKUP 4WD—V8—Truck Equipment Schedule T1						
F150 Lariat 5 1/2'	W145	36220	15350	16150	17500	22300
F150 Lariat 6 1/2'	W145	36520	15550	16350	17650	22400
F150 KingRnch 5 1/2'	W14V	39420	14450	15250	16900	21800
2WD	2		(2400)	(2400)	(3025)	(3025)

TRUCKS & VANS

Body Type	VIN	List	Trade-In Good	Very Good	Pvt-Party Good	Retail Excellent
SUPERCREW PICKUP 4WD—V8—Truck Equipment Schedule T1						
F150 FX4 4D 5 1/2'	W145	35320	13100	13800	15050	19150
F150 FX4 4D 6 1/2'	W145	35620	13100	13800	15050	19100
SUPERCREW PICKUP AWD—V8—Truck Equipment Schedule T1						
F150 Harley 5 1/2'	W145	37425	15300	16100	17400	22100
2WD			(725)	(725)	(920)	(920)
SUPER DUTY REGULAR CAB PICKUP—V8—Truck Equipment Schedule T1						
F250 XL 2D 8'	F205	24795	5225	5625	6400	8525
F350 XL 2D 8'	F305	25515	4175	4500	5550	7625
4WD	1,3		2125	2125	2705	2705
V8, Turbo Dsl 6.4L	R		3925	3925	4965	4965
V10, 6.8 Liter	Y		500	500	625	625
SUPER DUTY REGULAR CAB 4WD—V8—Truck Equipment Schedule T1						
F250 XLT 2D 8'	F215	28480	8000	8600	9700	12950
2WD	0,2		(2400)	(2400)	(3050)	(3050)
V8, Turbo Dsl 6.4L	R		3925	3925	4980	4980
V10, 6.8 Liter	Y		500	500	625	625
SUPER DUTY REGULAR CAB 4WD—V8—Turbo Diesel—Truck Equip Sch T1						
F350 XLT 2D 8'	F31R	29535	12700	13650	14800	19450
2WD	0,2		(2400)	(2400)	(2980)	(2980)
V8, 5.4 Liter	5		(3900)	(3900)	(4850)	(4850)
V10, 6.8 Liter	Y		(3900)	(3900)	(4850)	(4850)
SUPER DUTY SUPER CAB PICKUP—V8—Truck Equipment Schedule T1						
F250 XL 4D 6 3/4'	X205	26920	6200	6675	7850	10650
F250 XL 4D 8'	X205	27115	5725	6175	7350	10000
F350 XL 4D 8'	X305	28155	6300	6800	7950	10750
F350 XLT 4D 8'	X305	32900	7800	8375	9550	12850
F350 Lariat 4D 8'	X305	35420	8225	8850	10000	13400
4WD	1,3		2125	2125	2780	2780
V8, Turbo Dsl 6.4L	R		3925	3925	5100	5100
V10, 6.8 Liter	Y		500	500	640	640
SUPER DUTY SUPER CAB 4WD—V8—Truck Equipment Schedule T1						
F250 XLT 4D 6 3/4'	X215	31320	10550	11350	12450	16550
F250 XLT 4D 8'	X215	34545	10150	10900	12050	16050
F350 Lariat 4D 8'	X215	35870	10350	11150	12250	16300
F350 XLT 4D 6 3/4'	X315	32705	10750	11550	12700	16900
F350 Lariat 4D 6 3/4'	X315	35220	10450	11250	12400	16500
2WD	0,2		(2400)	(2400)	(3025)	(3025)
V8, Turbo Dsl 6.4L	R		3925	3925	4945	4945
V10, 6.8 Liter	Y		500	500	620	620
SUPER DUTY SUPER CAB 4WD—V8 Turbo Diesel—Truck Equip Sch T1						
F250 Lariat 4D 6 3/4'	X21R	34200	15700	16850	17950	23600
2WD	0,2		(2400)	(2400)	(2975)	(2975)
V8, 5.4 Liter	5		(3900)	(3900)	(4845)	(4845)
V10, 6.8 Liter	Y		(3900)	(3900)	(4845)	(4845)
SUPER DUTY SUPER CAB—V8 Turbo Diesel—Truck Equipment Sch T1						
F350 XL 4D 6 3/4'	X31R	33825	13750	14750	15850	20800
4WD	1,3		2125	2125	2665	2665
V8, 5.4 Liter	5		(3900)	(3900)	(4875)	(4875)
V10, 6.8 Liter	Y		(3900)	(3900)	(4875)	(4875)
SUPER DUTY SUPER CAB 4WD—V8—Truck Equipment Schedule T1						
F250 FX4 4D 6 3/4'	X215	36040	10650	11450	12650	16800
F250 FX4 4D 8'	X215	36240	10500	11300	12400	16500
F350 FX4 4D 6 3/4'	X315	37370	11000	11850	13000	17300
F350 FX4 4D 8'	X315	30830	10800	11650	12850	17100
V8, Turbo Dsl 6.4L	R		3925	3925	4945	4945
V10, 6.8 Liter	Y		500	500	620	620
SUPER DUTY CREW CAB PICKUP—V8—Truck Equipment Schedule T1						
F250 XL 4D 6 3/4'	W205	28280	7750	8325	9500	12800
F250 King Ranch 8'	W205	40575	9550	10250	11450	15250
F350 XL 4D 8'	W305	29400	7750	8325	9500	12800
F350 XLT 4D 8'	W305	35015	10500	11300	12350	16300
F350 Lariat 4D 8'	W305	37825	11450	12300	13250	17300
4WD	1,3		2125	2125	2705	2705
V8, Turbo Dsl 6.4L	R		3925	3925	4965	4965
V10, 6.8 Liter	Y		500	500	625	625
SUPER DUTY CREW CAB 4WD—V8—Truck Equipment Schedule T1						
F250 XLT 4D 8'	W215	33755	12100	13000	14050	18500
F350 King Ranch 8'	W315	41465	13300	14250	15450	20400
2WD	0,2		(2400)	(2400)	(3010)	(3010)
V8, Turbo Dsl 6.4L	R		3925	3925	4920	4920
V10, 6.8 Liter	Y		500	500	615	615

Body Type	VIN	List	Trade-In Good	Very Good	Pvt-Party Good	Retail Excellent

SUPER DUTY CREW CAB—V8 Turbo Diesel—Truck Equipment Sch T1

Body Type	VIN	List	Good	Very Good	Good	Excellent
F250 XL 4D 8'	W20R	28475	11500	12350	13450	17750
F250 Lariat 4D 8'	W20R	36935	14450	15550	16700	22000
F350 XL 4D 6 3/4'	W30R	29200	12350	13250	14350	19000
4WD	1,3		2125	2125	2650	2650
V8, 5.4 Liter	5		(3900)	(3900)	(4840)	(4840)
V10, 6.8 Liter	Y		(3900)	(3900)	(4840)	(4840)

SUPER DUTY CREW CAB 4WD—V8 Turbo Diesel—Truck Equip Sch T1

Body Type	VIN	List	Good	Very Good	Good	Excellent
F250 XLT 4D 6 3/4'	W21R	33570	16900	18150	19000	24800
F250 Lariat 4D 6 3/4'	W21R	36745	18800	20200	20900	27000
F250 KingRnch 6 3/4'	W21R	40385	18550	19900	20700	26900
F350 Lariat 4D 6 3/4'	W31R	37635	18200	19500	20400	26500
F350 XLT 4D 6 3/4'	W31R	34830	17100	18350	19250	25100
F350 KingRnch 6 3/4'	W31R	41275	18400	19750	20500	26600
2WD	0,2		(2400)	(2400)	(2950)	(2950)
V8, 5.4 Liter	5		(3900)	(3900)	(4805)	(4805)
V10, 6.8 Liter	Y		(3900)	(3900)	(4805)	(4805)

SUPER DUTY CREW CAB PICKUP 4WD—V8—Truck Equipment Schedule T1

Body Type	VIN	List	Good	Very Good	Good	Excellent
F250 FX4 4D 8'	W215	38495	12450	13350	14500	19200
F350 FX4 4D 6 3/4'	W315	39255	13100	14050	15250	20200
F350 FX4 4D 8'	W315	39445	12700	13650	14900	19700
V8, Turbo Dsl 6.4L	R		3925	3925	4910	4910
V10, 6.8 Liter	Y		500	500	615	615

SUPER DUTY CREW CAB 4WD—V8 Turbo Diesel—Truck Equipment Sch T1

Body Type	VIN	List	Good	Very Good	Good	Excellent
F250 FX4 4D 6 3/4'	W21R	38295	17800	19050	19950	26000
V8, 5.4 Liter	5		(3900)	(3900)	(4820)	(4820)
V10, 6.8 Liter	Y		(3900)	(3900)	(4820)	(4820)

SUPER DUTY CREW CAB 4WD—V8 Turbo Diesel—Truck Equipment Schedule T1

Body Type	VIN	List	Good	Very Good	Good	Excellent
F250 Harley 6 3/4'	W21R	52425	23600	24900	25300	31100
F250 Harley 8'	W21R	52620	23400	24700	25100	31000
F350 Harley 6 3/4'	W31R	53075	24000	25300	25700	31600
F350 Harley 8'	W31R	53270	23800	25100	25500	31400
V10, 6.8 Liter	Y		(525)	(525)	(615)	(615)

SUPER DUTY CREW CAB—V8 Turbo Diesel—Truck Equipment Schedule T1

Body Type	VIN	List	Good	Very Good	Good	Excellent
F450 4D 8'	W42R	41620	17600	18550	19100	23500
F450 XLT 4D 8'	W42R	47395	19200	20200	20700	25500
F450 King Ranch 8'	W42R	53715	22200	23300	23700	29100
4WD	1,3		2125	2125	2470	2470

SUPER DUTY CREW CAB 4WD—V8 Turbo Diesel—Truck Equip Sch T1

Body Type	VIN	List	Good	Very Good	Good	Excellent
F450 Lariat 4D 8'	W43R	50075	22400	23600	24000	29500
2WD	0,2		(2400)	(2400)	(2770)	(2770)

2009 FORD (1,2or3)F(D,MorT)—U027-9-#

ESCAPE—4-Cyl.—Truck Equipment Schedule T1

Body Type	VIN	List	Good	Very Good	Good	Excellent
XLS Sport Utility 4D	U027	21620	4925	5225	6275	8075
4WD			1150	1150	1510	1510

ESCAPE 4WD—4-Cyl. Hybrid—Truck Equipment Schedule T1

Body Type	VIN	List	Good	Very Good	Good	Excellent
Sport Utility 4D	U593	30750	8550	9050	10550	13750
Limited Sport Util	U593	33080	10750	11350	12800	16400
2WD	0,4		(825)	(825)	(1080)	(1080)

ESCAPE 4WD—V6—Truck Equipment Schedule T1

Body Type	VIN	List	Good	Very Good	Good	Excellent
XLT Sport Utility 4D	U93G	26185	7375	7800	8950	11450
Limited Sport Util	U94G	27640	8575	9075	10150	12900
2WD	0,4		(825)	(825)	(1085)	(1085)
4-Cyl, 2.5 Liter	7		(575)	(575)	(740)	(740)

EDGE—V6—Truck Equipment Schedule T1

Body Type	VIN	List	Good	Very Good	Good	Excellent
SE Sport Utility 4D	K36C	26905	8175	8550	9800	12150
SEL Sport Utility 4D	K38C	29810	9325	9725	11000	13550
Limited Sport Util	K39C	32565	10150	10600	11900	14700
Sport SUV 4D	K30C	34020	13200	13800	15150	18450
AWD	4		625	625	770	770

TAURUS X—V6—Truck Equipment Schedule T1

Body Type	VIN	List	Good	Very Good	Good	Excellent
SEL Sport Utility	K03W	28400	5500	5850	7050	9200
AWD	5,8,6		900	900	1200	1200

TAURUS X AWD—V6—Truck Equipment Schedule T1

Body Type	VIN	List	Good	Very Good	Good	Excellent
Eddie Bauer Spt Utl	K08W	33310	7925	8400	9675	12450
Limited Sport Util	K06W	34305	8150	8625	9950	12850
FWD	2,3,7		(1200)	(1200)	(1600)	(1600)

EXPLORER 4WD—V6—Truck Equipment Schedule T1

Body Type	VIN	List	Good	Very Good	Good	Excellent
XLT Sport Utility 4D	U73E	30130	8075	8600	9650	12450
Eddie Bauer Spt Util	U74E	33275	9575	10200	11350	14650
Third Row Seat			450	450	580	580
2WD	6		(1275)	(1275)	(1650)	(1650)

TRUCKS & VANS

Body Type	VIN	List	Trade-In Good	Very Good	Pvt-Party Good	Retail Excellent
AWD	8		0	0	0	0
V8, 4.6 Liter	8		350	350	440	440
EXPLORER 4WD—V8—Truck Equipment Schedule T1						
Limited Sport Util	U758	38520	11200	11900	13050	16750
2WD	6		(1275)	(1275)	(1630)	(1630)
AWD	8		0	0	0	0
V6, 4.0 Liter	E		(225)	(225)	(295)	(295)
EXPLORER SPORT TRAC—V6—Truck Equipment Schedule T1						
XLT Utility Pickup	U31E	26810	12600	13050	14350	17100
4WD	5		1275	1275	1490	1490
V8, 4.6 Liter	8		350	350	400	400
EXPLORER SPORT TRAC 4WD—V6—Truck Equipment Schedule T1						
Limited Util Pickup	U53E	34650	16200	16750	18150	21500
2WD	6		(1275)	(1275)	(1495)	(1495)
AWD	8		0	0	0	0
V8, 4.6 Liter	8		350	350	400	400
FLEX—V6—Truck Equipment Schedule T1						
SE Sport Utility 4D	K51C	28995	8650	9150	10000	12500
SEL Sport Utility 4D	K52C	32770	9375	9925	10950	13750
Limited Sport Util	K53C	35405	11450	12100	13000	16150
AWD	6		625	625	780	780
EXPEDITION 4WD—V8—Truck Equipment Schedule T1						
XLT Sport Utility 4D	U165	36645	11150	11800	12750	16050
Power Third Row			325	325	415	415
2WD	5,7,9		(825)	(825)	(1035)	(1035)
EXPEDITION 4WD—V8—Truck Equipment Schedule T1						
Eddie Bauer Spt Util	U185	41980	14050	14850	16050	20200
Limited Sport Util	U205	46140	15400	16300	17050	20900
King Ranch Spt Util	U185	46750	15800	16700	17400	21400
2WD	5,7,9		(825)	(825)	(1035)	(1035)
EXPEDITION EL 4WD—V8—Truck Equipment Schedule T1						
XLT Sport Utility 4D	K165	40170	12350	13100	14050	17650
Power Third Row			325	325	415	415
2WD	5,7,9		(825)	(825)	(1035)	(1035)
EXPEDITION EL 4WD—V8—Truck Equipment Schedule T1						
Eddie Bauer Spt Util	K185	44630	14850	15700	16950	21400
Limited Sport Util	K205	48790	15900	16800	17550	21600
King Ranch Spt Util	K185	49200	16350	17250	18000	22100
2WD	5,7,9		(825)	(825)	(1035)	(1035)
ECONOLINE WAGON—V8—Truck Equipment Schedule T1						
E150 XL Super Duty	E11W	29145	8650	9175	9925	12500
E150 XLT S.D.	E11W	31935	9825	10450	11300	14350
E350 XL Super Duty	E31L	31505	9400	10000	10750	13500
E350 XLT S.D.	E31L	35170	10950	11600	12500	15900
E350 XL S.D. Ext	S31L	33895	10300	10950	11850	15050
E350 XLT S.D. Ext	S31L	36515	11850	12600	13550	17150
V8, 5.4 Liter (E150)	L		225	225	280	280
V10, 6.8 Liter	S		625	625	760	760
ECONOLINE VAN—V8—Truck Equipment Schedule T1						
E150 Cargo Van	E14W	26040	8700	9475	10100	13100
E150 Extended	S14W	27040	9350	10150	10900	14150
E250 Cargo Van	E24W	27075	9700	10550	11150	14400
E250 Extended	S24W	28225	10900	11850	12450	16050
E350 Super Cargo	E34L	29865	10300	11200	11750	15200
E350 SD Extended	S34L	30795	11400	12400	13000	16750
Crew Van Pkg			225	225	295	295
V8, 5.4L (E150/E250)	L		225	225	295	295
V8, Turbo Dsl 6.0L	P		2425	2425	3035	3035
V10, 6.8 Liter	S		625	625	795	795
RANGER REGULAR CAB PICKUP—4-Cyl.—Truck Equipment Schedule T2						
XL 2D 7'	R10D	18400	4025	4375	5350	7375
XLT 2D 7'	R10D	19525	4650	5025	5975	8200
V6, 4.0 Liter	E		400	400	495	495
RANGER REGULAR CAB PICKUP—4-Cyl.—Truck Equipment Schedule T1						
XL 2D 6'	R10D	17555	4700	5100	6050	8300
Sport 2D 6'	R10D	19145	5675	6150	7225	9825
XLT 2D 6'	R10D	18820	5500	5975	7075	9625
RANGER SUPER CAB PICKUP—4-Cyl.—Truck Equipment Schedule T1						
XL 2D 6'	R14D	19045	6475	7000	8075	10950
4WD	1,5		1425	1425	1755	1755
V6, 4.0 Liter	E		400	400	490	490
RANGER SUPER CAB PICKUP—V6—Truck Equipment Schedule T1						
XLT 2D 6'	R14E	20235	8150	8825	9725	12900

1015

Body Type	VIN	List	Trade-In Good	Very Good	Pvt-Party Good	Retail Excellent
4WD	1,5		**1425**	**1425**	**1725**	**1725**
4-Cyl, 2.3 Liter	D		**(300)**	**(300)**	**(350)**	**(350)**
RANGER SUPER CAB PICKUP—V6—Truck Equipment Schedule T1						
Sport 2D 6'	R14E	21555	**8250**	**8925**	**10200**	**13950**
Sport 4D 6'	R44E	22825	**9025**	**9750**	**10850**	**14600**
XLT 4D 6'	R44E	22202	**8825**	**9550**	**10650**	**14300**
4WD	1,5		**1425**	**1425**	**1720**	**1720**
RANGER SUPER CAB PICKUP 4WD—V6—Truck Equipment Schedule T2						
FX4 Off-Road 2D 6'	R15E	25255	**10700**	**11550**	**12200**	**15850**
RANGER SUPER CAB PICKUP 4WD—V6—Truck Equipment Schedule T1						
FX4 Off-Road 4D 6'	R45E	26955	**11300**	**12200**	**12850**	**16700**
REGULAR CAB PICKUP—V8—Truck Equipment Schedule T1						
F150 XL 2D 6 1/2'	F12W	22965	**7650**	**8125**	**9175**	**11850**
F150 XL 2D 8'	F12W	23265	**7225**	**7700**	**8750**	**11250**
F150 STX 2D 6 1/2'	F12W	25765	**8375**	**8900**	**9950**	**12800**
F150 XLT 2D 6 1/2'	F12W	26935	**8950**	**9500**	**10550**	**13600**
F150 XLT 2D 8'	F12W	27235	**8475**	**9000**	**10050**	**12950**
4WD	4		**2475**	**2475**	**3010**	**3010**
V8, 24V, 4.6 Liter (XL)	8		**150**	**150**	**185**	**185**
V8, 5.4 Liter	V		**325**	**325**	**385**	**385**
SUPER CAB PICKUP—V8—Truck Equipment Schedule T1						
F150 XL 4D 6 1/2'	X12W	25670	**8200**	**8575**	**9875**	**12300**
F150 STX 4D 5 1/2'	X12W	27170	**9125**	**9525**	**10800**	**13300**
F150 STX 4D 6 1/2'	X12W	27470	**10300**	**10750**	**12200**	**15250**
F150 XLT 4D 5 1/2'	X12W	29160	**10250**	**10700**	**12000**	**14700**
F150 XLT 4D 6 1/2'	X12W	29460	**10700**	**11200**	**12500**	**15350**
4WD	4		**2475**	**2475**	**3020**	**3020**
V8, 5.4 Liter	V		**325**	**325**	**385**	**385**
SUPER CAB PICKUP—V8—Truck Equipment Schedule T1						
F150 XLT 4D 8'	X12V	25970	**8650**	**9050**	**10300**	**12750**
F150 XLT 4D 8'	X12V	29760	**9325**	**9750**	**11350**	**14350**
F150 Lariat 4D 5 1/2'	X12V	33160	**11150**	**11600**	**12950**	**15950**
F150 Lariat 4D 6 1/2'	X12V	33460	**11300**	**11800**	**13200**	**16250**
4WD	4		**2475**	**2475**	**2990**	**2990**
SUPER CAB PICKUP 4WD—V8—Truck Equipment Schedule T1						
F150 FX4 4D 5 1/2'	X14V	34605	**13800**	**14400**	**15900**	**19500**
F150 FX4 4D 6 1/2'	X14V	34905	**14550**	**15200**	**16650**	**20400**
SUPERCREW PICKUP—V8—Truck Equipment Schedule T1						
F150 XL 4D 5 1/2'	W12W	29380	**11600**	**12100**	**13500**	**16650**
F150 XL 4D 6 1/2'	W12W	33340	**11400**	**11900**	**13300**	**16400**
F150 XLT 4D 5 1/2'	W128	31820	**12650**	**13200**	**14600**	**17950**
4WD	4		**2475**	**2475**	**2970**	**2970**
V8, 24V, 4.6 Liter (XL)	8		**150**	**150**	**180**	**180**
V8, 5.4 Liter	V		**325**	**325**	**380**	**380**
SUPERCREW PICKUP 4WD—V8—Truck Equipment Schedule T1						
F150 XLT 4D 6 1/2'	W148	35265	**15500**	**16200**	**17700**	**21700**
2WD	2		**(2600)**	**(2600)**	**(3100)**	**(3100)**
V8, 5.4 Liter	V		**325**	**325**	**380**	**380**
SUPERCREW PICKUP—V8—Truck Equipment Schedule T1						
F150 KingRnch 6 1/2'	W12V	40115	**16650**	**17350**	**19000**	**23400**
F150 Platinum 6 1/2'	W12V	42185	**17450**	**18200**	**19800**	**24200**
4WD	4		**2475**	**2475**	**2975**	**2975**
SUPERCREW PICKUP 4WD—V8—Truck Equipment Schedule T1						
F150 Lariat 5 1/2'	W14V	38965	**18750**	**19550**	**21200**	**25900**
F150 Lariat 6 1/2'	W14V	39265	**18600**	**19400**	**20900**	**25600**
F150 KingRnch 5 1/2'	W14V	43260	**19100**	**19900**	**21600**	**26600**
F150 Platinum 5 1/2'	W14V	44560	**19450**	**20300**	**21900**	**26900**
2WD	2		**(2600)**	**(2600)**	**(3105)**	**(3105)**
SUPERCREW PICKUP 4WD—V8—Truck Equipment Schedule T1						
F150 FX4 4D 5 1/2'	W14V	37265	**16700**	**17400**	**19000**	**23300**
F150 FX4 4D 6 1/2'	W14V	37565	**16700**	**17400**	**19000**	**23300**
SUPER DUTY REGULAR CAB PICKUP—V8—Truck Equipment Schedule T1						
F250 XL 2D 8'	F205	27060	**7025**	**7450**	**8425**	**10700**
F350 XL 2D 8'	F305	27780	**5850**	**6200**	**7400**	**9625**
4WD	1,3		**2475**	**2475**	**2965**	**2965**
V8, Turbo Dsl 6.4L	R		**4150**	**4150**	**4985**	**4985**
V10, 6.8 Liter	Y		**525**	**525**	**640**	**640**
SUPER DUTY REGULAR CAB PICKUP—V8—Truck Equipment Schedule T1						
F250 XL 2D 8'	F215	30610	**10300**	**10850**	**12150**	**15500**
2WD	0,2		**(2600)**	**(2600)**	**(3085)**	**(3085)**
V8, Turbo Dsl 6.4L	R		**4150**	**4150**	**4935**	**4935**
V10, 6.8 Liter	Y		**525**	**525**	**635**	**635**

TRUCKS & VANS

Body Type	VIN	List	Trade-In Good	Very Good	Pvt-Party Good	Retail Excellent
SUPER DUTY REGULAR CAB 4WD—V8 Turbo Diesel—Truck Equip Sch T1						
F350 XLT 2D 8'	F31R	31665	15300	16150	17450	22000
2WD	0,2		(2600)	(2600)	(3045)	(3045)
V8, 5.4 Liter	5		(4150)	(4150)	(4875)	(4875)
V10, 6.8 Liter	Y		(4125)	(4125)	(4850)	(4850)
SUPER DUTY SUPER CAB PICKUP—V8—Truck Equipment Schedule T1						
F250 XL 4D 6 3/4'	X205	29185	8175	8675	9950	12800
F250 XL 4D 8'	X205	29380	7700	8175	9450	12200
F350 XLT 4D 6 3/4'	X215	38595	12750	13500	15000	19100
F350 XL 4D 8'	X305	30420	8075	8575	9850	12750
F350 XLT 4D 8'	X305	35030	10100	10650	12200	15350
F350 Lariat 4D 8'	X305	38145	10550	11150	12550	16050
4WD	1,3		2475	2475	2980	2980
V8, Turbo Dsl 6.4L	R		4150	4150	5010	5010
V10, 6.8 Liter	Y		525	525	645	645
SUPER DUTY SUPER CAB PICKUP 4WD—V8—Truck Equipment Schedule T1						
F250 XLT 4D 6 3/4'	X215	33450	12550	13300	14800	18900
F250 XLT 4D 8'	X215	33635	12450	13150	14550	18500
F350 XLT 4D 6 3/4'	X315	34835	12750	13500	15000	19200
F350 XLT 4D 8'	X315	37945	13000	13750	15250	19400
2WD	0,2		(2600)	(2600)	(3090)	(3090)
V8, Turbo Dsl 6.4L	R		4150	4150	5030	5030
V10, 6.8 Liter	Y		525	525	645	645
SUPER DUTY SUPER CAB—V8 Turbo Diesel—Truck Equipment Sch T1						
F350 XL 4D 6 3/4'	X31R	40025	15650	16550	17900	22700
4WD	1,3		2475	2475	2920	2920
V8, 5.4 Liter	5		(4150)	(4150)	(4910)	(4910)
V10, 6.8 Liter	Y		(4125)	(4125)	(4880)	(4880)
SUPER DUTY SUPER CAB 4WD—V8 Turbo Diesel—Truck Equipment Sch T1						
F250 Lariat 4D 6 3/4'	X21R	36925	18100	19100	20500	26000
2WD	0,2		(2600)	(2600)	(3045)	(3045)
V8, 5.4 Liter	5		(4150)	(4150)	(4875)	(4875)
V10, 6.8 Liter	Y		(4125)	(4125)	(4850)	(4850)
SUPER DUTY SUPER CAB PICKUP 4WD—V8—Truck Equipment Schedule T1						
F250 FX4 4D 6 3/4'	X215	38720	13350	14100	15600	19850
F250 FX4 4D 8'	X215	38920	13150	13900	15400	19600
F350 FX4 4D 6 3/4'	X315	40050	14150	14950	16450	20900
F350 FX4 4D 8'	X315	40235	13550	14350	15850	20200
V8, Turbo Dsl 6.4L	R		4150	4150	4930	4930
V10, 6.8 Liter	Y		525	525	635	635
SUPER DUTY CREW CAB PICKUP—V8—Truck Equipment Schedule T1						
F250 XL 4D 6'	W205	30545	9650	10200	11550	14800
F250 King Ranch 8'	W205	43055	12450	13150	14600	18600
F350 XL 4D 6'	W305	31665	9650	10200	11550	14800
F350 XLT 4D 8'	W305	37460	12700	13650	14350	19050
F350 Lariat 4D 8'	W305	41240	13450	14200	15500	19500
4WD	1,3		2475	2475	2935	2935
V8, Turbo Dsl 6.4L	R		4150	4150	4935	4935
V10, 6.8 Liter	Y		525	525	635	635
SUPER DUTY CREW CAB PICKUP 4WD—V8—Truck Equipment Schedule T1						
F250 XLT 4D 8'	W215	35885	14500	15350	16700	21100
F350 King Ranch 8'	W315	45330	16400	17300	18700	23600
2WD	0,2		(2600)	(2600)	(3070)	(3070)
V8, Turbo Dsl 6.4L	R		4150	4150	4910	4910
V10, 6.8 Liter	Y		525	525	630	630
SUPER DUTY CREW CAB—V8 Turbo Diesel—Truck Equipment Sch T1						
F250 XL 4D 8'	W20R	30740	13600	14350	15750	20000
F250 Lariat 4D 8'	W20R	39660	17050	18000	19450	24700
F350 XL 4D 6 3/4'	W30R	31465	15100	15950	17300	21900
4WD	1,3		2475	2475	2895	2895
V8, 5.4 Liter	5		(4150)	(4150)	(4870)	(4870)
V10, 6.8 Liter	Y		(4125)	(4125)	(4845)	(4845)
SUPER DUTY CREW CAB 4WD—V8 Turbo Diesel—Truck Equipment Sch T1						
F250 XLT 4D 6 3/4'	W21R	35700	19600	20700	21900	27500
F250 Lariat 4D 6 3/4'	W21R	39470	21400	22600	23800	29800
F250 KingRnch 6 3/4'	W21R	42865	21600	22800	24000	30000
F350 XL 4D 6 3/4'	W31R	36960	19550	20700	22000	27600
F350 Lariat 4D 6 3/4'	W31R	40360	20300	21500	22800	28700
F350 KingRnch 6 3/4'	W31R	43755	21400	22600	23600	29400
2WD	0,2		(2600)	(2600)	(3030)	(3030)
V8, 5.4 Liter	5		(4150)	(4150)	(4855)	(4855)
V10, 6.8 Liter	Y		(4125)	(4125)	(4830)	(4830)

Body Type	VIN	List	Trade-In Good	Very Good	Pvt-Party Good	Retail Excellent
SUPER DUTY CREW CAB 4WD—V8—Truck Equipment Schedule T1						
F250 FX4 4D 8'	W215	41175	15100	15950	17400	22100
F350 FX4 4D 6 3/4'	W315	41935	15850	16750	18250	23100
F350 FX4 4D 8'	W315	42125	15450	16350	17800	22600
V8, Turbo Dsl 6.4L	R		4150	4150	4910	4910
V10, 6.8 Liter	Y		525	525	630	630
SUPER DUTY CREW CAB 4WD—V8 Turbo Diesel—Truck Equipment Sch T1						
F250 FX4 4D 6 3/4'	W21R	40975	20500	21600	23000	28900
V8, 5.4 Liter	5		(4150)	(4150)	(4855)	(4855)
V10, 6.8 Liter	Y		(4125)	(4125)	(4825)	(4825)
SUPER DUTY CREW CAB 4WD—V8 Turbo Diesel—Truck Equipment Sch T1						
F250 Harley 6 3/4'	W21R	55465	28700	29900	30600	36300
F250 Harley 8'	W21R	55660	28500	29700	30500	36100
F350 Harley 6 3/4'	W31R	56310	29300	30500	31200	37000
F350 Harley 8'	W31R	56115	29100	30300	31000	36800
SUPER DUTY CREW CAB—V8 Turbo Diesel—Truck Equipment Sch T1						
F450 XL 4D 8'	W42R	43785	22500	23400	24000	28400
F450 XLT 4D 8'	W42R	48370	23900	24900	25600	30200
F450 King Ranch 8'	W42R	56005	27300	28400	29000	34300
4WD	3		2475	2475	2705	2705
SUPER DUTY CREW CAB 4WD—V8 Turbo Diesel—Truck Equipment Sch T1						
F450 Lariat 4D 8'	W43R	51810	27800	29000	29600	35000
2WD			(2600)	(2600)	(2830)	(2830)
SUPER DUTY CREW CAB 4WD—V8 Turbo Diesel—Truck Equip Sch T1						
F450 Harley 8'	W43R	60425	29700	31000	31500	37300

Body Type	VIN	List	Trade-In Good	Very Good	Pvt-Party Good	Retail Excellent
2010 FORD (1,2orN)(ForM)(0,D,MorT)–U027–A–#						
ESCAPE—4-Cyl.—Truck Equipment Schedule T1						
XLS Sport Utility 4D	U027	21240	6650	6975	8150	10100
4WD	9,5		1250	1250	1560	1560
ESCAPE 4WD—4-Cyl. Hybrid—Truck Equipment Schedule T1						
Sport Utility 4D	U5K3	32225	12350	12900	14250	17350
Limited Sport Util	U5K3	34735	13700	14300	15750	19200
2WD	0,4		(950)	(950)	(1110)	(1110)
ESCAPE 4WD—V6—Truck Equipment Schedule T1						
XLT Sport Util 4D	U9DG	27015	9100	9550	10800	13250
Limited Sport Util	U9EG	28745	10550	11050	12350	15200
2WD	0,4		(950)	(950)	(1175)	(1175)
4-Cyl, 2.5 Liter	7		(675)	(675)	(815)	(815)
EDGE—V6—Truck Equipment Schedule T1						
SE Sport Utility 4D	K3GC	27695	9300	9625	11150	13450
SEL Sport Utility 4D	K3JC	30695	11100	11500	13100	15750
Limited Sport Util	K3KC	33495	11800	12200	13850	16650
Sport SUV 4D	K3AC	34695	14050	14500	16350	19650
AWD	4		700	700	870	870
EXPLORER 4WD—V6—Truck Equipment Schedule T1						
XLT Sport Utility	U7DE	32015	9475	9925	11150	13750
Eddie Bauer Spt Utl	U7EE	36015	12100	12650	14000	17300
Third Row Seat			525	525	645	645
2WD	6		(1350)	(1350)	(1675)	(1675)
AWD	8		0	0	0	0
V8, 4.6 Liter	8		275	275	350	350
EXPLORER 4WD—V8—Truck Equipment Schedule T1						
Limited Sport Util	U758	40325	12600	13150	14500	17900
2WD	6		(1350)	(1350)	(1680)	(1680)
AWD			0	0	0	0
V6, 4.0 Liter	E		(275)	(275)	(350)	(350)
EXPLORER SPORT TRAC—V6—Truck Equipment Schedule T1						
XLT Utility Pickup	U3BE	28625	15100	15550	17100	19800
4WD			1350	1350	1560	1560
EXPLORER SPORT TRAC 4WD—V6—Truck Equipment Schedule T1						
Limited Util Pickup	U5DE	36005	19350	19900	21500	24700
2WD	3		(1350)	(1350)	(1565)	(1565)
AWD	2		0	0	0	0
V8, 4.6 Liter	8		275	275	325	325
FLEX—V6—Truck Equipment Schedule T1						
SE Sport Utility 4D	K5BC	29325	10250	10700	12000	14750
SEL Sport Util 4D	K5CC	32100	11350	11850	13300	16350
Limited Sport Util	K5DC	37995	12850	13400	14950	18300
AWD	6		700	700	880	880
V6, 3.5L, EcoBoost	T		1525	1525	1915	1915
EXPEDITION 4WD—V8—Truck Equipment Schedule T1						
XLT Sport Utility 4D	U1G5	38910	13750	14350	15650	18900

Body Type	VIN	List	Trade-In Good	Very Good	Pvt-Party Good	Retail Excellent
Power Third Row		......	375	375	465	465
2WD	F,H,K		(950)	(950)	(1160)	(1160)
EXPEDITION 4WD—V8—Truck Equipment Schedule T1						
Eddie Bauer Spt Util	U1J5	44715	17300	18050	19450	23500
Limited Sport Util	U2A5	46485	20300	21200	21900	25900
King Ranch Spt Util	U1J5	49015	20800	21600	22400	26500
2WD	F,H,K		(950)	(950)	(1160)	(1160)
EXPEDITION EL 4WD—V8—Truck Equipment Schedule T1						
XLT Sport Utility 4D	K1G5	42435	15600	16250	17500	21000
Power Third Row		......	375	375	460	460
2WD	F,H,K		(950)	(950)	(1150)	(1150)
EXPEDITION EL 4WD—V8—Truck Equipment Schedule T1						
Eddie Bauer Spt Util	K1J5	46895	18000	18750	20300	24600
Limited Sport Util	K2A5	49135	21100	22000	22800	27000
King Ranch Spt Util	K1J5	51665	21400	22300	23100	27200
2WD	F,H,K		(950)	(950)	(1165)	(1165)
TRANSIT CONNECT CARGO VAN—4-Cyl.—Truck Equipment Sch T2						
XL Cargo Van 4D	S6AN	21475	8550	8950	10250	12700
XLT Cargo Van 4D	S6BN	22535	9250	9675	11100	13750
TRANSIT CONNECT PASSENGER VAN—4-Cyl.—Truck Equipment Sch T1						
XL Passenger Van	S9AN	21830	8350	8850	9650	12100
XLT Passenger Van	S9BN	23045	8850	9400	10200	12750
ECONOLINE WAGON—V8—Truck Equipment Schedule T1						
E150 XL Super Duty	E1BW	28450	10100	10550	11500	13950
E150 XLT S.D.	E1BW	31145	11250	11750	12750	15450
E350 XL Super Duty	E3BL	31545	10800	11300	12250	14800
E350 XLT S.D. Ext	S3BL	33850	11600	12150	13150	15900
E350 XLT S.D.	E3BL	34265	12200	12750	13800	16700
E350 XLT S.D. Ext	S3BL	35565	13150	13750	14900	18100
V8, 5.4 Liter (E150)	L		275	275	315	315
ECONOLINE VAN—V8—Truck Equipment Schedule T1						
E150 Cargo Van	E1EW	26230	10600	11450	12100	15200
E150 Extended	S1EW	27195	11200	12100	12800	16100
E250 Cargo Van	E2EW	27230	11550	12500	13100	16400
E250 Extended	S2EW	28340	12900	13900	14500	18150
E350 Super Cargo	E3EL	29920	12150	13150	13750	17200
E350 Super Extended	S3EL	30820	13300	14350	15050	18800
Crew Van Pkg			275	275	325	325
V8, 5.4L (E150/E250)	L		275	275	325	325
V8, Turbo Dsl 6.0L	P		2675	2675	3235	3235
V10, 6.8 Liter	S		675	675	810	810
RANGER REGULAR CAB PICKUP—4-Cyl.—Truck Equipment Schedule T2						
XL 2D 7'	R1AD	19445	5350	5725	6775	8825
V6, 4.0 Liter	E		475	475	565	565
RANGER REGULAR CAB PICKUP—4-Cyl.—Truck Equipment Schedule T1						
XL 2D 6'	R1AD	19160	6550	6975	7950	10250
XLT 2D 6'	R1AD	20300	7500	8000	9075	11700
RANGER SUPER CAB PICKUP—4-Cyl.—Truck Equipment Schedule T1						
XL 2D 6'	R1ED	20235	8125	8675	9775	12600
4WD	F		1625	1625	1930	1930
V6, 4.0 Liter	E		475	475	560	560
RANGER SUPER CAB PICKUP—V6—Truck Equipment Schedule T1						
XLT 2D 6'	R1EE	22300	9675	10300	11350	14500
4-Cyl, 2.3 Liter	D		(325)	(325)	(390)	(390)
RANGER SUPER CAB PICKUP—V6—Truck Equipment Schedule T1						
Sport 2D 6'	R1EE	23875	10150	10800	12000	15500
Sport 4D 6'	R4EE	24940	10700	11400	12600	16200
XLT 4D 6'	R4EE	24205	10350	11050	12250	15750
4WD	F		1625	1625	1915	1915
REGULAR CAB PICKUP—V8—Truck Equipment Schedule T1						
F150 XL 2D 6 1/2'	F1CW	22555	8300	8675	9925	12400
F150 XL 2D 8'	F1CW	22655	8200	8575	9800	12200
F150 STX 2D 6 1/2'	F1CW	25380	9450	9875	11200	13900
F150 XLT 2D 6 1/2'	F1CW	26550	10250	10700	12050	14950
F150 XLT 2D 8'	F1CW	26850	9650	10100	11400	14150
4WD	E		2725	2725	3350	3350
V8, 24V, 4.6 Liter	8		150	150	195	195
V8, Flex Fuel, 5.4 Liter	V		350	350	420	420
SUPER CAB PICKUP—V8—Truck Equipment Schedule T1						
F150 XL 4D 6 1/2'	X1CW	26180	9725	10050	11600	13950
F150 STX 4D 6 1/2'	X1CW	27980	11750	12150	13700	16400
4WD	E		2725	2725	3370	3370
V8, 24V, 4.6 Liter	8		150	150	195	195

Body Type	VIN	List	Trade-In Good	Very Good	Pvt-Party Good	Retail Excellent
V8, Flex Fuel, 5.4 Liter	V		350	350	420	420
SUPER CAB PICKUP—V8—Truck Equipment Schedule T1						
F150 XLT 4D 6 1/2'	X1C8	29970	12250	12650	14250	17050
4WD	E		2725	2725	3305	3305
V8, Flex Fuel, 5.4 Liter	V		350	350	410	410
SUPER CAB PICKUP—V8—Truck Equipment Schedule T1						
F150 XL 4D 8'	X1CV	26480	10100	10450	11950	14300
F150 XLT 4D 8'	X1CV	30270	12000	12400	13950	16700
F150 Lariat 4D 6 1/2'	X1CV	34180	13150	13600	15350	18400
4WD	E		2725	2725	3345	3345
SUPER CAB PICKUP 4WD—V8—Truck Equipment Schedule T1						
F150 FX4 4D 6 1/2'	X1EV	36065	16650	17250	19100	22800
F150 SVT Rptr 5 1/2'	X1EV	38995	27400	28600	28400	32700
V8, 6.2 Liter	6		775	775	840	840
SUPERCREW PICKUP—V8—Truck Equipment Schedule T1						
F150 XL 4D 5 1/2'	W1CV	29590	13150	13600	15350	18350
F150 XLT 4D 5 1/2'	W1CV	32330	14000	14500	16250	19450
F150 Kng Rnch 6 1/2'	W1CV	41475	18900	19500	21500	25600
F150 Platinum 6 1/2'	W1CV	43350	19050	19700	21700	25900
F150 Harley 5 1/2'	W1CV	43665	20000	20700	22700	27100
4WD	E		2725	2725	3290	3290
V8, 24V, 4.6 Liter	8		150	150	195	195
V8, Flex Fuel, 5.4L (XL)	V		350	350	415	415
SUPERCREW PICKUP—V8—Truck Equipment Schedule T1						
F150 XL 4D 6 1/2'	W1CV	33850	13150	13650	15350	18300
4WD	E		2725	2725	3310	3310
V8, 16V, 4.6 Liter	W		(325)	(325)	(405)	(405)
V8, 24V, 4.6 Liter	8		(175)	(175)	(215)	(215)
SUPERCREW PICKUP 4WD—V8—Truck Equipment Schedule T1						
F150 XLT 4D 6 1/2'	W1EV	35775	17200	17800	19700	23500
F150 Lariat 4D 5 1/2'	W1EV	39685	20200	20900	22800	27200
F150 Lariat 4D 5 1/2'	W1EV	39985	20200	20800	22800	27100
F150 Kng Rnch 5 1/2'	W1EV	44320	21400	22100	24200	28800
F150 Platinum 5 1/2'	W1EV	46195	21100	21800	23800	28500
2WD	C		(2775)	(2775)	(3350)	(3350)
V8, 24V, 4.6 Liter	8		(175)	(175)	(215)	(215)
SUPERCREW PICKUP 4WD—V8—Truck Equipment Schedule T1						
F150 FX4 4D 5 1/2'	W1EV	38425	18000	18600	20600	24600
F150 FX4 4D 5 1/2'	W1EV	38725	18050	18650	20600	24600
SUPER DUTY REGULAR CAB PICKUP—V8—Truck Equipment Schedule T1						
F250 XL 2D 8'	F2A5	26275	9200	9600	10700	13000
F350 XL 2D 8'	F3A5	26995	7375	7725	9050	11300
4WD	1,3		2725	2725	3190	3190
V8, Turbo Dsl 6.4L	R		4375	4375	5105	5105
V10, 6.8 Liter	Y		575	575	660	660
SUPER DUTY REGULAR CAB 4WD—V8—Truck Equipment Schedule T1						
F250 XLT 2D 8'	F215	29820	11950	12450	13950	17200
2WD	0,2		(2775)	(2775)	(3285)	(3285)
V8, Turbo Dsl 6.4L	R		4375	4375	5175	5175
V10, 6.8 Liter	Y		575	575	670	670
SUPER DUTY REGULAR CAB 4WD—V8 Turbo Diesel—Truck Equip Sch T1						
F350 XLT 2D 8'	F31R	43240	16850	17600	19250	23600
2WD	0,2		(2775)	(2775)	(3250)	(3250)
V8, 5.4 Liter	5		(4375)	(4375)	(5120)	(5120)
V10, 6.8 Liter	Y		(4350)	(4350)	(5095)	(5095)
SUPER DUTY SUPER CAB PICKUP—V8—Truck Equipment Schedule T1						
F250 XL 4D 6 3/4'	X2A5	29655	9575	10000	11450	14250
F250 XL 4D 8'	X2A5	29850	9200	9625	11050	13750
F250 XLT 4D 8'	X2A5	34100	11100	11600	13150	16300
F250 Lariat 4D 8'	X2A5	40555	17350	18100	19800	24400
F350 XL 4D 8'	X3A5	30890	9675	10100	11600	14400
F350 XLT 4D 8'	X3A5	35500	11450	11950	13500	16750
F350 Lariat 4D 8'	X3A5	38615	12250	12750	14300	17700
4WD	1,3		2725	2725	3275	3275
V8, Turbo Dsl 6.4L	R		4375	4375	5240	5240
V10, 6.8 Liter	Y		575	575	675	675
SUPER DUTY SUPER CAB PICKUP 4WD—V8—Truck Equipment Schedule T1						
F350 XLT 4D 6 3/4'	X3B5	35300	14200	14900	16600	20500
F350 Lariat 4D 6 3/4'	X3B5	38415	14250	14900	16600	20500
2WD	0,2		(2775)	(2775)	(3290)	(3290)
V8, Turbo Dsl 6.4L	R		4375	4375	5185	5185
V10, 6.8 Liter	Y		575	575	670	670

Body Type	VIN	List	Trade-In Good	Very Good	Pvt-Party Good	Retail Excellent
SUPER DUTY SUPER CAB 4WD—V8 Turbo Diesel—Truck Equipment Sch T1						
F250 XLT 4D 6 3/4'	X2BR	45010	19300	20100	21800	26700
F250 Lariat 4D 6 3/4'	X2BR	37395	20200	21100	22900	28100
2WD	0,2		(2775)	(2775)	(3250)	(3250)
V8, 5.4 Liter	5		(4375)	(4375)	(5125)	(5125)
V10, 6.8 Liter	Y		(4350)	(4350)	(5100)	(5100)
SUPER DUTY SUPER CAB—V8 Turbo Diesel—Truck Equipment Sch T1						
F350 XL 4D 6 3/4'	X3BR	40005	16150	16900	18650	23000
4WD	1,3		2725	2725	3250	3250
V8, 5.4 Liter	5		(4375)	(4375)	(5200)	(5200)
V10, 6.8 Liter	Y		(4350)	(4350)	(5175)	(5175)
SUPER DUTY CREW CAB PICKUP—V8—Truck Equipment Schedule T1						
F250 XL 4D 6 3/4'	W2A5	31015	11400	11900	13450	16650
F250 King Ranch 8'	W2A5	44120	14850	15500	17150	21100
F350 XLT 4D 8'	W3A5	37615	14050	14700	16300	20000
F350 XLT 4D 8'	W3A5	32135	11400	11900	13450	16650
F350 Lariat 4D 8'	W3A5	41020	15900	16600	18050	22000
4WD	1,3		2725	2725	3225	3225
V8, Turbo Dsl 6.4L	R		4375	4375	5160	5160
V10, 6.8 Liter	Y		575	575	665	665
SUPER DUTY CREW CAB PICKUP 4WD—V8—Truck Equipment Schedule T1						
F250 XLT 4D 8'	W2B5	36350	16050	16750	18400	22600
F350 King Ranch 8'	W3B5	45010	18850	19700	21600	26500
2WD	0,2		(2775)	(2775)	(3270)	(3270)
V8, Turbo Dsl 6.4L	R		4375	4375	5155	5155
V10, 6.8 Liter	Y		575	575	665	665
SUPER DUTY CREW CAB—V8 Turbo Diesel—Truck Equipment Sch T1						
F250 XLT 4D 8'	W2AR	31210	15350	16050	17650	21700
F250 Lariat 4D 8'	W2AR	40130	18750	19550	21300	26100
F350 XLT 4D 6 3/4'	W3AR	42980	16750	17500	19100	23400
4WD	1,3		2725	2725	3210	3210
V8, 5.4 Liter	5		(4375)	(4375)	(5135)	(5135)
V10, 6.8 Liter	Y		(4350)	(4350)	(5110)	(5110)
SUPER DUTY CREW CAB 4WD—V8 Turbo Diesel—Truck Equipment Sch T1						
F250 XLT 4D 6 3/4'	W2BR	47265	21300	22300	24000	29300
F250 Lariat 4D 8'	W21R	39940	23800	24900	26600	32300
F250 KingRnch 6 3/4'	W21R	43930	23900	25000	26700	32500
F350 XLT 4D 8'	W3BR	48300	21700	22600	24300	29600
F350 Lariat 4D 3/4'	W3BR	40830	22200	23200	24900	30500
F350 King Ranch 6'	W3BR	44820	23200	24200	25900	31500
2WD	0,2		(2775)	(2775)	(3235)	(3235)
V8, 5.4 Liter	5		(4375)	(4375)	(5100)	(5100)
V10, 6.8 Liter	Y		(4350)	(4350)	(5075)	(5075)
SUPER DUTY CREW CAB PICKUP 4WD—V8—Truck Equipment Schedule T1						
F250 CABELA'S 6'	W2B5	43630	27000	27900	29100	33700
F250 CABELA'S 8'	W2B5	43830	26600	27500	28700	33300
F350 CABELA'S 8'	W3B5	44590	27400	28300	29600	34300
F350 CABELA'S 8'	W3B5	44780	26800	27700	29000	33600
V8, Turbo Dsl 6.4L	R		4375	4375	4705	4705
V10, 6.8 Liter	Y		575	575	610	610
SUPER DUTY CREW CAB 4WD—V8 Turbo Diesel—Truck Equip Sch T1						
F250 Harley 6 3/4'	W2BR	59390	30200	31200	32600	37800
F250 Harley 8'	W2BR	59585	30000	31000	32400	37700
F350 Harley 6 3/4'	W3BR	60040	30800	31800	33200	38400
F350 Harley 8'	W3BR	60235	30600	31600	33000	38200
SUPER DUTY CREW CAB—V8 Turbo Diesel—Truck Equipment Schedule T1						
F450 XL 4D 8'	W4CR	45120	23400	24200	25300	29300
F450 XLT 4D 8'	W4CR	50500	25200	26000	27300	31700
F450 King Ranch 8'	W4CR	57930	28600	29500	30900	35800
4WD	D		2725	2725	2945	2945
SUPER DUTY CREW CAB 4WD—V8 Turbo Diesel—Truck Equipment Sch T1						
F450 Lariat 4D 8'	W4DR	53940	28700	29600	30900	35700
2WD	C		(2775)	(2775)	(2980)	(2980)
SUPER DUTY CREW CAB 4WD—V8 Turbo Diesel—Truck Equipment Sch T1						
F450 Harley 8'	W4DR	63785	31100	32100	33400	38600

2011 FORD (1,2orN)(ForM)(0,D,MorT)—U027–B–#

Body Type	VIN	List	Trade-In Good	Very Good	Pvt-Party Good	Retail Excellent
ESCAPE—4-Cyl.—Truck Equipment Schedule T1						
XLS Sport Util 4D	U027	21785	7525	7850	9350	11450
4WD	9		1400	1400	1715	1715
ESCAPE 4WD—4-Cyl. Hybrid—Truck Equipment Schedule T1						
Sport Utility 4D	U5K3	32340	14450	14950	16400	19350
Limited Sport Util	U5K3	34850	16150	16650	18000	21000

TRUCKS & VANS

Body Type	VIN	List	Trade-In Good	Very Good	Pvt-Party Good	Retail Excellent
2WD	4		**(1075)**	**(1075)**	**(1235)**	**(1235)**
ESCAPE 4WD—V6—Truck Equipment Schedule T1						
XLT Sport Util 4D	U9DG	26525	**10500**	**10900**	**12300**	**14750**
Limited Sport Util	U9EG	28105	**11300**	**11750**	**13150**	**15600**
2WD	0		**(1075)**	**(1075)**	**(1290)**	**(1290)**
4-Cyl, 2.5 Liter	7		**(775)**	**(775)**	**(925)**	**(925)**
EDGE—V6—Truck Equipment Schedule T1						
SE Sport Util 4D	K3GC	28195	**11150**	**11500**	**13000**	**15100**
SEL Sport Util 4D	K3JC	30995	**13700**	**14050**	**15650**	**17950**
Limited Sport Util 4D	K3KC	36495	**15200**	**15650**	**17250**	**19750**
Sport SUV 4D	K3AK	36995	**17850**	**18300**	**20000**	**23000**
AWD	4		**775**	**775**	**895**	**895**
EXPLORER 4WD—V6—Truck Equipment Schedule T1						
Sport Utility 4D	K8B8	30995	**14900**	**15350**	**16550**	**19300**
XLT Sport Utility	K8D8	33995	**17550**	**18100**	**19350**	**22600**
Limited Sport Util	K8F8	39995	**19100**	**19700**	**21000**	**24600**
Third Row Seat			**575**	**575**	**670**	**670**
2WD	7		**(1450)**	**(1450)**	**(1655)**	**(1655)**
FLEX—V6—Truck Equipment Schedule T1						
SE Sport Util 4D	K5BC	29850	**11400**	**11800**	**13300**	**15900**
SEL Sport Util 4D	K5CC	32650	**13050**	**13500**	**15150**	**18050**
Limited Sport Util	K5DC	38620	**14750**	**15250**	**16950**	**20200**
AWD	6		**775**	**775**	**935**	**935**
V6, EcoBoost, 3.5L	T		**1600**	**1600**	**1945**	**1945**
FLEX AWD—V6 EcoBoost—Truck Equipment Schedule T1						
Titanium Spt Util	K6DT	45960	**18400**	**19000**	**20900**	**24900**
2WD	5		**(825)**	**(825)**	**(990)**	**(990)**
V6, 3.5 Liter	C		**(1600)**	**(1600)**	**(1925)**	**(1925)**
EXPEDITION 4WD—V8—Truck Equipment Schedule T1						
XLT Sport Utility 4D	U1J5	42025	**18400**	**18950**	**20200**	**23400**
Power Third Row			**425**	**425**	**500**	**500**
2WD	H		**(1075)**	**(1075)**	**(1230)**	**(1230)**
EXPEDITION 4WD—V8—Truck Equipment Schedule T1						
XL Sport Utility 4D	U1G5	40485	**15900**	**16400**	**17750**	**20600**
Limited Sport Util	U2A5	48695	**22100**	**22800**	**23800**	**27300**
King Ranch Spt Util	U1J5	49965	**22500**	**23300**	**24200**	**27900**
Third Row Seat			**(400)**	**(400)**	**(450)**	**(450)**
2WD	H		**(1075)**	**(1075)**	**(1230)**	**(1230)**
EXPEDITION EL 4WD—V8—Truck Equipment Schedule T1						
XLT Sport Utility 4D	K1J5	44735	**19500**	**20100**	**21400**	**24700**
Power Third Row			**425**	**425**	**500**	**500**
2WD	H		**(1075)**	**(1075)**	**(1230)**	**(1230)**
EXPEDITION EL 4WD—V8—Truck Equipment Schedule T1						
XL Sport Utility 4D	K1G5	43135	**18750**	**19350**	**20600**	**23900**
Limited Sport Util	K2A5	51345	**23100**	**23800**	**24800**	**28400**
King Ranch Spt Util	K1J5	52615	**23500**	**24200**	**25100**	**28800**
2WD	H		**(1075)**	**(1075)**	**(1230)**	**(1230)**
TRANSIT CONNECT CARGO VAN—4-Cyl.—Truck Equipment Sch T2						
XL Van 4D	S6AN	21895	**10150**	**10500**	**12050**	**14450**
XLT Van 4D	S6BN	22955	**10850**	**11200**	**12850**	**15450**
TRANSIT CONNECT PASSENGER VAN—4-Cyl.—Truck Equipment Sch T1						
XLT Van 4D	S9BN	23745	**10150**	**10600**	**11700**	**14150**
XLT Premium Van	S9CN	23895	**10250**	**10600**	**12000**	**14250**
ECONOLINE WAGON—V8—Truck Equipment Schedule T1						
E150 XL	E1BW	28950	**11500**	**11850**	**13150**	**15500**
E150 XLT	E1BW	31405	**12650**	**13050**	**14350**	**17000**
E350 XL Super Duty	E3BL	32045	**12150**	**12550**	**13800**	**16350**
E350 XL S.D. Ext	S3BL	34350	**12800**	**13200**	**14600**	**17250**
E350 XLT S.D.	E3BL	34525	**13150**	**13550**	**15400**	**18200**
E350 XLT S.D. Ext.	S3BL	35825	**14750**	**15200**	**16700**	**19750**
V8, 5.4 Liter (E150)	L		**300**	**300**	**345**	**345**
V10, 6.8 Liter	S		**700**	**700**	**820**	**820**
ECONOLINE VAN—V8—Truck Equipment Schedule T1						
E150 Cargo Van	E1EW	26820	**12300**	**13250**	**13950**	**17150**
E150 Extended	S1EW	28030	**12900**	**13850**	**14700**	**18150**
E250 Cargo Van	E2EW	27820	**13050**	**14050**	**14800**	**18150**
E250 Extended	S2EW	29175	**14400**	**15450**	**16200**	**19900**
E350 Super Cargo	E3EL	30750	**13750**	**14750**	**15500**	**18950**
E350 SD Extended	S3EL	31650	**15050**	**16150**	**16900**	**20700**
E350 Cab-Ch DR	E3FL	26800	**18400**	**18950**	**20600**	**24300**
Crew Van Pkg			**300**	**300**	**350**	**350**
V8, 5.4L (E150/E250)	L		**300**	**300**	**350**	**350**
V10, 6.8 Liter	S		**700**	**700**	**830**	**830**

TRUCKS & VANS

Body Type	VIN	List	Trade-In Good	Very Good	Pvt-Party Good	Retail Excellent
RANGER REGULAR CAB PICKUP—4-Cyl.—Truck Equipment Schedule T2						
XL 2D 7'	R1AD	19825	6900	7275	8550	10900
V6, 4.0 Liter	E		525	525	635	635
RANGER REGULAR CAB PICKUP—4-Cyl.—Truck Equipment Schedule T1						
XL 2D 6'	R1AD	19655	8100	8550	9825	12450
XLT 2D 6'	R1AD	20795	9025	9525	10800	13600
RANGER SUPER CAB PICKUP—4-Cyl.—Truck Equipment Schedule T1						
XL 2D 6'	R1ED	21350	9550	10100	11500	14600
4WD	F		1825	1825	2125	2125
V6, 4.0 Liter	E		525	525	620	620
RANGER SUPER CAB PICKUP—V6—Truck Equipment Schedule T1						
XLT 2D 6'	R1EE	22415	11850	12500	13650	16950
4-Cyl, 2.3 Liter	D		(675)	(675)	(770)	(770)
RANGER SUPER CAB PICKUP—V6—Truck Equipment Schedule T2						
Sport 2D 6'	R1EE	24100	12150	12800	14200	17850
Sport 4D 6'	R4EE	25170	12100	12750	14200	17850
4WD	F		1825	1825	2115	2115
RANGER SUPER CAB PICKUP—V6—Truck Equipment Schedule T1						
XLT 4D 6'	R4EE	24315	12250	12900	14350	18050
REGULAR CAB PICKUP—V8—Truck Equipment Schedule T1						
F150 XL 2D 6 1/2'	F1CF	23390	10600	10950	12350	14850
F150 XL 2D 8'	F1CF	23690	10300	10650	12050	14450
F150 STX 2D 6 1/2'	F1CF	27220	12000	12400	13950	16800
F150 XLT 2D 6 1/2'	F1CF	27840	12200	12600	14150	17050
F150 XLT 2D 8'	F1CF	28145	11650	12050	13600	16350
4WD	E		2925	2925	3500	3500
V6, EcoBoost, 3.5L	T		1600	1600	1915	1915
V6, Flex Fuel, 3.7 Liter	M		(650)	(650)	(775)	(775)
SUPER CAB PICKUP—V8—Truck Equipment Schedule T1						
F150 XL 4D 6 1/2'	X1CF	27215	12100	12400	14150	16550
F150 XL 4D 8'	X1CF	29390	11800	12100	13800	16100
F150 STX 4D 6 1/2'	X1CF	30005	14200	14550	16450	19150
F150 XLT 4D 6 1/2'	X1CF	30430	14250	14650	16450	19150
F150 XLT 4D 8'	X1CF	32800	13550	13900	15750	18400
F150 FX2 4D 6 1/2'	X1CF	34050	14000	14400	16250	19000
F150 Lariat 4D 6 1/2'	X1CF	35085	15400	15850	17700	20600
Luxury Pkg			500	500	580	580
4WD	E		2925	2925	3490	3490
V6, EcoBoost, 3.5L	T		1600	1600	1915	1915
V6, Flex Fuel, 3.7 Liter	M		(650)	(650)	(770)	(770)
SUPER CAB PICKUP 4WD—V8—Truck Equipment Schedule T1						
F150 FX4 4D 6 1/2'	X1EF	37600	18400	18900	21000	24500
F150 SVT Raptor 5'	X1R6	42525	30500	31500	32000	36100
Luxury Pkg			500	500	575	575
V6, EcoBoost, 3.5L	T		1600	1600	1890	1890
SUPERCREW PICKUP—V8—Truck Equipment Schedule T1						
F150 XL 4D 5 1/2'	W1CF	30755	14800	15200	17150	20000
F150 XL 4D 6 1/2'	W1CF	34810	14750	15150	17050	19900
F150 XLT 4D 5 1/2'	W1CF	32785	16300	16750	18700	21800
F150 FX4 4D 5 1/2'	W1CF	36410	17850	18350	20400	23700
F150 FX4 4D 6 1/2'	W1CF	36710	17100	17600	19600	22800
F150 Kng Rnch 6 1/2'	W1CF	43065	21600	22100	24300	28200
F150 Platinum 6 1/2'	W1CF	44875	21700	22300	24500	28400
Luxury Pkg			500	500	575	575
4WD	E		2925	2925	3470	3470
V6, EcoBoost, 3.5L	T		1600	1600	1900	1900
V6, Flex Fuel, 3.7 Liter	M		(650)	(650)	(770)	(770)
V8, 6.2 Liter	6		375	375	435	435
SUPERCREW PICKUP 4WD—V8—Truck Equipment Schedule T1						
F150 XLT 4D 5 1/2'	W1EF	37170	18950	19450	21600	25200
F150 Lariat 4D 5 1/2'	W1EF	40590	22600	23200	25400	29500
F150 Lariat 4D 6 1/2'	W1EF	40890	22500	23100	25400	29500
F150 Kng Rnch 5 1/2'	W1EV	45910	24300	25000	27300	31700
F150 Platinum 5 1/2'	W1EF	47720	23900	24500	27000	31500
2WD	C		(2950)	(2950)	(3490)	(3490)
V6, EcoBoost, 3.5L	T		1600	1600	1900	1900
V8, 6.2 Liter	6		375	375	435	435
SUPERCREW PICKUP—V8—Truck Equipment Schedule T1						
F150 Harley 5 1/2'	W1C6	48970	22400	23000	25300	29400
4WD			2925	2925	3460	3460
SUPERCREW PICKUP 4WD—V8—Truck Equipment Schedule T1						
F150 Lariat Ltd 5'	W1E6	51315	26000	26700	29100	33900
2WD			(2950)	(2950)	(3470)	(3470)

TRUCKS & VANS

Body Type	VIN	List	Trade-In Good	Trade-In Very Good	Pvt-Party Good	Retail Excellent
SUPERCREW PICKUP 4WD—V8—Truck Equipment Schedule T1						
F150 FX4 4D 5 1/2'	W1EF	39960	20700	21300	23500	27400
F150 FX4 4D 6 1/2'	W1EF	40260	20700	21300	23500	27300
F150 SVT Raptor 5'	W1R6	45290	34100	35200	35500	40200
Luxury Pkg			500	500	580	580
V6, EcoBoost, 3.5L	T		1600	1600	1895	1895
SUPER DUTY REGULAR CAB PICKUP—V8—Truck Equipment Schedule T1						
F250 XL 2D 8'	F2A6	28995	12850	13300	14650	17150
F350 XL 2D 8'	F3A6	29715	13050	13500	14850	17400
4WD	B		2925	2925	3445	3445
V8, Turbo Diesel, 6.7L	T		4600	4600	5400	5400
SUPER DUTY REGULAR CAB 4WD—V8—Truck Equipment Schedule T1						
F250 XLT 2D 8'	F2B6	32275	17800	18400	19800	23200
2WD	A		(2950)	(2950)	(3450)	(3450)
V8, Turbo Diesel, 6.7L	T		4600	4600	5370	5370
SUPER DUTY REGULAR CAB 4WD—V8 Turbo Diesel—Truck Equip Sch T1						
F350 XLT 2D 8'	F3BT	44205	23600	24300	25800	30100
2WD	E		(2950)	(2950)	(3440)	(3440)
V8, Flex Fuel, 6.2 Liter	6		(4400)	(4400)	(5105)	(5105)
SUPER DUTY SUPER CAB PICKUP—V8—Truck Equipment Schedule T1						
F250 XL 4D 6 3/4'	X2A6	31120	15500	16050	17450	20500
F250 XL 4D 8'	X2A6	31315	14350	14850	16300	19200
F350 XL 4D 6 3/4'	X3B6	40055	19200	19850	21200	24800
F350 XL 4D 8'	X3A6	32360	15350	15850	17250	20200
F350 Lariat 4D 8'	X3A6	40600	17700	18300	19700	23100
4WD	B		2925	2925	3440	3440
V8, Turbo Diesel, 6.7L	T		4600	4600	5395	5395
SUPER DUTY SUPER CAB PICKUP 4WD—V8—Truck Equipment Schedule T1						
F250 XLT 4D 6 3/4'	X2B6	34885	20400	21100	22500	26400
F250 XLT 4D 8'	X2B6	35070	20300	20900	22300	26100
F250 Lariat 4D 6 3/4'	X2B6	39380	25500	26300	27900	32700
F350 Lariat 4D 6 3/4'	X3B6	36500	20800	21400	23200	27400
F350 Lariat 4D 6 3/4'	X3B6	40400	20200	20900	22300	26100
2WD	A		(2950)	(2950)	(3465)	(3465)
V8, Turbo Diesel, 6.7L	T		4600	4600	5455	5455
SUPER DUTY SUPER CAB—V8 Turbo Diesel—Truck Equipment Schedule T1						
F350 XLT 4D 8'	X3AT	36695	21800	22500	23900	28000
4WD			2925	2925	3440	3440
V8, Flex Fuel, 6.2 Liter	6		(4400)	(4400)	(5145)	(5145)
SUPER DUTY SUPER CAB 4WD—V8 Turbo Diesel—Truck Equip Sch T1						
F250 Lariat 4D 8'	X2BT	39580	28800	29700	31400	36800
2WD	A		(2950)	(2950)	(3455)	(3455)
V8, Flex Fuel, 6.2 Liter	6		(4400)	(4400)	(5125)	(5125)
SUPER DUTY CREW CAB PICKUP—V8—Truck Equipment Schedule T1						
F250 XL 4D 6 3/4'	W2AT	32480	17350	17900	19350	22700
F250 King Ranch 8'	W2A6	46880	20500	21200	22600	26500
F350 XL 4D 6 3/4'	W3A6	33400	18200	18800	20200	23700
4WD	B		2925	2925	3420	3420
V8, Turbo Diesel, 6.7L	T		4600	4600	5390	5390
SUPER DUTY CREW CAB PICKUP 4WD—V8—Truck Equipment Schedule T1						
F250 XLT 4D 8'	W2B6	37320	22100	22800	24300	28500
F350 XLT 4D 6 3/4'	W3B6	41425	23200	23900	25700	30300
F350 KingRnch 6 3/4'	W3B6	50385	25300	26200	27800	32600
2WD			(2950)	(2950)	(3460)	(3460)
V8, Turbo Diesel, 6.7L	T		4600	4600	5365	5385
SUPER DUTY CREW CAB—V8 Turbo Diesel—Truck Equipment Schedule T1						
F250 XL 4D 8'	W2AT	40510	19950	20600	22200	26000
F250 Lariat 4D 8'	W2AT	49950	26300	27200	28700	33500
F350 XL 4D 8'	W3AT	41435	21200	21900	23500	27600
F350 XL 4D 8'	W3AT	38810	24500	25300	26900	31400
4WD			2925	2925	3430	3430
V8, Flex Fuel, 6.2 Liter	6		(4400)	(4400)	(5130)	(5130)
SUPER DUTY CREW CAB 4WD—V8 Turbo Diesel—Truck Equip Sch T1						
F250 XLT 4D 6 3/4'	W2BT	48230	27300	28200	29700	34800
F250 Lariat 4D 6 3/4'	W2BT	41925	30400	31400	33000	38400
F250 King Ranch 6'	W2BT	46690	30400	31400	33000	38500
F350 Lariat 4D 6 3/4'	W3BT	42815	29200	30100	31800	37200
F350 King Ranch 8'	W3BT	47670	29900	30900	32600	38100
F350 Lariat 4D 8'	W3AT	43005	26700	27600	29000	33800
2WD	A		(2950)	(2950)	(3430)	(3430)
V8, Flex Fuel, 6.2 Liter	6		(4400)	(4400)	(5090)	(5090)
SUPER DUTY CREW CAB 4WD—V8 Turbo Diesel—Truck Equip Sch T1						
F450 XL 4D 8'	W4DT	49325	27900	28600	30100	33900

Body Type	VIN	List	Trade-In Good	Very Good	Pvt-Party Good	Retail Excellent
F450 XLT 4D 8'	W4DT	54680	30700	31500	33100	37400
F450 Lariat 4D 8'	W4DT	58370	35000	35900	37400	42100
F450 King Ranch 8'	W4DT	63350	36500	37400	39000	43900

2012 FORD (1,2orN)(ForM)(0,D,MorT)—(U027)—C–#

Body Type	VIN	List	Trade-In Good	Very Good	Pvt-Party Good	Retail Excellent
ESCAPE—4-Cyl.—Truck Equipment Schedule T1						
XLS Sport Utility 4D	U027	21995	9900	10250	11750	13900
4WD	9		1475	1475	1810	1810
ESCAPE 4WD—4-Cyl. Hybrid—Truck Equipment Schedule T1						
Sport Utility 4D	U5K3	33145	15900	16350	17900	20600
Limited Sport Util	U5K3	35655	16300	16700	18350	21200
2WD	4		(1500)	(1500)	(1700)	(1700)
ESCAPE 4WD—V6—Truck Equipment Schedule T1						
XLT Sport Utility	U9DG	27245	12750	13150	14850	17350
Limited Sport Util	U9EG	28745	13950	14450	15850	18300
2WD	0		(1500)	(1500)	(1765)	(1765)
4-Cyl, 2.5 Liter	7		(875)	(875)	(1020)	(1020)
EDGE—V6—Truck Equipment Schedule T1						
SE Sport Utility 4D	K3GC	28465	12450	12700	14600	16850
SEL Sport Utility 4D	K3JC	31770	15300	15650	17700	20300
Limited Sport Util	K3KC	35625	16550	16900	19000	21800
Sport SUV 4D	K3AK	37800	19600	20100	22300	25500
AWD	4		850	850	1010	1010
4-Cyl, EcoBoost 2.0L	9		1025	1025	1225	1225
EXPLORER 4WD—V6—Truck Equipment Schedule T1						
Sport Utility 4D	K8B8	30995	16600	16950	18250	20800
XLT Sport Utility	K8D8	34805	20100	20500	21900	24900
Limited Sport Util	K8F8	40565	21700	22200	23600	26900
Third Row Seat			625	625	710	710
2WD	7		(1525)	(1525)	(1710)	(1710)
FLEX—V6—Truck Equipment Schedule T1						
SE Sport Util 4D	K5BC	29995	13850	14200	16000	18750
SEL Sport Util 4D	K5CC	32625	16750	17200	19050	22200
Limited Sport Util	K5DC	38640	18200	18650	20600	24000
Titanium Spt Util	K5DC	45980	22000	22500	24600	28700
AWD	6		850	850	1000	1000
V6, EcoBoost, 3.5L	7		1700	1700	2005	2005
EXPEDITION 4WD—V8—Truck Equipment Schedule T1						
XLT Sport Utility 4D	U1J5	42810	21900	22400	23900	27100
Power Third Row			475	475	550	550
2WD	H		(1500)	(1500)	(1705)	(1705)
EXPEDITION 4WD—V8—Truck Equipment Schedule T1						
XL Sport Utility 4D	U1G5	41270	20300	20700	22300	25300
Limited Sport Util	U2A5	48940	25800	26500	27800	31500
King Ranch Spt Util	U1J5	50450	27000	27700	29000	32800
2WD	F		(1500)	(1500)	(1710)	(1710)
EXPEDITION EL 4WD—V8—Truck Equipment Schedule T1						
XLT Sport Utility 4D	K1J5	45520	22800	23300	24900	28200
Power Third Row			475	475	550	550
2WD	H		(1500)	(1500)	(1705)	(1705)
EXPEDITION EL 4WD—V8—Truck Equipment Schedule T1						
XL Sport Utility 4D	K1G5	43920	22200	22700	24400	27600
Limited Spt Util 4D	K2A5	51590	27100	27800	29100	32900
King Ranch Spt Util	K1J5	53100	27600	28300	29500	33300
2WD	F		(1500)	(1500)	(1705)	(1705)
TRANSIT CONNECT CARGO VAN—4-Cyl.—Truck Equipment Sch T2						
XL Van 4D	S6AN	22525	11900	12200	13900	16200
XLT Van 4D	S6BN	23585	12650	12950	14700	17150
TRANSIT CONNECT PASSENGER VAN—4-Cyl.—Truck Equipment Sch T2						
XLT Van 4D	S9BN	24260	11800	12200	13550	15900
XLT Premium Van	S9CN	24410	12050	12350	13950	16100
ECONOLINE WAGON—V8—Truck Equipment Schedule T1						
E150 XL	E1BW	29165	13600	13850	15400	17800
E150 XLT	E1BW	31620	14700	15050	16600	19200
E350 XL Super Duty	E3BL	32260	14250	14550	16100	18650
E350 XL S.D. Ext	S3BL	34565	15050	15400	17000	19600
E350 XLT S.D.	E3BL	34740	15450	15750	17400	20100
E350 XLT S.D. Ext	S3BL	36040	17400	17750	19450	22500
V8, 5.4 Liter (E150)	L		325	325	370	370
V10, 6.8 Liter	S		725	725	830	830
ECONOLINE VAN—V8—Truck Equipment Schedule T1						
E150 Cargo Van	E1EW	27510	13600	14550	15400	18550
E150 Extended	S1EW	28720	14850	15900	16700	20200

TRUCKS & VANS

Body	Type	VIN	List	Trade-In Good	Very Good	Pvt-Party Good	Retail Excellent
E250 Cargo Van	E2EW	28510	14400	15400	16250	19600
E250 Extended	S2EW	29865	15700	16800	17600	21200
Crew Van Pkg			325	325	375	375
V8, Flex Fuel, 5.4 Liter	L		325	325	375	375
V10, 6.8 Liter	S		725	725	845	845
ECONOLINE VAN—V8—Truck Equipment Schedule T1						
E350 Super Cargo	E3EL	31555	15150	16200	16950	20500
E350 SD Extended	S3EL	32455	16650	17800	18600	22400
Crew Van Pkg			325	325	370	370
V10, 6.8 Liter	S		725	725	845	845
REGULAR CAB PICKUP—V8—Truck Equipment Schedule T1						
F150 XL 2D 6 1/2'	F1CF	24985	11550	11850	13450	15850
F150 XL 2D 8'	F1CF	25290	12100	12350	13950	16300
F150 STX 2D 6 1/2'	F1CF	28650	13400	13650	15500	18150
F150 XLT 2D 6 1/2'	F1CF	29685	14100	14400	16250	19050
F150 XLT 2D 8'	F1CF	29990	13400	13700	15550	18250
4WD			3125	3125	3675	3675
V6, EcoBoost, 3.5L	T		1700	1700	1975	1975
V6, Flex Fuel, 3.7 Liter	M		(725)	(725)	(850)	(850)
SUPER CAB PICKUP—V8—Truck Equipment Schedule T1						
F150 XL 4D 6 1/2'	X1CF	28810	14650	15000	16900	19250
F150 XL 4D 8'	X1CF	28110	14300	14600	16500	18800
F150 STX 4D 6 1/2'	X1CF	31435	16350	16700	18750	21500
F150 XLT 4D 6 1/2'	X1CF	32275	17200	17550	19550	22200
F150 XLT 4D 8'	X1CF	31575	16550	16900	18850	21400
F150 FX2 4D 6 1/2'	X1CF	34895	17000	17350	19350	22000
F150 Lariat 4D 6 1/2'	X1CF	36005	18200	18600	20700	23500
Luxury Pkg			500	500	575	575
4WD	E		3125	3125	3615	3615
V6, EcoBoost, 3.5L	T		1700	1700	1960	1960
V6, Flex Fuel, 3.7 Liter	M		(725)	(725)	(835)	(835)
SUPER CAB PICKUP 4WD—V8—Truck Equipment Schedule T1						
F150 FX4 4D 6 1/2'	X1EF	38475	22200	22700	25000	28500
F150 SVT Raptor 5'	X1R6	43565	34300	35100	35900	39900
Luxury Pkg			500	500	580	580
V6, EcoBoost, 3.5L	T		1700	1700	1965	1965
SUPERCREW PICKUP—V8—Truck Equipment Schedule T1						
F150 XL 4D 5 1/2'	W1CF	32470	17150	17550	19550	22300
F150 XL 4D 6 1/2'	W1CF	32685	17100	17500	19450	22100
F150 XLT 4D 5 1/2'	W1CF	34755	19250	19650	21700	24700
F150 FX2 4D 5 1/2'	W1CF	37380	21400	21900	24100	27400
F150 FX2 4D 6 1/2'	W1CF	37675	21000	21500	23600	26800
F150 Kng Rnch 6 1/2'	W1CF	43810	24500	25000	27500	31200
F150 Platinum 6 1/2'	W1CF	45620	24600	25100	27500	31300
Luxury Pkg			500	500	575	575
4WD	E		3125	3125	3615	3615
V6, EcoBoost, 3.5L	T		1700	1700	1960	1960
V6, Flex Fuel, 3.7 Liter	M		(725)	(725)	(835)	(835)
V8, 6.2 Liter	6		400	400	450	450
SUPERCREW PICKUP 4WD—V8—Truck Equipment Schedule T1						
F150 XLT 4D 6 1/2'	W1EF	38265	22100	22600	24800	28200
F150 Lariat 4D 5 1/2'	W1EF	41760	25600	26200	28700	32600
F150 Lariat 4D 6 1/2'	W1EF	42060	25600	26200	28400	32600
F150 Kng Rnch 5 1/2'	W1EF	46785	27300	27900	30400	34600
F150 Platinum 5 1/2'	W1EF	48595	27400	28000	30600	34900
2WD	C		(3150)	(3150)	(3620)	(3620)
V6, EcoBoost, 3.5L	T		1700	1700	1960	1960
V8, 6.2 Liter	6		400	400	450	450
SUPERCREW PICKUP—V8—Truck Equipment Schedule T1						
F150 Harley 5 1/2'	W1C6	49715	26100	26600	29100	33200
4WD	E		3125	3125	3600	3600
SUPERCREW PICKUP 4WD—V8—Truck Equipment Schedule T1						
F150 FX4 4D 5 1/2'	W1EF	40955	26100	26700	29200	33300
F150 FX4 4D 6 1/2'	W1EF	41255	26800	27400	29900	34000
F150 SVT Raptor 5'	W1R6	46465	38000	38900	39500	43800
Luxury Pkg			500	500	575	575
V6, EcoBoost, 3.5L	T		1700	1700	1965	1965
SUPER DUTY REGULAR CAB PICKUP—V8—Truck Equipment Schedule T1						
F250 XL 2D 8'	F2A6	29830	14150	14500	16100	18600
4WD	B		3125	3125	3660	3660
V8, Turbo Dsl, 6.7L	T		4825	4825	5640	5640
SUPER DUTY REGULAR CAB 4WD—V8—Truck Equipment Schedule T1						
F250 XLT 2D 8'	F2B6	33160	18500	19000	20700	23800

Body Type	VIN	List	Trade-In Good	Very Good	Pvt-Party Good	Retail Excellent
2WD	A	......	(3150)	(3150)	(3610)	(3610)
V8, Turbo Dsl, 6.7L	T	......	4825	4825	5545	5545
SUPER DUTY REGULAR CAB PICKUP—V8 Flex Fuel—Truck Equip Sch T1						
F350 XL 2D 8'	F3A6	30550	14350	14700	16250	18800
4WD	B	......	3125	3125	3655	3655
V8, Turbo Diesel, 6.7L	T	......	4825	4825	5630	5630
SUPER DUTY REGULAR CAB 4WD—V8 Turbo Diesel—Truck Equip Sch T1						
F350 XLT 2D 8'	F3BT	45090	25200	25800	27700	31900
2WD	A	......	(3150)	(3150)	(3635)	(3635)
V8, Flex Fuel, 6.2 Liter	6	......	(4650)	(4650)	(5395)	(5395)
SUPER DUTY SUPER CAB PICKUP—V8—Truck Equipment Schedule T1						
F250 XL 4D 6 3/4'	X2A6	31955	17050	17500	19150	22100
F250 XL 4D 8'	X2A6	32150	16600	17000	18700	21700
F350 XL 4D 6 3/4'	X3B6	36210	20100	20600	22300	25800
F350 XL 4D 8'	X3A6	33195	16150	16550	18250	21100
F350 Lariat 4D 8'	X3A6	41630	18950	19400	21200	24400
4WD	B	......	3125	3125	3660	3660
V8, Turbo Dsl, 6.7L	T	......	4825	4825	5640	5640
SUPER DUTY SUPER CAB PICKUP 4WD—V8—Truck Equipment Schedule T1						
F250 XLT 4D 6 3/4'	X2B6	35770	20900	21400	23200	26800
F250 XLT 4D 8'	X2B6	35955	21000	21500	23300	26900
F250 Lariat 4D 6 3/4'	X2B6	40410	26900	27500	29500	34000
F350 XLT 4D 8'	X3B6	37385	22000	22500	24500	28500
F350 Lariat 4D 6 3/4'	X3B6	41430	21700	22200	24000	27700
2WD	A	......	(3150)	(3150)	(3615)	(3615)
V8, Turbo Dsl, 6.7L	T	......	4825	4825	5635	5635
SUPER DUTY SUPER CAB PICKUP—V8 Turbo Diesel—Truck Equip Sch T1						
F350 XLT 4D 8'	X3AT	45415	23000	23600	25400	29300
4WD	B	......	3125	3125	3635	3635
V8, Flex Fuel, 6.2 Liter	6	......	(4650)	(4650)	(5410)	(5410)
SUPER DUTY SUPER CAB 4WD—V8 Turbo Diesel—Truck Sch T1						
F250 Lariat 4D 8'	X2BT	40610	31100	31900	34000	39200
2WD	A	......	(3100)	(3150)	(3640)	(3640)
V8, Flex Fuel, 6.2 Liter	6	......	(4650)	(4650)	(5405)	(5405)
SUPER DUTY CREW CAB PICKUP—V8—Truck Equipment Schedule T1						
F250 King Ranch 8'	W2A6	48370	25400	26000	27900	32100
4WD	B	......	3125	3125	3635	3635
V8, Turbo Diesel, 6.7L	T	......	4825	4825	5600	5600
SUPER DUTY CREW CAB PICKUP 4WD—V8—Truck Equip Sch T1						
F250 XL 4D 6 3/4'	W2A6	33315	18000	18500	20200	23300
F250 XLT 4D 8'	W2B6	42055	24000	24600	26500	30500
F350 XLT 4D 8'	W3B6	42310	24200	24800	27000	31300
F350 KingRnch 6 3/4'	W3B6	51415	26400	27100	29100	33600
2WD	A	......	(3150)	(3150)	(3610)	(3610)
V8, Turbo Diesel, 6.7L	T	......	4825	4825	5545	5545
SUPER DUTY CREW CAB PICKUP—V8 Flex Fuel—Truck Equip Sch T1						
F350 XL 4D 6 3/4'	W3A6	34235	19250	19700	21500	24800
4WD	B	......	3125	3125	3650	3650
V8, Turbo Dsl, 6.7L	T	......	4825	4825	5620	5620
SUPER DUTY CREW CAB—V8 Turbo Diesel—Truck Equipment Sch T1						
F250 XL 4D 8'	W2AT	41700	20900	21400	23200	26900
F250 Lariat 4D 8'	W2AT	51440	29900	30600	32700	37700
F350 XL 4D 8'	W3AT	42625	22200	22700	24600	28500
F350 XLT 4D 8'	W3AT	47530	26400	25500	27400	31700
F350 Lariat 4D 8'	W3AT	51870	30900	31700	33600	38600
4WD	B	......	3125	3125	3640	3640
V8, Flex Fuel, 6.2 Liter	6	......	(4650)	(4650)	(5415)	(5415)
SUPER DUTY CREW CAB PICKUP 4WD—V8 Turbo Diesel—Truck Sch T1						
F250 XLT 4D 6 3/4'	W2BT	49815	29000	29700	31700	36400
F250 KngRnch 6 3/4'	W2BT	59285	37100	38100	39900	45500
F250 Lariat 4D 6 3/4'	W2BT	54520	36000	36900	39100	44900
F350 Lariat 4D 8'	W3BT	55170	32300	34000	36100	41600
F350 King Ranch 8'	W3BT	59445	32400	33200	35300	40500
2WD	A	......	(3150)	(3150)	(3520)	(3520)
V8, Flex Fuel, 6.2 Liter	6	......	(4650)	(4650)	(5225)	(5225)
SUPER DUTY CREW CAB 4WD—V8 Turbo Diesel—Truck Equip Sch T1						
F450 XL 4D 8'	W4DT	50160	34200	35000	36800	40800
F450 XLT 4D 8'	W4DT	55565	38100	38900	40800	45200
F450 Lariat 4D 8'	W4DT	59440	41000	41900	43900	48700
F450 King Ranch 8'	W4DT	64380	43900	44800	46800	51900

Body Type	VIN	List	Trade-In Good	Trade-In Very Good	Pvt-Party Good	Retail Excellent

2013 FORD (1,2orN)(ForM)(0,D,MorT)–(U0F7)–D–#

ESCAPE—4-Cyl.—Truck Equipment Schedule T1

Body Type	VIN	List	Good	Very Good	Good	Excellent
S Sport Utility 4D	U0F7	23295	12150	12500	14400	16900

ESCAPE 4WD—4-Cyl. EcoBoost—Truck Equipment Schedule T1

SE Sport Utility 4D	U9GX	27645	14200	14650	16600	19300
SEL Sport Utility	U9HX	30445	15350	15850	17600	20300
Titanium Sport Util	U9J9	32945	17650	18200	20100	23200
2WD		0	(1275)	(1275)	(1510)	(1510)

EDGE—V6—Truck Equipment Schedule T1

SE Sport Utility 4D	K3GC	28350	14450	14750	16850	19100
SEL Sport Utility 4D	K3JC	31905	18000	18350	20600	23200
Limited Sport Util	K3KC	38750	18750	19100	21500	24400
Sport SUV 4D	K3AK	37935	22100	22500	25000	28300
AWD		4	925	925	1090	1090
4-Cyl, EcoBoost, 2.0L		9	450	450	520	520

EXPLORER 4WD—V6—Truck Equipment Schedule T1

Sport Utility 4D	K8B8	31695	18900	19200	20800	23500
XLT Sport Utility 4D	K8D8	35170	22600	23000	24500	27500
Limited Sport Util	K8F8	40680	23600	24000	25800	29100
Sport SUV 4D	K8GT	41545	28400	28900	30800	34700
Third Row Seat			675	675	770	770
2WD		7	(1600)	(1600)	(1815)	(1815)
4-Cyl, EcoBoost 2.0L		9	525	525	605	605

FLEX—V6—Truck Equipment Schedule T1

SE Sport Utility 4D	K5B8	31710	16300	16650	18300	20800
SEL Sport Util 4D	K5C8	34050	20600	21000	22600	25600
Limited Sport 4D	K5D8	40055	21100	21500	23500	26800
AWD			925	925	1055	1055
V6, EcoBoost, 3.5L		T	1800	1800	2045	2045

EXPEDITION 4WD—V8 Flex Fuel—Truck Equipment Schedule T1

XLT Sport Utility 4D	U1J5	43925	23800	24200	26300	29700
Power Third Row			525	525	610	610
2WD		H	(1275)	(1275)	(1450)	(1450)

EXPEDITION 4WD—V8 Flex Fuel—Truck Equipment Schedule T1

XL Sport Utility 4D	U1G5	40825	22000	22400	24400	27500
Limited Sport Util	U2A5	50200	28700	29300	30800	34400
King Ranch Spt Util	U1J5	51775	29200	29800	31300	35000
2WD		K	(1275)	(1275)	(1415)	(1415)

EXPEDITION EL 4WD—V8—Truck Equipment Schedule T1

XLT Sport Utility 4D	K1J5	46635	25200	25700	27800	31400
Power Third Row			525	525	610	610
2WD		H	(1275)	(1275)	(1450)	(1450)

EXPEDITION EL 4WD—V8—Truck Equipment Schedule T1

XL Sport Utility 4D	K1G5	44350	24400	24800	27000	30400
Limited Spt Util 4D	K2A5	52850	30600	31200	32700	36500
King Ranch Spt Util	K1J5	54425	30900	31500	33000	36800
2WD		H	(1275)	(1275)	(1450)	(1450)

TRANSIT CONNECT CARGO VAN—4-Cyl.—Truck Equipment Sch T2

| XL Van 4D | S7AN | 23200 | 13650 | 13900 | 15750 | 18000 |
| XLT Van 4D | S7BN | 24260 | 14450 | 14700 | 16650 | 19000 |

TRANSIT CONNECT PASSENGER VAN—4-Cyl.—Truck Equipment Sch T1

| XLT Van 4D | S9BN | 24825 | 13750 | 14050 | 15650 | 17950 |
| XLT Premium Van | S9CN | 24975 | 13950 | 14200 | 16050 | 18200 |

ECONOLINE WAGON—V8—Truck Equipment Schedule T1

E150 XL	E1BW	29925	15750	16000	17800	20300
E150 XLT	E1BW	32370	16850	17150	18950	21700
V8, 5.4 Liter		L	350	350	395	395

ECONOLINE WAGON—V8—Truck Equipment Schedule T1

E350 XL Super Duty	E3BL	33255	16400	16650	18450	21100
E350 XL S.D. Ext	S3BL	35555	17150	17400	19300	22100
E350 XLT S.D.	E3BL	35715	17700	17950	19850	22700
E350 XLT S.D. Ext	S3BL	37015	19750	20100	22100	25300
V10, 6.8 Liter		S	750	750	860	860

ECONOLINE VAN—V8—Truck Equipment Schedule T1

E150 Cargo Van	E1EW	27795	14900	15950	16700	19800
E150 Extended	S1EW	29010	16250	17350	18050	21400
E250 Cargo Van	E2EW	29780	15800	16850	17550	20900
E250 Extended	S2EW	31140	17600	18800	19500	23200
Crew Van Pkg			350	350	395	395
V8, Flex Fuel, 5.4 Liter		L	350	350	395	395

ECONOLINE VAN—V8 Flex Fuel—Truck Equipment Sch T1

| E350 Super Cargo | E3EL | 31955 | 17000 | 18200 | 18850 | 22400 |

Body Type	VIN	List	Trade-In Good	Trade-In Very Good	Pvt-Party Good	Retail Excellent
E350 SD Extended	S3EL	32855	18450	19700	20400	24300
Crew Van Pkg			350	350	395	395
V10, 6.8 Liter	S		750	750	860	860
REGULAR CAB PICKUP—V8—Truck Equipment Schedule T1						
F150 XL 2D 6 1/2'	F1CF	24665	13650	13850	15350	17400
F150 XL 2D 8'	F1CF	24965	13350	13550	15050	17050
F150 STX 2D 6 1/2'	F1CF	28180	15900	16150	17700	20000
F150 XLT 2D 6 1/2'	F1CF	29680	16150	16450	18050	20500
F150 XLT 2D 8'	F1CF	29985	15600	15850	17450	19800
4WD	E		3275	3275	3670	3670
V6, EcoBoost, 3.5L	T		1800	1800	2010	2010
V6, Flex Fuel, 3.7 Liter	M		(775)	(775)	(880)	(880)
SUPER CAB PICKUP—V8—Truck Equipment Schedule T1						
F150 XL 4D 6 1/2'	X1CF	28400	16100	16400	18400	20800
F150 XL 4D 8'	X1CF	28790	15950	16250	18250	20500
F150 STX 4D 6 1/2'	X1CF	30965	18250	18600	20800	23600
F150 XLT 4D 6 1/2'	X1CF	32270	18400	18750	20900	23500
F150 XLT 4D 8'	X1CF	32570	17750	18100	20200	22800
F150 FX2 4D 6 1/2'	X1CF	36180	20100	20400	22700	25600
F150 Lariat 4D 6 1/2'	X1CF	36830	21900	22300	24700	27800
Luxury Pkg			500	500	575	575
4WD	E		3275	3275	3745	3745
V6, EcoBoost, 3.5L	T		1800	1800	2055	2055
V6, Flex Fuel, 3.7 Liter	M		(775)	(775)	(900)	(900)
V8, 6.2 Liter	6		1075	1075	1225	1225
SUPER CAB PICKUP 4WD—V8—Truck Equipment Schedule T1						
F150 FX4 4D 6 1/2'	X1EF	39760	24500	24900	27700	31500
F150 SVT Raptor 5'	X1R6	44335	37800	38500	39500	43500
Luxury Pkg			500	500	580	580
V6, EcoBoost, 3.5L	T		1800	1800	2085	2085
SUPERCREW PICKUP 4WD—V6 EcoBoost—Truck Equipment Sch T1						
F150 Limited 5 1/2'	W1CT	53450	29900	30500	33400	37700
2WD	C		(3275)	(3275)	(3745)	(3745)
SUPERCREW PICKUP—V8—Truck Equipment Schedule T1						
F150 XL 4D 5 1/2'	W1CF	32150	19200	19550	21800	24500
F150 XL 4D 6 1/2'	W1CF	33485	18500	18900	21000	23700
F150 XLT 4D 5 1/2'	W1CF	34750	20500	20800	23100	26000
F150 FX2 4D 5 1/2'	W1CF	38660	22600	23000	25400	28600
F150 Kng Rnch 6 1/2'	W1CF	46810	26000	26400	29100	32800
F150 Platinum 6 1/2'	W1CF	47395	26400	26900	29600	33400
Luxury Pkg			500	500	575	575
4WD	E		3275	3275	3755	3755
V6, EcoBoost, 3.5L	T		1800	1800	2055	2055
V6, Flex Fuel, 3.7 Liter	M		(775)	(775)	(900)	(900)
V8, 6.2 Liter	6		400	400	460	460
SUPERCREW PICKUP 4WD—V8—Truck Equipment Schedule T1						
F150 XLT 4D 5 1/2'	W1EF	39260	22700	23200	25600	29000
F150 Lariat 4D 5 1/2'	W1EF	42585	28400	29000	31800	35800
F150 Lariat 4D 6 1/2'	W1EF	42885	27300	27800	30500	34400
F150 Kng Rnch 5 1/2'	W1EF	47785	30000	30600	33400	37600
F150 Platinum 5 1/2'	W1EF	50370	29100	29600	32700	37000
Luxury Pkg			500	500	575	575
2WD	C		(3275)	(3275)	(3745)	(3745)
V6, EcoBoost, 3.5L	T		1800	1800	2050	2050
V8, 6.2 Liter	6		400	400	460	460
SUPERCREW PICKUP 4WD—V8—Truck Equipment Schedule T1						
F150 FX4 4D 5 1/2'	W1EF	42240	27400	27900	30800	34900
F150 FX4 4D 6 1/2'	W1EF	42540	28200	28700	31600	35700
Luxury Pkg			500	500	580	580
V6, EcoBoost, 3.5L	T		1800	1800	2080	2080
V8, 6.2 Liter	6		400	400	465	465
SUPERCREW PICKUP 4WD—V8—Truck Equipment Schedule T1						
F150 SVT Raptor 5'	W1R6	47235	43300	44200	44900	49200
SUPER DUTY REGULAR CAB PICKUP—V8—Truck Equipment Schedule T1						
F250 XL 2D 8'	F2A6	30380	13750	14050	16050	18650
F350 XL 2D 8'	F3A6	31280	14250	14550	16450	19000
4WD	B		3275	3275	3810	3810
V8, Turbo Diesel, 6.7L	T		5025	5025	5870	5870
SUPER DUTY REGULAR CAB 4WD—V8—Truck Equipment Schedule T1						
F250 XLT 2D 8'	F2B6	37215	18250	18600	20800	24100
2WD	A		(3275)	(3275)	(3800)	(3800)
V8, Turbo Diesel, 6.7L	T		5025	5025	5855	5855

Body Type	VIN	List	Trade-In Good	Very Good	Pvt-Party Good	Retail Excellent
SUPER DUTY REGULAR CAB PICKUP 4WD—V8 Turbo Diesel—Truck Sch T1						
F350 XLT 2D 8'	F3BT	46032	26000	26600	29200	33800
2WD	A,C		(3275)	(3275)	(3720)	(3720)
V8, Flex Fuel, 6.2 Liter	6		(4925)	(4925)	(5615)	(5615)
SUPER DUTY SUPER CAB PICKUP—V8—Truck Equipment Schedule T1						
F250 XL 4D 6 3/4'	X2A6	32580	17350	17700	19650	22600
F250 XL 4D 8'	X2A6	32680	17050	17450	19400	22300
F350 XL 4D 8'	X3A6	33680	16500	16850	18900	21900
F350 Lariat 4D 8'	X3A6	43175	20100	20500	22600	26100
4WD			3275	3275	3790	3790
V8, Turbo Dsl, 6.7L	T		5025	5025	5840	5840
SUPER DUTY SUPER CAB PICKUP—V8 Turbo Diesel—Truck Sch T1						
F350 XLT 4D 8'	X3AT	45975	23900	24400	26900	31100
4WD	B,D		3275	3275	3730	3730
V8, Flex Fuel, 6.2 Liter	6		(4925)	(4925)	(5635)	(5635)
SUPER DUTY SUPER CAB PICKUP 4WD—V8—Truck Equipment Schedule T1						
F250 XLT 4D 6 3/4'	X2B6	39715	21900	22300	24600	28400
F250 XLT 4D 8'	X2B6	39915	21700	22100	24400	28200
F250 Lariat 4D 6 3/4'	X2B6	45265	27300	27900	30500	35400
F350 XL 4D 6 3/4'	X3B6	36480	20700	21100	23400	27000
F350 XL 4D 8'	X3B6	40615	22900	23400	25700	29700
F350 Lariat 4D 6 3/4'	X3B6	46165	22800	23300	25600	29600
2WD	A		(3275)	(3275)	(3785)	(3785)
SUPER DUTY SUPER CAB PICKUP 4WD—V8 Turbo Diesel—Truck Sch T1						
F250 Lariat 4D 8'	X2BT	53425	32000	32700	35400	40800
2WD	A		(3275)	(3275)	(3715)	(3715)
V8, Flex Fuel, 6.2 Liter	6		(4925)	(4925)	(5610)	(5610)
SUPER DUTY CREW CAB PICKUP—V8 Turbo Diesel—Truck Equip Sch T1						
F250 Lariat 8'	W2A6	52770	32000	32700	35500	41000
4WD	B		3275	3275	3705	3705
V8, Flex Fuel, 6.2 Liter	6		(4925)	(4925)	(5595)	(5595)
SUPER DUTY CREW CAB PICKUP—V8 Flex Fuel—Truck Equip Sch T1						
F250 King Ranch 8'	W2A6	50065	29500	30100	32800	37800
F350 XL 4D 6 3/4'	W3A6	35080	20200	20600	22800	26300
4WD			3275	3275	3720	3720
V8, Turbo Dsl, 6.7L	T		5025	5025	5730	5730
SUPER DUTY CREW CAB PICKUP—V8 Flex Fuel—Truck Equip Sch T1						
F250 XL 6 3/4'	W2B6	34465	18800	19200	21500	25000
4WD	B		3275	3275	3735	3735
V8, Turbo Dsl, 6.7L	T		5025	5025	5760	5760
SUPER DUTY CREW CAB PICKUP 4WD—V8 Flex Fuel—Truck Equip Sch T1						
F250 XLT 8'	W2B6	41815	24500	25000	27400	31700
F250 Platinum 6 3/4'	W2B6	53750	33100	33800	36400	41700
F250 Platinum 8'	W2B6	53950	32900	33600	36200	41500
2WD	A		(3275)	(3275)	(3720)	(3720)
V8, Turbo Dsl, 6.7L	T		5025	5025	5730	5730
SUPER DUTY CREW CAB PICKUP 4WD—V8 Turbo Diesel—Truck Sch T1						
F250 XLT 6 3/4'	W2BT	49575	29600	30200	32900	37800
2WD	A		(3275)	(3275)	(3715)	(3715)
V8, Flex Fuel, 6.2 Liter	6		(4925)	(4925)	(5615)	(5615)
SUPER DUTY CREW CAB—V8 Turbo Diesel—Truck Equipment Schedule T1						
F350 XL 4D 8'	W3AT	43040	24200	24700	27200	31400
F350 XLT 4D 8'	W3AT	47875	26100	26700	29400	34100
F350 Lariat 4D 8'	W3AT	53535	33400	34100	36900	42500
4WD	B,D		3275	3275	3725	3725
V8, Flex Fuel, 6.2 Liter	6		(4925)	(4925)	(5630)	(5630)
SUPER DUTY CREW CAB 4WD—V8—Truck Equipment Schedule T1						
F350 XL 4D 6 3/4'	W3B6	42715	25200	25700	28400	32900
F350 KingRnch 6 3/4'	W3B6	54155	31100	31700	34400	39700
F350 Platinum 6 3/4'	W3B6	54850	35500	36200	38700	44300
2WD	A		(3275)	(3275)	(3720)	(3720)
V8, Turbo Dsl, 6.7L	T		5025	5025	5735	5735
SUPER DUTY CREW CAB—V8 Turbo Diesel—Truck Equipment Sch T1						
F250 XL 8'	W2BT	43555	22300	22700	25000	28900
4WD			3275	3275	3750	3750
V8, Flex Fuel, 6.2 Liter	6		(4925)	(4925)	(5665)	(5665)
SUPER DUTY CREW CAB 4WD—V8 Turbo Diesel—Truck Equip Sch T1						
F350 Lariat 4D 6 3/4'	W3BT	56525	37500	38300	41000	47000
F350 King Ranch 8'	W3BT	62115	36500	37200	39700	45400
F250 Lariat 6 3/4'	W2BT	55625	37500	38200	40800	46600
F350 KingRnch 6'	W3BT	61015	38300	39100	41500	47200
F350 Platinum 8'	W3BT	62810	40500	41300	43700	49600
2WD	A		(3275)	(3275)	(3710)	(3710)

TRUCKS & VANS

Body Type	VIN	List	Trade-In Good	Trade-In Very Good	Pvt-Party Good	Retail Excellent
V8, Flex Fuel, 6.2 Liter	6		(4925)	(4925)	(5605)	(5605)

SUPER DUTY CREW CAB 4WD—V8 Turbo Diesel—Truck Equip Sch T1

Body Type	VIN	List	Good	Very Good	Good	Excellent
F450 XL 4D 8'	W4DT	50580	39200	39900	42800	47700
F450 XLT 4D 8'	W4DT	55415	43500	44300	47100	52300
F450 Lariat 4D 8'	W4DT	61465	47300	48100	50800	56200
F450 King Ranch 8'	W4DT	66735	48100	49000	52000	57400
F450 Platinum 8'	W4DT	67550	49000	49900	52900	58400

2014 FORD (1,2orN)(ForM)(0,D,MorT)–(U0F7)–E–#

ESCAPE—4-Cyl.—Truck Equipment Schedule T1

Body Type	VIN	List	Good	Very Good	Good	Excellent
S Sport Utility 4D	U0F7	23595	13000	13400	15500	18150

ESCAPE 4WD—4-Cyl. EcoBoost—Truck Equipment Schedule T1

SE Sport Utility 4D	U9GX	28195	16250	16750	18750	21700
Titanium Sport Util	U9JX	31745	18800	19400	21400	24600
2WD	0		(1375)	(1375)	(1610)	(1610)

EDGE—V6—Truck Equipment Schedule T1

SE Sport Utility 4D	K3GC	28995	16900	17200	19400	21900
SEL Sport Utility 4D	K3JC	32195	18900	19250	21600	24300
Limited Sport Util	K3KC	35995	20400	20800	23300	26300
Sport SUV 4D	K3AK	38495	25200	25700	28300	31800
AWD	4		1000	1000	1175	1175
4-Cyl, EcoBoost, 2.0L	9		475	475	550	550

EXPLORER 4WD—V6—Truck Equipment Schedule T1

Sport Utility 4D	K8B8	32495	21100	21400	23000	25800
XLT Sport Utility 4D	K8D8	35495	24800	25100	26800	30100
Limited Sport Util	K8F8	40995	25600	26000	27900	31300
Sport SUV 4D	K8GT	41675	30800	31200	33200	37200
2WD	7		(1700)	(1700)	(1895)	(1895)
4-Cyl EcoBoost 2.0L	9		575	575	630	630

FLEX—V6—Truck Equipment Schedule T1

SE Sport Util 4D	K5B8	31995	17800	18150	20200	23200
SEL Sport Util 4D	K5C8	34395	21700	22100	24200	27600
Limited Sport Util	K5D8	40295	23200	23700	26100	30000
AWD	6		1000	1000	1180	1180
V6, EcoBoost, 3.5L	T		1875	1875	2225	2225

EXPEDITION 4WD—V8 Flex Fuel—Truck Equipment Schedule T1

XLT Sport Utility 4D	U1J5	45075	27800	28300	30400	33900
Power Third Row			575	575	640	640
2WD	H		(1375)	(1375)	(1550)	(1550)

EXPEDITION 4WD—V8 Flex Fuel—Truck Equipment Schedule T1

XL Sport Utility 4D	U1G5	41975	23900	24300	26500	29800
Limited Sport Util	U2A5	51350	32200	32800	34400	38300
King Ranch Spt Util	U1J5	55610	33100	33700	35300	39300
2WD	K		(1375)	(1375)	(1520)	(1520)

EXPEDITION EL 4WD—V8 Flex Fuel—Truck Equipment Schedule T1

| XLT Sport Utility 4D | K1J5 | 47785 | 29800 | 30300 | 32600 | 36300 |
| Power Third Row | | | 575 | 575 | 640 | 640 |

EXPEDITION EL 4WD—V8 Flex Fuel—Truck Equipment Schedule T1

XL Sport Utility 4D	K1G5	45500	28300	28800	31000	34600
Limited Spt Util 4D	K2A5	54000	33600	34300	35800	39800
King Ranch Spt Util	K1J5	58260	34400	35100	36600	40600
2WD	F		(1375)	(1375)	(1520)	(1550)

TRANSIT CONNECT CARGO VAN—4-Cyl.—Truck Equipment Sch T2

XL Van Van 4D	S6E7	22995	15700	15950	17750	20000
XLT Van Van 4D	S6F7	24520	16550	16850	18650	21000
4-Cyl EcoBoost 1.6L	X		150	150	165	165

TRANSIT CONNECT PASSENGER VAN—4-Cyl.—Truck Equipment Sch T1

XL Van Van 4D	S9E7	25995	15600	15850	17550	19700
XLT Van Van 4D	S8F7	25520	16250	16550	18250	20600
Titanium Van 4D	E9G7	29995	18700	19050	20800	23400
4-Cyl EcoBoost 1.6L	X		150	150	165	165

E150 PASSENGER VAN—V8 Flex Fuel—Truck Equipment Schedule T1

XL Van 3D	E1BW	30725	17700	17950	19850	22600
XLT Van 3D	E1BW	33170	18950	19250	21100	23900
V8, Flex Fuel, 5.4 Liter	L		375	375	425	425

E350 PASSENGER VAN—V8 Flex Fuel—Truck Equipment Schedule T1

XL Super Duty	E3BL	34555	18500	18750	20600	23400
XL SD Extended	S3BL	36855	19250	19550	21400	24200
XLT Super Duty	E3BL	37015	19850	20200	21900	24800
XLT SD Extended	S3BL	38315	21700	22100	24000	27200
V10, 6.8 Liter	S		775	775	880	880

E150 CARGO VAN—V8 Flex Fuel—Truck Equipment Schedule T1

| Cargo Van | E1EW | 28595 | 16650 | 17800 | 18300 | 21500 |

Body Type	VIN	List	Trade-In Good	Very Good	Pvt-Party Good	Retail Excellent
Extended Van	S1EW	29810	17650	18850	19350	22800
Crew Van Pkg			375	375	420	420
V8, Flex Fuel, 5.4 Liter	L		375	375	420	420
E250 CARGO VAN—V8 Flex Fuel—Truck Equipment Schedule T1						
Cargo Van	E2EW	30055	17150	18300	18900	22440
Extended Cargo	S2EW	31415	19000	20300	20800	24600
Crew Van Pkg			375	375	420	420
V8, Flex Fuel, 5.4 Liter	L		375	375	420	420
E350 CARGO VAN—V8 Flex Fuel—Truck Equipment Schedule T1						
Super Duty Cargo	E3EL	32755	18350	19600	20200	23900
SD Extended Van	S3EL	33655	20000	21400	21800	25700
Crew Van Pkg			375	375	425	425
V10, 6.8 Liter	S		775	775	885	885
REGULAR CAB PICKUP—V6 EcoBoost Twin Turbo—Truck Sch T1						
F150 FX2 2D 6 1/2'	1FCT	35130	22800	23100	24600	27500
REGULAR CAB PICKUP 4WD—V6 EcoBoost Twin Turbo—Truck Sch T1						
F150 FX4 2D 6 1/2'	F1ET	39245	26400	26800	28400	31700
REGULAR CAB PICKUP—V8—Truck Equipment Schedule T1						
F150 XL 2D 6 1/2'	F1CF	25310	15050	15300	16800	18850
F150 XL 2D 8'	F1CF	25610	14850	15100	16550	18550
F150 STX 2D 6 1/2'	F1CF	29040	14400	14600	16300	18500
F150 XLT 2D 6 1/2'	F1CF	30615	17250	17500	18950	21200
F150 XLT 2D 8'	F1CF	30915	16650	16900	18450	20800
4WD	E		3500	3500	3880	3880
V6, Flex Fuel, 3.7 Liter	M		(825)	(825)	(920)	(920)
V6, EcoBoost, 3.5L	T		1875	1875	2100	2100
REGULAR CAB PICKUP—V8 Flex Fuel—Truck Equipment Sch T1						
F250 XL 2D 8'	F2A6	31230	17900	18300	20100	22900
4WD	B		3500	3500	3955	3955
V8, Turbo Diesel, 6.7L	T		5225	5225	5915	5915
REGULAR CAB PICKUP 4WD—V8 Flex Fuel—Truck Equipment Sch T1						
F250 XLT 2D 8'	F2B6	38060	21700	22100	24200	27600
2WD	A		(3500)	(3500)	(3985)	(3985)
V8, Turbo Diesel, 6.7L	T		5225	5225	5960	5960
SUPER CAB PICKUP—V8 Flex Fuel—Truck Equipment Schedule T1						
F150 XL 4D 6 1/2'	X1CF	30225	19450	19800	21800	24200
F150 XL 4D 8'	X1CF	30525	19300	19650	21600	24000
F150 STX 4D 6 1/2'	X1CF	32740	21100	21500	23700	26600
F150 XLT 4D 6 1/2'	X1CF	34315	21100	21500	23600	26300
F150 XLT 4D 8'	X1CF	34615	20700	21100	23200	25900
F150 FX2 4D 6 1/2'	X1CF	36735	23800	24300	26500	29500
F150 Lariat 4D 6 1/2'	X1CF	37920	24800	25300	27700	31000
Luxury Equip Group			500	500	565	565
4WD	E		3500	3500	3955	3955
V6, Flex Fuel, 3.7 Liter	M		(825)	(825)	(940)	(940)
V6, EcoBoost, 3.5L	T		1875	1875	2120	2120
V8, 6.2 Liter	6		1175	1175	1320	1320
SUPER CAB PICKUP 4WD—V8 Flex Fuel—Truck Equipment Sch T1						
F150 FX4 4D 6 1/2'	X1EF	40850	28800	29300	32100	36000
V6, EcoBoost, 3.5L	T		1875	1875	2145	2145
V8, 6.2 Liter	6		1175	1175	1335	1335
SUPER CAB PICKUP 4WD—V8—Truck Equipment Schedule T1						
F150 SVT Raptor 5'	X1R6	45275	40400	41200	42300	46500
SUPERCREW PICKUP—V8 Flex Fuel—Truck Equipment Schedule T1						
F150 XL 4D 5 1/2'	W1CF	34205	22000	22400	24600	27400
F150 XL 4D 6 1/2'	W1CF	34505	21800	22200	24300	27100
F150 XLT 4D 5 1/2'	W1CF	36150	23400	23800	26000	29000
F150 STX 4D 5 1/2'	W1CF	37460	23500	24000	27100	31100
F150 Kng Rnch 6 1/2'	W1EF	45795	29400	29900	32600	36400
F150 Platinum 6 1/2'	W1CF	48820	31000	31600	34200	38100
4WD	E		3500	3500	3965	3965
V6, EcoBoost, 3.5L	T		1875	1875	2130	2130
V6, Flex Fuel, 3.7 Liter	M		(825)	(825)	(940)	(940)
V8, 6.2 Liter	6		400	400	450	450
SUPERCREW PICKUP—V8 Flex Fuel—Truck Equipment Schedule T1						
F150 FX2 4D 5 1/2'	W1CF	39570	25100	25600	28100	31400
V6, EcoBoost, 3.5L	T		1875	1875	2145	2145
V8, 6.2 Liter	6		400	400	455	455
SUPERCREW PICKUP 4WD—V6 EcoBoost—Truck Equipment Schedule T1						
F150 Limited 5 1/2'	W1ET	53830	34300	34900	37900	42300
2WD	C		(3500)	(3500)	(3990)	(3990)
SUPERCREW PICKUP 4WD—V8 Flex Fuel—Truck Equipment Schedule T1						
F150 XLT 4D 6 1/2'	W1EF	40875	24800	25200	27800	31300

Body Type	VIN	List	Trade-In Good	Very Good	Pvt-Party Good	Retail Excellent
F150 Lariat 4D 5 1/2'	W1EF	44185	31800	32400	35200	39200
F150 Lariat 4D 6 1/2'	W1EF	44480	32300	32800	35500	39600
F150 Kng Rnch 5 1/2'	W1EF	48920	33300	33900	36700	40900
F150 Platinum 5 1/2'	W1EF	51945	33300	33900	36900	41300
2WD	C		(3500)	(3500)	(4010)	(4010)
V6, EcoBoost, 3.5L	T		1875	1875	2155	2155
V8, 6.2 Liter	6		400	400	450	450
SUPERCREW PICKUP 4WD—V8 Flex Fuel—Truck Equipment Schedule T1						
F150 FX4 4D 5 1/2'	W1EF	43690	32900	33500	36400	40600
F150 FX4 4D 6 1/2'	W1EF	43985	32700	33300	36100	40400
V6, EcoBoost, 3.5L	T		1875	1875	2130	2130
V8, 6.2 Liter	6		400	400	455	455
SUPERCREW PICKUP 4WD—V8—Truck Equipment Schedule T1						
F150 SVT Raptor 5'	W1R6	48510	48000	49000	49700	54300
SUPER DUTY REGULAR CAB PICKUP—V8 Flex Fuel—Truck Equip Sch T1						
F350 XL 2D 8'	F3A6	32125	19950	20300	22000	24800
4WD	B,D		3500	3500	3880	3880
V8, Turbo Diesel, 6.7L	T		5225	5225	5800	5800
SUPER DUTY REGULAR CAB PICKUP 4WD—V8 Turbo Diesel—Truck Equip Sch T1						
F350 XLT 2D 8'	F3BT	47275	30100	30700	33200	38000
2WD	A,C		(3500)	(3500)	(3920)	(3920)
V8, Flex Fuel, 6.2 Liter	6		(5200)	(5200)	(5835)	(5835)
SUPER DUTY SUPER CAB PICKUP—V8 Flex Fuel—Truck Equipment Sch T1						
F250 XL 4D 6 3/4'	X2A6	33425	21100	21500	23300	26400
F250 XL 4D 8'	X2A6	33625	20900	21300	23100	26200
4WD	B		3500	3500	3970	3970
V8, Turbo Diesel, 6.7L	T		5225	5225	5935	5935
SUPER DUTY SUPER CAB PICKUP 4WD—V8 Flex Fuel—Truck Sch T1						
F250 XLT 4D 6 3/4'	X2B6	40565	25600	26100	28400	32400
F250 XLT 4D 8'	X2B6	40765	25400	25900	28200	32200
F250 Lariat 4D 6 3/4'	X2B6	46110	31100	31700	34300	39300
2WD	A		(3500)	(3500)	(3995)	(3995)
V8 Turbo Diesel 6.7L	T		5225	5225	5950	5950
SUPER DUTY SUPER CAB PICKUP 4WD—V8 Turbo Diesel—Truck Sch T1						
F250 Lariat 4D 8'	X2BT	54630	36000	36700	39400	44900
2WD	A		(3500)	(3500)	(3930)	(3930)
V8, Flex Fuel, 6.2 Liter	6		(5200)	(5200)	(5845)	(5845)
SUPER DUTY SUPER CAB—V8 Flex Fuel—Truck Equipment Sch T1						
F350 XL 4D 8'	X3A6	34525	21900	22400	24200	27400
F350 XLT 4D 8'	X3AT	47175	33900	34600	36600	41300
F350 Lariat 4D 8'	X3A6	44020	31500	32100	33800	37800
4WD	B,D		3500	3500	3890	3890
V8, Turbo Diesel, 6.7L	T		5225	5225	5820	5820
SUPER DUTY SUPER CAB PICKUP 4WD—V8 Flex Fuel—Truck Equipment Sch T1						
F350 XL 4D 6 3/4'	X3B6	37125	24200	24700	26900	30700
F350 XLT 4D 6 3/4'	X3B6	41465	29200	29800	32000	36200
F350 Lariat 4D 6 3/4'	X3B6	47010	33300	34000	35900	40400
2WD	A		(3500)	(3500)	(3935)	(3935)
V8, Turbo Diesel, 6.7L	T		5225	5225	5885	5885
SUPER DUTY CREW CAB PICKUP—V8 Flex Fuel—Truck Equip Sch T1						
F250 XL 6 3/4'	W2A6	34825	22200	22700	24800	28500
F250 King Ranch 8'	W2A6	50910	34900	35600	38100	43400
F350 XL 4D 6 3/4'	W3A6	35725	23600	24100	26300	30000
4WD	B		3500	3500	3990	3990
V8, Turbo Diesel, 6.7L	T		5225	5225	5965	5965
SUPER DUTY CREW CAB PICKUP—V8 Turbo Diesel—Truck Sch T1						
F250 XL 8'	W2AT	43340	28600	29200	31300	35500
F250 Lariat 8'	W2AT	53840	38000	38700	41400	47100
F350 XL 4D 8'	W3AT	44240	28800	29400	31700	36100
F350 XLT 4D 8'	W3AT	49075	31700	32300	34800	39800
F350 Lariat 4D 8'	W3AT	54735	39600	40400	43000	48900
4WD	B		3500	3500	3930	3930
V8, Flex Fuel, 6.2 Liter	6		(5200)	(5200)	(5845)	(5845)
SUPER DUTY CREW CAB PICKUP 4WD—V8 Turbo Diesel—Truck Sch T1						
F250 XLT 6 3/4'	W2BT	50775	34700	35400	37800	43000
F250 Lariat 6 3/4'	W2BT	56825	42400	43200	45700	51700
F350 Lariat 4D 6 3/4'	W3BT	57725	41900	42700	45300	51400
F350 King Ranch 8'	W3BT	63315	46100	47000	49100	55100
F350 Platinum 8'	W3BT	64010	46200	47100	49200	55300
2WD	A		(3500)	(3500)	(3945)	(3945)
V8, Flex Fuel, 6.2 Liter	6		(5200)	(5200)	(5870)	(5870)
SUPER DUTY CREW CAB PICKUP 4WD—V8 Flex Fuel—Truck Equip Sch T1						
F250 XLT 8'	W2B6	42660	28500	29100	31500	35900

Body Type	VIN	List	Trade-In Good	Very Good	Pvt-Party Good	Retail Excellent
F250 KingRnch 6'	W2BT	62220	44000	44800	47100	53000
F250 Platinum 6 3/4'	W2B6	54595	40100	40900	43200	48800
F250 Platinum 8'	W2B6	63110	40800	41600	43900	49500
F350 XLT 4D 6 3/4'	W3B6	43365	29200	29800	32400	37100
F350 KingRnch 6 3/4'	W3B6	54805	40100	40900	43200	48800
F350 Platinum 6 3/4'	W3B6	55495	39600	40400	42900	48500
2WD	A		(3500)	(3500)	(3955)	(3955)
V8, Turbo Diesel, 6.7L	T		5225	5225	5910	5910

GMC — See CHEVROLET TRUCKS

HONDA

2000 HONDA–(JHL,2HKor4S6)(RD174)–Y–#

CR-V 4WD—4-Cyl.—Truck Equipment Schedule T2						
LX Sport Utility 4D	RD174	19465	1275	1450	2000	3425
EX Sport Utility 4D	RD176	20965	1675	1900	2550	4225
SE Sport Utility 4D	RD187	23015	2175	2450	3100	5150
2WD	2		(275)	(275)	(355)	(355)
PASSPORT 4WD—V6—Truck Equipment Schedule T1						
LX Sport Utility 4D	CM58V	27515	1225	1350	1875	3100
EX Sport Utility 4D	CM58V	29465	1700	1875	2425	3975
2WD	K		(275)	(275)	(355)	(355)
ODYSSEY—V6—Truck Equipment Schedule T1						
LX Minivan 4D	RL185	23815	725	875	1300	2250
EX Minivan 4D	RL186	26415	1100	1300	1700	2900

2001 HONDA–(JHL,2HKor4S6)(RD174)–1–#

CR-V 4WD—4-Cyl.—Truck Equipment Schedule T2						
LX Sport Utility 4D	RD174	19590	1500	1700	2250	3750
EX Sport Utility 4D	RD176	21190	2025	2275	2900	4750
SE Sport Utility 4D	RD187	23240	2375	2675	3300	5375
2WD	2		(300)	(300)	(385)	(385)
PASSPORT 4WD—V6—Truck Equipment Schedule T1						
LX Sport Util 4D	CM58W	27740	1550	1700	2200	3550
EX Sport Utility 4D	CM58W	29690	2050	2250	2850	4525
2WD	K		(300)	(300)	(385)	(385)
ODYSSEY—V6—Truck Equipment Schedule T1						
LX Minivan 4D	RL185	24340	800	950	1425	2525
EX Minivan 4D	RL186	26840	1175	1375	1775	3000

2002 HONDA–(JHL,2HKor4S6)(RD784)–2–#

CR-V 4WD—4-Cyl.—Truck Equipment Schedule T2						
LX Sport Utility 4D	RD784	19640	2800	3100	3425	5225
EX Sport Utility 4D	RD784	21940	3525	3900	4200	6375
2WD	2		(350)	(350)	(465)	(465)
PASSPORT 4WD—V6—Truck Equipment Schedule T1						
LX Sport Util 4D	CM58W	28040	2025	2225	2800	4375
EX Sport Utility 4D	CM58W	29990	2650	2900	3475	5375
2WD	K		(350)	(350)	(465)	(465)
ODYSSEY—V6—Truck Equipment Schedule T1						
LX Minivan 4D	RL185	24690	1075	1250	1650	2800
EX Minivan 4D	RL186	27190	1600	1825	2225	3675

2003 HONDA–(Jor5)HorJ(L,Kor6)(YH272)–3–#

ELEMENT 4WD—4-Cyl.—Truck Equipment Schedule T2						
DX Sport Utility 4D	YH272	18760	2650	2875	3350	4975
EX Sport Utility 4D	YH285	21310	3850	4200	4875	7225
2WD	1		(425)	(425)	(565)	(565)
CR-V 4WD—4-Cyl.—Truck Equipment Schedule T2						
LX Sport Utility 4D	RD774	19760	3250	3625	3900	5875
EX Sport Utility 4D	RD788	22060	4050	4500	4950	7475
2WD	2		(425)	(425)	(565)	(565)
PILOT 4WD—V6—Truck Equipment Schedule T1						
LX Sport Utility 4D	YF181	27380	2600	2950	3350	5175
EX Sport Utility 4D	YF184	29730	3225	3650	4125	6425
ODYSSEY—V6—Truck Equipment Schedule T1						
LX Minivan 4D	RL185	24860	1425	1650	2025	3275
EX Minivan 4D	RL186	27360	1850	2125	2550	4100

TRUCKS & VANS

Body Type	VIN	List	Trade-In Good	Trade-In Very Good	Pvt-Party Good	Retail Excellent

2004 HONDA–(J,2or5)F,HorJ(K,L,Nor6)(YH183)–4–#

ELEMENT—4-Cyl.—Truck Equipment Schedule T2

Body Type	VIN	List	Good	Very Good	Good	Excellent
LX Sport Utility 4D	YH183	18990	3500	3800	4250	6175
4WD	2		525	525	705	705

ELEMENT 4WD—4-Cyl.—Truck Equipment Schedule T2

DX Sport Utility 4D	YH272	17990	3450	3750	4200	6100
EX Sport Utility 4D	YH225	20790	4650	5025	5675	8250
2WD	1		(500)	(500)	(665)	(665)

CR-V 4WD—4-Cyl.—Truck Equipment Schedule T2

LX Sport Utility 4D	RD774	19890	3650	4050	4525	6750
EX Sport Utility 4D	RD788	22240	4550	5025	5575	8375
2WD	2		(500)	(500)	(665)	(665)

PILOT 4WD—V6—Truck Equipment Schedule T1

LX Sport Utility 4D	YF181	27590	3225	3600	3950	5925
EX Sport Utility 4D	YF184	29960	4025	4525	5000	7500

ODYSSEY—V6—Truck Equipment Schedule T1

LX Minivan 4D	RL185	24980	1600	1825	2250	3650
EX Minivan 4D	RL186	27480	2175	2475	2950	4725

2005 HONDA–(J,2or5)F,HorJ(K,L,Nor6)(YH283)–5–#

ELEMENT—4-Cyl.—Truck Equipment Schedule T2

LX Sport Utility 4D	YH283	18990	3825	4150	4900	6900
4WD			575	575	775	775

ELEMENT 4WD—4-Cyl.—Truck Equipment Schedule T2

EX Sport Utility 4D	YH286	20790	5125	5550	6425	8975
2WD	1		(575)	(575)	(765)	(765)

CR-V 4WD—4-Cyl.—Truck Equipment Schedule T2

LX Sport Utility 4D	RD774	21710	4650	5125	5825	8475
EX Sport Utility 4D	RD788	22865	5125	5650	6575	9675
SE Sport Utility 4D	RD779	25565	5725	6300	7200	10550
2WD	6		(575)	(575)	(765)	(765)

PILOT 4WD—V6—Truck Equipment Schedule T1

LX Sport Utility 4D	YF181	27865	3350	3775	4575	6825
EX Sport Utility 4D	YF184	30435	4325	4850	5650	8425

ODYSSEY—V6—Truck Equipment Schedule T1

LX Minivan 4D	RL382	25510	3100	3500	4125	6400
EX Minivan 4D	RL384	28510	3650	4125	4825	7375
Touring Minivan 4D	RL388	35015	5325	6000	6875	10500

2006 HONDA–(J,2or5)(F,HorJ)(J,K,L,Nor6)(YH283)–6–#

ELEMENT—4-Cyl.—Truck Equipment Schedule T1

LX Sport Utility 4D	YH283	19700	5050	5425	6025	8150
4WD			625	625	825	825

ELEMENT 4WD—4-Cyl.—Truck Equipment Schedule T2

EX-P Sport Util 4D	YH277	22920	6600	7100	7800	10550
EX Sport Utility 4D	YH286	21575	6500	6975	7700	10400
2WD	1		(625)	(625)	(820)	(820)

CR-V 4WD—4-Cyl.—Truck Equipment Schedule T2

LX Sport Utility 4D	RD774	22145	5625	6175	7075	10100
SE Sport Utility 4D	RD779	26000	7125	7800	8775	12550
2WD	6		(625)	(625)	(845)	(845)

CR-V 4WD—4-Cyl.—Truck Equipment Schedule T1

EX Sport Utility 4D	RD788	24300	6275	6850	7750	11050
2WD			(625)	(625)	(845)	(845)

PILOT 4WD—V6—Truck Equipment Schedule T1

LX Sport Utility 4D	YF181	28745	5050	5600	6225	8875
EX Sport Utility 4D	YF184	31295	5925	6575	7325	10400
EX-L Sport Utility 4D	YF185	33640	7125	7900	8675	12300
2WD	2		(1025)	(1025)	(1375)	(1375)

ODYSSEY—V6—Truck Equipment Schedule T1

LX Minivan 4D	RL382	25895	3700	4150	4750	7000
EX Minivan 4D	RL384	28945	4500	5025	5575	8225
Touring Minivan 4D	RL388	37145	6850	7650	8250	12100

RIDGELINE 4WD—V6—Truck Equipment Schedule T1

RT Short Bed	YK162	28250	6850	7375	7875	10450
RTS Short Bed	YK164	30625	7375	7950	8450	11150
RTL Short Bed	YK165	32040	8900	9550	10050	13300

2007 HONDA–(J,2or5)(F,HorJ)(J,K,L,Nor6)YH283–7–#

ELEMENT—4-Cyl. VTEC—Truck Equipment Schedule T1

LX Sport Utility 4D	YH283	21695	5725	6125	6975	9250

Body Type	VIN	List	Trade-In Good	Very Good	Pvt-Party Good	Retail Excellent
4WD			975	975	1255	1255

ELEMENT 4WD—4-Cyl. VTEC—Truck Equipment Schedule T1
| EX Sport Utility 4D | YH287 | 23705 | 7025 | 7525 | 8450 | 11300 |
| 2WD | 1 | | (675) | (675) | (875) | (875) |

ELEMENT—4-Cyl. VTEC—Truck Equipment Schedule T1
| SC Sport Utility 4D | YH189 | 24090 | 7700 | 8225 | 9100 | 12100 |

CR-V 4WD—4-Cyl. VTEC—Truck Equipment Schedule T2
LX Sport Utility 4D	RE483	22395	6950	7550	8600	12050
EX Sport Utility 4D	RE485	24645	8225	8925	9875	13750
EX-L Sport Utility	RE487	26635	8775	9500	10600	14850
2WD	3		(675)	(675)	(910)	(910)

PILOT 4WD—V6 VTEC—Truck Equipment Schedule T1
LX Sport Utility 4D	YF181	28990	6375	7000	7575	10300
EX Sport Utility 4D	YF184	31540	7300	8000	8600	11650
EX-L Sport Utility	YF185	33840	8150	8925	9525	12950
2WD	2		(1100)	(1100)	(1480)	(1480)

ODYSSEY—V6 VTEC—Truck Equipment Schedule T1
LX Minivan 4D	RL382	26240	4575	5050	5625	8000
EX Minivan 4D	RL384	29290	5275	5825	6475	9175
Touring Minivan 4D	RL388	37490	7825	8625	9275	13100

RIDGELINE 4WD—V6 VTEC—Truck Equipment Schedule T1
RT Short Bed	YK162	28395	7975	8525	9225	12050
RTX Short Bed	YK163	28895	8625	9200	9850	12850
RTS Short Bed	YK164	30870	8825	9425	10100	13200
RTL Short Bed	YK165	35535	10650	11350	11950	15550

2008 HONDA—(J,2or5)(F,HorJ)(J,K,L,Nor6)YH283-8-#

ELEMENT—4-Cyl. VTEC—Truck Equipment Schedule T1
| LX Sport Utility 4D | YH283 | 21015 | 6900 | 7275 | 8225 | 10450 |
| 4WD | | | 1075 | 1075 | 1365 | 1365 |

ELEMENT 4WD—4-Cyl. VTEC—Truck Equipment Schedule T1
| EX Sport Utility 4D | YH287 | 23025 | 8950 | 9425 | 10400 | 13200 |
| 2WD | 1 | | (725) | (725) | (925) | (925) |

ELEMENT—4-Cyl. VTEC—Truck Equipment Schedule T1
| SC Sport Utility 4D | YH189 | 23410 | 9600 | 10100 | 11100 | 14050 |

CR-V 4WD—4-Cyl. VTEC—Truck Equipment Schedule T2
LX Sport Utility 4D	RE483	23155	8350	8950	9825	12850
EX Sport Utility 4D	RE485	24785	9200	9850	10850	14300
EX-L Sport Utility	RE487	27370	10000	10700	11750	15500
2WD	3		(725)	(725)	(955)	(955)

PILOT 4WD—V6 VTEC—Truck Equipment Schedule T1
VP Sport Utility 4D	YF182	29630	8025	8625	9275	11900
EX Sport Utility 4D	YF184	31780	9125	9800	10450	13400
EX-L Sport Utility	YF185	34080	10150	10900	11500	14800
SE Sport Utility 4D	YF183	33630	9475	10200	10850	13950
2WD	2		(1200)	(1200)	(1485)	(1485)

ODYSSEY—V6 VTEC—Truck Equipment Schedule T1
LX Minivan 4D	RL382	26495	5575	6025	6825	9200
EX Minivan 4D	RL384	29595	6750	7300	8050	10750
Touring Minivan 4D	RL388	40645	9325	10050	10900	14600

RIDGELINE 4WD—V6 VTEC—Truck Equipment Schedule T1
RT Short Bed	YK162	28635	8625	9100	10050	12650
RTX Short Bed	YK163	29135	9575	10100	11000	13800
RTS Short Bed	YK164	31060	10400	10950	11850	14850
RTL Short Bed	YK165	33725	12600	13300	14100	17550

2009 HONDA—(J,2or5)(F,HorJ)(J,K,L,Nor6)YH283-9-#

ELEMENT—4-Cyl. VTEC—Truck Equipment Schedule T2
| LX Sport Utility 4D | YH283 | 22145 | 8800 | 9200 | 10250 | 12550 |
| 4WD | | | 1150 | 1150 | 1330 | 1330 |

ELEMENT 4WD—4-Cyl. VTEC—Truck Equipment Schedule T1
| EX Sport Utility 4D | YH287 | 24255 | 10750 | 11200 | 12300 | 15000 |
| 2WD | 1 | | (825) | (825) | (955) | (955) |

ELEMENT—4-Cyl. VTEC—Truck Equipment Schedule T1
| SC Sport Utility 4D | YH189 | 24740 | 11250 | 11750 | 12900 | 15700 |

CR-V 4WD—4-Cyl. VTEC—Truck Equipment Schedule T1
LX Sport Utility 4D	RE483	23155	9750	10350	11300	14150
EX Sport Utility 4D	RE485	25405	11050	11700	12800	16100
EX-L Sport Utility	RE487	27955	11900	12600	13700	17300
2WD	3		(825)	(825)	(1050)	(1050)

PILOT 4WD—V6 VTEC—Truck Equipment Schedule T1
| LX Sport Utility 4D | YF285 | 29965 | 10550 | 11150 | 11850 | 14600 |

TRUCKS & VANS

2009 HONDA

Body Type	VIN	List	Trade-In Good	Trade-In Very Good	Pvt-Party Good	Retail Excellent
EX Sport Utility 4D	YF184	32765	12100	12800	13450	16500
EX-L Sport Utility	YF485	36005	13800	14600	15350	18800
Touring Sport Util	YF183	37565	15200	16050	16700	20400
2WD		2	(1275)	(1275)	(1545)	(1545)
ODYSSEY—V6 VTEC—Truck Equipment Schedule T1						
LX Minivan 4D	RL382	27025	7100	7525	8375	10650
EX Minivan 4D	RL384	30125	8650	9175	10050	12750
Touring Minivan 4D	RL388	41115	11600	12300	13350	17000
RIDGELINE 4WD—V6 VTEC—Truck Equipment Schedule T1						
RT Short Bed	YK162	28870	10900	11400	12400	15000
RTS Short Bed	YK164	31975	12850	13400	14500	17450
RTL Short Bed	YK165	34850	14750	15400	16500	19800

2010 HONDA — 5(ForJ)(N,Por6)(YH2H3)–A–#

Body Type	VIN	List	Good	Very Good	Good	Excellent
ELEMENT—4-Cyl. VTEC—Truck Equipment Schedule T2						
LX Sport Util 4D	YH2H3	22485	10650	11050	12150	14900
4WD			1250	1250	1460	1460
ELEMENT 4WD—4-Cyl. VTEC—Truck Equipment Schedule T1						
EX Sport Utility 4D	YH2H7	23795	13000	13450	15050	17900
2WD		1	(950)	(950)	(1115)	(1115)
ELEMENT—4-Cyl. VTEC—Truck Equipment Schedule T1						
SC Sport Utility 4D	YH1H9	24230	13350	13800	15350	18150
CR-V 4WD—4-Cyl. VTEC—Truck Equipment Schedule T2						
LX Sport Utility 4D	RE4H3	23505	11250	11800	12950	15650
EX Sport Utility	RE4H5	25805	12350	12950	14200	17250
EX-L Sport Utility	RE4H7	28455	13100	13750	15150	18450
2WD		3	(950)	(950)	(1175)	(1175)
PILOT 4WD—V6 VTEC—Truck Equipment Schedule T1						
LX Sport Utility	YF4H2	30205	12400	12950	14000	16800
EX Sport Utility 4D	YF4H4	33055	13550	14150	15300	18400
EX-L Sport Utility	YF4H5	38155	15250	15900	17150	20600
Touring Sport Utility	YF4H8	39355	17200	17950	19000	22700
2WD		2	(1350)	(1350)	(1615)	(1615)
ACCORD CROSSTOUR—V6 VTEC—Truck Equipment Schedule T1						
EX Sport Utility 4D	TF1H3	30380	11100	11450	12700	14950
EX-L Spt Util 4D	TF1H5	33280	11550	11950	13250	15650
4WD			1175	1175	1385	1385
ODYSSEY—V6 VTEC—Truck Equipment Schedule T1						
LX Minivan 4D	RL3H2	27515	9175	9575	10750	13200
EX Minivan 4D	RL3H4	30615	10950	11450	12650	15500
EX-L Minivan 4D	RL3H6	34115	13300	13900	15400	18900
Touring Minivan	RL3H9	41465	14550	15200	16750	20600
RIDGELINE 4WD—V6 VTEC—Truck Equipment Schedule T1						
RT Short Bed	YK1F2	29160	13450	13900	15250	17850
RTS Short Bed	YK1F4	32265	15450	16000	17300	20200
RTL Short Bed	YK1F5	35140	17450	18050	19400	22700

2011 HONDA — (5orJ)(F,HorJ)(6,L,NorP)(YH2H3)–B–#

Body Type	VIN	List	Good	Very Good	Good	Excellent
ELEMENT—4-Cyl. VTEC—Truck Equipment Schedule T2						
LX Sport Utility	YH2H3	22855	14150	14500	16050	18350
4WD			1400	1400	1585	1585
ELEMENT 4WD—4-Cyl. VTEC—Truck Equipment Schedule T2						
EX Sport Utility 4D	YH2H7	24965	15950	16400	17950	20500
2WD			(1075)	(1075)	(1210)	(1210)
CR-V 4WD—4-Cyl. VTEC—Truck Equipment Schedule T2						
LX Sport Utility	RE4H3	23725	12350	12850	14050	16550
SE Sport Utility	RE4H4	24425	12600	13100	14350	16850
EX Sport Utility	RE4H5	26025	13400	13950	15300	18050
EX-L Spt Utility	RE4H7	28675	14650	15250	16650	19650
2WD		3	(1075)	(1075)	(1260)	(1260)
PILOT 4WD—V6 VTEC—Truck Equipment Schedule T1						
LX Sport Utility 4D	YF4H2	30425	14500	15000	16250	19000
EX Sport Utility 4D	YF4H4	33275	15700	16200	17550	20500
EX-L Sport Utility	YF4H5	36375	17800	18350	19700	23000
Touring Sport Util	YF4H9	41175	19400	20000	21300	24800
2WD		3	(1450)	(1450)	(1670)	(1670)
ACCORD CROSSTOUR—V6 VTEC—Truck Equipment Schedule T1						
EX Sport Utility 4D	TF1H3	30570	12400	12750	14350	16600
EX-L Sport Utility	TF1H5	33470	12850	13200	14800	17050
4WD		2	1325	1325	1530	1530
ODYSSEY—V6 VTEC—Truck Equipment Schedule T1						
LX Minivan 4D	RL5H2	27585	12150	12550	14050	16750

Body Type	VIN	List	Trade-In Good	Very Good	Pvt-Party Good	Retail Excellent
EX Minivan 4D	RL5H4	30685	13900	14350	16000	19000
EX-L Minivan 4D	RL5H6	34185	16700	17200	18850	22300
Touring Minivan	RL5H9	41535	18750	19350	21200	25200
Touring Elite 4D	RL5H9	44030	20100	20800	22700	27000
RIDGELINE 4WD—V6 VTEC—Truck Equipment Schedule T1						
RT Short Bed	YK1F2	29680	15800	16200	17650	20100
RTS Short Bed	YK1F4	32385	17350	17800	19300	21900
RTL Short Bed	YK1F5	35260	20600	21200	22600	25600

Body Type	VIN	List	Trade-In Good	Very Good	Pvt-Party Good	Retail Excellent
CR-V AWD—4-Cyl. i-VTEC—Truck Equipment Schedule T2						
LX Sport Utility	RM4H3	24355	13850	14350	15950	18500
EX Sport Utility	RM4H5	26455	15350	15900	17700	20700
EX-L Spt Utility	RM4H7	29105	17000	17550	19450	22800
2WD		3	(1500)	(1500)	(1730)	(1730)
PILOT 4WD—V6 i-VTEC—Truck Equipment Schedule T1						
LX Sport Utility 4D	YF4H2	30880	16150	16550	18150	20900
EX Sport Utility 4D	YF4H4	33730	17500	17950	19600	22600
EX-L Sport Utility	YF4H5	36980	19850	20400	22000	25200
Touring Sport Util	YF4H9	41630	21900	22500	24000	27500
2WD		3	(1525)	(1525)	(1760)	(1760)
CROSSTOUR—V6 VTEC—Truck Equipment Schedule T1						
EX Sport Util 4D	TF1H3	31150	13250	13500	15300	17400
EX-L Sport Util 4D	TF1H5	33800	14800	15150	16950	19250
4WD		2	1500	1500	1705	1705
4-Cyl, i-VTEC, 2.4 Liter			(875)	(875)	(995)	(995)
ODYSSEY—V6 i-VTEC—Truck Equipment Schedule T1						
LX Minivan 4D	RL5H2	29035	13350	13700	15450	17950
EX Minivan 4D	RL5H4	32285	15650	16000	17850	20700
EX-L Minivan 4D	RL5H6	35685	18450	18850	20800	24000
Touring Minivan	RL5H9	41990	21400	21900	24000	27800
Touring Elite 4D	RL5H9	44485	21900	22400	24600	28600
RIDGELINE 4WD—V6 VTEC—Truck Equipment Schedule T1						
RT Short Bed	YK1F2	30060	18900	19300	21100	23600
Sport Short Bed	YK1F7	30805	19600	20000	21800	24400
RTS Short Bed	YK1F4	32765	21000	21400	23200	25900
RTL Short Bed	YK1F5	35640	23000	23500	25300	28200

Body Type	VIN	List	Trade-In Good	Very Good	Pvt-Party Good	Retail Excellent
CR-V AWD—4-Cyl. i-VTEC—Truck Equipment Schedule T2						
LX Sport Utility	RM4H3	24775	16050	16550	18000	20400
EX Sport Utility	RM4H5	26875	17250	17800	19300	21900
EX-L Sport Utility	RM4H7	29525	19200	19800	21300	24200
2WD		3	(1500)	(1500)	(1670)	(1670)
PILOT 4WD—V6 i-VTEC—Truck Equipment Schedule T1						
LX Sport Utility 4D	YF4H2	31850	19450	19850	21500	24400
EX Sport Utility 4D	YF4H4	34100	21100	21500	23200	26300
EX-L Sport Utility	YF4H5	37350	23800	24300	25900	29300
Touring Sport Util	YF4H9	42000	25500	26000	27700	31100
2WD		3	(1600)	(1600)	(1810)	(1810)
CROSSTOUR—V6 i-VTEC—Truck Equipment Schedule T1						
EX Sport Util 4D	TF1H3	31720	15600	15900	17850	20000
EX-L Sport Util 4D	TF1H5	34370	17700	18050	20000	22300
4-Cyl, i-VTEC, 2.4 Liter			(975)	(975)	(1100)	(1100)
4WD			1625	1625	1835	1835
ODYSSEY—V6 i-VTEC—Truck Equipment Schedule T1						
LX Minivan 4D	RL5H2	29405	16750	17050	18900	21500
EX Minivan 4D	RL5H4	32555	19050	19400	21300	24200
EX-L Minivan 4D	RL5H6	35955	22200	22600	24600	27900
Touring Minivan	RL5H9	42200	24900	25300	27600	31300
Touring Elite	RL5H9	44755	25500	26000	28300	32200
RIDGELINE 4WD—V6 VTEC—Truck Equipment Schedule T1						
RT Short Bed	YK1F2	30180	20600	21000	22900	25400
Sport Short Bed	YK1F7	30925	22700	23200	25000	27700
RTS Short Bed	YK1F4	32885	23600	24100	26000	28900
RTL Short Bed	YK1F5	35760	26500	27000	27500	30500

Body Type	VIN	List	Trade-In Good	Very Good	Pvt-Party Good	Retail Excellent
CR-V AWD—4-Cyl. i-VTEC—Truck Equipment Schedule T2						
LX Sport Utility	RM4H3	25025	17700	18200	19700	22200
EX Sport Utility	RM4H5	27125	19000	19550	21100	23800
EX-L Sport Utility	RM4H7	29775	20800	21500	23000	26000

Body Type	VIN	List	Trade-In Good	Very Good	Pvt-Party Good	Retail Excellent
2WD			(1500)	(1500)	(1675)	(1675)
PILOT 4WD—V6 i-VTEC—Truck Equipment Schedule T1						
LX Sport Utility 4D	YF4H2	32100	21500	21900	23600	26500
EX Sport Utility 4D	YF4H4	34350	23300	23800	25400	28500
EX-L Sport Utility	YF4H5	37600	25900	26400	28100	31500
Touring Sport Util	YF4H9	42250	28400	28900	30600	34100
2WD			(1700)	(1700)	(1895)	(1895)
CROSSTOUR—V6 i-VTEC—Truck Equipment Schedule T1						
EX Sport Utility 4D	TF1H3	31870	18550	18900	20600	22800
EX-L Sport Utility	TF1H5	34520	20700	21100	22800	25000
4WD			1750	1750	1940	1940
4-Cyl, i-VTEC, 2.4 Liter			(1075)	(1075)	(1190)	(1190)
ODYSSEY—V6 i-VTEC—Truck Equipment Schedule T1						
LX Minivan 4D	RL5H2	29655	19650	20000	21900	24600
EX Minivan 4D	RL5H4	32955	22000	22400	24300	27200
EX-L Minivan 4D	RL5H6	36455	25200	25700	27700	31000
Touring Minivan	RL5H9	42710	28100	28600	30800	34500
Touring Elite	RL5H9	48320	29100	29600	32000	35900
RIDGELINE 4WD—V6 VTEC—Truck Equipment Schedule T1						
RT Short Bed	YK1F2	30405	22100	22500	24400	27000
Sport Short Bed	YK1F7	31550	23800	24200	26200	28900
RTS Short Bed	YK1F4	33210	26100	26600	28500	31400
RTL Short Bed	YK1F5	35985	27100	27600	29700	32900
SE Short Bed	YK1F6	38335	28600	29200	31200	34300

HUMMER

2002 HUMMER — 137(ZA85)--2-#

H1 4WD—V8 Turbo Diesel—Truck Equipment Schedule T3						
Open Top 4D	ZA85	98681	49300	52700	48300	57900
Wagon 4D	ZA84	109834	52700	56300	51500	61800
Winch			450	450	500	500

2003 HUMMER — 5GR-(N23U)-3-#

H2 4WD—V8—Truck Equipment Schedule T3						
Sport Utility 4D	N23U	50200	13300	14200	14300	18000
Third Row Seat			275	275	320	320
Adventure Pkg			150	150	190	190
Lux Pkg			150	150	190	190
Air Suspension			300	300	375	375
H1 4WD—V8 Turbo Diesel—Truck Equipment Schedule T3						
Open Top 4D	A903	106185	57300	61100	55600	66000
Wagon 4D	A843	117508	60600	64600	58900	70000
Winch			525	525	580	580

2004 HUMMER — 5GR-(N23U)-4-#

H2 4WD—V8—Truck Equipment Schedule T3						
Sport Utility 4D	N23U	51395	14300	15250	15350	19150
Limited Ed Spt Util	N23U	59840	16300	17400	17300	21500
Third Row Seat			300	300	350	350
Adventure Pkg			175	175	210	210
Lux Pkg			175	175	210	210
Air Suspension			325	325	390	390
H1 4WD—V8 Turbo Diesel—Truck Equipment Schedule T3						
Open Top 4D	A903	106185	64000	68000	61900	72800
Wagon 4D	ZA84	117508	68400	72800	66200	77900
Winch			575	575	640	640
Adventure Pkg			175	175	190	190

2005 HUMMER — 5GR-(N23U)-5-#

H2 4WD—V8—Truck Equipment Schedule T3						
Sport Utility 4D	N23U	52000	16850	17900	18050	22100
Third Row Seat			325	325	375	375
Adventure Pkg			200	200	225	225
Lux Pkg			200	200	225	225
Air Suspension			350	350	405	405
H2 SUT 4WD—V8—Truck Equipment Schedule T3						
Sport Utility Pickup	N22U	53055	18400	19600	19450	23600
Adventure Pkg			200	200	225	225
Victory Red Ltd Ed			200	200	225	225

Body Type	VIN	List	Trade-In Good	Trade-In Very Good	Pvt-Party Good	Retail Excellent
Lux Pkg			200	200	225	225
Air Suspension			350	350	400	400

2006 HUMMER — 5G(RorT)-(N136)-6-#

H3 4WD—5-Cyl.—Truck Equipment Schedule T3
Sport Utility 4D	N136	31195	9200	9675	10650	13300
Adventure Pkg			200	200	250	250
Luxury Pkg			200	200	250	250
Off-Road Suspension			350	350	430	430

H2 4WD—V8—Truck Equipment Schedule T3
Sport Utility 4D	N23U	53855	19650	20800	20800	25100
Third Row Seat			350	350	395	395
Adventure Pkg			200	200	245	245
Limited Edition			200	200	245	245
Luxury Pkg			200	200	245	245
Air Suspension			350	350	420	420

H2 SUT 4WD—V8—Truck Equipment Schedule T3
Sport Utility Pickup	N22U	53910	21100	22300	22200	26800
Adventure Pkg			200	200	240	240
Limited Edition			200	200	240	240
Luxury Pkg			200	200	240	240
Air Suspension			350	350	420	420

H1 4WD—V8 Turbo Diesel—Truck Equipment Schedule T3
Open Top 4D	PH90	129399	106500	112600	102700	117900
Wagon 4D	PH84	140796	113000	119500	108700	124500
Winch			675	675	730	730
Adventure Pkg			200	200	225	225

2007 HUMMER — 5G(RorT)-(N13E)-7-#

H3 4WD—5-Cyl.—Truck Equipment Schedule T3
Sport Utility 4D	N13E	31640	10350	10800	11750	14450
Adventure Pkg			225	225	265	265
Luxury Pkg			225	225	265	265
H3X Pkg			225	225	265	265
Off-Road Suspension			375	375	445	445

H2 4WD—V8—Truck Equipment Schedule T3
Sport Utility 4D	N23U	54255	22600	23900	23900	28500
Third Row Seat			375	375	425	425
Adventure Pkg			225	225	260	260
Luxury Pkg			225	225	260	260
Special Edition			225	225	260	260
Air Suspension			375	375	440	440

H2 SUT 4WD—V8—Truck Equipment Schedule T3
Sport Utility Pickup	N22U	54300	23600	24900	24800	29500
Adventure Pkg			225	225	260	260
Luxury Pkg			225	225	260	260
Special Edition			225	225	260	260
Air Suspension			375	375	435	435

2008 HUMMER — 5G(RorT)-(N13E)-8-#

H3 4WD—5-Cyl.—Truck Equipment Schedule T3
Sport Utility 4D	N13E	32390	11600	12100	13150	15800
Adventure Pkg	3		250	250	280	280
Luxury Pkg			250	250	280	280
Off-Road Suspension	4		400	400	455	455

H3x 4WD—5-Cyl.—Truck Equipment Schedule T3
Sport Utility 4D	N53E	40685	13900	14450	15550	18550
Luxury Pkg	4		250	250	280	280

H3 ALPHA 4WD—V8—Truck Equipment Schedule T3
Sport Utility 4D	N63L	39260	14250	14800	15850	18900
Luxury Pkg	4		250	250	275	275
Off-Road Suspension			400	400	450	450

H2 4WD—V8—Truck Equipment Schedule T3
Sport Utility 4D	N238	56410	29800	31200	31100	36000
Third Row Seat			400	400	440	440
Adventure Pkg	7		250	250	275	275
Luxury Pkg	8		250	250	275	275
Air Suspension			400	400	445	445

H2 SUT 4WD—V8—Truck Equipment Schedule T3
Sport Utility Pickup	N928	56455	31100	32600	32300	37300
Adventure Pkg			250	250	275	275
Luxury Pkg	0		250	250	275	275

TRUCKS & VANS

Body Type	VIN	List	Trade-In Good	Very Good	Pvt-Party Good	Retail Excellent
Air Suspension			400	400	440	440

2009 HUMMER — 5G(R,TorN)–(N13E)–9–#

H3T 4WD—5-Cyl.—Truck Equipment Schedule T3
Sport Utility Pickup	N13E	33190	18750	19400	20700	24300
Adventure Pkg			275	275	330	330
Luxury Pkg			275	275	330	330
Off-Road Suspension			400	400	465	465

H3T ALPHA—V8—Truck Equipment Schedule T3
Sport Utility Pickup	N63L	36760	20800	21600	22700	26500
Adventure Pkg			275	275	325	325
Off-Road Suspension			400	400	460	460

H3 4WD—5-Cyl.—Truck Equipment Schedule T3
Sport Utility 4D	N13E	34785	13750	14300	15700	18550
Adventure Pkg			275	275	335	335
Luxury Pkg			275	275	335	335
Off-Road Suspension			400	400	470	470

H3x 4WD—5-Cyl.—Truck Equipment Schedule T3
| Sport Utility 4D | N53E | 42830 | 18700 | 19400 | 20700 | 24300 |
| H3X Pkg | | | 275 | 275 | 330 | 330 |

H3 ALPHA 4WD—V8—Truck Equipment Schedule T3
Sport Utility 4D	N63L	41405	18250	18900	20300	23800
H3X Pkg			275	275	330	330
Off-Road Suspension			400	400	465	465

H2 4WD—V8—Truck Equipment Schedule T3
Sport Utility 4D	N238	57590	38900	40500	40100	45200
Third Row Seat			450	450	495	495
Adventure Pkg			275	275	310	310
Luxury Pkg			275	275	310	310
Air Suspension			400	400	440	440

H2 SUT 4WD—V8—Truck Equipment Schedule T3
Sport Utility Pickup	N228	57635	41000	42700	42100	47300
Adventure Pkg			275	275	310	310
Luxury Pkg			275	275	310	310
Air Suspension			400	400	440	440

2010 HUMMER — 5G(R,TorN)–(NGDE)–A–#

H3T 4WD—5-Cyl.—Truck Equipment Schedule T3
Sport Util Pickup	NGDE	33390	22100	22800	24100	27600
Adventure Pkg			325	325	380	380
Luxury Pkg			325	325	380	380
Off-Road Suspension			400	400	455	455

H3T ALPHA 4WD—V8 Flex Fuel—Truck Equipment Schedule T3
| Sport Util Pickup | NKDP | 36460 | 23500 | 24200 | 25700 | 29500 |

H3 4WD—5-Cyl.—Truck Equipment Schedule T3
Sport Utility 4D	NGDE	35865	16650	17150	18700	21600
Adventure Pkg			325	325	385	385
Luxury Pkg			325	325	385	385
Off-Road Suspension			400	400	460	460

H3 ALPHA 4WD—V8—Truck Equipment Schedule T3
Sport Utility 4D	NLDP	42485	20800	21400	22900	26400
Adventure Pkg			325	325	380	380
Off-Road Suspension			400	400	455	455

HYUNDAI

2001 HYUNDAI — KM8S(B72D)–1–#

SANTA FE 4WD—V6—Truck Equipment Schedule T2
GL Sport Utility 4D	B72D	20234	775	925	1150	1800
GLS Sport Utility 4D	C72D	21234	1125	1325	1625	2675
LX Sport Utility 4D	C72D	22434	1450	1725	2050	3400
2WD	8		(300)	(300)	(385)	(385)
4-Cyl, 2.4 Liter	B		(225)	(225)	(300)	(300)

2002 HYUNDAI — KM8S(B82D)–2–#

SANTA FE—4-Cyl.—Equipment Schedule T2
| Sport Utility 4D | B82B | 17694 | 800 | 950 | 1275 | 2150 |

SANTA FE 4WD—V6—Truck Equipment Schedule T2
| GLS Sport Utility 4D | C72D | 21594 | 1325 | 1550 | 1925 | 3175 |
| LX Sport Utility 4D | C72D | 23794 | 1900 | 2225 | 2650 | 4325 |

Body Type	VIN	List	Trade-In Good	Very Good	Pvt-Party Good	Retail Excellent
2WD	8		(350)	(350)	(465)	(465)

2003 HYUNDAI — KM8S(B82B)-3-#

SANTA FE—4-Cyl.—Truck Equipment Schedule T2
Sport Utility 4D	B82B	17894	1025	1200	1575	2575

SANTA FE 4WD—V6—Truck Equipment Schedule T2
GLS Sport Utility 4D	C72D	21894	1750	2025	2425	3875
LX Sport Utility 4D	C72E	24394	2425	2800	3175	5050
2WD	8		(425)	(425)	(565)	(565)
V6, 3.5 Liter	E		325	325	420	420

2004 HYUNDAI — KM8S(B82B)-4-#

SANTA FE—4-Cyl.—Truck Equipment Schedule T2
Sport Utility 4D	B82B	18589	1200	1400	1800	2950

SANTA FE 4WD—V6—Truck Equipment Schedule T2
GLS Sport Utility 4D	C72D	23089	1825	2100	2600	4200
LX Sport Utility 4D	C72E	26089	2775	3175	3750	6025
2WD	8		(500)	(500)	(665)	(665)
V6, 3.5 Liter	8		350	350	465	465

2005 HYUNDAI — KM8(SC73D)-5-#

SANTA FE 4WD—V6—Truck Equipment Schedule T2
GLS Sport Util 4D	SC73D	23594	2500	2875	3525	5475
LX Sport Utility 4D	SC73E	26594	3375	3875	4500	6900
2WD	1		(575)	(575)	(765)	(765)
V6, 3.5 Liter (GLS)	E		375	375	510	510

TUCSON—4-Cyl.—Truck Equipment Schedule T2
GL Sport Utility 4D	JM12B	18894	2250	2475	3050	4350
4WD	6		575	575	765	765

TUCSON 4WD—V6—Truck Equipment Schedule T1
GLS Sport Util 4D	JN72D	22094	3150	3425	4050	5825
LX Sport Utility 4D	JN72D	23344	3800	4150	4900	7050
2WD	1		(575)	(575)	(715)	(715)

2006 HYUNDAI — KM8(SC73D)-6-#

SANTA FE 4WD—V6—Truck Equipment Schedule T2
GLS Sport Util 4D	SC73D	23795	3575	4050	4725	6975
Limited Sport Util	SC73E	26495	4225	4750	5550	8300
2WD	1		(625)	(625)	(845)	(845)
V6, 3.5 Liter (GLS)	E		425	425	560	560

TUCSON—4-Cyl.—Truck Equipment Schedule T1
GL Sport Utility 4D	JM12B	19345	2800	3025	3575	5000
4WD	7		625	625	820	820

TUCSON 4WD—V6—Truck Equipment Schedule T1
GLS Sport Util 4D	JN72D	22495	3700	4025	4675	6475
Limited Sport Util	JN72D	22845	3950	4300	4875	6850
2WD	1		(625)	(625)	(810)	(810)

2007 HYUNDAI — KM8(JM72B)-7-#

TUCSON 4WD—4-Cyl.—Truck Equipment Schedule T1
GLS Sport Util 4D	JM72B	18995	4225	4550	5200	7075
2WD	1		(675)	(675)	(875)	(875)

TUCSON—V6—Truck Equipment Schedule T1
Limited Sport Util	JN12D	22845	4300	4650	5275	7325
4WD	7		975	975	1280	1280

TUCSON 4WD—V6—Truck Equipment Schedule T1
SE Sport Utility 4D	JN72D	22995	4800	5200	5800	8050
2WD	1		(675)	(675)	(885)	(885)

SANTA FE—V6—Truck Equipment Schedule T2
Limited Sport Util	SH13E	26595	6200	6900	7525	10600
Third Row Seat			250	250	325	325
AWD	7		775	775	1020	1020

SANTA FE AWD—V6—Truck Equipment Schedule T1
GLS Sport Utility 4D	SG73D	24795	5475	6100	6700	9400
Third Row Seat			250	250	325	325
2WD	1		(675)	(675)	(910)	(910)

SANTA FE AWD—V6—Truck Equipment Schedule T2
SE Sport Utility 4D	SH73E	26295	5975	6625	7225	10100
Third Row Seat			250	250	325	325
2WD	1		(675)	(675)	(910)	(910)

TRUCKS & VANS

Body Type	VIN	List	Trade-In Good	Very Good	Pvt-Party Good	Retail Excellent
VERACRUZ—V6—Truck Equipment Schedule T1						
GLS Sport Util 4D	NU13C	28695	6550	7275	7375	9900
SE Sport Utility 4D	NU13C	30395	7075	7875	7950	10650
Limited Sport Util	NU73C	34695	7475	8300	8500	11500
AWD	7		525	525	640	640
ENTOURAGE—V6—Truck Equipment Schedule T1						
GLS Minivan	MC233	24495	3450	3850	4775	7175
SE Minivan	MC233	26995	3775	4200	5125	7700
Limited Minivan	MC233	29495	4375	4875	5800	8650

2008 HYUNDAI — KM8(JM12B)-8-#

Body Type	VIN	List	Trade-In Good	Very Good	Pvt-Party Good	Retail Excellent
TUCSON—4-Cyl.—Truck Equipment Schedule T1						
GLS Sport Util 4D	JM12B	20195	5025	5350	6100	8100
TUCSON—V6—Truck Equipment Schedule T1						
Limited Sport Util	JN12D	23545	5625	6075	6850	9300
4WD	7		1075	1075	1400	1400
TUCSON 4WD—V6—Truck Equipment Schedule T1						
SE Sport Utility 4D	JN72D	23645	6450	6925	7650	10400
2WD	1		(725)	(725)	(950)	(950)
SANTA FE—V6—Truck Equipment Schedule T2						
Limited Sport Util	SH13E	28945	7475	8100	8825	11700
Third Row Seat			250	250	330	330
AWD	7		800	800	1055	1055
SANTA FE AWD—V6—Truck Equipment Schedule T2						
GLS Sport Util 4D	SG73D	24995	6550	7100	7675	10100
SE Sport Utility 4D	SH73E	26495	7075	7675	8425	11150
Third Row Seat			250	250	330	330
2WD	1		(725)	(725)	(945)	(945)
VERACRUZ—V6—Truck Equipment Schedule T1						
GLS Sport Util 4D	NU13C	27595	7775	8425	8700	11100
SE Sport Utility 4D	NU13C	29295	7975	8650	8950	11450
Limited Sport Util	NU13C	34745	9075	9825	10100	12950
AWD	7		550	550	665	665
ENTOURAGE—V6—Truck Equipment Schedule T1						
GLS Minivan	MC233	24595	4675	5075	5950	8325
Limited Minivan	MC233	30495	5600	6100	7125	9875

2009 HYUNDAI — KM8(JM12B)-9-#

Body Type	VIN	List	Trade-In Good	Very Good	Pvt-Party Good	Retail Excellent
TUCSON—4-Cyl.—Truck Equipment Schedule T1						
GLS Sport Util 4D	JM12B	20695	5850	6200	7350	9575
TUCSON—V6—Truck Equipment Schedule T1						
Limited Sport Util	JN12D	24645	7175	7650	8725	11600
4WD	7		1150	1150	1545	1545
TUCSON 4WD—V6—Truck Equipment Schedule T1						
SE Sport Utility 4D	JN72D	24195	7525	8025	9125	12150
2WD	1		(825)	(825)	(1110)	(1110)
SANTA FE—V6—Truck Equipment Schedule T2						
Limited Sport Util	SH13E	29595	9050	9625	10600	13550
Third Row Seat			275	275	365	365
AWD	7		900	900	1160	1160
SANTA FE AWD—V6—Truck Equipment Schedule T2						
GLS Sport Util 4D	SG73D	25445	8025	8525	9400	11950
SE Sport Utility 4D	SH73E	27345	8625	9150	10100	12850
Third Row Seat			275	275	360	360
2WD	1		(825)	(825)	(1060)	(1060)
VERACRUZ—V6—Truck Equipment Schedule T1						
GLS Sport Util 4D	NU13C	29595	8875	9450	10250	12950
Limited Sport Util	NU13C	36745	9825	10450	11350	14350
AWD	7		625	625	770	770

2010 HYUNDAI — KM8(JT3AC)-A-#

Body Type	VIN	List	Trade-In Good	Very Good	Pvt-Party Good	Retail Excellent
TUCSON AWD—4-Cyl.—Truck Equipment Schedule T1						
GLS Sport Util 4D	JT3AC	20790	9475	9975	10750	13050
2WD	3		(950)	(950)	(1115)	(1115)
TUCSON—V6—Truck Equipment Schedule T1						
Limited Sport Util	JU3AC	25140	10500	11100	11650	14300
AWD	C		975	975	1145	1145
SANTA FE—V6—Truck Equipment Schedule T2						
Limited Sport Util	SKDAG	29390	11300	11850	13100	16100
AWD	D		975	975	1245	1245
4-Cyl, 2.4 Liter	B		(475)	(475)	(605)	(605)

Body Type	VIN	List	Trade-In Good	Very Good	Pvt-Party Good	Retail Excellent
SANTA FE AWD—4-Cyl.—Truck Equipment Schedule T2						
GLS Sport Util 4D	SGDAB	25490	**10400**	**10850**	**12050**	**14800**
2WD	3	......	(950)	(950)	(1200)	(1200)
SANTA FE AWD—V6—Truck Equipment Schedule T2						
SE Sport Util 4D	SHDAG	28690	**10850**	**11300**	**12550**	**15550**
2WD	3	......	(950)	(950)	(1200)	(1200)
VERACRUZ—V6—Truck Equipment Schedule T1						
GLS Sport Util 4D	NU4CC	30795	**9950**	**10400**	**11350**	**13800**
Limited Sport Util	NU4CC	36645	**11750**	**12300**	**13300**	**16150**
AWD	7	......	700	700	845	845

2011 HYUNDAI — KM8(JT3AB)-B-#

Body Type	VIN	List	Trade-In Good	Very Good	Pvt-Party Good	Retail Excellent
TUCSON—4-Cyl.—Truck Equipment Schedule T1						
GL Sport Utility	JT3AB	20540	**9850**	**10300**	**11350**	**13700**
GLS Sport Util 4D	JTCAC	24290	**11500**	**12050**	**13050**	**15900**
2WD	3	......	(1075)	(1075)	(1260)	(1260)
TUCSON—V6—Truck Equipment Schedule T1						
Limited Sport Util	JU3AC	25490	**12250**	**12900**	**13750**	**16750**
AWD	C	......	975	975	1145	1145
SANTA FE—V6—Truck Equipment Schedule T2						
Limited Sport Util	ZK4AG	29790	**12450**	**12850**	**14450**	**17300**
AWD	D	......	975	975	1150	1150
4-Cyl, 2.4 Liter	B	......	(475)	(475)	(575)	(575)
SANTA FE AWD—V6—Truck Equipment Schedule T2						
GLS Sport Util 4D	ZGDAG	25490	**11800**	**12150**	**13550**	**16150**
2WD	3	......	(1075)	(1075)	(1250)	(1250)
4-Cyl, 2.4 Liter	B	......	(475)	(475)	(570)	(570)
SANTA FE AWD—V6—Truck Equipment Schedule T2						
SE Sport Util 4D	ZHDAG	28690	**12050**	**12400**	**13900**	**16600**
2WD	3	......	(1075)	(1075)	(1250)	(1250)
VERACRUZ—V6—Truck Equipment Schedule T1						
GLS Sport Util 4D	NU4CC	30840	**11750**	**12100**	**13650**	**16350**
Limited Sport Util	NU4CC	36690	**13250**	**13650**	**15400**	**18500**
AWD	7	......	775	775	950	950

2012 HYUNDAI — 5(NMorXY)orKM8(JT3AB)-C-#

Body Type	VIN	List	Trade-In Good	Very Good	Pvt-Party Good	Retail Excellent
TUCSON—4-Cyl.—Truck Equipment Schedule T1						
GL Sport Utility 4D	JT3AB	20855	**10800**	**11300**	**12450**	**14750**
TUCSON—V6—Truck Equipment Schedule T1						
Limited Sport Util	JU3AC	25705	**13150**	**13750**	**14950**	**17900**
AWD	D	......	1075	1075	1250	1250
TUCSON AWD—4-Cyl.—Truck Equipment Schedule T1						
GLS Sport Utility	JUCAC	24655	**12650**	**13250**	**14450**	**17300**
2WD	3	......	(1500)	(1500)	(1730)	(1730)
SANTA FE—4-Cyl.—Truck Equipment Schedule T2						
Limited Sport Util	ZK4AG	30035	**13700**	**14000**	**15800**	**18550**
AWD	D	......	1075	1075	1260	1260
V6, 3.5 Liter	G	......	500	500	580	580
SANTA FE AWD—V6—Truck Equipment Schedule T2						
GLS Sport Util 4D	ZGDAG	27635	**13700**	**14000**	**15700**	**18250**
2WD	3,4	......	(1500)	(1500)	(1725)	(1725)
4-Cyl, 2.4 Liter	B	......	(500)	(500)	(565)	(565)
SANTA FE AWD—V6—Truck Equipment Schedule T2						
SE Sport Util 4D	ZHDAG	28920	**13650**	**13900**	**15650**	**18300**
2WD	4	......	(1500)	(1500)	(1735)	(1735)
VERACRUZ—V6—Truck Equipment Schedule T1						
GLS Sport Util 4D	NU4CC	29155	**13900**	**14200**	**16050**	**18850**
Limited Sport Util	NU4CC	35305	**15100**	**15450**	**17350**	**20400**
AWD	D	......	850	850	1025	1025

2013 HYUNDAI — 5(NMorXY)orKM8(JT3AB)-D-#

Body Type	VIN	List	Trade-In Good	Very Good	Pvt-Party Good	Retail Excellent
TUCSON—4-Cyl.—Truck Equipment Schedule T1						
GL Sport Utility 4D	JT3AB	21070	**12900**	**13450**	**14700**	**17250**
TUCSON AWD—4-Cyl.—Truck Equipment Schedule T1						
GLS Sport Utility	JU3AC	24920	**14050**	**14650**	**15900**	**18750**
Limited Sport Util	JUCAC	27770	**15350**	**15950**	**17250**	**20300**
2WD	3	......	(1275)	(1275)	(1455)	(1455)
SANTA FE SPORT AWD—4-Cyl.—Truck Equipment Schedule T2						
Sport Utility 4D	ZTDLB	27025	**16750**	**17000**	**18750**	**21400**
2WD	3	......	(1275)	(1275)	(1435)	(1435)
SANTA FE SPORT AWD—4-Cyl. Turbo—Truck Equipment Schedule T2						
2.0T Sport Util 4D	ZUDLA	30275	**18950**	**19250**	**21100**	**24000**

TRUCKS & VANS

TRUCKS & VANS

Body Type	VIN	List	Trade-In Good	Very Good	Pvt-Party Good	Retail Excellent
2WD	3		(1275)	(1275)	(1445)	(1445)
SANTA FE AWD—V6—Truck Equipment Schedule T2						
GLS Sport Util	SMDHF	30945	19250	19550	21100	23600
FWD	4		(1500)	(1500)	(1645)	(1645)
SANTA FE—V6—Truck Equipment Schedule T2						
Limited Sport Util	SR4HF	33945	21200	21500	22800	25400
AWD	D		1200	1200	1310	1310

2014 HYUNDAI — 5(NMorXY)orKM8(JUDAF)-E-#

Body Type	VIN	List	Trade-In Good	Very Good	Pvt-Party Good	Retail Excellent
TUCSON AWD—4-Cyl.—Truck Equipment Schedule T1						
GLS Sport Utility	JUDAF	23805	15800	16450	17450	20100
SE Sport Utility	JUDAG	25855	16400	17050	18050	20800
Limited Sport Utility	JUDAG	28555	18050	18800	19650	22500
2WD	3,4		(1500)	(1500)	(1675)	(1675)
SANTA FE SPORT AWD—4-Cyl.—Truck Equipment Schedule T1						
Sport Utility 4D	ZUDLB	27385	17450	17700	19700	22600
2WD	3		(1375)	(1375)	(1570)	(1570)
SANTA FE SPORT AWD—4-Cyl. Turbo—Truck Equipment Schedule T1						
2.0T Sport Utility	ZWDLA	33085	20800	21100	23100	26400
2WD	3		(1375)	(1375)	(1575)	(1575)
SANTA FE AWD—V6—Truck Equipment Schedule T1						
GLS Sport Util	SMDHF	32405	21900	22200	23700	26400
FWD	4		(1500)	(1500)	(1640)	(1640)
SANTA FE—V6—Truck Equipment Schedule T1						
Limited Sport Util	SN4HF	34555	23100	23500	25000	28000
AWD	D		1325	1325	1460	1460

INFINITI

2000 INFINITI — JNR(AR05Y)-Y-#

Body Type	VIN	List	Trade-In Good	Very Good	Pvt-Party Good	Retail Excellent
QX4 4WD—V6—Truck Equipment Schedule T3						
Sport Utility 4D	AR05Y	36075	2175	2500	3000	4850

2001 INFINITI — JNR(DR07Y)-1-#

Body Type	VIN	List	Trade-In Good	Very Good	Pvt-Party Good	Retail Excellent
QX4 4WD—V6—Truck Equipment Schedule T3						
Sport Utility 4D	DR07Y	36075	2400	2775	3225	5175
2WD	X		(625)	(625)	(820)	(820)

2002 INFINITI — JNR(DR07Y)-2-#

Body Type	VIN	List	Trade-In Good	Very Good	Pvt-Party Good	Retail Excellent
QX4 4WD—V6—Truck Equipment Schedule T3						
Sport Utility 4D	DR07Y	36095	2825	3200	3600	5600
2WD	X		(700)	(700)	(935)	(935)

2003 INFINITI — JNR(AS08W)-3-#

Body Type	VIN	List	Trade-In Good	Very Good	Pvt-Party Good	Retail Excellent
FX35 AWD—V6—Truck Equipment Schedule T3						
Sport Utility 4D	AS08W	36245	6125	6600	7125	9675
Intelligent Cruise Ctrl			250	250	320	320
Sport Pkg			325	325	420	420
2WD	U		(775)	(775)	(1040)	(1040)
FX45 AWD—V8—Truck Equipment Schedule T3						
Sport Utility 4D	BS08W	44770	6175	6600	7400	9850
Intelligent Cruise Ctrl			250	250	320	320
QX4 4WD—V6—Truck Equipment Schedule T3						
Sport Utility 4D	DR09Y	36695	3450	3875	4225	6425
2WD	X		(775)	(775)	(1040)	(1040)

2004 INFINITI — JNR(AS08W)-4-#

Body Type	VIN	List	Trade-In Good	Very Good	Pvt-Party Good	Retail Excellent
FX35 AWD—V6—Truck Equipment Schedule T3						
Sport Utility 4D	AS08W	36395	6800	7275	7750	10400
Intelligent Cruise Ctrl			275	275	350	350
Sport Pkg			350	350	450	450
2WD	U		(875)	(875)	(1140)	(1140)
FX45 AWD—V8—Truck Equipment Schedule T3						
Sport Utility 4D	BS08W	44920	6800	7275	8200	10950
Intelligent Cruise Ctrl			275	275	355	355
QX56 4WD—V8—Truck Equipment Schedule T3						
Sport Utility 4D	AA08C	51080	6525	7125	7525	10600
Intelligent Cruise Ctrl			275	275	355	355
2WD			(875)	(875)	(1155)	(1155)

Body Type	VIN	List	Trade-In Good	Very Good	Pvt-Party Good	Retail Excellent
2005 INFINITI — JNR(AS08W)-5-#						
FX35 AWD—V6—Truck Equipment Schedule T3						
Sport Utility 4D	AS08W	37060	7350	7850	8650	11450
Adaptive Cruise Control			300	300	380	380
Sport Pkg			375	375	480	480
2WD	U		(950)	(950)	(1235)	(1235)
FX45 AWD—V8—Truck Equipment Schedule T3						
Sport Utility 4D	BS08W	46060	6950	7425	8675	11450
Adaptive Cruise Control			300	300	385	385
QX56 4WD—V8—Truck Equipment Schedule T3						
Sport Utility 4D	AA08C	51700	7675	8350	9000	12550
Adaptive Cruise Control			300	300	385	385
2WD			(950)	(950)	(1260)	(1260)
2006 INFINITI — JNR(AS08W)-6-#						
FX35 AWD—V6—Truck Equipment Schedule T3						
Sport Utility 4D	AS08W	40050	9625	10250	11000	14250
Adaptive Cruise Control			325	325	400	400
Sport Pkg			400	400	495	495
2WD	U		(625)	(625)	(800)	(800)
FX45 AWD—V8—Truck Equipment Schedule T3						
Sport Utility 4D	BS08W	50500	10450	11100	12150	15400
Adaptive Cruise Control			325	325	400	400
QX56 4WD—V8—Truck Equipment Schedule T3						
Sport Utility 4D	AA08C	53250	9625	10400	10850	14650
Adaptive Cruise Control			325	325	410	410
2WD	A		(625)	(625)	(820)	(820)
2007 INFINITI — JNR(AS08W)-7-#						
FX35 AWD—V6—Truck Equipment Schedule T3						
Sport Utility 4D	AS08W	40000	10750	11350	12100	15400
Adaptive Cruise Control			350	350	425	425
Sport Pkg			425	425	515	515
RWD	U		(675)	(675)	(850)	(850)
FX45 AWD—V8—Truck Equipment Schedule T3						
Sport Utility 4D	BS08W	50550	12250	12950	14000	17450
Adaptive Cruise Control			350	350	420	420
QX56 4WD—V8—Truck Equipment Schedule T3						
Sport Utility 4D	AA08C	53850	11600	12450	12750	16750
Adaptive Cruise Control			350	350	425	425
2WD	A		(675)	(675)	(855)	(855)
2008 INFINITI — JNR(AJ09E)-8-#						
EX35—V6—Truck Equipment Schedule T3						
Journey Sport Util	AJ09E	35665	11750	12650	12750	15850
Adaptive Cruise Control			375	375	420	420
AWD	F		800	800	925	925
EX35 AWD—V6—Truck Equipment Schedule T3						
Sport Utility 4D	AJ09F	33415	11750	12600	12700	15800
RWD			(725)	(725)	(845)	(845)
FX35 AWD—V6—Truck Equipment Schedule T3						
Sport Utility 4D	AS08W	40365	12350	13050	13700	16950
Adaptive Cruise Control			375	375	440	440
Sport Pkg			450	450	550	550
RWD	U		(725)	(725)	(880)	(880)
FX45 AWD—V8—Truck Equipment Schedule T3						
Sport Utility 4D	BS08W	50915	13200	13850	15050	18200
Adaptive Cruise Control			375	375	440	440
QX56 4WD—V8—Truck Equipment Schedule T3						
Sport Utility 4D	AA08C	56165	14450	15400	15600	19850
Adaptive Cruise Control			375	375	440	440
2WD	D		(725)	(725)	(885)	(885)
2009 INFINITI — JNR(AJ09E)-9-#						
EX35—V6—Truck Equipment Schedule T3						
Journey Sport Util	AJ09E	36865	12900	13650	14350	17500
Intelligent Cruise Ctrl			375	375	430	430
AWD	F		900	900	1035	1035
EX35 AWD—V6—Truck Equipment Schedule T3						
Sport Utility 4D	AJ09F	36065	12650	13350	14050	17150

Body Type	VIN	List	Trade-In Good	Very Good	Pvt-Party Good	Retail Excellent
RWD			(825)	(825)	(960)	(960)
FX35 AWD—V6—Truck Equipment Schedule T3						
Sport Utility 4D	AS18W	44465	16400	17100	17900	21300
Premium Pkg			700	700	805	805
Adaptive Cruise Control			375	375	435	435
RWD	U		(825)	(825)	(965)	(965)
FX50 AWD—V8—Truck Equipment Schedule T3						
Sport Utility 4D	BS18W	59265	18950	19800	20700	24000
Adaptive Cruise Control			375	375	430	430
Sport Pkg			500	500	585	585
QX56 4WD—V8—Truck Equipment Schedule T3						
Sport Utility 4D	AA08C	59015	17100	18000	18500	22700
Adaptive Cruise Control			375	375	445	445
2WD	D		(825)	(825)	(985)	(985)

2010 INFINITI — (5orJ)N(1,3or8)(AJOHP)–A–#

Body Type	VIN	List	Trade-In Good	Very Good	Pvt-Party Good	Retail Excellent
EX35—V6—Truck Equipment Schedule T3						
Journey Sport Util	AJOHP	36895	15850	16550	17250	20300
Intelligent Cruise Ctrl			400	400	440	440
Premium Pkg			750	750	835	835
AWD	R		975	975	1105	1105
EX35 AWD—V6—Truck Equipment Schedule T3						
Sport Utility 4D	AJOHR	36065	15700	16350	17050	20000
Intelligent Cruise Ctrl			400	400	440	440
Premium Pkg			750	750	835	835
RWD	P		(950)	(950)	(1075)	(1075)
FX35 AWD—V6—Truck Equipment Schedule T3						
Sport Utility 4D	AS1MW	44715	18150	18800	19850	23100
Premium Pkg			750	750	855	855
Adaptive Cruise Control			400	400	450	450
RWD	U		(950)	(950)	(1100)	(1100)
FX50 AWD—V8—Truck Equipment Schedule T3						
Sport Utility 4D	BS1MW	59265	23100	24000	24900	28300
Adaptive Cruise Control			400	400	440	440
Sport Pkg			550	550	630	630
QX56 4WD—V8—Truck Equipment Schedule T3						
Sport Utility 4D	ZA0NE	60015	20300	21100	21800	25800
Adaptive Cruise Control			400	400	450	450
2WD	F		(950)	(950)	(1110)	(1110)

2011 INFINITI — (5orJ)N(1or8)(AJOHP)–B–#

Body Type	VIN	List	Trade-In Good	Very Good	Pvt-Party Good	Retail Excellent
EX35—V6—Truck Equipment Schedule T3						
Journey Sport Util	AJOHP	37300	18350	18950	19800	22600
Intelligent Cruise Ctrl			425	425	460	460
Premium Pkg			800	800	870	870
AWD	R		975	975	1075	1075
EX35 AWD—V6—Truck Equipment Schedule T3						
Sport Utility 4D	AJOHR	36425	18000	18600	19500	22300
Intelligent Cruise Ctrl			425	425	460	460
Premium Pkg			800	800	870	870
RWD	P		(1075)	(1075)	(1175)	(1175)
FX35 AWD—V6—Truck Equipment Schedule T3						
Sport Utility 4D	AS1MW	43925	22200	22800	24000	27200
Adaptive Cruise Control			425	425	465	465
Premium Pkg			800	800	890	890
RWD	U		(1075)	(1075)	(1200)	(1200)
FX50 AWD—V8—Truck Equipment Schedule T3						
Sport Utility 4D	BS1MW	57275	25400	26300	27300	30600
Adaptive Cruise Control			425	425	460	460
Sport Pkg			600	600	675	675
QX56 4WD—V8—Truck Equipment Schedule T3						
Sport Utility 4D	AZ2NE	60665	30600	31600	32100	36300
Adaptive Cruise Control			425	425	460	460
2WD	F		(1075)	(1075)	(1185)	(1185)

2012 INFINITI — (5orJ)N(1or8)(AJOHP)–C–#

Body Type	VIN	List	Trade-In Good	Very Good	Pvt-Party Good	Retail Excellent
EX35—V6—Truck Equipment Schedule T3						
Journey Sport Util	AJOHP	38850	20900	21400	22400	25100
Intelligent Cruise Ctrl			450	450	480	480
Premium Pkg			850	850	915	915
AWD	R		1075	1075	1180	1180

Body Type	VIN	List	Trade-In Good	Very Good	Pvt-Party Good	Retail Excellent
EX35 AWD—V6—Truck Equipment Schedule T3						
Sport Utility 4D	AJ0HR	37895	20800	21300	22300	25000
Intelligent Cruise Ctrl			450	450	480	480
RWD	P		(1175)	(1175)	(1270)	(1270)
FX35 AWD—V6—Truck Equipment Schedule T3						
Sport Utility 4D	AS1MW	45795	25000	25600	27100	30200
Limited Edition	AS1MW	52445	27400	28000	29700	32800
Adaptive Cruise Control			450	450	490	490
Premium Pkg	U		850	850	935	935
RWD	U		(1175)	(1175)	(1300)	(1300)
FX50 AWD—V8—Truck Equipment Schedule T3						
Sport Utility 4D	BS1MW	60245	32200	33200	34200	37700
Adaptive Cruise Control			450	450	480	480
Sport Pkg			675	675	735	735
QX56 4WD—V8—Truck Equipment Schedule T3						
Sport Utililty 4D	AZ2NE	62790	35600	36600	37400	41400
Adaptive Cruise Control			450	450	480	480
2WD	F		(1500)	(1500)	(1640)	(1640)

Body Type	VIN	List	Trade-In Good	Very Good	Pvt-Party Good	Retail Excellent
JX35 AWD—V6—Truck Equipment Schedule T1						
Sport Utility 4D	AL0MM	42500	30100	30900	31900	35600
FWD	N		(1275)	(1275)	(1385)	(1385)
EX37—V6—Truck Equipment Schedule T3						
Journey Sport Util	BJ0HP	39600	24200	24700	26500	30000
Intelligent Cruise Ctrl			475	475	520	520
Premium Pkg			875	875	990	990
AWD	F,L,R		1200	1200	1350	1350
EX37 AWD—V6—Truck Equipment Schedule T3						
Sport Utility 4D	BJ0HR	38700	23500	23900	25800	29200
Intelligent Cruise Ctrl			475	475	520	520
RWD	E,K,P		(1275)	(1275)	(1420)	(1420)
FX37 AWD—V6—Truck Equipment Schedule T3						
Sport Utility 4D	CS1MW	46700	25800	26400	28100	31100
Limited Edition	CS1MW	53700	29600	30100	32100	35100
Adaptive Cruise Control			475	475	515	515
Premium Pkg			875	875	980	980
RWD	U,N,7,P		(1275)	(1275)	(1400)	(1400)
FX50 AWD—V8—Truck Equipment Schedule T3						
Sport Utility 4D	BS1MW	61600	35500	36600	37800	41600
Adaptive Cruise Control			475	475	510	510
QX56 4WD—V8—Truck Equipment Schedule T3						
Sport Utility 4D	AZ2NE	64740	37300	38100	39500	43200
Adaptive Cruise Control			475	475	505	505
Technology Pkg			450	450	480	480
Touring Pkg			900	900	965	965
2WD	D,F		(1500)	(1500)	(1630)	(1630)

Body Type	VIN	List	Trade-In Good	Very Good	Pvt-Party Good	Retail Excellent
QX50 AWD—V6—Truck Equipment Schedule T3						
Sport Utility 4D	BJ0HR	36795	27600	28100	29700	33300
RWD	P		(1375)	(1375)	(1510)	(1510)
QX50—V6—Truck Equipment Schedule T3						
Journey Sport Util	BJ0HP	38045	28500	29000	30700	34300
Premium Pkg			925	925	1025	1025
Technology Pkg			475	475	515	515
AWD	R		1325	1325	1465	1465
QX60 AWD—4-Cyl. Supercharged Hybrid—Truck Equipment Sch T3						
Sport Utility 4D	CL0MM	47495	35200	35900	36900	40600
Intelligent Cruise Ctrl			500	500	530	530
FWD	N		(1500)	(1500)	(1620)	(1620)
QX60 AWD—V6—Truck Equipment Schedule T3						
3.5 Sport Utility	AL0MM	43945	32200	32800	34000	37600
Intelligent Cruise Ctrl			500	500	535	535
Technology Pkg			475	475	510	510
Touring Pkg			925	925	1020	1020
FWD	N		(1500)	(1500)	(1635)	(1635)
QX70 AWD—V6—Truck Equipment Schedule T3						
3.7 Sport Utility	CS1MW	47395	30300	30900	32900	36000
Intelligent Cruise Ctrl			500	500	540	540
Technology Pkg			475	475	515	515
Touring Pkg			925	925	1025	1025

Body Type	VIN	List	Trade-In Good	Very Good	Pvt-Party Good	Retail Excellent
QX70 AWD—V8—Truck Equipment Schedule T3						
5.0 Sport Utility	BS1MW	62495	39000	40100	41200	45000
Technology Pkg			475	475	505	505
QX80 AWD—V8—Truck Equipment Schedule T3						
Sport Utility 4D	AZ2NE	66645	48700	49600	51400	55600
Intelligent Cruise Ctrl			500	500	525	525
Technology Pkg			475	475	500	500
Deluxe Touring Pkg			925	925	1000	1000
2WD	D,F		(1500)	(1500)	(1600)	(1600)

ISUZU

2000 ISUZU — (JAC,4S2or1GG)–(M57D)–Y–#

Body Type	VIN	List	Trade-In Good	Very Good	Pvt-Party Good	Retail Excellent
AMIGO 4WD—4-Cyl.—Truck Equipment Schedule T2						
S Sport Utility 2D	M57D	20190	1600	1825	2425	4125
Hard Top			50	50	65	65
2WD	K		(275)	(275)	(355)	(355)
V6, 3.2 Liter	W		350	350	460	460
RODEO 4WD—V6—Truck Equipment Schedule T1						
S Sport Utility 4D	M58W	24935	1225	1400	2075	3625
LS Sport Utility 4D	M58W	27615	1425	1625	2125	3575
LSE Sport Util 4D	M58W	31760	2000	2300	2900	4825
2WD	K		(525)	(525)	(715)	(715)
4-Cyl, 2.2 Liter	D		(300)	(300)	(400)	(400)
VEHICROSS 4WD—V6—Truck Equipment Schedule T1						
Sport Utility 2D	N57X	31045	4375	5000	5150	7800
TROOPER 4WD—V6—Truck Equipment Schedule T1						
S Sport Utility 4D	J58X	29445	1050	1225	1800	3100
LS Sport Utility 4D	J58X	31145	1725	2000	2650	4550
Limited Spt Utl 4D	J58X	35193	1825	2100	2875	4925
2WD			(325)	(325)	(425)	(425)
HOMBRE—4-Cyl.—Truck Equipment Schedule T2						
S Short Bed	S144	11855	1425	1575	2300	3925
XS Short Bed	S144	13355	1650	1825	2625	4475
S Spacecab	S194	14180	1825	2025	2925	4975
XS Spacecab	S194	16005	2200	2425	3425	5850
Third Door			100	100	135	135
4WD	T		400	400	535	535
V6, 4.3 Liter	W		125	125	165	165

2001 ISUZU — (JACor4S2)–(M57W)–1–#

Body Type	VIN	List	Trade-In Good	Very Good	Pvt-Party Good	Retail Excellent
RODEO SPORT 4WD—V6—Truck Equipment Schedule T2						
Soft Top 2D	M57W	20270	2650	3050	3450	5425
Hard Top 2D	M57W	20880	2750	3150	3550	5600
2WD	K		(625)	(625)	(820)	(820)
4-Cyl, 2.2 Liter	D		(300)	(300)	(400)	(400)
RODEO 4WD—V6—Truck Equipment Schedule T1						
S Sport Utility 4D	M58W	26025	1600	1825	2525	4350
LS Sport Utility 4D	M58W	27480	1650	1875	2375	3950
LSE Sport Util 4D	M58W	31950	2250	2575	3175	5200
2WD	K		(625)	(625)	(820)	(820)
4-Cyl, 2.2 Liter	D		(300)	(300)	(400)	(400)
VEHICROSS 4WD—V6—Truck Equipment Schedule T1						
Sport Utility 2D	N57X	31045	5225	5950	5925	8800
TROOPER 4WD—V6—Truck Equipment Schedule T1						
S Sport Utility 4D	J58X	29690	1300	1500	2025	3350
LS Sport Utility 4D	J58X	31285	2075	2375	3025	5000
Limited Spt Util 4D	J58X	35333	2200	2525	3300	5525
2WD			(375)	(375)	(490)	(490)

2002 ISUZU — (JACor4S2)–(M57W)–2–#

Body Type	VIN	List	Trade-In Good	Very Good	Pvt-Party Good	Retail Excellent
RODEO SPORT 4WD—V6—Truck Equipment Schedule T2						
Soft Top 2D	M57W	22655	2975	3375	3675	5650
Hard Top 2D	M57W	22380	3475	3950	4225	6475
2WD			(700)	(700)	(935)	(935)
4-Cyl, 2.2 Liter	D		(325)	(325)	(445)	(445)
RODEO 4WD—V6—Truck Equipment Schedule T1						
S Sport Utility 4D	M58W	25305	1850	2100	2775	4600
LS Sport Utility 4D	M58W	28355	2025	2325	2875	4650
LSE Sport Util 4D	M58W	32340	2725	3100	3650	5825
2WD	K		(700)	(700)	(935)	(935)

Body Type	VIN	List	Trade-In Good	Trade-In Very Good	Pvt-Party Good	Retail Excellent
4-Cyl, 2.2 Liter	D		(325)	(325)	(445)	(445)
AXIOM 4WD—V6—Truck Equipment Schedule T1						
Sport Utility 4D	F58X	29625	1925	2200	2750	4400
XS Sport Utility 4D	F58X	31945	2325	2650	3200	5100
2WD			(700)	(700)	(935)	(935)
TROOPER 4WD—V6—Truck Equipment Schedule T1						
S Sport Utility 4D	J58X	30015	1625	1850	2350	3825
LS Sport Utility 4D	J58X	33300	2425	2775	3400	5525
Limited Spt Util 4D	J58X	37270	2625	3000	3825	6350
2WD			(425)	(425)	(550)	(550)

2003 ISUZU — (4NUor4S2)–(K57D)–3–#

Body Type	VIN	List	Trade-In Good	Trade-In Very Good	Pvt-Party Good	Retail Excellent
RODEO SPORT—4-Cyl.—Truck Equipment Schedule T2						
S Soft Top 2D	K57D	14624	3275	3700	3975	5975
RODEO SPORT 4WD—V6—Truck Equipment Schedule T2						
S Hard Top 2D	M57W	20040	4600	5200	5525	8275
2WD	K		(775)	(775)	(1040)	(1040)
4-Cyl, 2.2 Liter	D		(375)	(375)	(485)	(485)
RODEO 4WD—V6—Truck Equipment Schedule T1						
S Sport Utility 4D	M58W	22004	2125	2425	3175	5200
2WD	K		(775)	(775)	(1040)	(1040)
4-Cyl, 2.2 Liter	D		(375)	(375)	(485)	(485)
AXIOM 4WD—V6—Truck Equipment Schedule T1						
S Sport Utility 4D	F58X	27620	2600	2950	3375	5250
XS Sport Utility 4D	F58X	30620	3050	3450	4000	6300
2WD	E		(775)	(775)	(1040)	(1040)
ASCENDER 4WD—6-Cyl.—Truck Equipment Schedule T1						
S Sport Utility 4D	T16S	31974	1975	2250	2825	4525
LS			325	325	445	445
Limited			575	575	760	760
2WD	S		(475)	(475)	(645)	(645)
V8, 5.3 Liter	T		200	200	275	275

2004 ISUZU — (4NUor4S2)–(M58W)–4–#

Body Type	VIN	List	Trade-In Good	Trade-In Very Good	Pvt-Party Good	Retail Excellent
RODEO 4WD—V6—Truck Equipment Schedule T1						
S Sport Utility 4D	M58W	23479	2500	2825	3650	5950
2WD	K		(875)	(875)	(1155)	(1155)
V6, 3.5 Liter	Y		350	350	460	460
AXIOM 4WD—V6—Truck Equipment Schedule T1						
S Sport Utility 4D	F58X	28149	3275	3675	4225	6500
XS Sport Utility 4D	F58X	31149	3700	4150	4850	7500
2WD	E		(875)	(875)	(1155)	(1155)
ASCENDER 4WD—6-Cyl.—Truck Equipment Schedule T1						
S Sport Utility 4D	T16S	31849	2300	2600	3300	5300
Third Row Seat	3		675	675	895	895
LS			375	375	485	485
Limited			625	625	845	845
2WD	S		(525)	(525)	(710)	(710)
V8, 5.3 Liter	P		225	225	300	300

2005 ISUZU — 4NU–(T16S)–5–#

Body Type	VIN	List	Trade-In Good	Trade-In Very Good	Pvt-Party Good	Retail Excellent
ASCENDER 4WD—6-Cyl.—Truck Equipment Schedule T1						
S Sport Utility 4D	T16S	32083	2700	3050	3875	5950
Third Row Seat	3		725	725	950	950
LS			400	400	530	530
Limited			700	700	925	925
2WD	S		(575)	(575)	(775)	(775)
V8, 5.3 Liter	M		250	250	320	320

2006 ISUZU — (1GGor4NU)–(S198)–6–#

Body Type	VIN	List	Trade-In Good	Trade-In Very Good	Pvt-Party Good	Retail Excellent
i280 EXTENDED CAB PICKUP—4-Cyl.—Truck Equipment Schedule T2						
S Short Bed	S198	17649	3850	4300	4950	7250
LS Short Bed	S198	19649	4500	5025	5625	8225
i350 CREW CAB PICKUP 4WD—5-Cyl.—Truck Equipment Schedule T2						
LS Short Bed	T136	28018	6175	6875	7550	11000
ASCENDER 4WD—6-Cyl.—Truck Equipment Schedule T1						
S Sport Utility 4D	T16S	31878	3325	3700	4550	6675
Third Row Seat	3		750	750	1010	1010
LS			425	425	570	570
Limited			750	750	1005	1005
2WD	S		(625)	(625)	(845)	(845)
V8, 5.3 Liter	M		250	250	345	345

Body Type	VIN	List	Trade-In Good	Very Good	Pvt-Party Good	Retail Excellent
2007 ISUZU — (1GGor4NU)–(S199)–7–#						
i290 EXTENDED CAB PICKUP—4-Cyl.—Truck Equipment Schedule T2						
S Short Bed	S199	17674	4550	5025	5700	8150
LS Short Bed	S199	20613	5250	5825	6625	9450
i370 EXTENDED CAB PICKUP—5-Cyl.—Truck Equipment Schedule T2						
LS Short Bed	S19E	21763	6175	6800	7575	10750
i370 CREW CAB PICKUP—5-Cyl.—Truck Equipment Schedule T2						
LS Short Bed	S13E	28043	6850	7550	8325	11800
4WD	T	......	1075	1075	1405	1405
ASCENDER 4WD—6-Cyl.—Truck Equipment Schedule T1						
S Sport Utility 4D	T13S	28694	4000	4425	5250	7425
LS		......	450	450	610	610
2WD	S	......	(675)	(675)	(910)	(910)
2008 ISUZU — (1GGor4NU)–(S199)–8–#						
i290 EXTENDED CAB PICKUP—4-Cyl.—Truck Equipment Schedule T2						
S Short Bed	S199	18084	5800	6275	7175	9650
i370 EXTENDED CAB PICKUP—5-Cyl.—Truck Equipment Schedule T2						
LS Short Bed	S19E	23084	7525	8125	9100	12200
i370 CREW CAB PICKUP—5-Cyl.—Truck Equipment Schedule T2						
LS Short Bed	S13E	25214	8325	9000	9950	13350
4WD	T	......	1225	1225	1530	1530
ASCENDER 4WD—6-Cyl.—Truck Equipment Schedule T1						
S Sport Utility 4D	T13S	29884	4475	4825	5675	7625
LS		......	500	500	640	640
2WD	S	......	(725)	(725)	(960)	(960)

JEEP

Body Type	VIN	List	Trade-In Good	Very Good	Pvt-Party Good	Retail Excellent
2000 JEEP — 1J4–(A29P)–Y–#						
WRANGLER 4WD—4-Cyl.—Truck Equipment Schedule T2						
SE Sport Utility 2D	A29P	16305	5100	5425	6275	8750
Rear Seat		......	50	50	65	65
Hard Top		......	250	250	335	335
WRANGLER 4WD—6-Cyl.—Truck Equipment Schedule T2						
Sport Utility 2D	A49S	18995	5675	6025	7150	10000
Sahara Spt Util 2D	A59S	20925	6175	6550	7725	10800
Rear Seat		......	50	50	65	65
Hard Top		......	250	250	335	335
CHEROKEE 4WD—6-Cyl.—Truck Equipment Schedule T1						
SE Sport Utility 2D	F27S	21285	1625	1800	2525	4225
SE Sport Utility 4D	F28S	22320	1675	1850	2700	4500
Sport 2D	F47S	21860	1900	2100	2975	4950
Sport 4D	F48S	22895	1950	2150	3050	5050
Classic Spt Ut 4D	F58S	23420	2150	2375	3300	5500
Limited Spt Ut 4D	F68S	25745	2625	2900	3825	6275
2WD	T	......	(525)	(525)	(715)	(715)
4-Cyl, 2.5 Liter		......	(300)	(300)	(400)	(400)
GRAND CHEROKEE 4WD—6-Cyl.—Truck Equipment Sch T1						
Laredo Sport Util 4D	W48S	29075	1225	1375	2100	3700
2WD	X	......	(525)	(525)	(715)	(715)
V8, 4.7 Liter	N	......	175	175	235	235
GRAND CHEROKEE 4WD—V8—Truck Equipment Schedule T3						
Limited Sport Util 4D	258N	35950	1675	1900	2825	4975
2WD	X	......	(525)	(525)	(715)	(715)
6-Cyl, 4.0 Liter	S	......	(150)	(150)	(200)	(200)
2001 JEEP — 1J4–(A29P)–1–#						
WRANGLER 4WD—4-Cyl.—Truck Equipment Schedule T2						
SE Sport Utility 2D	A29P	16095	5325	5650	6450	8875
Rear Seat		......	50	50	65	65
Hard Top		......	250	250	335	335
WRANGLER 4WD—6-Cyl.—Truck Equipment Schedule T2						
Sport Utility 2D	A49S	19615	6125	6500	7500	10300
Sahara Spt Util 2D	A59S	22895	6925	7325	8400	11550
Hard Top		......	250	250	335	335
CHEROKEE 4WD—6-Cyl.—Truck Equipment Schedule T1						
SE Sport Utility 2D	F27S	21780	2125	2325	3050	4900
SE Sport Utility 4D	F28S	22815	2275	2500	3225	5175

Body Type	VIN	List	Trade-In Good	Trade-In Very Good	Pvt-Party Good	Retail Excellent
Sport Utility 2D	F47S	22410	2475	2750	3500	5600
Sport Utility 4D	F48S	23445	2525	2800	3575	5700
Classic Spt Ut 4D	F58S	23835	2775	3075	3875	6175
Limited Spt Ut 4D	F68S	23970	3375	3700	4500	7075
2WD			(625)	(625)	(820)	(820)
GRAND CHEROKEE 4WD—6-Cyl.—Truck Equipment Sch T1						
Laredo Sport Util 4D	W48S	29855	1400	1575	2250	3850
2WD	X		(625)	(625)	(820)	(820)
V8, 4.7 Liter	N		200	200	260	260
GRAND CHEROKEE 4WD—V8—Truck Equipment Schedule T3						
Limited Spt Ut 4D	W58N	35870	1950	2175	3050	5200
2WD	X		(625)	(625)	(820)	(820)
6-Cyl, 4.0 Liter	S		(150)	(150)	(200)	(200)

Body Type	VIN	List	Trade-In Good	Trade-In Very Good	Pvt-Party Good	Retail Excellent
WRANGLER 4WD—4-Cyl.—Truck Equipment Schedule T2						
SE Sport Utility 2D	A29P	16410	5475	5800	6750	9175
Rear Seat			75	75	85	85
Hard Top			275	275	355	355
WRANGLER 4WD—6-Cyl.—Truck Equipment Schedule T2						
X Sport Utility 2D	A49S	18895	6575	6950	7825	10550
Sport Utility 2D	A49S	20665	6975	7375	8275	11100
Sahara Spt Util 2D	A59S	24035	7650	8100	9050	12150
Hard Top			275	275	355	355
LIBERTY 4WD—V6—Truck Equipment Schedule T1						
Sport Utility 4D	L48K	21070	1800	2025	2800	4700
Limited Utility 4D	L58K	23305	2400	2675	3475	5725
Renegade Utility 4D	L38K	23855	2475	2775	3550	5850
2WD	K		(700)	(700)	(935)	(935)
4-Cyl, 2.4 Liter	1		(250)	(250)	(345)	(345)
GRAND CHEROKEE 4WD—6-Cyl.—Truck Equipment Schedule T1						
Laredo Sport Util 4D	W48S	27995	1575	1750	2575	4375
Sport Utility 4D	W38S	29140	1675	1875	2700	4575
2WD	X		(700)	(700)	(935)	(935)
V8, 4.7 Liter	N		200	200	280	280
GRAND CHEROKEE 4WD—V8—Truck Equipment Schedule T3						
Limited Spt Ut 4D	W58N	33300	2275	2550	3425	5750
Overland Spt Utl 4D	W68N	37430	2350	2625	3525	5900
2WD	X		(700)	(700)	(935)	(935)
6-Cyl, 4.0 Liter	S		(200)	(200)	(265)	(265)

Body Type	VIN	List	Trade-In Good	Trade-In Very Good	Pvt-Party Good	Retail Excellent
WRANGLER 4WD—4-Cyl.—Truck Equipment Schedule T2						
SE Sport Utility 2D	A291	16910	6525	6900	7600	9975
Rear Seat			100	100	120	120
Hard Top			300	300	380	380
WRANGLER 4WD—6-Cyl.—Truck Equipment Schedule T2						
X Sport Utility 2D	A39S	19295	8050	8500	9250	12100
"Sport" Spt Util 2D	A49S	21930	8575	9050	9850	12900
Sahara Spt Util 2D	A59S	24695	9075	9575	10350	13600
Rubicon Spt Utl 2D	A59S	24995	9575	10100	10950	14300
Hard Top			300	300	375	375
LIBERTY 4WD—V6—Truck Equipment Schedule T1						
Sport Utility 4D	L48K	21880	2500	2775	3450	5525
Limited Utility 4D	L58K	24045	3075	3400	4100	6500
Renegade Utility 4D	L38K	24630	3175	3500	4175	6625
2WD	K		(775)	(775)	(1040)	(1040)
4-Cyl, 2.4 Liter	1		(300)	(300)	(405)	(405)
GRAND CHEROKEE 4WD—6-Cyl.—Truck Equipment Schedule T1						
Laredo Sport Util 4D	W48S	28640	2425	2700	3325	5325
2WD	X		(775)	(775)	(1040)	(1040)
V8, 4.7 Liter	N		325	325	435	435
GRAND CHEROKEE 4WD—V8—Truck Equipment Schedule T3						
Limited Spt Util 4D	W58N	34920	3400	3775	4475	7100
Overland Spt Utl 4D	W68J	37975	3500	3875	4600	7275
2WD	X		(775)	(775)	(1040)	(1040)
6-Cyl, 4.0 Liter	S		(275)	(275)	(365)	(365)

Body Type	VIN	List	Trade-In Good	Trade-In Very Good	Pvt-Party Good	Retail Excellent
WRANGLER 4WD—4-Cyl.—Truck Equipment Schedule T2						
SE Sport Utility 2D	A291	17515	7350	7750	8325	10650
Rear Seat			100	100	125	125

TRUCKS & VANS

Body Type	VIN	List	Trade-In Good	Very Good	Pvt-Party Good	Retail Excellent
Hard Top	....	....	325	325	395	395
WRANGLER 4WD—6-Cyl.—Truck Equipment Schedule T2						
X Sport Utility 2D	A39S	19945	9375	9875	10500	13400
"Sport" SUV 2D	A49S	22755	9625	10150	10850	13900
Unlimited Util LWB	A29S	24995	9850	10400	11150	14350
Sahara Spt Util 2D	A59S	25520	9800	10300	11100	14300
Rubicon Spt Utl 2D	A69S	25695	10550	11100	11800	15100
Hard Top	....	....	325	325	390	390
LIBERTY 4WD—V6—Truck Equipment Schedule T1						
Sport Utility 4D	L48K	21855	2925	3250	3925	6150
Limited Utility 4D	L58K	24870	3500	3850	4525	7050
Renegade Utility 4D	L38K	25455	3550	3925	4675	7250
2WD	K	....	(875)	(875)	(1155)	(1155)
4-Cyl, 2.4 Liter	1	....	(350)	(350)	(465)	(465)
GRAND CHEROKEE 4WD—6-Cyl.—Truck Equipment Schedule T1						
Laredo Sport Util 4D	W48S	29875	2825	3100	3825	6025
2WD	X	....	(875)	(875)	(1155)	(1155)
V8, 4.7 Liter	N,J	....	250	250	325	325
GRAND CHEROKEE 4WD—V8—Truck Equipment Schedule T3						
Limited Spt Util 4D	W58N	35655	3475	3850	4775	7500
Overland Spt Util 4D	W68J	39920	3900	4325	5250	8225
2WD	X	....	(875)	(875)	(1155)	(1155)
6-Cyl, 4.0 Liter	S	....	(325)	(325)	(445)	(445)

2005 JEEP — 1J(4or8)-(A291)-5-#

Body Type	VIN	List	Trade-In Good	Very Good	Pvt-Party Good	Retail Excellent
WRANGLER 4WD—4-Cyl.—Truck Equipment Schedule T2						
SE Sport Utility 2D	A291	18510	7875	8300	9050	11300
Rear Seat	....	....	100	100	120	120
6-Cyl, 4.0 Liter	S	....	775	775	935	935
WRANGLER 4WD—6-Cyl.—Truck Equipment Schedule T2						
X Sport Utility 2D	A39S	20820	10050	10550	11250	14000
"Sport" SUV 2D	A49S	24725	11200	11750	12550	15750
Unlimited Util LWB	A44S	25480	11700	12300	13100	16400
Rubicon Spt Utl 2D	A69S	27825	12100	12750	13550	17050
Rubicon LWB Util 2D	A69S	29025	14600	15350	15950	19800
Unltd Rubicon LWB	A69S	29195	10400	11250	11400	15150
Hard Top	....	....	350	350	405	405
LIBERTY 4WD—V6—Truck Equipment Schedule T1						
Sport Utility 4D	L48K	22985	3350	3700	4625	6950
Renegade Utility 4D	L38K	24920	4100	4550	5450	8150
Limited Utility 4D	L58K	25645	4025	4450	5375	8025
2WD	K	....	(950)	(950)	(1260)	(1260)
4-Cyl, 2.4 Liter	1	....	(400)	(400)	(520)	(520)
4-Cyl, 2.8L, Turbo Dsl	5	....	1425	1425	1905	1905
GRAND CHEROKEE 4WD—V6—Truck Equipment Schedule T1						
Laredo Sport Util 4D	R48K	28745	3950	4375	5300	7925
2WD	S	....	(950)	(950)	(1260)	(1260)
V8, 4.7 Liter	N	....	250	250	345	345
GRAND CHEROKEE 4WD—V8—Truck Equipment Schedule T3						
Limited Spt Util 4D	R58N	34690	5150	5700	6800	10100
2WD	S	....	(950)	(950)	(1260)	(1260)
V8, HEMI, 5.7 Liter	2	....	250	250	345	345

2006 JEEP — 1J(4or8)-(A291)-6-#

Body Type	VIN	List	Trade-In Good	Very Good	Pvt-Party Good	Retail Excellent
WRANGLER 4WD—4-Cyl.—Truck Equipment Schedule T2						
SE Sport Utility 2D	A291	18730	8375	8800	9550	11800
Rear Seat	....	....	100	100	120	120
6-Cyl, 4.0 Liter	S	....	825	825	975	975
WRANGLER 4WD—6-Cyl.—Truck Equipment Schedule T2						
X Sport Utility 2D	A39S	21040	10900	11400	12150	15000
"Sport" SUV 2D	A49S	24725	11650	12250	13100	16300
Unlimited LWB Util.	A44S	25480	12400	13000	13800	17100
Rubicon Spt Utl 2D	A69S	28125	12800	13400	14250	17650
Unltd Rubicon LWB	A69S	29125	11200	12050	12400	16250
Hard Top	....	....	375	375	435	435
LIBERTY 4WD—V6—Truck Equipment Schedule T1						
Sport Utility 4D	L48K	23965	4400	4825	5625	8125
Renegade Utility 4D	L38K	25855	5050	5525	6500	9375
Limited Utility 4D	L58K	27405	5100	5600	6525	9375
2WD	K	....	(1025)	(1025)	(1375)	(1375)
4-Cyl, 2.8L, Turbo Dsl	5	....	1550	1550	2050	2050

Body Type	VIN	List	Trade-In Good	Very Good	Pvt-Party Good	Retail Excellent

COMMANDER 4WD—V6—Truck Equipment Schedule T1
Sport Utility 4D	G48K	29985	5150	5550	6475	8900
2WD	H		(1025)	(1025)	(1375)	(1375)
V8, 4.7 Liter	N		525	525	700	700

COMMANDER 4WD—V8—Truck Equipment Schedule T1
Limited Spt Util 4D	G58N	38900	6950	7475	8550	11850
2WD	H		(1025)	(1025)	(1375)	(1375)
V8, HEMI, 5.7 Liter	2		275	275	370	370

GRAND CHEROKEE 4WD—V6—Truck Equipment Schedule T1
Laredo Sport Util 4D	R48K	29830	4925	5400	6150	8850
2WD	S		(1025)	(1025)	(1375)	(1375)
V8, 4.7 Liter	N		275	275	370	370

GRAND CHEROKEE 4WD—V8—Truck Equipment Schedule T3
Limited Spt Util 4D	R58N	36700	6525	7150	8150	11750
2WD	S		(1025)	(1025)	(1375)	(1375)
V8, HEMI, 5.7 Liter	2		275	275	370	370

GRAND CHEROKEE 4WD—V8 HEMI—Truck Equipment Schedule T3
SRT8 Sport Util 4D	R783	39995	14350	15050	16250	20400
Overland Spt Utl 4D	R682	42925	7250	7925	8975	12950
2WD	S		(1025)	(1025)	(1375)	(1375)

PATRIOT 4WD—4-Cyl.—Truck Equipment Schedule T1
Sport Utility 4D	F28W	17785	4700	4925	6225	8300
Limited Spt Util 4D	F48W	22785	5350	5625	7200	9625
2WD	T		(1100)	(1100)	(1480)	(1480)

COMPASS 4WD—4-Cyl.—Truck Equipment Schedule T1
Sport SUV 4D	F47W	17585	4225	4675	5250	7375
Limited Spt Util 4D	F57W	21740	4750	5250	5850	8300
2WD	T		(1100)	(1100)	(1480)	(1480)

WRANGLER 4WD—V6—Truck Equipment Schedule T2
X Sport Utility 2D	A241	19970	12050	12600	13400	16250
Unlimited X Spt Util	A391	23235	14650	15300	16100	19550
Sahara Spt Util 2D	A541	24785	13950	14600	15450	18750
Unltd Sahara Util 4D	A591	27560	15950	16700	17500	21300
Rubicon Spt Util 2D	A641	26750	14650	15350	16200	19650
Unltd Rubicon 4D	A691	29720	16250	17300	17300	21900
Hard Top			400	400	460	460
2WD	B		(1100)	(1100)	(1300)	(1300)

LIBERTY 4WD—V6—Truck Equipment Schedule T1
Sport Utility 4D	L48K	23460	5275	5750	6575	9100
Limited Utility 4D	L58K	27045	6350	6900	7700	10600
2WD	K		(1100)	(1100)	(1480)	(1480)

COMMANDER 4WD—V6—Truck Equipment Schedule T1
Sport Utility 4D	G48K	31080	6375	6825	7675	10250
2WD	H		(1100)	(1100)	(1480)	(1480)
V8, 4.7 Liter	N		625	625	845	845

COMMANDER 4WD—V8—Truck Equipment Schedule T1
Limited Sport Util	G58N	39215	8900	9500	10450	13850
2WD	H		(1100)	(1100)	(1480)	(1480)
V8, HEMI, 5.7 Liter	2		300	300	390	390

COMMANDER 4WD—V8 HEMI—Truck Equipment Schedule T1
| Overland Sport Util | G682 | 44545 | 9775 | 10450 | 11100 | 14500 |
| 2WD | H | | (1100) | (1100) | (1405) | (1405) |

GRAND CHEROKEE 4WD—V6—Truck Equipment Schedule T1
Laredo Sport Util 4D	R48K	30205	5900	6425	7300	10100
2WD	S		(1100)	(1100)	(1480)	(1480)
V8, 4.7 Liter	N		300	300	390	390

GRAND CHEROKEE 4WD—V8—Truck Equipment Schedule T3
Limited Sport Util 4D	R58N	37890	7525	8150	9225	12950
2WD	S		(1100)	(1100)	(1480)	(1480)
V6, Turbo Dsl 3.0L	M		875	875	1175	1175
V8, HEMI, 5.7 Liter	2		300	300	390	390

GRAND CHEROKEE 4WD—V8 HEMI—Truck Equipment Schedule T3
SRT8 Sport Util 4D	R783	40675	16750	17500	18550	22800
Overland Spt Util 4D	R682	43260	8625	9350	10350	14400
2WD	S		(1100)	(1100)	(1480)	(1480)
V6, Turbo Dsl 3.0L	M		875	875	1175	1175

PATRIOT 4WD—4-Cyl.—Truck Equipment Schedule T1
| Sport SUV 4D | F28W | 18885 | 4875 | 5100 | 6750 | 8850 |

Body Type	VIN	List	Trade-In Good	Very Good	Pvt-Party Good	Retail Excellent
Limited Spt Util 4D	F48W	23605	6225	6500	8275	10800
2WD	T		(1200)	(1200)	(1595)	(1595)
COMPASS 4WD—4-Cyl.—Truck Equipment Schedule T1						
Sport SUV 4D	F47W	20905	5225	5650	6400	8450
Limited Utility 4D	F57W	24885	6225	6725	7450	9850
2WD	T		(1200)	(1200)	(1555)	(1555)
WRANGLER 4WD—V6—Truck Equipment Schedule T2						
X Sport Utility 2D	A241	20195	13400	13950	14950	17800
Unlimited X Spt Util	A391	24115	15650	16300	17300	20600
Sahara Spt Util 2D	A541	25650	15350	15950	17000	20200
Unltd Sahara Util 4D	A591	29025	17900	18600	19650	23400
Rubicon Spt Utl 2D	A641	27880	16000	16600	17650	21000
Unltd Rubicon 4D	A691	31020	18950	19950	20300	24700
Hard Top			400	400	450	450
2WD	B		(1200)	(1200)	(1350)	(1350)
LIBERTY 4WD—V6—Truck Equipment Schedule T1						
Sport Utility 4D	N28K	23425	7650	8200	9150	12050
Limited Utility 4D	N58K	26785	8925	9550	10650	14100
2WD			(1200)	(1200)	(1595)	(1595)
COMMANDER 4WD—V6—Truck Equipment Schedule T1						
Sport Utility 4D	G48K	30095	7475	7900	8950	11450
2WD	H		(1200)	(1200)	(1580)	(1580)
V8, 4.7 Liter	N		675	675	900	900
COMMANDER 4WD—V8—Truck Equipment Schedule T1						
Limited Sport Util	G58N	39620	10350	10900	12000	15200
2WD	H		(1200)	(1200)	(1555)	(1555)
V8, HEMI, 5.7 Liter	2		475	475	610	610
COMMANDER 4WD—V8 HEMI—Truck Equipment Schedule T1						
Overland Sport Util	G682	44545	12250	12900	13800	17300
2WD	H		(1200)	(1200)	(1460)	(1460)
GRAND CHEROKEE 4WD—V6—Truck Equipment Schedule T1						
Laredo Sport Util	R48K	31085	7300	7825	8625	11250
2WD	S		(1200)	(1200)	(1520)	(1520)
V6, Turbo Dsl 3.0L	M		2000	2000	2530	2530
V8, Flex Fuel, 4.7 Liter	N		675	675	870	870
GRAND CHEROKEE 4WD—V8 HEMI—Truck Equipment Schedule T3						
Limited Spt Util 4D	R582	39930	10350	11050	11850	15350
2WD	S		(1200)	(1200)	(1525)	(1525)
V6, Turbo Dsl 3.0L	M		250	250	315	315
V8, Flex Fuel, 4.7 Liter	N		(650)	(650)	(820)	(820)
GRAND CHEROKEE 4WD—V8 HEMI—Truck Equipment Schedule T3						
SRT8 Sport Util 4D	R783	41220	18400	19150	20200	24100
Overland Sport Util	R682	44135	11500	12300	13150	17050
2WD	S		(1200)	(1200)	(1535)	(1535)
V6, Turbo Dsl 3.0L	M		925	925	1200	1200

2009 JEEP — 1J(4or8)-(F28B)-9-#

Body Type	VIN	List	Trade-In Good	Very Good	Pvt-Party Good	Retail Excellent
PATRIOT 4WD—4-Cyl.—Truck Equipment Schedule T1						
Sport SUV 4D	F28B	20220	6300	6525	8175	10300
Limited Spt Util 4D	F48B	24910	7650	7925	9725	12250
2WD	T		(1275)	(1275)	(1695)	(1695)
COMPASS 4WD—4-Cyl.—Truck Equipment Schedule T1						
Sport SUV 4D	F47B	21945	6725	7125	8075	10200
Limited Util 4D	F57B	26305	7325	7775	8950	11550
2WD	T		(1275)	(1275)	(1615)	(1615)
WRANGLER 4WD—V6—Truck Equipment Schedule T2						
X Sport Utility 2D	A241	21385	14000	14500	15700	18400
Unlimited X Spt Util	A391	24915	16850	17450	18600	21600
Sahara Spt Util 2D	A541	27195	16100	16650	17750	20600
Unltd Sahara Util 4D	A591	29845	19500	20200	21400	24900
Rubicon Spt Utl 2D	A641	28890	17350	18000	19150	22300
Unltd Rubicon 4D	A691	32990	21000	21900	22500	26500
Hard Top			450	450	505	505
2WD	B		(1275)	(1275)	(1410)	(1410)
LIBERTY 4WD—V6—Truck Equipment Schedule T1						
Sport SUV 4D	N28K	24520	9100	9625	10850	13850
Limited Utility 4D	N58K	27625	11000	11650	12900	16350
2WD			(1275)	(1275)	(1675)	(1675)
COMMANDER 4WD—V6—Truck Equipment Schedule T1						
Sport Utility 4D	G48K	32140	10050	10450	11700	14400
2WD			(1275)	(1275)	(1590)	(1590)
V8, 4.7 Liter	P		725	725	910	910

1015

Body Type	VIN	List	Trade-In Good	Very Good	Pvt-Party Good	Retail Excellent
COMMANDER 4WD—V8—Truck Equipment Schedule T1						
Limited Sport Util	G58P	41335	12200	12750	14200	17500
2WD	H	......	(1275)	(1275)	(1595)	(1595)
V8, HEMI, 5.7 Liter	T	......	625	625	770	770
COMMANDER 4WD—V8 HEMI—Truck Equipment Schedule T1						
Overland Sport Util	G68T	45940	14100	14750	16100	19600
2WD	H	......	(1275)	(1275)	(1560)	(1560)
GRAND CHEROKEE 4WD—V6—Truck Equipment Schedule T1						
Laredo Sport Util 4D	R48K	33200	9075	9600	10600	13250
2WD	S	......	(1275)	(1275)	(1580)	(1580)
V6, Turbo Dsl 3.0L	M	......	2100	2100	2605	2605
V8, Flex Fuel, 4.7 Liter	P	......	625	625	765	765
GRAND CHEROKEE 4WD—V8 HEMI—Truck Equipment Schedule T3						
Limited Spt Util 4D	R58T	41435	13250	14000	15250	19200
2WD	S	......	(1275)	(1275)	(1590)	(1590)
V6, Turbo Dsl 3.0L	M	......	225	225	285	285
V8, Flex Fuel, 4.7 Liter	P	......	(700)	(700)	(860)	(860)
GRAND CHEROKEE 4WD—V8 HEMI—Truck Equipment Schedule T3						
SRT8 Sport Util 4D	R78W	43745	23500	24300	25300	29300
GRAND CHEROKEE 4WD—V8 HEMI—Truck Equipment Schedule T3						
Overland Sport Util	R68T	45625	14050	14800	15900	19800
2WD	S	......	(1275)	(1275)	(1580)	(1580)
V6, Turbo Dsl 3.0L	M	......	975	975	1215	1215

2010 JEEP — 1J4–(F1GB)–A–#

Body Type	VIN	List	Trade-In Good	Very Good	Pvt-Party Good	Retail Excellent
PATRIOT 4WD—4-Cyl.—Truck Equipment Schedule T1						
Sport SUV 4D	F1GB	21176	7400	7650	9075	10900
Limited Spt Util 4D	F4GB	26280	9725	10050	11500	13650
2WD	T	......	(1350)	(1350)	(1635)	(1635)
COMPASS 4WD—4-Cyl.—Truck Equipment Schedule T1						
Sport SUV 4D	F1FB	18595	7875	8225	9500	11750
Limited SUV	F5FB	26865	10100	10550	11800	14450
2WD	T	......	(1350)	(1350)	(1695)	(1695)
WRANGLER 4WD—V6—Truck Equipment Schedule T2						
"Sport" SUV 2D	A2D1	22680	14850	15300	16700	19250
Unlimited "Sport" 4D	A3H1	26100	18950	19550	20700	23600
Sahara Spt Util 2D	A5D1	27770	17850	18450	19650	22500
Unltd Sahara Util 4D	A5H1	30420	21000	21700	22900	26200
Unlimited Spt RHD	Z3H1	28680	18100	18650	19900	22800
Rubicon Spt Util 2D	A6D1	29525	19150	19800	20900	23800
Unltd Rubicon 4D	A6H1	33565	22400	23200	24200	27900
Hard Top		......	525	525	585	585
2WD	B	......	(1350)	(1350)	(1485)	(1485)
LIBERTY 4WD—V6—Truck Equipment Schedule T1						
Sport SUV 4D	N2GK	25609	10500	11000	12150	14750
Renegade Spt Util	N3GK	28605	11750	12300	13500	16450
Limited Util 4D	N5GK	29480	12250	12800	14050	17100
2WD	P	......	(1350)	(1350)	(1675)	(1675)
COMMANDER 4WD—V6—Truck Equipment Schedule T1						
Sport Utility 4D	G4GK	34295	11550	11950	13300	15750
2WD	H	......	(1350)	(1350)	(1615)	(1615)
V8, HEMI, 5.7 Liter	T	......	925	925	1085	1085
COMMANDER 4WD—V8 HEMI—Truck Equipment Schedule T1						
Limited Sport Util	G5GT	43610	15950	16500	17950	21100
2WD	H	......	(1350)	(1350)	(1595)	(1595)
GRAND CHEROKEE 4WD—V6—Truck Equipment Schedule T1						
Laredo Sport Util	R4GK	33460	10900	11400	12600	15300
2WD	S	......	(1350)	(1350)	(1665)	(1665)
V8, HEMI, 5.7 Liter	T	......	700	700	855	855
GRAND CHEROKEE 4WD—V8 HEMI—Truck Equipment Schedule T3						
Limited Spt Util 4D	R5GT	42540	15350	16050	17450	21200
2WD	S	......	(1350)	(1350)	(1670)	(1670)
V6, 3.7 Liter	K	......	(750)	(750)	(935)	(935)
GRAND CHEROKEE 4WD—V8 HEMI—Truck Equipment Schedule T3						
SRT8 Sport Util 4D	R7GW	44105	24900	25700	26900	30600

2011 JEEP — 1J4–(F1GB)–B–#

Body Type	VIN	List	Trade-In Good	Very Good	Pvt-Party Good	Retail Excellent
PATRIOT 4WD—4-Cyl.—Truck Equipment Schedule T1						
Sport SUV 4D	F1GB	19495	9125	9400	10850	12600
Latitude X Spt Util	F4GB	25695	10750	11050	12600	14600
2WD	T	......	(1450)	(1450)	(1680)	(1680)

2011 JEEP

Body Type	VIN	List	Trade-In Good	Very Good	Pvt-Party Good	Retail Excellent
COMPASS 4WD—4-Cyl.—Truck Equipment Schedule T1						
Sport SUV 4D	F1FB	22795	10050	10350	11750	13950
Limited Spt Util 4D	F5FB	26695	11850	12200	13650	16050
2WD	T		(1450)	(1450)	(1710)	(1710)
WRANGLER 4WD—V6—Truck Equipment Schedule T2						
"Sport" SUV 2D	A2D1	23620	16650	17150	18500	21000
Unlimited "Sport" 4D	A3H1	27120	21500	22100	23300	26100
Sahara Spt Util 2D	A5D1	28820	19450	20000	21400	24100
70th Annv Spt Util	A7D1	29805	21000	21600	22800	25600
Rubicon Spt Util 2D	A6D1	29995	21300	21900	23100	26000
Unlimited Spt RHD	Z3H1	29660	20400	21000	22300	25100
Unltd Sahara Util 4D	A5H1	31520	23500	24200	25400	28600
Unltd 70th Annv Util	A7H1	32505	22900	23600	24900	28000
Unltd Rubicon 4D	A6H1	34320	24800	25500	26700	29800
Hard Top			575	575	640	640
LIBERTY 4WD—V6—Truck Equipment Schedule T1						
Sport SUV 4D	N2GK	25610	11800	12250	13650	16250
Renegade Spt Util	N3GK	27995	12650	13150	14750	17600
Limited Util 4D	N5GK	28995	13400	13950	15500	18400
2WD	N		(1450)	(1450)	(1755)	(1755)
GRAND CHEROKEE 4WD—V6—Truck Equipment Schedule T1						
Laredo Sport Util	R4GG	32995	16800	17500	18700	21700
70th Anniversary			625	625	750	750
Off-Road Adventure I			175	175	200	200
Off-Road Adventure II			425	425	500	500
2WD	S		(1450)	(1450)	(1705)	(1705)
V8, 5.7 Liter	T		775	775	915	915
GRAND CHEROKEE 4WD—V6—Truck Equipment Schedule T3						
Limited Sport Util	R5GG	39600	19700	20500	21800	25400
Adaptive Cruise Control			425	425	495	495
Off-Road Adventure I			175	175	200	200
Off-Road Adventure II			425	425	500	500
2WD	S		(1450)	(1450)	(1710)	(1710)
V8, 5.7 Liter	T		775	775	920	920
GRAND CHEROKEE 4WD—V8—Truck Equipment Schedule T3						
Overland Sport Util	R6GT	41095	20700	21500	22800	26500
Adaptive Cruise Control			425	425	490	490
Summit Edition			875	875	1040	1040
2WD	S		(1450)	(1450)	(1705)	(1705)
V6, Flex Fuel, 3.6 Liter	G		(850)	(850)	(1020)	(1020)

2012 JEEP — (1,2or3)C4–(JPBB)–C–#

Body Type	VIN	List	Trade-In Good	Very Good	Pvt-Party Good	Retail Excellent
PATRIOT—4-Cyl.—Truck Equipment Schedule T1						
Sport SUV 4D	JPBB	17875	9225	9500	11050	12900
4WD	R		1525	1525	1775	1775
PATRIOT 4WD—4-Cyl.—Truck Equipment Schedule T1						
Latitude SUV 4D	JRFB	23560	11650	11950	13700	15850
Limited SUV 4D	JRCB	26110	11900	12250	14000	16250
2WD	P		(1525)	(1525)	(1785)	(1785)
COMPASS 4WD—4-Cyl.—Truck Equipment Schedule T1						
Sport SUV 4D	JDBB	21825	11200	11450	13250	15550
Latitude Spt Util 4D	JDEB	24225	11850	12100	13950	16350
Limited Spt Util 4D	JDCB	26825	12850	13150	15150	17750
2WD	C		(1525)	(1525)	(1845)	(1845)
WRANGLER 4WD—V6—Truck Equipment Schedule T2						
Sport SUV 2D	JWAG	23970	18400	18900	20200	22500
Unlimited Sport 4D	JWDG	27470	22700	23300	24400	26900
Unlimited Spt RHD	JWKG	30235	21300	21900	23300	26100
Sahara Spt Util 2D	JWBG	29895	21700	22300	23400	25900
Rubicon Spt Utl 2D	JWCG	30795	23300	23900	25200	28100
Hard Top			625	625	700	700
Call of Duty MW3			850	850	930	930
LIBERTY 4WD—V6—Truck Equipment Schedule T1						
Sport SUV 4D	JMAK	25770	13250	13750	15400	17950
Limited Ed SUV 4D	JMCK	29155	15400	15950	17650	20600
Limited Jet Ed SUV	JMFK	29355	16800	17350	19100	22200
2WD	L		(1525)	(1525)	(1825)	(1825)
GRAND CHEROKEE 4WD—V6—Truck Equipment Schedule T1						
Laredo Sport Util	JFAG	29820	18350	18950	20300	23300
Limited Sport Util	JFBG	40120	20700	21400	22900	26300
Altitude Edition			1625	1625	1905	1905
Off-Road Adventure I			175	175	205	205
Off-Road Adventure II			450	450	515	515

Body Type	VIN	List	Trade-In Good	Very Good	Pvt-Party Good	Retail Excellent
2WD	E		(1525)	(1525)	(1780)	(1780)
V8, 5.7 Liter	T		850	850	990	990
GRAND CHEROKEE 4WD—V8—Truck Equipment Schedule T1						
Overland Sport Util	JFCT	42330	23200	24000	25600	29300
Summit Edition			925	925	1090	1090
2WD	E		(1525)	(1525)	(1785)	(1785)
V6, Flex Fuel, 3.6 Liter	G		(900)	(900)	(1065)	(1065)
GRAND CHEROKEE 4WD—V8 HEMI—Truck Equipment Schedule T3						
SRT8 Sport Util 4D	JFDJ	55295	34200	35100	36400	40200

2013 JEEP — (1,2or3)C4—(JRBB)—D—#

Body Type	VIN	List	Trade-In Good	Very Good	Pvt-Party Good	Retail Excellent
PATRIOT 4WD—4-Cyl.—Truck Equipment Schedule T1						
Sport SUV 4D	JRBB	18770	11850	12200	13950	16100
Latitude SUV 4D	JRFB	23805	13100	13450	15400	17700
Limited SUV 4D	JRCB	26355	13850	14200	16200	18600
2WD	P		(1600)	(1600)	(1895)	(1895)
COMPASS 4WD—4-Cyl.—Truck Equipment Schedule T1						
Sport SUV 4D	JDBB	23270	12300	12550	14600	16850
Latitude Spt Util 4D	JDEB	24370	12750	13000	15100	17500
Limited Spt Util 4D	JDCB	27070	13950	14200	16350	18950
2WD	C		(1600)	(1600)	(1920)	(1920)
WRANGLER 4WD—V6—Truck Equipment Schedule T2						
Sport SUV 2D	JWAG	23120	19200	19650	21000	23100
Sport S SUV 2D	JWAG	25320	19950	20500	21800	24000
Spt Freedom 2D	JWBG	28620	23000	23600	24700	27100
Spt Freedom 2D	JWAG	28990	21700	22200	23400	25700
Rubicon Spt Utl 2D	JWCG	31420	24300	25000	26300	28900
Rubicon 10th Anniv	JPFG	36990	29100	29600	31200	33900
Sahara Moab 2D	JWBG	33990	24100	24600	26100	28300
Unlimited Sport 4D	JWDG	26620	23600	24200	25400	27800
Unlimited Sport S	JWDG	29020	23800	24400	25700	28200
Unlimited Spt RHD	JWKG	30920	23400	24000	25200	27800
Unltd Sahara Util	JWEG	32120	25900	26600	27800	30500
Unltd Spt Freedom	JWDG	32490	24200	24700	26100	28300
Unltd Rubicon 4D	JWFG	34920	30000	30600	32000	34700
Unltd Rubicon 10th	JWFG	40490	33000	33600	35100	38100
Unltd Sahara Moab	JWEG	37490	27200	27700	29200	31600
Hard Top			675	675	750	750
GRAND CHEROKEE 4WD—V6 Flex Fuel—Truck Equipment Schedule T1						
Laredo Sport Util	JFAG	30420	20400	21000	22400	25300
Laredo X Sport Util	JFAG	41420	23000	23700	25300	28700
Altitude Sport Util	JFAG	37220	22800	23500	25000	28300
Limited Sport Util	JFAG	40220	23400	24100	25600	29000
TrailHawk Spt Util	JFAG	41191	23200	23900	25500	28900
Overland Sport Util	JFCG	46215	26600	27400	29000	32700
Overland Summit	JFCG	50215	27100	27900	29500	33200
Adaptive Cruise Control			475	475	535	535
Off-Road Adventure I			175	175	210	210
Off-Road Adventure II			450	450	525	525
Advanced Technology			675	675	780	780
2WD	E		(1600)	(1600)	(1835)	(1835)
V8, 5.7 Liter	T		925	925	1060	1060
GRAND CHEROKEE 4WD—V8 HEMI—Truck Equipment Schedule T3						
SRT8 Sport Util 4D	JFDJ	60921	40000	41000	42100	46100
SRT8 Alpine Spt Util	JFDJ	63785	40900	41900	43000	47000
SRT8 Vapor Spt Util	JFDJ	63785	40900	41900	43000	47000

2014 JEEP — (1,2or3)C4—(JPBA)—E—#

Body Type	VIN	List	Trade-In Good	Very Good	Pvt-Party Good	Retail Excellent
PATRIOT—4-Cyl.—Truck Equipment Schedule T1						
Altitude Ed Spt Util	JPBA	17385	11500	11800	14050	16700
High Altitude Ed 4D	JPBA	22185	14200	14550	17000	19950
PATRIOT 4WD—4-Cyl.—Truck Equipment Schedule T1						
Sport SUV 4D	JRBB	20290	13100	13450	15850	18700
Latitude SUV 4D	JRFB	24390	14700	15050	17500	20400
Limited SUV 4D	JRCB	26890	15350	15750	18100	21000
2WD	P		(1700)	(1700)	(2115)	(2115)
COMPASS—4-Cyl.—Truck Equipment Schedule T1						
Altitude Ed Spt Util	JCEA	20285	11850	12050	14550	17300
High Altitude 4D	JCEA	24685	14400	14650	17600	21000
COMPASS 4WD—4-Cyl.—Truck Equipment Schedule T1						
Sport SUV 4D	JDBB	21390	13800	14050	16600	19450
Latitude Spt Util 4D	JDEB	24990	14900	15150	17700	20700

Body Type	VIN	List	Trade-In Good	Very Good	Pvt-Party Good	Retail Excellent
Limited Spt Util 4D	JDCB	28090	16200	16500	18950	22000
2WD	C		(1700)	(1700)	(2100)	(2100)

WRANGLER 4WD—V6—Truck Equipment Schedule T2
Sport SUV 2D	JWAG	23590	20600	21100	22300	24300
Sport S SUV 2D	JWAG	25790	21400	21900	23100	25400
Willys Wheeler 2D	JWAG	26790	22200	22700	23900	26200
Willys Wheeler W 2D	JWAG	28890	23800	24400	25600	28000
Sahara Spt Util 2D	JWBG	28990	24100	24700	25900	28300
Freedom SUV 2D	JWAG	29090	23100	23700	24900	27300
Unlimited Spt RHD	JWKG	31390	25600	26300	27400	30000
Rubicon Spt Util 2D	JWCG	31890	25900	26600	27800	30300
Rubicon X Util 2D	JWCG	36090	29800	30300	31600	34000
Unlimited Sport 4D	JWDG	26990	25100	25700	26600	28900
Unlimited Sport S	JWDG	29590	24400	25100	26300	28800
Unltd Willys Whlr	JWDG	30590	25800	26200	27500	29600
Unltd Sahara 4D	JWEG	32590	27100	27700	28900	31600
UnltdWillysWhr W	JWDG	32690	27500	28000	29200	31300
Unltd Freedom Ed	JWDG	32890	26000	26700	28100	30900
Unltd Rubicon X 4D	JWDG	39790	33200	33800	35000	37400
Hard Top			725	725	800	800

WRANGLER 4WD—V6—Truck Equipment Schedule T2
Altitude Spt Util 2D	JWBG	32690	25600	26300	27600	30400
Polar SUV 2D	JWBG	33490	27700	28400	29700	32500
Unltd Rubicon 4D	JWFG	35490	31500	32100	33200	35400
Unltd Altitude 4D	JWFG	36490	30200	30700	32000	34400
Unltd Dragon Ed	JWEG	37290	30900	31400	32700	35100
Unlimited Polar Ed	JWEG	37290	31100	31700	32900	35300

CHEROKEE 4WD—4-Cyl.—Truck Equipment Schedule T1
Sport SUV 4D	JMAB	25990	15550	15850	17950	20200
Latitude Spt Util	JMCB	27490	17050	17350	19450	21900
Altitude Sport Util	JMCB	27990	17250	17550	19600	21900
TrailHawk Spt Utl	JMBB	30490	22800	23300	25300	28000
Limited Sport Util	JMDB	30990	20800	21200	23300	26000
Adaptive Cruise Control			500	500	545	545
Technology Pkg			1025	1025	1125	1125
2WD	L		(1700)	(1700)	(1930)	(1930)
V6, 3.2 Liter	S		725	725	835	835

GRAND CHEROKEE 4WD—V6 Flex Fuel—Truck Equipment Schedule T1
Laredo Spt Util 4D	JFAG	31790	22600	23300	24400	27000
Laredo E Spt Util 4D	JFAG	33490	23900	24600	25700	28500
Altitude Spt Util 4D	JFAG	38585	24100	24900	26300	29400
Limited Spt Util 4D	JFBG	38790	26600	27400	28600	31800
Overland Spt Util 4D	JFCT	49185	28100	28900	30200	33600
Summit Spt Util 4D	JFJT	54685	32400	33400	34700	38600
Off-Road Adventure I			200	200	210	210
Off-Road Adventure II			475	475	530	530
Advanced Technology			725	725	815	815
2WD	E		(1700)	(1700)	(1875)	(1875)
V6, EcoDiesel, 3.0T			2925	2925	3250	3250
V8, 5.7 Liter	T		1000	1000	1115	1115

GRAND CHEROKEE 4WD—V8 HEMI—Truck Equipment Schedule T3
SRT Sport Util 4D	JFDJ	63990	47300	48500	49300	53500

KIA

2000 KIA — KNM(JA623)-Y-#

SPORTAGE 4WD—4-Cyl.—Truck Equipment Schedule T2
Sport Util Conv 2D	JA623	14945	400	475	1100	2075
Sport Utility 4D	JA723	16745	575	675	1350	2500
EX Sport Utility 4D	JA723	19045	1125	1275	2075	3750
2WD			(275)	(275)	(355)	(355)

2001 KIA — KND(JB623)-1-#

SPORTAGE 4WD—4-Cyl.—Truck Equipment Schedule T2
Sport Util Conv 2D	JB723	15345	425	500	1150	2125
Sport Utility 4D	JB723	17245	600	700	1450	2700
EX Sport Utility 4D	JB723	19545	1225	1375	2125	3775
Limited Spt Util 4D	JB723	20090	1325	1500	2225	3875
2WD	B		(300)	(300)	(385)	(385)

2002 KIA

Body Type	VIN	List	Trade-In Good	Very Good	Pvt-Party Good	Retail Excellent

2002 KIA — KND(JA623)-2-#

SPORTAGE 4WD—4-Cyl.—Truck Equipment Schedule T2

Body Type	VIN	List	Good	Very Good	Good	Excellent
Sport Util Conv 2D	JA623	15640	475	550	1350	2600
Sport Utility 4D	JA723	18715	675	775	1625	3025
2WD	B		(350)	(350)	(465)	(465)

SEDONA—V6—Truck Equipment Schedule T1

LX Minivan	UP131	19590	500	625	1075	1875
EX Minivan	UP131	21590	975	1150	1700	2975

2003 KIA — KND(UP131)-3-#

SEDONA—V6—Truck Equipment Schedule T1

LX Minivan	UP131	19965	725	850	1325	2250
EX Minivan	UP131	22180	1250	1450	2000	3450

SORENTO 4WD—V6—Truck Equipment Schedule T1

LX Sport Utility 4D	JC733	21795	2075	2450	2725	4250
EX Sport Utility 4D	JC733	24595	2725	3200	3600	5750
2WD			(475)	(475)	(645)	(645)

2004 KIA — KND(UP131)-4-#

SEDONA—V6—Truck Equipment Schedule T1

LX Minivan	UP131	20615	800	925	1400	2375
EX Minivan	UP131	22725	1325	1550	2125	3575

SORENTO 4WD—V6—Truck Equipment Schedule T1

LX Sport Utility 4D	JC733	23290	2875	3325	3325	5275
EX Sport Utility 4D	JC733	25490	3275	3800	4350	7000
2WD	D		(525)	(525)	(710)	(710)

2005 KIA — KND(JE723)-5-#

SPORTAGE 4WD—V6—Truck Equipment Schedule T2

LX Sport Utility 4D	JE723	20290	2925	3250	4000	6025
EX Sport Utility 4D	JE723	21990	3300	3650	4500	6725
2WD	F		(575)	(575)	(765)	(765)
4-Cyl, 2.0 Liter	4		(325)	(325)	(420)	(420)

SEDONA—V6—Truck Equipment Schedule T1

LX Minivan	UP131	20840	1275	1475	2125	3475
EX Minivan	UP131	23240	1850	2125	2950	4800

SORENTO 4WD—V6—Truck Equipment Schedule T1

LX Sport Utility 4D	JC733	23840	2975	3425	3975	6050
EX Sport Utility 4D	JC733	26140	3575	4150	4800	7275
2WD	D		(575)	(575)	(775)	(775)

2006 KIA — KND(JE723)-6-#

SPORTAGE 4WD—V6—Truck Equipment Schedule T1

LX Sport Utility 4D	JE723	20890	3650	4000	4700	6700
2WD	F		(625)	(625)	(845)	(845)
4-Cyl, 2.0 Liter	4		(350)	(350)	(455)	(455)

SPORTAGE 4WD—V6—Truck Equipment Schedule T2

EX Sport Utility 4D	JE723	22590	4100	4475	5225	7475
2WD	F		(625)	(625)	(845)	(845)

SEDONA—V6—Truck Equipment Schedule T1

LX Minivan	MB233	23665	2475	2800	3600	5675
EX Minivan	MB233	26265	3200	3600	4450	6975

SORENTO 4WD—V6—Truck Equipment Schedule T1

LX Sport Utility 4D	JC733	24470	3650	4175	4825	7125
EX Sport Utility 4D	JC733	26770	4300	4925	5525	8150
2WD	D		(625)	(625)	(845)	(845)

2007 KIA — KND(JE723)-7-#

SPORTAGE 4WD—V6—Truck Equipment Schedule T1

LX Sport Utility 4D	JE723	21790	4250	4625	5300	7300
2WD	F		(675)	(675)	(910)	(910)
4-Cyl, 2.0 Liter	4		(375)	(375)	(485)	(485)

SPORTAGE 4WD—V6—Truck Equipment Schedule T2

EX Sport Utility 4D	JE723	23490	4900	5350	6150	8500
2WD	F		(675)	(675)	(910)	(910)

SEDONA—V6—Truck Equipment Schedule T1

Minivan 4D	MB133	21195	2550	2850	3575	5375
LX Minivan 4D	MB233	24295	3150	3500	4250	6325
EX Minivan 4D	MB233	26895	3825	4250	5100	7600

Body Type	VIN	List	Trade-In Good	Very Good	Pvt-Party Good	Retail Excellent
SORENTO—V6—Truck Equipment Schedule T1						
Sport Utility 4D	JD736	20665	**3400**	3850	4600	6675
SORENTO 4WD—V6—Truck Equipment Schedule T1						
LX Sport Utility 4D	JC736	25265	**4400**	4950	5575	7975
EX Sport Utility 4D	JC736	26865	**5525**	6225	6850	9650
2WD	D		**(675)**	(675)	(910)	(910)

2008 KIA — KND(JE723)-8-#

Body Type	VIN	List	Trade-In Good	Very Good	Pvt-Party Good	Retail Excellent
SPORTAGE 4WD—V6—Truck Equipment Schedule T1						
LX Sport Utility 4D	JE723	21970	**4975**	5350	6350	8475
2WD	F		**(725)**	(725)	(975)	(975)
4-Cyl, 2.0 Liter	4		**(400)**	(400)	(520)	(520)
SPORTAGE 4WD—V6—Truck Equipment Schedule T2						
EX Sport Utility 4D	JE723	23520	**5950**	6375	7450	10000
2WD	F		**(725)**	(725)	(975)	(975)
SEDONA—V6—Truck Equipment Schedule T1						
Minivan 4D	MB133	21420	**3325**	3625	4675	6750
LX Minivan 4D	MB233	24320	**4000**	4350	5425	7775
EX Minivan 4D	MB233	26920	**4800**	5200	6300	8975
SORENTO—V6—Truck Equipment Schedule T1						
Sport Utility 4D	JD735	21695	**4900**	5375	6125	8225
SORENTO 4WD—V6—Truck Equipment Schedule T1						
LX Sport Utility 4D	JC735	24895	**5525**	6050	6925	9425
EX Sport Utility 4D	JC736	26895	**6575**	7200	8050	10950
2WD	D		**(725)**	(725)	(970)	(970)

2009 KIA — KND(JE723)-9-#

Body Type	VIN	List	Trade-In Good	Very Good	Pvt-Party Good	Retail Excellent
SPORTAGE 4WD—V6—Truck Equipment Schedule T1						
LX Sport Utility 4D	JE723	22670	**6425**	6800	7700	9675
2WD	F		**(825)**	(825)	(1030)	(1030)
4-Cyl, 2.0 Liter	4		**(450)**	(450)	(555)	(555)
SPORTAGE 4WD—V6—Truck Equipment Schedule T2						
EX Sport Utility 4D	JE723	24075	**7950**	8425	9400	11800
2WD	F		**(825)**	(825)	(1030)	(1030)
SEDONA—V6—Truck Equipment Schedule T1						
Minivan 4D	MB133	21995	**4250**	4525	5700	7850
LX Minivan 4D	MB333	24995	**4725**	5025	6225	8525
EX Minivan 4D	MB233	28495	**5750**	7500	9025	12200
SORENTO—V6—Truck Equipment Schedule T1						
Sport Utility 4D	JD735	22295	**5800**	6200	7200	9400
SORENTO—V6—Truck Equipment Schedule T1						
EX Sport Utility 4D	JD736	26095	**7525**	8050	9175	12050
4WD	C		**1150**	1150	1545	1545
SORENTO 4WD—V6—Truck Equipment Schedule T1						
LX Sport Utility 4D	JC735	25395	**6850**	7350	8325	10850
2WD	D		**(825)**	(825)	(1105)	(1105)
BORREGO—V6—Truck Equipment Schedule T1						
LX Sport Utility 4D	JJ741	26995	**7500**	7950	8925	11250
EX Sport Utility 4D	JJ741	28745	**8150**	8625	9575	12050
4WD	H		**1275**	1275	1610	1610
V8, 4.6 Liter	2		**1525**	1525	1935	1935
BORREGO 4WD—V8—Truck Equipment Schedule T1						
Limited Sport Util	JH742	40745	**11900**	12550	13650	17150
2WD			**(1275)**	(1275)	(1615)	(1615)

2010 KIA — KND(KGCA3)-A-#

Body Type	VIN	List	Trade-In Good	Very Good	Pvt-Party Good	Retail Excellent
SPORTAGE 4WD—V6—Truck Equipment Schedule T1						
LX Sport Utility 4D	KGCA3	23190	**8450**	8850	10200	12700
2WD	3		**(950)**	(950)	(1210)	(1210)
4-Cyl, 2.0 Liter	2,4		**(525)**	(525)	(665)	(665)
SPORTAGE 4WD—V6—Truck Equipment Schedule T2						
EX Sport Utility 4D	KHCA3	24190	**9525**	9975	11500	14350
2WD	3		**(950)**	(950)	(1220)	(1220)
SEDONA—V6—Truck Equipment Schedule T1						
Minivan 4D	MF4A3	22990	**6125**	6400	7800	10100
LX Minivan 4D	MG4A3	24990	**6575**	6875	8275	10700
EX Minivan 4D	MH4A3	29490	**8900**	9300	10900	14000

2011 KIA — 5XYorKND(PA3A2)-B-#

Body Type	VIN	List	Trade-In Good	Very Good	Pvt-Party Good	Retail Excellent
SPORTAGE—4-Cyl.—Truck Equipment Schedule T2						
Sport Utility 4D	PA3A2	18990	**9750**	10150	11300	13350

Body Type	VIN	List	Trade-In Good	Very Good	Pvt-Party Good	Retail Excellent
SPORTAGE—4-Cyl.—Truck Equipment Schedule T2						
EX Sport Utility	PC3A2	23990	12100	12600	13800	16200
AWD	C		975	975	1135	1135
SPORTAGE AWD—4-Cyl.—Truck Equipment Schedule T2						
LX Sport Utility	PBCA2	22490	11000	11400	12650	14950
2WD	3		(1075)	(1075)	(1245)	(1245)
SPORTAGE AWD—4-Cyl. Turbo—Truck Equipment Schedule T2						
SX Sport Utility	PECA2	27990	14500	15050	16550	19550
2WD	3		(1075)	(1075)	(1255)	(1255)
SORENTO—4-Cyl.—Truck Equipment Schedule T1						
Sport Utility 4D	KT3A1	20790	10650	11000	12250	14700
SORENTO—V6—Truck Equipment Schedule T1						
EX Sport Utility	KU3A2	28190	13500	13950	15250	18250
AWD	C,D		975	975	1140	1140
4-Cyl, 2.4 Liter	1		(475)	(475)	(545)	(545)
SORENTO AWD—V6—Truck Equipment Schedule T1						
LX Sport Utility	KTCA2	27890	12400	12850	14050	16850
SX Sport Utility	KWDA2	34490	14350	14850	16250	19550
2WD	3		(1075)	(1075)	(1250)	(1250)
4-Cyl, 2.4 Liter	1		(475)	(475)	(545)	(545)
SEDONA—V6—Truck Equipment Schedule T1						
LX Minivan 4D	MG4A7	25390	7950	8200	9850	12300
EX Minivan 4D	MH4A7	29990	10300	10650	12450	15400

2012 KIA — 5XYorKND(PA3A2)-C-#

Body Type	VIN	List	Trade-In Good	Very Good	Pvt-Party Good	Retail Excellent
SPORTAGE—4-Cyl.—Truck Equipment Schedule T2						
Sport Utility 4D	PA3A2	19300	10900	11250	12700	14800
SPORTAGE—4-Cyl.—Truck Equipment Schedule T2						
EX Sport Utility	PC3A2	24700	13850	14350	15850	18350
AWD	C		1075	1075	1265	1265
SPORTAGE AWD—4-Cyl.—Truck Equipment Schedule T2						
LX Sport Utility	PBCA2	23100	12450	12900	14400	16650
2WD	3		(1500)	(1500)	(1755)	(1755)
SPORTAGE AWD—4-Cyl. Turbo—Truck Equipment Schedule T2						
SX Sport Utility 4D	PCCA6	29200	15750	16300	18000	20900
2WD	3		(1500)	(1500)	(1775)	(1775)
SORENTO—4-Cyl.—Truck Equipment Schedule T1						
Sport Utility 4D	KT3A1	22050	11850	12150	13550	15950
SORENTO—V6—Truck Equipment Schedule T1						
EX Sport Utility 4D	KU3A2	28750	14800	15150	16500	19200
AWD	C,D		1075	1075	1265	1265
4-Cyl, GDI, 2.4 Liter	6		(500)	(500)	(585)	(585)
SORENTO AWD—V6—Truck Equipment Schedule T1						
LX Sport Utility	KTCA1	26150	13650	13950	15350	17850
SX Sport Utility	KWDA1	35650	17400	17800	19250	22400
FWD	3		(1175)	(1175)	(1350)	(1350)
4-Cyl, GDI, 2.4 Liter	6		(500)	(500)	(580)	(580)
SEDONA—V6—Truck Equipment Schedule T1						
LX Minivan 4D	MG4A7	25700	9775	9975	11800	14250
EX Minivan 4D	MH4A7	29990	12150	12450	14450	17400

2013 KIA — 5XYorKND(PB3A2)-D-#

Body Type	VIN	List	Trade-In Good	Very Good	Pvt-Party Good	Retail Excellent
SPORTAGE—4-Cyl.—Truck Equipment Schedule T2						
Sport Utility 4D	PB3A2	19800	12300	12650	14200	16350
SPORTAGE AWD—4-Cyl.—Truck Equipment Schedule T2						
LX Sport Utility	PBCA2	23500	13450	13900	15700	18150
EX Sport Utility	PCCA2	26500	16450	16950	18600	21300
2WD	3		(1500)	(1500)	(1755)	(1755)
SPORTAGE AWD—4-Cyl. Turbo—Truck Equipment Schedule T2						
SX Sport Utility 4D	PCCA6	29200	17700	18200	19900	22700
2WD	3		(1500)	(1500)	(1730)	(1730)
SORENTO AWD—V6—Truck Equipment Schedule T1						
LX Sport Utility	KTDA2	28220	15400	15650	17150	19800
EX Sport Utility	KU3A2	28750	17400	17700	19200	22000
SX Sport Utility	KWDA2	34200	19550	19850	21500	24800
FWD	3		(1275)	(1275)	(1440)	(1440)
4-Cyl, GDI, 2.4 Liter	6		(575)	(575)	(645)	(645)

2014 KIA — 5XYorKND(PBCAC)-E-#

Body Type	VIN	List	Trade-In Good	Very Good	Pvt-Party Good	Retail Excellent
SPORTAGE AWD—4-Cyl.—Truck Equipment Schedule 1						
LX Sport Utility	PBCAC	23950	15050	15500	17450	20200
EX Sport Utility	PCCAC	27350	17550	18050	19900	22800

TRUCKS & VANS

Body Type	VIN	List	Trade-In Good	Very Good	Pvt-Party Good	Retail Excellent
SX Sport Utility	PCCA6	29250	19550	20100	21800	24800
FWD	3		(1500)	(1500)	(1780)	(1780)

SORENTO AWD—V6—Truck Equipment Schedule T1

Body Type	VIN	List	Good	Very Good	Good	Excellent
LX Sport Utility	KTDA7	28250	17000	17250	19500	23000
EX Sport Utility	KU3A7	30850	19900	20200	22400	26300
SX Sport Utility	KWDA7	37550	22600	22900	25100	29400
Limited Sport Utility 4D		40550	23500	23900	26100	30400
FWD	3,4		(1375)	(1375)	(1650)	(1650)
4-Cyl, GDI, 2.4 Liter	6		(675)	(675)	(805)	(805)

LAND ROVER

2000 LAND ROVER — SAL(TY124)-Y-#

DISCOVERY SERIES II 4WD—V8—Truck Equipment Schedule T3

Body Type	VIN	List	Good	Very Good	Good	Excellent
SD Spt Util 4D	TY124	36725	750	900	1525	2825
SD7 Spt Util 4D	TY124	35725	1025	1200	1875	3450
Sport Utility 4D	TY124	36725	1025	1200	1875	3450
Rear Seats			200	200	265	265
Air Conditioning, Rear			100	100	135	135
Dual Moon Roofs			475	475	620	620
Performance Pkg			275	275	375	375

RANGE ROVER 4WD—V8—Truck Equipment Schedule T3

Body Type	VIN	List	Good	Very Good	Good	Excellent
County Spt Ut 4D	PA124	58925	925	1025	1525	2475
4.0 Sport Util 4D	PA124	59625	550	625	1175	2025
4.0 SE Sport Util 4D	PV124	59625	500	550	1100	1925
4.6 HSE Spt Util 4D	PF164	67625	950	1050	1625	2750
4.6 HSE Spt Util 4D	PV144	67925	1375	1525	2150	3600
4.6 Vitesse Util 4D	PF164	68625	1725	1925	2650	4350
4.6 Holland Holland	PV164	79625	2450	3525	3875	5825

2001 LAND ROVER — SAL(TY124)-1-#

DISCOVERY SERIES II 4WD—V8—Truck Equipment Schedule T3

Body Type	VIN	List	Good	Very Good	Good	Excellent
SD Sport Util 4D	TY124	33975	950	1100	1800	3300
SD7 Sport Util 4D	TY124	35725	1075	1250	2025	3725
LE Sport Util 4D	TY124	34975	975	1150	1875	3500
LE7 Sport Util 4D	TY124	36725	1375	1600	2400	4400
SE Sport Util 4D	TY124	36975	1700	2000	2950	5375
SE7 Sport Util 4D	TY124	38725	1375	1600	2300	4125
Rear Jump Seats			200	200	265	265
Air Conditioning, Rear			100	100	145	145
Dual Moon Roofs			500	500	655	655
Performance Pkg			325	325	425	425

RANGE ROVER 4WD—V8—Truck Equipment Schedule T3

Body Type	VIN	List	Good	Very Good	Good	Excellent
4.6 SE Sport Util 4D	PV164	62625	650	750	1275	2150
4.6 HSE Sport Util	PV164	68665	1600	1775	2375	3875

2002 LAND ROVER — SAL(NM222)-2-#

FREELANDER AWD—V6—Truck Equipment Schedule T3

Body Type	VIN	List	Good	Very Good	Good	Excellent
S Sport Utility 4D	NM222	25600	825	1000	1450	2475
SE Sport Utility 4D	NY222	28400	1375	1625	2125	3625
HSE Sport Util 4D	NE222	28400	1375	1625	2150	3650

DISCOVERY SERIES II 4WD—V8—Truck Equipment Schedule T3

Body Type	VIN	List	Good	Very Good	Good	Excellent
SD Sport Util 4D	TL144	33995	1025	1200	1875	3375
SD7 Sport Util 4D	TK144	34995	1500	1725	2425	4275
SE Sport Util 4D	TY144	37795	2050	2375	3200	5575
SE7 Sport Util 4D	TW124	38875	1800	2075	2850	4925
Rear Jump Seats			225	225	310	310
Air Conditioning, Rear			125	125	170	170
Dual Moon Roofs			525	525	710	710
Performance Pkg			350	350	480	480

RANGE ROVER 4WD—V8—Truck Equipment Schedule T3

Body Type	VIN	List	Good	Very Good	Good	Excellent
4.6 HSE Sport Util	PL162	68665	1825	2000	2625	4150

2003 LAND ROVER — SAL(NM222)-3-#

FREELANDER AWD—V6—Truck Equipment Schedule T3

Body Type	VIN	List	Good	Very Good	Good	Excellent
S Sport Util 4D	NM222	25600	1025	1200	1625	2750
SE3 Sport Util 2D	NY122	26995	1375	1625	2050	3375
SE Sport Util 4D	NY222	28400	1625	1925	2325	3825
HSE Sport Util 4D	NE222	32200	1750	2050	2550	4200

2003 LAND ROVER

Body Type	VIN	List	Trade-In Good	Trade-In Very Good	Pvt-Party Good	Retail Excellent
DISCOVERY 4WD—V8—Truck Equipment Schedule T3						
S Sport Util 4D	TL144	34995	1175	1350	2000	3475
SE Sport Util 4D	TY144	38995	2700	3100	3900	6575
SE7 Sport Util 4D	TW124	39995	2625	3000	3725	6225
HSE Spt Util 4D	TP144	40995	3700	4225	5050	8275
HSE7 Spt Ut 4D	TR144	41995	3825	4350	5150	8475
Rear Jump Seats			275	275	355	355
Air Conditioning, Rear			150	150	190	190
Dual Moon Roofs			575	575	755	755
Suspension Pkg			400	400	525	525
RANGE ROVER 4WD—V8—Truck Equipment Schedule T3						
HSE Sport Util 4D	MB114	71865	4475	4875	5475	8075

2004 LAND ROVER — SAL(NY222)-4-#

Body Type	VIN	List	Trade-In Good	Trade-In Very Good	Pvt-Party Good	Retail Excellent
FREELANDER AWD—V6—Truck Equipment Schedule T3						
SE Sport Util 4D	NY222	25995	1875	2200	2800	4600
SE3 Spt Util 2D	NY222	28195	2025	2375	2975	4875
HSE Sport Util 4D	NE222	28995	2175	2525	2975	4750
DISCOVERY 4WD—V8—Truck Equipment Schedule T3						
S Sport Utility 4D	TL194	34995	1825	2100	2750	4550
SE Sport Utility 4D	TY194	39250	3550	4025	4950	8100
SE7 Spt Util 4D	TW194	40350	3500	3975	4600	7400
HSE Spt Util 4D	TP194	41250	4650	5250	5950	9425
HSE7 Spt Util 4D	TR194	42250	4750	5375	6050	9575
G4 Sport Utility 4D	TL194	39995	3700	4200	5075	8275
Rear Jump Seats			300	300	385	385
Air Conditioning, Rear			175	175	220	220
Dual Moon Roofs			600	600	785	785
Suspension Pkg			425	425	575	575
RANGE ROVER 4WD—V8—Truck Equipment Schedule T3						
HSE Sport Util 4D	ME114	72250	5000	5400	5925	8500
Westminister Util	MH114	84700	7725	8375	9000	12750
Luxury Pkg			675	675	885	885

2005 LAND ROVER — SAL(NY222)-5-#

Body Type	VIN	List	Trade-In Good	Trade-In Very Good	Pvt-Party Good	Retail Excellent
FREELANDER AWD—V6—Truck Equipment Schedule T3						
SE Sport Utility 4D	NY222	27495	2025	2375	3225	5150
SE3 Sport Util 2D	NM122	27495	1925	2250	3150	5075
LR3 4WD—V8—Truck Equipment Schedule T3						
SE Sport Util 4D	AD254	44995	6425	6950	7525	10200
Third Row Seat			325	325	415	415
V6, 4.0 Liter			(1150)	(1150)	(1500)	(1500)
LR3 4WD—V8—Truck Equipment Schedule T3						
HSE Sport Util 4D	AF254	49995	7450	8075	8625	11700
Third Row Seat			325	325	415	415
RANGE ROVER 4WD—V8—Truck Equipment Schedule T3						
HSE Sport Util 4D	ME114	73750	5925	6425	7400	10400
Westminister Util	MH114	86000	9050	9775	10700	14850
Luxury Pkg			725	725	970	970

2006 LAND ROVER — SAL(AB244)-6-#

Body Type	VIN	List	Trade-In Good	Trade-In Very Good	Pvt-Party Good	Retail Excellent
LR3 4WD—V6—Truck Equipment Schedule T3						
Sport Utility 4D	AB244	38950	6050	6500	7225	9725
Third Row Seat	C,E		350	350	445	445
LR3 4WD—V8—Truck Equipment Schedule T3						
SE Sport Utility 4D	AD254	45450	7450	8000	8750	11800
Third Row Seat	C,E		350	350	445	445
LR3 4WD—V8—Truck Equipment Schedule T3						
HSE Sport Util 4D	AG254	53450	8425	9050	9775	13150
Third Row Seat	G		350	350	445	445
Luxury Pkg			375	375	505	505
RANGE ROVER SPORT 4WD—V8—Truck Equipment Schedule T3						
HSE Sport Util 4D	SF254	56750	11200	12000	12350	16250
Luxury Pkg			800	800	995	995
RANGE ROVER SPORT 4WD—V8 Supercharged—Truck Equipment Sch T3						
Sport Utility 4D	SD234	69750	11900	12750	13200	17500
Adaptive Cruise Control			325	325	405	405
RANGE ROVER 4WD—V8—Truck Equipment Schedule T3						
HSE Sport Util 4D	ME154	74950	9100	9775	10500	14100
Luxury Pkg			800	800	1045	1045
RANGE ROVER 4WD—V8 Supercharged—Truck Equipment Sch T3						
Sport Utility 4D	MF134	89950	12750	13650	14200	18850

SEE BACK PAGES FOR TRUCK EQUIPMENT

2006 LAND ROVER

Body Type	VIN	List	Trade-In Good	Very Good	Pvt-Party Good	Retail Excellent
Westminster 4D	MH134	98150	13800	14800	15400	20500

2007 LAND ROVER — SAL(AD244)-7-#

Body Type	VIN	List	Good	Very Good	Good	Excellent
LR3 4WD—V8—Truck Equipment Schedule T3						
SE Sport Utility 4D	AD244	42150	9975	10650	11200	14450
Third Row Seat			375	375	455	455
V6, 4.0 Liter	4		(1350)	(1350)	(1690)	(1690)
LR3 4WD—V8—Truck Equipment Schedule T3						
HSE Sport Util 4D	AG254	53950	11400	12150	12700	16350
Luxury Pkg			400	400	500	500
Third Row Seat			375	375	455	455
RANGE ROVER SPORT 4WD—V8—Truck Equipment Schedule T3						
HSE Sport Util 4D	SF254	57950	12900	13750	14100	18050
Luxury Pkg			850	850	1060	1060
RANGE ROVER SPORT 4WD—V8 Supercharged—Truck Equipment Sch T3						
Sport Utility 4D	SD234	71250	13700	14600	14900	19000
Adaptive Cruise Control			350	350	420	420
RANGE ROVER 4WD—V8—Truck Equipment Schedule T3						
HSE Sport Util 4D	ME154	77250	12350	13200	13650	17550
Luxury Pkg			850	850	1075	1075
RANGE ROVER 4WD—V8 Supercharged—Truck Equipment Schedule T3						
Sport Utility 4D	MF134	92750	15700	16700	17050	21800

2008 LAND ROVER — SAL(FP24N)-8-#

Body Type	VIN	List	Good	Very Good	Good	Excellent
LR2 AWD—6-Cyl.—Truck Equipment Schedule T3						
SE Sport Utility 4D	FP24N	34700	7100	7750	8325	11000
HSE Sport Utility 4D	FR24N	36150	8275	9050	9500	12450
LR3 4WD—V8—Truck Equipment Schedule T3						
SE Sport Utility 4D	AE254	49300	11450	12100	12750	15750
HSE Sport Util 4D	AG254	54800	12850	13550	14400	17900
Third Row Seat			400	400	470	470
Luxury Pkg			425	425	520	520
RANGE ROVER SPORT 4WD—V8—Truck Equipment Schedule T3						
HSE Sport Util 4D	SF254	58500	14100	14850	15500	19100
Luxury Pkg			925	925	1105	1105
RANGE ROVER SPORT 4WD—V8 Supercharged—Truck Equipment Sch T3						
Sport Utility 4D	SH234	71950	14800	15600	16250	20000
Adaptive Cruise Control			375	375	440	440
RANGE ROVER 4WD—V8—Truck Equipment Schedule T3						
HSE Sport Util 4D	ME154	77950	15100	15950	16600	20400
Luxury Pkg			925	925	1100	1100
RANGE ROVER 4WD—V8 Supercharged—Truck Equipment Schedule T3						
Sport Utility 4D	MF134	93600	19800	20800	21100	25700
Westminster Util	MH134	105600	24300	25600	25600	31200

2009 LAND ROVER — SAL(FR24N)-9-#

Body Type	VIN	List	Good	Very Good	Good	Excellent
LR2 AWD—6-Cyl.—Truck Equipment Schedule T3						
HSE Sport Util 4D	FR24N	36150	10650	11400	11850	14750
LR3 4WD—V8—Truck Equipment Schedule T3						
Sport Utility 4D	AE254	46750	18000	18750	19550	23200
Third Row Seat			450	450	525	525
HSE Lux Pkg			450	450	525	525
RANGE ROVER SPORT 4WD—V8—Truck Equipment Schedule T3						
HSE Sport Util 4D	SF254	59150	17550	18250	19250	22900
Luxury Pkg			975	975	1160	1160
RANGE ROVER SPORT 4WD—V8 Supercharged—Truck Equipment Sch T3						
Sport Utility 4D	SH234	72600	20100	21000	21900	26000
Adaptive Cruise Control			375	375	445	445
RANGE ROVER 4WD—V8—Truck Equipment Schedule T3						
HSE Sport Util 4D	ME154	78450	19450	20300	21200	25400
Luxury Pkg			975	975	1165	1165
RANGE ROVER 4WD—V8 Supercharged—Truck Equipment Schedule T3						
Sport Utility 4D	MF134	94100	26000	27100	27700	32700
Autobiography Pkg			5775	5775	6730	6730

2010 LAND ROVER — SAL(FR2BN)-A-#

Body Type	VIN	List	Good	Very Good	Good	Excellent
LR2 AWD—6-Cyl.—Truck Equipment Schedule T3						
HSE Sport Util 4D	FR2BN	36350	12650	13250	14150	17200
LR4 4WD—Truck Equipment Schedule T3						
Sport Utility 4D	AB2D4	48100	26700	27600	28300	32300
Third Row Seat			525	525	590	590
HSE Pkg			1500	1500	1670	1670

Body Type	VIN	List	Trade-In Good	Very Good	Pvt-Party Good	Retail Excellent
HSE Lux Pkg			3050	3050	3405	3405
RANGE ROVER SPORT 4WD—V8—Truck Equipment Schedule T3						
HSE Sport Util 4D	SF2D4	60495	24400	25200	26200	30000
Luxury Pkg			1000	1000	1135	1135
RANGE ROVER SPORT 4WD—V8 Supercharged—Truck Equipment Sch T3						
Sport Utility 4D	SH2E4	74195	27000	27900	28900	33200
Luxury Pkg			1000	1000	1140	1140
Adaptive Cruise Control			400	400	445	445
RANGE ROVER 4WD—V8—Truck Equipment Schedule T3						
HSE Sport Util 4D	ME1D4	79275	26400	27300	28400	32700
Vision Assist Pack			375	375	435	435
Adaptive Cruise Control			400	400	450	450
Luxury Pkg			1000	1000	1145	1145
RANGE ROVER 4WD—V8 Supercharged—Truck Equipment Schedule T3						
Sport Utility 4D	MF1E4	95125	32300	33400	34300	39400
Luxury Pkg			1000	1000	1135	1135
Adaptive Cruise Control			400	400	445	445

LR2 AWD—6-Cyl.—Truck Equipment Schedule T3						
Sport Utility 4D	FR2BN	36550	17950	18550	19450	22800
HSE Pkg			1600	1600	1770	1770
HSE Lux Pkg			3225	3225	3585	3585
LR4 4WD—V8—Truck Equipment Schedule T3						
Sport Utility 4D	AB2D4	48500	29200	30000	31200	34800
Third Row Seat			575	575	640	640
HSE Pkg			1600	1600	1740	1740
HSE Lux Pkg			3225	3225	3535	3535
Metropolis Black Ltd Ed			550	550	615	615
Metropolis Limited Ed			550	550	615	615
RANGE ROVER SPORT 4WD—V8—Truck Equipment Schedule T3						
HSE Sport Util 4D	SF2D4	60495	26900	27600	29000	32700
Luxury Pkg			1000	1000	1130	1130
RANGE ROVER SPORT 4WD—V8 Supercharged—Truck Equipment Sch T3						
Sport Utility 4D	SH2E4	75395	30300	31100	32700	36800
Autobiography Pkg			3250	3250	3670	3670
Luxury Pkg			1000	1000	1130	1130
Adaptive Cruise Control			425	425	470	470
RANGE ROVER 4WD—V8—Truck Equipment Schedule T3						
HSE Sport Util 4D	ME1E4	79685	30900	31700	33200	37500
Luxury Pkg			1000	1000	1130	1130
RANGE ROVER 4WD—V8 Supercharged—Truck Equipment Schedule T3						
Sport Utility 4D	MF1E4	95465	37900	38900	40400	45300
Autobiography Pkg			6475	6475	7255	7255
Luxury Pkg			1000	1000	1120	1120

LR2 AWD—6-Cyl.—Truck Equipment Schedule T3						
Sport Utility 4D	FR2BN	36550	19550	20000	21100	24300
HSE Pkg			1675	1675	1860	1860
HSE Lux Pkg			3400	3400	3760	3760
LR4 4WD—V8—Truck Equipment Schedule T3						
Sport Utility 4D	AB2D4	50600	35600	36300	37800	41500
Third Row Seat			625	625	690	690
HSE Pkg			1675	1675	1835	1835
HSE Lux Pkg			3400	3400	3710	3710
RANGE ROVER EVOQUE 4WD—4-Cyl. Turbo—Truck Equipment Sch T3						
Sport Utility 4D	VN2BG	43995	28700	29300	30200	34200
Spt Util Coupe 2D	VN1BG	44995	28500	29100	30000	34000
Dynamic Spt Util	VS2BG	58995	33100	33800	34400	38800
Dynamic Coupe 2D	VS1BG	60795	32300	33000	33700	38100
Prestige Sport Util	VU2BG	60795	33100	33800	34400	38900
Adaptive Dynamics Susp			575	575	630	630
RANGE ROVER SPORT 4WD—V8—Truck Equipment Schedule T3						
HSE Sport Util 4D	SF2D4	61745	34500	35300	37000	40800
Luxury Pkg			1000	1000	1115	1115
RANGE ROVER SPORT 4WD—V8 Supercharged—Truck Equipment Sch T3						
Sport Utility 4D	SH2E4	76945	40000	40900	42600	47100
Autobiography Pkg			3425	3425	3810	3810
Adaptive Cruise Control			450	450	490	490
RANGE ROVER 4WD—V8—Truck Equipment Schedule T3						
HSE Sport Util 4D	ME1D4	81125	39200	40000	42000	46600

Body Type	VIN	List	Trade-In Good	Trade-In Very Good	Pvt-Party Good	Retail Excellent
Luxury Pkg			1000	1000	1120	1120
RANGE ROVER 4WD—V8 Supercharged—Truck Equipment Schedule T3						
Sport Utility 4D	MH1E4	96520	45900	46800	48500	53300
Autobiography Pkg			6825	6825	7580	7580

2013 LAND ROVER — SAL(FP28G)–D–#

LR2 AWD—4-Cyl. Turbo—Truck Equipment Schedule T3
Body Type	VIN	List	Good	Very Good	Good	Excellent
Sport Utility 4D	FP2BG	37250	21500	21900	23500	27100
HSE Sport Util 4D	FR2BG	39795	23500	23900	25600	29400
HSE LUX Spt Utl	FT2BG	42395	26400	26800	28400	32600

LR4 4WD—V8—Truck Equipment Schedule T3
Sport Utility 4D	AB2D4	49995	39800	40500	42100	45700
HSE Sport Util 4D	AF2D4	54220	41000	41700	43400	47100
HSE LUX Spt Util	AK2D4	55220	44100	44900	46400	50300

RANGE ROVER EVOQUE 4WD—4-Cyl. Turbo—Truck Equip Schedule T3
Pure Sport Utility 4D	VN2BG	41995	29800	30300	31400	35200
Pure Plus Util 4D	VP2BG	43995	31500	32000	33000	36900
Pure Plus Cpe 2D	VP1BG	44995	30200	30700	31800	35800
Pure Premium 4D	VR2BG	48195	31900	32400	33500	37600
Pure Premium 2D	VR1BG	49595	32300	32800	33900	38100
Dynamic Spt 4D	VT2BG	51695	38000	38600	39300	43800
Prestige Spt Util	VV2BG	52595	36000	36600	37400	41800
Dynamic Spt 2D	VT1BG	53095	35300	35900	36800	41100

RANGE ROVER SPORT 4WD—V8—Truck Equipment Schedule T3
HSE Sport Utility 4D	SF2D4	60895	40900	41700	43500	47400
HSE Lux Sport 4D	SK2D4	65595	41600	42400	44300	48500
GT Limited Ed 4D	SF2D4	70995	50000	50900	52800	57200
Adaptive Cruise Control			475	475	505	505

RANGE ROVER SPORT 4WD—V8 Supercharged—Truck Equipment Sch T3
Sport Utility 4D	SH2E4	76495	52800	53700	55800	60700
Limited Ed Spt Util	SH2E4	80040	56100	57100	59000	64000
Autobiography 4D	SP2E4	87195	60000	61100	63000	68100
Adaptive Cruise Control			475	475	505	505

RANGE ROVER 4WD—V8—Truck Equipment Schedule T3
Sport Utility 4D	GR2DF	84350	60200	61300	63100	68200
HSE Sport Util 4D	GS2DF	89350	69500	70700	72100	77600
Adaptive Cruise Control			475	475	505	505

RANGE ROVER 4WD—V8 Supercharged—Truck Equipment Schedule T3
Sport Utility 4D	GS2EF	100800	76000	77400	78500	84100
Adaptive Cruise Control			475	475	495	495

RANGE ROVER 4WD—V8 Supercharged—Truck Equipment Schedule T3
Autobiography 4D	GV2EF	131800	99600	101500	102000	108400

2014 LAND ROVER — SAL(FP2BG)–E–#

LR2 AWD—4-Cyl. Turbo—Truck Equipment Schedule T1
Sport Utility 4D	FP2BG	37495	25800	26200	27600	31400
HSE Sport Util 4D	FR2BG	39995	27600	28100	29500	33400
HSE LUX Spt Utl	FT2BG	42595	30400	30800	32300	36500

LR4 4WD—V6 Supercharged—Truck Equipment Schedule T1
Sport Utility 4D	AB2V6	50595	43300	44100	45400	48800
HSE Sport Util 4D	AG2V6	55495	45400	46200	47400	50800
HSE LUX Spt Util	AK2V6	60795	49000	49900	51300	54800

RANGE ROVER EVOQUE 4WD—4-Cyl. Turbo—Truck Equipment Sch T3
Pure Sport Utility 4D	VN2BG	41995	33100	33600	34700	38800
Pure Plus Util 4D	VP2BG	44995	33900	34400	35500	39600
Pure Plus Cpe 2D	VP1BG	45040	32900	33400	34500	38600
Pure Premium 4D	VR2BG	49595	35600	36100	37000	41300
Pure Premium 2D	VR1BG	50595	35800	36300	37200	41500
Prestige Spt Util	VU2BG	56295	41900	42500	43000	47600
Dynamic Spt 4D	VT2BG	57195	43300	44000	44400	49100
Dynamic Spt 2D	VT1BG	58195	39100	39700	40400	44800
Adaptive Cruise Control			500	500	525	525

RANGE ROVER SPORT 4WD—V6 Supercharged—Truck Equipment Sch T3
SE Sport Util 4D	WJ2VF	63495	52500	53400	55100	59300
HSE Sport Util 4D	WG2VF	68495	59700	60800	62200	66600

RANGE ROVER SPORT 4WD—V8 Supercharged—Truck Equipment Sch T3
Sport Utility 4D	WR2EF	79995	66700	67900	69000	73600
Autobiography 4D	WV2EF	93295	72800	74100	74900	79700

RANGE ROVER 4WD—V6 Supercharged—Truck Equipment Schedule T3
Sport Utility 4D	GR2VF	83545	72000	73300	74100	78800

RANGE ROVER 4WD—V6 Supercharged—Truck Equipment Schedule T3
HSE Sport Util 4D	GS2VF	88545	75600	76900	77600	82400

Body Type	VIN	List	Trade-In Good	Very Good	Pvt-Party Good	Retail Excellent
Adaptive Cruise Control			500	500	515	515
RANGE ROVER 4WD—V8 Supercharged—Truck Equipment Schedule T3						
Sport Utility 4D	GS2EF	99995	85600	87200	87400	92600
Adaptive Cruise Control			500	500	515	515
RANGE ROVER 4WD—V8 Supercharged—Truck Equipment Schedule T3						
Autobiography 4D	GV2EF	135995	114300	116300	116500	123300
AutobiographyBlk	GV3TF	185000	149300	152000	150800	158900

LEXUS

2000 LEXUS — JT6(HF10U)-Y-#

RX 300 4WD—V6—Truck Equipment Schedule T3

Body Type	VIN	List	Good	Very Good	Good	Excellent
Sport Utility 4D	HF10U	35680	3325	3650	4000	6000
2WD			(325)	(325)	(445)	(445)
LX 470 4WD—V8—Truck Equipment Schedule T3						
Sport Utility 4D	HT00W	59500	7075	7650	8275	11550

2001 LEXUS — JTJ(HF10U)-1-#

RX 300 4WD—V6—Truck Equipment Schedule T3

Body Type	VIN	List	Good	Very Good	Good	Excellent
Sport Utility 4D	HF10U	37430	4025	4425	4775	6975
Silversport Edition			125	125	170	170
2WD			(375)	(375)	(510)	(510)
LX 470 4WD—V8—Truck Equipment Schedule T3						
Sport Utility 4D	HT00W	61950	7900	8525	9175	12650

2002 LEXUS — JTJ(HF10U)-2-#

RX 300 4WD—V6—Truck Equipment Schedule T3

Body Type	VIN	List	Good	Very Good	Good	Excellent
Sport Utility 4D	HF10U	37580	4375	4800	5125	7375
Coach Edition			175	175	245	245
2WD	G		(425)	(425)	(575)	(575)
LX 470 4WD—V8—Truck Equipment Schedule T3						
Sport Utility 4D	HT00W	63051	9375	10050	10600	14300

2003 LEXUS — JTJ(HF10U)-3-#

RX 300 4WD—V6—Truck Equipment Schedule T3

Body Type	VIN	List	Good	Very Good	Good	Excellent
Sport Utility 4D	HF10U	38800	4725	5150	5550	7975
2WD	G		(475)	(475)	(645)	(645)
GX 470 4WD—V8—Truck Equipment Schedule T3						
Sport Utility 4D	BT20X	45500	7825	8375	9150	12450
Third Row Seat			625	625	840	840
LX 470 4WD—V8—Truck Equipment Schedule T3						
Sport Utility 4D	HT00W	63700	11900	12750	13000	17100

2004 LEXUS — JTJ(HA31U)-4-#

RX 330 AWD—V6—Truck Equipment Schedule T3

Body Type	VIN	List	Good	Very Good	Good	Excellent
Sport Utility 4D	HA31U	39195	7850	8525	8975	12550
Dynamic Cruise Control			275	275	355	355
Performance Pkg			1700	1700	2280	2280
2WD	G		(525)	(525)	(710)	(710)
GX 470 4WD—V8—Truck Equipment Schedule T3						
Sport Utility 4D	BT20X	45700	8925	9525	10300	13850
Third Row Seat			675	675	855	855
LX 470 4WD—V8—Truck Equipment Schedule T3						
Sport Utility 4D	HT00W	64800	13350	14200	14450	18700

2005 LEXUS — JTJ(HA31U)-5-#

RX 330 AWD—V6—Truck Equipment Schedule T3

Body Type	VIN	List	Good	Very Good	Good	Excellent
Sport Utility 4D	HA31U	37800	8375	9050	9850	13600
Dynamic Cruise Control			300	300	385	385
Performance Pkg			1850	1850	2475	2475
2WD	G		(575)	(575)	(775)	(775)
GX 470 4WD—V8—Truck Equipment Schedule T3						
Sport Utility 4D	BT20X	46425	10500	11200	11950	15550
Third Row Seat			700	700	855	855
LX 470 4WD—V8—Truck Equipment Schedule T3						
Sport Utility 4D	HT00W	65400	14300	15200	15800	20200

2006 LEXUS

Body Type	VIN	List	Trade-In Good	Very Good	Pvt-Party Good	Retail Excellent

2006 LEXUS — JTJ(HA31U)-6-#

RX 330 AWD—V6—Truck Equipment Schedule T3
Sport Utility 4D	HA31U	38420	9100	9775	10450	14050
Dynamic Cruise Control			325	325	415	415
Performance Pkg			2000	2000	2630	2630
2WD	G		(625)	(625)	(830)	(830)

RX 400h AWD—V6 Hybrid—Truck Equipment Schedule T3
Sport Utility 4D	HW31U	49060	9300	10000	10650	14200
Dynamic Cruise Control			325	325	420	420
2WD	G		(625)	(625)	(835)	(835)

GX 470 4WD—V8—Truck Equipment Schedule T3
Sport Utility 4D	BT20X	47185	11600	12250	13050	16550
Third Row Seat			725	725	860	860

LX 470 4WD—V8—Truck Equipment Schedule T3
Sport Utility 4D	HT00W	67945	16850	17850	18250	22800

2007 LEXUS — JTJ(HK31U)-7-#

RX 350 AWD—V6—Truck Equipment Schedule T3
Sport Utility 4D	HK31U	39495	10800	11550	12050	15600
Dynamic Cruise Control			350	350	430	430
Performance Pkg			2150	2150	2715	2715
2WD	G		(675)	(675)	(860)	(860)

RX 400h AWD—V6 Hybrid—Truck Equipment Schedule T3
Sport Utility 4D	HW31U	43275	11150	11900	12600	16400
Dynamic Cruise Control			350	350	430	430
2WD	G		(675)	(675)	(865)	(865)

GX 470 4WD—V8—Truck Equipment Schedule T3
Sport Utility 4D	BT20X	47330	14250	15000	15700	19400
Third Row Seat			750	750	885	885

LX 470 4WD—V8—Truck Equipment Schedule T3
Sport Utility 4D	HT00W	68090	19800	20800	21100	25900

2008 LEXUS — JTJ(HK31U)-8-#

RX 350 AWD—V6—Truck Equipment Schedule T3
Sport Utility 4D	HK31U	39565	11950	12600	13400	16700
Dynamic Cruise Control			375	375	450	450
Performance Pkg			2300	2300	2820	2820
FWD	G		(725)	(725)	(900)	(900)

RX 400h AWD—V6 Hybrid—Truck Equipment Schedule T3
Sport Utility 4D	HW31U	43345	13150	13850	14750	18350
Dynamic Cruise Control			375	375	455	455
2WD	G		(725)	(725)	(915)	(915)

GX 470 4WD—V8—Truck Equipment Schedule T3
Sport Utility 4D	BT20X	47580	17450	18200	19100	22900
Third Row Seat			800	800	900	900

LX 570 4WD—V8—Truck Equipment Schedule T3
Sport Utility 4D	HY00W	74565	31300	32700	32400	37700
Dynamic Cruise Control			375	375	455	455

2009 LEXUS — JTJ(HK31U)-9-#

RX 350 AWD—V6—Truck Equipment Schedule T3
Sport Utility 4D	HK31U	42765	14200	14850	16100	19500
Dynamic Cruise Control			375	375	445	445
Premium Pkg			700	700	830	830
Performance Pkg			2450	2450	2925	2925
FWD	G		(1200)	(1200)	(1430)	(1430)

GX 470 4WD—V8—Truck Equipment Schedule T3
Sport Utility 4D	BT20X	48380	19550	20200	21400	25000
Third Row Seat			800	800	920	920

LX 570 4WD—V8—Truck Equipment Schedule T3
Sport Utility 4D	HY00W	76530	32700	33800	34200	39000

2010 LEXUS — JT(Jor2)(BK1BA)-A-#

RX 350 AWD—V6—Truck Equipment Schedule T3
Sport Utility 4D	BK1BA	39025	18800	19450	20700	24100
Premium Pkg			750	750	860	860
FWD	Z		(1075)	(1075)	(1250)	(1250)

RX 450h AWD—V6 Hybrid—Truck Equipment Schedule T3
Sport Utility 4D	BC1BA	44125	21700	22400	23600	27300
Premium Pkg			750	750	845	845

Body Type	VIN	List	Trade-In Good	Very Good	Pvt-Party Good	Retail Excellent
FWD	Z		(1075)	(1075)	(1230)	(1230)
GX 460 4WD—V8—Truck Equipment Schedule T3						
Sport Utility 4D	BM7FX	52845	26900	27700	28800	32500
Premium Spt Util	JM7FX	57640	28000	28800	29800	33700
Power Third Row			800	800	890	890
LX 570 4WD—V8—Truck Equipment Schedule T3						
Sport Utility 4D	HY7AX	77280	36300	37300	38200	42900

2011 LEXUS — (JTor2T)(Jor2)(BK1BA)-B-#

Body Type	VIN	List	Trade-In Good	Very Good	Pvt-Party Good	Retail Excellent
RX 350 AWD—V6—Truck Equipment Schedule T3						
Sport Utility 4D	BK1BA	40250	20900	21500	23000	26200
Premium Pkg			800	800	900	900
FWD	Z		(1200)	(1200)	(1360)	(1360)
RX 450h AWD—V6 Hybrid—Truck Equipment Schedule T3						
Sport Utility 4D	BC1BA	45700	23900	24500	26100	29600
Premium Pkg			800	800	890	890
FWD	Z		(1200)	(1200)	(1345)	(1345)
GX 460 4WD—V8—Truck Equipment Schedule T3						
Sport Utility 4D	BM7FX	53220	29400	30100	31500	35000
Premium Utility	JM7FX	58015	32700	33500	34800	38500
LX 570 4WD—V8—Truck Equipment Schedule T3						
Sport Utility 4D	HY7AX	78630	41300	42300	43600	48100

2012 LEXUS — (JTor2T)(Jor2)(BK1BA)-C-#

Body Type	VIN	List	Trade-In Good	Very Good	Pvt-Party Good	Retail Excellent
RX 350 AWD—V6—Truck Equipment Schedule T3						
Sport Utility 4D	BK1BA	41350	24300	24800	26600	29700
Premium Pkg			850	850	940	940
FWD	Z		(1275)	(1275)	(1420)	(1420)
RX 450h AWD—V6 Hybrid—Truck Equipment Schedule T3						
Sport Utility 4D	BC1BA	47700	27600	28200	30000	33300
Premium Pkg			850	850	930	930
FWD	Z		(1275)	(1275)	(1405)	(1405)
GX 460 4WD—V8—Truck Equipment Schedule T3						
Sport Utility 4D	BM7FX	54120	32600	33300	35000	38500
Premium Spt Util	JM7FX	58915	36600	37400	38900	42400

2013 LEXUS — (JTor2T)(Jor2)(BK1BA)-D-#

Body Type	VIN	List	Trade-In Good	Very Good	Pvt-Party Good	Retail Excellent
RX 350 AWD—V6—Truck Equipment Schedule T3						
Sport Utility 4D	BK1BA	41585	28800	29300	31300	34500
FWD	Z		(1325)	(1325)	(1470)	(1470)
RX 350 F SPORT AWD—V6—Truck Equipment Schedule T3						
Sport Utility 4D	BK1BA	47875	31000	31600	33500	36800
RX 450h AWD—V6 Hybrid—Truck Equipment Schedule T3						
Sport Utility 4D	BC1BA	48185	33000	33600	35500	38900
FWD	Z		(1325)	(1325)	(1460)	(1460)
GX 460 4WD—V8—Truck Equipment Schedule T3						
Sport Utility 4D	BM7FX	54320	37200	37900	39500	42800
Premium Spt Util	JM7FX	59115	40000	40700	42500	46000
LX 570 AWD—V8—Truck Equipment Schedule T3						
Sport Utility 4D	HY7AX	81805	53300	54300	56400	61100

2014 LEXUS — (JTor2T)(Jor2)(BK1BA)-E-#

Body Type	VIN	List	Trade-In Good	Very Good	Pvt-Party Good	Retail Excellent
RX 350 AWD—V6—Truck Equipment Schedule T3						
Sport Utility 4D	BK1BA	43170	33100	33700	35400	38500
Comfort Pkg			500	500	530	530
Luxury Pkg			500	500	530	530
Dynamic Cruise Control			500	500	520	520
FWD	Z		(1400)	(1400)	(1495)	(1495)
RX 350 F SPORT AWD—V6—Truck Equipment Schedule T3						
Sport Utility 4D	BK1BA	48360	37500	38200	39700	42900
RX 450h AWD—V6 Hybrid—Truck Equipment Schedule T3						
Sport Utility 4D	BC1BA	49820	38800	39500	41100	44300
Comfort Pkg			500	500	525	525
Luxury Pkg			500	500	525	525
Premium Pkg			925	925	985	985
Dynamic Cruise Control			500	500	515	515
FWD	Z		(1400)	(1400)	(1480)	(1480)
GX 460 4WD—V8—Truck Equipment Schedule T3						
Sport Utility	BM7FX	49995	42900	43700	45100	48400
Premium Pkg			1775	1775	1895	1895
GX 460 4WD—V8—Truck Equipment Schedule T3						
Luxury Sport Util	JM7FX	61625	47600	48400	50200	53800

Body Type	VIN	List	Trade-In Good	Very Good	Pvt-Party Good	Retail Excellent
Driver Support Pkg			1175	1175	1245	1245
LX 570 AWD—V8—Truck Equipment Schedule T3						
Sport Utility 4D	HY7AX	82690	64700	65800	67300	72000
Sensing Cruise Control			500	500	525	525
Luxury Pkg			500	500	535	535

LINCOLN

2000 LINCOLN — 5LM–(U28A)–Y–#

NAVIGATOR 4WD—V8—Truck Equipment Schedule T3
Sport Utility 4D	U28A	46500	1325	1525	1925	3175
Air Conditioning, Rear			100	100	135	135
2WD	7		(325)	(325)	(445)	(445)

2001 LINCOLN — 5LM–(U28A,R)–1–#

NAVIGATOR 4WD—V8—Truck Equipment Schedule T3
Sport Utility 4D	U28A,R	48085	1525	1750	2225	3675
2WD	7		(375)	(375)	(510)	(510)

2002 LINCOLN — 5LM–(U28R)–2–#

NAVIGATOR 4WD—V8—Truck Equipment Schedule T3
Sport Utility 4D	U28R	48680	2050	2325	3000	4925
2WD	7		(425)	(425)	(575)	(575)

BLACKWOOD—V8—Truck Equipment Schedule T3
Sport Util Pickup 4D	W05A	52500	10850	12300	11200	15600

2003 LINCOLN — 5LM–(U88H)–3–#

AVIATOR AWD—V8—Truck Equipment Schedule T3
Sport Utility 4D	U88H	42945	3025	3450	3725	5850
2WD	6		(475)	(475)	(645)	(645)

NAVIGATOR 4WD—V8—Truck Equipment Schedule T3
Sport Utility 4D	U28R	52425	2900	3275	3975	6375
2WD			(475)	(475)	(645)	(645)

2004 LINCOLN — 5LM–(U88H)–4–#

AVIATOR AWD—V8—Truck Equipment Schedule T3
Sport Utility 4D	U88H	43400	3525	3975	4325	6700
2WD	6		(525)	(525)	(710)	(710)

NAVIGATOR 4WD—V8—Truck Equipment Schedule T3
Sport Utility 4D	U28R	52775	3725	4200	4900	7575
2WD	7		(525)	(525)	(710)	(710)

2005 LINCOLN — 5LM–(U88H)–5–#

AVIATOR AWD—V8—Truck Equipment Schedule T3
Sport Utility 4D	U88H	44150	3900	4400	4925	7325
2WD	6		(575)	(575)	(775)	(775)

NAVIGATOR 4WD—V8—Truck Equipment Schedule T3
Sport Utility 4D	U285	53985	5025	5625	6275	9150
2WD	7		(575)	(575)	(775)	(775)

2006 LINCOLN —5L(MorT)–(W165)–6–#

MARK LT 4WD—V8—Truck Equipment Schedule T3
Super Crew Pickup	W165	43595	12150	13450	13300	17950
2WD	6		(2000)	(2000)	(2420)	(2420)

NAVIGATOR 4WD—V8—Truck Equipment Schedule T3
Sport Utility 4D	U285	53075	6275	6975	7625	10750
Limited Edition			300	300	400	400
2WD	7		(625)	(625)	(845)	(845)

2007 LINCOLN — 5L(MorT)–(U68C)–7–#

MKX AWD—V6—Truck Equipment Schedule T3
Sport Utility 4D	U68C	36445	8925	9450	10450	13050
Elite Pkg			325	325	385	385
FWD			(575)	(575)	(700)	(700)

MARK LT—V8—Truck Equipment Schedule T3
Super Crew 6 1/2'	W165	42395	11700	12800	12900	17100
4WD	8		1875	1875	2200	2200

MARK LT 4WD—V8—Truck Equipment Schedule T3
Super Crew 5 1/2'	W165	42095	14800	16150	16050	21100

2007 LINCOLN

Body Type	VIN	List	Trade-In Good	Very Good	Pvt-Party Good	Retail Excellent
2WD	6	____	(2175)	(2175)	(2565)	(2565)
NAVIGATOR 4WD—V8—Truck Equipment Schedule T3						
Sport Utility 4D	U285	49475	9875	10800	11150	14950
Élite Pkg		____	325	325	420	420
2WD	6	____	(675)	(675)	(900)	(900)
NAVIGATOR L 4WD—V8—Truck Equipment Schedule T3						
Sport Utility 4D	L285	52475	11250	12350	12600	16800
Élite Pkg		____	325	325	415	415
2WD	6	____	(675)	(675)	(890)	(890)

2008 LINCOLN — 5L(MorT)-(U68C)-8-#

Body Type	VIN	List	Trade-In Good	Very Good	Pvt-Party Good	Retail Excellent
MKX AWD—V6—Truck Equipment Schedule T3						
Sport Utility 4D	U68C	37845	10750	11250	12400	15150
Limited Edition		____	325	325	405	405
FWD	6	____	(650)	(650)	(800)	(800)
MARK LT—V8—Truck Equipment Schedule T3						
Super Crew 6 1/2'	W165	39565	15150	16250	16450	20700
4WD	8	____	2125	2125	2460	2460
MARK LT 4WD—V8—Truck Equipment Schedule T3						
Super Crew 5 1/2'	W165	42365	18500	19850	19800	24900
2WD	6	____	(2400)	(2400)	(2745)	(2745)
NAVIGATOR 4WD—V8—Truck Equipment Schedule T3						
Sport Utility 4D	U285	51555	12250	13150	13500	17050
Élite Pkg		____	325	325	415	415
2WD	7	____	(725)	(725)	(900)	(900)
NAVIGATOR L 4WD—V8—Truck Equipment Schedule T3						
Sport Utility 4D	L285	54555	13200	14200	14650	18600
Élite Pkg		____	325	325	420	420
2WD	7	____	(725)	(725)	(910)	(910)

2009 LINCOLN — 5L(MorT)-(U68C)-9-#

Body Type	VIN	List	Trade-In Good	Very Good	Pvt-Party Good	Retail Excellent
MKX AWD—V6—Truck Equipment Schedule T3						
Sport Utility 4D	U68C	40035	12650	13200	14600	17350
Limited Edition		____	350	350	425	425
FWD	6	____	(700)	(700)	(840)	(840)
NAVIGATOR 4WD—V8—Truck Equipment Schedule T3						
Sport Utility 4D	U285	56265	15650	16500	17100	20800
Élite Pkg		____	350	350	420	420
2WD	7	____	(825)	(825)	(980)	(980)
NAVIGATOR L 4WD—V8—Truck Equipment Schedule T3						
Sport Utility 4D	L285	57955	17150	18100	18550	22500
Élite Pkg		____	350	350	415	415
2WD	7	____	(825)	(825)	(975)	(975)

2010 LINCOLN — (2or5)LM-(J6JC)-A-#

Body Type	VIN	List	Trade-In Good	Very Good	Pvt-Party Good	Retail Excellent
MKX AWD—V6—Truck Equipment Schedule T3						
Sport Utility 4D	J6JC	41045	14650	15200	16600	19250
Limited Edition		____	375	375	435	435
FWD	6	____	(750)	(750)	(870)	(870)
MKT—V6—Truck Equipment Schedule T3						
Sport Utility 4D	J5FR	44995	13150	13600	15200	17800
AWD	A	____	700	700	825	825
MKT AWD—V6 EcoBoost Twin Turbo—Truck Equipment Sch T3						
Sport Utility 4D	J5AT	49995	14500	14950	16700	19700
NAVIGATOR 4WD—V8—Truck Equipment Schedule T3						
Sport Utility 4D	J2J5	58225	18050	18800	19650	23300
Élite Pkg		____	375	375	435	435
2WD	H	____	(950)	(950)	(1110)	(1110)
NAVIGATOR L 4WD—V8—Truck Equipment Schedule T3						
Sport Utility 4D	J3J5	60390	19100	19900	20800	24500
Élite Pkg		____	375	375	430	430
2WD	H	____	(950)	(950)	(1105)	(1105)

2011 LINCOLN — (2or5)LM-(J6JK)-B-#

Body Type	VIN	List	Trade-In Good	Very Good	Pvt-Party Good	Retail Excellent
MKX AWD—V6—Truck Equipment Schedule T3						
Sport Utility 4D	J6JK	41845	17600	18200	19650	22400
Limited Edition		____	400	400	455	455
FWD	6	____	(1000)	(1000)	(1175)	(1175)
MKT—V6—Truck Equipment Schedule T3						
Sport Utility 4D	J5FR	44995	15900	16400	18150	21000
AWD	A	____	775	775	905	905

2011 LINCOLN

Body Type	VIN	List	Trade-In Good	Very Good	Pvt-Party Good	Retail Excellent
MKT AWD—V6 EcoBoost Twin Turbo—Truck Equipment Schedule T3						
Sport Utility 4D	J5AT	49995	**16850**	**17350**	**19400**	**22600**
NAVIGATOR 4WD—V8—Truck Equipment Schedule T3						
Sport Utility 4D	J2J5	60980	**22500**	**23300**	**24200**	**27900**
2WD	H		(1075)	(1075)	(1205)	(1205)
NAVIGATOR L 4WD—V8—Truck Equipment Schedule T3						
Sport Utility 4D	J3J5	63145	**22100**	**22800**	**23900**	**27500**
2WD	H		(1075)	(1075)	(1205)	(1205)

2012 LINCOLN — (2or5)LM–(J6JK)–C–#

Body Type	VIN	List	Trade-In Good	Very Good	Pvt-Party Good	Retail Excellent
MKX AWD—V6—Truck Equipment Schedule T3						
Sport Utility 4D	J6JK	42140	**20300**	**20900**	**22600**	**25500**
Limited Edition			400	400	460	460
FWD	6		(1075)	(1075)	(1240)	(1240)
MKT—V6—Truck Equipment Schedule T3						
Sport Utility 4D	J5FR	45095	**17300**	**17750**	**19450**	**22100**
AWD	A		850	850	960	960
MKT AWD—V6 EcoBoost Twin Turbo—Truck Equipment Schedule T3						
Sport Utility 4D	J5AT	47090	**19500**	**20000**	**21800**	**24800**
NAVIGATOR 4WD—V8—Truck Equipment Schedule T3						
Sport Utility 4D	J2J5	61670	**26600**	**27200**	**28400**	**32000**
2WD	H		(1500)	(1500)	(1680)	(1680)
NAVIGATOR L 4WD—V8—Truck Equipment Schedule T3						
Sport Utility 4D	J3J5	63835	**29700**	**30500**	**31500**	**35300**
2WD	H		(1500)	(1500)	(1665)	(1665)

2013 LINCOLN — (2or5)LM–(J6JK)–D–#

Body Type	VIN	List	Trade-In Good	Very Good	Pvt-Party Good	Retail Excellent
MKX AWD—V6—Truck Equipment Schedule T3						
Sport Utility 4D	J6JK	42270	**24700**	**25400**	**26900**	**30000**
Elite Pkg			400	400	445	445
Limited Edition Pkg			400	400	445	445
FWD	6		(1075)	(1075)	(1205)	(1205)
MKT—V6—Truck Equipment Schedule T3						
Sport Utility 4D	J5FK	46160	**19250**	**19750**	**21500**	**24100**
AWD	N,L		925	925	1035	1035
MKT AWD—V6 EcoBoost Twin Turbo—Truck Equipment Schedule T3						
Sport Utility 4D	J5AT	48155	**23800**	**24400**	**26300**	**29600**
NAVIGATOR 4WD—V8 Flex Fuel—Truck Equipment Schedule T3						
Sport Utility 4D	J2J5	61670	**29900**	**30500**	**32200**	**36200**
2WD	H		(1275)	(1275)	(1430)	(1430)
NAVIGATOR L 4WD—V8 Flex Fuel—Truck Equipment Schedule T3						
Sport Utility 4D	J3J5	63835	**33500**	**34200**	**35800**	**39900**
2WD	H		(1275)	(1275)	(1410)	(1410)

2014 LINCOLN — (2or5)LM–(J8JK)–E–#

Body Type	VIN	List	Trade-In Good	Very Good	Pvt-Party Good	Retail Excellent
MKX AWD—V6—Truck Equipment Schedule T3						
Sport Utility 4D	J8JK	41420	**28900**	**29700**	**31100**	**34300**
Adaptive Cruise Control			500	500	535	535
Elite Pkg			400	400	440	440
Limited Edition Pkg			400	400	440	440
FWD	6		(1100)	(1100)	(1195)	(1195)
MKT—V6—Truck Equipment Schedule T3						
Sport Utility 4D	J5FK	46180	**24900**	**25500**	**27000**	**29800**
AWD	L,N		1000	1000	1090	1090
4-Cyl, EcoBoost, 2.0L			475	475	510	510
MKT AWD—V6 EcoBoost Twin Turbo—Truck Equipment Schedule T3						
Sport Utility 4D	J5AT	48175	**27700**	**28400**	**29900**	**33000**
NAVIGATOR 4WD—V8 Flex Fuel—Truck Equipment Schedule T3						
Sport Utility 4D	J2J5	59845	**36000**	**36700**	**38300**	**42600**
2WD	H		(1375)	(1375)	(1515)	(1515)
NAVIGATOR L 4WD—V8 Flex Fuel—Truck Equipment Schedule T3						
Sport Utility 4D	J3J5	62010	**39000**	**39700**	**41200**	**45600**
2WD	H		(1375)	(1375)	(1510)	(1510)

MAZDA

2000 MAZDA–(JM3,4F2or4F4)–(LW28)–Y–#

Body Type	VIN	List	Trade-In Good	Very Good	Pvt-Party Good	Retail Excellent
MPV—V6—Truck Equipment Schedule T1						
DX Minivan 4D	LW28	20475	**725**	**925**	**1300**	**2375**
LX Minivan 4D	LW28	22530	**925**	**1175**	**1575**	**2825**

Body Type	VIN	List	Trade-In Good	Very Good	Pvt-Party Good	Retail Excellent
ES Minivan 4D	LW28	26030	1300	1600	1975	3500
B2500 PICKUP—4-Cyl.—Truck Equipment Schedule T2						
SX Short Bed	R12C	12005	750	825	1475	2625
SE Short Bed	R12C	14315	1175	1300	2050	3600
SE Cab Plus 2D	R16C	16505	1625	1775	2675	4650
B3000 PICKUP—V6—Truck Equipment Schedule T2						
SX Short Bed	R12V	12400	950	1050	1775	3100
SE Short Bed	R12V	14710	1175	1300	2050	3600
SE Cab Plus 2D	R16V	16975	1800	2000	3025	5225
SE Cab Plus 4D	R16V	17965	1950	2175	3250	5625
TroyLee Cb Plus 4D	R16V	19120	2150	2375	3500	6075
B3000 PICKUP 4WD—V6—Truck Equipment Schedule T2						
SE Short Bed	R13V	18235	1700	1875	2875	5000
SE Cab Plus 4D	R17V	20970	2350	2600	3725	6400
B4000 PICKUP—V6—Truck Equipment Schedule T2						
SE Cab Plus 4D	R16X	21390	2650	2925	4200	7225
B4000 PICKUP 4WD—V6—Truck Equipment Schedule T2						
SE Cab Plus 4D	R17X	23300	2700	2975	4275	7350
TroyLee Cb Plus 4D	R17X	24150	2875	3175	4525	7800

Body Type	VIN	List	Trade-In Good	Very Good	Pvt-Party Good	Retail Excellent
TRIBUTE 4WD—V6—Truck Equipment Schedule T1						
DX Sport Utility 4D	U061	21055	850	975	1600	2850
LX Sport Utility 4D	U081	22535	1250	1425	2100	3650
ES Sport Utility 4D	U081	23540	1475	1650	2375	4100
2WD			(375)	(375)	(510)	(510)
4-Cyl, 2.0 Liter	B		(225)	(225)	(285)	(285)
MPV—V6—Truck Equipment Schedule T1						
DX Minivan 4D	LW28	21155	800	1025	1400	2475
LX Minivan 4D	LW28	23280	1150	1425	1775	3150
ES Minivan 4D	LW28	26760	1550	1900	2250	3950
B2300 PICKUP—4-Cyl.—Truck Equipment Schedule T2						
SX Short Bed	R12D	12930	1100	1200	1825	3075
SE Short Bed	R12D	15130	1575	1725	2425	4050
B2500 PICKUP—4-Cyl.—Truck Equipment Schedule T2						
SX Short Bed	R12C	12785	1000	1100	1700	2875
SE Short Bed	R12C	14985	1500	1650	2325	3875
B3000 PICKUP—V6—Truck Equipment Schedule T2						
SE Short Bed	R12U	15575	1675	1850	2650	4400
Dual Spt Short Bed	R12U	15315	1700	1875	2675	4450
SE Cab Plus 2D	R16U	17810	2175	2400	3275	5450
SE Cab Plus 4D	R16U	18180	2400	2625	3550	5900
Dual Sport Cab + 4D	R16U	17735	2475	2725	3650	6050
B3000 PICKUP 4WD—V6—Truck Equipment Schedule T2						
4WD SE Short Bed	R13U	15575	2075	2275	3100	5100
SE Cab Plus 4D	R13U	20615	2600	2850	3900	6500
B4000 PICKUP—V6—Truck Equipment Schedule T2						
Dual Sport Cab + 4D	R17X	19935	2825	3125	4100	6800
B4000 PICKUP 4WD—V6—Truck Equipment Schedule T2						
SE Cab Plus 4D	R17X	22780	3175	3500	4525	7475

Body Type	VIN	List	Trade-In Good	Very Good	Pvt-Party Good	Retail Excellent
TRIBUTE 4WD—V6—Truck Equipment Schedule T1						
DX Sport Utility 4D	U061	22575	975	1100	1725	2975
LX Sport Utility 4D	U081	23225	1450	1600	2325	3975
ES Sport Utility 4D	U081	24455	1825	2050	2800	4675
2WD			(425)	(425)	(575)	(575)
4-Cyl, 2.0 Liter	B		(250)	(250)	(345)	(345)
MPV—V6—Truck Equipment Schedule T1						
LX Minivan 4D	LW28	22770	1500	1825	2225	3875
ES Minivan 4D	LW28	27712	2025	2450	2900	5025
B2300 PICKUP—4-Cyl.—Truck Equipment Schedule T2						
Short Bed	R12D	13240	1475	1625	2250	3650
B3000 PICKUP—V6—Truck Equipment Schedule T2						
Dual Spt Short Bed	R12U	15870	2150	2350	3125	5075
Dual Spt Cab + 2D	R16U	18290	3100	3400	4275	6850
B3000 PICKUP 4WD—V6—Truck Equipment Schedule T2						
Cab Plus 2D	R13U	20775	3300	3600	4500	7225
B4000 PICKUP—V6—Truck Equipment Schedule T2						
Dual Spt Cab + 4D	R17E	20085	3350	3650	4550	7325
B4000 PICKUP 4WD—V6—Truck Equipment Schedule T2						
Cab Plus 4D	R17E	22830	3600	3950	5000	8025

TRUCKS & VANS

Body Type	VIN	List	Trade-In Good	Very Good	Pvt-Party Good	Retail Excellent
2003 MAZDA–(JM3,4F2or4F4)–(Z92B)–3–#						
TRIBUTE 4WD—4-Cyl.—Truck Equipment Schedule T1						
DX Sport Utility 4D	Z92B	20440	1000	1125	1775	3000
2WD	0		(475)	(475)	(645)	(645)
TRIBUTE 4WD—V6—Truck Equipment Schedule T2						
LX Sport Utility 4D	Z941	22125	1700	1900	2650	4375
ES Sport Utility 4D	Z961	24885	2075	2300	3100	5125
2WD	0		(475)	(475)	(645)	(645)
MPV—V6—Truck Equipment Schedule T1						
LX S-V Minivan 4D	LW28A	21895	1575	1900	2250	3825
LX Minivan 4D	LW28A	23120	1850	2250	2650	4475
ES Minivan 4D	LW28A	26520	2400	2900	3225	5425
B2300 PICKUP—4-Cyl.—Truck Equipment Schedule T2						
Short Bed	R12D	13740	1875	2050	2700	4275
SE Cab Plus	R16D	17960	2900	3175	3875	6075
B3000 PICKUP—V6—Truck Equipment Schedule T2						
Dual Spt Short Bed	R12U	16590	2675	2925	3625	5675
Dual Spt Cab + 2D	R16V	18700	3650	4000	4875	7575
SE Cab Plus 4D	R46V	18935	3600	3925	4825	7500
B4000 PICKUP—V6—Truck Equipment Schedule T2						
Dual Spt Cab + 4D	R17E	20495	3900	4275	5175	8025
B4000 PICKUP 4WD—V6—Truck Equipment Schedule T2						
Cab Plus 2D	R17X	20260	3825	4175	5075	7875
SE Cab Plus 2D	R17X	21705	4175	4550	5475	8500
SE Cab Plus 4D	R17X	23240	4450	4750	5675	8800
2004 MAZDA–(JM3,4F2or4F4)–(Z92B)–4–#						
TRIBUTE 4WD—4-Cyl.—Truck Equipment Schedule T2						
DX Sport Utility 4D	Z92B	21087	1150	1275	1900	3150
2WD	0		(525)	(525)	(710)	(710)
TRIBUTE 4WD—V6—Truck Equipment Schedule T1						
LX Sport Utility 4D	Z941	23972	2025	2250	3000	4825
ES Sport Utility 4D	Z961	25562	2275	2525	3325	5375
2WD	0		(525)	(525)	(710)	(710)
MPV—V6—Truck Equipment Schedule T1						
LX Minivan 4D	W28A	23780	2325	2775	3125	5150
ES Minivan 4D	W28A	28750	3025	3600	3875	6325
B2300 PICKUP—4-Cyl.—Truck Equipment Schedule T2						
Short Bed	R12D	14840	2275	2500	3200	5025
SE Cab Plus	R16D	18980	3475	3775	4550	7025
B3000 PICKUP—V6—Truck Equipment Schedule T2						
Dual Sport 6'	R12U	17915	3175	3475	4225	6550
Dual Sport Cab + 2D	R16V	19871	4350	4725	5675	8725
SE Cab Plus 4D	R46V	20140	4450	4850	5800	8900
B4000 PICKUP—V6—Truck Equipment Schedule T2						
Dual Sport Cab + 4D	R17E	21865	4650	5075	6025	9250
B4000 PICKUP 4WD—V6—Truck Equipment Schedule T2						
Cab Plus 2D	R17X	20850	4575	4975	5900	9100
SE Cab Plus 2D	R17X	22350	5025	5450	6450	9850
SE Cab Plus 4D	R17X	24090	5225	5700	6700	10250
2005 MAZDA–(JM3,4F2or4F4)–(Z02Z)–5–#						
TRIBUTE—4-Cyl.—Truck Equipment Schedule T1						
i Sport Utility 4D	Z02Z	20515	1350	1525	2325	3650
4WD			575	575	775	775
TRIBUTE—V6—Truck Equipment Schedule T1						
s Sport Utility 4D	Z941	24980	2250	2500	3350	5175
2WD	0		(575)	(575)	(775)	(775)
MPV—V6—Truck Equipment Schedule T1						
LX-SV Minivan 4D	W28A	22665	2375	2825	3400	5550
LX Minivan 4D	W28A	23485	2875	3400	3925	6375
ES Minivan 4D	W28J	29050	3625	4300	4900	7850
B2300 PICKUP—4-Cyl.—Truck Equipment Schedule T2						
Short Bed	R12D	15935	2625	2875	3725	5575
B3000 PICKUP—V6—Truck Equipment Schedule T2						
Extended Cab 4D	R46U	19480	5900	6425	7300	10450
Dual Sport 6'	R12U	20120	3675	4025	5000	7425
Dual Sport Ext 4D	R46U	21870	6025	6550	7525	10850
B4000 PICKUP 4WD—V6—Truck Equipment Schedule T2						
Extended Cab 4D	R47E	22220	6350	6875	7750	11100
SE Extended Cab 4D	R47E	26765	6600	7150	8350	12250

Body Type	VIN	List	Trade-In Good	Very Good	Pvt-Party Good	Retail Excellent

2006 MAZDA–(JM1or3,4F2or4)(CR293)–6–#

MAZDA5—4-Cyl.—Truck Equipment Schedule T1
| Sport Minivan 4D | CR293 | 18895 | 2950 | 3350 | 4025 | 6300 |
| Touring Minivan 4D | CR193 | 20410 | 3450 | 3925 | 4575 | 7100 |

TRIBUTE—4-Cyl.—Truck Equipment Schedule T1
| i Sport Utility 4D | Z02Z | 21525 | 1625 | 1800 | 2600 | 3925 |
| 4WD | 9 | | 625 | 625 | 845 | 845 |

TRIBUTE 4WD—V6—Truck Equipment Schedule T1
| s Sport Utility 4D | Z941 | 25290 | 2975 | 3275 | 4150 | 6225 |
| 2WD | 0 | | (625) | (625) | (845) | (845) |

MPV—V6—Truck Equipment Schedule T1
LX-SV Minivan 4D	W28A	22675	3200	3725	4400	7100
LX Minivan 4D	W28A	23510	3550	4150	4950	7900
ES Minivan 4D	W28J	29075	4550	5300	6050	9600

B2300 PICKUP—4-Cyl.—Truck Equipment Schedule T2
| Short Bed | R12D | 15690 | 3300 | 3575 | 4425 | 6475 |

B3000 PICKUP—V6—Truck Equipment Schedule T2
Extended Cab 4D	R46U	19510	6525	7050	8000	11300
Dual Sport 6'	R12U	20145	4775	5150	6125	8850
Dual Sport Ext 4D	R46U	21900	7650	8250	9150	12800

B4000 PICKUP 4WD—V6—Truck Equipment Schedule T2
| Extended Cab 4D | R47E | 22515 | 7425 | 8025 | 8925 | 12500 |
| SE Extended Cab 4D | R47E | 27060 | 7875 | 8525 | 9750 | 13950 |

2007 MAZDA–(JM1or3,4F2or4)(CR193)–7–#

MAZDA5—4-Cyl.—Truck Equipment Schedule T1
Sport Minivan 4D	CR193	19130	3725	4200	4925	7400
Touring Minivan 4D	CR193	20645	4425	4975	5675	8500
Grand Touring 4D	CR193	21895	4625	5175	5875	8775

CX-7—4-Cyl. Turbo—Truck Equipment Schedule T1
"Sport" SUV 4D	ER293	26010	4150	4525	5250	7325
Touring Sport Util	ER293	27760	4200	4575	5425	7675
AWD			525	525	685	685

CX-7 AWD—4-Cyl. Turbo—Truck Equipment Schedule T1
| Grand Touring Util | ER293 | 28560 | 4700 | 5100 | 5925 | 8350 |
| FWD | | | (575) | (575) | (775) | (775) |

CX-9—V6—Truck Equipment Schedule T1
"Sport" SUV 4D	TB28Y	30830	5800	6525	6775	9425
Grand Touring 4D	TB28Y	34470	7200	8075	8325	11700
AWD	3		525	525	685	685

CX-9 AWD—V6—Truck Equipment Schedule T1
| Touring Sport Util | TB38Y | 32930 | 7000 | 7850 | 8025 | 11200 |
| FWD | | | (575) | (575) | (775) | (775) |

B2300 PICKUP—4-Cyl.—Truck Equipment Schedule T2
| Short Bed | R12D | 16170 | 4000 | 4325 | 5175 | 7250 |

B3000 PICKUP—V6—Truck Equipment Schedule T2
Extended Cab 4D	R46U	19675	8150	8775	9525	12850
Dual Sport 6'	R12U	20310	5725	6175	7175	9925
Dual Sport Ext 4D	R46U	22065	8650	9300	10100	13750

B4000 PICKUP 4WD—V6—Truck Equipment Schedule T2
| Extended Cab 4D | R47E | 22680 | 8600 | 9250 | 9975 | 13500 |
| SE Extended Cab 4D | R47E | 27225 | 8625 | 9275 | 10450 | 14550 |

2008 MAZDA–(JM1or3,4F2or4)(CR293)–8–#

MAZDA5—4-Cyl.—Truck Equipment Schedule T1
Sport Minivan 4D	CR293	19580	4175	4600	5425	7800
Touring Minivan 4D	CR293	21245	4975	5475	6250	8925
Grand Touring 4D	CR293	23000	5150	5650	6425	9175

TRIBUTE—4-Cyl. Hybrid—Truck Equipment Schedule T1
| HEV Touring | Z49H | 28535 | 6275 | 6725 | 7875 | 10650 |
| 4WD | | | 1075 | 1075 | 1425 | 1425 |

TRIBUTE 4WD—4-Cyl. Hybrid—Truck Equipment Schedule T1
| HEV Grand Touring | Z59H | 31045 | 9050 | 9700 | 10950 | 14650 |
| 2WD | | | (725) | (725) | (975) | (975) |

TRIBUTE—4-Cyl.—Truck Equipment Schedule T1
i Sport Utility 4D	Z02Z	20910	3950	4250	5125	6875
i Grand Touring Util	Z02Z	23875	5525	5950	7025	9425
4WD	9		1075	1075	1425	1425

TRIBUTE 4WD—4-Cyl.—Truck Equipment Schedule T1
| i Touring Spt Util | Z02Z | 23435 | 5400 | 5775 | 6850 | 9175 |
| 2WD | 0 | | (725) | (725) | (975) | (975) |

TRUCKS & VANS

Body Type	VIN	List	Trade-In Good	Trade-In Very Good	Pvt-Party Good	Retail Excellent
TRIBUTE 4WD—V6—Truck Equipment Schedule T1						
s Sport Utility 4D	Z961	23900	5675	6100	7125	9525
s Touring Spt Util	Z961	24675	5825	6250	7300	9775
s Grand Touring Util	Z961	26865	6750	7225	8375	11300
2WD	0		(725)	(725)	(975)	(975)
CX-7—4-Cyl. Turbo—Truck Equipment Schedule T1						
"Sport" SUV 4D	ER293	24345	4375	4700	5575	7525
Touring Sport Util	ER293	26095	5025	5400	6425	8600
AWD			550	550	720	720
CX-7 AWD—4-Cyl. Turbo—Truck Equipment Schedule T1						
Grand Touring Util	ER293	28595	5175	5575	6625	8900
FWD			(650)	(650)	(880)	(880)
CX-9—V6—Truck Equipment Schedule T1						
"Sport" SUV 4D	TB28A	29995	7100	7825	7975	10450
Grand Touring Util	TB28A	33950	8725	9575	9575	12500
AWD	3		550	550	670	670
CX-9 AWD—V6—Truck Equipment Schedule T1						
Touring Sport Util	TB38A	32930	8300	9150	9175	12000
FWD			(650)	(650)	(815)	(815)
B2300 PICKUP—4-Cyl.—Truck Equipment Schedule T2						
Short Bed	R12D	16170	4900	5225	6150	8300
B4000 PICKUP 4WD—V6—Truck Equipment Schedule T2						
Extended Cab 4D	R47E	22680	9425	10050	11050	14500
SE Extended Cab 4D	R47E	27225	12000	12800	13850	18200

2009 MAZDA–(JM1or3,4F2or4)(CR293)–9–#

Body Type	VIN	List	Trade-In Good	Trade-In Very Good	Pvt-Party Good	Retail Excellent
MAZDA5—4-Cyl.—Truck Equipment Schedule T1						
Sport Minivan 4D	CR293	19775	5075	5500	6450	8750
Touring Minivan 4D	CR293	21590	6150	6675	7575	10200
Grand Touring 4D	CR293	23345	6575	7100	8000	10750
TRIBUTE—4-Cyl. Hybrid—Truck Equipment Schedule T1						
HEV Touring	Z493	28845	8050	8500	9650	12300
4WD			1150	1150	1505	1505
TRIBUTE 4WD—4-Cyl. Hybrid—Truck Equipment Schedule T1						
HEV Grand Touring	Z593	33195	10300	10900	12000	15200
2WD			(825)	(825)	(1060)	(1060)
TRIBUTE—4-Cyl.—Truck Equipment Schedule T1						
i Sport Utility 4D	Z027	22460	4600	4875	5825	7550
i Grand Touring Util	Z027	25290	6800	7225	8250	10550
4WD	9		1150	1150	1520	1520
TRIBUTE 4WD—4-Cyl.—Truck Equipment Schedule T1						
i Touring Spt Util	Z927	25360	6875	7300	8375	10650
2WD			(825)	(825)	(1070)	(1070)
TRIBUTE 4WD—V6—Truck Equipment Schedule T1						
s Sport Utility 4D	Z96G	23605	6725	7125	8100	10300
s Touring Spt Util	Z96G	26620	7325	7750	8800	11150
s Grand Touring Util	Z96G	28305	8325	8825	9950	12650
2WD	0		(825)	(825)	(1075)	(1075)
CX-7—4-Cyl. Turbo—Truck Equipment Schedule T1						
"Sport" SUV 4D	ER293	24550	5500	5850	6950	8950
Touring Sport Util	ER293	26450	6325	6700	7850	10100
AWD			625	625	815	815
CX-7 AWD—4-Cyl. Turbo—Truck Equipment Schedule T1						
Grand Touring Util	ER293	29050	6600	7000	8275	10800
FWD			(700)	(700)	(935)	(935)
CX-9—V6—Truck Equipment Schedule T1						
"Sport" SUV 4D	TB28A	30490	8625	9325	9725	12400
Grand Touring Util	TB28A	34475	10700	11550	11800	15000
AWD	3		625	625	760	760
CX-9 AWD—V6—Truck Equipment Schedule T1						
Touring Sport Util	TB38A	33785	10150	10950	11300	14350
FWD			(700)	(700)	(855)	(855)
B2300 PICKUP—4-Cyl.—Truck Equipment Schedule T2						
Short Bed	R12D	16780	5750	6100	7175	9300
SE-5 Pkg			125	125	145	145
B4000 PICKUP 4WD—V6—Truck Equipment Schedule T2						
Extended Cab 4D	R47E	22870	10350	10950	12000	15300

2010 MAZDA–(JM1or3,4F2or4)(CR293)–A–#

Body Type	VIN	List	Trade-In Good	Trade-In Very Good	Pvt-Party Good	Retail Excellent
MAZDA5—4-Cyl.—Truck Equipment Schedule T1						
Sport Minivan 4D	CR293	18745	6600	7050	7850	10050
Touring Minivan 4D	CR293	22000	7700	8225	9125	11700

Body Type	VIN	List	Trade-In Good	Very Good	Pvt-Party Good	Retail Excellent
Grand Touring 4D	CR293	23755	**8050**	**8575**	**9475**	**12150**
TRIBUTE—4-Cyl.—Truck Equipment Schedule T1						
i Sport Utility 4D	Y0C7	22880	**5825**	**6125**	**7400**	**9350**
i Grand Touring Util	Y0C7	25985	**7700**	**8075**	**9375**	**11650**
4WD	9		**1250**	**1250**	**1580**	**1580**
TRIBUTE 4WD—4-Cyl.—Truck Equipment Schedule T1						
i Touring Spt Util	Y9C7	25780	**7575**	**7925**	**9225**	**11450**
2WD	0		**(950)**	**(950)**	**(1200)**	**(1200)**
TRIBUTE 4WD—4-Cyl.—Truck Equipment Schedule T1						
s Grand Touring	Y9GG	29350	**9350**	**9800**	**11100**	**13650**
2WD	0		**(950)**	**(950)**	**(1175)**	**(1175)**
CX-7—4-Cyl.—Truck Equipment Schedule T1						
i SV Sport Util 4D	ER2W5	22480	**7750**	**8125**	**9625**	**12150**
i Sport SUV 4D	ER2W5	22300	**7350**	**7700**	**9225**	**11700**
CX-7—4-Cyl. Turbo—Truck Equipment Schedule T1						
s Grand Touring	ER2W3	33815	**8675**	**9100**	**10750**	**13600**
AWD	0		**700**	**700**	**925**	**925**
CX-7 AWD—4-Cyl. Turbo—Truck Equipment Schedule T1						
s Touring Spt Util	ER4W3	28250	**9150**	**9600**	**11150**	**14000**
FWD	2		**(750)**	**(750)**	**(970)**	**(970)**
CX-9—V6—Truck Equipment Schedule T1						
"Sport" SUV 4D	TB28A	29385	**10150**	**10800**	**11700**	**14800**
Grand Touring Util	TB28A	33395	**11750**	**12500**	**13400**	**16900**
AWD	3		**700**	**700**	**885**	**885**
CX-9 AWD—V6—Truck Equipment Schedule T1						
Touring Sport Util	TB38A	32705	**11400**	**12150**	**13050**	**16500**
FWD			**(750)**	**(750)**	**(940)**	**(940)**

2011 MAZDA — (4F2orJM3)-(Y0C7)-B-#

Body Type	VIN	List	Good	Very Good	Good	Excellent
TRIBUTE—4-Cyl.—Truck Equipment Schedule T1						
i Sport Utility 4D	Y0C7	23225	**6675**	**6950**	**8350**	**10250**
i Grand Touring Util	Y0C7	26330	**8475**	**8825**	**10100**	**12100**
4WD	9		**1400**	**1400**	**1725**	**1725**
TRIBUTE 4WD—4-Cyl.—Truck Equipment Schedule T1						
i Touring Spt Util	Y9C7	26125	**8325**	**8675**	**9975**	**11950**
2WD	0		**(1075)**	**(1075)**	**(1285)**	**(1285)**
TRIBUTE 4WD—V6—Truck Equipment Schedule T1						
s Grand Touring	Y9GG	29695	**11300**	**11750**	**13150**	**15600**
2WD	0		**(1075)**	**(1075)**	**(1270)**	**(1270)**
CX-7—4-Cyl.—Truck Equipment Schedule T1						
i SV Sport Utility	ER2A5	22785	**9550**	**9925**	**11350**	**13600**
i Sport Utility	ER2B5	23590	**10100**	**10550**	**11850**	**14100**
i Touring Sport Util	ER2C5	27185	**11100**	**11550**	**12900**	**15300**
CX-7—4-Cyl. Turbo—Truck Equipment Schedule T1						
s Grand Touring	ER2D3	32435	**12050**	**12550**	**14000**	**16650**
AWD	4		**775**	**775**	**920**	**920**
CX-7 AWD—4-Cyl. Turbo—Truck Equipment Schedule T1						
s Touring Spt Util	ER4C3	28750	**11800**	**12250**	**13600**	**16150**
FWD	2		**(1000)**	**(1000)**	**(1200)**	**(1200)**
CX-9 AWD—V6—Truck Equipment Schedule T1						
"Sport" SUV 4D	TB2BA	31320	**12450**	**13100**	**13900**	**16900**
Touring Sport Util	TB2CA	33240	**13950**	**14700**	**15400**	**18500**
Grand Touring Util	TB2DA	35330	**16100**	**16950**	**17600**	**21100**
FWD	2		**(1000)**	**(1000)**	**(1145)**	**(1145)**

2012 MAZDA — 4F(2or3)JM(2or3)-(W2BL)-C-#

Body Type	VIN	List	Good	Very Good	Good	Excellent
MAZDA5—4-Cyl.—Truck Equipment Schedule T1						
Sport Minivan 4D	W2BL	20990	**8800**	**9200**	**10300**	**12650**
Touring Minivan 4D	W2CL	21990	**9975**	**10400**	**11550**	**14100**
Grand Touring 4D	W2DL	24670	**10800**	**11300**	**12450**	**15150**
CX-7—4-Cyl.—Truck Equipment Schedule T1						
i SV Sport Utility	ER2A5	22985	**10100**	**10450**	**12050**	**14350**
i Sport Utility	ER2B5	23790	**11450**	**11800**	**13400**	**15750**
i Touring Sport Util	ER2C5	27385	**12600**	**13000**	**14750**	**17350**
CX-7—4-Cyl. Turbo—Truck Equipment Schedule T1						
s Grand Touring	ER2D3	32635	**14750**	**15300**	**17000**	**19850**
AWD	4		**850**	**850**	**1000**	**1000**
CX-7 AWD—4-Cyl. Turbo—Truck Equipment Schedule T1						
s Touring Spt Util	ER4C3	28950	**13700**	**14200**	**15950**	**18700**
FWD	2		**(1075)**	**(1075)**	**(1265)**	**(1265)**
CX-9 AWD—V6—Truck Equipment Schedule T1						
"Sport" SUV 4D	TB2BA	31570	**14700**	**15350**	**16450**	**19600**

Body Type	VIN	List	Trade-In Good	Very Good	Pvt-Party Good	Retail Excellent
Touring Sport Util	TB2CA	33490	16300	17050	17950	21200
Grand Touring Util	TB2DA	35580	18900	19750	20600	24300
FWD			(1075)	(1075)	(1230)	(1230)

2013 MAZDA — 4F(2or3)JM(2or3)-(CW2BL)-D-#

MAZDA5—4-Cyl.—Truck Equipment Schedule T1
Sport Minivan 4D	CW2BL	21735	10000	10400	12000	14900
Touring Minivan	CW2CL	22865	11200	11650	13350	16500
Grand Touring 4D	CW2DL	25265	12050	12500	14200	17550

CX-5—4-Cyl. SKYACTIV—Truck Equipment Schedule T1
Sport SUV 4D	KE2BE	22890	12700	13050	14750	17150
Touring Sport Util	KE2CE	24690	15000	15500	17250	19850
Grand Touring	KE2DE	27840	17300	17850	19750	22700
AWD	4		925	925	1080	1080

CX-9 AWD—V6—Truck Equipment Schedule T1
"Sport" SUV 4D	TB3BA	32170	16700	17350	18600	21900
Touring Sport Util	TB3CA	34615	18100	18800	19900	23300
Grand Touring Util	TB3DA	37170	21300	22100	22900	26500
FWD	2		(1075)	(1075)	(1230)	(1230)

2014 MAZDA — 4F(2or3)JM(2or3)-(CW2BL)-E-#

MAZDA5—4-Cyl—Truck Equipment Schedule T1
Sport Minivan 4D	CW2BL	21935	11600	12050	13600	16550
Touring Minivan	CW2CL	23065	12950	13450	15150	18400
Grand Touring 4D	CW2DL	25465	15150	15700	17300	20800

CX-5—4-Cyl. SKYACTIV—Truck Equipment Schedule T1
Sport SUV 4D	KE2BE	23390	15250	15700	17350	19750
Touring Sport Util	KE2CY	25410	16300	16800	18400	20900
Grand Touring	KE2DY	28415	19050	19650	21400	24400
AWD	4		1000	1000	1140	1140

CX-9 AWD—V6—Truck Equipment Schedule T1
"Sport" SUV 4D	TB3BA	32370	17800	18500	19500	22700
Touring Sport Util	TB3CA	34865	19600	20400	21300	24700
Grand Touring Util	TB3DA	37420	23500	24400	25100	28800
FWD	2		(1100)	(1100)	(1230)	(1230)

MERCEDES-BENZ

2000 MERCEDES-BENZ — 4JG(AB54E)-Y-#

ML-CLASS 4WD—V6—Truck Equipment Schedule T3
ML320 Spt Util 4D	AB54E	36895	1575	1700	2425	3825
Third Row Seat			150	150	195	195

ML-CLASS 4WD—V8—Truck Equipment Schedule T3
ML430 Spt Util 4D	AB72E	44345	2100	2275	3150	4925
ML55 Spt Util 4D	AB74E	65495	2375	2575	3525	5525
Third Row Seat			150	150	195	195

2001 MERCEDES-BENZ — 4JG(AB54E)-1-#

ML-CLASS 4WD—V6—Truck Equipment Schedule T3
ML320 Spt Util 4D	AB54E	38045	1700	1825	2625	4050
Sport Pkg			350	350	475	475
Third Row Seat			175	175	215	215
designo Edition			450	450	605	605

ML-CLASS 4WD—V8—Truck Equipment Schedule T3
ML430 Spt Util 4D	AB72E	44845	2725	2925	3775	5750
ML55 Spt Util 4D	AB74E	66545	2825	3050	4100	6350
Sport Pkg			350	350	475	475
Third Row Seat			175	175	215	215
designo Edition			450	450	605	605

2002 MERCEDES-BENZ — WDCor4JG(AB54E)-2-#

ML-CLASS 4WD—V6—Truck Equipment Schedule T3
ML320 Spt Util 4D	AB54E	36945	2125	2300	2975	4400
designo Edition			500	500	665	665
Third Row Seat			175	175	240	240
Sport Pkg			400	400	535	535

ML-CLASS 4WD—V8—Truck Equipment Schedule T3
ML500 Spt Util 4D	AB75E	45595	3000	3225	4000	5925
ML55 Spt Util 4D	AB74E	66545	3050	3275	4500	7050
Sport Pkg			400	400	535	535

TRUCKS & VANS

Body Type	VIN	List	Trade-In Good	Very Good	Pvt-Party Good	Retail Excellent
Third Row Seat			175	175	240	240
designo Edition			500	500	665	665
G-CLASS 4WD—V8—Truck Equipment Schedule T3						
G500 Sport Util 4D	YR49E	73145	**21900**	**23400**	**22400**	**28700**
designo Edition			500	500	595	595

2003 MERCEDES-BENZ — WDCor4JG(AB54E)-3-#

ML-CLASS 4WD—V6—Truck Equipment Schedule T3						
ML320 Spt Util 4D	AB54E	40315	**2650**	**2850**	**3625**	**5350**
ML350 Spt Util 4D	AB57E	40665	**2825**	**3025**	**3925**	**5950**
Sport Pkg			450	450	595	595
Inspiration Edition			400	400	540	540
designo Edition			550	550	725	725
Third Row Seat			200	200	260	260
ML-CLASS 4WD—V8—Truck Equipment Schedule T3						
ML500 Spt Util 4D	AB75E	46015	**3275**	**3525**	**4500**	**6725**
ML55 Spt Util 4D	AB74E	66565	**5525**	**5925**	**7100**	**10150**
Sport Pkg			450	450	595	595
Inspiration Edition			400	400	540	540
designo Edition			550	550	725	725
Third Row Seat			200	200	260	260
G-CLASS 4WD—V8—Truck Equipment Schedule T3						
G500 Spt Util 4D	YR49	74265	**23600**	**25200**	**24300**	**31200**
G55 Spt Util 4D	YR46	90565	**26900**	**28700**	**26800**	**33400**
designo Edition			550	550	640	640

2004 MERCEDES-BENZ — WDCor4JG(AB57E)-4-#

ML-CLASS 4WD—V6—Truck Equipment Schedule T3						
ML350 Sport Util	AB57E	39720	**3425**	**3675**	**4600**	**6725**
Inspiration Edition			450	450	585	585
designo Edition			600	600	785	785
Third Row Seat			225	225	285	285
ML-CLASS 4WD—V8—Truck Equipment Schedule T3						
ML500 Spt Util 4D	AB75E	46470	**3775**	**4025**	**5050**	**7325**
Inspiration Edition			450	450	585	585
designo Edition			600	600	785	785
Third Row Seat			225	225	285	285
G-CLASS 4WD—V8—Truck Equipment Schedule T3						
G500 Sport Util	YR49	76870	**25500**	**27100**	**26100**	**32900**
G55 Sport Util	YR46	93420	**32700**	**34800**	**32300**	**39700**
designo Edition			600	600	665	665

2005 MERCEDES-BENZ — WDCor4JG(AB57E)-5-#

M-CLASS 4WD—V6—Truck Equipment Schedule T3						
ML350 Sport Util	AB57E	40370	**4175**	**4475**	**5600**	**7900**
Special Edition			475	475	635	635
designo Edition			625	625	845	845
Third Row Seat			250	250	320	320
M-CLASS 4WD—V8—Truck Equipment Schedule T3						
ML500 Spt Util 4D	AB75E	47120	**4550**	**4850**	**6050**	**8475**
Special Edition			475	475	635	635
designo Edition			625	625	845	845
Third Row Seat			250	250	320	320
G-CLASS 4WD—V8—Truck Equipment Schedule T3						
G500 Sport Util	YR49E	78420	**30200**	**32000**	**30700**	**37800**
G500 Grand Ed Util	YR49C	80420	**31800**	**33700**	**32200**	**39700**
designo Edition			625	625	710	710
G-CLASS 4WD—V8 Supercharged—Truck Equipment Schedule T3						
G55 Spt Util 4D	YR46E	100620	**35700**	**37800**	**35500**	**43100**
G55 Grand Ed Util	YR46C	103720	**37200**	**39500**	**36900**	**44700**

2006 MERCEDES-BENZ — 4JG(BB86E)-6-#

M-CLASS 4WD—V6—Truck Equipment Schedule T3						
ML350 Spt Util 4D	BB86E	40525	**7975**	**8500**	**9575**	**12800**
Premium Pkg			650	650	870	870
Sport Pkg			575	575	775	775
M-CLASS 4WD—V8—Truck Equipment Schedule T3						
ML500 Spt Util 4D	BB75E	49275	**8475**	**9000**	**10150**	**13300**
Premium Pkg			650	650	870	870
Sport Pkg			575	575	775	775
G-CLASS 4WD—V8—Truck Equipment Schedule T3						
G500 Sport Util 4D	YR49E	78420	**33100**	**34900**	**33700**	**41100**

SEE BACK PAGES FOR TRUCK EQUIPMENT

Body Type	VIN	List	Trade-In Good	Very Good	Pvt-Party Good	Retail Excellent
G-CLASS AWD—V8 Supercharged—Truck Equipment Sch T3						
G55 Sport Util 4D	YR71E	100620	**38400**	**40500**	**38300**	**46100**
R-CLASS AWD—V6—Truck Equipment Schedule T3						
R350 Sport Wagon	CB65E	48775	**6450**	**6950**	**7500**	**9950**
Premium Pkg			650	650	840	840
Sport Pkg			425	425	560	560
R-CLASS AWD—V8—Truck Equipment Schedule T3						
R500 Sport Wagon	CB75E	56275	**7075**	**7625**	**8375**	**11250**
KEYLESS-GO			200	200	250	250
Premium Pkg			650	650	865	865
Sport Pkg			425	425	575	575

2007 MERCEDES-BENZ — 4JG(BB22E)-7-#

Body Type	VIN	List	Trade-In Good	Very Good	Pvt-Party Good	Retail Excellent
M-CLASS 4WD—V6 Turbo Diesel—Truck Equipment Schedule T3						
ML320 CDI Spt Util	BB22E	44455	**11800**	**12500**	**13200**	**16750**
Adaptive Cruise Control			350	350	415	415
P1 Pkg			300	300	355	355
P2 Pkg			275	275	345	345
P3 Pkg			500	500	610	610
Sport Pkg			625	625	775	775
M-CLASS 4WD—V6—Truck Equipment Schedule T3						
ML350 Spt Util 4D	BB86E	43455	**9450**	**10000**	**10750**	**13700**
Adaptive Cruise Control			350	350	415	415
P1 Pkg			300	300	355	355
P2 Pkg			275	275	345	345
P3 Pkg			500	500	610	610
Sport Pkg			625	625	775	775
M-CLASS 4WD—V8—Truck Equipment Schedule T3						
ML500 Spt Util 4D	BB75E	49975	**10650**	**11200**	**12200**	**15350**
Adaptive Cruise Control			350	350	415	415
P1 Pkg			300	300	355	355
P2 Pkg			275	275	345	345
P3 Pkg			500	500	610	610
Sport Pkg			625	625	775	775
M-CLASS 4WD—V8—Truck Equipment Schedule T3						
ML63 Sport Util 4D	BB77E	86275	**16000**	**16850**	**17650**	**21900**
G-CLASS 4WD—V8—Truck Equipment Schedule T3						
G500 Sport Util 4D	YR49E	81675	**35900**	**37800**	**36700**	**44000**
G-CLASS 4WD—V8 Supercharged—Truck Equipment Sch T3						
G55 Spt Util 4D	YR71E	105275	**43800**	**46000**	**43700**	**51600**
GL-CLASS 4WD—V6 Turbo Diesel—Truck Equipment Schedule T3						
GL320 CDI Spt Utl	BF22E	53175	**14500**	**15400**	**16350**	**20400**
Adaptive Cruise Control			350	350	425	425
Premium Pkg			675	675	840	840
GL-CLASS 4WD—V8—Truck Equipment Schedule T3						
GL450 Spt Util 4D	BF71E	55675	**12650**	**13450**	**14150**	**17600**
Adaptive Cruise Control			350	350	420	420
Premium Pkg			675	675	830	830
R-CLASS 4WD—V6 Turbo Diesel—Truck Equipment Schedule T3						
R320 CDI Spt Wag	CB22E	44775	**10000**	**10650**	**11400**	**14950**
Adaptive Cruise Control			350	350	440	440
Premium Pkg 1			300	300	375	375
Premium Pkg 2			275	275	365	365
R-CLASS 4WD—V6—Truck Equipment Schedule T3						
R350 Sport Wagon	CB65E	43775	**7800**	**8350**	**9100**	**11950**
Adaptive Cruise Control			350	350	445	445
Premium Pkg 1			300	300	380	380
Premium Pkg 2			275	275	370	370
Sport Pkg			475	475	630	630
R-CLASS 4WD—V8—Truck Equipment Schedule T3						
R500 Sport Wagon	CB75E	51275	**9150**	**9775**	**10550**	**13800**
KEYLESS-GO			200	200	255	255
Adaptive Cruise Control			350	350	440	440
Premium Pkg 1			300	300	380	380
Premium Pkg 2			275	275	365	365
Sport Pkg			475	475	625	625
R-CLASS 4WD—V8—Truck Equipment Schedule T3						
R63 Sport Wagon	CB77E	88175	**26000**	**27700**	**26300**	**32500**
KEYLESS-GO			200	200	230	230
Adaptive Cruise Control			350	350	395	395

Body Type	VIN	List	Trade-In Good	Trade-In Very Good	Pvt-Party Good	Retail Excellent
2008 MERCEDES-BENZ — 4JG(BB22E)-8-#						
M-CLASS 4WD—V6 Turbo Diesel—Truck Equipment Schedule T3						
ML320 CDI Spt Util	BB22E	45425	**13200**	**13900**	**14650**	**18200**
KEYLESS-GO			200	200	235	235
Adaptive Cruise Control			375	375	435	435
Premium Pkg 1			300	300	355	355
Premium Pkg 2			300	300	360	360
Premium Pkg 3			500	500	595	595
M-CLASS 4WD—V6—Truck Equipment Schedule T3						
ML350 Spt Util 4D	BB86E	44425	**11700**	**12300**	**12900**	**15900**
KEYLESS-GO			200	200	235	235
Adaptive Cruise Control			375	375	430	430
Premium Pkg 1			300	300	350	350
Premium Pkg 2			300	300	355	355
Premium Pkg 3			500	500	585	585
M-CLASS 4WD—V8—Truck Equipment Schedule T3						
ML350 Edition Util	BB86E	52705	**11750**	**12300**	**13350**	**16200**
M-CLASS 4WD—V8—Truck Equipment Schedule T3						
ML550 Spt Util 4D	BB72E	53175	**14000**	**14600**	**15700**	**19050**
KEYLESS-GO			200	200	235	235
Adaptive Cruise Control			375	375	435	435
Premium Pkg 1			300	300	355	355
Premium Pkg 2			300	300	360	360
Premium Pkg 3			500	500	595	595
M-CLASS 4WD—V8—Truck Equipment Schedule T3						
ML63 Spt Util 4D	BB77E	87425	**20100**	**21000**	**22000**	**26400**
KEYLESS-GO			200	200	235	235
G-CLASS 4WD—V8—Truck Equipment Schedule T3						
G500 Sport Util 4D	YR49E	86975	**43800**	**45700**	**44600**	**51800**
G-CLASS 4WD—V8 Supercharged—Truck Equipment Sch T3						
G55 Spt Util 4D	YR71E	110675	**50700**	**52900**	**51300**	**59100**
GL-CLASS 4WD—V6 Turbo Diesel—Truck Equipment Schedule T3						
GL320 CDI Spt Util	BF22E	55975	**15900**	**16800**	**17650**	**21700**
KEYLESS-GO			200	200	245	245
Adaptive Cruise Control			375	375	445	445
Premium Pkg 1			300	300	365	365
Premium Pkg 2			300	300	370	370
GL-CLASS 4WD—V8—Truck Equipment Schedule T3						
GL450 Spt Util 4D	BF71E	58475	**15200**	**16100**	**16800**	**20400**
KEYLESS-GO			200	200	240	240
Adaptive Cruise Control			375	375	435	435
Premium Pkg 1			300	300	360	360
Premium Pkg 2			300	300	360	360
GL-CLASS 4WD—V8—Truck Equipment Schedule T3						
GL550 Spt Util 4D	BF86E	77850	**16450**	**17400**	**18250**	**22400**
KEYLESS-GO			200	200	240	240
R-CLASS 4WD—V6 Turbo Diesel—Truck Equipment Schedule T3						
R320 CDI Spt Wag	CB22E	46175	**11450**	**12100**	**13050**	**16400**
KEYLESS-GO			200	200	250	250
Distronic Cruise Control			375	375	460	460
P1 Pkg			300	300	375	375
P2 Pkg			300	300	380	380
P3 Pkg			500	500	630	630
R-CLASS 4WD—V6—Truck Equipment Schedule T3						
R350 Sport Wagon	CB65E	45175	**9325**	**9850**	**10650**	**13350**
KEYLESS-GO			200	200	250	250
Distronic Cruise Control			375	375	455	455
P1 Pkg			300	300	370	370
P2 Pkg			300	300	375	375
P3 Pkg			500	500	620	620
2WD	56		(725)	(725)	(910)	(910)
2009 MERCEDES-BENZ — 4JG(BB25E)-9-#						
M-CLASS 4WD—V6 Turbo Diesel—Truck Equipment Schedule T3						
ML320 BLUETEC	BB25E	48125	**16400**	**17150**	**17900**	**21300**
KEYLESS-GO			200	200	230	230
Full Leather			225	225	270	270
Premium Pkg 1			325	325	385	385
Premium Pkg 2			325	325	370	370
M-CLASS 4WD—V6—Truck Equipment Schedule T3						
ML350 Sport Util	BB86E	46625	**14900**	**15550**	**16200**	**19250**

Body Type	VIN	List	Trade-In Good	Very Good	Pvt-Party Good	Retail Excellent
KEYLESS-GO			200	200	230	230
Full Leather			225	225	265	265
Premium Pkg 1			325	325	380	380
Premium Pkg 2			325	325	370	370
2WD			(1025)	(1025)	(1185)	(1185)
M-CLASS 4WD—V8—Truck Equipment Schedule T3						
ML550 Sport Util	BB72E	55325	17200	17800	18950	22200
KEYLESS-GO			200	200	230	230
Full Leather			225	225	270	270
Premium Pkg 1			325	325	385	385
Premium Pkg 2			325	325	370	370
M-CLASS AWD—V8—Truck Equipment Schedule T3						
ML63 Sport Util	BB77E	89225	24200	25100	26300	30800
G-CLASS 4WD—V8—Truck Equipment Schedule T3						
G550 Sport Utility	YR36E	101125	51300	53100	52700	59700
G-CLASS AWD—V8 Supercharged—Truck Equipment Schedule T3						
G55 Sport Utility	YR71E	120325	53700	55600	55000	62100
GL-CLASS AWD—V6 Turbo Diesel—Truck Equipment Schedule T3						
GL320 BLUETEC	BF25E	59755	19550	20500	21300	25400
KEYLESS-GO			200	200	235	235
Premium Pkg 1			325	325	395	395
Premium Pkg 2			325	325	385	385
GL-CLASS AWD—V8—Truck Equipment Schedule T3						
GL450 Sport Util	BF71E	60755	18850	19800	20500	24200
KEYLESS-GO			200	200	235	235
Premium Pkg 1			325	325	390	390
Premium Pkg 2			325	325	375	375
GL-CLASS AWD—V8—Truck Equipment Schedule T3						
GL550 Sport Util	BF86E	80375	21600	22600	23300	27500
R-CLASS 4WD—V6 Turbo Diesel—Truck Equipment Schedule T3						
R320 BLUETEC	CB25E	48825	15100	15750	16700	19900
KEYLESS-GO			200	200	230	230
Premium Pkg 1			325	325	385	385
Premium Pkg 2			325	325	375	375
R-CLASS 4WD—V6—Truck Equipment Schedule T3						
R350 Sport Wagon	CB65E	47325	14200	14850	15650	18500
KEYLESS-GO			200	200	230	230
Premium Pkg 1			325	325	380	380
Premium Pkg 2			325	325	375	375

Body Type	VIN	List	Trade-In Good	Very Good	Pvt-Party Good	Retail Excellent
GLK-CLASS—V6—Truck Equipment Schedule T3						
GLK350 Spt Util	GG5GB	37225	15400	16050	16850	19900
KEYLESS-GO			200	200	230	230
Full Leather			575	575	655	655
Appearance Pkg			125	125	135	135
Multimedia Pkg			425	425	485	485
Premium Pkg 1			800	800	925	925
GLK-CLASS 4MATIC AWD—V6—Truck Equipment Schedule T3						
GLK350 Spt Util	GG8HB	39225	16300	17000	17750	21000
KEYLESS-GO			200	200	230	230
Full Leather			575	575	655	655
Appearance Pkg			125	125	135	135
Multimedia Pkg			425	425	485	485
Premium Pkg 1			800	800	925	925
M-CLASS AWD—V6 Turbo Diesel—Truck Equipment Schedule T3						
ML350 BLUETEC	BB2FB	50575	19600	20300	21400	25000
KEYLESS-GO			200	200	230	230
Full Leather			575	575	650	650
Premium Pkg 1			375	375	440	440
Premium Pkg 2			350	350	395	395
M-CLASS—V6—Truck Equipment Schedule T3						
ML350 Sport Util	BB5GB	46575	16300	16900	17950	20900
KEYLESS-GO			200	200	230	230
Full Leather			575	575	645	645
Premium Pkg 1			375	375	435	435
Premium Pkg 2			350	350	390	390
M-CLASS 4MATIC AWD—V6—Truck Equipment Schedule T3						
ML350 Sport Util	BB8GB	49075	17850	18500	19550	22800
KEYLESS-GO			200	200	230	230
Full Leather			575	575	645	645
Premium Pkg 1			375	375	435	435
Premium Pkg 2			350	350	390	390

Body Type	VIN	List	Trade-In Good	Very Good	Pvt-Party Good	Retail Excellent
M-CLASS—V6 Hybrid—Truck Equipment Schedule T3						
ML450 Sport Util	BB9FB	55875	21300	22000	23500	27000
KEYLESS-GO			200	200	230	230
Full Leather			575	575	645	645
Premium Pkg 1			375	375	435	435
Premium Pkg 2			350	350	390	390
Distronic Cruise Control			400	400	445	445
M-CLASS AWD—V8—Truck Equipment Schedule T3						
ML550 Spt Util 4D	BB7CB	57625	20500	21100	22600	26000
KEYLESS-GO			200	200	230	230
Full Leather			575	575	650	650
Premium Pkg 1			375	375	440	440
Premium Pkg 2			350	350	395	395
M-CLASS AWD—V8—Truck Equipment Schedule T3						
ML63 AMG SUV	BB7HB	91925	29200	30000	31300	35500
R-CLASS 4MATIC AWD—V6 Turbo Diesel—Truck Equipment Sch T3						
R350 BLUETEC	CB2FE	51675	18300	18900	20100	23300
KEYLESS-GO			200	200	230	230
Premium Pkg 1			375	375	435	435
Premium Pkg 2			350	350	390	390
R-CLASS 4MATIC AWD—V6—Truck Equipment Schedule T3						
R350 Sport Wagon	CB6FE	50175	17000	17550	18700	21600
KEYLESS-GO			200	200	225	225
Premium Pkg 1			375	375	435	435
Premium Pkg 2			350	350	390	390
GL-CLASS AWD—V6 Turbo Diesel—Truck Equipment Schedule T3						
GL350 BLUETEC	BF2FB	62725	23800	24900	25700	29800
KEYLESS-GO			200	200	230	230
Premium Pkg 1			375	375	435	435
Premium Pkg 2			350	350	390	390
GL-CLASS AWD—V8—Truck Equipment Schedule T3						
GL450 Spt Util 4D	BF7BB	63725	23600	24600	25200	28900
KEYLESS-GO			200	200	225	225
Premium Pkg 1			375	375	430	430
Premium Pkg 2			350	350	385	385
GL-CLASS AWD—V8—Truck Equipment Schedule T3						
GL550 Spt Util 4D	BF8GB	83725	27200	28300	28900	33200
G-CLASS AWD—V8—Truck Equipment Schedule T3						
G550 Sport Util 4D	YC3HF	104875	55100	56700	57200	63600
G-CLASS AWD—V8 Supercharged—Truck Equipment Schedule T3						
G55 Sport Util	YC7BF	123575	62500	64300	64100	70900

Body Type	VIN	List	Trade-In Good	Very Good	Pvt-Party Good	Retail Excellent
GLK-CLASS—V6—Truck Equipment Schedule T3						
GLK350 Spt Util	GG5GB	36375	18100	18700	19700	22600
KEYLESS-GO			200	200	225	225
Full Leather			600	600	665	665
AMG Styling Pkg			500	500	555	555
Appearance Pkg			125	125	135	135
Multimedia Pkg			425	425	490	490
Premium Pkg 1			850	850	950	950
GLK-CLASS 4MATIC AWD—V6—Truck Equipment Schedule T3						
GLK350 Spt Util	GG8HB	38375	18550	19150	20200	23400
KEYLESS-GO			200	200	225	225
Full Leather			600	600	670	670
AMG Styling Pkg			500	500	555	555
Appearance Pkg			125	125	135	135
Multimedia Pkg			425	425	490	490
Premium Pkg 1			850	850	955	955
M-CLASS AWD—V6 Turbo Diesel—Truck Equipment Schedule T3						
ML350 BLUETEC	BB2FB	53145	22200	22800	24200	27600
KEYLESS-GO			200	200	230	230
Full Leather			600	600	675	675
Premium Pkg 1			425	425	495	495
Premium Pkg 2			375	375	415	415
designo Edition			875	875	985	985
Distronic Cruise Control			425	425	475	475
M-CLASS—V6—Truck Equipment Schedule T3						
ML350 Sport Util	BB5GB	49145	19900	20500	21700	24700
KEYLESS-GO			200	200	225	225
Full Leather			600	600	670	670
Premium Pkg 1			425	425	490	490
Premium Pkg 2			350	350	390	390

TRUCKS & VANS

TRUCKS & VANS

Body Type	VIN	List	Trade-In Good	Very Good	Pvt-Party Good	Retail Excellent
designo Edition			875	875	980	980
Distronic Cruise Control			425	425	470	470
M-CLASS 4MATIC AWD—V6—Truck Equipment Schedule T3						
ML350 Sport Util	BB8GB	51645	21200	21900	23100	26300
KEYLESS-GO			200	200	225	225
Full Leather			600	600	670	670
Premium Pkg 1			425	425	490	490
Premium Pkg 2			350	350	390	390
designo Edition			875	875	980	980
Off-Road Pkg			375	375	410	410
Distronic Cruise Control			425	425	470	470
M-CLASS AWD—V6 Hybrid—Truck Equipment Schedule T3						
ML450 Sport Util	BB9FB	58445	25900	26600	28300	31900
KEYLESS-GO			200	200	225	225
Full Leather			600	600	665	665
Premium Pkg 1			425	425	490	490
Premium Pkg 2			350	350	390	390
designo Edition			875	875	975	975
M-CLASS AWD—V8—Truck Equipment Schedule T3						
ML550 Spt Util 4D	BB7CB	60245	24600	25200	27100	30600
KEYLESS-GO			200	200	225	225
Full Leather			600	600	670	670
Premium Pkg 1			425	425	490	490
Premium Pkg 2			350	350	395	395
designo Edition			875	875	980	980
Off-Road Pkg			375	375	410	410
Distronic Cruise Control			425	425	470	470
M-CLASS AWD—V8—Truck Equipment Schedule T3						
ML63 AMG SUV	BB7HB	93465	36000	36900	38400	42700
Distronic Cruise Control			425	425	445	445
R-CLASS 4MATIC AWD—V6 Turbo Diesel—Truck Equipment Sch T3						
R350 BLUETEC	CB2FE	52615	23200	23800	25400	28800
KEYLESS-GO			200	200	225	225
Premium Pkg 1			425	425	485	485
Premium Pkg 2			375	375	405	405
R-CLASS 4MATIC AWD—V6—Truck Equipment Schedule T3						
R350 Sport Wagon	CB6FE	51115	22700	23300	24700	27900
KEYLESS-GO			200	200	225	225
Premium Pkg 1			425	425	485	485
Premium Pkg 2			375	375	405	405
GL-CLASS AWD—V6 Turbo Diesel—Truck Equipment Schedule T3						
GL350 BLUETEC	BF2FE	63755	25500	26500	27800	32000
KEYLESS-GO			200	200	230	230
Full Leather			325	325	385	385
Premium Pkg 1			425	425	500	500
Premium Pkg 2			375	375	420	420
Distronic Cruise Control			425	425	480	480
GL-CLASS AWD—V8—Truck Equipment Schedule T3						
GL450 Spt Util 4D	BF7BE	64755	26700	27700	28600	32600
KEYLESS-GO			200	200	225	225
Full Leather			325	325	375	375
Premium Pkg 1			425	425	490	490
Premium Pkg 2			375	375	410	410
Off-Road Pkg			375	375	410	410
Distronic Cruise Control			425	425	470	470
GL-CLASS AWD—V8—Truck Equipment Schedule T3						
GL550 Spt Util 4D	BF8GE	85325	31800	33000	33900	38400
Full Leather			325	325	375	375
Off-Road Pkg			375	375	410	410
G-CLASS AWD—V8—Truck Equipment Schedule T3						
G550 Sport Util 4D	YC3HF	106625	58900	60300	61500	67400
G-CLASS AWD—V8 Supercharged—Truck Equipment Schedule T3						
G55 Sport Utility	YC7BF	125325	69400	71000	71400	77800

2012 MERCEDES-BENZ — (4JGorWDC)(GG5HB)-C-#

Body Type	VIN	List	Trade-In Good	Very Good	Pvt-Party Good	Retail Excellent
GLK-CLASS—V6—Truck Equipment Schedule T3						
GLK350 Spt Util	GG5HB	36775	20100	20600	22000	24800
KEYLESS-GO			200	200	225	225
Full Leather			625	625	685	685
AMG Styling Pkg			525	525	575	575
Appearance Pkg			125	125	145	145
Multimedia Pkg			450	450	500	500
Premium Pkg 1			875	875	990	990

2012 MERCEDES-BENZ

Body	Type	VIN	List	Trade-In Good	Very Good	Pvt-Party Good	Retail Excellent
GLK-CLASS 4MATIC AWD—V6—Truck Equipment Schedule T3							
GLK350 Spt Util		GG8HB	38755	20500	21000	22500	25400
KEYLESS-GO				200	200	225	225
Full Leather				625	625	690	690
AMG Styling Pkg				525	525	575	575
Appearance Pkg				125	125	145	145
Multimedia Pkg				450	450	505	505
Premium Pkg 1				875	875	990	990
M-CLASS 4MATIC AWD—V6 Turbo Diesel—Truck Equipment Sch T3							
ML350 BLUETEC		DA2EB	51365	30300	31000	32400	35800
KEYLESS-GO				200	200	215	215
DISTRONIC PLUS				450	450	470	470
Driver Assistance Pkg				625	625	660	660
Premium Pkg 1				475	475	515	515
Premium Pkg 2				375	375	410	410
designo Edition				900	900	955	955
M-CLASS 4MATIC AWD—V6—Truck Equipment Schedule T3							
ML350 Sport Util		DA5HB	49865	29000	29700	31000	34200
KEYLESS-GO				200	200	215	215
DISTRONIC PLUS				450	450	470	470
Driver Assistance Pkg				625	625	660	660
Premium Pkg 1				475	475	515	515
Premium Pkg 2				375	375	410	410
designo Edition				900	900	955	955
M-CLASS 4MATIC AWD—V8 Twin Turbo—Truck Equip Sch T3							
ML550 Spt Util		DA7DB	58465	33600	34300	35900	39300
KEYLESS-GO				200	200	215	215
DISTRONIC PLUS				450	450	470	470
Driver Assistance Pkg				625	625	660	660
Premium Pkg 1				475	475	515	515
Premium Pkg 2				375	375	410	410
designo Edition				900	900	955	955
M-CLASS 4MATIC AWD—V8—Truck Equipment Schedule T3							
ML63 AMG SUV		DA7EB	95865	49700	50700	52600	57400
DISTRONIC PLUS				450	450	465	465
AMG Performance Pkg				3900	3900	4110	4110
Driver Assistance Pkg				625	625	650	650
R-CLASS 4MATIC AWD—V6 Turbo Diesel—Truck Equipment Sch T3							
R350 BLUETEC		CB2FE	54715	25800	26400	28200	31400
KEYLESS-GO				200	200	220	220
DISTRONIC Cruise				450	450	485	485
Premium Pkg 1				475	475	530	530
Premium Pkg 2				375	375	420	420
R-CLASS 4MATIC AWD—V6—Truck Equipment Schedule T3							
R350 Sport Wagon		CB5HE	53565	24900	25400	27100	30100
KEYLESS-GO				200	200	220	220
DISTRONIC Cruise				450	450	480	480
Premium Pkg 1				475	475	530	530
Premium Pkg 2				375	375	420	420
GL-CLASS AWD—V6 Turbo Diesel—Truck Equipment Schedule T3							
GL350 BlueTEC		BF2FE	63320	35200	36300	37200	41500
KEYLESS-GO				200	200	220	220
DISTRONIC Cruise				450	450	480	480
Premium Pkg 1				475	475	530	530
Premium Pkg 2				375	375	420	420
GL-CLASS AWD—V8—Truck Equipment Schedule T3							
GL450 Spt Util 4D		BF7BE	64320	32600	33700	34600	38400
KEYLESS-GO				200	200	220	220
DISTRONIC Cruise				450	450	480	480
Premium Pkg 1				475	475	525	525
Premium Pkg 2				375	375	415	415
Off-Road Pkg				375	375	415	415
GL-CLASS AWD—V8—Truck Equipment Schedule T3							
GL550 Spt Util 4D		BF8GE	87050	38700	40000	40700	45200
Off-Road Pkg				375	375	420	420
G-CLASS AWD—V8—Truck Equipment Schedule T3							
G550 Sport Util 4D		YC3HF	107975	68200	69600	71200	77300

2013 MERCEDES-BENZ — (4JGorWDC)(GG0EB)–D–#

Body	Type	VIN	List	Trade-In Good	Very Good	Pvt-Party Good	Retail Excellent
GLK-CLASS 4MATIC AWD—4-Cyl. Turbo Diesel—Truck Equip Sch T3							
GLK250 BlueTec		GG0EB	39495	26000	26600	28300	31400
KEYLESS-GO				200	200	220	220
DISTRONIC PLUS				475	475	515	515

SEE BACK PAGES FOR TRUCK EQUIPMENT

TRUCKS & VANS

Body Type	VIN	List	Trade-In Good	Very Good	Pvt-Party Good	Retail Excellent
AMG Styling Pkg			550	550	600	600
Appearance Pkg			125	125	150	150
Driver Assistance Pkg			650	650	710	710
Multimedia Pkg			475	475	515	515
Premium Pkg 1			900	900	1000	1000
GLK-CLASS—V6—Truck Equipment Schedule T3						
GLK350 Spt Util	GG5HB	37995	24900	25400	27000	29900
KEYLESS-GO			200	200	220	220
DISTRONIC PLUS			475	475	515	515
AMG Styling Pkg			550	550	595	595
Appearance Pkg			125	125	150	150
Driver Assistance Pkg			650	650	705	705
Multimedia Pkg			475	475	510	510
Premium Pkg			900	900	990	990
GLK-CLASS 4MATIC AWD—V6—Truck Equipment Schedule T3						
GLK350 Spt Util	GG8JB	39995	24600	25200	26900	30000
KEYLESS-GO			200	200	225	225
DISTRONIC PLUS			475	475	520	520
AMG Styling Pkg			550	550	605	605
Appearance Pkg			125	125	150	150
Driver Assistance Pkg			650	650	715	715
Multimedia Pkg			475	475	520	520
Premium Pkg			900	900	1005	1005
M-CLASS—V6—Truck Equipment Schedule T3						
ML350 Sport Util	DA5JB	48175	31400	32100	33400	36300
KEYLESS-GO			200	200	210	210
DISTRONIC PLUS			475	475	495	495
Driver Assistance Pkg			650	650	680	680
Premium Pkg 2			900	900	955	955
M-CLASS 4MATIC AWD—V6 Turbo Diesel—Truck Equipment Schedule T3						
ML350 BLUETEC	DA2EB	52175	34600	35300	36700	40000
KEYLESS-GO			200	200	210	210
DISTRONIC PLUS			475	475	495	495
Driver Assistance Pkg			650	650	680	680
designo Edition			900	900	950	950
Premium Pkg 1			900	900	950	950
M-CLASS 4MATIC AWD—V6—Truck Equipment Schedule T3						
ML350 Sport Util	DA5HB	50675	34000	34700	36000	39000
KEYLESS-GO			200	200	210	210
DISTRONIC PLUS			475	475	490	490
Driver Assistance Pkg			650	650	675	675
designo Edition			900	900	950	950
M-CLASS 4MATIC AWD—V8 Twin Turbo—Truck Equip Sch T3						
ML550 Sport Util	DA7DB	59705	39500	40200	41700	45000
KEYLESS-GO			200	200	210	210
Driver Assistance Pkg			650	650	675	675
designo Edition			900	900	950	950
Premium Pkg			900	900	950	950
M-CLASS 4MATIC AWD—V8—Truck Equipment Schedule T3						
ML63 AMG SUV	DA7EB	97005	62500	63700	65300	70100
GL-CLASS 4MATIC AWD—V6 Turbo Diesel—Truck Equipment Sch T3						
GL350 BlueTEC	DF2EB	63275	47300	48800	49100	53700
KEYLESS-GO			200	200	215	215
DISTRONIC PLUS			475	475	500	500
Bang & Olufsen Sound			2825	2825	3040	3040
Premium Pkg 1			525	525	570	570
GL-CLASS 4MATIC AWD—V8 Twin Turbo—Truck Equipment Sch T3						
GL450 Spt Util 4D	DF7CB	64775	40300	41500	42300	46400
KEYLESS-GO			200	200	215	215
Bang & Olufsen Sound			2825	2825	3060	3060
Driver Assistance Pkg			650	650	690	690
Premium Pkg 1			525	525	575	575
GL-CLASS 4MATIC AWD—V8 Twin Turbo—Truck Equipment Schedule T3						
GL550 Spt Util 4D	DF7DB	87775	53700	55400	55700	60600
Bang & Olufsen Sound			2825	2825	3020	3020
GL-CLASS 4MATIC AWD—V8 Twin Turbo—Truck Equipment Schedule T3						
GL63 AMG Spt Util	DF7EE	117800	83400	85100	84800	90200
Bang & Olufsen Sound			2825	2825	2945	2945
DISTRONIC PLUS			475	475	485	485
G-CLASS 4MATIC AWD—V8—Truck Equipment Schedule T3						
G550 Sport Utility	YC3HF	113905	76500	77900	79600	85700
G63 AMG Spt Util	YC7DF	135205	99900	101700	102500	108900

Body Type	VIN	List	Trade-In Good	Very Good	Pvt-Party Good	Retail Excellent

2014 MERCEDES-BENZ — (4JGorWDC)(GG0EB)-E-#

GLK-CLASS 4MATIC AWD—4-Cyl. Turbo Diesel—Truck Equip Sch T3

Body Type	VIN	List	Good	Very Good	Good	Excellent
GLK250 BlueTEC	GG0EB	39905	30300	30900	33000	36300
KEYLESS-GO			200	200	220	220
DISTRONIC PLUS			500	500	545	545
Driver Assistance Pkg			675	675	740	740
Multimedia Pkg			475	475	530	530
AMG Styling Pkg			575	575	630	630
Premium Pkg 1			900	900	1000	1000

GLK-CLASS—V6—Truck Equipment Schedule T3

GLK350 Spt Util	GG5HB	38405	27400	28000	29900	33100
KEYLESS-GO			200	200	220	220
DISTRONIC PLUS			500	500	545	545
AMG Styling Pkg			575	575	630	630
Multimedia Pkg			475	475	535	535
AMG Styling Pkg			575	575	630	630
Premium Pkg 1			900	900	1000	1000

GLK-CLASS 4MATIC AWD—V6—Truck Equipment Schedule T3

GLK350 Sport Util	GG8JB	40405	31500	32100	34200	37800
KEYLESS-GO			200	200	220	220
DISTRONIC PLUS			500	500	540	540
Driver Assistance Pkg			675	675	735	735
Multimedia Pkg			475	475	530	530
AMG Styling Pkg			575	575	625	625
Premium Pkg 1			900	900	995	995

M-CLASS—V6—Truck Equipment Schedule T3

ML350 Sport Util	DA5JB	48715	36100	36800	38200	41100
KEYLESS-GO			200	200	210	210
DISTRONIC PLUS			500	500	520	520
Premium Pkg 1			900	900	950	950

M-CLASS 4MATIC AWD—V6 Turbo Diesel—Truck Equipment Schedule T3

ML350 BlueTEC	DA2EB	52715	40800	41500	42900	46200
KEYLESS-GO			200	200	210	210
DISTRONIC PLUS			500	500	515	515
designo Edition			900	900	945	945
Premium Pkg 1			900	900	945	945

M-CLASS 4MATIC AWD—V6—Truck Equipment Schedule T3

ML350 Sport Util	DA5HB	51215	40100	40900	42200	45300
KEYLESS-GO			200	200	210	210
DISTRONIC PLUS			500	500	515	515
designo Edition			900	900	945	945
Premium Pkg 1			900	900	945	945

M-CLASS 4MATIC AWD—V8 Twin Turbo—Truck Equip Sch T3

ML550 Sport Util	DA7DB	60375	47000	47900	49100	52500
KEYLESS-GO			200	200	210	210
DISTRONIC PLUS			500	500	515	515
designo Edition			900	900	940	940
Premium Pkg 1			900	900	940	940

M-CLASS 4MATIC AWD—V8 Twin Turbo—Truck Equipment Schedule T3

ML63 AMG Util	DA7EB	98175	70900	72200	73600	78500
DISTRONIC PLUS			500	500	510	510
Bang & Olufsen Sound			2950	2950	3065	3065

GL-CLASS 4MATIC AWD—V6 Turbo Diesel—Truck Equipment Sch T3

GL350 BlueTEC	DF2EE	63925	52900	54400	54600	58700
KEYLESS-GO			200	200	210	210
DISTRONIC PLUS			500	500	520	520
Driver Assistance Pkg			675	675	705	705
Premium Pkg 1			575	575	600	600

GL-CLASS 4MATIC AWD—V8 Twin Turbo—Truck Equipment Sch T3

GL450 Sport Util	DF7CE	65475	56900	58600	58600	63000
KEYLESS-GO			200	200	210	210
DISTRONIC PLUS			500	500	520	520
Driver Assistance Pkg			675	675	705	705
Premium Pkg 1			575	575	600	600

GL-CLASS 4MATIC AWD—V8 Twin Turbo—Truck Equipment Sch T3

GL550 Sport Util	DF7DE	89525	67900	69900	69600	74800
Bang & Olufsen Sound			2950	2950	3130	3130
DISTRONIC PLUS			500	500	520	520
Driver Assistance Pkg			675	675	705	705

GL-CLASS 4MATIC AWD—V8 Twin Turbo—Truck Equipment Sch T3

GL63 AMG Spt Utl	DF7EE	119085	89100	90700	91000	96400
Bang & Olufsen Sound			2950	2950	3085	3085

Body Type	VIN	List	Trade-In Good	Very Good	Pvt-Party Good	Retail Excellent
G-CLASS 4MATIC AWD—V8—Truck Equipment Schedule T3						
G550 Sport Utility	YC3HF 115125	**87200**	**88800**	**90200**	**96500**	
G-CLASS 4MATIC AWD—V8 Twin Turbo—Truck Equipment Schedule T3						
G63 AMG Spt Util	YC7DF 136625	**112700**	**114600**	**115100**	**121800**	

MERCURY

2000 MERCURY — 4M2-(U86P)-Y-#

MOUNTAINEER AWD—V8—Truck Equipment Schedule T1						
Sport Utility 4D	U86P	30360	900	1075	1625	2950
Premier	6		250	250	345	345
2WD	6		(525)	(525)	(715)	(715)
4WD	7		0	0	0	0
V8, 4.0 Liter	E		(125)	(125)	(160)	(160)
VILLAGER—V6—Truck Equipment Schedule T1						
Minivan 4D	V11T	22995	575	750	1325	2550
Sport Minivan 4D	V12T	25995	1175	1475	2050	3825
Estate Minivan 4D	V14T	27695	1250	1550	2150	3975

2001 MERCURY — 4M2-(U86P)-1-#

MOUNTAINEER AWD—V8—Truck Equipment Schedule T1						
Sport Utility 4D	U86P	30695	950	1125	1650	2950
Premier			300	300	400	400
2WD	6		(625)	(625)	(820)	(820)
4WD	7		0	0	0	0
V6, 4.0 Liter	E		(150)	(150)	(185)	(185)
VILLAGER—V6—Truck Equipment Schedule T1						
Minivan 4D	V11T	23140	775	1000	1550	2925
Sport Minivan 4D	V12T	26365	1475	1825	2375	4350
Estate Minivan 4D	V14T	27840	1550	1900	2475	4500

2002 MERCURY — 4M2-(U86W)-2-#

MOUNTAINEER AWD—V8—Truck Equipment Schedule T1						
Sport Utility 4D	U86W	31310	1550	1800	2525	4475
Premier			350	350	455	455
Third Row Seat			600	600	790	790
2WD	6		(700)	(700)	(935)	(935)
V6, 4.0 Liter	E		(150)	(150)	(205)	(205)
VILLAGER—V6—Truck Equipment Schedule T1						
Minivan 4D	V11T	19995	925	1150	1650	3025
Sport Minivan 4D	V12T	24995	1700	2100	2625	4625
Estate Minivan 4D	V14T	26995	1775	2175	2725	4800

2003 MERCURY — 4M2-(U86W)-3-#

MOUNTAINEER AWD—V8—Truck Equipment Schedule T1						
Sport Utility 4D	U86W	32605	2000	2325	2925	4850
Premier Sport Util	U86W	34750	2275	2650	3250	5400
Third Row Seat			625	625	830	830
2WD	6		(775)	(775)	(1040)	(1040)
V6, Flex Fuel, 4.0 Liter	K		(175)	(175)	(225)	(225)

2004 MERCURY — (2MRor4M2)-(A202)-4-#

MONTEREY—V6—Truck Equipment Schedule T1						
Minivan	A202	29995	1600	1825	2625	4550
Premier			325	325	440	440
MOUNTAINEER AWD—V8—Truck Equipment Schedule T1						
Sport Utility 4D	U86W	32855	2450	2800	3600	6025
Premier			425	425	560	560
Third Row Seat			650	650	870	870
2WD	6		(875)	(875)	(1155)	(1155)
V6, Flex Fuel, 4.0 Liter	K		(200)	(200)	(255)	(255)

2005 MERCURY — (2MRor4M2)-(A222)-5-#

MONTEREY—V6—Truck Equipment Schedule T1						
Minivan	A222	29695	2000	2275	3200	5275
Premier Minivan	A222	35665	2425	2750	3725	6100
MARINER 4WD—V6—Truck Equipment Schedule T1						
Sport Utility 4D	U571	25245	2850	3150	4050	6175
2WD	6		(575)	(575)	(775)	(775)

Body Type	VIN	List	Trade-In Good	Very Good	Pvt-Party Good	Retail Excellent
4-Cyl, 2.3 Liter	Z		(400)	(400)	(540)	(540)
MOUNTAINEER AWD—V8—Truck Equipment Schedule T1						
Sport Utility 4D	U86W	33505	2850	3275	4225	6800
Premier Sport Util	U86W	39625	3150	3600	4600	7400
Third Row Seat			675	675	910	910
2WD	6		(950)	(950)	(1260)	(1260)
V6, Flex Fuel 4.0L	E,K		(225)	(225)	(285)	(285)

2005 MERCURY — (1,2or3)ME-(A222)-6-#

Body Type	VIN	List	Trade-In Good	Very Good	Pvt-Party Good	Retail Excellent
MONTEREY—V6—Truck Equipment Schedule T1						
Minivan	A222	29325	2800	3150	4050	6375
MARINER 4WD—4-Cyl. Hybrid—Truck Equipment Schedule T1						
Sport Utility 4D	U98H	29840	3975	4350	5400	8025
MARINER 4WD—V6—Truck Equipment Schedule T1						
Sport Utility 4D	U571	25650	3450	3800	4825	7225
Premier Sport Util	U571	27400	3700	4050	5100	7625
2WD	6		(625)	(625)	(845)	(845)
4-Cyl, 2.3 Liter	Z		(450)	(450)	(585)	(585)
MOUNTAINEER AWD—V6—Truck Equipment Schedule T1						
Sport Utility 4D	U468	31995	4125	4650	5525	8350
Third Row Seat			700	700	945	945
2WD	3		(1025)	(1025)	(1375)	(1375)
V8, 4.6 Liter	8		275	275	370	370
MOUNTAINEER AWD—V8—Truck Equipment Schedule T1						
Premier Sport Util	U38E	36145	4525	5075	5975	9075
Third Row Seat			700	700	945	945
2WD	3		(1025)	(1025)	(1375)	(1375)

2007 MERCURY — (2MRor4M2)-(A222)-7-#

Body Type	VIN	List	Trade-In Good	Very Good	Pvt-Party Good	Retail Excellent
MONTEREY—V6—Truck Equipment Schedule T1						
Minivan	A222	29350	3525	3900	5025	7700
MARINER 4WD—4-Cyl. Hybrid—Truck Equipment Schedule T1						
Sport Utility 4D	U39H	28615	5550	6025	6950	9700
MARINER 4WD—V6—Truck Equipment Schedule T1						
Sport Utility 4D	U901	25420	4575	4975	5800	8175
Premier Sport Util	U901	27515	5225	5675	6425	8950
2WD	8		(675)	(675)	(910)	(910)
4-Cyl, 2.3 Liter	Z		(475)	(475)	(620)	(620)
MOUNTAINEER AWD—V6—Truck Equipment Schedule T1						
Sport Utility 4D	U478	30270	5375	5975	6650	9375
Third Row Seat			750	750	985	985
2WD	3		(1100)	(1100)	(1480)	(1480)
V8, 4.6 Liter	8		300	300	400	400
MOUNTAINEER AWD—V8—Truck Equipment Schedule T1						
Premier Spt Util	U388	34740	6125	6800	7400	10350
Third Row Seat			750	750	985	985
2WD	3		(1100)	(1100)	(1480)	(1480)

2008 MERCURY — (2MRor4M2)-(U39H)-8-#

Body Type	VIN	List	Trade-In Good	Very Good	Pvt-Party Good	Retail Excellent
MARINER 4WD—4-Cyl. Hybrid—Truck Equipment Schedule T1						
Sport Utility 4D	U39H	28370	6950	7425	8600	11600
2WD	2		(725)	(725)	(975)	(975)
MARINER 4WD—V6—Truck Equipment Schedule T1						
Sport Utility 4D	U911	24335	5825	6250	7250	9675
Premier Spt Util	U971	26235	6400	6850	7875	10500
4-Cyl, 2.3 Liter	8		(500)	(500)	(655)	(655)
MOUNTAINEER AWD—V6—Truck Equipment Schedule T1						
Sport Utility 4D	U47E	32850	6475	7025	7750	10300
2WD	3		(1200)	(1200)	(1570)	(1570)
Third Row Seat			775	775	1030	1030
MOUNTAINEER AWD—V8—Truck Equipment Schedule T1						
Premier Spt Util 4D	U488	32410	6675	7250	8025	10750
Third Row Seat			775	775	1040	1040
2WD	3		(1200)	(1200)	(1590)	(1590)
V6, 4.0 Liter	E		(300)	(300)	(385)	(385)

2009 MERCURY — (2MRor4M2)-(U393)-9-#

Body Type	VIN	List	Trade-In Good	Very Good	Pvt-Party Good	Retail Excellent
MARINER 4WD—4-Cyl. Hybrid—Truck Equipment Schedule T1						
Sport Utility 4D	U393	31195	8800	9325	10350	13100
2WD	2		(825)	(825)	(1060)	(1060)

Body Type	VIN	List	Trade-In Good	Very Good	Pvt-Party Good	Retail Excellent
MARINER 4WD—V6—Truck Equipment Schedule T1						
Sport Utility 4D	U91G	25380	7225	7650	8725	11050
Premier Spt Util 4D	U97G	26485	7600	8050	9100	11550
2WD	8		(825)	(825)	(1065)	(1065)
4-Cyl, 2.5 Liter	3		(700)	(700)	(895)	(895)
MOUNTAINEER AWD—V6—Truck Equipment Schedule T1						
Sport Utility 4D	U47E	30360	8250	8775	9900	12800
2WD	3		(1275)	(1275)	(1655)	(1655)
Third Row Seat			800	800	1035	1035
MOUNTAINEER AWD—V8—Truck Equipment Schedule T1						
Premier Spt Util 4D	U388	34535	9500	10100	11250	14500
Third Row Seat			800	800	1030	1030
2WD	3		(1275)	(1275)	(1645)	(1645)
V6, 4.0 Liter	E		(325)	(325)	(430)	(430)

2010 MERCURY–(2MRor4M2)–(N3K3)–A–#

Body Type	VIN	List	Trade-In Good	Very Good	Pvt-Party Good	Retail Excellent
MARINER 4WD—4-Cyl. Hybrid—Truck Equipment Schedule T1						
Sport Utility 4D	N3K3	32470	11400	11950	13300	16300
2WD	2		(950)	(950)	(1170)	(1170)
MARINER 4WD—V6—Truck Equipment Schedule T1						
Sport Utility 4D	N9BG	26510	8975	9425	10650	13150
Premier Sport Util	N9HG	28580	9775	10250	11550	14150
2WD	8		(950)	(950)	(1180)	(1180)
4-Cyl, 2.5 Liter	7		(775)	(775)	(955)	(955)
MOUNTAINEER AWD—V6—Truck Equipment Schedule T1						
Sport Utility 4D	N4HE	32215	9775	10200	11450	14200
2WD	3		(1350)	(1350)	(1680)	(1680)
MOUNTAINEER AWD—V8—Truck Equipment Schedule T1						
Premier Sport Util	N4J8	37995	12300	12800	14200	17600
Third Row Seat			800	800	995	995
2WD	3		(1350)	(1350)	(1690)	(1690)
V6, 4.0 Liter	E		(375)	(375)	(475)	(475)

2011 MERCURY — 4M2–(N3K3)–B–#

Body Type	VIN	List	Trade-In Good	Very Good	Pvt-Party Good	Retail Excellent
MARINER 4WD—4-Cyl. Hybrid—Truck Equipment Schedule T1						
Sport Utility 4D	N3K3	32590	12050	12500	14000	16750
2WD	2		(1075)	(1075)	(1280)	(1280)
MARINER 4WD—V6—Truck Equipment Schedule T1						
Sport Utility 4D	N9BG	27040	9975	10400	11900	14400
Premier Sport Util	N9HG	29110	10550	10950	12450	15000
2WD	8		(1075)	(1075)	(1300)	(1300)
4-Cyl, 2.5 Liter	7		(850)	(850)	(1035)	(1035)

MITSUBISHI

2000 MITSUBISHI — JA4–(S21H)–Y–#

Body Type	VIN	List	Trade-In Good	Very Good	Pvt-Party Good	Retail Excellent
MONTERO SPORT 2WD—V6—Truck Equipment Schedule T1						
ES Utility 4D	S21H	22982	500	625	1000	1750
MONTERO SPORT 4WD—V6—Truck Equipment Schedule T1						
LS Utility 4D	T31H	27262	1150	1375	1825	3175
XLS Utility 4D	T31H	29782	1325	1575	2025	3525
Limited Utility 4D	T41R	31812	1750	2050	2650	4575
2WD	S		(525)	(525)	(715)	(715)
MONTERO 4WD—V6—Truck Equipment Schedule T1						
Sport Utility 4D	R51R	32262	1550	1825	2325	4100
Endeavor Pkg			125	125	160	160

2001 MITSUBISHI — JA4–(T21H)–1–#

Body Type	VIN	List	Trade-In Good	Very Good	Pvt-Party Good	Retail Excellent
MONTERO SPORT 4WD—V6—Truck Equipment Schedule T1						
ES Utility 4D	T21H	25467	925	1150	1550	2700
LS Utility 4D	T31H	28177	1400	1650	2125	3625
XS Sport Utility 4D	T31H	29187	1550	1825	2300	3925
XLS Utility 4D	T31H	29827	1575	1850	2325	3975
Limited Utility 4D	T41R	33297	2050	2400	2975	5025
2WD	S		(625)	(625)	(820)	(820)
MONTERO 4WD—V6—Truck Equipment Schedule T1						
XLS Spt Util 4D	W31R	31817	1475	1725	2200	3850
Limited Spt Util 4D	W51R	35817	1950	2300	2825	4825

2002 MITSUBISHI

Body Type	VIN	List	Trade-In Good	Very Good	Pvt-Party Good	Retail Excellent

2002 MITSUBISHI — JA4-(T21H)-2-#

MONTERO SPORT 4WD—V6—Truck Equipment Schedule T1

Body Type	VIN	List	Good	Very Good	Good	Excellent
ES Utility 4D	T21H	25647	**1225**	1425	1850	3125
LS Utility 4D	T31H	28337	**1675**	1950	2450	4075
XLS Utility 4D	T31H	30187	**1825**	2150	2650	4400
Limited Utility 4D	T41R	33447	**2500**	2925	3400	5625
2WD	S		**(700)**	(700)	(935)	(935)

MONTERO 4WD—V6—Truck Equipment Schedule T1

| XLS Spt Util 4D | W31R | 32247 | **1650** | 1925 | 2425 | 4125 |
| Limited Spt Util 4D | W51R | 36357 | **2300** | 2675 | 3125 | 5225 |

2003 MITSUBISHI — JA4-(Z31G)-3-#

OUTLANDER AWD—4-Cyl.—Truck Equipment Schedule T1

LS Sport Utility 4D	Z31G	19877	**1825**	2100	2725	4425
XLS Sport Utility 4D	Z41G	21370	**2275**	2600	3225	5200
2WD			**(475)**	(475)	(645)	(645)

MONTERO SPORT 4WD—V6—Truck Equipment Schedule T1

ES Utility 4D	T21H	25802	**1650**	1925	2375	3925
LS Utility 4D	T21H	28362	**2125**	2450	3000	4925
XLS Utility 4D	T31H	30212	**2300**	2650	3175	5225
Limited Utility 4D	T41R	33472	**3000**	3475	4000	6525
2WD	S		**(775)**	(775)	(1040)	(1040)

MONTERO 4WD—V6—Truck Equipment Schedule T1

XLS Spt Util 4D	W31S	33072	**2300**	2675	3075	5025
Limited Spt Util 4D	W51S	37182	**3025**	3525	3850	6250
20th Annv Ed Spt Ut	W51S	39022	**3575**	4125	4475	7150

2004 MITSUBISHI — (Jor4)A4-(Z31G)-4-#

OUTLANDER AWD—4-Cyl.—Truck Equipment Schedule T1

LS Sport Utility 4D	Z31G	20692	**2300**	2600	3325	5350
XLS Spt Utility 4D	Z41G	22792	**2700**	3050	3825	6150
2WD	X		**(525)**	(525)	(710)	(710)

MONTERO SPORT 4WD—V6—Truck Equipment Schedule T1

LS Utility 4D	T31R	26392	**2600**	3000	3600	5850
XLS Utility 4D	T31R	28592	**2825**	3225	3850	6225
2WD	S		**(875)**	(875)	(1155)	(1155)

ENDEAVOR AWD—V6—Truck Equipment Schedule T1

LS Sport Utility 4D	N21S	28192	**2050**	2300	2900	4575
XLS Sport Utility 4D	N31S	30492	**3025**	3400	3950	6100
Limited Spt Utl 4D	N41S	33792	**3325**	3750	4300	6625
2WD	M		**(875)**	(875)	(1155)	(1155)

MONTERO 4WD—V6—Truck Equipment Schedule T1

| Limited Spt Util 4D | W51S | 35624 | **3575** | 4125 | 4500 | 7100 |

2005 MITSUBISHI — (Jor4)A4(LZ31F)-5-#

OUTLANDER AWD—4-Cyl.—Truck Equipment Schedule T1

LS Sport Utility 4D	LZ31F	21244	**2450**	2775	3675	5700
XLS Spt Utl 4D	LZ41F	23724	**2975**	3325	4325	6725
Limited Sport Util	LZ81F	25774	**3650**	4100	5100	7775
2WD	X		**(575)**	(575)	(775)	(775)

ENDEAVOR AWD—V6—Truck Equipment Schedule T1

LS Sport Utility 4D	MN21S	28294	**2675**	3025	3725	5550
XLS Sport Utility 4D	MN31S	30894	**3500**	3950	4775	7100
Limited Sport Util	MN41S	33794	**3875**	4350	5150	7675
2WD	M		**(950)**	(950)	(1260)	(1260)

MONTERO 4WD—V6—Truck Equipment Schedule T1

| Limited Spt Utl | NW51S | 36424 | **4575** | 5250 | 5575 | 8350 |

2006 MITSUBISHI — (Jor4)A(3,4or7)(LX41F)-6-#

OUTLANDER—4-Cyl.—Truck Equipment Schedule T1

| SE Sport Utility 4D | LX41F | 22624 | **3200** | 3575 | 4725 | 7325 |
| AWD | Z | | **700** | 700 | 920 | 920 |

OUTLANDER AWD—4-Cyl.—Truck Equipment Schedule T1

LS Sport Utility 4D	LZ31F	24094	**3075**	3425	4575	7125
Limited Sport Util	LZ81F	26544	**4450**	4950	6025	9000
2WD	X		**(625)**	(625)	(845)	(845)

ENDEAVOR AWD—V6—Truck Equipment Schedule T1

LS Sport Utility 4D	MN21S	28594	**3400**	3800	4550	6600
Limited Sport Util	MN41S	32894	**4625**	5125	5925	8600
2WD	M		**(1025)**	(1025)	(1375)	(1375)

Body Type	VIN	List	Trade-In Good	Very Good	Pvt-Party Good	Retail Excellent
MONTERO 4WD—V6—Truck Equipment Schedule T1						
Limited Spt Utl	MW51S	36784	5425	6175	6650	9725
RAIDER EXTENDED CAB—V6—Truck Equipment Schedule T1						
LS Short Bed	HC22K	22400	3600	3900	4575	6400
4WD	T	------	975	975	1290	1290
V8, 4.7 Liter	N	------	350	350	455	455
RAIDER EXTENDED CAB—V8—Truck Equipment Schedule T1						
DuroCross Short	HC32K	26085	5850	6350	7050	9725
4WD	T	------	975	975	1290	1290
V6, 3.7 Liter	K	------	(350)	(350)	(475)	(475)
RAIDER DOUBLE CAB—V6—Truck Equipment Schedule T1						
LS Short Bed	HC28K	24325	5175	5600	6475	9075
DuroCross Short	HC38K	26010	5500	5950	6800	9550
4WD	T	------	975	975	1290	1290
V8, 4.7 Liter	N	------	350	350	455	455
RAIDER DOUBLE CAB—V8—Truck Equipment Schedule T1						
XLS Short Bed	HC48K	31320	6425	6925	7750	10800
AWD	T	------	975	975	1290	1290

Body Type	VIN	List	Trade-In Good	Very Good	Pvt-Party Good	Retail Excellent
OUTLANDER—V6—Truck Equipment Schedule T1						
ES Sport Utility 4D	MS31X	21995	3775	4150	5000	7100
Third Row Seat		------	250	250	325	325
OUTLANDER 4WD—V6—Truck Equipment Schedule T1						
ES Sport Utility 4D	MT31X	23033	4725	5175	6075	8650
XLS Sport Util 4D	MT41X	25635	5475	6000	7100	10100
Third Row Seat		------	250	250	325	325
2WD	X	------	(675)	(675)	(910)	(910)
ENDEAVOR AWD—V6—Truck Equipment Schedule T1						
LS Sport Utility 4D	MN21S	29624	4450	4900	5475	7550
SE Sport Utility 4D	MN31S	31374	5400	5950	6750	9350
2WD	M	------	(1100)	(1100)	(1480)	(1480)
RAIDER EXTENDED CAB—V6—Truck Equipment Schedule T1						
LS Short Bed	HC22K	23665	3775	4075	4950	6975
RAIDER DOUBLE CAB—V6—Truck Equipment Schedule T1						
LS Short Bed	HC28K	24650	5700	6125	7250	10200
DuroCross Short	HC38K	27395	6275	6750	7900	11100
4WD	T	------	1075	1075	1420	1420
V8, 4.7 Liter	N,P	------	375	375	485	485
RAIDER DOUBLE CAB—V8—Truck Equipment Schedule T1						
SE Sport Utility	HC28N	27355	7000	7550	8675	12150

Body Type	VIN	List	Trade-In Good	Very Good	Pvt-Party Good	Retail Excellent
OUTLANDER—4-Cyl.—Truck Equipment Schedule T1						
ES Sport Utility	MS21W	20640	4725	5100	6000	8100
SE Sport Utility	MS31W	23880	6000	6450	7625	10350
Third Row Seat		------	250	250	330	330
4WD		------	1075	1075	1410	1410
OUTLANDER 4WD—V6—Truck Equipment Schedule T1						
LS Sport Utility	MT31X	24520	6500	7000	8275	11300
XLS Sport Utility	MT41X	25760	7775	8350	9625	13000
Third Row Seat		------	250	250	330	330
2WD	S	------	(725)	(725)	(975)	(975)
ENDEAVOR AWD—V6—Truck Equipment Schedule T1						
LS Sport Utility 4D	MN21S	29724	5225	5625	6500	8575
SE Sport Utility 4D	MN31S	31524	6450	6950	7925	10500
2WD	M	------	(1200)	(1200)	(1565)	(1565)
RAIDER EXTENDED CAB—V6—Truck Equipment Schedule T1						
LS Short Bed	HC22K	23735	4375	4675	5550	7475
RAIDER DOUBLE CAB—V6—Truck Equipment Schedule T1						
LS Short Bed	HC28K	25795	6650	7100	8175	11000
4WD	T	------	1225	1225	1645	1645

Body Type	VIN	List	Trade-In Good	Very Good	Pvt-Party Good	Retail Excellent
OUTLANDER—4-Cyl.—Truck Equipment Schedule T1						
ES Sport Utility	MS21W	20905	5425	5750	6775	8650
SE Sport Utility	MS31W	24305	6575	6950	8075	10400
Third Row Seat		------	275	275	355	355
4WD		------	1150	1150	1440	1440
OUTLANDER 4WD—V6—Truck Equipment Schedule T1						
XLS Sport Util	MT31X	26325	8725	9225	10400	13300
Third Row Seat	4	------	275	275	350	350

Body Type	VIN	List	Trade-In Good	Very Good	Pvt-Party Good	Retail Excellent
2WD	L		(825)	(825)	(1035)	(1035)
RAIDER EXTENDED CAB—V6—Truck Equipment Schedule T1						
LS Short Bed	HC22K	24950	5200	5525	6575	8675
RAIDER DOUBLE CAB—V6—Truck Equipment Schedule T1						
LS Short Bed	HC28K	27010	7425	7850	9275	12250
4WD	T		1425	1425	1910	1910

2010 MITSUBISHI—(Jor4)A4(AS2AW)-A-#

Body Type	VIN	List	Trade-In Good	Very Good	Pvt-Party Good	Retail Excellent
OUTLANDER—4-Cyl.—Truck Equipment Schedule T1						
ES Sport Utility	AS2AW	21580	6400	6700	7825	9675
SE Sport Utility	JS3AW	23280	7550	7900	9175	11400
Third Row Seat			325	325	405	405
4WD			1250	1250	1505	1505
OUTLANDER 4WD—V6—Truck Equipment Schedule T1						
XLS Sport Utility	JT4AX	27110	9925	10350	11750	14500
GT Sport Util 4D	JT5AX	30300	10950	11400	12850	15750
Third Row Seat			325	325	400	400
2WD	S		(950)	(950)	(1150)	(1150)
ENDEAVOR AWD—V6—Truck Equipment Schedule T1						
LS Sport Utility 4D	JN2AS	30239	7850	8200	9675	12150
SE Sport Utility 4D	JN3AS	32214	9100	9500	11100	13950
2WD	M		(1350)	(1350)	(1775)	(1775)

2011 MITSUBISHI—(Jor4)A4(AP3AU)-B-#

Body Type	VIN	List	Trade-In Good	Very Good	Pvt-Party Good	Retail Excellent
OUTLANDER SPORT—4-Cyl.—Truck Equipment Schedule T1						
ES Sport Utility	AP3AU	20275	8100	8375	9825	11950
OUTLANDER SPORT 4WD—4-Cyl.—Truck Equipment Schedule T1						
SE Sport Utility	AR4AU	23775	9925	10250	11850	14400
2WD	P		(1075)	(1075)	(1345)	(1345)
OUTLANDER—4-Cyl.—Truck Equipment Schedule T1						
ES Sport Utility	AS2AW	22775	7975	8250	9725	11800
OUTLANDER—4-Cyl.—Truck Equipment Schedule T1						
SE Sport Utility	AS3AW	23775	8550	8825	10350	12600
4WD	T		1400	1400	1715	1715
OUTLANDER—V6—Truck Equipment Schedule T1						
XLS Sport Utility	JS4AX	26575	10850	11250	12900	15650
OUTLANDER 4WD—V6—Truck Equipment Schedule T1						
GT Sport Utility	JT5AX	28575	12000	12400	14100	16950
ENDEAVOR AWD—V6—Truck Equipment Schedule T1						
LS Sport Utility 4D	JN2AS	30525	9250	9850	11300	13600
SE Sport Utility 4D	JN3AS	34364	11100	11450	13000	15550
2WD	M		(1450)	(1450)	(1730)	(1730)

2012 MITSUBISHI—(4orJ)A4(AP3AU)-C-#

Body Type	VIN	List	Trade-In Good	Very Good	Pvt-Party Good	Retail Excellent
OUTLANDER SPORT—4-Cyl.—Truck Equipment Schedule T1						
ES Sport Utility	AP3AU	20605	9200	9450	10950	12900
OUTLANDER SPORT 4WD—4-Cyl.—Truck Equipment Schedule T1						
SE Sport Utility	AR4AU	24105	11800	12100	13750	16150
2WD	P		(1500)	(1500)	(1735)	(1735)
OUTLANDER—4-Cyl.—Truck Equipment Schedule T1						
ES Sport Utility	AS2AW	23155	9225	9475	10950	12900
OUTLANDER—4-Cyl.—Truck Equipment Schedule T1						
SE Sport Utility	AS3AW	24155	9925	10200	11700	13750
4WD	T		1475	1475	1745	1745
OUTLANDER 4WD—V6—Truck Equipment Schedule T1						
GT Sport Utility	AT5AX	28705	13250	13600	15400	18050
2WD	S		(1500)	(1500)	(1770)	(1770)

2013 MITSUBISHI—(4orJ)A4(P3AU)-D-#

Body Type	VIN	List	Trade-In Good	Very Good	Pvt-Party Good	Retail Excellent
OUTLANDER SPORT—4-Cyl.—Truck Equipment Schedule T1						
ES Sport Utility	P3AU	21195	10450	10650	12100	14000
4WD	R		1475	1475	1715	1715
OUTLANDER SPORT 4WD—4-Cyl.—Truck Equipment Schedule T1						
SE Sport Utility	R4AU	24520	12800	13050	14850	17150
LE Sport Utility	R5AU	25720	13550	13800	15650	18050
2WD	P		(1275)	(1275)	(1470)	(1470)
OUTLANDER—4-Cyl.—Truck Equipment Schedule T1						
ES Sport Utility	S2AW	23520	11050	11300	12850	14800
OUTLANDER—4-Cyl.—Truck Equipment Schedule T1						
SE Sport Utility	T3AW	24820	11400	11650	13200	15200
4WD	T		1475	1475	1750	1750

SEE BACK PAGES FOR TRUCK EQUIPMENT

Body Type	VIN	List	Trade-In Good	Very Good	Pvt-Party Good	Retail Excellent
OUTLANDER 4WD—V6—Truck Equipment Schedule T1						
GT Sport Utility	T5AX	29420	**15450**	**15750**	**17600**	**20200**
2WD	S		**(1275)**	**(1275)**	**(1485)**	**(1485)**

2014 MITSUBISHI—(4orJ)A4(P3AU)—E-#

Body Type	VIN	List	Trade-In Good	Very Good	Pvt-Party Good	Retail Excellent
OUTLANDER SPORT—4-Cyl.—Truck Equipment Schedule T1						
ES Sport Utility 4D	P3AU	21495	**11250**	**11450**	**13200**	**15300**
4WD	R		**1500**	**1500**	**1730**	**1730**
OUTLANDER SPORT 4WD—4-Cyl.—Truck Equipment Schedule T1						
SE Sport Utility 4D	R4AU	24820	**14300**	**14550**	**16250**	**18450**
2WD	P		**(1375)**	**(1375)**	**(1540)**	**(1540)**
OUTLANDER—4-Cyl.—Truck Equipment Schedule T1						
ES Sport Utility	D2A3	23820	**12700**	**12950**	**14700**	**16900**
OUTLANDER 4WD—4-Cyl.—Truck Equipment Schedule T1						
SE Sport Utility	Z3A3	25795	**14600**	**14900**	**16550**	**18800**
2WD	D		**(1375)**	**(1375)**	**(1555)**	**(1555)**
OUTLANDER 4WD—V6—Truck Equipment Schedule T1						
GT Sport Utility	Z4AX	28620	**18450**	**18800**	**20500**	**23300**

NISSAN

2000 NISSAN—(1N6,4N2,5N1orJN8)(ED28Y)-Y-#

Body Type	VIN	List	Trade-In Good	Very Good	Pvt-Party Good	Retail Excellent
XTERRA 4WD—V6—Truck Equipment Schedule T1						
XE Sport Utility 4D	ED28Y	22019	**1350**	**1525**	**2075**	**3475**
SE Sport Utility 4D	ED28Y	26069	**1900**	**2150**	**2825**	**4725**
2WD	T		**(275)**	**(275)**	**(355)**	**(355)**
4-Cyl, 2.4 Liter	D		**(200)**	**(200)**	**(275)**	**(275)**
PATHFINDER 4WD—V6—Truck Equipment Schedule T1						
XE Sport Utility 4D	AR05Y	28919	**1000**	**1175**	**1900**	**3425**
SE Sport Utility 4D	AR05Y	30869	**1500**	**1750**	**2500**	**4375**
LE Sport Utility 4D	AR05Y	31819	**1775**	**2050**	**2875**	**5025**
2WD	S		**(525)**	**(525)**	**(715)**	**(715)**
QUEST—V6—Truck Equipment Schedule T1						
GXE Minivan	XN11T	22779	**900**	**1125**	**1700**	**3225**
SE Minivan	XN11T	24919	**1500**	**1850**	**2425**	**4500**
GLE Minivan	XN11T	26919	**1725**	**2125**	**2800**	**5125**
FRONTIER—4-Cyl.—Truck Equipment Schedule T2						
XE Short Bed	DD21S	12110	**525**	**550**	**1075**	**1750**
XE King Cab	DD26S	14060	**1100**	**1175**	**1750**	**2700**
4WD	Y		**400**	**400**	**535**	**535**
V6, 3.3 Liter	Y		**125**	**125**	**165**	**165**
FRONTIER—V6—Truck Equipment Schedule T2						
Desrt Rnr XE King	ED26S	16260	**1450**	**1575**	**2175**	**3300**
Desrt Rnr SE King	ED26S	18410	**1825**	**1950**	**2700**	**4050**
XE Crew Cab 4D	ED27S	17810	**1925**	**2050**	**2800**	**4200**
SE Crew Cab 4D	ED27S	19110	**2250**	**2425**	**3200**	**4775**
4WD	Y		**400**	**400**	**535**	**535**
FRONTIER 4WD—V6—Truck Equipment Schedule T2						
SE King Cab	DD26Y	21010	**1850**	**1975**	**2725**	**4075**

2001 NISSAN—(1N6,4N2,5N1orJN8)(ED28Y)-1-#

Body Type	VIN	List	Trade-In Good	Very Good	Pvt-Party Good	Retail Excellent
XTERRA 4WD—V6—Truck Equipment Schedule T1						
XE Sport Utility 4D	ED28Y	22569	**1675**	**1875**	**2350**	**3725**
SE Sport Utility 4D	ED28Y	26619	**2275**	**2550**	**3125**	**5050**
2WD	T		**(300)**	**(300)**	**(385)**	**(385)**
4-Cyl, 2.4 Liter	D		**(225)**	**(225)**	**(300)**	**(300)**
PATHFINDER 4WD—V6—Truck Equipment Schedule T1						
XE Sport Utility 4D	DR0TY	30169	**1375**	**1575**	**2200**	**3800**
SE Sport Utility 4D	DR0TY	30869	**1725**	**2000**	**2675**	**4525**
LE Sport Utility 4D	DR0TY	31819	**2100**	**2425**	**3250**	**5475**
2WD	X		**(625)**	**(625)**	**(820)**	**(820)**
AWD			**0**	**0**	**0**	**0**
QUEST—V6—Truck Equipment Schedule T1						
GXE Minivan	ZN16T	22959	**1100**	**1350**	**1925**	**3575**
SE Minivan	ZN16T	24919	**1750**	**2175**	**2825**	**5100**
GLE Minivan	ZN17T	27569	**2075**	**2550**	**3175**	**5700**
FRONTIER—4-Cyl.—Truck Equipment Schedule T2						
XE Short Bed	DD21S	12219	**750**	**825**	**1350**	**2100**
XE King Cab	DD26S	14169	**1325**	**1425**	**2000**	**3025**
4WD	Y		**400**	**400**	**535**	**535**
V6, 3.3 Liter	E		**125**	**125**	**165**	**165**

Body Type	VIN	List	Trade-In Good	Very Good	Pvt-Party Good	Retail Excellent
FRONTIER—V6—Truck Equipment Schedule T2						
Desrt Rnr XE King	ED26T	16469	1725	1850	2475	3700
Desrt Rnr SE King	ED26T	18619	2150	2300	3050	4525
XE Crew Cab 4D	ED27T	18569	2350	2500	3275	4875
SE Crew Cab 4D	ED27T	20719	2725	2925	3725	5500
4WD	Y		400	400	535	535
FRONTIER 4WD—V6—Truck Equipment Schedule T2						
SE King Cab	ED26Y	21219	2125	2275	3025	4500
FRONTIER—V6 Supercharged—Truck Equipment Schedule T2						
King Cab	MD26T	20519	2200	2350	3100	4625
Crew Cab 4D	MD27T	21969	2725	2925	3725	5500
4WD	Y		400	400	535	535

2002 NISSAN—(1N6,5N1orJN8)(ED28Y)-2-#

Body Type	VIN	List	Trade-In Good	Very Good	Pvt-Party Good	Retail Excellent
XTERRA 4WD—V6—Truck Equipment Schedule T1						
XE Sport Utility 4D	ED28Y	22739	1925	2175	2575	4000
SE Sport Utility 4D	ED28Y	26739	2500	2800	3275	5175
2WD	T		(350)	(350)	(465)	(465)
4-Cyl, 2.4 Liter	D		(250)	(250)	(335)	(335)
XTERRA 4WD—V6 Supercharged—Truck Equipment Schedule T1						
XE S/C Spt Util 4D	MD28T	26239	2050	2275	2750	4350
SE S/C Spt Util 4D	MD28T	28039	2975	3325	3800	5950
2WD	T		(350)	(350)	(465)	(465)
PATHFINDER 4WD—V6—Truck Equipment Schedule T1						
SE Sport Utility 4D	DR07Y	29189	1900	2175	2875	4775
LE Sport Utility 4D	DR07Y	32039	2475	2825	3600	5925
2WD	X		(700)	(700)	(935)	(935)
QUEST—V6—Truck Equipment Schedule T1						
GXE Minivan	ZN15T	23279	1350	1650	2125	3825
SE Minivan	ZN16T	25039	2125	2575	3100	5400
GLE Minivan	ZN17T	27689	2425	2950	3450	6000
FRONTIER KING CAB—4-Cyl.—Truck Equipment Schedule T2						
Short Bed	ED27S	13339	1675	1800	2375	3500
XE Short Bed	DD26S	14339	1725	1850	2425	3600
4WD	Y		500	500	665	665
V6, 3.3 Liter	E		150	150	185	185
FRONTIER KING CAB—V6—Truck Equipment Schedule T2						
Desert Runner XE	ED26T	16539	2100	2250	2975	4375
Desert Runner SE	ED26T	19739	2625	2800	3575	5225
FRONTIER KING CAB 4WD—V6—Truck Equipment Schedule T2						
SE Short Bed	ED26Y	22339	2650	2825	3600	5275
FRONTIER CREW CAB—V6—Truck Equipment Schedule T2						
XE Short Bed	ED27T	18739	2900	3100	3900	5675
XE Long Bed	ED27T	19299	2800	3000	3775	5525
SE Short Bed	ED27T	22239	3375	3600	4425	6450
SE Long Bed	ED27T	22799	3200	3425	4250	6200
4WD	Y		500	500	665	665
FRONTIER KING CAB—V6 Supercharged—Truck Equipment Schedule T2						
Short Bed	MD26T	20889	2700	2875	3650	5350
4WD	Y		500	500	665	665
FRONTIER CREW CAB—V6 Supercharged—Truck Equipment Schedule T2						
Short Bed	MD27T	23739	3300	3500	4350	6325
Long Bed	MD27T	24299	3125	3350	4175	6075
4WD	Y		500	500	665	665

2003 NISSAN—(1N6,5N1orJN8)(ED28Y)-3-#

Body Type	VIN	List	Trade-In Good	Very Good	Pvt-Party Good	Retail Excellent
XTERRA 4WD—V6—Truck Equipment Schedule T1						
XE Sport Utility 4D	ED28Y	23939	2575	2875	3200	4850
SE Sport Utility 4D	ED28Y	27239	3200	3550	3950	6025
2WD	T		(425)	(425)	(565)	(565)
4-Cyl, 2.4 Liter	D		(275)	(275)	(360)	(360)
XTERRA 4WD—V6 Supercharged—Truck Equipment Schedule T1						
SE S/C Spt Util 4D	MD28T	28539	3600	4025	4525	6850
2WD	T		(425)	(425)	(565)	(565)
MURANO AWD—V6—Truck Equipment Schedule T1						
SL Sport Utility 4D	AZ08W	30339	3225	3650	4000	6125
SE Sport Utility 4D	AZ08W	31139	3525	4000	4450	6775
2WD	T		(475)	(475)	(645)	(645)
PATHFINDER 4WD—V6—Truck Equipment Schedule T1						
SE Sport Utility 4D	DR09Y	29339	2475	2800	3400	5450
LE Sport Utility 4D	DR09Y	34339	3075	3475	4125	6575
2WD	X		(775)	(775)	(1040)	(1040)

Body Type	VIN	List	Trade-In Good	Very Good	Pvt-Party Good	Retail Excellent
FRONTIER KING CAB—4-Cyl.—Truck Equipment Schedule T2						
Short Bed	ED27S	13529	2200	2350	3100	4550
DD26S Short Bed	DD26S	14579	2300	2475	3225	4725
4WD	Y		625	625	820	820
V6, 3.3 Liter	E		175	175	220	220
FRONTIER KING CAB—V6—Truck Equipment Schedule T2						
Desert Runner XE	ED26T	16709	2750	2925	3725	5450
Desert Runner SE	ED26T	21109	3700	3925	4975	7225
FRONTIER KING CAB 4WD—V6—Truck Equipment Schedule T2						
SE Short Bed	ED26Y	23709	3750	4000	5025	7300
FRONTIER CREW CAB—V6—Truck Equipment Schedule T2						
XE Short Bed	ED27T	18979	3575	3825	4700	6825
XE Long Bed	ED27T	19529	3475	3700	4575	6650
SE Short Bed	ED27T	22829	4350	4650	5750	8300
SE Long Bed	ED27T	23379	4175	4450	5550	8025
4WD	Y		625	625	820	820
FRONTIER KING CAB—V6 Supercharged—Truck Equipment Schedule T2						
Short Bed	MD26T	21359	3400	3625	4500	6525
4WD	Y		625	625	820	820
FRONTIER CREW CAB—V6 Supercharged—Truck Equipment Schedule T2						
Short Bed	MD27T	24329	4275	4550	5650	8175
Long Bed	MD27T	24879	4100	4375	5450	7900
4WD	Y		625	625	820	820

2004 NISSAN—(1N6,5N1orJN8)(ED28Y)-4-#

Body Type	VIN	List	Trade-In Good	Very Good	Pvt-Party Good	Retail Excellent
XTERRA 4WD—V6—Truck Equipment Schedule T1						
XE Sport Utility 4D	ED28Y	22940	3050	3375	3775	5675
SE Sport Utility 4D	ED28Y	27240	3550	3925	4475	6750
2WD	T		(500)	(500)	(665)	(665)
4-Cyl, 2.4 Liter	T		(200)	(200)	(255)	(255)
XTERRA 4WD—V6 Supercharged—Truck Equipment Schedule T1						
SE S/C Spt Util 4D	MD28T	28540	4150	4600	5125	7700
2WD	T		(500)	(500)	(665)	(665)
MURANO AWD—V6—Truck Equipment Schedule T1						
SL Sport Utility 4D	AZ08W	30340	3750	4225	4775	7200
SE Sport Utility 4D	AZ08W	31290	4025	4525	5100	7725
2WD	T		(525)	(525)	(710)	(710)
QUEST—V6—Truck Equipment Schedule T1						
S Minivan	BV28U	24780	2575	2975	3300	5250
SL Minivan	BV28U	27280	3075	3525	3825	6050
SE Minivan	BV28U	32780	3550	4100	4450	7000
PATHFINDER 4WD—V6—Truck Equipment Schedule T1						
SE Sport Utility 4D	DR09Y	29540	3150	3550	4125	6400
LE Sport Utility 4D	DR09Y	34590	3850	4325	5025	7750
2WD	X		(875)	(875)	(1155)	(1155)
PATHFINDER ARMADA 4WD—V8—Truck Equipment Schedule T1						
SE Sport Utility 4D	AA08B	36750	5300	5650	6325	8650
SE Off-Rd Spt Utl	AA08B	39900	6175	6575	7400	10100
LE Sport Utility 4D	AA08B	41250	6175	6575	7400	10100
2WD	A		(525)	(525)	(710)	(710)
FRONTIER KING CAB—4-Cyl.—Truck Equipment Schedule T2						
Short Bed	ED27S	13830	3400	3625	4400	6275
XE Short Bed	DD26S	14880	3575	3800	4600	6550
4WD	Y		750	750	1000	1000
V6, 3.3 Liter	E		200	200	255	255
FRONTIER KING CAB—V6—Truck Equipment Schedule T2						
Desert Runner XE	ED26T	17030	3875	4150	5125	7275
FRONTIER KING CAB 4WD—V6 Supercharged—Truck Equip Sched T2						
Short Bed	MD26T	25430	4825	5125	6200	8825
FRONTIER CREW CAB—V6—Truck Equipment Schedule T2						
XE Short Bed	ED27T	19360	4900	5200	6300	8950
XE Long Bed	ED27T	19910	4775	5075	6150	8750
LE Short Bed	ED27T	24900	5450	5800	7125	10100
LE Long Bed	ED27T	25450	5425	5775	7125	10100
4WD	Y		750	750	1000	1000
FRONTIER CREW CAB—V6 Supercharged—Truck Equipment Schedule T2						
Short Bed	MD27T	24810	5450	5800	7125	10100
Long Bed	MD27T	25360	5500	5850	6975	9925
4WD	Y		750	750	1000	1000
TITAN KING CAB—V8—Truck Equipment Schedule T1						
XE Short Bed	AA06A	23050	4475	5025	5100	7275
SE Short Bed	AA06A	25050	5300	5950	5950	8475
LE Short Bed	AA06A	29450	5375	6025	6050	8675

TRUCKS & VANS

Body Type	VIN	List	Trade-In Good	Very Good	Pvt-Party Good	Retail Excellent
4WD	B		1175	1175	1545	1545
TITAN CREW CAB—V8—Truck Equipment Schedule T1						
XE Short Bed	AA07A	25750	5900	6650	6750	9600
SE Short Bed	AA07A	27350	6500	7300	7350	10450
LE Short Bed	AA07A	31750	6750	7575	7625	10900
4WD	B		1175	1175	1540	1540

2005 NISSAN—(1N6,5N1orJN8)(AN08W)-5-#

Body Type	VIN	List	Trade-In Good	Very Good	Pvt-Party Good	Retail Excellent
XTERRA 4WD—V6—Truck Equipment Schedule T1						
S Sport Utility 4D	AN08W	24280	4225	4650	5325	7775
Off-Road Spt Utl	AN08W	27280	4775	5275	5925	8600
SE Spt Utl 4D	AN08W	27880	4975	5475	6150	8900
2WD	U		(575)	(575)	(765)	(765)
MURANO AWD—V6—Truck Equipment Schedule T1						
S Sport Utility 4D	AZ08W	29180	3500	3950	4550	6600
SL Sport Utility 4D	AZ08W	30680	4475	5025	5575	8025
SE Sport Utility 4D	AZ08W	31630	5125	5725	6225	8950
2WD	T		(575)	(575)	(775)	(775)
QUEST—V6—Truck Equipment Schedule T1						
Minivan	BV28U	23910	2050	2375	3025	4850
S Minivan	BV28U	25110	2775	3200	3850	6175
SL Minivan	BV28U	26810	3250	3750	4350	6900
SE Minivan	BV28U	32810	3675	4225	4975	7900
PATHFINDER 4WD—V6—Truck Equipment Schedule T1						
XE Spt Utl 4D	AR19W	27300	4100	4600	5300	7775
SE Spt Utl 4D	AR18W	28500	4750	5300	5975	8725
SE Off-Road Utl	AR18W	31850	5025	5625	6250	9125
LE Spt Utl 4D	AR18W	35400	5625	6300	7025	10200
2WD	U		(950)	(950)	(1260)	(1260)
ARMADA—V8—Truck Equipment Schedule T1						
SE Sport Utility 4D	AA08A	34670	5400	5775	6975	9525
4WD	B		575	575	775	775
ARMADA 4WD—V8—Truck Equipment Schedule T1						
SE Off-Rd Spt Utl	AA08B	40420	6950	7400	8725	11900
ARMADA 4WD—V8—Truck Equipment Schedule T1						
LE Sport Utility 4D	AA08B	42150	6950	7400	8775	12000
2WD	A		(575)	(575)	(775)	(775)
FRONTIER KING CAB—4-Cyl.—Truck Equipment Schedule T2						
XE Short Bed	BD06T	16080	4650	4975	5950	8050
FRONTIER KING CAB—V6—Truck Equipment Schedule T2						
SE Short Bed	AD06U	20130	5400	5750	6925	9350
LE Short Bed	AD06U	22880	6725	7150	8350	11250
Nismo Short Bed	AD06U	22680	6700	7125	8300	11200
4WD	W		875	875	1110	1110
FRONTIER CREW CAB—V6—Truck Equipment Schedule T2						
SE Short Bed	AD07U	22180	6725	7175	8300	11250
LE Short Bed	AD07U	24480	7400	7875	9150	12300
Nismo Short Bed	AD07U	24630	9150	9725	11100	14900
4WD	W		875	875	1105	1105
TITAN KING CAB—V8—Truck Equipment Schedule T1						
XE Short Bed	AA06A	23300	5525	6175	6500	9050
SE Short Bed	AA06A	25450	5850	6550	7025	9925
LE Short Bed	AA07B	30220	6100	6825	7400	10550
4WD	B		1275	1275	1620	1620
TITAN CREW CAB—V8—Truck Equipment Schedule T1						
XE Short Bed	AA07A	26150	6750	7550	7900	11100
SE Short Bed	AA07A	27950	7525	8400	8800	12400
LE Short Bed	AA07A	32700	7775	8675	9125	12900
4WD	B		1275	1275	1690	1690

2006 NISSAN—(1N6,5N1orJN8)(AN08W)-6-#

Body Type	VIN	List	Trade-In Good	Very Good	Pvt-Party Good	Retail Excellent
XTERRA 4WD—V6—Truck Equipment Schedule T1						
X Sport Utility 4D	AN08W	23330	4875	5350	6100	8725
S Sport Utility 4D	AN08W	25530	5275	5775	6500	9275
Off-Rd Spt Utl	AN08W	27630	5575	6100	6975	9950
SE Spt Utl 4D	AN08W	28230	5600	6150	7050	10100
2WD	U		(625)	(625)	(845)	(845)
MURANO AWD—V6—Truck Equipment Schedule T1						
S Sport Utility 4D	AZ08W	29805	4600	5100	5600	7850
SL Sport Utility 4D	AZ08W	31355	5600	6225	6775	9425
SE Sport Utility 4D	AZ08W	32305	6225	7225	7750	10800
2WD	T		(625)	(625)	(845)	(845)

Body Type	VIN	List	Trade-In Good	Very Good	Pvt-Party Good	Retail Excellent
QUEST—V6—Truck Equipment Schedule T1						
Minivan	BV28U	24580	2800	3175	3800	5900
S Special Edition	BV28U	25880	3425	3875	4475	6900
SL Minivan	BV28U	27480	4150	4725	5375	8250
SE Minivan	BV28U	34080	4650	5275	6025	9300
PATHFINDER 4WD—V6—Truck Equipment Schedule T1						
S Spt Utl 4D	AR18W	27830	5050	5600	6325	8925
SE Spt Utl 4D	AR18W	29080	5600	6225	6850	9625
SE Off-Road Util	AR18W	31880	6475	7200	7750	10850
LE Spt Utl 4D	AR18W	36130	7025	7775	8375	11650
2WD	U		(1025)	(1025)	(1375)	(1375)
ARMADA—V8—Truck Equipment Schedule T1						
SE Spt Utl 4D	AA08A	35435	6175	6550	7800	10450
4WD	B		625	625	845	845
ARMADA 4WD—V8—Truck Equipment Schedule T1						
SE Off-Road Util	AA08W	41505	8150	8625	9975	13350
LE Spt Utl 4D	AA08W	43270	7500	7950	9400	12700
2WD	A		(625)	(625)	(845)	(845)
FRONTIER KING CAB—4-Cyl.—Truck Equipment Schedule T2						
XE Short Bed	BD06T	16480	5100	5425	6450	8675
FRONTIER KING CAB—V6—Truck Equipment Schedule T1						
SE Short Bed	AD06U	20730	5925	6300	7500	10050
Nismo Short Bed	AD06U	23030	8350	8875	10200	13650
4WD	W		975	975	1240	1240
FRONTIER KING CAB—V6—Truck Equipment Schedule T2						
LE Short Bed	AD06T	23230	8450	8975	10000	13050
4WD	Y		975	975	1195	1195
FRONTIER CREW CAB—V6—Truck Equipment Schedule T1						
SE Short Bed	AD07U	22580	8600	9150	10350	13800
4WD	W		975	975	1240	1240
FRONTIER CREW CAB—V6—Truck Equipment Schedule T1						
LE Short Bed	AD07T	24930	9025	9600	11000	14700
Nismo Short Bed	AD07U	25080	9475	10050	11450	15250
4WD	W		975	975	1240	1240
TITAN KING CAB—V8—Truck Equipment Schedule T1						
XE Short Bed	AA06A	23920	5775	6400	6850	9425
SE Short Bed	AA06A	26070	6450	7150	7675	10650
LE Short Bed	BA06A	31085	6750	7500	8050	11250
4WD	B		1500	1500	1965	1965
TITAN CREW CAB—V8—Truck Equipment Schedule T1						
XE Short Bed	AA07A	26770	7350	8150	8650	12000
SE Short Bed	AA07A	28570	8175	9025	9525	13250
LE Short Bed	BA07A	33555	8950	9875	10350	14450
4WD	B		1500	1500	1985	1985

Body Type	VIN	List	Trade-In Good	Very Good	Pvt-Party Good	Retail Excellent
XTERRA 4WD—V6—Truck Equipment Schedule T1						
X Sport Utility 4D	AN08W	23505	5450	5925	6775	9350
S Sport Utility 4D	AN08W	25755	5900	6400	7225	9975
Off-Road Spt Utl	AN08W	27805	6400	6950	7725	10600
SE Spt Utl 4D	AN08W	28555	6625	7200	7950	10950
2WD	U		(675)	(675)	(910)	(910)
MURANO AWD—V6—Truck Equipment Schedule T1						
S Sport Utility 4D	AZ08W	30000	5725	6225	6775	9100
SL Sport Utility 4D	AZ08W	31550	6775	7450	7850	10500
SE Sport Utility 4D	AZ08W	32500	7350	8075	8650	11700
2WD	T		(675)	(675)	(890)	(890)
QUEST—V6—Truck Equipment Schedule T1						
Minivan	BV28U	25350	3175	3575	4225	6400
S Minivan	BV28U	26300	3800	4275	5000	7525
SL Minivan	BV28U	28500	4825	5425	6100	9075
SE Minivan	BV28U	35300	5900	6625	7700	11650
PATHFINDER 4WD—V6—Truck Equipment Schedule T1						
S Sport Utility 4D	AR18W	28250	6175	6775	7450	10200
SE Sport Utility	AR18W	29500	6800	7450	8175	11150
SE Off-Rd Utl	AR18W	32300	7675	8425	9050	12300
LE Spt Utl 4D	AR18W	36650	8150	8925	9475	12850
2WD	U		(1100)	(1100)	(1480)	(1480)
ARMADA—V8—Truck Equipment Schedule T1						
SE Sport Utility 4D	AA08W	35695	7350	7750	9100	11950
4WD	W		975	975	1310	1310
ARMADA 4WD—V8—Truck Equipment Schedule T1						
LE Sport Utility 4D	AA08B	43785	8675	9150	10600	14000

1015

Body Type	VIN	List	Trade-In Good	Trade-In Very Good	Pvt-Party Good	Retail Excellent
2WD	A		(675)	(675)	(910)	(910)
FRONTIER KING CAB—4-Cyl.—Truck Equipment Schedule T2						
XE Short Bed	BD06T	16700	5425	5775	6900	9075
FRONTIER KING CAB—V6—Truck Equipment Schedule T2						
SE Short Bed	AD06U	20785	6650	7075	8175	10700
Nismo Short Bed	AD06U	23305	9375	9925	11200	14600
4WD	W		1075	1075	1325	1325
FRONTIER KING CAB—V6—Truck Equipment Schedule T2						
LE Short Bed	AD06U	23550	8775	9300	10500	13700
4WD	W		1075	1075	1335	1335
FRONTIER CREW CAB—V6—Truck Equipment Schedule T1						
SE Short Bed	AD07U	22555	9225	9800	11000	14400
SE Long Bed	AD09U	23355	9000	9550	10700	14000
4WD	W		1075	1075	1325	1325
FRONTIER CREW CAB—V6—Truck Equipment Schedule T2						
LE Short Bed	AD07U	25250	9875	10500	11750	15250
LE Long Bed	AD09U	25750	9825	10450	11500	14800
Nismo Short Bed	AD07U	25300	10900	11550	12800	16650
4WD	W		1075	1075	1320	1320
TITAN KING CAB—V8—Truck Equipment Schedule T1						
XE Short Bed	AA06A	24435	5400	5950	6600	8975
SE Short Bed	AA06A	26585	6700	7350	7975	10850
LE Short Bed	BA06A	31595	7250	7950	8600	11700
4WD	B		1875	1875	2440	2440
TITAN CREW CAB—V8—Truck Equipment Schedule T1						
XE Short Bed	AA07A	27285	7900	8650	9200	12450
SE Short Bed	AA07A	29085	8650	9475	10050	13700
LE Short Bed	BA07A	35855	9775	10700	11250	15300
4WD	B		1875	1875	2405	2405

2008 NISSAN—(J,1or5)N(1,6or8)(AS58V)-8-#

Body Type	VIN	List	Trade-In Good	Trade-In Very Good	Pvt-Party Good	Retail Excellent
ROGUE AWD—4-Cyl.—Truck Equipment Schedule T1						
S Sport Utility 4D	AS58V	21195	6525	7200	7275	9675
SL Sport Utility 4D	AS58V	22615	7200	7950	8050	10750
2WD	T		(725)	(725)	(875)	(875)
XTERRA 4WD—V6—Truck Equipment Schedule T1						
X Sport Utility 4D	AN08W	24725	7625	8175	8925	11550
S Sport Utility 4D	AN08W	26425	7975	8550	9250	11950
Off-Road Spt Utl	AN08W	27075	8425	9025	9750	12600
SE Spt Utl 4D	AN08W	29375	8525	9125	9875	12750
2WD	U		(725)	(725)	(915)	(915)
QUEST—V6—Truck Equipment Schedule T1						
Minivan	BV28U	25725	4125	4550	5075	7050
S Minivan	BV28U	26425	5150	5675	6400	8900
SL Minivan	BV28U	30325	6725	7400	8025	11100
SE Minivan	BV28U	35825	7450	8175	9025	12650
PATHFINDER 4WD—V6—Truck Equipment Schedule T1						
S Sport Utility 4D	AR18B	28405	8300	8950	9600	12400
SE Sport Utility 4D	AR18B	31705	9050	9750	10450	13450
SE Off-Road Util	AR18B	34605	9175	9850	10600	13750
LE Sport Utility 4D	AR18B	37705	10000	10750	11500	14850
2WD	A		(1200)	(1200)	(1495)	(1495)
V8, 5.6 Liter	B		250	250	310	310
ARMADA—V8—Truck Equipment Schedule T1						
SE Sport Utility 4D	AA08B	36075	9550	9975	11350	14200
4WD	B		1075	1075	1340	1340
ARMADA 4WD—V8—Truck Equipment Schedule T1						
LE Sport Utility 4D	AA08C	45295	11250	11750	13200	16500
2WD	D		(725)	(725)	(915)	(915)
FRONTIER KING CAB—4-Cyl.—Truck Equipment Schedule T2						
XE Short Bed	BD06T	16895	6350	6725	7750	9850
FRONTIER KING CAB—V6—Truck Equipment Schedule T2						
SE Short Bed	AD06U	20705	7675	8125	9225	11700
Nismo Short Bed	AD06U	23305	10200	10800	12000	15100
4WD	W		1225	1225	1540	1540
4-Cyl, 2.5 Liter	B		(225)	(225)	(280)	(280)
FRONTIER KING CAB—V6—Truck Equipment Schedule T2						
LE Short Bed	AD06U	24095	9625	10150	11350	14300
4WD	W		1225	1225	1545	1545
FRONTIER CREW CAB—V6—Truck Equipment Schedule T1						
SE Short Bed	AD07U	22555	10150	10800	11750	15000
SE Long Bed	AD09U	23355	9925	10500	11500	14700
4WD	W		1225	1225	1540	1540

Body Type	VIN	List	Trade-In Good	Very Good	Pvt-Party Good	Retail Excellent
FRONTIER CREW CAB—V6—Truck Equipment Schedule T2						
LE Short Bed	AD07U	25795	**10600**	**11200**	**12400**	**15650**
LE Long Bed	AD09U	26295	**10450**	**11050**	**12250**	**15450**
Nismo Short Bed	AD07U	25495	**11600**	**12250**	**13500**	**17000**
4WD	W		**1225**	**1225**	**1545**	**1545**
TITAN KING CAB—V8—Truck Equipment Schedule T1						
XE Short Bed	AA06A	25135	**6925**	**7450**	**8075**	**10400**
XE Long Bed	AA06E	25545	**6825**	**7350**	**7950**	**10250**
SE Short Bed	AA06A	27395	**8325**	**8950**	**9600**	**12350**
SE Long Bed	AA06E	27805	**8225**	**8850**	**9500**	**12250**
LE Short Bed	BA06A	33365	**8775**	**9450**	**10100**	**13000**
LE Long Bed	AA06E	33775	**8825**	**9500**	**10150**	**13050**
4WD	C,F		**2125**	**2125**	**2655**	**2655**
TITAN KING CAB 4WD—V8—Truck Equipment Schedule T1						
Pro-4X Short Bed	AA06C	32725	**10950**	**11800**	**12500**	**16100**
TITAN CREW CAB—V8—Truck Equipment Schedule T1						
XE Short Bed	AA07D	28065	**9775**	**10500**	**11100**	**14200**
XE Long Bed	AA07G	28475	**9425**	**10150**	**10750**	**13800**
SE Short Bed	AA07D	29965	**10600**	**11350**	**12000**	**15500**
SE Long Bed	BA07A	30385	**10400**	**11150**	**11800**	**15200**
LE Long Bed	BA07A	35935	**11550**	**12450**	**13150**	**17000**
4WD	C,F		**2125**	**2125**	**2635**	**2635**
TITAN CREW CAB 4WD—V8—Truck Equipment Schedule T1						
LE Long Bed	AA07B	39275	**14550**	**15650**	**16300**	**21000**
2WD	A		**(2400)**	**(2400)**	**(2985)**	**(2985)**
TITAN CREW CAB 4WD—V8—Truck Equipment Schedule T1						
Pro-4X Short Bed	BA07B	34925	**14500**	**15550**	**16200**	**20800**
Pro-4X Long Bed	BA07B	35525	**13650**	**14650**	**15350**	**19800**

Body Type	VIN	List	Trade-In Good	Very Good	Pvt-Party Good	Retail Excellent
ROGUE AWD—4-Cyl.—Truck Equipment Schedule T1						
S Sport Utility 4D	AS58V	22200	**7400**	**8000**	**8425**	**10850**
SL Sport Utility 4D	AS58V	23790	**8000**	**8650**	**9050**	**11650**
2WD	T		**(825)**	**(825)**	**(990)**	**(990)**
XTERRA 4WD—V6—Truck Equipment Schedule T1						
X Sport Utility 4D	AN08W	25940	**10100**	**10700**	**11550**	**14350**
X Sport Utility 4D	AN08W	27640	**10500**	**11100**	**11900**	**14750**
Off-Rd Spt Uti	AN08W	30120	**11000**	**11600**	**12400**	**15300**
SE Spt Util 4D	AN08W	30120	**11050**	**11650**	**12550**	**15600**
2WD	U		**(825)**	**(825)**	**(1000)**	**(1000)**
MURANO AWD—V6—Truck Equipment Schedule T1						
S Sport Utility 4D	AZ18W	28675	**9825**	**10400**	**11200**	**13850**
SL Sport Utility 4D	AZ18U	30225	**11000**	**11650**	**12450**	**15300**
LE Sport Utility 4D	AZ18U	36655	**11100**	**11750**	**12650**	**15650**
2WD	U		**(825)**	**(825)**	**(1020)**	**(1020)**
QUEST—V6—Truck Equipment Schedule T1						
Minivan	BV28U	26370	**5500**	**5950**	**6750**	**8975**
S Minivan	BV28U	27430	**6725**	**7275**	**8000**	**10600**
SL Minivan	BV28U	31330	**8625**	**9325**	**10050**	**13250**
SE Minivan	BV28U	36430	**9925**	**10700**	**11600**	**15400**
PATHFINDER 4WD—V6—Truck Equipment Schedule T1						
S Sport Utility 4D	AR18B	29990	**10750**	**11350**	**12300**	**15300**
SE Sport Utility 4D	AR18B	33290	**11500**	**12200**	**13100**	**16300**
SE Off-Road Util	AR18B	36190	**11900**	**12600**	**13500**	**16850**
LE Sport Utility 4D	AR18B	39290	**12700**	**13400**	**14300**	**17650**
2WD	A		**(1275)**	**(1275)**	**(1590)**	**(1590)**
V8, 5.6 Liter	B		**275**	**275**	**345**	**345**
ARMADA—V8—Truck Equipment Schedule T1						
SE Sport Utility 4D	AA08D	36910	**11100**	**11500**	**13100**	**15900**
4WD	C		**1150**	**1150**	**1395**	**1395**
ARMADA 4WD—V8—Truck Equipment Schedule T1						
LE Sport Utility 4D	AA08D	47525	**13350**	**13850**	**15700**	**19000**
2WD	D		**(825)**	**(825)**	**(1005)**	**(1005)**
FRONTIER KING CAB—4-Cyl.—Truck Equipment Schedule T2						
XE Short Bed	BD06T	18240	**7300**	**7725**	**8700**	**10650**
FRONTIER KING CAB—V6—Truck Equipment Schedule T1						
SE Short Bed	AD06W	22190	**9175**	**9675**	**10800**	**13250**
4WD	W		**1425**	**1425**	**1735**	**1735**
4-Cyl, 2.5 Liter	B		**(250)**	**(250)**	**(290)**	**(290)**
FRONTIER KING CAB—V6—Truck Equipment Schedule T2						
LE Short Bed	AD06U	25620	**10750**	**11350**	**12400**	**15200**
4WD	W		**1425**	**1425**	**1730**	**1730**

546   DEDUCT FOR RECONDITIONING

Body Type	VIN	List	Trade-In Good	Very Good	Pvt-Party Good	Retail Excellent
FRONTIER KING CAB 4WD—V6—Truck Equipment Schedule T1						
Pro-4X Short Bed	AD06W	28410	13400	14100	15350	18800
2WD	T		(2200)	(2200)	(2650)	(2650)
FRONTIER CREW CAB—V6—Truck Equipment Schedule T1						
SE Short Bed	AD07U	24940	11050	11700	12650	15700
SE Long Bed	AD09U	24840	10950	11600	12550	15550
LE Short Bed	AD07U	27320	11850	12500	13600	16650
LE Long Bed	AD09U	27820	11750	12350	13500	16550
4WD	W		1425	1425	1730	1730
FRONTIER CREW CAB 4WD—V6—Truck Equipment Schedule T2						
Pro-4X Short Bed	AD07W	29760	14650	15450	16700	20500
2WD	U		(2200)	(2200)	(2655)	(2655)
TITAN KING CAB—V8—Truck Equipment Schedule T1						
XE Short Bed	AA06A	26930	9125	9650	10400	12900
XE Long Bed	AA06E	27530	9075	9600	10350	12750
SE Short Bed	AA06A	28930	10800	11450	12250	15150
SE Long Bed	AA06E	29530	10550	11150	11950	14800
LE Short Bed	BA06A	34405	11200	11850	12750	15800
4WD	C,F		2475	2475	2880	2880
TITAN KING CAB 4WD—V8—Truck Equipment Schedule T1						
Pro-4X Short Bed	AA06C	34460	13400	14200	15150	18800
TITAN CREW CAB—V8—Truck Equipment Schedule T1						
XE Short Bed	AA07D	29480	11950	12650	13450	16600
XE Long Bed	AA07G	30080	11750	12450	13250	16350
SE Short Bed	AA07D	31130	12850	13550	14550	18000
SE Long Bed	BA07D	31505	12550	13250	14150	17500
LE Short Bed	BA07D	36605	14100	14950	15950	19800
4WD	C,F		2475	2475	2875	2875
TITAN CREW CAB 4WD—V8—Truck Equipment Schedule T1						
LE Long Bed	AA07C	39905	17300	18300	19200	23800
2WD	D		(2600)	(2600)	(3035)	(3035)
TITAN CREW CAB 4WD—V8—Truck Equipment Schedule T1						
Pro-4X Short Bed	BA07C	36435	16550	17600	18550	23200
Pro-4X Long Bed	BA07C	37035	16300	17200	18100	22400

2010 NISSAN—(J,1or5)N(1,6or8)(AS5MV)—A—#

Body Type	VIN	List	Trade-In Good	Very Good	Pvt-Party Good	Retail Excellent
ROGUE AWD—4-Cyl.—Truck Equipment Schedule T1						
S Sport Utility	AS5MV	22340	8925	9450	10350	12950
SL Sport Utility	AS5MV	23930	9400	9975	10900	13700
S Krom Ed Util	AS5MV	26110	9800	10250	11500	14100
2WD	T		(950)	(950)	(1195)	(1195)
XTERRA 4WD—V6—Truck Equipment Schedule T1						
X Sport Utility 4D	AN0NW	26100	11150	11650	12650	15200
S Sport Utility 4D	AN0NW	28270	11350	11900	12950	15550
Off-Road Spt Util	AN0NW	31200	12550	13150	14100	16900
SE Sport Util 4D	AN0NW	31200	12200	12800	13800	16550
2WD	N,U		(950)	(950)	(1140)	(1140)
MURANO AWD—V6—Truck Equipment Schedule T1						
S Sport Utility 4D	AZ1MW	30450	11450	11950	13150	15900
SL Sport Utility	AZ1MW	32000	13050	13600	14850	17900
LE Sport Utility	AZ1MW	38980	13000	13600	14950	18100
2WD	N,U		(950)	(950)	(1170)	(1170)
PATHFINDER 4WD—V6—Truck Equipment Schedule T1						
S Sport Util 4D	AR1NB	30240	12750	13300	14250	17050
SE Sport Util 4D	AR1NB	33410	13400	14000	15100	18000
LE Sport Util 4D	AR1NB	39910	14950	15600	16700	19950
2WD	N		(1350)	(1350)	(1615)	(1615)
V8, 5.6 Liter	B		325	325	400	400
ARMADA—V8—Truck Equipment Schedule T1						
SE Spt Util 4D	AA0ND	38310	13700	14100	15850	18600
Titanium Spt Util	BA0ND	43240	14550	15000	16750	19650
4WD	C,E		1250	1250	1465	1465
ARMADA—V8—Truck Equipment Schedule T1						
Platinum Spt Util	AA0NC	52970	16250	16700	18650	21900
2WD	D,F		(950)	(950)	(1125)	(1125)
FRONTIER KING CAB—4-Cyl.—Truck Equipment Schedule T2						
XE Short Bed	BD0CT	18340	8450	8925	9850	11800
FRONTIER KING CAB—V6—Truck Equipment Schedule T1						
SE Short Bed	AD0CU	22290	10850	11450	12550	15050
4WD	V,W		1625	1625	1895	1895
4-Cyl, 2.5 Liter	B		(250)	(250)	(290)	(290)
FRONTIER KING CAB—V6—Truck Equipment Schedule T2						
LE Short Bed	AD0CU	25720	12100	12750	13800	16500

Body Type	VIN	List	Trade-In Good	Very Good	Pvt-Party Good	Retail Excellent
4WD			1625	1625	1890	1890
FRONTIER KING CAB 4WD—V6—Truck Equipment Schedule T1						
Pro-4X Short Bed	AD0CW	28510	15300	16100	17300	20700
2WD	R,U		(2200)	(2200)	(2545)	(2545)
FRONTIER CREW CAB—V6—Truck Equipment Schedule T1						
SE Short Bed	AD0EU	24140	12750	13450	14300	17250
SE Long Bed	AD0FU	24940	12650	13350	14200	17150
4WD	V,W		1625	1625	1890	1890
FRONTIER CREW CAB—V6—Truck Equipment Schedule T2						
LE Short Bed	AD0EU	27420	13550	14250	15450	18450
LE Long Bed	AD0FU	27920	13450	14150	15300	18300
4WD			1625	1625	1895	1895
FRONTIER CREW CAB 4WD—V6—Truck Equipment Schedule T2						
Pro-4X Short Bed	AD0EW	29860	16550	17400	18550	22100
2WD	R,U		(2200)	(2200)	(2545)	(2545)
TITAN KING CAB—V8—Truck Equipment Schedule T1						
XE Short Bed	AA0CA	27120	9775	10200	11300	13650
SE Short Bed	AA0CA	29120	11250	11750	12900	15650
4WD	C,J		2725	2725	3100	3100
TITAN KING CAB 4WD—V8—Truck Equipment Schedule T1						
Pro-4X Short Bed	AA0CC	34850	14850	15550	16850	20400
TITAN CREW CAB—V8—Truck Equipment Schedule T1						
XE Short Bed	AA0ED	29670	12450	13000	14150	17050
SE Short Bed	AA0ED	31320	13450	14050	15350	18500
SE Long Bed	AA0FD	31770	13250	13850	15100	18200
LE Short Bed	AA0ED	37220	15050	15750	17000	20500
4WD	C,J		2725	2725	3085	3085
TITAN CREW CAB 4WD—V8—Truck Equipment Schedule T1						
Pro-4X Short Bed	AA0EC	37050	18300	19100	20400	24500

2011 NISSAN—(J,1or5)N(1,6or8)(AF5MV)—B—#

Body Type	VIN	List	Trade-In Good	Very Good	Pvt-Party Good	Retail Excellent
JUKE—4-Cyl. Turbo—Truck Equipment Schedule T1						
S Sport Util 4D	AF5MV	21260	9525	9850	11050	13000
SV Sport Util 4D	AF5MV	23060	9775	10100	11250	13200
SL Sport Util 4D	AF5MV	25350	10100	10450	11450	13300
AWD	V		1000	1000	1125	1125
ROGUE AWD—4-Cyl.—Truck Equipment Schedule T1						
S Sport Utility 4D	AS5MV	22860	10150	10600	11550	13850
SV Spt Util 4D	AS5MV	25270	10850	11350	12400	14900
S Krom Ed Util	AS5MV	26460	10350	10700	12100	14350
2WD	T		(1075)	(1075)	(1230)	(1230)
XTERRA 4WD—V6—Truck Equipment Schedule T1						
X Sport Utility 4D	AN0NW	26700	12700	13200	14500	17050
S Sport Util 4D	AN0NW	28690	13100	13600	14950	17600
Pro-4X Spt Util	AN0NW	30900	14350	14950	16200	18950
2WD	N,U		(1075)	(1075)	(1275)	(1275)
MURANO AWD—V6—Truck Equipment Schedule T1						
S Sport Util 4D	AZ1MW	30900	12000	12400	13750	16250
SV Sport Util 4D	AZ1MW	34310	13150	13600	15100	17800
SL Sport Util 4D	AZ1MW	37850	14700	15200	16650	19600
LE Sport Util 4D	AZ1MW	39940	15300	15800	17400	20600
2WD	N,U		(1075)	(1075)	(1265)	(1265)
QUEST—V6—Truck Equipment Schedule T1						
S Minivan	AE2KU	28550	11550	12200	13050	15950
SV Minivan	AE2KU	31700	12700	13400	14250	17400
SL Minivan	AE2KU	35150	14400	15150	16150	19850
LE Minivan	AE2KU	42150	15100	15900	17000	20900
PATHFINDER 4WD—V6—Truck Equipment Schedule T1						
S Sport Utility 4D	AR1NB	30640	14250	14700	16050	18750
SV Sport Util 4D	AR1NB	33990	14800	15300	16650	19500
Silver Ed Spt Util	AR1NB	38290	16050	16600	18000	21100
LE Sport Utility	AR1NB	40470	16800	17350	18800	22000
2WD	N		(1450)	(1450)	(1710)	(1710)
V8, 5.6 Liter	B		375	375	450	450
ARMADA—V8—Truck Equipment Schedule T1						
SL Spt Util 4D	AA0ND	43835	17050	17500	19350	22100
4WD	C,E		1400	1400	1625	1625
ARMADA 4WD—V8—Truck Equipment Schedule T1						
SV Spt Util 4D	AA0NC	44460	17100	17550	19300	21900
Platinum Spt Util	AA0NC	53840	19850	20300	22200	25300
2WD	D		(1075)	(1075)	(1240)	(1240)
FRONTIER KING CAB—4-Cyl.—Truck Equipment Schedule T2						
S Short Bed	BD0CT	19600	9800	10300	11350	13400

Body Type	VIN	List	Trade-In Good	Trade-In Very Good	Pvt-Party Good	Retail Excellent
FRONTIER KING CAB—V6—Truck Equipment Schedule T1						
SV Short Bed	AD0CU	23370	**12150**	**12800**	**13900**	**16500**
4WD	V,W		1825	1825	2135	2135
4-Cyl, 2.5 Liter	B		(275)	(275)	(310)	(310)
FRONTIER KING CAB 4WD—V6—Truck Equipment Schedule T1						
Pro-4X Short Bed	AD0CW	29670	**18000**	**18900**	**20200**	**23800**
2WD	R,U		(2800)	(2800)	(3265)	(3265)
FRONTIER CREW CAB—V6—Truck Equipment Schedule T1						
S Short Bed	AD0EU	23610	**12800**	**13450**	**14550**	**17150**
SV Short Bed	AD0EU	25040	**13850**	**14600**	**15700**	**18650**
4WD	V,W		1825	1825	2135	2135
FRONTIER CREW CAB—V6—Truck Equipment Schedule T2						
SV Long Bed	AD0FU	25040	**13800**	**14500**	**15550**	**18450**
SL Short Bed	AD0EU	29230	**15450**	**16250**	**17450**	**20600**
SL Long Bed	AD0FU	29730	**15150**	**15950**	**17150**	**20200**
4WD	V,W		1825	1825	2130	2130
FRONTIER CREW CAB 4WD—V6—Truck Equipment Schedule T1						
Pro-4X Short Bed	AD0EW	30410	**19300**	**20200**	**21500**	**25400**
2WD	R,U		(2800)	(2800)	(3260)	(3260)
TITAN KING CAB—V8—Truck Equipment Schedule T1						
S Short Bed	BA0CD	27815	**11150**	**11500**	**12800**	**15100**
4WD	C,J		2925	2925	3340	3340
TITAN KING CAB 4WD—V8—Truck Equipment Schedule T1						
SV Short Bed	AA0CC	32665	**15650**	**16200**	**17650**	**20800**
2WD	D,K		(2950)	(2950)	(3375)	(3375)
TITAN KING CAB 4WD—V8—Truck Equipment Schedule T1						
Pro-4X Short Bed	AA0CC	35500	**16600**	**17150**	**18750**	**22100**
TITAN CREW CAB—V8—Truck Equipment Schedule T1						
S Short Bed	AA0ED	30320	**14000**	**14500**	**15900**	**18700**
SV Short Bed	BA0ED	32015	**15050**	**15550**	**17000**	**20000**
SV Long Bed	BA0FD	32465	**14850**	**15350**	**16850**	**19850**
SL Short Bed	BA0ED	37915	**17150**	**17750**	**19250**	**22600**
4WD	C		2925	2925	3335	3335
TITAN CREW CAB 4WD—V8—Truck Equipment Schedule T1						
Pro-4X Short Bed	AA0CC	37700	**20100**	**20800**	**22400**	**26300**

Body Type	VIN	List	Trade-In Good	Trade-In Very Good	Pvt-Party Good	Retail Excellent
JUKE—4-Cyl. Turbo—Truck Equipment Schedule T1						
S Sport Utility 4D	AF5MU	20530	**10550**	**10850**	**12100**	**13950**
SV Sport Utility	AF5MU	22340	**11200**	**11500**	**12800**	**14750**
SL Sport Utility	AF5MU	24660	**11450**	**11750**	**13050**	**14950**
AWD	V		1050	1050	1195	1195
ROGUE AWD—4-Cyl.—Truck Equipment Schedule T1						
S Sport Utility 4D	AS5MV	23590	**11650**	**12000**	**13250**	**15500**
SV Sport Utility	AS5MV	26030	**12650**	**13050**	**14350**	**16750**
2WD	T		(1500)	(1500)	(1730)	(1730)
XTERRA 4WD—V6—Truck Equipment Schedule T1						
X Sport Utility 4D	AN0NW	27120	**14500**	**15000**	**16500**	**19100**
S Sport Utility 4D	AN0NW	29110	**15000**	**15500**	**17050**	**19700**
Pro-4X Spt Util	AN0NW	31530	**15850**	**16400**	**17900**	**20700**
2WD	N,U		(1500)	(1500)	(1775)	(1775)
MURANO AWD—V6—Truck Equipment Schedule T1						
S Sport Util 4D	AZ1MW	31700	**13550**	**13900**	**15500**	**17950**
SV Sport Util 4D	AZ1MW	35270	**14950**	**15300**	**16950**	**19650**
SL Sport Util 4D	AZ1MW	38810	**17150**	**17550**	**19150**	**22100**
LE Sport Util 4D	AZ1MW	44190	**18100**	**18600**	**20300**	**23400**
CrossCabriolet 2D	AZ1FW	45350	**20200**	**20700**	**22100**	**25100**
2WD	N,P,U		(1500)	(1500)	(1730)	(1730)
QUEST—V6—Truck Equipment Schedule T1						
S Minivan	AE2KU	28560	**12250**	**12800**	**13800**	**16550**
SV Minivan	AE2KU	31860	**13400**	**14000**	**15200**	**18300**
SL Minivan	AE2KU	35310	**15850**	**16550**	**17750**	**21400**
LE Minivan	AE2KU	42160	**16200**	**16900**	**18200**	**22000**
PATHFINDER 4WD—V6—Truck Equipment Schedule T1						
S Sport Utility 4D	AR1NB	31380	**15700**	**16100**	**17650**	**20300**
SV Sport Utility	AR1NB	34730	**16450**	**16850**	**18450**	**21200**
Silver Ed Spt Util	AR1NB	38720	**17950**	**18400**	**20000**	**23000**
LE Sport Utility	AR1NB	42530	**18450**	**18900**	**20500**	**23600**
2WD	N		(1525)	(1525)	(1800)	(1800)
V8, 5.6 Liter	B		425	425	490	490
ARMADA—V8—Truck Equipment Schedule T1						
SL Sport Utility	AA0ND	44935	**19500**	**19900**	**22000**	**24700**
4WD	C,E		1475	1475	1700	1700

TRUCKS & VANS

Body Type	VIN	List	Trade-In Good	Very Good	Pvt-Party Good	Retail Excellent
ARMADA 4WD—V8—Truck Equipment Schedule T1						
SV Sport Utility	AA0NC	45065	20300	20700	22700	25500
Platinum Spt Util	AA0NC	54925	24900	25400	27300	30400
2WD	D,F		(1500)	(1500)	(1720)	(1720)
NV1500 CARGO VAN—V6—Truck Equipment Schedule T1						
S Van 3D		26045	13050	13500	14600	17100
SV Van 3D		27645	14450	14950	16100	18900
NV2500 CARGO VAN—V6—Truck Equipment Schedule T1						
S Van 3D		27045	14150	14650	15750	18400
SV Van 3D		28645	15300	15800	16950	19850
High Ceiling Roof			1450	1450	1695	1695
V8, 5.6 Liter			525	525	600	600
NV3500 CARGO VAN—V6—Truck Equipment Schedule T1						
S Van 3D		29645	15850	16350	17550	20600
SV Van 3D		31245	16600	17150	18350	21600
High Ceiling Roof			1450	1450	1705	1705
NV3500 PASSENGER VAN—V8—Truck Equipment Schedule T1						
S Van 3D	AF0AA	33585	18500	19100	20100	23400
SV Van 3D	AF0AA	35785	20300	21000	22100	25700
V6, 4.0 Liter	B		(625)	(625)	(705)	(705)
NV3500 PASSENGER VAN—V8—Truck Equipment Schedule T1						
SL Van 3D	AF0AA	38385	21700	22500	23500	27300
FRONTIER KING CAB—4-Cyl.—Truck Equipment Schedule T2						
S Short Bed	BD0CT	20075	10900	11400	12600	14900
FRONTIER KING CAB—V6—Truck Equipment Schedule T1						
SV Short Bed	AB0CU	23845	13600	14250	15550	18200
4WD	V,W		2100	2100	2475	2475
4-Cyl, 2.5 Liter	B		(275)	(275)	(330)	(330)
FRONTIER KING CAB 4WD—V6—Truck Equipment Schedule T1						
Pro-4X Short Bed	AD0CW	30130	19000	19950	21200	24800
FRONTIER CREW CAB—V6—Truck Equipment Schedule T1						
S Short Bed	AD0EU	24085	14250	14950	16200	18900
SV Short Bed	AD0EU	25095	15600	16400	17500	20600
4WD	V,W		2100	2100	2475	2475
FRONTIER CREW CAB—V6—Truck Equipment Schedule T2						
SV Long Bed	AD0FU	25500	15400	16150	17250	20300
SL Short Bed	AD0EU	29690	16650	17450	18650	21800
SL Long Bed	AD0FU	30190	16100	16900	18100	21100
4WD	V,W		2100	2100	2470	2470
FRONTIER CREW CAB 4WD—V6—Truck Equipment Schedule T2						
Pro-4X Short Bed	AD0EW	29820	20400	21400	22700	26600
TITAN KING CAB—V8—Truck Equipment Schedule T1						
S Short Bed	BA0CA	28405	13100	13450	15000	17350
4WD	C,J		3125	3125	3515	3515
TITAN KING CAB 4WD—V8—Truck Equipment Schedule T1						
SV Short Bed	AA0CC	33255	17750	18200	19850	22900
2WD	A		(3150)	(3150)	(3515)	(3515)
TITAN KING CAB 4WD—V8—Truck Equipment Schedule T1						
Pro-4X Short Bed	AA0CC	36115	18600	19050	20800	23900
TITAN CREW CAB—V8—Truck Equipment Schedule T1						
S Short Bed	AA0ED	30935	16450	16900	18450	21300
SV Short Bed	BA0ED	32605	17050	17500	19150	22100
SV Long Bed	BA0FD	33055	16850	17300	18950	21900
SL Short Bed	AA0ED	38485	19200	19650	21400	24600
4WD	C		3125	3125	3505	3505
TITAN CREW CAB 4WD—V8—Truck Equipment Schedule T1						
Pro-4X Short Bed	AA0EC	38315	21200	21700	23500	27200
2013 NISSAN—(J,1or5)(NorB)(1,6,8orZ)(AF5MR)–D–#						
JUKE—4-Cyl. Turbo—Truck Equipment Schedule T1						
S Sport Utility 4D	AF5MR	20770	11650	11900	13500	15550
SV Sport Utility	AF5MR	22890	12050	12300	13950	16000
NISMO Spt Util	AF5MR	23780	12500	12800	14400	16500
SL Sport Utility	AF5MR	25780	12600	12850	14500	16600
AWD	V		1125	1125	1245	1245
ROGUE AWD—4-Cyl.—Truck Equipment Schedule T1						
S Sport Utility 4D	AS5MV	24435	12900	13200	14950	17300
SV Sport Utility	AS5MV	26875	13950	14300	16200	18800
2WD	T		(1275)	(1275)	(1490)	(1490)
XTERRA 4WD—V6—Truck Equipment Schedule T1						
X Sport Utility 4D	AN0NW	25835	16150	16600	18250	20800
S Sport Utility 4D	AN0NW	27745	16500	17050	18600	21200
PRO-4X Spt Util	AN0NW	31335	16700	17200	18850	21500

Body Type	VIN	List	Trade-In Good	Trade-In Very Good	Pvt-Party Good	Retail Excellent
MURANO AWD—V6—Truck Equipment Schedule T1						
S Sport Util 4D	AZ1MW	32955	15350	15700	17450	19950
SV Sport Util 4D	AZ1MW	35305	15900	16250	18050	20650
SL Sport Util 4D	AZ1MW	40115	19700	20100	21800	24800
LE Sport Util 4D	AZ1MW	41195	20900	21300	23200	26500
CrossCabriolet 2D	AZ1FW	45385	22400	22800	24300	27300
2WD	U,N,P		(1500)	(1500)	(1725)	(1725)
QUEST—V6—Truck Equipment Schedule T1						
S Minivan	AE2KP	26835	15350	15950	16900	19850
SV Minivan	AE2KP	30585	16950	17600	18650	22000
SL Minivan	AE2KP	34365	19150	19900	21000	24700
LE Minivan	AE2KP	43485	19500	20300	21400	25300
PATHFINDER 4WD—V6—Truck Equipment Schedule T1						
S Sport Utility 4D	AR2MM	30695	17700	18050	19700	22400
SV Sport Utility	AR2MM	33955	18250	18600	20300	23100
SL Sport Utility	AR2MM	36895	20200	20700	22400	25500
Platinum Spt Util	AR2MM	41595	21100	21500	23300	26500
2WD	U,N,P		(1600)	(1600)	(1875)	(1875)
ARMADA 4WD—V8—Truck Equipment Schedule T1						
SL Sport Utility	AA0NC	46995	22000	22400	24500	27300
SV Sport Utility	AA0NC	47205	22100	22500	24500	27200
Platinum Sport Util	AA0NC	57175	26400	26900	29000	32100
2WD	D,F		(1500)	(1500)	(1685)	(1685)
NV200—4-Cyl.—Truck Equipment Schedule T2						
S Van 4D	CM0KN	20850	12500	12850	14100	16400
SV Van 4D	CM0KN	21840	13000	13350	14750	17150
NV1500 CARGO VAN—V6—Truck Equipment Schedule T1						
S Van 3D		26415	14700	15100	16300	18750
SV Van 3D		28055	16150	16600	17800	20500
NV2500 HD CARGO VAN—V6—Truck Equipment Schedule T1						
S Van 3D		27415	15850	16250	17400	20000
SV Van 3D		29055	17250	17700	18900	21700
High Ceiling Roof			1525	1525	1765	1765
V8, 5.6 Liter			550	550	625	625
NV3500 HD CARGO VAN—V8—Truck Equipment Schedule T1						
S Van 3D		30015	17850	18300	19550	22500
SV Van 3D		31655	18550	19000	20400	23700
High Ceiling Roof			1525	1525	1785	1785
NV3500 HD PASSENGER VAN—V8—Truck Equipment Schedule T1						
S Van 3D	AF0AA	33885	20400	20900	22100	25400
SV Van 3D	AF0AA	36085	22300	22900	24000	27600
SL Van 3D	AF0AA	38685	24000	24600	25800	29600
V6, 4.0 Liter	B		(650)	(650)	(725)	(725)
FRONTIER KING CAB—4-Cyl.—Truck Equipment Schedule T2						
S Short Bed	BD0CT	20835	11600	12200	13750	16500
FRONTIER KING CAB—V6—Truck Equipment Schedule T2						
SV Short Bed	AD0CU	23885	14450	15150	16700	19700
Desert Runner	AD0CU	24605	15250	16000	17850	21300
4WD	V,W		2400	2400	2775	2775
4-Cyl, 2.5 Liter	B		(300)	(300)	(340)	(340)
FRONTIER KING CAB 4WD—V6—Truck Equipment Schedule T2						
Pro-4X Short Bed	AD0CW	31375	20000	21000	22800	27000
FRONTIER CREW CAB—V6—Truck Equipment Schedule T2						
S Short Bed	AD0EU	23925	15300	16050	17750	21100
SV Short Bed	AD0EU	24835	16550	17350	18900	22400
SV Long Bed	AD0FU	25555	16350	17150	18700	22200
Desert Runner 5'	AD0EU	25855	16200	17000	18850	22500
SL Short Bed	AD0EU	31435	18200	19050	20700	24400
SL Long Bed	AD0FU	31935	17700	18550	20100	23700
4WD	V,W		2400	2400	2760	2760
FRONTIER CREW CAB 4WD—V6—Truck Equipment Schedule T2						
Pro-4X Short Bed	AD0EW	31065	21000	22000	23900	28300
TITAN KING CAB—V8—Truck Equipment Schedule T1						
S Short Bed	AA0CA	29815	14050	14350	16400	19100
4WD	C,J		3275	3275	3685	3685
TITAN KING CAB 4WD—V8—Truck Equipment Schedule T1						
SV Short Bed	AA0CC	35095	18850	19250	21700	25300
2WD	A,H		(3275)	(3275)	(3685)	(3685)
TITAN KING CAB 4WD—V8—Truck Equipment Schedule T1						
Pro-4X Short Bed	AA0CC	38035	19650	20100	22500	26300
TITAN CREW CAB—V8—Truck Equipment Schedule T1						
S Short Bed	AA0ED	32365	16950	17300	19500	22800
SV Short Bed	AA0ED	34445	18200	18600	20900	24400

TRUCKS & VANS

Body Type	VIN	List	Trade-In Good	Trade-In Very Good	Pvt-Party Good	Retail Excellent
SV Long Bed	AA0FD	34895	18000	18400	20700	24100
SL Short Bed	AA0ED	41035	19850	20300	22700	26500
4WD	C,J		3275	3275	3680	3680
TITAN CREW CAB 4WD—V8—Truck Equipment Schedule T1						
Pro-4X Short Bed	AA0EC	40235	22700	23100	25600	29800

2014 NISSAN—(J,1or5)(NorB)(1,6,8orZ)(AF5MR)—E—#

Body Type	VIN	List	Trade-In Good	Trade-In Very Good	Pvt-Party Good	Retail Excellent
JUKE—4-Cyl. Turbo—Truck Equipment Schedule T1						
S Sport Utility 4D	AF5MR	19800	12650	12900	14600	16750
SV Sport Utility	AF5MR	22850	13550	13800	15450	17650
NISMO Sport Util	AF5MR	23800	14150	14450	16050	18250
SL Sport Utility	AF5MR	25100	14250	14500	16150	18350
NISMO RS 4D	DF5MR	26930	16050	16350	17850	20100
AWD	V		1175	1175	1310	1310
ROGUE SELECT AWD—4-Cyl.—Truck Equipment Schedule T1						
S Sport Utility 4D	AS5MV	22200	13450	14600	16400	18600
FWD	L,T		(1375)	(1375)	(1520)	(1520)
ROGUE AWD—4-Cyl.—Truck Equipment Schedule T1						
S Sport Utility	AT2MV	24700	17100	17400	19050	21300
SV Sport Utility	AT2MV	26440	18450	18750	20400	22700
SL Sport Utility	AT2MV	30280	19550	19900	21500	23900
FWD	T		(1375)	(1375)	(1500)	(1500)
XTERRA 4WD—V6—Truck Equipment Schedule T1						
X Sport Utility 4D	AN0NW	26020	17700	18250	19800	22400
S Sport Utility 4D	AN0NW	27930	17900	18450	20000	22600
2WD	U		(1500)	(1500)	(1735)	(1735)
XTERRA 4WD—V6—Truck Equipment Schedule T1						
PRO-4X Spt Util	AN0NW	31950	19150	19750	21200	23900
MURANO AWD—V6—Truck Equipment Schedule T1						
S Sport Util 4D	AZ1MW	31090	17700	18050	19850	22600
SV Sport Util 4D	AZ1MW	33990	19700	20100	21900	24800
SL Sport Util 4D	AZ1MU	37850	22600	23000	24700	27800
LE Sport Util 4D	AZ1MW	40340	24000	24500	26400	29900
FWD	U		(1500)	(1500)	(1710)	(1710)
MURANO AWD—V6—Truck Equipment Schedule T1						
CrossCabriolet 2D	AZ1FY	42840	26500	27000	28400	31500
QUEST—V6—Truck Equipment Schedule T1						
S Minivan	AE2K	26850	16750	17400	18400	21500
SV Minivan	AE2K	30600	18550	19250	20200	23600
SL Minivan	AE2K	34380	20900	21700	22700	26400
LE Minivan	AE2K	43500	21800	22600	23600	27600
PATHFINDER 4WD—4-Cyl. Supercharged Hybrid—Truck Equip Sch T1						
SV Sport Utility	CR2MM	37570	23400	23900	25700	29000
SL Sport Utility	CR2MM	40510	25500	26000	27800	31300
Platinum Spt Util	CR2MM	45210	27200	27700	29500	33200
2WD	N		(1700)	(1700)	(1925)	(1925)
PATHFINDER 4WD—V6—Truck Equipment Schedule T1						
S Sport Utility 4D	AR2MM	31145	20300	20700	22300	25100
SV Sport Utility	AR2MM	34405	20800	21200	22900	25900
SL Sport Utility	AR2MM	37345	23900	24400	26100	29400
Platinum Spt Util	AR2MM	42045	25200	25700	27400	30800
2WD	N		(1700)	(1700)	(1945)	(1945)
ARMADA—V8—Truck Equipment Schedule T1						
SL Sport Utility	AA0ND	43175	26400	26900	28900	31800
4WD	C,E		1500	1500	1650	1650
ARMADA 4WD—V8—Truck Equipment Schedule T1						
SV Sport Utility	AA0NE	43385	24900	25400	27500	30300
Platinum Spt Util	AA0NE	53355	31100	31600	33600	36700
2WD	D,F		(1500)	(1500)	(1665)	(1665)
NV200—4-Cyl—Truck Equipment Schedule T1						
S Van 4D	CM0KN	21100	14150	14500	15750	18150
SV Van 4D	CM0KN	22090	14900	15300	16600	19050
NV1500 CARGO VAN—V6—Truck Equipment Schedule T1						
S Van 3D	BF0KL	26665	16700	17100	18250	20800
SV Van 3D	BF0KL	27655	17900	18400	19550	22300
NV2500 CARGO VAN—V6—Truck Equipment Schedule T1						
S Van 3D	BF0KX	27665	18350	18850	19900	22600
SV Van 3D	BF0KX	28655	19350	19850	21000	23900
High Ceiling Roof			1600	1600	1820	1820
V8, 5.6 Liter	A		575	575	645	645
NV3500 HD CARGO VAN—V8—Truck Equipment Schedule T1						
S Van 3D	AF0KX	30565	20100	20600	21700	24800
SV Van 3D	AF0KX	31555	20800	21300	22600	26000

Body Type	VIN	List	Trade-In Good	Very Good	Pvt-Party Good	Retail Excellent
High Ceiling Roof	....	....	1600	1600	1845	1845
NV3500 HD PASSENGER VAN—V8—Truck Equipment Schedule T1						
S Van 3D	AF0AA	34435	23000	23600	24600	28000
SV Van 3D	AF0AA	36635	24900	25500	26600	30200
SL Van 3D	AF0AA	39235	26700	27300	28400	32200
V6, 4.0 Liter	B	....	(675)	(675)	(745)	(745)
FRONTIER KING CAB—4-Cyl.—Truck Equipment Schedule T1						
S Pickup 2D 6'	BD0CT	21130	12750	13400	15000	17750
FRONTIER KING CAB—V6—Truck Equipment Schedule T2						
SV Pickup 2D 6'	AD0CU	24060	15750	16500	18000	21100
Desert Runner 6'	AD0CU	24780	16150	16950	18750	22300
4WD	W	....	2700	2700	3130	3130
4-Cyl, 2.5 Liter	B	....	(300)	(300)	(345)	(345)
FRONTIER KING CAB 4WD—V6—Truck Equipment Schedule T2						
PRO-4X Pickup 6'	AD0CW	31900	21400	22500	24100	28400
FRONTIER CREW CAB—V6—Truck Equipment Schedule T2						
S Pickup 4D 5'	AD0ER	24220	16400	17200	18800	22100
SV Pickup 4D 5'	AD0ER	25320	17850	18750	20300	23800
SV Pickup 4D 6'	AD0FR	26040	17650	18500	20000	23500
Desert Runner 5'	AD0ER	26100	17800	18700	20400	24200
SL Pickup 4D 5'	AD0ER	31830	19100	20000	21600	25300
SL Pickup 4D 6'	AD0FR	32330	18600	19450	21000	24600
4WD	V,W	....	2700	2700	3145	3145
FRONTIER CREW CAB 4WD—V6—Truck Equipment Schedule T2						
PRO-4X Pickup 5'	AD0EV	31660	21900	23000	24800	29200
TITAN KING CAB—V8—Truck Equipment Schedule T1						
S Short Bed	AA0CH	30265	16350	16700	18800	21700
4WD	C	....	3500	3500	3905	3905
TITAN KING CAB 4WD—V8—Truck Equipment Schedule T1						
SV Short Bed	AA0C4	35545	21600	22000	24500	28300
2WD	H	....	(3500)	(3500)	(3910)	(3910)
TITAN KING CAB 4WD—V8—Truck Equipment Schedule T1						
Pro-4X Short Bed	AA0C4	38485	22600	23100	25500	29500
TITAN CREW CAB—V8—Truck Equipment Schedule T1						
S Short Bed	AA0ED	32815	18650	19000	21300	24700
SV Short Bed	AA0ED	34895	20800	21300	23600	27300
SV Long Bed	AA0FD	35345	20600	21100	23400	27000
SL Short Bed	AA0ED	41485	22600	23100	25500	29500
4WD	C,J	....	3500	3500	3920	3920
TITAN CREW CAB 4WD—V8—Truck Equipment Schedule T1						
PRO-4X Short Bed	AA0EC	40685	25400	25800	28400	32800

OLDSMOBILE

2000 OLDSMOBILE — 1GH-(X03E)-Y-#

Body Type	VIN	List	Trade-In Good	Very Good	Pvt-Party Good	Retail Excellent
SILHOUETTE—V6—Truck Equipment Schedule T1						
GL Extended	X03E	25530	1125	1350	1800	3125
GLS Extended	X03E	29220	1525	1800	2250	3900
Premiere Extended	X03E	32130	1725	2025	2500	4300
BRAVADA AWD—V6—Truck Equipment Schedule T3						
Sport Utility 4D	T13W	31923	1175	1375	2700	5200

2001 OLDSMOBILE — 1GH-(X03E)-1-#

Body Type	VIN	List	Trade-In Good	Very Good	Pvt-Party Good	Retail Excellent
SILHOUETTE—V6—Truck Equipment Schedule T1						
GL Extended	X03E	26920	1450	1700	2125	3625
GLS Extended	X03E	31055	1875	2200	2725	4575
Premiere Extended	X03E	33855	2025	2375	2900	4850
BRAVADA AWD—V6—Truck Equipment Schedule T3						
Sport Utility 4D	T13W	32335	1450	1675	2875	5375

2002 OLDSMOBILE — 1GH-(X23E)-2-#

Body Type	VIN	List	Trade-In Good	Very Good	Pvt-Party Good	Retail Excellent
SILHOUETTE—V6—Truck Equipment Schedule T1						
GL Extended	X23E	27560	1800	2125	2600	4300
GLS Extended	X03E	31635	2325	2700	3175	5225
Premiere Extended	X13E	33535	2475	2900	3350	5500
AWD	V	....	275	275	375	375
BRAVADA AWD—6-Cyl.—Truck Equipment Schedule T3						
Sport Utility 4D	T13W	34967	1725	2025	2550	4225
2WD	S	....	(700)	(700)	(935)	(935)

SEE BACK PAGES FOR TRUCK EQUIPMENT

TRUCKS & VANS

TRUCKS & VANS

Body Type	VIN	List	Trade-In Good	Very Good	Pvt-Party Good	Retail Excellent

2003 OLDSMOBILE — 1GH–(X23E)–3–#

SILHOUETTE—V6—Truck Equipment Schedule T1

GL Extended	X23E	28510	2275	2650	3125	5100
GLS Extended	X03E	32175	2850	3275	3725	5975
Premiere Extended	X13E	34225	3150	3625	4075	6525
AWD	V		325	325	445	445

BRAVADA AWD—6-Cyl.—Truck Equipment Schedule T3

Sport Utility 4D	T13S	35145	2450	2825	3425	5675
2WD	S		(775)	(775)	(1040)	(1040)

2004 OLDSMOBILE — 1GH–(X23E)–4–#

SILHOUETTE—V6—Truck Equipment Schedule T1

GL Extended	X23E	28790	2900	3325	3700	5775
GLS Extended	X03E	32450	3100	3550	3900	6100
Premiere Extended	X13E	34510	3475	3975	4300	6700
AWD	V		375	375	505	505

BRAVADA AWD—6-Cyl.—Truck Equipment Schedule T3

Sport Utility 4D	T13S	36245	2900	3300	3875	6225
2WD	S		(875)	(875)	(1155)	(1155)

PLYMOUTH — See DODGE TRUCKS

PONTIAC

2000 PONTIAC — 1GM–(U03E)–Y–#

MONTANA—V6—Truck Equipment Schedule T1

Minivan	U03E	24255	850	1025	1375	2325
Extended Minivan	X03E	25365	1075	1275	1650	2800

2001 PONTIAC — (1GMor3G7)–(A03E)–1–#

AZTEK—V6—Truck Equipment Schedule T1

Sport Utility 4D	A03E	21995	800	925	1525	2675
GT Sport Utility 4D	A03E	24995	1200	1400	2075	3625
AWD	B		350	350	470	470

MONTANA—V6—Truck Equipment Schedule T1

Minivan 4D	U03E	24810	1075	1300	1750	2975
Ext Minivan 4D	X03E	27150	1375	1650	2150	3725

2002 PONTIAC — (1GMor3G7)–(A03E)–2–#

AZTEK—V6—Truck Equipment Schedule T1

Sport Utility 4D	A03E	20545	1050	1200	1850	3200
AWD	B		375	375	505	505

MONTANA—V6—Truck Equipment Schedule T1

Minivan 4D	U03E	24990	1250	1475	1975	3350
Ext Minivan 4D	X03E	27390	1650	1950	2450	4125

2003 PONTIAC — (1GMor3G7)–(A03E)–3–#

AZTEK—V6—Truck Equipment Schedule T1

Sport Utility 4D	A03E	20870	1300	1475	2125	3625
AWD	B		400	400	545	545

MONTANA—V6—Truck Equipment Schedule T1

Minivan 4D	U03E	24845	1500	1750	2225	3725
Ext Minivan 4D	X03E	26645	1850	2200	2775	4650
AWD	V		700	700	920	920

2004 PONTIAC — (1GMor3G7)–(A03E)–4–#

AZTEK—V6—Truck Equipment Schedule T1

Sport Utility 4D	A03E	21595	1700	1925	2625	4375
AWD	B		425	425	580	580

MONTANA—V6—Truck Equipment Schedule T1

Minivan 4D	U03E	23845	1775	2075	2675	4425
Ext Minivan 4D	X03E	26220	2175	2525	3200	5275
AWD	V		750	750	1000	1000

Body Type	VIN	List	Trade-In Good	Trade-In Very Good	Pvt-Party Good	Retail Excellent

2005 PONTIAC — (1GMor3G7)–(A03E)–5–#

AZTEK—V6—Truck Equipment Schedule T1
| Sport Utility 4D | A03E | 22060 | 1875 | 2125 | 3075 | 4850 |
| AWD | B | | 475 | 475 | 615 | 615 |

MONTANA—V6—Truck Equipment Schedule T1
| Ext Minivan 4D | V23E | 26755 | 2500 | 2900 | 3650 | 5800 |

MONTANA SV6 AWD—V6—Truck Equipment Schedule T1
Minivan 4D	X23L	28415	2750	3175	3850	6075
5-Passenger Seating			(325)	(325)	(420)	(420)
FWD			(775)	(775)	(1025)	(1025)

2006 PONTIAC — (1GMor3G7)–(L63F)–6–#

TORRENT—V6—Truck Equipment Schedule T1
| Sport Utility 4D | L63F | 22990 | 3300 | 3750 | 4475 | 6800 |
| AWD | 7 | | 575 | 575 | 765 | 765 |

MONTANA SV6 AWD—V6—Truck Equipment Schedule T1
Minivan 4D	X23L	28760	3225	3675	4375	6725
4-Passenger Seating			(350)	(350)	(455)	(455)
FWD	U		(525)	(525)	(715)	(715)

2007 PONTIAC — (1GMor3G7)–(L63F)–7–#

TORRENT—V6—Truck Equipment Schedule T1
| Sport Utility 4D | L63F | 24395 | 3775 | 4225 | 4950 | 7150 |
| AWD | 7 | | 600 | 600 | 810 | 810 |

2008 PONTIAC — (1GMor3G7)–(L33F)–8–#

TORRENT—V6—Truck Equipment Schedule T1
Sport Utility 4D	L33F	23470	4175	4550	5350	7300
GXP Sport Utility 4D	L537	27995	4900	5350	6125	8175
AWD	4,7		650	650	850	850

2009 PONTIAC — (1GMor3G7)–(L33F)–9–#

TORRENT—V6—Truck Equipment Schedule T1
Sport Utility 4D	L33F	24740	5050	5375	6300	8075
GXP Sport Utility 4D	L537	29340	6150	6550	7275	9175
AWD	4,6		675	675	815	815

PORSCHE

2003 PORSCHE — WP1–(AB29P)–3–#

CAYENNE AWD—V8—Truck Equipment Schedule T3
| S Sport Utility 4D | AB29P | 56665 | 5650 | 6075 | 6825 | 9400 |

CAYENNE AWD—V8 Turbo—Truck Equipment Schedule T3
| Sport Utility 4D | AC29P | 89665 | 6475 | 6925 | 7625 | 10400 |

2004 PORSCHE — WP1–(AA29P)–4–#

CAYENNE AWD—V6—Truck Equipment Schedule T3
| Sport Utility 4D | AA29P | 43665 | 6025 | 6425 | 7225 | 9825 |

CAYENNE AWD—V8—Truck Equipment Schedule T3
| S Sport Utility 4D | AB29P | 56665 | 6700 | 7150 | 7975 | 10900 |

CAYENNE AWD—V8 Twin Turbo—Truck Equipment Schedule T3
| Sport Utility 4D | AC29P | 89665 | 8700 | 9275 | 9900 | 13200 |

2005 PORSCHE — WP1–(AA29P)–5–#

CAYENNE AWD—V6—Truck Equipment Schedule T3
| Sport Utility 4D | AA29P | 44995 | 6950 | 7400 | 8350 | 11100 |

CAYENNE AWD—V8—Truck Equipment Schedule T3
| S Sport Utility 4D | AB29P | 57195 | 7975 | 8500 | 9525 | 12650 |

CAYENNE AWD—V8 Twin Turbo—Truck Equipment Schedule T3
| Sport Utility 4D | AC29P | 90195 | 9600 | 10200 | 11200 | 14800 |

2006 PORSCHE — WP1–(AA29P)–6–#

CAYENNE AWD—V6—Truck Equipment Schedule T3
Sport Utility 4D	AA29P	46015	8400	8925	9850	12750
SportDesign			1175	1175	1505	1505
Off-Road Tech			1175	1175	1505	1505
Off-Road Design			1175	1175	1505	1505

TRUCKS & VANS

Body Type	VIN	List	Trade-In Good	Very Good	Pvt-Party Good	Retail Excellent
CAYENNE AWD—V8—Truck Equipment Schedule T3						
S Sport Utility 4D	AB29P	58015	11100	11750	12600	16200
S Titanium Spt Util	AB29P	65715	15950	16900	17550	22200
SportDesign			1175	1175	1485	1485
Off-Road Tech			1175	1175	1485	1485
Off-Road Design			1175	1175	1485	1485
CAYENNE AWD—V8 Twin Turbo—Truck Equipment Schedule T3						
Sport Utility 4D	AC29P	91015	13150	13950	14750	18750
S Sport Utility 4D	AC29P	112415	22600	23900	23900	29800
SportDesign			1175	1175	1395	1395
Off-Road Tech			1175	1175	1395	1395
Off-Road Design			1175	1175	1395	1395

2007 PORSCHE — No Production

2008 PORSCHE — WP1(AA29P)-8-#

Body Type	VIN	List	Trade-In Good	Very Good	Pvt-Party Good	Retail Excellent
CAYENNE AWD—V6—Truck Equipment Schedule T3						
Sport Utility 4D	AA29P	47295	14100	14750	15650	18800
SportDesign			1300	1300	1485	1485
Off-Road Tech			1300	1300	1485	1485
CAYENNE AWD—V8—Truck Equipment Schedule T3						
S Sport Utility 4D	AB29P	58795	15300	16000	17000	20500
GTS Sport Util 4D	AD29P	73195	21300	22200	22900	27300
SportDesign			1300	1300	1495	1495
Off-Road Tech			1300	1300	1495	1495
CAYENNE AWD—V8 Twin Turbo—Truck Equipment Schedule T3						
Sport Utility 4D	AC29P	94595	20500	21400	22400	26900
SportDesign			1300	1300	1475	1475
Off-Road Tech			1300	1300	1475	1475

2009 PORSCHE — WP1(AA29P)-9-#

Body Type	VIN	List	Trade-In Good	Very Good	Pvt-Party Good	Retail Excellent
CAYENNE AWD—V6—Truck Equipment Schedule T3						
Sport Utility 4D	AA29P	48975	17000	17600	18750	21900
Full Leather			550	550	610	610
SportDesign			1350	1350	1525	1525
Off-Road Tech			1350	1350	1525	1525
CAYENNE AWD—V8—Truck Equipment Schedule T3						
S Sport Utility 4D	AB29P	60295	18450	19150	20400	23900
GTS Sport Util 4D	AD29P	75575	26200	27100	28000	32500
Full Leather			550	550	610	610
SportDesign			1350	1350	1530	1530
Off-Road Tech			1350	1350	1530	1530
CAYENNE AWD—V8 Twin Turbo—Equipment Schedule T3						
Sport Utility 4D	AC29P	98595	29200	30200	31400	36700
S Sport Utility 4D	AC29P	124495	36600	37900	38400	44200
Full Leather			550	550	595	595
SportDesign			1350	1350	1490	1490
Off-Road Tech			1350	1350	1490	1490

2010 PORSCHE — WP1(AA2AP)-A-#

Body Type	VIN	List	Trade-In Good	Very Good	Pvt-Party Good	Retail Excellent
CAYENNE AWD—V6—Truck Equipment Schedule T3						
Sport Utility 4D	AA2AP	49475	21100	21700	23000	26100
Full Leather			575	575	625	625
SportDesign			1425	1425	1565	1565
Off-Road Tech			1425	1425	1565	1565
CAYENNE AWD—V8—Truck Equipment Schedule T3						
S Sport Utility 4D	AB2AP	61675	24100	24800	26200	29800
GTS Sport Util 4D	AD2AP	76375	32600	33500	34700	39200
Full Leather			575	575	630	630
SportDesign			1425	1425	1570	1570
Off-Road Tech			1425	1425	1570	1570
CAYENNE AWD—V8 Twin Turbo—Truck Equipment Schedule T3						
Sport Utility 4D	AC2AP	100875	37300	38400	39600	44700
S Sport Utility 4D	AC2AP	127275	47100	48400	49000	54800
Full Leather			575	575	615	615
SportDesign			1425	1425	1535	1535
Off-Road Tech			1425	1425	1535	1535

2011 PORSCHE — WP1(AA2A2)-B-#

Body Type	VIN	List	Trade-In Good	Very Good	Pvt-Party Good	Retail Excellent
CAYENNE AWD—V6—Truck Equipment Schedule T3						
Sport Utility 4D	AA2A2	49475	30400	31100	32500	36000

Body Type	VIN	List	Trade-In Good	Trade-In Very Good	Pvt-Party Good	Retail Excellent
Full Leather		----	600	600	645	645
Adaptive Cruise Control		----	425	425	455	455
Premium Pkg		----	1575	1575	1720	1720
Premium Pkg Plus		----	2475	2475	2715	2715
Convenience Pkg		----	1250	1250	1365	1365
CAYENNE AWD—V6 Supercharged Hybrid—Truck Equipment Sch T3						
S Sport Utility 4D	AE2A2	68675	35100	35900	37500	41700
Full Leather		----	600	600	650	650
Adaptive Cruise Control		----	425	425	455	455
Convenience Pkg		----	1250	1250	1370	1370
Premium Pkg		----	1575	1575	1725	1725
Premium Pkg Plus		----	2475	2475	2725	2725
CAYENNE AWD—V8—Truck Equipment Schedule T3						
S Sport Utility 4D	AB2A2	64675	33400	34200	35800	39900
Full Leather		----	600	600	650	650
Adaptive Cruise Control		----	425	425	455	455
Convenience Pkg		----	1250	1250	1370	1370
Premium Pkg		----	1575	1575	1725	1725
Premium Pkg Plus		----	2475	2475	2725	2725
CAYENNE AWD—V8 Twin Turbo—Truck Equipment Schedule T3						
Sport Utility 4D	AC2A2	105775	45700	46800	48300	53700
Adaptive Cruise Control		----	425	425	450	450
Premium Pkg Plus		----	2475	2475	2675	2675
Sport Pkg		----	1275	1275	1385	1385

2012 PORSCHE — WP1(AA2A2)-C-#

Body Type	VIN	List	Trade-In Good	Trade-In Very Good	Pvt-Party Good	Retail Excellent
CAYENNE AWD—V6—Truck Equipment Schedule T3						
Sport Utility 4D	AA2A2	49175	34600	35300	36800	40000
Full Leather		----	625	625	665	665
25 Years Exclusive		----	900	900	985	985
Convenience Pkg		----	1325	1325	1435	1435
Premium Pkg		----	1650	1650	1775	1775
Premium Plus Pkg		----	2575	2575	2790	2790
SportDesign Pkg		----	1325	1325	1435	1435
CAYENNE AWD—V6 Supercharged Hybrid—Truck Equipment Sch T3						
S Sport Utility 4D	AE2A2	69975	39600	40500	42300	46400
Full Leather		----	625	625	670	670
Adaptive Cruise Control		----	450	450	480	480
25 Years Exclusive		----	900	900	995	995
Convenience Pkg		----	1325	1325	1445	1445
Premium Pkg		----	1650	1650	1790	1790
Premium Plus Pkg		----	2575	2575	2815	2815
SportDesign Pkg		----	1325	1325	1445	1445
CAYENNE AWD—V8—Truck Equipment Schedule T3						
S Sport Utility 4D	AB2A2	65975	40800	41600	43300	47300
Full Leather		----	625	625	670	670
Adaptive Cruise Control		----	450	450	480	480
25 Years Exclusive		----	900	900	990	990
Convenience Pkg		----	1325	1325	1435	1435
Premium Pkg		----	1650	1650	1780	1780
Premium Plus Pkg		----	2575	2575	2795	2795
SportDesign Pkg		----	1325	1325	1435	1435
CAYENNE AWD—V8 Twin Turbo—Truck Equipment Schedule T3						
Sport Utility 4D	AC2A2	108075	51300	52400	54500	59800
Adaptive Cruise Control		----	450	450	475	475
25 Years Exclusive		----	900	900	980	980
Premium Plus Pkg		----	2575	2575	2770	2770
Sport Pkg		----	1325	1325	1430	1430
SportDesign Pkg		----	1325	1325	1425	1425

2013 PORSCHE — WP1(AA2A2)-D-#

Body Type	VIN	List	Trade-In Good	Trade-In Very Good	Pvt-Party Good	Retail Excellent
CAYENNE AWD—V6—Truck Equipment Schedule T3						
Sport Utility 4D	AA2A2	49825	41300	42000	43300	46500
Full Leather		----	650	650	685	685
Convenience Pkg		----	1400	1400	1500	1500
Premium Pkg		----	1700	1700	1830	1830
Premium Pkg Plus		----	2675	2675	2865	2865
SportDesign Pkg		----	1400	1400	1500	1500
CAYENNE AWD—V6 Diesel—Truck Equipment Schedule T3						
Sport Utility 4D	AF2A2	56725	43800	44600	45800	49100
Full Leather		----	650	650	685	685
Adaptive Cruise Control		----	475	475	500	500

SEE BACK PAGES FOR TRUCK EQUIPMENT

TRUCKS & VANS

Body Type	VIN	List	Trade-In Good	Trade-In Very Good	Pvt-Party Good	Retail Excellent
Convenience Pkg			1400	1400	1500	1500
Premium Pkg			1700	1700	1830	1830
Premium Pkg Plus			2675	2675	2860	2860
SportDesign Pkg			1400	1400	1500	1500
CAYENNE AWD—V6 Supercharged Hybrid—Truck Equipment Sch T3						
S Sport Utility	AE2A2	70825	54300	55300	56400	60100
Full Leather			650	650	675	675
Adaptive Cruise Control			475	475	490	490
Convenience Pkg			1400	1400	1480	1480
Premium Pkg			1700	1700	1805	1805
Premium Pkg Plus			2675	2675	2825	2825
SportDesign Pkg			1400	1400	1480	1480
CAYENNE AWD—V8—Truck Equipment Schedule T3						
S Sport Utility 4D	AB2A2	66825	53700	54700	55800	59300
Full Leather			650	650	675	675
Adaptive Cruise Control			475	475	490	490
Convenience Pkg			1400	1400	1480	1480
Premium Pkg			1700	1700	1805	1805
Premium Pkg Plus			2675	2675	2825	2825
SportDesign Pkg			1400	1400	1480	1480
CAYENNE AWD—V8—Truck Equipment Schedule T3						
GTS Sport Utility	AD2A2	83025	62900	64000	64900	69000
Sensing Cruise Control			475	475	490	490
CAYENNE AWD—V8 Twin Turbo—Truck Equipment Schedule T3						
Sport Utility 4D	AC2A2	109725	66600	67800	69800	75400
Full Leather			650	650	680	680
Adaptive Cruise Control			475	475	495	495
Premium Pkg Plus			2675	2675	2835	2835
Sport Pkg			1375	1375	1465	1465
SportDesign Pkg			1400	1400	1485	1485

2014 PORSCHE — WP1(AA2A2)-E-#

Body Type	VIN	List	Trade-In Good	Trade-In Very Good	Pvt-Party Good	Retail Excellent
CAYENNE AWD—V6—Truck Equipment Schedule T3						
Sport Utility 4D	AA2A2	50575	47900	48800	49700	52900
Full Leather			500	500	530	530
Premium Pkg			1775	1775	1880	1880
Premium Pkg Plus			2775	2775	2930	2930
SportDesign Pkg			1475	1475	1560	1560
Ceramic Brakes			4075	4075	4305	4305
CAYENNE AWD—V6—Truck Equipment Schedule T3						
Platinum Edition	AA2A2	64295				
Adaptive Cruise Control						
Burmester Sound						
Full Leather						
SportDesign Pkg						
Ceramic Brakes						
CAYENNE AWD—V6 Diesel—Truck Equipment Schedule T3						
Sport Utility 4D	AF2A2	57575	51300	52200	53600	57100
Full Leather			500	500	530	530
Adaptive Cruise Control			500	500	520	520
Premium Pkg			1775	1775	1880	1880
Premium Plus Pkg			2775	2775	2930	2930
SportDesign Pkg			1475	1475	1560	1560
Ceramic Brakes			4075	4075	4305	4305
CAYENNE AWD—V6 Diesel—Truck Equipment Schedule T3						
Platinum Edition	AF2A2	67895				
Adaptive Cruise Control						
Burmester Sound						
Full Leather						
SportDesign Pkg						
Ceramic Brakes						
CAYENNE AWD—V6 Supercharged Hybrid—Truck Equipment Sch T3						
S Sport Utility 4D	AE2A2	71875	60000	61000	62000	65800
Adaptive Cruise Control			500	500	515	515
Premium Pkg			1775	1775	1875	1875
Premium Plus Pkg			2775	2775	2920	2920
SportDesign Pkg			1475	1475	1555	1555
Ceramic Brakes			4075	4075	4290	4290
CAYENNE AWD—V8—Truck Equipment Schedule T3						
S Sport Utility 4D	AB2A2	67775	57800	58800	59900	63600
Adaptive Cruise Control			500	500	515	515
Premium Pkg			1775	1775	1870	1870
Premium Plus Pkg			2775	2775	2915	2915

Body Type	VIN	List	Trade-In Good	Trade-In Very Good	Pvt-Party Good	Retail Excellent
SportDesign Pkg			1475	1475	1555	1555
Ceramic Brakes			4075	4075	4285	4285
CAYENNE AWD—V8—Truck Equipment Schedule T3						
GTS Sport Utility	AD2A2	84275	71000	72300	73000	77200
Adaptive Cruise Control			500	500	515	515
Ceramic Brakes			4075	4075	4265	4265
CAYENNE AWD—V8 Twin Turbo—Truck Equipment Schedule T3						
Sport Utility 4D	AC2A2	111375	87200	88700	90000	96100
S Sport Utility	AC2A2	146975	99100	100800	102100	108500
Adaptive Cruise Control			500	500	515	515
Premium Plus Pkg			2775	2775	2900	2900
Sport Pkg			1425	1425	1500	1500
SportDesign Pkg			1475	1475	1545	1545
Ceramic Brakes			4075	4075	4260	4260

RAM

2011 RAM — (1or3)D7–(E2BK)–B–#

Body Type	VIN	List	Trade-In Good	Trade-In Very Good	Pvt-Party Good	Retail Excellent
DAKOTA EXTENDED CAB PICKUP—V6—Truck Equipment Schedule T1						
ST 4D 6 1/2'	E2BK	23850	9350	10050	10750	13200
Big Horn/Lone Star	E3BK	24725	10700	11500	12150	14900
4WD	W		1825	1825	2215	2215
V8, Flex Fuel, 4.7 Liter	P		800	800	965	965
DAKOTA CREW CAB PICKUP—V6—Truck Equipment Schedule T1						
Big Horn/Lone Star	E3GK	27420	13150	14150	14850	18150
Laramie 4D 5 1/4'	E5GK	31275	13500	14550	15700	19650
4WD	W		1825	1825	2205	2205
V8, Flex Fuel, 4.7 Liter	P		800	800	960	960
DAKOTA CREW CAB PICKUP 4WD—V8—Truck Equipment Schedule T1						
TRX 4D 5 1/4'	W7BP	32460	14500	15550	16250	19800
RAM REGULAR CAB PICKUP—V6—Truck Equipment Schedule T1						
1500 ST 2D 6 1/3'	B1EP	21510	9400	9725	11000	13000
1500 ST 2D 8'	B1EP	22185	8775	9075	10350	12300
1500 SLT 2D 6 1/3'	B1EP	25755	10250	10550	11850	14100
1500 SLT 2D 8'	B1EP	26055	9775	10100	11350	13450
4WD	V		2925	2925	3450	3450
V6, 3.7 Liter	C		(650)	(650)	(765)	(765)
V8, HEMI, 5.7 Liter	T		1000	1000	1175	1175
RAM REGULAR CAB PICKUP—V8 HEMI—Truck Equipment Schedule T1						
1500 Sport 2D 6 1/3'	B1ET	31440	11750	12150	13550	16100
2500 ST 2D 8'	P2ET	28495	12400	12800	14050	16450
2500 SLT 2D 8'	P2ET	31275	13000	13450	14800	17400
4WD	V		2925	2925	3465	3465
6-Cyl, Turbo Dsl 6.7L	L		5400	5400	6150	6150
RAM REGULAR CAB PICKUP—6-Cyl. Turbo Diesel—Truck Equip Sch T1						
3500 ST 2D 8' DR	M4EL	36070	19000	19650	20900	24300
3500 SLT 2D 8' DR	M4EL	39245	21100	21800	23100	26800
4WD	V		2925	2925	3250	3250
RAM QUAD CAB PICKUP—V8—Truck Equipment Schedule T1						
1500 ST 4D 6 1/3'	B1GP	25940	12850	13300	14850	17550
1500 SLT 4D 6 1/3'	B1GP	29835	13400	13850	15350	18200
4WD	V		2925	2925	3450	3450
V6, 3.7 Liter	K		(650)	(650)	(765)	(765)
V8, HEMI, 5.7 Liter	T		1000	1000	1175	1175
RAM QUAD CAB PICKUP—V8—Truck Equipment Schedule T1						
1500 Sport 4D 6 1/3'	B1GT	34800	15350	15850	17450	20600
1500 Laramie 6 1/3'	B1GT	37580	15500	16000	17700	21100
4WD	V		2925	2925	3465	3465
RAM CREW CAB PICKUP—V8—Truck Equipment Schedule T1						
1500 ST 4D 5 1/2'	B1CP	29910	14800	15300	16850	19950
1500 SLT 4D 5 1/2'	B1CP	32490	15600	16100	17800	21100
4WD	V		2925	2925	3455	3455
V8, HEMI, 5.7 Liter	T		1000	1000	1185	1185
RAM CREW CAB PICKUP—V8 HEMI—Truck Equipment Schedule T1						
1500 Sport 4D 5 1/2'	B1CT	36955	17150	17700	19550	23300
1500 Laramie 4D 5'	B1CT	39340	18450	19050	20900	24900
1500 Laramie Lghrn	B1CT	43160	20700	21400	23000	27000
2500 ST 4D 6 1/3'	P2CT	31980	16150	16700	17900	20800
2500 ST 4D 8'	P2CT	32180	15700	16200	17450	20300
2500 SLT 4D 6 1/3'	P2CT	36135	17350	17900	19200	22400
2500 SLT 4D 8'	P2CT	36335	16700	17250	18950	22500

Body Type	VIN	List	Trade-In Good	Very Good	Pvt-Party Good	Retail Excellent
2500 Laramie 6 1/3'	P2CT	40770	19000	19650	20900	24300
2500 Laramie 8'	P2CT	40970	18650	19250	20500	23800
2500 Lrmie Lghrn 6'	P2CT	45420	23500	24300	25500	29600
2500 Lrmie Lghrn 8'	P2CT	45620	23700	24400	25700	29800
4WD	V		2925	2925	3490	3490
6-Cyl, Turbo Dsl 6.7L	L		5400	5400	6030	6030
RAM CREW CAB PICKUP 4WD—V8 HEMI—Truck Equipment Sch T1						
2500 Power Wagon 6'	T2CT	45930	23500	24200	25600	29700
RAM CREW CAB PICKUP—6-Cyl. Turbo Diesel—Truck Equipment Sch T1						
3500 ST 4D 6 1/3'	M3CL	39990	22500	23300	24500	28400
3500 ST 4D 8' DR.	M3CL	40190	22400	23100	24300	28300
3500 SLT 4D 6 1/3'	M3CL	44765	23200	23900	25300	29400
3500 SLT 4D 8' DR.	M3CL	44965	22900	23700	25000	29200
3500 Laramie 6 1/3'	M3CL	48780	25100	25900	27200	31500
3500 Laramie 8' DR.	M3CL	48980	25000	25800	27100	31300
3500 Lrmie Lghrn 6'	M3CL	53380	29100	30000	31300	36300
3500 Lrmie Lghrn 8'	M3CL	53580	28800	29700	31100	36000
4WD			2925	2925	3240	3240
RAM MEGA CAB PICKUP—V8 HEMI—Truck Equipment Schedule T1						
2500 SLT 4D 6 1/3'	P2HT	36835	20500	21200	22400	25900
2500 Laramie 6 1/3'	P2HT	41470	22500	23200	24400	28200
2500 Laramie Lghrn	P2HT	46120	24200	25000	26300	30500
4WD	T		2925	2925	3255	3255
6-Cyl, Turbo Dsl 6.7L	L		5400	5400	6005	6005
RAM MEGA CAB PICKUP—6-Cyl. Turbo Diesel—Truck Equipment Sch T1						
3500 SLT 6 1/3'	M3HL	45465	27000	27900	29100	33700
3500 Laramie 6 1/3'	M3HL	49480	28300	29200	30440	35100
3500 Laramie Lghrn 6'	M3HL	55480	30600	31600	32800	37900
4WD	Y		2925	2925	3230	3230

2012 RAM — (1,2or3)C6–(DGAG)–C–#

Body Type	VIN	List	Trade-In Good	Very Good	Pvt-Party Good	Retail Excellent
RAM C/V—V6—Truck Equipment Schedule T2						
Van 4D	DGAG	23975	8950	9150	11100	13550
RAM REGULAR CAB PICKUP—V8—Truck Equipment Schedule T1						
1500 ST 2D 6 1/3'	D6AP	22470	11700	12000	13550	15800
1500 Outdrsman 6'	D6BP	29245	14300	14650	16450	19200
1500 Outdrsman 8'	D6EP	29545	14150	14500	16250	18900
1500 SLT 2D 6 1/3'	D6BP	26650	12200	12500	14100	16500
1500 SLT 2D 8'	D6EP	26950	11850	12150	13700	16000
RamBox			475	475	550	550
4WD	7		3125	3125	3720	3720
V6, 3.7 Liter	K		(725)	(725)	(860)	(860)
V8, HEMI, 5.7 Liter	T		1275	1275	1515	1515
RAM REGULAR CAB PICKUP—V8 Flex Fuel—Truck Equipment Schedule T1						
1500 Tradesman 6'	D6AT	23335	12750	13100	14700	17050
1500 Tradesman 8'	D6DT	23635	12400	12700	14200	16500
4WD	7		3125	3125	3690	3690
RamBox			475	475	550	550
V8, HEMI, 5.7 Liter	T		1275	1275	1505	1505
RAM REGULAR CAB PICKUP—V8—Truck Equipment Schedule T1						
2500 ST 2D 8'	D4AT	29425	15250	15650	17000	19450
2500 SLT 2D 8'	D4BT	32205	16550	16950	18400	21000
2500 Outdrsman 8'	D4BT	34900	18850	19350	20800	23700
4WD	5		3125	3125	3515	3515
6-Cyl, Turbo Dsl, 6.7L	L		5625	5625	6310	6310
RAM REGULAR CAB PICKUP—V8 HEMI—Truck Equipment Schedule T1						
1500 Express 6 1/3'	D6AT	24075	12550	12900	14550	16950
1500 Tradesman HD	D4RT	29900	15500	15900	17650	20600
1500 Sport 2D 6 1/3'	D6CT	32335	14850	15200	17000	19800
RamBox			475	475	550	550
4WD	7		3125	3125	3700	3700
RAM REGULAR CAB PICKUP—6-Cyl. Turbo Diesel—Truck Equip Sch T1						
3500 ST 2D 8' DR.	DPAL	37795	21300	21800	23100	26300
3500 SLT 2D 8' DR.	DPBL	40570	23700	24300	25700	29100
4WD	R		3125	3125	3465	3465
RAM QUAD CAB PICKUP—V8—Truck Equipment Schedule T1						
1500 ST 4D 6 1/3'	D6FP	26645	14750	15100	16850	19600
1500 Tradesman 6'	D6FP	27630	14000	14350	16050	18650
1500 SLT 4D 6 1/3'	D6GP	30865	15100	15500	17250	20100
1500 Outdoorsman	D6GP	33660	14800	15200	17000	19800
RamBox			475	475	550	550
4WD	7		3125	3125	3690	3690
V6, 3.7 Liter	K		(725)	(725)	(860)	(860)

Body Type	VIN	List	Trade-In Good	Trade-In Very Good	Pvt-Party Good	Retail Excellent
V8, HEMI, 5.7 Liter	T		1275	1275	1500	1500
RAM QUAD CAB PICKUP—V8 HEMI—Truck Equipment Schedule T1						
1500 Express 6 1/3'	D6PT	29045	14950	15300	17050	19900
1500 Big Horn 6 1/3'	D6GT	33015	17200	17650	19500	22700
1500 Lone Star 61/3'	D6GT	33015	18150	18600	20400	23700
1500 Sport 6 1/3'	D6HT	35830	19000	19450	21400	24800
1500 Laramie 6 1/3'	D6JT	39410	18800	19250	21200	24700
RamBox		......	475	475	540	540
4WD	7	......	3125	3125	3625	3625
RAM CREW CAB PICKUP—V8—Truck Equipment Schedule T1						
1500 Tradesman 5'	D6LP	30110	15550	15950	17700	20500
4WD	7	......	3125	3125	3675	3675
V8, HEMI, 5.7 Liter	T		1275	1275	1495	1495
RAM CREW CAB PICKUP—V8—Truck Equipment Schedule T1						
1500 ST 4D 5 1/2'	D6KP	30640	16150	16550	18700	22100
1500 SLT 4D 5 1/2'	D6LP	33220	17450	17850	19800	23200
1500 Outdoorsman	D6LP	35215	17400	17850	19750	23000
RamBox		......	475	475	550	550
4WD	7	......	3125	3125	3710	3710
V8, HEMI, 5.7 Liter	T		1275	1275	1510	1510
RAM CREW CAB PICKUP—V8 HEMI—Truck Equipment Schedule T1						
1500 Express 5 1/2'	D6LT	31205	16550	16950	18800	21900
1500 SLT 5 1/2'	D6LT	34570	18550	19050	21000	24400
1500 Lone Star 5 1/2'	D6LT	34570	18800	19250	21100	24400
1500 Sport 5 1/2'	D6MT	37685	20600	21100	23100	26900
1500 Laramie 5 1/2'	D6NT	40870	23400	24000	26000	30200
1500 Laramie Lghrn	D6PT	44120	23100	23600	25700	29900
1500 Laramie Ltd	D6NT	45720	24200	24800	26900	31200
2500 ST 4D 6 1/3'	D4CT	33140	18300	18750	20000	22700
2500 ST 4D 8'	D4HT	33340	17300	17700	19050	21700
2500 SLT 4D 6 1/3'	D4DT	37295	19800	20300	21800	25000
2500 SLT 4D 8'	D4JT	37495	18700	19150	21000	24300
2500 Big Horn 6 1/3'	D4DT	39090	20800	21300	23100	26600
2500 Big Horn 8'	D4JT	39290	20600	21100	22900	26400
2500 Lone Star 6 1/3'	D4DT	39090	20800	21100	22900	26600
2500 Lone Star 8'	D4JT	39290	20800	21300	23100	26600
2500 Outdoorsmn 6'	D4DT	39090	22300	22800	24600	28300
2500 Outdoorsmn 8'	D4JT	40190	22400	23000	24800	28600
2500 Laramie 6 1/3'	D4FT	42730	24900	25500	26900	30600
2500 Laramie 8'	D4KT	42930	24800	25500	26800	30400
2500 Lrmie Lghrn 6'	D4FT	46925	27600	28300	29700	33700
2500 Lrmie Lghrn 8'	D4LT	47125	27800	28500	29900	33900
2500 LtdLrmLghn 6	D4GT	47980	28500	29200	30700	34700
2500 LtdLrmLghn 8	D4LT	48180	28600	29300	30800	34900
RamBox		......	475	475	550	550
4WD	7	......	3125	3125	3690	3690
6-Cyl, Turbo Dsl 6.7L	L		5625	5625	6230	6230
RAM CREW CAB PICKUP 4WD—V8 HEMI—Truck Equipment Sch T1						
2500 Power Wagon 6'	D5ET	46790	30300	31000	32500	36800
RAM 3500 CREW CAB PICKUP—6-Cyl. Turbo Diesel—Truck Equip Sch T1						
ST 4D 6 1/3'	D2CL	42265	26000	26600	28000	31700
ST 4D 8' DR	DPGL	42890	26400	27000	28500	32400
SLT 4D 6 1/3'	D2DL	47040	27700	28400	29900	34100
SLT 4D 8' DR	DPHL	47665	27500	28100	29700	33800
Big Horn 4D 6 1/3'	D2DL	48135	28500	29200	30700	34800
Big Horn 4D 8'	DPHL	48760	29200	29900	31400	35600
Lone Star 4D 6 1/3'	D2DL	48135	28600	29300	30800	34900
Lone Star 4D 8'	DPHL	48760	29100	29800	31300	35500
Outdoorsman 4D 6'	D2DL	49335	29700	30500	32000	36200
Outdoorsman 4D 8'	DPHL	48665	29200	29900	31400	35600
Laramie 4D 6 1/3'	D2EL	51855	30800	31500	33000	37400
Laramie 4D 8' DR	DPJL	52480	30900	31700	33100	37400
Laramie Longhorn 6'	D2FL	54630	32700	33500	35000	39700
Lrmie Lnghrn 8'	DPKL	55255	32700	33500	34900	39600
Lrmie Lnghrn Ltd 6'	D2FL	56535	35600	36400	37800	42600
Lrmie Lnghrn Ltd 8'	DPKL	57460	35800	36600	37900	42800
RamBox		......	475	475	515	515
4WD	3	......	3125	3125	3465	3465
RAM 2500 MEGA CAB PICKUP—V8 HEMI—Truck Equipment Schedule T1						
SLT 4D 6 1/3'	D4MT	38065	23100	23700	25000	28400
Big Horn 4D 6 1/3'	D4MT	39860	21800	22300	23700	27000
Lone Star 4D 6 1/3'	D4MT	39860	22000	22500	23900	27200
Outdoorsman 6 1/3'	D4MT	40760	24000	24600	25900	29400

2012 RAM

Body Type	VIN	List	Trade-In Good	Very Good	Pvt-Party Good	Retail Excellent
Laramie 4D 6 1/3'	D4NT	43500	27500	28100	29500	33500
Lrmie Lnghrn Ltd 6'	D4PT	48780	29400	30200	31700	35900
RamBox			475	475	520	520
4WD	5		3125	3125	3485	3485
6-Cyl, Turbo Dsl 6.7L	L		5625	5625	6260	6260
RAM 3500 MEGA CAB PICKUP—6-Cyl. Turbo Diesel—Truck Equip Sch T1						
SLT 4D 6 1/3' DR	D2LL	48465	29900	30700	32200	36400
Outdoorsman 6 1/3'	D2LL	49465	30300	31000	32500	36800
Big Horn 4D 6 1/3'	D2LL	49560	30400	31100	32600	36900
Lone Star 4D 6 1/3'	D2LL	49560	30400	31100	32600	36900
Laramie 4D 6 1/3'	D2ML	53280	32600	33400	34800	39300
Lrmie Longhorn 6'	D2NL	56055	33900	34700	36200	40900
Lrmie Lnghrn Ltd 6'	D2NL	57960	36400	37300	38800	43900
Lrmie Lnghrn Ltd 8'	DPKL	57460	35800	36600	37900	42800
RamBox			475	475	515	515
4WD	3		3125	3125	3460	3460

2013 RAM — (1,2or3)C6-(RGAG)-D-#

Body Type	VIN	List	Trade-In Good	Very Good	Pvt-Party Good	Retail Excellent
RAM C/V TRADESMAN—V6—Truck Equipment Schedule T2						
Van 4D	RGAG	23460	10850	11000	13050	15500
RAM REGULAR CAB PICKUP—V6 Flex Fuel—Truck Equipment Sch T1						
1500 RFE 2D 6 1/3'	R6RG	29195	15850	16200	18000	20700
RAM REGULAR CAB PICKUP—V6—Truck Equipment Schedule T1						
1500 Tradesman 6'	R6AP	23585	13950	14250	16050	18450
1500 Tradesman 8'	R6DP	23970	14000	14300	16050	18400
1500 SLT 2D 6 1/3'	R6BP	28445	15450	15800	17600	20200
1500 SLT 2D 8'	R6EP	28745	14800	15100	16900	19400
4WD			3275	3275	3780	3780
V6, Flex Fuel, 3.6 Liter	G		(775)	(775)	(905)	(905)
V8, HEMI, 5.7 Liter	T		1275	1275	1485	1485
RAM REGULAR CAB PICKUP—V8 HEMI—Truck Equipment Schedule T1						
1500 Express 6 1/3'	R6AT	25820	14550	14850	16650	19150
4WD			3275	3275	3760	3760
RAM REGULAR CAB PICKUP—V8 HEMI—Truck Equipment Schedule T1						
1500 R/T 2D 6 1/3'	R6CT	33930	20100	20500	22400	25700
RAM REGULAR CAB PICKUP 4WD—V8 HEMI—Truck Equipment Sch T1						
1500 Sport 2D 6 1/3'	R7CT	36850	20500	21000	23000	26400
RAM REGULAR CAB PICKUP—V8 HEMI—Truck Equipment Schedule T1						
2500 SLT 2D 8'	R4BT	33895	17300	17650	19600	22600
2500 Tradesman 8'	R4AT	30215	14600	14900	16950	19800
4WD	5		3275	3275	3700	3700
6-Cyl Turbo Diesel 6.6L	T		5825	5825	6605	6605
RAM REGULAR CAB PICKUP—6-Cyl. Turbo Diesel—Truck Equip Sch T1						
3500 ST Trdsmn 8	R2AL	39195	21900	22400	24500	28200
3500 SLT 2D 8'	R2BL	42905	24900	25400	27700	31900
4WD	3,R		3275	3275	3620	3620
V8, HEMI, 5.7 Liter	T		(5825)	(5825)	(6465)	(6465)
RAM QUAD CAB PICKUP—V8 Flex Fuel—Truck Equipment Schedule T1						
1500 Tradesman 6'	R6FP	28180	16650	17000	18800	21500
1500 SLT 4D 6 1/3'	R6GP	31900	17650	18000	19950	22900
RamBox			500	500	560	560
4WD	7		3275	3275	3750	3750
V6, Flex Fuel, 3.6 Liter	G		(775)	(775)	(900)	(900)
V8, HEMI, 5.7 Liter	T		1275	1275	1470	1470
RAM QUAD CAB PICKUP—V6 Flex Fuel—Truck Equipment Sch T1						
1500 Outdoorsman	R6GG	34555	17750	18100	20100	23100
4WD			3275	3275	3730	3730
V8, HEMI, 5.7 Liter	T		1275	1275	1465	1465
RAM QUAD CAB PICKUP—V8 HEMI—Truck Equipment Schedule T1						
1500 Express 6 1/3'	R6FT	30740	17350	17750	19550	22400
1500 Big Horn 6 1/3'	R6GT	34205	18550	18950	21000	24100
1500 Lone Star 6 1/3'	R6GT	34205	19850	20300	22200	25500
1500 Sport 6 1/3'	R6HT	37425	20700	21100	23200	26600
1500 Laramie 6 1/3'	R6JT	39610	21500	22000	24000	27500
RamBox			500	500	560	560
4WD	7		3275	3275	3720	3720
RAM CREW CAB PICKUP—V6 Flex Fuel—Truck Equipment Schedule T1						
1500 Outdrsman 5'	R6LG	36710	20000	20400	22500	26000
RamBox			500	500	565	565
4WD	7		3275	3275	3755	3755
V8, HEMI, 5.7 Liter	T		1275	1275	1475	1475
RAM CREW CAB PICKUP—V8 Flex Fuel—Truck Equipment Schedule T1						
1500 Tradesman 5'	R6KP	30760	18650	19000	20800	23800

Body Type	VIN	List	Trade-In Good	Very Good	Pvt-Party Good	Retail Excellent
1500 Tradesman 6'	R6SP	31370	17550	17900	19700	22500
1500 SLT 4D 5 1/2'	R6LP	34515	20300	20700	22800	26100
RamBox			500	500	555	555
4WD	7		3275	3275	3750	3750
V6, Flex Fuel, 3.6 Liter	G		(775)	(775)	(900)	(900)
V8, HEMI, 5.7 Liter	T		1275	1275	1470	1470
RAM CREW CAB PICKUP—V8 HEMI—Truck Equipment Schedule T1						
1500 Express 5 1/2'	R6KT	32870	19500	19900	22000	25300
1500 Big Horn 5 1/2'	R6LT	36360	20400	20800	22900	26500
1500 Big Horn 6 1/3'	R6TT	37220	20300	20800	22800	26300
1500 Lone Star 5 1/2'	R6LT	36360	20800	21200	23200	26600
1500 Lone Star 6 1/3'	R6TT	37220	20600	21100	23100	26500
1500 Outdrsmn 6'	R6TT	37570	19800	20200	22300	25600
1500 Sport 4D 5 1/2'	R6MT	39280	23600	24100	26200	30100
1500 Sport 4D 6 1/3'	R6UT	39890	23600	24100	26300	30300
1500 SLT 4D 6 1/3'	R7TT	40045	24500	25000	27300	31300
1500 Laramie 5 1/2'	R6NT	41465	25800	26300	28700	33100
1500 Laramie 6 1/3'	R6VT	42075	25700	26200	28500	32700
1500 Lrmie Lghrn 5'	R6PT	45270	26700	27200	29500	33900
1500 Lrmie Lghrn 6'	R6WT	45880	27000	27600	29900	34300
1500 Laramie Ltd 5'	R6PT	48675	27800	28300	30700	35200
1500 Laramie Ltd 6'	R6WT	48975	27700	28300	30600	35000
RamBox			500	500	565	565
4WD	7		3275	3275	3770	3770
RAM CREW CAB PICKUP—V8 HEMI—Truck Equipment Schedule T1						
2500 Tradesman 6'	R4CT	33640	17800	18150	20100	23100
2500 Tradesman 8'	R4HT	37715	17750	18100	20000	23100
2500 SLT 4D 6 1/3'	R4CT	37715	20700	21100	23200	26800
2500 SLT 4D 8'	R4JT	37915	20800	21200	23200	26800
2500 Big Horn 6 1/3'	R4DT	39550	22400	22900	24900	28500
2500 Lone Star 6 1/3'	R4DT	39550	22200	22700	24700	28400
2500 Big Horn 8'	R4JT	39750	22200	22700	24700	28400
2500 Lone Star 8'	R4JT	39750	22400	22900	24900	28500
2500 Laramie 6 1/3'	R4FT	43490	25900	26500	28600	32700
2500 Laramie 8'	R4KT	43690	25700	26200	28400	32500
2500 Lrmie Lghrn 6'	R4GT	48785	29500	30100	32400	37000
2500 Lrmie Lghrn 8'	R4LT	48985	29700	30300	32600	37200
2500 LrmLghnLtd 6	R4GT	53675	33600	34200	36700	41800
2500 LrmLghnLtd 8	R4LT	53875	33800	34400	36800	42000
RamBox			500	500	555	555
4WD	5		3275	3275	3695	3695
6-Cyl Turbo Diesel 6.7L	L		5825	5825	6605	6605
RAM 2500 CREW CAB PICKUP 4WD—V8 HEMI—Truck Equipment Sch T1						
Power Wagon 6'	R5ET	57760	31500	32200	34400	39100
Trdsmn Pwr Wag 6'	R5CT	50200	30300	30900	33200	37800
Laramie Power Wag	R5ST	59530	34700	35400	37700	42900
RamBox			500	500	535	535
RAM 2500 CREW CAB PICKUP 4WD—V8 HEMI—Truck Equipment Sch T1						
2500 Outdrsman 6'	R5DT	43855	25800	26300	28500	32500
2500 Outdoorsman 8'	R5JT	44055	26000	26500	28700	32700
RamBox			500	500	535	535
6-Cyl Turbo Diesel, 6.7L	L		5825	5825	6360	6360
RAM 3500 CREW CAB—6-Cyl. Turbo Diesel—Truck Equip Sch T1						
ST Tradesman 6'	R2CL	43300	26100	26700	28900	33200
ST Tradesman 4D 8'	R2GL	43500	27200	27800	30000	34200
SLT 4D 6 1/3'	R2DL	47615	29000	29600	32100	36800
SLT 4D 8'	R2HL	47815	29200	29800	32300	37000
Big Horn 4D 6 1/3'	R2DL	48750	29900	30500	32800	37500
Big Horn 4D 8'	R2HL	48950	30100	30700	33100	37800
Lone Star 4D 6 1/3'	R2DL	48750	29900	30500	32800	37500
Lone Star 4D 8'	R2HL	48950	30100	30700	33100	37800
Laramie 4D 6 1/3'	R2EL	53590	34500	35100	37700	43100
Laramie 4D 8'	R2JL	53790	34300	34900	37500	42900
Laramie Lnghrn 6'	R2FL	59145	36400	37100	38800	43400
Laramie Longhorn 8'	R2KL	59345	36200	36900	38600	43200
Lrme Lnghrn Ltd 6'	R2FL	62240	40300	41100	42600	47500
Lrme Lnghrn Ltd 8'	R3KL	62240	40500	41300	42800	47700
RamBox			500	500	540	540
4WD	3		3275	3275	3610	3610
V8, HEMI, 5.7 Liter	T		(5825)	(5825)	(6450)	(6450)
RAM MEGA CAB PICKUP—V8 HEMI—Truck Equipment Schedule T1						
2500 SLT 4D 6 1/3'	R4MT	38715	23600	24000	26100	29900
2500 Big Horn 6 1/3'	R4MT	40550	23000	23500	25500	29200

Body Type	VIN	List	Trade-In Good	Very Good	Pvt-Party Good	Retail Excellent
2500 Lone Star 6 1/3'	R4MT	40550	23000	23500	25500	29200
2500 Laramie 6 1/3'	R4NT	44685	28000	28600	30900	35400
2500 Laramie Lghrn	R4PT	50025	29600	30200	32600	37300
2500 LrmLnghrnLtd	R4PT	54915	31400	32100	34400	39200
RamBox			500	500	535	535
4WD	5		3275	3275	3630	3630
6-Cyl Turbo Diesel, 6.7L	L		5825	5825	6480	6480

RAM MEGA CAB PICKUP—6-Cyl. Turbo Diesel—Truck Equip Sch T1

Body Type	VIN	List	Trade-In Good	Very Good	Pvt-Party Good	Retail Excellent
3500 SLT 6 1/3' DR	R2LL	48615	30900	31500	33800	38500
3500 Big Horn 6 1/3'	R2LL	49750	30900	31500	33400	37800
3500 Lone Star 6 1/3'	R2LL	49750	30900	31500	33400	37800
3500 Laramie 6'	R2ML	54590	32000	32700	35000	39800
3500 Lrmie Lnghrn 6	R2NL	60145	37200	37900	39600	44300
3500 LrmLnghrnLtd	R2NL	60245	40000	40800	42700	47900
RamBox			500	500	540	540
4WD	3,R		3275	3275	3590	3590
V8, HEMI, 5.7 Liter	T		(5825)	(5825)	(6410)	(6410)

RAM C/V TRADESMAN—V6 Flex Fuel—Truck Equipment Schedule T2

Body Type	VIN	List	Trade-In Good	Very Good	Pvt-Party Good	Retail Excellent
Van 4D	RGAG	22355	12700	12900	14950	17500

PROMASTER 1500 CARGO VAN—4-Cyl. Turbo Diesel—Truck Sch T1

Tradesman Van 3D		30515	19750	20100	21600	24000

PROMASTER 2500 CARGO VAN—V6—Truck Equipment Schedule T1

Tradesman Van 3D		33870	21700	22100	23600	26100
Tradesman Window Van		34250	22000	22400	23900	26500
4-Cyl, Turbo Dsl, 3.0L			2225	2225	2490	2490

PROMASTER 3500 CARGO VAN—V6—Truck Equipment Schedule T1

Tradesman Van 3D		36345	24400	24800	26200	28900
Tradesman Extended		37145	24900	25300	26800	29500
4-Cyl, Turbo Dsl, 3.0L			2225	2225	2470	2470

RAM REGULAR CAB PICKUP—V6 Flex Fuel—Truck Equipment Sch T1

1500 HFE 2D 6 1/3'	R6RG	29805	17400	17750	19750	22600
RamBox			525	525	585	585
V8, HEMI, 5.7 Liter	T		1300	1300	1460	1460

RAM REGULAR CAB PICKUP—V6 Flex Fuel—Truck Equipment Schedule T1

1500 Tradesman 6'	R6AG	25295	14850	15150	17000	19450
1500 Express 6 1/3'	R6AT	27105	15950	16250	18050	20600
1500 SLT 2D 6 1/3'	R6BG	29455	17050	17400	19150	21800
1500 HFE 2D 6 1/3'	R6RG	29805	17400	17750	19750	22600
1500 Big Horn 6 1/3'	R6BG	30650	18150	18550	20500	23500
1500 Lone Star 6'	R6BG	30650	18150	18550	20500	23500
RamBox			525	525	595	595
4WD	7		3500	3500	4045	4045
V8, HEMI, 5.7 Liter	T		1300	1300	1490	1490

RAM REGULAR CAB PICKUP—V6 Flex Fuel—Truck Equipment Schedule T1

1500 Tradesman 8'	R6DG	25680	14900	15200	17000	19400
1500 SLT 2D 8'	R6EG	29755	16600	16950	18650	21200
1500 Big Horn 2D 8'	R6EG	30950	17850	18200	20200	23200
1500 Lone Star 2D 8'	R6EG	30950	17850	18200	20200	23200
4WD	7		3500	3500	4020	4020
V6, EcoDiesel, 3.0T	M		2925	2925	3350	3350
V8, HEMI, 5.7 Liter	T		1300	1300	1480	1480

RAM REGULAR CAB PICKUP—V8 HEMI—Truck Equipment Schedule T1

1500 R/T 6 1/3'	R6CT	35850	21700	22100	24100	27400
RamBox			525	525	585	585

RAM REGULAR CAB PICKUP 4WD—V8 HEMI—Truck Equipment Sch T1

1500 Sport 2D 6 1/3'	R6CT	38260	23700	24200	26100	29500
RamBox			525	525	580	580
2WD	6		(3500)	(3500)	(3945)	(3945)

RAM REGULAR CAB PICKUP—V8 HEMI—Truck Equipment Sch T1

2500 SLT 8'	R4BT	34720	19400	19750	22000	25400
2500 Tradesman 8'	R4AT	30695	16600	16950	19200	22300
4WD	5		3500	3500	3975	3975
6-Cyl Turbo Diesel 6.7L	L		6025	6025	6855	6855
V8, HEMI, 6.4 Liter	J		575	575	650	650

RAM REGULAR CAB PICKUP—6-Cyl. Turbo Diesel—Truck Equip Sch T1

3500 Tradesman 8'	R2AL	39785	24400	24900	27300	31300
3500 SLT 2D 8'	R2BL	43845	27200	27700	30000	34300
4WD	3,R		3500	3500	3830	3830
V8, HEMI, 5.7 Liter	T		(5900)	(5900)	(6460)	(6460)
V8, HEMI, 6.4 Liter	J		(4950)	(4950)	(5420)	(5420)

Body Type	VIN	List	Trade-In Good	Very Good	Pvt-Party Good	Retail Excellent
RAM QUAD CAB PICKUP—V8 HEMI—Truck Equipment Schedule T1						
1500 Tradesman 6'	R6HT	31140	17950	18300	20200	23000
1500 SLT 4D 6 1/3'	R6HT	38835	22700	23200	25200	28700
RamBox			525	525	590	590
4WD	7		3500	3500	3990	3990
V6, Flex Fuel, 3.6 Liter	G		(825)	(825)	(950)	(950)
V6, Turbo Diesel, 3.0L	M		2925	2925	3325	3325
RAM QUAD CAB PICKUP—V6 Flex Fuel—Truck Equipment Sch T1						
1500 Outdorsman	R6GG	35365	19850	20300	22200	25400
RamBox			525	525	585	585
4WD	7		3500	3500	3965	3965
V6, Turbo EcoDsl, 3.0L	M		2925	2925	3300	3300
V8, HEMI, 5.7 Liter	T		1300	1300	1460	1460
RAM QUAD CAB PICKUP—V8 HEMI—Truck Equipment Schedule T1						
1500 Express 6 1/3'	R6FT	31800	19250	19650	21500	24500
1500 SLT 4D 6 1/3'	R6GT	34320	19950	20400	22200	25300
1500 Big Horn 6 1/3'	R6GT	35515	20700	21100	23100	26400
RamBox			525	525	585	585
4WD	7		3500	3500	3960	3960
V6, Turbo EcoDsl, 3.0L	M		2925	2925	3285	3285
V6, Flex Fuel, 3.6 Liter	G		(825)	(825)	(940)	(940)
RAM CREW CAB PICKUP—V6 Flex Fuel—Truck Equipment Schedule T1						
1500 Outdrsman 5'	R6LG	37670	22200	22600	24700	28300
1500 Tradesman 5'	R6LG	33620	21000	21400	23200	26200
1500 SLT 4D 5 1/2'	R6LG	37790	21300	21800	23800	27300
1500 Big Horn 5 1/2'	R6LG	36670	21000	21400	23600	27200
1500 Lone Star 5 1/2'	R6LG	36670	23100	23600	25600	29200
RamBox			525	525	610	610
4WD	7		3500	3500	4125	4125
V6, Turbo, EcoDsl, 3.0L	M		2925	2925	3440	3440
V8, HEMI, 5.7 Liter	T		1300	1300	1520	1520
RAM CREW CAB PICKUP—V8 HEMI—Truck Equipment Schedule T1						
1500 Tradesman 6'	R6ST	33080	20200	20600	22400	25500
1500 Express 5 1/2'	R6KT	34280	20900	21300	23300	26700
1500 SLT 4D 6 1/3'	R6TT	37425	24900	25400	27800	31900
1500 Big Horn 6 1/3'	R9TT	38620	22400	22800	24900	28400
1500 Lone Star 6 1/3'	R6TT	38620	23900	24400	26400	30100
1500 Outdrsman 6'	R6MT	40690	27100	27600	29700	33700
1500 Sport 4D 5 1/2'	R6MT	40990	27300	27800	29900	34000
1500 Sport 4D 6 1/3'	R6UT	40990	27300	27800	29900	34000
1500 Laramie 5 1/2'	R6NT	42875	28100	28600	31000	35400
1500 Laramie 6 1/3'	R6VT	43175	26900	27400	30100	34700
1500 Lrme Lnghrn 5'	R6PT	46680	30900	31500	33800	38400
1500 Lrme Lnghrn 6'	R6WT	46980	30700	31300	33700	38200
1500 Lrme Ltd 5 1/2'	R6PT	49175	31100	31700	34000	38700
1500 Lrme Ltd 6 1/3'	R6WT	49475	31300	31900	34200	38800
RamBox			525	525	595	595
4WD	7		3500	3500	4035	4035
V6, Turbo, EcoDsl, 3.0L	M		2925	2925	3310	3310
RAM CREW CAB PICKUP—V8 HEMI—Truck Equipment Schedule T1						
2500 Tradesman 6'	R4CT	34265	19700	20100	22000	25100
2500 Tradesman 8'	R4HT	34845	19650	20000	22000	25100
2500 SLT 4D 6 1/3'	R4DT	38740	22900	23300	25500	29300
2500 SLT 4D 8'	R4JT	38940	22500	23000	25300	29200
2500 Big Horn 6 1/3'	R4DT	40575	24600	25100	27200	30900
2500 Lone Star 6 1/3'	R4DT	40575	24600	25100	27200	30900
2500 Big Horn 8'	R4JT	40775	24400	24900	27000	30700
2500 Lone Star 8'	R4JT	40775	24800	25300	27400	31100
2500 Laramie 6 1/3'	R4FT	44460	30000	30600	32800	37100
2500 Laramie 8'	R4KT	44660	30600	31200	33400	37800
2500 Lrmie Lghrn 6'	R4GT	49875	31700	32300	34600	39200
2500 Lrmie Lghrn 8'	R4LT	50075	32100	32700	35000	39600
2500 Laramie Ltd 6'	R4GT	52170	32500	33200	35200	39700
2500 Laramie Ltd 8'	R4LT	51870	32300	33000	35000	39500
RamBox			525	525	580	580
4WD	5		3500	3500	3935	3935
6-Cyl Turbo Diesel 6.7L	L		6025	6025	6785	6785
V8, CNG, HEMI 5.7L	2		4275	4275	4805	4805
V8, HEMI, 6.4 Liter	J		575	575	645	645
RAM CREW CAB PICKUP 4WD—V8 HEMI—Truck Equipment Sch T1						
2500 Outdorsmn 6	R5DT	44605	28200	28700	30900	35100
2500 Outdorsman 8'	R5JT	44805	28400	28900	31100	35300
RamBox			525	525	565	565

TRUCKS & VANS

2014 RAM

Body Type	VIN	List	Trade-In Good	Very Good	Pvt-Party Good	Retail Excellent
6-Cyl Turbo Diesel 6.7L	L		6025	6025	6585	6585
V8, HEMI, 6.4 Liter	J		575	575	625	625
RAM CREW CAB PICKUP 4WD—V8 HEMI—Truck Equipment Sch T1						
2500 Power Wag 6 1/3'	R5EJ	50340	34100	34800	36900	41800
2500 TrdsmnPwrWag 6	R5CJ	45690	32900	33500	35700	40500
2500 Lrmie PwrWag 6	R5FJ	56215	37400	38200	40300	45500
RAM CREW CAB PICKUP—6-Cyl. Turbo Diesel—Truck Equip Sch T1						
3500 Tradesman 6'	R2CL	43800	28800	29300	31800	36400
3500 Tradesman 8'	R2GL	44000	29800	30400	32800	37400
3500 SLT 4D 6 1/3'	R2DL	48415	31300	31900	34500	39400
3500 SLT 4D 8'	R2HL	48615	31500	32100	34600	39500
3500 Big Horn 6 1/3'	R2DL	49550	32400	33000	35500	40500
3500 Big Horn 8'	R2HL	49750	32600	33200	35700	40700
3500 Lone Star 6 1/3'	R2DL	49550	32400	33000	35500	40500
3500 Lone Star 8'	R2HL	49750	32600	33200	35700	40700
3500 Laramie 6 1/3'	R2EL	54185	36700	37400	40000	45300
3500 Laramie 8'	R2JL	54385	37200	37900	40400	45900
3500 Lrmie Lghrn 6'	R2FL	59645	39300	40100	42300	47700
3500 Lrmie Lghrn 8'	R2KL	59845	39100	39800	42100	47400
3500 Laramie Ltd 8'	R2KL	62140	43200	44100	46300	52100
3500 Laramie Ltd 6'	R2FL	62440	43400	44200	46400	52200
RamBox			525	525	565	565
4WD	3		3500	3500	3820	3820
V8, HEMI, 5.7 Liter	T		(5900)	(5900)	(6440)	(6440)
V8, HEMI, 6.4 Liter	J		(4950)	(4950)	(5405)	(5405)
RAM MEGA CAB PICKUP—V8 HEMI—Truck Equipment Schedule T1						
2500 SLT 4D 6 1/3'	R4MT	39740	25800	26300	28500	32500
2500 Big Horn 6 1/3'	R4MT	41575	25000	25500	27900	32000
2500 Lone Star 6 1/3'	R4MT	41575	25000	25500	27900	32000
2500 Laramie 6 1/3'	R4NT	45460	30700	31300	33600	38300
2500 LrmeLnghrn 6'	R4PT	50875	31800	32500	35100	40200
2500 Laramie Ltd 6'	R4PT	53670	34400	35000	37000	41500
RamBox			525	525	565	565
4WD	5		3500	3500	3820	3820
6-Cyl Turbo Diesel 6.7L	L		6025	6025	6585	6585
V8, HEMI, 6.4 Liter	J		575	575	625	625
RAM MEGA CAB PICKUP—6-Cyl. Turbo Diesel—Truck Equipment Sch T1						
3500 SLT 6 1/3' DR	R2LL	49615	32700	33300	35900	40900
3500 Big Horn 6 1/3'	R2LL	50750	33300	33900	36400	41400
3500 Lone Star 6 1/3'	R2LL	50750	33300	33900	36400	41400
3500 Laramie 6 1/3'	R2ML	55385	37800	38500	40800	46100
3500 LrmieLnghrn 6	R2NL	60845	42200	43100	45000	50300
3500 Laramie Ltd 6'	R2NL	63640	45100	46000	48100	54000
RamBox			525	525	580	580
4WD	3,R		3500	3500	3940	3940
V8, HEMI, 5.7 Liter	T		(5900)	(5900)	(6645)	(6645)
V8, HEMI, 6.4 Liter	J		(4950)	(4950)	(5575)	(5575)

SAAB

2005 SAAB — 5S3E(T13S)-5-#

9-7X AWD—6-Cyl.—Truck Equipment Schedule T3						
Linear Sport Util 4D	T13S	38990	2350	2675	3425	5225
9-7X AWD—V8—Truck Equipment Schedule T3						
Arc Sport Utility 4D	T13M	40990	2675	3000	3875	5950

2006 SAAB — 5S3-(T13S)-6-#

9-7X AWD—6-Cyl.—Truck Equipment Schedule T3						
4.2i Sport Utility 4D	T13S	39240	2850	3200	3900	5750
9-7X AWD—V8—Truck Equipment Schedule T3						
5.3i Sport Utility 4D	T13M	41240	3625	4025	4825	7000

2007 SAAB — 5S3-(T13S)-7-#

9-7X AWD—6-Cyl.—Truck Equipment Schedule T3						
4.2i Sport Utility 4D	T13S	39735	3350	3700	4575	6525
9-7X AWD—V8—Truck Equipment Schedule T3						
5.3i Sport Utility 4D	T13M	41735	4475	4900	5650	7950

1015

Body Type	VIN	List	Trade-In Good	Very Good	Pvt-Party Good	Retail Excellent

2008 SAAB — 5S3-(T13S)-8-#

9-7X AWD—6-Cyl.—Truck Equipment Schedule T3
4.2i Sport Utility 4D T13S 39935 **5075 5475 6250 8325**
9-7X AWD—V8—Truck Equipment Schedule T3
5.3i Sport Util 4D T13M 42035 **6225 6700 7825 10600**
Aero Sport Util 4D T23H 45750 **8350 8975 9775 12800**

2009 SAAB — 5S3-(T13S)-9-#

9-7X AWD—6-Cyl.—Truck Equipment Schedule T3
4.2i Sport Utility 4D T13S 41710 **6975 7400 8150 10100**
9-7X AWD—V8—Truck Equipment Schedule T3
5.3i Sport Util 4D T13M 44440 **7550 8000 9075 11550**
Aero Sport Util 4D T23H 48200 **9300 9850 10900 13700**

2011 SAAB — 3G0-(NREY)-B-#

9-4X AWD—V6—Truck Equipment Schedule T3
Sport Utility .... NREY 36700 **13900 14350 15850 18700**
Prem Sport Utility .... NTEY 41070 **17250 17800 19400 22900**
9-4X AWD—V6 Turbo—Truck Equipment Schedule T3
Aero Sport Utility NUE6 48835 **18650 19300 20900 24600**

SATURN

2002 SATURN — 5GZ-(Z23D)-2-#

VUE—4-Cyl.—Truck Equipment Schedule T1
Sport Utility 4D Z23D 17775 **625 750 1450 2725**
AWD **375 375 505 505**
V6, 3.0 Liter .... B **250 250 335 335**

2003 SATURN — 5GZ-(Z23D)-3-#

VUE—4-Cyl.—Truck Equipment Schedule T1
Sport Utility 4D Z33D 18295 **800 950 1775 3300**
AWD 4,6 **400 400 545 545**
V6, 3.0 Liter .... B **275 275 365 365**

2004 SATURN — 5GZ-(Z23D)-4-#

VUE—4-Cyl.—Truck Equipment Schedule T1
Sport Utility 4D Z33D 19135 **1075 1225 2100 3825**
AWD 4,6 **425 425 580 580**
V6, 3.5 Liter .... B **300 300 395 395**

2005 SATURN — 5GZ-(Z23D)-5-#

VUE—4-Cyl.—Truck Equipment Schedule T1
Sport Utility 4D Z23D 21190 **1350 1550 2525 4250**
AWD 4,6 **475 475 615 615**
V6, 3.5 Liter 4 **325 325 425 425**
RELAY—V6—Truck Equipment Schedule T1
2 Minivan V03L 24485 **1675 1925 2600 4125**
3 Minivan V23L 27580 **2350 2675 3425 5475**
AWD .... X **550 550 715 715**

2006 SATURN — 5GZ-(Z23D)-6-#

VUE—4-Cyl.—Truck Equipment Schedule T1
Sport Utility 4D Z23D 19345 **1975 2250 3250 5200**
AWD 4,6 **500 500 655 655**
V6, 3.5 Liter .... B **350 350 455 455**
RELAY—V6—Truck Equipment Schedule T1
2 Minivan V03L 23590 **2175 2450 3150 4850**
3 Minivan V23L 27490 **2850 3225 3925 6025**
AWD .... X **575 575 765 765**

2007 SATURN — 5GZ-(Z33Z)-7-#

VUE—4-Cyl. Hybrid—Truck Equipment Schedule T1
Sport Utility 4D Z33Z 22995 **3050 3425 4225 6325**
VUE—4-Cyl.—Truck Equipment Schedule T1
Sport Utility 4D Z23D 19770 **2675 2975 3775 5625**
AWD 4,6 **525 525 685 685**

Body Type	VIN	List	Trade-In Good	Very Good	Pvt-Party Good	Retail Excellent
V6, 3.5 Liter	L		375	375	485	485
RELAY—V6—Truck Equipment Schedule T1						
Minivan	V531	22210	2750	3075	3750	5600
2 Minivan	V031	24540	3475	3875	4550	6750
3 Minivan	V231	28625	4100	4550	5575	8450
OUTLOOK—V6—Truck Equipment Schedule T1						
XE Sport Utility 4D	R137	27990	5400	6000	6550	9100
XR Sport Utility 4D	R237	30290	5975	6625	7225	10100
AWD	V		675	675	850	850

2008 SATURN — 5GZor3GS(L03Z)-8-#

Body Type	VIN	List	Trade-In Good	Very Good	Pvt-Party Good	Retail Excellent
VUE—4-Cyl. Hybrid—Truck Equipment Schedule T1						
Green Line Spt Util	L03Z	24795	4850	5275	5925	7975
VUE—4-Cyl.—Truck Equipment Schedule T1						
XE Sport Utility 4D	L33P	21395	4500	4875	5550	7500
AWD	4,7		550	550	695	695
V6, 3.5 Liter	N		400	400	505	505
VUE—V6—Truck Equipment Schedule T1						
XR Sport Utility 4D	L537	24895	4975	5400	6050	8125
Red Line Spt Util	L937	27395	6100	6625	7525	10150
AWD	4,7		550	550	695	695
OUTLOOK—V6—Truck Equipment Schedule T1						
XE Sport Utility 4D	R137	28340	6375	6900	7675	10250
XR Sport Utility 4D	R237	30640	7300	7925	8750	11700
AWD	V		700	700	895	895

2009 SATURN — 5GZor3GS(L93Z)-9-#

Body Type	VIN	List	Trade-In Good	Very Good	Pvt-Party Good	Retail Excellent
VUE—4-Cyl. Hybrid—Truck Equipment Schedule T1						
Sport Utility 4D	L93Z	27650	5900	6275	7050	8925
VUE—4-Cyl.—Truck Equipment Schedule T1						
XE Sport Utility 4D	L33P	22770	5650	6025	6850	8675
AWD	4,6,0		625	625	730	730
V6, 3.5 Liter	N		450	450	530	530
VUE—V6—Truck Equipment Schedule T1						
XR Sport Utility 4D	L537	26095	6525	6925	7650	9625
AWD	6		625	625	715	715
4-Cyl, 2.4 Liter	P		(550)	(550)	(650)	(650)
VUE—V6—Truck Equipment Schedule T1						
Red Line Sport Util	L137	28595	7550	8025	8775	11000
AWD	4,6,0		625	625	710	710
OUTLOOK—V6—Truck Equipment Schedule T1						
XE Sport Utility 4D	R137	31055	7925	8450	9525	12300
XR Sport Utility 4D	R237	34880	9200	9775	10850	13950
AWD	V		750	750	910	910

2010 SATURN — 5GZor3GS(LAE1)-A-#

Body Type	VIN	List	Trade-In Good	Very Good	Pvt-Party Good	Retail Excellent
VUE—4-Cyl.—Truck Equipment Schedule T1						
XE Sport Utility 4D	LAE1	23580	7375	7725	8900	11050
VUE—V6—Truck Equipment Schedule T1						
XR Sport Utility 4D	LEE7	26965	7950	8325	9600	12000
XR-L Sport Util	LKE7	29430	9050	9475	10850	13550
AWD	F		700	700	810	810
4-Cyl, 2.4 Liter	1		(500)	(500)	(590)	(590)
OUTLOOK—V6—Truck Equipment Schedule T1						
XE Spt Util 4D	RTED	31905	9575	10000	11200	13750
XR-L Spt Util 4D	RVED	37705	11400	11900	13150	16200
AWD	V		775	775	930	930

SUBARU

2000 SUBARU — JF1(SF635)-Y-#

Body Type	VIN	List	Trade-In Good	Very Good	Pvt-Party Good	Retail Excellent
FORESTER AWD—4-Cyl.—Truck Equipment Schedule T1						
L Sport Utility 4D	SF635	21390	1000	1200	1575	2675
S Sport Utility 4D	SF655	23890	1350	1600	1975	3300

2001 SUBARU — JF1(SF635)-1-#

Body Type	VIN	List	Trade-In Good	Very Good	Pvt-Party Good	Retail Excellent
FORESTER AWD—4-Cyl.—Truck Equipment Schedule T1						
L Sport Utility 4D	SF635	21590	1225	1450	1800	2975
S Sport Utility 4D	SF655	24190	1650	1925	2325	3825

Body Type	VIN	List	Trade-In Good	Very Good	Pvt-Party Good	Retail Excellent

2002 SUBARU — JF1(SF635)-2-#

FORESTER AWD—4-Cyl.—Truck Equipment Schedule T1
| L Sport Utility 4D | SF635 | 21625 | 1550 | 1800 | 2175 | 3575 |
| S Sport Utility 4D | SF655 | 24220 | 2050 | 2375 | 2775 | 4525 |

2003 SUBARU—(JF1or4S4)(BorS)(G636)-3-#

FORESTER AWD—4-Cyl.—Truck Equipment Schedule T1
| X Sport Utility 4D | G636 | 21870 | 1900 | 2225 | 2650 | 4300 |
| XS Sport Utility 4D | G656 | 24220 | 2475 | 2850 | 3200 | 5050 |

BAJA AWD—4-Cyl.—Truck Equipment Schedule T1
| Sport Util Pickup 4D | T61C | 24520 | 4650 | 5075 | 5575 | 8250 |

2004 SUBARU-(JF1or4S4)(BorS)(G636)-4-#

FORESTER AWD—4-Cyl.—Truck Equipment Schedule T1
| X Sport Utility 4D | G636 | 22245 | 2325 | 2650 | 3100 | 4950 |
| XS Sport Utility 4D | G656 | 24495 | 3000 | 3450 | 3825 | 5975 |

FORESTER AWD—4-Cyl. Turbo—Truck Equipment Schedule T1
| XT Sport Utility 4D | G696 | 26320 | 4050 | 4650 | 4950 | 7575 |

BAJA AWD—4-Cyl.—Truck Equipment Schedule T1
| "Sport" SUT | T61C | 22545 | 5350 | 5825 | 6500 | 9475 |

BAJA AWD—4-Cyl. Turbo—Truck Equipment Schedule T1
| Sport Util Pickup 4D | T63C | 24545 | 6000 | 6525 | 7225 | 10550 |

2005 SUBARU-(JF1or4S4)(BorS)(G636)-5-#

FORESTER AWD—4-Cyl.—Truck Equipment Schedule T1
X Sport Utility 4D	G636	22670	3200	3675	4400	6725
XS Sport Utility 4D	G656	25070	3350	3850	4650	7175
XS LL Bean Spt Util	G676	26970	4175	4775	5425	8200

FORESTER AWD—4-Cyl. Turbo—Truck Equipment Schedule T1
| XT Sport Utility 4D | G696 | 27070 | 5000 | 5700 | 6150 | 9100 |

BAJA AWD—4-Cyl.—Truck Equipment Schedule T1
| "Sport" SUT | T62C | 22770 | 5875 | 6375 | 7175 | 10150 |

BAJA AWD—4-Cyl. Turbo—Truck Equipment Schedule T1
| Sport Util Pickup 4D | T63C | 24770 | 6725 | 7300 | 8025 | 11350 |

2006 SUBARU-(JF1or4S4)(B,SorW)(G636)-6-#

FORESTER AWD—4-Cyl.—Truck Equipment Schedule T1
| X Sport Utility 4D | G636 | 23220 | 4150 | 4675 | 5225 | 7600 |
| X LL Bean Spt Util | G676 | 27521 | 4950 | 5575 | 6000 | 8625 |

FORESTER AWD—4-Cyl. Turbo—Truck Equipment Schedule T1
| XT Limited Spt Util | G696 | 29320 | 6900 | 7750 | 8000 | 11250 |

BAJA AWD—4-Cyl.—Truck Equipment Schedule T1
| "Sport" SUT | T62C | 23920 | 7275 | 7850 | 8500 | 11650 |

BAJA AWD—4-Cyl. Turbo—Truck Equipment Schedule T1
| Sport Util Pickup 4D | T63C | 26220 | 8475 | 9150 | 9725 | 13300 |

B9 TRIBECA AWD—H6—Truck Equipment Schedule T1
Sport Utility 4D	X82D	31920	5625	6050	6875	9350
Limited Sport Util	X82D	32910	6425	6925	7800	10700
Third Row Seat			225	225	305	305

2007 SUBARU-(JF1or4S4)(B,SorW)(G636)-7-#

FORESTER AWD—4-Cyl.—Truck Equipment Schedule T1
X Sport Utility 4D	G636	22620	5000	5550	6000	8400
Sports X Spt Util	G636	22320	5025	5575	6050	8450
X LL Bean Spt Util	G676	27320	7625	8450	8725	11900

FORESTER AWD—4-Cyl. Turbo—Truck Equipment Schedule T1
| XT Sports X Spt Util | G696 | 26620 | 7775 | 8625 | 8825 | 11950 |
| XT Limited Spt Util | G696 | 29320 | 9200 | 10200 | 10150 | 13650 |

B9 TRIBECA AWD—H6—Truck Equipment Schedule T1
Sport Utility 4D	X82D	30620	6425	6875	7700	10250
Limited Sport Util	X82D	33120	7650	8175	9200	12350
Third Row Seat			250	250	305	305

2008 SUBARU-(JF1or4S4)(B,SorW)(G636)-8-#

FORESTER AWD—4-Cyl.—Truck Equipment Schedule T1
X Sport Utility 4D	G636	22640	6125	6650	7400	9875
Sports X Spt Util	G666	23140	7275	7875	8475	11100
X LL Bean Spt Util	G676	27340	8850	9575	10200	13350

Body Type	VIN	List	Trade-In Good	Very Good	Pvt-Party Good	Retail Excellent
FORESTER AWD—4-Cyl. Turbo—Truck Equipment Schedule T1						
Sports XT Spt Util	G696	28640	**9450**	**10250**	**10750**	**14100**
XT Limited Spt Util	G696	29540	**10100**	**10950**	**11400**	**14800**
TRIBECA AWD—H6—Truck Equipment Schedule T1						
Sport Utility 4D	X91D	30640	**7225**	**7650**	**8750**	**11200**
Limited Sport Util	X92D	33240	**8500**	**8975**	**10300**	**13400**
Third Row Seat			250	250	305	305

2009 SUBARU—(JF1or4S4)(B,SorW)(G636)-9-#

Body Type	VIN	List	Trade-In Good	Very Good	Pvt-Party Good	Retail Excellent
FORESTER AWD—4-Cyl.—Truck Equipment Schedule T1						
X Sport Utility 4D	G636	20660	**8025**	**8550**	**9450**	**12000**
X Limited Spt Util	G636	26660	**9150**	**9725**	**10700**	**13600**
X LL Bean Spt Util	G676	26660	**9250**	**9825**	**10800**	**13750**
FORESTER AWD—4-Cyl. Turbo—Truck Equipment Schedule T1						
XT Sport Utility 4D	G696	26860	**9550**	**10150**	**11100**	**14150**
XT Limited Spt Util	G696	28860	**10250**	**10900**	**11850**	**15050**
TRIBECA AWD—H6—Truck Equipment Schedule T1						
Sport Utility 4D	X91D	30640	**9475**	**9875**	**10950**	**13300**
Limited Sport Util	X92D	33260	**10700**	**11150**	**12250**	**14900**
Third Row Seat			275	275	325	325

2010 SUBARU—(JF1or4S4)(B,SorW)(H6AC)-A-#

Body Type	VIN	List	Trade-In Good	Very Good	Pvt-Party Good	Retail Excellent
FORESTER AWD—4-Cyl.—Truck Equipment Schedule T1						
2.5X Sport Utility	H6AC	20990	**10250**	**10750**	**11750**	**14250**
2.5X Premium 4D	H6CC	23490	**11050**	**11550**	**12550**	**15150**
2.5X Limited 4D	H6DC	26690	**11850**	**12400**	**13350**	**16100**
FORESTER AWD—4-Cyl. Turbo—Truck Equipment Schedule T1						
2.5XT Premium 4D	H6EC	27190	**11950**	**12450**	**13450**	**16250**
2.5XT Limited 4D	H6FC	29190	**12750**	**13350**	**14400**	**17400**
TRIBECA AWD—H6—Truck Equipment Schedule T1						
3.6R Premium 4D	X9FD	31190	**10350**	**10700**	**12050**	**14350**
3.6R Limited 4D	X9GD	33190	**11700**	**12100**	**13550**	**16050**
3.6R Touring 4D	X9GD	36490	**13500**	**14000**	**15600**	**18500**
Third Row Seat			325	325	380	380

2011 SUBARU—(JF2or4S4)(B,SorW)(SHBAC)-B-#

Body Type	VIN	List	Trade-In Good	Very Good	Pvt-Party Good	Retail Excellent
FORESTER AWD—4-Cyl.—Truck Equipment Schedule T1						
2.5X Sport Utility	SHBAC	22420	**12050**	**12450**	**13650**	**16100**
2.5X Premium Util	HBCC	23920	**12600**	**12950**	**14350**	**16900**
2.5X Limited 4D	HBDC	27720	**13250**	**13650**	**15000**	**17650**
2.5X Touring 4D	HBHC	28720	**13650**	**14100**	**15450**	**18200**
FORESTER AWD—4-Cyl. Turbo—Truck Equipment Schedule T1						
2.5XT Premium Util	HGAC	27720	**13350**	**13800**	**15150**	**17800**
2.5XT Touring 4D	HGGC	30720	**15600**	**16100**	**17350**	**20300**
TRIBECA AWD—H6—Truck Equipment Schedule T1						
3.6R Premium 4D	X9FD	31220	**12650**	**13000**	**14600**	**16850**
3.6R Limited 4D	X9HD	33220	**15150**	**15550**	**17250**	**19850**
3.6R Touring 4D	X9GD	36520	**16350**	**16800**	**18550**	**21400**
Third Row Seat			375	375	445	445

2012 SUBARU—(JF2or4S4)(B,SorW)(SHBAC)-C-#

Body Type	VIN	List	Trade-In Good	Very Good	Pvt-Party Good	Retail Excellent
FORESTER AWD—4-Cyl.—Truck Equipment Schedule T1						
2.5X Sport Utility	SHBAC	22570	**13600**	**13850**	**15400**	**17750**
2.5X Premium Util	HBCC	24070	**14600**	**14900**	**16350**	**18800**
2.5X Limited 4D	HBEC	27370	**15500**	**15850**	**17300**	**19850**
2.5X Touring 4D	HBGC	28670	**16450**	**16800**	**18150**	**20700**
FORESTER AWD—4-Cyl. Turbo—Truck Equipment Schedule T1						
2.5XT Premium 4D	HGAC	27870	**16050**	**16400**	**17700**	**20200**
2.5XT Touring 4D	HGGC	30670	**18250**	**18650**	**20100**	**22900**
TRIBECA AWD—H6—Truck Equipment Schedule T1						
3.6R Premium 4D	X9FD	31370	**16550**	**16900**	**18800**	**21300**
3.6R Limited 4D	X9GD	33370	**17950**	**18350**	**20000**	**22500**
3.6R Touring 4D	X9GD	36670	**19350**	**19750**	**21500**	**24100**
Third Row Seat			425	425	480	480

2013 SUBARU—(JF2or4S4)(B,SorW)(GPABC)-D-#

Body Type	VIN	List	Trade-In Good	Very Good	Pvt-Party Good	Retail Excellent
XV CROSSTREK AWD—4-Cyl.						
Premium Spt Util	GPABC	23790	**15550**	**15850**	**17350**	**19650**
Limited Sport Util	GPAGC	25290	**16450**	**16800**	**18350**	**20800**
FORESTER AWD—4-Cyl.—Truck Equipment Schedule T1						
2.5X Sport Utility	SHAAC	22090	**15400**	**15650**	**17300**	**19700**

Body Type	VIN	List	Trade-In Good	Very Good	Pvt-Party Good	Retail Excellent
2.5X Premium Util	SHADC	25090	16450	16700	18250	20700
2.5X Limited 4D	SHAEC	27790	17400	17650	19150	21600
2.5X Touring 4D	SHAGC	29190	18700	19000	20500	22900
FORESTER AWD—4-Cyl. Turbo—Truck Equipment Schedule T1
2.5XT Premium	SHGAC	28000	18050	18350	19800	22300
2.5XT Touring	SHGGC	30790	20300	20600	22000	24600
TRIBECA AWD—H6—Truck Equipment Schedule T1
3.6R Limited 4D	WX9FD	33390	21100	21500	23300	25800
Third Row Seat			450	450	485	485

Body Type	VIN	List	Good	Very Good	Good	Excellent
XV CROSSTREK AWD—4-Cyl.—Truck Equipment Schedule T1
Premium Spt Util	GPACC	23820	17200	17450	19100	21600
Limited Spt Util	GPACG	25320	17350	17650	19350	21900
XV CROSSTREK AWD—4-Cyl. Hybrid—Truck Equipment Schedule T1
Sport Utility 4D	GPBKC	26820	17550	17850	19500	22000
Touring Sport Util	GPBKC	30120	17350	17650	19250	21800
FORESTER AWD—4-Cyl.—Truck Equipment Schedule T1
2.5i Sport Utility	SJAAC	23820	17750	18000	19650	22200
2.5i Premium Util	SJACC	24320	19000	19250	20800	23200
2.5i Limited 4D	SJAHC	28820	19900	20200	21700	24200
2.5i Touring 4D	SJALC	30820	21600	21900	23200	25800
FORESTER AWD—4-Cyl. Turbo—Truck Equipment Schedule T1
2.0XT Premium 4D	SJGDC	28820	20600	20900	22200	24700
2.0XT Touring 4D	SJGLC	33820	23700	24100	25400	28000
TRIBECA AWD—H6—Truck Equipment Schedule T1
3.6R Ltd Spt Util	WX9FD	34920	25200	25600	27600	30500

SUZUKI

Body Type	VIN	List	Good	Very Good	Good	Excellent
VITARA—4-Cyl.—Truck Equipment Schedule T2
JS Convertible 2D	TC03C	13939	850	1000	1600	2850
JS Hard Top 4D	TE52V	15949	925	1100	1725	3025
JLS Convertible 2D	TC52C	15439	1050	1200	1850	3300
JLS Hard Top 4D	TE52V	16749	1175	1350	2050	3625
VITARA 4WD—4-Cyl.—Truck Equipment Schedule T2
JX Convertible 2D	TA03C	15739	875	1025	1650	2900
JX Hard Top 4D	TD52V	17549	1100	1275	1925	3425
JLX Convertible 2D	TA52C	17239	1175	1350	2050	3625
JLX Hard Top 4D	TD52V	18349	1275	1475	2200	3875
GRAND VITARA—V6—Truck Equipment Schedule T1
JLS Hard Top 4D	TE62V	19749	575	700	1125	2025
Ltd Hard Top 4D	TE62V	22149	1000	1200	1725	3100
GRAND VITARA 4WD—V6—Truck Equipment Schedule T1
JLX Hard Top 4D	TD62V	20749	800	950	1450	2625
Ltd Hard Top 4D	TD62V	23149	1150	1375	1925	3450

Body Type	VIN	List	Good	Very Good	Good	Excellent
VITARA—4-Cyl.—Truck Equipment Schedule T2
JS Convertible 2D	TC03C	14369	1175	1350	1925	3325
JS Hard Top 4D	TE52V	16079	1250	1450	2050	3500
JLS Convertible 2D	TC52C	15869	1175	1350	1925	3325
JLS Hard Top 2D	TE52V	16869	1450	1675	2325	3975
JLS Hard Top 4D	TE52V	17019	1475	1700	2350	4025
VITARA 4WD—4-Cyl.—Truck Equipment Schedule T2
JX Convertible 2D	TA03C	15969	1200	1375	1975	3400
JX Hard Top 4D	TD52V	17579	1400	1625	2250	3850
JLX Convertible 2D	TA52C	17469	1450	1675	2325	3975
JLX Hard Top 2D	TD52V	18469	2575	2900	3500	5675
JLX Hard Top 4D	TD52V	18579	1500	1725	2400	4075
GRAND VITARA—V6—Truck Equipment Schedule T1
JLS Hard Top 4D	TE62V	19879	650	800	1225	2175
Ltd Hard Top 4D	TE62V	22279	1175	1400	1925	3400
GRAND VITARA 4WD—V6—Truck Equipment Schedule T1
JLX Hard Top 4D	TD62V	21079	975	1175	1675	2950
Ltd Hard Top 4D	TD62V	23479	1400	1650	2175	3875
XL-7 4WD—V6—Truck Equipment Schedule T1
Sport Utility 4D	TX92V	21499	800	925	1275	2050
Plus Sport Util 4D	TX92V	23999	925	1050	1475	2475
Touring Spt Utl 4D	TX92V	24999	1150	1300	1750	2900

SEE BACK PAGES FOR TRUCK EQUIPMENT

Body Type	VIN	List	Trade-In Good	Very Good	Pvt-Party Good	Retail Excellent
Limited Spt Utl 4D	TX92V	26499	1425	1600	2050	3375
2WD	Y		(625)	(625)	(820)	(820)

2002 SUZUKI — (Jor2)S3(TC52C)-2-#

VITARA—4-Cyl.—Truck Equipment Schedule T2
Body Type	VIN	List	Good	Very Good	Good	Excellent
JLS Convertible 2D	TC52C	16089	1600	1825	2425	4050
JLS Hard Top 4D	TE52V	17299	1925	2200	2925	4875

VITARA 4WD—4-Cyl.—Truck Equipment Schedule T2
| JLX Convertible 2D | TA52C | 17489 | 1950 | 2225 | 2975 | 4950 |
| JLX Hard Top 4D | TD52V | 18699 | 1950 | 2225 | 2975 | 4950 |

GRAND VITARA—V6—Truck Equipment Schedule T1
| JLS Hard Top 4D | TE62V | 19099 | 900 | 1050 | 1500 | 2650 |
| Ltd Hard Top 4D | TE62V | 22299 | 1525 | 1800 | 2300 | 3950 |

GRAND VITARA 4WD—V6—Truck Equipment Schedule T1
| JLX Hard Top 4D | TD62V | 20299 | 1300 | 1525 | 2000 | 3475 |
| Ltd Hard Top 4D | TD62V | 23499 | 1700 | 2000 | 2600 | 4475 |

XL-7 4WD—V6—Truck Equipment Schedule T1
Sport Utility 4D	TX92V	22319	850	975	1375	2250
Plus Spt Util 4D	TX92V	23819	925	1075	1575	2650
Touring Spt Utl 4D	TX92V	25319	1175	1325	1850	3125
Limited Spt Utl 4D	TX92V	26519	1475	1650	2200	3650
2WD	Y		(700)	(700)	(935)	(935)

2003 SUZUKI — (Jor2)S3(TA52C)-3-#

VITARA 4WD—4-Cyl.—Truck Equipment Schedule T2
Convertible 2D	TA52C	17509	2425	2750	3400	5475
Hard Top 4D	TD52V	18719	2375	2700	3400	5550
2WD	C,E		(425)	(425)	(565)	(565)

GRAND VITARA 4WD—V6—Truck Equipment Schedule T1
| Hard Top 4D | TD62V | 20319 | 1725 | 2025 | 2550 | 4275 |
| 2WD | E | | (425) | (425) | (565) | (565) |

XL-7 4WD—V6—Truck Equipment Schedule T1
Touring Spt Utl 4D	TX92V	22339	1200	1375	1925	3250
Limited Spt Utl 4D	TX92V	25399	1525	1725	2225	3675
Third Row Seat			200	200	260	260
2WD	Y		(775)	(775)	(1040)	(1040)

2004 SUZUKI — (Jor2)S3(TD52V)-4-#

VITARA 4WD—V6—Truck Equipment Schedule T2
| LX Hard Top 4D | TD62V | 17999 | 2725 | 3050 | 3675 | 5750 |
| 2WD | E | | (500) | (500) | (665) | (665) |

GRAND VITARA—V6—Truck Equipment Schedule T1
| LX Hard Top 4D | TE62V | 18999 | 1875 | 2175 | 2725 | 4475 |
| 4WD | D | | 525 | 525 | 705 | 705 |

GRAND VITARA 4WD—V6—Truck Equipment Schedule T1
| EX Hard Top 4D | TD62V | 22499 | 2750 | 3150 | 3900 | 6575 |
| 2WD | E | | (500) | (500) | (665) | (665) |

XL-7 4WD—V6—Truck Equipment Schedule T1
LX Sport Utility 4D	TX92V	22899	2250	2525	3150	5075
EX Sport Utility 4D	TY92V	23699	1600	1800	2350	3850
Third Row Seat			300	300	385	385
2WD	Y		(875)	(875)	(1155)	(1155)

2005 SUZUKI — JS3(TE62V)-5-#

GRAND VITARA—V6—Truck Equipment Schedule T1
| LX Hard Top 4D | TE62V | 19994 | 2175 | 2525 | 3200 | 5075 |
| 4WD | D | | 575 | 575 | 775 | 775 |

GRAND VITARA 4WD—V6—Truck Equipment Schedule T1
| EX Hard Top 4D | TD62V | 23194 | 3125 | 3600 | 4450 | 7175 |
| 2WD | E | | (575) | (575) | (765) | (765) |

XL-7 4WD—V6—Truck Equipment Schedule T1
LX Sport Utility 4D	TX92V	25394	2275	2575	3350	5200
EX Sport Utility 4D	TY92V	24694	1825	2075	2850	4425
Third Row Seat			325	325	420	420
2WD	Y		(950)	(950)	(1260)	(1260)

2006 SUZUKI — JS3(TE944)-6-#

GRAND VITARA—V6—Truck Equipment Schedule T1
| XSport Spt Util 4D | TE944 | 21694 | 2200 | 2550 | 3225 | 5000 |
| 4WD | D | | 625 | 625 | 845 | 845 |

Body Type	VIN	List	Trade-In Good	Very Good	Pvt-Party Good	Retail Excellent

GRAND VITARA 4WD—V6—Truck Equipment Schedule T1
Sport Utility 4D	TD941	21794	2775	3175	3700	5575
Premium Sport Util	TD943	22894	2675	3050	3725	5750
Luxury Sport Util	TD947	25194	3600	4100	4775	7250
2WD	E		(625)	(625)	(845)	(845)

XL-7 4WD—V6—Truck Equipment Schedule T1
Sport Utility 4D	TX92V	25194	3225	3600	4200	6175
Premium Spt Util	TX92V	27294	3650	4100	4800	7025
Third Row Seat			350	350	455	455
2WD	Y		(1025)	(1025)	(1375)	(1375)

2007 SUZUKI — (2orJ)S3(TE944)-7-#

GRAND VITARA—V6—Truck Equipment Schedule T1
| XSport Spt Util 4D | TE944 | 22119 | 3250 | 3675 | 4250 | 6175 |
| 4WD | D | | 975 | 975 | 1310 | 1310 |

GRAND VITARA 4WD—V6—Truck Equipment Schedule T1
Sport Utility 4D	TD941	22519	3575	4050	4500	6425
Luxury Sport Util	TD947	25649	4850	5450	5925	8575
2WD	E		(675)	(675)	(910)	(910)

XL7 4WD—V6—Truck Equipment Schedule T1
Sport Utility 4D	DA217	26584	3500	3900	4650	6750
Special Sport Util	DA117	27999	3550	3950	4725	6850
Luxury Sport Util	DA517	28199	3550	3950	4750	6900
Limited Sport Util	DA717	30199	4250	4725	5450	7850
Third Row Seat			375	375	485	485
2WD	B		(1100)	(1100)	(1480)	(1480)

2008 SUZUKI — (2orJ)S3(TE944)-8-#

GRAND VITARA—V6—Truck Equipment Schedule T1
| XSport Util 4D | TE944 | 22999 | 4250 | 4700 | 5325 | 7350 |
| 4WD | D | | 1075 | 1075 | 1425 | 1425 |

GRAND VITARA 4WD—V6—Truck Equipment Schedule T1
| Sport Utility 4D | TD941 | 23099 | 4225 | 4675 | 5075 | 6800 |
| 2WD | E | | (725) | (725) | (925) | (925) |

XL7—V6—Truck Equipment Schedule T1
| Sport Utility 4D | DB117 | 22294 | 1950 | 2175 | 3050 | 4475 |

XL7 4WD—V6—Truck Equipment Schedule T1
Premium Sport Util	DA217	25499	4050	4450	5300	7400
Luxury Sport Util	DA317	27444	4200	4625	5550	7825
Limited Sport Util	DA717	29844	4700	5175	6100	8575
Third Row Seat			400	400	520	520
2WD	B		(1200)	(1200)	(1595)	(1595)

2009 SUZUKI — (2orJ)S3(TE041)-9-#

GRAND VITARA—4-Cyl.—Truck Equipment Schedule T1
| Sport Utility 4D | TE041 | 20649 | 4500 | 4875 | 5425 | 7100 |

GRAND VITARA 4WD—4-Cyl.—Truck Equipment Schedule T1
| Premium Sport Util | TD041 | 22499 | 5150 | 5600 | 6350 | 8325 |
| 2WD | E | | (825) | (825) | (1045) | (1045) |

GRAND VITARA—4-Cyl.—Truck Equipment Schedule T1
XSport Util 4D	TE144	22799	4600	5000	5650	7475
4WD	D		1150	1150	1475	1475
V6, 3.2 Liter	1,B		550	550	700	700

GRAND VITARA 4WD—V6—Truck Equipment Schedule T1
Luxury Sport Util	TD149	27349	7675	8300	9025	11800
2WD	E		(825)	(825)	(1040)	(1040)
4-Cyl, 2.4 Liter	0,A		(475)	(475)	(580)	(580)

XL7 4WD—V6—Truck Equipment Schedule T1
Sport Utility 4D	DA217	27995	6050	6600	7325	9575
Luxury Sport Util	DA317	29829	6900	7525	8250	10750
Limited Spt Util	DA717	30430	7450	8125	8800	11400
Third Row Seat			450	450	600	600
FWD			(1275)	(1275)	(1700)	(1700)

EQUATOR EXTENDED CAB—4-Cyl.—Truck Equipment Schedule T2
| Short Bed | BD09U | 17995 | 6075 | 6450 | 7175 | 8975 |
| Prem Short Bed | BD09U | 22450 | 8200 | 8675 | 9425 | 11750 |

EQUATOR EXTENDED CAB—V6—Truck Equipment Schedule T2
| Sport Short Bed | AD09U | 23670 | 8750 | 9275 | 10000 | 12450 |
| 4WD | | | 1425 | 1425 | 1765 | 1765 |

EQUATOR CREW CAB—V6—Truck Equipment Schedule T2
| Short Bed | AD07U | 23985 | 8925 | 9450 | 10200 | 12700 |
| Sport Short Bed | AD07U | 25150 | 10500 | 11100 | 11800 | 14700 |

TRUCKS & VANS

Body Type	VIN	List	Trade-In Good	Very Good	Pvt-Party Good	Retail Excellent
Sport Long Bed	AD09U	25500	10250	10850	11550	14400
4WD			1425	1425	1755	1755
EQUATOR CREW CAB 4WD—V6—Truck Equipment Schedule T2						
RMZ Short Bed	AD07W	29325	12650	13400	14100	17550

2010 SUZUKI — (2orJ)S3or5Z6(TE0D1)—A-#

Body Type	VIN	List	Trade-In Good	Very Good	Pvt-Party Good	Retail Excellent
GRAND VITARA—4-Cyl.—Truck Equipment Schedule T1						
Sport Utility 4D	TE0D1	19794	4725	5050	5750	7325
GRAND VITARA 4WD—4-Cyl.—Truck Equipment Schedule T1						
Premium Spt Util	TD0D2	22794	6425	6875	7450	9250
2WD	E		(950)	(950)	(1100)	(1100)
GRAND VITARA 4WD—4-Cyl.—Truck Equipment Schedule T1						
XSport Util 4D	TE1D8	23244	5450	5825	6575	8275
4WD	D		1250	1250	1475	1475
V6, 3.2 Liter			600	600	695	695
GRAND VITARA 4WD—V6—Truck Equipment Schedule T1						
Limited Sport Util	TD1D9	27794	7800	8325	9000	11200
2WD	E		(950)	(950)	(1105)	(1105)
4-Cyl, 2.4 Liter	0		(525)	(525)	(610)	(610)
EQUATOR EXTENDED CAB—4-Cyl.—Truck Equipment Schedule T2						
Pickup 2D 6'	2D0CT	18315	6750	7100	7925	9700
Premium 2D 6'	2D0CT	22870	8850	9300	10250	12500
EQUATOR EXTENDED CAB—V6—Truck Equipment Schedule T2						
Sport 2D 6'	1D0CT	24040	9425	9925	10850	13250
4WD	V		1625	1625	1960	1960
EQUATOR CREW CAB—V6—Truck Equipment Schedule T2						
Sport 4D 5'	1D0EU	25570	11150	11750	12700	15500
Sport 4D 6'	1D0FU	25920	10800	11350	12300	15000
4WD			1625	1625	1955	1955
EQUATOR CREW CAB 4WD—V6—Truck Equipment Schedule T2						
RMZ 4D 5'	1D0FW	29645	13300	13950	14950	18200

2011 SUZUKI — JS3or5Z6(TE0D1)—B-#

Body Type	VIN	List	Trade-In Good	Very Good	Pvt-Party Good	Retail Excellent
GRAND VITARA—4-Cyl.—Truck Equipment Schedule T1						
SVE Sport Util	TE0D1	19794	4900	5175	6000	7500
Sport Utility 4D	TE0D1	19994	5150	5425	6200	7700
GRAND VITARA 4WD—4-Cyl.—Truck Equipment Schedule T1						
Premium Spt Util	TD0D2	23244	7750	8175	8925	10800
Limited Sport Util	TD0D7	25644	9050	9550	10300	12450
2WD	E		(1075)	(1075)	(1215)	(1215)
EQUATOR EXTENDED CAB—4-Cyl.—Truck Equipment Schedule T2						
Pickup 2D 6'	2D0CT	18390	7650	8000	8950	10750
Premium 2D 6'	2D0CT	23174	9750	10200	11200	13400
EQUATOR EXTENDED CAB 4WD—V6—Truck Equipment Schedule T2						
Sport 2D 6'	1D0CV	26574	10300	10800	11750	14050
EQUATOR CREW CAB—V6—Truck Equipment Schedule T2						
Sport 4D 5'	1D0EU	25874	12000	12550	13600	16250
EQUATOR CREW CAB 4WD—V6—Truck Equipment Schedule T2						
Sport 4D 6'	1D0FW	28874	11650	12200	13200	15800
RMZ 4D 5'	1D0EW	29745	14000	14650	15750	18800

2012 SUZUKI — JS3or5Z6(TE0D1)—C-#

Body Type	VIN	List	Trade-In Good	Very Good	Pvt-Party Good	Retail Excellent
GRAND VITARA—4-Cyl.—Truck Equipment Schedule T1						
Sport Utility 4D	TE0D1	20314	5950	6225	7425	9225
Ultimate Advntr	TE0D3	23114	9325	9750	11150	13700
GRAND VITARA 4WD—4-Cyl.—Truck Equipment Schedule T1						
Premium Spt Util	TD0D2	23664	8825	9250	10500	12950
Limited Sport Util	TD0D7	26064	10650	11100	12450	15250
2WD	E		(1500)	(1500)	(1810)	(1810)
EQUATOR EXTENDED CAB—4-Cyl.—Truck Equipment Schedule T2						
Pickup 2D 6'	2D0CT	18714	7850	8200	9325	11200
Comfort 2D 6'	2D0CT	20114	8350	8725	9850	11800
Premium 2D 6'	2D0CT	23614	9900	10350	11550	13750
EQUATOR EXTENDED CAB 4WD—V6—Truck Equipment Schedule T2						
Sport 2D 6'	1D0CW	27114	10650	11100	12400	14750
EQUATOR CREW CAB—V6—Truck Equipment Schedule T2						
Sport 4D 5'	1D0EU	26514	12550	13050	14450	17200
EQUATOR CREW CAB 4WD—V6—Truck Equipment Schedule T2						
Sport 4D 6'	1D0FW	29514	12150	12650	13950	16600
RMZ 4D 5'	1D0EW	30365	15050	15700	17100	20300

Body Type	VIN	List	Trade-In Good	Very Good	Pvt-Party Good	Retail Excellent
2013 SUZUKI — JS3or5Z6(TE0D5)–D–#						
GRAND VITARA—4-Cyl.—Truck Equipment Schedule T1						
Sport Utility 4D	TE0D5	20799	7350	7650	8900	10850
GRAND VITARA 4WD—4-Cyl.—Truck Equipment Schedule T1						
Premium Spt Utl	TD0D6	24649	10000	10400	11750	14200
Limited Sport Util	TD0D7	26799	11750	12200	13600	16400
2WD	E	......	(1500)	(1500)	(1695)	(1695)

TOYOTA

Body Type	VIN	List	Trade-In Good	Very Good	Pvt-Party Good	Retail Excellent
2000 TOYOTA–(4,5orJ)T(3,AorB)(HP10V)–Y–#						
RAV4 4WD—4-Cyl.—Truck Equipment Schedule T2						
Sport Utility 4D	HP10V	18558	1675	1850	2375	3800
2WD	G,X	......	(325)	(325)	(445)	(445)
4RUNNER 4WD—4-Cyl.—Truck Equipment Schedule T1						
Sport Utility 4D	HM84R	26046	2425	2700	3050	4600
2WD	G	......	(525)	(525)	(715)	(715)
4RUNNER 4WD—V6—Truck Equipment Schedule T1						
SR5 Sport Util 4D	HN86R	29786	3250	3575	3950	5925
Limited Spt Ut 4D	HN87R	36948	3825	4225	4700	7050
2WD	G	......	(525)	(525)	(715)	(715)
LAND CRUISER 4WD—V8—Truck Equipment Schedule T3						
Sport Utility 4D	HT05J	51308	6375	6775	7900	11000
Third Row Seat		......	225	225	285	285
SIENNA—V6—Truck Equipment Schedule T1						
CE Minivan	ZF19C	23338	1325	1475	1950	3125
LE Minivan	ZF13C	25378	1650	1825	2300	3700
XLE Minivan	ZF13C	27414	2075	2275	2875	4600
Second Sliding Door		......	50	50	60	60
TACOMA—4-Cyl.—Truck Equipment Schedule T2						
Short Bed	NL42N	12208	1925	2125	2575	3975
Xtra Cab	VL52N	14458	2825	3100	3525	5425
PreRunner Short	NM92N	14298	2775	3050	3475	5350
PreRunner Xtra	SM92N	17418	3575	3925	4325	6625
4WD		......	400	400	535	535
V6, 3.4 Liter	N	......	100	100	130	130
TACOMA 4WD—V6—Truck Equipment Schedule T2						
Limited Xtra Cab	WN74N	24758	4425	4850	5250	7875
TUNDRA—V6—Truck Equipment Schedule T2						
Long Bed	JN321	15475	1050	1250	1925	3525
TUNDRA 4WD—V8—Truck Equipment Schedule T2						
SR5 Long Bed	KT441	23190	2350	2750	3350	5750
V6, 3.4 Liter	N	......	(300)	(300)	(405)	(405)
TUNDRA—V8—Truck Equipment Schedule T2						
SR5 Access Cab 4D	RT341	22730	2950	3425	3975	6675
Ltd Access Cab 4D	RT381	24975	3550	4125	4625	7700
4WD	4	......	625	625	820	820
V6, 3.4 Liter	N	......	(300)	(300)	(405)	(405)
2001 TOYOTA–(4,5orJ)T(3,B,DorE)(HH20V)–1–#						
RAV4 4WD—4-Cyl.—Truck Equipment Schedule T1						
Sport Utility 4D	HH20V	19175	2850	3125	3500	5225
2WD	G	......	(375)	(375)	(510)	(510)
HIGHLANDER—V6—Truck Equipment Schedule T1						
Sport Utility 4D	GF21A	25605	3225	3425	3975	5475
AWD	H	......	575	575	775	775
4-Cyl, 2.4 Liter	D	......	(225)	(225)	(285)	(285)
HIGHLANDER 4WD—V6—Truck Equipment Schedule T1						
Limited Spt Util 4D	HF21A	30445	4000	4250	4925	6725
2WD	G	......	(625)	(625)	(820)	(820)
4-Cyl, 2.4 Liter	D	......	(225)	(225)	(285)	(285)
4RUNNER 4WD—V6—Truck Equipment Schedule T1						
SR5 Sport Util 4D	HN86R	29375	3725	4100	4475	6550
Limited Spt Ut 4D	HN87R	38085	4450	4875	5250	7675
2WD	G	......	(625)	(625)	(820)	(820)
SEQUOIA—V8—Truck Equipment Schedule T1						
SR5 Spt Util 4D	ZT34A	31330	2625	2925	3100	4650
4WD	B,4	......	575	575	775	775
SEQUOIA 4WD—V8—Truck Equipment Schedule T1						
Limited Sport Util 4D	BT48A	42755	3475	3900	4125	6300

TRUCKS & VANS

Body Type	VIN	List	Trade-In Good	Very Good	Pvt-Party Good	Retail Excellent
2WD			(625)	(625)	(820)	(820)
LAND CRUISER 4WD—V8—Truck Equipment Schedule T3						
Sport Utility 4D	HT05J	53375	7575	8025	9150	12500
Third Row Seat			250	250	335	335
SIENNA—V6—Truck Equipment Schedule T1						
CE Minivan	ZF19C	24385	1550	1700	2275	3675
LE Minivan	ZF13C	26235	1800	1975	2625	4250
XLE Minivan	ZF13C	28916	2250	2500	3200	5150
TACOMA—4-Cyl.—Truck Equipment Schedule T2						
Short Bed	NL42N	12325	2150	2375	2775	4250
Xtra Cab	VL52N	14965	3175	3475	3875	5850
PreRunner Short	NM92N	14215	3050	3350	3725	5650
PreRunner Xtra	SM92N	16815	3850	4225	4700	7075
PreRunner 4D	GM92N	18335	5500	5925	6750	9500
PreRunner Ltd 4D	GM92N	22690	6300	6800	7625	10750
4WD			400	400	530	530
V6, 3.4 Liter	N		100	100	130	130
TACOMA—V6—Truck Equipment Schedule T2						
S-Runner Xtra Cab	VN52N	18385	3275	3600	3975	6000
TACOMA 4WD—V6—Truck Equipment Schedule T2						
Limited Xtra Cab	WN74N	24895	5150	5625	5875	8600
Double Cab 4D	HN72N	22345	6900	7425	7825	10600
Ltd Double Cab 4D	HN72N	25840	7150	7700	8150	11100
4-Cyl, 2.7 Liter	M		(225)	(225)	(285)	(285)
TUNDRA—V6—Truck Equipment Schedule T2						
Long Bed	JN321	16085	1075	1250	1950	3550
TUNDRA 4WD—V6—Truck Equipment Schedule T2						
SR5 Long Bed	KT441	23885	2350	2725	3375	5775
TUNDRA—V6—Truck Equipment Schedule T2						
SR5 Access Cab 4D	RT341	23455	3200	3700	4250	7075
Ltd Access Cab 4D	RT381	26205	3725	4325	4850	7925
4WD	4		725	725	955	955
V6, 3.4 Liter	N		(325)	(325)	(435)	(435)

2002 TOYOTA—(4,5orJ)T(3,B,DorE)(HH20V)-2-#

Body Type	VIN	List	Trade-In Good	Very Good	Pvt-Party Good	Retail Excellent
RAV4 4WD—4-Cyl.—Truck Equipment Schedule T2						
Sport Utility 4D	HH20V	19485	3150	3450	3900	5850
2WD	G		(425)	(425)	(575)	(575)
HIGHLANDER—V6—Truck Equipment Schedule T1						
Sport Utility 4D	GF21A	25970	3775	4000	4800	6650
Limited Spt Utl 4D	GF21A	29905	4500	4750	5575	7675
AWD	H		675	675	900	900
4-Cyl, 2.4 Liter	D		(250)	(250)	(345)	(345)
4RUNNER 4WD—V6—Truck Equipment Schedule T1						
SR5 Sport Util 4D	HN86R	29385	4225	4625	4925	7050
Limited Spt Ut 4D	HN87R	36615	5050	5525	5775	8275
2WD	G		(700)	(700)	(935)	(935)
SEQUOIA—V8—Truck Equipment Schedule T1						
SR5 Spt Util 4D	ZT34A	31780	3525	3925	4125	6175
4WD	B,4		675	675	900	900
SEQUOIA 4WD—V8—Truck Equipment Schedule T1						
Limited Spt Util 4D	BT48A	43235	4450	4950	5325	8075
2WD	Z		(700)	(700)	(935)	(935)
LAND CRUISER 4WD—V8—Truck Equipment Schedule T3						
Sport Utility 4D	HT05J	53105	8550	9050	10250	13950
SIENNA—V6—Truck Equipment Schedule T1						
CE Minivan	ZF19C	24415	1825	2000	2650	4225
LE Minivan	ZF13C	26265	2200	2425	3075	4900
XLE Minivan	ZF13C	28522	2700	2950	3650	5750
TACOMA—4-Cyl.—Truck Equipment Schedule T2						
Short Bed	NL42N	12410	2425	2675	3100	4700
Xtra Cab	VL52N	15050	3625	3975	4375	6575
PreRunner Short	NM92N	14400	3550	3900	4300	6450
PreRunner Xtra	SM92N	17000	4275	4700	5175	7750
PreRunner 4D	GM92N	18620	6975	7500	7950	10750
4WD			500	500	665	665
V6, 3.4 Liter	N		150	150	200	200
TACOMA—V6—Truck Equipment Schedule T2						
S-Runner Xtra Cab	VN52N	18570	3625	3975	4475	6725
PreRunner Ltd 4D	GM92N	23000	7825	8425	8950	12100
TACOMA 4WD—V6—Truck Equipment Schedule T2						
Limited Xtra Cab	WN72N	23655	5875	6425	6675	9575
Double Cab 4D	HN72N	22630	7925	8500	9025	12200

Body Type	VIN	List	Trade-In Good	Very Good	Pvt-Party Good	Retail Excellent
Ltd Double Cab 4D	HN72N	26150	8675	9325	9925	13550
TUNDRA—V6—Truck Equipment Schedule T2						
Long Bed	JN321	16115	2125	2475	2900	4750
TUNDRA 4WD—V8—Truck Equipment Schedule T2						
SR5 Long Bed	KT441	23915	3550	4050	4375	6975
TUNDRA—V8—Truck Equipment Schedule T2						
SR5 Access Cab 4D	RT341	23485	4250	4875	5225	8300
Ltd Access Cab 4D	RT381	27230	5050	5775	5925	9200
4WD	4		850	850	1135	1135
V6, 3.4 Liter	N		(350)	(350)	(465)	(465)

2003 TOYOTA—(4,5orJ)T(B,DorE)(HH20V)—3—#

Body Type	VIN	List	Trade-In Good	Very Good	Pvt-Party Good	Retail Excellent
RAV4 4WD—4-Cyl.—Truck Equipment Schedule T2						
Sport Utility 4D	HH20V	19515	3625	3950	4475	6650
2WD	G		(475)	(475)	(645)	(645)
HIGHLANDER—V6—Truck Equipment Schedule T1						
Sport Utility 4D	GF21A	26000	4125	4375	5350	7475
Limited Spt Utl 4D	GF21A	29935	4950	5225	6225	8600
AWD	H		775	775	1020	1020
4-Cyl, 2.4 Liter	D		(300)	(300)	(405)	(405)
4RUNNER 4WD—V6—Truck Equipment Schedule T1						
SR5 Sport Util 4D	BU14R	29990	5625	6150	6550	9275
Sport SUV 4D	BU14R	31785	6225	6800	7200	10200
Limited Spt Ut 4D	BU17R	36190	6925	7550	7900	11150
2WD	Z		(775)	(775)	(1040)	(1040)
V8, 4.7 Liter	T		200	200	250	250
SEQUOIA—V8—Truck Equipment Schedule T1						
SR5 Spt Util 4D	ZT34A	32170	3900	4325	4700	7000
4WD	B,4		775	775	1020	1020
SEQUOIA 4WD—V8—Truck Equipment Schedule T1						
Limited Spt Util 4D	BT48A	44030	4900	5450	5850	8750
2WD	Z		(775)	(775)	(1040)	(1040)
LAND CRUISER 4WD—V8—Truck Equipment Schedule T3						
Sport Utility 4D	HT05J	53915	11600	12250	13150	17200
SIENNA—V6—Truck Equipment Schedule T1						
CE Minivan	ZF19C	24415	2100	2300	2900	4500
LE Minivan	ZF13C	26265	2525	2750	3350	5175
XLE Minivan	ZF13C	28522	3175	3475	4075	6250
TACOMA PICKUP—4-Cyl.—Truck Equipment Schedule T2						
Short Bed	NL42N	12610	2775	3025	3475	5225
Xtra Cab	VL52N	15250	3925	4275	4825	7150
PreRunner Short	NM92N	14525	3775	4125	4650	6925
PreRunner Xtra	SM92N	17200	5000	5450	5950	8775
PreRunner 4D	GM92N	18820	7600	8125	8600	11450
4WD	P		625	625	820	820
V6, 3.4 Liter	N		225	225	300	300
TACOMA PICKUP—V6—Truck Equipment Schedule T2						
PreRunner Ltd 4D	GN92N	23430	8550	9150	9600	12750
TACOMA PICKUP 4WD—V6—Truck Equipment Schedule T2						
Limited Xtra Cab	WN72N	24085	6750	7375	7700	11050
Double Cab 4D	HN72N	22830	9025	9650	10100	13500
Ltd Double Cab 4D	HN72N	26580	9525	10200	10800	14500
TUNDRA—V6—Truck Equipment Schedule T2						
Long Bed	JN321	17308	2925	3325	3550	5475
TUNDRA 4WD—V8—Truck Equipment Schedule T2						
SR5 Long Bed	KT441	24265	4225	4825	5000	7675
TUNDRA—V8—Truck Equipment Schedule T2						
SR5 Access Cab 4D	RT341	23865	5125	5850	6000	9200
Ltd Access Cab 4D	RT381	27465	5725	6525	6650	10050
4WD	B,4		1025	1025	1380	1380
V6, 3.4 Liter	N		(375)	(375)	(495)	(495)

2004 TOYOTA—(5orJ)T(B,DorE)(HD20V)—4—#

Body Type	VIN	List	Trade-In Good	Very Good	Pvt-Party Good	Retail Excellent
RAV4 4WD—4-Cyl.—Truck Equipment Schedule T2						
Sport Utility 4D	HD20V	19940	4550	4925	5625	8250
2WD	G		(525)	(525)	(710)	(710)
HIGHLANDER—V6—Truck Equipment Schedule T1						
Sport Utility 4D	GP21A	25680	4750	5000	6000	8275
Limited Spt Utl 4D	GP21A	30520	5550	5850	7075	9700
Third Row Seat			300	300	385	385
AWD	E,H		850	850	1135	1135
4-Cyl, 2.4 Liter	D		(350)	(350)	(465)	(465)

TRUCKS & VANS

Body Type	VIN	List	Trade-In Good	Very Good	Pvt-Party Good	Retail Excellent
4RUNNER 4WD—V6—Truck Equipment Schedule T1						
SR5 Sport Util 4D	BU14R	29985	6700	7275	7700	10800
Sport SUV 4D	BU14R	31225	7300	7925	8325	11650
Limited Spt Util	BU17R	36260	8350	9050	9400	13050
Third Row Seat			200	200	275	275
2WD	Z		(875)	(875)	(1155)	(1155)
V8, 4.7 Liter	T		200	200	265	265
SEQUOIA—V8—Truck Equipment Schedule T1						
SR5 Spt Util 4D	ZT34A	32170	4675	5150	5450	7950
4WD	B,4		850	850	1135	1135
SEQUOIA 4WD—V8—Truck Equipment Schedule T1						
Limited Spt Util 4D	BT48A	44760	6550	7225	7650	11150
2WD	Z		(875)	(875)	(1155)	(1155)
LAND CRUISER 4WD—V8—Truck Equipment Schedule T3						
Sport Utility 4D	HT05J	54765	12750	13400	14200	18250
SIENNA—V6—Truck Equipment Schedule T1						
CE Minivan	ZA23C	23495	3325	3600	4175	6300
LE Minivan	ZA23C	24800	3650	3975	4675	7025
XLE Minivan	ZA22C	28800	4750	5175	5950	8925
XLE Limited	ZA22C	35020	5275	5750	6650	10100
AWD	B		375	375	510	510
TACOMA PICKUP—4-Cyl.—Truck Equipment Schedule T2						
Short Bed	NL42N	12800	3800	4150	4675	6825
Xtra Cab	VL52N	15460	5425	5900	6575	9575
PreRunner Short	NM92N	14715	5075	5525	5850	8325
PreRunner Xtra	SM92N	17410	6800	7400	7925	11400
PreRunner 4D	GM92N	19030	8575	9150	9450	12250
4WD	W,H		750	750	970	970
V6, 3.4 Liter	N		300	300	385	385
TACOMA PICKUP—V6—Truck Equipment Schedule T2						
S-Runner Xtra Cab	VN52N	20700	5850	6350	6925	10000
PreRunner Ltd 4D	GN92N	23640	8975	9575	9975	13050
TACOMA PICKUP 4WD—V6—Truck Equipment Schedule T2						
Limited Xtra Cab	WN72N	24295	9550	10350	10800	15300
Double Cab 4D	HN72N	23040	10400	11100	11450	14950
Ltd Double Cab 4D	HN72N	26790	10900	11600	11900	15550
TUNDRA—V6—Truck Equipment Schedule T2						
Long Bed	JN321	17335	4225	4775	4675	6750
TUNDRA 4WD—V8—Truck Equipment Schedule T2						
SR5 Long Bed	KT441	24415	5375	6075	5925	8650
TUNDRA—V8—Truck Equipment Schedule T2						
SR5 Access Cab 4D	RN341	23995	5550	6300	6175	8875
Ltd Access Cab 4D	ET381	27615	7075	7975	7825	11400
SR5 Double Cab 4D	ET341	26185	6875	7750	7500	10850
Ltd Double Cab 4D	BT481	33140	10800	12200	11500	16450
4WD	B,4		1175	1175	1535	1535
V6, 3.4 Liter	N		(400)	(400)	(520)	(520)
2005 TOYOTA—(5orJ)T(B,DorE)(HD20V)—5-#						
RAV4 4WD—4-Cyl.—Truck Equipment Schedule T2						
Sport Utility 4D	HD20V	21565	5200	5625	6225	8575
2WD	G		(575)	(575)	(755)	(755)
HIGHLANDER—V6—Truck Equipment Schedule T1						
Sport Utility 4D	GP21A	25705	5200	5475	6675	8825
Limited Spt Util 4D	DP21A	30545	6150	6500	7725	10200
Third Row Seat			325	325	420	420
AWD	E,H		925	925	1245	1245
4-Cyl, 2.4 Liter	D		(400)	(400)	(520)	(520)
4RUNNER 4WD—V6—Truck Equipment Schedule T1						
SR5 Sport Util 4D	BU14R	30335	7425	8050	8625	11700
Sport SUV 4D	BU14R	31605	8325	9000	9550	12950
Limited Spt Util	BU17R	36610	8775	9475	10100	13700
Third Row Seat			225	225	285	285
2WD	Z		(950)	(950)	(1230)	(1230)
V8, 4.7 Liter	T		200	200	275	275
SEQUOIA—V8—Truck Equipment Schedule T1						
SR5 Spt Util 4D	ZT34A	33035	6300	6925	7350	10300
4WD	B,4		925	925	1185	1185
SEQUOIA 4WD—V8—Truck Equipment Schedule T1						
Limited Spt Util 4D	BT48A	45525	8400	9225	9600	13450
2WD	Z		(950)	(950)	(1215)	(1215)
LAND CRUISER 4WD—V8—Truck Equipment Schedule T3						
Sport Utility 4D	HT05J	55590	14500	15200	16250	20500

TRUCKS & VANS

Body Type	VIN	List	Trade-In Good	Very Good	Pvt-Party Good	Retail Excellent
SIENNA—V6—Truck Equipment Schedule T1						
CE Minivan	ZA23C	23790	3700	4025	4775	6950
LE Minivan	ZA23C	25295	4225	4600	5325	7725
XLE Minivan	ZA22C	29590	5400	5875	6775	9825
XLE Limited	ZA22C	35860	6725	7300	8475	12500
AWD	B		425	425	575	575
TACOMA PICKUP—4-Cyl.—Truck Equipment Schedule T2						
Short Bed	NX22N	14880	5200	5650	6100	8425
Access Cab	UX42N	17925	8350	9050	9500	13100
PreRunner Short	NX62N	14850	5850	6350	6900	9550
4WD	P4		875	875	1135	1135
V6, 4.0 Liter	U		375	375	485	485
TACOMA PICKUP—V6—Truck Equipment Schedule T2						
PreRunner Access	TU62N	20515	9575	10350	10650	14550
4-Cyl, 2.7 Liter	M		(1625)	(1625)	(2115)	(2115)
TACOMA PICKUP—V6—Truck Equipment Schedule T2						
X-Runner Access	TU22N	23650	10050	10900	11050	14950
PreRunner Dbl 5'	JU62N	22240	9075	9650	10250	13150
PreRunner Dbl 6'	KU72N	22740	8975	9550	10150	13000
TACOMA PICKUP 4WD—V6—Truck Equipment Schedule T2						
Double Cab 5'	LU42N	22240	11800	12550	12800	16100
Double Cab 6'	MU52N	25815	11900	12650	13050	16600
TUNDRA—V6—Truck Equipment Schedule T2						
Long Bed	JU321	17360	3725	4200	4575	6625
TUNDRA—V8—Truck Equipment Schedule T2						
Work Truck Long	JT321	18995	4225	4750	4925	6975
SR5 Access Cab 4D	RT341	24700	6850	7700	7675	10800
Ltd Access Cab 4D	RT381	27640	6900	7750	7875	11250
SR5 Double Cab 4D	ET341	26685	8225	9250	9100	12800
Ltd Double Cab 4D	DT481	33640	11300	12700	12300	17250
4WD	4		1275	1275	1665	1665
V6, 4.0 Liter	T		(425)	(425)	(545)	(545)

Body Type	VIN	List	Trade-In Good	Very Good	Pvt-Party Good	Retail Excellent
RAV4 4WD—4-Cyl.—Truck Equipment Schedule T1						
SUV 4D	BD33V	22345	6150	6625	7350	9925
Sport SUV 4D	BD32V	23920	6825	7350	8150	11000
Limited SUV 4D	BD31V	24600	7450	8000	8825	12000
Third Row Seat			225	225	295	295
2WD	Z		(625)	(625)	(800)	(800)
V6, 3.5 Liter	K		575	575	715	715
HIGHLANDER—V6—Truck Equipment Schedule T1						
SUV 4D	GP21A	26235	5975	6275	7375	9475
Limited SUV 4D	DP21A	31105	7675	8075	9350	12050
Third Row Seat			350	350	450	450
AWD	E,H		1025	1025	1340	1340
4-Cyl, 2.4 Liter	D		(425)	(425)	(570)	(570)
HIGHLANDER 4WD—V6—Truck Equipment Schedule T1						
Sport SUV 4D	HD21A	29840	7175	7550	8825	11400
Limited SUV 4D	DP21A	31105	7675	8075	9350	12050
2WD	D,G		(1025)	(1025)	(1365)	(1365)
4-Cyl, 2.4 Liter	D		(425)	(425)	(575)	(575)
HIGHLANDER 4WD—V6 Hybrid—Truck Equipment Sch T1						
SUV 4D	EW21A	34995	5700	6000	7475	10000
Limited SUV 4D	EW21A	39855	7250	7625	9225	12400
Third Row Seat			350	350	455	455
2WD	D,G		(1025)	(1025)	(1375)	(1375)
4RUNNER 4WD—V6—Truck Equipment Schedule T1						
SR5 Sport Util 4D	BU14R	30475	9150	9825	10350	13700
Sport SUV 4D	BU14R	32815	10150	10900	11300	14950
Limited Spt Util 4D	BU17R	37190	10850	11650	12000	15750
Third Row Seat			225	225	290	290
2WD	Z		(1025)	(1025)	(1280)	(1280)
V8, 4.7 Liter	T		225	225	275	275
SEQUOIA—V8—Truck Equipment Schedule T1						
SR5 Spt Util 4D	ZT34A	33465	8075	8825	9000	12150
4WD	B,4		1025	1025	1250	1250
SEQUOIA 4WD—V8—Truck Equipment Schedule T1						
Limited Spt Util 4D	BT48A	45875	10200	11150	11300	15350
2WD	Z		(1025)	(1025)	(1275)	(1275)
LAND CRUISER AWD—V8—Truck Equipment Schedule T3						
Sport Utility 4D	HT05J	56680	16300	17100	18100	22600

Body Type	VIN	List	Trade-In Good	Very Good	Pvt-Party Good	Retail Excellent
SIENNA—V6—Truck Equipment Schedule T1						
CE Minivan	ZA23C	24190	4725	5100	5775	8200
LE Minivan	ZA23C	25695	5200	5600	6275	8875
XLE Minivan	ZA22C	29990	7275	7875	8800	12400
XLE Limited	ZA22C	36445	7950	8600	9675	13800
AWD	B		475	475	645	645
TACOMA PICKUP—4-Cyl.—Truck Equipment Schedule T1						
Short Bed	NX22N	15325	5400	5850	6525	8975
4WD	P,4		975	975	1245	1245
TACOMA PICKUP—4-Cyl.—Truck Equipment Schedule T2						
PreRunner Short	NX62N	15215	6100	6600	7250	10000
TACOMA PICKUP 4WD—4-Cyl.—Truck Equipment Schedule T2						
Access Cab	UX42N	21660	10050	10800	11100	14850
2WD	T,2		(1075)	(1075)	(1365)	(1365)
V6, 4.0 Liter	U		450	450	565	565
TACOMA PICKUP—V6—Truck Equipment Schedule T1						
PreRunner Access	TU62N	20920	10550	11400	11600	15550
4-Cyl, 2.7 Liter	X		(1725)	(1725)	(2200)	(2200)
TACOMA PICKUP—V6—Truck Equipment Schedule T2						
X-Runner Access	TU22N	24110	11100	12000	12200	16300
PreRunner Dbl 5'	JU62N	22605	11000	11650	12200	15350
PreRunner Dbl 6'	KU72N	23105	10900	11550	12050	15100
TACOMA PICKUP 4WD—V6—Truck Equipment Schedule T1						
Double Cab 5'	LU42N	25760	13650	14450	14750	18150
TACOMA PICKUP 4WD—V6—Truck Equipment Schedule T2						
Double Cab 6'	MU52N	26180	13300	14100	14600	18200
TUNDRA—V6—Truck Equipment Schedule T1						
Long Bed	JU321	17640	4475	5000	5350	7550
TUNDRA—V8—Truck Equipment Schedule T1						
SR5 Access Cab 4D	RT341	24957	7825	8725	8925	12500
4WD	B,4		1500	1500	1915	1915
V6, 4.0 Liter	U		(450)	(450)	(565)	(565)
TUNDRA—V8—Truck Equipment Schedule T2						
Work Truck Long	JT321	19195	4975	5550	5825	8175
Ltd Access Cab 4D	RT381	27820	7900	8800	8875	12350
SR5 Double Cab 4D	ET341	27185	9125	10150	10100	14000
Darrell Waltrip Ed.	ET341	30260	9275	10300	10400	14550
4WD	4		1500	1500	1935	1935
TUNDRA 4WD—V8—Truck Equipment Schedule T2						
Ltd Double Cab 4D	DT481	34220	12400	13750	13500	18750
2WD	E,3		(2000)	(2000)	(2555)	(2555)

Body Type	VIN	List	Trade-In Good	Very Good	Pvt-Party Good	Retail Excellent
RAV4 4WD—4-Cyl.—Truck Equipment Schedule T2						
SUV 4D	BD33V	22855	6600	7050	7875	10450
Sport SUV 4D	BD32V	24470	7700	8225	9100	12050
Limited SUV 4D	BD31V	25110	8150	8700	9600	12800
Third Row Seat			250	250	305	305
2WD	Z		(675)	(675)	(850)	(850)
V6, 3.5 Liter	K		600	600	760	760
FJ CRUISER 4WD—V6—Truck Equipment Schedule T1						
Sport Utility 2D	BU11F	24150	13400	14200	14700	17600
TRD Special Edition			1100	1100	1250	1250
2WD	Z		(1100)	(1100)	(1270)	(1270)
HIGHLANDER—V6—Truck Equipment Schedule T1						
SUV 4D	GP21A	26585	6925	7275	8625	11050
Limited SUV 4D	DP21A	31455	9325	9750	11300	14450
Third Row Seat			375	375	485	485
AWD	E		1100	1100	1470	1470
4-Cyl, 2.4 Liter	D		(475)	(475)	(620)	(620)
HIGHLANDER 4WD—V6—Truck Equipment Schedule T1						
Sport SUV 4D	HD21A	30190	8850	9250	10700	13750
Third Row Seat			375	375	485	485
2WD	D,G		(1100)	(1100)	(1480)	(1480)
HIGHLANDER 4WD—V6 Hybrid—Truck Equipment Schedule T1						
Sport Utility 4D	EW21A	34495	7875	8250	9625	12300
Limited Utility 4D	EW21A	36615	8675	9125	10550	13700
Third Row Seat			375	375	480	480
2WD	D,G		(1100)	(1100)	(1455)	(1455)
4RUNNER 4WD—V6—Truck Equipment Schedule T1						
SR5 Sport Util 4D	BU14R	30515	10500	11200	11650	15000
Sport SUV 4D	BU14R	32855	10950	11650	12200	15700
Limited Spt Util	BU17R	37230	12000	12800	13250	17050

TRUCKS & VANS

Body Type	VIN	List	Trade-In Good	Very Good	Pvt-Party Good	Retail Excellent
Third Row Seat			250	250	295	295
2WD	Z		(1100)	(1100)	(1340)	(1340)
V8, 4.7 Liter	T		225	225	280	280
SEQUOIA—V8—Truck Equipment Schedule T1						
SR5 Spt Util 4D	ZT34A	33805	9425	10200	10550	13950
4WD	B,4		1100	1100	1335	1335
SEQUOIA 4WD—V8—Truck Equipment Schedule T1						
Limited Spt Util 4D	BT48A	46265	12500	13550	13700	18100
2WD			(1100)	(1100)	(1340)	(1340)
LAND CRUISER AWD—V8—Truck Equipment Schedule T3						
Sport Utility 4D	HT05J	56820	18950	19800	20700	25300
SIENNA—V6—Truck Equipment Schedule T1						
CE Minivan	ZK23C	24800	5325	5725	6475	8875
LE Minivan	ZK23C	26325	5850	6300	7025	9600
XLE Minivan	ZK22C	30770	8175	8775	9650	13250
XLE Limited	ZK22C	36110	8900	9575	10550	14550
AWD	B		525	525	685	685
TACOMA PICKUP—4-Cyl.—Truck Equipment Schedule T1						
Short Bed	NX22N	15665	5975	6450	7125	9625
4WD	P,4		1075	1075	1365	1365
TACOMA PICKUP—4-Cyl.—Truck Equipment Schedule T2						
PreRunner Short	NX62N	15555	6650	7150	7900	10700
TACOMA PICKUP 4WD—4-Cyl.—Truck Equipment Schedule T2						
Access Cab	TX22N	21960	10950	11750	12050	15950
2WD	T		(1625)	(1625)	(2020)	(2020)
V6, 4.0 Liter	U		525	525	655	655
TACOMA PICKUP—V6—Truck Equipment Schedule T2						
PreRunner Access	TX62N	21220	11450	12250	12550	16500
4-cyl, 2.7 Liter	X		(1825)	(1825)	(2320)	(2320)
TACOMA PICKUP 4WD—V6—Truck Equipment Schedule T2						
X-Runner Access	TU22N	24450	11950	12800	13100	17200
PreRunner Dbl 5'	JU62N	22945	12150	12800	13400	16600
PreRunner Dbl 6'	KU72N	23445	11950	12550	13200	16300
TACOMA PICKUP 4WD—V6—Truck Equipment Schedule T1						
Double Cab 5'	LU42N	26100	15100	15900	16200	19700
TACOMA PICKUP 4WD—V6—Truck Equipment Schedule T2						
Double Cab 6'	MU52N	26520	14850	15600	16100	19700
TUNDRA PICKUP—V8—Equipment Schedule T1						
Short Bed	JT521	24075	8425	9275	9250	12300
Long Bed	LT521	24405	8125	8950	8950	11900
SR5 Double 6 1/2'	RT541	27495	11300	12450	12200	16300
SR5 Double 8'	ST541	27825	10800	11850	11700	15500
SR5 CrewMax 4D	ET541	42535	13900	15250	14850	19750
4WD	M		1875	1875	2265	2265
V6, 4.0 Liter	U		(475)	(475)	(565)	(565)
V8, 4.7 Liter	T		(475)	(475)	(565)	(565)
TUNDRA PICKUP 4WD—V8—Equipment Schedule T1						
Ltd Double Cab 4D	DV581	39235	17150	18850	18050	24000
Limited CrewMax 4D	BV581	38185	19750	21700	20400	26900
2WD	E		(2175)	(2175)	(2585)	(2585)
V8, 4.7 Liter	T		(475)	(475)	(555)	(555)

Body Type	VIN	List	Trade-In Good	Very Good	Pvt-Party Good	Retail Excellent
RAV4 4WD—4-Cyl.—Truck Equipment Schedule T2						
SUV 4D	BD33V	23185	7425	7825	8875	11300
Sport SUV 4D	BD32V	24760	8275	8725	9725	12350
Limited SUV 4D	BD31V	25440	8950	9450	10500	13350
Third Row Seat			250	250	310	310
2WD	Z		(725)	(725)	(910)	(910)
V6, 3.5 Liter	K		650	650	815	815
FJ CRUISER 4WD—V6—Truck Equipment Schedule T1						
Sport Utility 2D	BU11F	24820	15750	16500	16950	19750
2WD	Z		(1200)	(1200)	(1340)	(1340)
HIGHLANDER AWD—V6—Truck Equipment Schedule T1						
SUV 4D	ES41A	29435	11100	11600	13050	16100
Sport SUV 4D	ES43A	32085	12800	13300	15000	18650
Limited SUV 4D	ES42A	34835	14600	15200	17100	21200
Third Row Seat			400	400	490	490
2WD	D		(1200)	(1200)	(1500)	(1500)
HIGHLANDER AWD—V6 Hybrid—Truck Equipment Schedule T1						
SUV 4D	EW41A	34385	10850	11300	13000	16250
Limited SUV 4D	EW44A	40635	13050	13650	15300	19350
Third Row Seat			400	400	500	500

TRUCKS & VANS

Body Type	VIN	List	Trade-In Good	Very Good	Pvt-Party Good	Retail Excellent
4RUNNER 4WD—V6—Truck Equipment Schedule T1						
SR5 SUV 4D	BU14R	30975	13100	13850	14500	17800
Sport SUV 4D	BU14R	31010	13700	14450	15100	18550
Limited SUV 4D	BU17R	35385	14700	15500	16150	19900
Third Row Seat			250	250	285	285
2WD	Z		(1200)	(1200)	(1365)	(1365)
V8, 4.7 Liter	T		250	250	280	280
SEQUOIA 4WD—V8—Truck Equipment Schedule T1						
SR5 Spt Util 4D	BT44A	39185	15350	16350	16350	20300
Limited Spt Util 4D	BY68A	49135	18250	19500	19300	24000
Platinum Spt Util	BY67A	56285	23500	25000	24300	29900
2WD	Z		(1200)	(1200)	(1405)	(1405)
LAND CRUISER 4WD—V8—Truck Equipment Schedule T3						
Sport Utility 4D	HY05J	63885	30800	32000	32100	37300
SIENNA—V6—Truck Equipment Schedule T1						
CE Minivan	ZK23C	25025	6025	6450	7300	9700
LE Minivan	ZK23C	26550	6775	7225	8100	10750
XLE Minivan	ZK22C	30210	9150	9750	10800	14400
XLE Limited	ZK22C	36150	10450	11100	12150	16150
AWD	B		550	550	695	695
TACOMA PICKUP—4-Cyl.—Truck Equipment Schedule T1						
Short Bed	NX22N	15980	6800	7275	8025	10500
4WD	P4		1225	1225	1555	1555
TACOMA PICKUP—4-Cyl.—Truck Equipment Schedule T2						
PreRunner Short	NX62N	15835	7350	7850	8725	11450
TACOMA PICKUP 4WD—4-Cyl.—Truck Equipment Schedule T2						
Access Cab	UX42N	22240	12050	12850	13300	16950
2WD	T,2		(1650)	(1650)	(2030)	(2030)
V6, 4.0 Liter	U		575	575	720	720
TACOMA PICKUP—V6—Truck Equipment Schedule T1						
PreRunner Access	TU62N	21500	12750	13600	14000	17850
4-Cyl, 2.7 Liter	X		(1925)	(1925)	(2420)	(2420)
TACOMA PICKUP—V6—Truck Equipment Schedule T2						
X-Runner Access	TU22N	24730	12950	13800	14400	18450
PreRunner Dbl 5'	JU62N	23225	13200	13800	14900	18050
PreRunner Dbl 6'	KU72N	23725	13000	13550	14750	17950
TACOMA PICKUP 4WD—V6—Truck Equipment Schedule T1						
Double Cab 5'	LU42N	26415	16150	16850	17550	20900
TACOMA PICKUP 4WD—V6—Truck Equipment Schedule T2						
Double Cab 6'	MU52N	26800	15800	16500	17300	20600
TUNDRA PICKUP—V8—Truck Equipment Schedule T1						
Short Bed	JT521	24115	9975	10750	10900	13800
Long Bed	LT521	24445	9575	10300	10550	13350
Double 6 1/2'	RU541	25545	11800	12750	12850	16300
SR5 Double 6 1/2'	RT541	27535	12900	13900	14000	17750
SR5 Double 8'	ST541	27865	12400	13350	13400	17000
SR5 CrewMax 4D	ET541	30360	15800	17000	16850	21300
4WD	K,M		2125	2125	2530	2530
V6, 4.0 Liter	U		(500)	(500)	(580)	(580)
V8, 4.7 Liter	T		(500)	(500)	(580)	(580)
TUNDRA PICKUP 4WD—V8—Truck Equipment Schedule T1						
Double 8'	CV541	29910	14300	15400	15400	19500
Ltd Double Cab 4D	BV581	39570	19450	20900	20600	26200
CrewMax 4D	DV541	32735	18650	20100	19600	24600
Limited CrewMax	DV581	42870	21600	23200	22700	28700
2WD	E		(2400)	(2400)	(2790)	(2790)
V8, 4.7 Liter	T		(500)	(500)	(580)	(580)

Body Type	VIN	List	Trade-In Good	Very Good	Pvt-Party Good	Retail Excellent
RAV4 4WD—4-Cyl.—Truck Equipment Schedule T2						
SUV 4D	BF33V	23585	9275	9700	10800	13200
Sport SUV 4D	BF32V	25160	10200	10650	11800	14400
Limited SUV 4D	BF31V	25840	11100	11600	12800	15600
Third Row Seat	Z		275	275	335	335
2WD	Z		(825)	(825)	(985)	(985)
V6, 3.5 Liter	K		700	700	825	825
FJ CRUISER 4WD—V6—Truck Equipment Schedule T1						
Sport Utility 2D	BU11F	25710	18250	19050	19550	22300
2WD	Z		(1275)	(1275)	(1405)	(1405)
VENZA—4-Cyl.—Truck Equipment Schedule T1						
Sport Utility 4D	ZE11A	28145	11300	11950	12500	15350
AWD	B		625	625	725	725
V6, 3.5 Liter	K		700	700	820	820

Body Type	VIN	List	Trade-In Good	Very Good	Pvt-Party Good	Retail Excellent
HIGHLANDER AWD—V6—Truck Equipment Schedule T1						
SUV 4D	ES41A	29795	13200	13650	15050	17750
Sport SUV 4D	ES43A	14550	14550	15050	16650	19900
Limited SUV 4D	ES42A	35265	16700	17300	19000	22700
Third Row Seat			450	450	540	540
2WD	D		(1275)	(1275)	(1530)	(1530)
4-Cyl, 2.7 Liter			(575)	(575)	(680)	(680)
HIGHLANDER AWD—V6 Hybrid—Truck Equipment Schedule T1						
SUV 4D	EW41A	35445	12950	13450	15200	18350
Limited SUV 4D	EW44A	41765	15350	15950	17650	21600
Third Row Seat			450	450	550	550
4RUNNER 4WD—V6—Truck Equipment Schedule T1						
SR5 SUV 4D	BU14R	31660	16300	17000	17700	20900
Sport SUV 4D	BU14R	33970	16300	17000	17750	21000
Limited SUV 4D	BU17R	38345	17550	18300	19050	22600
Third Row Seat			275	275	315	315
2WD	Z		(1275)	(1275)	(1415)	(1415)
V8, 4.7 Liter	T		275	275	315	315
SEQUOIA 4WD—V8—Truck Equipment Schedule T1						
SR5 Spt Util 4D	BT44A	39445	16700	17650	18100	21900
Limited Spt Util 4D	BY68A	49395	21300	22500	22500	27000
Platinum Spt Util	BY67A	56545	25600	27000	26900	32300
2WD	Z		(1275)	(1275)	(1480)	(1480)
LAND CRUISER 4WD—V8—Truck Equipment Schedule T3						
Sport Utility 4D	HY05J	65440	32800	34000	34600	39700
SIENNA—V6—Truck Equipment Schedule T1						
CE Minivan	ZK23C	25225	7700	8150	9075	11600
LE Minivan	ZK23C	26750	8475	8950	9850	12550
XLE Minivan	ZK22C	30410	11500	12150	13250	16950
XLE Limited	ZK22C	36350	12700	13400	14650	18750
AWD	B		625	625	765	765
TACOMA PICKUP—4-Cyl.—Truck Equipment Schedule T1						
Short Bed	NX22N	16870	8025	8500	9350	11750
4WD	P4		1425	1425	1730	1730
TACOMA PICKUP—4-Cyl.—Truck Equipment Schedule T2						
PreRunner Short	NX62N	16800	8750	9250	10150	12850
TACOMA PICKUP 4WD—4-Cyl.—Truck Equipment Schedule T2						
Access Cab	UX42N	23840	12750	13500	14300	17750
2WD	T,2		(2200)	(2200)	(2640)	(2640)
V6, 4.0 Liter	U		675	675	800	800
TACOMA PICKUP—V6—Truck Equipment Schedule T1						
PreRunner Access	TX62N	23100	13550	14300	15050	18650
4-Cyl, 2.7 Liter	X		(2050)	(2050)	(2445)	(2445)
TACOMA PICKUP—V6—Truck Equipment Schedule T2						
X-Runner Access	TU22N	26030	14100	14900	15700	19600
PreRunner Dbl 5'	JU62N	24245	15050	15600	16850	19750
PreRunner Dbl 6'	KU72N	24745	14850	15400	16700	19650
TACOMA PICKUP 4WD—V6—Truck Equipment Schedule T1						
Double Cab 5'	LU42N	27375	17950	18600	19600	22800
TACOMA PICKUP 4WD—V6—Truck Equipment Schedule T1						
Double Cab 6'	MU52N	27820	17550	18150	19200	22300
TUNDRA PICKUP—V8—Truck Equipment Schedule T1						
Short Bed	JT521	24375	10100	10700	11450	14200
Long Bed	LT521	24705	9625	10200	11000	13650
Double 6 1/2'	RU541	25835	12350	13050	13750	17000
SR5 Double 6 1/2'	RT541	27795	13500	14300	15050	18600
SR5 CrewMax 4D	EV541	30620	18650	19700	20300	25100
4WD	M		2475	2475	2945	2945
V6, 4.0 Liter	U		(550)	(550)	(655)	(655)
V8, 4.7 Liter	T		(500)	(500)	(595)	(595)
TUNDRA PICKUP 4WD—V8—Truck Equipment Schedule T1						
Double 8'	CV541	30240	15100	16000	16650	20600
Ltd Double Cab 4D	BV581	39870	21000	22200	22500	27600
CrewMax 4D	DV541	35085	20200	21400	21600	26200
Limited CrewMax	DV581	42405	23700	25100	25300	30900
2WD	E		(2600)	(2600)	(3000)	(3000)
V8, 4.7 Liter	T		(500)	(500)	(595)	(595)

2010 TOYOTA—(3,4,5orJ)T(D,E,ForM)(BF4DV)—A—#

Body Type	VIN	List	Trade-In Good	Very Good	Pvt-Party Good	Retail Excellent
RAV4 4WD—4-Cyl.—Truck Equipment Schedule T2						
SUV 4D	BF4DV	23700	10450	10800	12250	14600
Sport SUV 4D	RF4DV	25400	11600	12000	13500	16050
Limited SUV 4D	DF4DV	26680	12550	13000	14500	17250

TRUCKS & VANS

Body Type	VIN	List	Trade-In Good	Very Good	Pvt-Party Good	Retail Excellent
Third Row Seat			325	325	385	385
2WD	Z		(950)	(950)	(1105)	(1105)
V6, 3.5 Liter	K		750	750	855	855
FJ CRUISER 4WD—V6—Truck Equipment Schedule T1						
Sport Utility 2D	BU4BF	26070	21300	22100	22700	25300
2WD			(1350)	(1350)	(1480)	(1480)
X-SP Pkg			625	625	665	665
Trail Team Special Ed			1125	1125	1225	1225
VENZA—4-Cyl.—Truck Equipment Schedule T1						
Sport Utility 4D	ZE11A	28475	12050	12550	13500	16100
AWD	B		700	700	825	825
V6, 3.5 Liter	K		750	750	875	875
HIGHLANDER AWD—V6—Truck Equipment Schedule T1						
SUV 4D	BK3EH	29850	14800	15250	16750	19450
Sport SUV 4D	EK3EH	32250	16700	17200	18800	21900
SE SUV 4D	BK3EH	34730	16950	17500	19100	22300
Limited SUV 4D	DK3EH	35320	18800	19400	21100	24500
Third Row Seat			525	525	600	600
2WD	X,Y,Z		(1350)	(1350)	(1560)	(1560)
4-Cyl, 2.7 Liter	A		(675)	(675)	(765)	(765)
HIGHLANDER AWD—V6 Hybrid—Truck Equipment Schedule T1						
SUV 4D	BW3EH	35500	14500	15000	16800	19850
Limited SUV 4D	JW3EH	41820	18900	19600	21300	25300
Third Row Seat			525	525	630	630
4RUNNER 4WD—V6—Truck Equipment Schedule T1						
SR5 Spt Util 4D	BU5JR	31715	21800	22500	23200	26300
Trail Sport Util	BU5JR	36500	22500	23300	23900	27200
Limited Spt Util	BU5JR	40600	24000	24800	25500	28900
Third Row Seat			325	325	360	360
2WD	Z		(1350)	(1350)	(1475)	(1475)
4-Cyl, 2.7 Liter	X		(675)	(675)	(725)	(725)
SEQUOIA 4WD—V8—Truck Equipment Schedule T1						
SR5 Spt Util 4D	BY5G1	43180	19850	20800	21300	24900
Limited Spt Util	JY5G1	52665	24700	25900	26200	30500
Platinum Spt Util	DY5G1	59705	28600	29900	30100	35000
2WD	K,Y,Z		(1350)	(1350)	(1535)	(1535)
LAND CRUISER 4WD—V8—Truck Equipment Schedule T3						
Sport Utility 4D	HY7AJ	66770	36300	37500	38200	43000
SIENNA—V6—Truck Equipment Schedule T1						
CE Minivan	KK4CC	25340	9600	10100	11200	13950
LE Minivan	KK4CC	26865	10400	10900	12000	14950
XLE Minivan	YK4CC	30525	14000	14700	16050	19950
XLE Limited	YK4CC	36465	15250	16050	17300	21500
AWD	J		700	700	850	850
TACOMA PICKUP—4-Cyl.—Truck Equipment Schedule T1						
Short Bed	NX4CN	16880	9150	9625	10550	12950
4WD	U,E		1625	1625	1905	1905
TACOMA PICKUP—4-Cyl.—Truck Equipment Schedule T2						
PreRunner Short	NX4GN	16855	9975	10500	11500	14150
TACOMA PICKUP 4WD—4-Cyl.—Truck Equipment Schedule T2						
Access Cab	UX4EN	23840	14100	14800	15800	19200
2WD	T,C		(2200)	(2200)	(2560)	(2560)
V6, 4.0 Liter	U		775	775	890	890
TACOMA PICKUP—V6—Truck Equipment Schedule T1						
PreRunner Access	TU4GN	23100	14650	15350	16300	19700
4-Cyl, 2.7 Liter	X		(2150)	(2150)	(2495)	(2495)
TACOMA PICKUP—V6—Truck Equipment Schedule T2						
X-Runner Access	TU4CN	26085	15250	16050	17500	20800
PreRunner Dbl 5'	JU4GN	24300	17400	17950	19400	22300
PreRunner Dbl 6'	KU4HN	24800	17000	17500	19000	21800
TACOMA PICKUP 4WD—V6—Truck Equipment Schedule T1						
Double Cab 5'	LI4EN	27385	20200	20800	22200	25400
TACOMA PICKUP 4WD—V6—Truck Equipment Schedule T2						
Double Cab 6'	LX4CN	27875	19450	20000	21400	24500
TUNDRA PICKUP—V8—Truck Equipment Schedule T1						
Short Bed	JM5F1	25155	13300	13900	14850	17650
Long Bed	LM5F1	25485	12700	13300	14300	17000
Double Cab 6 1/2'	RM5F1	27890	15800	16500	17400	20600
4WD	M		2725	2725	3135	3135
V6, 4.0 Liter	U		(625)	(625)	(715)	(715)
V8, 4.6 Liter	M		(500)	(500)	(575)	(575)
TUNDRA PICKUP 4WD—V8—Truck Equipment Schedule T1						
Double Cab 8'	CY5F1	30800	19550	20400	21200	25000

Body Type	VIN	List	Trade-In Good	Trade-In Very Good	Pvt-Party Good	Retail Excellent
Ltd Double Cab 4D	BY5F1	40430	23500	24500	25300	30000
CrewMax 4D 5 1/2'	DY5F1	33625	22500	23500	23900	28000
Limited 4D 5 1/2'	HY5F1	42965	25600	26700	27500	32600
2WD	E		(2775)	(2775)	(3110)	(3110)
V8, 4.6 Liter	M		(500)	(500)	(570)	(570)

TRUCKS & VANS

2011 TOYOTA—(2,3,4,5orJ)T(3,D,E,ForM)(BF4DV)—B—#

RAV4 4WD—4-Cyl.—Truck Equipment Schedule T2

Body Type	VIN	List	Good	Very Good	Good	Excellent
SUV 4D	BF4DV	24135	11800	12150	13800	16150
Sport SUV 4D	RF4DV	25835	13150	13500	15300	17850
Limited SUV 4D	DF4DV	27115	14250	14650	16500	19250
Third Row Seat			375	375	445	445
2WD	Z,K		(1075)	(1075)	(1250)	(1250)
V6, 3.5 Liter	K		775	775	920	920

FJ CRUISER 4WD—V6—Truck Equipment Schedule T1

Sport Utility 2D	BU4BF	27690	23200	24000	24600	27200
2WD	Z		(1450)	(1450)	(1570)	(1570)

VENZA—4-Cyl.—Truck Equipment Schedule T1

Sport Utility 4D	BA3B3B	28685	13000	13450	14800	17200
AWD	B		775	775	900	900
V6, 3.5 Liter	K		775	775	910	910

HIGHLANDER AWD—V6—Truck Equipment Schedule T1

Sport Utility 4D	BK3EH	30805	17850	18400	19800	22500
SE Spt Utl 4D	BK3EH	35410	19300	19850	21300	24100
Limited Spt Utl	DK3EH	37155	22300	23000	24500	27800
Third Row Seat			575	575	655	655
2WD	Y,Z		(1450)	(1450)	(1620)	(1620)
4-Cyl, 2.7 Liter	A		(775)	(775)	(865)	(865)

HIGHLANDER AWD—V6 Hybrid—Truck Equipment Schedule T1

Sport Utility 4D	BC3EH	38100	19150	19700	22000	25800
Limited Spt Utl	DC3EH	43755	23600	24400	26300	30800
Third Row Seat			575	575	675	675

4RUNNER 4WD—V6—Truck Equipment Schedule T1

SR5 Spt Util 4D	BU5J2	31/?25	23500	24100	25100	27900
Trail Sport Util	BU5JR	36510	25100	25800	26900	29900
Limited Sport Util	BU5JR	40610	25800	26500	27500	30700
Third Row Seat			375	375	415	415
2WD	Z		(1450)	(1450)	(1565)	(1565)

SEQUOIA 4WD—V8—Truck Equipment Schedule T1

SR5 Spt Util 4D	BY5G1	44405	24400	25400	26000	29500
Limited Spt Util	JY5G1	50580	30500	31700	32300	36700
Platinum Spt Util	DY5G1	60930	33400	34700	35100	39900
2WD	Z		(1450)	(1450)	(1615)	(1615)
V8, 4.6 Liter	M		375	375	430	430

LAND CRUISER 4WD—V8—Truck Equipment Schedule T3

Sport Utility 4D	HY7AJ	68180	39200	40300	41500	46300

SIENNA—4-Cyl.—Truck Equipment Schedule T1

Minivan 4D	KA3DC	25870	12250	12800	13750	16500

SIENNA—V6—Truck Equipment Schedule T1

CE Minivan 4D	ZK3DC	26310	13050	13650	14650	17450
SE Minivan 4D	XK3DC	31360	17550	18350	19450	23300
LE Minivan 4D	KK3DC	29710	13900	14550	15600	18700
XLE Minivan 4D	YK3DC	32975	17650	18450	19700	23700
Limited Minivan	YK3DC	39310	19550	20500	21500	25700
AWD	J		775	775	920	920
4-Cyl, 2.7 Liter	A		(950)	(950)	(1140)	(1140)

TACOMA PICKUP—4-Cyl.—Truck Equipment Schedule T1

Short Bed	NX4CN	18075	10650	11150	12150	14550
4WD	E,P		1825	1825	2100	2100

TACOMA PICKUP—4-Cyl.—Truck Equipment Schedule T2

PreRunner Dbl 5'	JU4GN	24760	18900	19350	21100	23900
4WD	E,P		1825	1825	2100	2100

TACOMA PICKUP 4WD—4-Cyl.—Truck Equipment Schedule T2

Access Cab	UX4EN	24300	15700	16450	17550	20900
2WD	C,T		(2800)	(2800)	(3170)	(3170)
V6, 4.0 Liter	U		875	875	980	980

TACOMA PICKUP 4WD—V6—Truck Equipment Schedule T2

Double Cab 5'	LU4EN	26735	21800	22300	23900	26900
2WD	C,J		(2500)	(2500)	(2865)	(2865)
4-Cyl, 2.7 Liter	X		(2250)	(2250)	(2580)	(2580)

TACOMA PICKUP—V6—Truck Equipment Schedule T2

PreRunner Access	TU4GN	23560	16200	16900	17950	21400
4-Cyl, 2.7 Liter	X		(2250)	(2250)	(2540)	(2540)

Body Type	VIN	List	Trade-In Good	Very Good	Pvt-Party Good	Retail Excellent
TACOMA PICKUP—V6—Truck Equipment Schedule T2						
X-Runner Access	TU4CN	26535	16950	17700	18800	22400
PreRunner Dbl 6'	KU4HN	25260	18150	18600	20300	23000
TACOMA PICKUP 4WD—V6—Truck Equipment Schedule T2						
Double Cab 6'	MU4FN	28335	21000	21500	22300	26100
TUNDRA PICKUP—V8—Truck Equipment Schedule T1						
Short Bed	JM5F1	26110	14700	15200	16450	19000
Long Bed	LY5F1	27385	14150	14600	15900	18400
Double Cab 6 1/2'	RY5F1	28640	17600	18150	19450	22400
4WD	K		2925	2925	3320	3320
V6, 4.0 Liter	U		(700)	(700)	(790)	(790)
V8, 4.6 Liter	M		(500)	(500)	(565)	(565)
TUNDRA PICKUP 4WD—V8—Truck Equipment Schedule T1						
Double Cab 8'	CY5F1	31525	20800	21500	22800	26300
Limited Dbl Cab	BY5F1	40730	25500	26300	27700	31900
CrewMax 4D	DY5F1	34350	23700	24400	25500	29200
Limited CrewMax	HY5F1	43265	27100	27900	29300	33800
2WD	F		(2950)	(2950)	(3320)	(3320)
V8, 4.6 Liter	M		(500)	(500)	(550)	(550)

Body Type	VIN	List	Trade-In Good	Very Good	Pvt-Party Good	Retail Excellent
RAV4 4WD—4-Cyl.—Truck Equipment Schedule T2						
SUV 4D	BF4DV	24860	12700	13000	14950	17200
Sport SUV 4D	RF4DV	26560	15150	15500	17600	20200
Limited SUV 4D	DF4DV	27530	15800	16150	18300	21100
Third Row Seat			425	425	490	490
2WD	K,Z		(1500)	(1500)	(1770)	(1770)
V6, 3.5 Liter	K		800	800	945	945
RAV4—AC—Equipment Schedule T2						
EV SUV 4D	YL4DV	50610	21000	21400	24000	27700
FJ CRUISER 4WD—V6—Truck Equipment Schedule T1						
Sport Utility 2D	BU4BF	28390	26300	27100	27800	30400
2WD	Z		(1525)	(1525)	(1635)	(1635)
VENZA—4-Cyl.—Truck Equipment Schedule T1						
LE Wagon 4D	ZA3BB	29635	13900	14200	15950	18400
XLE Wagon 4D	ZA3BB	31985	15600	15950	17800	20500
AWD	B		850	850	985	985
V6, 3.5 Liter	K		800	800	925	925
HIGHLANDER AWD—V6—Truck Equipment Schedule T1						
Sport Utility 4D	BK3EH	31505	20100	20700	22100	24700
SE Spt Util 4D	BK3EH	36110	21100	21700	23100	25900
Limited Spt Util	DK3EH	37855	24400	25000	26600	29800
2WD	Y,Z		(1525)	(1525)	(1690)	(1690)
4-Cyl, 2.7 Liter	A		(875)	(875)	(960)	(960)
HIGHLANDER AWD—V6 Hybrid—Truck Equipment Schedule T1						
Sport Utility 4D	BC3EH	38950	21800	22400	24000	27100
Limited Spt Util	DC3EH	44605	26000	26800	28600	32700
4RUNNER 4WD—V6—Truck Equipment Schedule T1						
SR5 Sport Util 4D	BU5JR	33640	24900	25400	26900	29700
Trail Sport Util	BU5JR	37565	26600	27100	28700	31700
Limited Sport Util	BU5JR	41440	28600	29200	30800	34000
2WD			(1525)	(1525)	(1665)	(1665)
SEQUOIA 4WD—V8—Truck Equipment Schedule T1						
SR5 Spt Util 4D	BY5G1	45765	27400	28300	29300	32900
Limited Spt Util	JY5G1	55250	33400	34500	35500	39900
Platinum Spt Util	DY5G1	62790	36700	38000	38800	43500
2WD	Z		(1525)	(1525)	(1705)	(1705)
V8, 4.6 Liter	M		475	475	540	540
SIENNA—4-Cyl.—Truck Equipment Schedule T1						
Minivan 4D	KA3DC	25870	14150	14750	15850	18650
V6, 3.5 Liter	K		575	575	660	660
SIENNA 4WD—V6—Truck Equipment Schedule T1						
LE Minivan 4D	KK3DC	30510	15750	16450	17500	20600
SE Minivan 4D	XK3DC	34250	19550	20400	21500	25300
XLE Minivan 4D	YK3DC	36967	19650	20500	21700	25700
Limited Minivan	YK3DC	40110	21700	22600	23800	28000
AWD	J		850	850	1015	1015
4-Cyl, 2.7 Liter	A		(1025)	(1025)	(1215)	(1215)
TACOMA PICKUP—4-Cyl.—Truck Equipment Schedule T1						
Pickup 2D 6'	NX4CN	18585	11700	12200	13150	15400
4WD			2100	2100	2430	2430
TACOMA PICKUP 4WD—4-Cyl.—Truck Equipment Schedule T2						
Access Cab 4D 6'	UX4EN	24310	17050	17750	18950	22300

2012 TOYOTA

Body Type	VIN	List	Trade-In Good	Very Good	Pvt-Party Good	Retail Excellent
2WD	C,T	....	(3000)	(3000)	(3425)	(3425)
V6, 4.0 Liter	U	....	975	975	1105	1105
TACOMA PICKUP—V6—Truck Equipment Schedule T2
PreRunner Access	TU4GN	23570	17900	18650	19750	23100
4-Cyl, 2.7 Liter	X	....	(2350)	(2350)	(2685)	(2685)
TACOMA PICKUP—V6—Truck Equipment Schedule T2
X-Runner Access	TU4CN	27190	19550	20300	21400	25100
PreRunner Dbl 6'	TU4GN	25570	19650	20100	22100	24900
TACOMA PICKUP—V6—Truck Equipment Schedule T2
PreRunner Dbl 5'	JU4GN	25070	20400	20800	22800	25600
4-Cyl, 2.7 Liter	X	....	(2350)	(2350)	(2720)	(2720)
TACOMA PICKUP 4WD—V6—Truck Equipment Schedule T1
Double Cab 4D 5'	LU4EN	28645	23100	23500	25500	28400
TACOMA PICKUP 4WD—V6—Truck Equipment Schedule T2
Double Cab 4D 6'	MU4FN	28645	22600	23000	24900	27800
TUNDRA PICKUP—V8—Truck Equipment Schedule T1
Short Bed	JM5F1	27340	17350	17750	19200	21700
Long Bed	LY5F1	28615	16600	16950	18500	21000
Double Cab 6 1/2'	RM5F1	29490	19650	20100	21600	24500
SR5			150	150	155	155
Sport Appearance			150	150	155	155
TRD Off-Road Pkg			150	150	155	155
4WD	C,U	....	3125	3125	3475	3475
V6, 4.0 Liter	U	....	(775)	(775)	(860)	(860)
V8, 4.6 Liter	M	....	(500)	(500)	(555)	(555)
TUNDRA PICKUP 4WD—V8—Truck Equipment Schedule T1
Double Cab 8'	CY5F1	32365	22700	23200	24800	28100
Limited Dbl Cab	BY5F1	41620	28100	28800	30500	34400
CrewMax 4D	DY5F1	35190	26900	27500	28900	32500
Limited CrewMax	HY5F1	44155	29900	30600	32500	36800
2WD	E	....	(3150)	(3150)	(3440)	(3440)
V8, 4.6 Liter	M	....	(500)	(500)	(545)	(545)

2013 TOYOTA—(3,4,5orJ)T(3,D,E,ForM)(BFREV)-D-#

Body Type	VIN	List	Good	Very Good	Good	Excellent
RAV4 AWD—4-Cyl.—Truck Equipment Schedule T2
LE SUV 4D	BFREV	25545	15900	16200	18100	20300
XLE SUV 4D	RFREV	26535	17800	18100	20000	22300
Limited SUV 4D	DFREV	29255	19350	19700	21700	24300
2WD	Z	....	(1500)	(1500)	(1690)	(1690)
RAV4—AC Electric—Truck Equipment Schedule T2
EV SUV 4D	YL4DV	50645	24300	24800	27500	31200
FJ CRUISER 4WD—V6—Truck Equipment Schedule T1
Sport Utility 2D	BU4BF	29315	27400	28200	29100	31700
2WD	Z	....	(1600)	(1600)	(1720)	(1720)
VENZA—4-Cyl.—Truck Equipment Schedule T1
LE Wagon 4D	ZA3BB	28510	15150	15400	17650	20300
XLE Wagon 4D	ZA3BB	32170	18550	18900	21000	23800
AWD	B	....	925	925	1095	1095
V6, 3.5 Liter	K	....	800	800	920	920
VENZA—V6—Truck Equipment Schedule T1
Limited Wagon 4D	ZK3BB	38230	20600	21000	23200	26400
AWD	B	....	925	925	1060	1060
HIGHLANDER AWD—V6—Truck Equipment Schedule T1
Sport Utility 4D	BK3EH	32540	22000	22600	24500	27700
Plus Sport Util 4D	BK3EH	33995	22400	23000	24900	28100
SE Sport Utility	BK3EH	36705	24500	25100	27200	30600
Limited Sport Util	DK3EH	40095	27200	27900	29800	33500
2WD	Z	....	(1600)	(1600)	(1820)	(1820)
4-Cyl, 2.7 Liter	A	....	(975)	(975)	(1095)	(1095)
HIGHLANDER AWD—V6 Hybrid—Truck Equipment Schedule T1
Sport Utility 4D	BC3EH	40815	23800	24400	26200	29300
Limited Spt Util	DC3EH	47015	28700	29400	31100	34700
4RUNNER 4WD—V6—Truck Equipment Schedule T1
SR5 Sport Utility	BU5JR	34060	26300	26800	28600	31500
Trail Sport Utility	BU5JR	37850	28100	28600	30400	33400
Limited Sport Util	BU5JR	41725	30400	30900	32900	36100
2WD	Z	....	(1600)	(1600)	(1775)	(1775)
SEQUOIA 4WD—V8—Truck Equipment Schedule T1
SR5 Sport Util 4D	BY5G1	46175	30300	31200	32400	36000
Limited Sport Util	JY5G1	55660	37200	38300	39500	43900
Platinum Spt Util	DY5G1	63565	40600	41800	42700	47300
2WD	Z	....	(1600)	(1600)	(1785)	(1785)

SEE BACK PAGES FOR TRUCK EQUIPMENT

Body Type	VIN	List	Trade-In Good	Very Good	Pvt-Party Good	Retail Excellent
SIENNA—V6—Truck Equipment Schedule T1						
L Minivan 4D	ZK3DC	27280	15350	16000	17050	19850
LE Minivan 4D	KK3DC	30830	17250	17950	19000	22100
SE Minivan 4D	XK3DC	34420	21800	22600	23700	27500
XLE Minivan 4D	YK3DC	34205	22300	23100	24300	28300
Limited Minivan 4D	YK3DC	40800	23900	24800	26100	30300
AWD	J	......	925	925	1075	1075
LAND CRUISER 4WD—V8—Truck Equipment Schedule T3						
Sport Utility 4D	HY7AJ	78940	50300	51600	53000	57900
TACOMA PICKUP—4-Cyl.—Truck Equipment Schedule T1						
Pickup 2D 6'	NX4CN	19270	12850	13350	14600	17000
4WD	P	......	2400	2400	2895	2895
TACOMA PICKUP 4WD—4-Cyl.—Truck Equipment Schedule T2						
Access Cab 4D 6'	UX4EN	24995	18400	19100	20500	24000
2WD	T	......	(3000)	(3000)	(3440)	(3440)
V6, 4.0 Liter	U	......	1075	1075	1225	1225
TACOMA PICKUP—V6—Truck Equipment Schedule T2						
PreRunner Access	TU4GN	24255	18750	19500	20900	24500
4-Cyl, 2.7 Liter	X	......	(2450)	(2450)	(2815)	(2815)
TACOMA PICKUP—V6—Truck Equipment Schedule T2						
X-Runner Access	TU4CN	27520	20800	21600	23000	26900
PreRunner Dbl 6'	KU4HN	25855	20800	21200	23200	25900
Limited Pkg		......	450	450	510	510
TACOMA PICKUP—V6—Truck Equipment Schedule T2						
PreRunner Dbl 5'	JU4GN	25355	21700	22100	24200	26900
Limited Pkg		......	450	450	505	505
4-Cyl, 2.7 Liter	X	......	(2450)	(2450)	(2825)	(2825)
TACOMA PICKUP 4WD—V6—Truck Equipment Schedule T1						
Double Cab 4D 5'	LU4EN	28430	24400	24900	27100	30000
Limited Pkg		......	450	450	500	500
2WD	J	......	(2725)	(2725)	(3090)	(3090)
4-Cyl, 2.7 Liter	X	......	(2450)	(2450)	(2785)	(2785)
TACOMA PICKUP 4WD—V6—Truck Equipment Schedule T1						
Double Cab 4D 6'	MU4FN	28930	24400	24900	26900	29800
Limited Pkg		......	450	450	500	500
TUNDRA PICKUP—V8—Truck Equipment Schedule T1						
Short Bed	JU5F1	27550	19050	19400	21500	24300
Long Bed	LY5F1	28825	18800	19100	21100	23800
Double Cab 6 1/2'	RY5F1	29950	21600	22000	24100	27300
4WD	U	......	3275	3275	3720	3720
V6, 4.0 Liter	U	......	(850)	(850)	(970)	(970)
V8, 4.6 Liter	M	......	(500)	(500)	(570)	(570)
TUNDRA PICKUP 4WD—V8—Truck Equipment Schedule T1						
Double Cab 8'	CY5F1	33990	24900	25400	27500	31000
Limited Dbl Cab	BY5F1	42255	30700	31300	33600	37600
CrewMax 4D	DY5F1	35825	29300	29800	32000	35900
Limited CrewMax	HY5F1	44790	32200	32800	35100	39300
2WD	T	......	(3275)	(3275)	(3725)	(3725)
V8, 4.6 Liter	M	......	(500)	(500)	(560)	(560)

Body Type	VIN	List	Trade-In Good	Very Good	Pvt-Party Good	Retail Excellent
RAV4 AWD—4-Cyl.—Truck Equipment Schedule T1						
LE Sport Utility	ZFREV	25810	18200	18550	20300	22400
XLE Sport Utility	WFREV	27260	19900	20300	22000	24100
Limited Sport Util	YFREV	30580	22100	22500	24100	26400
2WD	Z	......	(1500)	(1500)	(1660)	(1660)
RAV4—AC Electric—Truck Equipment Schedule T2						
EV Sport Utility 4D	YL4DV	50660	28800	29300	31000	33600
FJ CRUISER 4WD—V6—Truck Equipment Schedule T1						
Sport Utility 2D	BU4BF	29580	28000	28800	29700	32300
2WD	Z	......	(1700)	(1700)	(1805)	(1805)
VENZA—4-Cyl.—Truck Equipment Schedule T1						
LE Wagon 4D	ZA3BB	28760	17150	17450	19600	22300
XLE Wagon 4D	ZA3BB	32620	20100	20400	22500	25300
AWD	B	......	1000	1000	1160	1160
V6, 3.5 Liter	K	......	800	800	930	930
VENZA—V6—Truck Equipment Schedule T1						
Limited Wagon 4D	ZK3BB	38930	23300	23700	25700	28600
AWD	B	......	1000	1000	1120	1120
HIGHLANDER AWD—V6—Truck Equipment Schedule T1						
LE Sport Util 4D	BKRFH	32840	26100	26800	28700	32100
LE Plus Sport Util	BKRFH	35060	26600	27300	29100	32500
XLE Sport Util 4D	JKRFH	38360	29600	30300	32100	35600

TRUCKS & VANS

Body Type	VIN	List	Trade-In Good	Very Good	Pvt-Party Good	Retail Excellent
Limited Spt Util	DKRFH	41960	32300	33200	34700	38400
Ltd Platinum 4D	DKRFH	44810	34200	35100	36600	40300
4-Cyl, 2.7 Liter	A		(1075)	(1075)	(1185)	(1185)
HIGHLANDER AWD—V6 Hybrid—Truck Equipment Schedule T1						
Limited Spt Util	DCRFH	48160	36400	37300	38600	42400
Ltd Platinum 4D	DCRFH	50650	37000	38000	39300	43100
4RUNNER 4WD—V6—Truck Equipment Schedule T1						
SR5 Sport Utility	BU5JR	35555	27300	27800	29400	32000
SR5 Premium 4D	BU5JR	38475	29400	29900	31700	34500
Trail Sport Utility	BU5JR	36585	29300	29800	31600	34400
Trail Premium 4D	BU5JR	39505	30400	31000	32800	35700
Limited Sport Util	BU5JR	44260	32800	33300	35100	38100
KDSS Suspension			675	675	725	725
2WD	Z		(1700)	(1700)	(1840)	(1840)
SEQUOIA 4WD—V8—Truck Equipment Schedule T1						
SR5 Sport Utility	BY5G1	47815	33500	34500	35600	39300
Limited Sport Util	JY5G1	56775	39900	41000	42200	46600
Platinum Spt Util	DY5G1	64515	43800	45000	45900	50500
2WD	Z		(1700)	(1700)	(1860)	(1860)
SIENNA—V6—Truck Equipment Schedule T1						
L Minivan 4D	ZK3DC	27780	17700	18400	19400	22300
LE Minivan 4D	KK3DC	31350	19700	20500	21400	24600
XLE Minivan 4D	YK3DC	34505	24900	25800	26800	30800
SE Minivan 4D	XK3DC	34720	24700	25600	26600	30600
Limited Minivan	YK3DC	41100	26500	27600	28600	32900
AWD	J		1000	1000	1145	1145
LAND CRUISER 4WD—V8—Truck Equipment Schedule T3						
Sport Utility 4D	HY7AJ	79750	57000	58400	59500	64600
TACOMA PICKUP—4-Cyl.—Truck Equipment Schedule T1						
Pickup 2D 6 ft	NX4CN	19635	14500	15100	16200	18700
4WD	P		2700	2700	3095	3095
TACOMA PICKUP 4WD—4-Cyl.—Truck Equipment Schedule T2						
Access Cab 4D 6'	UX4EN	25210	20400	21200	22400	26000
2WD	T		(3000)	(3000)	(3425)	(3425)
V6, 4.0 Liter	U		1175	1175	1335	1335
TACOMA PICKUP—V6—Truck Equipment Schedule T2						
PreRunner Access	TU4GN	24420	20700	21500	22800	26500
4-Cyl, 2.7 Liter	X		(2575)	(2575)	(2935)	(2935)
TACOMA PICKUP—V6—Truck Equipment Schedule T2						
PreRunner Dbl 6'	KU4HN	26020	22500	22900	25000	27600
Limited Pkg			475	475	535	535
TACOMA PICKUP—V6—Truck Equipment Schedule T2						
PreRunner Dbl 5'	JU4GN	25520	23000	23500	25600	28300
Limited Pkg			475	475	530	530
4-Cyl, 2.7 Liter	X		(2575)	(2575)	(2930)	(2930)
TACOMA PICKUP 4WD—V6—Truck Equipment Schedule T1						
Double Cab 4D 5'	LU4EN	28645	26700	27200	29400	32400
Limited Pkg			475	475	525	525
2WD	J		(2850)	(2850)	(3200)	(3200)
4-Cyl, 2.7 Liter	X		(2575)	(2575)	(2885)	(2885)
TACOMA PICKUP 4WD—V6—Truck Equipment Schedule T1						
Double Cab 4D 6'	MU4FN	29145	25900	26400	28600	31600
Limited Pkg			475	475	525	525
TUNDRA PICKUP—V8—Truck Equipment Schedule T1						
SR Long Bed	NY5F1	29460	20300	20600	22600	25300
SR Double 6 1/2'	RY5F1	30350	23400	23800	25900	29100
SR5 Double 8'	CY5F1	35340	26200	26600	29300	33400
4WD	U		3500	3500	4065	4065
V6, 4.0 Liter	U		(925)	(925)	(1075)	(1075)
V8, 4.6 Liter	M		(500)	(500)	(580)	(580)
TUNDRA PICKUP 4WD—V8—Truck Equipment Schedule T1						
SR Double 8'	CY5F1	33730	26600	27000	29200	32700
SR5 Double 6 1/2'	UY5F1	35010	26700	27200	29800	33800
Limited Double 6'	BY5F1	40985	32500	33000	35400	39500
SR5 CrewMax 4D	DY5F1	37755	30700	31200	33900	38200
Limited CrewMax	HY5F1	43275	33600	34100	36500	40800
1794 Pickup 5 1/2'	AY5F1	48315	36800	37400	39600	43900
Platinum CrewMax	AY5F1	48700	37000	37600	39900	44400
2WD	T		(3500)	(3500)	(3975)	(3975)
V8, 4.6 Liter	M		(500)	(500)	(580)	(580)

1015   **SEE BACK PAGES FOR TRUCK EQUIPMENT**   589

Body Type	VIN	List	Trade-In Good	Trade-In Very Good	Pvt-Party Good	Retail Excellent

TRUCKS & VANS

VOLKSWAGEN

2000 VOLKSWAGEN — WV2(KH270)–Y–#

EUROVAN—V6—Truck Equipment Schedule T1

GLS Minivan	KH270	31890	3700	4525	4575	7575
MV Minivan	MH270	33390	3925	4825	4825	7950
Weekender Pkg		....	7000	7000	9335	9335

2001 VOLKSWAGEN — WV2(KH270)–1–#

EUROVAN—V6—Truck Equipment Schedule T1

Minivan	KH470	26815	4200	5100	5050	8250
MV Minivan	MH470	28315	4625	5625	5500	8950
Weekender Pkg		....	7000	7000	9335	9335

2002 VOLKSWAGEN — WV2(KB470)–2–#

EUROVAN—V6—Truck Equipment Schedule T1

GLS Minivan	KB470	26815	4925	5950	5900	9575
MV Minivan	MB470	28315	5425	6525	6400	10350
Weekender Pkg		....	7000	7000	9335	9335

2003 VOLKSWAGEN — WV2(KB470)–3–#

EUROVAN—V6—Truck Equipment Schedule T1

GLS Minivan	KB470	26815	5725	6875	6750	10600
MV Minivan	MB470	28315	6250	7500	7275	11400
Weekender Pkg		....	7000	7000	9335	9335

2004 VOLKSWAGEN — WVG(BC67L)–4–#

TOUAREG 4WD—V6—Truck Equipment Schedule T3

Sport Utility 4D	BC67L	35515	3050	3450	3750	5775
4-Corner Suspension		....	975	975	1305	1305
V8, 4.2 Liter		....	1000	1000	1340	1340

TOUAREG 4WD—V10 Turbo Diesel—Truck Equipment Schedule T3

TDI Sport Util 4D	GH67L	58415	7575	8575	8300	11950

2005 VOLKSWAGEN — WVG(BG77L)–5–#

TOUAREG 4WD—V6—Truck Equipment Schedule T3

Sport Utility 4D	BG77L	37795	3875	4400	4950	7400
4-Corner Suspension		....	1050	1050	1410	1410
V8, 4.2 Liter	M	....	1100	1100	1460	1460

2006 VOLKSWAGEN — WVG(BG67L)–6–#

TOUAREG 4WD—V6—Truck Equipment Schedule T3

Sport Utility 4D	BG67L	37975	5175	5750	6125	8725
4-Corner Suspension		....	1150	1150	1515	1515
V8, 4.2 Liter		....	1200	1200	1585	1585

TOUAREG 4WD—V10—Truck Equipment Schedule T3

TDI Sport Util 4D	PT77L	68420	11200	12450	12250	16900

2007 VOLKSWAGEN — WVG(BE77L)–7–#

TOUAREG 4WD—V6—Truck Equipment Schedule T3

Sport Utility 4D	BE77L	38660	6450	7100	7600	10500
4-Corner Suspension		....	1225	1225	1605	1605
V8, 4.2 Liter		....	1275	1275	1695	1695

TOUAREG 4WD—V10 Turbo Diesel—Truck Equipment Schedule T3

TDI Sport Util 4D	PT77L	59690	12050	13200	13050	17450

2008 VOLKSWAGEN — WVG(BE77L)–8–#

TOUAREG 2 4WD—V6—Truck Equipment Schedule T3

Sport Utility 4D	BE77L	49080	9050	9775	10100	12900
4-Corner Suspension		....	1300	1300	1505	1505
V8, 4.2 Liter		....	1375	1375	1600	1600

TOUAREG 2 4WD—V10 Turbo Diesel—Truck Equipment Schedule T3

TDI Sport Util 4D	PT77L	69000	12750	13750	14000	17850
4-Corner Suspension		....	1300	1300	1525	1525

Body Type	VIN	List	Trade-In Good	Very Good	Pvt-Party Good	Retail Excellent

2009 VOLKSWAGEN — WVG(AV75N)-9-#

TIGUAN—4-Cyl. Turbo—Truck Equipment Schedule T3
S Sport Utility 4D	AV75N	24990	7425	7875	8700	10850
SE Sport Utility 4D	AV75N	29025	8300	8775	9550	11850
SEL Sport Util 4D	AV75N	31740	9875	10450	11300	14100
Manual, 6-Spd	C		(350)	(350)	(430)	(430)

TIGUAN 4MOTION 4WD—4-Cyl. Turbo—Truck Equipment Sch T3
SE Sport Utility 4D	BV75N	29565	9700	10300	11050	13650
SEL Sport Util 4D	BV75N	33630	10800	11450	12300	15250

TOUAREG 2 4WD—V6—Truck Equipment Schedule T3
Sport Utility 4D	BE77L	39990	12000	12750	13150	16050
4-Corner Suspension			1375	1375	1570	1570
V8, 4.2 Liter			1475	1475	1680	1680

TOUAREG 2 4WD—V6 Turbo Diesel—Truck Equipment Schedule T3
TDI Sport Utility	AM77L	43490	16850	17800	18200	22300
4-Corner Suspension			1375	1375	1565	1565

ROUTAN—V6—Truck Equipment Schedule T3
S Minivan	HW441	25390	5600	6100	6750	8875
SE Minivan 4D	HW341	30290	7100	7725	8350	10950
SEL Minivan 4D	HW54X	33890	8250	8975	9550	12500
SEL Prem Minivan	HW64X	35290	9050	9825	10550	13900

2010 VOLKSWAGEN — WVGor2V4(CV7AX)-A-#

TIGUAN—4-Cyl. Turbo—Truck Equipment Schedule T3
S Sport Utility 4D	CV7AX	25050	9350	9775	10850	13050
SE Sport Utility 4D	AV7AX	29000	10000	10450	11550	14000
Wolfsburg Edition	AV7AX	28550	9575	10000	11100	13500
SEL Sport Util 4D	AV7AX	32015	12050	12600	13800	16700
Manual, 6-Spd	C		(375)	(375)	(450)	(450)

TIGUAN 4MOTION AWD—4-Cyl. Turbo—Truck Equipment Sch T3
S Sport Utility 4D	BV7AX	27050	10000	10450	11500	13850
SE Sport Utility 4D	BV7AX	31250	11850	12350	13500	16300
Wolfsburg Ed SUV	BV7AX	30500	11000	11500	12650	15300
SEL Sport Util 4D	BV7AX	33965	12950	13500	14900	18100

TOUAREG AWD—V6—Truck Equipment Schedule T3
VR6 Sport Utility	BF7A9	41190	14300	14950	15900	18850

TOUAREG AWD—V6 Turbo Diesel—Truck Equipment Schedule T3
TDI Sport Utility	AK7A9	44710	18600	19400	20000	23500
4-Corner Suspension			1475	1475	1650	1650

ROUTAN—V6—Truck Equipment Schedule T3
S Minivan 4D	RW4D1	26650	6975	7425	8325	10600
SE Minivan 4D	RW3D1	30420	8825	9400	10350	13150
SEL Minivan 4D	RW5DX	37250	10100	10700	11750	15000
SEL Premium	RW6DX	43300	10800	11450	12600	16200

2011 VOLKSWAGEN — WVGor2V4(AV7AX)-B-#

TIGUAN—4-Cyl. Turbo—Truck Equipment Schedule T3
S Sport Utility 4D	AV7AX	25405	10450	10800	12000	14150
SE Sport Utility 4D	AV7AX	28765	11900	12300	13550	15950
SEL Sport Util 4D	AV7AX	33640	13450	13900	15600	18650
Manual, 6-Spd	C		(450)	(450)	(530)	(530)

TIGUAN 4MOTION AWD—4-Cyl. Turbo—Truck Equipment Sch T3
S Sport Utility 4D	BV7AX	27360	11200	11550	12850	15100
SE Sport Utility 4D	BV7AX	30720	13300	13800	15300	18100
SEL Sport Util 4D	BV7AX	35595	14350	14850	16600	19850

TOUAREG AWD—V6 Supercharged Hybrid—Truck Equipment Sch T3
Sport Utility 4D	FG9BP	61385	23600	24300	25500	29200

TOUAREG AWD—V6—Truck Equipment Schedule T3
VR6 Sport Util	FF9BP	45270	19200	19800	20900	23900
VR6 Lux Spt Util	FF9BP	49120	19050	19650	20900	24100
VR6 Exec Spt Utl	FF9BP	54820	21900	22600	23800	27400

TOUAREG AWD—V6 Turbo Diesel—Truck Equipment Schedule T3
TDI Sport Util	FK9BP	48770	24200	24900	26100	30000
TDI Lux Spt Utl	FK9BP	52620	25200	26000	27200	31300
TDI Exec Spt Utl	FK9BP	58320	26400	27200	28600	33000
4-Corner Suspension			1575	1575	1810	1810

ROUTAN—V6—Truck Equipment Schedule T3
S Minivan 4D	RW4DG	26720	9250	9700	10500	12650
SE Minivan 4D	RW3DG	30430	11500	12050	12950	15700
SEL Minivan 4D	RW5DG	37420	12900	13500	14550	17550
SEL Premium	RW6DG	43320	13650	14250	15450	18800

TRUCKS & VANS

Body Type	VIN	List	Trade-In Good	Very Good	Pvt-Party Good	Retail Excellent

2012 VOLKSWAGEN — WVWGor2C4(AV7AX)-C-#

TIGUAN—4-Cyl. Turbo—Truck Equipment Schedule T3
2.0T S Sport Util	AV7AX	25210	11100	11400	12950	15200
2.0T LE Sport Util	AV7AX	25995	11050	11350	12900	15150
2.0T SE Sport Util	AV7AX	29505	12550	12900	14600	17050
2.0T SEL Spt Util	AV7AX	34845	14950	15300	17250	20200
Manual, 6-Spd	C		(425)	(425)	(495)	(495)

TIGUAN 4MOTION AWD—4-Cyl. Turbo—Truck Equipment Sch T3
2.0T S Sport Util	BV7AX	27165	12150	12450	14050	16400
2.0T SE Sport Util	BV7AX	31460	15000	15400	17150	20000
2.0T SEL Spt Util	BV7AX	36800	15900	16350	18400	21700

TOUAREG—V6—Truck Equipment Schedule T3
VR6 Sport SUV 4D	FF9BP	44245	22100	22600	24100	27200
VR6 Lux Spt Utl	FF9BP	50265	22500	23000	24700	28000
VR6 Exec Spt Utl	FF9BP	55965	25000	25600	27300	30900

TOUAREG AWD—V6 Supercharged Hybrid—Truck Equipment Sch T3
| Sport Utility 4D | FG9BP | 62865 | 28300 | 29000 | 30500 | 34200 |

TOUAREG AWD—V6 Turbo Diesel—Truck Equipment Schedule T3
TDI Sport SUV 4D	FK9BP	47745	27600	28200	30000	34100
TDI Lux Spt Utl	FK9BP	53765	28600	29300	31300	35600
TDI Exec Spt Utl	FK9BP	59465	30400	31100	33300	38000

ROUTAN—V6—Truck Equipment Schedule T3
S Minivan 4D	RVAAG	27840	11550	11950	12950	15200
SE Minivan 4D	RVABG	32830	14450	14900	16050	18850
SEL Minivan 4D	RVACG	38710	16100	16650	17750	20800
SEL Premium	RVADG	45100	16650	17200	18500	21900

2013 VOLKSWAGEN — WVWGor2C4(AV7AX)-D-#

TIGUAN—4-Cyl. Turbo—Truck Equipment Schedule T3
2.0T S Sport Util	AV7AX	25525	12050	12350	14150	16550
2.0T SE Sport Util	AV7AX	29985	14850	15200	17200	19950
2.0T SEL Spt Util	AV7AX	35690	16400	16750	18950	22100
Manual, 6-Spd	C		(475)	(475)	(565)	(565)

TIGUAN 4MOTION AWD—4-Cyl. Turbo—Truck Equipment Sch T3
2.0T S Sport Util	BV7AX	27480	13000	13300	15250	17800
2.0T SE Sport Util	BV7AX	31940	16900	17250	19300	22300
2.0T SEL Spt Util	BV7AX	37645	17250	17600	19850	23100

TOUAREG—V6—Truck Equipment Schedule T3
VR6 Sport SUV 4D	EF9BP	44300	23200	23600	25400	28400
VR6 Lux Spt Utl	EF9BP	50305	25300	25700	27600	30800
VR6 Exec Spt Utl	EF9BP	56030	26900	27400	29300	32700

TOUAREG AWD—V6 Supercharged Hybrid—Truck Equipment Sch T3
| Sport Utility 4D | EG9BP | 62930 | 31500 | 32000 | 33800 | 37400 |

TOUAREG AWD—V6 Turbo Diesel—Truck Equipment Schedule T3
TDI Sport SUV 4D	EP9BP	47800	30900	31500	33700	37700
TDI Lux Spt Utl	EP9BP	53805	33200	33800	36100	40500
TDI Exec Spt Utl	EP9BP	59530	34500	35100	37600	42300

ROUTAN—V6—Truck Equipment Schedule T3
S Minivan 4D	RVAAG		13900	14300	15500	17900
SE Minivan 4D	RVABG		17100	17550	18800	21700
SEL Premium	RVADG		19350	19850	21300	24700

2014 VOLKSWAGEN — WVWGor2C4(AV3AX)-E-#

TIGUAN—4-Cyl.—Truck Equipment Schedule T3
2.0T S Sport Util	AV3AX	26195	13950	14250	16400	19150
2.0T SE Sport Util	AV3AX	28205	16650	17000	18950	21800
2.0T SEL Spt Util	AV3AX	33860	19750	20100	22000	25000
2.0T R-Line Spt Utl	AV3AX	37745	19550	19950	21800	24800

TIGUAN 4MOTION AWD—4-Cyl. Turbo—Truck Equipment Sch T3
2.0T S Sport Util	BV3AX	28150	15350	15650	17750	20600
2.0T SE Sport Util	BV3AX	30160	18700	19100	21000	23900
2.0T SEL Spt Util	BV3AX	35815	20300	20700	22500	25500
2.0T R-Line Spt Utl	BV3AX	39700	22400	22800	24500	27600

TOUAREG AWD—V6—Truck Equipment Schedule T3
V6 Sport SUV 4D	EF9BP	44905	26200	26700	28500	31600
V6 Exec Spt Utl	EF9BP	58270	31600	32200	34000	37500
V6 Lux Spt Utl	EF9BP	52385	29100	29600	31500	34900
V6 R-Line Spt Utl	DF9BP	55025	30600	31200	33000	36400

TOUAREG AWD—V6 Supercharged Hybrid—Truck Equipment Sch T3
| Sport Utility 4D | EG9BP | 65080 | 37300 | 38000 | 39500 | 43200 |

Body Type	VIN	List	Trade-In Good	Trade-In Very Good	Pvt-Party Good	Retail Excellent
TOUAREG AWD—V6 Turbo Diesel—Truck Equipment Schedule T3						
TDI Sport SUV 4D	EP9BP	51945	33100	33700	36000	40100
TDI Exec Spt Utl	EP9BP	61770	36900	37500	40100	44900
TDI Lux Spt Utl	EP9BP	55685	34100	34700	37100	41500
X Sport Utility 4D	EP9BP	57080	31900	32500	34200	37600
TDI R-Line Spt Utl	DP9BP	58525	36300	36900	39300	43900
ROUTAN—V6—Truck Equipment Schedule T3						
S Minivan 4D	RVAAG	27840				
SE Minivan 4D	RVABG	35310				
SEL Premium 4D	RVADG	45100				

VOLVO

2003 VOLVO — YV1(CM59H)-3-#

XC90 AWD—5-Cyl. Turbo—Truck Equipment Schedule T3						
Sport Utility 4D	CM59H	35760	2900	3300	3775	6075
Versatility Pkg			300	300	395	395
Third Row Seat			225	225	290	290
FWD	N,Y		(750)	(750)	(1010)	(1010)
XC90 AWD—6-Cyl. Twin Turbo—Truck Equipment Schedule T3						
T6 Sport Utility 4D	CM91H	40660	2550	2900	3400	5500
Versatility Pkg			300	300	395	395
Third Row Seat			225	225	290	290

2004 VOLVO — YV1(CM59H)-4-#

XC90 AWD—5-Cyl. Turbo—Truck Equipment Schedule T3						
Sport Utility 4D	CM59H	36875	3550	4000	4450	7000
Versatility Pkg			325	325	420	420
Third Row Seat			225	225	310	310
FWD	N,Y		(850)	(850)	(1120)	(1120)
XC90 AWD—6-Cyl. Twin Turbo—Truck Equipment Schedule T3						
T6 Sport Utility 4D	CM91H	41650	3250	3675	4125	6525
Versatility Pkg			325	325	420	420
Third Row Seat			225	225	310	310

2005 VOLVO — YV1(CM592)-5-#

XC90 AWD—5-Cyl. Turbo—Truck Equipment Schedule T3						
Sport Utility 4D	CM592	37300	3700	4175	4975	7675
Versatility Pkg			350	350	455	455
Third Row Seat	Y		250	250	330	330
FWD	N,Y		(925)	(925)	(1225)	(1225)
XC90 AWD—6-Cyl. Twin Turbo—Truck Equipment Schedule T3						
T6 Sport Utility 4D	CM911	41700	3325	3775	4600	7125
Versatility Pkg			350	350	455	455
Third Row Seat	Y		250	250	330	330
XC90 AWD—V8—Truck Equipment Schedule T3						
Sport Utility 4D	CM852	46080	4175	4725	5525	8450
Versatility Pkg			350	350	455	455
Third Row Seat	Z		250	250	330	330

2006 VOLVO — YV1(CM592)-6-#

XC90 AWD—5-Cyl. Turbo—Truck Equipment Schedule T3						
2.5T Sport Util 4D	CM592	38110	4525	5050	5650	8275
Versatility Pkg			375	375	485	485
Third Row Seat	Y		275	275	350	350
FWD	N,Y		(1000)	(1000)	(1335)	(1335)
XC90 AWD—V8—Truck Equipment Schedule T3						
Sport Utility 4D	CM852	46535	5025	5600	6325	9375
Ocean Race Spt Utl	CM852	50555	6775	7550	8375	12300
Third Row Seat	Z		275	275	350	350

2007 VOLVO — YV1(CN982)-7-#

XC90—6-Cyl.—Truck Equipment Schedule T3						
3.2 Sport Utility 4D	CN982	36830	4950	5475	6175	8675
Versatility Pkg			400	400	520	520
Third Row Seat	Y,Z		275	275	370	370
AWD	M		1100	1100	1460	1460
XC90 AWD—V8—Truck Equipment Schedule T3						
Sport Utility 4D	CT852	47120	6375	7025	7850	11200
Sport SUV 4D	CZ852	49995	7775	8575	9350	13200

Body Type	VIN	List	Trade-In Good	Very Good	Pvt-Party Good	Retail Excellent
Third Row Seat	T,Z		275	275	370	370

2008 VOLVO — YV4(CN982)-8-#

XC90—6-Cyl.—Truck Equipment Schedule T3
3.2 Sport Utility 4D	CN982	36955	7050	7625	8350	11000
Versatility Pkg			425	425	515	515
Third Row Seat	Y,Z		300	300	365	365
AWD	M		1175	1175	1450	1450

XC90 AWD—V8—Truck Equipment Schedule T3
Sport Utility 4D	CZ852	49250	10450	11300	12000	15750
Sport SUV 4D	CT852	50615	12550	13500	13950	18100
Third Row Seat	T,Z		300	300	365	365

2010 VOLVO — YV(1or4)(960DL)-A-#

XC60—6-Cyl.—Truck Equipment Schedule T3
3.2 Sport Utility 4D	960DL	33245	12500	13050	14100	16900
Adaptive Cruise Control			400	400	460	460
AWD	Z		925	925	1080	1080

XC60 AWD—6-Cyl. Turbo—Truck Equipment Schedule T3
T6 Sport Utility 4D	992DZ	38050	15000	15650	16600	19700
R-Design Sport Util	992DZ	42400	14600	15250	16350	19500
Adaptive Cruise Control			400	400	450	450

XC90—6-Cyl.—Truck Equipment Schedule T3
3.2 Sport Utility 4D	982CY	38550	12500	13050	14150	17000
AWD	Z		950	950	1085	1085
Third Row Seat	F,Y		375	375	435	435

XC90 AWD—6-Cyl.—Truck Equipment Schedule T3
| 3.2 R-Design SUV | 982CT | 42350 | 15650 | 16300 | 17450 | 20900 |
| FWD | F | | (1200) | (1200) | (1345) | (1345) |

XC90 AWD—V8—Truck Equipment Schedule T3
| Sport Utility 4D | 852CZ | 48350 | 18450 | 19250 | 20300 | 24200 |
| Third Row Seat | T,Z | | 375 | 375 | 425 | 425 |

2011 VOLVO — YV(1or4)(952DL)-B-#

XC60—6-Cyl.—Truck Equipment Schedule T3
3.2 Sport Utility	952DL	33250	14900	15400	16700	19400
3.2 R-Design Util	952DL	38900	16600	17150	18500	21600
Adaptive Cruise Control			425	425	475	475
AWD	Z		1075	1075	1220	1220

XC60 AWD—6-Cyl. Turbo—Truck Equipment Schedule T3
T6 Sport Utility	902DZ	39250	18300	18900	20000	23100
T6 R-Design Util	902DZ	42400	18600	19200	20300	23500
Adaptive Cruise Control			425	425	465	465

XC90—6-Cyl.—Truck Equipment Schedule T3
3.2 Sport Utility 4D	982CY	39050	15400	15850	17300	20200
Third Row Seat	F,Y		425	425	485	485
AWD	Z		1075	1075	1190	1190

XC90 AWD—6-Cyl.—Truck Equipment Schedule T3
3.2 R-Design Util	952CT	42850	18700	19300	20700	24000
Third Row Seat	F,Y		425	425	475	475
FWD	F		(1200)	(1200)	(1320)	(1320)

XC90 AWD—V8—Truck Equipment Schedule T3
| Sport Utility 4D | 852CZ | 48850 | 21300 | 22000 | 23400 | 27100 |
| Third Row Seat | T,Z | | 425 | 425 | 475 | 475 |

2012 VOLVO — YV4(952DL)-C-#

XC60—6-Cyl.—Truck Equipment Schedule T3
3.2 Sport Utility 4D	952DL	33775	17400	17850	19200	21900
Adaptive Cruise Control			450	450	500	500
AWD	Z		1025	1025	1170	1170

XC60 AWD—6-Cyl. Turbo—Truck Equipment Schedule T3
T6 Sport Utility	902DZ	39825	20700	21300	22700	26000
T6 R-Design Util	902DZ	44025	20800	21400	22900	26300
Adaptive Cruise Control			450	450	500	500

XC90—6-Cyl.—Truck Equipment Schedule T3
| 3.2 Sport Utility | 952CY | 39275 | 18600 | 19000 | 20600 | 23400 |
| AWD | Z | | 1175 | 1175 | 1300 | 1300 |

XC90 AWD—6-Cyl.—Truck Equipment Schedule T3
| 3.2 R-Design Util | 952CT | 44075 | 22400 | 23000 | 24600 | 27800 |
| FWD | F | | (1200) | (1200) | (1330) | (1330) |

Body Type	VIN	List	Trade-In Good	Very Good	Pvt-Party Good	Retail Excellent

2013 VOLVO — YV4(952DL)-D-#

XC60—6-Cyl.—Truck Equipment Schedule T3

Body Type	VIN	List	Good	Very Good	Good	Excellent
3.2 Sport Utility 4D	952DL	35245	20600	21000	22600	25600
3.2 Premier SUV	952DL	38195	20500	20900	22700	25900
3.2 Premier Plus	952DL	40095	21300	21700	23400	26600
3.2 Platinum SUV	952DL	42795	23100	23600	25300	28600
Sensing Cruise Control			475	475	530	530
AWD	Z		1075	1075	1230	1230

XC60 AWD—6-Cyl. Turbo—Truck Equipment Schedule T3

Body Type	VIN	List	Good	Very Good	Good	Excellent
T6 Sport Utility 4D	902DZ	41345	23500	24000	25600	28900
T6 Premier Plus	902DZ	43445	24400	24900	26500	29900
T6 R-Design SUV	902DZ	45745	25000	25500	27200	30700
T6 Platinum SUV	902DZ	46145	25700	26200	28000	31500
T6 R-DsgnPrmr +	902DZ	47145	26300	26800	28600	32200
T6 R-Dsgn Pltnm	902DZ	49845	26800	27300	29200	33000
Sensing Cruise Control			475	475	520	520

XC90 3.2—6-Cyl.—Truck Equipment Schedule T3

Body Type	VIN	List	Good	Very Good	Good	Excellent
Sport Utility 4D	952CY	40375	23300	23700	25500	28300
Premier Plus 4D	952CY	42875	24300	24700	26500	29600
R-Design Spt Util	952CT	43395	25900	26300	28100	31200
R-Design Premier +	952CF	43575	25900	26400	28100	31200
Platinum Spt Util	952CY	45575	26000	26400	28200	31300
R-Design Platinum	952CF	46275	26600	27100	28800	32000
AWD	Z		1200	1200	1335	1335

2014 VOLVO — YV4(952DL)-E-#

XC60—6-Cyl.—Truck Equipment Schedule T3

Body Type	VIN	List	Good	Very Good	Good	Excellent
3.2 Sport Utility 4D	952DL	35765	24500	25000	26700	30000
3.2 Premier Spt Util	952DL	38865	24800	25300	27000	30300
3.2 Premier Plus 4D	952DL	40165	24300	24800	26500	29800
3.2 Platinum SUV	952DL	42865	27100	27700	29200	32600
Technology Pkg			650	650	715	715
AWD	Z		1175	1175	1290	1290

XC60 AWD—6-Cyl. Turbo—Truck Equipment Schedule T3

Body Type	VIN	List	Good	Very Good	Good	Excellent
T6 Sport Utility 4D	902DZ	42465	26400	26900	28600	31900
T6 Premier Plus 4D	902DZ	43765	27200	27800	29300	32700
T6 Platinum SUV	902DZ	46465	28100	28700	30200	33700
T6 R-Design SUV	902DZ	46715	28400	29000	30600	34000
T6 R-Dsgn Premr +	902DZ	48015	28800	29400	31000	34500
T6 R-Dsgn Pltnm	902DZ	50715	30000	30600	32100	35700
Technology Pkg			650	650	710	710

XC90 3.2—6-Cyl.—Truck Equipment Schedule T3

Body Type	VIN	List	Good	Very Good	Good	Excellent
Sport Utility 4D	952CY	40615	26000	26500	28200	31100
Premier Plus 4D	952CY	42115	26900	27400	29100	32200
R-Design Spt Util	952CF	43615	28600	29100	30900	34000
Platinum Spt Util	952CY	44815	28800	29300	31100	34200
R-Design Platinum	952CF	46315	29900	30400	32100	35300
AWD	Z		1200	1200	1325	1325

Equipment	00-02	03	04	05	06	07	08
MODEL PACKAGES (Truck Schedules T1 & T2)							
(Add Only If Not Listed on Individual Vehicle Listing)							
CHEVROLET/GMC:							
LTZ, SLT	275	—	—	—	—	—	—
LT, Xtreme	115	140	—	—	—	—	—
LS, SLE, ZR2 Suspension							
	100	115	140	—	—	—	—
DODGE:							
SLT, SXT	75	—	—	—	—	—	—
FORD:							
Limited, Chateau	300	375	—	—	—	—	—
Lariat, Adrenalin	145	200	275	350	—	—	—
XLT, XLT Sport, XLT NBX, FX4, Edge Plus, Amarillo							
	115	140	—	—	—	—	—
STX, EDGE	—	115	—	—	—	—	—
ALL MAKES:							
(All Other Model Packages Not Listed)							
	75	75	75	75	75	90	115
TRUCK SCHEDULE T1 (Deduct For)							
Manual Trans	(250)	(265)	(290)	(315)	(340)	(360)	(390)
TRUCK SCHEDULE T2 (Add For)							
Auto Trans	200	215	240	265	290	315	340
w/o Pwr Steering	(75)	(75)	(75)	(75)	(75)	(75)	(75)
w/o Air Cond	(175)	(190)	(200)	(200)	(200)	(200)	(200)
TRUCK SCHEDULE T3 (This Equipment Only)							
Premium Sound	75	90	115	140	150	150	150
Video/DVD	—	100	100	135	165	190	—
NavigationSystm	—	—	285	300	335	365	390
Grille Guard	50	50	50	50	50	50	50
Running Boards	200	200	200	200	200	200	200
Premium Wheels	150	165	190	215	240	265	290
Oversize Premium Wheels (20" Plus)							
	340	380	415	450	485	525	560
Towing Pkg	125	140	165	190	200	200	200
w/o Leather	(100)	(100)	(100)	(115)	(140)	(165)	(190)
OTHER OPTIONS (Truck Schedules T1 & T2)							
w/o Pwr Windows	(75)	(90)	(100)	(100)	(100)	(100)	(100)
w/o Power Locks	(50)	(50)	(50)	(50)	(50)	(50)	(50)
w/o Tilt Wheel	(50)	(65)	(75)	(75)	(75)	(75)	(75)
Premium Sound	50	50	50	50	50	50	50
Video/DVD	—	100	100	135	165	190	—
NavigationSystm	—	—	285	300	335	365	390
Leather	100	100	100	115	140	165	190

2000-2008 TRUCK FACTORY EQUIPMENT

Equipment	00-02	03	04	05	06	07	08
Quad Seating							
(4 Buckets)	125	140	150	150	150	150	150
Van Seating Pkgs							
(11/12 Pass)	275	290	315	340	365	390	400
(15 Passenger)	525	540	565	590	615	640	650
Privacy Glass (Vans/Wagons/Sport Utilities)							
	50	50	50	50	50	50	50
Sliding Rear Window (Pickups)							
	25	25	25	25	25	25	25
Roof Rack	25	25	25	25	25	25	25
Pickup Shell/Cap	75	90	100	100	100	100	100
Bed Liner	50	50	50	50	50	65	90
Grille Guard	50	50	50	50	50	50	50
Winch	50	50	50	65	90	115	140
Custom Bumper	50	50	50	50	50	50	50
Stepside							
(Short Bed PU)	50	65	90	115	140	150	150
(Long Bed PU)	(250)	(250)	—	—	—	—	—
Running Boards	200	200	200	200	200	200	200
Alloy Wheels	75	90	115	140	150	150	150
Premium Wheels	150	165	190	215	240	265	290
Oversize Premium Wheels (20" Plus)							
	305	380	415	450	485	525	560
Wide Tires or Oversize Off-Road Tires							
	50	50	50	50	50	65	90
Opt Fuel Tank	50	50	—	—	—	—	—
Towing Pkg	125	140	165	190	200	200	200
Dual Rear Wheels (Add Only on Models Not Listed as DR)							
(Pickups)	600	635	685	715	740	765	—
(Cab/Ch, Vans)	225	240	265	290	300	300	—
Single Rear Wheels (Deduct Only on Models Listed as DR)							
(Cab/Ch, Vans)	(225)	(240)	(265)	(290)	(300)	(300)	(300)
Snow Plow	300	350	425	500	575	650	725
Hydraulic Lift	350	350	350	350	350	350	350
Underbody Hoist/Dump Bed							
	350	350	350	350	350	350	350
Cab & Chassis Bodies							
9' Stake	450	465	490	515	540	565	590
12' Stake	500	515	540	565	590	615	640
14' Stake	550	565	590	615	640	665	690
16' Stake	600	615	640	665	690	715	740
12' x 8' Box	500	500	500	500	500	500	500
14' x 8' Box	550	550	550	550	550	550	550
16' x 8' Box	600	600	600	600	600	600	600
Utility	800	800	800	800	800	800	800
Aluminum Box	400	400	400	400	400	400	400

TRUCKS & VANS

SEE PAGE 9 FOR PVT PARTY & RETAIL EQUIPMENT

Equipment	09	10	11	12	13	14
ALL MAKES:						
(All Other Model Packages Not Listed)						
	125	125	125	140	165	190
TRUCK SCHEDULE T1 (Deduct For)						
5-Spd Manual	(450)	(525)	(585)	(635)	(685)	(735)
6-Spd Manual	(285)	(335)	—	(500)	—	—
TRUCK SCHEDULE T2 (Add For)						
Auto Trans	385	435	485	535	585	635
w/o Pwr Steering	(90)	(115)	(140)	(150)	(150)	(150)
w/o Air Cond	(235)	(285)	(335)	(385)	(435)	(465)
TRUCK SCHEDULE T3 (This Equipment Only)						
Premium Sound	185	235	285	315	340	365
Video/DVD	235	265	290	315	340	365
NavigationSystm	435	465	490	515	540	565
Panorama Roof	390	435	485	535	585	635
Premium Wheels	335	365	390	415	440	465
Oversize Premium Wheels (20" Plus)						
	595	630	670	705	740	775
Grille Guard	65	75	75	75	75	75
Parking Sensors	50	65	90	115	140	165
Backup Camera	65	90	115	140	200	190
Running Boards	200	200	200	200	200	200
Power Sliding Doors (Minivan)						
Single	25	25	25	25	40	65
Dual	50	65	90	115	140	165
Towing Pkg	215	240	265	290	300	300
w/o Leather	(235)	(285)	(335)	(385)	(435)	(500)
OTHER OPTIONS (Truck Schedules T1 & T2)						
w/o Pwr Windows	(115)	(140)	(165)	(190)	(215)	(240)
w/o Power Locks	(65)	(90)	(115)	(140)	(165)	(175)
w/o Tilt Wheel	(90)	(115)	(140)	(165)	(190)	(200)
Premium Sound	85	115	140	165	190	215
Video/DVD	235	265	290	315	340	365
NavigationSystm	435	465	490	515	540	565
Leather	235	285	335	385	435	500
Quad Seating						
(4 Buckets)	185	235	285	315	340	365
Van Seating Packages						
(11/12 Pass)	435	485	535	585	—	685
(14/15 Pass)	750	900	1050	1185	1310	—
Power Sliding Doors (Minivans)						
Single	25	25	25	25	40	65
Dual	50	65	90	115	140	165
Privacy Glass (Vans/Wagons/Sport Utilities)						
	65	90	100	100	100	100

TRUCKS & VANS

TRUCKS & VANS

Equipment	09	10	11	12	13	14
Sliding Rear Window (Pickups)						
	40	65	75	75	75	75
Power Sliding Rear Window (Pickups)						
	140	165	175	175	175	175
Roof Rack	40	65	90	100	100	100
Panorama Roof	390	435	485	535	585	635
Pickup Shell/Cap	135	165	190	215	240	265
Hard Tonneau	100	115	140	165	190	215
Bed Liner	100	100	100	115	140	165
Grille Guard	65	75	75	75	75	75
Winch	150	165	190	215	240	265
Custom Bumper	65	90	100	100	100	100
Parking Sensors	50	65	90	115	140	165
Backup Camera	65	90	115	140	200	190
Custom Paint	25	25	40	65	90	115
Two-Tone Paint	25	25	40	65	90	115
Stepside Bed	185	235	285	315	340	365
Running Boards	200	200	200	200	200	200
Alloy Wheels	165	190	215	240	265	290
Premium Wheels	335	365	390	415	440	465
Oversize Premium Wheels (20" Plus)						
	595	630	670	705	740	775
Wide Tires or Oversize Off-Road Tires						
	100	100	100	115	140	165
Towing Pkg	215	240	265	290	300	300
Dual Rear Wheels (Add Only on Models Not Listed as DR)						
(Pickups)	885	1010	1135	1260	1385	1510
(Cab/Ch, Vans)	350	425	485	535	585	635
Single Rear Wheels (Deduct Only on Models Listed as DR)						
(Cab/Ch, Vans)	(350)	(425)	(485)	(535)	(585)	(635)
Snow Plow	815	915	1015	1115	1215	1335
Hydraulic Lift	385	435	485	535	585	615
Underbody Hoist/Dump Bed						
	385	435	485	535	585	615
Cab & Chassis Bodies						
9' Stake	665	765	865	950	1025	1100
12' Stake	715	815	915	1015	1115	1200
14' Stake	765	865	965	1065	1165	1265
16' Stake	835	960	1065	1165	1265	1365
12' x 8' Box	550	625	685	735	785	835
14' x 8' Box	600	675	750	825	885	935
16' x 8' Box	665	750	825	900	975	1050
Utility	865	965	1065	1165	1265	1365
Aluminum Box	465	550	625	700	775	850

SEE PAGE 9 FOR PVT PARTY & RETAIL EQUIPMENT 599